GOLF
Magazine's
Encyclopedia
of Golf

GOLF
Magazine's Encyclopedia of Golf
The Complete Reference

SECOND EDITION

The Editors of
GOLF
MAGAZINE

HarperCollins*Publishers*

FIRST EDITION

Library of Congress Cataloging-in-Publication Data

GOLF magazine's encyclopedia of golf : the complete reference / the
    editors of GOLF magazine.—2nd ed.
        p.   cm.
    Includes index.
    ISBN 0-06-270019-7
    1. Golf.   I. GOLF magazine (New York, N.Y.)   II. Title:
Encyclopedia of golf.
GV965.G5455   1993
796.352—dc20   92-16293

93 94 95 96 97 PS/MPC 10 9 8 7 6 5 4 3 2 1

C O N T E N T S

The History of Golf

THE ROYAL AND ancient game of golf is one of the oldest of our modern sports. But its exact beginnings are lost in antiquity. Some historians trace golf back to the Stone Age, while others tell us that the sport had its origin with the idle antics of shepherd boys knocking small stones into holes in the ground with a crook while their flocks grazed nearby.

It is known, however, that the Romans, in their day of empire, played a game called *paganica*, which involved the use of a bent stick and a ball stuffed with wool in the open countryside. In the first century B.C., the Romans overran Europe, crossed the English Channel, and occupied parts of England and Scotland. They did not withdraw until the fourth century A.D. It is therefore assumed by most historians that their game of *paganica* was the forerunner not only of golf but of kindred games played in Holland, Belgium, France, and England. For instance, people in Holland and northern France played a game on a flat rectangular area, generally on ice, of 60 by 25 feet. Clubs shaped like hockey sticks with brass or wood heads were used to strike a ball at a post at each end of the field. It was much like croquet, but it was called *kolf*. French and Belgians played a similar game in the fields called *choulla* or *choulle*. The English also played a game in the fourteenth century called *cambuca*, which involved a club and a wooden ball.

Recent research by the Dutch golf historian Steven Van Hengel indicates that the Dutch may have played a much stronger role in golf's early history than had earlier been thought. Van Hengel found that, before the Dutch got involved in *kolf*, they played a form of golf called *colf* from the 13th century until the early 1700s. He traced the start of Dutch golf back to the village of Loenen aan de Vecht, which had four golf holes in 1297. Before 1400, the game was being played at Brussels, Brielle, Haarlem, and Utrecht as well as Loenen. Thirteen more cities joined the fold by 1500. By the end of the seventeenth century, *colf* was played in forty-seven Dutch communities. Although *colf* continued until at least 1830 at Loenen, it inexplicably vanished in other parts of the country at the beginning of the eighteenth century, and was replaced by *kolf*.

Colf is shown being played on grass with the players teeing the ball in a print by the artist Jan Luyken (1649–1712) and a painting by Pieter van de Borcht from about 1590 with a left-handed player at the top of his swing at a ball perched on a peg-type tee). Some historians doubt that the Dutch played at a hole, the object of the game as it has come down to us today. Some of the confusion no doubt stems from the Dutch playing *colf* on ice in the winter, usually toward a post. However, Van Hengel cites as evidence the well-known picture from the Flemish

1

Book of Hours, which dates from about 1500, that shows a foursome putting at a hole. Moreover, modern golf terminology shows some evidence for this and also of the Dutch influence on the game. A hole in Dutch is a *put*, which certainly sounds familiar. For instance, when a player found an obstacle impeded his play, he would say, *Stuit mij* (pronounced "sty my"). It's not a far cry from this to the "stymie," an old match play situation where one player's ball blocked the line of putt of another player. A Dutch player would also tee his ball on a *tuitje* (pronounced "toitee"). If his drive would hit someone, he would shout "*Voor!*" We also know, from a Dutch poem of 1657, that forecaddies were known as *ballemerkers*.

Fortunately, we also know something of the balls and clubs used by the Dutch. Recent excavations in Amsterdam for the city's subway system cut through a rubbish dump in use from 1565–1650. Among the objects unearthed was a beechwood golf ball dated around 1590, and some fragments of clubs. The ball has a diameter of two inches and weighs eighty-five grams. Solid wooden balls, which were also made from elm, are believed to have been in use until well into the seventeenth century. More than a dozen clubheads, some with broken hazel shafts, were also excavated. Apparently, the clubmaker looked for a straight hazel shaft with one branch. He then cut the branch back to about one and one half inches, and cast the clubhead around it. The metal most commonly used was lead.

The Dutch also used a leather-covered ball. White sheepskin balls stuffed with cow's hair were made from around 1425. Although the ball was originally made for the Dutch game of *kaatsen* (hand tennis), Van Hengel again cites the painting in the Book of Hours as evidence that *colfers* had adopted them before 1500. The painting shows three wooden and one leather-covered ball. The first traceable shipment of Dutch leather balls to Scotland was made in 1486 when a tradesman named Ritsaert Clays paid six groats to the toll-station at Bergen op Zoom for exporting one barrel of balls. Van Hengel states that a conservative estimate of Holland's annual production of leather balls between 1500 and 1600 is 500,000 a year for *colf* and *kaatsen* jointly.

Leather balls as well as clubs can clearly be seen in many seventeenth century Dutch paintings. Landscape painting did not start until early in the sixteenth century, but by the end of the century, Dutch and Flemish artists had painted dozens of landscapes,

some of which included the game of *colf*. Also, toward the end of the sixteenth century, a number of children's portraits with clubs and balls were executed. The earliest of these is a pencil sketch by Jacob Willemsz from 1587 for a life-size painting; it shows the great lawyer Hugh Grotius at the age of four with a leaden *colf* club in his right hand and a leather ball. Later portraits show leather-covered balls that look exactly like the "featherie" balls used in Scotland. A portrait of Marie Allegonda van Campstra at age nine painted by Julius de Geest in 1670 shows her with a leaden *colf* club and a wooden ball.

Recent research has also revealed that in 1552, the town documents of Goirle, Holland, mention a ball maker who obviously was making leather-covered balls because he is described as a "stuffer" of balls. This is interesting because the Gourlay family became prominent featherie ball makers in Scotland. Were they Dutch immigrants who brought their craft with them and took a last name after their town of origin? At present, the answer isn't known.

We do know that the Dutch traded extensively with Scotland during the fifteenth and sixteenth centuries. Most of this trade consisted of the export of wool from the Scottish East Coast ports to Holland, and was mainly carried in Dutch ships. At that time, mariners hadn't mastered the art of tacking against the wind. Without a favorable wind, ships' crews could find themselves stranded for months at a time on foreign shores.

Although only conjecture, it could be that Dutch seamen began taking their clubs along on the voyages to Scotland, and that this is how golf came to Scotland. A big inducement could have been the seaside linksland, ideal for the game, on the east coast of Scotland, the area where the first Scottish courses came into play. Recently, the wreck of a sixteenth-century Dutch ship was found off the Scottish East Coast. Its cargo included Dutch-made iron clubheads.

While there is still controversy over whether golf originated in Holland or in Scotland, the latter must be credited with fostering the development and growth of the game, as we know it today, from the fifteenth century onward.

EARLY DAYS OF GOLF IN THE BRITISH ISLES

The sport as played in the fifteenth century by the Scots was by no means as refined as the modern game of golf. Their equipment was still crude: a leather bag stuffed with feathers for a ball and a club cut from a bent tree branch. Nor did they have any set golf courses. But the Scots enjoyed their "golfe" so much that, in 1457, Scotland's Parliament of King James II declared it illegal. Anyone caught playing the game was fined and imprisoned because the King was afraid skill at golf would replace skill with the bow and arrow, which was necessary to the defense of the realm. Remember that this was a time when men went to war with bows and arrows, and hitting a bull's-eye was more important than sinking a golf shot.

But you cannot keep a game like golf down. In spite of the ban, the noblemen continued to play in pastures by the sea, and the game continued to be a popular amusement in Scotland. The proscription against golf apparently remained in effect until the introduction of gunpowder near the end of the fifteenth century lessened the importance of archery and restored golf as legal sport to the people in the mid-1500s.

Golf was the sport of the people, and there appear to have been no social barriers among those who played. Royalty and commoners often played together. As proof, we may cite the first international match of record. Back in 1682, when the then Prince

of Wales, later James II, was living at Holyrood, he engaged certain English noblemen in a controversy over the game's historic background and as an outcome challenged them to a foursome. He chose as his partner a poor Edinburgh shoemaker, John Paterson by name. The battle was staged at Links of Leith, near Edinburgh. The Prince and John were the winners. There are no details of how much the Prince contributed to the victory, but he did give the stakes to Paterson, with which John built a house in Canongate, Edinburgh, which stood until 1961, when it was demolished to make way for a housing project.

The first known organized golf club was founded in 1744 with the establishment of the Honourable Company of Edinburgh Golfers. The same year this golf society held its first annual tournament and awarded to the winner a silver club. The winner was also designated as the Captain of Golf for the coming year. The Honourable Company used the famous Links of Leith (the same course the Prince and John played their match on) and survived until 1831, when it ceased operations. In 1836, the society was reactivated, this time using the Musselburgh links as its course and headquarters for its tournaments.

Ten years after the Honourable Company was formed, the St. Andrews Society of Golfers came into existence. This organization, now known as the

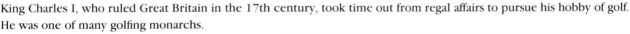

King Charles I, who ruled Great Britain in the 17th century, took time out from regal affairs to pursue his hobby of golf. He was one of many golfing monarchs.

The Royal and Ancient Golf Club of St. Andrews, Scotland, was founded in 1754. This engraving shows the St. Andrews links in 1798. *The Bettmann Archive.*

Royal and Ancient Golf Club of St. Andrews, has been in continuous operation since its activation in 1754. This, combined with other circumstances, obviously contributed to the recognition of the Royal and Ancient Golf Club as the Mecca of golf.

While during the latter half of the eighteenth century the rules, standards, and fashions of golf were set by the Honourable Company of Edinburgh Golfers, this leadership was gradually taken over by the members of the Royal and Ancient Golf Club. Here are basic rules, translated from the archaic English, as originally played at St. Andrews:

1. You must tee your ball within a club length of the hole.
2. Your tee must be upon the ground.
3. You are not to change the ball which you strike off the tee.
4. You are not to remove stones, bones, or any break-club for the sake of playing your ball, except upon the fair green, and that only within a club length of your ball.
5. If your ball come among water or any watery filth, you are at liberty to take out your ball and throw it behind the hazard six yards at least: you may play it with any club, and allow your adversary a stroke for so getting out your ball.
6. If your balls be found anywhere touching one another, you are to lift the first ball until you play the last.
7. At holing you are to play your ball honestly for the hole, and not to play upon your adversary's ball, not lying in your way to the hole.
8. If you should lose your ball by its being taken up or any other way, you are to go back to the spot where you struck last and drop another ball and allow your adversary a stroke for the misfortune.
9. No man at holing his ball is to be allowed to mark his way to the hole with his club or anything else.
10. If a ball is stopped by any person, horse, dog, or anything else, the ball so stopped must be played where it lies.

11. If you draw your club in order to strike and proceed so far with your stroke as to be bringing down your club, if then your club should break in any way, it is to be accounted a stroke.

12. He whose ball lies farthest from the hole is obliged to play first.

13. Neither trench, ditch, nor dike made for the preservation of the links, nor the Scholars' Holes, nor the Soldiers' Lines, shall be accounted a hazard, but the ball is to be taken out, teed, and played with any iron club.

Many of these early regulations are still in the *Rules of Golf.*

Many other traditions of golf can be traced to St. Andrews. Until the middle of the eighteenth century, for instance, golf had been played over courses of no established length. Leith, for example, had only five holes. Blackheath, another ancient club, had seven, which was the most fashionable number; but other courses had as many as twenty-five. Possibly seven would have remained as the traditional number for a round had it not been for the example of St. Andrews.

At the time the members of the Society of St. Andrews Golfers laid down the rules previously mentioned, the course at St. Andrews—what would now be the famous Old Course—had twelve holes. The first eleven traveled straight out to the end of a small peninsula. After playing these, the golfers returned to the clubhouse by playing the first ten greens backward, plus a solitary green by the clubhouse. Thus, a "round" of golf at St. Andrews consisted of twenty-two holes. That is, the golfers played "out" until they reached the End Hole. There they turned around and played "in" to the same holes. If two groups approached a green simultaneously, preference was given to those playing "out." The outgoing holes were marked with a small iron pin with white flags, while the incoming holes were marked with a red flag.

In 1764, however, the Royal and Ancient resolved that the first four holes should be converted into two. Since this change automatically converted the same four holes into two on the way back, the "round" was reduced from twenty-two holes to eighteen. And since St. Andrews was soon to become the arbiter of all that was correct about golf, eighteen holes soon came to be accepted as standard through-

out Scotland and England and eventually throughout the world.

Golf, of course, found its way down into England. It is written that the game was played at Blackheath, near London, in 1608. Actually, the Honourable Company of Golfers at Blackheath was established in 1766 and became the first club formed outside of Scotland. During the first half of the nineteenth century, through the 1850s, approximately thirty-five golf clubs were started in the British Isles. Some of these organizations soon disbanded, while others grew to great prominence. The first golf society founded on the European continent was the Pau Golf Club of France in 1856.

The history of golf is closely integrated with the history of its equipment. Actually, the history of golf, as we know it, could be divided into three periods, based on the type of ball used. The standard missiles during the early times were the wooden ball and the leather-covered ball stuffed with either wool or feathers. Apparently these balls co-existed for many years, with the featherie ultimately becoming the ball of choice. In 1554, the Royal Burgess Society noted a dispute between the cobblers of the Canongate and golf ball makers of North Leith. From this we can infer that the cobblers were then stitching leather golf balls. However, we still don't know for certain whether they stuffed the balls with wool or feathers. In 1585, there is a letter from a James Dickson to one Andrew Martin, asking for one dozen "commoun golf ballis." A little later, in 1614, the Earl of Caithness, describing the siege of Kirkwall, wrote, "Cannon balls of the besiegers were broken like golf balls and cloven in two halves." Since wooden golf balls would break into halves, but leather-covered balls wouldn't, these references seem to indicate that the Scots, like the Dutch, played with a "common" ball made of wood as well as leather-covered balls. It is not until 1743, in Thomas Mathison's poem "The Goff," that we find the first reference to the making of leather-covered balls stuffed with feathers. "Featheries," as these balls were known, required a great deal of tedious and skillful craftsmanship, and most ball makers could only make four to six top-quality ones a day. In addition, quite frequently even the best balls would burst on club-head impact, and the feathers would fly off in all directions. The "feather-ball period" of golf came to an end in about 1848 with the introduction of the gutta-percha ball. Gutta-percha is a resin or gum from certain types of Malaysian trees of the sapodilla family; it is generally brownish in color and resembles rubber in many ways. The "gutties," as these balls were called, popularized the game greatly. They were much lower in price, lasted longer, gave improved flight, and ran a great deal truer on the greens. The "gutta-percha ball period" lasted until the turn of the century, when we entered the "rubber-ball period," or the present era of golf. (More details on the evolution of the golf ball, as well as the clubs, may be found in Section IV.)

During the first half of the nineteenth century, clubs came to be divided into four classes: drivers, spoons, irons, and putters. Drivers were distinguished by their long, tapering, and flexible shafts and their small, raking heads. They comprised "play clubs," which had the least loft and were designed for use over safe ground only, and "grassed drivers,"

which had more loft and were designed to lift a ball from a heavy or downhill lie or over a hazard. Spoons were of four types: long spoons, middle spoons, short spoons, and baffing spoons, the distinctions being in the degree of loft. For a time there was also a fifth spoon, the niblick, a well-lofted club with a small head designed to drive a ball out of a rut or cup. Irons were three in number: driving irons, cleek, and bunker irons. There were two types of putters: driving putters, for approach work over unencumbered terrain, and green putters, for use on putting greens. With these sets, players negotiated their feather balls over holes measuring 80 to 400 yards.

In the era of the feather ball there were no championships as we now know them, but four of the great professional players of the period returned this card in a feather-ball match at St. Andrews in 1849:

	Out									
Willie and Jamie Dunn		6	5	4	6	6	6	4	4	5—46
Allan Robertson and Tom Morris, Sr.		6	5	6	5	5	5	5	4	4—45
	In									
Willie and Jamie Dunn		5	3	5	6	5	5	5	6	6—46—92
Allan Robertson and Tom Morris, Sr.		6	4	5	6	5	5	5	6	6—48—93

The Dunns represented the Honourable Company of Edinburgh Golfers, while Allan Robertson and Tom Morris were the professionals at St. Andrews. Incidentally, the score above was part of a four-ball match held over three courses—Musselburgh, St. Andrews, and North Berwick—in which Robertson and Morris defeated the Dunns by a single hole and won the imposing sum of £400.

Most golf clubs in the 1850s had professional golfers present. Their duties were greenkeeping, instructing, custodial, and even, in some cases, caddying. Occasionally, these early pros played in challenge matches for prizes offered by the "gentlemen golfers" of the various clubs. It was these amateurs who helped finance early golf competition.

While several so-called national championships were held previously, the first British Open Championship was organized at the Prestwick Golf Club in Ayrshire, Scotland, on October 17, 1860. Eight professionals formed the first field, which was won by Willie Park of Musselburgh. He played three rounds, all in one day, over the twelve-hole course in 174

strokes. Below are the names, *estimated* par, and length of the holes at Prestwick:

Hole No.	Name	Length	Modern-day Par
1	Start	577	5
2	Alps	385	4
3	Tunnel Out	169	3
4	Stone Dike	447	4
5	Sea He'therick	440	4
6	Tunnel In	314	4
7	Green Hollow	145	3
8	Station	167	3
9	Burn	396	4
10	Sauch House	213	3
11	Short Hole	132	3
12	Home Hole	418	4
		3,803	44

Ironically, Willie Park received no money for his triumph. His prize was the Championship Challenge Belt, fashioned of red morocco leather and silver, donated by the Earl of Eglinton. However, Park, his brother Mungo, and his son, Willie, Jr., who accounted for seven British Open titles among them, became a legendary trio of winners of money matches for large private stakes.

The Belt remained the championship trophy until 1870, when Tom Morris, Jr., earned permanent possession of it by scoring his third consecutive triumph. The British Open, which was by now "open" to the world, including amateurs, was held in abeyance for the year 1871. Competition for a new trophy, The Championship Challenge Cup, was resumed in 1872. Young Tom Morris, Jr. (at the age of twenty-one), won that, too, the only golfer in British Open history to win four in succession. His father, "old" Tom Morris, also won it four times, but not in succession.

Soon after Young Tom's death in 1875, two other professionals came close to duplicating his feat of four successive victories in the British Open, which was now being rotated between Prestwick, St. Andrews, and Musselburgh. Jamie Anderson of St. Andrews won it from 1877 to 1879. He was succeeded by Bob Ferguson, from Musselburgh, who won it three times and lost a fourth title in a row in a playoff. Peter Thomson of Australia duplicated Anderson's and Ferguson's feat from 1954 to 1956.

Scotland had exclusive possession of the British Open for the first thirty-four years. In 1894, the championship was held at the Royal St. George's Golf Club in Sandwich, England. The first Englishman to win the British Open, as well as the first amateur, was John Ball, Jr., in 1890. The only other amateur to win this event was an Englishman, Harold H. Hilton, who captured it in 1892 and 1897. The three dominant professionals in the British Isles at the turn of the century were John Henry Taylor, Harry Vardon, and James Braid. This famed trio, better known as the "Great Triumvirate" won sixteen British Opens among them. The first international professional match was held at Prestwick in 1903, where Scotland defeated England by 9 and 8.

While each club held its own amateur championship and there were numerous interclub matches, the first British Amateur championship was conducted by the Royal Liverpool Golf Club at Hoylake, England, with an informal competition in the summer of 1885. The success of this first competition prompted the host club to suggest that St. Andrews sponsor an annual amateur championship. A. E. MacFie, the 1885 winner over a field of forty-four, was

finally recognized in 1922 by the Royal and Ancient Club at St. Andrews as the first official champion.

The early years of the British Amateur were dominated by one golfer, John Ball, Jr., who grew up near the Royal Liverpool links and took part in the British Open at fifteen. Ball won the Amateur crown eight times between 1888 and 1912. He played in his last Amateur in 1921, reaching the sixth round at the age of sixty-one.

In the 1880s and 1890s golf courses, clubs, and facilities improved greatly and club membership increased rapidly in both Scotland and England. The game expanded into Ireland, Canada, and some of the British colonies. It was inevitable that golf would migrate to the United States.

GOLF BEGINS IN THE UNITED STATES

Golf was played in the United States before 1888, but it was not until that year that the St. Andrew's Golf Club of Yonkers, the first permanent American golf club, was organized. Actually, the legendary beginnings of golf in the United States go back to the 1780s at Harleston Green in Charleston, South Carolina. In the *South Carolina and Georgia Almanac* of 1793 there is reference to formation of a golf club in Charleston in 1786. Newspaper reference to golf in Charleston appears in 1788. Biographical material mentions the playing of golf at Harleston Green in 1791. Historians, among them H. B. Martin in his exhaustive study of *Fifty Years of American Golf*, pinpoint golf as lasting about twenty-five years at Harleston Green, ending at about the time of the War of 1812.

A golf club also came into being in Savannah, Georgia, before 1800—probably about 1795—and references to it continue until 1811. Apparently, the War of 1812 served to kill off the desire to continue play because not until after the Civil War was interest rekindled in the Americas.

The oldest continuous club in North America is the Royal Montreal Golf Club, organized in 1873. By 1880, four other Canadian golf clubs had been formed: Royal Quebec in 1874, Toronto Golf Club and Niagara-on-the-Lake Golf Club in 1876, and Brantford Golf Club in 1879.

Charles Blair Macdonald, a great mover in early American golf, recalled playing golf in the Chicago area around 1875. In 1883 or 1884, Colonel J. Hamilton Gillespie, a Scotsman who went into the lumber business in Florida, hit golf balls in a field that now is the main street of Sarasota. In 1881, one Andrew Bell of Burlington, Iowa, went to Scotland to attend the University of Edinburgh and, returning home in 1883, laid out four informal golf holes and played a few rounds with his friends.

In 1884, Russell W. Montague, a New Englander, got together with four friends from Scotland, organized a club at his summer home at Oakhurst, West Virginia—some two miles from White Sulphur Springs—designed a course, and played for two or three summers.

Soldiers stationed near the Rio Grande in 1886 played golf on a course they laid out. In 1887 a Scotsman turned cowboy, Alex Findlay, spent some of his leisure time hitting a golf ball around the Ne-

braska prairies. Golf turned up at Rockwell's Woods, near Norwich, Connecticut, in 1888, but lasted only three years.

Records clearly establish the start of golf at the Tuxedo Club, Tuxedo, New York, in 1889; it was being played in 1890 at clubs in Newport, Rhode Island, the Lake Champlain Hotel Course at Bluff Point, New York, and Middlesboro, Kentucky, along the old Daniel Boone Trail. Middlesboro traces its beginning to 1889. Predating all of these was the St. Andrew's Golf Club of Yonkers, New York.

Although the actual formation of the golf club at Yonkers did not occur until November 14, 1888, golf at St. Andrew's had its beginning nearly nine months before: on Washington's Birthday, February 22,

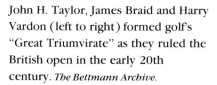

John H. Taylor, James Braid and Harry Vardon (left to right) formed golf's "Great Triumvirate" as they ruled the British open in the early 20th century. *The Bettmann Archive.*

Taken in November, 1888, at the St. Andrew's Golf Club in Yonkers, New York, this is the earliest known photograph of golf being played in the United States. John Reid, who founded St. Andrew's earlier that year, is at the right. J. B. Upham is putting, while Harry Holbrook (left) and A. P. Kinnan look on. The caddies are Warren and Frederick Holbrook.
The Bettmann Archive

1888, when John Reid invited some neighbors to his cow pasture across the road from his home in Yonkers-on-the-Hudson. Reid, born in Scotland, had come to the United States as a youth and had brought with him an interest in the game that was, by then, well established in his native land. In 1887, Bob Lockhart, a friend of Reid's, made a trip to Scotland and at Reid's request brought back with him a few golf clubs and some gutta-percha balls. Three improvised holes were laid out in the pasture, and on Washington's Birthday, Reid and neighbor John B. Upham gave an exhibition of the Scottish game. Watching as spectators—their interest soon to develop to the point of participation—were four other neighbors, Henry O. Tallmadge, Harry Holbrook, Kingman Putnam, and Alexander P. W. Kinnan.

Within a few months, more balls and clubs arrived from Scotland and the original three holes proved inadequate. The men of St. Andrew's made their first move, setting up their patch of recreation on a thirty-acre meadow owned by a local butcher, John C. Shotts. By the end of the summer of 1888, it became evident to Reid and his cronies that this was a game that would stay. That led to the dinner party at Reid's

home on November 14 at which St. Andrew's was formally organized. The minutes were kept by John B. Upham. Reid was elected President, with Upham as Secretary.

During the next three years, St. Andrew's made two more moves: to Grey Oaks, three miles distant, where the first United States championship, unofficial to be sure, was held in September 1894, and in 1897 to its present site, Mount Hope at Hastings-on-Hudson, where it was expanded to eighteen holes. All this, and more, of St. Andrew's early days was carefully documented in minutes kept by Upham, Reid, and their successors. This fact is most important in light of recent claims by the Dorset Field Club (Dorset, Vermont) and Foxburg Country Club (Foxburg, Pennsylvania). The Dorset Club claims to have had a golf course in 1886; the Foxburg Club maintains that their's was established in 1887. While either may well be the oldest golf club and course in the United States, no minutes or other documentation of date at the time has been unearthed.

In any event, by 1895 golf and golf clubs were flourishing throughout the country. As of the end of that year, at least seventy-five clubs were in opera-

Charles Blair Macdonald was one of the early giants in the game in the U.S. He won the first U.S. Amateur Championship in 1895. *Courtesy U.S.G.A.*

tion. The need for an organization to administer the game had been met with creation in 1894 of the Amateur Golf Association of the United States, later to become the United States Golf Association (USGA). The five charter member clubs were St. Andrew's, Newport, Shinnecock Hills on Long Island, the Chicago Golf Club, and The Country Club at Brookline, Massachusetts. The latter's role in early golf sometimes is misunderstood, since the Club was formed in 1882. Golf, however, was not played there until 1893.

It was really a mix-up involving championships that led to the creation of the USGA. In 1894, before there was a USGA, two different clubs in the East each held what it called the Amateur Championship of the United States. They were the Newport Golf Club in Rhode Island and the St. Andrew's Golf Club

of Yonkers. W.G. Lawrence won at Newport in September, with a score of 188 for 36 holes and, in October, L.B. Stoddard won at St. Andrew's, at match play. Thus, there were two so-called National Amateur Champions.

To avoid such an embarrassing condition thereafter, Henry O. Tallmadge, Secretary of the St. Andrew's Club, conceived the idea of a national association of clubs to establish uniform golf rules and to conduct championships. He invited representatives of the five clubs to a dinner in New York on December 22, 1894. This meeting led to the first official USGA Championships, both amateur and open, at the Newport Golf Club in October 1895.

Thirty-two players started in the Amateur Championship, entirely at match play, and the winner was Charles B. Macdonald, a Chicago Scotsman. One player, Richard Peters, carried a billiard cue and putted with it, in all seriousness. He went out in the first round before the more righteous play of a clergyman, the Rev. William Rainsford.

From a newspaper point of view, the social aspects of the Championship were perhaps more important than the golf, for the New York *Herald* published this thrilling account:

> At three o'clock society began to appear and fully 100 of the spectators were soon tramping over the hills. It was a bright scene; the ladies in their silks and the men in their red golfing coats made a scene of color seldom witnessed in outdoor sports. The game of the morning was C. B. Macdonald, the probable champion, against Laurence Curtis. The latter was not in any way in the game with Macdonald, for he has a low short drive compared to a long well directed drive of his opponent.

The first U.S. Open was played the day after the Amateur ended, also at Newport. It was at 36 holes, and the winner was the twenty-one-year-old assistant pro at Newport, Horace Rawlins. He scored 91-82-173 for the two rounds, which were held in a day. Ten professionals and one amateur competed. Horace Rawlins's prizes were a $50 gold medal and $150 in cash.

In November of the same year—1895—the USGA held its first women's amateur championships at Meadowbrook on Long Island. The winner, Mrs. Charles Brown, had 69 before lunch and 63 after lunch, and her 18-hole score of 132 made her the Champion. If this score sounds high, it must be remembered that the women were playing off the men's tees (there were no others) on one of the longest and toughest courses in the country. Few men, besides the imported Scots pros, could have broken 100 on Meadowbrook in those days, says Glenna Collett Vare in her 1927 book, *Ladies in the Rough.*

Thus, with the Amateur, the Open, and the Women's Amateur Championships, the USGA was launched. The USGA also drew up the Rules of the Game under which golf was to be played in the United States. Actually, the American rules followed those of the Royal and Ancient Golf Club of St. Andrews, Scotland, except for a few minor modifications.

The game of golf grew rapidly in America. In 1895 there were some seventy-five clubs in the United States; five years later there were more than 1,000. The state of New York had at least 160 courses, while Massachusetts boasted some 155.

While the USGA grew in stature on the national level, several sectional golf associations were formed and held district tournaments. Among the leading associations still in existence are: The Metropolitan Golf Association (1897), The Pacific Northwest Golf Association (1899), The Western Golf Association (1899), The Trans-Mississippi Golf Association (1901), and The Southern Golf Association (1902).

BEFORE WORLD WAR I

Because of the great popularity of golf in the United States, many professional golfers from the United Kingdom came to America to lend their technical skills to course construction and teaching. Many of them remained and formed the nucleus of the early professional competition. Harry Vardon, one of the famed "Great Triumvirate" and considered by many as the world's greatest player of this era, came to the United States in 1900 for exhibitions sponsored by A. G. Spalding & Bros., the sporting-goods firm, in hopes that his heroics might sell the public on the virtues of their new guttie golf ball, the *Vardon Flyer.* As far as the Spalding Brothers firm was concerned, the trip was not very successful because just about that time the rubber ball was introduced and the gutta-percha period of golf came to an end. However, Vardon's tour was no failure to American golf.

He won the United States Open in 1900, and his exhibitions created a great deal of interest in the game.

In the first decade of the twentieth century, American golf was ruled by foreign-born players. Willie Anderson, a native-born Scotsman, won four National Opens, three of them in a row (1903–1905), before he died at the age of thirty-two. His record of four victories has since been tied by Bobby Jones, Ben Hogan and Jack Nicklaus. Anderson's feat of three consecutive Open wins, however, has yet to be duplicated.

Alex Smith, one of five brothers, all fine professionals who migrated to America from Carnoustie, Scotland, captured the United States Open in 1906 and 1910. While Anderson, Smith, and the other winners—Aleck Ross, Fred McLeod, Lawrence Auchterlonie, and George Sargent—were by then United States residents, they were born in the British Isles. Johnny McDermott, who reputedly could pitch a mashie shot onto a handkerchief, was the first player born in the United States to win the Open. He did it in 1911 and again in 1912.

Then, in 1913, came the bombshell that literally made the game front page news in America. A twenty-year-old amateur, a former caddie, Francis Oiumet, defeated the great British professionals, Harry Vardon and Ted Ray, in a play-off for the Open Championship and thus became the first amateur to win the Open. As a matter of fact, an amateur won two of the next three Opens: Charles Evans won both the U.S. Open and the Amateur in 1916, to become the first golfer to accomplish this feat.

Of all America's early golfers, one of the most interesting was the amateur Walter J. Travis. Born in Australia, Travis, who came to be known as the "Old Man," came to the United States while still a boy and took up golf at the age of thirty-five. He won the United States Amateur three times and the British Amateur in his first and only attempt in 1904. Actually, he became the first "outsider" to win this British championship. Travis was one of the most accomplished putters in the game.

In the early part of our present century, amateur golf had a greater appeal to the imagination of Americans than professional golf. The reason was that the amateurs were homebred—not imported from the British Isles. Prior to the coming of Francis Ouimet and Charles Evans, Robert Gardner, Jerome Travers, Chandler Egan, and William Fownes were some of the amateurs along with Travis who held the amateur spotlight in the United States.

Women's competitive golf started in Britain with the first championship of the Ladies Golf Union in 1894. This event was won by Lady Margaret Scott. As a matter of fact, Lady Margaret won the championship two more consecutive times and then retired from competitive play. Other heroines of British golf were Rhona Adair, of Ireland; May Hezlet, also of Ireland; Dorothy Campbell, of Scotland, who won two British and two American championships between 1909 and 1911 and thirteen years later, as an American citizen married to a man named Hurd, won a third American amateur title; and Cecil Leitch, of England, who played golf like a man. Miss Leitch used a wide stance and played the ball well away from herself, had a strong palm grip, and did not consider it unfeminine to punch an iron shot. She won the first of her three championships of the Ladies Golf Union in 1914.

Beatrix Hoyt won three straight U.S. Women's Amateur Championships starting in 1896 before retiring from competition at age 21. *Courtesy U.S.G.A.*

Women's golf in America was dominated almost from its beginning by a teenager named Beatrix Hoyt. Starting with the second Women's Amateur in 1896, she won the title three straight times and was a medalist five straight times. She still remains the youngest winner, at age sixteen, of the Championship and retired from competition at the "old" age of twenty-one. The Misses Margaret and Harriot Curtis won four Amateur titles between them prior to World War I. Miss Campbell, as previously mentioned, was the first woman to win both the American and British Championships in the same year, 1909. Miss Gladys Ravenscroft won the British title in 1912 and the American title in 1913.

Before 1916, professional golfers were an obscure, poorly paid, lowly regarded lot. Unsuccessful attempts to organize the pros were made early in this century. In 1907, a regional association was formed in Chicago. It died shortly afterward. A New England association, organized in 1914, met the same fate. Then a Philadelphia department store magnate with $2,580 to spend finally got the show on the road. On January 16, 1916, Rodman Wanamaker, son of merchant John Wanamaker, called a meeting of professionals at the Taplow Club in New York. "Gentlemen," Wanamaker told the small gathering, "I think you should have a national organization. If you are interested, I will donate $2,580 as prize money for a tournament. I would suggest that the tournament be patterned after the News of the World Match Play Championship in Britain."

Among those at the meeting were John G. Anderson, A. H. Tillinghast, Joseph Appel, W. W. Harris, Jason Rogers, P. C. Pulver, and the eminent amateur Francis Ouimet. They were all enthusiastic. An organizing committee was selected with James Hepburn as Chairman, Herbert W. Strong as Secretary, and James Maiden, Robert White, Gilbert Nicholls, Jack Mackie, and Jack Hobens as other members. On January 24, 1916, they named Rogers, Hobens, Mackie, Strong, and G. C. Ennever to a committee to draft a constitution. The constitution was approved in New York on February 24, 1916. A total of 82 members, including 78 in Class A, were elected April 10, 1916. An additional 145 members—139 in Class A, 3 in Class C, and 3 in Class D—were added June 5, 1916.

The Association's first annual meeting was held June 26–28 at the Radisson Hotel in Minneapolis. Thirty-nine members were present. Robert White was elected the first President, George Fotheringham and James Maiden Vice-Presidents, and Herbert Strong Secretary and Treasurer. A twenty-four man Executive Committee was set up, consisting of nine members from the New York Metropolitan section, six from the Middle States, three from New England, three from the Southeast, one from the Central section, one from the Northwest, and one from the Pacific Southwest. Later that fall, the new organization decided to take Wanamaker up on his proposal to donate $2,580 as prize money for a tournament. A meeting was held at Garden City, New York, on July 14, 1916 at which it was decided that the tournament should be called the Championship of the Professional Golfers' Association of America. A trophy and a gold medal would go to the winner, a silver medal to the runner-up, and a bronze medal to each of the semi-finalists. The first tournament was staged at the Siwanoy Country Club in Bronxville, New York, October 10–16. Thirty-one PGA members competed. The winner was the late Long Jim Barnes, who beat Jock Hutchison, Sr., in the final match, 1 up. The winner's prize was $500.

BETWEEN THE WARS

In Britain no championships were held from 1915 to 1919, while in the United States championships were postponed during 1917 and 1918. Following the Armistice, the reign of the Great Triumvirate came to an end, and the brand of play of professionals and amateurs from the British Isles began to decline. On the other hand, America's golfers improved their game, and by 1923 it had become obvious even to the British that the leadership of the sport had passed to the United States.

The rise in the superiority of American golfers during the Roaring Twenties, sport's golden decade, was spectacular. One of the reasons for this increase in prestige of United States golf was Walter Hagen, undoubtedly the most colorful golfer of all time. He is considered by most experts as being the world's greatest match player. The Haig, as he was popularly known, won a record number of five PGA titles and a total of eleven major championships, plus capturing sixty-odd other tournaments and playing in more than 1,500 exhibitions. He was the first professional to win—and spend—a million dollars. The stories of his antics, both on the golf course and off, could fill many books.

One of the greatest accomplishments of Hagen is

The PGA of America was founded in 1916.

that he almost singlehandedly lifted the pro out of the caddie shack and into the clubhouse and first-class status. When The Haig went overseas for the British Open in 1922, he was informed coolly that he would have to dress in the pro shop, where it was necessary to hang his fancy knickers, silk shirts, and fleecy sweaters on a hook. Because he was a professional—and thus not a gentleman—he could not sully the sanctity of the clubhouse. Hagen met the situation by having his chauffeur drive his black limousine up to the front of the clubhouse and changing clothes in the back seat of the car. The stuffy British soon got the message. Barriers to the pros came down.

When Hagen won the British Open that year, he became the first native-born American to win this famed prize. (In 1921, Jock Hutchison, an American citizen, was the first person from the United States to win the Open.) Incidentally, The Haig won three more British Opens before he gave up tournament play just before World War II. The last tournament he won was the Gasparilla Open in 1935.

The twenties had other pros of great renown. Tommy Armour, Gene Sarazen, Macdonald Smith, Joe Kirkwood, Bobby Cruickshank, Leo Diegel, Jim Barnes, Jock Hutchison, Johnny Farrell, Al Espinosa, Horton Smith, Ted Ray, Denny Shute, and Joe Turnesa are a few of the more prominent names. The British professionals, during this period of time, could not make a dent in America. When Ted Ray won the National Open in 1920, that occasion marked the second time (Harry Vardon won it in 1900) that the trophy ever left the United States. Gary Player, of South Africa, in 1965, became the third foreign winner. On the other hand, except for

Walter Hagen (left), accompanied in practice for the 1926 British Open by caddie Jimmy McDonald, was largely responsible for increasing golf's prestige in the 1920s.
AP/Wide World Photos

1923, the Championship Challenge Cup—symbol of the British Open—remained in American hands from 1921 to 1933.

In the amateur ranks, the greatest amateur of all times, Robert Tyre Jones, Jr., blossomed forth in the early twenties. From 1923 to 1930, he won thirteen national Championships: four United States National Opens, three British Opens, five United States National Amateurs, and one British Amateur. His skill is pointed up most sharply by the fact that in eight out of nine straight United States Opens he was first or second; he won four and was runner-up in four. The climax of his career came in 1930, when he scored his Grand Slam by winning the four leading major golf championships of the world—the British and the American Opens and Amateurs—all in the same year. This record, as well as his thirteen major cham-

pionship wins, is unmatched. In 1930, after his Grand Slam, he retired from competitive golf at the age of twenty-eight.

In 1922, the Walker Cup Match came into being between selected British and American amateur teams. Possession of the Walker Cup was decided by four foursome matches and eight singles matches. The Americans won the trophy the first three years, and thereafter the matches were held every other year. Ten matches were held before the British finally took the cup in 1938. The only other times the trophy left the shores of the United States were in 1971 and 1979. The format of the Walker Cup competition was later used for both the Ryder Cup, among the professionals, and the Curtis Cup, among women amateurs.

During the twenties the only phase of the sport

where Britain had seeming superiority was in women's golf. In the early part of the decade Cecil Leitch carried on her domination of the game from the mid-1910s. Then, the incomparable Lady Heathcoat-Amory, nee Joyce Wethered, came along to become perhaps the finest female player in the history of the game. A flawless swinger, Miss Wethered at her prime was thought to be the equal of all but half a dozen men in the British Isles.

The number one woman golfer in America during this period was Glenna Collett, who later married Edwin H. Vare, Jr. In their only face-to-face meeting, Miss Wethered defeated Miss Collett 3 and 1 in the final round of the 1929 British Ladies' Amateur at St. Andrews. However, she won four United States Amateur Championships as Miss Collett and two more as Mrs. Vare. Most of Glenna's competition was furnished by Alexa Stirling, Edith Cummings, Marion Hollins, Maureen Orcutt, Miriam Burns, Virginia Van Wie, Mary K. Browne, and Helen Hicks.

In 1920, 477 golf clubs belonged to the USGA. At the end of sport's golden decade, there were more than 5,700 golf courses in the United States, including approximately 4,500 private clubs, 500 municipal courses, and 700 privately owned public fee courses. There were an estimated 9,000 courses throughout the world, of which better than 2,000 were in the British Isles. The USGA membership grew to 1,154 clubs. In 1922 the USGA started the National Amateur Public Links Championship for nonmember clubs. Also in that year, for the first time, admission fees were charged to spectators at the Open. This resulted partly from the need for controlling curiosity seekers at the Amateur the previous year.

The Depression years had their effect on golf. The club members of the USGA dropped to a low of 767 in 1935. At the same time, many of the professional tournaments cut their prize purses, and some were even suspended or dropped. But, with the upturn in the country's economy in 1936, golf's popularity was on the rise, too.

The pro tours, as we know them today, really got under way. History is cloudy on exactly how and when the Tour started. Most golfers of the period traced it to informal tournaments staged in Florida before and after World War I. The prize for the first such tournaments, as recalled by Long Jim Barnes just before his untimely passing, was a layer cake. Long Jim said that he and such players as Jock Hutchison, Tommy McNamara, Alex Smith, and Walter Hagen frequently got together in the days immediately following World War I—in 1919 and 1920—and played each other as if the world were at stake. "The prize," Long Jim said, "was a huge layer cake put up by one of the hotels. We washed it down with soda pop and whatever else was available."

Two of the professionals' wives—Estelle Armour, wife of Tommy Armour, and Jo Espinosa, wife of Al Espinosa—are credited with giving the Tour as much early impetus as anybody. They did it on the telephone.

Mrs. Espinosa telephoned friends in El Paso, Texas, and said that Armour, Espinosa, and Bobby Cruickshank would be happy to compete in a tournament there if sponsors could raise enough money to make the event worthwhile. El Paso golf enthusiasts were delighted. They got up the purse. The tournament was staged on greens of cottonseed hulls. Pros and amateurs of the area tried their skill against the three big-name competitors. The gallery was negligible. The total purse amounted to $1,000. But, the next year, the tournament was canceled. The ladies persevered. This time Mrs. Armour got on the phone. She called an influential friend from Chicago who was taking health baths in Hot Springs, Arkansas. With a towel wrapped around him in the steam room, the friend said, certainly, he would be glad to hold a tournament in Chicago.

That was the format of the early days of pro golf. A call to influential and wealthy golf enthusiasts in some far-off city, usually a resort area. Guarantee of a purse. Big-name pros. Such was the tournament life of the pros—fly-by-night events with small reward—until the circuit got under way. Actually, the pioneer of the winter circuit was the Texas Open, played on the public Brackenridge Course at San Antonio in 1922. A newspaperman, Jack O'Brien, got a group of wealthy Texans to put up $5,000 in prize money. Then scattered tournaments began popping up elsewhere. There was one at Sacramento, California, with $2,500 in prize money, and another in San Diego, six hundred miles to the south. The Los Angeles Open was started in 1927 with a total purse of $10,000, regarded as an earth-shaking figure.

The late Horton Smith once recalled that when he turned pro in 1926, the only other playing pros were Hagen and Joe Kirkwood, the transplanted Australian who later became famous as a trick-shot artist. Armour, Espinosa, and Cruickshank were teaching pros who made periodic forays to resort areas, where their appearances were mostly exhibitions. "Leo Diegel joined us later as the private professional for millionaire Edward B. McLean," Smith said. "Then came Wild Bill Mehlhorn. We played in the LaGorce Open in 1929 and I got a check for $1,000 for winning."

The summer circuit was started in 1930. The St. Paul Junior Chamber of Commerce raised $10,000 for a tournament to follow the National Open. Much more popular than the 72-hole tournaments were exhibitions by such players as Walter Hagen. Hagen was handled by Bob Harlow, a newspaperman who served as advance agent, publicity director, and promoter.

The first actual tournament bureau organizer was Hal Sharkey, sports editor of the Newark (New Jersey) *Evening News*. Working for nothing, he lined up pro tournaments while on assignment for other events, such as the Rose Bowl game in California and the baseball training camps in Florida. It was not until January, 1936, that the PGA hired a full-time tournament director. He was Fred Corcoran, an Irishman out of Boston with a flair for promotional gimmicks. He took the job for $75 a week and $5 a day expenses. When he started, there were eleven tournaments with prize money ranging between $3,000 and $10,000. When he left ten years later, there were more than thirty tournaments with prize money totaling $750,000. Currently, the touring pros play for over $40 million.

One of the most important tournaments in the United States, the Masters, was inaugurated in 1934 at the Augusta National Golf Club. This course was designed by Bobby Jones and Dr. Alister Mackenzie. Horton Smith won the first Masters with a 284, beating Craig Wood by a stroke. Over the years the Augusta club has become a shrine, symbolic of beauty, dignity, good manners, and superlative golf.

The better-known professionals in the early thirties were Gene Sarazen, Tommy Armour, Leo Diegel, Denny Shute, Ed Dudley, Harry Cooper, Macdonald Smith, Olin Dutra, Horton Smith, Craig Wood, and Billy Burke. The latter part of the decade also brought to the fore the names of such pros as Jimmy Demaret, Ralph Guldahl, Jimmy Thomson, Sam Snead, Ben Hogan, Byron Nelson, John Revolta, Paul

Horton Smith (right) receives the first place check of $1,500 from Col. Robert T. Jones, Sr., father of Bobby Jones, for winning the first Masters Tournament in 1934.
UPI/Bettmann

Runyan, Henry Picard, Harold McSpaden, E. J. Harrison, Vic Ghezzi, and a host of others.

In the British Isles, the American monopoly of their Open came to an end after Denny Shute's victory in 1933. The British pros, with Henry Cotton leading the way, kept the trophy in England until after World War II.

The leading amateurs after the retirement of Bobby Jones were Johnny Goodman, Lawson Little, and Bud Ward. A former caddie from Omaha, Johnny Goodman upset Bobby Jones in the first round of the 1929 National Amateur and four years later won the National Open to become the last amateur to take this event. In 1937 he added the National Amateur to his record. Lawson Little, Jr., won both the British and United States Amateurs back to back in 1934 and 1935. After this feat, he turned professional and captured the United States National Open in 1940 in a play-off with Gene Sarazen. Bud Ward won the United States Amateur title in both 1939 and 1941.

In women's golf, Virginia Van Wie, Helen Hicks, Maureen Orcutt, and Mrs. Edwin Vare still ruled the American scene in the first half of the 1930s, while Patty Berg and Betty Jameson led the way in the later half. In Great Britain, Enid Wilson, Diana Fishwick, and Pam Barton were the leaders. Miss Barton, who lost her life in World War II, won the British Ladies' Championship twice and was the last from foreign soil to win the United States Women's Amateur.

One of the most important developments in golf during the 1930s was the replacement of hickory by steel shafts. The superiority of the steel shafts showed up in the improvement of the play of the so-called "average golfer." Pro scores also improved.

During the early years of the Depression, the miniature golf course idea was started in Chattanooga, Tennessee, and spread rapidly throughout the United States. Garnet Carter is generally conceded to have thought up "Tom Thumb" golf, which required only a putter to play. But the fabulous rise of miniature golf was exceeded only by the quickness of its decline.

THE MODERN ERA

While golf in Great Britain came to a halt during the war years, competition continued in the United States, although in a limited fashion. All USGA events—the Open, Amateur, Women's Amateur, and Amateur Public Links Championship—were suspended from 1942 to 1945. However, there were plenty of tour events for those who were not in service.

The war years in golf were often called the era of Byron Nelson. His performances in 1944 and 1945, in which he swept twenty-six of fifty-one starts, should convince anyone of his greatness even though they were the war years and many of his colleagues were in the military service. Some competed now and then, however. He captured eight tournament victories in 1944 and eighteen the next year, depending on how you count the San Francisco Open, which was played in January and December of 1944. Some insist the December event was part of the 1945 tour. In any case, he took both of them. Eleven of his successes came in a row in 1945. In 1944, he also was second six times, third five times, fourth once, and sixth once. In 1945, he also was second seven times, third once, fourth twice, sixth once, and ninth once. Simple arithmetic will reveal that he placed first or second almost four of every five times he went to bat. His biggest prize in those years came in the Tam O'Shanter Open, forerunner of George S. May's so-called World Championships. It paid $13,462 in bonds in 1944 and $13,600 in bonds in 1945. Lord Byron annexed both, of course. No other tournament paid off in five figures during that time. He received only $1,000 for one victory, $1,333 for five others, $1,500 for another, $1,600 for one, and $2,000 for nine—all in bonds. By comparison, first money averaged $20,900 in thirty-seven official tourneys in 1967; in 1991, with forty-four events, it averaged $190,159. Harold "Jug" McSpaden was Nelson's major rival for money-winning honors, and the two became known as golf's "Gold Dust" twins. In other words, McSpaden won almost everything Nelson didn't during the war years.

With the end of the war and the return of golf to its prewar status, the sport entered the "modern era." In Sections II and III of the *Encyclopedia of Golf* are found records of major championships and Tour tournaments from 1941 to the present. Therefore, it is not necessary to dwell heavily on individuals and winners of various events. There were—and are—some professionals who dominate the modern era. These include, of course, such players as Ben Hogan, Sam Snead, Jimmy Demaret, Lloyd Mangrum, Julius Boros, Dr. Cary Middlecoff, Doug Ford, Tommy Bolt,

Gene Littler, Ken Venturi, Billy Casper, Arnold Palmer, Gary Player, Doug Sanders, Jack Nicklaus, Lee Trevino, Johnny Miller, Ray Floyd, Hubert Green, Hale Irwin, Lanny Wadkins, Tom Watson, Seve Ballesteros, Curtis Strange, and Nick Faldo.

What must be recorded is the tremendous growth of the Tour and the game itself, both spurred by television. The rights fees received from the networks sent Tour purses rocketing upward, while many of the millions who saw the golf broadcasts were inspired to try the game.

In 1956, a visionary entrepreneur named Walter Schwimmer conceived, produced, and sold to ABC a golf match between Sam Snead and Cary Middlecoff at Chicago's Cog Hill course. The golfers were paid $2,000 each, an excellent fee at the time. Snead won, 67 to 68. *All Star Golf*, as the program was called, gave birth to a host of other such shows, including *Celebrity Golf*, Shell's *Wonderful World of Golf*, *Challenge Golf*, the CBS *Golf Classic*, *Big Three Golf*, and others. Probably the most famous televised match was played in 1965 at the Houston Country Club between Ben Hogan and Snead on the *Wonderful World of Golf*. Hogan had previously lost to Snead in three play-offs, but this time he prevailed 69 to 72. Meanwhile, the popularity of these programs was not lost on the television networks, who began showing the Tour in 1959. Today, most tournaments on the PGA Tour are carried by a broadcast or cable network. In 1992, only seven out of fifty events were *not* on television in some shape or form.

Back in 1930, Bobby Jones's Grand Slam consisted of victories in the U.S. and British Opens and Amateurs all within one calendar year. Today, with the professional game dominating public interest, the Grand Slam consists of the Masters, U.S. Open, British Open, and the PGA Championship. To date, the nearest anyone has come to this holy grail of golf has been to win three out of four. In 1953, Ben Hogan won the Masters, U.S. Open, and British Open, but did not compete in the PGA, because its dates that year conflicted with the British Open. However, the attempts of the greats at the modern Grand Slam have been a major fuel to the publicity for the game, especially in the TV age. For example, in 1960, Arnold Palmer won the Masters and U.S. Open, then went over to St. Andrews to play in his first British Open, but finished second to Kel Nagle by one stroke. However, Palmer returned to win the British Open in 1961 and 1962, and in so doing almost

Ben Hogan holds the British Open trophy in 1953. He also won the Masters and U.S. Open that year, the closest any player has come to achieving the modern Grand Slam in a single year. *UPI/Bettmann*

singlehandedly put this oldest of championships back on the map after years of neglect by top U.S. golfers. Since the end of World War II up to 1961, the only victories by U.S. golfers in the British Open had been by Sam Snead in 1946 and, of course, by Hogan in 1953. Then, in 1972, Jack Nicklaus won both the Masters and U.S. Open, but, like Palmer, finished second in the British Open. Not until 1986 did it again appear that one golfer could actually pull off the Grand Slam. The Australian Greg Norman led every major going into the last round, but in the end only won one of them, the British Open. Perhaps because of the near impossibility, given the present level of competition, of anyone winning all four majors in one year, a player who has simply won all four is considered to be in a class by himself. Only four golfers have achieved this feat: Gene Sarazen, Ben Hogan, Gary Player, and Jack Nicklaus. The number of majors won in a golfer's career is another yardstick of greatness. Here Nicklaus is again pre-eminent, with his twentieth major (18 as a professional) coming in the 1986 Masters. He is followed by Jones with thirteen, Walter Hagen with eleven, and Gary Player and Hogan with nine each. Like Hogan, Lee Trevino achieved a unique "triple" in 1971, winning the U.S., Canadian, and British Opens in one year.

Another factor in the growth of the Tour has been the proliferation of celebrity or corporate sponsored tournaments. In the 1960s, the pros played in the Azalea, Rubber City, Oklahoma City, Baton Rouge, Mobil Sertoma, Lucky International, and other now defunct events. Today, they play the Infiniti Tournament of Champions, the Bob Hope Chrysler Classic, the AT&T Pebble Beach National Pro-Am (formerly the Bing Crosby), the Nestlé Invitational, the Canon Greater Hartford Open, and the NEC World Series of Golf. In 1992, more than two-thirds of the events on the PGA Tour had the name of a corporate sponsor as part of their official titles.

This change from largely community-sponsored events to big business is shown in the growth in prize money. First prize in the U.S. Open of 1895 was just $150. By the middle thirties, tournament winners could expect to earn about $1,500. The $10,000 of the forties was considered a major advance, but in the early fifties, when George S. May put his All-American and World Championships in operation, the winner took $50,000 out of Chicago for four days' work and earned $50,000 more for a series of exhibitions. This signaled the start of the big money era of modern golf. In 1958, the PGA Tour passed the $1 million mark in total prize money. In 1978, it crested $10 million; in 1987, it topped $30 million; in 1992 it topped $50 million.

The average purse in an official PGA event was $12,183 in 1945. In 1955, it had grown to $21,722, in 1965 to $79,125, in 1975 to $154,812, in 1985 to $538,096, and in 1991 to $1,058,182. First prize money in 1991 averaged over $190,000.

Another landmark in the PGA Tour's history occurred late in 1968. Up to that time the Professional Golfers' Association of America had run the Tour. However, for a long time the tournament players had become dissatisfied with the way the Tour was being managed, and wanted a larger share of the decision-making process. After a brief period when they broke away from the parent body, an amicable agreement was reached that set up the PGA Tour as a self-governing body within the PGA family. The first

Commissioner of what was then called the Tournament Players Division of the PGA was Joseph C. Dey; he took office early in 1969 and served until February 28, 1974. He was succeeded by Deane R. Beman, who is currently commissioner of the PGA Tour.

Under Beman's administration, not only has the value of tournament purses escalated at an unprecedented rate, but PGA Tour assets have increased from $730,000 in 1974 to $178 million today, while total revenues have increased from $3.9 million to $195 million.

The Tour made many innovations during this period. It began its own "near major" event in 1974, the Tournament Players Championship (now known as the Players Championship). Every year, this event has one of the strongest fields in golf and today is

Gene Sarazen was the first player to win all four major professional championships in his career. Only Ben Hogan, Gary Player and Jack Nicklaus have joined him. *Courtesy PGA*

considered just a rung below "major" status. The PGA Tour moved to its present headquarters in Ponte Vedra, Florida, in October 1980. Less than two years later, the Tournament Players Club at nearby Sawgrass (owned and operated by the Tour) hosted the TPC. The Club's course was the first to embody a new concept, conceived by Beman, of "Stadium" golf, the intent of which is to make the tournament experience as pleasurable as possible for the galleries of spectators. To do this, large spectator mounds and amphitheatres are constructed throughout the course that afford fans the best vantage points for viewing the action. At last count fourteen such courses have been built, with others in the planning stages. All of these new Tournament Players Club (also known as TPC) courses have been used for PGA Tour or PGA Senior Tour events.

The PGA Senior Tour began in 1980 with two events and $250,000 in prize money. However, its beginnings lie farther back in time. The PGA of America has long had an outstanding winter program for its members, including the PGA Seniors Championship, which started in 1937. More recently, Fred Raphael dreamed up a great idea for a tournament—why not get together the living "legends" of golf, and have them compete as two-man better ball teams at stroke play? The idea became reality in 1978, and the inaugural Liberty Mutual Legends of Golf event, played at the Onion Creek Country Club in Austin, Texas, was won by Sam Snead and Gardner Dickinson. The following year Julius Boros, playing with Roberto De Vicenzo, holed a birdie putt on the last hole to force a play-off with Tommy Bolt and Art Wall. The telecast of the play-off was one of the most

Deane Beman took over as Commissioner of the PGA Tour and has presided over a period of rapid growth. *Courtesy PGA*

thrilling in golf history, with Boros and De Vicenzo finally winning on the sixth extra hole. With such an exciting brand of golf on display, it was no accident that the PGA Senior Tour started the following year. Since then it has grown by leaps and bounds. In 1985, it had grown to twenty-seven events with official prize money of $6,076,000. In 1992, there were forty-two events with $21 million in prize money. Now, instead of old Tour players "fading away" in their forties, they keep honing their skills to be ready to compete as seniors. Arnold Palmer and Gary Player, two of the "Big Three" of the 1960s, were big senior drawing cards in the 1980s. The Senior Tour received a boost in 1990 from "rookies" Lee Trevino and Jack Nicklaus.

Other recent innovations by the PGA Tour include PGA Tour Properties (a joint venture of the Tour with the PGA of America), electronic scoreboards at tournaments, fitness training centers for the pros, PGA Tour Productions for in-house television programs, a professional Agronomy department, the Player Retirement Plan, and the Official Statistics Program. This last is a computerized program keeping track of players' performances in ten categories: scoring average; driving distance; driving accuracy, total driving, greens hit in regulation; putting, sand saves, eagle leaders and birdie leaders, plus a ranking which combines all of these in an attempt to designate the Tour's best all-around player.

GROWTH OF THE WOMEN'S TOUR

Interest in women golf professionals started after World War II. Certainly there were women professionals before that time. Helen Hicks was teaching; Babe Didrikson toured with Gene Sarazen in exhibition matches in 1935 (she applied for reinstatement as an amateur in 1943); and Joyce Wethered embarked on a tour of the United States, also in 1935, when deprived of her amateur status by the Ladies' Golf Union while working for a London sporting-goods store.

For the record, it is interesting to note that Miss Wethered and the Babe did oppose each other on two occasions that year in four-ball matches—once at Oak Park, Chicago, where the Babe shot 88 to the Briton's 78, and again at Meadowbrook, New York, where Miss Wethered's 77 was four strokes better than the former Olympic Games gold medalist. How-

Nancy Lopez put a charge into the LPGA Tour when she won nine tournaments, including five in a row, as a rookie in 1978. *UPI/Bettmann*

ever, it must be borne in mind that the Babe's power had not been properly harnessed at that early stage of her golfing career and that since she did not really come into her own until almost two decades after Joyce Wethered had quit tournament golf, no true comparison of these two tremendous competitors can ever be drawn. The Babe was reinstated to her former amateur status in 1943.

A Women's Professional Golfers' Association (WPGA) was eventually formed in 1946 by a pioneer woman pro named Hope Seignious, with the help of her father. A Women's Open championship was inaugurated, and Miss Seignious also initiated a golf publication that was tantamount to a house organ for the Association. But neither the Association nor the publication was flourishing when Fred Corcoran, manager for the Babe since she turned pro again in 1948, was summoned to meet with seven of the leading female pros in 1949. The women wanted leadership, proper promotion, more tournaments, and further

exposure. But Miss Seignious would not relinquish the reins of the WPGA, and so there came into being a rival body, which called itself the Ladies' Professional Golf Association (LPGA) and soon became the ruling body it is to this day.

Corcoran describes how in the first tournament he set up for the women at Essex Fells, New Jersey, everyone finished in the money—even Helen Dettweiler, who received $350 without ever teeing off. Her dog was sick! But Fred gives proper credit to Alvin Handmacher, entrepreneur of Wethervane clothing, as the man who "put the LPGA in business." Handmacher, eager to promote his merchandise coast to coast, agreed to a four-stop transcontinental tournament for a total purse of $15,000, with a further bonus of $5,000 to the winner. The tournament was to start in San Francisco, with stopovers in Chicago and Cleveland, before finishing in New York.

Helen Lengfield, publisher of the *National Golfer* and for many years one of the most admirable benefactors of the game of golf, then stepped into the picture. She augmented a spring tour on the coast to the extent of a further $15,000, and the women were on their way. As the tour expanded and the prize money grew over the years, more and more golfers were tempted to join the paid ranks, but in the formative years it was the Babe and personality "gal" Patty Berg who were the drawing cards at every event, with the diminutive Bauer sisters, Marlene and Alice, adding the change of pace in glamour and approach.

The untimely passing of Babe Didrikson in 1956 robbed golf of one of its most dynamic personalities and was a distinct, if temporary, setback to the women's tour. The Babe was not merely a prodigious hitter, a player who often brought off the impossible recovery, and one who amazed everyone with her delicate touch around the greens; she was also an inveterate performer. She loved the limelight, and she entertained her audience to the full. Had she not been stricken at the peak of her career, there is no knowing to what further heights she might have risen as a competitor or what paths she might have opened up for her fellow LPGA members in "fringe benefits." The Babe was the most promotable star women's golf has ever known.

Besides Zaharias, other fine players from the 1950s were Betsy Rawls, Louise Suggs, Marilynn Smith, Betty Jameson, and Mickey Wright. Of these Wright was in a class by herself, and became the LPGA's next superstar. Wright owned one of the great golf swings of all time, and was so formidable a striker of the ball, she invited favorable comparisons with Ben Hogan. With seventy-nine of her eighty-two wins coming between 1959 and 1968 (an incredible average of 7.9 victories a year), Wright dominated the Tour and set standards during that period—such as her thirteen victories in 1963 and her total of thirteen major victories—that may never be equalled.

Writing of her golf at Baltusrol in 1961, when she shot 69–72 on the final day to win her third U.S. Open title in four years, famed golf writer Herbert Warren Wind said:

"It is seriously to be doubted if Joyce Wethered or Babe Didrikson or any woman golfer has ever played a stretch of thirty-six holes with the power, accuracy, and overall command that Mickey did on that balmy July day. Her morning round was a lesson in how to score; she had no fewer than six birdies on her card. Her afternoon round was a lesson in shotmaking . . . I wonder if any golfer has ever made the game seem easier than she did that day. With the sole exception of Hogan's historic double-round at Oakland Hills in the 1951 Open, Mickey Wright's golf at Baltusrol strikes me as perhaps the finest sustained performance I have been privileged to watch in a championship."

In the LPGA's first year, 1950, the annual purse was $45,000, spread over nine events. By 1966, the purse had grown to $509,500, with thirty-seven events on the roster. This attracted many new outstanding golfers to the Tour, including Carol Mann, Sandra Haynie, Judy Rankin, Jane Blalock, and Donna Caponi. But the upswing didn't last. While Kathy Whitworth became the dominant player, eventually setting a new record of eighty-eight career wins, the schedule dropped to twenty-nine events in 1969, and then twenty-one in 1970 and 1971.

Up to this time, the LPGA's members were not only the golf show, but the staff and officials, too. They set up courses for play, made rulings, drummed up publicity, wrote the prize checks, even did the accounting. Following Corcoran as tournament director were J. Edwin Carter and Bob Renner in the 1950s, and Leonard Wirtz in the 1960s. However, it was obvious the Association lacked organization and direction, so in 1970 it appointed its first executive director, Bud Erickson. Two years later, the annual purse rebounded to $988,400 with thirty events, including the first Colgate–Dinah Shore Winners

Circle, the brainchild of David Foster, chairman of the board of Colgate-Palmolive and one of the Tour's big boosters. By 1973, the purse went to $1,471,000, and the first qualifying school was held.

However, also in 1973, the LPGA was hit by the biggest controversy in its history. Jane Blalock was suspended for alleged cheating and countersued for $2 million. She eventually settled out of court, but the LPGA lost nearly $300,000 in legal fees.

With its finances severely dented, the association had to push for profits. In 1975, Ray Volpe, a marketing expert, came over from the National Hockey League to become the Tour's first commissioner and secured television and publication rights, previously held by the individual tournaments. He contracted for minimum purses and multi-year contracts with sponsors and secured better venues.

Under his guidance, Tour purses went from $1,742,000 in 1975 to $6.4 million in 1982. The average tournament purse went from $50,000 to $176,000, and fields grew to 120 players. Television exposures increased from two to fourteen. Golf's first bonus points system—the Mazda LPGA Series—was set in place and the first non-team sport retirement system was approved and funded with a $400,000 1981 contribution. The LPGA moved its home to a permanent headquarters at the Sweetwater Country Club in Sugar Land, Texas. Most importantly, the association went from near-bankruptcy to being able to contribute approximately $2 million to charity from 1981 play.

Volpe also helped change the LPGA's image by selling the sex appeal of some players, over the objection of other LPGA members.

Laura Baugh, a beautiful blue-eyed blonde from Florida, was a sensation when she hit the Tour in 1973 at the age of eighteen. She became a star both in the United States and in Japan. Although to this day she has never won an LPGA event, she has finished second no less than seven times in her career and at the age of sixteen was U.S. Amateur champion in 1971.

Volpe's trump card, however, was not a stunning blonde but a dark, attractive brunette, Nancy Lopez.

In Lopez' first full season, 1978, she won a major, the LPGA Championship. She also won eight other events, five of them consecutively. She did for the LPGA what Arnold Palmer did for the PGA Tour. She was a great player who had great personal charm.

With a host of new talent from the post-war baby

boom, the Tour blossomed. In recent years, some of the outstanding players include Amy Alcott, Pat Bradley, JoAnne Carner, Beth Daniel, Juli Inkster, Betsy King, Patty Sheehan, and Hollis Stacy. The Tour has also attracted talented players from abroad, most notably Sally Little from South Africa, Jan Stephenson from Australia, and Ayako Okamoto from Japan.

Under Commissioner John D. Laupheimer, who took office early in 1982, the LPGA total annual purse topped $10 million in 1986. During that year, eighteen out of thirty-six events were televised. Like the men's tour, the old community-sponsored tournaments such as the Sandhills, Richmond, Ardmore, Oklahoma City, St. Louis, and Arkansas Opens gave way to events sponsored by corporations such as the McDonald's Championship, the du Maurier Classic, and the Nabisco Dinah Shore. At last count, twenty-three of the thirty-six events on the LPGA Tour had a corporation's name as part of its title. After serving as Commissioner for nearly seven years, Laupheimer resigned in July 1988. He was succeeded by William A. Blue, who resigned after less than two years on the job. Charles S. Mechem, Jr. took over in November 1990.

Unlike the men's Tour, the LPGA's majors have had a checkered career. This makes comparing the achievements of players of different eras more difficult. Between 1937 and 1942 there were only two majors—the Titleholder's and the Western Open. For the next three years only the Western was played. In 1946, the Titleholder's returned, and the first U.S. Women's Open was held at Spokane, Washington, under the sponsorship of the WPGA. There were then three majors from 1946 to 1954. (The LPGA took over operation of the U.S. Women's Open in 1949, then in 1953 the USGA assumed its operation.) The first LPGA Championship was played in 1955, and so for the first time there were four majors in women's professional golf. This state of affairs continued through 1966. From 1967 to 1971, the Titleholder's wasn't played, and after 1967, the Western was not played. So, except for one year, 1972, when the Titleholder's was again played, there were only two majors from 1968 to 1978. In 1979, the du Maurier Classic became the third major. Finally, in 1983, the Nabisco Dinah Shore became the fourth major. Only two players have swept the majors since the LPGA was chartered in 1950. Babe Zaharias won the U.S. Open, the Titleholder's and the Western Open, in 1950, and Sandra Haynie won the two ma-

jors played in 1974, the U.S. Open and the LPGA Championship. The closest any player has come to sweeping four majors was Mickey Wright's 1961 bid when she took the LPGA, the U.S. Open, and the Titleholder's, but failed to win the Western, and Pat Bradley who, in 1986, won the Nabisco Dinah Shore, LPGA, and du Maurier, but failed in the U.S. Open.

THE USGA TODAY

When the United States Golf Association (USGA) was formed in 1894, it had five member clubs. Today, USGA membership stands at 5,500. There are two classes of membership:

1. Member clubs. This is open to any regularly organized golf club in the United States. A regularly organized club is a permanent club of individual dues-paying members who manage their own affairs through officers and committees whom they select. Thus, a Member Club can be not only a private club but also a club of golfers using a public course. Annual dues and fees for publications total $100.
2. Member courses. This class of membership is open to any course not eligible for membership as a member club. Annual dues and fees for publications total $70.

In 1895, the USGA conducted three national championships, the Amateur, the Open, and the Women's Amateur. Over the years, ten more have been introduced: In 1922, the Amateur Public Links; in 1946, the Women's Open; in 1948, the Junior Amateur; in 1949, the Girls' Junior; in 1955, the Senior Amateur; in 1962, the Senior Women's Amateur; in 1977, the Women's Amateur Public Links; in 1980, the Senior Open; in 1981, the Mid-Amateur (restricted to amateurs twenty-five years old or older); and in 1987, the Women's Mid-Amateur.

Since 1922, in cooperation with the Royal and Ancient Golf Club of St. Andrews, Scotland, the USGA has also conducted the International Match for the Walker Cup between a team of amateur golfers from the United States and with players from Great Britain and Ireland. Similarly, the USGA, with the British Ladies' Golf Union, has since 1932 sponsored the

International Match for the Curtis Cup between teams of amateur women golfers. The USGA, on behalf of the World Amateur Golf Council, also has conducted the World Amateur Team Championship for the Eisenhower Trophy since 1958 and the Women's World Amateur Team Championship for the Espirito Santo Trophy since 1964.

An executive committee of fifteen members, elected by member clubs, directs the association's affairs. Under it, thirty-four other committees, with about 800 members, deal with various policy and administrative matters. There is also a paid administrative staff, headed by David Fay, the Senior Executive Director.

The USGA's single most important objective is to preserve the values and integrity of the game. To do this, it is active in many areas.

One of its most important functions is, together with the Royal and Ancient Golf Club of Saint Andrews, to write and interpret the Rules of Golf. In 1984, the Rules were completely reorganized, to aid compliance and interpretation. The Rules are contained in Section VI of this book. A pocket edition of the Rules is available for $1.00 from the USGA, Golf House, Far Hills, N.J. 07931.

The USGA also has developed our national system of handicapping—the USGA Golf Handicap System. It administers and enforces the Rules of Amateur Status, which define who is and who is not an amateur golfer. One of its major concerns is to preserve the character of the game and its emphasis on individual skill. To do this, it has developed standards for equipment. It also continuously tests new balls, clubs, and other equipment. Finally, the USGA sees itself as the custodian of the game's history in the United States. To this end, it maintains one of the finest golf libraries in existence, with over 7,000 books and periodicals open to researchers or merely for browsing. It also has an excellent golf museum.

THE PGA TODAY

The Professional Golfer's Association of America (PGA) has come a long way from its thirty-five charter members in February 1916. Today, the PGA has some 18,000 members and apprentices. It proudly defines itself as the "world's largest working sports organization." By its own definition, the PGA is a voluntary, incorporated, nonprofit membership association of golf professionals banded together in mutual interests. It lists its objectives as follows: 1. To elevate the standards of the professional; 2. To promote interest in the game; 3. To protect the mutual interests of members; and 4. To promote tournaments.

To be eligible to apply for membership, an applicant must be twenty-one years of age, a citizen of the United States, a high school graduate or higher, a golf professional or employed as an assistant to a Class A member of the PGA, or an approved tournament player (one who has earned his eligibility to play the PGA Tour). He must have been employed as an assistant to a Class A professional for a period of six months and upon application become an apprentice. As an apprentice he must earn thirty-six credits over a period of three or more years by attending business schools, serving his apprenticeship, and receiving college credit. Prior to approval of his application he must also satisfactorily complete a playing test and oral examination.

The PGA is governed by its twenty-member Board of Directors. The daily affairs of the association are managed by a staff of around sixty people headquartered at the association's administrative center at Palm Beach Gardens, Florida.

The PGA doesn't merely run the PGA Championship. It annually awards the Vardon Trophy to the golfer who maintains the finest scoring average in official events on the PGA Tour; a minimum of sixty rounds is required. It selects and fields the U.S. team that competes against Europe in the biennial Ryder Cup matches. It does the same for the PGA Cup matches, pitting U.S. club pros against those of Great Britain and Ireland. It hosts the PGA National Junior Championship for girls and boys. It also maintains the PGA Academy of Golf, a one-week instruction course for girls and boys aged 12–17.

The PGA annually spends more than $3 million on the continuing education of its members. It organizes the annual PGA Merchandise Show every year at the end of January. This is the largest golf equipment and apparel exposition in the world. It also conducts workshops in teaching golf, the Rules of Golf, club repair, and fitting and merchandising, to name a few.

In 1983, the PGA took over the administration of the World Golf Hall of Fame in Pinehurst, N.C. Overlooking the fourth green of the Pinehurst Number

Two course, the Hall has a great collection of golf memorabilia, artifacts, and historical items.

INTERNATIONAL COMPETITIONS

Other international competitions, besides the amateur and professional internationals mentioned above, include the World Cup, the Asahi Glass Four Tours World Championship, the Dunhill Cup and the Nicherei International.

The World Cup (called the Canada Cup until 1967) has been played since 1953. Thirty-two two-man teams play 72-hole stroke play aggregate. There is also an individual prize for the lowest 72-hole score.

The Four Tours World Championship begun in 1985, is a replacement for the annual team matches between the U.S. and Japanese tour players. It pits six-man teams from the PGA, European, Japanese and Australia/New Zealand tours in round-robin individual stroke play competition. On the final day, the members of the two teams with the highest points totals play off for the championship.

The Dunhill Cup, begun in 1985, is played annually. Sixteen nations are represented. Eight are automatic entries, six earn their spots through regional qualifiers, and two are selected by a panel. Three-man teams play medal match-play, in which the low score between two competing golfers earns a point for his team. Like match play, the event uses a knock-out format.

The Nicherei International is the annual ladies' team matches between players from the United States and Japan. Each country fields a team of sixteen players. Match play foursomes, better-ball matches, and individual medal match play are played on successive days.

GROWTH OF AMATEUR GOLF

The most important increase in the sport has been in the number of golfers and courses. The following charts, developed from statistics supplied by the National Golf Foundation, shows the growth since 1950 in the United States. The chart also shows how the number of golfers per course has increased over the years: in 1950, there were 652 golfers per course; in 1960, 689; 1970, 952; in 1980, 1,259; and in 1991, 1,754.

Year	Number of Golfers	Number of Courses
1950	3,215,160	4,931
1951	3,237,000	4,970
1952	3,265,000	5,020
1953	3,335,632	5,056
1954	3,400,000	5,076
1956	3,500,000	5,218
1957	3,812,000	5,553
1958	3,970,000	5,745
1959	4,125,000	5,991
1960	4,400,000	6,385
1961	5,000,000	6,623
1962	5,500,000	7,070
1963	6,250,000	7,477
1964	7,000,000	7,983
1965	7,750,000	8,323
1966	8,525,000	8,672
1967	9,100,000	9,336
1968	9,300,000	9,615
1969	9,500,000	9,926
1970	9,700,000	10,188
1971	10,000,000	10,494
1972	10,400,000	10,665
1973	11,000,000	10,896
1974	11,660,000	11,134
1975	12,036,000	11,370
1976	12,328,000	11,562
1977	12,500,000	11,745
1978	14,025,000	11,885
1979	14,612,000	11,966
1980	15,112,000	12,005
1981	15,566,000	12,035
1982	16,003,000	12,140
1983	16,514,000	12,197
1984	17,009,000	12,278
1985	17,520,000	12,346
1986	20,200,000	12,384
1987	21,700,000	12,407
1988	23,400,000	12,582
1989	24,700,000	12,658
1990	27,800,000	13,951
1991	24,800,000	14,136

As can be seen from the following chart, 1955 was a most important year in golf course development. It ended the period of flat growth in daily fee courses and the steady decline in private clubs. Between 1955 and 1970, daily fee courses enjoyed excellent growth, much better than private courses. They have continued growing up to the present. However, while the number of private clubs did grow appreciably from 1955 to 1970, it has levelled off in recent

Year	Total Courses	Private	Public	Daily Fee	Municipal
1931	5,691	4,448	1,243	700	543
1934	5,727	4,155	1,572	1,006	566
1941	5,209	3,288	1,921	1,210	711
1946	4,817	3,018	1,799	1,076	723
1950	4,931	3,049	1,882	1,141	741
1955	5,218	2,807	2,411	1,534	877
1960	6,385	3,236	3,149	2,254	895
1965	8,323	3,887	4,436	3,368	1,068
1970	10,188	4,619	5,569	4,248	1,321
1975	11,370	4,770	6,600	5,014	1,586
1980	12,005	4,848	7,134	5,340	1,794
1985	12,346	4,861	7,485	5,573	1,912
1991	14,136	5,113	9,023	6,764	2,259

years. The number of municipal courses grew slowly through 1960, but has grown much faster since then.

THE WIDE WORLD OF GOLF

Golf has gone world-wide, and it is still growing. Enthusiasts in over seventy nations on every continent now play the game. Their involvement ranges from Israel and Luxembourg, each with one golf club, to the United States, with 14,136 courses. There are nearly thirty-five million golfers in the world and over 21,000 courses. By 1993, even Russia will have an 18-hole course at the Moscow Country Club.

AFRICA

Botswana: Of the six courses in the country, the best is at Gaborene, located on the edge of the Kalahari desert. The country has 1,100 golfers.

Egypt: The game was here introduced by the British during World War I. First, the Gezira Sporting Club (a horse racing and social club) laid out a course within and around its racetrack. The Alexandria Sporting Club followed suit about 1920. Until 1956, the time of the Suez conflict, Egypt was the leader of golf in the Middle East. From the early 1950s, the Egyptian Open (begun in 1921) and the Egyptian Match Play attracted international stars such as Bobby Locke, who won the Open in 1954, and Gary Player, whose win in the 1955 Match Play was his first victory outside South Africa. After the Suez conflict, Egyptian golf declined. Today, there are five courses and 1,100 golfers.

Ghana: There are ten courses in Ghana, a British legacy from the days before independence (1957).

Ivory Coast: A beginning was made just a few years ago when the first two courses were built.

Kenya: Golf in Kenya was introduced by British settlers who established clubs in Nairobi (1906) and Mombasa (1911). Today, there are twenty-five courses and 2,000 golfers. Before World War II, most of the greens were "browns." In the late 1940s, however, experiments proved the feasibility of grass greens, and today only a few of the smaller nine-hole courses still have "browns."

Malawi: The first course, a nine-holer with sand greens, was opened at Blantyre in 1911. Malawi now has ten courses (most of them have nine holes and sand greens) serving 600 golfers. Many of the courses were planned and built by local golfers. Mzuzu, for example, was literally hacked out of the bush in the late 1960s by fifteen such stalwarts.

Morocco: Islamic in religion and culture, with a golfing history of some sixty years, Morocco leads the way in golf among Arab nations. Strong interest on the part of King Hassan, himself a keen golfer, together with a developing tourist industry, have led to the building of thirteen courses, five of which are eighteen holes, and all of which are grass. There are about 2,000 golfers. The most famous course is the Royal Golf Club Dar-es-Salaam (near the nation's capital, Rabat), which boasts a forty-five hole complex designed by Robert Trent Jones.

Nigeria: The oldest club in Nigeria is the Ikoyi Club in Lagos. Founded in 1933, the club has an eighteen-hole course and around 1,000 members. Nigeria's sixteen other clubs have small memberships and only two have eighteen holes.

Sierra Leone: Sierra Leone has two clubs, the Freetown Golf Club, founded in 1904, and the Yengema Golf Club, 1942. Both have eighteen holes.

South Africa: The first recorded golf in South Africa was in 1882, when a six-hole course was started by British Army officers at Wynberg, near Cape Town. By the turn of the century there were over fifty courses. Today, there are 80,100 golfers playing 379 courses. Up to about 1910, only a minority of clubs had grass greens. The blue ground from the Kimberley diamond mines made a really good putting surface, and was in great demand throughout the country. Today, with modern watering systems, this is a thing of the past. The finest golfers to come from South Africa are Bobby Locke and Gary Player.

Zaire: A small but thriving golfing community consists of four courses and 400 golfers.

Zambia: The oldest club is the Livingstone, founded in 1908. The country now has nineteen courses and 4,000 golfers.

Zimbabwe: Bulawayo Golf Club was the first club to be established in 1895, followed by Royal Salisbury in 1899. Of the seventy-eight courses in the country, twelve lie within a twenty-mile radius of Salisbury. However, by no means all the golf is confined to urban centers such as Salisbury, Bulawayo, Gwelo and Umtali. For example, Troutbeck, a most attractive nine-holer, is set against the background of a lake and mountains in the Eastern Highlands, beautiful country that should make every Scot feel at home. There are 6,300 Zimbabwean golfers.

ASIA

China: The Communist China *golf* revolution began in 1984, when a course designed by Arnold Palmer was built in Southern Guangdong province. Two years later, the thirty-nine-hole Beijing Golf Club opened. (The "extra" three holes are a practice course.) In 1990, Beijing hosted the Asian games, in which golf was added as an event. Several other courses are in various phases of construction in the Shenzen Special Economic Zone near Hong Kong. A total of a dozen courses is planned. At present, there are about 1,000 golfers, most of whom are Japanese businessmen.

Golf was first established in China by the British before the end of the nineteenth century. At the beginning of World War II, there were nine courses. All were eliminated when the People's Republic was founded in 1949.

Hong Kong: The first golf club, the Royal Hong Kong Golf Club, was founded in 1889 with just thirteen, mostly Scottish, members. Today, it has fifty-four holes. There are another four courses in Hong Kong, and 4,700 golfers.

India: The oldest club in the world outside Britain is the Royal Calcutta, founded by the British in 1829. By the turn of the century, India had nearly a dozen clubs. Today, there are 150 courses and 16,000 golfers. India owns one of the highest courses in the world: In the Himalayas, near the border with Tibet, Indian Army golfers have laid out a nine-hole course at 12,800 feet above sea level.

Indonesia: The game has grown faster here than anywhere else in recent years. It has seventy courses and 11,600 golfers.

Japan: In 1901, Arthur Groom, an English tea merchant, built the first golf course in Japan, for foreigners only, and two years later the first club, the Kobe Golf Club, was formed. In 1904, one of the Kobe members formed another club at nearby Yokoya. Here it was that Kakujiro Fukui, the son of a local farmer whose home was used as the clubhouse, became Japan's first professional golfer. In 1913, the Nagasaki course opened in the crater of a still-active volcano. When Nagasaki became a public course in 1922, the Japanese started playing the "barbarians' sport." From 1933 to 1945, foreign "contamination" was ordered purged from Japanese society. Not until about 1950 did the Japanese return to golf. However, it was the surprising victory of Torakichi Nakamura and Koichi Ono at the Kasumigaseki Country Club, near Tokyo, in the 1957 Canada Cup (Nakamura also won the individual trophy) that caught the imagination of their nation. Since then the game has enjoyed unbelievable growth. There are now 12 million golfers, 1,452 courses, and 3,860 driving ranges in Japan. Unfortunately, most Japanese players are only "driving range golfers" because of the expense and difficulty of playing on courses.

Korea: Golf in Korea dates from about 1920, but it was not until the present Seoul Country Club was founded in 1931 that the country had an eighteen-hole course. The club suffered badly during World War II and the Korean War. Now fully restored, many think that its sandy soil, undulating terrain, and fine stands of pine trees make it one of the finest in the Far East. There are now thirty courses in Korea and 260,000 golfers.

Malaysia: Golf is thriving in Malaysia as elsewhere in the East. The country's oldest golf clubs are the Perak at Taiping (1888), and Royal Selangor in Kuala Lumpur (1893). However, many courses were damaged during World War II and expansion only really started in 1953. Previously, most golfers were European or other expatriates, but during recent years Malaysians have taken up the game enthusiastically. In 1962, the Malaysian Golf Association comprised eighteen clubs. By 1972, the number had grown to thirty-six, and today, there are forty-seven courses and 7,000 golfers.

Pakistan: Before partition from India in 1947, the British were the main influence on golf in Pakistan. After 1947, with the departure of many non-Muslims, the game declined. However, a handful of Pakistani players have not only kept the game alive, but they have attracted many new golfers. There are now sixteen courses, half of which are nine-holers. Most have grass greens. At present there are 1,200 golfers in the country.

Philippines: Golf started in the Philippines when the Manila Golf Club was founded soon after the Spanish-American War of 1898–1901. Today, there are sixty-one courses and 18,500 golfers.

Singapore: Organized golf in Singapore dates from 1891, when Mr. Justice Goldney founded the Singapore Golf Club. The judge drove the first ball clad in knickerbockers, stiff collar, white tie, red coat, and bowler hat, to much local curiosity. There are now eleven clubs in Singapore and 9,100 golfers.

Sri Lanka: The Royal Columbo club, founded in 1882, is the oldest club in Sri Lanka (formerly Ceylon). However, the game is limited to it and two other clubs. There are 700 golfers in the country.

Taiwan: Golf in Taiwan started at Tamsui in the mid-1920s when the country was known as Formosa and occupied by the Japanese. At the end of World War II, the Nationalist Chinese fled the mainland for Formosa. There they found the American forces establishing a golf course on a battle training area. The Americans ran caddies' competitions and out of this program came Chen Chin Po and other fine players. Chen played with Lu Liang Huan in the 1956 Canada Cup at Wentworth, England, the first time Taiwan broke through into international play. The climax came in 1972, when Lu and Hsieh Min Nan won for Taiwan. Thereafter, Taiwan has produced many talented players, including Tze-Chung (known as T.C.) Chen, who led the 1985 U.S. Open only to lose it after double-hitting a ball and taking eight. T.C. won

the 1987 Los Angeles Open. Taiwan now has 22,000 golfers playing thirty-eight courses.

Thailand: Golf in Thailand (formerly Siam) originated when the Royal Bangkok club was started in 1890. The King of Siam, who had learned the game in Europe, encouraged the British to get things rolling. Some engineers, building the railway from Siam to Malaya, founded the Hua Hin club at a seaside resort more than 100 miles from Bangkok. However, the most progress has come recently, long after Siam became Thailand in 1939. There are now nineteen courses and 10,300 golfers.

AUSTRALIA/NEW ZEALAND/PACIFIC

Australia: There's a great deal of doubt about the beginnings of golf in Australia. The one fact known is that a Scot was at the bottom of it. The general consensus is that the first man to hit a golf ball on the continent was the Hon. James Graham, who had brought back a supply of clubs and featherie balls from Fife to Melbourne in about 1847. He may even have started a golf club. His hopes of launching the Royal and Ancient game "down under" were dashed by the gold rush. However, in about 1851, another Scot, John Dunsmore, was reportedly hitting a golf ball around a paddock in Sydney. Other Scottish enthusiasts may have started a club at Geelong as well.

It was an inhospitable environment for golf. Royal Adelaide, which claims a start in 1870, dissolved for sixteen years in 1876. The Australian Golf Club, founded in 1882, ceased to function in 1888 for five years. The Brisbane Club was founded in 1890, but later changed its name and, much later, amalgamated. The Royal Melbourne, founded in 1891, is the oldest club with a continuous existence. In 1904, the first Australian Open was held at Melbourne. It was won by the Hon. Michael Scott.

From that time to this, Australia's golf development has been rapid. Today, there are 1,440 courses and 686,000 golfers. Not a little of this expansion is due to the emergence of Australian golfers of world rank. The first of note was Norman Von Nida, who invaded British competitive golf in 1947 and became a leading money-winner. He was quickly followed by Peter Thomson, then Bruce Crampton and Bruce Devlin. More recently, David Graham and Greg Norman have carried the Aussie standard with distinction. Australia owns the longest hole in the world:

the sixth hole at Koolan Island Golf Club, Western Australia, is 782 metres (860 yards) long with a par of 7.

Fiji: Discovered in 1643 by the Dutch navigator Tasman, the first European settlement dates from 1804. The islands are now known for their sugar, tropical fruits, and gold mining. There are two eighteen-hole courses out of a total of fifteen and about 700 golfers.

Guam: First visited in 1521 by Magellan, Guam belonged to Spain until the United States took it (1898) in the Spanish-American War. Guam is today a major American naval and air base. There are four golf courses and 4,000 golfers.

New Zealand: Although legend has it that golf was played in New Zealand as early as the 1860s, the first verifiable date was the founding of the Dunedin (later the Otago) club in 1871. The father of New Zealand golf was an Edinburgh Scot, Charles Ritchie Howden, who emigrated and worked on sheepruns in Otago. Howden took the chair at the first meeting of the club and was elected captain. He later founded the New Zealand Distillery Company in Dunedin. The Christchurch club followed two years later, founded by two more Scots, Messrs. Duncan and Jameson. However, both clubs ran into difficulties, and the game lapsed for almost twenty years. Golf revived at Dunedin in 1892, and North Otago and the Hutt clubs were founded. In 1893, the first New Zealand Amateur was played at Otago, and was won by another Scot, J.A. Somerville. Thereafter, golf grew apace. Four more clubs came into existence in 1894, three more in 1895. By 1929, there were 129 clubs. In 1939, registered golfers totaled 29,000 at 328 clubs. Today, there are more than 100,000 golfers playing at 335 clubs. New Zealand's most famed golfer is Bob Charles, who won the British Open in 1963.

Tahiti: Famed as the classic "island paradise" of the South Seas, and the place where Paul Gauguin did many of his paintings, Tahiti also boasts one golf course with around 100 golfers.

BRITAIN/IRELAND

Britain and Ireland now have more than 1½ million golfers playing at better than 2,000 golf courses, with the following distribution: England—892,000 golfers and 1,200 courses; Ireland—105,000 golfers and 257 courses; Scotland—500,000 golfers and 444 courses; Wales—38,400 golfers and 100 courses.

EUROPE

Austria: The game in Austria dates back to 1901, when the Emperor Franz Josef I gave land at the annual rent of one krone for the course at Wien-Krieau, which became the Vienna Golf Club. By 1931, when the Austrian Golf Federation was founded, the number of players had risen to 1,200 and the number of clubs to six. Golf is growing, albeit slowly, in Austria. The country now has twenty-three clubs and 5,000 golfers.

Belgium: Although Belgium's first golf course was Royal Antwerp, founded in 1888, the growth of golf was much encouraged by royalty's keen interest in the game. In 1903, Leopold II said, "When British businessmen come to Belgium, they must have the opportunity of playing one of their favorite sports, golf." He later made land available for courses at Tervuren (Royal Golf Club of Belgium), Ostend and in the Ardennes (Golf Club of the Royal Castle of Ardenne). Leopold III occasionally played in championships, and his son, Baudouin, had a handicap of three. Belgium's most notable professional was Flory Van Donck, who twice was runner-up in the British Open. Belgium now has eighteen clubs and 5,000 golfers.

Bulgaria: There is only one course, a few miles from Sofia, the capital city. Paul Tomita, the professional, assisted in the design. More courses, intended to attract tourists, are in the planning stage.

Czechoslovakia: In 1899, when Bohemia was still part of the Austro-Hungarian empire, golf was played on the old Imperial common in Prague. However, the first course was not built until 1904, when the management of the famous spa at Carlsbad built nine holes in the Tepla valley. Golfers had to play over the river five times during a round. Another well-known spa, Marienbad, also built nine holes, opened by King Edward VII of Britain. Golf continued to be a fashionable game up until the Russian invasion in 1968. Czechoslovakia now has eight courses and 1,200 golfers.

Cyprus: Cyprus has one golf club, the Joint Services, in Dhekelia. It has eighteen holes.

Denmark: Golf found its way to Denmark at the turn of the century when F. Hansen and his sister, Mrs. Ingeborg Aagesen, took back clubs and balls from a stay in England and played on public ground near the famous Tuborg breweries in Copenhagen. The Copenhagen Golf Club was founded soon afterward. The game progressed slowly, and by 1954, there were twelve clubs. From about 1965 onward, the game surged in popularity. There now are fifty-four clubs and 21,000 golfers.

Finland: Golf was brought to Finland in 1930 by a Dane, Charles P. Jensen, who had traveled widely in America. The Helsinki Golf Club was founded in 1932 as a nine-holer, but in 1952 expanded to eighteen holes. The season in the south of Finland is from mid-May to mid-October, and is even shorter in the north. However, in summer the long hours of daylight permit the Midnight Sun tournament to be held. There are now seventeen courses with 3,200 players.

France: Although France was one of the first countries outside Britain to have a golf club—Pau was founded in 1854—the game has remained a sport of the wealthy and confined for the most part to the Paris area, resorts along the Channel coast, and the Basque country. France's most famous golfers have been: Arnaud Massy, who won the British Open in 1907, beating Vardon, Taylor, and Braid, then the "big three" of British golf, and Catherine Lacoste, who, as an amateur, won the U.S. Women's Open in 1967. France has 150 courses and 70,000 golfers.

Germany: In 1891, some members of London "society" who frequented the German spas at Bad Homburg and Baden-Baden took their golf clubs with them and amazed the locals when they started "digging up" nearby parks. However, it was not until 1895 that the first two German courses were laid out at Bremen and Berlin. The first German Open was played at Baden-Baden in 1912. William Roosevelt, a nephew of Theodore Roosevelt, was then president of the club. J.H. Taylor was the winner. After World War II, German golf had to start again from scratch. By 1962, there were fifty-five clubs, and almost one hundred by 1970. Today, there are 185 clubs and 60,000 golfers. Germany's most famous golfer is Bernhard Langer, whose victory in the German Open of 1981 was the first by a German.

Gibraltar: The island has one course, a nine-holer at Campamento.

Greece: Golf is developing slowly in Greece, mostly as an additional attraction to tourists. Greece has four courses (at Athens, Corfu, Halkidiki, and Rhodes) and 2,500 golfers.

Iceland: Golf began in Iceland in 1934 when Gunnlauger Einarsson, a Reykajavik doctor, founded the Golf Club of Iceland. Today, there are twenty clubs and 2,500 golfers. Despite a short golf season—limited to about four months, from the beginning of June to the end of September—Iceland has sent teams to several amateur international events.

Israel: Israel has one course, the Caesarea Golf Club, which opened in 1961 with an exhibition match between Sam Snead and long-hitting Englishman Harry Weetman. There are some 700 golfers in Israel.

Italy: Although one view of the origins of golf in Italy is that it was played in Rome by officers who followed Bonnie Prince Charlie into exile from Scotland (1766), there also is a pen drawing by Dutch artist Cornelis Poelenburgh, dated 1622, showing fellow artists Bartolomeus Breenbergh and Paul Bril playing the Dutch game of *colf* in the countryside outside Rome. Whatever its origin, golf in Italy remains largely a pursuit for the rich. There are sixty-six courses and 20,000 golfers.

Luxembourg: Golf in the Grand Duchy of Luxembourg is restricted to the Country Club Grand-Ducal de Luxembourg, founded in 1935. There are 800 golfers. Each July the club holds the Luxembourg International Amateur Championship for Ladies and Men at match play. The winners have been from America, Austria, Belgium, Germany, and Portugal.

Malta: Malta has one course, the Marsa Sports Club, founded in 1888. It has eighteen holes.

Netherlands: Whether the old Dutch game of *colf* was the forerunner of the golf or merely something closely akin to it, we do know for certain that modern Dutch golf history dates from 1893, when the Haagsche Golf Club was founded at The Hague. By

1910, four more clubs were opened. Play came to a standstill in World War II, but since then the game has thrived. In 1971, there were twenty-two courses, and now there are thirty-five with 15,000 golfers.

Norway: Golf started in Norway in 1924 with the founding of the Oslo Golfklubb, which has played a leading role ever since. In 1974, there were seven courses. Today, there are fourteen courses and 5,800 golfers.

Portugal: British port wine shippers built the first Portugese golf course in Oporto. Until 1929, the game was sporadically played at several courses of nine holes or even fewer. The second phase of Portugese golf was marked by the founding of the Estoril Club in 1929. For the next forty years, practically all Portugese championships were played there. The third phase has come from the recent development of the Algarve into a major tourist area. There are now eighteen courses in Portugal (counting two in the Azores), and 3,000 golfers.

Romania: The Diplomatic Club, three miles outside Bucharest, is the country's only golf course.

Spain: Golf started in Spanish territory when the Las Palmas Golf Club was founded in the Canary Islands. However, it wasn't until thirteen years later that the Madrid Polo Club was founded on the mainland. Generally, the game developed slowly. One reason was because it was played only by the very wealthy, another was that it was interrupted in many places by the Civil War. By 1954, there were still only fourteen clubs. By 1970, the number had increased to thirty-five. Today, there are seventy-nine courses with 20,000 players. Spain's leading golfer is Seve Ballesteros.

Sweden: The pioneers of Swedish golf were two brothers, Robert and Edvard Sager, who built a private six-hole course on their estate at Ryfors in 1888. However, no club was formed, and the game didn't spread further. At about the same time an Anglican clergyman in Gothenburg, the Rev. A.V. Despard, started playing golf in fields near the city, and formed the Gothenburg Golf Club, which existed from 1891 to 1894. Among its members were Edward and James Carnegie. However, it was not until 1904, when the club found a permanent home south of the city was golf firmly established. The game developed slowly, but surely. As late as 1945, there were only twenty-two clubs. Today there are 167, and 90,000 golfers.

Switzerland: The first course was laid out at Crans in 1905 by Sir Arnold Lunn, one of the pioneers of international skiing. The course was closed during World War I, and in 1923 the present course, at Crans-Sur-Sierre, was built. The Swiss Open has been held there every year since then, except for war years. Switzerland now has thirty-two courses and 32,000 golfers. The highest known course in Europe is located in Switzerland, at Sestriere, in the Italian Alps; it is 6,500 feet above sea level.

Yugoslavia: Before World War II, there were courses at Belgrade and Zagreb. However, now there is only one course, at Bled. There are only about 200 native golfers.

NORTH AMERICA

Canada: Canadian golf is older than American. There's speculation that the first swings were taken by young Scottish factors, who came to Canada as fur traders for the Hudson's Bay Company (established in 1670). However, there is evidence, from an advertisement in a Montreal newspaper of 1824, that Scots played golf at Priests' Farm on December 25 and January 1. In about 1860, it is said that Scottish mariners played at a three-hole course on the farm of their countryman, James Logan. However, the official start of the game occurred in 1873, when Edinburgh-born Alexander Dennistoun, along with fellow Scots John and David Sidey, formed the Montreal Golf Club. Queen Victoria made it "Royal" in 1884. The game has since spread to 1,224 courses and 1.5 million golfers.

Mexico: Mexican golf goes back to 1897, when nine holes were built in Puebla, a suburb of Mexico City. In 1907, the Mexico City Country Club was founded. Willie Smith, the 1899 U.S. Open Champion, was the professional there until his death in 1915, when the clubhouse was shelled during a rebellion. Smith was found in critical condition, hiding in a cellar. In more recent times, the Club de Golf Mexico, which dates from 1947, hosted the World Cup (1958, 1967) and World Amateur Team Championship (1966). Mexico has 124 courses and 17,600 golfers.

United States: The U.S. now has 13,004 courses and 24.8 million golfers.

CENTRAL/SOUTH AMERICA

Argentina: The British brought golf to Argentina in the 1890s. The newspapers of the time commented on the strange antics of the foreigners, but by the time the Lomas Golf Club was founded in 1892, many Argentinians had taken up the sport. The Lomas was followed by the San Martin and the Flores clubs, and in 1900, the Mar del Plata. Well-known Argentinian professional golfers include Jose Jurado, who nearly won the British Open in 1931 at Carnoustie, and Tony Cerda. However, Argentina's greatest golfer is undoubtedly Roberto de Vicenzo, who won the British Open in 1967. Argentina has 123 courses and 18,700 golfers.

Bolivia: Although one of the more remote golfing nations, Bolivia has nine courses. The best are the La Paz and Los Pinos, both of which are near the country's capital, La Paz. Bolivian courses include some of the highest in the world; La Paz Golf Club is 13,500 feet above sea level.

Brazil: Brazil's oldest club, the Sao Paulo Golf Club, dates back to around the turn of the century. It was founded by British engineers working with the Sao Paulo Railway Company. In 1923, the Gavea Golf and Country Club was started in Rio de Janeiro. Since then the number of clubs has risen to thirty-seven, the main centers being Rio and Sao Paulo. There are 10,000 Brazilian golfers.

Chile: Los Leones in Santiago, according to Roberto de Vicenzo, is the finest course in Chile. The oldest course is Granadilla Country Club, Vino del Mar, which dates from the turn of the century. Today, there are thirty-one clubs and 5,000 golfers.

Colombia: Golf began in Colombia in 1917 when the Country Club of Bogota was established. One of the club's founders, Enrique Samper, was introduced to the game in London in a novel way. While shopping, he saw a man making a swing with his umbrella and naturally concluded the man was mad. When told the man was a golf enthusiast, he took up the game and, on his return to Colombia, took along clubs and balls. In those early days, there were no lawn mowers, so, as in Scotland, sheep were used to keep the grass short. There are now thirty-five courses in the country and 8,300 golfers.

Costa Rica: There's just one course in Costa Rica and 500 golfers.

Guatemala: Guatemala has four courses and about 700 golfers.

Panama: Panama's 1,200 golfers play on six courses.

Paraguay: In Paraguay, 400 golfers enjoy three courses.

Peru: Peru has sixteen courses, most of them around the capital, Lima, and some 3,800 golfers. Several of the courses are very good, especially the Los Inkas Country Club. The highest golf course in the world is the Tuctu Golf Club, which is 14,335 feet above sea level.

Uruguay: The Club de Golf del Uruguay in Montevideo is the leading club in a country with four courses and 500 golfers.

Venezuela: There are twenty-three courses in Venezuela and 4,000 golfers.

WEST INDIES

Antigua: The country has one golf course and 100 golfers.

Bahamas: In the early 1770s, Captain Alexander Campbell, a Scottish officer commanding the British military in Nassau, brought golf to the Bahamas. Campbell laid out a course near Fort Charlotte. However, it was not until the late 1920s that the first permanent club was formed, the Nassau Golf Club. However, the biggest growth came fairly recently in a drive to attract tourists. There are now twenty-six courses with 1,100 golfers.

Barbados: Barbados has two courses and around 500 golfers.

Bermuda: Bermuda, a British possession since 1684, has more golf courses per square mile than anywhere else in the world. On an island only twenty-one miles long there are nine courses, played by 9,000 golfers. The best-known golf course is Mid-Ocean, designed by American golf pioneer Charles Blair Macdonald in 1924.

Cayman: The islands have one golf course and 100 golfers.

Dominican Republic: There are five courses in the Republic, but local members still number only about 700.

Guadaloupe: Guadaloupe has one course and about 100 golfers.

Jamaica: Golf has been played in Jamaica longer than anywhere else in the West Indies. The Manchester Club at Mandeville was founded in 1868, making it one of the oldest clubs in the world outside of Scotland. Tryall Golf and Beach Club has recently been the site of an LPGA Tour event, the Jamaica Classic, and the Johnnie Walker World Championship, an international men's event. Jamaica has twelve courses and 1,600 golfers.

Puerto Rico: The two courses at Dorado Beach are the best of the seven in Puerto Rico. Conceived by Laurence Rockefeller as an aid to the economy, the resort is situated on the northern shore of the island about ten miles west of San Juan. It began with eighteen holes in the late 1950s, but now has thirty-six. Both courses were designed by Robert Trent Jones. Cerromar also has thirty-six holes, also designed by Jones. There are about 2,000 Puerto Rican golfers.

St. Martin: The island now has one course and around 100 golfers.

Trinidad & Tobago: Trinidad has nine courses, the most outstanding being Mount Irvine Bay. Tobago has one course. There are 3,100 golfers.

Virgin Islands: Discovered by Columbus in 1493, the islands have four courses and 500 golfers.

Major Championships and Other Significant Tournaments

THE MAJORS

THE MASTERS

Year	Winner	Score		Runner-Up	Score	
1934	Horton Smith	284		Craig Wood	285	
1935	Gene Sarazen	282	(144)	Craig Wood	282	(149)
1936	Horton Smith	285		Harry Cooper	286	
1937	Byron Nelson	283		Ralph Guldahl	285	
1938	Henry Picard	285		Ralph Guldahl	287	
				Harry Cooper	287	
1939	Ralph Guldahl	279		Sam Snead	280	
1940	Jimmy Demaret	280		Lloyd Mangrum	284	
1941	Craig Wood	280		Byron Nelson	283	
1942	Byron Nelson	280	(69)	Ben Hogan	280	(70)
1943–1945 Not played						
1946	Herman Keiser	282		Ben Hogan	283	
1947	Jimmy Demaret	281		Byron Nelson	283	
				Frank Stranahan	283	
1948	Claude Harmon	279		Cary Middlecoff	284	

35

Sam Snead, left, chats with tournament founder Robert T. Jones, Jr., after winning the 1954 Masters. *Morgan Fitz*

Arnold Palmer and Jack Nicklaus combined to win seven of the nine Masters from 1958 through 1966. Defending champion Palmer helped Nicklaus don his first green jacket in 1963 and Nicklaus returned the favor when Palmer won in 1964. Nicklaus went on to win six Masters titles; Palmer won four. *UPI/Bettmann*

THE MASTERS (continued)

Year	Winner	Score		Runner-Up	Score	
1949	Sam Snead	282		Lloyd Mangrum	285	
				Johnny Bulla	285	
1950	Jimmy Demaret	283		Jim Ferrier	285	
1951	Ben Hogan	280		Skee Riegel	282	
1952	Sam Snead	286		Jack Burke, Jr.	290	
1953	Ben Hogan	274		Ed Oliver	279	
1954	Sam Snead	289	(70)	Ben Hogan	289	(71)
1955	Cary Middlecoff	279		Ben Hogan	286	
1956	Jack Burke, Jr.	289		Ken Venturi	290	
1957	Doug Ford	283		Sam Snead	286	
1958	Arnold Palmer	284		Doug Ford	285	
				Fred Hawkins	285	
1959	Art Wall, Jr.	284		Cary Middlecoff	285	
1960	Arnold Palmer	282		Ken Venturi	283	
1961	Gary Player	280		Charles Coe	281	
				Arnold Palmer	281	
1962	Arnold Palmer	280	(68)	Gary Player	280	(71)
				Dow Finsterwald	280	(77)
1963	Jack Nicklaus	286		Tony Lema	287	
1964	Arnold Palmer	276		Dave Marr	282	
				Jack Nicklaus	282	
1965	Jack Nicklaus	271		Arnold Palmer	280	
				Gary Player	280	
1966	Jack Nicklaus	288	(70)	Tommy Jacobs	288	(72)
				Gay Brewer, Jr.	280	(78)
1967	Gay Brewer, Jr.	280		Bobby Nichols	281	
1968	Bob Goalby	277		Roberto De Vicenzo	278	
1969	George Archer	281		Billy Casper	282	
				George Knudson	282	
				Tom Weiskopf	282	
1970	Billy Casper	279	(69)	Gene Littler	279	(74)
1971	Charles Coody	279		Johnny Miller	281	
				Jack Nicklaus	281	
1972	Jack Nicklaus	286		Bruce Crampton	289	
				Bobby Mitchell	289	
				Tom Weiskopf	289	
1973	Tommy Aaron	283		J.C. Snead	284	
1974	Gary Player	278		Dave Stockton	280	
				Tom Weiskopf	280	
1975	Jack Nicklaus	276		Johnny Miller	277	
				Tom Weiskopf	277	
1976	Ray Floyd	271		Ben Crenshaw	279	
1977	Tom Watson	276		Jack Nicklaus	278	
1978	Gary Player	277		Rod Funseth	278	
				Hubert Green	278	
				Tom Watson	278	
1979	Fuzzy Zoeller*	280		Ed Sneed	280	
				Tom Watson	280	
1980	Seve Ballesteros	275		Gibby Gilbert	279	
				Jack Newton	279	
1981	Tom Watson	280		Johnny Miller	282	
				Jack Nicklaus	282	

THE MASTERS (continued)

Year	Winner	Score	Runner-Up	Score
1982	Craig Stadler*	284	Dan Pohl	284
1983	Steve Ballesteros	280	Ben Crenshaw	284
			Tom Kite	284
1984	Ben Crenshaw	277	Tom Watson	279
1985	Bernhard Langer	282	Seve Ballesteros	284
			Ray Floyd	284
			Curtis Strange	284
1986	Jack Nicklaus	279	Tom Kite	280
			Greg Norman	280
1987	Larry Mize*	285	Seve Ballesteros	285
			Greg Norman	285
1988	Sandy Lyle	281	Mark Calcavecchia	282
1989	Nick Faldo*	283	Scott Hoch	283
1990	Nick Faldo*	278	Ray Floyd	278
1991	Ian Woosnam	277	Jose Maria Olazabal	278
1992	Fred Couples	275	Ray Floyd	277

Site every year: Augusta National GC, Augusta, Ga.

Figures in parentheses indicate playoff scores.

*Won sudden-death playoff.

TOURNAMENT RECORDS

Lowest score, 18 holes: 63, Nick Price, 1986, third round.

Lowest score, 36 holes: 131, Ray Floyd (65–66), 1976, first and second rounds; Johnny Miller (65–66), 1975, third and fourth rounds.

Lowest score, 54 holes: 201, Ray Floyd (65–66–70), 1976, first through third rounds.

Lowest score, 72 holes: 271, Jack Nicklaus (67–71–64–69), 1965; Ray Floyd (65–66–70–70), 1976.

Largest winning margin: 9 shots, Jack Nicklaus, 1965.

Oldest champion: 46, Jack Nicklaus, 1986.

Youngest champion: 23, Seve Ballesteros, 1980.

Most victories: 6, Jack Nicklaus (1963, 1965, 1966, 1972, 1975, 1986).

Most times runner-up: 4, Jack Nicklaus (1964, 1971, 1977, 1981). Tom Weiskopf (1969, 1972, 1974, 1975).

Victories in consecutive years: Jack Nicklaus (1965, 1966); Nick Faldo (1989, 1990).

Horace Rawlins won the first U.S. Open in 1895.
Courtesy U.S.G.A.

U.S. OPEN

Year	Winner, Score	Runner-Up, Score	Site
1895	Horace Rawlins, 173	Willie Dunn, 175	Newport GC, Newport, R.I.
1896	James Foulis, 152	Horace Rawlins, 155	Shinnecock Hills GC, Southampton, N.Y.
1897	Joe Lloyd, 162	Willie Anderson, 163	Chicago GC, Wheaton, Ill.
1898	Fred Herd, 328	Alex Smith, 335	Myopia Hunt Club, S. Hamilton, Mass.
1899	Willie Smith, 315	George Low, Val Fitzjohn, W.H. Way, 326	Baltimore CC, Baltimore, Md.
1900	Harry Vardon, 313	J.H. Taylor, 315	Chicago GC, Wheaton, Ill.
1901	Willie Anderson, 331 (85)	Alex Smith, 331 (86)	Myopia Hunt Club, S. Hamilton, Mass.
1902	Lawrence Auchterlonie, 307	Stewart Gardner, Walter Travis, 313	Garden City GC, Garden City, N.Y.
1903	Willie Anderson, 307 (82)	David Brown, 307 (84)	Baltusrol GC, Springfield, N.J.
1904	Willie Anderson, 303	Gilbert Nicholls, 308	Glen View GC, Golf, Ill.
1905	Willie Anderson, 314	Alex Smith, 316	Myopia Hunt Club, S. Hamilton, Mass.
1906	Alex Smith, 295	William Smith, 302	Onwentsia Club, Lake Forest, Ill.

U.S. OPEN (continued)

Year	Winner, Score	Runner-Up, Score	Site
1907	Alex Ross, 302	Gilbert Nicholls, 304	Phila. Cricket Club, Philadelphia, Pa.
1908	Fred McLeod, 322 (77)	Willie Smith, 322 (83)	Myopia Hunt Club, S. Hamilton, Mass.
1909	George Sargent, 290	Tom McNamara, 294	Englewood GC, Englewood, N.J.
1910	Alex Smith, 298 (71)	John McDermott, 298 (75), Macdonald Smith, 298 (77)	Phila. Cricket Club, Philadelphia, Pa.
1911	John McDermott, 307 (80)	Michael Brady, 307 (85), George Simpson, 307 (85)	Chicago GC, Wheaton, Ill.
1912	John McDermott, 294	Tom McNamara, 296	CC of Buffalo, Buffalo, N.Y.
1913	Francis Oiumet, 304 (72)	Harry Vardon, 304 (77), Edward Ray, 304 (78)	The Country Club, Brookline, Mass.
1914	Walter Hagen, 290	Charles Evans, Jr. (291)	Midlothian CC, Blue Island, Ill.
1915	Jerome Travers, 297	Tom McNamara, 298	Baltusrol GC, Springfield, N.J.
1916	Charles Evans, Jr., 286	Jock Hutchison, 288	Minikahda Club, Minneapolis, Minn.
1917–1918 Not played			
1919	Walter Hagen, 301 (77)	Michael Brady, 301 (78)	Brae Burn CC, W. Newton, Mass.
1920	Edward Ray, 295	Harry Vardon, Jack Burke, Leo Diegel, Jock Hutchison, 296	Inverness Club, Toledo, Ohio
1921	Jim Barnes, 289	Walter Hagen, Fred McLeod, 298	Columbia CC, Chevy Chase, Md.
1922	Gene Sarazen, 288	R.T. Jones, Jr., John Black, 289	Skokie CC, Glencoe, Ill.
1923	R.T. Jones, Jr., 296 (76)	Bobby Cruickshank, 296 (78)	Inwood CC, Inwood, N.Y.
1924	Cyril Walker, 297	R.T. Jones, Jr., 300	Oakland Hills CC, Birmingham, Mich.
1925	William Macfarlane, 291 (75–72)	R.T. Jones, Jr., 291 (75–73)	Worcester CC, Worcester, Mass.
1926	R. T. Jones, Jr., 293	Joe Turnesa, 294	Scioto CC, Columbus, Ohio
1927	Tommy Armour, 301 (76)	Harry Cooper, 301 (79)	Oakmont CC, Oakmont, Pa.
1928	Johnny Farrell, 294 (143)	R.T. Jones, Jr. (144)	Olympia Fields CC, Mateson, Ill.
1929	R.T. Jones, Jr., 294 (141)	Al Espinosa, 294 (164)	Winged Foot GC, Mamaroneck, NY.
1930	R.T. Jones, Jr., 287	Macdonald Smith, 289	Interlachen CC, Minneapolis, Minn.
1931	Billy Burke, 292 (149–148)	George Von Elm, 292 (149–149)	Inverness Club, Toledo, Ohio
1932	Gene Sarazen, 286	Bobby Cruickshank, T. Philip Perkins, 289	Fresh Meadow CC, Flushing, N.Y.
1933	John Goodman, 287	Ralph Guldahl, 288	North Shore CC, Glenview, Ill.
1934	Olin Dutra, 293	Gene Sarazen, 294	Merion Cricket Club, Ardmore, Pa.
1935	Sam Parks, Jr., 299	Jimmy Thomson, 301	Oakmont CC, Oakmont, Pa.
1936	Tony Manero, 282	Harry Cooper, 284	Baltusrol CC, Springfield, N.J.
1937	Ralph Guldahl, 281	Sam Snead, 283	Oakland Hills CC, Birmingham, Mich.

U.S. OPEN (continued)

Year	Winner, Score	Runner-Up, Score	Site
1938	Ralph Guldahl, 284	Dick Metz, 290	Cherry Hills Club, Englewood, Colo.
1939	Byron Nelson, 284 (68–70)	Craig Wood, 284 (68–73), Denny Shute, 284 (76)	Philadelphia CC, W. Conshohocken, Pa.
1940	Lawson Little, 287 (70)	Gene Sarazen, 287 (73)	Canterbury GC, Cleveland, Ohio
1941	Craig Wood, 284	Denny Shute, 287	Colonial Club, Fort Worth, Tex.
1942–1945 Not played			
1946	Lloyd Mangrum, 284 (72–72)	Byron Nelson, 284 (72–73), Vic Ghezzi, 284 (72–73)	Canterbury CC, Cleveland, Ohio
1947	Lew Worsham, 282 (69)	Sam Snead, 282 (70)	St. Louis CC, Clayton, Mo.
1948	Ben Hogan, 276	Jimmy Demaret, 278	Riviera CC, Los Angeles, Cal.
1949	Cary Middlecoff, 286	Sam Snead, Clayton Heafner, 287	Medinah CC, Medinah, Ill.
1950	Ben Hogan, 287 (69)	Lloyd Mangrum, 287 (73), George Fazio, 287 (75)	Merion CC, Ardmore, Pa.
1951	Ben Hogan, 287	Clayton Heafner, 289	Oakland Hills CC, Birmingham, Mich.
1952	Julius Boros, 281	Ed Oliver, 285	Northwood Club, Dallas, Tex.
1953	Ben Hogan, 283	Sam Snead, 289	Oakmont CC, Oakmont, Pa.
1954	Ed Furgol, 284	Gene Littler, 285	Baltusrol GC, Springfield, N.J.
1955	Jack Fleck, 287 (69)	Ben Hogan, 287 (72)	Olympic Club, San Francisco, Cal.
1956	Cary Middlecoff, 281	Julius Boros, Ben Hogan, 282	Oak Hill CC, Rochester, N.Y.
1957	Dick Mayer, 282 (72)	Cary Middlecoff, 282 (79)	Inverness Club, Toledo, Ohio
1958	Tommy Bolt, 283	Gary Player, 287	Southern Hills CC, Tulsa, Okla.
1959	Billy Casper, 282	Bob Rosburg, 283	Winged Foot GC, Mamaroneck, N.Y.
1960	Arnold Palmer, 280	Jack Nicklaus, 282	Cherry Hills CC, Englewood, Colo.
1961	Gene Littler, 281	Doug Sanders, Bob Goalby, 282	Oakland Hills CC, Birmingham, Mich.
1962	Jack Nicklaus, 283 (71)	Arnold Palmer, 283 (74)	Oakmont CC, Oakmont, Pa.
1963	Julius Boros, 293 (70)	Jacky Cupit, 293 (73), Arnold Palmer, 293 (76)	The Country Club, Brookline, Mass.
1964	Ken Venturi, 278	Tommy Jacobs, 282	Congressional CC, Washington, D.C.
1965	Gary Player, 282 (71)	Kel Nagle, 282 (74)	Bellerive CC, St. Louis, Mo.
1966	Billy Casper, 278 (69)	Arnold Palmer, 278 (73)	Olympic Club, San Francisco, Cal.
1967	Jack Nicklaus, 275	Arnold Palmer, 279	Baltusrol GC, Springfield, N.J.
1968	Lee Trevino, 275	Jack Nicklaus, 279	Oak Hill CC, Rochester, N.Y.
1969	Orville Moody, 281	Deane Beman, Al Geiberger, Bob Rosburg, 282	Champions GC, Houston, Tex.
1970	Tony Jacklin, 281	Dave Hill, 288	Hazeltine National GC, Chaska, Minn.

Jack Nicklaus celebrates after winning his fourth U.S. Open title in 1980. Willie Anderson, Bobby Jones and Ben Hogan are the only players with four Open titles. *Wide World Photos*

U.S. OPEN (Continued)

Year	Winner, Score	Runner-Up, Score	Site
1971	Lee Trevino, 280 (68)	Jack Nicklaus, 280 (71)	Merion GC, Ardmore, Pa.
1972	Jack Nicklaus, 290	Bruce Crampton, 293	Pebble Beach GC, Pebble Beach, Cal.
1973	Johnny Miller, 279	John Schlee, 280	Oakmont CC, Oakmont, Pa.
1974	Hale Irwin, 287	Forrest Fezler, 289	Winged Foot GC, Mamaroneck, N.Y.
1975	Lou Graham, 287 (71)	John Mahaffey, 287 (73)	Medinah CC, Medinah, Ill.
1976	Jerry Pate, 277	Tom Weiskopf, Al Geiberger, 279	Atlanta AC, Duluth, Ga.
1977	Hubert Green, 278	Lou Graham, 279	Southern Hills CC, Tulsa, Okla.
1978	Andy North, 285	J.C. Snead, Dave Stockton, 286	Cherry Hills CC, Englewood, Colo.
1979	Hale Irwin, 284	Gary Player, Jerry Pate 286	Inverness Club, Toledo, Ohio
1980	Jack Nicklaus, 272	Isao Aoki, 274	Baltusrol GC, Springfield, N.J.
1981	David Graham, 273	Bill Rogers, George Burns, 276	Merion GC, Ardmore, Pa.
1982	Tom Watson, 282	Jack Nicklaus, 284	Pebble Beach GL, Pebble Beach, Cal.
1983	Larry Nelson, 280	Tom Watson, 281	Oakmont CC, Oakmont, Pa.

U.S. OPEN (continued)

Year	Winner, Score	Runner-Up, Score	Site
1984	Fuzzy Zoeller, 276 (67)	Greg Norman, 276 (75)	Winged Foot GC, Mamaroneck, N.Y.
1985	Andy North, 279	Denis Watson, Dave Barr, Tze-Chung Chen, 280	Oakland Hills CC, Birmingham, Mich.
1986	Ray Floyd, 279	Lanny Wadkins, Chip Beck, 281	Shinnecock Hills GC, Southampton, N.Y.
1987	Scott Simpson, 277	Tom Watson, 278	Olympic Club, San Francisco, Cal.
1988	Curtis Strange, 278 (71)	Nick Faldo, 278 (75)	The Country Club, Brookline, Mass.
1989	Curtis Strange, 278	Chip Beck, Mark McCumber, Ian Woosnam, 279	Oak Hill CC, Rochester, N.Y.
1990	Hale Irwin, 280 (74)*	Mike Donald, 280 (74)	Medinah CC, Medinah, Ill.
1991	Payne Stewart, 282 (75)	Scott Simpson (77)	Hazeltine National GC, Chaska, Minn.
1992	Tom Kite, 285	Jeff Sluman, 287	Pebble Beach GL, Pebble Beach, Cal.

Figures in parentheses indicate playoff scores.

* Won in sudden-death after eighteen-hole playoff was tied.

Note: In 1917, an Open Patriotic Tournament was conducted for the benefit of the American Red Cross at Whitemarsh Valley CC, Philadelphia, Pa. Winner: Jock Hutchison, 292; runner-up: Tom McNamara, 299. In 1942, a Hale America tournament was conducted for the benefit of the Navy Relief Society and the United Service Organization at Ridgemoor CC, Chicago, Ill. Winner: Ben Hogan, 271; runners-up: Jimmy Demaret and Mike Turnesa, 274.

TOURNAMENT RECORDS

Lowest score, 18 holes: 63, Johnny Miller, 1973, fourth round at Oakmont; Jack Nicklaus, 1980, first round at Baltusrol; Tom Weiskopf, 1980, first round at Baltusrol.

Lowest score, 36 holes: 132, Larry Nelson (65–67), 1983, third and fourth rounds at Oakmont.

Lowest score, 54 holes: 203, George Burns (69–66–68), 1981, first through third rounds at Baltusrol; Tze-Chung Chen (65–69–69), 1985, first through third rounds at Oakland Hills.

Lowest score, 72 holes: 272, Jack Nicklaus (63–71–70–68), 1980, Baltusrol.

Largest winning margin: 11, Willie Smith, 1899.

Oldest champion: 45, Hale Irwin, 1990.

Youngest champion: 19, John McDermott, 1911.

Most victories: 4, Willie Anderson (1901, 1903, 1904, 1905); R. T. Jones, Jr. (1923, 1926, 1929, 1930); Ben Hogan (1948, 1950, 1951, 1953); Jack Nicklaus (1962, 1967, 1972, 1980).

Most times runner-up: 4, Sam Snead (1937, 1947, 1949, 1953); T. Jones, Jr. (1922, 1924, 1925, 1928); Arnold Palmer (1962, 1963, 1966, 1967); Jack Nicklaus (1960, 1968, 1971, 1982).

Victories in consecutive years: Willie Anderson (1903–04–05); John McDermott (1911–1912); R. T. Jones, Jr. (1929–1930); Ralph Guldahl (1937–1938); Ben Hogan (1950–1951); Curtis Strange (1988–1989).

BRITISH OPEN

Year	Winner, Score	Runner-Up	Site
1860	Willie Park, 174	Tom Morris, Sr., 176	Prestwick, Scotland
1861	Tom Morris, Sr., 163	Willie Park, 167	Prestwick, Scotland
1862	Tom Morris, Sr., 163	Willie Park, 176	Prestwick, Scotland
1863	Willie Park, 168	Tom Morris, Sr., 170	Prestwick, Scotland
1864	Tom Morris, Sr., 167	Andrew Strath, 169	Prestwick, Scotland
1865	Andrew Strath, 162	Willie Park, 164	Prestwick, Scotland
1866	Willie Park, 169	David Park, 171	Prestwick, Scotland
1867	Tom Morris, Sr., 170	Willie Park, 172	Prestwick, Scotland
1868	Tom Morris, Jr., 157	Robert Andrew, 159	Prestwick, Scotland
1869	Tom Morris, Jr., 154	Tom Morris, Sr., 157	Prestwick, Scotland
1870	Tom Morris, Jr., 149	Bob Kirk, David Strath, 161	Prestwick, Scotland
1871	Not played		
1872	Tom Morris, Jr., 166	David Strath, 169	Prestwick, Scotland
1873	Tom Kidd, 179	Jamie Anderson, 180	St. Andrews, Scotland
1874	Mungo Park, 159	Tom Morris, Jr., 161	Musselburgh, Scotland
1875	Willie Park, 166	Bob Martin, 168	Prestwick, Scotland
1876	Bob Martin, 176	David Strath, 176 (refused playoff)	St. Andrews, Scotland
1877	Jamie Anderson, 160	Bob Pringle, 162	Musselburgh, Scotland
1878	Jamie Anderson, 157	Bob Kirk, 159	Prestwick, Scotland
1879	Jamie Anderson, 169	James Allan, Andrew Kirkaldy, 172	St. Andrews, Scotland
1880	Bob Ferguson, 162	Peter Paxton, 167	Musselburgh, Scotland
1881	Bob Ferguson, 170	Jamie Anderson, 173	Prestwick, Scotland
1882	Bob Ferguson, 171	Willie Fernie, 174	St. Andrews, Scotland
1883	Willie Fernie, 159 (158)	Robert Ferguson, 159 (159)	Musselburgh, Scotland
1884	Jack Simpson, 160	D. Rolland, Willie Fernie, 164	Prestwick, Scotland
1885	Bob Martin, 171	Archie Simpson, 172	St. Andrews, Scotland
1886	David Brown, 157	Willie Campbell, 159	Musselburgh, Scotland
1887	Willie Park, Jr., 161	Bob Martin, 172	Prestwick, Scotland
1888	Jack Burns, 171	D. Anderson, B. Sayers, 172	St. Andrews, Scotland
1889	Willie Park, Jr., 155 (158)	Andrew Kirkaldy, 155 (163)	Musselburgh, Scotland
1890	John Ball, 164	Willie Fernie, Archie Simpson, 167	Prestwick, Scotland
1891	Hugh Kirkaldy, 166	Andrew Kirkaldy, Willie Fernie, 168	St. Andrews, Scotland
1892	Harold Hilton, 305	John Ball, Hugh Kirkaldy, Alex Herd, 308	Murifield, Scotland
1893	Willie Auchterlonie, 322	John Laidlay, 324	Prestwick, Scotland
1894	John H. Taylor, 326	Douglas Rolland, 331	Royal St. George's, England
1895	John H. Taylor, 322	Alex Herd, 326	St. Andrews, Scotland
1896	Harry Vardon, 316 (157)	John H. Taylor, 316 (161)	Muirfield, Scotland
1897	Harold Hilton, 314	James Braid, 315	Hoylake, England
1898	Harry Vardon, 307	Willie Park, Jr., 308	Prestwick, Scotland
1899	Harry Vardon, 310	Jack White, 315	Royal St. George's, England
1900	John H. Taylor, 309	Harry Vardon, 317	St. Andrews, Scotland
1901	James Braid, 309	Harry Vardon, 313	Muirfield, Scotland
1902	Alex Herd, 307	Harry Vardon, James Braid, 308	Hoylake, England
1903	Harry Vardon, 300	Tom Vardon, 306	Prestwick, Scotland
1904	Jack White, 296	John H. Taylor, James Braid, 297	Royal St. George's, England
1905	James Braid, 318	Rowland Jones, John H. Taylor, 323	St. Andrews, Scotland
1906	James Braid, 300	John H. Taylor, 304	Muirfield, Scotland
1907	Arnaud Massy, 312	John H. Taylor, 314	Hoylake, England
1908	James Braid, 291	Tom Ball, 299	Prestwick, Scotland
1909	John H. Taylor, 295	James Braid, Tom Ball, 301	Deal, England
1910	James Braid, 299	Alex Herd, 303	St. Andrews, Scotland

BRITISH OPEN (continued)

Year	Winner, Score	Runner-Up	Site
1911	Harry Vardon, 303	Arnaud Massy, 303	Royal St. George's, England
	(Massy conceded playoff at 35th hole)		
1912	Edward Ray, 295	Harry Vardon, 299	Muirfield, Scotland
1913	John H. Taylor, 304	Edward Ray, 312	Hoylake, England
1914	Harry Vardon, 306	John H. Taylor, 309	Prestwick, Scotland
1915–1919 Not played			
1920	George Duncan, 303	Alex Herd, 305	Deal, England
1921	Jock Hutchison, 296 (150)	Roger Wethered, 296 (159)	St. Andrews, Scotland
1922	Walter Hagen, 300	George Duncan, Jim Barnes, 301	Royal St. George's, England
1923	Arthur Havers, 295	Walter Hagen, 296	Troon, Scotland
1924	Walter Hagen, 301	Ernest Whitcombe, 302	Hoylake, England
1925	Jim Barnes, 300	Edward Ray, Archie Compston, 301	Prestwick, Scotland
1926	R.T. Jones, Jr., 291	Al Watrous, 293	Royal Lytham, England
1927	R.T. Jones, Jr., 285	Aubrey Boomer, Fred Robson, 291	St. Andrews, Scotland
1928	Walter Hagen, 292	Gene Sarazen, 294	Royal St. George's, England
1929	Walter Hagen, 292	Johnny Farrell, 298	Muirfield, Scotland
1930	R.T. Jones, Jr., 291	Macdonald Smith, Leo Diegel, 293	Hoylake, England
1931	Tommy Armour, 296	J. Jurado, 297	Carnoustie, Scotland
1932	Gene Sarazen, 283	Macdonald Smith, 288	Prince's, England
1933	Denny Shute, 292 (149)	Craig Wood, 292 (154)	St. Andrews, Scotland
1934	Henry Cotton, 283	Sidney Brews, 288	Royal St. George's, England
1935	Alfred Perry, 283	Alfred Padgham, 287	Muirfield, Scotland
1936	Alfred Padgham, 287	J. Adams, 288	Hoylake, England
1937	Henry Cotton, 290	R.A. Whitcombe, 292	Carnoustie, Scotland
1938	R.A. Whitcombe, 295	James Adams, 297	Royal St. George's, England
1939	Richard Burton, 290	Johnny Bulla, 292	St. Andrews, Scotland
1940–1945 Not played			
1946	Sam Snead, 290	Bobby Locke, Johnny Bulla, 294	St. Andrews, Scotland
1947	Fred Daly, 293	R.W. Horne, Frank Stranahan, 294	Hoylake, England
1948	Henry Cotton, 284	Fred Daly, 289	Muirfield, Scotland
1949	Bobby Locke, 283 (135)	Harry Bradshaw, 283 (147)	Royal St. George's, England
1950	Bobby Locke, 279	Roberto De Vicenzo, 281	Troon, Scotland
1951	Max Faulkner, 285	Antonio Cerda, 287	Portrush, Ireland
1952	Bobby Locke, 287	Peter Thomson, 288	Royal Lytham, England
1953	Ben Hogan, 282	Frank Stranahan, Peter Thomson, Antonio Cerda, Dai Rees, 286	Carnoustie, Scotland
1954	Peter Thomson, 283	S.S. Scott, Dai Rees, Bobby Locke, 284	Royal Birkdale, England
1955	Peter Thomson, 281	John Fallon, 283	St. Andrews, Scotland
1956	Peter Thomson, 286	Flory van Donck, 289	Hoylake, England
1957	Bobby Locke, 279	Peter Thomson, 282	St. Andrews, Scotland
1958	Peter Thomson, 278 (139)	Dave Thomas, 278 (143)	Royal Lytham, England
1959	Gary Player, 284	Flory van Donck, Fred Bullock, 286	Muirfield, Scotland
1960	Kel Nagle, 278	Arnold Palmer, 279	St. Andrews, Scotland
1961	Arnold Palmer, 284	Dai Rees, 285	Royal Birkdale, England
1962	Arnold Palmer, 276	Kel Nagle, 282	Troon, Scotland
1963	Bob Charles, 277 (140)	Phil Rodgers, 277 (148)	Royal Lytham, England
1964	Tony Lema, 279	Jack Nicklaus, 284	St. Andrews, Scotland
1965	Peter Thomson, 285	Brian Huggett, Christy O'Connor, 287	Royal Birkdale, England
1966	Jack Nicklaus, 282	Dave Thomas, Doug Sanders, 283	Muirfield, Scotland
1967	Roberto De Vicenzo, 278	Jack Nicklaus, 280	Hoylake, England
1968	Gary Player, 289	Jack Nicklaus, Bob Charles, 291	Carnoustie, Scotland

Lee Trevino won consecutive British Opens in 1971 and
1972. *Wide World Photos*

Gary Player took the British Open in three decades,
winning in 1959, 1968 and 1974. *Wide World Photos*

BRITISH OPEN (continued)

Year	Winner, Score	Runner-Up	Site
1969	Tony Jacklin, 280	Bob Charles, 282	Royal Lytham, England
1970	Jack Nicklaus, 283 (72)	Doug Sanders, 283 (73)	St. Andrews, Scotland
1971	Lee Trevino, 278	Liang Huan Lu, 279	Royal Birkdale, England
1972	Lee Trevino, 278	Jack Nicklaus, 279	Muirfield, Scotland
1973	Tom Weiskopf, 276	Neil Coles, Johnny Miller, 279	Troon, Scotland
1974	Gary Player, 282	Peter Oosterhuis, 286	Royal Lytham, England
1975	Tom Watson, 279 (71)	Jack Newton, 279 (72)	Carnoustie, Scotland
1976	Johnny Miller, 279	Jack Nicklaus, Seve Ballesteros, 285	Royal Birkdale, England
1977	Tom Watson, 268	Jack Nicklaus, 269	Turnberry, Scotland
1978	Jack Nicklaus, 281	Simon Owen, Tom Kite, Raymond Floyd, Ben Crenshaw, 283	St. Andrews, Scotland
1979	Seve Ballesteros, 283	Ben Crenshaw, Jack Nicklaus, 286	Royal Lytham, England
1980	Tom Watson, 271	Lee Trevino, 275	Muirfield, Scotland
1981	Bill Rogers, 276	Bernhard Langer, 280	Royal St. George's, England
1982	Tom Watson, 284	Peter Oosterhuis, Nick Price, 285	Royal Troon, Scotland
1983	Tom Watson, 275	Hale Irwin, Andy Bean, 276	Royal Birkdale, England
1984	Seve Ballesteros, 276	Tom Watson, Bernhard Langer, 278	St. Andrews, Scotland
1985	Sandy Lyle, 282	Payne Stewart, 283	Royal St. George's, England
1986	Greg Norman, 280	Gordon J. Brand, 285	Turnberry, Scotland
1987	Nick Faldo, 279	Paul Azinger, Rodger Davis, 280	Muirfield, Scotland
1988	Seve Ballesteros, 273	Nick Price, 275	Royal Lytham, England
1989	Mark Calcavecchia, 275*	Wayne Grady, Greg Norman, 275	Royal Troon, Scotland
1990	Nick Faldo, 270	Payne Stewart, Mark McNulty, 275	St. Andrews, Scotland
1991	Ian Baker-Finch, 272	Mike Harwood, 274	Royal Birkdale, England
1992	Nick Faldo, 272	John Cook, 273	Muirfield, Scotland

Figures in parentheses indicate play-off scores.

* Won four-hole playoff.

TOURNAMENT RECORDS

Lowest score, 18 holes: 63, Mark Hayes, 1977, second round at Turnberry; Isao Aoki, 1980, third round at Muirfield; Greg Norman, 1986, second round at Turnberry; Jodie Mudd, fourth round at Birkdale, 1991.

Lowest score, 36 holes: 130, Tom Watson (65–65), 1977, third and fourth rounds at Turnberry; Nick Faldo (66–64), 1992, first and second rounds at Muirfield.

Lowest score, 54 holes: 199, Nick Faldo (67–65–67), 1990, first through third rounds at St. Andrews; Nick Faldo (66–64–69), 1992, first through third rounds at Muirfield.

Lowest score, 72 holes: 268, Tom Watson (68–70–65–65), 1977, Turnberry.

Largest winning margin: 13, Tom Morris, Sr., 1862.

Oldest champion: 46, Tom Morris, Sr., 1867.

Youngest champion: 17, Tom Morris, Jr., 1868.

Most victories: 6, Harry Vardon (1896, 1898, 1899, 1903, 1911, 1914).

Most times runner-up: 7, Jack Nicklaus (1964, 1967, 1968, 1972, 1976, 1977, 1979).

Victories in consecutive years: Tom Morris, Sr. (1861, 1862); Tom Morris, Jr. (1868, 1869, 1870); Jamie Anderson (1877, 1878, 1879); Robert Ferguson (1880, 1881, 1882); John H. Taylor (1894, 1895); Harry Vardon (1898, 1899); James Braid (1905, 1906); Robert T. Jones, Jr. (1926, 1927); Walter Hagen (1928, 1929); Bobby Locke (1949, 1950); Peter Thomson (1954, 1955, 1956); Arnold Palmer (1961, 1962); Lee Trevino (1971, 1972); Tom Watson (1982, 1983).

Byron Nelson (second from right) defeated Sam Byrd (third from left) to win the 1945 PGA Championship. *Courtesy PGA*

PGA CHAMPIONSHIP:

Match Play, 1916–1957

Year	Winner	Score	Runner-Up	Site
1916	James M. Barnes	1 up	Jock Hutchison	Siwanoy CC, Bronxville, N.Y.
1917–1918 Not played				
1919	James M. Barnes	6 & 5	Fred McLeod	Engineers CC, Roslyn, N.Y.
1920	Jock Hutchison	1 up	J. Douglas Edgar	Flossmoor CC, Flossmoor, Ill.
1921	Walter Hagen	3 & 2	James M. Barnes	Inwood CC, Inwood, N.Y.
1922	Gene Sarazen	4 & 3	Emmet French	Oakmont CC, Oakmont, Pa.
1923	Gene Sarazen	1 up (38)	Walter Hagen	Pelham CC, Pelham, N.Y.
1924	Walter Hagen	2 up	James M. Barnes	French Lick CC, French Lick, Ind.
1925	Walter Hagen	6 & 5	Wm. Mehlhorn	Olympia Fields CC, Olympia, Ill.
1926	Walter Hagen	5 & 3	Leo Diegel	Salisbury GC, Westbury, N.Y.
1927	Walter Hagen	1 up	Joe Turnesa	Cedar Crest CC, Dallas, Tex.
1928	Leo Diegel	6 & 5	Al Espinosa	Baltimore CC, Baltimore, Md.
1929	Leo Diegel	6 & 4	Johnny Farrell	Hillcrest CC, Los Angeles, Cal.
1930	Tommy Armour	1 up	Gene Sarazen	Fresh Meadow CC, Flushing, N.Y.
1931	Tom Creavy	2 & 1	Denny Shute	Wannamoisett CC, Rumford, R.I.
1932	Olin Dutra	4 & 3	Frank Walsh	Keller GC, St. Paul, Minn.
1933	Gene Sarazen	5 & 4	Willie Goggin	Blue Mound CC, Milwaukee, Wis.
1934	Paul Runyan	1 up (38)	Craig Wood	Park CC, Williamsville, N.Y.
1935	John Revolta	5 & 4	Tommy Armour	Twin Hills CC, Okla. City, Okla.
1936	Denny Shute	3 & 2	Jimmy Thomson	Pinehurst CC, Pinehurst, N.C.
1937	Denny Shute	1 up (37)	Harold McSpaden	Pittsburgh CC, Aspinwall, Pa.
1938	Paul Runyan	8 & 7	Sam Snead	Shawnee CC, Shawnee-on-Dela., Pa.
1939	Henry Picard	1 up (37)	Byron Nelson	Pomonok CC, Flushing, N.Y.
1940	Byron Nelson	1 up	Sam Snead	Hershey CC, Hershey, Pa.
1941	Vic Ghezzi	1 up (38)	Byron Nelson	Cherry Hills CC, Denver, Colo.

PGA CHAMPIONSHIP:

Match Play, 1916–1957 (continued)

Year	Winner	Score	Runner-Up	Site
1942	Sam Snead	2 & 1	Jim Turnesa	Seaview CC, Atlantic City, N.J.
1943 Not played				
1944	Bob Hamilton	1 up	Byron Nelson	Manito G&CC, Spokane, Wash.
1945	Byron Nelson	4 & 3	Sam Byrd	Morraine CC, Dayton, Ohio
1946	Ben Hogan	6 & 4	Ed Oliver	Portland GC, Portland, Ore.
1947	Jim Ferrier	2 & 1	Chick Harbert	Plum Hollow CC, Detroit, Mich.
1948	Ben Hogan	7 & 6	Mike Turnesa	Norwood Hills CC, St. Louis, Mo.
1949	Sam Snead	3 & 2	Johnny Palmer	Hermitage CC, Richmond, Va.
1950	Chandler Harper	4 & 3	Henry Williams	Scioto CC, Columbus, Ohio
1951	Sam Snead	7 & 6	Walter Burkemo	Oakmont CC, Oakmont, Pa.
1952	Jim Turnesa	1 up	Chick Harbert	Big Spring CC, Louisville, Ky.
1953	Walter Burkemo	2 & 1	Felice Torza	Birmingham CC, Birmingham, Mich.
1954	Chick Harbert	4 & 3	Walter Burkemo	Keller GC, St. Paul, Minn.
1955	Doug Ford	4 & 3	Cary Middlecoff	Meadowbrook CC, Detroit, Mich.
1956	Jack Burke, Jr.	3 & 2	Ted Kroll	Blue Hill CC, Boston, Mass.
1957	Lionel Hebert	2 & 1	Dow Finsterwald	Miami Valley GC, Dayton, Ohio

PGA CHAMPIONSHIP:

Stroke Play, 1958–1992

Year	Winner, Score	Runner-Up, Score	Site
1958	Dow Finsterwald, 276	Billy Casper, 278	Llanerch CC, Havertown, Pa.
1959	Bob Rosburg, 277	Jerry Barber, Doug Sanders, 278	Minneapolis CC, St. Louis, Minn.
1960	Jay Hebert, 281	Jim Ferrier, 282	Firestone CC, Akron, Ohio
1961	Jerry Barber, 277 (67)	Don January, 277 (68)	Olympia Fields CC, Olympia Fields, Ill.
1962	Gary Player, 278	Bob Goalby, 279	Aronimink GC, Newtown Square, Pa.
1963	Jack Nicklaus, 279	Dave Ragan, 281	Dallas AC, Dallas, Tx.
1964	Bobby Nichols, 271	Jack Nicklaus, Arnold Palmer, 274	Columbus CC, Columbus, Ohio
1965	Dave Marr, 280	Jack Nicklaus, Billy Casper, 282	Laurel Valley, GC, Ligonier, Pa.
1966	Al Geiberger, 280	Dudley Wysong, 284	Firestone CC, Akron, Ohio
1967	Don January, 281 (69)	Don Massengale, 281 (71)	Columbine CC, Denver, Colo.
1968	Julius Boros, 281	Bob Charles, 282	Pecan Valley CC, San Antonio, Tex.
1969	Ray Floyd, 276	Gary Player, 278	NCR Club, Dayton, Ohio
1970	Dave Stockton, 279	Arnold Palmer, Bob Murphy, 281	Southern Hills, CC, Tulsa, Okla.
1971	Jack Nicklaus, 281	Billy Casper, 283	PGA National GC, Palm Beach Gardens, Fla.
1972	Gary Player, 281	Jim Jamieson, Tommy Aaron, 283	Oakland Hills CC, Birmingham, Mich.
1973	Jack Nicklaus, 277	Bruce Crampton, 281	Canterbury GC, Cleveland, Ohio
1974	Lee Trevino, 276	Jack Nicklaus, 277	Tanglewood GC, Clemmons, N.C.
1975	Jack Nicklaus, 276	Bruce Crampton, 278	Firestone CC, Akron, Ohio
1976	Dave Stockton, 281	Ray Floyd, Don January, 282	Congressional CC, Washington, D.C.
1977	Lanny Wadkins, 282*	Gene Littler, 282	Pebble Beach GL, Pebble Beach, Cal.
1978	John Mahaffey, 276*	Tom Watson, Jerry Pate, 276	Oakmont CC, Oakmont, Pa.
1979	David Graham, 272*	Ben Crenshaw, 272	Oakland Hills CC, Birmingham, Mich.
1980	Jack Nicklaus, 274	Andy Bean, 281	Oak Hill CC, Rochester, N.Y.
1981	Larry Nelson, 273	Fuzzy Zoeller, 277	Atlanta AC, Duluth, Ga.
1982	Ray Floyd, 272	Lanny Wadkins, 275	Southern Hills CC, Tulsa, Okla.

PGA CHAMPIONSHIP:
Stroke Play, 1958–1992 (continued)

Year	Winner, Score	Runner-Up, Score	Site
1983	Hal Sutton, 274	Jack Nicklaus, 275	Riviera CC, Los Angeles, Cal.
1984	Lee Trevino, 273	Gary Player, Lanny Wadkins, 277	Shoal Creek CC, Birmingham, Ala.
1985	Hubert Green, 278	Lee Trevino, 280	Cherry Hills CC, Englewood, Colo.
1986	Bob Tway, 276	Greg Norman, 278	Inverness Club, Toledo, Ohio
1987	Larry Nelson, 287*	Lanny Wadkins, 287	PGA National GC, Palm Beach Gardens, Fla.
1988	Jeff Sluman, 272	Paul Azinger, 275	Oak Tree GC, Edmond, Okla.
1989	Payne Stewart, 276	Andy Bean, Mike Reid, Curtis Strange, 277	Kemper Lakes GC, Hawthorn Woods, Ill.
1990	Wayne Grady, 282	Fred Couples, 285	Shoal Creek CC, Birmingham, Ala.
1991	John Daly, 276	Bruce Lietzke, 279	Crooked Stick GC, Carmel, Ind.
1992	Nick Price, 278	John Cook, Nick Faldo, Jim Gallagher, Gene Sauers, 281	Bellerive CC, St. Louis, Mo.

Figures in parentheses indicate playoff scores.

* Won sudden-death playoff.

TOURNAMENT RECORDS

Lowest score, 18 holes: 63, Bruce Crampton, 1975, second round at Firestone; Ray Floyd, 1982, first round at Southern Hills; Gary Player, 1984, second round at Shoal Creek.

Lowest score, 36 holes: 131 (65–66), Hal Sutton, 1983, first and second rounds at Riviera.

Lowest score, 54 holes: 200, Ray Floyd (63–69–68), 1982, first through third rounds at Southern Hills.

Lowest score, 72 holes: 271, Bobby Nichols (64–71–69–67), 1964, Columbus.

Largest winning margin: 7, Jack Nicklaus, 1980.

Oldest champion: 48, Julius Boros, 1968.

Youngest champion: 20, Gene Sarazen, 1922.

Most victories: 5, Walter Hagen (1921, 1924–1927); Jack Nicklaus (1963, 1971, 1973, 1975, 1980).

Most times runner-up: 4, Jack Nicklaus (1964, 1965, 1974, 1983).

Victories in consecutive years: Gene Sarazen (1922–1923); Walter Hagen (1924–1927); Leo Diegel (1928–1929); Denny Shute (1936–1937).

PGA TOUR

Date	Event	Winner	Score	1st Place Money	Total Purse
		1941 Tour			
Jan. 3–6	Los Angeles Open	John Bulla	281	$ 3,500	$ 10,000
Jan. 9–12	Oakland Open	Leonard Dodson	276	$ 1,200	$ 5,000
Jan. 15–19	San Francisco Match Play Championship	John Revolta	7&6	$ 1,000	$ 5,000
Jan. 25–26	Bing Crosby Tournament	Sam Snead	136	$ 500	$ 3,000
Jan. 31–Feb. 2	Western Open	Ed Oliver	275	$ 1,000	$ 5,000
Feb. 6–9	Texas Open	Lawson Little	273	$ 1,200	$ 5,000
Feb. 13–16	New Orleans Open	Henry Picard	276	$ 1,200	$ 5,000
Feb. 22–23	Thomasville Open	Harold McSpaden	207	$ 700	$ 3,000
Feb. 26–28	St. Petersburg Open	Sam Snead	279	$ 1,200	$ 5,000

Some of the stars of the early 1940s gathered at the Goodall Round Robin Tournament. Front row, left to right, Ben Hogan, Byron Nelson, Jimmy Demaret, Dick Metz, Craig Wood, Paul Runyan and Clayton Heafner. Back row, left to right, Henry Picard, Martin Pose, Jimmy Hines, Horton Smith, Gene Sarazen, Lawson Little, Jimmy Thomson and Sam Snead. *UPI/Bettmann*

PGA TOUR (continued)

Date	Event	Winner	Score	1st Place Money	Total Purse
Mar. 2–5	Miami Biltmore C.C. International Four-Ball Matches	Gene Sarazen and Ben Hogan	4&3	$ 1,000	$ 5,000
Mar. 9–10	Bellair Open	Horton Smith	206		$ 3,000
Mar. 12–16	St. Augustine Pro-Am Championship	Snead and Wehrle	1 up	NR	$ 3,000
Mar. 18–20	North and South Open	Sam Snead	277	$ 1,000	$ 4,000
Mar. 21–23	Greensboro Open	Byron Nelson	276	$ 1,200	$ 5,000
Mar. 28–30	Asheville Open	Ben Hogan	284	$ 1,200	$ 5,000
April 3–6	Masters	Craig Wood	280	$ 1,500	$ 5,000
May 22–25	Goodall Round Robin	Paul Runyan	Plus 26[b]	$ 1,000	$ 5,000
June 5–7	U.S. Open	Craig Wood	284	$ 1,000	$ 6,000
June 13–15	Mahoning Open	Clayton Heafner	276	$ 1,200	$ 5,000
June 18–22	Inverness Four-Ball Tournament	Jimmie Demaret and Ben Hogan	Plus 11[b]	$ 2,000	$ 6,000
July 7–13	PGA Championship	Vic Ghezzi	38 holes	$ 1,000	$ 7,820
July 18–20	Chicago Open	Ben Hogan	274	$ 1,200	$ 5,000
July 24–27	St. Paul Open	Horton Smith	276	$ 1,600	$ 7,500
Aug. 7–9	Canadian Open	Sam Snead	274	$ 1,000	$ 3,000
Aug. 15–17	Rochester *Times Union* Open	Sam Snead	277	$ 1,200	$ 5,000
Aug. 28–31	Hershey Open	Ben Hogan	275	$ 1,200	$ 5,000
Sept. 4–7	Tam O'Shanter Open	Byron Nelson	278	$ 2,000	$ 11,000
Sept. 12–14	Atlantic City Open	Lloyd Mangrum	275	$ 1,200	$ 5,000
Sept. 19–21	Henry Hurst Invitational	Sam Snead	272	$ 1,500	$ 5,000
Sept. 26–28	Providence Open	Lou Barbaro	273	$ 1,200	$ 5,000
Dec. 11–14	Miami Open	Byron Nelson	269	$ 2,537	$ 10,000
Dec. 20–22	Harlingen Open	Henry Picard	266	$ 1,000	$ 5,000
Dec. 26–28	Beaumont Open	Chick Harbert	276	$ 1,000	$ 5,000

1942 Tour

Date	Event	Winner	Score	1st Place Money	Total Purse
Jan. 9–12	Los Angeles Open	Ben Hogan	282	$ 3,500	$ 10,000
Jan. 15–18	Oakland Open	Byron Nelson	274	$ 1,000	$ 5,000
Jan. 22–25	San Francisco Open	Ben Hogan	279	$ 1,000	$ 5,000
Jan. 31–Feb. 1	Bing Crosby Pro-Am	Lloyd Mangrum and Leland Gibson (tied for first)	136	$ 1,400	$ 5,000
Feb. 5–8	Western Open	Herman Barron	276	$ 1,000	$ 5,000
Feb. 13–15	Texas Open	Chick Harbert	272	$ 1,000	$ 5,000
Feb. 20–22	New Orleans Open	Lloyd Mangrum	281	$ 1,000	$ 5,000
Mar. 4–6	St. Petersburg Open	Sam Snead	286	$ 1,000	$ 5,000
Mar. 8–11	Miami Four-Ball Invitational	Chandler Harper and Herman Keiser	4&3	$ 1,000	$ 5,000
Mar. 24–26	North and South Open	Ben Hogan	271	$ 1,000	$ 5,000
Mar. 27–30	Greensboro Open	Sam Byrd	279	$ 1,000	$ 5,000
Apr. 2–5	Land of the Sky Open	Ben Hogan	276	$ 1,000	$ 5,000
Apr. 9–12	Masters	Byron Nelson	280	$ 1,500	$ 5,000
May 23–31	PGA Championship	Sam Snead	2&1	$ 1,000	$ 7,820
June 11–14	Inverness Four-Ball Tournament	Lawson Little and Lloyd Mangrum	Plus 14[b]	$ 1,200 each	$ 7,650

PGA TOUR (continued)

Date	Event	Winner	Score	1st Place Money	Total Purse
June 18–21	Hale America	Ben Hogan	271	$ 1,000	$ 6,000
June 26–28	Mahoning Valley Open	Clayton Heafner	264	$ 1,000	$ 5,000
July 25–28	Tam O'Shanter Open	Byron Nelson	280	$ 2,500	$ 15,000
Aug. 1–2	St. Paul Open	Chick Harbert	280	$ 1,000	$ 5,000
Aug. 6–8	Canadian Open	Craig Wood	275	$ 1,000	$ 3,000
Aug. 13–16	Rochester Open	Ben Hogan	278	$ 1,000	$ 5,000
	1943 Tour				
July 19–25	All-American Open	Harold McSpaden	NR	$ 2,000	$ 10,000
Aug. 19–22	Chicago Victory Open	Sam Byrd	277	$ 1,000	$ 2,000
Sept. 2–5	Golden Valley Invitational Four-Ball	Craig Wood and Jimmy Demaret	Plus 10[b]	NR	NR
Dec. 16–19	Miami Open	Steve Warga, Jr.	280	$ 1,000	$ 5,000
	1944 Tour				
Jan. 7–10	Los Angeles Open	Harold McSpaden	278	$ 4,375	$ 12,500
Jan. 14–16	San Francisco Victory Open	Byron Nelson	275	$ 2,400	$ 10,000
Feb. 4–6	Phoenix Open	Harold McSpaden	273	$ 2,000	$ 5,000
Feb. 12–14	Texas Open	Johnny Revolta	273	$ 1,000	$ 7,000
Feb. 25–28	New Orleans Open	Sam Byrd	285	$ 1,000	$ 5,000
Mar. 3–5	Gulfport Open	Harold McSpaden	276	$ 1,000	$ 6,000
Mar. 14–16	North and South Open	Bob Hamilton	286	$ 750	$ 3,000
Mar. 19–21	Charlotte Open	Sgt. E.J. Harrison	275	$ 2,000	$ 10,000
Mar. 23–26	Durham Open	Craig Wood	271	$ 1,000	$ 5,000
Mar. 31–Apr. 2	Knoxville War Bond	Byron Nelson	270	$ 1,333	$ 6,666
June 8–11	*Philadelphia Inquirer* Open	Sam Byrd	274	$ 6,700	$ 17,500
June 15–18	New York Red Cross Tourney	Byron Nelson	275	$ 2,666	$ 13,333
June 30–July 2	Chicago Victory Open	Harold McSpaden	273	$ 3,000	$ 10,000
July 6–9	Minneapolis Four-Ball	Byron Nelson and Harold McSpaden	Plus 13[b]	$ 1,600	$ 8,800
Aug. 14–20	PGA Championship	Bob Hamilton	1 up	$ 3,500	$ 14,500
Aug. 21–28	Tam O'Shanter Open	Byron Nelson	280	$ 13,462	$ 30,100
Sept. 1–4	Nashville Open	Byron Nelson	269	$ 2,400	$ 10,000
Sept. 7–10	Texas Victory Open	Byron Nelson	276	$ 2,000	$ 10,000
Nov. 23–26	Portland Open	Sam Snead	289	$ 2,675	$ 13,600
Dec. 1–4	San Francisco Open	Byron Nelson	281	$ 2,666	$ 13,333
Dec. 7–10	Miami Open	Sgt. E.J. Harrison	274	$ 2,500	$ 10,000
Dec. 7–10	Oakland Open	Jim Ferrier	277	$ 1,600	$ 7,500
Dec. 15–17	Richmond Open	Sam Snead	278	$ 1,600	$ 7,500
	1945 Tour				
Jan. 5–8	Los Angeles Open	Sam Snead	283	$ 2,666	$ 13,333
Jan. 12–14	Phoenix Open	Byron Nelson	274	$ 1,333	$ 6,666
Jan. 18–21	Tucson Open	Ray Mangrum	268	$ 1,000	$ 5,000
Jan. 26–28	Texas Open	Sam Byrd	268	$ 1,000	$ 5,000
Feb. 1–4	Corpus Christi Open	Byron Nelson	264	$ 1,000	$ 5,000

PGA TOUR (continued)

Date	Event	Winner	Score	1st Place Money	Total Purse
Feb. 9–11	New Orleans Open	Byron Nelson	284	$ 1,333	$ 6,666
Feb. 16–18	Gulfport Open	Sam Snead	275	$ 1,000	$ 5,000
Feb. 23–25	Pensacola Open	Sam Snead	267	$ 1,000	$ 5,000
Mar. 1–4	Jacksonville Open	Sam Snead	266	$ 1,333	$ 5,000
Mar. 8–11	Miami Four-Ball Invitational	Byron Nelson and Harold McSpaden	8&6	$ 1,500 each	$ 10,000
Mar. 16–19	Charlotte Open	Byron Nelson	272	$ 2,000	$ 10,000
Mar. 23–25	Greensboro Open	Byron Nelson	271	$ 1,333	$ 7,500
Mar. 30–Apr. 1	Durham Open	Byron Nelson	276	$ 1,333	$ 6,666
Apr. 5–8	Atlanta Open	Byron Nelson	263	$ 2,000	$ 10,000
June 7–10	Montreal Open	Byron Nelson	268	$ 2,000	$ 10,000
June 14–17	*Philadelphia Inquirer* Invitational	Byron Nelson	269	$ 3,333	$ 17,500
June 29–July 1	Chicago Victory National Open	Byron Nelson	275	$ 2,000	$ 12,300
July 9–15	PGA Championship	Byron Nelson	4&3	$ 3,750	$ 15,000
July 18–21	St. Paul Open	Sgt. E.J. Harrison	273	$ 2,000	$ 10,000
July 26–29	Tam O'Shanter Open	Byron Nelson	269	$ 13,600	$ 60,000
Aug. 2–4	Canadian Open	Byron Nelson	280	$ 2,000	$ 10,000
Aug. 16–19	Memphis Invitational	Fred Haas, Jr.[a]	270	$ 2,000	$ 10,000
Aug. 23–26	Knoxville Invitational	Byron Nelson	276	$ 2,000	$ 10,000
Aug. 31–Sept. 3	Nashville Invitational	Ben Hogan	265	$ 2,666	$ 13,333
Sept. 6–9	Dallas Open	Sam Snead	276	$ 2,000	$ 10,000
Sept. 13–16	Tulsa Open	Sam Snead	277	$ 2,000	$ 7,500
Sept. 19–23	Esmeralda Open	Byron Nelson	266	$ 2,000	$ 7,500
Sept. 27–30	Portland Invitational	Ben Hogan	261	$ 2,666	$ 14,500
Oct. 4–7	Tacoma Open	Jimmy Hines	275	$ 2,000	$ 7,500
Oct. 11–14	Seattle Open	Byron Nelson	259	$ 2,000	$ 10,250
Nov. 2–4	Richmond Invitational	Ben Hogan	289	$ 2,000	$ 10,000
Nov. 6–8	North and South Open	Lt. Cary Middlecoff[a]	280	$ 1,000	$ 5,000
Nov. 9–11	Durham Open	Frank Stranahan[a]	277	$ 1,333	$ 6,666
Nov. 15–18	Mobile Open	Sam Byrd	283	$ 2,000	$ 10,000
Nov. 22–25	Montgomery Invitational	Ben Hogan	282	$ 2,000	$ 7,500
Nov. 29–Dec. 2	Orlando Open	Ben Hogan	270	$ 2,000	$ 10,000
Dec. 6–9	Miami Open	Henry Picard	267	$ 2,000	$ 10,000
Dec. 14–16	Glen Garden Invitational	Byron Nelson	273	$ 2,000	$ 7,500

1946 Tour

Date	Event	Winner	Score	1st Place Money	Total Purse
Jan. 4–7	Los Angeles Open	Byron Nelson	284	$ 2,666	$ 13,333
Jan. 10–13	San Francisco Open	Byron Nelson	283	$ 3,000	$ 15,000
Jan. 17–20	Richmond Open	Toney Penna	280	$ 2,000	$ 10,000
Jan. 24–27	Phoenix Open	Ben Hogan	273	$ 1,500	$ 7,500
Jan. 31–Feb. 3	Tucson Open	Jimmy Demaret	268	$ 1,500	$ 7,500
Feb. 7–10	San Antonio Open	Ben Hogan	264	$ 1,500	$ 8,000
Feb. 14–17	New Orleans Open	Byron Nelson	277	$ 1,500	$ 7,500
Feb. 21–24	Pensacola Open	Ray Mangrum	277	$ 1,500	$ 7,500
Feb. 28–Mar. 3	St. Petersburg Open	Ben Hogan	269	$ 2,000	$ 10,000
Mar. 7–10	Miami Four-Ball Invitational	Ben Hogan and Jimmy Demaret	1 up	$ 1,000 each	$ 7,500
Mar. 14–17	Jacksonville Open	Sam Snead	264	$ 1,500	$ 7,500

PGA TOUR (continued)

Date	Event	Winner	Score	1st Place Money	Total Purse
Mar. 21–24	Greater Greensboro Open	Sam Snead	270	$ 1,500	$ 7,500
Mar. 28–31	Charlotte Open	Bob Hamilton	273	$ 1,500	$ 7,500
Apr. 4–7	Masters	Herman Keiser	282	$ 2,500	$ 10,000
May 9–12	Houston Open	Byron Nelson	274	$ 2,000	$ 10,000
May 16–19	Colonial Invitational	Ben Hogan	279	$ 3,000	$ 15,000
May 24–26	Western Open	Ben Hogan	271	$ 2,000	$ 10,000
May 30–June 2	Goodall Round-Robin	Ben Hogan	Plus 51[b]	$ 2,150	$ 10,000
June 6–9	*Philadelphia Inquirer* Open	Herman Barron	277	$ 2,500	$ 15,000
June 13–15	U.S. Open	Lloyd Mangrum	284	$ 1,500	$ 8,000
June 20–23	Inverness Four-Ball Tournament	Ben Hogan and Jimmy Demaret	Plus 20	$ 1,625 each	$ 10,000
June 27–30	Canadian Open	George Fazio	278	$ 2,000	$ 10,000
July 5–7	Columbus Invitational	Byron Nelson	276	$ 2,500	$ 10,500
July 11–14	Kansas City Invitational	Frank Stranahan[a]	274	$ 2,500	$ 15,000
July 17–21	Chicago Victory National Golf Championship	Byron Nelson	279	$ 2,000	$ 10,000
July 22–28	All-American Golf Tournament	Herman Barron	280	$ 10,500	$ 45,000
Aug. 1–4	St. Paul Open	Henry Ransom	268	$ 2,000	$ 10,000
Aug. 7–10	Winnipeg Open	Ben Hogan	281	$ 2,000	$ 10,000
Aug. 19–25	PGA Championship	Ben Hogan	6&4	$ 3,500	$ 17,950
Aug. 30–Sept. 2	Golden State Open	Ben Hogan	275	$ 2,500	$ 15,000
Sept. 7–8	World Championship of Golf	Sam Snead	138	$ 10,000	$ 10,000
Sept. 12–15	Nashville Invitational	Johnny Palmer	266	$ 2,000	$ 10,000
Sept. 19–22	Memphis Invitational	Buck White	277	$ 2,000	$ 10,000
Sept. 26–29	Dallas Invitational	Ben Hogan	284	$ 2,000	$ 10,000
Oct. 3–6	Fort Worth Invitational	Frank Stranahan[a]	270	$ 2,000	$ 10,000
Oct. 10–13	Montgomery Invitational	Ky Laffoon	271	$ 2,000	$ 10,000
Oct. 16–20	Knoxville Invitational	Herman Keiser	291	$ 2,000	$ 10,000
Oct. 24–27	Richmond Invitational	Herman Keiser	278	$ 2,000	$ 10,000
Nov. 5–7	North and South Open	Ben Hogan	282	$ 1,500	$ 7,500
Nov. 21–24	Atlanta Invitational	Lew Worsham	279	$ 2,200	$ 11,700
Nov. 28–Dec. 1	Orlando Open	Harry Todd	275	$ 2,000	$ 10,000
Dec. 5–8	Miami Open	Sam Snead	268	$ 2,000	$ 10,000

1947 Tour

Date	Event	Winner	Score	1st Place Money	Total Purse
Jan. 3–6	Los Angeles Open	Ben Hogan	280	$ 2,000	$ 10,000
Jan. 10–12	Bing Crosby Pro-Am	George Fazio	213	$ 1,625	$ 10,000
Jan. 16–19	Richmond Open	George Schoux	268	$ 2,000	$ 10,000
Jan. 23–26	Phoenix Open	Ben Hogan	270	$ 2,000	$ 10,000
Jan. 30–Feb. 2	Tucson Open	Jimmy Demaret	264	$ 2,000	$ 10,000
Feb. 6–9	San Antonio Open	Ed Oliver	265	$ 2,000	$ 10,000
Feb. 27–Mar. 2	St. Petersburg Open	Jimmy Demaret	280	$ 2,000	$ 10,000
Mar. 6–9	Miami Four-Ball Championship	Ben Hogan and Jimmy Demaret	3&2	$ 1,250	$ 10,000
Mar. 13–16	Jacksonville Open	Clayton Heafner	281	$ 2,000	$ 10,000
Mar. 21–23	Greater Greensboro Open	Vic Ghezzi	286	$ 2,000	$ 10,000
Mar. 27–30	Charlotte Open	Cary Middlecoff	277	$ 2,000	$ 10,000

PGA TOUR (continued)

Date	Event	Winner	Score	1st Place Money	Total Purse
Apr. 3–6	Masters	Jimmy Demaret	281	$ 2,500	$ 10,000
May 8–11	Houston Open	Bobby Locke	277	$ 2,000	$ 10,000
May 15–18	Colonial Invitational	Ben Hogan	279	$ 3,000	$ 15,000
May 22–25	*Philadelphia Inquirer* Open	Bobby Locke	277	$ 2,500	$ 15,000
May 29–June 1	Goodall	Bobby Locke	Plus 37[b]	$ 2,000	$ 10,000
June 5–8	National Capital Open	Lloyd Mangrum	269	$ 2,000	$ 10,000
June 12–14	U.S. Open	Lew Worsham	282	$ 2,500	$ 10,000
June 18–24	PGA Championship	Jim Ferrier	2&1	$ 3,500	$ 17,950
June 26–29	Chicago Victory Open	Ben Hogan	270	$ 2,000	$ 10,000
June 30–July 8	All-American Golf Tournament	Bobby Locke	276	$ 7,000	$ 30,000
July 10–13	Inverness Round-Robin Four-Ball	Ben Hogan and Jimmy Demaret	Plus 12[b]	$ 3,250	$ 10,000
July 16–19	Canadian Open	Bobby Locke	268	$ 2,000	$ 10,000
July 24–27	Columbus Invitational	Bobby Locke	274	$ 2,000	$ 10,000
July 31–Aug. 3	St. Paul Open	Jim Ferrier	272	$ 2,000	$ 10,000
Aug. 7–10	Esmeralda Open	Herman Keiser	273	$ 2,000	$ 10,000
Aug. 14–17	Portland Open	Charles Congdon	270	$ 2,000	$ 10,000
Aug. 21–24	Reno Open	E.J. Harrison	272	$ 2,500	$ 15,000
Aug. 29–Sept. 1	Western Open	Johnny Palmer	270	$ 2,200	$ 12,500
Sept. 4–7	Denver Open	Lew Worsham	276	$ 2,500	$ 15,000
Sept. 11–14	Albuquerque Open	Lloyd Mangrum	268	$ 2,000	$ 10,000
Sept. 18–21	Atlanta Open	Toney Penna	281	$ 2,000	$ 10,000
Sept. 27–28	World Championship of Golf	Ben Hogan	135	$ 5,000	$ 5,000
Oct. 2–5	Reading Invitational Open	E.J. Harrison	277	$ 2,000	$ 10,000
Nov. 8–11	Hawaiian Open	E.J. Harrison	275	$ 2,000	$ 10,000
Dec. 4–7	Orlando Open	Dave Douglas	274	$ 2,000	$ 10,000
Dec. 11–14	Miami Open	Jimmy Demaret	267	$ 2,000	$ 10,000

1948 Tour

Date	Event	Winner	Score	1st Place Money	Total Purse
Jan. 2–5	Los Angeles Open	Ben Hogan	275	$ 2,000	$ 10,000
Jan. 9–11	Bing Crosby Pro-Am	Lloyd Mangrum	205	$ 2,000	$ 7,000
Jan. 15–18	Richmond Open	E.J. Harrison	273	$ 2,000	$ 10,000
Jan. 22–25	Phoenix Open	Bobby Locke	268	$ 2,000	$ 10,000
Jan. 28–Feb. 1	Tucson Open	Skip Alexander	264	$ 2,000	$ 10,000
Feb. 5–8	Texas Open	Sam Snead	264	$ 2,000	$ 10,000
Feb. 12–15	Lower Rio Grande Open	Lloyd Mangrum	269	$ 2,000	$ 10,000
Feb. 19–22	New Orleans Open	Bob Hamilton	280	$ 2,000	$ 10,000
Feb. 26–29	St. Petersburg Open Invitational	Lawson Little	272	$ 2,000	$ 10,000
Mar. 6–9	23rd International Four-Ball Championship	Jim Ferrier and Cary Middlecoff	1 up	$ 1,250 each	$ 10,000
Mar. 11–14	Jacksonville Open Invitational	Chick Harbert	284	$ 2,000	$ 10,000
Mar. 19–21	Greater Greensboro Open	Lloyd Mangrum	278	$ 2,000	$ 10,000
Mar. 25–28	Charlotte Open	Chick Harbert	273	$ 2,000	$ 10,000
Apr. 8–11	Masters	Claude Harmon	279	$ 2,500	$ 10,000
Apr. 29–May 2	National Capital Open	Skip Alexander	271	$ 2,200	$ 14,000

PGA TOUR (continued)

Date	Event	Winner	Score	1st Place Money	Total Purse
May 6–9	Goodall Round-Robin	Herman Barron	Plus 38[b]	$ 2,000	$ 10,000
May 13–16	*Philadelphia Inquirer* Open	Johnny Palmer	281	$ 2,250	$ 15,000
May 19–25	PGA Championship	Ben Hogan	7&6	$ 3,500	$ 17,950
May 27–30	Colonial Invitational	Clayton Heafner	272	$ 3,000	$ 15,000
June 3–6	Albuquerque Open	Jimmy Demaret	268	$ 2,000	$ 10,000
June 10–12	U.S. Open	Ben Hogan	276	$ 2,000	$ 10,000
June 17–20	Chicago Victory National Golf Championship	Bobby Locke	266	$ 2,000	$ 10,000
June 24–27	Inverness Round-Robin Four-Ball Invitational	Ben Hogan and Jimmy Demaret	Plus 16[b]	$ 1,500	$ 10,000
July 1–4	Motor City Open	Ben Hogan	275	$ 2,600	$ 15,000
July 9–11	Zooligan's Open	Lloyd Mangrum	268	$ 2,000	$ 10,000
July 15–18	Dapper Dan–Alcoma Tournament	Vic Ghezzi	271	$ 2,600	$ 15,000
July 22–25	Reading Open	Ben Hogan	269	$ 2,600	$ 15,000
July 29–Aug. 1	Western Open	Ben Hogan	281	$ 2,500	$ 15,000
Aug. 3–6	All-American Open	Lloyd Mangrum	277	$ 5,000	$ 30,000
Aug. 7–8	World Championship of Golf	Lloyd Mangrum	135	$ 10,000	$ 10,000
Aug. 12–15	St. Paul Open Invitational	Jimmy Demaret	273	$ 2,450	$ 15,000
Aug. 19–22	Denver Open Invitational Championship	Ben Hogan	270	$ 2,150	$ 11,000
Aug. 26–29	Utah Open Invitational	Lloyd Mangrum	274	$ 2,150	$ 11,000
Sept. 3–6	Reno Open Invitational	Ben Hogan	269	$ 3,500	$ 25,000
Sept. 16–19	Tacoma Open Invitational	Ed Oliver	274	$ 2,150	$ 11,000
Sept. 22–25	Canadian Open	Chuck Congdon	280	$ 1,200	$ 10,000
Sept. 30–Oct. 3	Portland Open Invitational	Fred Haas, Jr.	270	$ 2,450	$ 15,000
Oct. 14–17	Glendale Open Invitational	Ben Hogan	275	$ 2,450	$ 15,000
Nov. 4–7	Hawaiian Open	Cary Middlecoff	274	$ 2,000	$ 10,000
Dec. 9–12	Miami Open	Frank Stranahan[a]	270	$ 2,000	$ 10,000
Dec. 14–16	Havana Invitational	Sam Snead	209	$ 2,401	$ 10,000

1949 Tour

Date	Event	Winner	Score	1st Place Money	Total Purse
Jan. 7–10	Los Angeles Open	Lloyd Mangrum	284	$ 2,600	$ 10,000
Jan. 14–16	Bing Crosby Pro-Am	Ben Hogan	208	$ 2,000	$ 7,000
Jan. 19–24	Long Beach Open	Ben Hogan	272	$ 2,000	$ 10,000
Jan. 27–30	Phoenix Open	Jimmy Demaret	278	$ 2,000	$ 10,000
Feb. 3–6	Tucson Open	Lloyd Mangrum	263	$ 2,000	$ 10,000
Feb. 10–13	Texas Open	Dave Douglas	268	$ 2,000	$ 10,000
Feb. 17–20	Houston Open	John Palmer	272	$ 2,000	$ 10,000
Feb. 24–27	Rio Grande Valley Open	Cary Middlecoff	267	$ 2,000	$ 10,000
Mar. 3–6	St. Petersburg Open	Pete Cooper	275	$ 2,000	$ 10,000
Mar. 10–13	Miami Four-Ball Invitational	Cary Middlecoff and Jim Ferrier	9&8	$ 1,250	$ 10,000
Mar. 15–16	Seminole Pro-Am Tournament	Henry Ransom	137	$ 1,500	$ 10,000
Mar. 18–21	Jacksonville Open	Cary Middlecoff	274	$ 2,000	$ 10,000
Mar. 24–26	Greater Greensboro Open	Sam Snead	276	$ 2,000	$ 10,000
Apr. 7–10	Masters	Sam Snead	282	$ 2,750	$ 10,000

PGA TOUR (continued)

Date	Event	Winner	Score	1st Place Money	Total Purse
Apr. 14–17	Cavalier Specialists Tournament	Bobby Locke	201	$ 1,500	$ 10,000
Apr. 21–24	Wilmington Open	Henry Ransom	276	$ 2,000	$ 10,000
May 5–8	Greenbriar Pro-Am Tournament	Cary Middlecoff	265	$ 1,200	$ 10,000
May 12–15	Goodall Round-Robin	Bobby Locke	Plus 66[b]	$ 3,000	$ 15,000
May 19–22	*Philadelphia Inquirer* Open	Joe Kirkwood, Jr.	276	$ 2600	$ 15,000
May 25–31	PGA Championship	Sam Snead	3&2	$ 3,500	$ 17,950
June 9–11	U.S. Open	Cary Middlecoff	286	$ 2,000	$ 10,000
June 16–19	Motor City Open	Lloyd Mangrum	273	$ 2,250	$ 15,000
June 22–25	Canadian Open	E.J. Harrison	271	$ 2,000	$ 10,000
July 1–4	Washington Star Open	Sam Snead	272	$ 2,600	$ 15,000
July 7–10	Reading Open	Cary Middlecoff	266	$ 2,600	$ 15,000
July 14–18	Dapper Dan Open	Sam Snead	274	$ 2,600	$ 15,000
July 21–24	Inverness Four-Ball Invitational	Bob Hamilton and Chick Harbert	Plus 19[b]	$ 4,000	$ 15,000
July 28–31	Western Open	Sam Snead	268	$ 2,600	$ 15,000
Aug. 5–9	All American Tournament	Lloyd Mangrum	276	$ 3,333	$ 20,000
Aug. 11–14	World Championship of Golf	John Palmer	275	$ 10,000	$ 35,200
Aug. 18–21	Grand Rapids Open	Jim Ferrier	263	$ 2,600	$ 15,000
Aug. 27–28	Cedar Rapids Open	Dick Metz	211	$ 1,000	$ 5,000
Sept. 3–5	Ozark Open	Dave Douglas	203	$ 1,000	$ 5,000
Sept. 8–11	Kansas City Open	Jim Ferrier	277	$ 1,000	$ 5,000
Dec. 8–11	Miami Open	Fred Haas, Jr.	264	$ 2,000	$ 10,000
Dec. 15–18	Havana Pro-Am	Claude Harmon	271	$ 1,200	$ 10,000

1950 Tour

Date	Event	Winner	Score	1st Place Money	Total Purse
Jan. 6–10	Los Angeles Open	Sam Snead	280	$ 2,600	$ 15,000
Jan. 12–15	Bing Crosby Pro-Am	Jack Burke, Jr., Dave Douglas, Sam Snead, and Smiley Quick (tied for first)	214	$ 2,000	$ 7,000
Jan. 19–23	Long Beach Open	Fred Haas, Jr.	268	$ 2,000	$ 10,000
Jan. 26–29	Ben Hogan Open	Jimmy Demaret	269	$ 2,000	$ 10,000
Feb. 2–5	Tucson Open	Chandler Harper	267	$ 2,000	$ 10,000
Feb. 9–12	Texas Open	Sam Snead	265	$ 2,000	$ 10,000
Feb. 16–19	Rio Grande Valley Open	Jack Burke, Jr.	264	$ 2,000	$ 10,000
Feb. 23–26	Houston Open	Cary Middlecoff	277	$ 2,000	$ 10,000
Mar. 2–5	St. Petersburg Open	Jack Burke, Jr.	272	$ 2,000	$ 10,000
Mar. 7	La Gorce Pro-Am	Johnny Palmer	63	$ 300	$ 725
Mar. 9–12	Miami Beach Open	Sam Snead	273	$ 2,000	$ 10,000
Mar. 13–15	Seminole Pro-Am	Cary Middlecoff	207	$ 1,500	$ 10,000
Mar. 17–20	Jacksonville Open	Cary Middlecoff	279	$ 2,000	$ 10,000
Mar. 22	Aiken Pro-Am	Lawson Little	66	$ 450	$ 5,000
Mar. 23–26	Greater Greensboro Open	Sam Snead	269	$ 2,000	$ 10,000
Mar. 30–Apr. 2	Wilmington Open	E.J. Harrison	280	$ 2,000	$ 10,000
Apr. 6–9	Masters	Jimmy Demaret	283	$ 2,400	$ 10,000
Apr. 13–16	North Fulton Open	Jimmy Demaret	270	$ 2,000	$ 10,000
Apr. 20–23	Cavalier Specialist Tournament	Fred Hawkins	200	$ 1,100	$ 9,500

PGA TOUR (continued)

Date	Event	Winner	Score	1st Place Money	Total Purse
May 4–7	Greenbriar Pro-Am	Ben Hogan	259	$ 1,250	$ 10,000
May 18–21	Western Open	Sam Snead	282	$ 2,600	$ 15,000
May 25–28	Colonial Invitational	Sam Snead	277	$ 3,000	$ 15,000
June 1–4	Fort Wayne Open	Lloyd Mangrum	271	$ 2,600	$ 15,000
June 8–10	U.S. Open	Ben Hogan	287	$ 4,000	$ 10,000
June 15–18	Palm Beach Round-Robin	Lloyd Mangrum	Plus 37[b]	$ 3,000	$ 15,000
June 21–27	PGA Championship	Chandler Harper	4&3	$ 3,500	$ 17,950
July 1–4	Motor City Open	Lloyd Mangrum	274	$ 2,600	$ 15,000
July 13–16	Inverness Four-Ball Invitational	Sam Snead and Jim Ferrier	Plus 18[b]	$ 4,000	$ 15,000
July 20–23	St. Paul Open	Jim Ferrier	276	$ 2,600	$ 15,000
July 27–30	Sioux City Open	Jack Burke, Jr.	268	$ 2,600	$ 15,000
Aug. 5–8	All-American Tournament	Bobby Locke	282	$ 2,500	$ 15,000
Aug. 10–13	World Championship of Golf	Henry Ransom	281	$ 11,000	$ 50,000
Aug. 17–20	Eastern Open	Lloyd Mangrum	279	$ 2,600	$ 15,000
Aug. 24–27	Canadian Open	Jim Ferrier	271	$ 2,000	$ 10,000
Sept. 1–4	Empire State Open	Skip Alexander	279	$ 2,600	$ 15,000
Sept. 7–10	Reading Open	Sam Snead	268	$ 2,600	$ 15,000
Sept. 14–17	St. Louis Open	Cary Middlecoff	270	$ 2,600	$ 15,000
Sept. 21–24	Kansas City Open	Lloyd Mangrum	271	$ 2,600	$ 15,000
Sept. 28–Oct. 1	Ozark Open	Joe Kirkwood, Jr.	201	$ 1,000	$ 5,000
Oct. 31–Nov. 3	North and South Open	Sam Snead	275	$ 1,500	$ 7,500
Nov. 9–12	Savannah Open	Willie Goggin	280	$ 2,000	$ 10,000
Nov. 30–Dec. 3	Miami Open	Sam Snead	267	$ 2,000	$ 10,000
Dec. 7–10	Miami Four-Ball	Pete Cooper and Claude Harmon	1 up	$ 1,250 each	$ 10,000
Dec. 14–17	Havana Pro-Am	Jim Turnesa	267	$ 1,500	$ 15,000

1951 Tour

Date	Event	Winner	Score	1st Place Money	Total Purse
Jan. 5–8	Los Angeles Open	Lloyd Mangrum	260	$ 2,600	$ 15,000
Jan. 12–14	Bing Crosby Pro-Am	Byron Nelson	209	$ 2,000	$ 7,000
Jan. 19–22	Lakewood Park Open	Cary Middlecoff	271	$ 2,000	$ 10,000
Jan. 25–28	Phoenix Open	Lew Worsham	272	$ 2,000	$ 10,000
Feb. 1–4	Tucson Open	Lloyd Mangrum	269	$ 2,000	$ 10,000
Feb. 8–11	Texas Open	E.J. Harrison	265	$ 2,000	$ 10,000
Feb. 15–18	Rio Grande Valley Open	Chuck Klein	269	$ 2,000	$ 10,000
Feb. 22–25	Houston Open	Marty Furgol	277	$ 2,000	$ 10,000
Mar. 1–4	St. Petersburg Open	Jim Ferrier	268	$ 2,000	$ 10,000
Mar. 6	La Force Pro-Am	Sam Snead	63	$ 500	$ 2,500
Mar. 8–11	Miami Beach Open	Jim Ferrier	273	$ 2,000	$ 10,000
Mar. 12–14	Seminole Pro-Am	Lloyd Mangrum	203	$ 1,500	$ 10,000
Mar. 16–19	Jacksonville Open Invitational	Jim Ferrier	272	$ 2,000	$ 10,000
Mar. 21	Aiken Pro-Am	Lew Worsham	67	$ 345	$ 6,000
Mar. 23–26	Greensboro Open	Art Doering	279	$ 2,000	$ 10,000
Mar. 29–Apr. 1	Wilmington Azalea Open	Lloyd Mangrum	281	$ 2,000	$ 10,000
April 5–8	Masters	Ben Hogan	280	$ 3,000	$ 10,000
May 24–27	Colonial National Invitational	Cary Middlecoff	282	$ 3,000	$ 15,000

PGA TOUR (continued)

Date	Event	Winner	Score	1st Place Money	Total Purse
June 7–10	Palm Beach Round-Robin Invitational	Roberto De Vicenzo	Plus 40[b]	$ 3,000	$ 15,000
June 14–16	U.S. Open	Ben Hogan	287	$ 4,000	$ 12,000
June 21–24	Inverness Four-Ball Invitational	R. De Vicenzo and H. Ransom	Plus 9[b]	$ 4,000	$ 15,000
June 27–July 3	PGA Championship	Sam Snead	7&6	$ 3,500	$ 17,950
July 4–7	Canadian Open	Jim Ferrier	273	$ 2,250	$ 15,000
July 12–15	Western Open	Marty Furgol	270	$ 2,250	$ 15,000
July 19–22	Blue Ribbon Open	Joe Kirkwood, Jr.	271	$ 2,750	$ 20,000
July 26–29	St. Paul Open	Lloyd Mangrum	266	$ 2,250	$ 15,000
Aug. 2–5	All-American Open	Cary Middlecoff	274	$ 2,250	$ 15,000
Aug. 9–12	World Championship of Golf	Ben Hogan	273	$ 12,500	$ 50,000
Aug. 16–19	Sioux City Open	Buck White	272	$ 2,400	$ 15,000
Aug. 23–26	Fort Wayne Open	Jim Ferrier	269	$ 2,400	$ 15,000
Sept. 6–9	Empire State Open	Buck White	284	$ 2,400	$ 15,000
Sept. 13–16	Eastern Open	Cary Middlecoff	279	$ 2,400	$ 15,000
Sept. 20–23	Reading Open	Jim Turnesa	280	$ 2,400	$ 15,000
Sept. 27–30	St. Louis Open	Cary Middlecoff	269	$ 2,400	$ 15,000
Oct. 4–7	Kansas City Open	Cary Middlecoff	278	$ 2,400	$ 15,000
Nov. 7–11	North and South Open	Tommy Bolt	283	$ 1,500	$ 7,500
Dec. 6–9	Miami Open	Sam Snead	268	$ 2,000	$ 10,000
Dec. 13–16	Havana Pro-Am	Jimmy Demaret	275	$ 1,500	$ 15,000

1952 Tour

Date	Event	Winner	Score	1st Place Money	Total Purse
Jan. 4–7	Los Angeles Open	Tommy Bolt	289	$ 4,000	$ 17,500
Jan. 10–13	Bing Crosby Pro-Am	Jimmy Demaret	145	$ 2,000	$ 7,000
Jan. 17–20	San Diego Open	Ted Kroll	276	$ 2,000	$ 10,000
Jan. 24–27	Phoenix Open	Lloyd Mangrum	274	$ 2,000	$ 10,000
Jan. 31–Feb. 3	Tucson Open	H. Williams, Jr.	274	$ 2,000	$ 10,000
Feb. 7–10	El Paso Open	Cary Middlecoff	269	$ 2,000	$ 10,000
Feb. 14–17	Texas Open	Jack Burke, Jr.	260	$ 2,000	$ 10,000
Feb. 21–24	Houston Open	Jack Burke, Jr.	277	$ 2,000	$ 10,000
Feb. 28–Mar. 2	Baton Rouge Open	Jack Burke, Jr.	281	$ 2,000	$ 10,000
Mar. 6–9	St. Petersburg Open	Jack Burke, Jr.	266	$ 2,000	$ 10,000
Mar. 11	La Gorce Pro-Am	Tommy Bolt	68	$ 500	$ 5,600
Mar. 18	Seminole Pro-Am	Bob Toski	129	$ 875	$ 10,000
Mar. 21–24	Jacksonville Open	Doug Ford	280	$ 2,000	$ 10,000
Mar. 25	Aiken Pro-Am	Sam Snead	65	$ 450	$ 6,000
Mar. 27–30	Wilmington Azalea Open	Jimmy Clark	272	$ 2,000	$ 10,000
Apr. 3–6	Masters	Sam Snead	286	$ 4,000	$ 10,000
Apr. 11–14	Greater Greensboro Open	Dave Douglas	277	$ 2,000	$ 10,000
May 8–11	Pan American Open	Lloyd Mangrum	279	$ 2,600	$ 15,000
May 8–11	Greenbriar Pro-Am	Sam Snead	264	$ 1,800	$ 7,000
May 13	Piping Rock Pro-Am	Max Faulkner	68	$ 1,000	$ 5,000
May 15–18	Palm Beach Round-Robin Invitational	Sam Snead	Plus 57[b]	$ 3,000	$ 15,000
May 22–25	Colonial National Invitational	Ben Hogan	279	$ 4,000	$ 15,000
May 29–June 1	Western Open	Lloyd Mangrum	274	$ 2,400	$ 15,000

PGA TOUR (continued)

Date	Event	Winner	Score	1st Place Money	Total Purse
June 5–8	Ardmore Open	Dave Douglas	279	$ 5,400	$ 15,000
June 12–14	U.S. Open	Julius Boros	281	$ 4,000	$ 15,000
June 18–25	PGA Championship	Jim Turnesa	1 up	$ 3,500	$ 17,950
June 26–29	Inverness Round-Robin Invitational	Sam Snead and Jim Ferrier	Plus 13b	$ 5,000	$ 18,000
July 3–6	Motor City Open	Cary Middlecoff	274	$ 2,400	$ 15,000
July 10–13	St. Paul Open	Cary Middlecoff	266	$ 2,400	$ 15,000
July 16–19	Canadian Open	Johnny Palmer	263	$ 2,400	$ 15,000
July 24–27	Sioux City Open	Al Besselink	266	$ 2,400	$ 15,000
July 31–Aug. 3	All-American Open	Sam Snead	271	$ 3,400	$ 25,000
Aug. 7–10	World Championship of Golf	Julius Boros	276	$ 25,000	$ 75,000
Aug. 14–17	Kansas City Open	Cary Middlecoff	272	$ 2,400	$ 15,000
Aug. 21–24	Fort Wayne Open	Jimmy Clark	272	$ 2,400	$ 15,000
Aug. 29–Sept. 1	Insurance City Open	Ted Kroll	273	$ 2,400	$ 15,000
Sept. 4–7	Empire State Open	Jim Ferrier	262	$ 2,400	$ 15,000
Sept. 11–14	Eastern Open	Sam Snead	275	$ 2,400	$ 15,000
Sept. 18–21	National Celebrities Open	Jimmy Demaret	282	$ 2,400	$ 15,000
Oct. 8–12	Northern California Reno Open	E.J. Harrison	271	$ 1,000	$ 5,000
Nov. 13–16	Southern California Open	Jerry Barber	278	$ 750	$ 3,000
Nov. 23–25	Julius Boros Open	Sam Snead	207	$ 1,000	$ 5,000
Dec. 3–6	Havana Pro-Am	E.J. Harrison	270	$ 1,500	$ 15,000

1953 Tour

Date	Event	Winner	Score	1st Place Money	Total Purse
Jan. 2–5	Los Angeles Open	Lloyd Mangrum	280	$ 2,750	$ 20,000
Jan. 9–12	Bing Crosby Pro-Am	Lloyd Mangrum	204	$ 2,000	$ 10,000
Jan. 15–18	San Diego Open	Tommy Bolt	274	$ 2,000	$ 10,000
Jan. 19–21	Thunderbird Professional–Member Invitational	Jimmy Demaret	201	$ 1,500	$ 10,000
Jan. 23–26	Phoenix Open	Lloyd Mangrum	272	$ 2,000	$ 10,000
Jan. 29–Feb. 1	Tucson Open	Tommy Bolt	265	$ 2,000	$ 10,000
Feb. 5–8	El Paso Open	Chandler Harper	278	$ 2,000	$ 10,200
Feb. 12–15	Texas Open	Tony Holguin	264	$ 2,000	$ 10,400
Feb. 26, 28, Mar. 1	Houston Open	Cary Middlecoff	283	$ 4,000	$ 20,000
Mar. 5–8	Baton Rouge Open	Sam Snead	275	$ 2,000	$ 10,000
Mar. 12–15	St. Petersburg Open	E.J. Harrison	266	$ 2,000	$ 10,400
Mar. 16	La Gorce Professional Member Invitational	E.J. Harrison	68	$ 500	$ 3,500
Mar. 17–18	Seminole Pro-Am Invitational	Pete Cooper	138	$ 1,800	$ 10,000
Mar. 20–23	Jacksonville Open	Lew Worsham	272	$ 2,000	$ 10,200
Mar. 25	Palmetto Pro-Am	Dave Douglas	67	$ 450	$ 1,500
Mar. 27–29	Greensboro Open	Earl Stewart, Jr.	275	$ 2,000	$ 10,100
Apr. 2–5	Azalea Open Invitational	Jerry Barber	276	$ 2,000	$ 10,000
Apr. 9–12	Masters	Ben Hogan	274	$ 4,000	$ 24,410
Apr. 16–19	Virginia Beach Open	Doug Ford	262	$ 2,000	$ 10,000
Apr. 23–26	Tournament of Champions	Al Besselink	280	$ 10,000	$ 35,000
Apr. 30, May 1–3	Pan American Open	Ben Hogan	286	$ 2,604	$ 15,000

PGA TOUR (continued)

Date	Event	Winner	Score	1st Place Money	Total Purse
May 7–10	Ardmore Open	Earl Stewart, Jr.	282	$ 6,900	$ 26,300
May 7–10	Greenbriar Pro-Am	Sam Snead	268	$ 2,000	$ 11,500
May 11	Piping Rock Pro-Am	Claude Harmon	70	$ 1,000	$ 5,000
May 13–17	Palm Beach Round-Robin Invitational	Cary Middlecoff	Plus 42b	$ 3,000	$ 17,000
May 21–24	Colonial Invitational Tournament	Ben Hogan	282	$ 5,000	$ 25,000
May 28–31	Western Open Champion-ship	E.J. Harrison	278	$ 2,400	$ 15,000
June 11–13	U.S. Open	Ben Hogan	283	$ 5,000	$ 20,100
June 18–21	Inverness Invitational	Jack Burke, Jr.	272	$ 3,400	$ 18,000
June 25–28	Carling's Open	Cary Middlecoff	275	$ 2,400	$ 15,000
July 1–7	PGA Championship	Walter Burkemo	2&1	$ 5,000	$ 20,950
July 8–11	Canadian Open	Dave Douglas	273	$ 3,000	$ 15,000
July 16–19	St. Paul Open	Shelley Mayfield	269	$ 2,400	$ 15,000
July 23–26	Kansas City Open	Ed Oliver	269	$ 3,000	$ 17,500
July 30–31	All-American Open	Lloyd Mangrum	275	$ 3,420	$ 25,000
Aug. 6–9	World Championship of Golf	Lew Worsham	278	$ 25,000	$ 75,000
Aug. 13–16	Fort Wayne Open	Art Wall, Jr.	265	$ 2,400	$ 15,000
Aug. 20–23	Labatt Open	Doug Ford	265	$ 5,000	$ 25,000
Aug. 27–30	Insurance City Open	Bob Toski	269	$ 2,400	$ 15,000
Sept. 3–6	National Celebrities Open	Ted Kroll	281	$ 2,400	$ 15,000
Sept. 10–13	Eastern Open	Dick Mayer	279	$ 2,400	$ 15,000
Nov. 26–29	Columbia Open	E.J. Harrison	274	$ 2,000	$ 10,000
Dec. 3–6	Havana Pro-Am Invitational	Bob Toski	272	$ 1,500	$ 15,000
Dec. 10–12	Miami Open	Doug Ford	272	$ 2,000	$ 10,000

1954 Tour

Date	Event	Winner	Score	1st Place Money	Total Purse
Jan. 8–11	Los Angeles Open	Fred Wampler	281	$ 4,000	$ 20,000
Jan. 15–17	Bing Crosby Pro-Am	E.J. Harrison	210	$ 2,000	$ 10,000
Jan. 21–24	San Diego Open	Gene Littlera	274	$ 2,400	$ 15,000
Jan. 28–31	Thunderbird Invitational	Fred Haas, Jr.	268	$ 2,000	$ 15,000
Feb. 4–7	Phoenix Open	Ed Furgol	272	$ 2,000	$ 10,000
Feb. 18–21	Texas Open	Chandler Harper	259	$ 2,200	$ 12,500
Feb. 25–28	Mexican National Open	Johnny Palmer	286	$ 2,910	$ 10,000
Mar. 4–7	Houston Open	Dave Douglas	277	$ 6,000	$ 30,000
Mar. 11–14	Baton Rouge Open	Bob Toski	279	$ 2,000	$ 10,000
Mar. 16	International Four-Ball Pro-Am	Fred Haas, Jr.	66	$ 400	$ 5,000
Mar. 18–21	Miami Beach International Four-Ball	Tommy Bolt and Dick Mayer	258	$ 3,000	$ 15,000
Mar. 23–24	Seminole Pro-Am	Lew Worsham	136	$ 1,800	$ 10,000
Mar. 26–28	Azalea Open Invitational	Bob Toski	273	$ 2,000	$ 10,000
Apr. 2–4	Greater Greensboro Open	Doug Ford	283	$ 2,000	$ 10,000
Apr. 8–11	Masters	Sam Snead	289	$ 5,000	$ 33,500
Apr. 22–25	Tournament of Champions	Art Wall, Jr.	278	$ 10,000	$ 35,000
Apr. 30–May 2	San Francisco Pro-Am	Shelley Mayfield	212	$ 1,400	$ 10,000
May 6–9	Ardmore Open	Julius Boros	279	$ 7,200	$ 31,860
May 20–23	Eastern Open	Bob Toski	277	$ 4,000	$ 20,000

PGA TOUR (continued)

Date	Event	Winner	Score	1st Place Money	Total Purse
May 27–30	Colonial Invitational Tournament	Johnny Palmer	280	$ 5,000	$ 25,000
May 12–16	Palm Beach Round-Robin Invitational	Sam Snead	Plus 62b	$ 3,000	$ 15,000
May 17	Piping Rock Pro-Am	Cary Middlecoff	68	$ 875	$ 5,350
June 3–6	Western Open Championship	Lloyd Mangrum	277	$ 2,400	$ 15,000
June 10–13	Virginia Beach Open	Pete Cooper	263	$ 2,400	$ 15,000
June 17–19	U.S. Open	Ed Furgol	284	$ 6,000	$ 23,280
June 24–28	Insurance City Open	Tommy Bolt	271	$ 2,400	$ 15,000
July 1–4	Motor City Open	Cary Middlecoff	278	$ 3,000	$ 17,500
July 15–18	Carling's Open	Julius Boros	280	$ 5,000	$ 25,000
July 21–27	PGA Championship	Chick Harbert	4&3	$ 5,000	$ 20,950
July 29, 30–Aug. 1	Kansas City Open	Wally Ulrich	268	$ 4,000	$ 20,000
Aug. 5–8	All-American Open	Jerry Barber	277	$ 3,420	$ 25,000
Aug. 12–15	World Championship of Golf	Bob Toski	272	$ 50,000	$ 100,000
Aug. 19–22	Fort Wayne Open	Doug Ford	270	$ 2,400	$ 15,000
Aug. 25–28	Labatt Open	Bud Holscher	269	$ 5,000	$ 25,000
Sept. 2–5	Rubber City Open	Tommy Bolt	265	$ 2,400	$ 15,000
Sept. 23–26	National Celebrities Open	Marty Furgol	273	$ 7,500	$ 15,000
Dec. 7	La Gorce Pro-Am	Sam Snead	66	$ 500	$ 3,500
Dec. 9–12	Miami Open	Bob Rosburg	273	$ 2,000	$ 10,000
Dec. 16–19	Havana Pro-Am	Ed Furgol	273	$ 2,000	$ 15,000

1955 Tour

Date	Event	Winner	Score	1st Place Money	Total Purse
Jan. 6–9	Los Angeles Open	Gene Littler	276	$ 5,000	$ 32,500
Jan. 14–16	Bing Crosby Pro-Am	Cary Middlecoff	209	$ 2,500	$ 15,000
Jan. 20–23	Convair–San Diego Open	Tommy Bolt	274	$ 2,400	$ 15,000
Jan. 27–30	Thunderbird Invitational	Shelley Mayfield	270	$ 2,000	$ 15,000
Jan. 27–30	Imperial Valley Open	Mike Fetchick	266	$ 1,000	$ 5,000
Feb. 3–6	Phoenix Open	Gene Littler	275	$ 2,400	$ 15,000
Feb. 10–13	Tucson Open	Tommy Bolt	266	$ 2,000	$ 10,000
Feb. 17–20	Texas Open	Mike Souchak	257	$ 2,000	$ 12,500
Feb. 24–27	Houston Open	Mike Souchak	273	$ 6,000	$ 30,000
Mar. 3–6	Baton Rouge Open	Bo Wininger	278	$ 2,200	$ 12,500
Mar. 17–20	St. Petersburg Open	Cary Middlecoff	274	$ 2,200	$ 12,500
Mar. 21–22	Seminole Pro-Am	Mike Souchak	139	$ 1,800	$ 10,000
Mar. 24–27	Miami Beach Open	Eric Monti	270	$ 2,200	$ 12,500
Mar. 31–Apr. 3	Azalea Open	Billy Maxwell	270	$ 2,200	$ 12,500
Apr. 7–10	Masters	Cary Middlecoff	279	$ 5,000	$ 10,000
Apr. 14–17	Greater Greensboro Open	Sam Snead	273	$ 2,200	$ 12,500
Apr. 21–24	Virginia Beach Open	Chandler Harper	260	$ 2,400	$ 15,000
Apr. 28–May 1	Tournament of Champions	Gene Littler	280	$ 10,000	$ 35,000
May 5–8	Colonial Invitational	Chandler Harper	276	$ 5,000	$ 25,000
May 12–15	Arlington Hotel Open	Bo Wininger	270	$ 2,400	$ 15,000
May 19–22	Kansas City Open	Dick Mayer	271	$ 4,000	$ 20,000
May 26–29	Fort Wayne Invitational	Dow Finsterwald	269	$ 2,400	$ 15,000
June 1–5	Palm Beach Invitational	Sam Snead	Plus 46	$ 3,000	$ 15,000

PGA TOUR (continued)

Date	Event	Winner	Score	1st Place Money	Total Purse
June 16–18	U.S. Open	Jack Fleck	287	$ 6,000	$ 20,000
June 23–26	Western Open	Cary Middlecoff	272	$ 2,400	$ 15,000
June 29–July 2	British Columbia Open	Dow Finsterwald	270	$ 2,400	$ 15,000
July 7–10	St. Paul Open	Tommy Bolt	269	$ 2,400	$ 15,000
July 14–17	Miller Open	Cary Middlecoff	265	$ 6,000	$ 35,000
July 28–31	Rubber City Open	Henry Ransom	272	$ 2,400	$ 15,000
Aug. 4–7	All-American Champion-ship	Doug Ford	277	$ 3,420	$ 25,000
Aug. 11–14	World Championship of Golf	Julius Boros	281	$ 50,000	$ 100,000
Aug. 17–20	Canadian Open	Arnold Palmer	265	$ 2,400	$ 15,000
Aug. 25–28	Labatt Open	Gene Littler	272	$ 5,000	$ 25,000
Sept. 8–11	Cavalcade of Golf	Cary Middlecoff	276	$ 10,000	$ 50,000
Sept. 15–18	Philadelphia *Daily News* Open	Ted Kroll	273	$ 4,000	$ 20,000
Sept. 22–25	Carling Golf Classic	Doug Ford	276	$ 7,000	$ 50,000
Sept. 25	Insurance City Open	Sam Snead	269	$ 4,000	$ 20,000
Sept. 29–Oct. 2	Long Island Rotary Open	Max Evans	273	$ 2,400	$ 15,000
Oct. 6–9	Eastern Open	Frank Stranahan	280	$ 3,000	$ 17,500
Dec. 1–4	Havana Invitational	Mike Souchak	273	$ 2,000	$ 15,000
Dec. 8–11	Miami Beach Open	Sam Snead	201	$ 2,200	$ 12,500
Dec. 15–18	Mayfair Inn Open	Al Balding	269	$ 2,400	$ 15,000

1956 Tour

Date	Event	Winner	Score	1st Place Money	Total Purse
Jan. 6–9	Los Angeles Open	Lloyd Mangrum	272	$ 6,000	$ 30,000
Jan. 13–15	Bing Crosby Pro-Am	Cary Middlecoff	202	$ 2,500	$ 15,000
Jan. 19–22	Caliente Open	Mike Souchak	281	$ 2,200	$ 12,500
Jan. 26–29	Thunderbird Invitational	Jimmy Demaret	269	$ 2,000	$ 15,200
Jan. 26–29	Imperial Valley Open	Paul O'Leary	271	$ 1,000	$ 5,000
Feb. 2–5	Phoenix Open	Cary Middlecoff	276	$ 2,400	$ 15,000
Feb. 9–12	Tucson Open	Ted Kroll	264	$ 2,000	$ 15,000
Feb. 16–19	Texas Open	Gene Littler	276	$ 3,750	$ 18,750
Feb. 23–26	Houston Open	Ted Kroll	277	$ 6,000	$ 30,000
Mar. 1–4	Baton Rouge Open	Shelley Mayfield	277	$ 2,200	$ 12,500
Mar. 8–11	Pensacola Open	Don Fairfield	275	$ 2,200	$ 12,500
Mar. 15–18	St. Petersburg Open	Mike Fetchick	275	$ 2,200	$ 12,500
Mar. 22–25	Miami Beach Open	Gardner Dickinson, Jr.	272	$ 2,400	$ 15,000
Mar. 29–Apr. 1	Azalea Open	Mike Souchak	273	$ 2,200	$ 12,500
Apr. 5–8	Masters	Jack Burke, Jr.	289	$ 6,000	$ 42,000
Apr. 12–15	Greater Greensboro Open	Sam Snead	279	$ 2,200	$ 12,500
Apr. 19–22	Arlington Hotel Open	Billy Maxwell	272	$ 2,400	$ 15,000
Apr. 26–29	Tournament of Champions	Gene Littler	281	$ 10,000	$ 38,500
May 3–6	Colonial Invitational	Mike Souchak	280	$ 5,000	$ 25,000
May 10–13	Carling Open	Dow Finsterwald	274	$ 5,000	$ 25,000
May 17–20	Kansas City Open	Bo Wininger	273	$ 4,300	$ 22,000
May 24–27	Dallas Open	Don January	268	$ 6,000	$ 30,000
June 1–4	Texas Open	Peter Thomson	267	$ 13,478	$ 67,500
June 14–16	U.S. Open	Cary Middlecoff	281	$ 6,000	$ 24,900
June 21–24	Philadelphia *Daily News* Open	Dick Mayer	269	$ 4,000	$ 20,000

PGA TOUR (continued)

Date	Event	Winner	Score	1st Place Money	Total Purse
June 28–July 1	Insurance City Open	Arnold Palmer	274	$ 4,000	$ 20,000
July 5–8	Canadian Open	Doug Sanders[a]	273	Amateur	$ 15,000
July 12–15	Labatt Open	Billy Casper, Jr.	274	$ 5,000	$ 25,000
July 26–29	Eastern Open	Arnold Palmer	277	$ 3,800	$ 19,000
Aug. 2–5	All-American Championship	E. J. Harrison	278	$ 3,420	$ 25,000
Aug. 9–12	World Championship of Golf	Ted Kroll	273	$ 50,000	$ 101,200
Aug. 16–19	Miller Open	Ed Furgol	265	$ 6,000	$ 35,000
Aug. 23–26	St. Paul Open	Mike Souchak	271	$ 4,000	$ 20,000
Aug. 30–Sept. 2	Motor City Open	Bob Rosburg	284	$ 4,000	$ 20,000
Sept. 6–9	Rubber City Open	Ed Furgol	271	$ 3,000	$ 19,000
Sept. 13–16	Fort Wayne Open	Art Wall, Jr.	269	$ 2,400	$ 15,000
Sept. 20–23	Oklahoma City Open	Fred Hawkins	279	$ 2,400	$ 15,000
Oct. 4–7	San Diego Open	Bob Rosburg	270	$ 2,400	$ 15,000
Oct. 11–14	Western Open	Mike Fetchick	284	$ 5,000	$ 22,720
Dec. 6–9	Havana Invitational	Al Besselink	276	$ 2,500	$ 17,400
Dec. 13–16	Mayfair Inn Open	Mike Fetchick	263	$ 2,400	$ 15,000

1957 Tour

Date	Event	Winner	Score	1st Place Money	Total Purse
Jan. 4–7	Los Angeles Open	Doug Ford	280	$ 7,000	$ 35,000
Jan. 11–13	Bing Crosby Pro-Am	Jay Hebert	213	$ 2,500	$ 15,000
Jan. 17–20	Caliente Open	Ed Furgol	280	$ 2,000	$ 15,000
Jan. 24–27	Thunderbird Invitational	Jimmy Demaret	273	$ 2,000	$ 15,300
Jan. 24–27	Imperial Valley Open	Tony Lema	276	$ 1,000	$ 5,000
Jan. 31–Feb. 3	Phoenix Open	Billy Casper, Jr.	271	$ 2,000	$ 15,000
Feb. 7–10	Tucson Open	Dow Finsterwald	269	$ 2,000	$ 15,000
Feb. 14–17	Texas Open	Jay Hebert	271	$ 2,800	$ 20,000
Feb. 21–25	Houston Open	Arnold Palmer	279	$ 7,500	$ 37,100
Feb. 28–Mar. 3	Baton Rouge Open	Jimmy Demaret	278	$ 2,000	$ 15,000
Mar. 7–16	Pensacola Open	Art Wall, Jr.	273	$ 2,000	$ 15,000
Mar. 14–17	St. Petersburg Open	Pete Cooper	269	$ 1,700	$ 12,500
Mar. 23–24	Miami Beach Open	Al Balding	137	$ 1,200	$ 7,500
Mar. 28–31	Azalea Open	Arnold Palmer	282	$ 1,700	$ 12,500
Apr. 4–7	Masters	Doug Ford	283	$ 8,750	$ 53,300
Apr. 11–14	Greater Greensboro Open	Stan Leonard	276	$ 2,000	$ 15,000
Apr. 18–21	Tournament of Champions	Gene Littler	285	$ 10,000	$ 40,000
Apr. 24–28	Kentucky Derby Open	Billy Casper, Jr.	277	$ 4,300	$ 30,000
May 2–5	Colonial Invitational	Roberto DeVicenzo	284	$ 5,000	$ 25,000
May 9–12	Arlington Hotel Open	Jimmy Demaret	276	$ 2,800	$ 20,000
May 16–19	Greenbriar Invitational	E. J. Harrison	266	$ 2,300	$ 10,000
May 23–26	Kansas Open	Al Besselink	279	$ 2,800	$ 22,000
May 30–June 2	Palm Beach Invitational	Sam Snead	Plus 41[b]	$ 3,000	$ 10,050
June 6–9	Rubber City Open	Arnold Palmer	272	$ 2,800	$ 22,000
June 13–15	U.S. Open	Dick Mayer	282	$ 7,200	$ 28,560
June 20–23	Carling Open	Paul Harney	275	$ 5,700	$ 30,000
June 27–30	Western Open	Doug Ford	279	$ 5,000	$ 25,200
July 4–7	Labatt Open	Paul Harney	278	$ 3,500	$ 29,000
July 10–13	Canadian Open	George Bayer	271	$ 3,500	$ 25,000
July 21	Erie Open	Paul O'Leary	137	$ 1,000	$ 5,000

PGA TOUR (continued)

Date	Event	Winner	Score	1st Place Money	Total Purse
July 25–28	Eastern Open	Tommy Bolt	276	$ 2,800	$ 20,000
Aug. 1–5	All-American Open	Roberto DeVicenzo	273	$ 3,500	$ 25,000
Aug. 8–11	World Championship of Golf	Dick Mayer	279	$ 50,000	$ 101,200
Aug. 15–18	St. Paul Open	Ken Venturi	266	$ 2,800	$ 20,000
Aug. 22–25	Miller Open	Ken Venturi	267	$ 6,000	$ 35,000
Aug. 29–Sept. 2	Insurance City Open	Gardner Dickinson, Jr.	272	$ 2,800	$ 20,000
Sept. 13–16	Dallas Open	Sam Snead	264	$ 8,000	$ 40,000
Oct. 24–27	Hesperia Open	Billy Maxwell	275	$ 2,000	$ 15,000
Oct. 30–Nov. 3	San Diego Open	Arnold Palmer	271	$ 2,800	$ 20,000
Nov. 8–10	Long Beach Open	Charles Sifford	203	$ 1,200	$ 10,000
Nov. 22–24	West Palm Beach Open	Al Balding	209	$ 1,200	$ 10,000
Nov. 28–Dec. 1	Caracas Open	Al Besselink	279	$ 4,000	$ 20,000
Dec. 5–8	Havana Invitational	Al Balding	281	$ 2,400	$ 14,700
Dec. 12–15	Mayfair Inn Open	Walter Burkemo	269	$ 2,000	$ 15,000

1958 Tour

Date	Event	Winner	Score	1st Place Money	Total Purse
Jan. 3–6	Los Angeles Open	Frank Stranahan	275	$ 7,000	$ 35,000
Jan. 9–12	Bing Crosby Pro-Am	Billy Casper, Jr.	277	$ 4,000	$ 50,000
Jan. 17–20	Tijuana Open	E. J. Harrison	280	$ 2,000	$ 15,000
Jan. 23–26	Thunderbird Invitational	Ken Venturi	269	$ 1,500	$ 15,000
Jan. 30–Feb. 2	Phoenix Open	Ken Venturi	274	$ 2,000	$ 15,000
Feb. 6–9	Tucson Open	Lionel Hebert	265	$ 2,000	$ 15,000
Feb. 13–16	Texas Open	Bill Johnston	274	$ 2,000	$ 15,000
Feb. 20–24	Houton Invitational	Ed Oliver	281	$ 4,300	$ 30,000
Feb. 27–Mar. 2	Baton Rouge Open	Ken Venturi	276	$ 2,000	$ 15,000
Mar. 1–2	Jackson Open	Fred Hawkins	140	$ 750	$ 5,000
Mar. 9–11	New Orleans Open	Billy Casper, Jr.	278	$ 2,800	$ 20,000
Mar. 13–16	Pensacola Open	Doug Ford	278	$ 2,000	$ 15,000
Mar. 20–23	St. Petersburg Open	Arnold Palmer	276	$ 2,000	$ 15,000
Mar. 28–30	Azalea Open	Howie Johnson	282	$ 2,000	$ 15,000
Apr. 3–6	Masters	Arnold Palmer	284	$ 11,250	$ 60,050
Apr. 11–13	Greater Greensboro Open	Bob Goalby	275	$ 2,000	$ 15,000
Apr. 17–20	Kentucky Derby Open	Gary Player	274	$ 2,800	$ 20,000
Apr. 24–27	Lafayette Open	Jay Hebert	273	$ 2,000	$ 15,000
May 1–4	Colonial Invitational	Tommy Bolt	282	$ 5,000	$ 25,000
May 8–11	Arlington Hotel Open	Julius Boros	273	$ 2,800	$ 20,000
May 15–18	Memphis Invitational	Billy Maxwell	267	$ 2,800	$ 20,000
May 15–18	Greenbrier Invitational	Sam Snead	264	$ 2,300	$ 10,000
May 22–25	Kansas City Open	Ernie Vossier	269	$ 2,800	$ 20,000
May 29–June 1	Western Open	Doug Sanders	275	$ 5,000	$ 25,000
June 5–8	Dallas Open	Sam Snead	272	$ 3,500	$ 25,000
June 13–15	U.S. Open	Tommy Bolt	283	$ 8,000	$ 35,000
June 19–23	Buick Open	Billy Casper, Jr.	285	$ 9,000	$ 50,000
June 26–29	Pepsi Open	Arnold Palmer	273	$ 9,000	$ 50,000
July 3–6	Rubber City Open	Art Wall, Jr.	269	$ 2,800	$ 20,000
July 10–13	Insurance City Open	Jack Burke, Jr.	268	$ 3,500	$ 25,000
July 17–20	PGA Championship	Dow Finsterwald	276	$ 5,500	$ 39,400
July 24–27	Eastern Open	Art Wall, Jr.	276	$ 2,800	$ 20,000
Aug. 1–4	Gleneagles-Chicago Open	Ken Venturi	272	$ 9,000	$ 50,000

PGA TOUR (continued)

Date	Event	Winner	Score	1st Place Money	Total Purse
Aug. 7–11	Miller Open	Cary Middlecoff	264	$ 5,300	$ 35,000
Aug. 14–17	St. Paul open	Mike Souchak	263	$ 3,500	$ 25,000
Aug. 20–23	Canadian Open	Wes Ellis, Jr.	269	$ 3,500	$ 25,000
Aug. 28–Sept. 1	Vancouver Open	Jim Ferree	270	$ 6,400	$ 40,000
Sept. 5–8	Utah Open	Dow Finsterwald	267	$ 2,000	$ 15,000
Sept. 11–14	Denver Open	Tommy Jacobs	266	$ 2,800	$ 20,000
Sept. 18–21	Hesperia Open	John McMullin	271	$ 2,000	$ 15,000
Nov. 5–9	Carling Open	Julius Boros	284	$ 3,500	$ 25,000
Nov. 13–16	Havana Invitational	George Bayer	286	$ 6,500	$ 40,000
Nov. 20–23	West Palm Beach Open	Pete Cooper	269	$ 2,000	$ 15,000
Dec. 4–7	Mayfair Inn Open	George Bayer	272	$ 2,000	$ 15,000

1959 Tour

Date	Event	Winner	Score	1st Place Money	Total Purse
Jan. 2–5	Los Angeles Open	Ken Venturi	278	$ 5,300	$ 35,000
Jan. 9–12	Tijuana Open	Ernie Vossler	273	$ 2,800	$ 20,000
Jan. 15–18	Bing Crosby Pro-Am	Art Wall, Jr.	279	$ 4,000	$ 34,999
Jan. 22–25	Thunderbird Invitational	Arnold Palmer	266	$ 1,500	$ 12,000
Jan. 29–Feb. 1	San Diego Open	Marty Furgol	274	$ 2,800	$ 20,000
Feb. 5–8	Phoenix Open	Gene Littler	268	$ 2,400	$ 17,500
Feb. 12–15	Tucson Open	Gene Littler	266	$ 2,000	$ 15,000
Feb. 19–22	Texas Open	Wes Ellis, Jr.	276	$ 2,800	$ 20,000
Feb. 27–Mar. 1	Baton Rouge Open	Howie Johnson	283	$ 2,000	$ 15,000
Mar. 6–9	New Orleans Open	Bill Collins	280	$ 2,800	$ 20,000
Mar. 12–15	Pensacola Open	Paul Harney	269	$ 2,000	$ 15,000
Mar. 20–23	St. Petersburg Open	Cary Middlecoff	275	$ 2,000	$ 15,000
Mar. 27–30	Azalea Open	Art Wall, Jr.	282	$ 2,000	$ 15,000
Apr. 2–5	Masters	Art Wall, Jr.	284	$ 15,000	$ 76,100
Apr. 9–12	Greater Greensboro Open	Dow Finsterwald	278	$ 2,000	$ 15,000
Apr. 16–19	Houston Classic	Jack Burke, Jr.	277	$ 4,300	$ 30,000
Apr. 23–26	Tournament of Champions	Mike Souchak	281	$ 10,000	$ 46,620
Apr. 30–May 1	Colonial National	Ben Hogan	285	$ 5,000	$ 27,300
May 7–11	Oklahoma City Open	Arnold Palmer	273	$ 3,500	$ 25,000
May 14–17	Arlington Hotel Open	Gene Littler	270	$ 2,800	$ 20,000
May 21–25	Memphis Open	Don Whitt	272	$ 3,500	$ 25,000
May 28–31	Kentucky Derby Open	Don Whitt	274	$ 2,800	$ 20,000
June 4–7	Eastern Open	Dave Ragan, Jr.	273	$ 2,800	$ 20,000
June 11–14	U.S. Open	Billy Casper, Jr.	282	$ 12,000	$ 49,200
June 18–21	Canadian Open	Doug Ford	276	$ 3,500	$ 25,000
June 25–28	Gleneagles-Chicago Open	Ken Venturi	273	$ 9,000	$ 50,000
July 2–5	Buick Open	Art Wall, Jr.	282	$ 9,000	$ 50,060
July 9–12	Western Open	Mike Souchak	272	$ 5,000	$ 25,000
July 16–19	Insurance City Open	Gene Littler	272	$ 3,500	$ 25,000
July 30–Aug. 2	PGA Championship	Bob Rosburg	277	$ 8,250	$ 51,175
Aug. 6–9	Carling Open	Dow Finsterwald	276	$ 3,500	$ 25,000
Aug. 13–16	Motor City Open	Mike Souchak	268	$ 3,500	$ 25,000
Aug. 20–23	Rubber City Open	Tom Nieporte	267	$ 2,800	$ 20,000
Aug. 27–30	Miller Open	Gene Littler	265	$ 5,300	$ 35,000
Sept. 4–7	Kansas City Open	Dow Finsterwald	275	$ 2,800	$ 20,000
Sept. 11–14	Dallas Open	Julius Boros	274	$ 3,500	$ 25,000
Sept. 17–20	El Paso Open	Marty Furgol	273	$ 2,800	$ 20,000

PGA TOUR (continued)

Date	Event	Winner	Score	1st Place Money	Total Purse
Sept. 24–27	Golden Gate Championship	Mason Rudolph, Jr.	275	$ 6,400	$ 40,000
Oct. 1–4	Portland Open	Billy Casper, Jr.	269	$ 2,800	$ 20,000
Oct. 8–11	Hesperia Open	Eric Monti	271	$ 2,000	$ 15,000
Oct. 15–18	Orange County Open	Jay Hebert	273	$ 2,000	$ 15,000
Nov. 12–15	Lafayette Open	Billy Casper, Jr.	273	$ 2,000	$ 15,000
Nov. 19–22	Mobile Open	Billy Casper, Jr.	280	$ 2,000	$ 15,000
Nov. 26–29	West Palm Beach Open	Arnold Palmer	281	$ 2,000	$ 15,000
Dec. 3–6	Coral Gables Open	Doug Sanders	273	$ 2,800	$ 20,000

1960 Tour

Date	Event	Winner	Score	1st Place Money	Total Purse
Jan. 8–9	Los Angeles Open	Dow Finsterwald	280	$ 5,500	$ 37,500
Jan. 15–18	Yorba Linda Open	Jerry Barber	278	$ 2,800	$ 20,000
Jan. 21–24	Bing Crosby Pro-am	Ken Venturi	286	$ 4,000	$ 35,002
Jan. 28–31	San Diego Open	Mike Souchak	269	$ 2,800	$ 20,000
Feb. 3–7	Palm Springs Classic	Arnold Palmer	338	$ 12,000	$ 70,000
Feb. 11–14	Panama Open	Ernie Vossler	269	$ 1,500	$ 10,000
Feb. 11–15	Phoenix Open	Jack Fleck	273	$ 3,150	$ 22,500
Feb. 18–21	Tucson Open	Don January	271	$ 2,800	$ 20,000
Feb. 25–28	Texas Open	Arnold Palmer	276	$ 2,800	$ 20,000
Mar. 3–6	Baton Rouge Open	Arnold Palmer	279	$ 2,000	$ 15,000
Mar. 10–13	Pensacola Open	Arnold Palmer	273	$ 2,000	$ 15,000
Mar. 19–21	St. Petersburg Open	George Bayer	282	$ 2,000	$ 15,000
Mar. 24–27	DeSoto Open	Sam Snead	276	$ 5,300	$ 35,000
Mar. 31–Apr. 3	Azalea Open	Tom Nieporte	277	$ 2,000	$ 15,000
Apr. 7–10	Masters	Arnold Palmer	282	$ 17,500	$ 87,050
Apr. 14–17	Greater Greensboro Open	Sam Snead	270	$ 2,800	$ 20,000
Apr. 21–24	New Orleans Open	Dow Finsterwald	270	$ 3,500	$ 25,000
Apr. 28–May 2	Houston Classic	Bill Collins	280	$ 5,300	$ 36,440
May 5–8	Tournament of Champions	Jerry Barber	268	$ 16,000	$ 42,400
May 12–15	Colonial National	Julius Boros	280	$ 5,000	$ 30,000
May 19–22	Hot Springs Open	Bill Collins	275	$ 2,800	$ 20,000
May 26–29	"500" Festival	Doug Ford	270	$ 9,000	$ 50,000
June 2–5	Memphis Open	Tommy Bolt	273	$ 4,300	$ 30,000
June 9–12	Oklahoma City Open	Gene Littler	273	$ 4,300	$ 30,000
June 16–18	U.S. Open	Arnold Palmer	280	$ 14,400	$ 60,720
July 1–4	Buick Open	Mike Souchak	282	$ 9,000	$ 50,000
July 6–9	Canadian Open	Art Wall, Jr.	269	$ 3,500	$ 25,000
July 14–17	Western Open	Stan Leonard	278	$ 5,000	$ 25,000
July 21–24	PGA Championship	Jay Hebert	281	$ 11,000	$ 63,130
July 28–31	Eastern Open	Gene Littler	273	$ 3,500	$ 25,000
Aug. 4–7	Insurance City Open	Arnold Palmer	270	$ 3,500	$ 25,000
Aug. 18–21	St. Paul Open	Don Fairchild	266	$ 4,300	$ 30,000
Aug. 25–28	Milwaukee Open	Ken Venturi	271	$ 4,300	$ 30,000
Sept. 2–5	Dallas Open	Johnny Pott	275	$ 3,500	$ 25,000
Sept. 9–12	Utah Open	Bill Johnson	262	$ 2,800	$ 20,000
Sept. 15–18	Carling Open	Ernie Vossler	272	$ 3,500	$ 25,000
Sept. 22–25	Portland Open	Billy Casper, Jr.	266	$ 2,800	$ 20,000
Sept. 30–Oct. 3	Hesperia Open	Billy Casper, Jr.	275	$ 2,000	$ 15,000
Oct. 13–16	Orange County Open	Billy Casper, Jr.	276	$ 2,000	$ 15,000
Nov. 17–20	Cajun Classic Open	Lionel Hebert	272	$ 2,000	$ 15,000

PGA TOUR (continued)

Date	Event	Winner	Score	1st Place Money	Total Purse
Nov. 24–27	Mobile Open	Arnold Palmer	274	$ 2,000	$ 15,000
Dec. 1–4	West Palm Beach Open	Johnny Pott	278	$ 2,000	$ 15,000
Dec. 8–11	Coral Gables Open	Bob Goalby	272	$ 2,800	$ 20,000

1961 Tour

Date	Event	Winner	Score	1st Place Money	Total Purse
Jan. 6–9	Los Angeles Open	Bob Goalby	275	$ 7,500	$ 45,000
Jan. 12–15	San Diego Open	Arnold Palmer	271	$ 2,800	$ 20,000
Jan. 19–22	Bing Crosby Pro-Am	Bob Rosburg	282	$ 5,300	$ 35,000
Jan. 26–29	Lucky International	Gary Player	272	$ 9,000	$ 50,000
Feb. 1–5	Palm Springs Classic	Billy Maxwell	345	$ 5,300	$ 35,000
Feb. 9–12	Phoenix Open	Arnold Palmer	270	$ 4,300	$ 30,000
Feb. 16–19	Tucson Open	Dave Hill	269	$ 2,800	$ 20,000
Feb. 24–26	Baton Rouge Open	Arnold Palmer	266	$ 2,800	$ 20,000
Mar. 2–5	New Orleans Open	Doug Sanders	272	$ 4,300	$ 30,000
Mar. 9–12	Pensacola Open	Tommy Bolt	275	$ 2,800	$ 20,000
Mar. 16–19	St. Petersburg Open	Bob Goalby	261	$ 2,800	$ 20,000
Mar. 23–26	Sunshine Open	Gary Player	273	$ 3,500	$ 25,000
Apr. 1–2	Azalea Open	Jerry Barber	213	$ 1,206	$ 12,000
Apr. 6–8, 10	Masters	Gary Player	280	$ 20,000	$ 99,500
Apr. 13–16	Greater Greensboro Open	Mike Souchak	276	$ 3,200	$ 22,500
Apr. 20–23	Houston Classic	Jay Hebert	276	$ 7,000	$ 43,570
Apr. 27–30	Texas Open	Arnold Palmer	270	$ 4,300	$ 30,000
May 4–7	Tournament of Champions	Sam Snead	273	$ 10,000	$ 52,000
May 11–14	Colonial National	Doug Sanders	281	$ 7,000	$ 40,000
May 18–21	Hot Springs Open	Doug Sanders	273	$ 2,800	$ 20,000
May 25–28	"500" Festival	Doug Ford	273	$ 9,000	$ 50,000
June 1–4	Memphis Open	Cary Middlecoff	266	$ 14,300	$ 30,000
June 15–17	U.S. Open	Gene Littler	281	$ 14,000	$ 60,500
June 22–25	Western Open	Arnold Palmer	271	$ 5,000	$ 30,560
June 29–July 2	Buick Open	Jack Burke, Jr.	284	$ 9,000	$ 50,000
July 6–9	St. Paul Open	Don January	269	$ 4,300	$ 30,000
July 12–15	Canadian Open	Jacky Cupit	270	$ 4,300	$ 30,000
July 20–23	Milwaukee Open	Bruce Crampton	272	$ 4,300	$ 30,000
July 27–30	PGA Championship	Jerry Barber	277	$ 11,000	$ 64,800
Aug. 3–6	Eastern Open	Doug Sanders	275	$ 5,300	$ 35,000
Aug. 10–31	Insurance City Open	Billy Maxwell	271	$ 4,300	$ 30,000
Aug. 17–20	Carling Open	Gay Brewer, Jr.	277	$ 5,300	$ 35,000
Aug. 24–27	American Classic	Jay Hebert	278	$ 9,000	$ 50,900
Sept. 1–4	Dallas Open	Earl Stewart, Jr.	278	$ 4,300	$ 30,000
Sept. 7–10	Denver Open	Dave Hill	263	$ 3,500	$ 25,000
Sept. 14–17	Seattle Open	Dave Marr	265	$ 3,500	$ 25,000
Sept. 21–24	Portland Open	Billy Casper, Jr.	273	$ 3,500	$ 25,000
Sept. 28–Oct. 1	Bakersfield Open	Jack Fleck	276	$ 3,500	$ 25,000
Oct. 8	Hesperia Open	Tony Lema	138	$ 1,200	$ 10,000
Oct. 12–15	Ontario Open	Eric Monti	277	$ 2,800	$ 20,000
Oct. 19–22	Orange County Open	Bob McCallister	278	$ 2,400	$ 17,500
Nov. 2–5	Almaden Open	Jim Ferrier	279	$ 1,200	$ 10,000
Nov. 9–12	Beaumont Open	Joe Campbell	277	$ 2,800	$ 20,000
Nov. 16–19	Cajun Classic	Doug Sanders	270	$ 2,000	$ 15,000
Nov. 23–26	Mobile Open	Gay Brewer, Jr.	275	$ 2,000	$ 15,000

Gary Player, Arnold Palmer and Jack Nicklaus (left to right) were golf's "big three" in early 1960s. *UPI/Bettmann*

PGA TOUR (continued)

Date	Event	Winner	Score	1st Place Money	Total Purse
Nov. 30–Dec. 3	West Palm Beach Open	Gay Brewer, Jr.	274	$ 2,800	$ 20,000
Dec. 7–10	Coral Gables Open	George Knudson	273	$ 2,800	$ 20,000
	1962 Tour				
Jan. 5–8	Los Angeles Open	Phil Rodgers	268	$ 7,500	$ 45,000
Jan. 11–14	San Diego Open	Tommy Jacobs	277	$ 3,500	$ 25,000
Jan. 18–20	Bing Crosby Pro-Am	Doug Ford	286	$ 5,300	$ 35,000
Jan. 25–28	Lucky International Open	Gene Littler	274	$ 9,000	$ 50,000
Jan. 31–Feb. 4	Palm Springs Classic	Arnold Palmer	342	$ 5,300	$ 35,000
Feb. 8–11	Phoenix Open	Arnold Palmer	269	$ 5,300	$ 35,000
Feb. 15–18	Tucson Open	Phil Rodgers	263	$ 2,800	$ 20,000
Feb. 22–25	New Orleans Open	Bo Wininger	281	$ 4,300	$ 30,000
Mar. 2–4	Baton Rouge Open	Joe Campbell	274	$ 2,800	$ 20,000
Mar. 8–11	Pensacola Open	Doug Sanders	270	$ 2,800	$ 20,000

PGA TOUR (continued)

Date	Event	Winner	Score	1st Place Money	Total Purse
Mar. 15–18	St. Petersburg Open	Bob Nichols	272	$ 2,800	$ 20,000
Mar. 22–25	Doral Open	Billy Casper, Jr.	283	$ 9,000	$ 50,000
Mar. 29–Apr. 1	Azalea Open	Dave Marr	281	$ 2,800	$ 20,000
Apr. 5–8	Masters	Arnold Palmer	280	$ 20,000	$ 109,000
Apr. 12–15	Greater Greensboro Open	Billy Casper, Jr.	275	$ 5,300	$ 35,000
Apr. 19–22	Houston Classic	Bob Nichols	278	$ 9,000	$ 53,420
Apr. 26–29	Texas Open	Arnold Palmer	273	$ 4,300	$ 30,000
May 3–6	Tournament of Champions	Arnold Palmer	276	$ 11,000	$ 58,000
May 10–13	Colonial National	Arnold Palmer	281	$ 7,000	$ 40,000
May 17–20	Hot Springs Open	Al Johnson	273	$ 2,800	$ 20,000
May 24–27	"500" Festival	Billy Casper, Jr.	264	$ 9,000	$ 50,000
May 31–June 3	Memphis Open	Lionel Hebert	267	$ 6,400	$ 40,000
June 7–10	Thunderbird Classic	Gene Littler	275	$ 25,000	$ 100,000
June 14–16	U.S. Open	Jack Nicklaus	283	$ 15,000	$ 68,800
June 21–24	Eastern Open	Doug Ford	279	$ 5,300	$ 35,000
June 28–July 1	Western Open	Jacky Cupit	281	$ 11,000	$ 55,000
July 5–8	Buick Open	Bill Collins	284	$ 9,000	$ 50,000
July 12–15	Motor City Open	Bruce Crampton	267	$ 5,300	$ 35,000
July 19–22	PGA Championship	Gary Player	278	$ 13,000	$ 72,500
July 26–29	Canadian Open	Ted Kroll	278	$ 4,300	$ 30,000
Aug. 2–5	Insurance City Open	Bob Goalby	271	$ 5,300	$ 35,000
Aug. 9–12	American Classic	Arnold Palmer	276	$ 9,000	$ 51,000
Aug. 16–19	St. Paul Open	Doug Sanders	269	$ 4,300	$ 30,000
Aug. 23–26	Oklahoma City Open	Doug Sanders	280	$ 5,300	$ 35,000
Aug. 31–Sept. 3	Dallas Open	Billy Maxwell	277	$ 5,300	$ 35,000
Sept. 6–9	Denver Open	Bob Goalby	277	$ 4,300	$ 30,000
Sept. 13–16	Seattle Open	Jack Nicklaus	265	$ 4,300	$ 30,000
Sept. 20–23	Portland Open	Jack Nicklaus	269	$ 3,500	$ 25,000
Sept. 28–30	Sahara Invitational	Tony Lema	270	$ 2,800	$ 20,000
Oct. 11–14	Bakersfield Open	Billy Casper, Jr.	272	$ 6,400	$ 40,000
Oct. 18–21	Ontario Open	Al Geiberger	276	$ 3,500	$ 25,000
Oct. 25–28	Orange County Open	Tony Lema	267	$ 2,800	$ 20,000
Nov. 1–4	Beaumont Open	Dave Ragan, Jr.	283	$ 2,800	$ 20,000
Nov. 8–11	Cajun Classic	John Barnum	270	$ 2,400	$ 17,500
Nov. 15–18	Mobile Open	Tony Lema	273	$ 2,000	$ 15,000
Nov. 22–25	Carling Open	Bo Wininger	274	$ 5,300	$ 35,000
Nov. 29–Dec. 2	West Palm Beach Open	Dave Ragan, Jr.	277	$ 2,800	$ 20,000
Dec. 6–9	Coral Gables Open	Gardner Dickinson, Jr.	274	$ 2,800	$ 20,000

1963 Tour

Date	Event	Winner	Score	1st Place Money	Total Purse
Jan. 4–7	Los Angeles Open	Arnold Palmer	274	$ 9,000	$ 50,000
Jan. 10–13	San Diego Open	Gary Player	270	$ 3,500	$ 25,000
Jan. 17–20	Bing Crosby Pro-Am	Billy Casper, Jr.	285	$ 5,300	$ 35,000
Jan. 24–27	Lucky International Open	Jack Burke, jr.	276	$ 9,000	$ 50,000
Jan. 30–Feb. 3	Palm Springs Classic	Jack Nicklaus	345	$ 9,000	$ 50,000
Feb. 7–12	Phoenix Open	Arnold Palmer	273	$ 5,300	$ 35,000
Feb. 14–17	Tucson Open	Don January	266	$ 3,500	$ 25,000
Feb. 21–24	Caracas Open	Art Wall, Jr.	274	$ 1,300	$ 11,000
Mar. 1–4	New Orleans Open	Bo Wininger	279	$ 6,400	$ 40,000
Mar. 7–10	Pensacola Open	Arnold Palmer	273	$ 3,500	$ 25,000

PGA TOUR (continued)

Date	Event	Winner	Score	1st Place Money	Total Purse
Mar. 14–17	St. Petersburg Open	Ray Floyd	274	$ 3,500	$ 25,000
Mar. 21–24	Doral Open	Dan Sikes, Jr.	283	$ 9,000	$ 50,000
Mar. 28–31	Azalea Open	Jerry Barber	274	$ 2,800	$ 20,000
Apr. 4–7	Masters	Jack Nicklaus	286	$ 20,000	$ 94,000
Apr. 11–14	Greater Greensboro Open	Doug Sanders	270	$ 5,500	$ 37,500
Apr. 18–21	Houston Classic	Bob Charles	268	$ 9,000	$ 50,000
Apr. 25–28	Texas Open	Phil Rodgers	268	$ 4,300	$ 30,000
May 2–5	Tournament of Champions	Jack Nicklaus	273	$ 13,000	$ 59,000
May 9–12	Colonial National	Julius Boros	279	$ 12,000	$ 60,000
May 16–19	Oklahoma City Open	Don Fairfield	280	$ 5,300	$ 35,000
May 23–27	Memphis Open	Tony Lema	270	$ 9,000	$ 50,000
May 31–June 3	"500" Festival	Dow Finsterwald	268	$ 10,000	$ 10,000
June 6–9	Buick Open	Julius Boros	274	$ 9,000	$ 50,000
June 13–16	Thunderbird Classic	Arnold Palmer	277	$ 25,000	$ 100,000
June 20–23	U.S. Open	Julius Boros	293	$ 16,000	$ 71,300
June 27–July 1	Cleveland Open	Arnold Palmer	273	$ 22,000	$ 110,000
July 3–6	Canadian Open	Doug Ford	280	$ 9,000	$ 50,000
July 11–14	Hot Springs Open	Dave Hill	277	$ 3,500	$ 25,000
July 18–21	PGA Championship	Jack Nicklaus	279	$ 13,000	$ 80,900
July 25–29	Western Open	Arnold Palmer	280	$ 11,000	$ 57,200
Aug. 1–4	St. Paul Open	Jack Burke, Jr.	266	$ 5,300	$ 35,000
Aug. 15–18	Insurance City Open	Billy Casper, Jr.	271	$ 6,400	$ 40,000
Aug. 22–25	American Classic	Johnny Pott	276	$ 9,000	$ 50,000
Aug. 29–Sept. 1	Denver Open	Juan Rodriguez	276	$ 5,300	$ 35,000
Sept. 5–8	Utah Open	Tommy Jacobs	272	$ 6,400	$ 40,000
Sept. 12–15	Seattle Open	Bob Nichols	272	$ 5,300	$ 35,000
Sept. 19–22	Portland Open	Geore Knudson	271	$ 4,300	$ 30,000
Oct. 3–6	Whitemarsh Open	Arnold Palmer	281	$ 26,000	$ 125,000
Oct. 17–20	Sahara Invitational	Jack Nicklaus	276	$ 13,000	$ 70,000
Oct. 24–27	Fig Garden Open	Mason Rudolph, Jr.	275	$ 3,500	$ 25,000
Oct. 31–Nov. 3	Almaden Open	Al Geiberger	277	$ 3,500	$ 25,000
Nov. 7–10	Frank Sinatra Open	Frank Beard	278	$ 9,000	$ 50,000
Nov. 21–24	Cajun Classic	Rex Baxter, Jr.	275	$ 2,800	$ 20,000

1964 Tour

Date	Event	Winner	Score	1st Place Money	Total Purse
Jan. 3–6	Los Angeles Open	Paul Harney	280	$ 7,500	$ 50,000
Jan. 9–12	San Diego	Art Wall, Jr.	274	$ 4,000	$ 30,000
Jan. 16–19	Bing Crosby Pro-Am	Tony Lema	284	$ 5,800	$ 40,000
Jan. 23–26	Lucky International Open	Juan Rodriguez	272	$ 7,500	$ 50,000
Jan. 29–Feb. 2	Palm Springs Classic	Tommy Jacobs	353	$ 7,500	$ 50,000
Feb. 6–9	Phoenix Open	Jack Nicklaus	271	$ 7,500	$ 50,000
Feb. 13–16	Tucson Open	Jacky Cupit	274	$ 4,000	$ 30,000
Feb. 20–23	Caracas Open	George Knudson	277	$ 1,400	$ 11,000
Feb. 27–Mar. 2	New Orleans Open	Mason Rudolph, Jr.	283	$ 7,500	$ 50,000
Mar. 5–8	Pensacola Open	Gary Player	274	$ 4,000	$ 30,000
Mar. 12–15	St. Petersburg Open	Bruce Devlin	272	$ 3,300	$ 25,000
Mar. 19–22	Doral Open	Billy Casper, Jr.	277	$ 7,500	$ 50,000
Mar. 26–30	Azalea Open	Al Besselink	282	$ 2,700	$ 20,000
Apr. 2–5	Greater Greensboro Open	Julius Boros	277	$ 6,600	$ 45,000
Apr. 9–12	Masters	Arnold Palmer	276	$ 20,000	$ 129,800

PGA TOUR (continued)

Date	Event	Winner	Score	1st Place Money	Total Purse
Apr. 16–19	Houston Classic	Mike Souchak	278	$ 7,619	$ 57,500
Apr. 23–26	Texas Open	Bruce Crampton	273	$ 5,800	$ 40,000
Apr. 30–May 3	Tournament of Champions	Jack Nicklaus	279	$ 12,000	$ 65,000
May 7–10	Colonial National	Billy Casper, Jr.	279	$ 14,000	$ 75,000
May 14–18	Oklahoma City Open	Arnold Palmer	277	$ 5,000	$ 40,000
May 21–24	Memphis Open	Mike Souchak	270	$ 7,500	$ 50,000
May 27–31	"500" Festival	Gary Player	273	$ 12,000	$ 70,000
June 4–7	Thunderbird Classic	Tony Lema	276	$ 20,000	$ 100,000
June 11–14	Buick Open	Tony Lema	277	$ 8,177	$ 66,000
June 18–20	U.S. Open	Ken Venturi	278	$ 17,000	$ 87,450
June 25–28	Cleveland Open	Tony Lema	270	$ 20,000	$ 100,000
July 2–5	Whitemarsh Open	Jack Nicklaus	276	$ 24,042	$ 122,653
July 16–19	PGA Championship	Bob Nichols	271	$ 18,000	$ 100,000
July 23–26	Insurance City Open	Ken Venturi	273	$ 7,500	$ 50,000
July 30–Aug. 2	Canadian Open	Kel Nagle	277	$ 7,500	$ 50,000
Aug. 6–9	Western Open	Juan Rodriguez	268	$ 11,000	$ 65,010
Aug. 13–16	St. Paul Open	Chuck Courtney	272	$ 11,500	$ 65,000
Aug. 20–23	American Classic	Ken Venturi	275	$ 7,500	$ 50,000
Aug. 27–30	Carling Open	Bob Nichols	278	$ 35,000	$ 201,600
Sept. 4–7	Dallas Open	Charles Coody	271	$ 5,800	$ 40,000
Sept. 17–20	Portland Open	Jack Nicklaus	275	$ 5,800	$ 40,000
Sept. 23–27	Seattle Open	Billy Casper, Jr.	265	$ 5,800	$ 40,000
Oct. 1–4	Fresno Open	George Knudson	280	$ 5,000	$ 35,000
Oct. 8–11	Sunset-Camellia Open	Bob McCallister	281	$ 3,300	$ 25,000
Oct. 15–18	Sahara Invitational	R. H. Sikes	275	$ 12,000	$ 70,000
Oct. 22–25	Mountain View Open	Jack McGowan	273	$ 5,800	$ 40,000
Oct. 29–Nov. 1	Almaden Open	Billy Casper, Jr.	279	$ 3,300	$ 25,000
Nov. 19–22	Cajun Classic	Miller Barber	277	$ 3,300	$ 25,000

1965 Tour

Date	Event	Winner	Score	1st Place Money	Total Purse
Jan 8–11	Los Angeles Open	Paul Harney	276	$ 12,500	$ 70,000
Jan. 14–17	San Diego Open	Wes Ellis, Jr.	267	$ 4,850	$ 34,500
Jan. 21–24	Bing Crosby Pro-Am	Bruce Crampton	284	$ 7,500	$ 50,000
Jan. 28–31	Lucky International	George Archer	278	$ 8,500	$ 57,500
Feb. 3–7	Bob Hope Classic	Billy Casper, Jr.	348	$ 15,000	$ 80,000
Feb. 11–14	Phoenix Open	Rod Funseth	274	$ 10,500	$ 67,500
Feb. 18–21	Tucson Open	Bob Charles	271	$ 6,800	$ 46,000
Feb. 25–28	Caracas Open	Al Besselink	273	$ 2,000	$ 13,500
Mar. 4–7	Pensacola Open	Doug Sanders	277	$ 10,000	$ 65,000
Mar. 11–14	Doral Open	Doug Sanders	274	$ 11,000	$ 70,000
Mar. 18–21	Jacksonville Open	Bert Weaver	285	$ 8,500	$ 57,500
Mar. 25–28	Azalea Open	Dick Hart	276	$ 3,850	$ 28,750
Apr. 1–4	Greater Greensboro Open	Sam Snead	273	$ 11,000	$ 70,000
Apr. 8–11	Masters	Jack Nicklaus	271	$ 20,000	$ 137,675
Apr. 15–18	Houston Classic	Bob Nichols	273	$ 12,000	$ 75,000
Apr. 22–25	Texas Open	Frank Beard	270	$ 7,500	$ 50,000
May 6–11	Colonial National	Bruce Crampton	276	$ 20,000	$ 100,000
May 13–16	New Orleans Open	Dick Mayer	273	$ 20,000	$ 100,000
May 20–23	Memphis Open	Jack Nicklaus	271	$ 9,000	$ 60,000
May 27–30	"500" Festival	Bruce Crampton	279	$ 15,200	$ 87,000

PGA TOUR (continued)

Date	Event	Winner	Score	1st Place Money	Total Purse
June 3–6	Buick Open	Tony Lema	280	$ 20,000	$ 100,000
June 10–13	Cleveland Open	Dan Sikes, Jr.	272	$ 25,000	$ 125.000
June 17–20	U.S. Open	Gary Player	282	$ 25,000	$ 121,890
June 24–27	St. Paul Open	Raay Floyd	270	$ 20,000	$ 100,000
July 1–4	Western Open	Billy Casper, Jr.	270	$ 11,000	$ 70,000
July 14–17	Canadian Open	Gene Littler	273	$ 20,000	$ 100,000
July 22–25	Insurance City Open	Billy Casper, Jr.	274	$ 11,000	$ 70,000
July 29–Aug. 1	Thunderbird Classic	Jack Nicklaus	270	$ 20,000	$ 100,000
Aug. 5–8	Philadelphia Classic	Jack Nicklaus	277	$ 24,300	$ 121,500
Aug. 12–15	PGA Championship	Dave Marr	280	$ 25,000	$ 149,700
Aug. 19–23	Carling Open	Tony Lema	279	$ 35,000	$ 200,800
Aug. 26–29	American Classic	Al Geiberger	280	$ 20,000	$ 100,000
Sept. 2–5	Oklahoma City Open	Jack Rule, Jr.	283	$ 10,000	$ 65,000
Sept. 16–19	Portland Open	Jack Nicklaus	273	$ 6,600	$ 45,000
Sept. 23–26	Seattle Open	Gay Brewer, Jr.	279	$ 6,600	$ 45,000
Oct. 20–23	Sahara Invitational	Billy Casper, Jr.	269	$ 20,000	$ 100,000
Oct. 28–31	Almaden Open	Bob Verwey	273	$ 6,000	$ 46,000
Nov. 4–7	Hawaiian Open	Gay Brewer, Jr.	281	$ 9,000	$ 60,300
Nov. 11–14	Mexican Open	Homero Blancas	284	$ 3,000	$ 15,000
Nov. 18–21	Caracas Open	Al Besselink	275	$ 2,500	$ 15,000
Nov. 25–28	Cajun Classic	Babe Hiskey	275	$ 4,250	$ 32,000
Dec. 8–11	PGA Four-Ball	Brewer and Baird	259	$ 10,000 each	$ 125,000

1966 Tour

Date	Event	Winner	Score	1st Place Money	Total Purse
Jan. 6–9	Los Angeles Open	Arnold Palmer	273	$ 11,000	$ 70,000
Jan. 13–16	San Diego Open	Billy Casper, Jr.	268	$ 5,800	$ 40,000
Jan. 20–23	Bing Crosby Pro-Am	Don Massengale	283	$ 11,000	$ 70,000

Billy Casper won 51 tournaments on the PGA Tour between 1956 and 1975.
UPI/Bettmann

PGA TOUR (continued)

Date	Event	Winner	Score	1st Place Money	Total Purse
Jan. 27–31	Lucky International	Ken Venturi	273	$ 8,500	$ 57,000
Feb. 2–6	Bob Hope Classic	Doug Sanders	349	$ 15,000	$ 80,000
Feb. 10–14	Phoenix Open	Dudley Wysong, Jr.	278	$ 9,000	$ 60,000
Feb. 17–20	Tucson Open	Joe Campbell	278	$ 9,000	$ 60,000
Mar. 3–7	Pensacola Open	Gay Brewer, Jr.	272	$ 10,000	$ 65,000
Mar. 10–13	Doral Open	Phil Rodgers	278	$ 20,000	$ 100,000
Mar. 17–20	Citrus Open	Lionel Hebert	279	$ 21,000	$ 110,000
Mar. 24–27	Jacksonville Open	Doug Sanders	273	$ 13,000	$ 82,000
Mar. 31–Apr. 3	Greater Greensboro Open	Doug Sanders	276	$ 20,000	$ 100,000
Apr. 7–11	Masters	Jack Nicklaus	288	$ 20,000	$ 152,880
Apr. 14–17	Azalea Open	Bert Yancey	278	$ 3,200	$ 22,800
Apr. 14–18	Tournament of Champions	Arnold Palmer	283	$ 20,000	$ 100,000
Apr. 21–26	Dallas Open	Roberto DeVicenzo	276	$ 15,000	$ 85,000
Apr. 28–May 1	Texas Open	Harold Henning	272	$ 13,000	$ 80,000
May 12–16	New Orleans Open	Frank Beard	276	$ 20,000	$ 100,000
May 19–22	Colonial National	Bruce Devlin	280	$ 22,000	$ 110,000
May 26–29	Oklahoma City Open	Tony Lema	271	$ 8,500	$ 57,000
June 2–5	Memphis Open	Bert Yancey	265	$ 20,000	$ 100,000
June 9–12	Buick Open	Phil Rodgers	284	$ 20,000	$ 100,000
June 16–20	U.S. Open	Billy Casper, Jr.	278	$ 25,000	$ 144,490
June 23–26	Western Open	Billy Casper, Jr.	283	$ 20,000	$ 101,800
July 14–17	Minnesota Classic	Bobby Nichols	270	$ 20,000	$ 100,000
July 21–24	PGA Championship	Al Geiberger	280	$ 25,000	$ 149,700
July 28–31	"500" Festival	Billy Casper, Jr.	277	$ 16,400	$ 92,000
Aug. 4–7	Cleveland Open	R. H. Sikes, Jr.	268	$ 20,000	$ 100,000
Aug. 11–14	Thunderbird Classic	Mason Rudolph, Jr.	278	$ 20,000	$ 100,000
Aug. 18–21	Insurance City Open	Art Wall, Jr.	266	$ 20,000	$ 100,000
Aug. 25–28	Philadelphia Classic	Don January	278	$ 21,000	$ 110,000
Aug. 31–Sept. 3	Carling Open	Bruce Devlin	286	$ 35,000	$ 204,800
Sept. 15–18	Portland Open	Bert Yancey	271	$ 6,800	$ 45,600
Sept. 22–25	Seattle-Everett Open	Homero Blancas	266	$ 6,600	$ 45,000
Sept. 29–Oct. 2	Canadian Open	Don Massengale	280	$ 18,300	$ 91,500
Oct. 12–15	Sahara Invitational	Jack Nicklaus	282	$ 20,000	$ 100,000
Oct. 27–30	Hawaiian Open	Ted Makalena	271	$ 8,500	$ 57,000
Nov. 3–6	Mexico Open	Bob McCallister	278	$ 3,000	$ 15,000
Nov. 10–13	Caracas Open	Art Wall, Jr.	276	$ 3,000	$ 15,000
Nov. 17–20	Houston International	Arnold Palmer	275	$ 21,000	$ 110,000
Nov. 24–27	Cajun Classic	Jacky Cupit	271	$ 4,850	$ 34,500
Dec. 7–10	PGA National Team Championship	Palmer and Nicklaus	256	$ 25,000 each	$ 280,000

1967 Tour

Date	Event	Winner	Score	1st Place Money	Total Purse
Jan. 12–15	San Diego Open	Bob Goalby	269	$ 13,200	$ 66,000
Jan. 19–22	Bing Crosby Pro-Am	Jack Nicklaus	284	$ 16,000	$ 80,000
Jan. 26–29	Los Angeles Open	Arnold Palmer	269	$ 20,000	$ 100,000
Feb. 1–5	Bob Hope Classic	Tom Nieporte	349	$ 17,600	$ 88,000
Feb. 9–12	Phoenix Open	Julius Boros	272	$ 14,000	$ 70,000
Feb. 16–19	Tucson Open	Arnold Palmer	273	$ 12,000	$ 60,000
Mar. 2–5	Doral Open	Doug Sanders	275	$ 20,000	$ 100,000
Mar. 9–12	Flroida Citrus Open	Julius Boros	274	$ 23,000	$ 115,000

PGA TOUR (continued)

Date	Event	Winner	Score	1st Place Money	Total Purse
Mar. 16–19	Jacksonville Open	Dan Sikes, Jr.	279	$ 20,000	$ 100,000
Mar. 23–26	Pensacola Open	Gay Brewer, Jr.	262	$ 15,000	$ 75,000
Mar. 30–Apr. 2	Greater Greensboro Open	George Archer	267	$ 25,000	$ 125,000
Apr. 6–9	Masters	Gay Brewer, Jr.	280	$ 20,000	$ 154,850
Apr. 13–16	Azalea Open	Randy Glover	278	$ 5,000	$ 35,000
Apr. 13–16	Tournament of Champions	Frank Beard	278	$ 20,000	$ 100,000
Apr. 20–23	Dallas Open	Bert Yancey	274	$ 20,000	$ 100,000
Apr. 27–30	Texas Open	Juan Rodriguez	277	$ 20,000	$ 100,000
May 4–7	Houston Championships International	Frank Beard	274	$ 23,000	$ 115,000
May 11–14	Greater New Orleans Open	George Knudson	277	$ 20,000	$ 100,000
May 18–21	Colonial National Invitational	Dave Stockton	278	$ 23,000	$ 115,000
May 25–28	Oklahoma City Open	Miller Barber	278	$ 13,200	$ 66,000
June 1–4	Memphis Open	Dave Hill	272	$ 20,000	$ 100,000
June 8–11	Buick Open	Julius Boros	283	$ 20,000	$ 100,000
June 15–18	U.S. Open	Jack Nicklaus	275	$ 30,000	$ 169,400
June 22–25	Cleveland Open	Gardner Dickinson, Jr.	271	$ 20,700	$ 103,500
June 29–July 2	Canadian Open	Billy Casper, Jr.	279	$ 27,840	$ 185,600
July 6–9	"500" Festival Open	Frank Beard	279	$ 20,000	$ 100,000
July 20–23	PGA Championship	Don January	281	$ 25,000	$ 149,100
July 27–30	Minnesota Golf Classic	Lou Graham	286	$ 20,000	$ 100,000
Aug. 3–6	Western Open	Jack Nicklaus	274	$ 20,000	$ 102,400
Aug. 10–13	American Golf Classic	Arnold Palmer	276	$ 20,000	$ 100,000
Aug. 17–20	Insurance City Open	Charlie Sifford	272	$ 20,000	$ 100,000
Aug. 24–27	Westchester Classic	Jack Nicklaus	272	$ 50,000	$ 250,000
Aug. 30–Sept. 2	Carling World Open	Billy Casper, Jr.	281	$ 35,000	$ 198,600
Sept. 14–17	Philadelphia Classic	Dan Sikes, Jr.	276	$ 22,000	$ 110,000
Sept. 21–24	Thunderbird Classic	Arnold Palmer	283	$ 30,000	$ 150,000
Sept. 28–Oct. 1	Atlanta Classic	Bob Charles	282	$ 22,000	$ 115,000
Oct. 26–29	Sahara Open	Jack Nicklaus	270	$ 20,000	$ 100,000
Nov. 2–4	Hawaiian Open	Dudley Wysong, Jr.	284	$ 20,000	$ 100,000
Nov. 30–Dec. 3	Cajun Classic	Marty Fleckman	275	$ 5,000	$ 35,000

1968 Tour

Date	Event	Winner	Score	1st Place Money	Total Purse
Jan. 11–14	Bing Crosby Pro-Am	Johnny Pott	285	$ 16,000	$ 80,000
Jan. 18–21	Kaiser International Open	Kermit Zarley	273	$ 25,000	$ 120,000
Jan. 25–28	Los Angeles Open	Billy Casper, Jr.	274	$ 20,000	$ 100,000
Jan 31–Feb 4	Bob Hope Classic	Arnold Palmer	348	$ 20,000	$ 100,000
Feb. 8–11	Andy Williams–San Diego Open	Tom Weiskopf	273	$ 30,000	$ 100,000
Feb. 15–18	Phoenix Open	George Knudson	272	$ 20,000	$ 100,000
Feb. 22–25	Tucson Open	George Knudson	273	$ 20,000	$ 100,000
Mar. 7–10	Doral Open	Gardner Dickinson, Jr.	275	$ 20,000	$ 100,000
Mar. 14–17	Florida Citrus Open	Dan Sikes, Jr.	274	$ 23,000	$ 115,000
Mar. 21–25	Pensacola Open	George Archer	268	$ 14,000	$ 80,000
Mar. 28–31	Jacksonville Open	Tony Jacklin	273	$ 20,000	$ 100,000
Apr. 4–7	Greater Greensboro Open	Billy Casper, Jr.	267	$ 27,500	$ 137,500
Apr. 11–14	Masters	Bob Goalby	277	$ 20,000	$ 172,475
Apr. 11–14	Rebel Yell Open	Larry Mowry	279	$ 2,800	$ 20,000

PGA TOUR (continued)

Date	Event	Winner	Score	1st Place Money	Total Purse
Apr. 18–21	Tournament of Champions	Don January	276	$ 30,000	$ 100,000
Apr. 18–21	Azalea Open	Steve Reid	271	$ 5,000	$ 35,000
Apr. 25–28	Byron Nelson Classic	Miller Barber	270	$ 20,000	$ 100,000
May 2–5	Houston International Championships	Roberto DeVicenzo	274	$ 20,000	$ 100,000
May 9–12	Greater New Orleans Open	George Archer	271	$ 20,000	$ 100,000
May 16–19	Colonial National	Billy Casper, Jr.	275	$ 25,000	$ 125,000
May 16–19	Magnolia State Classic	B. R. McLendon	269	$ 2,800	$ 20,000
May 23–25	Memphis Open	Bob Lunn	268	$ 20,000	$ 100,000
May 30–June 2	Atlanta Classic	Bob Lunn	280	$ 23,000	$ 115,000
June 6–9	"500" Festival	Billy Casper, Jr.	280	$ 20,000	$ 100,000
June 13–16	U.S. Open	Lee Trevino	275	$ 30,000	$ 190,000
June 20–23	Canadian Open	Bob Charles	274	$ 25,000	$ 125,000
June 27–30	Cleveland Open	Dave Stockton	276	$ 22,000	$ 110,000
July 4–7	Buick Open	Tom Weiskopf	280	$ 25,000	$ 125,000
July 11–14	Greater Milwaukee Open	Dave Stockton	275	$ 40,000	$ 200,000
July 18–21	PGA Championship	Julius Boros	281	$ 25,000	$ 200,000
July 25–28	Minnesota Classic	Dan Sikes, Jr.	272	$ 20,000	$ 100,000
Aug. 1–4	Western Open	Jack Nicklaus	273	$ 26,000	$ 130,000
Aug. 8–11	American Classic	Jack Nicklaus	280	$ 25,000	$ 125,000
Aug. 15–18	Westchester Classic	Julius Boros	272	$ 50,000	$ 250,000
Aug. 22–25	Philadelphia Classic	Bob Murphy	276	$ 20,000	$ 100,000
Aug. 30–Sept. 2	Thunderbird Classic	Bob Murphy	277	$ 30,000	$ 150,000
Sept. 5–8	Greater Hartford Open	Billy Casper, Jr.	266	$ 20,000	$ 100,000
Sept. 12–15	Kemper Open	Arnold Palmer	276	$ 20,000	$ 150,000
Sept. 19–22	National Team Champ.	Archer & Nichols	265	$ 20,000 each	$ 200,000
Sept. 26–29	Robinson Open	Dean Refram	279	$ 5,000	$ 25,000
Oct. 17–20	Sahara Invitational	Juan Rodriguez	274	$ 20,000	$ 100,000
Oct. 24–27	Haig Open	Bob Dickson	271	$ 22,000	$ 110,000
Oct. 31–Nov. 4	Lucky International Open	Billy Casper, Jr.	269	$ 20,000	$ 100,000
Nov. 7–10	Hawaiian Open	Lee Trevino	272	$ 25,000	$ 125,000
Nov. 21–24	Cajun Classic	Ron Cerrudo	270	$ 5,000	$ 35,000

1969 Tour

Date	Event	Winner	Score	1st Place Money	Total Purse
Jan. 9–12	Almeda Open	Dick Lotz	290	$ 10,000	$ 50,000
Jan. 9–12	Los Angeles Open	Charlie Sifford	276	$ 20,000	$ 100,000
Jan. 16–17	Kaiser International Open	Miller Barber	135	$ 13,500*	$ 135,000
Jan. 22–27	Bing Crosby Pro-Am	George Archer	283	$ 25,000	$ 125,000
Jan. 30–Feb. 2	Andy Williams–San Diego Open	Jack Nicklaus	284	$ 30,000	$ 150,000
Feb. 5–9	Bob Hope Desert Classic	Billy Casper, Jr.	345	$ 20,000	$ 100,000
Feb. 13–16	Phoenix Open	Gene Littler	263	$ 20,000	$ 100,000
Feb. 20–23	Tucson Open	Lee Trevino	271	$ 20,000	$ 100,000
Feb. 27–Mar. 2	Doral Open	Tom Shaw	276	$ 30,000	$ 150,000
Mar. 6–9	Florida Citrus Open	Ken Still	278	$ 23,000	$ 115,000
Mar. 13–18	Monsanto Open	Jim Colbert, Jr.	267	$ 20,000	$ 100,000
Mar. 20–23	Greater Jacksonville Open	Ray Floyd	278	$ 20,000	$ 100,000
Mar. 27–30	National Airlines Open	Bunky Henry	278	$ 40,000	$ 200,000
Apr. 3–6	Greater Greensboro Open	Gene Littler	274	$ 32,000	$ 160,000

PGA TOUR (continued)

Date	Event	Winner	Score	1st Place Money	Total Purse
Apr. 10–14	Magnolia Classic	Larry Mowry	272	$ 5,000	$ 35,000
Apr. 11–13	Masters	George Archer	281	$ 20,000	$ 149,975
Apr. 17–20	Tallahassee Open	Chuck Courtney	282	$ 5,000	$ 35,000
Apr. 17–20	Azalea Open	Dale Douglass	275	$ 5,000	$ 35,000
Apr. 17–20	Tournament of Champions	Gary Player	284	$ 30,000	$ 150,000
Apr. 24–27	Byron Nelson Classic	Bruce Devlin	277	$ 20,000	$ 100,000
May 1–4	Greater New Orleans Open	Larry Hinson	275	$ 20,000	$ 100,000
May 9–12	Texas Open	Deane Beman	274	$ 20,000	$ 100,000
May 15–18	Colonial National Invitational	Gardner Dickinson, Jr.	278	$ 25,000	$ 125,000
May 22–25	Atlanta Classic	Bert Yancey	277	$ 23,000	$ 115,000
May 29–June 1	Memphis Open	Dae Hill	265	$ 30,000	$ 150,000
June 5–8	Western Open	Billy Casper, Jr.	276	$ 26,000	$ 130,000
June 12–15	U.S. Open	Orville Moody	281	$ 30,000	$ 161,400
June 19–22	Kemper Open	Dale Douglass	274	$ 30,000	$ 150,000
June 26–29	Cleveland Open	Charles Coody	271	$ 22,000	$ 110,000
July 3–6	Buick Open	Dave Hill	277	$ 25,000	$ 125,000
July 10–13	Minnesota Classic	Frank Beard	269	$ 20,000	$ 100,000
July 17–20	Philadelphia Classic	Dave Hill	279	$ 30,000	$ 150,000
July 24–27	American Classic	Ray Floyd	268	$ 25,000	$ 125,000
July 24–27	Canadian Open	Tommy Aaron	275	$ 25,000	$ 125,000
July 31–Aug. 3	Westchester Classic	Frank Beard	275	$ 50,000	$ 250,000
Aug. 7–10	Greater Milwaukee Open	Ken Still	277	$ 20,000	$ 100,000
Aug. 14–17	PGA Championship	Ray Floyd	276	$ 35,000	$ 175,000
Aug. 14–17	Indian Ridge Hospital Open	Monty Kaser	274	$ 7,400	$ 35,000
Aug. 21–24	AVCO Classic	Tom Shaw	280	$ 30,000	$ 150,000

Frank Beard was Player of the Year on the
PGA Tour in 1969. *UPI/Bettmann*

PGA TOUR (continued)

Date	Event	Winner	Score	1st Place Money	Total Purse
Aug. 29–Sept. 1	Greater Hartford Open	Bob Lunn	268	$ 20,000	$ 100,000
Sept. 4–7	Michigan Classic	Larry Ziegler	272	$ 20,000	$ 100,000
Sept. 25–28	Robinson Open	Bob Goalby	273	$ 15,000	$ 75,000
Oct. 16–19	Sahara Invitational	Jack Nicklaus	272	$ 20,000	$ 100,000
Oct. 23–26	Lucky International Open	Steve Spray	269	$ 20,000	$ 100,000
Oct. 30–Nov. 2	Kaiser International Open	Jack Nicklaus	273	$ 28,000	$ 135,000
Nov. 6–9	Hawaiian Open	Bruce Crampton	274	$ 25,000	$ 125,000
Nov. 27–30	Heritage Golf Classic	Arnold Palmer	283	$ 20,000	$ 100,000
Dec. 4–7	Danny Thomas–Diplomat Classic	Arnold Palmer	270	$ 25,000	$ 125,000
Dec. 4–7	West End Classic	Jim Weichers	274	$ 5,000	$ 25,000

1970 Tour

Date	Event	Winner	Score	1st Place Money	Total Purse
Jan. 8–11	Los Angeles Open	Billy Casper, Jr.	278	$ 20,000	$ 100,000
Jan. 15–18	Phoenix Open	Dale Douglass	271	$ 20,000	$ 100,000
Jan. 22–25	Bing Crosby Pro-Am	Bert Yancey	278	$ 25,000	$ 125,000
Jan. 29–Feb. 1	Andy Williams–San Diego Open	Pete Brown	275	$ 30,000	$ 150,000
Feb. 4–8	Bob Hope Desert Classic	Bruce Devlin	339	$ 25,000	$ 125,000
Feb. 12–15	Tucson Open	Lee Trevino	275	$ 20,000	$ 100,000
Feb. 19–22	San Antonio–Texas Open	Ron Cerrudo	273	$ 20,000	$ 100,000
Feb. 26–Mar. 1	Doral-Eastern Open	Mike Hill	279	$ 30,000	$ 150,000
Mar. 3–6	Florida Citrus Open	Bob Stone	278	$ 5,000	$ 35,000
Mar. 5–8	Florida Citrus	Bob Lunn	271	$ 30,000	$ 150,000
Mar. 12–15	Monsanto Open	Dick Lotz	275	$ 30,000	$ 150,000
Mar. 19–22	Greater Jacksonville Open	Don January	279	$ 20,000	$ 100,000
Mar. 26–29	National Airlines Open	Lee Trevino	274	$ 40,000	$ 200,000
Apr. 2–5	Greater Greensboro Open	Gary Player	271	$ 36,000	$ 180,000
Apr. 9–12	Masters	Billy Casper, Jr.	279	$ 25,000	$ 203,801
Apr. 9–12	Magnolia Classic	Chris Blocker	271	$ 5,000	$ 35,000
Apr. 16–19	Greater New Orleans Open	Miller Barber	278	$ 25,000	$ 125,000
Apr. 23–26	Tournament of Champions	Frank Beard	273	$ 30,000	$ 150,000
Apr. 23–26	Tallahassee Open	Harold Henning	277	$ 10,000	$ 50,000
Apr. 30–May 3	Byron Nelson Golf Classic	Jack Nicklaus	274	$ 20,000	$ 100,000
May 7–10	Houston/Champions International	Gibby Gilbert	282	$ 23,000	$ 115,000
May 14–17	Colonial National	Homero Blancas	278	$ 25,000	$ 125,000
May 21–24	Atlanta Classic	Tommy Aaron	275	$ 25,000	$ 125,000
May 28–31	Danny Thomas–Memphis Classic	Dave Hill	267	$ 30,000	$ 150,000
June 4–7	Kemper Open	Dick Lotz	278	$ 30,000	$ 150,000
June 4–7	Kiwanis Peninsula Open	Jerry Barrier	281	$ 5,000	$ 25,000
June 11–14	Western Open	Hugh Royer, Jr.	273	$ 26,000	$ 130,000
June 18–21	U.S. Open Championship	Tony Jacklin	281	$ 30,000	$ 203,500
June 25–28	Cleveland Open	Bruce Devlin	268	$ 30,000	$ 150,000
July 2–5	Canadian Open	Kermit Zarley	279	$ 25,000	$ 125,000
July 9–12	Greater Milwaukee Open	Deane Beman	276	$ 22,000	$ 110,000
July 16–19	IVB-Philadelphia Golf Classic	Billy Casper, Jr.	274	$ 30,000	$ 150,000
July 23–26	National Four-Ball Championship	Nicklaus and Palmer	259	$ 20,000 each	$ 200,000

PGA TOUR (continued)

Date	Event	Winner	Score	1st Place Money	Total Purse
July 30—Aug. 2	Westchester Classic	Bruce Crampton	273	$ 50,000	$ 250,000
Aug. 6—9	American Golf Classic	Frank Beard	276	$ 30,000	$ 150,000
Aug. 13—16	PGA Championship	Dave Stockton	279	$ 40,000	$ 200,000
Aug. 20—23	AVCO Classic	Billy Casper, Jr.	277	$ 32,000	$ 160,000
Aug. 27—30	Dow Jones Open	Bobby Nichols	276	$ 60,000	$ 300,000
Sept. 4—7	Greater Hartford Open	Bob Murphy	267	$ 20,000	$ 100,000
Sept. 17—20	Robinson Open Golf Classic	George Knudson	268	$ 20,000	$ 100,000
Sept. 24—27	Green Island Open	Mason Rudolph	274	$ 12,000	$ 60,000
Oct. 1—4	Azalea Open	Cesar Sanudo	269	$ 12,000	$ 60,000
Oct. 22—25	Kaiser International Open	Ken Still	278	$ 30,000	$ 150,000
Oct. 29—Nov. 1	Sahara Invitational	Babe Hiskey	276	$ 20,000	$ 100,000
Nov. 26—29	Heritage Golf Classic	Bob Goalby	280	$ 20,000	$ 100,000
Nov. 26—28	Sea Pines Open	Larry Wood	282	$ 6,000	$ 30,000
Dec. 3—6	Coral Springs Open	Bill Garrett	272	$ 25,000	$ 125,000
Dec. 10—13	Bahama Islands Open	Doug Sanders	272	$ 26,000	$ 130,000

1971 Tour

Date	Event	Winner	Score	1st Place Money	Total Purse
Jan. 7—10	Glen Campbell—Los Angeles Open	Bob Lunn	274	$ 22,000	$ 110,000
Jan. 14—17	Bing Crosby Pro-Am	Tom Shaw	278	$ 27,000	$ 135,000
Jan. 21—24	Phoenix Open	Miller Barber	261	$ 25,000	$ 125,000
Jan. 28—31	Andy Williams—San Diego Open	George Archer	272	$ 30,000	$ 150,000
Feb. 4—7	Hawaiian Open	Tom Shaw	273	$ 40,000	$ 200,000
Feb. 10—14	Bob Hope Desert Classic	Arnold Palmer	342	$ 28,000	$ 140,000
Feb. 18—21	Tucson Open	J. C. Snead	273	$ 22,000	$ 110,000
Feb. 24—28	PGA Championship	Jack Nicklaus	281	$ 40,000	$ 200,000
Mar. 4—7	Doral-Eastern Open	J. C. Snead	275	$ 30,000	$ 150,000
Mar. 11—14	Florida Citrus Invitational	Arnold Palmer	270	$ 30,000	$ 150,000
Mar. 18—21	Greater Jacksonville Open	Gary Player	281	$ 25,000	$ 125,000
Mar. 25—28	National Airlines Open	Gary Player	274	$ 40,000	$ 200,000
Apr. 1—4	Greater Greensboro Open	Brian Allin	275	$ 38,000	$ 190,000
Apr. 8—11	Masters	Charles Coody	279	$ 25,000	$ 197,976
Apr. 15—18	Monsanto Open	Gene Littler	276	$ 30,000	$ 150,000
Apr. 22—25	Tournament of Champions	Jack Nicklaus	279	$ 33,000	$ 165,000
Apr. 22—25	Tallahassee Open	Lee Trevino	273	$ 12,000	$ 60,000
Apr. 29—May 2	Greater New Orleans Open	Frank Beard	276	$ 25,000	$ 125,000
May 6—9	Byron Nelson Golf Classic	Jack Nicklaus	274	$ 25,000	$ 125,000
May 13—16	Houston/Champions International	Hubert Green	280	$ 25,000	$ 125,000
May 27—30	Danny Thomas—Memphis Classic	Lee Trevino	268	$ 35,000	$ 175,000
June 3—6	Atlanta Classic	Gardner Dickinson	275	$ 25,000	$ 125,000
June 10—13	Kemper Open	Tom Weiskopf	277	$ 30,000	$ 150,000
June 17—20	U.S. Open	Lee Trevino	280	$ 30,000	$ 200,000
June 24—27	Cleveland Open	Bobby Mitchell	262	$ 30,000	$ 150,000
July 1—4	Canadian Open	Lee Trevino	275	$ 30,000	$ 150,000
July 8—11	Greater Milwaukee Open	Dave Eichelberger	270	$ 25,000	$ 125,000
July 15—18	Western Open	Bruce Crampton	279	$ 30,000	$ 150,000
July 22—25	Westchester Classic	Arnold Palmer	270	$ 50,000	$ 250,000
Aug. 5—8	American Golf Classic	Jerry Heard	275	$ 30,000	$ 150,000

PGA TOUR (continued)

Date	Event	Winner	Score	1st Place Money	Total Purse
Aug. 12–15	Massachusetts Classic	Dave Stockton	275	$ 33,000	$ 165,000
July 29–Aug. 1	National Team Champion-ship	Palmer and Nicklaus	257	$ 20,000 each	$ 200,000
Aug. 19–22	IVB-Philadelphia Golf Classic	Tom Weiskopf	274	$ 30,000	$ 150,000
Aug. 25–29	U.S. Professional Match Play Championship	DeWitt Weaver d. Phil Rodgers	71–77	$ 35,000	$ 200,000
Sept. 3–6	Greater Hartford Open	George Archer	268	$ 22,000	$ 110,000
Sept. 9–12	Southern Open	Johnny Miller	267	$ 20,000	$ 100,000
Sept. 23–26	Robinson Open Golf Classic	Labron Harris, Jr.	274	$ 20,000	$ 100,000
Oct. 21–24	Kaiser International Open	Billy Casper, Jr.	269	$ 30,000	$ 150,000
Oct. 28–31	Sahara Invitational	Lee Trevino	280	$ 27,000	$ 135,000
Nov. 18–21	Azalea Open	George Johnson	274	$ 7,000	$ 35,000
Nov. 25–28	Sea Pines Heritage Classic	Hale Irwin	279	$ 22,000	$ 10,000
Dec. 2–6	Walt Disney World Open	Jack Nicklaus	273	$ 30,000	$ 150,000
Dec. 9–12	Bahamas National Open	Bob Goalby	275	$ 26,000	$ 130,000

1972 Tour

Date	Event	Winner	Score	1st Place Money	Total Purse
Jan. 6–9	Glen Campbell–Los Angeles Open	George Archer	270	$ 25,000	$ 125,000
Jan. 13–16	Bing Crosby Pro-Am	Jack Nicklaus	284	$ 28,000	$ 140,000
Jan. 20–23	Dean Martin–Tucson Open	Miller Barber	273	$ 30,000	$ 150,000
Jan. 27–30	Andy Williams–San Diego Open	Paul Harney	275	$ 30,000	$ 150,000
Feb. 3–6	Hawaiian Open	Grier Jones	274	$ 40,000	$ 200,000
Feb. 9–13	Bob Hope Desert Classic	Bob Rosburg	344	$ 29,000	$ 145,000
Feb. 17–20	Phoenix Open	Homero Blancas	273	$ 25,000	$ 125,000
Feb. 24–27	Jackie Gleason–Inverrary Classic	Tom Weiskopf	278	$ 52,000	$ 260,000
Mar. 2–5	Doral-Eastern Open	Jack Nicklaus	276	$ 30,000	$ 150,000
Mar. 9–12	Florida Citrus Open	Jerry Heard	276	$ 30,000	$ 150,000
Mar. 16–19	Greater Jacksonville Open	Tony Jacklin	283	$ 25,000	$ 125,000
Mar. 23–26	Greater New Orleans Open	Gary Player	279	$ 25,000	$ 125,000
Mar. 30–Apr. 2	Greater Greensboro Open	George Archer	272	$ 40,000	$ 200,000
Apr. 6–9	Masters	Jack Nicklaus	286	$ 25,000	$ 204,649
Apr. 13–16	Monsanto Open	Dave Hill	271	$ 30,000	$ 150,000
Apr. 20–23	Tournament of Champions	Bobby Mitchell	280	$ 33,000	$ 165,000
Apr. 20–23	Tallahassee Open	Bob Shaw	273	$ 15,000	$ 75,000
Apr. 27–30	Byron Nelson Golf Classic	Juan Rodriguez	273	$ 25,000	$ 125,000
May 4–7	Houston Open	Bruce Devlin	278	$ 25,000	$ 125,000
May 11–14	Colonial National Invitation	Jerry Heard	275	$ 25,000	$ 125,000
May 18–21	Danny Thomas–Memphis Classic	Lee Trevino	281	$ 35,000	$ 175,000
May 25–28	Atlanta Classic	Bob Lunn	275	$ 26,000	$ 130,000
June 1–4	Kemper Open	Doug Sanders	275	$ 35,000	$ 175,000
June 8–11	IVB–Philadelphia Golf Classic	J. C. Snead	282	$ 30,000	$ 150,000
June 15–18	U.S. Open	Jack Nicklaus	290	$ 30,000	$ 200,000
June 22–25	Western Open	Jim Jamieson	271	$ 30,000	$ 150,000
June 29–July 2	Cleveland Open	David Graham	278	$ 30,000	$ 150,000

PGA TOUR (continued)

Date	Event	Winner	Score	1st Place Money	Total Purse
July 6–9	Canadian Open	Gay Brewer	275	$ 30,000	$ 150,000
July 13–16	Greater Milwaukee Open	Jim Colbert	271	$ 25,000	$ 125,000
July 20–23	American Golf Classic	Bert Yancey	276	$ 30,000	$ 150,000
July 27–30	National Team Champion-ship	Hiskey and Zarley	262	$ 20,000 (each)	$ 200,000
Aug. 3–6	PGA Championship	Gary Player	281	$ 45,000	$ 225,000
Aug. 10–13	Westchester Classic	Jack Nicklaus	270	$ 50,000	$ 250,000
Aug. 17–20	USI Classic	Bruce Devlin	275	$ 40,000	$ 200,000
Aug. 24–27	Liggett & Myers Open	Lou Graham	285	$ 20,000	$ 100,000
Aug. 24–27	U.S. Professional Match Play Championship	Jack Nicklaus d. Frank Beard	2&1	$ 40,000	$ 150,000
Sept. 1–4	Greater Hartford Open	Lee Trevino	269	$ 25,000	$ 125,000
Sept. 7–10	Southern Open	DeWitt Weaver	276	$ 20,000	$ 100,000
Sept. 14–17	Greater St. Louis Golf Classic	Lee Trevino	269	$ 30,000	$ 150,000
Sept. 21–24	Robinson's Fall Golf Classic	Grier Jones	273	$ 20,000	$ 100,000
Sept. 28–Oct. 1	Quad Cities Open	Deane Beman	279	$ 20,000	$ 100,000
Oct. 19–22	Kaiser International Open	George Knudson	271	$ 30,000	$ 150,000
Oct. 26–29	Sahara Invitational	Lanny Wadkins	273	$ 27,000	$ 135,000
Nov. 2–5	San Antonio Texas Open	Mike Hill	273	$ 25,000	$ 125,000
Nov. 23–26	Heritage Golf Classic	Johnny Miller	281	$ 25,000	$ 125,000
Nov. 30–Dec. 3	Walt Disney World Open	Jack Nicklaus	267	$ 30,000	$ 150,000

1973 Tour

Date	Event	Winner	Score	1st Place Money	Total Purse
Jan. 4–7	Los Angeles Open	Rod Funseth	276	$ 27,000	$ 135,000
Jan. 11–14	Phoenix Open	Bruce Crampton	268	$ 30,000	$ 150,000
Jan. 18–22	Dean Martin–Tucson Open	Bruce Crampton	277	$ 30,000	$ 150,000
Jan. 25–28	Bing Crosby Pro-Am	Jack Nicklaus	282	$ 36,000	$ 180,000
Feb. 1–4	Hawaiian Open	John Schlee	273	$ 40,000	$ 200,000
Feb. 7–11	Bob Hope Desert Classic	Arnold Palmer	343	$ 32,000	$ 160,000
Feb. 13–18	Andy Williams–San Diego Open	Bob Dickson	278	$ 34,000	$ 170,000
Feb. 22–25	Jackie Gleason–Inverrary Classic	Lee Trevino	279	$ 52,000	$ 260,000
Mar. 1–9	Florida Citrus Open	Brian Allin	265	$ 30,000	$ 150,000
Mar. 8–11	Doral-Eastern Open	Lee Trevino	276	$ 30,000	$ 150,000
Mar. 15–18	Greater Jacksonville Open	Jim Colbert	279	$ 26,000	$ 130,000
Mar. 22–25	Greater New Orleans Open	Jack Nicklaus	280	$ 25,000	$ 125,000
Mar. 24–Apr. 1	Greater Greensboro Open	Chi Chi Rodriguez	267	$ 42,000	$ 210,000
Apr. 5–8	Masters	Tommy Aaron	283	$ 30,000	$ 204,000
Apr. 12–15	Monsanto Open	Homero Blancas	277	$ 30,000	$ 150,000
Apr. 19–22	Tournament of Champions	Jack Nicklaus	276	$ 40,000	$ 200,000
Apr. 19–22	Tallahassee Open	Hubert Green	277	$ 15,000	$ 75,000
Apr. 26–29	Byron Nelson Classic	Lanny Wadkins	277	$ 30,000	$ 150,000
May 3–6	Houston Open	Bruce Crampton	277	$ 41,000	$ 205,000
May 10–13	Colonial National Invitation	Tom Weiskopf	276	$ 30,000	$ 150,000
May 17–20	Danny Thomas–Memphis Classic	Dave Hill	283	$ 35,000	$ 175,000
May 24–27	Atlanta Classic	Jack Nicklaus	272	$ 30,000	$ 150,000
May 31–June 3	Kemper Open	Tom Weiskopf	271	$ 40,000	$ 200,000

PGA TOUR (continued)

Date	Event	Winner	Score	1st Place Money	Total Purse
June 7–10	IVB–Philadelphia Golf Classic	Tom Weiskopf	274	$ 30,045	$ 150,000
June 14–17	U.S. Open	Johnny Miller	279	$ 35,000	$ 200,000
June 21–24	American Golf Classic	Bruce Crampton	273	$ 32,000	$ 160,000
June 28–July 1	Western Open	Billy Casper, Jr.	272	$ 35,000	$ 175,000
July 5–8	Greater Milwaukee Open	Dave Stockton	276	$ 26,000	$ 130,000
July 12–15	Shrine Robinson Classic	Deane Beman	271	$ 25,000	$ 125,000
July 19–22	St. Louis Classic	Gene Littler	268	$ 42,000	$ 210,000
July 26–29	Canadian Open	Tom Weiskopf	278	$ 35,000	$ 175,000
Aug. 2–5	Westchester Classic	Bobby Nichols	272	$ 50,000	$ 250,000
Aug. 9–12	PGA Championship	Jack Nicklaus	277	$ 45,000	$ 225,000
Aug. 16–19	USI Classic	Lanny Wadkins	279	$ 40,000	$ 200,000
Aug. 23–26	U.S. Professional Match Play Championships	John Schroeder	2 up	$ 40,000	$ 100,000
Aug. 25–26	Liggett & Myers Open	Bert Greene	278	$ 20,000	$ 150,000
Aug. 31–Sept. 3	Sammy Davis, Jr.–Greater Hartford Open	Billy Casper, Jr.	264	$ 40,000	$ 200,000
Sept. 6–9	Southern Open	Gary Player	270	$ 20,030	$ 100,000
Sept. 13–16	Heritage Classic	Hale Irwin	272	$ 30,000	$ 150,000
Sept. 20–23	B.C. Open	Hubert Green	266	$ 20,000	$ 100,000
Sept. 27–30	Quad Cities Open	Sam Adams	268	$ 20,000	$ 100,000
Oct. 4–7	Ohio Kings Island Open	Jack Nicklaus	271	$ 25,000	$ 125,000
Oct. 18–21	Kaiser International Open	Ed Sneed	275	$ 30,091	$ 150,000
Oct. 25–28	Sahara Invitational	John Mahaffey	271	$ 27,000	$ 135,000
Nov. 1–4	San Antonio–Texas Open	Ben Crenshaw	270	$ 25,000	$ 125,000

Ben Crenshaw won his PGA Tour debut at the San Antonio–Texas Open in 1973. *Wide World Photos*

PGA TOUR (continued)

Date	Event	Winner	Score	1st Place Money	Total Purse
Nov. 9–12	World Open Golf Championship	Miller Barber	270	$ 100,000	$ 500,000
Nov. 29–Dec. 2	Walt Disney World Open	Jack Nicklaus	275	$ 30,000	$ 150,000

1974 Tour

Date	Event	Winner	Score	1st Place Money	Total Purse
Jan. 3–6	Bing Crosby Pro-Am	Johnny Miller	208	$ 27,750	$ 185,000
Jan. 10–13	Phoenix Open	Johnny Miller	271	$ 30,000	$ 150,000
Jan. 17–20	Dean Martin–Tucson Open	Johnny Miller	272	$ 30,000	$ 150,000
Jan. 24–27	Andy Williams–San Diego Open	Bobby Nichols	275	$ 34,000	$ 170,000
Jan. 31–Feb. 3	Hawaiian Open	Jack Nicklaus	271	$ 44,000	$ 220,000
Feb. 6–10	Bob Hope Desert Classic	Hubert Green	341	$ 32,048	$ 160,000
Feb. 14–17	Glen Campbell–Los Angeles Open	Dave Stockton	276	$ 30,000	$ 150,000
Feb. 21–24	Jackie Gleason–Inverrary Classic	Leonard Thompson	278	$ 52,000	$ 260,000
Feb. 28–Mar. 3	Florida Citrus Open	Jerry Heard	273	$ 30,000	$ 150,000
Mar. 7–10	Doral–Eastern Open	Brian Allin	272	$ 30,000	$ 150,000
Mar. 14–17	Greater Jacksonville Open	Hubert Green	276	$ 30,000	$ 150,000
Mar. 21–24	Heritage Classic	Johnny Miller	276	$ 40,000	$ 200,000
Mar. 28–31	Greater New Orleans Open	Lee Trevino	267	$ 30,000	$ 140,000
Apr. 4–7	Greater Greensboro Open	Bob Charles	270	$ 44,066	$ 220,000
Apr. 11–14	Masters	Gary Player	278	$ 35,000	$ 229,549
April 18–21	Monsanto Open	Lee Elder	274	$ 30,045	$ 150,000
Apr. 25–28	Tournament of Champions	Johnny Miller	280	$ 40,000	$ 200,000
Apr. 25–28	Tallahassee Open	Allen Miller	274	$ 18,000	$ 90,000
May 2–5	Byron Nelson Golf Classic	Brian Allin	269	$ 30,045	$ 150,000
May 9–12	Houston Open	Dave Hill	276	$ 30,000	$ 150,000
May 16–19	Colonial National Invitation	Rod Curl	276	$ 50,000	$ 150,000
May 23–26	Danny Thomas–Memphis Classic	Gary Player	273	$ 35,000	$ 175,000
May 30–June 2	Kemper Open	Bob Menne	270	$ 50,000	$ 200,000
June 6–9	IVB–Philadelphia Golf Classic	Hubert Green	271	$ 30,000	$ 150,000
June 13–16	U.S. Open	Hale Irwin	287	$ 35,000	$ 219,900
June 20–23	American Golf Classic	Jim Colbert	281	$ 34,000	$ 160,000
June 27–30	Western Open	Tom Watson	287	$ 40,000	$ 200,000
July 3–6	Greater Milwaukee Open	Ed Sneed	276	$ 26,000	$ 130,000
July 11–14	Quad Cities Open	Dave Stockton	271	$ 20,000	$ 100,000
July 18–21	B.C. Open	Richie Karl	273	$ 30,000	$ 100,000
July 25–28	Canadian Open	Bobby Nichols	270	$ 40,000	$ 200,000
Aug. 1–4	Pleasant Valley Classic	Victor Regalado	278	$ 40,000	$ 200,000
Aug. 8–11	PGA Championship	Lee Trevino	276	$ 45,000	$ 225,000
Aug. 15–18	Sammy Davis, Jr.–Greater Hartford Open	Dave Stockton	268	$ 40,000	$ 200,000
Aug. 22–25	Westchester Classic	Johnny Miller	269	$ 50,000	$ 250,000
Aug. 29–Sept. 1	Tournament Players Championship	Jack Nicklaus	272	$ 40,000	$ 200,000

PGA TOUR (continued)

Date	Event	Winner	Score	1st Place Money	Total Purse
Sept. 5–8	Southern Open	Forrest Fezler	271	$ 20,000	$ 100,000
Sept. 7–8	World Series of Golf	Lee Trevino	139	$ 50,000	$ 77,500
Sept. 12–15	World Open	Johnny Miller	281	$ 60,000	$ 325,000
Sept. 19–22	Ohio Kings Island Open	Miller Barber	277	$ 30,000	$ 125,000
Sept. 26–29	Kaiser International Open	Johnny Miller	271	$ 30,000	$ 150,000
Oct. 3–8	Sahara Invitational	Al Geiberger	273	$ 27,000	$ 135,000
Oct. 17–20	San Antonio–Texas Open	Terry Diehl	269	$ 25,000	$ 125,000
Oct. 31–Nov. 3	Disney World Team Championship	Hubert Green and B. R. McLendon	255	$ 25,000 each	$ 250,000

1975 Tour

Date	Event	Winner	Score	1st Place Money	Total Purse
Jan. 9–12	Phoenix Open	Johnny Miller	260	$ 30,000	$ 150,000
Jan. 16–19	Dean Martin–Tucson Open	Johnny Miller	263	$ 40,000	$ 200,000
Jan. 23–28	Bing Crosby Pro-Am	Gene Littler	280	$ 37,000	$ 185,000
Jan. 30–Feb. 2	Hawaiian Open	Gary Groh	274	$ 44,000	$ 220,000
Feb. 5–9	Bob Hope Desert Classic	Johnny Miller	339	$ 32,000	$ 160,000
Feb. 13–16	Andy Williams–San Diego Open	J. C. Snead	279	$ 34,000	$ 170,000
Feb. 20–23	Glen Campbell–Los Angeles Open	Pat Fitzsimons	275	$ 30,000	$ 150,000
Feb. 27–Mar. 2	Jackie Gleason–Inverrary Classic	Bob Murphy	273	$ 52,000	$ 260,000
Mar. 6–9	Florida Citrus Open	Lee Trevino	276	$ 40,000	$ 200,000
Mar. 13–16	Doral–Eastern Open	Jack Nicklaus	276	$ 30,000	$ 150,000
Mar. 20–23	Greater Jacksonville Open	Larry Ziegler	276	$ 30,000	$ 150,000
Mar. 27–30	Heritage Classic	Jack Nicklaus	271	$ 40,000	$ 200,000
Apr. 3–6	Greater Greensboro Open	Tom Weiskopf	275	$ 45,000	$ 225,000
Apr. 10–13	Masters	Jack Nicklaus	276	$ 40,000	$ 242,750
Apr. 17–20	Pensacola Open	Jerry McGee	271	$ 25,000	$ 125,000
Apr. 24–27	MONY Tournament of Champions	Al Geiberger	277	$ 40,000	$ 200,000
Apr. 24–27	Tallahassee Open	Rik Massengale	274	$ 12,000	$ 60,000
May 1–4	Houston Open	Bruce Crampton	273	$ 30,000	$ 150,000
May 8–11	Byron Nelson Golf Classic	Tom Watson	269	$ 35,000	$ 175,000
May 15–18	Greater New Orleans Open	Billy Casper, Jr.	271	$ 30,000	$ 150,000
May 22–25	Danny Thomas–Memphis Classic	Gene Littler	270	$ 35,000	$ 175,000
May 29–June 1	Atlanta Classic	Hale Irwin	271	$ 45,000	$ 225,000
June 5–8	Kemper Open	Ray Floyd	278	$ 50,000	$ 250,000
June 12–15	IVB–Philadelphia Golf Classic	Tom Jenkins	275	$ 30,000	$ 150,000
June 19–22	U.S. Open	Lou Graham	287	$ 40,000	$ 236,200
June 26–29	Western Open	Hale Irwin	283	$ 40,000	$ 200,000
July 2–5	Greater Milwaukee Open	Art Wall	271	$ 26,000	$ 130,000
July 10–13	Quad Cities Open	Roger Maltbie	275	$ 15,000	$ 125,000
July 17–20	Pleasant Valley Classic	Roger Maltbie	276	$ 40,000	$ 200,000
July 24–27	Canadian Open	Tom Weiskopf	274	$ 40,000	$ 200,000
July 31–Aug. 3	Westchester Classic	Gene Littler	271	$ 50,000	$ 250,000
Aug. 7–10	PGA Championship	Jack Nicklaus	276	$ 45,000	$ 225,000

PGA TOUR (continued)

Date	Event	Winner	Score	1st Place Money	Total Purse
Aug. 14–17	Sammy Davis, Jr.–Greater Hartford Open	Don Bies	267	$ 40,000	$ 200,000
Aug. 21–24	Tournament Players Championship	Al Geiberger	270	$ 50,000	$ 250,000
Aug. 29–Sept. 1	B.C. Open	Don Iverson	274	$ 35,000	$ 175,000
Sept. 4–7	Southern Open	Hubert Green	264	$ 20,000	$ 100,000
Sept. 6–7	World Series of Golf	Tom Watson	140	$ 50,000	$ 77,500
Sept. 11–14	World Open	Jack Nicklaus	280	$ 40,000	$ 200,000
Sept. 25–28	Sahara Invitational	Dave Hill	270	$ 27,000	$ 135,000
Oct. 2–5	Kaiser International Open	Johnny Miller	272	$ 35,000	$ 175,000
Oct. 16–19	San Antonio–Texas Open	Don January	275	$ 25,000	$ 125,000
Oct. 23–26	Disney World Team Championship	Jim Colbert and Dean Refram	252	$ 20,000 each	$ 200,000

1976 Tour

Date	Event	Winner	Score	1st Place Money	Total Purse
Jan. 8–11	NBC–Tucson Open	Johnny Miller	274	$ 40,000	$ 200,000
Jan. 15–18	Phoenix Open	Bob Gilder	268	$ 40,000	$ 200,000
Jan. 22–25	Bing Crosby Pro-Am	Ben Crenshaw	281	$ 37,000	$ 185,000
Jan. 29–Feb. 1	Hawaiian Open	Ben Crenshaw	270	$ 46,000	$ 230,000
Feb. 4–8	Bob Hope Desert Classic	Johnny Miller	344	$ 36,000	$ 180,000
Feb. 12–15	Andy Williams–San Diego Open	J. C. Snead	272	$ 36,000	$ 180,000
Feb. 19–22	Glen Campbell–Los Angeles Open	Hale Irwin	272	$ 37,000	$ 185,000
Feb. 26–Mar. 1	Tournament Players Championship	Jack Nicklaus	269	$ 60,000	$ 300,000
Mar. 4–7	Florida Citrus Open	Hale Irwin	270	$ 40,000	$ 200,000
Mar. 11–14	Doral–Eastern Open	Hubert Green	270	$ 40,000	$ 200,000
Mar. 18–21	Greater Jacksonville Open	Hubert Green	276	$ 35,000	$ 175,000
Mar. 25–28	Sea Pines Heritage Classic	Hubert Green	274	$ 43,000	$ 215,000
Apr. 1–4	Greater Greensboro Open	Al Geiberger	268	$ 46,000	$ 230,000
Apr. 8–11	Masters	Raymond Floyd	271	$ 40,000	$ 254,852
Apr. 15–18	MONY Tournament of Champions	Don January	277	$ 45,000	$ 225,000
Apr. 15–18	Tallahassee Open	Gary Koch	277	$ 16,000	$ 80,000
Apr. 22–25	NBC–New Orleans Open	Larry Ziegler	274	$ 35,000	$ 175,000
Apr. 29–May 2	Houston Open	Lee Elder	278	$ 40,000	$ 200,000
May 6–9	Byron Nelson Golf Classic	Mark Hayes	273	$ 40,000	$ 200,000
May 13–16	Colonial National Invitation	Lee Trevino	273	$ 40,000	$ 200,000
May 20–23	Danny Thomas–Memphis Classic	Gibby Gilbert	273	$ 40,000	$ 200,000
May 27–30	Memorial Tournament	Roger Maltbie	288	$ 40,000	$ 200,000
June 3–6	IVB–Bicentennial Classic	Tom Kite	277	$ 40,000	$ 200,000
June 10–13	Kemper Open	Joe Inman	277	$ 50,000	$ 250,000
June 14–20	U.S. Open	Jerry Pate	277	$ 42,000	$ 268,000
June 24–27	Western Open	Al Geiberger	288	$ 40,000	$ 200,000
July 1–4	Greater Milwaukee Open	Dave Hill	270	$ 26,000	$ 130,000
July 8–11	Ed McMahon–Quad Cities Open	John Lister	268	$ 20,000	$ 100,000

PGA TOUR (continued)

Date	Event	Winner	Score	1st Place Money	Total Purse
July 15–18	American Express Westchester Classic	David Graham	272	$ 60,000	$ 300,000
July 22–25	Canadian Open	Jerry Pate	267	$ 40,000	$ 200,000
July 29–Aug. 1	Pleasant Valley Classic	Bud Allin	277	$ 40,000	$ 200,000
Aug. 5–8	B.C. Open	Bob Wynn	271	$ 40,000	$ 200,000
Aug. 12–15	PGA Championship	Dave Stockton	281	$ 45,000	$ 250,000
Aug. 19–22	Sammy Davis, Jr.–Greater Hartford Open	Rik Massengale	266	$ 42,000	$ 210,000
Aug. 26–29	American Golf Classic	David Graham	274	$ 40,000	$ 200,000
Sept. 2–5	World Series of Golf	Jack Nicklaus	275	$ 100,000	$ 300,000
Sept. 9–12	World Open	Ray Floyd	274	$ 40,000	$ 200,000
Sept. 16–19	Ohio Kings Island Open	Ben Crenshaw	271	$ 30,000	$ 150,000
Sept. 23–26	Kaiser International Open	J. C. Snead	274	$ 35,000	$ 175,000
Sept. 20–Oct. 3	Sahara Invitational	George Archer	271	$ 27,000	$ 135,000
Oct. 14–17	San Antonio–Texas Open	Butch Baird	273	$ 25,000	$ 125,000
Oct. 21–24	Southern Open	B. R. McLendon	274	$ 25,000	$ 125,000
Oct. 28–Nov. 1	Pensacola Open	Mark Hayes	275	$ 25,000	$ 125,000
Nov. 4–7	Disney World Team Championship	Woody Blackburn and Bill Kratzert	260	$ 20,000 each	$ 200,000

1977 Tour

Date	Event	Winner	Score	1st Place Money	Total Purse
Jan. 6–9	Phoenix Open	Jerry Pate	277	$ 40,000	$ 200,000
Jan. 13–16	Joe Garagiola–Tucson Open	Bruce Lietzke	275	$ 40,000	$ 200,000
Jan. 20–23	Bing Crosby Pro-Am	Tom Watson	273	$ 40,000	$ 200,000
Jan. 27–30	Andy Williams–San Diego Open	Tom Watson	269	$ 36,000	$ 180,000
Feb. 3–6	Hawaiian Open	Bruce Lietzke	273	$ 48,000	$ 240,000
Feb. 19–13	Bob Hope Desert Classic	Rik Massengale	337	$ 40,000	$ 200,000
Feb. 17–20	Glen Campbell–Los Angeles Open	Tom Purtzer	273	$ 40,000	$ 200,000
Feb. 24–27	Jackie Gleason–Inverrary Classic	Jack Nicklaus	275	$ 50,000	$ 250,000
Mar. 3–6	Florida Citrus Open	Gary Koch	274	$ 40,000	$ 200,000
Mar. 10–13	Doral–Eastern	Andy Bean	277	$ 40,000	$ 200,000
Mar. 17–20	Tournament Players Championship	Mark Hayes	289	$ 60,000	$ 300,000
Mar. 24–27	Heritage Classic	Graham Marsh	273	$ 45,000	$ 225,000
Mar. 31–Apr. 3	Greater Greensboro Open	Danny Edwards	276	$ 47,000	$ 235,000
Apr. 7–10	Masters	Tom Watson	276	$ 40,000	$ 254,000
Apr. 14–17	Tournament of Champions	Jack Nicklaus	281	$ 45,000	$ 225,000
Apr. 14–17	Tallahassee Open	Ed Sneed	276	$ 16,000	$ 80,000
Apr. 21–24	NBC–New Orleans Open	Jim Simons	273	$ 35,000	$ 175,000
Apr. 28–May 1	Houston Open	Gene Littler	276	$ 40,000	$ 200,000
May 5–8	Byron Nelson Golf Classic	Raymond Floyd	276	$ 40,000	$ 200,000
May 12–15	Colonial National Invitation	Ben Crenshaw	272	$ 40,000	$ 200,000
May 19–22	Memorial Tournament	Jack Nicklaus	281	$ 45,000	$ 225,000
May 26–29	Atlanta Classic	Hale Irwin	273	$ 40,000	$ 200,000
June 2–5	Kemper Open	Tom Weiskopf	277	$ 50,000	$ 250,000

PGA TOUR (continued)

Date	Event	Winner	Score	1st Place Money	Total Purse
June 9–12	Memphis Classic	Al Geiberger	273	$ 40,000	$ 200,000
June 16–19	U.S. Open	Hubert Green	278	$ 45,000	$ 250,000
June 23–26	Western Open	Tom Watson	283	$ 40,000	$ 200,000
June 30–July 3	Greater Milwaukee Open	Dave Eichelberger	278	$ 26,000	$ 130,000
July 7–10	Quad Cities Open	Mike Morley	267	$ 25,000	$ 125,000
July 14–17	Pleasant Valley Classic	Raymond Floyd	271	$ 50,000	$ 250,000
July 21–24	Canadian Open	Lee Trevino	280	$ 45,000	$ 225,000
July 28–31	IVB-Philadelphia Golf Classic	Jerry McGee	272	$ 40,000	$ 200,000
Aug. 4–7	Greater Hartford Open	Bill Kratzert	265	$ 42,000	$ 210,000
Aug. 11–14	PGA Championship	Lanny Wadkins	282	$ 45,000	$ 250,000
Aug. 18–21	Westchester Classic	Andy North	272	$ 60,000	$ 300,000
Aug. 25–28	Colgate–Hall of Fame	Hale Irwin	264	$ 50,000	$ 250,000
Sept. 2–5	World Series of Golf	Lanny Wadkins	267	$ 100,000	$ 300,000
Sept. 1–4	Buick Open	Bobby Cole	271	$ 20,000	$ 100,000
Sept. 8–11	B.C. Open	Gil Morgan	270	$ 40,000	$ 200,000
Sept. 22–25	Kings Island Open	Mike Hill	269	$ 30,000	$ 150,000
Sept. 29–Oct. 2	Anheuser-Busch	Miller Barber	272	$ 40,000	$ 200,000
Oct. 13–16	San Antonio–Texas Open	Hale Irwin	266	$ 30,000	$ 150,000
Oct. 20–23	Southern Open	Jerry Pate	266	$ 25,000	$ 125,000
Oct. 27–30	Pensacola Open	Leonard Thompson	268	$ 25,000	$ 125,000
Nov. 3–6	Disney World Team Championship	Gibby Gilbert and Grier Jones	253	$ 20,000 each	$ 200,000

1978 Tour

Date	Event	Winner	Score	1st Place Money	Total Purse
Jan. 5–8	Joe Garagiola–Tucson Open	Tom Watson	274	$ 40,000	$ 200,000
Jan. 12–15	Phoenix Open	Miller Barber	272	$ 40,000	$ 200,000
Jan. 20–23	Bing Crosby National Pro-Am	Tom Watson	280	$ 45,000	$ 225,000
Jan. 26–29	Andy Williams–San Diego Open	Jay Haas	278	$ 40,000	$ 200,000
Feb. 2–5	Hawaiian Open	Hubert Green	274	$ 50,000	$ 250,000
Feb. 8–11	Bob Hope Desert Classic	Bill Rogers	339	$ 45,000	$ 225,000
Feb. 16–19	The Glen Campbell–Los Angeles Open	Gil Morgan	278	$ 40,000	$ 200,000
Feb. 23–26	Jackie Gleason–Inverrary Classic	Jack Nicklaus	276	$ 50,000	$ 250,000
Mar. 2–6	Florida Citrus Open	Mac McLendon	271	$ 40,000	$ 200,000
Mar. 9–12	Doral–Eastern Open	Tom Weiskopf	272	$ 40,000	$ 200,000
Mar. 16–19	Tournament Players Championship	Jack Nicklaus	289	$ 60,000	$ 344,270
Mar. 23–26	Heritage Classic	Hubert Green	277	$ 45,000	$ 255,000
Mar. 30–Apr. 2	Greater Greensboro Open	Seve Ballesteros	282	$ 48,000	$ 240,000
Apr. 6–9	Masters	Gary Player	277	$ 45,000	$ 262,402
Apr. 13–16	MONY Tournament of Champions	Gary Player	281	$ 45,000	$ 225,000
Apr. 13–16	Tallahassee Open	Barry Jaeckel	273	$ 16,000	$ 80,000
Apr. 20–23	Houston Open	Gary Player	270	$ 40,000	$ 200,000
Apr. 27–30	NBC–New Orleans	Lon Hinkle	271	$ 40,000	$ 200,000

PGA TOUR (continued)

Date	Event	Winner	Score	1st Place Money	Total Purse
May 4–7	Byron Nelson Golf Classic	Tom Watson	272	$ 40,000	$ 200,000
May 11–14	Colonial National Invitation	Lee Trevino	268	$ 40,000	$ 200,000
May 18–21	Memorial Tournament	Jim Simons	284	$ 50,000	$ 259,960
May 25–28	Atlanta Classic	Jerry Heard	269	$ 40,000	$ 200,000
June 1–4	Kemper Open	Andy Bean	273	$ 60,000	$ 300,000
June 8–11	Danny Thomas–Memphis Classic	Andy Bean	277	$ 50,000	$ 250,000
June 15–18	U.S. Open	Andy North	285	$ 45,000	$ 310,200
June 15–18	Buick–Goodwrench Open	Jack Newton	280	$ 20,000	$ 100,000
June 22–25	Canadian Open	Bruce Lietzke	283	$ 50,000	$ 250,000
June 29–July 2	Western Open	Andy Bean	282	$ 45,000	$ 225,000
July 6–9	Greater Milwaukee Open	Lee Elder	275	$ 30,000	$ 150,000
July 13–16	Ed McMahon–Quad Cities Open	Victor Regalado	269	$ 30,000	$ 150,000
July 20–23	IVB–Philadelphia Golf Classic	Jack Nicklaus	270	$ 50,000	$ 250,000
July 27–30	Sammy Davis, Jr.–Greater Hartford Open	Rod Funseth	264	$ 42,000	$ 210,000
Aug. 3–6	PGA Championship	John Mahaffey	270	$ 50,000	$ 300,000
Aug. 10–13	American Optical Classic	John Mahaffey	270	$ 45,000	$ 225,000
Aug. 17–20	American Express West-chester Classic	Lee Elder	274	$ 60,000	$ 300,000
Aug. 24–27	Colgate Hall of Fame Classic	Tom Watson	277	$ 50,000	$ 250,000
Aug. 31–Sept. 4	B.C. Open	Tom Kite	267	$ 45,000	$ 225,000
Sept. 7–10	Southern Open	Jerry Pate	269	$ 35,000	$ 175,000
Sept. 13–17	San Antonio–Texas Open	Ron Streck	265	$ 40,000	$ 200,000
Sept. 21–24	Anheuser-Busch Golf Classic	Tom Watson	270	$ 40,000	$ 200,000
Sept. 28–Oct. 1	World Series of Golf	Gil Morgan	278	$ 100,000	$ 300,000
Oct. 26–29	Pensacola Open	Mac McLendon	272	$ 25,000	$ 125,000
Nov. 2–5	Walt Disney World National Team Championship	Wayne Levi and Bob Mann	254	$ 20,000 each	$ 200,000

1979 Tour

Date	Event	Winner	Score	1st Place Money	Total Purse
Jan. 10–14	Bob Hope Desert Classic	John Mahaffey	343	$ 50,000	$ 275,000
Jan. 18–22	Phoenix Open	Ben Crenshaw	199	$ 33,750*	$ 250,000
Jan. 25–28	Andy Williams–San Diego Open	Fuzzy Zoeller	282	$ 45,000	$ 250,000
Feb. 1–4	Bing Crosby National Pro-Am	Lon Hinkle	284	$ 54,000	$ 300,000
Feb. 8–11	Hawaiian Open	Hubert Green	267	$ 54,000	$ 300,000
Feb. 15–18	Joe Garagiola–Tucson Open	Bruce Lietzke	265	$ 45,000	$ 250,000
Feb. 22–25	Glen Campbell–Los Angeles Open	Lanny Wadkins	276	$ 45,000	$ 250,000
Mar. 1–4	Bay Hill Citrus Classic	Bob Byman	278	$ 45,000	$ 250,000
Mar. 8–11	Jackie Gleason–Inverrary Classic	Larry Nelson	274	$ 54,000	$ 300,000

PGA TOUR (continued)

Date	Event	Winner	Score	1st Place Money	Total Purse
Mar. 15–18	Doral-Eastern Open	Mark McCumber	279	$ 45,000	$ 250,000
Mar. 22–25	Tournament Players Championship	Lanny Wadkins	283	$ 72,000	$ 437,292
Mar. 29–Apr. 1	Sea Pines Heritage Classic	Tom Watson	270	$ 54,000	$ 300,000
Apr. 5–8	Greater Greensboro Open	Ray Floyd	282	$ 45,000	$ 250,000
Apr. 12–15	Masters	Fuzzy Zoeller	280	$ 50,000	$ 299,625
Apr. 19–22	MONY Tournament of Champions	Tom Watson	270	$ 54,000	$ 300,000
Apr. 19–22	Tallahassee Open	Chi Chi Rodriguez	269	$ 18,000	$ 100,000
Apr. 26–29	First NBC New Orleans Open	Hubert Green	273	$ 45,000	$ 250,000
May 3–6	Houston Open	Wayne Levi	268	$ 54,000	$ 300,000
May 10–13	Byron Nelson Golf Classic	Tom Watson	275	$ 54,000	$ 300,000
May 17–20	Colonial National Invitation	Al Geiberger	274	$ 54,000	$ 300,000
May 24–27	Memorial Tournament	Tom Watson	285	$ 54,000	$ 329,885
May 31–June 3	Kemper Open	Jerry McGee	272	$ 63,000	$ 350,000
June 7–10	Atlanta Classic	Andy Bean	265	$ 54,000	$ 300,000
June 14–17	U.S. Open	Hale Irwin	284	$ 50,000	$ 325,000
June 21–24	Canadian Open	Lee Trevino	281	$ 63,000	$ 350,000
June 28–July 1	Danny Thomas–Memphis Classic	Gil Morgan	278	$ 54,000	$ 300,000
July 5–8	Western Open	Larry Nelson	286	$ 54,000	$ 300,000
July 12–15	Greater Milwaukee Open	Calvin Peete	269	$ 36,000	$ 200,000
July 19–22	Ed McMahon–Quad Cities Open	D.A. Weibring	266	$ 36,000	$ 200,000
July 26–29	IVB–Philadelphia Classic	Lou Graham	273	$ 45,000	$ 250,000
Aug. 2–5	PGA Championship	David Graham	272	$ 60,000	$ 350,000
Aug. 9–12	Sammy Davis, Jr.–Greater Hartford Open	Jerry McGee	267	$ 54,000	$ 300,000
Aug. 16–19	Manufacturers Hanover Westchester Classic	Jack Renner	277	$ 72,000	$ 400,000
Aug. 23–26	Colgate–Hall of Fame Classic	Tom Watson	272	$ 45,000	$ 250,000
Aug. 30–Sept. 2	B.C. Open	Howard Twitty	270	$ 49,500	$ 275,000
Sept. 6–9	American Optical Classic	Lou Graham	275	$ 45,000	$ 250,000
Sept. 13–16	Buick–Goodwrench Open	John Fought	280	$ 27,000	$ 150,000
Sept. 20–23	Anheuser-Busch Classic	John Fought	277	$ 54,000	$ 300,000
Sept. 27–30	World Series of Golf	Lon Hinkle	272	$ 100,000	$ 400,000
Oct. 4–7	San Antonio–Texas Open	Lou Graham	268	$ 45,000	$ 250,000
Oct. 11–14	Southern Open	Ed Fiori	274	$ 36,000	$ 200,000
Oct. 18–21	Pensacola Open	Curtis Strange	271	$ 36,000	$ 200,000
Oct. 25–28	Walt Disney World National Team Championship	George Burns and Ben Crenshaw	255	$ 22,500 each	$ 250,000

1980 Tour

Date	Event	Winner	Score	1st Place Money	Total Purse
Jan. 9–13	Bob Hope Desert Classic	Craig Stadler	343	$ 50,000	$ 304,000
Jan. 17–20	Phoenix Open	Jeff Mitchell	272	$ 54,000	$ 300,000
Jan. 24–27	Andy Williams–San Diego Open	Tom Watson	275	$ 45,000	$ 250,000

PGA TOUR (continued)

Date	Event	Winner	Score	1st Place Money	Total Purse
Jan. 31–Feb. 3	Bing Crosby Pro-Am	George Burns	280	$ 54,000	$ 300,000
Feb. 7–10	Hawaiian Open	Andy Bean	266	$ 58,500	$ 325,000
Feb. 14–17	Joe Garagiola–Tucson Open	Jim Colbert	270	$ 54,000	$ 300,000
Feb. 21–24	Glen Campbell–Los Angeles Open	Tom Watson	276	$ 45,000	$ 250,000
Feb. 27–Mar. 2	Bay Hill Classic	Dave Eichelberger	279	$ 54,000	$ 300,000
Mar. 6–9	Jackie Gleason–Inverrary Classic	Johnny Miller	274	$ 54,000	$ 300,000
Mar. 13–16	Doral–Eastern Open	Ray Floyd	279	$ 45,000	$ 250,000
Mar. 20–23	Tournament Players Championship	Lee Trevino	278	$ 72,000	$ 440,000
Mar. 27–30	Sea Pines Heritage Classic	Doug Tewell	280	$ 54,000	$ 300,000
Apr. 3–6	Greater Greensboro Open	Craig Stadler	275	$ 45,000	$ 250,000
Apr. 10–13	Masters	Seve Ballesteros	275	$ 55,000	$ 359,949
Apr. 10–13	Magnolia Classic	Roger Maltbie	65	$ 4,500	$ 50,000
Apr. 17–20	MONY Tournament of Champions	Tom Watson	276	$ 54,000	$ 300,000
Apr. 17–20	Tallahassee Open	Mark Pfeil	277	$ 18,000	$ 100,000
Apr. 24–29	Greater New Orleans Open	Tom Watson	273	$ 45,000	$ 250,000
May 1–4	Michelob–Houston Open	Curtis Strange	266	$ 63,000	$ 350,000

Curtis Strange was one of the leading players of the 1980s.

PGA TOUR (continued)

Date	Event	Winner	Score	1st Place Money	Total Purse
May 8–11	Byron Nelson Classic	Tom Watson	274	$ 54,000	$ 300,000
May 15–18	Colonial National Invitation	Bruce Lietzke	271	$ 54,000	$ 300,000
May 21–25	Memorial Tournament	David Graham	280	$ 54,000	$ 345,485
May 19–June 1	Kemper Open	John Mahaffey	275	$ 72,000	$ 400,000
June 5–8	Atlanta Classic	Larry Nelson	270	$ 54,000	$ 300,000
June 12–15	U.S. Open	Jack Nicklaus	272	$ 55,000	$ 356,700
June 19–22	Canadian Open	Bob Gilder	274	$ 63,000	$ 350,000
June 26–29	Danny Thomas–Memphis Classic	Lee Trevino	272	$ 54,000	$ 300,000
July 3–6	Western Open	Scott Simpson	281	$ 54,000	$ 300,000
July 10–13	Greater Milwaukee Open	Bill Kratzert	266	$ 36,000	$ 200,000
July 17–20	Quad Cities Open	Scott Hoch	266	$ 36,000	$ 200,000
July 23–27	Sammy Davis, Jr.–Greater Hartford Open	Howard Twitty	266	$ 54,000	$ 300,000
July 31–Aug. 3	IVB Golf Classic	Doug Tewell	272	$ 45,000	$ 250,000
Aug. 7–10	PGA Championship	Jack Nicklaus	274	$ 60,000	$ 375,000
Aug. 14–17	Manufacturers Hanover Westchester Classic	Curtis Strange	273	$ 72,000	$ 400,000
Aug. 21–24	World Series of Golf	Tom Watson	270	$ 100,000	$ 421,900
Aug. 21–24	Buick–Goodwrench Open	Peter Jacobsen	276	$ 45,000	$ 250,000
Aug. 28–31	B.C. Open	Don Pooley	271	$ 49,500	$ 275,000
Sept. 4–7	Jimmy Fund Pleasant Valley Classic	Wayne Levi	273	$ 54,000	$ 300,000
Sept. 11–14	Hall of Fame Tournament	Phil Hancock	275	$ 45,000	$ 250,000
Sept. 18–21	San Antonio–Texas Open	Lee Trevino	265	$ 45,000	$ 250,000
Sept. 25–28	Anheuser-Busch Classic	Ben Crenshaw	272	$ 54,000	$ 300,000
Oct. 2–5	Southern Open	Mike Sullivan	269	$ 36,000	$ 200,000
Oct. 9–12	Pensacola Open	Dan Halldorson	275	$ 36,000	$ 200,000
Oct. 16–19	Walt Disney World National Team Championship	Danny Edwards and David Edwards	253	$ 31,500	$ 350,000

1981 Tour

Date	Event	Winner	Score	1st Place Money	Total Purse
Jan. 8–11	Joe Garagiola–Tucson Open	Johnny Miller	265	$ 54,000	$ 300,000
Jan. 14–18	Bob Hope Desert Classic	Bruce Lietzke	335	$ 50,000	$ 304,000
Jan. 21–24	Phoenix Open	David Graham	268	$ 54,000	$ 300,000
Jan. 29–Feb. 1	Bing Crosby Pro-Am	John Cook	209	$ 40,500*	$ 304,500
Feb. 5–8	Wickes–Andy Williams– San Diego Open	Bruce Lietzke	278	$ 45,000	$ 250,000
Feb. 11–14	Hawaiian Open	Hale Irwin	265	$ 58,500	$ 325,000
Feb. 19–22	Glen Campbell–Los Angeles Open	Johnny Miller	270	$ 54,000	$ 300,000
Feb. 26–Mar. 1	Bay Hill Classic	Andy Bean	266	$ 54,000	$ 300,000
Mar. 5–8	American Motors Inverrary Classic	Tom Kite	274	$ 54,000	$ 300,000
Mar. 12–15	Doral–Eastern Open	Ray Floyd	273	$ 45,000	$ 250,000
Mar. 19–22	Tournament Players Championship	Ray Floyd	285	$ 72,000	$ 435,620
Mar. 26–29	Sea Pines Heritage Classic	Bill Rogers	278	$ 54,000	$ 300,000

PGA TOUR (continued)

Date	Event	Winner	Score	1st Place Money	Total Purse
Apr. 2–5	Greater Greensboro Open	Larry Nelson	281	$ 54,000	$ 300,000
Apr. 9–12	Masters	Tom Watson	280	$ 60,000	$ 362,587
Apr. 9–12	Magnolia Classic	Tom Jones	268	$ 13,500	$ 75,000
Apr. 16–19	MONY Tournament of Champions	Lee Trevino	273	$ 54,000	$ 300,000
Apr. 16–19	Tallahassee Open	Dave Eichelberger	271	$ 18,000	$ 100,000
Apr. 23–26	USF&G New Orleans Open	Tom Watson	270	$ 63,000	$ 350,000
Apr. 30–May 2	Michelob Houston Open	Ron Streck	198	$ 47,250*	$ 350,000
May 7–10	Byron Nelson Golf Classic	Bruce Lietzke	281	$ 54,000	$ 300,000
May 14–17	Colonial National Invitation	Fuzzy Zoeller	274	$ 54,000	$ 300,000
May 21–24	Memorial Tournament	Keith Fergus	284	$ 63,000	$ 380,445
May 28–31	Kemper Open	Craig Stadler	270	$ 72,000	$ 400,000
June 4–7	Atlanta Classic	Tom Watson	277	$ 54,000	$ 300,000
June 11–14	Manufacturers Hanover Westchester Classic	Ray Floyd	275	$ 72,000	$ 400,000
June 18–21	U.S. Open	David Graham	273	$ 55,000	$ 361,730
June 25–28	Danny Thomas–Memphis Classic	Jerry Pate	274	$ 54,000	$ 300,000
July 2–5	Western Open	Ed Fiori	277	$ 54,000	$ 300,000
July 9–12	Greater Milwaukee Open	Jay Haas	274	$ 45,000	$ 250,000
July 16–19	Quad Cities Open	Dave Barr	270	$ 36,000	$ 200,000
July 23–26	Anheuser-Busch Golf Classic	John Mahaffey	276	$ 54,000	$ 300,000
July 30–Aug. 2	Canadian Open	Peter Oosterhuis	280	$ 76,500	$ 425,000
Aug. 6–9	PGA Championship	Larry Nelson	273	$ 60,000	$ 401,050
Aug. 13–16	Sammy Davis, Jr.–Greater Hartford Open	Hubert Green	264	$ 54,000	$ 300,000
Aug. 20–23	Buick Open	Hale Irwin	277	$ 63,000	$ 350,000
Aug. 27–30	World Series of Golf	Bill Rogers	275	$ 100,000	$ 403,900
Sept. 3–6	B.C. Open	Jay Haas	270	$ 49,500	$ 275,000
Sept. 10–13	Pleasant Valley Jimmy Fund Classic	Jack Renner	273	$ 54,000	$ 300,000
Sept. 17–20	LaJet Classic	Tom Weiskopf	278	$ 63,000	$ 350,000
Sept. 24–27	Hall of Fame Tournament	Morris Hatalsky	275	$ 45,000	$ 250,000
Oct. 1–4	Texas Open	Bill Rogers	266	$ 45,000	$ 250,000
Oct. 8–11	Southern Open	J.C. Snead	271	$ 36,000	$ 200,000
Oct. 15–18	Pensacola Open	Jerry Pate	271	$ 36,000	$ 200,000
Oct. 22–25	Walt Disney World National Team Championship	Vance Heafner and Mike Holland	246	$ 36,000	$ 400,000

1982 Tour

Date	Event	Winner	Score	1st Place Money	Total Purse
Jan. 7–10	Joe Garagiola–Tucson Open	Craig Stadler	266	$ 54,000	$ 300,000
Jan. 13–17	Bob Hope Desert Classic	Ed Fiori	335	$ 50,000	$ 304,500
Jan. 21–25	Phoenix Open	Lanny Wadkins	263	$ 54,000	$ 300,000
Jan. 27–31	Wickes–Andy Williams– San Diego Open	Johnny Miller	270	$ 54,000	$ 300,000
Feb. 4–7	Bing Crosby Pro-Am	Jim Simons	274	$ 54,000	$ 300,000
Feb. 11–14	Hawaiian Open	Wayne Levi	277	$ 58,500	$ 325,000

PGA TOUR (continued)

Date	Event	Winner	Score	1st Place Money	Total Purse
Feb. 18–21	Glen Campbell–Los Angeles Open	Tom Watson	271	$ 54,000	$ 300,000
Feb. 25–28	Doral–Eastern Open	Andy Bean	278	$ 54,000	$ 300,000
Mar. 4–7	Bay Hill Classic	Tom Kite	278	$ 54,000	$ 300,000
Mar. 11–14	Honda–Inverrary Classic	Hale Irwin	269	$ 72,000	$ 400,000
Mar. 18–21	Tournament Players Championship	Jerry Pate	280	$ 90,000	$ 500,000
Mar. 25–28	Sea Pines Heritage Classic	Tom Watson	280	$ 54,000	$ 300,000
Apr. 2–5	Greater Greensboro Open	Danny Edwards	285	$ 54,000	$ 300,000
Apr. 8–11	Masters	Craig Stadler	284	$ 64,000	$ 367,152
Apr. 8–11	Magnolia Classic	Payne Stewart	270	$ 13,500	$ 75,000
Apr. 15–18	MONY Tournament of Champions	Lanny Wadkins	280	$ 63,000	$ 350,000
Apr. 15–18	Tallahassee Open	Bob Shearer	272	$ 18,000	$ 100,000
Apr. 22–25	USF&G Classic	Scott Hoch	206	$ 54,000*	$ 400,000
Apr. 29–May 2	Byron Nelson Golf Classic	Bob Gilder	266	$ 63,000	$ 350,000
May 6–9	Michelob–Houston Open	Ed Sneed	275	$ 63,000	$ 350,000
May 13–16	Colonial National Invitation	Jack Nicklaus	273	$ 63,000	$ 350,000
May 20–23	Georgia-Pacific–Atlanta Classic	Keith Fergus	273	$ 54,000	$ 300,000
May 27–30	Memorial Tournament	Ray Floyd	281	$ 63,000	$ 380,445
June 3–6	Kemper Open	Craig Stadler	275	$ 72,000	$ 400,000
June 10–13	Danny Thomas–Memphis Classic	Ray Floyd	271	$ 72,000	$ 400,000
June 17–20	U.S. Open	Tom Watson	282	$ 60,000	$ 375,000
June 24–27	Manufacturers Hanover Westchester Classic	Bob Gilder	261	$ 72,000	$ 400,000
July 1–4	Western Open	Tom Weiskopf	276	$ 63,000	$ 350,000
July 8–11	Greater Milwaukee Open	Calvin Peete	274	$ 45,000	$ 250,000
July 15–18	Miller High Life QCO	Payne Stewart	268	$ 36,000	$ 200,000
July 22–25	Anheuser-Busch Golf Classic	Calvin Peete	203	$ 63,000ᵃ	$ 350,000
July 29–Aug. 1	Canadian Open	Bruce Lietzke	277	$ 76,500	$ 425,000
Aug. 5–8	PGA Championship	Ray Floyd	272	$ 65,000	$ 450,000
Aug. 12–15	Sammy Davis, Jr.–Greater Hartford Open	Tim Norris	259	$ 54,000	$ 300,000
Aug. 19–22	Buick Open	Lanny Wadkins	273	$ 63,000	$ 350,000
Aug. 26–29	World Series of Golf	Craig Stadler	278	$ 100,000	$ 400,000
Sept. 2–5	B.C. Open	Calvin Peete	265	$ 49,500	$ 275,000
Sept. 9–12	Bank of Boston Classic	Bob Gilder	271	$ 54,000	$ 300,000
Sept. 16–19	Hall of Fame Tournament	Jay Haas	276	$ 45,000	$ 250,000
Sept. 23–26	Southern Open	Bobby Clampett	266	$ 45,000	$ 250,000
Sept. 30–Oct. 3	Texas Open	Jay Haas	262	$ 45,000	$ 250,000
Oct. 7–10	LaJet Classic	Wayne Levi	271	$ 63,000	$ 350,000
Oct. 21–24	Pensacola Open	Calvin Peete	268	$ 36,000	$ 200,000
Oct. 28–31	Walt Disney World Golf Classic	Hal Sutton	269	$ 72,000	$ 400,000

1983 Tour

Date	Event	Winner	Score	1st Place Money	Total Purse
Jan. 6–9	Joe Garagiola–Tucson Open	Gil Morgan	271	$ 54,000	$ 300,000

PGA TOUR (continued)

Date	Event	Winner	Score	1st Place Money	Total Purse
Jan. 13–16	Glen Campbell–Los Angeles Open	Gil Morgan	270	$ 54,000	$ 300,000
Jan. 19–23	Bob Hope Classic	Keith Fergus	335	$ 67,500	$ 375,000
Jan. 27–30	Phoenix Open	Bob Gilder	271	$ 63,000	$ 350,000
Feb. 3–6	Bing Crosby Pro-Am	Tom Kite	276	$ 58,500	$ 325,000
Feb. 10–13	Hawaiian Open	Isao Aoki	268	$ 58,500	$ 325,000
Feb. 17–20	Isuzu–Andy Williams–San Diego Open	Gary Hallberg	271	$ 54,000	$ 300,000
Feb. 24–27	Doral–Eastern Open	Gary Koch	271	$ 54,000	$ 300,000
Mar. 3–6	Honda–Inverrary Classic	Johnny Miller	278	$ 72,000	$ 400,000
Mar. 10–13	Bay Hill Classic	Mike Nicolette	283	$ 63,000	$ 350,000
Mar. 17–20	USF&G Classic	Bill Rogers	274	$ 72,000	$ 400,000
Mar. 25–28	Tournament Players Championship	Hal Sutton	283	$ 126,000	$ 700,000
Mar. 31–Apr. 3	Greater Greensboro Open	Lanny Wadkins	275	$ 72,000	$ 400,000
Apr. 7–10	Masters	Seve Ballesteros	280	$ 90,000	$ 500,000
Apr. 14–18	Sea Pines Heritage Classic	Fuzzy Zoeller	275	$ 63,000	$ 350,000
Apr. 21–24	MONY Tournament of Champions	Lanny Wadkins	280	$ 72,000	$ 400,000
Apr. 28–May 1	Byron Nelson Golf Classic	Ben Crenshaw	273	$ 72,000	$ 400,000
May 5–8	Houston–Coca-Cola Open	David Graham	275	$ 72,000	$ 400,000
May 12–15	Colonial National Invitation	Jim Colbert	278	$ 72,000	$ 400,000
May 19–22	Georgia-Pacific–Atlanta Classic	Calvin Peete	206	$ 72,000§	$ 400,000
May 26–29	Memorial Tournament	Hale Irwin	281	$ 72,000	$ 430,000
June 2–5	Kemper Open	Fred Couples	287	$ 72,000	$ 400,000
June 9–12	Manufacturers Hanover– Westchester Classic	Seve Ballesteros	276	$ 81,000	$ 450,000
June 16–19	U.S. Open	Larry Nelson	280	$ 72,000	$ 500,000
June 23–26	Danny Thomas–Memphis Classic	Larry Mize	274	$ 72,000	$ 400,000
June 30–July 3	Western Open	Mark McCumber	284	$ 72,000	$ 400,000
July 7–10	Greater Milwaukee Open	Morris Hatalsky	275	$ 45,000	$ 250,000
July 14–17	Miller High Life QCO	Danny Edwards	266	$ 36,000	$ 200,000
July 21–24	Anheuser-Busch Golf Classic	Calvin Peete	276	$ 63,000	$ 350,000
July 28–31	Canadian Open	John Cook	277	$ 63,000	$ 425,000
Aug. 4–7	PGA Championship	Hal Sutton	274	$ 100,000	$ 600,000
Aug. 11–14	Buick Open	Wayne Levi	272	$ 63,000	$ 350,000
Aug. 18–21	Sammy Davis, Jr.–Greater Hartford Open	Curtis Strange	268	$ 54,000	$ 300,000
Aug. 25–28	World Series of Golf	Nick Price	270	$ 100,000	$ 500,000
Sept. 1–4	B.C. Open	Pat Lindsey	268	$ 54,000	$ 300,000
Sept. 8–11	Bank of Boston Classic	Mark Lye	273	$ 63,000	$ 350,000
Sept. 14–18	Panasonic Las Vegas Pro Celebrity Classic	Fuzzy Zoeller	340	$ 135,000	$ 750,000
Sept. 22–15	LaJet–Coors Classic	Rex Caldwell	282	$ 63,000	$ 350,000
Sept. 29–Oct. 2	Texas Open	Jim Colbert	261	$ 54,000	$ 300,000
Oct. 6–9	Southern Open	Ronnie Black	271	$ 45,000	$ 250,000
Oct. 20–23	Walt Disney World Golf Classic	Payne Stewart	269	$ 72,000	$ 400,000

PGA TOUR (continued)

Date	Event	Winner	Score	1st Place Money	Total Purse
Oct. 27–30	Pensacola Open	Mark McCumber	266	$ 45,000	$ 250,000

1984 Tour

Date	Event	Winner	Score	1st Place Money	Total Purse
Jan. 2–8	Seiko–Tucson Match Play Championship	Tom Watson	2&1	$ 100,000	$ 708,000
Jan. 11–15	Bob Hope Classic	John Mahaffey	340	$ 72,000	$ 400,000
Jan. 19–22	Phoenix Open	Tom Purtzer	268	$ 72,000	$ 400,000
Jan. 26–29	Isuzu–Andy Williams–San Diego Open	Gary Koch	272	$ 72,000	$ 400,000
Feb. 2–5	Bing Crosby Pro-Am	Hale Irwin	278	$ 72,000	$ 400,000
Feb. 9–12	Hawaiian Open	Jack Renner	271	$ 90,000	$ 500,000
Feb. 16–19	Los Angeles Open	David Edwards	279	$ 72,000	$ 400,000
Mar. 1–4	Honda Classic	Bruce Lietzke	280	$ 90,000	$ 500,000
Mar. 8–11	Doral–Eastern Open	Tom Kite	272	$ 72,000	$ 400,000
Mar. 15–18	Bay Hill Classic	Gary Koch	272	$ 72,000	$ 400,000
Mar. 22–25	USF&G Classic	Bob Eastwood	272	$ 72,000	$ 400,000
Mar. 29–Apr. 1	Tournament Players Championship	Fred Couples	277	$ 144,000	$ 800,000
Apr. 6–8	Greater Greensboro	Andy Bean	280	$ 72,000	$ 400,000
Apr. 12–15	Masters	Ben Crenshaw	277	$ 108,000	$ 612,900
Apr. 19–22	Sea Pines Heritage Classic	Nick Faldo	270	$ 72,000	$ 400,000
Apr. 26–29	Houston Coca-Cola Open	Corey Pavin	274	$ 90,000	$ 500,000
May 3–6	MONY Tournament of Champions	Tom Watson	274	$ 72,000	$ 400,000
May 10–13	Byron Nelson Golf Classic	Craig Stadler	276	$ 90,000	$ 500,000
May 17–20	Colonial National Invitation	Peter Jacobsen	270	$ 90,000	$ 500,000
May 24–27	Memorial Tournament	Jack Nicklaus	280	$ 90,000	$ 565,500
May 31–June 3	Kemper Open	Greg Norman	280	$ 72,000	$ 400,000
June 7–10	Manufacturers Hanover–Westchester Classic	Scott Simpson	269	$ 90,000	$ 500,000
June 14–17	U.S. Open	Fuzzy Zoeller	276	$ 94,000	$ 602,324
June 21–24	Georgia-Pacific–Atlanta Classic	Tom Kite	269	$ 72,000	$ 400,000
June 28–July 1	Canadian Open	Greg Norman	278	$ 72,000	$ 525,000
July 5–8	Western Open	Tom Watson	280	$ 72,000	$ 400,000
July 12–15	Anheuser-Busch Golf Classic	Ronnie Black	267	$ 63,000	$ 350,000
July 19–22	Miller High Life QCO	Scott Hoch	266	$ 36,000	$ 200,000
July 26–29	Sammy Davis, Jr.–Greater Hartford Open	Peter Jacobsen	269	$ 72,000	$ 400,000
Aug. 2–5	Danny Thomas–Memphis Classic	Bob Eastwood	280	$ 90,000	$ 500,000
Aug. 9–12	Buick Open	Denis Watson	271	$ 72,000	$ 400,000
Aug. 16–19	PGA Championship	Lee Trevino	273	$ 125,000	$ 700,000
Aug. 23–26	NEC World Series of Golf	Denis Watson	271	$ 126,000	$ 700,000
Aug. 30–Sept. 2	B.C. Open	Wayne Levi	275	$ 54,000	$ 300,000
Sept. 6–9	Bank of Boston Classic	George Archer	270	$ 63,000	$ 350,000
Sept. 13–16	Greater Milwaukee Open	Mark O'Meara	272	$ 54,000	$ 300,000

PGA TOUR (continued)

Date	Event	Winner	Score	1st Place Money	Total Purse
Sept. 19–23	Panasonic Las Vegas Invitational	Denis Watson	341	$ 162,000	$ 900,000
Sept. 27–30	LaJet Golf Classic	Curtis Strange	273	$ 63,000	$ 350,000
Oct. 4–7	Texas Open	Calvin Peete	266	$ 63,000	$ 350,000
Oct. 11–14	Southern Open	Hubert Green	265	$ 54,000	$ 300,000
Oct. 18–21	Walt Disney World Golf Classic	Larry Nelson	266	$ 72,000	$ 400,000
Oct. 25–28	Pensacola Open	Bill Kratzert	270	$ 54,000	$ 300,000
Dec. 6–9	JC Penney Classic	Mike Donald and Vicki Alvarez	270	$ 50,000	$ 550,000
Dec. 13–16	Chrysler Team Invitational	Phil Hancock and Ron Streck	255	$ 50,000	$ 400,000

1985 Tour

Date	Event	Winner	Score	1st Place Money	Total Purse
Jan. 9–13	Bob Hope Classic	Lanny Wadkins	333	$ 90,000	$ 500,000
Jan. 17–20	Phoenix Open	Calvin Peete	270	$ 81,000	$ 450,200
Jan. 24–27	Los Angeles Open	Lanny Wadkins	264	$ 72,000	$ 400,000
Jan. 31–Feb. 3	Bing Crosby Pro-Am	Mark O'Meara	283	$ 90,000	$ 500,000
Feb. 7–10	Hawaiian Open	Mark O'Meara	267	$ 90,000	$ 500,000
Feb. 14–17	Isuzu–Andy Williams San Diego Open	Woody Blackburn	269	$ 72,000	$ 400,000
Feb. 21–24	Doral–Eastern Open	Mark McCumber	284	$ 72,000	$ 400,000
Feb. 28–Mar. 3	Honda Classic	Curtis Strange	275	$ 90,000	$ 500,000
Mar. 7–10	Hertz Bay Hill Classic	Fuzzy Zoeller	275	$ 90,000	$ 500,000
Mar. 14–17	USF&G Classic	Seve Ballesteros	205	$ 72,000§	$ 400,000
Mar. 20–24	Panasonic–Las Vegas Invitational	Curtis Strange	338	$ 171,000	$ 950,000
Mar. 28–31	Tournament Players Championship	Calvin Peete	274	$ 162,000	$ 900,000
Apr. 4–7	Greater Greensboro Open	Joey Sindelar	285	$ 72,000	$ 400,000
Apr. 11–14	Masters	Bernhard Langer	282	$ 126,000	$ 700,793
Apr. 18–21	Sea Pines Heritage Classic	Bernhard Langer	273	$ 72,000	$ 400,000
Apr. 25–28	Houston Open	Ray Floyd	277	$ 90,000	$ 500,000
May 2–5	MONY Tournament of Champions	Tom Kite	275	$ 72,000	$ 400,000
May 9–12	Byron Nelson Golf Classic	Bob Eastwood	272	$ 90,000	$ 500,000
May 16–19	Colonial National Invitation	Corey Pavin	266	$ 90,000	$ 500,000
May 23–26	Memorial Tournament	Hale Irwin	281	$ 100,000	$ 579,230
May 30–June 2	Kemper Open	Bill Glasson	278	$ 90,000	$ 500,000
June 6–9	Manufacturers Hanover–Westchester Classic	Roger Maltbie	275	$ 90,000	$ 500,000
June 13–16	U.S. Open	Andy North	279	$ 103,000	$ 650,000
June 20–23	Georgia-Pacific–Atlanta Classic	Wayne Levi	273	$ 90,000	$ 500,000
June 27–30	St. Jude Memphis Classic	Hal Sutton	279	$ 90,000	$ 500,000
July 4–7	Canadian Open	Curtis Strange	279	$ 86,506	$ 480,000
July 11–14	Anheuser-Busch Golf Classic	Mark Wiebe	273	$ 90,000	$ 500,000
July 17–21	Lite–Quad Cities Open	Dan Forsman	267	$ 54,000	$ 300,000
July 25–28	Canon–Sammy Davis, Jr.–Greater Hartford Open	Phil Blackmar	271	$ 108,000	$ 600,000

PGA TOUR (continued)

Date	Event	Winner	Score	1st Place Money	Total Purse
Aug. 1–4	Western Open	Scott Verplank[a]	279	$ 90,000	$ 500,000
Aug. 8–11	PGA Championship	Hubert Green	278	$ 125,000	$ 700,000
Aug. 15–18	Buick Open	Ken Green	268	$ 81,000	$ 450,000
Aug. 22–25	NEC World Series of Golf	Roger Maltbie	268	$ 126,000	$ 700,000
Aug. 28–Sept. 1	B.C. Open	Joey Sindelar	274	$ 54,000	$ 300,000
Sept. 5–8	Bank of Boston Classic	George Burns	267	$ 72,000	$ 400,000
Sept. 12–15	Greater Milwaukee Open	Jim Thorpe	274	$ 54,000	$ 300,000
Sept. 19–22	Southwest Golf Classic	Hal Sutton	273	$ 72,000	$ 400,000
Sept. 26–29	Texas Open	John Mahaffey	268	$ 63,000	$ 350,000
Oct. 3–6	Southern Open	Tim Simpson	264	$ 63,000	$ 350,000
Oct. 10–13	Walt Disney World–Oldsmobile Classic	Lanny Wadkins	267	$ 72,000	$ 400,000
Oct. 17–20	Pensacola Open	Danny Edwards	269	$ 54,000	$ 300,000
Oct. 24–27	Seiko–Tucson Match Play Championship	Jim Thorpe	4&3	$ 150,000	$ 700,000
Nov. 13–16	Isuzu–Kapalua International	Mark O'Meara	275	$ 125,000	$ 500,000
Nov. 30–Dec. 1	Skins Game	Fuzzy Zoeller	NA	$ 245,000	$ 360,000
Dec. 5–8	JC Penney Classic	Larry Rinker and Laurie Rinker	267	$ 120,000	$ 550,000
Dec. 12–15	Chrysler Team Invitational	Ray Floyd and Hal Sutton	260	$ 90,000	$ 500,000

1986 Tour

Date	Event	Winner	Score	1st Place Money	Total Purse
Jan. 2–5	Bahamas Classic	Hale Irwin	269	$ 72,000	$ 300,000
Jan. 8–11	MONY Tournament of Champions	Calvin Peete	267	$ 90,000	$ 500,000
Jan. 15–19	Bob Hope–Chrysler Classic	Donnie Hammond	335	$ 108,000	$ 600,000
Jan. 23–26	Phoenix Open	Hal Sutton	267	$ 90,000	$ 500,000
Jan. 30–Feb. 2	AT&T Pebble Beach National Pro-Am	Fuzzy Zoeller	205	$ 108,000§	$ 600,000
Feb. 6–9	Shearson Lehman Brothers–Andy Williams Open	Bob Tway	204	$ 81,000§	$ 450,000
Feb. 13–16	Hawaiian Open	Corey Pavin	272	$ 90,000	$ 500,000
Feb. 20–23	Los Angeles Open	Doug Tewell	270	$ 81,000	$ 450,000
Feb. 27–Mar. 2	Honda Classic	Kenny Knox	287	$ 90,000	$ 500,000
Mar. 6–9	Doral–Eastern Open	Andy Bean	276	$ 90,000	$ 500,000
Mar. 13–16	Hertz Bay Hill Classic	Dan Forsman	202	$ 90,000§	$ 500,000
Mar. 20–23	USF&G Classic	Calvin Peete	269	$ 90,000	$ 500,000
Mar. 27–30	Tournament Players Championship	John Mahaffey	275	$ 162,000	$ 900,000
Apr. 3–6	Greater Greensboro Open	Sandy Lyle	275	$ 90,000	$ 500,000
Apr. 10–13	Masters	Jack Nicklaus	279	$ 144,000	$ 758,600
Apr. 10–13	Deposit Guaranty Golf Classic	Dan Halldorson	263	$ 36,000	$ 200,000
Apr. 17–20	Sea Pines Heritage Golf Classic	Fuzzy Zoeller	276	$ 81,000	$ 450,000
Apr. 24–27	Houston Open	Curtis Strange	274	$ 90,000	$ 500,000
Apr. 30–May 4	Pansonic Las Vegas Invitational	Greg Norman	333	$ 207,000	$1,140,000
May 8–11	Byron Nelson Golf Classic	Andy Bean	269	$ 108,000	$ 600,000
May 15–18	Colonial National Invitation	Dan Pohl	205	$ 108,000[a]	$ 600,000
May 22–25	Memorial Tournament	Hal Sutton	271	$ 100,000	$ 577,730

PGA TOUR (continued)

Date	Event	Winner	Score	1st Place Money	Total Purse
May 29–June 1	Kemper Open	Greg Norman	277	$ 90,000	$ 500,000
June 5–8	Manufacturers Hanover–Westchester Classic	Bob Tway	272	$ 108,000	$ 600,000
June 12–15	U.S. Open	Ray Floyd	279	$ 115,000	$ 700,000
June 12–15	Provident Classic	Brad Faxon	261	$ 54,000	$ 300,000
June 19–22	Georgia-Pacific–Atlanta Classic	Bob Tway	269	$ 90,000	$ 500,000
June 26–29	Canadian Open	Bob Murphy	280	$ 108,000	$ 600,000
July 3–6	Canon–Sammy Davis, Jr.–Greater Hartford Open	Mac O'Grady	269	$ 126,000	$ 700,000
July 10–13	Anheuser-Busch Golf Classic	Fuzzy Zoeller	274	$ 90,000	$ 500,000
July 17–20	Hardee's Golf Classic	Mark Wiebe	268	$ 72,000	$ 400,000
July 24–27	Buick Open	Ben Crenshaw	270	$ 90,000	$ 500,000
July 31–Aug. 3	Western Open	Tom Kite	286	$ 90,000	$ 500,000
Aug. 7–10	PGA Championship	Bob Tway	276	$ 140,000	$ 800,000
Aug. 13–17	The International	Ken Green	12[b]	$ 180,000	$1,002,300
Aug. 21–24	NEC World Series of Golf	Dan Pohl	277	$ 126,000	$ 700,000
Aug. 28–31	Federal Express–St. Jude Classic	Mike Hulbert	280	$ 109,064	$ 605,912
Sept. 4–7	B.C. Open	Rick Fehr	267	$ 72,000	$ 400,000
Sept. 11–14	Bank of Boston Classic	Gene Sauers	274	$ 81,000	$ 450,000
Sept. 18–21	Greater Milwaukee Open	Corey Pavin	272	$ 72,000	$ 400,000
Sept. 25–28	Southwest Golf Classic	Mark Calcavecchia	275	$ 72,000	$ 400,000
Oct. 2–5	Southern Open	Fred Wadsworth	269	$ 63,000	$ 350,000
Oct. 9–12	Pensacola Open	Ernie Gonzalez	128	$ 40,500	$ 300,000
Oct. 16–19	Walt Disney World–Oldsmobile Golf Classic	Ray Floyd	275	$ 90,000	$ 500,000
Oct. 23–26	Vantge Championship	Ben Crenshaw	196	$ 180,000§	$1,000,000
Oct. 30–Nov. 2	Seiko–Tucson Match Play	Jim Thorpe	67	$ 150,000	$ 700,000
Oct. 30–Nov. 2	Tallahassee Open	Mark Hayes	273	$ 36,000	$ 200,000
Nov. 13–16	Isuzu Kapalua International	Andy Bean	278	$ 150,000	$ 600,000
Nov. 29–30	Skins Game	Fuzzy Zoeller	NA	$ 370,000	$ 450,000
Dec. 4–7	JC Penney Classic	Tom Purtzer and Juli Inkster	265	$ 65,000	$ 600,000
Dec. 11–14	Chrysler Team Invitational	Scott Hoch and Gary Hallberg	251	$ 70,000 each	$ 600,000

1987 Tour

Date	Event	Winner	Score	1st Place Money	Total Purse
Jan. 7–10	MONY Tournament of Champions	Mac O'Grady	278	$ 90,000	$ 500,000
Jan. 14–18	Bob Hope–Chrysler Classic	Corey Pavin	341	$ 162,000	$ 900,000
Jan. 22–25	Phoenix Open	Paul Azinger	268	$ 108,000	$ 600,000
Jan. 29–Feb. 1	AT&T–Pebble Beach National Pro-Am	Johnny Miller	278	$ 108,000	$ 600,000
Feb. 5–8	Hawaiian Open	Corey Pavin	270	$ 108,000	$ 600,000
Feb. 12–15	Shearson Lehman Bros.–Andy Williams Open	George Burns	266	$ 90,000	$ 500,000
Feb. 19–22	Los Angeles Open	T.C. Chen	275	$ 108,000	$ 600,000
Feb. 26–Mar. 1	Doral Ryder Open	Lanny Wadkins	277	$ 180,000	$1,000,000
Mar. 5–8	Honda Classic	Mark Calcavecchia	279	$ 108,000	$ 600,000

PGA TOUR (continued)

Date	Event	Winner	Score	1st Place Money	Total Purse
Mar. 12–15	Hertz Bay Hill Classic	Payne Stewart	264	$ 108,000	$ 600,000
Mar. 19–22	USF&G Classic	Ben Crenshaw	268	$ 90,000	$ 500,000
Mar. 26–29	Tournament Players Championship	Sandy Lyle	274	$ 180,000	$1,000,000
Apr. 2–5	Greater Greensboro Open	Scott Simpson	282	$ 108,000	$ 600,000
Apr. 9–12	Masters	Larry Mize	285	$ 162,000	$ 867,100
Apr. 9–12	Deposit Guaranty Classic	David Ogrin	267	$ 36,000	$200,000
Apr. 16–19	MCI Heritage Classic	Davis Love	271	$ 117,000	$ 650,000
Apr. 23–26	Big "I" Houston Open	Jay Haas	276	$ 108,000	$ 600,000
Apr. 29–May 3	Panasonic Las Vegas Invitational	Paul Azinger	271	$ 225,000	$1,250,000
May 7–10	Byron Nelson Golf Classic	Fred Couples	266	$ 108,000	$ 600,000
May 14–17	Colonial National Invitation	Keith Clearwater	266	$ 108,000	$ 600,000
May 21–24	Georgia-Pacific–Atlanta Classic	Dave Barr	265	$ 108,000	$ 600,000
May 28–31	Memorial Tournament	Don Pooley	272	$ 140,000	$ 849,290
June 4–7	Kemper Open	Tom Kite	270	$ 126,000	$ 700,000
June 11–14	Manufacturers Hanover–Westchester Classic	J.C. Snead	276	$ 108,000	$ 600,000
June 18–21	U.S. Open	Scott Simpson	277	$ 150,000	$ 825,000
June 25–28	Canon–Sammy Davis, Jr.–Greater Hartford Open	Paul Azinger	269	$ 126,000	$ 700,000
July 2–5	Canadian Open	Curtis Strange	276	$ 108,000	$ 600,000
July 9–12	Anheuser-Busch Golf Classic	Mark McCumber	267	$ 110,160	$ 612,000
July 16–19	Hardee's Golf Classic	Kenny Knox	265	$ 90,000	$ 500,000
July 23–26	Buick Open	Robert Wrenn	262	$ 108,000	$ 600,000
July 30–Aug. 2	Federal Express–St. Jude Classic	Curtis Strange	275	$ 130,328	$ 724,043
Aug. 6–9	PGA Championship	Larry Nelson	287	$ 150,000	$ 900,000
Aug. 12–16	The International	John Cook	11[b]	$ 180,000	$1,115,280
Aug. 20–23	Beatrice Western Open	D.A. Weibring	207	$ 144,000	$ 800,000
Aug. 27–30	NEC World Series of Golf	Curtis Strange	275	$ 144,000	$ 800,000
Aug. 27–30	Provident Classic	John Inman	265	$ 81,000	$ 450,000
Sept. 3–6	B.C. Open	Joey Sindelar	266	$ 72,000	$ 400,000
Sept. 10–13	Bank of Boston Classic	Sam Randolph	199	$ 90,000§	$ 500,000
Sept. 17–20	Greater Milwaukee Open	Gary Hallberg	269	$ 108,000	$ 600,000
Sept. 24–27	Southwest Golf Classic	Steve Pate	273	$ 72,000	$ 400,000
Oct. 1–4	Southern Open	Ken Brown	266	$ 72,000	$ 400,000
Oct. 8–11	Pensacola Open	Doug Tewell	269	$ 54,000	$ 300,000
Oct. 15–18	Walt Disney World–Oldsmobile Classic	Larry Nelson	268	$ 108,000	$ 600,000
Oct. 22–25	Seiko Tucson Open	Mike Reid	268	$ 108,000	$ 600,000
Oct. 29–Nov. 1	Nabisco Championships of Golf	Tom Watson	268	$ 360,000	$2,000,000
Oct. 29–Nov. 1	Centel Classic	Keith Clearwater	278	$ 90,000	$ 500,000
Nov. 12–15	Isuzu–Kapalua International	Andy Bean	267	$ 150,000	$ 600,000
Nov. 29–30	Skins Game	Lee Trevino	NA	$ 310,000	$ 450,000
Dec. 3–6	JC Penney Classic	Steve Jones and Jane Crafter	268	$ 65,000 each	$ 650,000

PGA TOUR (continued)

Date	Event	Winner	Score	1st Place Money	Total Purse
Dec. 10–13	Chrysler Team Championship	Bob Tway and Mike Hulbert	250	$ 50,000 each	$ 600,000

1988 Tour

Date	Event	Winner	Score	1st Place Money	Total Purse
Jan. 14–17	MONY Tournament of Champions	Steve Pate	202[a]	$ 90,000	$ 500,000
Jan. 20–24	Bob Hope Chrysler Classic	Jay Haas	338	$ 180,000	$1,000,000
Jan. 28–31	Phoenix Open	Sandy Lyle	269	$ 117,000	$ 650,000
Feb. 4–7	AT&T–Pebble Beach National Pro-Am	Steve Jones	280	$ 126,000	$ 700,000
Feb. 11–14	Hawaiian Open	Lanny Wadkins	271	$ 108,000	$ 600,000
Feb. 18–21	Shearson Lehman Hutton–Andy Williams Open	Steve Pate	269	$ 117,000	$ 650,000
Feb. 25–28	Los Angeles Open	Chip Beck	267	$ 135,000	$ 750,000
Mar. 3–6	Doral Ryder Open	Ben Crenshaw	274	$ 180,000	$1,000,000
Mar. 10–13	Honda Classic	Joey Sindelar	276	$ 126,000	$ 700,000
Mar. 17–20	Hertz Bay Hill Classic	Paul Azinger	271	$ 135,000	$ 750,000
Mar. 24–27	Players Championship	Mark McCumber	273	$ 225,000	$1,250,000
Mar. 30–Apr. 2	K mart–Greater Greensboro Open	Sandy Lyle	271	$ 180,000	$1,000,000
Apr. 7–10	Masters	Sandy Lyle	281	$ 183,800	$1,000,000
Apr. 7–10	Deposit Guaranty Golf Classic	Frank Conner	267	$ 36,000	$ 200,000
Apr. 14–17	MCI Heritage Classic	Greg Norman	271	$ 126,000	$ 700,000
Apr. 21–24	USF&G Classic	Chip Beck	262	$ 135,000	$ 750,000
Apr. 28–May 1	Independent Insurance Agent Open	Curtis Strange	270	$ 126,000	$ 700,000
May 4–8	Panasonic–Las Vegas Invitational	Gary Koch	274	$ 250,000	$1,388,889
May 12–15	GTE–Byron Nelson Classic	Bruce Lietzke	271	$ 135,000	$ 750,000
May 19–22	Colonial National Invitation	Lanny Wadkins	270	$ 135,000	$ 750,000
May 26–29	Memorial Tournament	Curtis Strange	274	$ 160,000	$ 950,250
June 2–5	Kemper Open	Morris Hatalsky	274	$ 144,000	$ 800,000
June 9–12	Manufacturers Hanover–Westchester Classic	Seve Ballesteros	276	$ 126,000	$ 700,000
June 16–19	U.S. Open	Curtis Strange	278	$ 180,000	$1,000,000
June 23–26	Georgia-Pacific–Atlanta Classic	Larry Nelson	268	$ 126,000	$ 700,000
June 30–July 3	Beatrice Western Open	Jim Benepe	278	$ 162,000	$ 900,000
July 7–10	Anheuser-Busch Golf Classic	Tom Sieckmann	270	$ 117,000	$ 650,000
July 14–17	Hardee's Golf Classic	Blaine McCallister	261	$ 108,000	$ 600,000
July 21–24	Canon–Sammy Davis, Jr.–Greater Hartford Open	Mark Brooks	269	$ 126,000	$ 700,000
July 28–31	Buick Open	Scott Verplank	268	$ 126,000	$ 700,000
Aug. 4–7	Federal Express–St. Jude Classic	Jodie Mudd	273	$ 171,692	$ 953,844
Aug. 11–14	PGA Championship	Jeff Sluman	272	$ 160,000	$1,000,000
Aug. 17–21	The International	Joey Sindelar	17[b]	$ 180,000	$1,115,280
Aug. 25–28	NEC World Series of Golf	Mike Reid	275	$ 162,000	$ 900,000

PGA TOUR (continued)

Date	Event	Winner	Score	1st Place Money	Total Purse
Aug. 25–28	Provident Classic	Phil Blackmar	264	$ 81,000	$ 450,000
Sept. 1–4	Canadian Open	Ken Green	275	$ 135,000	$ 750,000
Sept. 8–11	Greater Milwaukee Open	Ken Green	268	$ 126,000	$ 700,000
Sept. 15–18	Bank of Boston Classic	Mark Calcavecchia	274	$ 108,000	$ 600,000
Sept. 22–25	B.C. Open	Bill Glasson	268	$ 90,000	$ 500,000
Sept. 29–Oct. 2	Southern Open	David Frost	270	$ 72,000	$ 400,000
Oct. 6–9	Gatlin Brothers Southwest Classic	Tom Purtzer	269	$ 72,000	$ 400,000
Oct. 13–16	Texas Open	Corey Pavin	259	$ 108,000	$ 600,000
Oct. 20–23	Pensacola Open	Andrew Magee	271	$ 72,000	$ 400,000
Oct. 26–29	Walt Disney World–Oldsmobile Classic	Bob Lohr	263	$ 126,000	$ 700,000
Nov. 3–6	Seiko–Tucson Open	David Frost	266	$ 108,000	$ 600,000
Nov. 10–13	Nabisco Championships of Golf	Curtis Strange	279	$ 360,000	$2,000,000
Nov. 10–13	Centel Classic	Bill Glasson	272	$ 90,000	$ 500,000
Nov. 16–19	Isuzu–Kapalua International	Bob Gilder	266	$ 150,000	$ 600,000
Nov. 26–27	Skins Game	Ray Floyd	NA	$ 290,000	$ 450,000
Dec. 1–4	JC Penney Classic	John Huston and Amy Benz	269	$ 80,000	$ 800,000
Dec. 8–11	Chrysler Team Championship	Wayne Levi and George Burns	252	$ 50,000 each	$ 600,000

1989 Tour

Date	Event	Winner	Score	1st Place Money	Total Purse
Jan. 5–8	MONY Tournament of Champions	Steve Jones	279	$ 135,000	$ 750,000
Jan. 11–15	Bob Hope Chrysler Classic	Steve Jones	343	$ 180,000	$1,000,000
Jan. 19–22	Phoenix Open	Mark Calcavecchia	263	$ 126,000	$ 700,000
Jan. 26–29	AT&T–Pebble Beach National Pro-Am	Mark O'Meara	277	$ 180,000	$1,000,000
Feb. 2–5	Nissan Los Angeles Open	Mark Calcavecchia	272	$ 180,000	$1,000,000
Feb. 9–12	Hawaiian Open	Gene Sauers	197	$ 135,000§	$ 750,000
Feb. 16–19	Shearson Lehman–Hutton Open	Greg Twiggs	271	$ 126,000	$ 700,000
Feb. 23–26	Doral Ryder Open	Bill Glasson	275	$ 234,000	$1,000,000
Mar. 2–5	Honda Classic	Blaine McCallister	266	$ 144,000	$ 800,000
Mar. 9–12	Nestlé Invitational	Tom Kite	278	$ 144,000	$ 800,000
Mar. 16–19	Players Championship	Tom Kite	279	$ 243,000	$1,350,000
Mar. 23–26	USF&G Classic	Tim Simpson	274	$ 135,000	$ 750,000
Mar. 29–Apr. 2	Independent Insurance Agent Open	Mike Sullivan	280	$ 144,000	$ 800,000
Apr. 6–9	Masters	Nick Faldo	283	$ 200,000	$1,000,000
Apr. 6–9	Deposit Guaranty Golf Classic	Jim Booros	199[a]	$ 36,000	$ 200,000
Apr. 13–16	MCI Heritage Classic	Payne Stewart	268	$ 144,000	$ 800,000
Apr. 20–23	K mart–Greater Greensboro Open	Ken Green	277	$ 180,000	$1,000,000
Apr. 26–30	Las Vegas Invitational	Scott Hoch	336	$ 225,000	$1,300,000
May 4–7	Byron Nelson Classic	Jodie Mudd	265	$ 180,000	$1,000,000
May 11–14	Memorial Tournament	Bob Tway	277	$ 160,000	$1,004,290
May 18–21	Southwestern Bell Colonial	Ian Baker-Finch	270	$ 180,000	$1,000,000
May 25–28	BellSouth–Atlanta Classic	Scott Simpson	278	$ 162,000	$ 900,000

PGA TOUR (continued)

Date	Event	Winner	Score	1st Place Money	Total Purse
June 1–4	Kemper Open	Tom Byrum	268	$ 162,000	$ 900,000
June 8–11	Manufacturers Hanover–Westchester Classic	Wayne Grady	277	$ 180,000	$1,000,000
June 15–18	U.S. Open	Curtis Strange	278	$ 200,000	$1,049,089
June 22–25	Canadian Open	Steve Jones	271	$ 162,000	$ 900,000
June 29–July 2	Beatrice Western Open	Mark McCumber	275	$ 180,000	$1,000,000
July 6–9	Canon Greater Hartford Open	Paul Azinger	267	$ 180,000	$1,000,000
July 13–16	Anheuser-Busch Classic	Mike Donald	268	$ 153,000	$ 850,000
July 20–23	Hardee's Classic	Curt Byrum	268	$ 126,000	$ 700,000
July 27–30	Buick Open	Leonard Thompson	273	$ 180,000	$1,000,000
Aug. 3–6	Federal Express–St. Jude Classic	John Mahaffey	272	$ 180,000	$1,000,000
Aug. 10–13	PGA Championship	Payne Stewart	276	$ 200,000	$1,200,000
Aug. 17–20	The International	Greg Norman	13[b]	$ 180,000	$1,000,000
Aug. 24–27	NEC World Series of Golf	David Frost	276	$ 180,000	$1,000,000
Aug. 24–27	Chattanooga Classic	Stan Utley	263	$ 90,000	$ 500,000
Aug. 31–Sept. 3	Greater Milwaukee Open	Greg Norman	269	$ 144,000	$ 800,000
Sept. 7–10	B.C. Open	Mike Hulbert	268	$ 90,000	$ 500,000
Sept. 14–17	Bank of Boston	Blaine McCallister	271	$ 126,000	$ 700,000
Sept. 21–24	Southern Open	Ted Schultz	266	$ 72,000	$ 400,000
Sept. 28–Oct.1	Centel Classic	Bill Britton	200	$ 135,000§	$ 750,000
Oct. 5–8	Texas Open Presented By Nabisco	Donnie Hammond	258	$ 108,000	$ 600,000
Oct. 18–21	Walt Disney World–Oldsmobile Classic	Tim Simpson	272	$ 144,000	$ 800,000
Oct. 26–29	Nabisco Championships	Tom Kite	276	$ 450,000	$2,500,000
Nov. 8–11	Isuzu–Kapalua	Peter Jacobsen	270	$ 150,000	$ 650,000
Nov. 17–19	RMCC Invitational	Curtis Strange and Mark O'Meara	190	$ 125,000 each	$1,000,000
Nov. 30–Dec. 3	JC Penney Classic	Bill Glasson and Pat Bradley	267	$ 100,000 each	$1,000,000
Dec. 7–10	Chrysler Team	David Ogrin and Ted Schulz	257	$ 50,000	$ 600,000

1990 Tour

Date	Event	Winner	Score	1st Place Money	Total Purse
Jan. 4–7	MONY Tournament of Champions	Paul Azinger	272	$ 135,000	$ 750,000
Jan. 11–14	Northern Telecom–Tucson Open	Robert Gamez	270	$ 162,000	$ 900,000
Jan. 17–21	Bob Hope–Chrysler Classic	Peter Jacobsen	339	$ 180,000	$1,000,000
Jan. 25–28	Phoenix Open	Tommy Armour III	267	$ 162,000	$ 900,000
Feb. 1–4	AT&T–Pebble Beach National Pro-Am	Mark O'Meara	281	$ 180,000	$1,000,000
Feb. 8–11	Hawaiian Open	David Ishii	279	$ 180,000	$1,000,000
Feb. 15–18	Shearson Lehman Hutton Open	Dan Forsman	275	$ 162,000	$ 900,000
Feb. 22–25	Nissan Los Angeles Open	Fred Couples	266	$ 180,000	$1,000,000
Mar. 1–4	Doral Ryder Open	Greg Norman	273	$ 252,000	$1,400,000
Mar. 8–11	Honda Classic	John Huston	282	$ 180,000	$1,000,000
Mar. 15–18	Players Championship	Jodie Mudd	278	$ 270,000	$1,500,000

PGA TOUR (continued)

Date	Event	Winner	Score	1st Place Money	Total Purse
Mar. 22–25	Nestlé Invitational	Robert Gamez	274	$ 162,000	$ 900,000
Mar. 28–Apr. 1	Independent Insurance Agent Open	Tony Sills	204	$ 180,000§	$1,000,000
Apr. 5–8	Masters	Nick Faldo	278	$ 225,000	$1,250,000
Apr. 5–8	Deposit Guaranty Golf Classic	Gene Sauers	268	$ 54,000	$ 300,000
Apr. 12–15	MCI Heritage Classic	Payne Stewart	276	$ 180,000	$1,000,000
Apr. 19–22	K mart–Greater Greensboro Open	Steve Elkington	282	$ 225,000	$1,250,000
Apr. 26–29	USF&G Classic	David Frost	276	$ 180,000	$1,000,000
May 3–6	GTE Byron Nelson Classic	Payne Stewart	202	$ 180,000§	$1,000,000
May 10–13	Memorial Tournament	Greg Norman	216	$ 180,000§	$1,000,000
May 17–20	Southwestern Bell Colonial	Ben Crenshaw	272	$ 180,000	$1,000,000
May 24–27	BellSouth–Atlanta Classic	Wayne Levi	275	$ 180,000	$1,000,000
May 31–June 3	Kemper Open	Gil Morgan	274	$ 180,000	$1,000,000
June 7–10	Centel Western Open	Wayne Levi	275	$ 180,000	$1,000,000
June 14–17	U.S. Open	Hale Irwin	280	$ 220,000	$1,200,000
June 21–24	Buick Classic	Hale Irwin	269	$ 180,000	$1,000,000
June 28–July 1	Canon Greater Hartford Open	Wayne Levi	267	$ 180,000	$1,000,000
July 5–8	Anheuser-Busch Classic	Lanny Wadkins	266	$ 180,000	$1,000,000
July 12–15	Bank of Boston Classic	Morris Hatalsky	275	$ 162,000	$ 900,000
July 26–29	Buick Open	Chip Beck	272	$ 180,000	$1,000,000
Aug. 2–5	Federal Express–St. Jude Classic	Tom Kite	269	$ 180,000	$1,000,000
Aug. 9–12	PGA Championship	Wayne Grady	282	$ 225,000	$1,350,000
Aug. 16–19	The International	Davis Love	14[b]	$ 180,000	$1,000,000
Aug. 23–26	NEC World Series of Golf	Jose Maria Olazabal	262	$ 198,000	$1,100,000
Aug. 23–26	Chattanooga Classic	Peter Persons	260	$ 108,000	$ 600,000
Aug. 30–Sept. 2	Greater Milwaukee Open	Jim Gallagher	271	$ 162,000	$ 900,000
Sept. 6–9	Hardee's Golf Classic	Joey Sindelar	268	$ 180,000	$1,000,000
Sept. 13–16	Canadian Open	Wayne Levi	278	$ 180,000	$1,000,000
Sept. 20–23	B.C. Open	Nolan Henke	268	$ 126,000	$ 700,000
Sept. 27–30	Buick Southern Open	Kenny Knox	265	$ 108,000	$ 600,000
Oct. 4–7	H.E.B. Texas Open	Mark O'Meara	261	$ 144,000	$ 800,000
Oct. 10–14	Las Vegas Invitational	Bob Tway	334	$ 234,000	$1,300,000
Oct. 17–20	Walt Disney World— Oldsmobile Classic	Tim Simpson	264	$ 180,000	$1,000,000
Oct. 25–28	Nabisco Championships	Jodie Mudd	273	$ 450,000	$2,500,000

1991 Tour

Date	Event	Winner	Score	1st Place Money	Total Purse
Jan. 3–6	Infiniti Tournament of Champions	Tom Kite	272	$ 144,000	$ 800,000
Jan. 10–13	Northern Telecom–Tucson Open	Phil Mickelson[a]	272	—	$1,000,000
Jan. 17–20	United Airlines–Hawaiian Open	Lanny Wadkins	270	$ 198,000	$1,100,000
Jan. 24–27	Phoenix Open	Nolan Henke	268	$ 180,000	$1,000,000
Jan. 31–Feb. 3	AT&T–Pebble Beach National Pro-Am	Paul Azinger	274	$ 198,000	$1,100,000

PGA TOUR (continued)

Date	Event	Winner	Score	1st Place Money	Total Purse
Feb. 6–10	Bob Hope–Chrysler Classic	Corey Pavin	331	$ 198,000	$1,100,000
Feb. 14–17	Shearson Lehman Brothers Open	Jay Don Blake	268	$ 180,000	$1,000,000
Feb. 21–24	Nissan–Los Angeles Open	Ted Schulz	272	$ 180,000	$1,000,000
Feb. 28–Mar. 3	Doral Ryder Open	Rocco Mediate	276	$ 252,000	$1,400,000
Mar. 7–10	Honda Classic	Steve Pate	279	$ 180,000	$1,000,000
Mar. 14–17	Nestle Invitational	Andrew Magee	203	$ 180,000§	$1,000,000
Mar. 21–24	USF&G Classic	Ian Woosnam	275	$ 180,000	$1,000,000
Mar. 28–31	Players Championship	Steve Elkington	276	$ 288,000	$1,600,000
Apr. 11–14	Masters	Ian Woosnam	277	$ 243,000	$1,600,000
Apr. 11–14	Deposit Guaranty Classic	Larry Silveira	266	$ 54,000	$ 300,000
Apr. 18–21	MCI Heritage Classic	Davis Love	271	$ 180,000	$1,000,000
Apr. 25–28	K mart–Greater Greensboro Open	Mark Brooks	275	$ 225,000	$1,250,000
May 2–5	GTE Byron Nelson Classic	Nick Price	270	$ 198,000	$1,100,000
May 9–12	BellSouth–Atlanta Classic	Corey Pavin	272	$ 180,000	$1,000,000
May 16–19	Memorial	Kenny Perry	273	$ 216,000	$1,200,000
May 23–26	Southwestern Bell Colonial	Tom Purtzer	267	$ 216,000	$1,200,000
May 30–June 2	Kemper Open	Billy Andrade	263	$ 180,000	$1,000,000
June 6–9	Buick Classic	Billy Andrade	273	$ 180,000	$1,000,000
June 13–16	U.S. Open	Payne Stewart	282	$ 235,000	$1,300,000
June 20–23	Anheuser-Busch Classic	Mike Hulbert	266	$ 180,000	$1,000,000
June 27–30	Federal Express–St. Jude Classic	Fred Couples	269	$ 180,000	$1,000,000
July 4–7	Centel Western Open	Russ Cochran	275	$ 180,000	$1,000,000
July 11–14	New England Classic	Bruce Fleisher	268	$ 180,000	$1,000,000
July 18–21	Chattanooga Classic	Dillard Pruitt	260	$ 126,000	$ 700,000
July 25–28	Canon–Greater Hartford Open	Billy Ray Brown	271	$ 180,000	$1,000,000
Aug. 1–4	Buick Open	Brad Faxon	271	$ 180,000	$1,000,000
Aug. 8–11	PGA Championship	John Daly	276	$ 230,000	$1,350,000
Aug. 15–18	International	Jose Maria Olazabal	10[b]	$ 198,000	$1,100,000
Aug. 22–25	NEC World Series of Golf	Tom Purtzer	279	$ 216,000	$1,200,000
Aug. 29–Sept. 1	Greater Milwaukee Open	Mark Brooks	270	$ 180,000	$1,000,000
Sept. 5–8	Canadian Open	Nick Price	273	$ 180,000	$1,000,000
Sept. 12–15	Hardee's Classic	D.A. Weibring	267	$ 180,000	$1,000,000
Sept. 19–22	B.C. Open	Fred Couples	269	$ 144,000	$ 800,000
Sept. 26–29	Buick Southern Open	David Peoples	278	$ 126,000	$ 700,000
Oct. 3–6	H.E.B. Texas Open	Blaine McCallister	269	$ 162,000	$ 900,000
Oct. 9–13	Las Vegas Invitational	Andrew Magee	329	$ 270,000	$1,500,000
Oct. 16–19	Walt Disney World–Oldsmobile Classic	Mark O'Meara	267	$ 180,000	$1,000,000
Oct. 23–26	Independent Insurance Agent Open	Fulton Allem	273	$ 144,000	$ 800,000
Oct. 31–Nov. 3	Tour Championship	Craig Stadler	279	$ 360,000	$2,000,000

PGA TOUR (continued)

Date	Event	Winner	Score	1st Place Money	Total Purse
		1992 Tour			
Jan. 9–12	Infiniti Tournament of Champions	Steve Elkington	279	$ 144,000	$ 800,000
Jan. 16–19	Bob Hope–Chrysler Classic	John Cook	336	$ 198,000	$1,100,000
Jan. 23–26	Phoenix Open	Mark Calcavecchia	264	$ 180,000	$1,000,000
Jan. 30–Feb. 2	AT&T–Pebble Beach National Pro-Am	Mark O'Meara	275	$ 198,000	$1,100,000
Feb. 6–9	United Airlines–Hawaiian Open	John Cook	265	$ 216,000	$1,200,000
Feb. 13–16	Northern Telecom Open	Lee Janzen	270	$ 198,000	$1,100,000
Feb. 20–23	Buick Invitational of California	Steve Pate	200§	$ 180,000	$1,000,000
Feb. 27–Mar. 1	Nissan–Los Angeles Open	Fred Couples	269	$ 180,000	$1,000,000
Mar. 5–8	Doral Rider Open	Ray Floyd	271	$ 252,000	$1,400,000
Mar. 12–15	Honda Classic	Corey Pavin	273	$ 198,000	$1,100,000
Mar. 19–22	Nestle Invitational	Fred Couples	269	$ 180,000	$1,100,000
Mar. 26–29	Players Championship	Davis Love	273	$ 324,000	$1,800,000
Apr. 2–5	Freeport–McMoRan Classic	Chip Beck	276	$ 180,000	$1,000,000
Apr. 9–12	Masters	Fred Couples	275	$ 270,000	$1,500,000
Apr. 16–19	MCI Heritage Classic	Davis Love	269	$ 180,000	$1,000,000
Apr. 23–26	Kmart–Greater Greensboro Open	Davis Love	272	$ 225,000	$1,250,000
Apr. 30–May 3	Shell Houston Open	Fred Funk	272	$ 216,000	$1,200,000
May 7–10	BellSouth Classic	Tom Kite	272	$ 180,000	$1,000,000
May 14–17	GTE Byron Nelson Classic	Billy Ray Brown	199§	$ 198,000	$1,000,000
May 21–24	Southwestern Bell Colonial	Bruce Lietzke	267	$ 234,000	$1,300,000
May 28–31	Kemper Open	Bill Glasson	276	$ 198,000	$1,100,000
June 4–7	Memorial	David Edwards	273	$ 234,000	$1,300,000
June 11–14	Federal Express–St. Jude Classic	Jay Haas	263	$ 198,000	$1,100,000
June 18–21	U.S. Open	Tom Kite	285	$ 275,000	$1,500,000
June 25–28	Buick Classic	David Frost	268	$ 180,000	$1,000,000
July 2–5	Centel Western Open	Ben Crenshaw	276	$ 198,000	$1,100,000
July 9–12	Anheuser-Busch Classic	David Peoples	271	$ 198,000	$1,100,000
July 16–19	Chattanooga Classic	Mark Carnevale	269	$ 144,000	$ 800,000
July 23–26	New England Classic	Brad Faxon	268	$ 180,000	$1,000,000
July 30–Aug. 2	Canon–Greater Hartford Open	Lanny Wadkins	274	$ 180,000	$1,000,000
Aug. 6–9	Buick Open	Dan Forsman	276	$ 180,000	$1,000,000
Aug. 13–16	PGA Championship	Nick Price	278	$ 280,000	$1,600,000
Aug. 20–23	International	Brad Faxon	14ᵇ	$ 216,000	$1,200,000
Aug. 27–30	NEC World Series of Golf	Craig Stadler	273	$ 252,000	$1,400,000

PGA TOUR (continued)

Date	Event	Winner	Score	1st Place Money	Total Purse
Sept. 3–6	Greater Milwaukee Open	Richard Zokol	269	$ 180,000	$1,000,000
Sept. 10–13	Canadian Open	Greg Norman	280	$ 180,000	$1,000,000
Sept. 17–20	Hardee's Classic	David Frost	266	$ 180,000	$1,000,000
Sept. 24–27	B.C. Open	John Daly	266	$ 144,000	$ 800,000
Oct. 1–4	Buick Southern Open	Gary Hallberg	206§	$ 126,000	$ 700,000
Oct. 8–11	Las Vegas Invitational	John Cook	334	$ 234,000	$1,300,000
Oct. 15–18	Walt Disney World–Oldsmobile Classic	John Huston	262	$ 216,000	$1,200,000
Oct. 22–25	H.E.B. Texas Open	Nick Price	263	$ 162,000	$ 900,000
Oct. 29–Nov. 1	Tour Championship	Paul Azinger	276	$ 360,000	$2,000,000

Notes

[a] Amateur.

[b] Events decided on points system.

NR = not recorded.

NA = not applicable.

* Event cut to three rounds due to bad weather—purse reduced.

† Event cut to two rounds due to bad weather—purse reduced.

‡ Event cut to one round due to bad weather—purse reduced.

§ Event cut to three rounds due to bad weather—sponsor paid full purse.

TOUR RECORDS

Lowest score, 18 holes: 59, Al Geiberger, 1977, second round of Memphis Classic, Colonial CC, Memphis, Tenn.; Chip Beck, 1991, third round of Las Vegas Invitational, Sunrise CC, Las Vegas, Nev.

Lowest score, 36 holes: 125, Ron Streck (63-62), 1978, third and fourth rounds of Texas Open, Oak Hills CC, San Antonio, Tex.; Blaine McCallister (62-63), second and third rounds of Hardee's Classic, Oakwood CC, Coal Valley, Ill.

Lowest score, 54 holes: 189, Chandler Harper (63-63-63), 1954, second through fourth rounds of Texas Open, Brackenridge Park GC, San Antonio, Tex.

Lowest score, 72 holes: 257, Mike Souchak (60-68-66-65), 1955, Texas Open, Brackenridge Park GC, San Antonio, Tex.

Most shots under par (72-hole tournament): 27, Mike Souchak, 1955 Texas Open; Ben Hogan, 1945 Portland Invitational.

Most victories (official): Sam Snead, 81; Jack Nicklaus, 70; Ben Hogan, 63; Arnold Palmer, 60; Byron Nelson, 52; Billy Casper, 51.

Most consecutive years winning at least one tournament: 17, Jack Nicklaus (1962–1978); Arnold Palmer (1955–1971).

Most consecutive victories: 11, Byron Nelson, 1945.

Most victories in a single event: 8, Sam Snead, Greater Greensboro Open (1938–1946, 1949, 1950, 1955, 1956, 1960, 1965).

Most victories in a year: 18, Byron Nelson, 1945.

Largest victory margin: 16 strokes, Bobby Locke, 1948 Chicago Victory National Championship.

Oldest winner: 52, Sam Snead, 1965 Greater Greensboro Open.

Youngest winner (since 1941): 20, Ray Floyd, 1963 St. Petersburg Open.

WOMEN'S MAJOR CHAMPIONSHIPS

U.S. WOMEN'S OPEN

Year	Winner, Score	Runner-Up, Score	Site
1946	Patty Berg, 5&4	Betty Jameson	Spokane CC, Spokane, Wash.
1947	Betty Jameson, 295	Sally Sessions, Polly Riley, 301	Starmount Forest CC, Greensboro, N.C.
1948	Babe Zaharias, 300	Betty Hicks, 308	Atlantic City CC, Northfield, N.J.
1949	Louise Suggs, 291	Babe Didrikson, 305	Prince Georges G&CC, Landover, Md.
1950	Babe Zaharias, 291	Betsy Rawls, 300	Rolling Hills CC, Witchita, Kan.
1951	Betsy Rawls, 293	Louise Suggs, 298	Druid Hills GC, Atlanta Ga.
1952	Louise Suggs, 284	Marlene Bauer, Betty Jameson, 291	Bala GC, Philadelphia, Pa.
1953	Betsy Rawls, 302 (71)	Jacqueline Pung, 302, (77)	CC of Rochester, Rochester, N.Y.
1954	Babe Zaharias, 291	Betty Hicks, 303	Salem CC, Peabody, Mass.
1955	Fay Crocker, 299	Louise Suggs, Mary Lena Faulk, 303	Wichita CC, Wichita, Kan.
1956	Kathy Cornelius, 302 (75)	Barbara McIntire, 302 (82)	Northland CC, Duluth, Minn.
1957	Betsy Rawls, 299	Patty Berg, 305	Winged Foot GC, Mamaroneck, N.Y.
1958	Mickey Wright, 290	Louise Suggs, 295	Forest Lake CC, Bloomfield Hills, Mich.
1959	Mickey Wright, 287	Louise Suggs, 295	Churchill Valley CC, Pittsburgh, Pa.
1960	Betsy Rawls, 292	Joyce Ziske, 293	Worcester CC, Worcester, Mass.
1961	Mickey Wright, 293	Betsy Rawls, 299	Baltusrol GC, Springfield, N.J.
1962	Murle Lindstrom, 301	Ruth Jessen, JoAnn Prentice, 303	Dunes G&BC, Myrtle Beach, S.C.
1963	Mary Mills, 289	Sandra Haynie, Louise Suggs, 292	Kenwood CC, Cincinnati, Ohio
1964	Mickey Wright, 290 (70)	Ruth Jessen, 290 (72)	San Diego CC, Chula Vista, Cal.
1965	Carol Mann, 290	Kathy Cornelius, 292	Atlantic City CC, Northfield, N.J.
1966	Sandra Spuzich, 297	Carol Mann, 298	Hazeltine National GC, Chaska, Minn.
1967	Catherine Lacoste, 294	Susie Maxwell, Beth Stone, 296	Virginia Hot Springs G&TC, Hot Springs, Va.

Catherine Lacoste of France won the U.S. Women's Open in 1967, the only amateur to claim that title.

U.S. WOMEN'S OPEN (continued)

Year	Winner, Score	Runner-Up, Score	Site
1968	Susie Maxwell Berning, 289	Mickey Wright, 292	Moselem Springs GC, Fleetwood, Pa.
1969	Donna Caponi, 294	Peggy Wilson, 295	Scenic Hills CC, Pensacola, Fla.
1970	Donna Caponi, 287	Sandra Haynie, Sandra Spuzich, 288	Muskogee CC, Muskogee, Okla.
1971	JoAnne Carner, 288	Kathy Whitworth, 295	Kahkwa Club, Erie, Pa.
1971	Susie Berning, 299	Kathy Ahern, Pam Barnett, Judy Rankin, 300	Winged Foot GC, Mamaroneck, N.Y.
1973	Susie Berning, 290	Shelley Hamlin, Gloria Ehret, 295	CC of Rochester, Rochester, N.Y.
1974	Sandra Haynie, 295	Beth Stone, Carol Mann, 296	LaGrange CC, LaGrange, Ill.
1975	Sandra Palmer, 295	Nancy Lopez, JoAnne Carner, Sandra Post, 299	Atlantic City CC, Northfield, N.J.
1976	JoAnne Carner, 292 (76)	Sandra Palmer, 292 (78)	Rolling Green GC, Springfield, Pa.
1977	Hollis Stacy, 292	Nancy Lopez, 294	Hazeltine National GC, Chaska, Minn.
1978	Hollis Stacy, 289	JoAnne Carner, Sally Little, 290	CC of Indianapolis, Indianapolis, Ind.

Hollis Stacy won the U.S. Women's Open in 1977, 1978 and 1984. *AP/Wide World Photos*

U.S. WOMEN'S OPEN

Year	Winner, Score	Runner-Up, Score	Site
1979	Jerilyn Britz, 284	Debbie Massey, Sandra Palmer, 286	Brooklawn CC, Fairfield, Conn.
1980	Amy Alcott, 280	Hollis Stacy, 289	Richland CC, Nashville, Tenn.
1981	Pat Bradley, 279	Beth Daniel, 280	LaGrange CC, LaGrange, Ill.
1982	Janet Alex, 283	Sandra Haynie, Donna White, Jo-Anne Carner, Beth Daniel, 289	Del Paso CC, Sacramento, Cal.
1983	Jan Stephenson, 290	JoAnne Carner, Patty Sheehan, 291	Cedar Ridge CC, Tulsa, Okla.
1984	Hollis Stacy, 290	Rosie Jones, 291	Salem CC, Peabody, Mass.
1985	Kathy Baker, 280	Judy Clark, 283	Baltusrol GC, Springfield, N.J.
1986	Jane Geddes, 287 (71)	Sally Little (73)	NCR CC, Dayton, Ohio
1987	Laura Davies, 285 (71)	Ayako Okamoto (73), JoAnne Carner (74)	Plainfield CC, Edison, N.J.
1988	Liselotte Neumann, 277	Patty Sheehan, 280	Baltimore CC, Baltimore, Md.
1989	Betsy King, 278	Nancy Lopez, 282	Indianwood G & CC, Lake Orion, Mich.
1990	Betsy King, 284	Patty Sheehan, 285	Atlanta AC, Duluth, Ga.
1991	Meg Mallon, 283	Pat Bradley, 285	Colonial CC, Forth Worth, Tex.
1992	Patty Sheehan, 280 (72)	Juli Inkster, 280 (74)	Oakmont CC, Oakmont, Pa.

Figures in parentheses are play-off scores.

TOURNAMENT RECORDS

Lowest score, 18 holes: 65, Sally Little, 1978, fourth round, CC of Indianapolis; Judy Clark, 1985, third round, Baltusrol GC; Ayako Okamoto, 1989, fourth round, Indianwood G&CC.

Lowest score, 36 holes: 134, Pat Bradley (68-66), 1981, third and fourth rounds, LaGrange CC; Patty Sheehan (66-68), 1990, first and second rounds, Atlanta AC.

Lowest score, 54 holes: 208, Marlene Bauer (70-67-71), 1952, second through fourth rounds, Bala GC; Amy Alcott (70-70-68), 1980, first through third rounds, Richland CC; Pat Bradley (74-68-66), second through fourth rounds, LaGrange CC; Liselotte Neumann (67-72-69), first through third rounds, Baltimore CC; Juli Inkster (68-71-69), 1992, second through fourth rounds, Oakmont CC.

Lowest score, 72 holes: 277, Liselette Neumann (67-72-69-69), 1988, Baltimore CC.

Largest winning margin: 14, Louise Suggs, 1949.

Oldest champion: 40, Fay Crocker, 1955.

Youngest champion: 22, Catherine Lacoste, 1967.

Most victories: 4, Mickey Wright (1958–1959, 1961, 1964); Betsy Rawls (1951, 1953, 1957, 1960).

Most times runner-up: 5, Louise Suggs (1951, 1958, 1959, 1963); JoAnne Carner (1975, 1978, 1982, 1983, 1987).

Victories in consecutive years: Mickey Wright (1958–1959); Donna Caponi (1969–1970); Susie Berning (1972–1973); Hollis Stacy (1977–1978); Betsy King (1989–1990).

LPGA CHAMPIONSHIP

Year	Winner, Score	Runner-Up, Score	Site
1955	Beverly Hanson, 220—4&3**	Louise Suggs, 223	Orchard Ridge CC, Ft. Wayne, Ind.
1956	Marlene Hagge, 291*	Patty Berg, 291	Forest Lake CC, Detroit, Mich.
1957	Louise Suggs, 285	Wiffi Smith, 288	Churchill Valley CC, Pittsburgh, Pa.
1958	Mickey Wright, 288	Fay Crocker, 294	Churchill Valley CC, Pittsburgh, Pa.
1959	Betsy Rawls, 288	Patty Berg, 289	Sheraton Hotel CC, French Lick, Ind.
1960	Mickey Wright, 292	Louise Suggs, 295	Sheraton Hotel CC, French Lick, Ind.
1961	Mickey Wright, 287	Louise Suggs, 296	Stardust CC, Las Vegas, Nev.
1962	Judy Kimball, 282	Shirley Spork, 286	Stardust CC, Las Vegas, Nev.
1963	Mickey Wright, 294	Mary Lena Faulk, Mary Mills, Louise Suggs, 296	Stardust CC, Las Vegas, Nev.
1964	Mary Mills, 278	Mickey Wright, 280	Stardust CC, Las Vegas, Nev.
1965	Sandra Haynie, 279	Clifford Ann Creed, 280	Stardust CC, Las Vegas, Nev.
1966	Gloria Ehret, 282	Mickey Wright, 285	Stardust CC, Las Vegas, Nev.
1967	Kathy Whitworth, 284	Shirley Englehorn, 285	Pleasant Valley CC, Sutton, Mass.
1968	Sandra Post, 294 (68)	Kathy Whitworth, 294 (75)	Pleasant Valley CC, Sutton, Mass.
1969	Betsy Rawls, 293	Susie Berning, Carol Mann, 297	Concord GC, Kiamesha Lake, N.Y.
1970	Shirley Englehorn, 285*	Kathy Whitworth, 285	Pleasant Valley CC, Sutton, Mass.
1971	Kathy Whitworth, 288	Kathy Ahern, 292	Pleasant Valley CC, Sutton, Mass.
1972	Kathy Ahern, 293	Jane Blalock, 299	Pleasant Valley CC, Sutton, Mass.
1973	Mary Mills, 288	Betty Burfeindt, 289	Pleasant Valley CC, Sutton, Mass.
1974	Sandra Haynie, 288	JoAnne Carner, 290	Pleasant Valley CC, Sutton, Mass.
1975	Kathy Whitworth, 288	Sandra Haynie, 279	Pine Ridge GC, Baltimore, Md.
1976	Betty Burfeindt, 287	Judy Rankin, 288	Pine Ridge GC, Baltimore, Md.
1977	Chako Higuchi, 279	Pat Bradley, Sandra Post, Judy Rankin, 282	Bay Tree Plantation, N. Myrtle Beach, S.C.
1978	Nancy Lopez, 275	Amy Alcott, 281	Jack Nicklaus GC, Kings Island, Ohio
1979	Donna Caponi, 279	Jerilyn Britz, 282	Jack Nicklaus GC, Kings Island, Ohio
1980	Sally Little, 285	Jane Blalock, 288	Jack Nicklaus GC, Kings Island, Ohio
1981	Donna Caponi, 280	Jerilyn Britz, Pat Meyers, 281	Jack Nicklaus GC, Kings Island, Ohio
1982	Jan Stephenson, 279	JoAnne Carner, 281	Jack Nicklaus GC, Kings Island, Ohio
1983	Patty Sheehan, 279	Sandra Haynie, 281	Jack Nicklaus GC, Kings Island, Ohio
1984	Patty Sheehan, 272	Beth Daniel, Pat Bradley, 282	Jack Nicklaus GC, Kings Island, Ohio
1985	Nancy Lopez, 273	Alice Miller, 281	Jack Nicklaus GC, Kings Island, Ohio
1986	Pat Bradley, 277	Patty Sheehan, 278	Jack Nicklaus GC, Kings Island, Ohio
1987	Jane Geddes, 275	Betsy King, 276	Jack Nicklaus GC, Kings Island, Ohio
1988	Sherri Turner, 281	Amy Alcott, 282	Jack Nicklaus GC, Kings Island, Ohio
1989	Nancy Lopez, 274	Ayako Okamoto, 277	Jack Nicklaus GC, Kings Island, Ohio
1990	Beth Daniel, 280	Rosie Jones, 281	Bethesda CC, Bethesda, Md.
1991	Meg Mallon, 274	Pat Bradley, Ayako Okamoto, 275	Bethesda CC, Bethesda, Md.
1992	Betsy King, 267	Karen Noble, Liselotte Neumann, JoAnne Carner, 278	Bethesda CC, Bethesda, Md.

* Won sudden-death playoff.
** At the end of 54 holes, the two low scorers played a 36-hole match to determine the winner.

TOURNAMENT RECORDS

Lowest score, 18 holes: 63, Patty Sheehan, 1984, third round.

Lowest score, 36 holes: 131, Patty Sheehan (63-68), 1984, third and fourth rounds.

Lowest score, 54 holes: 201, Patty Sheehan (70-63-68), 1984, second through fourth rounds.

Lowest score, 72 holes: 267, Betsy King (68-66-67-66), 1992.

Largest winning margin: 11 strokes, Betsy King, 1992.

Oldest champion: 36, Betsy King, 1992.

Youngest champion: 20, Sandra Post, 1968.

Most victories: 4, Mickey Wright (1958, 1960, 1961, 1963).

Most times runner-up: 4, Louise Suggs (1955, 1960, 1961, 1963).

Victories in consecutive years: Mickey Wright (1960–1961); Patty Sheehan (1983–1984).

NABISCO DINAH SHORE

Year	Winner	Score	Runner-Up	Score
1972	Jane Blalock	213	Carol Mann, Judy Rankin	216
1973	Mickey Wright	284	Joyce Kazmierski	286
1974	Jo Ann Prentice*	289	Jane Blalock, Sandra Haynie	289
1975	Sandra Palmer	283	Kathy McMullen	284
1976	Judy Rankin	285	Betty Burfeindt	288
1977	Kathy Whitworth	289	JoAnne Carner, Sally Little	290
1978	Sandra Post*	283	Penny Pulz	283
1979	Sandra Post	276	Nancy Lopez	277
1980	Donna Caponi	275	Amy Alcott	277
1981	Nancy Lopez	277	Carolyn Hill	279
1982	Sally Little	278	Hollis Stacy, Sandra Haynie	281
1983	Amy Alcott	282	Beth Daniel, Kathy Whitworth	284
1984	Juli Inkster*	280	Pat Bradley	280
1985	Alice Miller	275	Jan Stephenson	278
1986	Pat Bradley	280	Val Skinner	282
1987	Betsy King*	283	Patty Sheehan	283
1988	Amy Alcott	274	Colleen Walker	276
1989	Juli Inkster	279	Tammie Green, JoAnne Carner	284
1990	Betsy King	283	Shirley Furlong, Kathy Postlewait	285
1991	Amy Alcott	273	Dottie Mochrie	281
1992	Dottie Mochrie*	279	Juli Inkster	279

Site every year: Mission Hills CC, Rancho Mirage, Cal.

Designated major in 1983. Named Colgate–Dinah Shore, 1972–1981.

* Won sudden death playoff.

TOURNAMENT RECORDS

Lowest score, 18 holes: 64, Nancy Lopez, 1981, fourth round; Sally Little, 1982, fourth round.

Lowest score, 36 holes: 132, Amy Alcott (65-67), 1980, second and third rounds; Amy Alcott (66-66), 1988, second and third rounds.

Lowest score, 54 holes: 202, Sally Little (67-71-64), 1982, second through fourth rounds.

Lowest score, 72 holes: 273, Amy Alcott (67-70-68-68), 1991.

Largest winning margin: 8 strokes, Amy Alcott, 1991.

Oldest champion: 38, Mickey Wright, 1973.

Youngest champion: 23, Juli Inkster, 1984.

Most victories: 3, Amy Alcott (1983, 1988, 1981).

Most times runner-up: 2, Sandra Haynie (1974–1982); JoAnne Carner (1977–1989).

Victories in consecutive years: Sandra Post (1978–1979).

DU MAURIER CLASSIC

Year	Winner, Score	Runner-Up, Score	Site
1973	Jocelyn Bourassa, 214*	Sandra Haynie, Judy Rankin, 214	Montreal GC, Montreal, Quebec
1974	Carole Jo Skala, 208	JoAnne Carner, 211	Candiac GC, Montreal, Quebec
1975	JoAnne Carner, 214*	Carol Mann, 214	St. George's CC, Toronto, Ontario
1976	Donna Caponi, 212*	Judy Rankin, 212	Cedar Brae G&CC, Toronto, Ontario
1977	Judy Rankin, 214	Pat Meyers, Sandra Palmer, 215	Lachute G&CC, Montreal, Quebec
1978	JoAnne Carner, 278	Hollis Stacy, 286	St. George's CC, Toronto, Ontario
1979	Amy Alcott, 285	Nancy Lopez, 288	Richelieu Valley CC, Montreal Quebec
1980	Pat Bradley, 277	JoAnne Carner, 278	St. George's CC, Montreal Quebec
1981	Jan Stephenson, 278	Nancy Lopez, Pat Bradley, 279	Summerlea CC, Dorion, Quebec
1982	Sandra Haynie, 280	Beth Daniel, 281	St. George's CC, Toronto, Ontario
1983	Hollis Stacy, 277	JoAnne Carner, Alice Miller, 279	Beaconsfield GC, Montreal Quebec
1984	Juli Inkster, 279	Ayako Okamoto, 280	St. George's G&CC, Toronto, Ontario
1985	Pat Bradley, 278	Jane Geddes, 279	Beaconsfield CC, Montreal Quebec
1986	Pat Bradley, 276*	Ayako Okamoto, 276	Board of Trade CC, Toronto, Ontario
1987	Jody Rosenthal, 272	Ayako Okamoto, 274	Islemere GC, Laval, Quebec
1988	Sally Little, 279	Laura Davies, 280	Vancouver GC, Coquitlam, British Columbia
1989	Tammie Green, 279	Pat Bradley, Betsy King, 280	Beaconsfield GC, Point Claire, Quebec
1990	Cathy Johnston, 276	Patty Sheehan, 278	Westmount G&CC, Kitchener, Ontario
1991	Nancy Scranton, 279	Debbie Massey, 282	Vancouver GC, Coquitlam, British Columbia
1992	Sherri Steinhauer, 277	Judy Dickinson, 279	St. Charles CC, Winnipeg, Manitoba

Designated major in 1979. Named La Canadienne, 1973; Peter Jackson Classic, 1974–82.

* Won sudden-death play-off.

TOURNAMENT RECORDS

Lowest score, 18 holes: 64, JoAnne Carner, 1978, fourth round; Jane Geddes, 1985, second round; Nancy Scranton, 1986, second round; Ayako Okamoto, 1986, fourth round; Robin Walton, 1987, third round; Nancy Scranton, 1991, third round.

Lowest score, 36 holes: 132, Nancy Scranton (64-68), 1991, third and fourth rounds.

Lowest score, 54 holes: 200, Ayako Okamoto (65-69-66), 1987, first through third rounds.

Lowest score, 72 holes: 272, Jody Rosenthal, 1987.

Largest winning margin: Eight strokes, JoAnne Carner, 1978.

Oldest champion: 39, JoAnne Carner, 1978.

Youngest champion: 23, Amy Alcott, 1979.

Most victories: 3, Pat Bradley (1980, 1985, 1986).

Most times runner-up: 3, JoAnne Carner (1974, 1980, 1983); Ayako Okamoto (1984, 1986, 1987).

Victories in consecutive years: Pat Bradley (1985–1986).

LPGA TOUR

Date	Event	Winner	Score	1st Place Money	Total Purse
		1950 Tour			
Jan. 19–22	Tampa Open	Polly Riley	295	NA	$ 3,500
Mar. 16–19	Titleholders Championship	Babe Zaharias	295	$ 700	$ 1,500
Mar. 24	Pro-Ladies Championship	Gracie de Moss[a]	NA	NA	NA
Apr. 29–30	Weathervane Women's Open, Pebble Beach, Cal.	Babe Zaharias	158	NA	NA
May 6–7	Weathervane Women's Open, Skycrest, Chicago, Ill.	Louise Suggs	160	NA	NA
May 13–14	Weathervane Women's Open, Ridgewood, Cleveland, Ohio	Babe Zaharias	145	NA	NA
May 20–21	Weathervane Women's Open, White Plains, N.Y.	Louise Suggs	155	NA	NA
May 26–28	New England Open	Patty Berg	217	NA	NA
June 19–24	Western Women's Open	Babe Zaharias	NA	NA	NA
Sept. 21–23	Sunset Hills Open	Patty Berg	217	$ 750	$ 3,000
Sept. 28–Oct.1	U.S. Women's Open	Babe Zaharias	291	$ 1,250	$ 5,000
		1951 Tour			
Jan. 5–7	Ponte Vedra Beach Women's Open	Babe Zaharias	223	$ 750	$ 3,000
Jan. 18–21	Tampa Women's Open	Babe Zaharias	288	$ 1,000	$ 3,500
Feb. 20–25	Orlando, Fla. Two-ball	Babe Zaharias and George Bolesta	6&5	NA	NA
Mar. 15–18	Titleholders Championship	Pat O'Sullivan[a]	301	NA	$ 1,500
Mar. 24–26	Sandhills Women's Open	Patty Berg	221	$ 750	$ 3,000
Apr. 14–15	Weathervane Women's Open, Dallas, Tex.	Babe Zaharias	147	$ 750	$ 3,000
Apr. 21–23	Richmond Women's Open	Babe Zaharias	224	$ 750	$ 3,000
Apr. 24	Sacramento Women's Invitational Open	Betsy Rawls	72	$ 225	$ 2,000
Apr. 29–May 1	Weathervane Women's Open, Fresno, Cal.	Babe Zaharias	225	$ 750	$ 3,000
May 5–6	Weathervane Women's Open, Pebble Beach, Cal.	Patty Berg	152	$ 750	$ 3,000
May 19–20	Weathervane Women's Open, Indianapolis, Ind.	Babe Zaharias	145	$ 750	$ 3,000
May 26–27	Weathervane Women's Open, Westchester, N.Y.		149	$ 1,250	$ 5,000
June 15–21	Women's Western Open	Patty Berg	2 up	NA	NA
June 29–July 1	Eastern Open	Beverly Hanson	215	$ 1,000	$ 2,775
Sept. 7–9	Carrollton Georgia Open	Louise Suggs	221	$ 750	$ 3,000
Sept. 13–16	U.S. Women's Open	Betsy Rawls	293	NA	$ 7,500
		1952 Tour			
NA	Jacksonville Open	Louise Suggs	227	$ 750	$ 3,300
Jan. 17–20	Tampa Open	Louise Suggs	293	$ 1,000	$ 3,500
NA	Weathervane Tournament	Betsy Rawls	71	NA	NA
Feb. 19–24	Orlando Mixed	Betty MacKinnon and Sam Snead	64	NA	NA

LPGA TOUR (continued)

Date	Event	Winner	Score	1st Place Money	Total Purse
Mar. 12–15	Titleholders Championship	Babe Zaharias	299	$ 1,000	$ 2,100
Mar. 26–30	New Orleans Women's Open	Patty Berg	299	$ 1,000	$ 3,925
Apr. 26–28	Richmond Open	Patty Berg	210	$ 750	$ 3,000
May 2–4	Fresno Open	Babe Zaharias	226	$ 1,175	$ 5,000
June 16–21	Women's Western Open	Betsy Rawls	NA	$ 1,000	$ 1,500
June 26–29	U.S. Women's Open	Louise Suggs	284	$ 1,750	$ 7,008
Aug. 7–10	All American Women	Louise Suggs	300	$ 1,000	$ 2,550
Aug. 14–17	World Championship	Betty Jameson	303	$ 5,000	NA
Sept. 5–7	Carrollton Tournament	Betsy Rawls	214	$ 750	NA
Sept. 10	Mary Lena Faulk Tourney	Betsy Rawls	74	$ 375	NA
Oct. 15–19	Betty Jameson Open	Louise Suggs	212	$ 875	NA
Oct. 23–28	Women's Texas Open	Babe Zaharias	7&6	NA	NA

1953 Tour

Date	Event	Winner	Score	1st Place Money	Total Purse
Jan. 15–18	Tampa Open	Louise Suggs	288	$ 1,250	$ 5,000
Feb. 6–8	Miami Beach Open	Betty Jameson	222	$ 875	$ 5,000
Feb. 17–22	Orlando Mixed Foursome	NA	NA	NA	$ 7,500
Feb. 27–Mar. 1	Sarasota Open	Babe Zaharias	217	$ 875	$ 3,517
Mar. 6–8	Jacksonville Open	Patty Berg	214	$ 875	NA
Mar. 12–15	Titleholders Championship	Patty Berg	294	$ 1,000	$ 2,200
Mar. 20–22	Peach Blossom	Louise Suggs	216	$ 875	$ 3,500
Mar. 27–29	New Orleans Women's Open	Patty Berg	227	$ 875	$ 3,500
Apr. 3–5	Babe Zaharias Open	Babe Zaharias	217	$ 875	NA
Apr. 15–16	Tamarisk Women's Open	Jackie Pung	145	$ 750	$ 3,000
NA	San Diego Open	Louise Suggs	144	$ 750	NA
May 9–10	Barbara Romack Invitational	Betsy Rawls	145	$ 875	$ 3,236
May 16–17	Nevada Open	Patty Berg	151	$ 875	$ 3,500
NA	Weathervane Women's Open	Louise Suggs	146	$ 750	$ 5,000
June 4–7	Eastern Open	Betsy Rawls	293	$ 1,250	$ 5,000
June 15–20	Western Open	Louise Suggs	NA	$ 1,000	NA
June 20–23	All-American Women	Patty Berg	308	$ 1,000	NA
June 25–27	U.S. Women's Open	Betsy Rawls	302	$ 2,000	$ 7,500
July 2–5	Triangle Round-Robin	Jackie Pung	382	$ 1,500	$ 7,200

1954 Tour

Date	Event	Winner	Score	1st Place Money	Total Purse
Jan. 15–17	Sea Island	Louise Suggs	231	$ 875	$ 3,500
Jan. 21–24	Tampa Women's Open	Betsy Rawls	311	$ 1,200	$ 5,000
Feb. 12–14	St. Petersburg Open	Beverly Hanson	216	$ 875	$ 3,500
Feb. 17–20	Serbin Open	Babe Zaharias	294	$ 1,200	$ 5,000
Mar. 5–7	Sarasota Open	Babe Zaharias	223	$ 875	$ 3,500
Mar. 11–14	Titleholders Championship	Louise Suggs	293	$ 1,000	$ 3,000
Mar. 26–28	Betsy Rawls Open	Louise Suggs	220	$ 875	$ 3,500
Apr. 2–4	Carrollton Georgia Open	Louise Suggs	218	$ 875	$ 3,500
Apr. 8–11	New Orleans Open	Marlene Bauer	297	$ 1,200	$ 5,000
Apr. 15–18	Babe Zaharias Open	Louise Suggs	224	$ 700	$ 3,500
May 13–16	National Capital Open	Babe Zaharias	299	$ 1,000	$ 5,000
June 3–6	Triangle Round-Robin	Patty Berg	372	$ 1,500	$ 7,500
June 14–19	Western Open	Betty Jameson	NA	$ 1,375	NA

LPGA TOUR (continued)

Date	Event	Winner	Score	1st Place Money	Total Purse
July 1–3	U.S. Women's Open	Babe Zaharias	291	$ 2,000	$ 7,500
July 23–25	Fort Wayne Open	Marilynn Smith	216	$ 700	$ 3,500
Aug. 2–5	World Championship	Patty Berg	298	$ 5,000	$ 12,000
Sept. 16–19	Wichita	Beverly Hanson	295	$ 1,000	NA
Sept. 23–26	Ardmore Open	Patty Berg	299	$ 1,816	NA
NA	Texas Open	Betsy Rawls	NA	$ 700	NA
	1955 Tour				
Jan. 13–16	Sea Island Open	Jackie Pung	151	$ 700	$ 3,000
Jan. 20–23	Tampa Open	Babe Zaharias	298	$ 1,000	$ 5,000
Feb. 10–13	St. Petersburg Open	Patty Berg	292	$ 1,000	$ 5,000
Feb. 17–20	Serbin Open	Fay Crocker	296	$ 1,000	$ 5,000
Feb. 24–27	Sarasota Open	Betty Jameson	285	$ 1,000	$ 5,000
Mar. 3–6	Jacksonville Open	Jackie Pung	297	$ 1,000	$ 5,000
Mar. 10–13	Titleholders Championship	Patty Berg	291	$ 1,000	$ 5,000
Apr. 8–10	Oklahoma City Open	Louise Suggs	229	$ 1,000	$ 5,000
Apr. 14–17	Babe Zaharias Open	Betty Jameson	210	$ 1,000	$ 5,000
Apr. 21–23	Carrollton Open	Betsy Rawls	218	$ 1,000	$ 5,000
Apr. 28–May 1	Peach Blossom	Babe Zaharias	293	$ 1,000	$ 5,000
May 26–28	Wolverine Open	Fay Crocker	291	$ 1,000	$ 5,000
June 2–5	Eastern Open	Louise Suggs	291	$ 1,000	$ 5,000
June 14–16	Triangle Round Robin	Louise Suggs	366	$ 1,800	$ 3,500
June 23–26	Western Open	Patty Berg	292	$ 1,000	$ 5,000
July 1–4	U.S. Women's Open	Fay Crocker	299	$ 2,000	$ 7,000
July 14–17	LPGA Championship	Beverly Hanson	220	$ 1,200	$ 5,000
July 21–24	Virginia Hot Springs Four-Ball	Betty Jameson and Mary Lena Faulk	280	$ 1,450	$ 6,500
July 28–31	Battle Creek Open	Beverly Hanson	220	$ 1,000	$ 5,000
Aug. 21–23	White Mountains Open	Betty Jameson	218	$ 900	$ 4,000
Aug. 26–28	Heart of America Open	Marilynn Smith	220	$ 900	$ 4,500
Sept. 9–12	St. Louis Open	Louise Suggs	289	$ 900	$ 4,300
Sept. 16–18	Denver Open	Marilynn Smith	221	$ 900	$ 4,500
Sept. 22–25	Clock Open	Patty Berg	288	$ 900	$ 4,500
	1956 Tour				
Jan. 14–15	Sea Island Open	Marlene Bauer	152	NA	$ 3,000
Jan. 19–22	Tampa Open	Betsy Rawls	293	NA	$ 4,500
Feb. 3–5	Havana Invitational	Louise Suggs	227	NA	$ 4,500
Feb. 9–12	Serbin Open	Fay Crocker	144	NA	$ 3,000
Feb. 16–19	St. Petersburg Open	Kathy Cornelius	287	NA	$ 5,000
Feb. 23–26	Babe Zaharias Cancer Fund Open	Betsy Rawls	291	NA	$ 5,000
Mar. 2–5	Jacksonville Open	Mickey Wright	294	NA	$ 4,500
Mar. 8–11	Titleholders Championship	Louise Suggs	302	NA	$ 5,000
Apr. 12–15	Babe Zaharias Open	Marlene Bauer Hagge	219	NA	$ 4,000
Apr. 19–22	Dallas Open	Patty Berg	291	NA	$ 7,500
Apr. 26–29	Betsy Rawls Open	Betsy Rawls	292	NA	$ 4,000
May 31–June 3	Pittsburgh Open	Marlene Bauer Hagge	293	NA	$ 6,000
June 6–10	Triangle Round-Robin	Marlene Bauer Hagge	359	$ 2,000	$ 10,000

LPGA TOUR (continued)

Date	Event	Winner	Score	1st Place Money	Total Purse
June 21–24	LPGA Championship	Marlene Bauer Hagge	293	$ 1,350	$ 6,500
June 28–July 1	Western Open	Beverly Hanson	304	$ 1,000	$ 5,000
July 5–8	Syracuse Open	Joyce Ziske	221	$ 1,316	$ 6,500
July 12–15	Hot Springs Four-Ball Invitational	Beverly Hanson and Kathy Cornelius	278	$ 725 each	$ 6,600
July 26–28	U.S. Women's Open	Kathy Cornelius	302	$ 1,500	$ 6,000
Aug. 2–5	All-American Open	Louise Suggs	301	$ 1,000	$ 5,000
Aug. 9–12	World Championship	Marlene Bauer Hagge	298	$ 6,000	$ 14,000
Aug. 16–19	St. Louis Open	Fay Crocker	288	$ 880	$ 4,000
Aug. 23–26	Mile High Open	Marlene Bauer Hagge	284	$ 800	$ 4,000
Sept. 13–16	Clock Open	Marlene Bauer Hagge	292	$ 900	$ 4,500
NA	Kansas City Open	Mary Lena Faulk	214	NA	NA
Oct. 11–14	Arkansas Open	Patty Berg	287	$ 880	$ 4,000
Oct. 21–22	Oklahoma Open	Betty Dodd	214	$ 880	$ 4,000
	1957 Tour				
Jan. 11–13	Sea Island Open	Mickey Wright	220	$ 880	$ 4,488
Jan. 17–20	Tampa Open	Betsy Rawls	298	$ 880	$ 4,488
Jan. 25–27	Lake Worth Open	Betsy Rawls	214	$ 880	$ 4,488
Feb. 1–3	Havana Open	Patty Berg	210	$ 880	$ 4,488
Feb. 9–10	Miami Open	Fay Crocker	143	$ 630	$ 3,500
Feb. 14–17	St. Petersburg Open	Mary Lena Faulk	279	$ 880	$ 4,488
Mar. 1–4	Jacksonville Open	Mickey Wright	295	$ 880	$ 5,000
Mar. 13–16	Titleholders Championship	Patty Berg	296	$ 1,000	$ 5,000
Apr. 11–14	Dallas Open	Wiffi Smith	285	$ 1,316	$ 6,670
Apr. 18–21	Babe Zaharias Open	Marlene Hagge	222	$ 882	$ 4,640
NA	Lawton Open	Marlene Hagge	216	$ 880	$ 4,489
Apr. 25–28	Western Open	Patty Berg	291	$ 1,000	$ 5,000
NA	Peach Blossom Open	Betsy Rawls	213	$ 880	$ 4,488
May 9–12	Gatlinburg Open	Beverly Hanson	295	$ 1,350	$ 7,500
May 23–26	Asheville Open	Beverly Hanson	286	$ 1,316	$ 6,478
May 29–June 2	Triangle Round-Robin	Fay Crocker	NA	$ 1,500	$ 9,600
June 6–9	LPGA Championship	Louise Suggs	285	$ 1,316	$ 6,750
June 30–July 3	U.S. Women's Open	Betsy Rawls	298	$ 1,800	$ 6,820
July 18–21	Hot Springs Four-Ball	Marilynn Smith and Fay Crocker	281	$ 1,500	$ 7,500
July 25–28	Wolverine Open	Mickey Wright	284	$ 1,391	$ 7,500
Aug. 8–11	All-American Open	Patty Berg	302	$ 6,000	$ 15,000
Aug. 16–18	Jackson Open	Betty Dodd	215	$ 880	$ 4,587
Aug. 22–25	Kansas City Open	Louise Suggs	220	$ 880	$ 4,382
Oct. 4–6	San Francisco Open	Wiffi Smith	221	$ 831	$ 4,744
	1958 Tour				
Jan. 10–12	Sea Island Open	Mickey Wright	224	$ 831	$ 4,750
Jan. 16–20	Tampa Open	Betsy Rawls	302	$ 1,247	$ 7,500
Jan. 24–26	Lake Worth Open	Marlene Hagge	218	$ 831	$ 4,744
NA	Havana Open	Fay Crocker	222	NA	NA
Feb. 13–16	St. Petersburg Open	Betsy Rawls	291	$ 1,248	$ 7,000
Feb. 27–Mar. 2	Jacksonville Open	Marilynn Smith	299	$ 875	$ 5,000

LPGA TOUR (continued)

Date	Event	Winner	Score	1st Place Money	Total Purse
Mar. 13–16	Titleholders Championship	Beverly Hanson	299	$ 1,000	$ 5,275
Apr. 17–20	Babe Zaharias Open	Louise Suggs	214	$ 831	$ 4,487
May 9–11	Lawton Open	Beverly Hanson	212	$ 831	$ 4,000
May 16–18	Betsy Rawls Peach Blossom Open	Wiffi Smith	216	$ 831	$ 4,000
May 22–28	Land of Sky Open	Marlene Hagge	213	$ 831	$ 4,750
May 30–June 1	Gatlinburg Open	Louise Suggs	222	$ 831	$ 4,750
June 5–8	LPGA Championship	Mickey Wright	288	$ 1,247	$ 7,000
June 12–15	Triangle Round-Robin	Louise Suggs	NA	$ 1,975	$ 9,000
June 19–22	Western Open	Patty Berg	293	$ 950	$ 4,750
June 26–28	U.S. Women's Open	Mickey Wright	290	$ 1,800	$ 7,200
July 10–15	American Women's Open	Patty Berg	288	$ 1,225	$ 7,000
July 17–20	Homestead Four-Ball	Betty Jameson and Mary Lena Faulk	290	$ 1,520	$ 7,500
July 24–27	French Lick Open	Louise Suggs	300	$ 1,247	$ 7,000
Aug. 8–10	Rockton Open	Mary Lena Faulk	216	$ 988	$ 6,500
Aug. 15–17	Heart of America Open	Bonnie Randolph	219	$ 831	$ 4,750
Aug. 21–24	Waterloo Open	Fay Crocker	287	$ 1,247	$ 7,000
NA	Opie Turner Open	Mickey Wright	222	NA	NA
Sept. 5–8	Dallas Open	Mickey Wright	284	$ 1,247	$ 8,500
Sept. 12–14	Jackson Open	Jackie Pung	220	$ 831	$ 4,748

1959 Tour

Date	Event	Winner	Score	1st Place Money	Total Purse
Jan. 9–11	Mayfair Open	Marlene Hagge	225	$ 831	$ 4,750
Jan. 16–18	Tampa Open	Ruth Jessen	301	$ 1,247	$ 7,500
Jan. 29–Feb. 1	Havana	Wiffi Smith	220	$ 697	$ 5,000
Feb. 12–15	St. Petersburg	Louise Suggs	282	$ 1,247	$ 7,500
Feb. 20–23	Lake Worth Open	Betsy Rawls	285	$ 1,247	$ 7,500
Feb. 28–Mar. 3	Golden Triangle Festival	Beverly Hanson	146	$ 475	$ 3,500
Mar. 3–6	Jacksonville Open	Mickey Wright	286	$ 997	$ 5,710
Mar. 12–15	Titleholder's Championship	Louise Suggs	297	$ 1,000	$ 5,000
Mar. 19–22	Nehi Open	Betsy Rawls	294	$ 997	$ 5,747
Apr. 10–12	Babe Zaharias Open	Betsy Rawls	215	$ 997	$ 5,500
Apr. 16–19	Dallas Civitan Open	Louise Suggs	287	$ 1,662	$ 10,000
Apr. 24–26	Betsy Rawls Open	Wiffi Smith	211	$ 997	$ 5,628
May 1–3	Land of the Sky Open	Betsy Rawls	215	$ 997	$ 5,000
May 8–10	Howard Johnson Invitational	Joyce Ziske	210	$ 997	$ 5,000
May 29–31	Cavalier Open	Mickey Wright	207	$ 997	$ 5,500
June 4–7	Triangle Round-Robin	Betsy Rawls	NA	$ 1,425	$ 9,000
June 11–14	American Women's Open	Beverly Hanson	297	$ 1,247	$ 7,000
June 25–27	U.S. Women's Open	Mickey Wright	287	$ 1,800	$ 7,200
July 3–6	LPGA Championship	Betsy Rawls	288	$ 1,247	$ 7,000
July 7–9	Hoosier Open	Marlene Hagge	141	$ 700	$ 4,000
July 9	Hoosier Celebrity	Mickey Wright	68	NA	$ 2,300
July 16–19	Alliance Machine International Open	Mickey Wright	291	$ 2,090	$ 10,000
July 24–26	Western Open	Betsy Rawls	291	$ 6,175	$ 17,539
Aug. 13–16	Seattle Open	Betsy Rawls	293	$ 1,247	$ 7,000
Aug. 20–23	Spokane Open	Beverly Hanson	287	$ 1,247	$ 7,000
Aug. 27–30	Waterloo Open	Betsy Rawls	282	$ 1,247	$ 7,000

LPGA TOUR (continued)

Date	Event	Winner	Score	1st Place Money	Total Purse
Sept. 3–6	Cosmopolitan Open	Kathy Cornelius	214	$ 997	$ 5,700
Sept. 10–13	Memphis Open	Marilynn Smith	295	NA	$ 7,000
Sept. 24–27	Opie Turner Open	Betsy Rawls	221	$ 1,247	$ 7,500
	1960 Tour				
Jan. 15–17	Sea Island Open	Mickey Wright	219	$ 997	$ 5,700
Feb. 11–14	St. Petersburg Open	Beverly Hanson	287	$ 1,247	$ 7,000
Feb. 18–21	Lake Worth Open	Fay Crocker	285	$ 1,247	$ 7,000
Feb. 25–28	Tampa Open	Mickey Wright	217	$ 1,247	$ 7,000
Mar. 10–13	Titleholders Championship	Fay Crocker	303	$ 1,140	$ 6,000
NA	Royal Crown Open	Wiffi Smith	298	$ 1,330	$ 7,600
Apr. 7–10	Babe Zaharias Open	Betsy Rawls	211	$ 1,083	$ 6,000
Apr. 21–24	Civitan Open	Louise Suggs	281	$ 1,662	$ 9,500
May 5–8	Betsy Rawls Peach Blossom Open	Wiffi Smith	212	$ 997	$ 5,500
June 2–5	Wolverine Open	Joyce Ziske	299	$ 1,247	$ 7,000
June 8–12	Triangle Round-Robin	Louise Suggs	NA	$ 1,245	NA
June 17–19	Cosmopolitan Open	Betsy Rawls	208	$ 1,247	$ 7,000
June 22–29	Western Open	Joyce Ziske	301	$ 1,247	$ 7,000
July 1–4	French Lick Open	Mickey Wright	292	$ 1,425	$ 8,000
July 6–10	Youngstown Kitchens Open	Louise Suggs	288	$ 2,500	$ 11,000
July 12	Hoosier Celebrity	Joyce Ziske	69	$ 350	$ 4,000
July 13–14	Leesburg Pro-Am	Barbara Romack	139	$ 350	$ 5,000
July 21–23	U.S. Women's Open	Betsy Rawls	292	$ 1,800	$ 7,200
July 28–31	American Women's Open	Patty Berg	292	$ 1,247	$ 7,000
Aug. 4–7	Waterloo Open	Wiffi Smith	286	$ 1,247	$ 7,000
Aug. 20–22	Asheville Open	Betsy Rawls	211	$ 1,247	$ 7,000
Aug. 24–27	Grossinger Open	Mickey Wright	218	$ 1,247	$ 7,000
Aug. 30–Sept. 1	Eastern Open	Mickey Wright	213	$ 1,247	$ 7,500
Sept. 15–18	Memphis Open	Mickey Wright	278	$ 1,247	$ 7,500
Sept. 29–Oct. 2	San Antonio Civitan Open	Louise Suggs	215	$ 1,068	$ 5,662
Oct. 2	Civitan Open				
	1961 Tour				
Jan. 24–25	Naples Pro-Am	Louise Suggs	138	$ 475	$ 3,500
Feb. 9–12	St. Petersburg Open	Mickey Wright	277	$ 1,247	$ 7,500
Feb. 14	Royal Poinciana Invitational	Louise Suggs	156	$ 1,200	$ 4,000
Mar. 10–12	LPGA Championship	Mickey Wright	220	$ 1,247	$ 7,500
Mar. 23–26	Golden Circle of Golf Festival	Louise Suggs	293	$ 1,247	$ 7,500
Apr. 13–16	Dallas Civitan Open	Louise Suggs	291	$ 1,662	$ 9,500
Apr. 20–23	Babe Zaharias Open	Mary Lena Faulk	211	$ 1,200	$ 7,000
Apr. 27–30	Titleholder's Championship	Mickey Wright	299	$ 1,200	$ 7,000
May 4–7	Peach Blossom Open	Ruth Jessen	212	$ 1,083	$ 7,000
May 11–14	Columbus Open	Mickey Wright	292	$ 997	$ 5,700
June 1–4	Western Open	Mary Lena Faulk	290	$ 1,313	$ 7,500
June 8–11	Triangle Round-Robin	Mary Lena Faulk	365	$ 1,100	$ 8,000
June 15–18	Eastern Open	Mary Lena Faulk	214	$ 1,247	$ 7,500
June 29–July 1	U.S. Women's Open	Mickey Wright	293	$ 1,800	$ 8,000
July 14–16	Tippecanoe Open	Kathy Cornelius	204	$ 997	$ 5,700

LPGA TOUR (continued)

Date	Event	Winner	Score	1st Place Money	Total Purse
July 21–23	Cosmopolitan Open	Betsy Rawls	213	$ 1,247	$ 7,500
July 27–30	American Women's Open	Judy Kimball	295	$ 1,247	$ 7,500
Aug. 3–6	Waterloo Open	Mickey Wright	286	$ 1,247	$ 7,500
Aug. 10–13	Kansas City Open	Louise Suggs	295	$ 1,247	$ 7,500
Aug. 24–27	Spokane Women's Open	Mickey Wright	280	$ 1,247	$ 7,500
Sept. 22–24	Sacramento Valley Open	Mickey Wright	223	$ 1,450	$ 8,000
Sept. 28–Oct. 1	Mickey Wright Open	Mickey Wright	290	$ 1,450	$ 8,000
Oct. 6–8	Bill Branin's Swing Parade	Betsy Rawls	221	$ 1,247	$ 7,500
Oct. 12–15	LPGA Las Vegas	Mickey Wright	287	$ 2,500	$ 14,000
Oct. 19–22	San Antonia Civitan Open	Louise Suggs	212	$ 1,247	$ 7,500

1962 Tour

Date	Event	Winner	Score	1st Place Money	Total Purse
Jan. 23–24	Naples Pro-Am	Mickey Wright and Marilynn Smith	143	$ 612	$ 4,000
Feb. 15–18	St. Petersburg Open	Louise Suggs	280	$ 1,200	$ 7,000
Apr. 20–22	Sunshine Open	Marilynn Smith	214	$ 1,200	$ 7,000
Apr. 26–29	Titleholders Championship	Mickey Wright	295	$ 1,330	$ 7,500
May 6–9	Peach Blossom	Mary Lena Faulk	217	$ 1,100	$ 7,500
May 10–13	Western Open	Mickey Wright	295	$ 1,200	$ 7,000
May 17–20	Muskogee Civitan Open	Patty Berg	290	$ 1,200	$ 7,000
May 24–27	Dallas Civitan Open	Ruth Jessen	292	$ 1,500	$ 9,300
June 1–3	Babe Zaharias Open	Betsy Rawls and Kathy Cornelius	146	$ 1,075	$ 7,000
June 7–10	Austin Civitan	Sandra Haynie	289	$ 1,200	$ 7,000
June 15–17	Cosmopolitan Open	Sandra Haynie	210	$ 1,200	$ 7,000
June 21–24	J.E. McAuliffe Memorial	Betsy Rawls	295	$ 1,250	$ 7,500
June 28–30	U.S. Women's Open	Murle Lindstrom	301	$ 1,800	$ 8,000
July 6–8	Kelly Girls Open	Kathy Whitworth	215	$ 1,300	$ 7,000
July 12–15	Milwaukee Open	Mickey Wright	289	$ 1,350	$ 10,000
July 20–22	Lady Carling	Shirley Englehorn	226	$ 1,450	$ 9,000
Aug. 2–5	Waterloo Open	Marilynn Smith	279	$ 1,200	$ 7,000
Aug. 10–12	Heart of America Invitational	Mickey Wright	286	$ 1,000	$ 7,500
Aug. 17–19	Albuquerque Swing Parade	Mickey Wright	219	$ 1,000	$ 5,700
Aug. 23–26	Salt Lake City Open	Mickey Wright	292	$ 1,200	$ 7,000
Aug. 31–Sept. 3	Spokane Open	Mickey Wright	275	$ 1,200	$ 7,000
Sept. 6–9	Eugene Open	Shirley Englehorn	292	$ 1,250	$ 7,500
Sept. 14–16	Sacramento Open	Ruth Jessen	218	$ 1,300	$ 7,500
Sept. 20–23	Visalia Open	Mary Lena Faulk	289	$ 1,350	$ 7,500
Sept. 27–30	San Diego Open	Mickey Wright	286	$ 1,300	$ 5,000
Oct. 4–7	LPGA Championship	Judy Kimball	282	$ 2,300	$ 14,000
Oct. 11–14	Thunderbird Tourney	Kathy Whitworth	213	$ 1,350	$ 8,400
Oct. 19–21	Carlsbad Cavern Open	Mickey Wright	219	$ 1,200	$ 7,000
Nov. 2–4	San Antonio Civitan Open	Murle Lindstrom	214	$ 1,200	$ 7,000

1963 Tour

Date	Event	Winner	Score	1st Place Money	Total Purse
Jan. 21–22	Naples Professional	Ruth Jessen	146	$ 500	$ 4,200
Feb. 1–3	Sea Island Women's Invitational	Mickey Wright	212	$ 1,000	$ 6,000
Feb. 7–10	St. Petersburg Open	Mickey Wright	288	$ 2,325	$ 15,000

LPGA TOUR (continued)

Date	Event	Winner	Score	1st Place Money	Total Purse
Apr. 19–21	Sunshine Women's Open	Betsy Rawls	220	$ 1,200	$ 7,500
Apr. 25–28	Titleholders Championship	Marilynn Smith	292	$ 1,235	$ 7,500
May 3–5	Peach Blossom Open	Marilynn Smith	216	$ 1,200	$ 7,500
May 10–12	Alpine Civitan Open	Mickey Wright	219	$ 1,200	$ 7,500
May 16–19	Muskogee Civitan Open	Mickey Wright	285	$ 1,250	$ 8,000
May 23–26	Dallas Civitan Open	Mickey Wright	283	$ 2,000	$ 13,000
May 31–June 2	Babe Zaharias Open	Mickey Wright	209	$ 1,250	$ 8,000
June 7–9	Rock City Ladies' Open	Barbara Romack	212	$ 1,500	$ 10,000
June 14–16	Cosmopolitan Women's Open	Ruth Jessen	213	$ 1,200	$ 7,500
June 20–23	Western Open	Mickey Wright	292	$ 1,200	$ 7,500
June 28–30	Carvel Ladies' Open	Kathy Whitworth	217	$ 1,350	$ 9,000
July 5–7	Lady Carling Eastern Open	Shirley Englehorn	221	$ 1,500	$ 10,000
July 12–14	Sight Open	Marlene Hagge	208	$ 1,500	$ 10,000
July 18–20	U.S. Women's Open	Mary Mills	289	$ 2,000	$ 9,000
July 26–28	Wolverine Open	Kathy Whitworth	198	$ 1,250	$ 8,000
Aug. 1–4	Milwaukee Jaycee Open	Kathy Whitworth	286	$ 2,000	$ 12,000
Aug. 9–11	Waterloo Women's Open Invitational	Mickey Wright	208	$ 1,200	$ 7,500
Aug. 16–18	Albuquerque Swing Parade	Mickey Wright	211	$ 1,350	$ 10,000
Aug. 23–25	Ogden Ladies' Open	Kathy Whitworth	214	$ 1,300	$ 8,500
Aug. 31–Sept. 2	Idaho Centennial Ladies' Open	Mickey Wright	210	$ 1,200	$ 7,500
Sept. 6–8	Spokane Women's Open	Kathy Whitworth	210	$ 1,250	$ 9,000
Sept. 12–15	Eugene Ladies' Open	Marilynn Smith	295	$ 1,350	$ 10,000
Sept. 19–22	Visalia Ladies' Open	Mickey Wright	285	$ 1,350	$ 10,200
Sept. 27–29	Mickey Wright Invitational	Mickey Wright	222	$ 1,300	$ 9,000
Oct. 10–13	LPGA Championship	Mickey Wright	294	$ 2,450	$ 16,000
Oct. 18–20	Hillside Open	Kathy Whitworth	219	$ 1,200	$ 7,500
Oct. 24–27	Phoenix Thunderbirds Ladies' Open	Sandra Haynie	286	$ 1,350	$ 10,000
Nov. 1–3	Cavern City Open	Marilynn Smith	212	$ 1,200	$ 7,500
Nov. 7–10	San Antonio Civitan Open	Kathy Whitworth	299	$ 1,300	$ 8,500
Nov. 15–17	Mary Mills Mississippi Gulf Coast Invitational	Kathy Whitworth	219	$ 3,325	$ 15,600
Dec. 5–8	Haig and Haig Mixed Four-some Invitational	Mickey Wright and Dave Ragan, Jr.	273	$ 5,600	$ 40,000

1964 Tour

Date	Event	Winner	Score	1st Place Money	Total Purse
Mar. 19–22	Western Open	Carol Mann	308	$ 1,200	$ 7,500
Apr. 2–5	St. Petersburg Women's Open Invitational	Mary Lena Faulk	289	$ 1,500	$ 10,000
Apr. 10–12	Baton Rouge Ladies' Open Invitational	Sandra Haynie	211	$ 1,200	$ 7,500
Apr. 17–19	Peach Blossom Invitational	Mickey Wright	215	$ 1,200	$ 7,500
Apr. 23–26	Titleholders Championship	Marilynn Smith	289	$ 1,235	$ 7,500
May 1–3	Alexandria Ladies' Open Invitational	Mickey Wright	214	$ 1,240	$ 8,000
May 8–10	Squirt Ladies' Open Invitational	Mickey Wright	215	$ 2,000	$ 12,500

LPGA TOUR (continued)

Date	Event	Winner	Score	1st Place Money	Total Purse
May 15–17	Muskogee Civitan Open	Mickey Wright	213	$ 1,250	$ 8,000
May 21–25	Dallas Civitan Open Invitational	Betsy Rawls	282	$ 2,100	$ 13,500
May 29–31	Babe Zaharias Open Invitational	Ruth Jessen	214	$ 1,300	$ 8,500
June 12–14	Lady Carling Open	Clifford Ann Creed	217	$ 1,500	$ 10,000
June 19–21	Lady Carling Eastern Open	Mickey Wright	220	$ 1,500	$ 10,000
June 26–28	Waldemar Open	Mickey Wright	215	$ 1,350	$ 9,200
July 9–11	U.S. Women's Open	Mickey Wright	290	$ 2,200	$ 9,900
July 17–19	Yankee Women's Open	Ruth Jessen	213	$ 1,500	$ 10,000
July 24–26	Cosmopolitan Women's Open	Clifford Ann Creed	211	$ 1,300	$ 8,500
July 30–Aug. 2	Milwaukee Jaycee Open	Mickey Wright	289	$ 2,000	$ 12,000
Aug. 7–9	Waterloo Women's Open Invitational	Shirley Englehorn	211	$ 1,300	$ 8,500
Aug. 14–16	Omaha Jaycee Open Invitational	Ruth Jessen	200	$ 1,350	$ 9,000
Aug. 21–23	Albuquerque Professional Amateur	Marilynn Smith	216	$ 1,350	$ 9,000
Aug. 27–30	Riverside Ladies' Open	Clifford Ann Creed	286	$ 1,350	$ 9,000
Sept. 4–7	Valhalla Open	Betsy Rawls	290	$ 1,500	$ 10,000
Sept. 10–13	Eugene Ladies' Open	Mary Mills	289	$ 1,350	$ 9,000
Sept. 24–27	Visalia Ladies' Open	Mickey Wright	284	$ 1,350	$ 9,000
Oct. 1–4	LPGA Championship	Mary Mills	278	$ 2,450	$ 16,500
Oct. 9–11	Hillside House Ladies' Open	Ruth Jessen	209	$ 1,300	$ 8,500
Oct. 15–18	Mickey Wright Invitational	Marlene Hagge	287	$ 1,300	$ 8,500
Oct. 22–25	Phoenix Thunderbirds Ladies Open	Ruth Jessen	289	$ 1,350	$ 9,000
Oct. 30–Nov. 1	Las Cruces Ladies' Open	Sandra Haynie	208	$ 1,300	$ 8,500
Nov. 6–8	Tall City Open	Mickey Wright	207	$ 1,350	$ 9,000
Nov. 12–15	San Antonio Civitan Open	Kathy Whitworth	283	$ 1,500	$ 10,000
Nov. 20–22	Mary Mills Mississippi Gulf Coast Invitational	Mickey Wright	215	$ 2,550	$ 17,000
Dec. 10–13	Haig and Haig Scotch Mixed Foursome Invitational	Shirley Englehorn and Sam Snead	272	$ 2,400	$ 40,000

1965 Tour

Date	Event	Winner	Score	1st Place Money	Total Purse
Mar. 18–21	St. Petersburg Open	Kathy Whitworth	281	$ 1,500	$ 9,600
Apr. 2–4	Baton Rouge Invitational	Mickey Wright	214	$ 1,275	$ 8,000
Apr. 23–25	Pensacola Invitational	Betsy Rawls	218	$ 1,275	$ 8,000
Apr. 29–May 2	Peach Blossom Open	Marilynn Smith	213	$ 1,275	$ 8,000
Apr. 30–May 2	Shreveport Kiwanis Invitational	Kathy Whitworth	210	$ 1,275	$ 8,000
May 14–16	Muskogee Civitan Open	Susie Maxwell	213	$ 1,275	$ 8,000
May 20–23	Dallas Civitan Open	Mickey Wright	283	$ 2,100	$ 13,396
May 28–30	Babe Zaharias Open	Marlene Hagge	215	$ 1,275	$ 8,000
June 4–6	Bluegrass Invitational	Kathy Whitworth	213	$ 1,350	$ 8,500
June 10–13	Western Open	Susie Maxwell	290	$ 1,500	$ 9,600
June 18–20	Cosmopolitan Open	Sandra Haynie	210	$ 1,275	$ 8,000
June 25–27	Carling Open	Carol Mann	211	$ 1,500	$ 9,600

LPGA TOUR (continued)

Date	Event	Winner	Score	1st Place Money	Total Purse
July 1–4	U.S. Women's Open	Carol Mann	290	$ 4,000	$ 17,780
July 9–11	Lady Carling Midwest Open	Kathy Whitworth	219	$ 1,500	$ 8,500
July 16–18	Yankee Open	Kathy Whitworth	213	$ 2,250	$ 14,000
July 23–25	Buckeye Savings Invitational	Kathy Whitworth	207	$ 1,500	$ 9,500
July 30–Aug. 1	Waterloo Open	Betsy Rawls	214	$ 1,275	$ 8,000
Aug. 5–8	Milwaukee Open	Marlene Hagge	287	$ 1,875	$ 12,000
Aug. 13–15	St. Louis Open	Mary Mills	216	$ 1,875	$ 12,500
Aug. 20–22	Omaha Jaycee Open	Clifford Ann Creed	208	$ 1,500	$ 11,500
Sept. 9–12	Eugene Open	Mary Mills	294	$ 1,350	$ 10,000
Sept. 16–19	Visalia Open	Clifford Ann Creed	289	$ 1,350	$ 8,500
Sept. 23–26	LPGA Championship	Sandra Haynie	279	$ 2,475	$ 15,830
Sept. 30–Oct. 3	Mickey Wright Invitational	Kathy Whitworth	283	$ 1,350	$ 8,600
Oct. 21–24	Phoenix Thunderbirds	Marlene Hagge	290	$ 1,350	$ 8,600
Oct. 28–30	Las Cruces Open	Clifford Ann Creed	215	$ 1,350	$ 9,000
Nov. 5–7	LPGA Tall City Open	Marlene Hagge	206	$ 1,350	$ 10,000
Nov. 11–14	Alamo Open	Marlene Hagge	216	$ 1,500	$ 8,800
Nov. 25–28	Titleholder's Championship	Kathy Whitworth	287	$ 1,500	$ 10,000

1966 Tour

Date	Event	Winner	Score	1st Place Money	Total Purse
Mar. 11–13	Lagunita Invitational	Kathy Whitworth	144	$ 800	$ 4,000
Mar. 17–20	St. Petersburg Women's Open	Marilynn Smith	285	$ 1,650	$ 11,000
Mar. 25–27	Louise Suggs Delray Beach Invitational	Marilynn Smith	211	$ 1,275	$ 8,500
Apr. 1–3	Venice Ladies' Open	Mickey Wright	217	$ 1,275	$ 8,500
Apr. 15–17	Raleigh Ladies' Invitational	Carol Mann	216	$ 1,500	$ 10,000
Apr. 22–24	Peach Blossom Invitational	Carol Mann	216	$ 1,275	$ 8,500
Apr. 29–May 1	Shreveport Kiwanis Club Invitational	Mickey Wright	217	$ 1,350	$ 9,000
May 6–8	Tall City Open	Kathy Whitworth	208	$ 1,875	$ 12,500
May 12–15	Dallas Civitan Invitational	Clifford Ann Creed	285	$ 2,250	$ 15,000
May 20–22	Babe Zaharias Open	Shirley Englehorn	209	$ 1,350	$ 9,000
May 27–29	Baton Rouge Ladies' Invitational	Carol Mann	209	$ 1,500	$ 10,000
June 3–5	Clayton Federal Invitational	Kathy Whitworth	208	$ 1,875	$ 12,500
June 10–12	Bluegrass Ladies' Invitational	Mickey Wright	210	$ 1,500	$ 10,000
June 16–19	Milwaukee Jaycee Open	Kathy Whitworth	273	$ 1,950	$ 13,000
June 24–26	Waterloo Women's Open Invitational	Carol Mann	214	$ 1,500	$ 10,000
June 30–July 3	U.S. Women's Open	Sandra Spuzich	297	$ 4,000	$ 20,680
July 8–10	Buckeye Savings Invitational	Sandra Haynie	205	$ 1,950	$ 13,000
July 15–17	Lady Carling Open (Ohio)	Clifford Ann Creed	221	$ 2,625	$ 17,500
July 22–24	Yankee Women's Open	Gloria Ehret and Judy Kimball	199	$ 2,000 each	$ 20,000
July 28–30	Supertest Ladies' Open	Kathy Whitworth	213	$ 2,250	$ 15,000
Aug. 5–7	Lady Carling Open (Mass.)	Kathy Whitworth	217	$ 2,250	$ 15,000
Aug. 12–14	Lady Carling Open (Md.)	Kathy Whitworth	214	$ 1,875	$ 12,500
Aug. 18–21	Western Open	Mickey Wright	302	$ 1,500	$ 10,000
Aug. 26–28	Glass City Classic	Sandra Haynie	213	$ 3,750	$ 25,000

LPGA TOUR (continued)

Date	Event	Winner	Score	1st Place Money	Total Purse
Sept. 1–2	Ladies' World Series of Golf	Mickey Wright	136	$ 9,500	$ 32,000
Sept. 8–11	Pacific Ladies' Classic	Mickey Wright	284	$ 1,500	$ 10,000
Sept. 16–18	Shirley Englehorn Invitational	Mickey Wright	203	$ 1,500	$ 10,000
Sept. 22–25	PGA Championship	Gloria Ehret	282	$ 2,475	$ 16,500
Sept. 29–Oct. 2	Mickey Wright Invitational	Mickey Wright	289	$ 1,500	$ 10,000
Oct. 20–23	Haig & Haig Scotch Mixed Foursome	Sandra Spuzich and Jack Rule	276	$ 3,550	$ 60,000
Oct. 28–30	Las Cruces Ladies' Open	Kathy Whitworth	214	$ 1,350	$ 9,000
Nov. 4–6	Amarillo Ladies' Open	Kathy Whitworth	215	$ 1,500	$ 10,000
Nov. 11–13	Alamo Ladies' Open	Kathy Whitworth	213	$ 1,875	$ 12,500
Nov. 18–20	The Success Open	Clifford Ann Creed	207	$ 1,500	$ 10,000
Nov. 24–27	Titleholders Championship	Kathy Whitworth	291	$ 1,500	$ 10,000
Dec. 2–4	Pensacola Ladies' Invitational	Sandra Haynie	218	$ 1,500	$ 10,000

1967 Tour

Date	Event	Winner	Score	1st Place Money	Total Purse
Mar. 16–19	St. Petersburg Orange Classic	Marilynn Smith	283	$ 1,875	$ 12,500
Mar. 23, 25–26	Venice Ladies' Open	Kathy Whitworth	217	$ 1,500	$ 10,000
Mar. 31–Apr. 2	Louise Suggs Invitational	Susie Maxwell	224	$ 1,500	$ 10,000
Apr. 21–23	Raleigh Ladies' Invitational	Kathy Whitworth	215	$ 1,800	$ 12,000
Apr. 28–30	Shreveport Kiwanis Club Invitational	Mickey Wright	219	$ 1,500	$ 10,000
May 5–7	Tall City Open	Carol Mann	214	$ 1,875	$ 12,500
May 11–13, 15	Dallas Civitan Open	Jo Ann Prentice	281	$ 2,475	$ 16,800
May 19–21	Babe Zaharias Open	Marilynn Smith	210	$ 1,500	$ 10,000
June 2–4	St. Louis Women's Invitational	Kathy Whitworth	209	$ 2,025	$ 13,500
June 9–11	Bluegrass Invitational	Mickey Wright	208	$ 1,500	$ 10,000
June 16–18	Milwaukee Jaycee Open	Susie Maxwell	216	$ 2,250	$ 15,000
June 23–25	Buckeye Savings Invitational	Carol Mann	207	$ 2,100	$ 14,000
June 29–July 2	U.S. Women's Open	Catherine Lacoste[a]	294	$ 5,000	$ 25,000
July 7–9	Lady Carling Open (Md.)	Mickey Wright	207	$ 2,250	$ 15,000
July 13–16	LPGA Championship	Kathy Whitworth	284	$ 2,625	$ 17,500
July 20–22	Supertest Ladies' Open	Carol Mann	210	$ 2,700	$ 18,000
July 28–30	Yankee Ladies' Team Championship	Clifford Ann Creed and Margie Masters	202	$ 4,000	$ 21,000
Aug. 4–6	Lady Carling Open (Ohio)	Kathy Whitworth	212	$ 3,075	$ 20,500
Aug. 17–20	Western Open	Kathy Whitworth	289	$ 1,500	$ 10,000
Aug. 25–27	Amarillo Ladies' Open	Sandra Haynie	212	$ 1,950	$ 13,000
Sept. 2–3	Ladies' World Series of Golf	Kathy Whitworth	137	$ 10,000	$ 32,000
Sept. 8–10	Pacific Golf Classic	Clifford Ann Creed	211	$ 1,575	$ 10,750
Sept. 15–17	Shirley Englehorn Invitational	Shirley Englehorn	210	$ 1,650	$ 11,000
Sept. 22–24	Mickey Wright Invitational	Sandra Haynie	212	$ 1,725	$ 11,500
Sept. 29–Oct. 1	Ladies' Los Angeles Open	Kathy Whitworth	212	$ 2,325	$ 16,000
Oct. 20–22	Carlsbad Jaycee Open	Murle Lindstrom	216	$ 1,650	$ 11,000
Oct. 27–29	Alamo Ladies' Open	Kathy Whitworth	213	$ 1,875	$ 12,500
Nov. 3–5	Corpus Christi Civitan Open	Clifford Ann Creed	214	$ 1,725	$ 11,500
Nov. 10–12	Quality Chek'd Classic	Margie Masters	214	$ 1,725	$ 11,500
Nov. 17–19	Pensacola Ladies' Invitational	Mickey Wright	210	$ 1,500	$ 10,000

LPGA TOUR (continued)

Date	Event	Winner	Score	1st Place Money	Total Purse
		1968 Tour			
Mar. 14–17	St. Petersburg Orange Blossom Open	Kathy Whitworth	213	$ 1,875	$ 12,500
Mar. 21–24	Port Malabar Invitational	Mickey Wright	215	$ 1,500	$ 10,000
Mar. 28–31	Palm Beach County Open	Mickey Wright	215	$ 1,875	$ 12,500
Apr. 11–14	O'Sullivan Open	Marilynn Smith	216	$ 1,875	$ 12,500
Apr. 18–21	Lady Carling Open (Ga.)	Carol Mann	200	$ 2,250	$ 15,000
Apr. 25–28	Raleigh Ladies' Invitational	Carol Mann	214	$ 2,250	$ 15,000
May 2–5	Shreveport Kiwanis Club Invitational	Carol Mann	217	$ 1,725	$ 11,500
May 9–12	Tall City Open	Mickey Wright	204	$ 2,625	$ 17,500
May 23–26	Dallas Civitan Open	Kathy Whitworth	209	$ 2,775	$ 18,500
June 5–9	Bluegrass Ladies Invitational	Carol Mann	210	$ 2,100	$ 14,250
June 13–16	"500" Ladies' Classic	Mickey Wright	212	$ 2,250	$ 15,500
June 20–23	LPGA Championship	Sandra Post	294	$ 3,000	$ 20,000
June 27–30	Lady Carling Open (Md.)	Kathy Whitworth	214	$ 3,000	$ 20,000
July 4–7	U.S. Women's Open	Susie Berning	289	$ 5,000	$ 24,950
July 11–14	Pabst Ladies' Classic	Carol Mann	206	$ 4,200	$ 28,000
July 18–21	Buckeye Savings Invitational	Carol Mann	209	$ 2,775	$ 18,500
July 25–27	Supertest Canadian Open	Carol Mann	213	$ 3,000	$ 20,500
Aug. 2–4	Gino Paoli Open	Kathy Whitworth	215	$ 2,250	$ 15,000
Aug. 10–12	Concord Open	Shirley Englehorn	229	$ 4,275	$ 28,500
Aug. 16–18	Holiday Inn Classic	Kathy Whitworth	206	$ 2,260	$ 15,685
Aug. 24–25	Ladies' World Series of Golf	Kathy Whitworth	138	$ 10,000	$ 35,000
Aug. 30–Sept. 1	Willow Park Ladies' Invitational	Carol Mann	205	$ 2,250	$ 15,000
Sept. 6–8	Pacific Ladies' Classic	Sandra Haynie	213	$ 1,875	$ 12,500
Sept. 13–15	Shirley Englehorn Invitational	Carol Mann	208	$ 1,725	$ 11,500
Sept. 19–22	Kings River Open	Kathy Whitworth	208	$ 2,250	$ 15,000
Sept. 26–29	Mickey Wright Invitational	Betsy Rawls	208	$ 2,025	$ 13,500
Oct. 18–20	Quality Chek'd Classic	Carol Mann	212	$ 1,875	$ 12,500
Oct. 25–27	River Plantation Invitational	Kathy Whitworth	205	$ 1,875	$ 12,500
Nov. 1–3	Canyon Ladies Classic	Kathy Whitworth	218	$ 3,300	$ 22,750
Nov. 8–10	Corpus Christi Civitan Open	Judy Rankin	213	$ 1,875	$ 12,500
Nov. 15–17	Pensacola Ladies' Invitational	Kathy Whitworth	216	$ 1,875	$ 12,500
Nov. 22–24	Louise Suggs Invitational	Kathy Whitworth	210	$ 1,875	$ 12,500
Nov. 29–Dec. 1	Hollywood Lakes Open	Peggy Wilson	209	$ 1,875	$ 12,500
		1969 Tour			
Jan. 16–19	Burdine's Invitational	JoAnne Carner[a]	216	$ 5,250	$ 35,000
Mar. 13–17	Orange Blossom Open	Kathy Whitworth	216	$ 2,250	$ 15,000
Mar. 20–23	Port Charlotte Invitational	Kathy Whitworth	218	$ 2,250	$ 15,000
Mar. 27–30	Port Malabar Invitational	Kathy Whitworth	210	$ 2,625	$ 17,500
Apr. 17–20	Lady Carling Open (Ga.)	Kathy Whitworth	212	$ 2,625	$ 17,500
Apr. 24–27	Raleigh Ladies Invitational	Carol Mann	212	$ 2,250	$ 15,000
May 1–4	Shreveport Kiwanis Club Invitational	Sandra Haynie	214	$ 2,250	$ 15,000
May 8–11	Dallas Civitan Open	Carol Mann	209	$ 3,225	$ 22,000

LPGA TOUR (continued)

Date	Event	Winner	Score	1st Place Money	Total Purse
May 15–18	St. Louis Women's Invitational	Sandra Haynie	208	$ 2,400	$ 16,000
May 21–25	Bluegrass Invitational	Mickey Wright	216	$ 2,325	$ 15,750
May 29–June 2	O'Sullivan Ladies' Open	Murle Lindstrom	208	$ 2,250	$ 15,000
June 5–8	Lady Carling Open (Md.)	Susie Berning	213	$ 3,000	$ 20,000
June 12–15	Patty Berg Classic	Kathy Whitworth	214	$ 3,750	$ 25,000
June 18–22	Pabst Ladies' Classic	Susie Berning	211	$ 4,500	$ 30,000
June 26–29	U.S. Women's Open	Donna Caponi	294	$ 5,000	$ 31,040
July 10–13	Ladies' Supertest Open	Sandra Haynie	216	$ 3,300	$ 22,000
July 17–20	Danbury Lady Carling Open	Carol Mann	215	$ 3,000	$ 20,000
July 23–27	LPGA Championship	Betsy Rawls	293	$ 5,250	$ 35,000
July 31–Aug. 3	Buckeye Savings Invitational	Sandra Spuzich	213	$ 3,000	$ 20,000
Aug. 8–10	Stroh's–WBLY Open	Marlene Hagge	216	$ 3,000	$ 20,000
Aug. 14–17	Southgate Ladies' Open	Carol Mann	217	$ 3,000	$ 20,000
Aug. 21–24	Tournament of Champs	Carol Mann	216	$ 3,000	$ 20,000
Sept. 4–7	Molson's Canadian Open	Carol Mann	212	$ 3,750	$ 25,500
Sept. 11–14	Wendell-West Open	Kathy Whitworth	213	$ 3,225	$ 22,000
Sept. 18–21	Lincoln-Mercury Open	Donna Caponi	214	$ 3,000	$ 20,500
Oct. 1–5	Mickey Wright Invitational	Carol Mann	212	$ 3,000	$ 20,000
Oct. 16–19	Quality Chek'd Classic	Mary Mills	213	$ 2,250	$ 15,000
Oct. 23–26	Corpus Christi Civitan Open	Carol Mann	212	$ 2,250	$ 15,000
Oct. 30–Nov. 2	River Plantation Women's Open	Kathy Whitworth	213	$ 2,625	$ 17,500

1970 Tour

Date	Event	Winner	Score	1st Place Money	Total Purse
Feb. 17–19	Burdine's Invitational	Carol Mann	216	$ 6,000	$ 40,000
Mar. 20–22	Orange Blossom Classic	Kathy Whitworth	216	$ 2,775	$ 18,000
Mar. 17–19	Raleigh Ladies' Invitational	Sandra Haynie	212	$ 2,475	$ 15,000
May 1–3	Shreveport Kiwanis Invitational	Sandra Haynie	214	$ 2,250	$ 15,000
May 8–10	Dallas Civitan Open	Betsy Rawls	214	$ 3,750	$ 25,000
May 14–17	Londoff Chevrolet Invitational	Shirley Englehorn	216	$ 3,000	$ 20,000
May 22–24	Bluegrass Invitational	Donna Caponi	214	$ 3,000	$ 20,000
May 29–31	O'Sullivan Open	Shirley Englehorn	210	$ 2,250	$ 15,000
June 5–7	Lady Carling Open	Shirley Englehorn	210	$ 3,375	$ 22,000
June 11–14	LPGA Championship	Shirley Englehorn	285	$ 4,500	$ 30,000
June 19–21	George Washington Classic	Judy Rankin	212	$ 3,750	$ 25,000
June 26–28	Len Immke Buick Open	Mary Mills	216	$ 3,000	$ 30,000
July 2–5	USGA Women's Open	Donna Caponi	287	$ 5,000	$ 31,000
July 16–19	Springfield Jaycee Open	Judy Rankin	209	$ 3,000	$ 20,000
Aug. 6–9	Lady Carling Open	Jane Blalock	221	$ 3,000	$ 20,000
Aug. 13–18	Cincinnati Open	Betsy Rawls	210	$ 3,000	$ 20,000
Aug. 20–23	Southgate Ladies' Open	Kathy Ahern	211	$ 3,000	$ 20,000
Sept. 10–13	Wendell West Open	JoAnne Carner	214	$ 6,000	$ 40,000
Sept. 24–27	Lincoln Mercury Open	Judy Rankin	217	$ 3,450	$ 23,000
Oct. 15–18	Quality Chek'd Classic	Kathy Whitworth	205	$ 2,250	$ 15,000
Oct. 22–25	Women's Charity Open	Marilynn Smith	214	$ 2,625	$ 17,500

1971 Tour

Date	Event	Winner	Score	1st Place Money	Total Purse
Feb. 18–21	Sears Women's World Classic of St. Lucie	Ruth Jessen	220	$ 10,000	$ 60,000

LPGA TOUR (continued)

Date	Event	Winner	Score	1st Place Money	Total Purse
Mar. 18–21	Orange Blossom Classic	Jan Ferraris	218	$ 3,000	$ 20,000
Apr. 15–18	Raleigh Ladies' Golf Classic	Kathy Whitworth	212	$ 3,000	$ 20,000
Apr. 22–25	Burdine's Invitational	Sandra Haynie	219	$ 4,500	$ 30,000
Apr. 29–May 2	Dallas Civitan Open	Sandra Haynie	201	$ 4,725	$ 31,500
May 6–9	San Antonio Open	Sandra Haynie	206	$ 3,000	$ 20,000
May 13–16	Sealy LPGA Classic	Sandra Palmer	289	$ 10,000	$ 50,000
May 20–23	Suzuki Golf International	Kathy Whitworth	217	$ 5,700	$ 38,000
June 4–6	Lady Carling Open	Kathy Whitworth	210	$ 3,750	$ 25,000
June 10–13	Eve–LPGA Championship	Kathy Whitworth	288	$ 7,950	$ 53,000
June 18–20	Heritage Open	Sandra Palmer	211	$ 3,750	$ 25,000
June 24–27	U.S. Women's Open	JoAnne Carner	288	$ 5,000	$ 31,000
July 9–11	George Washington Classic	Jane Blalock	208	$ 3,750	$ 25,000
July 15–17	LPGA Four-Ball Championship	Kathy Whitworth	206	$ 1,600	$ 20,000
July 23–25	O'Sullivan Ladies' Open	Judy Kimball	211	$ 3,000	$ 20,000
July 30–Aug. 1	Bluegrass Invitational	JoAnne Carner	210	$ 3,750	$ 25,000
Aug. 5–8	Lady Pepsi Open	Jane Blalock	214	$ 3,000	$ 20,000
Aug. 13–15	Len Immke Buick Open	Sandra Haynie	206	$ 3,750	$ 25,000
Aug. 20–22	Southgate Open	Pam Barnett	210	$ 3,000	$ 20,000
Sept. 24–26	Lincoln-Mercury Open	Pam Higgins	215	$ 3,750	$ 25,000
Oct. 15–17	Quality-First Classic	Judy Rankin	214	$ 3,000	$ 20,000

1972 Tour

Date	Event	Winner	Score	1st Place Money	Total Purse
Jan. 7–9	Burdine's Invitational	Marlene Hagge	211	$ 4,500	$ 30,000
Mar. 10–12	Lady Eve Open	Judy Rankin	210	$ 3,750	$ 25,000
Mar. 17–19	Orange Blossom Classic	Carol Mann	213	$ 3,000	$ 20,000
Mar. 24–26	Sears Women's World Classic	Betsy Cullen	72	$ 12,000	$ 85,000
Apr. 14–16	Colgate–Dinah Shore Winner's Circle	Jane Blalock	213	$ 20,000	$ 110,000
Apr. 21–23	Birmingham Centennial Open	Betty Burfeindt	212	$ 4,500	$ 30,000
Apr. 28–30	Alamo Ladies' Open	Kathy Whitworth	209	$ 3,750	$ 25,000
May 4–7	Sealy-LPGA Classic	Betty Burfeindt	282	$ 10,000	$ 50,000
May 12–14	Suzuki Golf International	Jane Blalock	208	$ 5,700	$ 38,000
May 19–21	Bluegrass Invitational	Kathy Cornelius	211	$ 3,750	$ 25,000
May 26–29	Titleholders Championship	Sandra Palmer	283	$ 3,000	$ 20,000
June 2–4	Lady Carling Open	Carol Mann	210	$ 4,500	$ 30,000
June 8–11	LPGA Championship	Kathy Ahern	293	$ 7,500	$ 50,000
June 29–July 2	USGA Women's Open	Susie Berning	299	$ 6,000	$ 38,350
July 7–9	George Washington Classic	Kathy Ahern	213	$ 4,500	$ 30,000
July 13–15	Angelo's LPGA Four-Ball Championship	Jane Blalock and Sandra Palmer	130	$ 1,600 each	$ 20,000
July 21–23	Raleigh Golf Classic	Kathy Whitworth	212	$ 3,000	$ 20,000
July 28–30	Lady Pepsi Open	Jan Ferraris	221	$ 3,750	$ 25,000
Aug. 4–6	Knoxville Ladies' Open	Kathy Whitworth	210	$ 3,750	$ 25,000
Aug. 11–13	Columbus Ladies' Open	Marilynn Smith	210	$ 4,500	$ 30,000
Aug. 18–20	Southgate Ladies' Open	Kathy Whitworth	216	$ 3,000	$ 20,000
Aug. 25–27	National Jewish Hospital Open	Sandra Haynie	207	$ 3,750	$ 25,000
Sept. 8–10	Dallas Civitan Open	Jane Blalock	211	$ 4,950	$ 33,000
Sept. 15–17	Waco Quality-First Classic	Sandra Haynie	206	$ 3,000	$ 20,000
Sept. 22–24	Lincoln-Mercury Open	Sandra Haynie	215	$ 4,200	$ 30,000
Sept. 29–Oct. 1	Portland Classic	Kathy Whitworth	212	$ 3,750	$ 25,000
Oct. 5–9	Heritage Village Open	Judy Rankin	212	$ 3,750	$ 25,000

LPGA TOUR (continued)

Date	Event	Winner	Score	1st Place Money	Total Purse
Oct. 20–22	GAC Classic	Betsy Rawls	141	$ 4,500	$ 30,000
Oct. 27–29	Corpus Christi Civitan	JoAnn Prentice	210	$ 3,000	$ 20,000
Nov. 3–5	Lady Errol Open	Jane Blalock	214	$ 4,500	$ 30,000
	1973 Tour				
Jan. 5–7	Burdine's Invitational	JoAnn Prentice	212	$ 4,500	$ 30,000
Feb. 9–11	Naples-Lely Classic	Kathy Whitworth	219	$ 3,750	$ 25,000
Feb. 16–18	Pompano Beach Open	Sandra Palmer	215	$ 5,250	$ 35,000
Mar. 9–11	S&H Green Stamp Classic	Kathy Whitworth	214	$ 20,000	$ 100,000
Mar. 16–18	Orange Blossom Classic	Sandra Haynie	216	$ 3,750	$ 25,000
Mar. 23–25	Sears Women's Open	Carol Mann	68	$ 15,000	$ 100,000
Mar. 30–Apr. 1	Alamo Ladies' Open	Betsy Cullen	218	$ 4,500	$ 30,000
Apr. 12–15	Colgate–Dinah Shore Winner's Circle	Mickey Wright	284	$ 25,000	$ 135,000
Apr. 27–29	Birmingham Classic	Gloria Ehret	217	$ 4,950	$ 33,000
May 4–6	America Defender–Raleigh Classic	Judy Rankin	217	$ 4,500	$ 30,000
May 11–13	Lady Carling Open	Judy Rankin	215	$ 4,500	$ 30,000
May 24–27	Bluegrass Open	Donna Young	216	$ 4,500	$ 30,000
May 31–June 3	Sealy-Fabergé	Kathy Cornelius	217	$ 25,000	$ 100,000
June 7–10	LPGA Championship	Mary Mills	288	$ 5,250	$ 50,000
June 14–17	La Canadienne Championship	Jocelyne Bourassa	214	$ 100,000	$ 50,000
June 22–24	Heritage Village Open	Susie Berning	207	$ 4,500	$ 50,000
June 29–July 1	Lady Tara Classic	Mary Mills	217	$ 4,500	$ 50,000
July 6–8	Marc Equity Classic	Mary Lou Crocker	210	$ 5,250	$ 35,000
July 13–15	George Washington Classic	Carole Jo Skala	214	$ 4,500	$ 30,000
July 19–22	U.S. Women's Open	Susie Berning	290	$ 6,000	$ 60,000
July 26–28	Angelo's LPGA Four-Ball Championship	Jane Blalock and Sandra Palmer	206	$ 2,400 each	$ 30,000
Aug. 3–5	Columbus Ladies' Open	Judy Rankin	212	$ 2,400	$ 30,000
Aug. 10–12	Child and Family Service Open	Betty Burfeindt	212	$ 4,500	$ 30,000
Aug. 17–19	St. Paul Open	Sandra Palmer	209	$ 4,500	$ 30,000
Aug. 24–26	National Jewish Hospital Open	Sandra Palmer	210	$ 4,500	$ 30,000
Aug. 31–Sept. 2	Charity Golf Classic	Sandra Haynie	208	$ 4,500	$ 30,000
Sept. 7–9	Dallas Civitan Open	Kathy Whitworth	213	$ 4,950	$ 30,000
Sept. 14–16	Southgate Ladies' Open	Kathy Whitworth	142	$ 3,750	$ 25,000
Sept. 21–23	Portland Classic	Kathy Whitworth	144	$ 4,500	$ 30,000
Sept. 28–30	Cameron Park Open	Sandra Palmer	212	$ 4,500	$ 30,000
Oct. 5–7	Lincoln-Mercury Open	Sandra Haynie	212	$ 4,500	$ 30,000
Oct. 12–14	GAC Classic	Judy Rankin	215	$ 5,250	$ 30,000
Oct. 19–21	Waco Open	Kathy Whitworth	209	$ 3,750	$ 25,000
Oct. 26–28	Corpus Christi Civitan	Sharon Miller	210	$ 3,750	$ 25,000
Nov. 2–4	Lady Errol Open	Kathy Whitworth	213	$ 7,500	$ 50,000
Nov. 30–Dec. 1	LPGA–Japan Classic	Jan Ferraris	216	$ 7,500	$ 50,000
	1974 Tour				
Feb. 1–3	Burdine's Invitational	Sandra Palmer	215	$ 4,950	$ 33,000
Feb. 8–10	Sears Women's Classic	Gail Denenberg	71	$ 15,000	$ 100,000
Feb. 15–17	Naples-Lely Classic	Carol Mann	209	$ 5,400	$ 35,000

LPGA TOUR (continued)

Date	Event	Winner	Score	1st Place Money	Total Purse
Mar. 1–3	Orange Blossom Classic	Kathy Whitworth	209	$ 4,250	$ 30,000
Mar. 8–10	S&H Green Stamp Classic	Carol Mann	219	$ 20,000	$ 100,000
Mar. 15–17	Bing Crosby International	Jane Blalock	215	$ 4,250	$ 30,000
Apr. 18–21	Colgate–Dinah Shore Winner's Circle	JoAnn Prentice	289	$ 32,000	$ 100,000
Apr. 26–28	Birmingham Classic	Jane Blalock	211	$ 5,000	$ 35,000
May 3–5	Lady Tara Classic	Sandra Spuzich	219	$ 5,000	$ 35,000
May 10–12	American Defender–Raleigh Classic	JoAnn Prentice	137	$ 5,000	$ 35,000
May 17–19	Bluegrass Invitational	JoAnne Carner	215	$ 5,000	$ 35,000
May 24–26	Hoosier Classic	JoAnne Carner	213	$ 5,000	$ 35,000
May 31–June 2	Baltimore Championship	Judy Rankin	144	$ 5,700	$ 40,000
June 6–9	Desert Inn Classic	JoAnne Carner	284	$ 20,000	$ 100,000
June 14–16	Medina Open	Sandra Haynie	215	$ 5,700	$ 40,000
June 20–23	LPGA Championship	Sandra Haynie	288	$ 7,000	$ 50,000
June 28–30	Peter Jackson Classic	Carole Jo Skala	208	$ 12,000	$ 60,000
July 5–7	Niagara Frontier Classic	Sue Roberts	213	$ 5,000	$ 35,000
July 12–13	Borden Classic	Sharon Miller	211	$ 5,700	$ 40,000
July 18–21	U.S. Women's Open	Sandra Haynie	295	$ 6,073	$ 40,000
July 26–28	Wheeling Classic	Carole Jo Skala	212	$ 5,000	$ 35,000
Aug. 2–4	George Washington Classic	Sandra Haynie	213	$ 5,700	$ 40,000
Aug. 8–10	Colgate-European Open	Judy Rankin	218	$ 10,000	$ 50,000
Aug. 16–18	St. Paul Open	JoAnne Carner	212	$ 5,000	$ 35,000
Aug. 23–25	National Jewish Hospital Open	Sandra Haynie	213	$ 5,000	$ 35,000
Aug. 30–Sept. 1	Southgate Ladies' Open	Jane Blalock and Sue Roberts	142	$ 4,375 each	$ 35,000
Sept. 6–8	Dallas Civitan Open	JoAnne Carner	217	$ 5,700	$ 40,000
Sept. 13–15	Charity Golf Classic	Sandra Haynie	208	$ 5,700	$ 40,000
Sept. 27–29	Portland Classic	JoAnne Carner	211	$ 5,000	$ 35,000
Oct. 4–6	Sacramento Union Classic	Carole Jo Skala	213	$ 5,000	$ 35,000
Oct. 18–21	Cubic Classic	Sandra Palmer	215	$ 5,000	$ 35,000
Nov. 1–3	Japan Classic	Chako Higuchi	209	$ 5,700	$ 40,000
Nov. 15–17	Bill Branch Classic	Bonnie Bryant	215	$ 5,000	$ 35,000
Nov. 22–24	Lady Errol Classic	Jane Blalock	218	$ 15,000	$ 100,000
Dec. 6–8	Colgate–Far East Open	Sandra Post	218	$ 13,300	$ 72,000

1975 Tour

Date	Event	Winner	Score	1st Place Money	Total Purse
Jan. 18–19	Colgate Triple Crown	Kathy Whitworth	144	$ 15,000	$ 50,000
Jan. 31–Feb. 2	Burdine's Invitational	Donna Young	208	$ 5,700	$ 40,000
Feb. 7–9	Naples-Lely Classic	Sandra Haynie	211	$ 5,700	$ 40,000
Feb. 21–23	Orange Blossom Classic	Amy Alcott	207	$ 5,000	$ 35,000
Mar. 21–23	Bing Crosby International	Sue Roberts	214	$ 6,400	$ 45,000
Mar. 27–29	Karsten Ping Classic	Jane Blalock	209	$ 10,000	$ 70,000
Apr. 18–21	Colgate–Dinah Shore Winner's Circle	Sandra Palmer	283	$ 32,000	$ 180,000
Apr. 25–27	Charity Golf Classic	Sandra Haynie	212	$ 6,400	$ 45,000
May 2–4	Birmingham Classic	Maria Astrologies	210	$ 5,700	$ 40,000
May 9–11	Lady Tara Classic	Donna Young	214	$ 5,700	$ 40,000
May 23–25	American Defender Classic	JoAnne Carner	206	$ 5,700	$ 40,000
May 30–June 1	LPGA Championship	Kathy Whitworth	288	$ 8,000	$ 55,000

LPGA TOUR (continued)

Date	Event	Winner	Score	1st Place Money	Total Purse
June 6–8	Girl Talk Classic	JoAnne Carner	213	$ 7,000	$ 50,000
June 13–15	Lawson's LPGA Classic	Carol Mann	217	$ 7,000	$ 50,000
June 20–22	Hoosier Classic	Betsy Cullen	215	$ 5,700	$ 40,000
June 27–29	Peter Jackson Classic	JoAnne Carner	214	$ 12,000	$ 60,000
July 4–6	Wheeling Classic	Sue McAllister	212	$ 5,700	$ 40,000
July 11–13	Borden Classic	Carol Mann	209	$ 9,200	$ 65,000
July 17–20	U.S. Women's Open	Sandra Palmer	295	$ 8,044	$ 55,000
July 25–27	George Washington Classic	Carol Mann	206	$ 5,700	$ 40,000
Aug. 2–3	Lady Keystone Open	Susie B. Maxwell	142	$ 4,200	$ 30,000
Aug. 7–9	Colgate–European Open	Donna Young	283	$ 11,700	$ 72,000
Aug. 15–17	Patty Berg Classic	JoAnn Washam	206	$ 6,400	$ 45,000
Aug. 22–24	National Jewish Hospital Open	Judy Rankin	207	$ 5,700	$ 40,000
Sept. 5–7	Dallas Civitan Open	Carol Mann	208	$ 6,200	$ 43,000
Sept. 12–14	Southgate Ladies' Open	Kathy Whitworth	213	$ 5,700	$ 40,000
Sept. 19–21	Portland Classic	JoAnn Washam	215	$ 5,700	$ 40,000
Oct. 17–19	Japan Classic	Shelley Hamlin	218	$ 15,000	$ 100,000
Oct. 23–26	Golf Inns of America	Mary Bea Porter	287	$ 5,700	$ 40,000
Nov. 14–16	Jacksonville Open	Sandra Haynie	223	$ 7,000	$ 50,000
Nov. 21–23	Greater Fort Myers Classic	Sandra Haynie	210	$ 5,700	$ 40,000
Dec. 5–7	Colgate Far East Open	Pat Bradley	216	$ 12,560	$ 75,000
Dec. 13–14	Colgate Triple Crown	Jane Blalock	142	$ 15,000	$ 50,000

1976 Tour

Date	Event	Winner	Score	1st Place Money	Total Purse
Jan. 30–Feb. 1	Burdine's Invitational	Judy Rankin	213	$ 5,700	$ 40,000
Feb. 6–8	Sarah Coventry–Naples Classic	Jan Stephenson	218	$ 8,500	$ 60,000
Feb. 13–15	Orange Blossom Classic	JoAnne Carner	209	$ 6,400	$ 45,000
Feb. 20–22	Bent Tree Classic	Kathy Whitworth	209	$ 8,500	$ 60,000
Apr. 1–4	Colgate–Dinah Shore Winner's Circle	Judy Rankin	285	$ 32,000	$ 185,000
Apr. 15–17	Karsten-Ping Open	Judy Rankin	205	$ 14,000	$ 80,000
Apr. 23–25	Birmingham Classic	Jan Stephenson	203	$ 5,700	$ 40,000
Apr. 30–May 2	Lady Tara Classic	JoAnne Carner	209	$ 7,000	$ 50,000
May 6–9	Ladies' Masters	Sally Little	281	$ 10,000	$ 70,000
May 14–16	American Defender Classic	Sue Roberts	211	$ 6,400	$ 45,000
May 21–23	'76 LPGA Classic	Amy Alcott	209	$ 14,000	$ 76,000
May 27–30	LPGA Championship	Betty Burfeindt	287	$ 8,000	$ 55,300
June 4–6	Girl Talk Classic	Pat Bradley	217	$ 14,000	$ 76,000
June 11–13	Peter Jackson Classic	Donna C. Young	212	$ 12,000	$ 60,000
June 18–20	Hoosier Classic	JoAnne Carner	210	$ 7,000	$ 50,000
June 24–27	Babe Zaharias Invitational	Judy Rankin	287	$ 15,000	$ 100,000
July 2–4	Bloomington Bicentennial Classic	Sandra Palmer	209	$ 7,000	$ 50,000
July 8–11	U.S. Open	JoAnne Carner	292	$ 9,054	$ 60,000
July 16–18	Borden Classic	Judy Rankin	205	$ 10,000	$ 70,000
July 23–25	Lady Keystone Open	Susie Berning	215	$ 7,000	$ 50,000
Aug. 4–7	Colgate–European Open	Chako Higuchi	284	$ 15,000	$ 100,000

LPGA TOUR (continued)

Date	Event	Winner	Score	1st Place Money	Total Purse
Aug. 13–15	Wheeling Classic	Jane Blalock	217	$ 7,000	$ 50,000
Aug. 20–22	Patty Berg	Kathy Whitworth	212	$ 8,000	$ 55,000
Aug. 27–29	National Jewish Hospital Open	Sandra Palmer	206	$ 7,000	$ 50,000
Sept. 3–5	Jerry Lewis Muscular Dystrophy Classic	Sandra Palmer	213	$ 15,000	$ 100,000
Sept. 10–12	Dallas Civitan Open	Jane Blalock	205	$ 7,000	$ 50,000
Sept. 17–19	Portland Classic	Donna C. Young	217	$ 6,400	$ 45,000
Sept. 23–26	Carlton	Donna C. Young	282	$ 35,000	$ 205,000
Nov. 1–3	LPGA/Japan Mizuno	Donna C. Young	217	$ 15,000	$ 100,000
Nov. 18–20	Colgate–Hong Kong Open	Judy Rankin	216	$ 10,000	$ 50,000
Nov. 25–27	Colgate–Far East Championship	Amy Alcott	211	$ 15,000	$ 100,000
Dec. 17–19	Pepsi-Cola Mixed Team Championship	Jo Ann Washam/ Chi Chi Rodrigues	275	$ 40,000	$ 200,000

1977 Tour

Date	Event	Winner	Score	1st Place Money	Total Purse
Jan. 14–15	Colgate Triple Crown	Jane Blalock	143	$ 15,000	$ 50,000
Feb. 11–13	Cancer Society Classic	Pam Higgins	212	$ 7,500	$ 50,000
Feb. 18–20	Orange Blossom Classic	Judy Rankin	208	$ 7,500	$ 50,000
Feb. 25–28	Bent Tree Classic	Judy Rankin	209	$ 15,000	$ 100,000
Mar. 24–27	Honda Civic Classic	Sandra Palmer	281	$ 22,500	$ 150,000
Mar. 31–Apr. 3	Colgate–Dinah Shore Winner's Circle	Kathy Whitworth	289	$ 36,000	$ 240,000
Apr. 14–17	Women's International	Sandra Palmer	281	$ 12,000	$ 80,000
Apr. 22–24	American Defender Classic	Kathy Whitworth	206	$ 7,500	$ 50,000
Apr. 29–May 1	Birmingham Classic	Debbie Austin	207	$ 9,000	$ 60,000
May 6–8	Lady Tara Classic	Hollis Stacy	209	$ 7,500	$ 50,000
May 13–15	Baltimore Classic	Jane Blalock	209	$ 8,250	$ 55,000
May 20–22	Coca-Cola Classic	Kathy Whitworth	202	$ 11,500	$ 77,000
May 27–29	Keystone Classic	Sandra Spuzich	201	$ 7,500	$ 50,000
June 2–5	Talk Tournament	JoAnne Carner	284	$ 15,000	$ 100,000
June 9–12	LPGA Championship	Chako Higuchi	279	$ 22,500	$ 150,000
June 17–19	Mayflower Classic	Judy Rankin	212	$ 7,500	$ 50,000
June 25–27	Hoosier Classic	Debbie Austin	207	$ 7,500	$ 50,000
July 1–3	Peter Jackson Classic	Judy Rankin	212	$ 12,000	$ 80,000
July 8–10	Bankers Trust Classic	Pat Bradley	213	$ 11,000	$ 75,000
July 15–17	Borden Classic	JoAnne Carner	207	$ 12,000	$ 80,000
July 21–24	U.S. Women's Open	Hollis Stacy	292	$ 11,040	$ 80,000
July 29–31	Pocono Northeast Classic	Debbie Austin	213	$ 11,000	$ 80,000
Aug. 3–6	Colgate–European Open	Judy Rankin	281	$ 15,000	$ 100,000
Aug. 11–14	Long Island	Debbie Austin	279	$ 15,000	$ 100,000
Aug. 19–21	Wheeling Classic	Debbie Austin	209	$ 7,500	$ 50,000
Aug. 26–29	Patty Berg Classic	Bonnie Lauer	212	$ 8,250	$ 55,000
Sept. 2–4	Springfield Classic	Hollis Stacy	271	$ 15,000	$ 100,000
Sept. 9–11	National Jewish Hospital Open	JoAnne Carner	210	$ 7,500	$ 50,000
Sept. 16–18	LPGA Team Championship	Judy Rankin JoAnne Carner	202	$ 12,000	$ 60,000
Sept. 22–25	Sarah Coventry	Jane Blalock	282	$ 15,000	$ 100,000

LPGA TOUR (continued)

Date	Event	Winner	Score	1st Place Money	Total Purse
Sept. 30–Oct. 2	Dallas Civitan Open	Vivian Brownlee	217	$ 7,500	$ 50,000
Oct. 7–9	Houston Exchange Clubs Classic	Amy Alcott	208	$ 7,500	$ 50,000
Nov. 1–3	Mizuno Classic	Debbie Massey	220	$ 15,000	$ 100,000
Nov. 10–13	Colgate–Far East Open	Silvia Bertolaccinni	214	$ 15,000	$ 100,000
Dec. 1–4	Pepsi-Cola Mixed Team Championship	Hollis Stacey and Jerry Pate	270	$ 40,000	$ 200,000
	1978 Tour				
Jan. 25–29	Colgate–Triple Crown	JoAnne Carner	1 up	$ 21,000	$ 100,000
Feb. 10–12	American Cancer Society Classic	Debbie Austin	212	$ 7,500	$ 50,000
Feb. 17–20	Orange Blossom Classic	Jane Blalock	212	$ 9,000	$ 60,000
Feb. 23–26	Bent Tree Classic	Nancy Lopez	289	$ 15,000	$ 100,000
Mar. 9–12	Sunstar Classic	Nancy Lopez	285	$ 15,000	$ 100,000
Mar. 16–19	Kathryn Crosby–Honda Civic Classic	Sally Little	282	$ 22,500	$ 150,000
Mar. 30–Apr. 2	Colgate–Dinah Shore Winner's Circle	Sandra Post	283	$ 36,000	$ 240,000
Apr. 14–16	Birmingham Classic	Hollis Stacy	207	$ 9,000	$ 60,000
Apr. 21–23	American Defender Classic	Amy Alcott	206	$ 8,250	$ 55,000
Apr. 28–30	Natural Light Lady Tara Classic	Janet Coles	211	$ 11,250	$ 75,000
May 5–8	Women's International	Jan Stephenson	283	$ 12,000	$ 80,000
May 12–14	Greater Baltimore Classic	Nancy Lopez	212	$ 9,750	$ 65,000
May 19–21	Coca-Cola Classic	Nancy Lopez	210	$ 15,000	$ 100,000
May 26–29	Golden Lights Championship	Nancy Lopez	277	$ 15,000	$ 100,000
June 1–4	Peter Jackson Classic	JoAnne Carner	278	$ 15,000	$ 100,000
June 8–11	LPGA Championship	Nancy Lopez	275	$ 22,500	$ 150,000
June 16–18	Bankers Trust Classic	Nanct Lopez	214	$ 11,250	$ 75,000
June 23–25	Lady Keystone Open	Pat Bradley	206	$ 7,500	$ 50,000
July 1–3	Mayflower Classic	Jane Blalock	209	$ 11,250	$ 75,000
July 7–9	Wheeling Classic	Jane Blalock	207	$ 11,250	$ 75,000
July 14–16	Borden Classic	JoAnne Carner	209	$ 12,750	$ 85,000
July 20–23	U.S. Women's Open	Hollis Stacy	289	$ 15,000	$ 105,199
July 28–30	Hoosier Classic	Pat Bradley	206	$ 9,000	$ 60,000
Aug. 3–6	Colgate–European Open	Nancy Lopez	289	$ 15,000	$ 100,000
Aug. 10–13	WUI Classic	Judy Rankin	283	$ 15,000	$ 100,000
Aug. 17–20	Lady Stroh's Open	Sandra Post	286	$ 22,500	$ 150,000
Aug. 25–27	Patty Berg Classic	Shelley Hamlin	208	$ 11,250	$ 75,000
Sept. 1–4	Rail Charity Classic	Pat Bradley	276	$ 15,000	$ 100,000
Sept. 8–10	National Jewish Hospital Open	Kathy Whitworth	211	$ 9,000	$ 60,000
Sept. 14–17	The Sarah Coventry	Donna Caponi	282	$ 15,000	$ 100,000
Sept. 22–24	Ping Classic Team Championship	Donna Caponi and Kathy Whitworth	203	$ 20,000	$ 100,000
Sept. 28–Oct. 1	Golden Lights Championship	Jane Blalock	276	$ 15,000	$ 100,000
Oct. 13–15	Civitan Open	Silvia Bertolaccinni	213	$ 11,250	$ 75,000
Oct. 20–22	Houston Exchange Clubs Classic	Donna Caponi	207	$ 7,500	$ 50,000
Nov. 1–3	Mizuno–Japan Classic	Michiko Okada	216	$ 18,750	$ 125,000
Nov. 9–12	Colgate Far East Open	Nancy Lopez	216	$ 15,000	$ 100,000

LPGA TOUR (continued)

Date	Event	Winner	Score	1st Place Money	Total Purse
Nov. 30–Dec. 3	JC Penney Classic	Pat Bradley and Lon Hinkle	267	$ 60,000	$ 300,000

1979 Tour

Date	Event	Winner	Score	1st Place Money	Total Purse
Feb. 1–4	Colgate Triple Crown	JoAnne Carner	4&3	$ 23,000	$ 100,000
Feb. 15–18	Elizabeth Arden Classic	Amy Alcott	285	$ 15,000	$ 100,000
Feb. 23–25	Orange Blossom Classic	Jane Blalock	205	$ 11,250	$ 75,000
Mar. 1–4	Bent Tree Classic	Sally Little	278	$ 15,000	$ 100,000
Mar. 8–11	Sunstar Classic	Nancy Lopez	280	$ 15,000	$ 100,000
Mar. 15–18	Honda Civic Classic	JoAnne Carner	281	$ 22,500	$ 150,000
Mar. 22–25	Sahara National Pro-Am	Nancy Lopez	274	$ 15,000	$ 100,000
Mar. 29–Apr. 1	Women's Kemper Open	JoAnne Carner	286	$ 22,500	$ 150,000
Apr. 5–8	Colgate–Dinah Shore Winner's Circle	Sandra Post	276	$ 37,500	$ 250,000
Apr. 18–22	Florida Lady Citrus	Jane Blalock	286	$ 15,000	$ 100,000
Apr. 27–29	Otey Crisman Classic	Jane Blalock	205	$ 15,000	$ 100,000
May 3–6	Women's International	Nancy Lopez	282	$ 12,000	$ 80,000
May 11–13	Lady Michelob	Sandra Post	210	$ 15,000	$ 100,000
May 18–20	Coca-Cola Classic	Nancy Lopez	216	$ 15,000	$ 100,000
May 24–27	Corning Classic	Penny Pulz	284	$ 15,000	$ 100,000
May 31–June 3	Golden Lights Championship	Nancy Lopez	280	$ 15,000	$ 100,000
June 7–10	LPGA Championship	Donna Caponi	279	$ 22,500	$ 150,000
June 14–17	The Sarah Coventry	Jane Blalock	280	$ 15,000	$ 100,000
June 21–24	Lady Keystone Open	Nancy Lopez	212	$ 15,000	$ 100,000
June 28–July 1	Lady Stroh's Open	Vicki Fergon	284	$ 22,500	$ 150,000
July 6–8	Mayflower Classic	Hollis Stacy	213	$ 15,000	$ 100,000
July 12–15	U.S. Women's Open	Jerilyn Britz	284	$ 19,000	$ 127,270
July 20–22	Greater Baltimore Classic	Pat Meyers	210	$ 11,250	$ 75,000
July 26–29	Peter Jackson Classic	Amy Alcott	285	$ 22,500	$ 150,000
Aug. 2–5	Colgate–European Open	Nancy Lopez	282	$ 16,500	$ 150,000
Aug. 9–12	WUI Classic	Judy Rankin	288	$ 15,000	$ 100,000
Aug. 17–19	Barth Classic	Sally Little	208	$ 15,000	$ 100,000
Aug. 23–26	Patty Berg Classic	Beth Daniel	208	$ 15,000	$ 100,000
Aug. 31–Sept. 3	Rail Charity Classic	Jo Ann Washam	275	$ 15,000	$ 100,000
Sept. 7–9	Columbia Savings Classic	Sally Little	209	$ 15,000	$ 100,000
Sept. 14–16	Portland-Ping Team Championship	Nancy Lopez and Jo Ann Washam	198	$ 20,000	$ 110,000
Sept. 20–23	ERA Real Estate Classic	Sandra Post	284	$ 15,000	$ 100,000
Sept. 27–30	Mary Kay Classic	Nancy Lopez	274	$ 19,500	$ 125,000
Oct. 5–7	Wheeling Classic	Debbie Massey	219	$ 15,000	$ 100,000
Oct. 11–14	United Virginia Bank Classic	Amy Alcott	286	$ 15,000	$ 100,000
Oct. 26–29	Colgate–Far East Open	Silvia Bertolaccini	213	$ 16,500	$ 150,000
Nov. 1–3	Mizuno Japan Classic	Amy Alcott	211	$ 18,750	$ 125,000
Dec. 6–9	JC Penney Classic	Murle Breer and Dave Eichelberger	267	$ 72,000	$ 400,000

1980 Tour

Date	Event	Winner	Score	1st Place Money	Total Purse
Feb. 1–4	Whirlpool Championship of Deer Creek	JoAnne Carner	282	$ 15,000	$ 100,000

LPGA TOUR (continued)

Date	Event	Winner	Score	1st Place Money	Total Purse
Feb. 7–10	Elizabeth Arden Classic	Jane Blalock	283	$ 15,000	$ 100,000
Feb. 15–17	S&H Golf Classic	Dot Germain	209	$ 15,000	$ 100,000
Feb. 21–24	Bent Tree Ladies' Classic	JoAnne Carner	280	$ 15,000	$ 100,000
Feb. 28–Mar. 2	Sun City Classic	Jan Stephenson	275	$ 15,000	$ 100,000
Mar. 6–9	Sunstar '80	JoAnne Carner	207	$ 18,750	$ 125,000
Mar. 13–16	Honda Civic Golf Classic	JoAnne Carner	279	$ 22,500	$ 150,000
Mar. 20–23	LPGA National Pro-Am	Donna Caponi	286	$ 30,000	$ 200,000
Mar. 27–30	Women's Kemper Open	Nancy Lopez	284	$ 22,500	$ 150,000
Apr. 3–6	Colgate–Dinah Shore	Donna Caponi	275	$ 37,500	$ 250,000
Apr. 11–13	American Defender WRAL Classic	Amy Alcott	206	$ 15,000	$ 100,000
Apr. 17–20	Florida "Lady Citrus"	Donna White	283	$ 15,000	$ 100,000
Apr. 25–27	Birmingham Classic	Barbara Barrow	210	$ 15,000	$ 100,000
May 1–4	CPC Women's International	Hollis Stacy	279	$ 14,700	$ 100,000
May 9–11	Lady Michelob	Pam Higgins	208	$ 15,000	$ 100,000
May 15–18	Coca-Cola Classic	Donna White	217	$ 18,750	$ 125,000
May 22–25	Corning Classic	Donna Caponi	281	$ 15,000	$ 100,000
May 29–June 1	Golden Lights Championship	Beth Daniel	287	$ 18,750	$ 125,000
June 5–8	LPGA Championship	Sally Little	285	$ 22,500	$ 150,000
June 12–15	The Boston Five Classic	Dale Lundquist	276	$ 22,500	$ 150,000
June 20–22	Lady Keystone Open	JoAnne Carner	207	$ 15,000	$ 100,000
June 26–29	Sarah Coventry	Nancy Lopez	283	$ 18,750	$ 125,000
July 3–6	Mayflower Classic	Amy Alcott	275	$ 22,500	$ 150,000
July 10–13	U.S. Women's Open	Amy Alcott	280	$ 20,047	$ 140,000
July 18–20	Greater Baltimore Golf Classic	Pat Bradley	206	$ 15,000	$ 100,000
July 24–27	WUI Classic	Sally Little	284	$ 18,750	$ 125,000
Aug. 1–3	West Virginia LPGA Classic	Sandra Post	211	$ 15,000	$ 100,000
Aug. 7–10	Peter Jackson Classic	Pat Bradley	277	$ 22,500	$ 150,000
Aug. 14–17	Patty Berg Classic	Beth Daniel	210	$ 15,000	$ 100,000
Aug. 21–24	Columbia Savings LPGA Classic	Beth Daniel	276	$ 22,500	$ 150,000
Aug. 29–Sept.1	Rail Charity Golf Classic	Nancy Lopez	275	$ 18,750	$ 125,000
Sept. 5–7	Barth Classic	Sandra Spuzich	212	$ 15,000	$ 100,000
Sept. 5–7	World Series of Women's Golf	Beth Daniel	282	$ 46,500	$ 150,000
Sept. 11–14	United Virginia Bank Classic	Donna Caponi	277	$ 15,000	$ 100,000
Sept. 18–21	ERA Real Estate Classic	Donna Caponi	283	$ 15,000	$ 100,000
Sept. 26–28	Mary Kay Classic	Jerilyn Britz	139	$ 22,500	$ 150,000
Oct. 2–5	Portland Ping Team Championship	Kathy Whitworth and Donna Caponi	195	$ 21,000	$ 115,000
Oct. 6–12	Inamori Golf Classic	Amy Alcott	280	$ 22,500	$ 150,000
Nov. 7–9	Mazda Japan Classic	Tatsuko Ohsako	213	$ 26,250	$ 225,000
Dec. 11–14	JC Penney Classic	Nancy Lopez and Curtis Strange	268	$ 72,000	$ 400,000
	1981 Tour				
Jan. 29–Feb. 1	Whirlpool Championship of Deer Creek	Sandra Palmer	284	$ 15,000	$ 100,000
Feb. 5–8	Elizabeth Arden Classic	Sally Little	283	$ 18,750	$ 125,000
Feb. 13–15	S&H Golf Classic	JoAnne Carner	215	$ 15,000	$ 100,000

LPGA TOUR (continued)

Date	Event	Winner	Score	1st Place Money	Total Purse
Feb. 19–22	Bent Tree Ladies' Classic	Amy Alcott	276	$ 22,500	$ 150,000
Feb. 26–Mar. 1	Olympia Gold Classic	Sally Little	142	$ 22,500	$ 150,000
Mar. 5–8	Arizona Copper Classic	Nancy Lopez	278	$ 18,750	$ 125,000
Mar. 12–15	Sun City Classic	Patty Hayes	277	$ 15,000	$ 100,000
Mar. 19–22	LPGA Desert Inn Pro-Am	Donna Caponi	286	$ 30,000	$ 200,000
Mar. 26–29	Women's Kemper Open	Pat Bradley	284	$ 26,250	$ 175,000
Apr. 2–5	Colgate–Dinah Shore	Nancy Lopez	277	$ 37,500	$ 250,000
Apr. 10–12	American Defender–WRAL Classic	Donna Caponi	208	$ 18,750	$ 125,000
Apr. 16–19	Florida Lady Citrus	Beth Daniel	281	$ 15,000	$ 100,000
Apr. 24–26	Birmingham Classic	Beth Solomon	206	$ 15,000	$ 100,000
Apr. 30–May 3	CPC Women's International	Sally Little	287	$ 18,750	$ 125,000
May 8–10	Lady Michelob	Amy Alcott	209	$ 18,750	$ 125,000
May 15–17	Coca-Cola Classic	Kathy Whitworth	211	$ 18,750	$ 125,000
May 21–24	Corning Classic	Kathy Hite	282	$ 18,750	$ 125,000
May 28–31	Golden Lights Championship	Cathy Reynolds	285	$ 18,750	$ 125,000
June 4–7	MacDonald's Classic	Sandra Post	282	$ 22,500	$ 150,000
June 11–14	LPGA Championship	Donna Caponi	280	$ 22,500	$ 150,000
June 19–21	Lady Keystone Open	JoAnne Carner	203	$ 18,750	$ 125,000
June 25–28	The Sarah Coventry	Nancy Lopez	285	$ 18,750	$ 125,000
July 2–5	Peter Jackson Classic	Jan Stephenson	278	$ 30,000	$ 200,000
July 9–12	Mayflower Classic	Debbie Austin	279	$ 22,500	$ 150,000
July 16–19	WUI Classic	Donna Caponi	282	$ 18,750	$ 125,000
July 23–26	U.S. Women's Open	Pat Bradley	279	$ 22,000	$ 148,670
July 30–Aug. 2	Boston Five Classic	Donna Caponi	276	$ 22,500	$ 150,000
Aug. 7–9	West Virginia Bank Classic	Hollis Stacy	212	$ 18,750	$ 125,000
Aug. 14–16	Mary Kay Classic	Jan Stephenson	198	$ 23,250	$ 155,000
Aug. 20–23	World Championship of Women's Golf	Beth Daniel	284	$ 50,000	$ 150,000
Aug. 27–30	Columbia Savings LPGA Classic	JoAnne Carner	278	$ 22,500	$ 150,000
Sept. 4–7	Rail Charity Golf Classic	JoAnne Carner	205	$ 18,750	$ 125,000
Sept. 11–13	United Virginia Bank Classic	Jan Stephenson	205	$ 18,750	$ 125,000
Sept. 17–20	Henredon Classic	Sandra Haynie	281	$ 24,750	$ 165,000
Oct. 1–4	Portland Ping Team Championship	Donna Caponi and Kathy Whitworth	203	$ 21,600	$ 120,000
Oct. 8–11	Inamori Classic	Hollis Stacy	286	$ 22,500	$ 150,000
Oct. 30–Nov. 1	Pioneer Cup	Chako Higuchi	180	$ 15,000	$ 125,000
Nov. 6–8	Mazda Japan Classic	Patty Sheehan	213	$ 30,000	$ 250,000
Dec. 3–6	JC Penney Classic	Beth Daniel and Tom Kite	270	$ 100,000	$ 500,000

1982 Tour

Date	Event	Winner	Score	1st Place Money	Total Purse
Jan. 28–31	Whirlpool Championship of Deer Creek	Hollis Stacy	282	$ 18,750	$ 125,000
Feb. 4–7	Elizabeth Arden Classic	JoAnne Carner	283	$ 18,750	$ 125,000
Feb. 12–14	S&H Golf Classic	Hollis Stacy	204	$ 18,750	$ 125,000
Feb. 18–21	Bent Tree Ladies' Classic	Beth Daniel	276	$ 22,500	$ 150,000
Feb. 22–28	Arizona Copper Classic	Ayako Okamoto	281	$ 18,750	$ 125,000
Mar. 4–7	American Express Sun City Classic	Beth Daniel	278	$ 15,000	$ 100,000

LPGA TOUR (continued)

Date	Event	Winner	Score	1st Place Money	Total Purse
Mar. 11–14	Olympia Gold Classic	Sally Little	288	$ 22,500	$ 150,000
Mar. 18–21	J&B Scotch Pro-Am	Nancy Lopez	279	$ 30,000	$ 200,000
Mar. 25–28	Women's Kemper Open	Amy Alcott	286	$ 26,250	$ 175,000
Apr. 1–4	Nabisco–Dinah Shore Invitational	Sally Little	278	$ 45,000	$ 300,000
Apr. 15–18	CPC Women's International	Kathy Whitworth	281	$ 22,500	$ 150,000
Apr. 23–25	Orlando Lady Classic	Patty Sheehan	209	$ 22,500	$ 150,000
Apr. 30–May 2	Birmingham Classic	Beth Daniel	203	$ 15,000	$ 100,000
May 7–9	United Virginia Bank Classic	Sally Little	208	$ 18,750	$ 125,000
May 14–16	Lady Michelob	Kathy Whitworth	207	$ 22,500	$ 150,000
May 21–23	Chrysler-Plymouth Charity Classic	Cathy Morse	216	$ 18,750	$ 125,000
May 27–30	Corning Classic	Sandra Spuzich	280	$ 18,750	$ 125,000
June 3–6	McDonald's Classic	JoAnne Carner	276	$ 37,500	$ 250,000
June 10–13	LPGA Championship	Jan Stephenson	279	$ 30,000	$ 200,000
June 18–20	Lady Keystone Open	Jan Stephenson	211	$ 30,000	$ 200,000
June 24–27	Rochester International	Sandra Haynie	276	$ 30,000	$ 200,000
July 1–4	Peter Jackson Classic	Sandra Haynie	280	$ 30,000	$ 200,000
July 9–11	West Virginia LPGA Classic	Hollis Stacy	209	$ 18,750	$ 125,000
July 15–18	Mayflower Classic	Sally Little	275	$ 30,000	$ 200,000
July 22–25	U.S. Women's Open	Janet Anderson	283	$ 27,315	$ 174,250
July 29–Aug. 1	Columbia Savings Classic	Beth Daniel	276	$ 30,000	$ 200,000
Aug. 5–8	Boston Five Classic	Sandra Palmer	281	$ 26,250	$ 175,000
Aug. 12–15	WUI Classic	Beth Daniel	276	$ 18,750	$ 125,000
Aug. 19–22	World Championship of Women's Golf	JoAnne Carner	284	$ 50,000	$ 150,000
Aug. 26–29	Henredon Classic	JoAnne Carner	282	$ 24,750	$ 165,000
Sept. 4–6	Rail Charity Golf Classic	JoAnne Carner	202	$ 18,750	$ 125,000
Sept. 10–12	May Kay Classic	Sandra Spuzich	206	$ 23,250	$ 155,000
Sept. 17–19	Portland Ping Team Championship	Sandra Haynie and Kathy McMullen	196	$ 21,600	$ 120,000
Sept. 30–Oct. 3	Inamori Classic	Patty Sheehan	277	$ 22,500	$ 150,000
Oct. 31–Nov. 2	Pioneer Cup	Nayoko Yoshikawa	141	$ 10,000	$ 125,000
Nov. 5–7	Mazda Japan Classic	Nancy Lopez	207	$ 30,000	$ 250,000
Dec. 9–12	JC Penney Classic	JoAnne Carner and John Mahaffey	268	$ 93,000	$ 500,000

1983 Tour

Date	Event	Winner	Score	1st Place Money	Total Purse
Jan. 27–30	Mazda Classic of Deer Creek	Pat Bradley	272	$ 22,500	$ 150,000
Feb. 3–6	Elizabeth Arden Classic	Nancy Lopez	285	$ 22,500	$ 150,000
Feb. 10–13	Sarasota Classic	Donna White	284	$ 26,250	$ 175,000
Feb. 25–27	Tucson Conquistadores LPGA	Jan Stephenson	207	$ 22,500	$ 150,000
Mar. 3–6	Samaritan Turquoise Classic	Anne-Marie Palli	205	$ 22,500	$ 150,000
Mar. 17–20	Women's Kemper Open	Kathy Whitworth	288	$ 30,000	$ 200,000
Mar. 31–Apr. 3	Nabisco–Dinah Shore Invitational	Amy Alcott	282	$ 55,000	$ 400,000
Apr. 7–10	J&B Scotch Pro-Am	Nancy Lopez	283	$ 30,000	$ 200,000
Apr. 15–17	Combanks Orlando Classic	Lynn Adams	208	$ 22,500	$ 150,000
Apr. 21–24	S&H Golf Classic	Hollis Stacy	277	$ 22,500	$ 150,000
Apr. 29–May 1	CPC International	Hollis Stacy	285	$ 27,250	$ 175,000

LPGA TOUR (continued)

Date	Event	Winner	Score	1st Place Money	Total Purse
May 6–8	Lady Michelob	Janet Coles	206	$ 22,500	$ 150,000
May 13–15	United Virginia Bank Classic	Lenore Muraoka	212	$ 22,500	$ 150,000
May 20–22	Chrysler-Plymouth Charity	Pat Bradley	212	$ 18,750	$ 125,000
May 26–29	Corning Classic	Patty Sheehan	272	$ 22,500	$ 150,000
June 3–5	West Virginia LPGA Classic	Alice Miller	216	$ 22,500	$ 150,000
June 9–12	LPGA Championship	Patty Sheehan	279	$ 30,000	$ 200,000
June 17–19	Lady Keystone Open	Jan Stephenson	205	$ 30,000	$ 200,000
June 23–26	Rochester International	Ayako Okamoto	282	$ 30,000	$ 200,000
June 30–July 3	Peter Jackson Classic	Hollis Stacy	277	$ 37,500	$ 250,000
July 14–17	McDonald's Kids Classic	Beth Daniel	286	$ 52,500	$ 350,000
July 21–24	Mayflower Classic	Lauren Howe	280	$ 30,000	$ 200,000
July 28–31	U.S. Women's Open	Jan Stephenson	290	$ 32,780	$ 200,000
Aug. 4–7	Boston Five Classic	Patti Rizzo	277	$ 26,250	$ 175,000
Aug. 11–14	Henredon Classic	Patty Sheehan	272	$ 27,000	$ 180,000
Aug. 18–21	Chevrolet World Champion- ship of Women's Golf	JoAnne Carner	282	$ 65,000	$ 200,000
Aug. 25–28	Columbia Savings Classic	Pat Bradley	277	$ 30,000	$ 200,000
Sept. 3–5	Rail Charity Classic	Lauri Peterson	210	$ 22,500	$ 150,000
Sept. 9–11	Portland Ping Championship	JoAnne Carner	212	$ 22,500	$ 175,000
Sept. 15–18	Safeco Classic	Juli Inkster	283	$ 26,250	$ 175,000
Sept. 23–26	Inamori Classic	Patty Sheehan	209	$ 26,250	$ 175,000
Sept. 29–Oct. 2	San Jose Classic	Kathy Postlewait	213	$ 26,250	$ 175,000
Nov. 4–6	Sports Nippon Team Match	Chako Higuchi	142	$ 20,000	$ 175,000
Nov. 11–13	Mazda Japan Classic	Pat Bradley	206	$ 37,500	$ 300,000
Dec. 8–11	JC Penney Classic	Jan Stephenson and Fred Couples	264	$ 46,500	$ 550,000

1984 Tour

Date	Event	Winner	Score	1st Place Money	Total Purse
Jan. 26–29	Mazda Classic of Deer Creek	Silvia Bertolaccinni	280	$ 30,000	$ 200,000
Feb. 2–5	Elizabeth Arden Classic	Patty Sheehan	280	$ 26,250	$ 175,000
Feb. 9–12	Sarasota Classic	Alice Miller	280	$ 26,250	$ 175,000
Mar. 1–4	Uniden LPGA Invitational	Nancy Lopez	284	$ 45,000	$ 300,000
Mar. 8–11	Samaritan Turquoise Classic	Chris Johnson	276	$ 22,500	$ 150,000
Mar. 15–18	Tucson Conquistadores Open	Chris Johnson	272	$ 22,500	$ 150,000
Mar. 22–25	Women's Kemper Open	Betsy King	283	$ 30,000	$ 200,000
Apr. 5–8	Nabisco–Dinah Shore	Juli Inkster	280	$ 55,000	$ 400,000
Apr. 12–15	J&B Scotch Pro-Am	Ayako Okamoto	275	$ 30,000	$ 200,000
Apr. 19–22	S&H Golf Classic	Vicki Fergon	275	$ 22,500	$ 150,000
Apr. 27–29	Freedom–Orlando Classic	Betsy King	202	$ 22,500	$ 150,000
May 5–7	Potamkin Cadillac Classic	Sharon Barrett	213	$ 30,000	$ 200,000
May 11–13	United Virginia Bank Classic	Amy Alcott	210	$ 26,250	$ 175,000
May 18–20	Chrysler-Plymouth Charity Classic	Barb Bunkowsky	209	$ 26,250	$ 175,000
May 24–27	Corning Classic	JoAnne Carner	281	$ 22,500	$ 150,000
May 31–June 3	LPGA Championship	Patty Sheehan	272	$ 37,500	$ 250,000
June 7–10	McDonald's Kids Classic	Patty Sheehan	281	$ 52,500	$ 350,000
June 14–17	Mayflower Classic	Ayako Okamoto	281	$ 37,500	$ 250,000
June 21–24	Boston Five Classic	Laurie Rinker	286	$ 33,750	$ 225,000
June 29–July 1	Lady Keystone Open	Amy Alcott	208	$ 30,000	$ 200,000
July 5–8	Jamie Farr Toledo Classic	Lauri Peterson	278	$ 26,250	$ 175,000

LPGA TOUR (continued)

Date	Event	Winner	Score	1st Place Money	Total Purse
July 12–15	U.S. Women's Open	Hollis Stacy	290	$ 36,000	$ 225,000
July 19–22	Rochester International	Kathy Whitworth	281	$ 30,000	$ 200,000
July 26–29	du Maurier Classic	Juli Inkster	279	$ 41,250	$ 275,000
Aug. 3–5	West Virginia LPGA Classic	Alice Miller	209	$ 22,500	$ 150,000
Aug. 9–12	Henredon Classic	Patty Sheehan	277	$ 27,000	$ 180,000
Aug. 16–19	Chevrolet World Champion- ship of Women's Golf	Nancy Lopez	281	$ 65,000	$ 200,000
Aug. 16–19	MasterCard International Pro-Am	Sally Quinlan	284	$ 15,287	$ 100,000
Aug. 23–26	Columbia Savings Classic	Betsy King	281	$ 30,000	$ 200,000
Aug. 31–Sept. 3	Rail Charity Classic	Cindy Hill	207	$ 26,250	$ 175,000
Sept. 7–9	Portland Ping Championship	Amy Alcott	212	$ 22,500	$ 150,000
Sept. 13–16	Safeco Classic	Kathy Whitworth	279	$ 26,250	$ 175,000
Sept. 21–23	San Jose Classic	Amy Alcott	211	$ 26,250	$ 175,000
Oct. 3–6	Hitachi Ladies' British Open	Ayako Okamoto	289	$ 30,039	$ 200,000
Oct. 11–14	Smirnoff Ladies' Irish Open	Kathy Whitworth	285	$ 22,500	$ 150,000
Oct. 26–28	Nichirei Cup Team Match	Hollis Stacy	138	$ 20,000	$ 154,000
Nov. 2–4	Mazda Japan Classic	Nayoko Yoshikawa	210	$ 41,250	$ 300,000
Dec. 6–9	JC Penney Classic	Vicki Alvarez and Mike McDonald	270	$ 46,500	$ 550,000

1985 Tour

Date	Event	Winner	Score	1st Place Money	Total Purse
Jan. 24–27	Mazda Classic	Hollis Stacy	280	$ 30,000	$ 200,000
Jan. 31–Feb. 3	Elizabeth Arden Classic	JoAnne Carner	280	$ 30,000	$ 200,000
Feb. 7–10	Sarasota Classic	Patty Sheehan	278	$ 30,000	$ 200,000
Feb. 21–24	Circle K Tucson Open	Amy Alcott	279	$ 26,250	$ 175,000
Feb. 28–Mar. 3	Samaritan Turquoise Classic	Betsy King	280	$ 22,500	$ 150,000
Mar. 7–10	Uniden LPGA Invitational	Bonnie Lauer	277	$ 49,500	$ 330,000
Mar. 14–17	Women's Kemper Open	Jane Blalock	287	$ 45,000	$ 300,000
Mar. 21–24	GNA Classic	Jan Stephenson	290	$ 37,500	$ 250,000
Apr. 4–7	Nabisco–Dinah Shore	Alice Miller	275	$ 55,000	$ 400,000
Apr. 11–14	Kyocera Inamori Classic	Beth Daniel	286	$ 26,250	$ 175,000
Apr. 18–21	J&B Scotch Pro-Am	Patty Sheehan	275	$ 30,000	$ 200,000
Apr. 25–28	S&H Golf Classic	Alice Miller	272	$ 26,250	$ 175,000
May 2–5	Moss Creek Women's Invitational	Amy Alcott	284	$ 30,000	$ 200,000
May 10–12	United Virginia Bank Classic	Kathy Whitworth	207	$ 30,000	$ 200,000
May 17–19	Chrysler-Plymouth Classic	Nancy Lopez	210	$ 26,250	$ 175,000
May 23–26	LPGA Corning Classic	Patty Rizzo	272	$ 37,500	$ 250,000
May 30–June 2	LPGA Championship	Nancy Lopez	273	$ 37,500	$ 250,000
June 6–9	McDonald's Championship	Alice Miller	272	$ 60,000	$ 400,000
June 13–16	Rochester International	Pat Bradley	280	$ 38,250	$ 255,000
June 20–23	Mayflower Classic	Alice Miller	280	$ 37,500	$ 250,000
June 28–30	Lady Keystone Open	Juli Inkster	209	$ 37,500	$ 250,000
July 4–7	Mazda Hall of Fame Championship	Nancy Lopez	281	$ 45,000	$ 300,000
July 11–14	U.S. Women's Open	Kathy Baker	280	$ 41,975	$ 250,000
July 18–21	Boston Five Classic	Judy Clark	280	$ 33,750	$ 225,000
July 25–28	du Maurier Classic	Pat Bradley	278	$ 45,000	$ 300,000
Aug. 1–4	Jamie Farr Toledo Classic	Penny Hammel	278	$ 26,250	$ 175,000

LPGA TOUR (continued)

Date	Event	Winner	Score	1st Place Money	Total Purse
Aug. 8–11	Henredon Classic	Nancy Lopez	268	$ 31,500	$ 210,000
Aug. 15–18	Nestlé World Championship of Women's Golf	Amy Alcott	274	$ 65,000	$ 200,000
Aug. 15–18	MasterCard International Pro-Am	Muffin Spencer-Devlin	209	$ 30,000	$ 200,000
Aug. 22–25	LPGA National Pro-Am	Pat Bradley	284	$ 45,000	$ 300,000
Aug. 31–Sept. 2	Rail Charity Classic	Betsy King	205	$ 27,750	$ 185,000
Sept. 6–8	Portland Ping Championship	Nancy Lopez	215	$ 26,250	$ 175,000
Sept. 12–15	Safeco Classic	JoAnne Carner	279	$ 30,000	$ 200,000
Sept. 20–22	Konica San Jose Classic	Val Skinner	209	$ 37,500	$ 250,000
Nov. 1–3	Nichirei Cup Team Match	Jan Stephenson	138	$ 16,600	$ 175,000
Nov. 8–10	Mazda Japan Classic	Jane Blalock	206	$ 45,000	$ 300,000

1986 Tour

Date	Event	Winner	Score	1st Place Money	Total Purse
Jan. 23–26	Mazda Classic	Val Skinner	280	$ 30,000	$ 200,000
Jan. 30–Feb. 2	Elizabeth Arden Classic	Ayako Okamoto	280	$ 30,000	$ 200,000
Feb. 6–9	Sarasota Classic	Patty Sheehan	279	$ 30,000	$ 200,000
Feb. 20–23	Standard Register–Samaritan Turquoise Classic	Mary Beth Zimmerman	278	$ 37,500	$ 250,000
Feb. 27–Mar. 2	Uniden LPGA Invitational	Mary Beth Zimmerman	281	$ 49,500	$ 330,000
Mar. 6–9	Women's Kemper Open	Juli Inkster	276	$ 45,000	$ 300,000
Mar. 13–16	GNA–Glendale Federal Classic	Chris Johnson	212	$ 37,500	$ 250,000
Mar. 20–23	Circle K Tucson Open	Penny Pulz	276	$ 30,000	$ 200,000
Apr. 3–6	Nabisco–Dinah Shore	Pat Bradley	280	$ 75,000	$ 430,000
Apr. 10–13	Kyocera Inamori Classic	Patty Sheehan	278	$ 30,000	$ 200,000
Apr. 24–27	S&H Golf Classic	Pat Bradley	272	$ 30,000	$ 200,000
May 9–11	United Virginia Bank Classic	Muffin Spencer-Devlin	214	$ 37,500	$ 250,000
May 16–18	Chrysler-Plymouth Classic	Becky Pearson	212	$ 30,000	$ 200,000
May 22–25	LPGA Corning Classic	Laurie Rinker	278	$ 37,500	$ 250,000
May 29–June 1	LPGA Championship	Pat Bradley	277	$ 45,000	$ 300,000
June 5–8	McDonald's Championship	Juli Inkster	282	$ 67,500	$ 450,000
June 13–15	Lady Keystone Open	Juli Inkster	210	$ 37,500	$ 250,000
June 19–22	Rochester International	Judy Dickinson	281	$ 38,250	$ 255,000
June 26–29	Mayflower Classic	Sandra Post	280	$ 52,500	$ 350,000
July 3–6	Mazda Hall of Fame Championship	Amy Alcott	284	$ 45,000	$ 300,000
July 10–13	U.S. Women's Open	Jane Geddes	287	$ 50,000	$ 300,000
July 17–20	Boston Five Classic	Jane Geddes	281	$ 41,250	$ 275,000
July 24–27	du Maurier Classic	Pat Bradley	276	$ 52,500	$ 350,000
July 31–Aug. 3	LPGA National Pro-Am	Amy Alcott	283	$ 45,000	$ 300,000
Aug. 7–10	Henredon Classic	Betsy King	277	$ 34,500	$ 230,000
Aug. 14–17	Nestlé World Championship	Pat Bradley	279	$ 78,000	$ 240,000
Aug. 14–17	MasterCard International Pro-Am	Cindy Mackey	276	$ 30,000	$ 200,000
Aug. 22–24	Atlantic City LPGA Classic	Juli Inkster	209	$ 33,750	$ 225,000
Aug. 30–Sept. 1	Rail Charity Classic	Betsy King	205	$ 30,000	$ 200,000
Sept. 1–7	Cellular One–Ping Golf Championship	Ayako Okamoto	207	$ 30,000	$ 200,000

LPGA TOUR (continued)

Date	Event	Winner	Score	1st Place Money	Total Purse
Sept. 11–14	Safeco Classic	Judy Dickinson	274	$ 30,000	$ 200,000
Sept. 19–21	Konica San Jose Classic	Patty Sheehan	212	$ 41,250	$ 275,000
Oct. 31–Nov. 2	Nichirei Cup Team Match	Ayako Okamoto	140	$ 16,000	$ 200,000
Nov. 7–9	Mazda Japan Classic	Ai-Yu Tu	213	$ 45,000	$ 300,000

1987 Tour

Date	Event	Winner	Score	1st Place Money	Total Purse
Jan. 29–Feb. 1	Mazda Classic	Kathy Postlewait	286	$ 30,000	$ 200,000
Feb. 5–8	Sarasota Classic	Nancy Lopez	281	$ 30,000	$ 200,000
Feb. 19–21	Tsumura Hawaiian Ladies' Open	Cindy Rarick	207	$ 45,000	$ 300,000
Feb. 26–Mar.1	Women's Kemper Open	Jane Geddes	276	$ 45,000	$ 300,000
Mar. 5–8	GNA–Glendale Federal Classic	Jane Geddes	286	$ 37,500	$ 250,000
Mar. 19–22	Circle K Tucson Open	Betsy King	281	$ 30,000	$ 200,000
Mar. 26–29	Standard Register Turquoise Classic	Pat Bradley	286	$ 45,000	$ 300,000
Apr. 2–5	Nabisco–Dinah Shore	Betsy King	283	$ 80,000	$ 500,000
Apr. 9–12	Kyocero Inamori Golf Classic	Ayako Okamoto	275	$ 30,000	$ 200,000
Apr. 17–19	Santa Barbara Open	Jan Stephenson	215	$ 45,000	$ 300,000
Apr. 30–May 3	S&H Golf Classic	Cindy Hill	271	$ 33,750	$ 225,000
May 8–10	United Virginia Bank Golf Classic	Jody Rosenthal	209	$ 37,500	$ 250,000
May 15–17	Chrysler-Plymouth Classic	Ayako Okamoto	215	$ 33,750	$ 225,000
May 21–24	Mazda LPGA Championship	Jane Geddes	275	$ 52,500	$ 350,00
May 28–31	LPGA Corning Classic	Cindy Rarick	275	$ 41,250	$ 275,000
June 4–7	McDonald's Championship	Betsy King	278	$ 75,000	$ 500,000
June 11–14	Mayflower Classic	Colleen Walker	278	$ 52,500	$ 350,000
June 19–21	Lady Keystone Open	Ayako Okamoto	208	$ 45,000	$ 300,000
June 25–28	Rochester International	Deb Richard	280	$ 45,000	$ 300,000
July 2–5	Jamie Farr Toledo Classic	Jane Geddes	280	$ 33,750	$ 225,000
July 9–12	du Maurier Classic	Jody Rosenthal	272	$ 60,000	$ 400,000
July 16–19	Boston Five Classic	Jane Geddes	277	$ 45,000	$ 300,000
July 23–26	U.S. Women's Open	Laura Davies	285	$ 55,000	$ 325,000
July 30–Aug. 2	Columbia Savings Pro-Am	Chris Johnson	277	$ 37,500	$ 250,000
Aug. 6–9	Henredon Classic	Mary Beth Zimmerman	206	$ 45,000	$ 300,000
Aug. 14–16	MasterCard International	Val Skinner	212	$ 33,750	$ 225,000
Aug. 21–23	Atlantic City LPGA Classic	Betsy King	207	$ 33,750	$ 225,000
Aug. 27–30	Nestlé World Championship	Ayako Okamoto	282	$ 81,500	$ 250,000
Sept. 5–7	Rail Charity Classic	Rosie Jones	208	$ 30,000	$ 200,000
Sept. 11–13	Cellular One–Ping Championship	Nancy Lopez	210	$ 33,750	$ 225,000
Sept. 17–20	Safeco Classic	Jan Stephenson	277	$ 33,750	$ 225,000
Sept. 25–27	Konica San Jose Classic	Jan Stephenson	205	$ 45,000	$ 300,000
Oct. 31–Nov. 1	Nichirei US–Japan Championship	Fukumi Tani	139	$ 25,000	$ 260,000
Nov. 6–8	Mazda Japan Classic	Yuko Moriguchi	206	$ 52,500	$ 350,000
Dec. 3–6	JC Penney Classic	Jane Crafter and Steve Jones	270	$ 68,000	$ 650,000

LPGA TOUR (continued)

Date	Event	Winner	Score	1st Place Money	Total Purse
		1988 Tour			
Feb. 4–7	Mazda Classic	Nancy Lopez	283	$ 30,000	$ 200,000
Feb. 11–14	Sarasota Classic	Patty Sheehan	282	$ 33,750	$ 225,000
Feb. 25–27	Hawaiian Ladies' Open	Ayako Okamoto	213	$ 45,000	$ 300,000
Mar. 3–6	Women's Kemper Open	Betsy King	280	$ 45,000	$ 300,000
Mar. 17–20	Circle K Tucson Open	Laura Davies	278	$ 45,000	$ 300,000
Mar. 24–27	Standard Register Turquoise Classic	Ok-Hee Ku	281	$ 52,500	$ 350,000
Mar. 31–Apr. 3	Nabisco–Dinah Shore	Amy Alcott	274	$ 80,000	$ 500,000
Apr. 7–10	San Diego Inamori Classic	Ayako Okamoto	272	$ 33,750	$ 225,000
Apr. 15–17	AI Star–Centinela	Nancy Lopez	210	$ 60,000	$ 400,000
Apr. 21–24	USX Classic	Rosie Jones	275	$ 33,750	$ 225,000
May 6–8	Crestar Classic	Juli Inkster	209	$ 45,000	$ 300,000
May 13–15	Chrysler-Plymouth Classic	Nancy Lopez	204	$ 37,500	$ 250,000
May 19–22	LPGA Championship	Sherri Turner	281	$ 52,500	$ 350,000
May 26–29	LPGA Corning Classic	Sherri Turner	273	$ 48,750	$ 325,000
June 2–5	Jamie Farr Toledo Classic	Laura Davies	277	$ 41,250	$ 275,000
June 9–12	Rochester International	Mei-Chi Cheng	287	$ 45,000	$ 300,000
June 17–19	Lady Keystone Open	Shirley Furlong	205	$ 45,000	$ 300,000
June 23–26	McDonald's Championship	Kathy Postlewait	276	$ 75,000	$ 500,000
June 30–July 3	du Maurier Classic	Sally Little	279	$ 75,000	$ 500,000
July 7–10	Mayflower Classic	Terry-Jo Myers	276	$ 60,000	$ 400,000
July 14–17	Boston Five Classic	Colleen Walker	274	$ 45,000	$ 300,000
July 21–24	U.S. Women's Open	Liselotte Neumann	277	$ 70,000	$ 400,000
July 29–31	Greater Washington Open	Ayako Okamoto	206	$ 33,750	$ 225,000
Aug. 4–7	Planters Pat Bradley International	Martha Nause	14*	$ 62,500	$ 400,000
Aug. 19–21	Atlantic City Classic	Juli Inkster	206	$ 33,750	$ 225,000
Aug. 25–28	Nestlé World Championship	Rosie Jones	279	$ 81,500	$ 265,000
Aug. 26–28	Ocean State Open	Patty Jordan	211	$ 22,500	$ 150,000
Sept. 3–5	Rail Charity Classic	Betsy King	207	$ 37,500	$ 250,000
Sept. 9–11	Cellular One–Ping Championship	Betsy King	213	$ 37,500	$ 250,000
Sept. 15–18	Safeco Classic	Juli Inkster	278	$ 33,750	$ 225,000
Sept. 22–25	Santa Barbara Open	Rosie Jones	212	$ 45,000	$ 300,000
Sept. 30–Oct. 2	Konica San Jose Classic	Kathy Guadagnino	207	$ 45,000	$ 300,000
Oct. 28–30	Nicherei US–Japan Championship	Beth Daniel	139	$ 20,000	$ 260,000
Nov. 4–6	Mazda Japan Classic	Patty Sheehan	206	$ 67,500	$ 450,000
Dec. 1–4	JC Penney Classic	Amy Benz and John Huston	269	$ 80,000 each	$ 800,000
		1989 Tour			
Jan. 13–15	Jamaica Classic	Betsy King	202	$ 75,000	$ 500,000
Jan. 26–29	Oldsmobile LPGA Classic	Dottie Mochrie	279	$ 45,000	$ 300,000
Feb. 16–18	Orix Hawaiian Ladies' Open	Sherri Turner	205	$ 45,000	$ 300,000
Feb. 24–26	Women's Kemper Open	Betsy King	202	$ 60,000	$ 400,000
Mar. 16–19	Circle K LPGA Tucson Open	Lori Garbacz	274	$ 45,000	$ 300,000

LPGA TOUR (continued)

Date	Event	Winner	Score	1st Place Money	Total Purse
Mar. 23–26	Standard Register Turquoise Classic	Allison Finney	282	$ 60,000	$ 400,000
Mar. 30–Apr. 2	Nabisco–Dinah Shore	Juli Inkster	279	$ 80,000	$ 500,000
Apr. 6–9	Red Robin Kyocera Inamori Classic	Patti Rizzo	277	$ 45,000	$ 300,000
Apr. 14–16	AI Star–Centinela Hospital Classic	Pat Bradley	208	$ 67,500	$ 450,000
Apr. 20–23	USX Golf Classic	Betsy King	275	$ 37,500	$ 250,000
Apr. 28–30	Sara Lee Classic	Kathy Postlewait	203	$ 63,750	$ 425,000
May 5–7	Crestar Classic	Juli Inkster	210	$ 45,000	$ 300,000
May 12–14	Chrysler-Plymouth Classic	Cindy Rarick	214	$ 41,250	$ 275,000
May 18–21	Mazda LPGA Championship	Nancy Lopez	274	$ 75,000	$ 500,000
May 25–28	LPGA Corning Classic	Ayako Okamoto	272	$ 48,750	$ 325,000
June 1–4	Rochester International	Patty Sheehan	278	$ 45,000	$ 300,000
June 9–11	Pat Bradley International	Robin Hood	16*	$ 62,500	$ 400,000
June 16–18	Lady Keystone Open	Laura Davies	207	$ 45,000	$ 300,000
June 22–25	McDonald's Championship	Betsy King	272	$ 82,500	$ 550,000
June 29–July 2	du Maurier Classic	Tammie Green	279	$ 90,000	$ 600,000
July 7–9	Jamie Farr Toledo Classic	Penny Hammel	206	$ 41,250	$ 275,000
July 13–16	U.S. Women's Open	Betsy King	278	$ 80,000	$ 450,000
July 20–23	Boston Five Classic	Amy Alcott	272	$ 52,500	$ 350,000
July 28–30	Atlantic City Classic	Nancy Lopez	206	$ 33,750	$ 225,000
Aug. 4–6	Greater Washington Open	Beth Daniel	205	$ 45,000	$ 300,000
Aug. 24–27	Nestle World Championship	Betsy King	275	$ 83,500	$ 265,000
Aug. 25–27	Mitsubishi Motors Ocean State Open	Tina Barrett	210	$ 22,500	$ 150,000
Sept. 2–4	Rail Charity Golf Classic	Beth Daniel	203	$ 41,250	$ 275,000
Sept. 8–10	Cellular One–Ping Golf Championship	Muffin Spencer-Devlin	214	$ 45,000	$ 300,000
Sept. 14–17	Safeco Classic	Beth Daniel	273	$ 45,000	$ 300,000
Sept. 21–24	Nippon Travel–MBS Classic	Nancy Lopez	277	$ 45,000	$ 300,000
Sept. 29–Oct. 1	Konica San Jose Classic	Beth Daniel	205	$ 48,750	$ 325,000
Oct. 27–29	Nicherei US–Japan Team Championship	Colleen Walker	210	$ 80,000	$ 350,000
Nov. 3–5	Mazda Japan Classic	Elaine Crosby	205	$ 75,000	$ 500,000
Nov. 30–Dec. 3	JC Penney Classic	Pat Bradley and Bill Glasson	267	$ 100,000 each	$1,000,000

1990 Tour

Date	Event	Winner	Score	1st Place Money	Total Purse
Jan. 19–21	Jamaica Classic	Patty Sheehan	212	$ 75,000	$ 500,000
Feb. 1–4	Oldsmobile LPGA Classic	Pat Bradley	281	$ 45,000	$ 300,000
Feb. 16–18	Phar-Mor at Inverrary	Jane Crafter	209	$ 60,000	$ 400,000
Feb. 22–24	Orix Hawaiian Ladies' Open	Beth Daniel	210	$ 52,500	$ 350,000
Mar. 1–4	Women's Kemper Open	Beth Daniel	283	$ 75,000	$ 500,000
Mar. 9–11	Desert Inn LPGA International	Maggie Will	214	$ 60,000	$ 400,000
Mar. 15–18	Circle K LPGA Tucson Open	Colleen Walker	276	$ 45,000	$ 300,000
Mar. 22–25	Standard Register Turquoise Classic	Pat Bradley	280	$ 75,000	$ 500,000
Mar. 29–Apr. 1	Nabisco–Dinah Shore	Betsy King	283	$ 90,000	$ 600,000
Apr. 5–8	Red Robin Kyocera Inamori Classic	Kris Monaghan	276	$ 45,000	$ 300,000

LPGA TOUR (continued)

Date	Event	Winner	Score	1st Place Money	Total Purse
May 3–6	Sara Lee Classic	Ayako Okamoto	210	$ 63,750	$ 425,000
May 11–13	Crestar Classic	Dottie Mochrie	200	$ 52,500	$ 350,000
May 17–20	Pat Bradley International	Cindy Rarick	25*	$ 60,000	$ 400,000
May 24–27	LPGA Corning Classic	Pat Bradley	274	$ 52,500	$ 350,000
June 1–3	Lady Keystone Open	Cathy Gerring	208	$ 45,000	$ 300,000
June 7–10	McDonald's Championship	Patty Sheehan	275	$ 97,500	$ 650,000
June 14–17	Atlantic City Classic	Chris Johnson	275	$ 45,000	$ 300,000
June 21–24	Rochester International	Patty Sheehan	271	$ 60,000	$ 400,000
June 28–July 1	du Maurier Classic	Cathy Johnson	276	$ 90,000	$ 600,000
July 6–9	Jamie Farr Toledo Classic	Tina Purtzer	205	$ 48,750	$ 325,000
July 12–15	U.S. Women's Open	Betsy King	284	$ 85,000	$ 500,000
July 20–22	Phar-Mor in Youngstown	Beth Daniel	207	$ 60,000	$ 400,000
July 26–29	Mazda LPGA Championship	Beth Daniel	280	$ 150,000	$1,000,000
Aug. 2–5	Boston Five Classic	Barb Mucha	277	$ 52,500	$ 350,000
Aug. 9–12	Stratton Mountain LPGA Classic	Cathy Gerring	281	$ 67,500	$ 450,000
Aug. 16–19	JAL Big Apple Classic	Betsy King	273	$ 60,000	$ 400,000
Aug. 24–26	Northgate Classic	Beth Daniel	203	$ 56,250	$ 375,000
Sept. 1–3	Rail Charity Golf Classic	Beth Daniel	203	$ 45,000	$ 300,000
Sept. 7–9	Ping–Cellular One LPGA Golf Championship	Patty Sheehan	208	$ 52,500	$ 350,000
Sept. 13–16	Safeco Classic	Patty Sheehan	270	$ 45,000	$ 300,000
Sept. 20–23	MBS LPGA Classic	Nancy Lopez	281	$ 48,750	$ 325,000
Oct. 4–7	Centel Classic	Beth Daniel	271	$ 150,000	$1,000,000
Oct. 11–14	Trophee Urban–World Championship	Cathy Gerring	278	$ 100,000	$ 325,000
Nov. 2–4	Mazda Japan Classic	Debbie Massey	133	$ 82,500	$ 550,000
Nov. 29–Dec. 2	JC Penney Classic	Beth Daniel and Davis Love	266	$ 100,000 each	$1,000,000
Dec. 6–9	Itoman LPGA World Match Play Championship	Betsy King	2 up	$ 100,000	$ 450,000

1991 Tour

Date	Event	Winner	Score	1st Place Money	Total Purse
Jan. 18–20	Jamaica Classic	Jane Geddes	207	$ 75,000	$ 500,000
Jan. 31–Feb. 3	Oldsmobile LPGA Classic	Meg Mallon	276	$ 60,000	$ 400,000
Feb. 8–10	Phar-Mor at Inverrary	Beth Daniel	209	$ 75,000	$ 500,000
Feb. 21–23	Orix Hawaiian Ladies' Open	Patty Sheehan	207	$ 52,500	$ 350,000
Feb. 27–Mar. 2	Women's Kemper Open	Deb Richard	275	$ 75,000	$ 500,000
Mar. 7–10	Inamori Classic	Laura Davies	277	$ 60,000	$ 400,000
Mar. 15–17	Desert Inn LPGA International	Penny Hammel	211	$ 60,000	$ 400,000
Mar. 21–24	Standard Register Ping	Danielle Ammaccapane	283	$ 82,500	$ 550,000
Mar. 28–31	Nabisco Dinah Shore	Amy Alcott	273	$ 90,000	$ 600,000
Apr. 4–7	Ping–Welch's Championship	Chris Johnson	273	$ 52,500	$ 350,000
May 3–5	Sara Lee Classic	Nancy Lopez	206	$ 63,700	$ 425,000
May 9–12	Crestar–Farm Fresh Classic	Hollis Stacy	282	$ 60,000	$ 400,000
May 16–19	Centel Classic	Pat Bradley	278	$ 165,000	$1,100,000
May 23–26	LPGA Corning Classic	Betsy King	273	$ 60,000	$ 400,000
May 30–June 2	Rochester International	Rosie Jones	276	$ 60,000	$ 400,000
June 7–9	Atlantic City Classic	Jane Geddes	208	$ 45,000	$ 300,000
June 14–16	Lady Keystone Open	Colleen Walker	207	$ 60,000	$ 400,000

LPGA TOUR (continued)

Date	Event	Winner	Score	1st Place Money	Total Purse
June 20–23	McDonald's Championship	Beth Daniel	273	$ 112,000	$ 750,000
June 27–30	Mazda LPGA Championship	Meg Malloon	274	$ 150,000	$1,000,000
July 5–7	Jamie Farr Toledo Classic	Alice Miller	205	$ 52,500	$ 350,000
July 11–14	U.S. Women's Open	Meg Mallon	283	$ 110,000	$ 600,000
July 18–21	JAL Big Apple Classic	Betsy King	279	$ 75,000	$ 500,000
July 25–28	LPGA Bay State Classic	Juli Inkster	275	$ 60,000	$ 400,000
Aug. 2–4	Phar-Mor in Youngstown	Deb Richard	207	$ 75,000	$ 500,000
Aug. 8–11	Stratton Mountain LPGA Classic	Melissa McNamara	278	$ 67,500	$ 450,000
Aug. 16–18	Northgate Computer Classic	Cindy Rarick	211	$ 60,000	$ 400,000
Aug. 22–25	Chicago *Sun-Times* Shootout	Martha Nause	275	$ 63,750	$ 425,000
Aug. 31–Sept. 2	Rail Charity Golf Classic	Pat Bradley	197	$ 60,000	$ 400,000
Sept. 6–8	Ping–Cellular One LPGA Golf Championship	Michelle Estill	208	$ 60,000	$ 400,000
Sept. 12–15	du Maurier Classic	Nancy Scranton	279	$ 105,000	$ 700,000
Sept. 19–22	Safeco Classic	Pat Bradley	280	$ 60,000	$ 400,000
Sept. 26–29	MBS LPGA Classic	Pat Bradley	277	$ 52,500	$ 350,000
Oct. 3–6	Daikyo World Championship	Meg Mallon	216	$ 100,000	$ 325,000
Nov. 8–10	Mazda Japan Classic	Liselotte Neumann	211	$ 82,500	$ 550,000

1992 Tour

Date	Event	Winner	Score	1st Place Money	Total Purse
Jan. 30–Feb. 2	Oldsmobile LPGA Classic	Colleen Walker	279	$ 60,000	$ 400,000
Feb. 7–9	Phar-Mor at Inverrary	Shelley Hamlin	206	$ 75,000	$ 500,000
Feb. 20–22	Itoki Hawaiian Ladies' Open	Lisa Walters	208	$ 60,000	$ 400,000
Feb. 26–29	Women's Kemper Open	Dawn Coe	275	$ 75,000	$ 500,000
March 5–8	Inamori Classic	Judy Dickinson	277	$ 63,750	$ 425,000
March 12–15	Ping–Welch's Championship	Brandie Burton	277	$ 60,000	$ 400,000
March 19–22	Standard Register Ping	Danielle Ammaccapane	279	$ 82,500	$ 550,000
March 26–29	Nabisco Dinah Shore	Dottie Mochrie	279	$ 105,000	$ 700,000
April 3–5	Las Vegas LPGA International	Dana Lofland	212	$ 67,500	$ 450,000
April 16–19	Sega Women's Championship	Dottie Mochrie	277	$ 90,000	$ 600,000
April 24–26	Sarah Lee Classic	Maggie Will	207	$ 78,750	$ 525,000
April 30–May 3	Centel Classic	Danielle Ammaccapane	275	$ 180,000	$1,200,000
May 8–10	Crester–Farm Fresh Classic	Jennifer Wyatt	208	$ 63,750	$ 425,000
May 14–17	Mazda LPGA Championship	Betsy King	267	$ 150,000	$1,000,000
May 21–24	LPGA Corning Classic	Colleen Walker	276	$ 67,500	$ 450,000
May 28–31	Oldsmobile Classic	Barb Mucha	276	$ 75,000	$ 500,000
June 4–7	McDonald's Championship	Ayako Okamoto	205	$ 112,500	$ 750,000
June 12–14	ShopRite LPGA Classic	Anne-Marie Palli	207	$ 60,000	$ 400,000
June 19–21	Lady Keystone Open	Danielle Ammaccapane	208	$ 60,000	$ 400,000
June 25–28	Rochester International	Patty Sheehan	269	$ 60,000	$ 400,000
July 3–5	Jamie Farr Toledo Classic	Patty Sheehan	209	$ 60,000	$ 400,000
July 10–12	Phar-Mor in Youngstown	Betsy King	209	$ 75,000	$ 500,000
July 16–19	JAL Big Apple Classic	Juli Inkster	273	$ 75,000	$ 500,000
July 23–26	U.S. Women's Open	Patty Sheehan	280	$ 130,000	$ 700,000
July 30–Aug. 2	Welch's Classic	Dottie Mochrie	278	$ 63,750	$ 425,000
Aug. 6–9	McCall's LPGA Classic at Stratton Mountain	Florence Descampe	278	$ 75,000	$ 500,000
Aug. 13–16	du Maurier Ltd. Classic	Sherri Steinhauer	277	$ 105,000	$ 700,000

LPGA TOUR (continued)

Date	Event	Winner	Score	1st Place Money	Total Purse
Aug. 21–23	Northgate Computer Classic	Kris Tschetter	211	$ 63,750	$ 425,000
Aug. 27–30	*Sun-Times* Classic	Dottie Mochrie	216	$ 67,500	$ 450,000
Sept. 5–7	Rail Charity Golf Classic	Nancy Lopez	199	$ 67,500	$ 450,000
Sept. 11–13	Ping–Cellular One LPGA Golf Championship	Nancy Lopez	209	$ 67,500	$ 450,000
Sept. 17–20	Safeco Classic	Colleen Walker	277	$ 67,500	$ 450,000
Sept. 24–27	Los Coyotes LPGA Classic	Nancy Scranton	279	$ 75,000	$ 500,000
Nov. 6–8	Mazda Japan Classic	Betsy King	205	$ 97,500	$ 650,000

a Amateur.

* Event decided on points system.

NA = Not available.

LPGA ALL-TIME RECORDS

Lowest score, 18 holes; 62, Mickey Wright, 1964, first round of Tall City Open, Hogan Park GC, Midland, Tex.; Vicki Fergon, 1984, second round of San Jose Classic, Almaden G&CC, San Jose, Cal.; Laura Davies, 1991, first round of Rail Charity Classic, Rail GC, Springfield, Ill.; Hollis Stacy, 1992, second round of Safeco Classic, Kent, Wash.

Lowest score, 36 holes: 129, Judy Dickinson (64-65), 1985 S&H Golf Classic, Pasadena Yacht & CC, St. Petersburg, Fla.

Lowest score, 54 holes: 197, Pat Bradley (67-65-65), 1991 Rail Charity Classic, Rail GC, Springfield, Ill.

Lowest score, 72 holes: 267, Betsy King (68-66-67-66), 1992 Mazda LPGA Championship, Bethesda CC, Bethesda, Md.

Most victories (official): Kathy Whitworth, 88; Mickey Wright, 82; Patty Berg, 57; Betsy Rawls, 55; Louise Suggs, 50.

Most consecutive years winning at least one tournament: 17, Kathy Whitworth (1962–1978).

Most consecutive victories: 5, Nancy Lopez, 1978.

Most victories in a year: 13, Mickey Wright, 1963.

Largest victory margin: 14 strokes, Louise Suggs, 1949 U.S. Women's Open; Cindy Mackey, 1986 MasterCard International Pro-Am.

Oldest winner: 46, JoAnne Carner, 1985 Safeco Classic.

Youngest winner: 18, Marlene Hagge, 1952 Sarasota Open.

SENIOR PGA TOUR

Date	Event	Winner	Score	1st Place Money	Total Purse
		1980 Tour			
Apr. 25–27	*Liberty Mutual Legends of Golf	Tommy Bolt and Art Wall	187	$ 35,000 each	$ 400,000
June 20–22	Atlantic City Sr. International	Don January	208	$ 20,000	$ 125,000
June 26–29	*U.S. Sr. Open	Roberto De Vicenzo	285	$ 20,000	$ 100,000
Sept. 26–28	*World Srs. Invitational	Gene Littler	211	$ 20,000	$ 150,000
Nov. 13–16	Suntree Sr. Classic	Charles Sifford	279	$ 20,000	$ 125,000
Dec. 4–7	*PGA Sr. Championship	Arnold Palmer	289	$ 20,000	$ 125,000
		1981 Tour			
Mar. 12–15	*Vintage Invitational	Gene Littler	271	$ 50,000	$ 300,000
Apr. 2–5	Michelob–Shrine Sr. Classic	Don January	280	$ 20,000	$ 125,000
Arp. 24–26	*Liberty Mutual Legends of Golf	Gene Littler and Bob Rosburg	257	$ 35,000 each	$ 410,000
June 5–7	Eureka Federal Savings Classic	Don January	208	$ 25,000	$ 150,000
June 12–14	Peter Jackson Champions	Miller Barber	204	$ 20,000	$ 125,000
June 26–28	Marlboro Classic	Bob Goalby	208	$ 25,000	$ 150,000
July 10–13	U.S. Sr. Open	Arnold Palmer	289	$ 26,000	$ 150,000
Sept. 17–20	*World Srs. Invitational	Miller Barber	282	$ 23,000	$ 125,000
Sept. 24–27	*Merrill Lynch–*Golf Digest* Commemorative	Doug Ford	208	$ 20,000	$ 100,000
Oct. 16–18	Suntree Classic	Miller Barber	204	$ 20,000	$ 125,000
Dec. 3–6	PGA Srs. Championship	Miller Barber	281	$ 20,000	$ 125,000
		1982 Tour			
Mar. 11–14	*Vintage Invitational	Miller Barber	282	$ 40,000	$ 300,000
Apr. 23–25	*Liberty Mutual Legends of Golf	Sam Snead and Don January	183	$ 50,000 each	$ 450,000
Apr. 1–4	Michelob Srs. Classic	Don January	278	$ 20,000	$ 125,000
June 10–13	Marlboro Classic	Arnold Palmer	276	$ 25,000	$ 150,000
June 24–27	Peter Jackson Champions	Bob Goalby	273	$ 31,500	$ 200,000
July 8–11	U.S. Sr. Open	Miller Barber	282	$ 28,648	$ 150,000
Aug. 12–15	*Denver Post* Champions of Golf	Arnold Palmer	275	$ 25,000	$ 150,000
Aug. 19–22	Greater Syracuse Srs.	Bill Collins	285	$ 25,000	$ 150,000
Aug. 25–28	Jeremy Ranch Srs.	Billy Casper	279	$ 25,000	$ 150,000
Sept. 17–19	Merrill Lynch–*Golf Digest* Commemorative	Billy Casper	206	$ 22,500	$ 125,000
Oct. 14–17	Suntree Classic	Miller Barber	264	$ 22,500	$ 135,000
Oct. 21–22	Hilton Head Srs. International	Miller Barber and Dan Sikes	138**	$ 15,000 each	$ 112,000
Dec. 3–6	PGA Srs. Championship	Don January	288	$ 25,000	$ 150,000
		1983 Tour			
Feb. 24–27	*Vintage Invitational	Gene Littler	280	$ 35,000	$ 300,000
Mar. 18–20	Daytona Beach Srs. Classic	Gene Littler	203	$ 25,000	$ 150,000
Apr. 22–24	*Doug Sanders Pro-Celebrity	Roberto De Vicenzo	140	$ 25,000	$ 140,000
Apr. 28–May 1	*Liberty Mutual Legends of Golf	Roberto De Vicenzo and Rod Funseth	258	$ 50,000 each	$ 475,000

SENIOR PGA TOUR (continued)

Date	Event	Winner	Score	1st Place Money	Total Purse
May 20–22	Hall of Fame Srs.	Rod Funseth	198	$ 25,000	$ 150,000
June 3–5	Gatlin Bros. Classic	Don January	208	$ 33,500	$ 225,000
June 9–12	Sr. Tournament Players Championship	Miller Barber	278	$ 40,000	$ 250,000
June 23–26	Peter Jackson Champions	Don January	274	$ 33,250	$ 200,000
June 30–July 2	Marlboro Classic	Don January	273	$ 25,000	$ 150,000
July 7–10	Greater Syracuse Srs. Classic	Gene Littler	275	$ 25,000	$ 150,000
July 15–17	Merrill Lynch–*Golf Digest* Commemorative	Miller Barber	200	$ 25,000	$ 150,000
July 21–24	U.S. Sr. Open	Billy Casper	288	$ 30,566	$ 175,000
Aug. 18–21	*Denver Post* Champions	Don January	217	$ 25,000	$ 150,000
Aug. 25–28	Shootout at Jeremy Ranch	Bob Goalby and Mike Reid	256	$ 25,000 each	$ 380,000
Sept. 1–4	Citizens Union Sr. Classic	Don January	269	$ 25,000	$ 150,000
Sept. 22–25	World Sr. Invitational	Doug Sanders	283	$ 25,000	$ 150,000
Sept. 30–Oct. 2	United Virginia Bank Srs.	Miller Barber	211	$ 25,000	$ 150,000
Oct. 13–16	Suntree Classic	Don January	274	$ 25,000	$ 135,000
Oct. 20–23	Hilton Head Srs. International	Miller Barber	281	$ 25,000	$ 150,000
Dec. 1–4	Boca Grove Srs. Classic	Arnold Palmer	271	$ 25,000	$ 150,000

1984 Tour

Date	Event	Winner	Score	1st Place Money	Total Purse
Jan. 5–8	Seiko–Tucson Sr. Match Play Championship	Gene Littler	2 up	$ 100,000	$ 306,000
Jan. 19–22	PGA Srs. Championship	Arnold Palmer	282	$ 35,000	$ 200,000
Jan. 27–29	*Viceroy Sr. Panama Open	Orville Moody	207	$ 20,000	$ 130,000
Mar. 22–25	Vintage Invitational	Don January	280	$ 50,000	$ 300,000
Apr. 6–8	Daytona Beach Srs. Classic	Orville Moody	213	$ 22,500	$ 150,000
Apr. 20–22	Sr. PGA Tour Roundup	Billy Casper	202	$ 30,000	$ 200,000
Apr. 26–29	*Liberty Mutual Legends of Golf	Gay Brewer and Billy Casper	258	$ 50,000 each	$ 500,000
May 3–6	MONY Tournament of Champions	Orville Moody	288	$ 30,000	$ 250,000
May 18–20	Doug Sanders Celebrity Classic	Arnold Palmer and Miller Barber**	134	$ 21,500 each	$ 150,000
June 1–3	Gatlin Bros. Sr. Classic	Dan Sikes	210	$ 33,750	$ 250,000
June 15–17	Roy Clark Sr. Challenge	Miller Barber	212	$ 30,000	$ 200,000
June 21–24	Sr. Tournament Players Championship	Arnold Palmer	276	$ 36,000	$ 250,000
June 28–July 1	U.S. Sr. Open	Miller Barber	286	$ 36,448	$ 200,000
July 6–8	Greater Syracuse Srs. Classic	Miller Barber	206	$ 30,000	$ 200,000
July 13–15	Merrill Lynch–*Golf Digest* Commemorative	Roberto De Vicenzo	206	$ 22,500	$ 150,000
July 27–29	*Denver Post* Champions	Miller Barber	208	$ 30,000	$ 200,000
Aug. 10–12	du Maurier Champions	Don January	194	$ 33,750	$ 200,000
Aug. 23–26	Shootout at Jeremy Ranch	Don January and Mike Sullivan	250	$ 30,000 each	$ 400,000
Sept. 1–3	Citizens Union Sr. Classic	Gay Brewer	204	$ 26,050	$ 175,000
Sept. 7–9	United Virginia Bank Srs.	Dan Sikes	207	$ 30,000	$ 200,000
Sept. 13–16	World Srs. Invitational	Peter Thomson	281	$ 25,000	$ 150,000
Sept. 21–23	Digital Middlesex Classic	Don January	209	$ 26,000	$ 175,000

SENIOR PGA TOUR (continued)

Date	Event	Winner	Score	1st Place Money	Total Purse
Sept. 27–30	*Coca-Cola Grand Slam	Lee Elder	281	$ 50,000	$ 320,000
Oct. 3–7	*Unionmutual Srs. Classic	Rod Funseth	2 up	$ 30,000	$ 125,000
Oct. 12–14	Suntree Sr. Classic	Lee Elder	200	$ 22,500	$ 150,000
Oct. 19–21	Hilton Head Srs. International	Lee Elder	203	$ 30,000	$ 200,000
Nov. 30–Dec. 2	Quadel Srs. Classic	Arnold Palmer	205	$ 30,060	$ 200,000
Dec. 6–9	PGA Srs. Championship	Peter Thomson	286	$ 40,000	$ 225,000
	1985 Tour				
Feb. 7–10	Sunrise Sr. Classic	Miller Barber	211	$ 30,000	$ 200,000
Mar. 14–17	Vintage Invitational	Peter Thomson	280	$ 40,000	$ 300,000
Mar. 22–24	Sr. PGA Tour Roundup	Don January	198	$ 30,000	$ 200,000
Mar. 29–31	Carta Blanca–Johnny Mathis Classic	Peter Thomson	205	$ 37,500	$ 250,000
Apr. 25–28	Liberty Mutual Legends of Golf	Don January and Gene Littler	257	$ 50,000 each	$ 500,000
May 2–5	MONY Tournament of Champions	Peter Thomson	284	$ 30,000	$ 100,000
May 10–12	Dominion Srs.	Don January	206	$ 30,000	$ 200,000
May 17–19	United Hospitals Sr. Championship	Don January	135	$ 30,000	$ 200,000
May 30–June 2	*Denver Post* Champions of Golf	Lee Elder	213	$ 30,000	$ 200,000
June 7–9	Champions Classic	Peter Thomson	210	$ 30,000	$ 200,000
June 14–16	Sr. Players Reunion	Peter Thomson	202	$ 26,000	$ 175,000
June 20–23	Sr. Tournament Players Championship	Arnold Palmer	274	$ 36,000	$ 300,000
June 27–30	U.S. Sr. Open	Miller Barber	285	$ 40,199	$ 225,000
July 4–6	Greenbrier–American Express Championship	Don January	200	$ 30,000	$ 200,000
July 19–21	Greater Syracuse Srs. Classic	Peter Thomson	204	$ 30,000	$ 200,000
July 26–28	Merrill Lynch–*Golf Digest* Commemorative	Lee Elder	133	$ 27,000	$ 175,000
Aug. 2–4	Digital Srs. Classic	Lee Elder	208	$ 30,000	$ 200,000
Aug. 16–18	du Maurier Champions	Peter Thomson	203	$ 23,794	$ 225,000
Aug. 22–25	Shootout at Jeremy Ranch	Miller Barber and Ben Crenshaw	257	$ 30,000	$ 400,000
Aug. 30–Sept. 1	United Virginia Bank Srs.	Peter Thomson	207	$ 37,500	$ 250,000
Sept. 19–22	PaineWebber World Srs. Invitational	Miller Barber	277	$ 30,000	$ 200,000
Oct. 10–13	Hilton Head Srs. International	Mike Fetchick	210	$ 30,000	$ 200,000
Oct. 18–20	Barnett Suntree Classic	Peter Thomson	207	$ 24,750	$ 165,000
Oct. 24–27	Seiko–Tucson Sr. Match Play	Harold Henning	4&3	$ 75,000	$ 300,000
Nov. 22–24	Quadel Srs. Classic	Gary Player	205	$ 30,000	$ 200,000
Dec. 20–21	Mazda Champions	Don January and Alice Miller	127	$ 250,000 each	$ 730,000
	1986 Tour				
Jan. 8–11	MONY Sr. Tournament of Champions	Miller Barber	282	$ 30,000	$ 100,000
Feb. 7–9	Treasure Coast Classic	Charles Owens	202	$ 33,750	$ 225,000

SENIOR PGA TOUR (continued)

Date	Event	Winner	Score	1st Place Money	Total Purse
Feb. 13–16	General Foods Sr. PGA Championship	Gary Player	281	$ 45,000	$ 250,000
Mar. 14–16	Sr. PGA Tour Roundup	Charles Owens	202	$ 30,000	$ 200,000
Mar. 20–23	Vintage Invitational	Dale Douglass	272	$ 40,500	$ 300,000
Mar. 28–30	Johnny Mathis Srs. Classic	Dale Douglass	202	$ 37,500	$ 250,000
Apr. 24–27	Liberty Mutual Legends of Golf	Gene Littler and Don January	255	$ 50,000 each	$ 500,000
May 2–4	Sunwest Bank–Charley Pride Sr. Classic	Gene Littler	202	$ 37,500	$ 250,000
May 9–11	Benson & Hedges Invitational at The Dominion	Bruce Crampton	202	$ 37,500	$ 250,000
May 16–18	United Hospitals Sr. Championship	Gary Player	206	$ 30,000	$ 200,000
May 30–June 1	*Denver Post* Champions	Gary Player	208	$ 37,500	$ 250,000
June 6–8	Sr. Players Reunion	Don January	203	$ 26,250	$ 175,000
June 19–22	Sr. Tournament Players Championship	Chi Chi Rodriguez	206	$ 45,000	$ 300,000
June 26–29	U.S. Sr. Open	Dale Douglass	279	$ 42,500	$ 275,000
July 11–13	Greenbrier–American Express Championship	Don January	207	$ 30,000	$ 200,000
July 18–20	Greater Grand Rapids Open	Jim Ferree	204	$ 37,500	$ 250,000
July 25–27	MONY Syracuse Srs. Classic	Bruce Crampton	206	$ 30,000	$ 200,000
Aug. 1–3	Merrill Lynch–*Golf Digest* Commemorative	Lee Elder	199	$ 37,500	$ 250,000
Aug. 8–10	Digital Srs. Classic	Chi Chi Rodriguez	203	$ 30,000	$ 200,000
Aug. 15–17	GTE Northwest Classic	Bruce Crampton	210	$ 37,500	$ 250,000
Aug. 21–24	Showdown Classic	Bobby Nichols and Curt Byrum	249	$ 33,750 each	$ 450,000
Aug. 29–31	Bank One Sr. Classic	Gene Littler	201	$ 30,000	$ 200,000
Sept. 12–14	United Virginia Bank Srs.	Chi Chi Rodriguez	202	$ 45,000	$ 300,000
Sept. 18–21	PaineWebber World Srs. Invitational	Bruce Crampton	279	$ 30,021	$ 20,000
Oct. 10–12	Fairfield Barnett Classic	Dale Douglass	203	$ 26,250	$ 175,000
Oct. 17–19	Cuyahoga Srs. International	Butch Baird	210	$ 30,000	$ 200,000
Oct. 24–26	Pepsi Sr. Challenge	Bruce Crampton	136	$ 37,500	$ 250,000
Oct. 30–Nov. 2	Seiko–Tucson Sr. Match Play Championship	Don January	70	$ 75,000	$ 300,000
Nov. 7–9	Las Vegas Sr. Classic	Bruce Crampton	206	$ 37,500	$ 250,000
Nov. 21–23	Shearson-Lehman Brothers Srs. Classic	Bruce Crampton	200	$ 30,000	$ 200,000
Dec. 19–21	Mazda Champions	Bob Charles and Amy Alcott	193	$ 250,000 each	$ 720,000

1987 Tour

Date	Event	Winner	Score	1st Place Money	Total Purse
Jan. 7–10	MONY Sr. Tournament of Champions	Don January	287	$ 30,000	$ 200,000
Feb. 11–15	General Foods Sr. PGA Championship	Chi Chi Rodriguez	282	$ 47,000	$ 260,000
Mar. 13–15	Del E. Webb Arizona Classic	Billy Casper	201	$ 30,000	$ 200,000
Mar. 19–22	Vintage Chrysler Invitational	Bob Charles	285	$ 40,500	$ 270,000
Mar. 26–29	GTE Classic	Bob Charles	208	$ 41,250	$ 275,000

SENIOR PGA TOUR (continued)

Date	Event	Winner	Score	1st Place Money	Total Purse
Apr. 23–26	Liberty Mutual Legends of Golf	Orville Moody and Bruce Crampton	251	$ 60,000 each	$ 600,000
May 1–3	Sunwest Bank–Charley Pride Sr. Classic	Bob Charles	208	$ 37,500	$ 250,000
May 8–10	Vantage at The Dominion	Chi Chi Rodriguez	203	$ 37,500	$ 250,000
May 15–17	United Hospitals Sr. Championship	Chi Chi Rodriguez	202	$ 33,750	$ 225,000
May 22–24	Silver Pages Classic	Chi Chi Rodriguez	200	$ 37,500	$ 250,000
May 29–31	Denver Champions	Bruce Crampton	204	$ 37,500	$ 250,000
June 5–7	Sr. Players Reunion	Chi Chi Rodriguez	201	$ 30,093	$ 200,000
June 11–14	Mazda Sr. Tournament Players Championship	Gary Player	280	$ 60,000	$ 400,000
June 26–28	Greater Grand Rapids Open	Billy Casper	200	$ 37,500	$ 250,000
July 3–5	Greenbrier–American Express Championship	Bruce Crampton	200	$ 33,750	$ 225,000
July 9–12	U.S. Sr. Open	Gary Player	270	$ 47,000	$ 300,000
July 17–19	MONY Syracuse Sr. Classic	Bruce Crampton	197	$ 37,500	$ 250,000
July 31–Aug. 2	NYNEX–*Golf Digest* Commemorative	Gene Littler	200	$ 37,500	$ 250,000
Aug. 6–9	Digital Srs. Classic	Chi Chi Rodriguez	198	$ 37,500	$ 250,000
Aug. 14–16	Rancho Murieta Sr. Gold Rush	Orville Moody	205	$ 45,000	$ 300,000
Aug. 21–23	GTE Northwest Classic	Chi Chi Rodriguez	206	$ 45,000	$ 300,000
Aug. 28–30	Showdown Classic	Miller Barber	210	$ 45,000	$ 300,000
Sept. 4–6	Vantage Presents Bank One Sr. Classic	Bruce Crampton	197	$ 33,750	$ 225,000
Sept. 11–13	PaineWebber World Srs. Invitational	Gary Player	207	$ 37,500	$ 250,000
Sept. 18–20	Crestar Classic	Larry Mowry	203	$ 48,750	$ 325,000
Sept. 25–27	Newport Cup	Miller Barber	202	$ 30,000	$ 200,000
Oct. 1–4	Vantage Championship	Al Geiberger	206	$ 135,000	$1,000,000
Oct. 9–11	Pepsi Sr. Challenge	Larry Mowry	203	$ 37,500	$ 250,000
Oct. 16–18	Hilton Head Srs. International	Al Geiberger	209	$ 37,500	$ 250,000
Oct. 23–25	Las Vegas Sr. Classic	Al Geiberger	203	$ 37,500	$ 250,000
Nov. 13–15	Fairfield Barnett St. Classic	Dave Hill	202	$ 30,000	$ 200,000
Nov. 20–22	Gus Machado Sr. Classic	Gene Littler	207	$ 45,000	$ 300,000
Dec. 11–13	GTE Kaanapali Sr. Classic	Orville Moody	132	$ 45,000	$ 300,000
Dec. 18–20	Mazda Champions	Miller Barber and Nancy Lopez	191	$ 250,000 each	$ 850,000

1988 Tour

Date	Event	Winner	Score	1st Place Money	Total Purse
Jan. 14–17	MONY Sr. Tournament of Champions	Dave Hill	211	$ 30,000	$ 100,000
Feb. 11–14	General Foods PGA Srs. Championship	Gary Player	284	$ 63,000	$ 350,000
Feb. 19–21	GTE Suncoast Sr. Classic	Dale Douglass	210	$ 45,000	$ 300,000
Feb. 26–28	Aetna Challenge	Gary Player	207	$ 45,000	$ 300,000
Mar. 3–6	Vintage Chrysler Invitational	Orville Moody	263	$ 48,000	$ 320,000
Mar. 11–13	GTE Classic	Harold Henning	214	$ 41,250	$ 275,000
Mar. 18–20	The Pointe/Del E. Webb Arizona Classic	Al Geiberger	199	$ 33,750	$ 225,000

SENIOR PGA TOUR (continued)

Date	Event	Winner	Score	1st Place Money	Total Purse
Apr. 14–17	Doug Sanders Kingwood Classic	Chi Chi Rodriguez	208	$ 37,500	$ 250,000
Apr. 28–May 1	Liberty Mutual Legends of Golf	Bruce Crampton and Orville Moody	254	$ 60,000	$ 650,000
May 6–8	Vantage at The Dominion	Billy Casper	205	$ 37,500	$ 250,000
May 13–15	United Hospitals Classic	Bruce Crampton	205	$ 33,750	$ 225,000
May 20–22	NYNEX–*Golf Digest* Commemorative	Bob Charles	196	$ 45,000	$ 300,000
May 27–29	Sunwest Bank–Charley Pride Sr. Classic	Bob Charles	206	$ 41,250	$ 275,000
June 3–5	Sr. Players Reunion	Orville Moody	206	$ 37,500	$ 250,000
June 9–12	Mazda Sr. Tournament Players Championship	Billy Casper	278	$ 60,000	$ 400,000
June 16–19	Northville Invitational	Don Bies	202	$ 52,500	$ 350,000
June 24–26	Southwestern Bell Classic	Gary Player	203	$ 37,500	$ 250,000
July 2–4	Rancho Murieta Sr. Gold Rush	Bob Charles	207	$ 52,500	$ 350,000
July 8–10	GTE Northwest Classic	Bruce Crampton	207	$ 45,000	$ 300,000
July 15–17	Showdown Classic	Miller Barber	207	$ 52,500	$ 350,000
July 22–24	Newport Cup	Walter Zembriski	132	$ 37,500	$ 250,000
July 29–31	Digital Srs. Classic	Chi Chi Rodriguez	202	$ 45,000	$ 300,000
Aug. 4–7	U.S. Sr. Open	Gary Player	288	$ 65,000	$ 325,000
Aug. 10–14	MONY Syracuse Srs. Classic	Dave Hill	200	$ 37,500	$ 250,000
Aug. 19–21	Greater Grand Rapids Open	Orville Moody	203	$ 37,500	$ 250,000
Aug. 26–28	Bank One Sr. Classic	Bob Charles	200	$ 37,500	$ 250,000
Sept. 9–11	GTE North Classic	Gary Player	201	$ 52,500	$ 350,000
Sept. 16–18	Crestar Classic	Arnold Palmer	203	$ 48,750	$ 325,000
Sept. 23–25	PaineWebber World Srs. Invitational	Dave Hill	206	$ 45,000	$ 300,000
Sept. 28–Oct. 2	Pepsi Sr. Challenge	Bob Charles	139	$ 45,000	$ 300,000
Oct. 6–9	Vantage Championship	Walter Zembriski	278	$ 135,000	$1,000,000
Oct. 28–30	General Tire Classic	Larry Mowry	204	$ 37,500	$ 250,000
Nov. 10–13	Fairfield Barnett Sr. Classic	Miller Barber	197	$ 33,750	$ 225,000
Nov. 18–20	Gus Machado Sr. Classic	Lee Elder	202	$ 45,000	$ 300,000
Dec. 1–4	GTE Kaanapali Classic	Don Bies	204	$ 45,000	$ 300,000
Dec. 16–18	Mazda Champions	Dave Hill and Colleen Walker	186	$ 250,000	$ 850,000

1989 Tour

Date	Event	Winner	Score	1st Place Money	Total Purse
Jan. 5–8	MONY Sr. Tournament of Champions	Miller Barber	280	$ 50,000	$ 250,000
Feb. 9–12	General Foods PGA Srs. Championship	Larry Mowry	281	$ 72,000	$ 400,000
Feb. 17–19	GTE Suncoast Classic	Bob Charles	207	$ 45,000	$ 300,000
Feb. 24–26	Aetna Challenge	Gene Littler	209	$ 45,000	$ 300,000
Mar. 2–5	Vintage Chrysler Invitational	Miller Barber	281	$ 55,500	$ 370,000
Mar. 10–12	MONY Arizona Classic	Bruce Crampton	200	$ 45,000	$ 300,000
Mar. 31–Apr. 2	Murata Srs. Reunion	Don Bies	208	$ 45,000	$ 300,000
Apr. 13–16	Tradition at Desert Mountain	Don Bies	275	$ 90,000	$ 600,000
Apr. 27–30	Liberty Mutual Legends of Golf	Al Geiberger and Harold Henning	251	$ 60,000 each	$ 650,000

SENIOR PGA TOUR (continued)

Date	Event	Winner	Score	1st Place Money	Total Purse
May 5–7	RJR at The Dominion	Larry Mowry	201	$ 37,500	$ 250,000
May 12–14	Bell Atlantic–St. Christopher's Classic	Dave Hill	206	$ 60,000	$ 400,000
May 19–21	NYNEX–*Golf Digest* Commemorative	Bob Charles	193	$ 45,000	$ 300,000
May 26–28	Southwestern Bell Classic	Bobby Nichols	209	$ 45,000	$ 300,000
June 2–4	Doug Sanders Kingwood Celebrity Classic	Homero Blancas	208	$ 45,000	$ 300,000
June 8–11	Mazda Sr. Tournament Players Championship	Orville Moody	271	$ 105,000	$ 700,000
June 16–18	Northville Long Island Classic	Butch Baird	183	$ 52,500	$ 350,000
June 23–25	MONY Syracuse Sr. Classic	Jim Dent	201	$ 45,000	$ 300,000
June 29–July 2	U.S. Sr. Open	Orville Moody	279	$ 80,000	$ 450,000
July 7–9	Digital Srs. Classic	Bob Charles	200	$ 45,000	$ 300,000
July 14–16	Greater Grand Rapids Open	John Paul Cain	203	$ 45,000	$ 300,000
July 21–23	Ameritech Sr. Open	Bruce Crampton	205	$ 75,000	$ 500,000
July 28–30	Newport Cup	Jim Dent	206	$ 41,500	$ 275,000
Aug. 4–6	Showdown Classic	Tom Shaw	207	$ 52,500	$ 350,000
Aug. 11–13	Rancho Murieta Sr. Gold Rush	Dave Hill	207	$ 52,500	$ 350,000
Aug. 18–20	GTE Northwest Classic	Al Geiberger	204	$ 52,500	$ 350,000
Aug. 25–27	Sunwest Bank–Charley Pride Sr. Golf Classic	Bob Charles	203	$ 45,000	$ 300,000
Sept. 1–3	RJR Bank One Classic	Rives McBee	202	$ 45,000	$ 300,000
Sept. 8–10	GTE North Classic	Gary Player	135	$ 52,500	$ 350,000
Sept. 15–17	Crestar Classic	Chi Chi Rodriguez	203	$ 52,500	$ 350,000
Sept. 29–Oct. 1	Fairfield-Barnett Space Coast Classic	Bob Charles	203	$ 45,000	$ 300,000
Oct. 6–8	RJR Championship	Gary Player	207	$ 202,500	$1,500,000
Oct. 13–15	Gatlin Brothers Southwest Classic	George Archer	209	$ 45,000	$ 300,000
Oct. 20–22	TransAmerica Sr. Golf Championship	Billy Casper	207	$ 60,000	$ 400,000
Nov. 10–12	General Tire Las Vegas Classic	Charles Coody	205	$ 45,000	$ 300,000
Nov. 30–Dec. 2	GTE West Classic	Walter Zembriski	197	$ 52,500	$ 350,000
Dec. 7–9	GTE Kaanapali Classic	Don Bies	132	$ 45,000	$ 300,000
Dec. 15–17	Mazda Champions	Mike Hill and Patti Rizzo	191	$ 250,000 each	$ 900,000

1990 Tour

Date	Event	Winner	Score	1st Place Money	Total Purse
Jan. 4–7	MONY Sr. Tournament of Champions	George Archer	283	$ 37,500	$ 250,000
Feb. 2–4	Royal Caribbean Classic	Lee Trevino	206	$ 60,000	$ 400,000
Feb. 9–11	GTE Suncoast Classic	Mike Hill	207	$ 67,500	$ 450,000
Feb. 16–18	Aetna Challenge	Lee Trevino	200	$ 60,000	$ 400,000
Mar. 2–4	Vintage Chrysler Invitational	Lee Trevino	205	$ 60,000	$ 400,000
Mar. 16–18	Vantage at The Dominion	Jim Dent	205	$ 45,000	$ 300,000
Mar. 29–Apr. 1	Tradition at Desert Mountain	Jack Nicklaus	206	$ 120,000	$ 800,000
Apr. 12–15	PGA Srs. Championship	Gary Player	281	$ 75,000	$ 450,000
Apr. 19–22	Liberty Mutual Legends of Golf	Dale Douglass and Charles Coody	249	$ 70,000 each	$ 750,000

SENIOR PGA TOUR (continued)

Date	Event	Winner	Score	1st Place Money	Total Purse
Apr. 27–29	Murata Reunion Pro-Am	Frank Beard	207	$ 60,000	$ 400,000
May 4–6	Las Vegas Sr. Classic	Chi Chi Rodriguez	204	$ 67,500	$ 450,000
May 11–13	Southwestern Bell Classic	Jimmy Powell	208	$ 67,500	$ 450,000
May 18–20	Doug Sanders Kingwood	Lee Trevino	203	$ 45,000	$ 300,000
May 25–27	Bell Atlantic Classic	Dale Douglass	206	$ 75,000	$ 500,000
June 1–3	NYNEX Commemorative	Lee Trevino	199	$ 52,500	$ 350,000
June 7–10	Mazda Sr. TPC	Jack Nicklaus	261	$ 150,000	$1,000,000
June 15–17	MONY Syracuse Sr. Classic	Jim Dent	199	$ 60,000	$ 400,000
June 22–24	Digital Srs. Classic	Bob Charles	203	$ 52,500	$ 350,000
July 6–8	Northville Long Island Classic	George Archer	208	$ 67,500	$ 450,000
July 13–15	Kroger Sr. Classic	Jim Dent	133	$ 90,000	$ 600,000
July 20–22	Ameritech Sr. Open	Chi Chi Rodriguez	203	$ 75,000	$ 500,000
July 27–29	Newport Cup	Al Kelley	134	$ 45,000	$ 300,000
Aug. 3–5	PaineWebber Invitational	Bruce Crampton	205	$ 67,500	$ 450,000
Aug. 10–12	Sunwest Bank–Charley Pride Sr. Golf Classic	Chi Chi Rodriguez	205	$ 52,500	$ 350,000
Aug. 17–19	Showdown Championship	Rives McBee	202	$ 52,500	$ 350,000
Aug. 24–26	GTE Northwest Classic	George Archer	205	$ 52,500	$ 350,000
Aug. 31–Sept. 2	GTE North Classic	Mike Hall	201	$ 67,500	$ 450,000
Sept. 7–9	Vantage Bank One Classic	Rives McBee	201	$ 45,000	$ 300,000
Sept. 14–16	Greater Grand Rapids Open	Don Massengale	134	$ 45,000	$ 300,000
Sept. 21–23	Crestar Classic	Jim Dent	202	$ 52,500	$ 350,000
Sept. 28–30	Fairfield Barnett Space Coast Classic	Mike Hill	200	$ 45,000	$ 300,000
Oct. 5–7	Vantage Championship	Charles Coody	202	$ 202,500	$1,500,000
Oct. 12–14	Gatlin Brothers Southwest Classic	Bruce Crampton	204	$ 45,000	$ 300,000
Oct. 19–21	TransAmerica Sr. Golf Championship	Lee Trevino	205	$ 75,000	$ 500,000
Oct. 26–28	Gold Rush at Rancho Murieta	George Archer	204	$ 60,000	$ 400,000
Nov. 2–4	Security Pacific Sr. Classic	Mike Hill	201	$ 75,000	$ 500,000
Dec. 7–9	GTE Kaanapali Classic	Bob Charles	206	$ 67,500	$ 450,000
Dec. 14–16	New York Life Champions	Mike Hill	201	$ 150,000	$1,000,000
	1991 Tour				
Jan. 3–6	Infiniti Sr. Tournament of Champions	Bruce Crampton	279	$ 80,000	$ 350,000
Feb. 1–3	Royal Caribbean Classic	Gary Player	200	$ 67,500	$ 450,000
Feb. 8–10	GTE Suncoast Classic	Bob Charles	210	$ 67,500	$ 450,000
Feb. 15–17	Aetna Challenge	Lee Trevino	205	$ 67,500	$ 450,000
Mar. 1–3	GTE West Classic	Chi Chi Rodriguez	132	$ 67,500	$ 450,000
Mar. 15–17	Vantage at The Dominion	Lee Trevino	137	$ 52,500	$ 350,000
Mar. 22–24	Vintage ARCO Invitational	Chi Chi Rodriguez	206	$ 75,000	$ 500,000
Apr. 4–7	Tradition at Desert Mountain	Jack Nicklaus	277	$ 120,000	$ 800,000
Apr. 18–21	PGA Srs. Championship	Jack Nicklaus	271	$ 85,000	$ 500,000
Apr. 26–28	Doug Sanders Kingwood Celebrity Classic	Mike Hill	203	$ 45,000	$ 300,000
May 3–5	Las Vegas Sr. Classic	Chi Chi Rodriguez	204	$ 67,500	$ 450,000
May 10–12	Murata Reunion Pro-Am	Chi Chi Rodriguez	208	$ 60,000	$ 400,000

SENIOR PGA TOUR (continued)

Date	Event	Winner	Score	1st Place Money	Total Purse
May 16–19	Liberty Mutual Legends of Golf	Lee Trevino and Mike Hill	252	$ 70,000 each	$ 750,000
May 24–26	Bell Atlantic Classic	Jim Ferree	208	$ 82,500	$ 550,000
May 31–June 2	NYNEX Commemorative	Charles Coody	193	$ 60,000	$ 400,000
June 6–9	Mazda Presents Sr. Players Championship	Jim Albus	279	$ 150,000	$1,000,000
June 14–16	MONY Syracuse Sr. Classic	Rocky Thompson	199	$ 60,000	$ 400,000
June 21–23	PaineWebber Invitational	Orville Moody	217	$ 67,500	$ 450,000
June 28–30	Southwestern Bell Classic	Jim Colbert	201	$ 67,500	$ 450,000
July 5–7	Kroger Sr. Classic	Al Geiberger	203	$ 90,000	$ 600,000
July 12–14	Newport Cup	Larry Ziegler	199	$ 48,750	$ 325,000
July 19–21	Ameritech Sr. Open	Mike Hill	200	$ 75,000	$ 500,000
July 25–28	U.S. Sr. Open	Jack Nicklaus	282	$ 100,000	$ 600,000
Aug. 2–4	Northville Long Island Classic	George Archer	204	$ 67,500	$ 450,000
Aug. 9–11	Showdown Classic	Dale Douglass	209	$ 52,500	$ 350,000
Aug. 16–18	GTE Northwest Classic	Mike Hill	200	$ 60,000	$ 400,000
Aug. 23–25	Sunwest Bank–Charley Pride Sr. Classic	Lee Trevino	200	$ 52,500	$ 350,000
Aug. 30–Sept. 1	GTE North Classic	George Archer	199	$ 67,500	$ 450,000
Sept. 6–8	First of America Classic	Harold Henning	202	$ 52,500	$ 350,000
Sept. 13–15	Digital Srs. Classic	Rocky Thompson	205	$ 60,000	$ 400,000
Sept. 20–22	Nationwide Championship	Mike Hill	212	$ 105,000	$ 700,000
Sept. 27–29	Bank One Classic	DeWitt Weaver	207	$ 45,000	$ 300,000
Oct. 4–6	Vantage Championship	Jim Colbert	205	$ 202,500	$1,500,000
Oct. 11–13	Raley's Sr. Gold Rush	George Archer	206	$ 67,500	$ 450,000
Oct. 18–20	TransAmerica Sr. Championship	Charles Coody	204	$ 75,000	$ 500,000
Oct. 25–27	Security Pacific Sr. Classic	John Brodie	200	$ 75,000	$ 500,000
Dec. 6–8	First Development– Kaanapali Classic	Jim Colbert	195	$ 90,000	$ 600,000
Dec. 13–15	New York Life Champions	Mike Hill	202	$ 150,000	$1,000,000

1992 Tour

Date	Event	Winner	Score	1st Place Money	Total Purse
Jan. 9–12	Infiniti Sr. Tournament of Champions	Al Geiberger	282	$ 52,500	$ 350,000
Jan. 31–Feb. 2	Royal Caribbean	Don Massengale	205	$ 75,000	$ 500,000
Feb. 6–9	Aetna Challenge	Jimmy Powell	197	$ 67,500	$ 450,000
Feb. 14–16	GTE Suncoast Classic	Jim Colbert	200	$ 67,500	$ 450,000
Mar. 6–8	GTE West Classic	Bruce Crampton	195	$ 67,500	$ 450,000
Mar. 13–15	Vantage at The Dominion	Lee Trevino	201	$ 60,000	$ 400,000
Mar. 20–22	Vintage ARCO Invitational	Mike Hill	203	$ 75,000	$ 500,000
Apr. 2–5	Tradition at Desert Mountain	Lee Trevino	274	$ 120,000	$ 800,000
Apr. 16–19	PGA Srs. Championship	Lee Trevino	278	$ 100,000	$ 700,000
Apr. 23–26	Liberty Mutual Legends of Golf	Lee Trevino and Mike Hill	251	$ 140,000	$ 750,000
May 1–3	Las Vegas Sr. Classic	Lee Trevino	206	$ 67,500	$ 450,000
May 8–10	Murata Reunion Pro-Am	George Archer	211	$ 60,000	$ 400,000
May 15–17	Doug Sanders Kingwood Celebrity Classic	Mike Hill	134	$ 52,500	$ 350,000

SENIOR PGA TOUR (continued)

Date	Event	Winner	Score	1st Place Money	Total Purse
May 22–24	Bell Atlantic Classic	Lee Trevino	205	$ 82,500	$ 550,000
May 29–31	NYNEX Commemorative	Dale Douglass	133	$ 60,000	$ 400,000
June 5–7	PaineWebber Invitational	Don Bies	203	$ 67,500	$ 450,000
June 11–14	Mazda Presents Sr. Players Championship	Dave Stockton	277	$ 150,000	$1,000,000
June 26–28	Southwestern Bell Classic	Gibby Gilbert	193	$ 67,500	$ 450,000
July 3–5	Kroger Sr. Classic	Gibby Gilbert	198	$ 90,000	$ 600,000
July 9–12	U.S. Sr. Open	Larry Laoretti	275	$ 130,000	$ 700,000
July 17–19	Ameritech Sr. Open	Dale Douglas	201	$ 75,000	$ 500,000
July 24–26	Newport Cup	Jim Dent	204	$ 60,000	$ 400,000
July 31–Aug. 2	Northville Long Island Classic	George Archer	205	$ 67,500	$ 450,000
Aug. 7–9	Digital Srs. Classic	Mike Hill	136	$ 75,000	$ 500,000
Aug. 14–16	Bruno's Memorial Classic	George Archer	208	$ 105,000	$ 700,000
Aug. 21–23	GTE Northwest Classic	Mike Joyce	204	$ 67,500	$ 450,000
Aug. 28–30	Franklin Showdown Classic	Orville Moody	137	$ 60,000	$ 400,000
Sept. 4–6	First of America Classic	Gibby Gilbert	202	$ 60,000	$ 400,000
Sept. 11–13	Bank One Classic	Terry Dill	203	$ 75,000	$ 500,000
Sept. 18–20	GTE North Classic	Ray Floyd	199	$ 67,500	$ 450,000
Sept. 25–27	Nationwide Championship	Isao Aoki	136	$ 120,000	$ 800,000
Oct. 2–4	Vantage Championship	Jim Colbert	132	$ 202,500	$1,500,000
Oct. 9–11	Raley's Sr. Gold Rush	Bob Charles	201	$ 75,000	$ 500,000
Oct. 16–18	TransAmerica Sr. Championship	Bob Charles	200	$ 75,000	$ 500,000
Oct. 23–25	Ralph's Sr. Classic	Ray Floyd	195	$ 90,000	$ 600,000
Oct. 30–Nov. 1	Kaanapali Classic	Tommy Aaron	198	$ 75,000	$ 500,000
Nov. 6–8	Ko Olina Sr. Invitational	Chi Chi Rodriguez	206	$ 75,000	$ 500,000

* Not an official Senior PGA Tour event.

** Tournament reduced to 36 holes by rain. Co-winners announced.

TOUR RECORDS

Lowest score, 18 holes; 61, Lee Elder, 1985, Merrill Lynch–Golf Digest Commemorative; Jim Colbert, 1991 First Development Kaanapali Classic.

Lowest score, 36 holes: 127, Bruce Crampton (63-64), 1987 Vantage Bank One Classic; Gibby Gilbert (62-65), 1992 Southwest Bell Classic.

Lowest score, 54 holes: 193, Bob Charles (63-65-65), 1989 NYNEX–*Golf Digest* Commemorative; Gibby Gilbert (62-65-66), 1992 Southwest Bell Classic.

Lowest score, 72 holes: 261, Jack Nicklaus (65-68-64-64), 1990 Mazda Senior TPC.

Most shots under par, 72-hole tournament: 27, Jack Nicklaus, 1990 Mazda Senior TPC.

Most victories (official): Miller Barber, 24; Don January, 22; Chi Chi Rodriguez, 21; Bruce Crampton, 19; Bob Charles, 18.

Most consecutive years winning at least one tournament: 9, Miller Barber (1981–1989).

Most consecutive victories: 4, Chi Chi Rodriguez, 1987

Most victories in a year: 9, Peter Thomson, 1985.

Largest victory margin: 11 strokes, Arnold Palmer, 1985 Senior Tournament Players Championship; Orville Moody, 1988 Vintage Chrysler Invitational.

Oldest winner: 63, Mike Fetchick, 1985 Hilton Head Seniors International.

Youngest winner: 50 years, 14 days; George Archer, 1989 Gatlin Brothers Southwest Classic.

AMATEUR

U.S. AMATEUR CHAMPIONSHIP

Match Play, 1895–1964

Year	Winner	Score	Runner-Up	Site
1895	Charles B. Macdonald	12 & 11	Charles Sands	Newport GC, Newport, R.I.
1896	H.J. Whigham	8 & 7	J.G. Thorp	Shinnecock Hills GC, Southampton, N.Y.
	Medalist: H.J. Whigham, 173			
1897	H.J. Whigham	8 & 6	W. Rossiter Betts	Chicago GC, Wheaton, Ill.
	Medalist: Charles B. Macdonald, 174			
1898	Findlay Douglas	5 & 3	Walter Smith	Morris County GC, Morristown, N.J.
	Medalist: J.H. Choate, Jr., 175			
1899	H.M. Harriman	3 & 2	Findlay Douglas	Onwentsia Club Lake Forest, Ill.
	Medalist: Charles B. Macdonald, 168			
1900	Walter Travis	2 up	Findlay Douglas	Garden City GC, Garden City, N.Y.
	Medalist: Walter Travis, 166			
1901	Walter Travis	5 & 4	Walter Egan	CC of Atlantic City, Atlantic City, N.J.
	Medalist: Walter Travis, 157			
1902	Louis James	4 & 2	Eben Byers	Glen View GC, Golf, Ill.
	Medalist: Walter Travis, 79			
1903	Walter Travis	5 & 4	Eben Byers	Nassau CC, Glen Cove, N.Y.
1904	H. Chandler Egan	8 & 6	Fred Herreshoff	Baltusrol, GC, Springfield, N.J.
	Medalist: H. Chandler Egan, 242			
1905	H. Chandler Egan	6 & 5	D.E. Sawyer	Chicago GC, Wheaton, Ill.
	Medalist: D.P. Fredericks, 155			
1906	Eben Byers	2 up	George Lyon	Englewood GC, Englewood, N.J.
	Medalist: Walter Travis, 152			
1907	Jerome Travers	6 & 5	Archibald Graham	Euclid Club, Cleveland, Ohio
	Medalist: Walter Travis, 146			
1908	Jerome Travers	8 & 7	Max Behr	Garden City GC, Garden City, N.Y.
	Medalist: Walter Travis, 153			
1909	Robert Gardner	4 & 3	H. Chandler Egan	Chicago GC, Wheaton, Ill.
	Medalist: Charles Evans, Jr., 151			
1910	William Fownes, Jr.	4 & 3	Warren Wood	The Country Club, Brookline, Mass.
	Medalist: Fred Herreshoff, 152			
1911	Harold Hilton	1 up (37)	Fred Herreshoff	Apawamis Club, Rye, N.Y.
	Medalist: Harold Hilton, 150			
1912	Jerome Travers	7 & 6	Charles Evans, Jr.	Chicago GC, Wheaton, Ill.
	Medalist: Charles Evans, Jr., 152			
1913	Jerome Travers	5 & 4	John Anderson	Garden City GC, Garden City, N.Y.
	Medalist: Charles Evans, Jr., 148			
1914	Francis Ouimet	6 & 5	Jerome Travers	Ekwanok CC, Manchester, Vt.
	Medalists: R.R. Gorton, W.C. Fownes, Jr., 144			
1915	Robert Gardner	5 & 4	John Anderson	CC of Detroit, Grosse Pte. Farms, Mich.
	Medalist: Dudley Mudge, 152			
1916	Charles Evans, Jr.	4 & 3	Robert Gardner	Merion Cricket Club, Ardmore, Pa.
	Medalist: W.C. Fownes, Jr., 153			
1917–18 Not played				
1919	S. Davidson Herron	5 & 4	R.T. Jones, Jr.	Oakmont CC, Oakmont, Pa.
	Medalists: S. Davidson Herron, J.B. Manion, Paul Tewksbury, 158			

U.S. AMATEUR CHAMPIONSHIP

Match Play, 1895–1964 (continued)

Year	Winner	Score	Runner-Up	Site
1920	Charles Evans, Jr. Medalist: Robert T. Jones, Jr., 154	7 & 6	Francis Ouimet	Engineers CC, Roslyn, N.Y.
1921	Jess Guilford Medalist: Francis Ouimet, 144	7 & 6	Robert Gardner	St. Louis CC, Clayton, Mo.
1922	Jess Sweetser Medalist: Jesse Guilford, 144	3 & 2	Charles Evans, Jr.	The Country Club, Brookline, Mass.
1923	Max Marston Medalists: C. Evans, Jr., R.T. Jones, Jr., 149	1 up (38)	Jess Sweetser	Flossmoor CC, Flossmoor, Ill.
1924	Robert T. Jones, Jr. Medalist: D. Clarke Corkran, 142	9 & 8	George Von Elm	Merion Cricket Club, Ardmore, Pa.
1925	Robert T. Jones, Jr. Medalist: Roland McKenzie, 145	8 & 7	Watts Gunn	Oakmont CC, Oakmont, Pa.
1926	George Von Elm Medalist: Robert T. Jones, Jr., 143	2 & 1	Robert T. Jones, Jr.	Baltusrol GC, Springfield, N.J.
1927	Robert T. Jones, Jr. Medalist: Robert T. Jones, Jr., 142	8 & 7	Charles Evans, Jr.	Minikahda Club, Minneapolis, Minn.
1928	Robert T. Jones, Jr. Medalist: George Voigt, 143	10 & 9	T. Philip Perkins	Brae Burn CC, West Newton, Mass.
1929	Harrison Johnston Medalists: Robert T. Jones, Jr., Eugene Homans, 145	4 & 3	O.F. Willing	Del Monte G&CC, Pebble Beach, Cal.
1930	Robert T. Jones, Jr. Medalist: Robert T. Jones, Jr., 142	8 & 7	Eugene Homans	Merion Cricket Club, Ardmore, Pa.
1931	Francis Ouimet Medalists: Arthur Yates, Charles Seaver, John Lehman, 148	6 & 5	Jack Westland	Beverly CC, Chicago, Ill.
1932	C. Ross Somerville Medalist: John Fischer, 142	2 & 1	John Goodman	Baltimore CC, Baltimore, Md.
1933	George Dunlap, Jr. Medalist: John Fischer, 141	6 & 5	Max Marston	Kenwood CC, Cincinnati, Ohio
1934	Lawson Little	8 & 7	David Goldman	The Country Club, Brookline, Mass.
1935	Lawson Little	4 & 2	Walter Emery	The Country Club, Cleveland, Ohio
1936	John Fischer	1 up (37)	Jack McLean	Garden City GC, Garden City, N.Y.
1937	John Goodman Medalist: Roger Kelly, 142	2 up	Raymond Billows	Alderwood CC, Portland, Ore.
1938	Willie Turnesa Medalist: Gus Moreland, 146	8 & 7	B. Patrick Abbott	Oakmont CC, Oakmont, Pa.
1939	Marvin Ward Medalist: Thomas Sheehan, 139	7 & 5	Raymond Billows	North Shore CC, Glenview, Ill.
1940	Richard Chapman Medalist: Richard Chapman, 140	11 & 9	W. B. McCullough	Winged Foot GC, Mamaroneck, N.Y.
1941	Marvin Ward Medalist: Stewart Alexander, 144	4 & 3	B. Patrick Abbott	Omaha Field Club, Omaha, Neb.
1942–45	Not played			
1946	Ted Bishop Medalist: Skee Riegel, 136	1 up (37)	Smiley Quick	Baltusrol GC, Springfield, N.J.

U.S. AMATEUR CHAMPIONSHIP

Match Play, 1895–1964 (continued)

Year	Winner	Score	Runner-Up	Site
1947	Skee Riegel	2 & 1	John Dawson	Del Monte G&CC, Pebble Beach, Cal.
1948	Willie Turnesa	2 & 1	Raymond Billows	Memphis CC, Memphis, Tenn.
1949	Charles Coe	11 & 10	Rufus King	Oak Hill CC, Rochester, N.Y.
1950	Sam Urzetta	1 up (39)	Frank Stranahan	Minneapolis GC, Minneapolis, Minn.
1951	Billy Maxwell	4 & 3	Joseph Gagliardi	Saucon Valley CC, Bethlehem, Pa.
1952	Jack Westland	3 & 2	Al Mengert	Seattle GC, Seattle, Wash.
1953	Gene Littler	1 up	Dale Morey	Oklahoma City G&CC, Oklahoma City, Okla.
1954	Arnold Palmer	1 up	Robert Sweeny	CC of Detroit, Grosse Pte. Farms, Mich.
1955	E. Harvie Ward	9 & 8	William Hyndman	CC of Virginia, Richmond, Va.
1956	E. Harvie Ward	5 & 4	Charles Kocsis	Knollwood Club, Lake Forest, Ill.
1957	Hillman Robbins	5 & 4	Frank Taylor	The Country Club, Brookline, Mass.
1958	Charles Coe	5 & 4	Tommy Aaron	Olympic Club, San Francisco, Cal.
1959	Jack Nicklaus	1 up	Charles Coe	Broadmoor GC, Colorado Springs, Colo.
1960	Deane Beman	6 & 4	Robert Gardner	St. Louis CC, Clayton, Mo.
1961	Jack Nicklaus	8 & 6	Dudley Wysong	Pebble Beach GL, Pebble Beach, Cal.
1962	Labron Harris	1 up	Downing Gray	Pinehurst CC, Pinehurst, N.C.
1963	Deane Beman	2 & 1	R. H. Sikes	Wakonda Club, Des Moines, Iowa
1964	William Campbell	1 up	Ed Tutwiler	Canterbury CC, Cleveland, Ohio

Stroke Play, 1965–1972

Year	Winner, Score	Runner-Up, Score	Site
1965	Bob Murphy, 291	Bob Dickson, 292	Southern Hills CC, Tulsa, Okla.
1966	Gary Cowan, 285 (75)	Deane Beman, 285 (76)	Merion GC, Ardmore, Pa.
1967	Bob Dickson, 285	Vinnie Giles, 286	Broadmoor GC, Colorado Springs, Colo.
1968	Bruce Fleisher, 284	Vinnie Giles, 285	Scioto CC, Columbus, Ohio
1969	Steve Melnyk, 286	Vinnie Giles, 291	Oakmont CC, Oakmont, Pa.
1970	Lanny Wadkins, 279	Tom Kite, 280	Waverly CC, Portland, Ore.
1971	Gary Cowan, 280	Eddie Pearce, 283	Wilmington CC, Wilmington, Del.
1972	Vinnie Giles, 285	Mark Hayes, Ben Crenshaw, 288	Charlotte CC, Charlotte, N.C.

Match Play, 1973–1992

Year	Winner	Score	Runner-Up	Site
1973	Craig Stadler	6 & 5	David Strawn	Inverness Club, Toledo, Ohio
1974	Jerry Pate	2 & 1	John Grace	Ridgewood CC, Ridgewood, N.J.
1975	Fred Ridley	2 up	Keith Fergus	CC of Virginia, Richmond, Va.
1976	Bill Sander	8 & 6	Parker Moore	Bel-Air CC, Los Angeles, Cal.
1977	John Fought	9 & 8	Doug Fischesser	Aronomink GC, Newtown Square, Pa.
1978	John Cook	5 & 4	Scott Hoch	Plainfield CC, Edison, N.J.

U.S. AMATEUR CHAMPIONSHIP

Match Play, 1973–1992 (continued)

Year	Winner	Score	Runner-Up	Site
1979	Mark O'Meara Medalist: Bobby Clampett, 134	8 & 7	John Cook	Canterbury GC, Cleveland, Ohio
1980	Hal Sutton Medalist: Fred Couples, 139	9 & 8	Bob Lewis	CC of North Carolina, Pinehurst, N.C.
1981	Nathaniel Crosby Medalist: Joe Rassett, 145	1 up (37)	Brian Lindley	Olympic Club, San Francisco, Cal.
1982	Jay Sigel Medalists: Bob Lewis, Bob Stanger, 141	8 & 7	David Tolley	The Country Club, Brookline, Mass.
1983	Jay Sigel Medalist: Clark Burroughs, 139	8 & 7	Chris Perry	North Shore CC, Glenview, Ill.
1984	Scott Verplank Medalist: Scott Verplank, 137	4 & 3	Sam Randolph	Oak Tree GC, Edmond, Okla.
1985	Sam Randolph Medalist: Sam Randolph, 134	1 up	Peter Persons	Montclair GC, West Orange, N.J.
1986	Buddy Alexander Medalist: Len Mattiace, 137	5 & 3	Chris Kite	Shoal Creek GC, Birmingham, Ala.
1987	Bill Mayfair Medalist: Scott Gump, 141	4 & 3	Eric Rebmann	Jupiter Hills Club, Jupiter, Fla.
1988	Eric Meeks Medalist: Tom McKnight, 137	7 & 6	Danny Yates	Virginia Hot Springs G&TC, Hot Springs, Va.
1989	Chris Patton Medalist: Eoghan O'Connell, 137	3 & 1	Danny Green	Merion GC, Ardmore, Pa.
1990	Phil Mickelson Medalist: Phil Mickelson, 135	5 & 4	Manny Zerman	Cherry Hills CC, Englewood, Colo.
1991	Mitch Voges Medalists: Allen Doyle, John Harris, 136	7 & 6	Manny Zerman	Honors Course, Ooltewah, Tenn.
1992	Justin Leonard Medalist: David Duval, 136	8 & 7	Tom Scherrer	Muirfield Village GC, Dublin, Ohio.

Note: In years where no medalist is listed, competition was all match play.

U.S. WOMEN'S AMATEUR CHAMPIONSHIP

Year	Winner	Score	Runner-Up	Site
1895	Mrs. C. S. Brown 18 holes, stroke play	132	Nellie Sargent	Meadow Brook Club, Hempstead, N.Y.
1896	Beatrix Hoyt Medalist: Beatrix Hoyt, 95	2 & 1	Mrs. Arthur Turnure	Morris County GC, Morristown, N.J.
1897	Beatrix Hoyt Medalist: Beatrix Hoyt, 108	5 & 4	Nellie Sargent	Essex CC, Manchester, Mass.
1898	Beatrix Hoyt Medalist: Beatrix Hoyt, 92	5 & 3	Maude Wetmore	Ardsley Club, Ardsley, N.Y.
1899	Ruth Underhill Medalist: Beatrix Hoyt, 97	2 & 1	Margaret Fox	Philadelphia CC, Philadelphia, Pa.
1900	Frances C. Griscom Medalist: Beatrix Hoyt, 97	6 & 5	Margaret Curtis	Shinnecock Hills GC, Southampton, N.Y.
1901	Genevieve Hecker Medalists: Margaret Curtis, Mary Adams, Mrs. E. A. Manice, Lucy Herron, 97	5 & 3	Lucy Herron	Baltusrol GC, Springfield, N.J.
1902	Genevieve Hecker Medalists: Louisa Wells, Margaret Curtis, 89	4 & 3	Louisa Wells	The Country Club, Brookline, Mass.
1903	Bessie Anthony Medalist: Margaret Fox, 94	7 & 6	J. Anna Carpenter	Chicago GC, Wheaton, Ill.
1904	Georgianna Bishop Medalists: Charlotte Dod, L. Vanderhoef, Harriot Curtis, 93	5 & 3	Mrs. E. F. Sanford	Merion Cricket Club, Ardmore, Pa.
1905	Pauline Mackay Medalists: Margaret Curtis, G. Bishop, 87	1 up	Margaret Curtis	Morris County GC, Morristown, N.J.
1906	Harriot Curtis Medalist: Pauline Mackay, 87	2 & 1	Mary Adams	Brae Burn CC, West Newton, Mass.
1907	Margaret Curtis Medalist: Margaret Curtis, 95	7 & 6	Harriot Curtis	Midlothian CC, Blue Island, Ill.
1908	Katherine Harley Medalist: Harriot Curtis, 85	6 & 5	Mrs. T. H. Polhemus	Chevy Chase Club, Chevy Chase, Md.

Margaret Curtis won the U.S. Women's Amateur in 1907, 1911 and 1912. *Courtesy PGA World Hall of Fame*

Alexa Stirling captured consecutive U.S. Women's Amateurs in 1916, 1919 and 1920 (the event was not held in 1917 and 1918).
Courtesy PGA World Hall of Fame

U.S. WOMEN'S AMATEUR CHAMPIONSHIP

Year	Winner	Score	Runner-Up	Site
1909	Dorothy Campbell Medalists: Margaret Fox, Anita Phipps, Margaret Curtis, 86	3 & 2	Nonna Barlow	Merion Cricket Club, Ardmore, Pa.
1910	Dorothy Campbell Medalist: Dorothy Campbell, 85	2 & 1	Mrs. G. M. Martin	Homewood CC, Flossmoor, Ill.
1911	Margaret Curtis Medalist: Nonna Barlow, 87	5 & 3	Lillian Hyde	Baltusrol GC, Springfield, N.J.
1912	Margaret Curtis Medalist: Margaret Curtis, 88	3 & 2	Nonna Barlow	Essex CC, Manchester, Mass.
1913	Gladys Ravenscroft Medalist: Gladys Ravenscroft, 88	2 up	Marion Hollins	Wilmington CC, Wilmington, Del.
1914	Katherine Harley Jackson Medalist: Georgianna Bishop, 85	1 up	Elaine Rosenthal	Nassau GC, Glen Cove, N.Y.
1915	Florence Vanderbeck Medalist: Florence Vanderbeck, 85	3 & 2	Margaret Gavin	Onwentsia Club, Lake Forest, Ill.
1916	Alexa Stirling Medalist: Dorothy Campbell Hurd, 86	2 & 1	Mildred Caverly	Belmont Springs CC, Waverly, Mass.

U.S. WOMEN'S AMATEUR CHAMPIONSHIP (continued)

Year	Winner	Score	Runner-Up	Site
1917–18 Not played				
1919	Alexa Stirling	6 & 5	Margaret Gavin	Shawnee CC, Shawnee, Pa.
	Medalists: Alexa Stirling, Margaret Gavin, 87			
1920	Alexa Stirling	5 & 4	Dorothy Campbell Hurd	Mayfield CC, Cleveland, Ohio
	Medalist: Marion Hollins, 82			
1921	Marion Hollins	5 & 4	Alexa Stirling	Hollywood GC, Deal, N.J.
	Medalist: Glenna Collett, 177			
1922	Glenna Collett	5 & 4	Margaret Gavin	Greenbrier GC, White Sulphur Springs, W. Va.
	Medalist: Glenna Collett, 81			
1923	Edith Cummings	3 & 2	Alexa Stirling	Westchester CC, Rye, N.Y.
	Medalist: Alexa Stirling, 84			
1924	Dorothy Campbell Hurd	7 & 6	Mary K. Browne	Rhode Island CC, Nyatt, R.I.
	Medalist: Glenna Collett, 79			
1925	Glenna Collett	9 & 8	Alexa Stirling Fraser	St. Louis CC, Clayton, Mo.
	Medalist: Alexa Stirling Fraser, 77			
1926	Helen Stetson	3 & 1	Elizabeth Goss	Merion Cricket Club, Ardmore, Pa.
	Medalist: Glenna Collett, 81			
1927	Miram Burns Horn	5 & 4	Maureen Orcutt	Cherry Valley Club, Garden City, N.Y.
	Medalist: Ada McKenzie, 77			
1928	Glenna Collett	13 & 12	Virginia Van Wie	Va. Hot Springs G&TC, Hot Springs, Va.
	Medalist: Maureen Orcutt, 80			
1929	Glenna Collett	4 & 3	Leona Pressler	Oakland Hills CC, Birmingham, Mich.
	Medalists: Helen Hicks, Virginia Van Wie, 79			
1930	Glenna Collett	6 & 5	Virginia Van Wie	Los Angeles CC, Beverly Hills, Cal.
	Medalist: Opal Hill, 79			
1931	Helen Hicks	2 & 1	Glenna Collett Vare	CC of Buffalo, Williamsville, N.Y.
	Medalists: Maureen Orcutt, Glenna C. Vare, Dorothy Higbie, Opal Hill, 82			
1932	Virginia Van Wie	10 & 8	Glenna Collett Vare	Salem CC, Peabody, Mass.
	Medalists: Maureen Orcutt, Virginia Van Wie, 77			
1933	Virginia Van Wie	4 & 3	Helen Hicks	Exmoor CC, Highland Park, Ill.
	Medalist: Enid Wilson, 76			
1934	Virginia Van Wie	2 & 1	Dorothy Traung	Whitemarsh Valley CC, Chestnut Hill, Pa.
	Medalists: Leona Pressler Cheney, Lucille Robinson, Glenna C, Vare, 82			
1935	Glenna Collett Vare	3 & 2	Patty Berg	Interlachen CC, Hopkins, Minn.
	Medalist: Jean Bauer, 79			
1936	Pamela Barton	4 & 3	Maureen Orcutt	Canoe Brook CC, Summit, N.J.
	Medalist: Estelle Lawson Page, 78			
1937	Estelle Lawson Page	7 & 6	Patty Berg	Memphis CC, Memphis, Tenn.
	Medalist: Estelle Lawson Page, 79			
1938	Patty Berg	6 & 5	Estelle Lawson Page	Westmoreland CC, Wilmette, Ill.
	Medalists: Dorothy Traung, Estelle L. Page, 80			
1939	Betty Jameson	3 & 2	Dorothy Kirby	Wee Burn Club, Darien, Conn.
	Medalist: Bea Barrett, 74			
1940	Betty Jameson	6 & 5	Jane Cothran	Del Monte G&CC, Pebble Beach, Cal.
	Medalist: Dorothy Traung, 78			
1941	Elizabeth Hicks Newell	5 & 3	Helen Sigel	The Country Club, Brookline, Mass.
	Medalists: Grace Amory, Alice Belanger, Jean Bauer, Betty Jameson, 76			

Virginia Van Wie won three straight U.S. Women's Amateurs in 1932 and 1934. *Courtesy U.S.G.A.*

U.S. WOMEN'S AMATEUR CHAMPIONSHIP (continued)

Year	Winner	Score	Runner-Up	Site
1942–1945 Not played				
1946	Babe Didrikson Zaharias	11 & 9	Clara Sherman	Southern Hills CC, Tulsa, Okla.
	Medalist: Dorothy Kirby, 152			
1947	Louise Suggs	2 up	Dorothy Kirby	Franklin Hills CC, Franklin, Mich.
	Medalist: Louise Suggs, 78			
1948	Grace Lenczyk	4 & 3	Helen Sigel	Del Monte G&CC, Pebble Beach, Cal.
	Medalist: Bettye Mims White, 77			
1949	Dorothy Porter	3 & 2	Dorothy Kielty	Merion GC, Ardmore, Pa.
1950	Beverly Hanson	6 & 4	Mae Murray	Atlanta AC, Atlanta, Ga.
1951	Dorothy Kirby	2 & 1	Claire Koran	Town & CC, St. Paul, Minn.
	Medalists: Carol Diringer, Barbara Romack, 74			

U.S. WOMEN'S AMATEUR CHAMPIONSHIP (continued)

Year	Winner	Score	Runner-Up	Site
1952	Jacqueline Pung Medalist: Dorothy Kirby, 76	2 & 1	Shirley McFedters	Waverly CC, Portland, Ore.
1953	Mary Lena Faulk	3 & 2	Polly Riley	Rhode Island CC, W. Barrington, R.I.
1954	Barbara Romack	4 & 2	Mickey Wright	Allegheny CC, Sewickley, Pa.
1955	Patricia Lesser	7 & 6	Jane Nelson	Myers Park CC, Charlotte, N.C.
1956	Marlene Stewart	2 & 1	JoAnne Gunderson	Meridian Hills CC, Indianapolis, Ind.
1957	JoAnne Gunderson	8 & 6	Ann Casey Johnstone	Del Paso CC, Sacramento, Cal.
1958	Anne Quast	3 & 2	Barbara Romack	Wee Burn CC, Darien, Conn.
1959	Barbara McIntire	4 & 3	Joanne Goodwin	Congressional CC, Washington, D.C.
1960	JoAnne Gunderson	6 & 5	Jean Ashley	Tulsa CC, Tulsa, Okla.
1961	Anne Quast Sander	14 & 13	Phyllis Pruess	Tacoma G&CC, Tacoma, Wash.
1962	JoAnne Gunderson	9 & 8	Ann Baker	CC of Rochester, Rochester, N.Y.
1963	Anne Quast Sander	2 & 1	Peggy Conley	Taconic GC, Williamstown, Mass.
1964	Barbara McIntire Medalists: JoAnne Gunderson, Polly Riley, Barbara McIntire, 151	3 & 2	JoAnne Gunderson	Prairie Dunes CC, Hutchinson, Kan.
1965	Jean Ashley Medalist: Lida Fee Matthews, 148	5 & 4	Anne Quast Sander	Lakewood CC, Denver, Colo.
1966	JoAnne Gunderson Carner Medalist: Shelley Hamlin, 143	1 up (41)	Marlene Stewart Streit	Sewickley Heights GC, Sewickley, Pa.
1967	Mary Lou Dill Medalist: Phyllis Preuss, 148	5 & 4	Jean Ashley	Annandale GC, Pasadena, Cal.
1968	JoAnne Gunderson Carner Medalist: Catherine Lacoste, 143	5 & 4	Anne Quast Sander	Birmingham CC, Birmingham, Mich.
1969	Catherine Lacoste Medalist: Barbara Boddie, 147	3 & 2	Shelley Hamlin	Las Colinas CC, Irving, Tex.
1970	Martha Wilkinson Medalist: Martha Wilkinson, 150	3 & 2	Cynthia Hill	Wee Burn CC, Darien, Conn.
1971	Laura Baugh Medalists: Connie Day, Jane Bastanchury, 150	1 up	Beth Barry	Atlanta CC, Marietta, Ga.
1972	Mary Budke Medalist: Carol Sorenson Flenniken, 148	5 & 4	Cynthia Hill	St. Louis CC, Clayton, Mo.
1973	Carol Semple Medalist: Kaye Potter, 74	1 up	Anne Quast Sander	Montclair GC, West Orange, N.J.
1974	Cynthia Hill Medalist: Debbie Massey, 70	5 & 4	Carol Semple	Broadmoor GC, Seattle, Wash.
1975	Beth Daniel Medalist: Nancy Roth Syms, 71	3 & 2	Donna Horton	Brae Burn CC, West Newton, Mass.
1976	Donna Horton Medalist: Beth Daniel, 70	2 & 1	Marianne Bretton	Del Paso CC, Sacramento, Cal.

U.S. WOMEN'S AMATEUR CHAMPIONSHIP (continued)

Year	Winner	Score	Runner-Up	Site
1977	Beth Daniel Medalist: Mary Lawrence, 72	3 & 1	Cathy Sherk	Cincinnati CC, Cincinnati, Ohio
1978	Cathy Sherk Medalist: Belle Robertson, 72	4 & 3	Judith Oliver	Sunnybrook GC, Plymouth Meeting, Pa.
1979	Carolyn Hill Medalist: Kathy Baker, 71	7 & 6	Patty Sheehan	Memphis CC, Memphis, Tenn.
1980	Juli Inkster Medalist: Dorothy Lasker, 147	2 up	Patti Rizzo	Prairie Dunes CC, Hutchinson, Kan.
1981	Juli Inkster Medalists: Patti Rizzo, Heather Farr, 147	1 up	Lindy Goggin	Waverly CC, Portland, Ore.
1982	Juli Inkster Medalist: Penny Hammell, 143	4 & 3	Cathy Hanlon	Broadmoor GC, Colorado Springs, Colo.
1983	Joanne Pacillo Medalist: Mary Anne Widman, 147	2 & 1	Sally Quinlan	Canoe Brook CC, Summit, N.J.
1984	Deb Richard Medalist: Claire Waite, 145	1 up (37)	Kim Williams	Broadmoor GC, Seattle, Wash.
1985	Michiko Hattori Medalist: Michiko Hattori, Cheryl Stacy, 151	5 & 4	Cheryl Stacy	Fox Chapel CC, Pittsburgh, Pa.
1986	Kay Cockerill Medalists: Pearl Sinn, Michiko Hattori, 148	9 & 7	Kathleen McCarthy	Pasatiempo GC, Santa Cruz, Cal.
1987	Kay Cockerill Medalists: Michiko Hattori, Tracy Kerdyk, 147	3 & 2	Tracy Kerdyk	Rhode Island CC, Barrington, R.I.
1988	Pearl Sinn Medalist: Pearl Sinn, 140	6 & 5	Karen Noble	Minikahda CC, Minneapolis, Minn.
1989	Vicki Goetze Medalist: Pat Hurst, 143	4 & 3	Brandie Burton	Pinehurst CC, Pinehurst, N.C.
1990	Pat Hurst Medalist: Vicki Goetze, 144	1 up (37)	Stephanie Davis	Canoe Brook CC, Summit, N.J.
1991	Amy Fruhwirth Medalist: Amy Fruhwirth, 144	5 & 4	Heidi Voorhees	Prairie Dunes CC, Hutchinson, Kan.
1992	Vicki Goetze Medalists: Emilee Klein, Debbie Parks, 143	1 up	Annika Sorenstam	Kemper Lakes, GC, Hawthorn Woods, Ill.

Note: In years where no medalist is listed, competition was all match play.

U.S. AMATEUR PUBLIC LINKS CHAMPIONSHIP

Year	Winner, Runner-Up	Score	Year	Winner, Runner-Up	Score
1922	Edmund Held, Richard Walsh	6 & 5	1959	William Wright, Frank Campbell	3 & 2
1923	Richard Walsh, J. Stewart Whitham	6 & 5	1960	Verne Callison, Tyler Caplin	7 & 6
1924	Joseph Coble, Henry Decker	2 & 1	1961	R. H. Sikes, John Molenda	4 & 3
1925	Raymond McAuliffe, William Serrick	6 & 5	1962	R. H. Sikes, Hung Soo Ahn	2 & 1
1926	Lester Bolstad, Carl Kauffman	3 & 2	1963	Bob Lunn, Steve Opperman	1 up
1927	Carl Kauffman, William Serrick	1 up (37)	1964	William McDonald, Dean Wilson	5 & 3
1928	Carl Kauffman, Phil Ogden	8 & 7	1965	Arne Dokka, Leo Zampedro	10 & 9
1929	Carl Kauffman, Milton Soncrant	4 & 3	1966	Lamont Kaser, Dave Ojala	6 & 5
1930	Robert Wingate, Joseph Greene	1 up	1967	Verne Callison, Ronald Stokley	287*
1931	Charles Ferrera, Joe Nichols	5 & 4	1968	Gene Towry, Bob Unger	292*
1932	R. L. Miller, Pete Miller	4 & 2	1969	John Jackson, 4 players tied for second	292*
1933	Charles Ferrera, R. L. Miller	3 & 2	1970	Bob Risch, Mike Zimmerman	293*
1934	David Mitchell, Arthur Armstrong	5 & 3	1971	Fred Haney, Bob Blomberg	290*
1935	Frank Strafaci, Joe Coria	1 up (37)	1972	Bob Allard, Rick Schultz	285*
1936	B. Patrick Abbott, Claude Rippy	4 & 3	1973	Stan Stopa; Gary Hitch, Philip Reichel (tie)	294*
1937	Bruce McCormick, Don Erickson	1 up	1974	Charles Baraneba, Frank Mazion	290*
1938	Al Leach, Louis Cyr	1 up	1975	Randy Baraneba, Alan Yamamoto	1 up (37)
1939	Andrew Szwedko, Phillip Gordon	1 up	1976	Eddie Mudd, Archie Dadian	1 up (37)
1940	Robert Clark, Michael Dietz	8 & 6	1977	Jerry Vidovic, Jeff Kern	4 & 2
1941	William Welch, Jack Kerns	6 & 5	1978	Dean Prince, Tony Figueredo	5 & 3
1942–1945 Not played			1979	Dennis Walsh, Eric Mork	4 & 3
1946	Smiley Quick, Louis Stafford	3 & 2	1980	Jodie Mudd, Rick Gordon	9 & 8
1947	Wilfred Crossley, Avery Beck	6 & 5	1981	Jodie Mudd, Billy Tuten	3 & 2
1948	Michael Ferentz, Ben Hughes	2 & 1	1982	Billy Tuten, Brad Heninger	6 & 5
1949	Kenneth Towns, William Betger	5 & 4	1983	Billy Tuten, David Hobby	3 & 1
1950	Stanley Bielat, John Dobro	7 & 5	1984	Bill Malley, Dirk Jones	2 & 1
1951	Dave Stanley, Ralph Branesic	1 up	1985	Jim Sorenson, Jay Cooper	12 & 11
1952	Omer Bogan, Robert Scherer	4 & 3	1986	Bill Mayfair, Jim Sorenson	3 & 2
1953	Ted Richards, Irving Cooper	1 up	1987	Kevin Johnson, Jimmy England	10 & 9
1954	Gene Andrews, Jack Zimmerman	1 up	1988	Ralph Howe, Kevin Johnson	1 up (37)
1955	Sam Kocsis, Lewis Bean	2 up	1989	Tim Hobby, Henry Cagigal	4 & 3
1956	James Buxbaum, W. C. Scarbrough	3 & 2	1990	Michael Combs, Terrence Miskell	4 & 3
1957	Don Essig, Gene Towry	6 & 5	1991	David Berganio, Jr., Michael Combs	4 & 2
1958	Dan Sikes, Bob Ludlow	3 & 2	1992	Warren Schutte, Richard Mayo	3 & 2

* Stroke play, 1967–1974. Score is winner's score.

WOMEN'S AMATEUR PUBLIC LINKS

Year	Winner, Runner-Up	Score	Year	Winner, Runner-Up	Score
1977	Kelly Fuiks, Kathy Williams	1 up	1985	Danielle Ammaccapane, Kristy Kolacny	6 & 5
1978	Kelly Fuiks, Diana Schwab	5 & 4	1986	Cindy Schreyer, Vicki Goetze	3 & 2
1979	Lori Castillo, Becky Pearson	2 up	1987	Tracy Kerdyk, Pearl Sinn	4 & 3
1980	Lori Castillo, Pam Miller	2 & 1	1988	Pearl Sinn, Tami Jo Henningsen	2 & 1
1981	Mary Enright, Lauri Merten	3 & 1	1989	Pearl Sinn, Kelli Akers	2 & 1
1982	Nancy Taylor, Kerri Clark	2 & 1	1990	Cathy Mockett, Barbara Blancher	5 & 4
1983	Kelli Antolock, Nancy Taylor	1 up	1991	Tracy Hanson, Carri Wood	1 up
1984	Heather Farr, Kristy Kolacny	3 & 2	1992	Amy Fruhwirth, Sara Evens	2 & 1

U.S. JUNIOR AMATEUR CHAMPIONSHIP

Year	Winner, Runner-Up	Score	Year	Winner, Runner-Up	Score
1948	Dean Lind, Ken Venturi	4 & 2	1971	Mike Brannan, Robert Steele	4 & 3
1949	Gay Brewer, Mason Rudolph	6 & 4	1972	Bob Byman, Scott Simpson	2 & 1
1950	Mason Rudolph, Charles Beville	2 & 1	1973	Jack Renner, Mike Brannan	1 up (20)
1951	Tommy Jacobs, Floyd Addington	4 & 2	1974	David Nevatt, Mark Tinder	4 & 3
1952	Don Bisplinghoff, Eddie Meyerson	2 up	1975	Brett Mullin, Scott Templeton	2 & 1
1953	Rex Baxter, George Warren	2 & 1	1976	Madden Hatcher, Doug Clarke	3 & 2
1954	Foster Bradley, Al Geiberger	3 & 1	1977	Willie Wood, David Games	4 & 3
1955	Billy Dunn, William Seanor	3 & 2	1978	Don Hurter, Keither Banes	1 up (21)
1956	Harlan Stevenson, Jack Rule	3 & 1	1979	Jack Larkin, Billy Tuten	1 up
1957	Larry Beck, David Leon	6 & 5	1980	Eric Johnson, Bruce Soulsby	4 & 3
1958	Gordon Baker, R. Douglas Lindsey	2 & 1	1981	Scott Erickson, Matt McCarley	4 & 3
1959	Larry Lee, Michael McMahon	2 up	1982	Rich Marik, Tim Straub	4 & 3
1960	William Tindall, Robert Hammer	2 & 1	1983	Tim Straub, John Mahon	1 up
1961	Charles McDowell, Jay Sigel	2 up	1984	Doug Martin, Brad Agee	4 & 2
1962	Jim Wiechers, James Sullivan	4 & 3	1985	Charles Rymer, Greg Lesher	1 up (19)
1963	Gregg McHatton, Richard Bland	4 & 3	1986	Brian Montgomery, Nicky Goetze	2 & 1
1964	Johnny Miller, Enrique Sterling	2 & 1	1987	Brett Quigley, Bill Heim	1 up
1965	Jim Masserio, Lloyd Liebler	3 & 2	1988	Jason Widener, Brandon Knight	1 up
1966	Gary Sanders, Ray Leach	2 up	1989	David Duval, Austin Maki	1 up
1967	John Crooks, Andy North	2 & 1	1990	Mathew Todd, Dennis Hillman	1 up
1968	Eddie Pearce, W. B. Harman	6 & 5	1991	Tiger Woods, Brad Zwetschke	1 up (19)
1969	Aly Trompas, Eddie Pearce	3 & 1	1992	Tiger Woods, Mark Wilson	1 up
1970	Gary Koch, Mike Nelms	8 & 6			

U.S. GIRLS' JUNIOR CHAMPIONSHIP

Year	Winner, Runner-Up	Score	Year	Winner, Runner-Up	Score
1949	Marlene Bauer, Barbara Bruning	2 up	1971	Hollis Stacy, Amy Alcott	1 up (19)
1950	Patricia Lesser, Mickey Wright	4 & 2	1972	Nancy Lopez, Cathy Morse	1 up
1951	Arlene Brooks, Barbara McIntire	1 up	1973	Amy Alcott, Mary Lawrence	6 & 5
1952	Mickey Wright, Barbara McIntire	1 up	1974	Nancy Lopez, Lauren Howe	7 & 5
1953	Mildred Myerson, Holly Jean Roth	4 & 2	1975	Dayna Benson, Kyle O'Brien	1 up
1954	Margaret Smith, Sue Driscoll	5 & 3	1976	Pilar Dorado, Kellii Doherty	3 & 2
1955	Carole Jo Kabler, JoAnne Gunderson	4 & 3	1977	Althea Tome, Missie McGeorge	3 & 2
1956	JoAnne Gunderson, Clifford Ann Creed	4 & 3	1978	Lori Castillo, Jenny Lidback	4 & 2
1957	Judy Eller, Beth Stone	1 up (20)	1979	Penny Hammell, Amy Benz	2 & 1
1958	Judy Eller, Sherry Wheeler	1 up	1980	Laurie Rinker, Libby Akers	5 & 4
1959	Judy Rand, Marcia Hamilton	5 & 3	1981	Kay Cornelius, Kim Simmons	2 & 1
1960	Carol Sorenson, Sharon Fladoos	2 & 1	1982	Heather Farr, Caroline Keggi	2 & 1
1961	Mary Lowell, Margaret Martin	1 up	1983	Kim Saiki, Buffy Klein	2 & 1
1962	Mary Lou Daniel, Mary Sawyer	2 up	1984	Cathy Mockett, Michiko Hattori	1 up
1963	Jan Ferraris, Peggy Conley	2 up	1985	Dana Lofland, Amy Fruhwirth	4 & 3
1964	Peggy Conley, Laura McIvor	6 & 5	1986	Pat Hurst, Adele Moore	1 up (20)
1965	Gail Sykes, Mary Louise Pritchett	5 & 4	1987	Michelle McGann, Lynne Mikulas	7 & 5
1966	Claudia Mayhew, Kathy Ahern	3 & 2	1988	Jamille Jose, Debbie Parks	5 & 4
1967	Elizabeth Story, Liana Zambresky	5 & 4	1989	Brandie Burton, Camie Hosino	1 up
1968	Margaret Harmon, Kaye Beard	3 & 2	1990	Sandrine Mendiburu, Vicki Goetze	3 & 2
1969	Hollis Stacy, Jane Fassinger	1 up	1991	Emilee Klein, Kimberly Marshall	3 & 2
1970	Hollis Stacy, Janet Aulisi	1 up	1992	Fumi Jamie Koizumi, Alicia Allison	5 & 4

U.S. SENIOR AMATEUR CHAMPIONSHIP

Year	Winner, Runner-Up	Score	Year	Winner, Runner-Up	Score
1955	J. Wood Platt, George Studinger	5 & 4	1974	Dale Morey, Lewis Oehmig	4 & 2
1956	Frederick Wright, J. Clark Espie	4 & 3	1975	William Colm, Stephen Stimac	4 & 3
1957	J. Clark Espie, Frederick Wright	2 & 1	1976	Lewis Oehmig, John Richardson	4 & 3
1958	Thomas Robbins, John Dawson	2 & 1	1977	Dale Morey, Lewis Oehmig	4 & 3
1959	J. Clark Espie, J. Wolcott Brown	3 & 1	1978	Keith Compton, John Kline	1 up
1960	Michael Cestone, David Rose	1 up (20)	1979	William Campbell, Lewis Oehmig	2 & 1
1961	Dexter Daniels, William Lanman	2 & 1	1980	William Campbell, Keith Compton	3 & 2
1962	Merrill Carlsmith, Willis Blakely	4 & 2	1981	Ed Updegraff, Dale Morey	2 & 1
1963	Merrill Carlsmith, William Higgins	3 & 2	1982	Alton Duhon, Ed Updegraff	2 up
1964	William Higgins, Edward Murphy	2 & 1	1983	William Hyndman, Richard Runkle	1 up
1965	Robert Kiersky, George Beechler	1 up (19)	1984	Robert Rawlins, Richard Runkle	1 up (19)
1966	Dexter Daniels, George Beechler	1 up	1985	Lewis Oehmig, Ed Hopkins	1 up
1967	Ray Palmer, Walter Bronson	3 & 2	1986	R.S. Williams, John Harbottle	3 & 2
1968	Curtis Person, Ben Goodes	2 & 1	1987	John Richardson, James Kite	5 & 4
1969	Curtis Person, David Goldman	1 up	1988	Clarence Moore, Bud Stevens	5 & 4
1970	Gene Andrews, James Ferris	1 up	1989	Bo Williams, Joe Simpson	1 up (19)
1971	Tom Draper, Ernest Pieper	3 & 1	1990	Jackie Cummings, Bobby Clark	3 & 2
1972	Lewis Oehmig, Ernest Pieper	1 up (20)	1991	Bill Bosshard, Morris Beecroft	5 & 4
1973	William Hyndman, Harry Welch	3 & 2	1992	Clarence Moore, Robert Harris	6 & 4

U.S. SENIOR WOMEN'S AMATEUR CHAMPIONSHIP

Year	Winner, Runner-Up	Score	Year	Winner, Runner-Up	Score
1962	Maureen Orcutt, Glenna Collett Vare	240	1978	Alice Dye, Ceil Maclaurin	232*
1963	Allison Choate, Maureen Orcutt	239*	1979	Alice Dye, Ceil Maclaurin	223
1964	Loma Smith, Mrs. William Kirkland	247	1980	Dorothy Porter, Ceil Maclaurin	236
1965	Loma Smith, Charlotte Haskell	242	1981	Dorothy Porter, Alice Dye	242
1966	Maureen Orcutt, Anelia Goldthwaite	242	1982	Edean Ihlanfeldt, Mary Ann Morrison	232
1967	Marge Mason, Loma Smith	236	1983	Dorothy Porter, Lois Hodge	234
1968	Carolyn Cudone, Loma Smith	236	1984	Constance Guthrie, Janice Calin	227
1969	Carolyn Cudone, Mrs. Lowell Brown	236*	1985	Marlene Streit, Louise Wilson	224
1970	Carolyn Cudone, Paulette Lee	231	1986	Constance Guthrie, 3 tied for second	225
1971	Carolyn Cudone, Ann Gregory	236	1987	Anne Quast Sander, Harriet Hart	228
1972	Carolyn Cudone, Mrs. Wayne Rutter	231	1988	Lois Hodge, Marlene Streit	228
1973	Gwen Hibbs, Mrs. Wayne Rutter	229	1989	Anne Quast Sander, Alice Dye	224
1974	Justine Cushing, Carolyn Cudone	231	1990	Anne Quast Sander, Marlene Streit	225*
1975	Alberta Bower, Carolyn Cudone	234	1991	Phyllis Preuss, Anne Quast Sander	221
1976	Ceil Maclaurin, Carol Bowman	230	1992	Rosemary Thompson, Anne Quast Sander	220
1977	Dorothy Porter, Alice Dye	230			

* Won playoff

U.S. MID-AMATEUR CHAMPIONSHIP

Year	Winner, Runner-Up	Score	Year	Winner, Runner-Up	Score
1981	Jim Holtgrieve, Bob Lewis	2 up	1987	Jay Sigel, David Lind	1 up (20)
1982	William Hoffer, Jeffrey Ellis	3 & 2	1988	David Eger, Scott Mayne	2 & 1
1983	Jay Sigel, Randy Sonnier	1 up	1989	James Taylor, James Hadden	4 & 3
1984	Michael Podolak, Bob Lewis	5 & 4	1990	Jim Stuart, Mark Sollenberger	1 up
1985	Jay Sigel, Gordon Brewer	3 & 2	1991	Jim Stuart, Bert Atkinson	1 up
1986	Bill Loeffler, Charles Pinkard	4 & 3	1992	Danny Yates, David Lind	1 up

U.S. WOMEN'S MID-AMATEUR CHAMPIONSHIP

Year	Winner, Runner-Up	Score	Year	Winner, Runner-Up	Score
1987	Cindy Scholefield, Pat Cornett	6 & 5	1990	Carol Semple Thompson, Page Marsh Lea	3 & 1
1988	Martha Lang, Mary Hanyak	4 & 3	1991	Sarah LaBrun Ingram, Martha Lang	6 & 5
1989	Robin Weiss, Page Marsh Lea	1 up (22)	1992	Marion Maney-McInerney, Carol Semple Thompson	1 up (19)

NCAA CHAMPIONSHIP

Year	Individual Champion	Team Champion
1897	Louis P. Bayard, Jr. (Princeton)	Yale
1898	John Reid, Jr. (Spring—Yale)	Harvard
	James F. Curtis (Harvard)—Fall	Yale
1899	Percy Pyne II (Princeton)	Harvard
1900	Not played	
1901	H. Lindsley (Harvard)	Harvard
1902	Charles Hitchcock Jr. (Yale)—Spring	Yale
	H. Chandler Egan (Harvard)—Fall	Harvard
1903	F.O. Reinhart (Princeton)	Harvard
1904	A.L. White (Harvard)	Harvard
1905	Robert Abbott (Yale)	Yale
1906	W.E. Clow (Yale)	Yale
1907	Ellis Knowles (Yale)	Yale
1908	H.H. Wilder (Harvard)	Yale
1909	Albert Seckel (Princeton)	Yale
1910	Robert E. Hunter (Yale)	Yale
1911	George C. Stanley (Yale)	Yale
1912	F.C. Davidson (Harvard)	Yale
1913	Nathaniel Wheeler (Yale)	Yale
1914	Edward P. Allis III (Harvard)	Princeton
1915	Francis R. Blossom (Yale)	Yale
1916	J.W. Hubbell (Harvard)	Princeton
1917–1918 Not played		
1919	A.L. Walker, Jr. (Columbia)	Princeton
1920	Jess W. Sweetser (Yale)	Princeton
1921	J. Simpson Dean (Princeton)	Dartmouth
1922	Pollock Boyd (Dartmouth)	Princeton
1923	Dexter Cummings (Yale)	Princeton
1924	Dexter Cummings (Yale)	Yale
1925	G. Fred Lamprecht (Tulane)	Yale
1926	G. Fred Lamprecht (Tulane)	Yale
1927	Watts Gunn (Georgia Tech)	Princeton
1928	Maurice J. McCarthy, Jr. (Georgetown)	Princeton
1929	Tom Aycock (Yale)	Princeton
1930	George T. Dunlap, Jr. (Princeton)	Princeton
1931	George T. Dunlap, Jr. (Princeton)	Yale
1932	John W. Fischer, Jr. (Michigan)	Yale
1933	Walter Emery (Oklahoma)	Yale
1934	Charles R. Yates (Georgia Tech)	Michigan
1935	Ed White (Texas)	Michigan
1936	Charles Kocsis (Michigan)	Yale
1937	Fred Haas, Jr. (Louisiana State)	Princeton
1938	John P. Burke (Georgetown)	Stanford
1939	Vincent D'Antoni (Tulane)	Stanford
1940	F. Dixon Brooke (Virginia)	Princeton & LSU
1941	Earl Stewart (Louisiana State)	Stanford
1942	Frank Tatum, Jr. (Stanford)	Stanford & LSU
1943	Wallace Ulrich (Carleton)	Yale
1944	Louis Lick (Minnesota)	Notre Dame
1945	John Lorms (Ohio State)	Ohio State
1946	George Hamer (Georgia)	Stanford

NCAA CHAMPIONSHIP (continued)

Year	Individual Champion	Team Champion
1947	Dave Barclay (Michigan)	Louisiana State
1948	Bob Harris (San Jose State)	San Jose State
1949	Harvie Ward (North Carolina)	North Texas State
1950	Fred Wampler (Purdue)	North Texas State
1951	Tom Nieporte (Ohio State)	North Texas State
1952	Jim Vickers (Oklahoma)	North Texas State
1953	Earl Moeller (Oklahoma A&M)	Stanford
1954	Hillman Robbins (Memphis State)	Southern Methodist
1955	Joe Campbell (Purdue)	Louisiana State
1956	Rick Jones (Ohio State)	Houston
1957	Rex Baxter, Jr. (Houston)	Houston
1958	Phil Rodgers (Houston)	Houston
1959	Dick Crawford (Houston)	Houston
1960	Dick Crawford (Houston)	Houston
1961	Jack Nicklaus (Ohio State)	Purdue
1962	Kermit Zarley (Houston)	Houston
1963	R.H. Sikes (Arkansas)	Oklahoma State
1964	Terry Small (San Jose State)	Houston
1965	Marty Fleckman (Houston)	Houston
1966	Bob Murphy (Florida)	Houston
1967	Hale Irwin (Colorado)	Houston
1968	Grier Jones (Oklahoma State)	Florida
1969	Bob Clark (Cal State-Los Angeles)	Houston
1970	Jack Mahaffey (Houston)	Houston
1971	Ben Crenshaw (Texas)	Texas
1972	Ben Crenshaw (Texas) Tom Kite (Texas)—tie	
1973	Ben Crenshaw (Texas)	Florida
1974	Curtis Strange (Wake Forest)	Wake Forest
1975	Jay Haas (Wake Forest)	Wake Forest
1976	Scott Simpson (Southern California)	Oklahoma State
1977	Scott Simpson (Southern California)	Houston
1978	David Edwards (Oklahoma State)	Oklahoma State
1979	Gary Hallberg (Wake Forest)	Ohio State
1980	Jay Don Blake (Utah State)	Oklahoma State
1981	Ron Commans (Southern California)	Brigham Young
1982	Billy Ray Brown (Houston)	Houston
1983	Jim Carter (Arizona State)	Oklahoma State
1984	John Inman (North Carolina)	Houston
1985	Clark Burroughs (Ohio State)	Houston
1986	Scott Verplank (Oklahoma State)	Wake Forest
1987	Brian Watts (Oklahoma State)	Oklahoma State
1988	E.J. Pfister (Oklahoma State)	UCLA
1989	Phil Mickelson (Arizona State)	Oklahoma
1990	Phil Mickelson (Arizona State)	Arizona State
1991	Warren Schutte (Nevada-Las Vegas)	Oklahoma State
1992	Phil Mickelson (Arizona State)	Arizona

WOMEN'S NATIONAL INTERCOLLEGIATE CHAMPIONSHIP

AIAW

Year	Winner
1941	Eleanor Dudley (Alabama)
1942–1945	Not played
1946	Phyllis Otto (Northwestern)
1947	Shirley Spork (Michigan State)
1948	Grace Lenczyk (Stetson)
1949	Marilynn Smith (Kansas)
1950	Betty Rowland (Rollins)
1951	Barbara Bruning (Wellesley)
1952	Mary Ann Villegas (Ohio State)
1953	Pat Lesser (Seattle)
1954	Nancy Reed (George Peabody)
1955	Jackie Yates (Redlands)
1956	Marlene Stewart (Rollins)
1957	Meriam Bailey (Northwestern)
1958	Carol Ann Pushing (Carleton)
1959	Judy Eller (Miami)
1960	JoAnne Gunderson (Arizona State)
1961	Judy Hoetmer (Miami)
1962	Carol Sorenson (Washington)
1963	Claudia Lindor (Arizona State)
1964	Patti Shook (Valparaiso)
1965	Roberta Albers (W. Washington State)
1966	Joyce Kazmierski (Michigan State)
1967	Martha Wilkinson (California State)
1968	Gail Sykes (Odessa)
1969	Jane Bastanchury (Arizona State)
1970	Cathy Gaughan (Arizona State)
1971	Shelley Hamlin (Stanford)

Year	Individual Champion	Team Champion
1972	Ann Laughlin (Miami)	Miami
1973	Bonnie Lauer (Michigan State)	North Carolina-Greensboro
1974	Mary Budke (Oregon State)	Rollins
1975	Barbara Barrow (San Diego State)	Arizona State
1976	Nancy Lopez (Tulsa)	Furman
1977	Cathy Morse (Miami)	Miami
1978	Debbie Petrizi (Texas)	Miami (Fla.)
1979	Kyle O'Brien (Southern Methodist)	Southern Methodist
1980	Patty Sheehan (San Jose State)	Tulsa
1981	Terri Moody (Georgia)	Florida State
1982	Amy Benz (Southern Methodist)	Tulsa

WOMEN'S NATIONAL INTERCOLLEGIATE CHAMPIONSHIP (continued)

NCAA

Year	Individual Champion	Team Champion
1982	Kathy Baker (Tulsa)	Tulsa
1983	Penny Hammell (Miami)	Texas Christian
1984	Cindy Schreyer (Georgia)	Miami (Fla.)
1985	Danielle Ammaccapane (Arizona State)	Florida
1986	Page Dunlap (Florida)	Florida
1987	Caroline Keggi (New Mexico)	San Jose State
1988	Melissa McNamara (Tulsa)	Tulsa
1989	Pat Hurst (San Jose State)	San Jose State
1990	Susan Slaughter (Arizona)	Arizona State
1991	Annika Sorenstam (Arizona)	UCLA
1992	Vicki Goetze (Georgia)	San Jose State

INTERNATIONAL TOURNAMENTS

PROFESSIONAL

Europe

BENSON & HEDGES INTERNATIONAL

1971	Tony Jacklin	1977	Antonio Garrido	1983	John Bland	1989	Gordon Brand, Jr.
1972	Jack Newton	1978	Lee Trevino	1984	Sam Torrance	1990	Jose Maria Olazabal
1973	Vince Baker	1979	Maurice Bembridge	1985	Sandy Lyle	1991	Bernhard Langer
1974	Philippe Toussaint	1980	Graham Marsh	1986	Mark James	1992	Peter Senior
1975	Vicente Fernandez	1981	Tom Weiskopf	1987	Noel Ratcliffe		
1976	Graham Marsh	1982	Greg Norman	1988	Peter Baker		

DUNHILL BRITISH MASTERS

1985	Lee Trevino	1987	Mark McNulty	1989	Nick Faldo	1991	Seve Ballesteros
1986	Seve Ballesteros	1988	Sandy Lyle	1990	Mark James	1992	Christy O'Conner, Jr.

DUTCH OPEN

1919	D. Oosterveer	1935	Sidney Brews	1962	Brian Huggett	1978	Bob Byman
1920	H. Burrows	1936	Flory van Donck	1963	R. Waltman	1979	Graham Marsh
1921	H. Burrows	1937	Flory van Donck	1964	Sewsunker Sewgolum	1980	Seve Ballesteros
1922	G. Panell	1938	Alf Padgham	1965	Angel Miguel	1981	Harold Henning
1923	H. Burrows	1939	Bobby Locke	1966	Ramon Sota	1982	Paul Way
1924	Aubrey Boomer	1940–1947	Not played	1967	Peter Townsend	1983	Ken Brown
1925	Aubrey Boomer	1948	Cecil Denny	1968	J. Cockin	1984	Bernhard Langer
1926	Aubrey Boomer	1953	Flory van Donck	1969	Guy Wolstenholme	1985	Graham Marsh
1927	Percy Boomer	1954	Ugo Grappasonni	1970	Vicente Fernandez	1986	Seve Ballesteros
1928	Ernest Whitcombe	1955	Alfonso Angelini	1971	Ramon Sota	1987	Gordon Brand, Jr.
1929	J.J. Taylor	1956	Antonio Cerda	1972	Jack Newton	1988	Mark Mouland
1930	J. Oosterveer	1957	John Jacobs	1973	Douglas McClelland	1989	Jose Maria Olazabal
1931	F. Dyer	1958	Dave Thomas	1974	Brian Barnes	1990	Stephen McAllister
1932	Auguste Boyer	1959	Sewsunker Sewgolum	1975	Hugh Baiocchi	1991	Payne Stewart
1933	Marcel Dallemagne	1960	Sewsunker Sewgolum	1976	Seve Ballesteros	1992	Bernhard Langer
1934	Sidney Brews	1961	B. Wilkes	1977	Bob Byman		

EUROPEAN MASTERS-SWISS OPEN

1923	Aleck Ross	1948	Ugo Grappasonni	1964	Harold Henning	1980	Nick Price
1924	Percy Boomer	1949	Marcel Dallemagne	1965	Harold Henning	1981	Manuel Pinero
1925	Aleck Ross	1950	Aldo Casera	1966	Alfonso Angelini	1982	Ian Woosnam
1926	Aleck Ross	1951	Eric Brown	1967	R. Vines	1983	Nick Faldo
1927–1928	Not played	1952	Ugo Grappasonni	1968	Roberto Bernardini	1984	Jerry Anderson
1929	A. Wilson	1953	Flory van Donck	1969	Roberto Bernardini	1985	Craig Stadler
1930	Auguste Boyer	1954	Bobby Locke	1970	Graham Marsh	1986	Jose Maria Olazabal
1931	Marcel Dallegmane	1955	Flory van Donck	1971	Peter Townsend	1987	Anders Forsbrand
1932–1933	Not played	1956	Dai Rees	1972	Graham Marsh	1988	Chris Moody
1934	Auguste Boyer	1957	Alfonso Angelini	1973	Hugh Baiocchi	1989	Seve Ballesteros
1935	Auguste Boyer	1958	Kenneth Bousfield	1974	Bob Charles	1990	Ronan Rafferty
1936	F. Francis	1959	Dai Rees	1975	Dale Hayes	1991	Jeff Hawkes
1937	Marcel Dallemagne	1960	Harold Henning	1976	Manuel Pinero	1992	James Spence
1938	J. Saubaber	1961	Kel Nagle	1977	Seve Ballesteros		
1939	F. Cavalo	1962	Bob Charles	1978	Seve Ballesteros		
1940–1947	Not played	1963	Dai Rees	1979	Hugh Baiocchi		

EUROPEAN OPEN

1978	Bobby Wadkins	1982	Manuel Pinero	1986	Greg Norman	1990	Peter Senior
1979	Sandy Lyle	1983	Isao Aoki	1987	Paul Way	1991	Mike Harwood
1980	Tom Kite	1984	Gordon Brand, Jr.	1988	Ian Woosnam	1992	Nick Faldo
1981	Graham Marsh	1985	Bernhard Langer	1989	Andrew Murray		

FRENCH OPEN

1906	Arnaud Massy	1930	Ernest Whitcombe	1955	Byron Nelson	1975	Brian Barnes
1907	Arnaud Massy	1931	Aubrey Boomer	1956	Angel Miguel	1976	Vincent Tshabalala
1908	John H. Taylor	1932	Arthur Lacey	1957	Flory van Donck	1977	Seve Ballesteros
1909	John H. Taylor	1933	B. Gadd	1958	Flory van Donck	1978	Dale Hayes
1910	James Braid	1934	Sidney Brews	1959	Dave Thomas	1979	Bernard Gallacher
1911	Arnaud Massy	1935	Sidney Brews	1960	Roberto De Vicenzo	1980	Greg Norman
1912	Jean Gassiat	1936	Marcel Dallemagne	1961	Kel Nagle	1981	Sandy Lyle
1913	George Duncan	1937	Marcel Dallemagne	1962	A. Murray	1982	Seve Ballesteros
1914	J. Douglas Edgar	1938	Marcel Dallemagne	1963	Bruce Devlin	1983	Nick Faldo
1915–1919	Not played	1939	M. Pose	1964	Roberto De Vicenzo	1984	Bernhard Langer
1920	Walter Hagen	1940–1945	Not played	1965	Ramon Sota	1985	Seve Ballesteros
1921	Aubrey Boomer	1946	Henry Cotton	1966	D. Hutchinson	1986	Seve Ballesteros
1922	Aubrey Boomer	1947	Henry Cotton	1967	Bernard Hunt	1987	Jose Rivero
1923	James Ockenden	1948	F. Cavalo	1968	Peter Butler	1988	Nick Faldo
1924	Cyril Tolley	1949	Ugo Grappasonni	1969	Jean Garaialde	1989	Nick Faldo
1925	Arnaud Massy	1950	Roberto De Vicenzo	1970	David Graham	1990	Philip Walton
1926	Aubrey Boomer	1951	H. Hassanein	1971	Liang Huan Lu	1991	Eduardo Romero
1927	George Duncan	1952	Bobby Locke	1972	Barry Jaeckel	1992	Miguel Angel Martin
1928	Cyril Tolley	1953	Bobby Locke	1973	Peter Oosterhuis		
1929	Aubrey Boomer	1954	Flory van Donck	1974	Peter Oosterhuis		

GERMAN OPEN

1911	Harry Vardon	1938	Henry Cotton	1963	Brian Huggett	1978	Seve Ballesteros
1912	John H. Taylor	1939	Henry Cotton	1964	Roberto De Vicenzo	1979	Tony Jacklin
1913–1925	Not played	1940–1950	Not played	1965	Harold Henning	1980	Mark McNulty
1926	Percy Alliss	1951	Antonio Cerda	1966	Bob Stanton	1981	Bernhard Langer
1927	Percy Alliss	1952	Antonio Cerda	1967	Donald Swaelens	1982	Bernhard Langer
1928	Percy Alliss	1953	Flory van Donck	1968	B. Franklin	1983	Corey Pavin
1929	Percy Alliss	1954	Bobby Locke	1969	Jean Garailde	1984	Wayne Grady
1930	Auguste Boyer	1955	Kenneth Bousfield	1970	Jean Garailde	1985	Bernhard Langer
1931	R. Golias	1956	Flory van Donck	1971	Neil Coles	1986	Bernhard Langer
1932	Auguste Boyer	1957	Harry Weetman	1972	Graham Marsh	1987	Mark McNulty
1933	Percy Alliss	1958	F. de Luca	1973	Francisco Abreu	1988	Seve Ballesteros
1934	Alf Padgham	1959	Kenneth Bousfield	1974	Simon Owen	1989	Craig Parry
1935	Auguste Boyer	1960	Peter Thomson	1975	Maurice Bembridge	1990	Mark McNulty
1936	Auguste Boyer	1961	Bernard Hunt	1976	Simon Hobday	1991	Mark McNulty
1937	Henry Cotton	1962	Bob Verwey	1977	Tienie Britz	1992	Vijay Singh

IRISH OPEN

1975	Christy O'Connor, Jr.	1980	Mark James	1985	Seve Ballesteros	1990	Jose Maria Olazabal
1976	Ben Crenshaw	1981	Sam Torrance	1986	Seve Ballesteros	1991	Nick Faldo
1977	Hubert Green	1982	John O'Leary	1987	Bernhard Langer	1992	Nick Faldo
1978	Ken Brown	1983	Seve Ballesteros	1988	Ian Woosnam		
1979	Mark James	1984	Bernhard Langer	1989	Ian Woosnam		

ITALIAN OPEN

1925	F. Pasquali	1938	Flory van Donck	1958	Peter Alliss	1980	M. Manelli
1926	Auguste Boyer	1939–1946	Not played	1959	Peter Thomson	1981	Jose Maria Canizares
1927	Percy Alliss	1947	Flory van Donck	1960	B. Wilkes	1982	Mark James
1928	Auguste Boyer	1948	Aldo Casera	1961–1970	Not played	1983	Bernhard Langer
1929	R. Golias	1949	H. Hassanein	1971	Ramon Sota	1984	Sandy Lyle
1930	Auguste Boyer	1950	Ugo Grappasonni	1972	Norman Wood	1985	Manuel Pinero
1931	Auguste Boyer	1951	James Adams	1973	Tony Jacklin	1986	David Feherty
1932	Aubrey Boomer	1952	Eric Brown	1974	Peter Oosterhuis	1987	Sam Torrance
1933	Not played	1953	Flory van Donck	1975	Billy Casper	1988	Greg Norman
1934	N. Nutley	1954	Ugo Grappasonni	1976	Baldovino Dassu	1989	Ronan Rafferty
1935	Percy Alliss	1955	Flory van Donck	1977	Angel Gallardo	1990	Richard Boxall
1936	Henry Cotton	1956	Antonio Cerda	1978	Dale Hayes	1991	Craig Parry
1937	M. Dallemagne	1957	Harold Henning	1979	Brian Barnes	1992	Sandy Lyle

LANCÔME TROPHY

1970	Tony Jacklin	1976	Seve Ballesteros	1982	David Graham	1987	Ian Woosnam
1971	Arnold Palmer	1977	Graham Marsh	1983	Seve Ballesteros	1988	Seve Ballesteros
1972	Tommy Aaron	1978	Lee Trevino	1984	Sandy Lyle	1989	Eduardo Romero
1973	Johnny Miller	1979	Johnny Miller	1985	Nick Price	1990	Jose Maria Olazabal
1974	Billy Casper	1980	Lee Trevino	1986	Seve Ballesteros,	1991	Frank Nobilo
1975	Gary Player	1981	David Graham		Bernhard Langer	1992	Mark Roe

VOLVO PGA CHAMPIONSHIP

1955	Kenneth Bousfield	1965	Peter Alliss	1975	Arnold Palmer	1985	Paul Way
1956	Charles Ward	1966	Guy Wolstenholme	1976	Neil Coles	1986	Rodger Davis
1957	Peter Alliss	1967	Malcolm Gregson	1977	Manuel Pinero	1987	Bernhard Langer
1958	Harry Bradshaw	1968	Peter Townsend	1978	Nick Faldo	1988	Ian Woosnam
1959	Dai Rees	1968	D. Talbot	1979	Vicente Fernandez	1989	Nick Faldo
1960	A.F. Stickley	1969	Bernard Gallacher	1980	Nick Faldo	1990	Mike Harwood
1961	B.J. Bamford	1970–1971	Not played	1981	Nick Faldo	1991	Seve Ballesteros
1962	Peter Alliss	1972	Tony Jacklin	1982	Tony Jacklin	1992	Tony Johnstone
1963	Peter Butler	1973	Peter Oosterhuis	1983	Seve Ballesteros		
1964	A.G. Grubb	1974	Maurice Bembridge	1984	Howard Clark		

SCANDINAVIAN OPEN

1973	Bob Charles	1978	Seve Ballesteros	1983	Sam Torrance	1988	Seve Ballesteros
1974	Tony Jacklin	1979	Sandy Lyle	1984	Ian Woosnam	1989	Ronan Rafferty
1975	George Burns	1980	Greg Norman	1985	Ian Baker-Finch	1990	Craig Stadler
1976	Hugh Baiocchi	1981	Seve Ballesteros	1986	Greg Turner	1991	Colin Montgomerie
1977	Bob Byman	1982	Bob Byman	1987	Gordon Brand, Jr.	1992	Nick Faldo

SPANISH OPEN

1912	Arnaud Massy	1933	G. Gonzalez	1955	H. de Lamaze	1974	Jerry Heard
1913–1915 Not played		1934	J. Bernardino	1956	Peter Alliss	1975	Arnold Palmer
1916	A. de la Torre	1935	A. de la Torre	1957	Max Faulkner	1976	Eddie Polland
1917	A. de la Torre	1936–1940 Not played		1958	Peter Alliss	1977	Bernard Gallacher
1918	Not played	1941	M. Provencio	1959	Peter Thomson	1978	Brian Barnes
1919	A. de la Torre	1942	G. Gonzalez	1960	Sebastian Miguel	1979	Dale Hayes
1920	Not played	1943	M. Provencio	1961	Angel Miguel	1980	Eddie Polland
1921	E. Lafitte	1944	N. Sagardia	1962	Not played	1981	Seve Ballesteros
1922	Not played	1945	C. Celles	1963	Ramon Sota	1982	Sam Torrance
1923	A. de la Torre	1946	M. Morcillio	1964	Angel Miguel	1983	Eamonn Darcy
1924	Not played	1947	M. Gonzalez,	1965	Not played	1984	Bernhard Langer
1925	A. de la Torre		M. Morcillo	1966	Roberto De Vicenzo	1985	Seve Ballesteros
1926	J. Bernardino	1948	M. Morcillo	1967	Sebastian Miguel	1986	Howard Clark
1927	Arnaud Massy	1949	M. Morcillo	1968	Bob Shaw	1987	Nick Faldo
1928	Arnaud Massy	1950	Antonio Cerda	1969	Jean Garaialde	1988	Mark James
1929	E. Lafitte	1951	M. Provencio	1970	Angel Gallardo	1989	Bernhard Langer
1930	J. Bernardino	1952	Max Faulkner	1971	Dale Hayes	1990	Rodger Davis
1931	Not played	1953	Max Faulkner	1972	Antonio Garrido	1991	Eduardo Romero
1932	G. Gonzalez	1954	Sebastian Miguel	1973	Neil Coles	1992	Andrew Sherborne

VOLVO MASTERS

1988	Nick Faldo	1990	Mike Harwood	1992	Sandy Lyle
1989	Ronan Rafferty	1991	Rodger Davis		

WORLD MATCH PLAY CHAMPIONSHIP

1964	Arnold Palmer	1972	Tom Weiskopf	1980	Greg Norman	1988	Sandy Lyle
1965	Gary Player	1973	Gary Player	1981	Seve Ballesteros	1989	Nick Faldo
1966	Gary Player	1974	Hale Irwin	1982	Seve Ballesteros	1990	Ian Woosnam
1967	Arnold Palmer	1975	Hale Irwin	1983	Greg Norman	1991	Seve Ballesteros
1968	Gary Player	1976	David Graham	1984	Seve Ballesteros	1992	Nick Faldo
1969	Bob Charles	1977	Graham Marsh	1985	Seve Ballesteros		
1970	Jack Nicklaus	1978	Isao Aoki	1986	Greg Norman		
1971	Gary Player	1979	Bill Rogers	1987	Ian Woosnam		

Australia/New Zealand

AUSTRALIAN MASTERS

1979	Barry Vivian	1983	Greg Norman	1987	Greg Norman	1991	Peter Senior
1980	Gene Littler	1984	Greg Norman	1988	Ian Baker-Finch	1992	Craig Parry
1981	Greg Norman	1985	Bernhard Langer	1989	Greg Norman		
1982	Graham Marsh	1986	Mark O'Meara	1990	Greg Norman		

AUSTRALIAN OPEN

1904	Michael Scott	1929	Ivo Whitton	1954	Ossie Pickworth	1974	Gary Player
1905	D. Soutar	1930	F.P. Eyre	1955	Bobby Locke	1975	Jack Nicklaus
1906	Carnegie Clark	1931	Ivo Whitton	1956	Bruce Crampton	1976	Jack Nicklaus
1907	Michael Scott	1932	M.J. Ryan	1957	Frank Phillips	1977	David Graham
1908	Clyde Pearce	1933	M.L. Kelly	1958	Gary Player	1978	Jack Nicklaus
1909	C. Felstead	1934	W.J. Bolger	1959	Kel Nagle	1979	Jack Newton
1910	Carnegie Clark	1935	F.W. McMahon	1960	Bruce Devlin	1980	Greg Norman
1911	Not played	1936	Gene Sarazen	1961	Frank Phillips	1981	Bill Rogers
1912	Ivo Whitton	1937	G. Naismith	1962	Gary Player	1982	Bob Shearer
1913	Ivo Whitton	1938	Jim Ferrier	1963	Gary Player	1983	Peter Fowler
1914–1919 Not played		1939	Jim Ferrier	1964	Jack Nicklaus	1984	Tom Watson
1920	Joe Kirkwood	1940–1945 Not played		1965	Gary Player	1985	Greg Norman
1921	A. LeFevre	1946	Ossie Pickworth	1966	Arnold Palmer	1986	Rodger Davis
1922	C. Campbell	1947	Ossie Pickworth	1967	Peter Thomson	1987	Greg Norman
1923	T.E. Howard	1948	Ossie Pickworth	1968	Jack Nicklaus	1988	Mark Calcavecchia
1924	A. Russell	1949	E. Cremin	1969	Gary Player	1989	Peter Senior
1925	F. Popplewell	1950	Norman von Nida	1970	Gary Player	1990	Peter Senior
1926	Ivo Whitton	1951	Peter Thomson	1971	Jack Nicklaus	1991	Wayne Riley
1927	R. Stewart	1952	Norman von Nida	1972	Peter Thomson		
1928	F. Popplewell	1953	Norman von Nida	1973	J.C. Snead		

AUSTRALIAN PGA

1906	D. Soutar	1939	E. Nesmith	1961	A. Murray	1978	Hale Irwin
1907	D. Soutar	1940–1945 Not played		1962	Bill Dunk	1979	Stewart Ginn
1908–1923 Not available		1946	Norman von Nida	1963	C. Johnston	1980	Sam Torrance
1924	T. Howard	1947	Ossie Pickworth	1964	C. Johnston	1981	Seve Ballesteros
1925	T. Howard	1948	Norman von Nida	1965	Kel Nagle	1982	Graham Marsh
1926	F. Eyre	1949	Kel Nagle	1966	Peter Thomson	1983	Bob Shearer
1927–1928 Not played		1950	Norman von Nida	1967	Bill Dunk	1984	Greg Norman
1929	R. Stewart	1951	Norman von Nida	1968	Kel Nagle	1985	Greg Norman
1930	J. Robertson	1952	W. Holder	1969	Bruce Devlin	1986	Michael Harwood
1931	J. Spence	1953	Ossie Pickworth	1970	Bruce Devlin	1987	Roger Mackay
1932	F. McMahon	1954	Kel Nagle	1971	Bill Dunk	1988	Wayne Grady
1933	V. Richardson	1955	Ossie Pickworth	1972	Randall Vines	1989	Peter Senior
1934	M. Kelly	1956	L. Wilson	1973	Randall Vines	1990	Brett Ogle
1935	V. Richardson	1957	Gary Player	1974	Bill Dunk	1991	Wayne Grady
1936	W. Clifford	1958	Kel Nagle	1975	Vic Bennetts		
1937	E. Cremin	1959	Kel Nagle	1976	Bill Dunk		
1938	E. Cremin	1960	J. Sullivan	1977	Mike Cahill		

NEW ZEALAND OPEN

1907	A.D.S. Duncan	1930	Andrew Shaw	1955	Peter Thomson	1975	Bill Dunk
1908	J.A. Clements	1931	Andrew Shaw	1956	N. Berwick	1976	Simon Owen
1909	J.A. Clements	1932	Andrew Shaw	1957	Kel Nagle	1977	Bob Byman
1910	A.D.S. Duncan	1933	E.J. Moss	1958	Kel Nagle	1978	Bob Shearer
1911	A.D.S. Duncan	1934	Andrew Shaw	1959	Peter Thomson	1979	Stewart Ginn
1912	J.A. Clements	1935	A. Murray	1960	Peter Thomson	1980	Brian Allin
1913	E.S. Douglas	1936	Andrew Shaw	1961	Peter Thomson	1981	Bob Shearer
1914	E.S. Douglas	1937	J.P. Hornabrook	1962	Kel Nagle	1982	Terry Gale
1915–1918 Not played		1938	Bobby Locke	1963	Bruce Devlin	1983	Ian Baker-Finch
1919	E.S. Douglas	1939	J.P. Hornabrook	1964	Kel Nagle	1984	Bruce Devlin
1920	Joe Kirkwood	1940–1945 Not played		1965	Peter Thomson	1985	Corey Pavin
1921	E.S. Douglas	1946	R.H. Glading	1966	Bob Charles	1986	Rodger Davis
1922	A. Brooks	1947	R.H. Glading	1967	Kel Nagle	1987	Ronan Rafferty
1923	A. Brooks	1948	A. Murray	1968	Kel Nagle	1988	Terry Gale
1924	E.J. Moss	1949	James Galloway	1969	Kel Nagle	1989	Greg Turner
1925	E.M. Macfarlane	1950	Peter Thomson	1970	Bob Charles	1990	Ian Stanley
1926	Andrew Shaw	1951	Peter Thomson	1971	Peter Thomson	1991	Rodger Davis
1927	E.J. Moss	1952	A. Murray	1972	Bill Dunk		
1928	S. Morpeth	1953	Peter Thomson	1973	Bob Charles		
1929	Andrew Shaw	1954	Bob Charles	1974	Bob Gilder		

Japan

BRIDGESTONE TOURNAMENT

1972	Hsieh Min Nan	1978	Hiroshi Ishii	1984	Masahiro Kuramoto	1990	Saburo Fujiki
1973	Hiroshi Ishii	1979	Lanny Wadkins	1985	Masahiro Kuramoto	1991	Isao Aoki
1974	Graham Marsh	1980	Bob Gilder	1986	Tateo Ozaki	1992	Masahiro Kuramoto
1975	Yoshitaka Yamamoto	1981	Hale Irwin	1987	David Ishii		
1976	Takashi Murakami	1982	Hsieh Min Nan	1988	Masashi Ozaki		
1977	Fujio Kobayashi	1983	Eitaro Deguchi	1989	Roger Mackay		

CHUNICHI CROWNS

1972	Peter Thomson	1978	Isao Aoki	1984	Scott Simpson	1990	Noboru Sugai
1973	Isao Aoki	1979	Isao Aoki	1985	Seiji Ebihara	1991	Seve Ballesteros
1974	Takashi Murakami	1980	Isao Aoki	1986	David Ishii	1992	Masashi Ozaki
1975	Isao Aoki	1981	Graham Marsh	1987	Masashi Ozaki		
1976	David Graham	1982	Gary Hallberg	1988	Scott Simpson		
1977	Graham Marsh	1983	Tze Ming Chen	1989	Greg Norman		

DUNLOP PHOENIX

1974	Johnny Miller	1979	Bobby Wadkins	1984	Scott Simpson	1989	Larry Mize
1975	Hubert Green	1980	Tom Watson	1985	Tsuneyuki Nakajima	1990	Larry Mize
1976	Graham Marsh	1981	Seve Ballesteros	1986	Bobby Wadkins	1991	Larry Nelson
1977	Seve Ballesteros	1982	Calvin Peete	1987	Craig Stadler		
1978	Andy Bean	1983	Tze Ming Chen	1988	Ken Green		

JAPAN OPEN

1927	R. Akahoshi	1942–1949	Not played	1964	Hideyo Sugimoto	1979	Kuo Chi Hsiung
1928	R. Asami	1950	Y. Hayashi	1965	T. Kitta	1980	Katsuji Kikuchi
1929	T. Miyamoto	1951	Son Shi Kin	1966	S. Sato	1981	Yutaka Hagawa
1930	T. Miyamoto	1952	Torakichi Nakamura	1967	T. Kitta	1982	Akira Yobe
1931	R. Asami	1953	Son Shi Kin	1968	Takaaki Kono	1983	Isao Aoki
1932	T. Miyamoto	1954	Y. Hayashi	1969	Hideyo Sugimoto	1984	Koichi Uehara
1933	K. Nakamura	1955	Koichi Ono	1970	M. Kitta	1985	Tsuneyuki Nakajima
1934	Not played	1956	Torakichi Nakamura	1971	Y. Fujii	1986	Tsuneyuki Nakajima
1935	T. Miyamoto	1957	H. Kobari	1972	Hahn Chang Sang	1987	Isao Aoki
1936	T. Miyamoto	1958	Torakichi Nakamura	1973	Ben Arda	1988	Masashi Ozaki
1937	Chin Sei Sui	1959	Chen Ching-Po	1974	Masashi Ozaki	1989	Masashi Ozaki
1938	R.M. Fuku	1960	H. Kobari	1975	Takashi Murakami	1990	Tsuneyuki Nakajima
1939	T. Toda	1961	K. Hosoishi	1976	Kosaku Shimada	1991	Tsuneyuki Nakajima
1940	T. Miyamoto	1962	Teruo Sugihara	1977	Seve Ballesteros	1992	Masahi Ozaki
1941	En Toku Shun	1963	T. Toda	1978	Seve Ballesteros		

JAPAN PGA

1931	R. Asami	1953	Chin Sei Sui	1967	S. Miyamoto	1981	Isao Aoki
1932	L. Montes	1954	S. Ishif	1968	K. Shimada	1982	Masahiro Kuramoto
1933	L. Montes	1955	Koichi Ono	1969	H. Ishii	1983	Tsuneyuki Nakajima
1934	T. Miyamoto	1956	Y. Hayashi	1970	S. Sato	1984	Tsuneyuki Nakajima
1935	T. Toda	1957	Torakichi Nakamura	1971	Masashi Ozaki	1985	Tateo Ozaki
1936	T. Miyamoto	1958	Torakichi Nakamura	1972	Seiichi Kanai	1986	Isao Aoki
1937	I. Uekata	1959	Torakichi Nakamura	1973	Isao Aoki	1987	David Ishii
1938	T. Toda	1960	R. Tanaami	1974	Masashi Ozaki	1988	Tateo Ozaki
1939	T. Toda	1961	Y. Hayashi	1975	Takashi Murakami	1989	Masashi Ozaki
1940	T. Toda	1962	Torakichi Nakamura	1976	Seiichi Kanai	1990	Hideki Kase
1941–49	Not played	1963	T. Kitta	1977	Tsuneyuki Nakajima	1991	Masashi Ozaki
1950	Y. Hayashi	1964	T. Kitta	1978	Fujio Kobayashi	1992	Masahiro Kuramoto
1951	T. Ishii	1965	M. Kono	1979	Hsieh Min Nan		
1952	S. Inoue	1966	M. Kono	1980	Yoshitaka Yamamoto		

TAIHEIYO MASTERS

1972	Gay Brewer	1977	Bill Rogers	1982	Scott Hoch	1988	Seve Ballesteros
1973	Masashi Ozaki	1978	Gil Morgan	1983–1984	Not played	1989	Jose Maria Olazabal
1974	Gene Littler	1979	Norio Suzuki	1985	Tsuneyuki Nakajima	1990	Jose Maria Olazabal
1975	Gene Littler	1980	Norio Suzuki	1986	Yasuhiro Funatogawa	1991	Roger Mackay
1976	Jerry Pate	1981	Danny Edwards	1987	Graham Marsh		

Africa

SOUTH AFRICAN OPEN

1905	A.G. Gray	1929	A. Tosh	1954	R.C. Taylor	1975	Bobby Cole
1906	A.G. Gray	1930	Sidney Brews	1955	Bobby Locke	1976	Dale Hayes
1907	L.B. Waters	1931	Sidney Brews	1956	Gary Player	1977	Gary Player
1908	G. Fotheringham	1932	C. McIlvenny	1957	Harold Henning	1978	Hugh Baiocchi
1909	J. Fotheringham	1933	Sidney Brews	1958	A.A. Stewart	1979	Gary Player
1910	G. Fotheringham	1934	Sidney Brews	1959	D.J. Hutchinson	1980	Bobby Cole
1911	G. Fotheringham	1935	Bobby Locke	1960	Gary Player	1981	Gary Player
1912	G. Fotheringham	1936	C.E. Olander	1961	R. Waltman	1982	Not played
1913	J.A.W. Prentice	1937	Bobby Locke	1962	Harold Henning	1983	Charles Bolling
1914	G. Fotheringham	1938	Bobby Locke	1963	R. Waltman	1984	Tony Johnstone
1915–1918 Not played		1939	Bobby Locke	1964	Alan Henning	1985	Gavin Levenson
1919	H.G. Stewart	1940	Bobby Locke	1965	Gary Player	1986	David Frost
1920	L.B. Waters	1941–1945 Not played		1966	Gary Player	1987	Mark McNulty
1921	J. Brews	1946	Bobby Locke	1967	Gary Player	1988	Wayne Westner
1922	F. Jangle	1947	R.W. Glennie	1968	Gary Player	1989	Fred Wadsworth
1923	J. Brews	1948	M. Janks	1969	Gary Player	1990	Trevor Dodds
1924	B.H. Elkin	1949	Sidney Brews	1970	Tommy Horton	1991	Wayne Westner
1925	Sidney Brews	1950	Bobby Locke	1971	Simon Hobday	1992	Ernie Els
1926	J. Brews	1951	Bobby Locke	1972	Gary Player		
1927	Sidney Brews	1952	Sidney Brews	1973	Gary Player		
1928	J. Brews	1953	J.R. Boyd	1974	Bob Charles		

Americas

CANADIAN OPEN

1904	J.H. Oke	1929	Leo Diegel	1952	John Palmer	1974	Bobby Nichols
1905	George Cumming	1930	Tommy Armour	1953	Dave Douglas	1975	Tom Weiskopf
1906	Charles Murray	1931	Walter Hagen	1954	Pat Fletcher	1976	Jerry Pate
1907	Percy Barrett	1932	Harry Cooper	1955	Arnold Palmer	1977	Lee Trevino
1908	Albert Murray	1933	Joe Kirkwood	1956	Doug Sanders	1978	Bruce Lietzke
1909	Karl Keffer	1934	Tommy Armour	1957	George Bayer	1979	Lee Trevino
1910	Daniel Kenny	1935	Gene Kunes	1958	Wesley Ellis	1980	Bob Gilder
1911	Charles Murray	1936	Lawson Little	1959	Doug Ford	1981	Peter Oosterhuis
1912	George Sargent	1937	Harry Cooper	1960	Art Wall	1982	Bruce Lietzke
1913	Albert Murray	1938	Sam Snead	1961	Jacky Cupit	1983	John Cook
1914	Karl Keffer	1939	Harold McSpaden	1962	Ted Kroll	1984	Greg Norman
1915–1918 Not played		1940	Sam Snead	1963	Doug Ford	1985	Curtis Strange
1919	J. Douglas Edgar	1941	Sam Snead	1964	Kel Nagle	1986	Bob Murphy
1920	J. Douglas Edgar	1942	Craig Wood	1965	Gene Littler	1987	Curtis Strange
1921	W.H. Trovinger	1943–1944 Not played		1966	Don Massengale	1988	Ken Green
1922	Al Watrous	1945	Byron Nelson	1967	Billy Casper	1989	Steve Jones
1923	C.W. Hackney	1946	George Fazio	1968	Bob Charles	1990	Wayne Levi
1924	Leo Diegel	1947	Bobby Locke	1969	Tommy Aaron	1991	Nick Price
1925	Leo Diegel	1948	C.W. Congdon	1970	Kermit Zarley	1992	Greg Norman
1926	Mac Smith	1949	Dutch Harrison	1971	Lee Trevino		
1927	Tommy Armour	1950	Jim Ferrier	1972	Gay Brewer		
1928	Leo Diegel	1951	Jim Ferrier	1973	Tom Weiskopf		

AMATEUR

BRITISH AMATEUR

1885	A.F. Macfie	1910	John Ball	1939	Alexander Kyle	1969	Michael Bonnallack
1886	Horace Hutchinson	1911	Harold Hilton	1940–1945	Not played	1970	Michael Bonnallack
1887	Horace Hutchinson	1912	John Ball	1946	James Bruen	1971	Steve Melnyk
1888	John Ball	1913	Harold Hilton	1947	Willie Turnesa	1972	Trevor Homer
1889	J.E. Laidlay	1914	J.L.C. Jenkins	1948	Frank Stranahan	1973	Richard Siderowf
1890	John Ball	1915–1919	Not played	1949	Samuel McCready	1974	Trevor Homer
1891	J.E. Laidlay	1920	Cyril Tolley	1950	Frank Stranahan	1975	Vinnie Giles
1892	John Ball	1921	William Hunter	1951	Richard Chapman	1976	Richard Siderowf
1893	P.C. Anderson	1922	Ernest Holderness	1952	E. Harvie Ward	1977	Peter McEvoy
1894	John Ball	1923	Roger Wethered	1953	Joe Carr	1978	Peter McEvoy
1895	Leslie Balfour-Melville	1924	Ernest Holderness	1954	Douglas Bachli	1979	Jay Sigel
1896	F.G. Tait	1925	Robert Harris	1955	Joe Conrad	1980	Duncan Evans
1897	A.J.T. Allan	1926	Jess Sweetser	1956	John Beharrell	1981	Phillippe Ploujoux
1898	F.G. Tait	1927	William Tweddell	1957	R. Reid Jack	1982	Martin Thompson
1899	John Ball	1928	Thomas Perkins	1958	Joe Carr	1983	Philip Parkin
1900	Harold Hilton	1929	Cyril Tolley	1959	Deane Beman	1984	Jose-Maria Olazabal
1901	Harold Hilton	1930	Bob Jones	1960	Joe Carr	1985	Garth McGimpsey
1902	C. Hutchings	1931	E. Martin Smith	1961	Michael Bonnallack	1986	David Curry
1903	R. Maxwell	1932	John de Forest	1962	Richard Davies	1987	Paul Mayo
1904	Walter Travis	1933	Michael Scott	1963	Michael Lunt	1988	Christian Hardin
1905	A.G. Barry	1934	Lawson Little	1964	Gordon Clark	1989	Stephen Dodd
1906	James Robb	1935	Lawson Little	1965	Michael Bonnallack	1990	Rolf Muntz
1907	John Ball	1936	Hector Thomson	1966	Bobby Cole	1991	Gary Wolstenholme
1908	E.A. Lassen	1937	Robert Sweeny	1967	Bob Dickson	1992	Stephen Dundas
1909	R. Maxwell	1938	Charles Yates	1968	Michael Bonnallack		

CANADIAN AMATEUR

1895	T.H. Harley	1921	Frank Thompson	1949	Richard Chapman	1972	Doug Roxburgh
1896	Stewart Gillespie	1922	C.C. Fraser	1950	William Mawhinney	1973	George Burns
1897	W.A.H. Kerr	1923	W.J. Thompson	1951	Walter McElroy	1974	Doug Roxburgh
1898	George Lyon	1924	Frank Thompson	1952	Larry Bouchey	1975	Jim Nelford
1899	Vere Brown	1925	Donald Carrick	1953	Don Cherry	1976	Jim Nelford
1900	George Lyon	1926	C. Ross Somerville	1954	E. Harvie Ward	1977	Rod Spittle
1901	W.A.H. Kerr	1927	Donald Carrick	1955	Moe Norman	1978	Rod Spittle
1902	F.R. Martin	1928	C. Ross Somerville	1956	Moe Norman	1979	Rafael Alarcon
1903	George Lyon	1929	Eddie Held	1957	Nick Weslock	1980	Greg Olson
1904	Percy Taylor	1930	C. Ross Somerville	1958	Bruce Castator	1981	Richard Zokol
1905	George Lyon	1931	C. Ross Somerville	1959	John Johnston	1982	Doug Roxburgh
1906	George Lyon	1932	Gordon Taylor	1960	R.K. Alexander	1983	Danny Mijovic
1907	George Lyon	1933	Albert Campbell	1961	Gary Cowan	1984	Bill Swarz
1908	Alex Wilson	1934	Albert Campbell	1962	Reg Taylor	1985	Brent Franklin
1909	E. Legge	1935	C. Ross Somerville	1963	Nick Weslock	1986	Brent Franklin
1910	Fritz Martin	1936	Fred Haas, Jr.	1964	Nick Weslock	1987	Brent Franklin
1911	G.H. Hutton	1937	C. Ross Somerville	1965	Bunky Henry	1988	Doug Roxburgh
1912	George Lyon	1938	Ted Adams	1966	Nick Weslock	1989	Warren Sye
1913	G.H. Turpin	1939	Kenneth Black	1967	S. Jones	1990	Peter Major
1914	George Lyon	1940–1945 Not played		1968	Jim Doyle	1991	Jeff Kraemer
1915–1918 Not played		1946	Henry Martell	1969	Wayne McDonald	1992	Darren Ritchie
1919	William McLuckie	1947	Frank Stranahan	1970	Allen Miller		
1920	C.B. Grier	1948	Frank Stranahan	1971	Richard Siderowf		

WOMEN

LADIES' BRITISH OPEN

1976	Jenny Lee Smith	1981	Debbie Massey	1986	Laura Davies	1991	Penny Grice-Whitaker
1977	Vivien Saunders	1982	Marta Figueras-Dotti	1987	Alison Nicholas	1992	Patty Sheehan
1978	Janet Melville	1983	Not played	1988	Corinne Dibnah		
1979	Alison Sheard	1984	Ayako Okamoto	1989	Jane Geddes		
1980	Debbie Massey	1985	Betsy King	1990	Helen Alfredsson		

LADIES' BRITISH AMATEUR

1893	Lady Margaret Scott	1921	Cecil Leitch	1949	Frances Stephens	1972	Michelle Walker
1894	Lady Margaret Scott	1922	Joyce Wethered	1950	Vicomtesse de Saint	1973	Ann Irvin
1895	Lady Margaret Scott	1923	Doris Chambers		Sauveur	1974	Ann Irvin
1896	A.B. Pascoe	1924	Joyce Wethered	1951	Mrs. P.G. Maccan	1975	Julia Greenhalgh
1897	E.C. Orr	1925	Joyce Wethered	1952	Moira Paterson	1976	Cathy Panton
1898	L. Thompson	1926	Cecil Leitch	1953	Marlene Stewart	1977	Angela Uzielli
1899	May Hezlet	1927	Thion de la Chaume	1954	Frances Stevens	1978	Edwina Kennedy
1900	Rhona K. Adair	1928	Nanette LeBlan	1955	Mrs. G. Valentine	1979	Maureen Madill
1901	Molly A. Graham	1929	Joyce Wethered	1956	Wiffi Smith	1980	Anne Sander
1902	May Hezlet	1930	Diana Fishwick	1957	Philomena Garvey	1981	Belle Robertson
1903	Rhona K. Adair	1931	Enid Wilson	1958	Mrs. G. Valentine	1982	Kitrina Douglas
1904	Lottie Dod	1932	Enid Wilson	1959	Elizabeth Price	1983	Jill Thornhill
1905	B. Thompson	1933	Enid Wilson	1960	Barbara McIntire	1984	Jody Rosenthal
1906	Mrs. W. Kennion	1934	Mrs. A.M. Holm	1961	Mrs. A.D. Spearman	1985	Lilian Behan
1907	May Hezlet	1935	Wanda Morgan	1962	Mrs. A.D. Spearman	1986	Marnie McGuire
1908	M. Titterton	1936	Pamela Barton	1963	Brigette Varangot	1987	Janet Collingham
1909	Dorothy Campbell	1937	Jessie Anderson	1964	Carol Sorenson	1988	Joanne Furby
1910	G. Suttie	1938	Mrs. A.W. Holm	1965	Brigette Varangot	1989	Helen Dobson
1911	Dorothy Campbell	1939	Pamela Barton	1966	Elizabeth Chadwick	1990	Julie Hall
1912	Gladys Ravenscroft	1940–1945	Not played	1967	Elizabeth Chadwick	1991	Valerie Michaud
1913	Muriel Dodd	1946	Mrs. G.W.	1968	Brigette Varangot	1992	Pernille Pedersen
1914	Cecil Leitch		Hetherington	1969	Catherine Lacoste		
1915–1919	Not played	1947	Babe Zaharias	1970	Dinah Oxley		
1920	Cecil Leitch	1948	Louise Suggs	1971	Michelle Walker		

CANADIAN WOMEN'S AMATEUR

1901	L. Young	1926	Ada Mackenzie	1954	Marlene Stewart	1975	Debbie Massey
1902	M. Thomson	1927	Helen Payson	1955	Marlene Stewart	1976	Debbie Massey
1903	F. Harvey	1928	Virginia Wilson	1956	Marlene Stewart	1977	Cathy Sherk
1904	F. Harvey	1929	Helen Hicks	1957	Betty Stanhope	1978	Cathy Sherk
1905	M. Thomson	1930	Maureen Orcutt	1958	Marlene Stewart Streit	1979	Stacey West
1906	M. Thomson	1931	Maureen Orcutt	1959	Marlene Stewart Streit	1980	Edwina Kennedy
1907	M. Thomson	1932	Margery Kirkham	1960	Judy Darling	1981	Jane Lock
1908	M. Thomson	1933	Ada Mackenzie	1961	Judy Darling	1982	Cindy Pleger
1909	V.H. Anderson	1934	Alexa Stirling Fraser	1962	Gayle Hitchens	1983	Dawn Coe
1910	Dorothy Campbell	1935	Ada Mackenzie	1963	Marlene Stewart Streit	1984	Kim Williams
1911	Dorothy Campbell	1936	Mrs. A.B. Darling	1964	Margaret Masters	1985	Kim Williams
1912	Dorothy Campbell	1937	Mrs. J. Rogers	1965	Jocelyn Bourassa	1986	Marilyn O'Connor
1913	M. Todd	1938	Mrs. F.J. Mulqueen	1966	Helene Gagnon	1987	Tracy Kerdyk
1914–1918	Not played	1939–1946	Not played	1967	Bridget Jackson	1988	Michiko Hattori
1919	Ada Mackenzie	1947	Grace Lenczyk	1968	Marlene Stewart Streit	1989	Cheryl Dasphone
1920	Alexa Stirling	1948	Grace Lenczyk	1969	Marlene Stewart Streit	1990	Sara LeBrun Ingram
1921	Cecil Leitch	1949	Grace DeMoss	1970	Mrs. G.H. Moore	1991	Adele Moore
1922	Mrs. W.A. Gavin	1950	Dorothy Kielty	1971	Jocelyn Bourassa	1992	Marie-Josee Roleau
1923	Glenna Collett	1951	Marlene Stewart	1972	Marlene Stewart Streit		
1924	Glenna Collett	1952	Edean Anderson	1973	Marlene Stewart Streit		
1925	Ada Mackenzie	1953	Barbara Romack	1974	Debbie Massey		

INTERNATIONAL TEAM MATCHES

MEN'S PROFESSIONAL

RYDER CUP MATCH

Year	Winner/Loser	Site
1927	United States, 9½ Great Britain, 2½	Worcester CC, Worcester, Mass.
1929	Great Britain, 7 United States, 5	Moortown, England
1931	United States, 9 Great Britain, 3	Scioto CC, Columbus, Ohio
1933	Great Britain, 6½ United States, 5½	Southport & Ainsdale Courses, England
1935	United States, 9 Great Britain, 3	Ridgewood CC, Ridgewood, N.J.
1937	United States, 8 Great Britain, 4	Southport & Ainsdale Courses, England

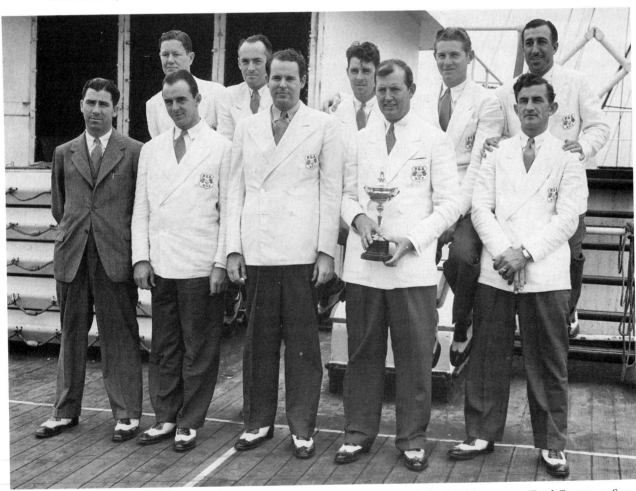

The 1937 U.S. Ryder Cup team was the first to win on British soil. Front row, left to right, manager Fred Corcoran, Sam Snead, Ralph Guldahl, Ed Dudley, Johnny Revolta. Back row, left to right, Byron Nelson, Denny Shute, Henry Picard, Horton Smith, Tony Manero. *Wide World Photos*

RYDER CUP MATCH (continued)

Year	Winner/Loser	Site
1947	United States, 11 Great Britain, 1	Portland GC, Portland, Ore.
1949	United States, 7 Great Britain, 5	Ganton GC, Scarborough, England
1949	United States, 7 Great Britain, 5	Ganton GC, Scarborough, England
1951	United States, 9$^1/_2$ Great Britain, 2$^1/_2$	Pinehurst CC, Pinehurst, N.C.
1953	United States, 6$^1/_2$ Great Britain, 5$^1/_2$	Wentworth, England
1955	United States, 8 Great Britain, 4	Thunderbird Ranch & CC, Palm Springs, Cal.
1957	Great Britain, 7$^1/_2$ United States, 4$^1/_2$	Lindrick GC, Yorkshire, England
1959	United States, 8$^1/_2$ Great Britain, 3$^1/_2$	Eldorado CC, Palm Desert, Cal.
1961	United States, 14$^1/_2$ Great Britain, 9$^1/_2$	Royal Lytham and St. Anne's GC, St. Anne's-On-The-Sea, England
1963	United States, 23 Great Britain, 9	East Lake CC, Atlanta, Ga.
1965	United States, 19$^1/_2$ Great Britain, 12$^1/_2$	Royal Birkdale GC, Southport, England
1967	United States, 23$^1/_2$ Great Britain, 8$^1/_2$	Champions GC, Houston, Tex.
1969	United States, 16 Great Britain, 16—Tie	Royal Birkdale GC, Southport, England
1971	United States, 18$^1/_2$ Great Britain, 13$^1/_2$	Old Warson CC, St. Louis, Mo.
1973	United States, 19 Great Britain, 13	Muirfield, Scotland
1975	United States, 21 Great Britain, 11	Laurel Valley GC, Ligonier, Pa.
1977	United States, 12$^1/_2$ Great Britain, 7$^1/_2$	Royal Lytham and St. Anne's GC, St. Anne's-On-The-Sea, England
1979	United States, 17 Europe, 11	Greenbrier, White Sulphur Springs, W. Va.
1981	United States, 18$^1/_2$ Europe, 9$^1/_2$	Walton Health GC, Surrey, England
1983	United States, 14$^1/_2$ Europe, 13$^1/_2$	PGA National GC, Palm Beach Gardens, Fla.
1985	Europe, 16$^1/_2$ United States, 11$^1/_2$	The Belfry GC, Sutton Coldfield, England
1987	Europe, 15 United States, 13	Muirfield Village GC, Dublin, Ohio
1989	Europe, 14 United States, 14—Tie	The Belfry GC, Sutton Coldfield, England
1991	United States, 14$^1/_2$ Europe, 13$^1/_2$	Kiawah Island Resort (Ocean Course), Kiawah Island, S.C.

WORLD CUP MATCH TEAM RESULTS

Year	Winner	Runner-Up	Site
1953	Argentina, 287 Antonio Cerda Roberto De Vicenzo	Canada, 297 Stan Leonard Bill Kerr	Beaconsfield, GC, Montreal, Canada
1954	Australia, 556 Peter Thomson Kel Nagle	Argentina, 560 Antonio Cerda Roberto De Vicenzo	Laval-sur-le-Lac, Montreal, Canada
1955	United States, 560 Ed Furgol Chick Harbert	Australia, 569 Peter Thomson Kel Nagle	Columbia CC, Washington, D.C.
1956	United States, 567 Ben Hogan Sam Snead	South Africa, 581 Bobby Locke Gary Player	Wentworth Club, Wentworth, England
1957	Japan, 557 Torakichi Nakamura Koichi Ono	United States, 566 Sam Snead Jimmy Demaret	Kasumigaseki GC, Tokyo, Japan
1958	Ireland, 579 Harry Bradshaw Christy O'Connor	Spain, 582 Angel Miguel Sebastian Miguel	Club de Golf Mexico, Mexico City, Mexico
1959	Australia, 563 Peter Thomson Kel Nagle	United States, 573 Sam Snead Cary Middlecoff	Royal Melbourne GC, Melbourne, Australia
1960	United States, 565 Sam Snead Arnold Palmer	England, 573 Harry Weetman Bernard Hunt	Portmarnock GC, Dublin, Ireland
1961	United States, 560 Sam Snead Jimmy Demaret	Australia, 572 Peter Thomson Kel Nagle	Dorado GC, Puerto Rico
1962	United States, 557 Arnold Palmer Sam Snead	Argentina, 559 Roberto De Vicenzo Fidel DeLuca	Jockey GC of San Isidro, Buenos Aires, Argentina
1963	United States, 482* Jack Nicklaus Arnold Palmer	Spain, 485 Sebastian Miguel Ramon Sota	Saint Nom la Breteche, Versailles, France
1964	United States, 554 Jack Nicklaus Arnold Palmer	Argentina, 564 Roberto De Vicenzo L. Ruiz	Royal Kaanapali GC, Maui, Hawaii
1965	South Africa, 571 Gary Player Harold Henning	Spain, 579 Angel Miguel Ramon Sota	Club de Campo, Madrid, Spain
1966	United States, 548 Arnold Palmer Jack Nicklaus	South Africa, 553 Gary Player Harold Henning	Yomiuri CC, Tokyo, Japan
1967	United States, 557 Arnold Palmer Jack Nicklaus	New Zealand, 570 Bob Charles Walter Godfrey	Club de Golf Mexico, Mexico City, Mexico
1968	Canada, 569 Al Balding George Knudson	United States, 571 Julius Boros Lee Trevino	Circolo Golf Olgiata, Rome, Italy
1969	United States, 552 Orville Moody Lee Trevino	Japan, 560 Takaaki Kono H. Yasuda	Singapore Island CC, Singapore

WORLD CUP MATCH TEAM RESULTS (continued)

Year	Winner	Runner-Up	Site
1970	Australia, 545 David Graham Bruce Devlin	Argentina, 555 Roberto De Vicenzo Vicente Fernandez	Jockey GC of San Isidro, Buenos Aires, Argentina
1971	United States, 555 Jack Nicklaus Lee Trevino	South Africa, 557 Gary Player Harold Henning	PGA National GC, Palm Beach Gardens, Fla.
1972	Taiwan, 438 Hsieh Min Nan Lu Liang-Huan	Japan, 444 Takaaki Kono Takashi Murakami	Royal Melbourne GC, Melbourne, Australia
1973	United States, 558 Johnny Miller Jack Nicklaus	South Africa, 564 Gary Player Hugh Baiocchi	Nueva Andalucia, Marbella, Spain
1974	South Africa, 554 Bobby Cole Dale Hayes	Japan, 559 Masashi Ozaki Isao Aoki	Lagunita CC, Caracas, Venezuela
1975	United States, 554 Johnny Miller Lou Graham	Taiwan, 564 Hsieh Min Nan Kuo Chi Hsiung	Navatanee GC, Bangkok, Thailand
1976	Spain, 574 Seve Ballesteros Manuel Pinero	United States, 576 Jerry Pate Dave Stockton	Mission Hills CC, Palm Springs, Cal.
1977	Spain, 591 Seve Ballesteros Antonio Garrido	Philippines, 594 Rudy Lavares Ben Arda	Wack Wack G&CC, Manila, Philippines
1978	United States, 564 John Mahaffey Andy North	Australia, 574 Greg Norman Wayne Grady	Princeville Makai GC, Kauai, Hawaii
1979	United States, 575 Hale Irwin John Mahaffey	Scotland, 580 Sandy Lyle Ken Brown	Glyfada GC, Athens, Greece
1980	Canada, 572 Dan Halldorson Jim Nelford	Scotland, 575 Sandy Lyle Steve Martin	El Rincon Club, Bogata, Columbia
1981	Not played		
1982	Spain, 563 Manuel Pinero Jose Maria Canizares	United States, 566 Bob Gilder Calvin Peete	Pierre Marques Cse., Acapulco, Mexico
1983	United States, 565 Rex Caldwell John Cook	Australia, 572 Peter Fowler Wayne Grady	Pondok G&CC, Jakarta, Indonesia
1984	Spain, 414 Jose Maria Canizares Jose Rivero	Scotland, 422 Gordon Brand, Jr. Sam Torrance	Olgiata GC, Rome, Italy
1985	Canada, 559 Dan Halldorson Dave Barr	England, 563 Howard Clark Paul Way	LaQuinta Hotel GC, LaQuinta, Cal.
1986	Not played		
1987	Wales, 574** Ian Woosnam David Llewellyn	Scotland, 574 Sandy Lyle Sam Torrance	Kapalua Resort, Maui, Hawaii

WORLD CUP MATCH TEAM RESULTS (continued)

Year	Winner	Runner-Up	Site
1988	United States, 560 Ben Crenshaw Mark McCumber	Japan, 561 Tateo Ozaki Masashi Ozaki	Royal Melbourne GC, Melbourne, Australia
1989	Australia, 278 Peter Fowler Wayne Grady	Spain, 281 Jose Maria Canizares Jose Maria Olazabal	Las Brisas GC, Marbella, Spain
1990	Germany, 556 Bernhard Langer Torsten Giedeon	England, 559 Mark James Richard Boxall Ireland, 559 David Feherty Ronan Rafferty	Grand Cypress GC, Orlando, Fla.
1991	Sweden, 563 Anders Forsbrand Per-Ulrik Johansson	Wales, 564 Ian Woosnam Phillip Price	La Querce GC, Rome, Italy
1992	United States, 548 Fred Couples Davis Love	Sweden, 549 Per-Ulrich Johansson Anders Forsbrand	La Moraleja GC, Madrid, Spain

* Play was limited to 63 holes because of fog.

** Won playoff.

INTERNATIONAL TROPHY

(Awarded to low individual in World Cup)

Year	Winner	Score	Year	Winner	Score
1954	Stan Leonard, Canada	275	1974	Bobby Cole, South Africa	271
1955	Ed Furgol, United States	279	1975	Johnny Miller, United States	275
1956	Ben Hogan, United States	277	1976	Ernesto Acosta, Mexico	282
1957	Torakichi Nakamura, Japan	274	1977	Gary Player, South Africa	289
1958	Angel Miguel, Spain	286	1978	John Mahaffey, United States	281
1959	Stan Leonard, Canada	275	1979	Hale Irwin, United States	285
1960	Flory Van Donck, Belgium	279	1980	Sandy Lyle, Scotland	282
1961	Sam Snead, United States	272	1981	Not played	
1962	Roberto de Vicenzo, Argentina	276	1982	Manuel Pinero, Spain	281
1963	Jack Nicklaus, United States	237*	1983	Dave Barr, Canada	276
1964	Jack Nicklaus, United States	276	1984	Jose Maria Canizares, Spain	205**
1965	Gary Player, South Africa	281	1985	Howard Clark, England	272
1966	George Knudson, Canada	272	1986	Not played	
1967	Arnold Palmer, United States	276	1987	Ian Woosnam, Wales	274
1968	Al Balding, Canada	274	1988	Ben Crenshaw, United States	275
1969	Lee Trevino, United States	275	1989	Peter Fowler, Australia	137**
1970	Roberto De Vicenzo, Argentina	269	1990	Payne Stewart, United States	271
1971	Jack Nicklaus, United States	271	1991	Ian Woosnam, Wales	273
1972	Hsieh Min Nan, Taiwan	217**	1992	Brett Ogle, Australia	270
1973	Johnny Miller, United States	277			

*Play was limited to 63 holes by fog.

**Play was limited top two rounds by bad weather.

FOUR TOURS WORLD CHAMPIONSHIP OF GOLF

Year	Winner	Score	Runner-Up	Site
1985	United States	10–2	Europe	Kapalua Resort, Maui, Haw.
1986	Japan	8–4	Europe	Yomiuri CC, Tokyo, Japan
1987	United States	10–2	Europe	Yomiuri CC, Tokyo, Japan
1988	United States	10–4	Europe	Kapalua Resort, Maui, Haw.
1989	United States	6–6*	Europe	Yomiuri CC, Tokyo, Japan
1990	Australia	0–0**	United States	Yomiuri CC, Tokyo, Japan
1991	Europe	8–4	Australia	Royal Adelaide GC, Adelaide, Aust.
1992	Not played			

* Winner determined by tiebreaker.
** Final rained out. Winner determined by tiebreaker.

ALFRED DUNHILL CUP

1985	Australia	3–0	United States	St. Andrews, Scotland
1986	Australia	3–0	Japan	St. Andrews, Scotland
1987	England	2–1	Scotland	St. Andrews, Scotland
1988	Ireland	2–1	Australia	St. Andrews, Scotland
1989	United States	3½–2½	Japan	St. Andrews, Scotland
1990	Ireland	3½–2½	England	St. Andrews, Scotland
1991	Sweden	2–1	South Africa	St. Andrews, Scotland
1992	England	2½–½	Scotland	St. Andrews, Scotland

Men's Amateur

WALKER CUP

Year	Winner/Loser	Site
1922	United States, 8 Great Britain, 4	National GL of America, Southampton, N.Y.
1923	United States, 6½ Great Britain, 5½	St. Andrews, Scotland
1924	United States, 9 Great Britain, 3	Garden City GC, Garden City, N.Y.
1926	United States, 6½ Great Britain, 5½	St. Andrews, Scotland
1928	United States, 11 Great Britain, 1	Chicago GC, Wheaton, Ill.
1930	United States, 10 Great Britain, 2	Royal St. George's GC, Sandwich, England
1932	United States, 9½ Great Britain, 2½	The Country Club, Brookline, Mass.
1934	United States, 9½ Great Britain, 2½	St. Andrews, Scotland
1936	United States, 10½ Great Britain, 1½	Pine Valley GC, Clementon, N.J.
1938	Great Britain, 7½ United States, 4½	St. Andrews, Scotland
1947	United States, 8 Great Britain, 4	St. Andrews, Scotland
1949	United States, 10 Great Britain, 2	Winged Foot GC, Mamaroneck, N.Y.
1951	United States, 7½ Great Britain, 4½	Birkdale GC, Southport, England
1953	United States, 9 Great Britain, 3	Kittansett Club, Marion, Mass.
1955	United States, 10 Great Britain, 2	St. Andrews, Scotland
1957	United States, 8½ Great Britain, 3½	Minikahda Club, Minneapolis, Minn.
1959	United States, 9 Great Britain, 3	Muirfield, Scotland
1961	United States, 11 Great Britain, 1	Seattle GC, Seattle, Wash.
1963	United States, 14 Great Britain, 10	Turnberry, Scotland
1965	Great Britain, 12 United States, 12—Tie	Baltimore CC, Baltimore, Md.
1967	United States, 15 Great Britain, 9	Royal St. George's GC, Sandwich, England
1969	United States, 13 Great Britain, 11	Milwaukee CC, Milwaukee, Wis.
1971	Great Britain, 13 United States, 11	St. Andrews, Scotland
1973	United States, 14 Great Britain, 10	The Country Club, Brookline, Mass.
1975	United States, 15½ Great Britain, 8½	St. Andrews, Scotland

WALKER CUP (continued)

Year	Winner/Loser	Site
1977	United States, 16 Great Britain, 8	Shinnecock Hills GC, Southampton, N.Y.
1979	United States, 16 Great Britain, 8	Muirfield, Scotland
1981	United States, 15 Great Britain, 9	Cypress Point GC, Pebble Beach, Cal.
1983	United States, 13½ Great Britain, 10½	Royal Liverpool GC, Hoylake, England
1985	United States, 13 Great Britain, 11	Pine Valley GC, Clementon, N.J.
1987	United States, 16½ Great Britain, 7½	Sunningdale GC, Berkshire, England
1989	Great Britain, 12½ United States, 11½	Peachtree GC, Atlanta, Ga.
1991	United States, 14 Great Britain, 10	Portmarnock GC, Dublin, Ireland

WORLD AMATEUR TEAM CHAMPIONSHIP

Year	Winner, Score	Runner-Up	Site
1958	Australia, 918*	United States, 918	St. Andrews, Scotland
1960	United States, 834	Australia, 876	Merion GC, Ardmore, Pa.
1962	United States, 854	Canada, 862	Fuji GC, Kawana, Japan
1964	Great Britain, 895	Canada, 897	Olgiata GC, Rome, Italy
1966	Australia, 877	United States, 879	Club de Golf Mexico, Mexico City, Mexico
1968	United States, 868	Great Britain, 869	Royal Melbourne GC, Melbourne, Aust.
1970	United States, 857	New Zealand, 869	Real Club de la Puerta de Hierro, Madrid, Spain
1972	United States, 865	Australia, 870	Olivos GC, Beunos Aires, Argentina
1974	United States, 888	Japan, 898	Campo de Golf, Cajuiles, Dominican Republic
1976	Great Britain, 892	Japan, 894	Penina GC, Portimao, Portugal
1978	United States, 873	Canada, 886	Pacific Harbour G&CC, Fiji
1980	United States, 848	South Africa, 875	Pinehurst CC, Pinehurst, N.C.
1982	United States, 859	Japan, 866	Lausanne GC, Lausanne, Switzerland
1984	Japan, 870	United States, 877	Royal Hong Kong GC, Hong Kong
1986	Canada, 838	United States, 841	Lagunita CC, Caracas, Venezuela
1988	Great Britain, 882	United States, 887	Ullna GC, Stockholm, Sweden
1990	Sweden, 879	United States, New Zealand, 892	Christchurch GC, Christchurch, N.Z.
1992	New Zealand, 823	United States, 830	Capilano G&CC, West Vancouver, B.C., Canada

* Won playoff.

WOMEN'S AMATEUR

CURTIS CUP

Year	Winner/Loser	Site
1932	United States, 5½ Great Britain, 3½	Wentworth GC, Wentworth, England
1934	United States, 6½ Great Britain, 2½	Chevy Chase Club, Chevy Chase, Md.
1936	United States, 4½ Great Britain, 4½—Tie	King's Course, Gleneagles, Scotland
1938	United States, 5½ Great Britain, 3½	Essex CC, Manchester, Mass.
1948	United States, 6½ Great Britain, 2½	Birkdale GC, Southport, England
1950	United States, 7½ Great Britain, 1½	CC of Buffalo, Williamsville, N.Y.
1952	Great Britain, 5 United States, 4	Muirfield, Scotland
1954	United States, 6 Great Britain, 3	Merion GC, Ardmore, Pa.
1956	Great Britain, 5 United States, 4	Prince's GC, Sandwich Bay, England
1958	Great Britain, 4½ United States, 4½—Tie	Brae Burn CC, West Newton, Mass.
1960	United States, 6½ Great Britain, 2½	Lindrick GC, Worksop, England
1962	United States, 8 Great Britain, 1	Broadmoor GC, Colorado Springs, Colo.
1964	United States, 10½ Great Britain, 7½	Royal Porthcawl GC, Porthcawl, S. Wales
1966	United States, 13 Great Britain, 5	Virginia Hot Springs G&TC, Hot Springs, Va.
1968	United States, 10½ Great Britain, 7½	Royal County Down GC, Newcastle, Northern Ireland
1970	United States, 11½ Great Britain, 6½	Brae Burn CC, West Newton, Mass.
1972	United States, 10 Great Britain, 8	Western Gailes, Ayrshire, Scotland
1974	United States, 13 Great Britain, 5	San Francisco GC, San Francisco, Cal.
1976	United States, 11½ Great Britain, 6½	Royal Lytham & St. Anne's GC, St. Anne's-On-The-Sea, England
1978	United States, 12 Great Britain, 6	Apawamis Club, Rye, N.Y.
1980	United States, 13 Great Britain, 5	St. Pierre G&CC, Chepstow, Wales
1982	United States, 14½ Great Britain, 3½	Denver CC, Denver, Colo.
1984	United States, 9½ Great Britain, 8½	Muirfield, Scotland
1986	Great Britain, 13 United States, 5	Prairie Dunes CC, Hutchinson, Kan.
1988	Great Britain, 11 United States, 7	Royal St. George's GC, Sandwich, England

CURTIS CUP (continued)

Year	Winner/Loser	Site
1990	United States, 14 Great Britain, 4	Somerset Hills CC, Bernardsville, N.J.
1992	Great Britain, 10 United States, 8	Royal Liverpool GC, Hoylake, England

WOMEN'S WORLD AMATEUR TEAM CHAMPIONSHIP

Year	Winner, Score	Runner-Up, Score	Site
1964	France, 589	United States, 589	St. Germain GC, Paris, France
1966	United States, 580	Canada, 589	Mexico City CC, Mexico City, Mexico
1968	United States, 616	Australia, 621	Victoria GC, Victoria, Australia
1970	United States, 598	France, 599	Club de Campo, Madrid, Spain
1972	United States, 583	France, 587	Hindu CC, Buenos Aires, Argentina
1974	United States, 620	Great Britain, South Africa, 636	Campo de Golf, Cajuiles, Dominican Republic
1976	United States, 605	France, 622	Vilamoura GC, Algarve, Portugal
1978	Australia, 596	Canada, 597	Pacific Harbour G&CC, Fiji
1980	United States, 588	Australia, 595	Pinehurst CC, Pinehurst, N.C.
1982	United States, 579	New Zealand, 596	Geneva GC, Geneva, Switzerland
1984	United States, 585	France, 597	Royal Hong Kong GC, Hong Kong
1986	Spain, 580	France, 583	Lagunita CC, Caracas, Venezuela
1988	United States, 587	Sweden, 588	Drottningholm GC, Stockholm, Sweden
1990	United States, 585	New Zealand, 597	Russley GC, Christchurch, N.Z.
1992	Spain, 588	Great Britain, 589	Marine Drive GC, Vancouver, B.C., Canada

Golfdom's Who's Who

In one form or another, golf has been played for more than half a millennium. At present it is played by about 35 million people on every continent in the world on which grass will grow. Over the years, certain golfers have come to be known as the "greats" of the game. The following biographies describe the lives and accomplishments of the outstanding players.

GREAT GOLFERS OF ALL TIME

AARON, TOMMY. Born in Gainesville, GA, February 22, 1937. With one of the most graceful swings in golf, Aaron dominated amateur events in his home state in the late 1950s. He won the Georgia Open three times, and the Georgia and Southeastern amateurs twice each. On the national scene, he was finalist in the 1958 U.S. Amateur and won the 1959 Sunnehanna and 1960 Western Amateurs. He was a member of the winning 1959 Walker Cup team before turning pro the following year. On the professional circuit, he became known as a perennial "bridesmaid" because he finished second nine times

before defeating Sam Snead in a playoff for the 1969 Canadian Open. The highlight of his career was in 1973 when he won the Masters, becoming the first native Georgian to do so. Aaron was a Ryder Cup team member in 1969 and 1973. He subsequently joined the Senior PGA Tour in 1987.

Tommy Aaron. *Wide World Photos*

Tournament Record: 1959: Winner of Sunnehanna Amateur. 1960: Winner of Western Amateur. 1969: Winner of Canadian Open. 1970: Winner of Atlanta Classic. 1972: Winner of Lancome Trophy, France. 1973: Winner of Masters. 1992: Winner of Kaanapali Classic.

ALCOTT, AMY. Born in Kansas City, MO, February 22, 1956. A top-rated amateur, Alcott won the U.S.G.A. Girls' Junior in 1973. After turning pro in 1975, she celebrated her nineteenth birthday by winning the Orange Blossom Classic, only her third event on Tour. She also won Rookie-of-the-Year honors. Since then, she has had only two winless years (1987 and 1990) and has racked up 29 victories. Amy has five majors to her credit: the 1979 Peter Jackson Classic, the 1980 U.S. Women's Open, which she won by nine strokes, and the 1983, 1988, and 1991 Nabisco–Dinah Shore Invitationals.

Alcott enjoys a good laugh. When she won the 1988 Nabisco–Dinah Shore, after she hadn't had a victory in almost two years, she celebrated by taking

Amy Alcott. *Courtesy LPGA*

a leaf out of Jerry Pate's book—she and her caddie, Bill Kurre, jumped into the lake surrounding the green at Mission Hills. She did the same thing in 1991.

Alcott has a brisk, no-nonsense swing and is known as one of the finest shotmakers on the LPGA Tour.

Tournament Record: 1973: Winner of USGA Girls' Junior Championship. 1975: Winner of Orange Blossom Classic. 1976: Winner of LPGA Classic, and Colgate Far East Open. 1977: Winner of Houston Exchange Clubs Classic. 1978: Winner of American Defender Classic. 1979: Winner of Elizabeth Arden Classic, Peter Jackson Classic, United Virginia Bank Classic, and Mizuno Japan Classic. 1980: Winner of American Defender–WRAL Classic, Mayflower Classic, U.S. Women's Open, and Inamori Classic. 1981: Winner of Bent Tree Ladies Classic, and Lady Michelob. 1982: Winner of Women's Kemper Open. 1983: Winner of Nabisco–Dinah Shore. 1984: Winner of United Virginia Bank Classic, Lady Keystone Open, Portland Ping Championship, and San Jose Classic. 1985: Winner of Circle K Tucson Open, Moss Creek Women's Invitational, and Nestle World Championship of Women's Golf. 1986: Winner of Mazda Hall of Fame Championship, LPGA National Pro-Am, and Mazda Champions (with Bob Charles). 1988: Winner of Nabisco–Dinah Shore. 1989: Winner of Boston Five Classic. 1991: Winner of Nabisco–Dinah Shore.

ANDERSON, WILLIE. Born in North Berwick, Scotland, in May 1880, died in 1910. He was among the first of the Scottish professionals to come to this country, arriving in the mid-1890's with his father, Tom, and his brother, Tom, Jr. He won the U.S. Open in 1901, and then put together three straight victories in 1903, 1904, and 1905 to become the first of the three men who have won four Open titles. He was runner-up in 1897 and finished in the top five on six other occasions—a remarkable record. He also scored four triumphs in the Western Open, which ranked second only to the U.S. Open in those days.

Anderson was the first great player to emerge in this country, but no one is sure just how great, since balls, clubs, and the condition of courses were far below today's standards. He hit the ball with a smooth, deliberate swing and was a good putter who never became rattled. Anderson was a dour man who

Willie Anderson.
Courtesy U.S.G.A.

ARCHER, GEORGE WILLIAM. Born in San Francisco, CA, October 1, 1939, Archer started playing golf when he was twelve years old, and grew up playing the Harding Park course in San Francisco, then the site of the Lucky International event on the PGA Tour. "People accused me of knowing every blade of grass on that course," he says. "It's not true. I didn't know at least a dozen of them." Archer had an outstanding amateur career, crowned by wins in the 1963 Trans-Mississippi, Northern California Open, and San Francisco City Championship. That year he was low amateur for the third straight year in the Lucky International, and reached the semifinals of the U.S. Amateur, losing to Deane Beman.

Archer turned pro in 1964, and his first win came at the Lucky the following year. Archer once described winning the Masters as "just like going to the moon . . . it's unthinkable." In 1969, the unthinkable became reality when Archer won the Masters, and within three months astronauts went to the moon. At

George Archer. *UPI/Bettmann*

attended strictly to business and displayed little sense of humor on the course, but he was a mixer off the course and was popular with his fellow golfers. He was pro at ten clubs in fourteen years, and in 1906 and 1910 he moved to the club that was to be host to the next Open championship, so he obviously cared a great deal about adding another title to his list.

A friend of Anderson's said that although Willie was not a glad-hander, "he went the route with his friends and probably his convivial habits had much to do with undermining his health and hastened his end." He died in 1910 of arteriosclerosis, and his death came as a shock because he presented the outward appearance of perfect health right up to the end. In fact, he played three 36-hole matches during the week preceding his death.

6'6", Archer is the tallest player to ever win a major. The last of Archer's 13 Tour wins came in the 1984 Bank of Boston Classic, his first victory in eight injury-riddled years. In 1975, he had surgery to repair a torn tendon in his left wrist. In 1977 he encountered back problems that required surgery two years later when two discs were fused.

In a game dominated by players of medium height, Archer almost seems too tall for golf. To reduce the arc of his swing to manageable width, he uses a deep knee bend. Archer's swing may be a little ungainly, but it is very effective, and he has excellent tempo. When golfers discuss great putters, Archer's name is sure to come up. His stroke has been held up as a model of proper "arm–shoulder" action ever since he came on the Tour.

Archer joined the Senior Tour in 1989 and won in his debut, the Gatlin Brothers Southwest Classic. He scored four wins in 1990 and two in 1991.

Tournament Record: 1963: Winner of Trans-Mississippi Amateur, Northern California Open, and San Francisco City Championship. 1965: Winner of Lucky International. 1967: Winner of Greensboro. 1968: Winner of Pensacola, New Orleans, and National Team (with Bobby Nichols). 1969: Winner of Masters, and Bing Crosby. 1971: Winner of Williams-San Diego, and Hartford. 1972: Winner of Campbell-Los Angeles, and Greensboro. 1976: Winner of Del Webb Sahara Invitational. 1984: Winner of Bank of Boston Classic. 1989: Winner of Gatlin Brothers Southwest Classic. 1990: Winner of MONY Tournament of Champions, Northville Long Island Classic, GTE Northwest Classic, and Gold Rush at Rancho Murieta. 1991: Winner of Northville Long Island Classic and GTE North Classic. 1992: Winner of Murata Reunion Pro-Am, Northville Long Island Classic and Bruno's Memorial Classic.

ARMOUR, THOMAS DICKSON. Born in Edinburgh, Scotland, September 24, 1895. Died September 13, 1968. One of the most colorful and legendary figures in the history of golf. There was never anything small about Armour's reputation. At one time or another he was known as the greatest iron player, the greatest raconteur, the greatest drinker, and the greatest and most expensive teacher in golf. He definitely was a great player, while the rest of his reputation, like most legends, contains much picturesque exaggeration. Not long after his playing career came to a close, the prematurely gray hair, the Scottish back-

ground, the tournament record, and the legend in general merged to give him an elder-statesmanlike quality, and he typified golf—or what golf was thought to be—to many Americans.

During World War I Armour was a machine gunner in the tank corps and quickly rose to the rank of major. He was wounded and lost the sight of one eye, and while convalescing, he decided to make a career in golf. He won the French Amateur in 1920 and a couple of years later decided to take up residence in the United States. After a few amateur successes Armour turned pro, and by 1927 he was at the top. In that year he won six tournaments, including the U.S. Open and the Canadian Open. He won four more events in 1928 and a couple in 1929, including the Western Open with what was then a record score of 273. Having proved himself to be a great stroke player, Armour beat Gene Sarazen in the final to win the 1930 PGA Championship on Sarazen's home course, demonstrating he could win matches, too. He completed his collection of major titles by winning the 1931 British Open. He was a contender through 1935, when he lost to Johnny Revolta in the final of the PGA, but after that he played in tournaments less often and less effectively.

As a teacher, which he then became almost exclu-

Tommy Armour.

sively, he was respected by everybody, and top players from Lawson Little to Babe Didrikson went to him for assistance. At one time he collected the highest teaching fees in golf while sitting under an umbrella at Boca Raton. Armour always enjoyed conversation (it was said he was the only man who could rival Hagen in oratory), and as he passed his seventieth birthday he could still be found in Florida in the winter and at Winged Foot in New York in the summer drinking coffee and holding court in the clubhouse.

Tournament Record: 1920: Winner of French Amateur, Gleneagles Amateur, and Shawnee Invitation. 1925: Winner of Florida West Coast Open. 1927: Winner of U.S. Open, Canadian Open, Oregon Open, El Paso Open, Long Beach Open, and Miami Four-Ball. 1928: Winner of Metropolitan Open, Philadelphia Open, Pennsylvania Open, and National Golf Links Invitational. 1929: Winner of Western Open, and Sacramento Open. 1930: Winner of PGA Championship, Canadian Open, and St. Louis Open. 1931: Winner of British Open. 1932: Winner of Miami Open, and Miami Four-Ball. 1934: Winner of Canadian Open. 1935: Winner of Miami Open; runner-up in PGA Championship.

AZINGER, PAUL. Born in Holyoke, MA, January 6, 1960. When Azinger broke through with three victories on the PGA Tour in 1987, it was the culmination of years of improvement that saw him climb from near the bottom of the Tour as a rookie in 1982, all the way to the top five years later. Azinger nipped Curtis Strange in the points race for PGA Player of the Year honors in 1987; Azinger also finished second on the money list with $822,481 and second in scoring average at 70.21.

Since then, he's remained one of the top players on Tour, finishing eleventh on the money list in 1988, third in 1989, and fourth in 1990, while winning one tournament each year.

Azinger's present status is quite a long way from his 1982 rookie season, when he finished 171st on the money list with $10,655 and lost his playing card. Azinger, who grew up in Bradenton, Fla., and went to school at Brevard Junior College and Florida State, was back on Tour in 1984, but lost his card again. Things started to turn around late that year when he earned medalist honors at the qualifying school.

Paul Azinger. *Fred Vuich*

Azinger was ninety-third on the money list in 1985 and improved all the way to twenty-ninth in 1986 when he finished second in the Hawaiian Open. Despite an unorthodox style—he uses a strong grip and hits his shots low—Azinger was developing a reputation as one of the better iron players on Tour, especially with the short irons.

When his putting, previously mediocre at best, improved in 1987, Azinger took off. He was the only player on the Tour to win in each year from 1987 through 1990, and a victory in early 1991 at the AT&T Pebble Beach National Pro-Am made it five years in a row. He came close to winning two major championships in that span, leading through three rounds before finishing second at both the 1987 British Open and 1988 PGA Championship.

Tournament Record: 1988: Winner of Phoenix Open, Panasonic Las Vegas Invitational, and Canon—

Sammy Davis Jr. Greater Hartford Open. 1988: Winner of Hertz Bay Hill Classic. 1989: Winner of Canon Greater Hartford Open. 1990: Winner of MONY Tournament of Champions. 1991: Winner of AT&T Pebble Beach National Pro-Am. 1992: Winner of Tour Championship.

BALL, JOHN. Born in Hoylake, England, December 24, 1861. Died in December 1940. He was England's greatest amateur and ranks among the best in the history of the game. Ball grew up on the Hoylake course and by the age of fifteen was good enough to finish sixth in the British Open. He won the British Open in 1890, the first amateur to do so.

Ball won the British Amateur a record eight times between 1888 and 1912 and was still able to reach the sixth round in 1921—at the age of sixty! The British Amateur was not begun until 1885, nearly ten years after Ball reached championship caliber, and most historians agree he would have won more than

John Ball. *Courtesy U.S.G.A.*

eight titles had the tournament been founded a decade earlier.

BALLESTEROS, SEVERIANO. Born in Pedrena, Santander, Spain, April 9, 1957. Seve Ballesteros started to play golf at age seven. He learned the game with a rusty 3-iron head fitted to a "shaft" whittled from a stick. Golf balls were hard to come by when Ballesteros was young, so he would search the beach for round stones of the right size and play with them instead. At age nine, he graduated to a real 3-iron, complete with steel shaft. But it was still his only club. Learning to manipulate the 3-iron for every type of shot was the major factor in his developing the shotmaking feel and inventiveness that is the trademark of his game. Following in the footsteps of his three elder brothers—Baldomero, Manuel, and Vicente—Seve also started caddying at Real Club de Golf de Pedrena. At age twelve, armed with a full set of clubs, he won a caddie tournament with a 79. At age thirteen, he played to scratch.

Ballesteros turned professional on January 1, 1974, when he was sixteen, and the same year won the Spanish Young Pro Open. At the age of nineteen, he led by two shots going into the final round of the 1976 British Open at Royal Birkdale, but ultimately finished second to Johnny Miller. That year he became the youngest golfer ever to top the European Order of Merit, winning three events. He went on to lead the Order of Merit in the next two years as well, and he led Spain to the World Cup title in 1976 and 1977. His victory in the Greater Greensboro Open in 1978 gave him victories on four continents (Europe, North America, Asia, and Africa) before his twenty-first birthday.

His first major victory came in the 1979 British Open at Royal Lytham. And he did it in typical swashbuckling fashion, hitting only two fairways during the last round. On the 16th, for example, he cut his drive into a parking lot, then proceeded to birdie the hole with a pitch and putt. Such exploits made comparisons to a young Arnold Palmer inevitable. However, it was a more controlled Ballesteros who won the 1980 Masters. He no longer gave the impression of trying to pulverize the ball, but now swung back shorter and more in control. At twenty-three, he became the youngest Masters champion. When he added the 1983 Masters and 1984 British Open, it seemed that the sky was the limit. Since then,

Seve Ballesteros. *Fred Vuich*

World Cup Team title (with Manuel Pinero). 1977: Winner of French Open, Braun International, Uniroyal International, Swiss Open, Japan Open, Dunlop Phoenix, Otago Charity Classic, and World Cup Team title (with Tony Garrido). 1978: Winner of Greater Greensboro Open, Swiss Open, Kenya Open, Martini International, German Open, and Scandinavian Open. 1979: Winner of British Open. 1980: Winner of Masters, Dutch Open, and Scandinavian Open. 1981: Winner of World Match Play, Scandinavian Open, Spanish Open, and Australian PGA. 1982: Winner of World Match Play and French Open. 1983: Winner of Masters, Manufacturers-Hanover Westchester Classic, British PGA, and Irish Open. 1984: Winner of British Open. 1985: Winner of USF&G Classic. 1986: Winner of British Masters, Irish Open, Monte Carlo Open, French Open, Dutch Open, and co-winner of Lancome Trophy (sudden-death play-off with Bernhard Langer discontinued after four holes due to darkness). 1987: Winner of Suze (Cannes) Open. 1988: Winner of Manufacturers-Hanover Westchester Classic, Mallorca Open, British Open, German Open, Lancome Trophy, Scandinavian Open, and Taiheiyo Masters. 1989: Winner of Madrid Open, Epson Grand Prix, and Ebel European Masters–Swiss Open. 1990: Winner of de Baleares Open. 1991: Winner of Volvo PGA Championship, Dunhill British Masters, Toyota World Match Play, and Chunichi Crowns Open. 1992: Winner of Dubal Desert Classic and de Balearas Open.

though, he's added only one more major title, the 1988 British Open, for a total of five.

Ballesteros has won six tournaments on the PGA Tour, but he has always preferred to play in Europe and was a full member of the U.S. Tour only in 1984 and 1985. He lost his membership after failing to fulfill his obligation of playing fifteen tournaments in 1985.

The Spaniard's best years in Europe in the 1980s were in 1986 and 1988 when he led the Order of Merit for the fourth and fifth times. In the latter year, besides the British Open, he won four more European events plus one each in the U.S. and Japan. Ballesteros was the key player on the European Ryder Cup teams that took the Cup away from the U.S. in 1985 and 1987 and held it with a tie in 1989. He also played in the 1979 and 1983 Ryder Cups.

Tournament Record: 1974: Winner of Spanish Young Pro Open. 1975: Winner of Spanish Young Pro Open. 1976: Winner of Dutch Open, Lancome Championship, Swaelens Memorial Challenge, and

BARBER, MILLER. Born in Shreveport, LA, March 31, 1931. Miller's family moved to Texarkana, Texas, when he was six. He first played golf as a high-school sophomore, and for three years was a member of the University of Arkansas golf team. He won the Southwest Conference Championship in 1951. During a three-year hitch in the military, he won the 1957 Air Force Championship. Barber had a lean start on Tour, after turning professional in 1958, when he earned an average of less than $3,000 a year from 1959–1961. For most of 1962, Barber worked at the Apawamis Club, Rye, New York. He won the 1962 Metropolitan Open. Barber's first Tour victory came in his home state at the 1964 Cajun Classic. Since then Barber has never looked back. Known as "Mr X" on Tour because "I always kept to myself and wore the large Air Force style glasses," Barber won one

Miller Barber.
Will Hertzberg

ner of USGA Senior Open, Suntree Senior Classic, and tied for first in Hilton Head Seniors International (last two rounds rained out). 1983: Winner of Senior Tournament Players Championship, Commemorative Pro-Am, United Virginia Bank, and Hilton Head Seniors International. 1984: Winner of Roy Clark Senior Challenge, USGA Senior Open, Greater Syracuse Seniors, and Denver Post Champions. 1985: Winner of Sunrise Senior Classic, USGA Senior Open, Shootout at Jeremy Ranch (with Ben Crenshaw), Paine Webber World Seniors Invitational, and Coca-Cola Grand Slam Champion (Japan). 1986: Winner of MONY Tournament of Champions. 1987: Winner of Showdown Classic, Newport Cup, and Mazda Champions. 1988: Winner of Showdown Classic, and Fairfield Barnett Senior Classic. 1989: Winner of MONY Tournament of Champions, and Vintage Chrysler Invitational.

tournament a year from 1967 through 1974, a record matched only by Jack Nicklaus during that period. He also played on the 1969 and 1971 Ryder Cup teams. The last of Barber's eleven Tour wins came in the 1978 Phoenix Open. Joining the Senior Tour in 1981, he has been even more successful, with twenty-four victories to his credit, including three USGA Senior Opens, one PGA Seniors, and one Tournament Players Championship.

Barber's swing is unique. In the takeaway, he turns the club counterclockwise, closing the blade, and at the top, has a flying right elbow. On the downswing, however, he reroutes the club back onto the correct plane and is a solid, long hitter. His old friend, Don January, recalls, "When Miller first came out on Tour, I tried to help him change to a more conventional action. He worked hard, but just couldn't play that way. In the end, I told him to stick with what he's got." Good advice. That swing has won Barber over $4 million.

Tournament Record: 1951: Winner of Southwest Conference Championship. 1962: Winner of Metropolitan Open. 1964: Winner of Cajun Classic. 1967: Winner of Oklahoma City Open. 1968: Winner of Byron Nelson Classic. 1969: Winner of Kaiser International. 1970: Winner of New Orleans Open. 1971: Winner of Phoenix Open. 1972: Winner of Tucson Open. 1973: Winner of World Open. 1974: Winner of Ohio Kings Island Open. 1977: Winner of Anheuser-Busch Classic. 1978: Winner of Phoenix Open. 1981: Winner of Peter Jackson Champions, Suntree Senior Classic, and PGA Seniors. 1982: Win-

Jim Barnes. *Courtesy PGA World Hall of Fame*

BARNES, JAMES M. Born in Lelant, Cornwall, England, in 1887. Died May 24, 1966. He was a caddie and apprentice club maker before coming to the United States in 1906. He stood 6 feet 3 inches and weighed about 170 and, not surprisingly, became known as Long Jim. Little was known of him until he popped up in second place in the Canadian Open of 1912. When he tied for fourth behind Vardon, Ray, and Ouimet in the 1913 U.S. Open, people began to take notice. Barnes won the Western Open in 1914 and then broke through with a victory in the 1916 PGA Championship, the first time the event was held. He repeated in 1919 and then won the U.S. Open, by nine strokes, in 1921. Although he continued to win occasional tournaments for several years, his victory in the 1925 British Open came as something of a surprise because it was felt his best years were behind him. Although he lived in the United States, he remained British at heart, and through those years he steadfastly refused to relinquish his British citizenship.

Tournament Record: 1913: Winner of Pacific-Northwest Open. 1914: Winner of Western Open. 1915: Winner of Connecticut Open. 1916: Winner of PGA Championship, North and South Open, Connecticut Open, and New York Newspaper Open. 1917: Winner of Western Open, and Philadelphia Open. 1919: Winner of PGA Championship, North and South Open, Western Open, Shawnee Open, and Southern Open. 1920: Winner of Shawnee Open. 1921: Winner of U.S. Open; runner-up in PGA. 1922: Winner of California Open. 1923: Winner of Corpus Christi Open. 1924: Runner-up in PGA Championship. 1925: Winner of British Open. 1930: Winner of Cape Cod Open. 1937: Winner of Long Island Open.

BEARD, FRANK. Born in Dallas, TX, May 1, 1939. Beard grew up in Louisville, Kentucky. As a youngster, Beard favored basketball, but developed such ability in golf that when he went to the University of Florida, he limited his athletic activity to the golf team. He won the Kentucky Amateur in 1960 and 1961.

Turning pro in 1962, Beard gained the reputation of being a colorless businessman whose main interest was earning money on Tour rather than winning. He certainly earned a lot of money, enjoying five

Frank Beard. *Fred Vuich*

$100,000-plus seasons from 1967 to 1971. In 1969, he was leading money-winner with $175,224. He also played on the 1969 and 1971 Ryder Cup teams. However, he didn't generate much fan interest because as Beard himself said, "I don't do anything spectacular, don't have any odd habits, and don't wear loud clothes." He did put the lie to his supposed lack of interest in winning, saying, "If I'm just a businessman, then surely I realize that they pay more for first place than second." He surely did, winning a total of eleven Tour events.

If he wasn't spectacular, his putting certainly was. In winning the 1970 Tournament of Champions, Beard scored a second-round 64 using just twelve putts per nine holes; he made nine birdies. In his American Golf Classic victory the same year, he needed only ten putts on the back nine for a third-round 67.

In 1972, however, he tried to change his compact but elegant swing. "I've always been a hooker," he said at the time, "but I felt that shot limited me. So, I straightened up and aimed right at the hole. I started to hit so many bad shots that it drained my confidence. When I went back to my old game, I couldn't do the things I used to."

He was never the same golfer again. He had a near-brush with destiny in 1975, when he led the U.S. Open at Medinah by three shots after the third round, but then took a final round 78 and tied for third. Beard joined the Senior Tour in 1989 and scored his first victory the next year.

Tournament Record: 1960: Winner of Kentucky Amateur. 1961: Winner of Kentucky Amateur. 1963: Winner of Frank Sinatra Open. 1965: Winner of Texas Open. 1966: Winner of New Orleans Open. 1967: Winner of Tournament of Champions, Houston Open, and "500" Festival Open. 1969: Winner of Minnesota Open, and Westchester Classic. 1970: Winner of Tournament of Champions and American Golf Classic. 1971: Winner of New Orleans Open. 1990: Winner of Murata Reunion Pro-Am.

BERG, PATRICIA JANE. Born in Minneapolis, MN, February 13, 1918. Berg took up the game at age thirteen, and three years later she won the 1934 Minneapolis City Championship. The following year, she was runner-up in the U.S. Women's Amateur. Her

Patty Berg. *Courtesy LPGA*

total of twenty-nine amateur wins include three Titleholders (1937-39) and victories in the U.S. and Western Amateurs in 1938. In 1936 and 1938 she played on the Curtis Cup teams and turned pro in 1940. Berg has had a long and distinguished career. She was a founder and charter member of the LPGA, and served as its first president for four years. She won 57 times as a pro (44 being LPGA titles), not including three unofficial titles. She won six events in both the 1953 and 1955 seasons. She was leading money winner in 1954, 1956, and 1957. Berg was inducted into the LPGA Hall of Fame in 1967. Besides her playing career, Berg has done much to boost the growth of the game both at home and abroad. She was the first woman pro to give an exhibition in Japan (1962). She is reputed to have staged more clinics than any other golfer in history.

Tournament Record: 1934: Winner of Minneapolis City Championship. 1937: Winner of Titleholders. 1938: Winner of Titleholders, U.S. Women's Amateur, and Western Women's Amateur. 1939: Winner of Titleholders. 1941: Winner of Western Open, North Carolina Open, and New York Invitational. 1943: Winner of Western Open, and All-American Open. 1944: Winner of Pro-Lady Victory National (with Johnny Revolta). 1945: Winner of All-American Open. 1946: Winner of Northern California Open, Northern California Medal Tournament, Pebble Beach Open, and U.S. Women's Open. 1947: Winner of Northern California Open, Pebble Beach Open, and Northern California Medal Tournament. 1948: Winner of Titleholders Championship, Western Open, and Hardscrabble Open. 1949: Winner of Tampa Open, Texas PGA Championship, and Hardscrabble Open. 1950: Winner of Eastern Open, Sunset Hills Open, Hardscrabble Open, and Orlando Two-Ball (with Earl Stewart). 1951: Winner of Western Open, Sandhills Open, Weathervane Pebble Beach, Weathervane Westchester, and Weathervane Playoff. 1952: Winner of New Orleans Open, Richmond Open, and New York Weathervane Open. 1953: Winner of Titleholders Championship, All-American Open, World Championship, Jacksonville Open, New Orleans Open, Reno Open, and Phoenix Weathervane Open (tied for first). 1954: Winner of World Championship, Triangle Round Robin, Ardmore Open, and Orlando Two-Ball (with Pete Cooper). 1955: Winner of Titleholders Championship, Western Open, All-American Open, World Champi-

Jane Blalock. *Courtesy LPGA*

onship, St. Petersburg Open, and Clock Open. 1956: Winner of Dallas Open, and Arkansas Open. 1957: Winner of Titleholders Championship, Western Open, All-American Open, World Championship, and Havana Open. 1958: Winner of Western Open, and American Women's Open. 1960: Winner of American Open. 1962: Winner of Muskogee Civitan Open.

BLALOCK, JANE. Born in Portsmouth, NH, September 19, 1945. Blalock had an excellent amateur career, winning the New Hampshire and New England Junior championships in 1963, and then four New Hampshire state titles (1965-68). She also took the 1965 Florida Intercollegiate and 1968 New England Amateur championships. Joining the LPGA Tour in 1969, Blalock got off the mark quickly with a tie for seventh in the Quality Chek'd Classic, took Rookie-of-the-Year honors, and never looked back. That year, she started a streak of 299 tournaments without

missing a cut; it ended at the last event of 1980. She also finished among the top ten money winners for ten consecutive seasons (1971-1980) and was the first LPGA professional to win $100,000 for four straight seasons (1977-80). After slipping a bit from 1982 to 1984, Blalock had one of her best seasons ever in 1985, finishing with $192,426 for the year and winning two events, giving her twenty-nine official LPGA victories. That was her last hurrah, though, before quitting the Tour in 1988.

Tournament Record: 1963: Winner of New Hampshire Junior, and New England Junior. 1965: Winner of New Hampshire Women's Amateur, and Florida Intercollegiate. 1966: Winner of New Hampshire Women's Amateur. 1967: Winner of New Hampshire Women's Amateur. 1968: Winner of New Hampshire Women's Amateur, and New England Women's Amateur. 1970: Winner of Atlanta Carling Open. 1971: Winner of George Washington Classic, and Lady Pepsi Open. 1972: Winner of Colgate-Dinah Shore Winner's Circle, Suzuki International, Angelo's Four-Ball Championship, Dallas Civitan Open, and Lady Errol. 1973: Winner of Angelo's Four-Ball Championship. 1974: Winner of Bing Crosby International, Birmingham Classic, Southgate Classic, and Lady Errol Classic. 1975: Winner of Karsten-Ping Open and Colgate Triple Crown. 1976: Winner of Wheeling Classic and Dallas Civitan Open. 1977: Winner of Greater Baltimore Classic, The Sarah Coventry, and Colgate Triple Crown. 1978: Winner of Orange Blossom Classic, Wheeling Classic, Mayflower Classic, and Golden Lights Championship. 1979: Winner of Orange Blossom Classic, Florida Lady Citrus, Otey Crisman Classic, and The Sarah Coventry. 1980: Winner of Elizabeth Arden Classic. 1985: Winner of Women's Kemper Open and Mazda Japan Classic.

BOROS, JULIUS NICHOLAS. Born in Fairfield, CT, March 30, 1920. After a successful amateur career, Boros gave up accountancy and turned pro at the age of twenty-nine. Until he won his second U.S. Open Championship in 1963, Boros was probably one of the most underrated golfers playing the Tour. He had won the Open in 1952, and had followed that with two victories in George May's rich "World" tournament. He was leading money winner in 1952 and 1955. But through all those years he seemed to be the forgotten man to the general public, and it always

Julius Boros. *Will Hertzberg*

seemed something of a surprise when he finished near the top of the U.S. Open every year. Perhaps it was his swing that put everybody to sleep. It appears effortless, with almost a lazy look. As the late Tony Lema described it, "It's all hands and wrists, like a man dusting the furniture." Nevertheless, Boros finished in the top ten of the Open eleven times, behind only Jack Nicklaus, Ben Hogan, and Arnold Palmer since World War II. He also played on four Ryder Cup teams (1959, 1963, 1965, and 1967).

Boros had some of his best years on Tour in his later forties, winning over $100,000 in 1967 and 1968. In 1968, he won the PGA Championship at the age of forty-eight and is still the oldest winner of the event.

As a senior, Boros won the 1971 and 1977 PGA Seniors Championship. However, his most memorable feat came in the 1979 Legends of Golf. Playing with Roberto De Vicenzo, Boros made a birdie at the last hole to force a playoff with Art Wall and Tommy Bolt. The telecast of the playoff was one of the most thrilling in golf history, with Boros and De Vicenzo winning on the sixth playoff hole. It did much to boost the credibility of senior golf, and it was no coincidence that the PGA Senior Tour started the following year.

Tournament Record: 1948: Winner of Shore Line Open. 1951: Winner of Massachusetts Open. 1952: Winner of U.S. Open, World Championship, and Canada Cup (with Jim Turnesa). 1954: Winner of Ardmore Open and Carling Open. 1955: Winner of World Championship. 1958: Winner of Carling Open and Arlington Open. 1959: Winner of Dallas Open. 1960: Winner of Colonial Invitation. 1963: Winner of U.S. Open, Colonial Invitation, and Buick Open. 1964: Winner of Greensboro Open and West Palm Beach Open. 1967: Winner of Phoenix Open, Florida Citrus Open, and Buick Open. 1968: Winner of PGA Championship, Westchester Classic, and World Cup (with Lee Trevino). 1971: Winner of PGA Seniors Championship. 1977: Winner of PGA Seniors Championship. 1979: Winner of Legends of Golf (with Roberto De Vicenzo).

BRADLEY, PAT. Born in Westford, MA, March 24, 1951. Bradley started playing golf at age eight, but was also a fine skier. In fact, she was a ski instructor for a time before deciding to concentrate solely on golf. During her amateur career she played mainly in New England, where she won the New Hampshire Amateur in 1967 and 1969, the Massachusetts Amateur in 1972, and the New England Amateur in 1972 and 1973. A member of the Florida International University golf team, Bradley was selected to the first All-American Women's Collegiate team in 1970. She was the Florida Women's Collegiate Champion in 1971.

Since joining the LPGA in 1974, Bradley has proved to be one of the most consistent players in the Tour's history. From 1976 through 1986, she never ranked worse than eleventh on the money list. Over her eighteen-year career she has racked up 30 official victories, including six major championships.

In 1986, she won three out of the four majors—the Nabisco–Dinah Shore, the LPGA Championship, and the du Maurier Classic. (This feat has only been achieved twice in LPGA Tour history; Mickey Wright won three out of four in 1961 and Babe Zaharias won three in a three-major year, 1950.) In the fourth major, the U.S. Open, Bradley finished in a tie for fifth, three strokes behind. Bradley also won two other Tour events that year and finished second six times for a then record money-winning year of $492,021.

Her other major wins have come in the 1980 Peter Jackson Classic, the 1981 U.S. Women's Open, and the 1985 du Maurier Classic. In the 1981 Open, she set a 72-hole scoring record, a 9-under par 279. She closed with a 66, another Open record.

After competing in eight events in 1988, it was discovered that Bradley was suffering from hyperthyroidism. While that was a lost season, she recovered to win a total of eight events in the next three years. Her four victories in 1991 enabled her to reach the LPGA Hall of Fame by meeting the standard of 30 victories. She was the Tour's leading money winner and Player of the Year, each for the second time.

Bradley draws the ball and is long off the tee. She is also an excellent player in a wind. Regardless of the time of day, her mother rings a bell on their back porch after each Bradley victory.

Tournament Record: 1967: Winner of New Hampshire Amateur. 1969: Winner of New Hampshire Amateur. 1971: Winner of Florida Women's Collegiate Championship. 1972: Winner of Massa-

chusetts Amateur, and New England Amateur. 1973: Winner of New England Amateur. 1975: Winner of Colgate Far East Open. 1976: Winner of Girl Talk Classic. 1977: Winner of Bankers Trust Classic. 1978: Winner of Lady Keystone, Hoosier Classic, Rail Charity Classic, and JC Penney Classic (with Lon Hinkle). 1980: Winner of Greater Baltimore Classic and Peter Jackson Classic. 1981: Winner of Women's Kemper Open and U.S. Women's Open. 1983: Winner of Mazda Classic of Deer Creek, Chrysler-Plymouth Charity Classic, Columbia Savings Classic, and Mazda Japan Classic. 1985: Winner of Rochester International, du Maurier Classic, and LPGA National Pro-Am. 1986: Winner of Nabisco–Dinah Shore, S&H Golf Classic, LPGA Championship, du Maurier Classic, and Nestlé World Championship of Women's Golf. 1987: Winner of Standard Register Turquoise Classic. 1989: Winner of AI Star–Centinela Hospital Classic, and JC Penney Classic (with Bill Glasson). 1990: Winner of Oldsmobile Classic, Standard Register Turquoise Classic, and Corning Classic. 1991: Winner of Centel Classic, Rail Charity Classic, Safeco Classic, and MBS Classic.

Pat Bradley. *Courtesy LPGA*

BRADY, MICHAEL JOSEPH. Born in Brighton, MA, April 15, 1887. Died December 3, 1972. Brady was one of the first of the American homebred professionals to become a championship player. Unfortunately, he is often best remembered for the championships he did not win. In 1911, carrying only six clubs, he tied Johnny McDermott and George Simpson for the U.S. Open title, but lost in a play-off. In 1912 he had a four-stroke lead, but closed with an 80 and tied for third. In 1915 he trailed Jerry Travers by a stroke going into the last round, but again had a final 80 and finished sixth. His most famous failure was in 1919, when he led by five strokes after three rounds and once again closed with an 80. Walter Hagen tied him with a 75 and won the play-off the next day by a stroke. Despite these unfortunate mishaps, Brady was a very fine golfer.

In 1917 he broke 100 for twenty-seven holes, and on Labor Day of the same year he made two holes in one during a single round. In 1922 he shot 291 and won the Western Open by ten strokes.

Tournament Record: 1911: Runner-up in U.S. Open. 1914: Winner of Massachusetts Open. 1916: Winner of Massachusetts Open. 1917: Winner of

Mike Brady. *Courtesy U.S.G.A.*

North and South Open. 1919: Runner-up in U.S. Open. 1922: Winner of Western Open. 1923: Winner of Massachusetts Open. 1924: Winner of Metropolitan Open. 1925: Winner of Westchester Open.

BRAID, JAMES. Born in Elie, Scotland, February 6, 1870. Died November 27, 1950. His is one of the most revered names in golf. Braid, along with Harry Vardon and J. H. Taylor, formed the "triumvirate" that dominated golf for twenty years prior to World War I. He was the first man to win the British Open five times, and he also won the British Match Play Championship four times and the French Open once. His record in the British Open is remarkable in that he won his five championships and was second three times all in the space of ten years. Braid was a tall, quiet man who hit the ball great distances, yet never appeared ruffled, no matter how he was playing. It was once said of him that no one could be as wise as

James Braid looked. He was one of the founding members of the British PGA and in his later years designed many courses.

BREWER, GAY ROBERT. Born in Middletown, OH, March 19, 1932. Brewer started playing golf at the age of eight, and by the time he turned professional and joined the Tour in 1956, he had collected some seventy trophies. He won the USGA Junior Championship in 1949. Brewer's finest year was undoubtedly 1967. After two second-place finishes and one third-place finish, Brewer shot a 26 under par 262 to win at Pensacola. His first three rounds of 66-64-61 (191) are still a PGA Tour record. He then won the Masters in dashing style, shooting a last round 67 to take the title. The Masters had eluded him the previous year when he missed a short putt on the last green to tie with Tommy Jacobs and Jack Nicklaus. Nicklaus won the play-off. In 1967 Brewer holed a putt of similar length for victory on the 72nd hole. Later in the year, Brewer went over to Scotland and won the Alcan Golfer of the Year event at St. An-

James Braid. *Courtesy U.S.G.A.*

Gay Brewer. *Wide World Photos*

drews. The $50,000 first prize was at that time the largest in golf history. Brewer was a member of the 1967 and 1971 Ryder Cup teams.

As a senior, Brewer's best year came in 1984, when he won two events, the Legends of Golf, partnered with Billy Casper, and the Citizens Union Senior Golf Classic. He took home prize money totaling $133,769.

Brewer owns one of the most peculiar swings in golf. He takes the club straight back from the ball, then lifts it up with a flying right elbow. Bringing the elbow back into his side, he reroutes the club back to the inside on his downswing. But as he says, "I've had this swing ever since I started golf. I'm not about to change it now."

Tournament Record: 1949: Winner of U.S.G.A. Junior Championship. 1961: Winner of Carling Open, Mobile Open, and West Palm Beach Open. 1963: Winner of Waco Turner Open. 1965: Winner of Seattle Open, Hawaiian Open, and National Team Championship (with Butch Baird). 1966: Winner of Pensacola Open. 1967: Winner of Pensacola Open, Masters, and Alcan Golfer of the Year. 1968: Winner of Alcan Golfer of the Year. 1972: Winner of Cana-

dian Open and Taiheiyo Masters (Japan). 1984: Winner of Legends of Golf (with Billy Casper) and Citizens Union Senior Golf Classic.

BURKE, JACK, JR. Born in Fort Worth, TX, January 29, 1923. One of America's top postwar golfers. He won four tournaments in a row, was runner-up in the Masters, and won the Vardon Trophy, all in 1952, and then was named golfer of the year in 1956 after winning the PGA Championship and Masters. Although his closing 71 was a fine round under the prevailing conditions, his 1956 Masters victory unfortunately is remembered as the one Ken Venturi lost. Burke also had to come from behind to win the PGA Championship. He was five down to Ed Furgol after 14 holes and three down to Ted Kroll after 19 in his last two matches. Burke, a fine putter, was a member of four Ryder Cup teams and won seven of eight matches. He won the 1952 Texas Open with a score of 260 (67-65-64-64).

Burke began playing at the age of seven under the tutelage of his father and was a good player by the time he reached his teens. He joined the tour in 1950 and won three tournaments in his first year. A wrist injury kept Burke out of the 1957 U.S. Open, and chronic trouble with his hand curtailed his play somewhat from then on.

Tournament Record: 1949: Winner of Metropolitan Open. 1950: Winner of Rio Grande Valley

Jack Burke, JR.
AP/Wide World Photos

Open, Bing Crosby Pro-Am, St. Petersburg Open, and Sioux City Open. 1951: Winner of Piping Rock Pro-Am. 1952: Winner of St. Petersburg Open, Texas Open, Houston Open, Baton Rouge Open, and Miami Open; runner-up in Masters. 1953: Winner of Inverness Invitational. 1956: Winner of Masters, and PGA Championship. 1958: Winner of Insurance City Open. 1959: Winner of Houston Classic. 1961: Winner of Buick Open. 1963: Winner of Lucky International Open, Texas State Open, and St. Paul Open.

CALCAVECCHIA, MARK JOHN. Born in Laurel, NE, June 12, 1960. Calcavecchia's PGA Tour career got off to a slow start, but after his first victory in the fall of 1986, he was on the road to success.

Calcavecchia quit the University of Florida to join the Tour at the age of 21 in the summer of 1981, but his game wasn't ready. He didn't crack the top 130 money winners until five years later. Always a long hitter and aggressive player, Calcavecchia often lacked control of both the ball and his temper. Eventually, he learned to keep his emotions in check and developed a short game that could bail him out of any trouble.

He scored what at the time seemed a stunning upset by winning the 1986 Southwest Classic, but that was only a sign of things to come. In the next four years, he ranked tenth, sixth, fifth, and seventh on the money list and won four more Tour events, earning at least $500,000 each year. Calcavecchia's best year was 1989. He won the Phoenix and Los Angeles Opens on the PGA Tour and added his first major championship by winning the British Open in

Donna Caponi. *UPI/Bettmann*

a play-off over Greg Norman and Wayne Grady. The next year proved frustrating, however, as Calcavecchia finished second five times without posting a victory.

Tournament Record: 1986: Winner of Southwest Classic. 1987: Winner of Honda Classic. 1988: Winner of Bank of Boston Classic and Australian Open. 1989: Winner of Phoenix Open, Nissan Los Angeles Open, and British Open. 1992: Winner of Phoenix Open.

CAPONI, DONNA. Born in Detroit, MI, January 29, 1945. Donna Caponi took to golf at age eight, instructed by her father, golf professional Harry Caponi. She won the 1956 Junior Los Angeles Open. Turning professional in 1965, Caponi had to wait four years before breaking through to victory in the 1969 U.S. Women's Open at Scenic Hills CC, Pensacola, Florida. It was quite a tester. After opening with scores of 74, 76, and 75, Caponi took the lead in the last round by eagling the par 5 15th hole. She made a par on 16, bogeyed 17, and then was delayed in playing the 18th hole by lightning. She had to wait in the clubhouse for fifteen minutes while play was suspended. Far from being unnerved by the delay, Caponi made a birdie 4 on the final hole for a one-stroke victory. Her final round of 69 was the lowest shot by a champion up to that time. The following year, the Open was held at Muskogee CC in Mus-

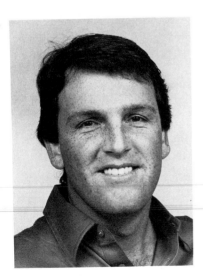

Mark Calcavecchia.
Courtesy PGA

kogee, Oklahoma. Caponi became the second woman to win back-to-back Opens, not only matching Mickey Wright's performance but also Wright's record score of 287, set in 1959. Caponi had rounds of 69, 70, 71, and 77. Although well ahead after a record score of 210 for three rounds, she had a scare on the last hole when Sandra Spuzich missed a six-footer for a tie. Caponi then holed her four-footer for the victory. Before retiring in 1989, Donna compiled twenty-four official Tour wins, including the LPGA Championship in 1979 and 1981. Although she never was leading money winner, she finished second in 1976 and 1980 and third in 1969. She finished among the top ten money winners ten times.

Tournament Record: 1956: Winner of Junior Los Angeles Open. 1969: Winner of U.S. Women's Open and Lincoln-Mercury Open. 1970: Winner of Bluegrass Invitational, and U.S. Women's Open. 1973: Winner of Bluegrass Invitational. 1975: Winner of Burdine's Invitational, Colgate European Open, and Lady Tara Classic. 1976: Winner of Peter Jackson Classic, Portland Classic, The Carlton, and Mizuno Japan Classic. 1978: Winner of The Sarah Coventry, Portland Ping Team Championship (with Kathy Whitworth), and Houston Classic. 1979: Winner of LPGA Championship. 1980: Winner of LPGA National Pro-Am, Colgate–Dinah Shore Winner's Circle, Corning Classic, United Virginia Bank Classic, Portland Ping Team Championship (with Kathy Whitworth), and ERA Real Estate Classic. 1981: Winner of LPGA Desert Inn Pro-Am, American Defender–WRAL Classic, LPGA Championship, WUI Classic, Portland Ping Team Championship (with Kathy Whitworth), and Boston Five Classic.

CARNER, JOANNE. Born in Kirkland, WA, April 4, 1939. Carner began playing golf at the age of ten and went on to compile a brilliant amateur record before joining the LPGA Tour. She graduated from Arizona State University with a B.A. in Physical Education, but did not turn professional until nine years later, in 1970. Few women have ever brought such impressive credentials into the pro ranks.

Known as "the Great Gundy" (from her maiden name, Gunderson), she won the U.S. Amateur five times, the National Collegiate title, and just about every other important amateur championship at least once. She played on four U.S. Curtis Cup teams (1958, 1960, 1962, 1964). In her last year before

Joanne Carner. *UPI/Bettmann*

turning pro, she won the 1969 Burdine's Invitational in Miami, the last amateur to win an LPGA event. She is also the only player to have won the U.S.G.A. Junior, U.S. Women's Amateur, and U.S. Women's Open.

Since joining the pro ranks as a thirty-year-old rookie, Carner has won more official tournaments (forty-two) and collected more Vare Trophies (five: 1974, 1975, 1981–1983) than anyone on Tour in that span. She was inducted into the LPGA Hall of Fame in 1982.

One of the longest hitters in the history of women's golf, Carner is known for her aggressive game. She is also a fine sand player.

Tournament Record: 1956: Winner of USGA Girls' Junior. 1957: Winner of U.S. Amateur. 1958: Winner of Pacific Northwest Amateur. 1959: Winner of Western Amateur and Pacific Northwest Amateur. 1960: Winner of U.S. Amateur, Southwest Amateur, and NCAA Championship. 1961: Winner of Trans-

Mississippi Amateur. 1962: Winner of U.S. Amateur. 1966: Winner of U.S. Amateur. 1967: Winner of Northwest Amateur. 1968: Winner of U.S. Amateur and Eastern Amateur. 1970: Winner of Wendell West Open. 1971: Winner of U.S. Open and Bluegrass Invitational. 1974: Winner of Bluegrass Invitational, Hoosier Classic, Desert Inn Classic, St. Paul Open, Dallas Civitan Open, and Portland Classic. 1975: Winner of American Defender Classic, All-American Classic, and Peter Jackson Classic. 1976: Winner of Orange Blossom Classic, Lady Tara Classic, and Hoosier Classic. 1977: Winner of Talk Tournament, Borden Classic, National Jewish Hospital Open, and LPGA Team Championship (with Judy Rankin). 1978: Winner of Peter Jackson Classic, Borden Classic, and Colgate Triple Crown. 1979: Winner of Honda Civic Classic, Women's Kemper Open, and Colgate Triple Crown. 1980: Winner of Whirlpool Championship of Deer Creek, Bent Tree Ladies Classic, Sunstar '80, Honda Civic Classic, and Lady Keystone Open. 1981: Winner of S&H Golf Classic, Lady Keystone Open, Columbia Savings LPGA Classic, and Rail Charity Golf Classic. 1982: Winner of Elizabeth Arden Classic, McDonald's LPGA Kids' Classic, Chevrolet World Championship of Women's Golf, Henredon Classic, and Rail Charity Golf Classic. 1983: Winner of Chevrolet World Championship of Women's Golf, and Portland Ping Championship. 1984: Winner of Corning Classic. 1985: Winner of Elizabeth Arden Classic, and Safeco Classic.

Billy Casper. *Leonard Kamsler*

CASPER, WILLIAM EARL, JR. Born in San Diego, CA, June 24, 1931. One of the giants of modern American golf, Billy Casper had a fine amateur career in the San Diego area. He briefly attended Notre Dame University (one semester), then put in a four-year hitch in the Navy before turning pro in 1954. He joined the PGA Tour the following year, and his first victory, in the Labatt Open, came in 1956. Casper then rose rapidly to the top.

He won his first major, the 1959 U.S. Open at Winged Foot (N.Y.), with a score of 282. He took just 114 putts enroute to victory, and this made his reputation as one of the finest putters ever. Soon, golfers everywhere were emulating his style on the greens—he keeps his left forearm against his left thigh as he strokes with his wrists, the clubface remaining square to the target line.

The praise he's gotten for his putting skill, although well deserved, has always bothered Casper a little, because he feels that his considerable skill with the other clubs is overlooked.

In his early years, Casper had unusual appeal to golfers everywhere in that he was overweight (at 5'11" and fluctuating between 200 and 215 lbs.) and preferred fishing to practice.

In mid-1964, Casper's appearance, if not his golf, underwent a massive change. Plagued by allergies during his career, Casper went to a Chicago allergist, who recommended an exotic diet that included buffalo, elephant and whale meat, as well as avocado. No-no's were such common foods as oranges, wheat, eggs, pork, peas, beans and chocolate. "Buffalo Billy," as Casper was known at that time, went on the diet and slimmed down to 175 pounds. He continued to win on Tour.

His most memorable victory came in the 1966 U.S. Open at the Olympic Club in San Francisco. In the final round, Casper caught Arnold Palmer after coming from seven strokes behind with nine holes to play. The next day, he beat Palmer in the play-off 69 to 73, after being two strokes behind after nine holes. He won his third major, the 1970 Masters, in another play-off, beating Gene Littler 69 to 74.

Casper's achievements while on the PGA Tour include: Fifty-one official victories; Player of the Year twice (1966 and 1970); Vardon Trophy winner five times (1960, 1963, 1965, 1966, 1968); Ryder Cup team member eight straight times (1961 through 1975), non-playing captain in 1979; induction into the World Golf Hall of Fame in 1978; and induction into the PGA Hall of Fame in 1982.

In the mid-1970s, Casper went into a sickening slump. His baffling loss of form led him to a hypnotist in Salt Lake City. He then went to sports psychologist Cliff Webb at Brigham Young University, where he studied videotapes of his swing when playing at his best as well as during the slump. It helped, but he did not come all the way back.

His third move proved best. He returned to San Diego and worked with Phil Rodgers, who, after his Tour career, had become an outstanding teacher. Rodgers completely revamped Casper's swing, changing him from a fader to the biggest drawer of the ball in top class golf since Bobby Locke.

In 1982, Casper proved the efficiency of his new swing by winning back-to-back victories on the Senior PGA Tour, the Shootout at Jeremy Ranch and the Merrill Lynch Commemorative. Since then, he has captured a total of seven Senior events, including the 1983 U.S. Senior Open and the 1988 Mazda Senior Players Championship. He's also made another comeback—to a comfortable 215 pounds.

Tournament Record: 1949: Winner of Southern California Interscholastic. 1950: Winner of San Diego Amateur. 1953: Winner of San Diego County Open. 1954: Winner of San Diego County Open, and 11th Naval District Tourney. 1956: Winner of Labatt Open. 1957: Winner of Phoenix Open and Kentucky Derby Open. 1958: Winner of Bing Crosby National, New Orleans Open, Buick Open, and Havana Invitational; runner-up in PGA. 1959: Winner of U.S. Open, Portland Open, Lafayette Open, Mobile Open, and Brazil Open. 1960: Winner of Portland Open, Hesperia Open, Orange County Open, and Bakersfield Open. 1961: Winner of Portland Open. 1962:

Winner of Doral Open, Greensboro Open, 500 Festival Open, and Bakersfield Open. 1963: Winner of Bing Crosby National and Insurance City Open. 1964: Winner of Doral Open, Colonial Invitational, Seattle Open, and Almaden Open. 1965: Winner of Bob Hope Classic, Insurance City Open, Western Open, and Sahara Invitational. 1966: Winner of U.S. Open, San Diego Open, 500 Festival Open, and Western Open. 1967: Winner of Canadian Open and Carling World Open. 1968: Winner of Southern California Open, Los Angeles Open, Greensboro Open, Colonial Invitational, 500 Festival Open, Greater Hartford Open, and Lucky International Open. 1969: Winner of Bob Hope Desert Classic, Western Open, and Alcan Golfer of the Year Championship. 1970: Winner of Los Angeles Open, Masters, IVB-Philadelphia Classic, and AVCO Classic. 1971: Winner of Kaiser International Open, and Miki Gold Cup. 1973: Winner of Western Open and Sammy Davis, Jr.–Greater Hartford Open. 1974: Winner of Lancome Trophy (France). 1975: Winner of New Orleans Open and Italian Open. 1977: Winner of Mexican Open. 1982: Winner of Shootout At Jeremy Ranch, and Merrill Lynch–*Golf Digest* Commemorative Pro-Am. 1983: Winner of USGA Senior Open. 1984: Winner of Senior PGA Tour Roundup and Legends of Golf (with Gay Brewer). 1987: Winner of Del E. Webb Arizona Classic and Greater Grand Rapids Open. 1988: Winner of Vantage at the Dominion, and Mazda Senior Players Championship. 1989: Winner of TransAmerica Senior Championship.

COLLETT, GLENNA (MRS. EDWIN H. VARE). Born in New Haven, CT, June 20, 1903. Died February 3, 1989. The greatest amateur player the United States ever produced. She won the U.S. Women's championship a record six times in addition to being runner-up twice and a semifinalist twice, all in the space of fourteen years. Glenna also won the North and South and the Eastern six times each in the course of dominating American women's golf during the 1920s. However, she had the misfortune to come on the scene at the same time as Joyce Wethered, the incomparable British star, who defeated Glenna in a great British final in 1929 at St. Andrews. Glenna also gained the British final in 1930 at Formby, but lost to Diana Fishwick. She had been beaten in the third round by Miss Wethered in 1925. Glenna took up the game at the age of fourteen and was a pupil of Alex

Glenna
Collett Vare.
*Courtesy PGA World
Hall of Fame*

Smith, the U.S. Open champion, who also tutored Jerry Travers.

COODY, BILLY CHARLES. Born in Stamford, TX, July 13, 1937. Charles Coody got his start in the game at age twelve by going to the course with his father. He never really had a special teaching professional. Coody was quite an athlete in his school days; he was quarterback for his high school team and was an all-state basketball player. He won the state high school golf championship in 1954, and during the next seven years won some thirty amateur golf titles around his native state, including the 1959 Texas and West Texas Amateur Championships. When Coody went to Texas Christian University, it was primarily to play golf. However, since TCU didn't have golf scholarships, he was given one for basketball. He graduated in 1960 with a degree in business. While serving a three-year hitch in the Air Force, he qualified for the 1960 and 1961 U.S. Opens. In 1962, he reached the semi-finals of the U.S. Amateur, earning his first invitation to the Masters. He turned pro the following year.

The Masters was to give Coody his greatest moments in the game. He led the 1969 Masters by one stroke with three holes to play, but then decided to play defensively and bogeyed in to drop to fifth place. Two years later, he closed with birdie–birdie–par–par, winning by two strokes over Jack Nicklaus and Johnny Miller. The title earned him a spot in the 1971 World Series of Golf at Firestone CC, Akron, Ohio, which was then a four-man unofficial event. He won it, taking home $50,000. He was a member of the 1971 Ryder Cup team.

Coody had a successful trip across the Atlantic in 1973. He won two tournaments in Great Britain, the Wills Open in England, and the John Player Classic in Turnberry, Scotland.

He was a steady, if not spectacular, performer on the PGA Tour. From 1965 through 1977, he put together thirteen straight years in the top sixty money-winners. His career winnings exceeded $1 million.

Although Coody's swing is eminently sound, it is distinguished by a distinctive little lurch forward in the follow-through. He normally draws the ball. His game is as steady as a rock. His peers cite his ability to hit any kind of trouble shot. He joined the Senior Tour in 1987. Much like his record on the regular Tour, he's been a steady player but not a big winner. Through 1991, he'd won four individual events.

Tournament Record: 1954: Winner of Texas State High School Championship. 1959: Winner of Texas

Charles Coody. *UPI/Bettmann*

Harry Cooper. *Courtesy U.S.G.A.*

burst on the national scene in 1926 by winning the Los Angeles and Del Monte Opens. He was in good position to win the 1927 U.S. Open, but three-putted the last green, was tied by Tommy Armour, and lost in a play-off. Over the next decade, Cooper won many tournaments and in 1937 was the leading money winner and took the Vardon Trophy. He seemed certain to win the Open at last in 1936 when he finished at 284, a tournament record, but Tony Manero came out of nowhere to win with 282. Cooper continued at the top until the advent of World War II. Since then he has been a respected club pro in the New York area.

Tournament Record: 1923, 1924: Winner of Texas PGA. 1926: Winner of Los Angeles Open and Del Monte Open. 1927: Winner of Oklahoma City Open; runner-up in U.S. Open. 1929: Winner of Oklahoma Open, Shawnee Open, Medinah Open, and Western New York PGA. 1930: Winner of Pasadena Open, St. Paul Open, Salt Lake City Open, and Medinah Open. 1931: Winner of Pasadena Open. 1932: Winner of Canadian Open and Tri-State Open. 1933: Winner of Illinois Open. 1934: Winner of Western Open, Illinois Open, and Illinois PGA. 1935: Winner of St. Paul Open, Medinah Open, and Illinois Open. 1936: Winner of Florida West Coast Open and St. Paul Open; runner-up in U.S. Open and Masters. 1937: Winner of Canadian Open, True Temper Open, Los Angeles Open, Houston Open, St. Petersburg Open, Oakland Open, and Oklahoma City Four-Ball. 1939: Winner of Goodall Round Robin, and Connecticut Open. 1942: Winner of Minnesota Open and Bing Crosby Pro-Am. 1955: Winner of PGA Quarter Century Club Tourney. 1962: Winner of Atlantic City Senior Open.

Amateur Championship and West Texas Amateur Championship. 1964: Winner of Dallas Open. 1969: Winner of Cleveland Open. 1971: Winner of Masters, and World Series of Golf. 1973: Winner of Wills Open (England), and John Player Classic (Scotland). 1989: Winner of General Tire Las Vegas Classic. 1990: Winner of Liberty Mutual Legends of Golf (with Dale Douglass), and Vantage Championship. 1991: Winner of NYNEX Commemorative and TransAmerica Senior Championship.

COOPER, HARRY E. Born in Leatherhead, England, August 4, 1904. He was rated one of the best tee-to-green players of all time and was the winner of many tournaments, but, despite his great skills, Cooper was destined never to win a major championship. He began playing in England, but his game developed in Texas, where he moved with his parents when still quite young. After considerable local success, he

COTTON, THOMAS HENRY. Born in Holmes Chapel, England, January 26, 1907. Died December 22, 1987. He was one of England's greatest players and just about its only one of world stature in the 1930s and 1940s. Although Cotton won the British Open three times and captured many titles on the Continent, he had little success in his occasional trips to the United States, with the result that Americans always slightly underrated him. Besides his abilities as a player, Cotton was an effective teacher who authored several fine books of golf instruction. In later years he turned to course architecture and was the designer of several layouts in England, France, and Portugal. Cotton

Henry Cotton.
Courtesy U.S.G.A.

was a member of three Ryder Cup teams and was captain twice.

Tournament Record: 1926, 1927: Winner of Kent Professional. 1928: Winner of Kent Professional and Croydon and District Professional. 1929: Winner of Kent Professional. 1930: Winner of Belgian Open, Mar-del-Plata Open, and Kent Professional. 1931: Winner of Dunlop-Southport Tourney. 1932: Winner of *News of the World* Tourney and Dunlop-Southport Tourney. 1934: Winner of British Open and Belgian Open. 1935: Winner of Yorkshire *Evening News* Tourney and Leeds Tourney. 1936: Winner of Italian Open and Dunlop Metropolitan Tourney. 1937: Winner of German Open, British Open, Czechoslovak Open, and Silver King Tourney. 1938: Winner of German Open, Czechoslovak Open, and Belgian Open. 1939: Winner of German Open and *Daily Mail* Tourney. 1940: Winner of *News of the World* Tourney. 1945: Winner of *News Chronicle* Tourney. 1946: Winner of French Open, *News of the World* Tourney, Star Tourney, and Vichy Open. 1947: Winner of French Open, Spalding Tourney,

and Yorkshire *Evening News* Tourney. 1948: Winner of British Open and White Sulphur Springs Invitational. 1953: Winner of Dunlop Tourney. 1954: Winner of Penfold Tourney.

CRENSHAW, BEN DANIEL. Born in Austin, TX, January 11, 1952. If ever a golfer came out on the PGA Tour marked for stardom, it was Crenshaw. At age eighteen, he tied for low amateur in the U.S. Open at Hazeltine, beating the likes of Arnold Palmer, Jack Nicklaus, and Gary Player. At the University of Texas, Crenshaw was practically unbeatable, winning the NCAA Championship three times in a row (1971, 1972, 1973), although he shared it with teammate Tom Kite in 1972. Crenshaw was a member of the 1972 World Cup team and the following year won both the medal and match phases of the prestigious Western Amateur. He also won the 1973 Sunnehanna Amateur. Crenshaw earned his Tour card in the fall of 1973, winning medalist honors at a walk; the runner-up, Gil Morgan, was twelve strokes behind.

In his first event on Tour, Crenshaw won the 1973 San Antonio–Texas Open by two strokes. It was the first time this had happened since Marty Fleckman won his first pro start in 1967. Crenshaw followed with a second-place finish in the 1973 World Open, a 144-hole, $500,000 tournament.

Crenshaw didn't win in 1974, however, and for perhaps the first time in his life he had doubts about the soundness of his swing. In those days, Crenshaw's swing had the enviably smooth tempo, which is still its trademark, but it was very long, the club going far beyond horizontal at the top. He also made a big lateral movement to the right going back. He hit the ball a long way, but he could miss, by his own admission, as many as ten fairways a round. He started tinkering with his swing, and went into a slump that lasted through 1975.

The slump ended only when he stopped tinkering and did what came naturally, as was urged by his father Charlie and teacher Harvey Penick.

The years from 1976 (his best with three victories) to 1981 were very good ones. He finished no worse than twenty-first on the money-winning list—he was second in 1976 and fifth in 1979 and 1980. However, he had only won eight times. For any other young man on the Tour, such a performance would have been outstanding, but for the "Gentle Ben" expected to dethrone the "Golden Bear," it almost seemed ordinary. Contributing to the feeling were five runner-up finishes in 1979 alone, and a record in playoffs of 0-5 (now 0-7).

In the majors, where the great golfers separate themselves from the merely very good, Crenshaw only knew heartbreak.

In the 1975 U.S. Open at Medinah, he finished only a shot back after a thinned tee shot at the par-3 71st hole found the lake fronting the green. He took a disastrous double-bogey 5 on the hole. In 1978, he finished second to Jack Nicklaus at the British Open at St. Andrews. The next year, he again was runner-up in the British Open, this time to Seve Ballesteros, after taking another double-bogey at the 71st hole. In 1976, he was second to Ray Floyd in the Masters.

Crenshaw started doubting his swing again, and by

Ben Crenshaw. *Fred Vuich*

late 1981, he had lost all confidence. After he missed the cut at the 1982 PGA Championship, he went home to his beloved golf books, his family and friends, and Harvey Penick.

Penick's advice was to revert to his natural swing, and he advised Crenshaw to work on getting set correctly at address, and then work principally on his balance and rhythm.

In 1983, Crenshaw had an excellent season, winning the Byron Nelson, where he finished with a brilliant 66. He was also runner-up in the Masters and Memorial. Overall, he had nine top-ten finishes for the year. He was selected to the Ryder Cup team a second time. (He had previously made the team in 1981.)

Crenshaw's finest hour came in the 1984 Masters. Going into the last round two strokes behind Tom Kite, Crenshaw played the round of his life. Birdies at the second and eighth holes tied him with Kite. Another birdie at the 9th put him one ahead. At the 10th, he holed a 60-footer for another birdie, which put him two ahead. He then showed his maturity by making sound strategic decisions down the stretch and finished with a 68 and a total of 277 for a two-shot victory.

After a problem with hyperactive thyroid, he returned to good form, winning two tournaments in 1986 and three more over the next four years.

By the end of the 1980s, Crenshaw had corrected his overly long swing and excess lateral movement by improving his setup, most notably by setting his right knee a little inwards at address. He is still a magician in extricating himself from trouble, and as a putter, he remains the best of this or arguably any other time.

Tournament Record: 1971: Winner of NCAA Championship. 1972: Co-Champion (with Tom Kite) of NCAA Championship. 1973: Winner of NCAA Championship, Western Amateur, Sunnehanna Amateur, and San Antonio–Texas Open. 1976: Winner of Bing Crosby National Pro-Am, Hawaiian Open, Ohio Kings Island Open, and Irish Open. 1977: Winner of Colonial National Invitation. 1979: Winner of Phoenix Open and Walt Disney World Team Championship (with George Burns). 1980: Winner of Anheuser-Busch Classic and Texas State Open. 1983: Winner of Byron Nelson Classic. 1984: Winner of Masters. 1986: Winner of Buick Open and Vantage Championship. 1987: Winner of

USF&G Classic. 1988: Winner of Doral Ryder Open. 1990: Winner of Southwestern Bell Colonial. 1992: Winner of Central Western Open.

CRUICKSHANK, ROBERT ALLAN. Born in Grantown-on-Spey, Scotland, November 16, 1894. Died August 27, 1975. Wee Bobby was one of the world's best players in the 1920s, was still a threat in every championship in the 1930s, was good enough to finish twenty-fifth in the U.S. Open at the age of fifty-five, and was still winning at the age of sixty. He finished fourth or better in the Open five times in fifteen years and twice reached the PGA semifinals, but never won a major title. In the 1923 Open at Inwood Country Club, he tied Bobby Jones on the 72nd hole, but lost in a play-off. In 1932 at Fresh Meadow he finished 69, 68, but Gene Sarazen was playing the last 28 holes in 100 strokes, and again Bobby was second.

Cruickshank began playing at the age of four and

Bobby Cruickshank. *UPI/Bettmann*

was a golfing rival of Tommy Armour in school. After heroic service in World War I, during which he was taken prisoner, he turned to golf for a living and moved to the United States in 1921. Almost immediately he was a consistent winner, and he captured many titles over the next three decades.

Tournament Record: 1919, 1920: Winner of Edinburgh Coronation Trophy. 1921: Winner of New York Open and St. Joseph Open. 1922: Winner of Spalding Tourney and Wykagyl Tourney. 1923: Runner-up in U.S. Open. 1924: Winner of Colorado Open and Mid-Continent Open. 1925: Winner of Miami Four-Ball and Oklahoma City Open. 1926: Winner of North and South Open, Westchester Open, and Mid-South Amateur-Pro; tied for first in Florida Open. 1927: Winner of North and South Open, Texas Open, Hot Springs Open, Miami Four-Ball, Los Angeles Open, and South Central Open. 1928: Winner of Maryland Open. 1929: Winner of Westchester Open; tied for first in Hot Springs Open. 1932: Tied for second in U.S. Open. 1933: Winner of Virginia Open. 1934: Winner of Virginia Open, National Capital City Open, and Nassau Open. 1935: Winner of Virginia Open, British Colonial Open, and Sarasota Open. 1936, 1937, 1939: Winner of Virginia Open. 1943: Winner of North and South Open. 1949, 1950: Winner of Tri-State PGA. 1954: Winner of Erie Open.

DANIEL, ELIZABETH ANN. Born in Charleston, SC, on October 14, 1956. Beth Daniel grew up in a golfing family and began to play when she was seven. She was playing in her first tournament at eight, and was a quarter-finalist in the USGA Junior Girls' Championship in 1973. She won the Twin States (North and South Carolina) Junior Girls' Championship in 1973, '74, and '75. In 1975, Daniel won the U.S. Women's Amateur at her first attempt—only seven other women have achieved this feat since the championship began, in 1895. Enroute to victory, she defeated Nancy Lopez in the second round. At the time, Daniel was about to enter her sophomore year at Furman University. She won the U.S. Women's Amateur again in 1977. She also was a member of the 1976 and 1978 Curtis Cup teams and the 1978 World Amateur Team.

Turning pro in 1978, she qualified for the LPGA Tour in January 1979 and that spring won the World Ladies' Championship in Japan. By the end of the

Beth Daniel.
Courtesy LPGA

year, she had bagged her first official event, the Patty Berg Classic, and run away with Rookie-of-the-Year honors, earning $97,027. In 1980, she won four tournaments and became the first LPGA player to earn more than $200,000 in one season. She was named Player of the Year. She led the Tour in earnings in 1981 for the second straight year and in 1982 became the first woman golfer to win over $200,000 in three straight seasons. In 1984, she was plagued by back problems, the first in a series of woes that combined to limit her to one victory in a five-year span. Daniel lost confidence in her game, especially her putting, and in 1988 was set back by mononucleosis.

In 1989 and 1990, Daniel roared back with a total of eleven victories. Seven of these came in 1990, when she was Player of the Year. She also won her first major title, the Mazda LPGA Championship, and earned a single-season record $863,578. She won the Vave Trophy for low scoring average in both 1989 and 1990.

Daniel is tall (5'10") and a very long hitter. Except for her slumping years, she's also been an excellent putter, as her two victories in the Golf Putter Award Playoff (1982 and 1985) attest. However, her medium irons may be the strongest part of her game.

Tournament Record: 1973: Winner of Twin States Junior Girls' Championship. 1974: Winner of Twin States Junior Girls' Championship. 1975: Winner of Twin States Junior Girls' Championship and U.S. Women's Amateur Championship. 1977: Winner of U.S. Women's Amateur Championship. 1979: Winner of World Ladies Championship (Japan) and Patty Berg Classic. 1980: Winner of Golden Lights Championship, Patty Berg Classic, Columbia Savings Classic, and Chevrolet World Championship of Women's Golf. 1981: Winner of Florida Lady Citrus, Chevrolet World Championship of Women's Golf, and JC Penney Classic (with Tom Kite). 1982: Winner of Bent Tree Ladies Classic, American Express Sun City Classic, Birmingham Classic, Columbia Savings Classic, and WUI Classic. 1983: Winner of McDonald's LPGA Kids Classic. 1985: Winner of Kyocera Inamori Classic. 1988: Nichirei Ladies Cup United States-Japan Team Championship. 1989: Winner of Greater Washington Open, Rail Charity Classic, Safeco Classic, and Konica San Jose Classic. 1990: Winner of Orix Hawaiian Ladies Open, Women's Kemper Open, Phar-Mor in Youngstown, Mazda LPGA Championship, Northgate Classic, Rail Charity Classic, Centel Classic, and JC Penney Classic (with Davis Love III). 1991: Winner of Phar-Mor at Inverrary and McDonald's Championship.

DEMARET, JAMES NEWTON. Born in Houston, TX, May 25, 1910. Died December 28, 1983. He was one of the game's most colorful personalities and an outstanding player for three decades. Demaret became the first man to win three Masters titles (1940, 1947, 1950), was semi-finalist in the PGA four times, finished fourth or better in the U.S. Open three times, was undefeated in six Ryder Cup matches, won the Vardon Trophy, and was a member of the winning U.S. team in the Canada Cup competition. The Texas native was identified with golf all his life, although he had a short career as a singer with a band in nightclubs. He was one of nine children of a carpenter, and two of his brothers were professionals. After several years of local success, which included winning the Texas PGA five straight times, Demaret joined the pro circuit full time in 1938 and quickly won the San Francisco Match Play tournament. He won the Los Angeles Open in 1939, and by 1940 he was one of the best. That year he won seven tournaments, including the Masters. Demaret was one of Ben Hogan's closest friends, and in 1941 the two won the Inverness Four-Ball, the first of six titles they were to win as partners. Many years later, Demaret wrote a book with Jimmy Breslin called *My Partner, Ben Hogan*. Demaret, a warm-hearted man, parlayed his engaging personality and eye-catching wardrobe into a bona fide gate attraction after World War II. In

Jimmy Demaret. *UPI/Bettmann*

later years he became a partner in the Champions Golf Club in Houston, vice-president of a club manufacturing company, and commentator on a TV golf series.

Tournament Record: 1934, 1935, 1936, 1937: Winner of Texas PGA. 1938: Winner of San Francisco Match Play and Texas PGA. 1939: Winner of Los Angeles Open. 1940: Winner of Masters, San Francisco Match Play, Western Open, New Orleans Open, St. Petersburg Open, Oakland Open, and Seminole Pro-Am. 1941: Winner of Inverness Four-Ball, Connecticut Open, and Argentine Open. 1943: Winner of Michigan PGA and Golden Valley Four-Ball. 1945: Winner of Texas PGA. 1946: Winner of Miami Four-Ball, Inverness Four-Ball, and Tucson Open. 1947: Winner of Masters, Miami Four-Ball, Inverness Four-Ball, Miami Open, St. Petersburg Open, and Tucson Open. 1948: Winner of Albuquerque Open, Inverness Four-Ball, and St. Paul Open; runner-up in

U.S. Open. 1949: Winner of Phoenix Open. 1950: Winner of Masters, Ben Hogan Open, and North Fulton Open. 1951: Winner of Havana Pro-Am. 1952: Winner of Bing Crosby National and National Celebrities Tourney. 1953: Winner of Seminole Pro-Am. 1956: Winner of Palm Springs Invitational. 1957: Winner of Thunderbird Invitational, Baton Rouge Open, and Arlington Hotel Open.

DIEGEL, Leo. Born in Detroit, MI, April 27, 1899. Died in 1951. One of the greatest, and at the same time most tragic, figures in the history of golf. It has been said that in his inspired moments Diegel was the equal of any player who ever lived, but in the end, all he had to show for it was two PGA Championships, four Canadian Open titles, and an assortment of lesser tournament victories. That list is impressive enough, but it represents nothing like what Diegel seemed capable of doing. He was eighth or better eleven times in the British and U.S. Opens and was fourth or better on seven of those occasions.

Leo Diegel. *AP/Wide World Photos*

Eight times he was in position to win right down to the closing holes. His temperament was his undoing, and none of the many remedies he tried had any lasting effect. By nature he was an impatient player and a worrier. He would bound forward after each shot, unable to walk down the fairway at a normal pace. Often, while waiting for another player to drive, Diegel would jump into the air or climb on a tee box in order to see from what lie he would be playing his next shot. The best-known, and most extreme, cure he tried was his famous spread-eagle putting stance in which he bent over with his chin almost touching the handle of the putter and stuck his elbows out in a fashion that looked like a car with both doors open. As early as 1922 he set a record for that time by winning the Shreveport Open with a 275. Later, Canadians called him "Eagle Diegel" after he won the Canadian Open with a 274 that included a 65. Once, at Columbia, he shot nine holes in 29 after betting he could break 30. Willie MacFarlane said he thought Diegel, given a week, could break the record at any course in the country. Often he broke 75 by hitting his shots while standing on one leg. Bernard Darwin once said Diegel was "in a way the greatest golfing genius I have ever seen."

Tournament Record: 1916: Winner of Michigan Open. 1920: Winner of Pinehurst Amateur-Pro; tied for second in U.S. Open. 1922: Winner of Shreveport Open; tied for first in Louisiana Open. 1924: Winner of Canadian Open, Shawnee Open, and Illinois Open. 1925: Winner of Canadian Open, Middle Atlantic Open, Mid-South Amateur-Pro, and Florida Open. 1926: Winner of Middle Atlantic Open and Maryland Open; runner-up in PGA. 1927: Winner of San Diego Open and Middle Atlantic Open. 1928: Winner of PGA Championship, Canadian Open, and Massachusetts Open; tied for first in Long Beach Open. 1929: Winner of PGA Championship, Canadian Open, San Diego Open, and Miami Four-Ball. 1930: Winner of Oregon Open, San Francisco Match Play, and Southern California Open; tied for second in British Open. 1933: Winner of Timber Point Open, Southern California Open, and California Open. 1934: Winner of Walter Hagen Tourney and New England PGA Open.

DUTRA, OLIN. Born in Monterey, CA, January 17, 1901. Died May 5, 1983. Dutra won the PGA Championship in 1932 and the U.S. Open in 1934, along

Olin Dutra. *Wide World Photos*

with several lesser titles, and was a member of two Ryder Cup teams. He worked in a hardware store in his teens and for several years practiced his golf by getting up at 4 A.M., three days a week. After turning pro he continued to get up at such an unlikely hour in order to hold two club jobs simultaneously. He became known as an indefatigable teacher, but still found time to hone a game that was one of the best in the early 1930s. In his Open victory, at Merion, Dutra, despite being ill, shot closing rounds of 71 and 72 to overtake Gene Sarazen, who met disaster at the 11th hole and finished with a 76. Dutra was still good enough in 1961, at the age of sixty, to shoot a 61 over the Jurupa Hills course, where he was professional.

Tournament Record: 1922: Winner of Del Monte Match Play. 1928, 1929, and 1930: Winner of Southern California PGA. 1931: Winner of Southern California PGA, Southwest Open, California State Match Play, and Pacific Southwest PGA. 1932: Winner of PGA Championship, Metropolitan Open, North Shore Open, St. Paul Open, and Southern California

Open. 1933: Winner of Southern California PGA. 1934: Winner of U.S. Open and Miami Biltmore Open. 1935: Winner of Sunset Fields Open and Santa Monica Open. 1936: Winner of True Temper Open. 1937: Winner of Sunset Fields Open. 1940: Winner of California Open.

ELDER, ROBERT LEE. Born in Dallas, TX, July 14, 1934. Lee Elder is to golf what Jackie Robinson was to baseball, Oscar Robertson to basketball and Jim Brown to football. Other blacks pioneered in golf—most notably Charlie Sifford—but Elder was the first to achieve star status and the material success that goes with it.

Elder turned pro in 1959, and played the black United Golf Association tour until 1967. That year, Elder won 21 out of 23 events he entered, and his winnings financed his successful attempt to qualify for the PGA Tour.

Elder first came to national prominence when he

Lee Elder. *UPI/Bettmann*

tied Jack Nicklaus in the 1968 American Golf Classic and then fought Nicklaus tooth and nail in the thrilling televised sudden-death play-off, Elder losing on the fifth hole.

In the fall of 1971, Gary Player invited Elder to play in Player's homeland, South Africa. Because of that country's apartheid policy, the incident attracted world-wide attention. During that trip, Elder distinguished himself, and won the Nigerian Open.

In 1974, Elder broke through on the PGA Tour, winning the Monsanto Open. He defeated Peter Oosterhuis on the fourth hole of the sudden-death play-off. This victory earned him the first Masters invitation ever extended to a black. His best year was 1978, when he tied Lee Trevino in the Greater Milwaukee Open and won yet another play-off on the eighth hole. Then a birdie on the last hole at the Westchester Classic gave him a one-stroke victory over Mark Hayes. In 1979, he became the first black to play in the Ryder Cup. He was then 45.

Elder joined the Senior PGA Tour in July 1984 and, in his sixth start, won the Suntree Senior Classic. He won again the following week at the Hilton Head Seniors International. In 1985, Elder finished second on the money list with three of his four victories coming in play-offs. That was his best campaign. He suffered a heart attack in November 1987, but, exactly a year later, came back to win the Gus Machado Senior Classic.

All in all, Elder's is an amazing record, considering he didn't make it to the big leagues until he was thirty-three.

Tournament Record: 1971: Winner of Nigerian Open. 1974: Winner of Monsanto Open. 1976: Winner of Houston Open. 1978: Winner of Greater Milwaukee Open and Westchester Classic. 1984: Winner of Suntree Senior Classic, Hilton Head Seniors International, and Coca-Cola Grand Slam (Japan). 1985: Winner of *Denver Post* Champions, Merrill Lynch/*Golf Digest* Commemorative, Digital Seniors Classic, and Citizens Union Senior Golf Classic. 1986: Winner of Merrill Lynch/*Golf Digest* Commemorative. 1988: Winner of Gus Machado Senior Classic.

EVANS, CHARLES (CHICK), JR. Born in Indianapolis, IN, July 18, 1890. Died November 6, 1979. One of America's great amateur golfers and a player whose competitive career spanned more than sixty years.

Chick Evans. *UPI/Bettmann*

tic. 1908: Winner of Chicago Amateur and Western Interscholastic. 1909: Winner of Western Amateur. 1910: Winner of Western Open. 1911: Winner of French Amateur, North and South Amateur, and Chicago Amateur. 1912: Winner of Western Amateur; runner-up in U.S. Amateur. 1914: Winner of Western Amateur and Chicago District Amateur; runner-up in U.S. Open. 1915: Winner of Western Amateur. 1916: Winner of U.S. Open and U.S. Amateur. 1920: Winner of U.S. Amateur and Western Amateur. 1921: Winner of Western Amateur. 1922: Winner of Western Amateur; runner-up in U.S. Amateur. 1923: Winner of Western Amateur. 1925: Winner of Kansas City Open. 1927: Runner-up in U.S. Amateur.

FALDO, NICK. Born in Hertfordshire, England, July 18, 1957. Faldo has been one of the leading European players ever since he was named Rookie of the Year on the European Tour in 1977, but it wasn't

Nick Faldo. *Fred Vuich*

After almost a decade of winning everything but championships, Evans took both the U.S. Open and Amateur in 1916, and his 286 in the Open was a record that stood for twenty years. Although no one had ever before taken both championships in a single year, Evans' feat evoked little surprise because experts had recognized for years that he was a player of infinite promise. Since his first tournament victory in 1907, at the age of seventeen, Evans had won more than twenty events, including the French Amateur and so many Western Amateurs that it appeared he held the franchise. After playing dozens of Red Cross exhibitions during World War I, he won the Amateur for the second time in 1920, and since he was only thirty, it appeared as if he might win it several more times. But although he was in the fight for another decade, during which he was runner-up twice, he never won again. Evans competed in the Amateur for more than fifty years, and it was unfortunate that he eventually began to meet players who never saw him during his prime. Evans was active in senior affairs for the rest of his career and was responsible for setting up the Evans Scholarship Foundation for caddies.

Tournament Record: 1907: Winner of Chicago Amateur, Western Junior, and Western Interscholas-

until the late 1980s that he staked his claim as one of the best players in the world. From 1987 through 1992, Faldo posted five victories in major championships, plus 2 seconds and two thirds. Nobody had a better record in the four majors during that period.

Faldo's rise to the top came after he reworked his swing with the help of teaching pro David Leadbetter. The transition period led to a two-year slump in 1985 and 1986, but that's something Faldo was willing to put up with in order to build a swing that would win major championships.

Winning majors was about the only thing Faldo lacked in the first phase of his career. He showed promise early when he took the British Youths' Championship and English Amateur in 1975. After a brief stay at the University of Houston, Faldo returned to England to turn pro at age 19.

Faldo finished eighth on the Order of Merit in 1977, his first full season. The next year he took the first of four European PGA Championships. He really emerged in 1983 when he won five European events and led the Order of Merit. He joined the PGA Tour and won the Heritage Classic in 1984. Still, he was unhappy with his game and felt he should do better in the majors.

The "new" Faldo emerged in 1987. He started off by winning the Madrid Open, his first victory in three years. Then, more importantly, he captured the British Open, where he churned out eighteen pars in the final round at Muirfield to finish one stroke ahead of Paul Azinger. Much like Jack Nicklaus in his prime, Faldo began to focus his game on the majors. He lost the U.S. Open in a play-off to Curtis Strange in 1988, but the next year he defeated Scott Hoch in a play-off to win the Masters. In 1990 he became only the second player to successfully defend the Masters title. This time he defeated Ray Floyd in a play-off. He also landed his second British Open in 1990, becoming the first player since Tom Watson in 1982 to win two majors in one year. He added a third British Open in 1992.

Straight hitting and mental toughness are probably Faldo's strongest attributes. He earned a reputation as a steady but unspectacular player with his all-par effort at Muirfield, but in 1989 and 1990, with improved putting, he began to produce some fireworks. He shot a 65 in the final round of the 1989 Masters, birdied four of the last six holes of the 1990 Masters and shot 18-under-par 270 for four rounds at the Old Course in winning the 1990 British Open by five

strokes. While more conservative than gambling by nature, he has shown that his game is strong enough to produce low numbers.

Tournament Record: 1975: Winner of British Youths' Amateur and English Amateur. 1977: Winner of Skol Lager. 1979: Winner of Colgate PGA Championship and ICL Tournament. 1980: Winner of Sun Alliance PGA Championship. 1981: Winner of Sun Alliance PGA Championship. 1982: Winner of Haig Whisky TPC. 1983: Winner of French Open, Martini International, Car Care Plan International, Lawrence Batley International, and Ebel European Masters–Swiss Open. 1984: Winner of Sea Pines Heritage Classic and Car Care Plan International. 1987: Winner of Spanish Open and British Open. 1988: Winner of French Open and Volvo Masters. 1989: Winner of The Masters, Volvo PGA Championship, Dunhill British Masters, French Open, and Suntory World Match-Play Championship. 1990: Winner of The Masters, British Open, and Johnnie Walker Classic. 1991: Winner of Carrolls Irish Open. 1992: Winner of Carrolls Irish Open, GA European Open, and Toyota World Match Play Championship.

FARRELL, JOHN J. Born in White Plains, NY, April 1, 1901. Died June 14, 1988. The U.S. Open champion in 1928 and one of the most colorful and most competent players during the 1920s and early 1930s. In addition to winning the Open, Farrell was in the top five on three other occasions, was runner-up in the British Open, and played on three Ryder Cup teams. In the PGA Championship from 1922 through 1937, he was runner-up once, a semi-finalist twice, and a quarter-finalist five times. Farrell started as a caddie in the Westchester area of New York and made his decision to stick with golf after watching the pros play in the first PGA tournament at Siwanoy in 1916. He burst on the scene in 1922 by winning the Shawnee Open, gaining the quarter-finals of the PGA and tying for eleventh in the U.S. Open as the playing partner of the equally unknown Gene Sarazen, who won the event. From that point Farrell was winning tournaments and knocking at the door of championships for more than a decade. During that time he gained the reputation of being the best-dressed pro in an era of snappy dressers, and he often won prizes for his dapper ensembles.

Tournament Record: 1922: Winner of Shawnee Open. 1925: Winner of Philadelphia Open and Miami

Johnny Farrell. *Courtesy U.S.G.A.*

Four-Ball. 1926: Winner of Shawnee Open, Westchester Open, Florida Open, Central Florida Open, Miami Four-Ball and Mid-South Pro Best-Ball. 1927: Winner of Shawnee Open, Philadelphia Open, Metropolitan Open, Pennsylvania Open, Massachusetts Open, Wheeling Open, Eastern Open, and Chicago Open. 1928: Winner of U.S. Open, LaGorce Open, Miami Open, and Miami Four-Ball. 1929: Runner-up in British Open; runner-up in PGA Championship. 1930: Winner of Pensacola Open and New York Open. 1931: Winner of Pensacola Open. 1936: Winner of New Jersey Open. 1940, 1941: Winner of Rhode Island Open.

FLOYD, Raymond Loran. Born in Fort Bragg, NC, September 4, 1942. Ray Floyd first won on the PGA Tour as a rookie at the age of twenty in 1963; twenty-nine years later he won the Doral Ryder Open within

a year of becoming eligible for the Senior Tour. Such career longevity has only been matched by Sam Snead in the history of the PGA Tour. Along the way, Floyd has collected twenty-two Tour victories, including two PGA Championships, one Masters and one U.S. Open. The British Open is the only major championship that has eluded him.

Floyd grew up in Fort Bragg, NC, where he learned the game from his father, L.B., a teaching pro. At the age of thirteen, he was scoring in the low 70s. He was soon involved in money matches, the usual game being a $100 Nassau. A major-league baseball prospect, Floyd decided on golf after winning the 1960 International Jaycee tournament. He entered the University of North Carolina, but only remained in college a few months. He then went into the Army, getting out in time to play the final Tour event of 1962.

Floyd's Tour career was off to a flying start when he won the St. Petersburg Open in March 1963. Despite his early success, Floyd did not show signs of greatness until 1969. A noted playboy, golf appeared to come in a poor second to his social life at that time. At any rate, at the start of 1967, Floyd announced that he was a changed man and had decided to concentrate on golf.

It took a couple of years, but in 1969 it must have seemed worthwhile. Floyd enjoyed his greatest year to date, winning three times, including the PGA Championship, his first major. It wasn't until 1975, however, that Floyd began winning with regularity. Peaking later than most players, he posted thirteen of his victories between 1975 and 1982.

He developed a reputation as a feared front-runner

Ray Floyd.
Courtesy PGA

because once he grabbed the lead, he usually stayed there. His most memorable performance came in the 1976 Masters, which he led throughout and won by eight strokes with a record-tying 271 total. He played the par-fives in 13 under par, thanks in large part to his 5-wood, which he put in the bag because he thought the greens on Augusta's par-fives demanded a higher, softer shot than was possible with long irons.

Floyd won three tournaments each in 1981 and 1982, finishing second on the money list each year. In 1981, he collected a bonus of $200,000 in unofficial money for winning the Doral Eastern Open and Tournament Players Championship back-to-back. He posted another wire-to-wire major championship victory in the 1982 PGA Championship at Southern Hills in Tulsa, Oklahoma, where he opened with a 63.

Floyd's finest hour came in the 1986 U.S. Open at Shinnecock Hills in Southampton, New York. Midway through the final round, he was one of eight players tied for the lead. Floyd birdied the 13th and 16th holes for a final-round 66 and a two-shot victory. Having become the oldest player to win the U.S. Open, four years later he nearly became the oldest to win the Masters. At age 47, Floyd led the 1990 Masters for the entire final round until a bogey at the 71st hole dropped him into a tie with Nick Faldo. Floyd lost at the second play-off hole. Floyd made yet another run at the Masters in 1992, finishing second to Fred Couples.

Floyd was selected to the Ryder Cup team seven times (1969, 1975, 1977, 1981, 1983, 1985 and 1991) and was a non-playing captain in 1989. He won the Vardon Trophy in 1983.

Floyd's swing is not pretty. He takes the club back to the inside too quickly, but then corrects this with a lifting of his left arm as he nears the top of the swing. He then makes as good a move through the ball as anyone who has ever played the game. He is also a great shotmaker and putter. Perhaps most important, he has an ability to repeat his swing under pressure. In the stretch, his concentration is awesome—on a par with Nicklaus at his best.

Tournament Record: 1960: Winner of International Jaycees Championship. 1963: Winner of St. Petersburg Open. 1965: Winner of St. Paul Open. 1969: Winner of Jacksonville Open, American Golf Classic, and PGA Championship. 1975: Winner of Kemper Open. 1976: Winner of Masters and World Open. 1977: Winner of Byron Nelson Classic and Pleasant Valley Classic. 1978: Winner of Brazilian Open. 1979: Winner of Greensboro Open and Costa Rica Cup. 1980: Winner of Doral–Eastern Open. 1981: Winner of Doral–Eastern Open, Tournament Players Championship, Manufacturers-Hanover Westchester Classic, and Canada PGA Championship. 1982: Winner of Memorial Tournament, Danny Thomas–Memphis Classic, PGA Championship, and $1 Million Sun City Challenge. 1985: Winner of Houston Open and Chrysler Team Invitational (with Hal Sutton). 1986: Winner of U.S. Open and Walt Disney–Oldsmobile Classic. 1992: Winner of Doral Ryder Open.

FORD, DOUGLAS. Born in West Haven, CT, August 6, 1922. One of the fastest and most consistent players in golf after World War II. Ford won the 1955 PGA, the 1957 Masters, played on four Ryder Cup teams, and banked more than a third of a million dollars during his career. He was second on the money list twice and was never out of the top twenty during his first dozen years on the circuit. Ford, a member of a golfing family whose name originally was Fortunato, has been described as "the guy who looks as if he is playing through the group he is playing with." Ford relied on a strong short game to offset the big hitters on the tour.

As a senior, Ford won the Commemorative Pro-Am and Doug Sanders Energy Classic in 1981. Both events were unofficial at the time.

Tournament Record: 1940: Winner of New York Junior. 1941: Winner of Westchester Junior. 1942: Winner of New York Junior. 1947: Winner of Westchester Amateur. 1948: Winner of Houston Invitational. 1952: Winner of Jacksonville Open. 1953: Winner of Virginia Beach Open, LaBatt Open, and Miami Open. 1954: Winner of Greensboro Open and Fort Wayne Open. 1955: Winner of PGA Championship, Carling Open, and All-American Open. 1957: Winner of Masters, Los Angeles Open, Western Open and Metropolitan PGA. 1958: Winner of Pensacola Open; tied for second in Masters. 1959: Winner of Canadian Open and Metropolitan PGA. 1960: Winner of 500 Festival Open and Metropolitan PGA. 1961: Winner of 500 Festival Open, Westchester Open, and Westchester PGA. 1962: Winner of Bing Crosby National and Eastern Open. 1963: Winner of Canadian Open and Metropolitan PGA. 1981: Winner of Commemorative Pro-Am, and Doug Sanders Energy Classic.

Jane Geddes. *Courtesy LPGA*

GEDDES, JANE. Born in Huntington, NY, February 5, 1960. Jane Geddes won seven tournaments in the span of just over a year from the summer of 1986 to the summer of 1987, but she has been unable to repeat that sort of dominance. Two of her victories were in women's majors: the U.S. Women's Open in 1986 and the LPGA Championship in 1987.

Those wins came in Geddes's third and fourth full seasons on the Tour, marking a rapid advancement from a relatively mediocre amateur career. Geddes didn't play golf at all until she was seventeen years old, turning to the sport after her family moved from Huntington, New York, to Summerville, South Carolina, where she was exposed to country club sports.

A year later, Geddes was playing golf at UNC–Charlotte. When the school dropped its women's golf program after her freshman season, Geddes transferred to Florida State, where she helped the Lady Seminoles capture the team championship as a junior. Still, Geddes wasn't ready for the Tour until she spent a year refining her game on the mini-tours.

Geddes finished seventeenth on the money list in 1985, her second full campaign, finishing second at a major, the du Maurier Classic. One of the longer hitters and better ball-strikers on Tour, Geddes seemed due to win.

Her first victory was a big one, the Women's Open. Geddes closed with rounds of 70 and 69 at the NCR Golf Club in Dayton, Ohio, then defeated Sally Little in an 18-hole play-off. Proving it was no fluke, Geddes won the next week at the Boston Five Classic.

Geddes won five times in 1987, the most of anyone on Tour that year, and earned $396,818 to rank third on the money list. She won the LPGA Championship in fine style by shooting a closing 67 to beat Betsy King by one shot. But it wasn't until the first event of 1991, the Jamaica Classic, that Geddes was able to score her next victory.

Tournament Record: 1986: U.S. Women's Open and Boston Five Classic. 1987: Women's Kemper Open, GNA–Glendale Federal Classic, Mazda LPGA Championship, Jamie Farr Toledo Classic, and Boston Five Classic. 1991: Winner of Jamaica Classic and Atlantic City Classic.

GEIBERGER, ALLEN LEE. Born in Red Bluff, CA, September 1, 1937. Al Geiberger has carved a unique niche for himself in golf's pantheon with just one round of golf. On June 10th, 1977, Geiberger shot a 13-under par 59 in the second round of the Memphis Classic, becoming the first player to break 60 in an official PGA Tour event (Chip Beck matched the feat in 1991). During the round, he produced 11 birdies and one eagle and took just twenty-three putts. He holed an eight-foot birdie putt on the last hole. He went on to win the tournament with rounds of 72, 59, 72, and 70 over the 7,249 yard Colonial Country Club course. Because of this feat, Geiberger is affectionately known on the Tour as "Mr. 59."

Geiberger joined the Tour in 1960 after an excellent junior and amateur career. He won the 1954 National Jaycee championship, and later that year traveled to Europe with the short-lived junior Walker Cup team, played in Great Britain and then took the French junior title. At the University of Southern California, he compiled a 34-2 record in collegiate matches while helping USC to an unbeaten streak of fifty-one victories. In his final two years in college (1958 and 1959), he won both the Pacific

Coast Conference and Southern California Intercollegiate titles.

At 6'2" and 165 pounds, Geiberger was known as the "human one-iron" when he first came out on Tour. Despite the joshing, the good-natured Geiberger immediately made the top sixty money winners and remained there until 1969. He was in the top sixty again from 1973 through 1977, and in 1979. He has a total of eleven Tour wins to his credit, including the 1966 PGA Championship. He played on the Ryder Cup team in 1967 and 1975.

At the 1965 American Golf Classic, he added another dimension to the variety of energy foods such as raisins, bananas, and the like, devoured by various professionals during a round. He revealed that he had been packing peanut butter and jelly sandwiches in his golf bag to beat mid-round "hungries." He had started the habit during the PGA Championship when, paired with Arnold Palmer, he had despaired of getting to a refreshment stand because of "Arnie's Army."

If there were an award for "most comebacks from surgery" on the Tour, Geiberger would win hands down. First it was a nervous stomach disorder that nearly ended his career in the 1960s and early 1970s. In 1978, he needed intestinal surgery. In 1979, he underwent knee surgery. In 1980, emergency surgery for the removal of his colon had to be performed. In all, he underwent three operations in just two months.

When he turned fifty on September 21, 1987, Geiberger quickly made his presence felt on the PGA Senior Tour. On October 4, he won the Vantage Championship, the $135,000 he earned in that event being nearly three times larger than his biggest previous paycheck ($54,000 in the 1979 Colonial). Two weeks later, he won the Hilton Head Seniors and the following week the Las Vegas Seniors. He won one tournament each in 1988 and 1989.

Johnny Miller has described Geiberger's swing as one of the best on Tour. "It's the simplest I've seen," Miller says. "If you want to copy one swing, copy his." At the top of his form, Geiberger's swing is a joy to watch, with its leisurely rhythm and superb timing. His money shot is a controlled fade.

Tournament Record: 1954: Winner of National Jaycee Championship and French Junior Championship. 1958: Winner of Pacific Coast Conference Championship and Southern California Intercollegiate Championship. 1959: Winner of Pacific Coast Conference Championship and Southern California Intercollegiate Championship. 1962: Winner of Ontario Open and Caracas Open. 1963: Winner of Almaden Open. 1965: Winner of American Golf Classic. 1966: Winner of PGA Championship. 1974: Winner of Sahara Invitational. 1975: Winner of Tournament of Champions and Tournament Players Championship. 1976: Winner of Greater Greensboro Open, and Western Open. 1977: Winner of Danny Thomas–Memphis Classic. 1979: Winner of Colonial National Invitation. 1982: Winner of Frontier Airline Open. 1985: Winner of Colorado Open. 1987: Winner of Vantage Championship, Hilton Head Seniors International, and Las Vegas Senior Classic. 1988: Winner of The Pointe–Del E. Webb Arizona Classic. 1989: Winner of Liberty Mutual Legends of Golf (with Harold Henning) and GTE Northwest Classic. 1991: Winner of Kroger Senior Classic. 1992: Winner of Infinity Senior Tournament of Champions.

Al Geiberger. *Will Hertzberg*

GRAHAM, ANTHONY DAVID. Born in Windsor, New South Wales, Australia, May 23, 1946. David Graham

David Graham.

was fourteen years old when he found a set of left-handed clubs in his garage. He played with them for two years before switching to right-handed clubs. In 1962, he turned professional and worked in a golf shop in Melbourne. After a three-year apprenticeship, he took the head pro job at a nine-hole course in Tasmania. Late in the 1960s, he went on the tournament circuit in Australia and the Far East. He qualified for the PGA Tour in 1971, and now makes his home in Dallas, Texas.

It was a long road for Graham, but he reached the top of his profession. He has won eight PGA Tour events, including two majors, the 1979 PGA Championship and 1981 U.S. Open. Abroad, he has won in Australia, Britain, Europe, Japan, Mexico, New Zealand, South America, South Africa, and Thailand.

By winning the 1979 PGA Championship, Graham became the first Australian since Peter Thomson to take a major. At Oakland Hills CC, Birmingham, Mich., Graham shot 69, 68, 70, then in the final round, needed a par 4 at the 459-yard 72nd hole for a 63. He took a 6, tieing with Ben Crenshaw. In the sudden-death play-off, Graham holed putts of twenty-five feet and ten feet to stay in the fight, then birdied the third hole for victory.

At the 1981 U.S. Open at Merion Golf Club, Ardmore, PA, Graham played one of the great tee-to-green rounds of all time. He shot a 67 in the final round, while hitting every green and missing just one fairway, to win by three strokes.

Graham added only one more victory in the U.S., in 1983, and has been an infrequent competitor since 1989.

Tournament Record: 1967: Winner of Queensland PGA. 1970: Winner of Tasmanian Open, Victoria Open, Thailand Open, Tokyo Yomiuri Open, French Open, and World Cup (with Bruce Devlin). 1971: Winner of Caracas Open and JAL Open. 1972: Winner of Cleveland Open. 1975: Winner of Wills Masters. 1976: Winner of Westchester Classic, American Golf Classic, Chunichi Crowns Invitational, and World Match Play. 1977: Winner of Australian Open and South African PGA Championship. 1978: Winner of Mexico Cup. 1979: Winner of PGA Championship, West Lakes Classic, and New Zealand Open. 1980: Winner of Memorial Tournament, Mexican Open, Rolex World Mixed Team Championship (with Jan Stephenson), and Brazilian Classic. 1981: Winner of Phoenix Open, U.S. Open, and Lancôme Trophy. 1982: Winner of Lancôme Trophy. 1983: Winner of Houston Coca-Cola Open. 1985: Winner of Queensland Open and Dunhill Nations Cup (with Greg Norman and Graham Marsh). 1986: Winner of Dunhill Nations Cup (with Greg Norman and Rodger Davis).

GRAHAM, Louis Krebs. Born in Nashville, TN, January 7, 1938. Graham took up golf when he was ten years old, and played well enough in the following years to earn a scholarship to Memphis State University. However, he quit school after three years and enlisted in the Army. For a time, he was a member of President Kennedy's honor guard. After his discharge in 1962, Graham worked at two clubs near Baltimore before finding the financial backing to head for the Tour in 1964.

For most of his career, Graham has been a steady, if unspectacular performer. From 1967, when he won his first tournament, the Minnesota Classic, to 1979, he was only out of the top sixty money winners once. However, he won just six Tour events.

The quintessential "percentage" player, Graham typically knocks the ball straight down the middle with his fundamentally excellent golf swing, then plops the ball on the "fat" part of the green, takes one or two putts, another routine birdie or par, and on to the next tee. Although blessed with a lot of golfing talent and a fine sense of humor, Graham almost manages to make his very good brand of golf seem dull.

Lou Graham. *UPI/Bettmann*

His biggest triumph—winning the 1975 U.S. Open—came as a complete surprise to the golfing world and even to Graham himself. Only a week before, he had opened with a 65 at Philadelphia, then finished in thirty-fourth place after playing some pretty bad golf. "I've got no business going to the U.S. Open this week and playing a hard course like Medinah," Graham told his wife, Patsy. He started with a 74, seven strokes off the pace, and his second round of 72 left him 11 strokes behind Tom Watson, who meanwhile had set a 36-hole U.S. Open record. Then Graham shot a 68, which pulled him up to four off the lead. Then, as most of the field rolled over and played dead, he finished with a 73, putting him into an 18-hole play-off with John Mahaffey at three-over par 287. Graham won by two strokes, 71 to 73.

After his U.S. Open win, Graham enjoyed his four most rewarding years on Tour. From 1976 through 1978, he exceeded $100,000 in prize money every year, and in 1979, went on a tear late in the season and won the IVB–Philadelphia Classic, American Optical Classic, and San Antonio–Texas Open, all in a matter of eight weeks. He finished the year with $190,827.

Graham was a member of the 1973, 1975 and 1979 Ryder Cup teams, and played for the U.S. in the 1975 World Cup. He joined the Senior Tour in 1988.

Tournament Record: 1967: Winner of Minnesota Classic. 1972: Winner of Liggett & Myers. 1975: Winner of U.S. Open. 1979: Winner of IVB–Philadelphia Classic, American Optical Classic, and San Antonio–Texas Open.

GREEN, HUBERT MYATT, II. Born in Birmingham, AL, December 28, 1946. The son of a general practitioner in Birmingham, Green started to swing a golf club at age five. As a teenager he played all sports, but he began to concentrate on golf in high school. While at Florida State University, he won the 1966 Southern Amateur. He also finished fourth in the 1968 U.S. Amateur, then a stroke play event. He repeated in the Southern the following year, and was selected to the Walker Cup team, but had to decline because he had decided to turn professional.

Hubert Green. *UPI/Bettmann*

In 1971, his first full year on Tour, Green won the Houston Open, and was Rookie of the Year. He was in the top sixty money winners every year through 1982, and from 1974 through 1979 was no worse than thirteenth on the money list. During one three-week stretch in 1976, he won three straight tournaments—the Doral-Eastern Open, Greater Jacksonville Open, and Sea Pines Heritage Classic. Green has nineteen Tour victories to his credit, including two majors, and played on the 1977, 1979, and 1985 Ryder Cup teams.

Green's first major came in 1977, when he led throughout in the U.S. Open at Southern Hills, Tulsa, Oklahoma. Starting with a one-under par 69 that tied him with six other players, he then shot 67, 72 to lead both rounds by one stroke. With just four holes left to play, he was told that an anonymous telephone caller had threatened to kill him. He was asked whether he would like a suspension of play, but decided to continue. Thankfully, the threat proved empty, and Green carded a 70, winning by a stroke over Lou Graham.

Green's second major, the 1985 PGA Championship at Cherry Hills, Denver, Colorado, came after he'd slumped in the early 1980s. Green outfought Lee Trevino to win a two-man duel by two strokes.

Since then, Green's game has slipped, and he's ranked no better than 73rd on the money list.

Green's game is highly individual. On the full swing, he leans well over the ball, his hands very low. He picks the club up quickly to the outside, then loops it back to the inside coming down. Although not a long hitter, he is a fine shotmaker. His style in chipping, with the ball played to the right of the right foot and the hands well forward, hooding the blade, is unique; he is deadly with it. Green uses a putter dating from 1930. He employs a split-handed technique, with his right forefinger down the shaft.

Tournament Record: 1966: Winner of Southern Amateur Championship. 1969: Winner of Southern Amateur Championship. 1971: Winner of Houston Open. 1973: Winner of Tallahassee Open and B.C. Open. 1974: Winner of Bob Hope Classic, Greater Jacksonville Open, IVB—Philadelphia Golf Classic, and Walt Disney World National Team Play (with Mac McLendon). 1975: Winner of Southern Open and Dunlop Phoenix (Japan). 1976: Winner of Doral—Eastern Open, Jacksonville Open, and Sea Pines Heritage Classic. 1977: Winner of U.S. Open

Ralph Guldahl. *AP/Wide World Photos*

and Irish Open. 1978: Winner of Hawaiian Open and Sea Pines Heritage Classic. 1979: Winner of Hawaiian Open and New Orleans Open. 1980: Co-winner of Jerry Ford Invitational. 1981: Winner of Sammy Davis, Jr.—Greater Hartford Open. 1984: Winner of Southern Open. 1985: Winner of PGA Championship.

GULDAHL, RALPH. Born in Dallas, TX, November 22, 1911. Died in 1987. Guldahl was a great stroke player who became one of the few to win consecutive U.S. Open championships when he triumphed in 1937 and 1938. However, his years at the top were few, and the story of his ups and downs is a strange one. He joined the tour in the early 1930s, won one tournament, and was runner-up in the Open when his game suddenly fell apart. He finally became so discouraged he quit golf completely in 1935. A few months later he tried again after making some revisions in his swing and putting in countless hours of practice. This time the effort bore fruit, and in the next five years he won ten tournaments, including the two Opens and the Masters of 1939. These also included three straight Western Opens, an event that ranked only behind the Open, PGA, and Masters in those days. Then, again, his skills left him, virtually overnight, and no one has ever been able to fathom the reason, least of all Guldahl. Dozens of players watched him hit practice balls; he had slow-motion movies taken of his swing and compared with earlier films; and people everywhere came up with theories and remedies—but nobody found the right answer. Guldahl left the tour in 1942 and, except for a brief return in 1949, never played the circuit again.

Tournament Record: 1932: Winner of Phoenix Open. 1933: Runner-up in U.S. Open. 1936: Winner of Western Open, Augusta Open, and Miami-Biltmore Open. 1937: Winner of U.S. Open and Western Open; runner-up in Masters. 1938: Winner of U.S. Open and Western Open; runner-up in Masters. 1939: Winner of Masters, Miami Four-Ball, Greensboro Open, and Dapper Dan Open. 1940: Winner of Milwaukee Open and Inverness Four-Ball.

HAGEN, WALTER CHARLES. Born in Rochester, NY, December 21, 1892. Died October 6, 1969. The most colorful personality in the history of golf and one of its greatest players. His record of winning eleven major championships would be more than enough to insure his lasting fame, but Hagen did far more than that. Because of his refusal to go second-class, he led the way in breaking down the social barrier between amateurs and professionals; he was the fashion plate everyone copied; he demanded—and got—large sums for exhibitions and tours, thus helping to raise considerably the prize money available to professionals; and above all, with his all-night parties just before a crucial match, his chauffeur-driven limousine, his sartorial splendor, his superior gamesmanship—plus his skill as a player—he imbued golf with a dash and color that put it increasingly in the public eye and gave it and him more newspaper space than it had won in all the years before he came on the scene.

Hagen was not a classic swinger, and he seldom had the consistency necessary to put four good rounds together. But he was a very good player, a great putter, and a man who had the almost uncanny ability to hit "impossible" recovery shots to the green, then sink a birdie putt to beat an opponent who was never out of the fairway. He also was a master of psychology and showmanship, and he used these tools along with his great ability as a scrambler to unnerve and defeat many a foe, even on days when his own game was not particularly sharp. "The Haig" won two U.S. Opens, four British Opens, and five PGA Championships—the last four in succession—

plus dozens of lesser titles. His total of career victories is estimated anywhere between 60 and 83, and he won hundreds of exhibitions during his many tours. Some of these were more or less formal ones, with Joe Kirkwood and others; and some consisted of a caravan of three limousines and an entourage that included chauffer, manager, personal caddie, and suitcases full of money collected at previous stops. The money was always something to be got rid of as quickly as possible, and Sir Walter used to take pride in saying he was the first golfer to make a million dollars and spend two.

Hagen's ability as a player and his contributions to the popularity and success of golf in general cannot be overestimated. As Bernard Darwin once wrote: "This difference, as there is so often between Hagen and the other man, is that Hagen just won and the other man just did not." Or, as A. C. M. Croome put it: "He makes more bad shots in a single season than Harry Vardon did from 1890 to 1914, but he beats more immaculate golfers because 'three of those and

Walter Hagen. *UPI/Bettmann*

one of them' counts 4 and he knows it." And Gene Sarazen once wrote: "All the professionals who have a chance to go after the big money today should say a silent thanks to Walter Hagen each time they stretch a check between their fingers. It was Walter who made professional golf what it is."

Tournament Record: 1914: Winner of U.S. Open and Pinehurst Amateur-Pro. 1915: Winner of Massachusetts Open and Panama Exposition Open. 1916: Winner of Western Open, Shawnee Open, and Metropolitan Open. 1918: Winner of North and South Open. 1919: Winner of U.S. Open and Metropolitan Open. 1920: Winner of French Open, Metropolitan Open, and Bellevue Open. 1921: Winner of PGA Championship, Western Open, Michigan Open, and Florida West Coast Open; tied for second in U.S. Open. 1922: Winner of British Open, New York Open, Deland Open, White Sulphur Springs Open, and Florida West Coast Open. 1923: Winner of North and South Open, Texas Open, Long Beach Open, Florida West Coast Open, and Asheville Open; tied for first in Wichita Open; runner-up in PGA Championship; runner-up in British Open. 1924: Winner of PGA Championship, British Open, Belgian Open, North and South Open, and Rockaway PGA. 1925: Winner of PGA Championship. 1926: Winner of PGA Championship, Western Open, and Eastern Open. 1927: Winner of PGA Championship and Western Open. 1928: Winner of British Open. 1929: Winner of British Open, Great Lakes Open, Miami Four-Ball, Long Beach Open, and Virginia Beach Open. 1930: Winner of Coral Gables Open and Michigan PGA. 1931: Winner of Canadian Open and Michigan PGA; tied for first in Coral Gables Open. 1932: Winner of Western Open and St. Louis Open. 1935: Winner of Gasparilla Open. 1936: Winner of Inverness Four-Ball.

HAGGE, MARLENE (BAUER). Born in Eureka, SD, February 16, 1934. Hagge started playing golf when she was three years old under the watchful eye of her father, Dave. She first attracted attention when she won the 1944 Long Beach *Boys'* Junior. In 1949, she won the first USGA Girls' Junior Championship and the Western Junior Championship. That year she was voted Athlete of the Year by the Associated Press, also Golfer of the Year, one of the Top Ten Women and Teenager of the Year. She also won the 1949 Helms Athletic Award.

Marlene Hagge.
Courtesy LPGA

The next year, she turned professional, being an LPGA Founder and Charter Member and the youngest player, at 16, to ever join the LPGA Tour. In 1952, she won her first event at age 18, 14 days; she is still the youngest to win on the Tour. In 1956, she was leading money-winner with $20,235. She had eight victories that year, including the LPGA Championship, in which she bested Patty Berg in a play-off. She also had five victories in 1965.

The last of Hagge's victories came in 1972, but she has continued to play the Tour. She is now the LPGA Tour's senior active member, playing in her forty-third season in 1992.

Tournament Record: 1944: Winner of Long Beach Boys' Junior City Championship. 1947: Winner of Palm Spring Invitational. 1948: Winner of Los Angeles Women's City Championship, Palm Spring Invitational, and North California Women's Open. 1952: Winner of Sarasota Open. 1954: Winner of New Orleans Open. 1956: Winner of Sea Island Open, Clock Open, Babe Zaharias Open, Denver Open, Pittsburgh Open, LPGA Championship, World Championship, and Triangle Round Robin. 1957: Winner of Babe Zaharias Open and Lawton Open. 1958: Winner of Lake Worth Open and Land of Sky Open. 1959: Winner of Mayfair Open and Hoosier Open. 1963: Winner of Sight Open. 1964: Winner of Mickey Wright Invitational. 1965: Winner of Babe Zaharias Open, Milwaukee Open, Phoenix Thunderbirds Open, Tall City Open, and Alamo Open. 1969: Winner of Strohs–WBLY Open. 1972: Winner of Burdine's Invitational.

HAYNIE, SANDRA. Born in Forth Worth, TX, June 4, 1943. Haynie took up golf when she was eleven years old. As an amateur, she won the 1957 and 1958 Texas State Women's Public Links and the 1958 and 1959 Texas Women's Amateur. She also took the 1960 Women's Trans-Mississippi. The following year she went on the LPGA Tour.

In her first year, her best finish was a tenth in the San Antonio Open. But in 1962, she started a remarkable string. From that year through 1975, she had at least one victory a year. She ran her total wins to thirty-nine, winning four times in 1966, 1971, and 1975 and six times in 1974. She also won three

Sandra Haynie.
Courtesy LPGA

majors. In 1965, she won the LPGA Championship. Then in 1974, she took both the LPGA Championship and U.S. Women's Open, a feat only equalled by Mickey Wright. From 1963 through 1975, she was never worse than ninth on the money list and was in the top five ten times. She was inducted into the LPGA Hall of Fame in 1977.

From 1977 through 1980, injuries and business interests curtailed her play to just seventeen events. However, in 1981 she returned to the Tour full time, and won her fourth major, the 1982 Peter Jackson Classic, and two other tournaments. This brought her tally up to forty-two official wins. She also won the unofficial Portland Ping Team Championship in 1982 (with Kathy McMullen).

At the end of the 1984 season, she retired from the Tour because of knee problems. However, in 1986 and 1988, she played the Tour part-time and pushed her career earnings over the $1 million mark. She retired again after playing a full schedule in 1989 and finishing fifty-seventh on the money list.

Tournament Record: 1957: Winner of Texas State Women's Public Links Championship. 1958: Winner of Texas State Women's Public Links Championship and Texas Women's Amateur Championship. 1959: Winner of Texas Women's Amateur Championship. 1960: Winner of Women's Trans-Mississippi Amateur. 1962: Winner of Austin Civitan Open and Cosmopolitan Open. 1963: Winner of Phoenix Thunderbird Open. 1964: Winner of Baton Rouge Open and Las Cruces Open. 1965: Winner of Cosmopolitan Open and LPGA Championship. 1966: Winner of Buckeye Savings Invitational, Glass City Classic, Alamo Open, and Pensacola Invitational. 1967: Winner of Amarillo Open and Mickey Wright Invitational. 1968: Winner of Pacific Classic. 1969: Winner of St. Louis Invitational, Supertest Open, and Shreveport Kiwanis Invitational. 1970: Winner of Raleigh Invitational and Shreveport Kiwanis Invitational. 1971: Winner of Burdines Invitational, Dallas Civitan Open, San Antonio Alamo Open, and Len Immke Buick Open. 1972: Winner of National Jewish Hospital Open, Quality First Classic, and Lincoln-Mercury Open. 1973: Winner of Orange Blossom Classic, Lincoln-Mercury Open, and Charity Golf Classic. 1974: Winner of Lawson's Open, LPGA Championship, U.S. Women's Open, George Washington Classic, National Jewish Hospital Open, and Charity Golf Classic. 1975: Winner of Naples-Lely

Harold Hilton. *Courtesy U.S.G.A.*

holes. Hilton scored 305 and won by three strokes. Five years later, he recorded his second British Open win at Hoylake, his home course, defeating James Braid by one shot and leaving the previous year's champion, Harry Vardon, six shots in his wake. Hilton played billiards while waiting to see if Braid could beat his score of 314. He then came out to see Braid, needing a three to tie, hit a great second shot which almost hit the flagstick but rolled well past. In 1898, he came in third, two strokes behind Vardon.

Hilton's finest year came in 1911. He won the British Amateur for the third time, then went to America to win the U.S. Amateur, beating Fred Herreshoff in the final on the 37th hole. He was first to win both Amateurs in one year. While in the U.S., he also won the amateur tournament at the opening of the National Golf Links, Southampton, New York. In the British Open, he finished a shot behind the Vardon–Arnaud Massy play-off.

Rather a small man at 5'6" and 154 lbs., Hilton had an extremely fast swing. So furiously did he hurl himself at the ball, he often lost his hat in the finish. Despite this, he was very accurate.

Hilton was the first editor of *Golf Monthly*, and also was editor of *Golf Illustrated* (both British magazines). He designed many golf courses.

Tournament Record: 1892: Winner of British Open. 1897: Winner of British Open and Irish Open Amateur. 1900: Winner of British Amateur and Irish Open Amateur. 1901: Winner of British Amateur and Irish Open Amateur. 1902: Winner of Irish Open Amateur. 1911: Winner of British Amateur and U.S. Amateur. 1913: Winner of British Amateur.

Classic, Charity Golf Classic, Jacksonville Classic, and Ft. Myers Classic. 1981: Winner of Henredon Classic. 1982: Winner of Rochester International, Peter Jackson Classic, and Portland Ping Team Championship (with Kathy McMullen).

HILTON, HAROLD HORSFALL. Born West Kirby, England, January 12, 1869. Died March 5, 1942. Hilton has the distinction of being the only Britisher to win the U.S. Amateur. He is also one of only three amateurs (John Ball and Bobby Jones being the other two) to have won the British Open. During a career that stretched from the early 1890s to the start of World War I, Hilton won two British Opens, four British Amateurs, one U.S. Amateur, and four Irish Open Amateurs.

His first victory in the British Open came at Muirfield in 1892, the first time the event was played at 72

HOGAN, WILLIAM BENJAMIN. Born in Dublin, TX, August 13, 1912. Ranks with Nicklaus, Vardon and Jones among history's greatest golfers and is considered by some to be the best of all. Hogan won four United States Opens, two PGA Championships, two Masters, and a British Open and came close to doubling that figure, at least. From 1940 through 1960, he was never out of the top ten in the U.S. Open. He was Masters runner-up four times and was never worse than seventh from 1941 through 1956. He won the British Open on his only attempt and broke the course record at Carnoustie in the process. He set the scoring record in the U.S. Open and Masters. He was undefeated in Ryder Cup play. He was PGA player of the year four times. He won the Vardon

Ben Hogan. *UPI/Bettmann*

Trophy four times. Impressive as all this was and is, Hogan doubtless would have done even better had it not been for the automobile accident in 1949 that nearly cost him his life. Everyone knows that Ben came back to win six of his nine major titles after the accident, but most persons feel he would have surpassed that had he been in top physical condition. They point to the many times he came down to the closing holes limping and visibly exhausted, finishing on guts and pride alone. Guts he had in abundance, and he needed every bit of it he could muster before becoming the great player everyone today remembers.

Hogan started out swinging left-handed as a youngster, but soon switched and became a promising young player. He turned pro while still in his teens, but attracted no national notice for almost a decade. Meanwhile, he probably hit more practice balls than anyone in history in the process of trying to cure a bad hook and become a winner on the pro tour. Ben began to win in 1940, and in the next three years he won three Vardon Trophies and was leading money winner three times. This success did not surprise those who had watched his hard work over the years, but it did not necessarily please all of them, either, for Ben was not the most popular player around. He was a grim competitor who had little to say on the course and whose determination to succeed was so great that he practiced putting in his hotel room at night and hit shots for hours before and after a round. After returning from World War II service, he immediately picked up where he left off, winning everything in sight in 1946, 1947, and 1948. By this time, his swing was so precise that someone described it as being like a machine stamping out bottle caps. One got the feeling, not without some justification, that he could put the ball exactly where he wanted. After the accident he was, if anything, a better player than ever, but he had to curtail his schedule drastically because of physical limitations. At about this time also, he became a little less sour—off the course, at least—and people began to say he had mellowed. Whether he had or not did not affect his golf game, which remained in a class by itself as long as his ailments permitted him to play. In the 1967 Masters, for example, Hogan set a record by shooting the back nine in 30 strokes, one of the most dramatic and heartwarming performances of his career.

Tournament Record: 1938: Winner of Hershey Four-Ball. 1940: Winner of North and South Open, Greensboro Open, Asheville Open, Goodall Round Robin, and Westchester Open. 1941: Winner of Miami Four-Ball, Asheville Open, Inverness Four-Ball, Chicago Open, and Hershey Open. 1942: Winner of Los Angeles Open, San Francisco Open, Hale America Open, North and South Open, Asheville Open, and Rochester Open; runner-up in Masters. 1945: Winner of Nashville Open, Portland Open, Richmond Open, Montgomery Open, and Orlando Open. 1946: Winner of PGA Championship, Phoenix Open, San Antonio Open, St. Petersburg Open, Miami Four-Ball, Colonial Invitational, Western Open, Goodall Round Robin, Inverness Four-Ball, Winnipeg Open, Golden State Open, Dallas Invitational, and North and South Open; runner-up in Masters. 1947: Winner of Los Angeles Open, Phoenix

Open, Miami Four-Ball, Colonial Invitational, Chicago Open, Inverness Four-Ball, International Invitational, and Seminole Pro-Amateur. 1948: Winner of U.S. Open, PGA Championship, Los Angeles Open, Motor City Open, Western Open, Inverness Four-Ball, Reading Open, Denver Open, Reno Open, and Glendale Open. 1949: Winner of Bing Crosby Invitational, and Long Beach Open. 1950: Winner of U.S. Open and Greenbrier Pro-Am. 1951: Winner of U.S. Open, Masters, and World Championship. 1952: Winner of Colonial Invitational. 1953: Winner of U.S. Open, Masters, British Open, Colonial Invitational, and Pan-American Open. 1954: Runner-up in Masters. 1955: Runner-up in U.S. Open and Masters. 1956: Winner of Canada Cup; tied for second in U.S. Open. 1959: Winner of Colonial Invitational.

INKSTER, JULI (SIMPSON). Born in Santa Cruz, CA, June 24, 1960. Few women have come to the LPGA Tour with such an imposing amateur record as Juli

Juli Inkster. Courtesy LPGA

Inkster. From 1979–1982, she was a collegiate All-American while at San Jose State University. In 1982, she won her third U.S. Women's Amateur in a row. The last time this feat was accomplished was in 1934 by Virginia Van Wie, and, before that, by only three other women—Glenna Collett Vare (1930), Alexa Stirling (1920), and Beatrix Hoyt (1898). Inkster was a Curtis Cup team member in 1982, winning both her matches, by 7 and 6. Later that year, she won the individual prize in the Women's World Amateur Team Championship by four strokes with 290. She also won the California State Amateur in 1981.

Inkster won her fifth professional start, the Safeco Classic; only Amy Alcott, in her third event, has won more quickly. This win qualified Inkster for the 1984 Nabisco–Dinah Shore, which she won on the first sudden-death hole, defeating Pat Bradley. In the last event of her rookie season, she shot a final-round 67 to win the du Maurier Classic by a stroke. This was Inkster's second major of the season; she is the only rookie to ever accomplish this feat. Inkster took Rookie-of-the-Year honors, setting a new money-winning record for a rookie of $217,424. Inkster won the Lady Keystone Open in 1985 and continued her winning ways in 1986, taking the Women's Kemper Open, the McDonald's Championship, and Lady Keystone Open back-to-back, the Atlantic City Classic, then won the JC Penney Classic with Tom Purtzer. She finished in third place on the money list, her best yet, with $285,293.

Inkster won three times in 1988 and added another Nabisco–Dinah Shore title in 1989. She gave birth to a daughter in February 1990, and had trouble regaining top form after the layoff, though she did post a victory in 1991 at the Bay State Classic. By 1992, she was back among the top ten money winners.

Inkster is a long hitter with a slow, measured action and an unusually upright arm swing. She is a very fine putter.

Tournament Record: 1980: Winner of U.S. Women's Amateur. 1981: Winner of U.S. Women's Amateur and California Women's Amateur. 1982: Winner of U.S. Women's Amateur. 1983: Winner of Safeco Classic. 1984: Winner of Nabisco–Dinah Shore, and du Maurier Classic. 1985: Winner of Safeco Classic. 1986: Winner of Women's Kemper Open, McDonald's Championship, Lady Keystone Open, Atlantic City Classic, and JC Penney Classic (with Tom Purtzer). 1988: Winner of Crestar Classic, Atlantic City Classic, and Safeco Classic. 1989: Winner of Nabisco–Dinah Shore and Crestar Classic. 1991: Winner of Bay State Classic. 1992: Winner of JAL Big Apple Classic.

IRWIN, HALE S. Born in Joplin, MO, June 3, 1945. Irwin is best known for winning three U.S. Opens, his only major championships, but he also was one of the most consistent and best players on the PGA Tour throughout the 1970s and 1980s. He ranked among the top sixty money winners in every year from 1970 through 1985, and from 1973 through 1978, Irwin always ranked in the top seven. After the 1975 Tucson Open, where he missed the 36-hole cut, he didn't do so again until the 1979 Bing Crosby, a run of eighty-six events. Only Byron Nelson (113 events) and Jack Nicklaus (105) have enjoyed longer streaks of finishing in the money. Irwin has nineteen Tour victories to his credit.

Irwin has scored many of his victories on the

Hale Irwin. *Fred Vuich*

toughest courses. That includes U.S. Opens at Winged Foot (1974), Inverness (1979), Medinah (1990), and also such regular Tour stops as Harbour Town (Heritage Classic), Butler National (Western Open), Riviera (Los Angeles Open), Pinehurst No. 2 (World Open), Muirfield Village (Memorial) and Pebble Beach (Bing Crosby Pro-Am). Not a birdie machine, Irwin is at his best on courses where par is a good score.

Irwin is an intense competitor, a fact which may go back to his days as an all-conference defensive back at the University of Colorado. He also played golf in college, winning the 1967 NCAA Championship. He won his first Tour event, the 1971 Heritage Classic, in his fourth year on Tour. He'd added another Heritage, in 1973, before stamping himself as a major performer by capturing the 1974 U.S. Open at Winged Foot, where the course set-up was so difficult that the winning score was seven over par. In 1979, he won with an even-par total at Inverness.

Irwin remained a steady performer until the late 1980s, when outside interests, including a golf-course management business, began to take time away from his game. He came back strong in 1990, at age forty-five, with his third Open victory and another win the next week at the Buick Classic. With four other top-five finishes, Irwin earned $838,249 for the year to push his career earnings over $4 million.

Tournament Record: 1967: Winner of NCAA Championship. 1971: Winner of Heritage Classic. 1973: Winner of Heritage Classic. 1974: Winner of U.S. Open and World Piccadilly Match Play. 1975: Winner of Western Open, Atlanta Classic, and World Piccadilly Match Play. 1976: Winner of Glen Campbell Los Angeles Open and Florida Citrus Open. 1977: Winner of Atlanta Classic, Hall of Fame Classic, and San Antonio–Texas Open. 1978: Winner of Australian PGA Championship. 1979: Winner of U.S. Open, South African PGA Championship, World Cup individual and team (with John Mahaffey). 1981: Winner of Hawaiian Open, Buick Open, and Bridgestone Classic (Japan). 1982: Winner of Honda–Inverrary Classic and Brazilian Open. 1983: Winner of Memorial Tournament. 1984: Winner of Bing Crosby Pro-Am. 1985: Winner of Memorial Tournament. 1986: Winner of Bahamas Classic. 1987: Winner of Fila Classic. 1990: Winner of U.S. Open and Buick Classic.

Don January. *Courtesy PGA*

JANUARY, DONALD RAY. Born in Plainview, TX, November 20, 1929. As an amateur, Don January won a flock of tournaments, including two victories apiece in the Texas Junior and Dallas City championship. At North Texas State, January played on the school's NCAA Championship teams of 1950, 1951, and 1952. He entered the Air Force following graduation and turned professional in 1955 while still in the service.

Joining the Tour in 1956, January still competed and won money through 1983. During that period January won eleven Tour events and made the top sixty twenty times. His best years were 1963 and 1976, when he finished ninth on the money list. He was selected to the 1965 Ryder Cup team.

The highlights of his career have come in the PGA Championship. In 1961, only a remarkable finish by Jerry Barber kept January from claiming victory. Barber holed long putts on the final three holes to tie January, then defeated him in the 18-hole play-off, 67

to 68. However, in 1967 January tied with Don Massengale at 281 and this time won the playoff, 69 to 71. In 1976, January again finished second, to Dave Stockton.

In 1972, January left the Tour to devote his time to golf course construction in the Dallas area. When financing became difficult due to the recession, he rejoined the Tour in 1975, soon after his forty-fifth birthday, and made a remarkable comeback. He won the Texas Open that year and went on to win the 1976 Tournament of Champions. 1976 was easily his best year on Tour; he earned $163,622. He also won the Vardon Trophy with a scoring average of 70.56, the oldest winner ever. His great form earned him a place on the 1977 Ryder Cup team; at nearly forty-eight years old, he is the oldest American player to be chosen.

When the Senior Tour started in 1980, January won the opener, the Atlantic City Seniors. He has gone on to win twenty-two official events.

The secrets of January's longevity as a player lie in four factors. First, while on the PGA Tour, he paced himself well, never competing in all the available events. He once was quoted as saying, "When I've won $60,000, I head for home." Second, he has to be one of the most deliberate players on record. He and Bobby Locke would probably tie for "most stately progression around a golf course." Third, he became financially stable early in his career, winning twice in his first season, and also picking up $50,000 for a hole-in-one at the Palm Springs Golf Classic in 1961. Fourth, his suppleness. Although he stands almost too erect, and therefore has to steepen his arm swing, January swings more slowly and longer as a senior than anyone, even Sam Snead. Long, slow swings last.

Tournament Record: 1956: Winner of Dallas Centennial Open and Apple Valley Clambake. 1959: Winner of Valencia Open. 1960: Winner of Tucson Open. 1961: Winner of St. Paul Open. 1963: Winner of Tucson Open. 1966: Winner of Philadelphia Classic. 1967: Winner of PGA Championship. 1968: Winner of Tournament of Champions. 1970: Winner of Jacksonville Open. 1975: Winner of San Antonio–Texas Open. 1976: Winner of MONY Tournament of Champions. 1980: Winner of Atlantic City Senior International and Australian Seniors. 1981: Winner of Michelob–Egypt Temple and Eureka Federal Savings. 1982: Winner of Michelob Classic and PGA

Seniors. 1983: Winner of Gatlin Brothers Senior Classic, Peter Jackson Champions, Marlboro Classic, *Denver Post* Champions, Citizens Union Senior Classic, and Suntree Seniors Classic. 1984: Winner of Vintage Invitational, du Maurier Champions, Shootout at Jeremy Ranch (with Mike Sullivan), and Digital Middlesex Classic. 1985: Winner of Senior Roundup, Legends of Golf (with Gene Littler), the Dominion Seniors, United Hospitals Senior Golf Championship, Greenbriar–American Express Championship, and Mazda Champions (with Alice Miller). 1986: Winner of Legends of Golf (with Gene Littler), Senior Players Reunion Pro-Am, Greenbriar–American Express Championship, and Seiko–Tucson Match Play Championship. 1987: Winner of MONY Senior Tournament of Champions.

JONES, ROBERT TYRE, JR. Born in Atlanta, GA, March 17, 1902. Died December 18, 1971. One of the two or three greatest golfers in history and considered by many to be the greatest of all. Jones won 13 major championships and climaxed his career with the Grand Slam in 1930, which consisted of winning the U.S. Open, British Open, U.S. Amateur, and British Amateur in a single season. George Trevor called it the "impregnable quadrilateral," and that is what it was. Aside from the record itself, which is remarkable, there are two things that make Jones's achievements all the more impressive. First, he was an amateur, and, unlike the pros, played in only a few tournaments each year. Second, he had compiled his amazing record and retired by the age of twenty-eight, an age when many other champions were just getting started. In all, Jones won four U.S. Opens (a feat performed earlier by Willie Anderson and later by Ben Hogan), five U.S. Amateurs, three British Opens, and one British Amateur.

Bob Jones was a child prodigy, having taken up the game early and patterned his swing more or less along the lines of Stewart Maiden, the Scottish pro who served at East Lake, Jone's course in Atlanta. By the time he reached his teens, Jones was outstanding: good enough, in fact, to play in the 1916 U.S. Amateur at the tender age of fourteen. This first appearance in a championship began what O. B. Keeler, his biographer, called the "seven lean years." During this period, Jones established himself as a great player and one who was overdue to win a major title. The lean years ended in 1923, and the seven years of plenty began when Jones won the U.S. Open at In-

wood. From that point it was Jones against the field, with Jones usually prevailing. His dominance is best understood by reviewing his record in the U.S. Open. After finishing eighth in 1920 and fifth in 1921, he embarked on a nine-year streak that saw him win the title four times, finish second three times, and tie for second once. Only in 1927, when he tied for eleventh, was he worse than second. Finally, the strain of getting keyed up for the championships proved not to be worth the effort, and Jones retired. Subsequently, he began a long association with Spalding, made a pioneering series of movie shorts on instruction, and conceived and helped design the Augusta National course in Augusta, Georgia. Jones and Clifford Roberts began the Masters tournament there in 1934 and saw it grow over a relatively short time into one of the world's most cherished titles. The Masters was Jones's only tournament appearance for many years. He had to quit after two rounds in 1947 because of what was diagnosed as bursitis in his shoulder. Later, the trouble was found to be a spinal ailment. Surgery failed to help, and his condition gradually deteriorated to such an extent that he was confined to a wheel chair. In later years, new young fans knew Jones as the gracious host of the Masters on television, and it was hard to realize that here was the man who was the hero of the Golden Age of sport. He had everything: wealth, good looks, tremendous talent, and the proper measure of both confidence and modesty. In short, Bobby Jones was the ideal All-American.

Tournament Record: 1916: Winner of Georgia Amateur. 1917: Winner of Southern Amateur. 1919: Runner-up in U.S. Amateur. 1920: Winner of Southern Amateur. 1922: Winner of Southern Amateur; tied for second in U.S. Open. 1923: Winner of U.S. Open. 1924: Winner of U.S. Amateur and Georgia-Alabama Open; runner-up in U.S. Open. 1925: Winner of U.S. Amateur; runner-up in U.S. Open. 1926: Winner of U.S. Open and British Open; runner-up in U.S. Amateur. 1927: Winner of U.S. Amateur, British Open, Southern Open, and Atlanta Open. 1928: Winner of U.S. Amateur; runner-up in U.S. Open. 1929: Winner of U.S. Open. 1930: Winner of U.S. Open, British Open, U.S. Amateur, British Amateur, and Augusta Open.

KING, BETSY. Born in Reading, PA, August 13, 1955. King's career on the LPGA Tour can be divided into two distinct parts. In her first seven years, 1977

Betsy King. *Courtesy LPGA*

through 1983, she didn't win a tournament. Ever since then, she's been one of the best women players in the game. From 1984 through 1990 she won more tournaments, twenty-three, than any other player on the Tour. She was Player of the Year in 1984 ad 1989, led the money list both of those years and won the Vare Trophy in 1987.

The long wait for success was unexpected considering King's fine amateur record. She was low amateur in the 1976 U.S. Women's Open, where she finished eighth, and she helped her Furman University team to the national championship that year.

King's early years on Tour weren't entirely undistinguished. She finished no worse than twenty-eighth on the money list in 1978, 1979, 1981, 1982, and 1983, finishing second four times in that span. But she couldn't break through with a victory.

That finally happened after three years of working with instructor Ed Oldfield, who reworked her swing to help her get rid of a nasty hook. Once King broke the barrier by winning the 1984 Women's Kemper Open, the floodgates opened. She won twice more

that year, and posted at least two victories in every year through 1992.

King captured her first major, the Nabisco–Dinah Shore, in 1987, then added the U.S. Women's Open in 1989. In 1990, she took both of those titles for a second time. Her best overall campaign was 1989, when she won six tournaments and $654,132. By the end of 1991, she'd passed $3.3 million in career earnings.

King is one of the best drivers on Tour, hitting her tee ball long and high. In recent years, she has also become known as an excellent putter.

Tournament Record: 1984: Winner of Women's Kemper Open, Freedom Orlando Classic, and Columbia Savings Classic. 1985: Winner of Samaritan Turquoise Classic, Rail Charity Classic, and Ladies British Open. 1986: Winner of Henredon Classic, Rail Charity Classic. 1987: Winner of Circle K Tucson Open, Nabisco–Dinah Shore, McDonald's Championship and Atlantic City Classic. 1988: Winner of Women's Kemper Open, Rail Charity Classic, and Cellular One-Ping Championship. 1989: Winner of Jamaica Classic, Women's Kemper Open, USX Classic, McDonald's Championship, U.S. Women's Open, and Nestlé World Championship. 1990: Nabisco–Dinah Shore, U.S. Women's Open, JAL Big Apple Classic, and Itoman World Match Play. 1991: Winner of Corning Classic and JAL Big Apple Classic. 1992: Winner of Mazda LPGA Championship and Mazda Japan Classic.

KITE, THOMAS O., JR. Born in McKinney, TX, December 9, 1949. Kite's first taste of golf took place when he was six years old. At age eleven, he won his first tournament, an age-group event at the Country Club of Austin, Texas, and began to play seriously three years later. As an amateur, Kite was first heard of in 1970 as medalist in the Western Amateur, runner-up in the Southern Amateur, and second to Lanny Wadkins in the U.S. Amateur. He played on the winning World Amateur team that year, and the following year on the Walker Cup team. In 1972, he shared the NCAA title with his University of Texas teammate, Ben Crenshaw.

Joining the Tour in the fall of 1972, Kite had a rookie year that was a model of consistency, a quality that has been the keynote of his career. In 1973, he missed just three cuts in thirty-five events, and was voted Rookie-of-the-Year. Ever since, other than in 1974, 1976 and 1991, he has been in the top twenty every year. He has fifteen Tour victories to his credit and has played on six Ryder Cup teams (1979, 1981, 1983, 1985, 1987, 1989). In 1981, the Golf Writers Association of America gave him their award for Player of the Year. That year he was the winner of the Vardon Trophy for best scoring average in 1981, then repeated in 1982. He was named PGA Player of the Year in 1989.

His first win came in the 1976 IVB-Philadelphia, his second in the 1978 B.C. Open, but 1981 set a pattern that Kite has followed fairly closely ever since. He won one Tour event, the Inverrary Classic, and had a spate of high finishes—second three times, third three times, fourth once, fifth once, and sixth five times. He finished first on the money list with $375,699. In 1984 and 1992, he won twice, in 1989 he won three times, and in 1988 he was winless; other than that, Kite has one once every year starting in 1981. Until he captured the 1992 U.S. Open, Kite was unable to win a major championship, a surprising gap considering his overall record. Perhaps his best previous chance came in the 1989 U.S. Open, where he led through three rounds, but closed with a 78. He did score two of his most significant victories that year. He won the Players Championship and the season-ending Nabisco Championship, where he locked up the season money title with $1,395,278.

Kite finally made his major breakthrough, at age 42, by winning the 1992 U.S. Open at Pebble Beach. His final-round 72, when most contenders were struggling to break 80 in the windy conditions, earned him a two-stroke victory over Jeff Sluman.

A look at the Tour statistics for 1981 reveals why Kite is so often a high finisher rather than a winner. He had the lowest stroke average, was fifth in hitting greens in regulation, second in number of birdies, sixth in getting up and down in two from sand, and fourteenth in putting. However, in driving, he was seventh in accuracy, but out of the top fifty in distance. It is difficult to overpower today's super-strong fields, where the longest hitters average close to 280 yards, when one is a 250–255-yard hitter, as Kite is.

Kite owns an exceptionally sound swing, honed by hours of practice that would daunt all but a Ben Hogan. He was one of the first Tour players to go to the "three-wedge" system in the short game, adding a very lofted sand wedge for short pitches and sand shots, and modifying the loft of his 3-, 4-, and 5-irons to fill the gap. Working with Dave Pelz, "Professor

Tom Kite.
Fred Vuich

Putt," Kite has made himself into one of the better putters on Tour.

Tournament Record: 1972: NCAA co-chairman with Ben Crenshaw. 1976: Winner of IVB–Bicentennial Golf Classic. 1978: Winner of B.C. Open. 1980: Winner of European Open. 1981: Winner of American Motors–Inverrary Classic. 1982: Winner of Bay Hill Classic. 1983: Winner of Bing Crosby National Pro-Am. 1984: Winner of Doral–Eastern Open and Georgia-Pacific Atlanta Classic. 1985: Winner of MONY Tournament of Champions. 1986: Winner of Western Open. 1987: Winner of Kemper Open. 1989: Winner of Nestle Invitational, Players Championship, and Nabisco Championship. 1990: Winner of Federal Express St. Jude Classic. 1991: Winner of Infiniti Tournament of Champions. 1992: Winner of Bell South Classic and U.S. Open.

LANGER, BERNHARD. Born in Anhausen, West Germany, August 27, 1957. The son of a Bavarian bricklayer, Langer started in the game as a caddie at age nine at the Augsburg Country Club in Anhausen. In 1972, he went to work as an assistant professional to Heinz Fehring at the Munich Golf and Country Club. When he had completed the apprenticeship program at age eighteen, Langer went on the European Tour.

In 1979, he had his first victory, in the World Under-25 Tournament. He won by seventeen strokes. Later that year, he won the German PGA title—and tied for second in the World Cup individual standings. In 1980, he became the first German to take a major European title, the Dunlop Masters. He won two other events, and again finished second in the World Cup. In 1981, Langer dominated the European golf circuit, taking the Bob Hope British Classic and German Open (the first German ever to win) and racking up fifteen top-ten finishes in nineteen events. He also was second to Bill Rogers in the British Open at Sandwich, and led the World Series at Firestone with nine holes to play, but faded to sixth place. He topped the Order of Merit and had a stroke average of 70.56. In 1982, he added another German Open to his total, but otherwise it was a poor year. He came back with a rush in 1983, with four victories in Europe and one in Japan. In 1984, he won four

Bernhard Langer. *Fred Vuich*

European events—the Irish, Dutch, French and Spanish Opens—and again finished first in the Order of Merit. His 69.42 scoring average was the best in Europe.

Langer reached world status in 1985, his first full year on the PGA Tour. He won the Masters in impressive fashion, coming from six strokes off the pace after two rounds. In the last round, he had birdies on the 13th and 15th holes to overtake Curtis Strange, who bogeyed both holes. Langer also made a clutch birdie putt of fifteen feet on 17 to wrap up his victory. He had rounds of 72, 74, 68, and 68 to beat Strange, Seve Ballesteros, and Ray Floyd by two strokes. The next week, he won the Sea Pines Heritage. Langer took the lead after the third round, but then was tied by Bobby Wadkins at 273. Langer won on the first play-off hole.

Twice in his career, Langer has had to battle the yips on short putts. In his first few years on the European Tour, he had a terrible case. But in 1980 he took the advice of Seve Ballesteros to use a heavier putter, and his putting turned around. Langer once again began to have serious trouble on the greens in 1988, but his putting has improved somewhat in recent years since he went to an unorthodox grip where his right hand holds his left forearm. Langer hasn't won in the U.S. since 1985, but he's won thirteen times in Europe since then. He quit the PGA Tour as a regular member in 1989.

Langer has played on six European Ryder Cup teams (1981, 1983, 1985, 1987, 1989, 1991).

Tournament Record: 1979: Winner of World Under-25 Tournament, and German Closed Pro Championship. 1980: Winner of Dunlop Masters and Columbian Open. 1981: Winner of German Open and Bob Hope British Classic. 1982: Winner of German Open. 1983: Winner of Italian Open, Glasgow Classic, TPC at St. Mellion, Johnnie Walker Tournament, and Casio World (Japan). 1984: Winner of Irish Open, Dutch Open, French Open, and Spanish Open. 1985: Winner of German Open, European Open, Australian Masters, Masters, Sea Pines Heritage Classic, and Sun City Challenge. 1986: Winner of German Open, and joint first with Seve Ballesteros in Lancôme Trophy (play-off stopped by darkness). 1987: Winner of Belgian Classic, British PGA Championship, and Irish Open. 1988: Winner of European Epson Match Play. 1989: Winner of Peugeot Spanish Open, and German Masters. 1990: Winner of Cepsa

Madrid Open, and Austrian Open. 1991: Winner of Benson & Hedges International Open and Mercedes German Masters. 1992: Winner of Heineken Dutch Open and Honda Open.

LITTLE, SALLY. Born in Sea Point, Capetown, South Africa, October 12, 1951. The best South African woman golfer of all time, Little took up the game at twelve years of age. Until she turned professional, she had no professional instruction, relying on her father, Percy. She compiled an excellent amateur record in South Africa. Among other events, she won the Western Province Match Play three times (1967, 1968, 1969) and the Transvaal Stroke Play three times (1968, 1969, 1970). In 1970, she was low individual scorer in the World Women's Amateur Team Championship at the Club de Campo, Madrid, Spain; she shot 299, the next best score being 302. The following year, she won the South African match and stroke titles.

Coming to America, she tied for fifth as an amateur in the Lady Carling at Baltimore in June 1971. She then joined the LPGA Tour and by August had earned her player's card. Although she only competed in

Sally Little. *UPI/Bettmann*

seven events, she was named Rookie of the Year. Little's first victory on the Tour took her, and everyone else, by surprise. Playing for a tie with Jan Stephenson at the 1976 Women's International at Moss Creek, Little holed a seventy-five-foot bunker shot for a birdie to win by a stroke. She then went on to establish herself as one of the Tour's top players, finishing among the top ten money winners from 1977 through 1982, her highest being third place in 1982. She has won fifteen Tour events, including three majors: the 1980 LPGA Championship, the 1982 Nabisco–Dinah Shore, and the 1988 du Maurier Classic. She became a U.S. citizen in 1982.

Little's career was put on hold in 1983. Abdominal surgery in late December prevented her playing until the fourth tournament of the season. Then, after playing in only five events, she underwent arthroscopic knee surgery and only rejoined the Tour for the last two events of the season. Little came close to another major in the 1986 U.S. Women's Open, losing the 18-hole play-off to Jane Geddes, 73 to 71. However, she was pretty convincing in the 1988 du Maurier, as she sank a thirty-foot putt on the last hole to defeat Britian's Laura Davies.

Tournament Record: 1967: Winner of Western Province Match Play. 1968: Winner of Western Province Match Play and Transvaal Stroke Play. 1969: Winner of Western Province Match Play, Transvaal Stroke Play, Trand Match, Eastern Province, and Natal Match Play. 1970: Winner of Transvaal Stroke Play and Trand Match. 1971: Winner of South African Women's Stroke Play and South African Women's Match Play. 1976: Winner of Women's International. 1978: Winner of Honda Civic Classic. 1979: Winner of Bent Tree Ladies Classic, Barth Classic, and Columbia Savings Classic. 1980: Winner of LPGA Championship and WVI Classic. 1981: Winner of Elizabeth Arden Classic, Olympia Gold Classic, and CPC Women's International. 1982: Winner of Olympia Gold Classic, Nabisco–Dinah Shore, United Virginia Bank Classic, and Mayflower Classic. 1988: Winner of du Maurier Classic.

LITTLE, WILLIAM LAWSON, JR. Born in Newport, RI, June 23, 1910. Died February 1, 1968. One of America's greatest amateurs and probably the greatest between the retirement of Bobby Jones and the advent of Jack Nicklaus. Little won the U.S. and British Amateurs in 1934, then won the same two events the

Lawson Little. *Wide World Photos*

British Amateur. 1935: Winner of U.S. Amateur and British Amateur. 1936: Winner of Canadian Open. 1937: Winner of Shawnee Open and San Francisco Match Play. 1940: Winner of U.S. Open and Los Angeles Open. 1941: Winner of Texas Open. 1942: Winner of Inverness Four-Ball. 1948: Winner of St. Petersburg Open.

LITTLER, GENE ALEC. Born July 21, 1930, San Diego, CA. The winner of both the U.S. Amateur and National Open and one of the smoothest swingers in golf. Littler turned pro early in 1954 and over the next fifteen years won more than twenty tournaments and well over one-half million dollars. So fluid was his swing that when he won the San Diego Open, people were predicting Littler would be the game's next superstar. When he finished second in the U.S. Open that year, then won five tournaments in 1955, the experts seemed justified in their predictions. Littler continued to win in 1956, but he was tapering off; and in 1957 and 1958, he fell into a slump that was broken only by his third straight victory in the Tournament of Champions. During this period he tinkered with his swing and, in the course of struggling to regain his old consistency, received a variety of confusing advice. However, it all came back in 1959, as Littler won five tournaments and finished the year as second money winner. He remained one of the Tour's steadiest money winners all the way through the mid-1970s. Littler's only major championship came in the 1961 U.S. Open; he lost the 1970 Masters in a playoff against Billy Casper.

next year in a feat that deserves to be ranked close to Jones's Grand Slam of 1930 and Ben Hogan's sweep of 1953. Although he turned professional in 1936 and later won the U.S. Open, Little's fame rests on that string of thirty-one consecutive match victories. Little first attracted real attention in the 1933 U.S. Amateur when he reached the semifinals, although he had created a stir back in 1929 when, as a teenager, he had beaten Johnny Goodman right after Goodman upset Jones in the first round at Pebble Beach. His performance in the 1933 Amateur earned Little a berth on the Walker Cup Team, and it was in those matches, against the British at St. Andrews in 1934, that his great streak began. He turned pro in 1936 amid great fanfare, but, although he was to win several tournaments, including the Open, he never really lived up to expectations.

Tournament Record: 1928, 1930: Winner of Northern California Amateur. 1932: Winner of Broadmoor Invitational. 1933: Winner of Colorado Closed Amateur. 1934: Winner of U.S. Amateur and

Gene Littler.
Courtesy PGA

In the spring of 1972, Littler underwent surgery for cancer of the lymph glands, and it was feared his career was over. He rejoined the Tour six months later and won five tour events from then through 1977.

He was awarded the Ben Hogan Trophy for his courageous comeback in 1973.

Littler has been a very successful senior, winning eight official Senior Tour events and eight other senior events. He also won the Australian Masters in 1980.

Tournament Record: 1948: Winner of U.S. Jaycee Junior. 1953: Winner of U.S. Amateur, California Open, and California Amateur. 1954: Winner of San Diego Open; runner-up in U.S. Open. 1955: Winner of Los Angeles Open, Pan-American Open, Phoenix Open, Tournament of Champions, and LaBatt Open. 1956: Winner of Texas Open, Tournament of Champions, Palm Beach Round Robin, and Arizona Open. 1957: Winner of Tournament of Champions. 1959: Winner of Phoenix Open, Tucson Open, Arlington Hotel Open, Insurance City Open, and Miller Open. 1960: Winner of Oklahoma City Open and Eastern Open. 1961: Winner of U.S. Open. 1962: Winner of Lucky International Open and Thunderbird Invitational. 1964: Winner of Southern California Open. 1965: Winner of Canadian Open. 1966: Winner of World Series of Golf. 1969: Winner of Phoenix Open and Greater Greensboro Open. 1971: Winner of Monsanto Open and Colonial National Invitational. 1973: Winner of St. Louis Classic. 1974: Winner of Taiheiyo Masters (Japan). 1975: Winner of Bing Crosby National Pro-Am, Danny Thomas–Memphis Classic, Westchester Classic, and Taiheiyo Masters (Japan). 1977: Winner of Houston Open. 1980: Winner of World Seniors Invitational and Australian Masters. 1981: Winner of Legends of Golf (with Bob Rosburg) and Vintage Invitational. 1982: Winner of World Seniors Invitational. 1983: Winner of Daytona Beach Senior Classic, Greater Syracuse Classic, Vintage Invitational and Coca-Cola Senior Grand Slam (Japan). 1984: Winner of Seiko–Tucson Match Play. 1985: Winner of Legends of Golf (with Don January). 1986: Winner of Legends of Golf (with Don January), Charlie Pride Seniors, and Bank One Senior Golf Classic. 1987: Winner of NYNEX/*Golf Digest* Commemorative and Gus Machado Senior Golf Classic. 1989: Winner of Aetna Challenge.

LOCKE, ARTHUR D'ARCY (BOBBY). Born in Germiston, Transvaal, South Africa, November 20, 1917. Died March 9, 1987. A four-time winner of the British Open and the first foreign player to become a consistent winner in the United States. Locke, the son of a successful sports outfitter in South Africa, took to the game early and was a champion while still in his teens. Then, after flying more than a hundred missions during World War II, he returned to golf and quickly became a player of world stature. He hit the United States circuit in 1947 and proceeded to win seven tournaments and finish second on the money-winning list. He made several subsequent appearances in the States and was in the top five in the U.S. Open five times. Locke was not a stylish player, but he had a fine short game and was a great putter. In appearance he was the very antithesis of the postwar professional. He wore knickers, a white shirt, and tie and displayed a swing that could hardly be said to compare with Vardon's. All this made his appearance on the American scene a refreshing one,

Bobby Locke. *Wide World Photos*

but he soon discovered that the important thing on the United States tour was money, and his attitude changed to a more businesslike one.

Tournament Record: 1931: Winner of South Africa Boys Championship. 1935: Winner of South Africa Open, South Africa Amateur, Natal Open, Natal Amateur, and Transvaal Amateur. 1936: Winner of Natal Open, Natal Amateur, and Lucifer Empire Trophy. 1937: Winner of South Africa Open, South Africa Amateur, Transvaal Amateur, and Orange Free State Amateur. 1938: Winner of South Africa Open, Irish Open, New Zealand Open, South Africa Professional, and Transvaal Open. 1939: Winner of South Africa Open, Dutch Open, South Africa Professional, and Transvaal Open. 1940: Winner of South Africa Open, Transvaal Open, and South Africa Professional. 1946: Winner of South Africa Open, South Africa Professional, Transvaal Open, Yorkshire *Evening News* Tournament, Dunlop Masters, and Brand Lochryn Tournament; runner-up in British Open. 1947: Winner of Canadian Open, Houston Invitational, Philadelphia *Inquirer* Open, All-American Open, Columbus Open, Goodall Round Robin, Carolinas PGA, and South Africa Dunlop Tournament. 1948: Winner of Phoenix Open, Chicago Victory Open, and Carolinas Open. 1949: Winner of British Open, Transvaal Open, Cavalier Invitational, Goodall Round Robin, and Greenbrier Pro-Am. 1950: Winner of British Open, South Africa Open, South Africa Professional, Transvaal Open, Dunlop Tournament, Spalding Tournament, All-America Open, and North British Tournament. 1951: Winner of South Africa Open, Transvaal Open, and South Africa Professional. 1952: Winner of British Open, French Open, Mexican Open, and Lotus Tournament. 1953: Winner of French Open and Natal Open. 1954: Winner of Egyptian Open, German Open, Swiss Open, Dunlop Tournament, Dunlop Masters, Egyptian Match Play, Transvaal Open, and Swallow-Harrogate Tournament; tied for second in British Open. 1955: Winner of Australian Open, Transvaal Open, South Africa Open, and South Africa Professional. 1957: Winner of British Open, Daks Tournament, and Bowmaker Amateur–Professional. 1958: Winner of Transvaal Open.

LOPEZ, NANCY. Born in Torrance, CA, January 6, 1957. Lopez took up the game at age eight under the guidance of her father, Domingo. She had a phenom-

Nancy Lopez.
Courtesy LPGA

enal amateur career. At twelve, she won the New Mexico Women's Amateur. She won two U.S. Junior Girls (1972 and 1974), three Western Juniors (1972, 1973, 1974) and the 1975 Mexican Amateur. That year she finished second in the U.S. Women's Open to Sandra Palmer. She attended Tulsa University for two years. In 1976, she won the Trans-National, Western Amateur, AIAW National Collegiate Championship, and four other collegiate titles. She was also a member of the 1976 Curtis Cup and World Amateur teams.

One week before the July 1977 LPGA Qualifying School, Lopez had another second place finish in the U.S. Women's Open. This was her first event as a professional. After finishing third in the school, she took two more seconds that year, in the Colgate European Open, Sunningdale, England, and Long Island Charity Classic. This was an impressive start, by any standards, but gave no hint of explosion of wins to come.

In 1978, Lopez won nine Tour events, including one major, the LPGA Championship, by six strokes. Seven of the wins were in the U.S., and she also won in Japan and England. She finished the year as leading money winner with a record $189,813 and won the Vare Trophy with a scoring average of 71.76. She was also Player of the Year as well as Rookie of the Year. However, what caused the media excitement, and the tripling of Tour attendance, was that five of the U.S. wins were consecutive, a new record. Lopez was also a player to whom other golfers could relate. Her sunny, outgoing personality, unusual swing and phenomenal putting made marvelous copy for the press and cocktail conversation for everyone else. She was, in effect, a one-woman promotion for the LPGA Tour.

Her second year was only a little less sensational. In 1979, she had eight wins and again was Player of the Year and leading money-winner. Her stroke average (71.20) stood as an all-time LPGA record until she surpassed it in 1985.

Lopez became a Tour millionaire in winnings at the 1983 Nabisco–Dinah Shore. It was at this tournament that she announced her first pregnancy. Only competing in twelve tournaments that year, she fell a little short of $100,000 in earnings ($91,477) for the first time since 1977. In 1984, despite playing in only sixteen events, Lopez still managed two wins.

In 1985, Lopez was back with a vengeance. She won five tournaments, including her second LPGA Championship. In twenty-five starts, she had twenty-one top ten finishes, including a string of twelve consecutive events where she was not out of the top five. She again was Player of the Year and leading money-winner with $416,472, becoming the first player to earn over $400,000 in one season. She set a new LPGA record for scoring average of 70.73. In winning the Henredon Classic, she set two other records: For lowest 72 holes, 268 (20 under par), and for most subpar holes—she recorded twenty-five birdies.

Lopez only played in four tournaments during the 1986 season because of the birth of her second child in May of that year. Nevertheless, she managed two second place finishes and a third late in the year. If it was a "quiet" year for Lopez, it was quite the reverse for her husband, Ray Knight, who, third baseman for the Mets, was the MVP in the 1986 World Series.

In July 1987, Lopez was inducted into the LPGA Hall of Fame after she had won her thirty-fifth official tournament, the Sarasota Classic, the event that provided her first Tour win in 1978. In 1988, she collected three more victories, and was Rolex Player of the Year for the fourth time in her LPGA career. In 1989, Lopez won the LPGA Championship for the third time, and by the end of 1991 she'd run her career victory total to forty-four.

Tournament Record: 1969: Winner of New Mexico Women's Amateur. 1972: Winner of U.S. Girls' Junior, and Western Junior Girls'. 1973: Winner of Western Junior Girls'. 1974: Winner of U.S. Girls' Junior, and Western Junior Girls'. 1975: Winner Mexican Women's Amateur. 1976: Winner of Trans-National, Western Women's Amateur, and AIAW National Collegiate Championship. 1978: Winner of Bent Tree Ladies Classic, Sunstar Classic, Greater Baltimore Classic, Coca-Cola Classic, Golden Lights Championship, LPGA Championship, Bankers Trust Classic, Colgate European Open, and Colgate Far East Open. 1979: Winner of Sunstar Classic, Sahara National Pro-Am, Women's International, Coca-Cola Classic, Golden Lights Championship, Lady Keystone Open, Colgate European Open, and Mary Kay Classic. 1980: Winner of Women's Kemper Open, Sarah Coventry, and Rail Charity Classic. 1981: Winner of Arizona Copper Classic, Colgate–Dinah Shore, and Sarah Coventry. 1982: Winner of J&B Scotch Pro-Am and Mazda Japan Classic. 1983: Winner of Elizabeth Arden Classic and J&B Scotch Pro-Am. 1984: Winner of Uniden LPGA Invitational and Chevrolet World Championship of Women's Golf. 1985: Winner of Chrysler-Plymouth Charity Classic, LPGA Championship, Mazda Hall of Fame Championship, Henredon Classic, and Portland–Ping Championship. 1987: Winner of Sarasota Classic, Cellular One–Ping Golf Championship, and Mazda Champions (with Miller Barber). 1988: Winner of Mazda Classic, AI Star–Centinela Hospital Classic, and Chrysler-Plymouth Classic. 1989: Winner of Mazda LPGA Championship, Atlantic City Classic, and MBS Classic. 1990: Winner of MBS Classic. 1991: Winner of Sara Lee Classic. 1992: Winner of Rail Charity Classic and Ping–Cellular One Championship.

LYLE, ALEXANDER WALTER BARR. Born in Shrewsbury, Scotland, February 9, 1958. With his father, Alex, being a golf professional, it was hardly surprising that Sandy Lyle took to the game when he was very young. By the time he was ten, he had broken 80, and he went on to have a good amateur career, playing for the British Walker Cup team in 1977, when he also got to the fifth round of the U.S. Amateur.

Turning professional in 1977, Lyle got off the mark quickly with a win in the 1978 Nigerian Open. After several more strong years on the European Tour, Lyle first came to American attention in 1984, when he won the Kapalua International, beating a field which included twelve players who had won that year on the PGA Tour. The long-hitting Scotsman made mincemeat of the 6,728 yard Kapalua Resort course, shooting 68, 64, 69, 65—266 to win by eight strokes over Bernhard Langer.

The following year, Lyle broke through into the top ranks by winning his first major, the British Open at Royal St. George's Golf Club, Sandwich, England. Before the Open began, Lyle said "I've served my apprenticeship. Now it's about time I won this title." His gutsy performance made him the first native Open champion since Tony Jacklin achieved the feat in 1969.

In 1986, Lyle showed he could win on the U.S. mainland, taking his first PGA Tour event, the Greensboro Open.

However, Lyle's finest year in the U.S. was yet to come. In 1988, he won the Phoenix Open in a playoff over Fred Couples, and won the Greensboro Open for the second time with another playoff win over Ken Green. Then came the Masters.

In the opening round, the gusting winds sent the field's average score soaring to 76.72. But Lyle quietly went about his business, and compiled a steady 71, just two strokes off the lead. In the second round, he took command with a 67, for a 6-under par 138, and his even par third round of 72 brought him in at 210, which gave him a two-stroke lead.

In the last round, he lost his rhythm around Amen Corner, squandering what had become a three-stroke lead by three-putting the par-4 11th hole for a bogey, and then dumping his 8-iron into the water on the small, but utterly treacherous, 12th hole, where he wound up with a double bogey 5. He then cooled off and regrouped, making birdies on the 16th and 18th to beat Mark Calcavecchia by one shot. His birdie on the final hole came when he hit a 7-iron from a fairway bunker to within ten feet of the pin.

Just as it seemed he'd arrived as a great player, Lyle fell into a horrible slump. He capped 1988 by winning the World Match Play Championship, but in the next two years he didn't post a single victory, or even pose a serious threat. He even asked to be left off the 1989 European Ryder Cup team because of his poor form. He had played on the Ryder Cup teams of 1979, 1981, 1983, 1985, and 1987. Lyle finally recovered with a victory at the 1991 BMW International Open, but he did not make the Ryder Cup team that year.

Tournament Record: 1978: Winner of Nigerian Open. 1979: Winner of Scandinavian Open, British Airways–Avis Open, and European Open. 1980: Winner of Coral Welsh Classic and World Cup individual, playing for Scotland. 1981: Winner of French Open and Lawrence Batley International. 1982: Winner of Lawrence Batley International. 1983: Winner of Madrid Open. 1984: Winner of Italian Open, Lancome Trophy, Kapalua International, and Casio World Open (Japan). 1985: Winner of Benson and Hedges International and British Open. 1986: Winner of Greater Greensboro Open. 1987: Winner of Tournament Players Championship, and German Masters. 1988: Winner of Phoenix Open, Kmart Greater Greensboro Open, Masters, Dunhill Masters, and Suntory World Match Play. 1991: Winner of BMW International Open. 1992: Winner of Italian Open and Volvo Masters.

MAHAFFEY, JOHN DRAYTON. Born in Kerrville, TX, May 9, 1948. An outstanding player at the University of Houston, where he took a degree in psychology in

John Mahaffey.

1970, John Mahaffey was All-American in 1969 and 1970. He won the NCAA in 1970, and tied for low amateur in that year's U.S. Open, finishing in thirty-sixth place along with Ben Crenshaw.

Since qualifying for the PGA Tour in 1971, Mahaffey has won ten Tour events, including one major, the 1978 PGA Championship. He also had two U.S. Opens on his line, but they got away.

At the 1975 U.S. Open at Medinah, he tied with Lou Graham. However, he couldn't buy a putt in the play-off, and lost 73–71. In 1976, at the Atlanta Athletic Club, his first three rounds were 70, 68, 69 for a two-stroke lead over Jerry Pate. In the final round, Mahaffey bogeyed the last three holes to lose the lead and finish fourth, three strokes behind Pate.

Mahaffey's single major came in the 1978 PGA Championship at Oakmont. Mahaffey started with a 75, but then put together rounds of 67 and 68. In the final round, Mahaffey came from seven strokes off the pace set by Tom Watson to shoot 66 for a total of 276, in a tie with Watson and Pate. Mahaffey birdied the second play-off hole to win.

Another important victory was the 1986 Tournament Players Championship at the TPC at Ponte Vedra, Fla. Mahaffey shot 69, 70, 65, and was four strokes behind Larry Mize going into the last round. However, while Mahaffey played steadily for a one-under par 71, Mize faded to a 76 to give Mahaffey a one-stroke victory. Since then, he's won only once, the 1989 Federal Express–St. Jude Classic.

Mahaffey played on the 1978 and 1979 World Cup teams, and was a medalist in 1978. He was also a member of the 1979 Ryder Cup team. Although not a long hitter at 5'9" and 160 lbs, Mahaffey is an accurate player.

Tournament Record: 1970: Winner of NCAA Championship. 1973: Winner of Sahara Invitational. 1978: Winner of PGA Championship and American Optical Classic. 1979: Winner of Bob Hope Desert Classic. 1980: Winner of Kemper Open. 1981: Winner of Anheuser-Busch Classic. 1984: Winner of Bob Hope Classic. 1985: Winner of Texas Open. 1986: Winner of Tournament Players Championship. 1989: Winner of Federal Express–St. Jude Classic.

MANGRUM, LLOYD EUGENE. Born in Trenton, TX, August 1, 1914. Died November 17, 1973. One of the most successful campaigners in postwar American golf. Mangrum won the U.S. Open in 1946 and tied for first in 1950, losing in a play-off. He also finished in the top five on four other occasions. In the Masters he was fourth or better seven times, and in the PGA he was a semi-finalist twice and a quarter-finalist twice. In a career that covered more than two decades, he won over fifty tournaments, played on three Ryder Cup Teams, and twice won the Vardon Trophy for low scoring average.

Mangrum grew up in Texas, where he learned the game along with such heroes as Ben Hogan, Byron Nelson, Ralph Guldahl, and Jimmy Demaret. He turned pro in 1929 at the age of fifteen and played in his first PGA-sponsored tournament at nineteen. The 1930s were lean years for him, like everyone else, but near the end of the decade he began to display the skills that were to make him one of the game's top all-time winners. Mangrum began to follow the tour in earnest in 1939, and by 1940 he had arrived.

Lloyd Mangrum.

That season he won the Thomasville Open, finished second in the Masters after opening with a course-record 64, and ran fifth in the U.S. Open. He was seventh money winner in 1941 and advanced to fourth in 1942 before entering the Army, where he attained the rank of staff sergeant. He was wounded twice in the Battle of the Bulge and spent part of his convalescent period at St. Andrews, where he won a GI tournament in 1945. Mangrum rejoined the tournament circuit in 1946 and launched a nine-year run, during which he won thirty-five tournaments and never was out of the top ten money winners. With his thin mustache and with black hair parted in the middle, he had the look of a river-boat gambler, and this, plus his obvious skills, quickly made him a gallery favorite.

Tournament Record: 1938: Winner of Pennsylvania Open. 1940: Winner of Thomasville Open; runner-up in Masters. 1941: Winner of Atlantic City Open. 1942: Winner of New Orleans Open, Inverness Four-Ball, and Seminole Pro-Amateur. 1945: Winner of Army Victory Tournament and GI Tournament. 1946: Winner of U.S. Open and Argentine Open. 1947: Winner of National Capital Open, Albuquerque Open, and Montebello Open. 1948: Winner of Bing Crosby Invitational, Rio Grande Valley Open, Greensboro Open, Columbus Open, All-American Open, World Tournament, Utah Open and Zooligans Open. 1949: Winner of Los Angeles Open, Tucson Open, and All-American Open; tied for first in Motor City Open. 1950: Winner of Eastern Open, Fort Wayne Open, Kansas City Open, Motor City Open; runner-up in U.S. Open. 1951: Winner of Los Angeles Open, Tucson Open, Seminole Pro-Amateur, Azalea Open, and St. Paul Open. 1952: Winner of Phoenix Open, Pan-American Open, Western Open, California Open, and Montebello Open. 1953: Winner of Los Angeles Open, Phoenix Open, Bing Crosby Invitational, and All-American Open. 1954: Winner of Western Open. 1956: Winner of Los Angeles Open. 1960: Winner of Southern California Open.

MANN, CAROL. Born in Buffalo, NY, February 3, 1941. Mann started playing golf at age eleven. She won the Western Junior and Chicago Junior in 1958. In 1960, she won the Chicago Women's Amateur, and then turned professional.

From 1961 to 1975, Mann had thirty-eight victo-

Carol Mann. *Courtesy LPGA*

ries, including two majors, the 1964 Western Open and 1965 U.S. Women's Open. Until 1978, she never was worse than twenty-ninth on the money list. Her best earning years were in 1969, when she was leading money winner; 1968, when she finished second; and 1965, 1967 and 1975, when she took third place. From 1964 to 1975, her only winless year was 1971.

In 1968, she challenged Kathy Whitworth for supremacy on the LPGA Tour. They both accounted for ten wins. Mann set a Vare Trophy record of 72.04 that stood until Nancy Lopez broke it with 71.76 in 1978. She finished second to Whitworth on the money list. The following year, their roles were reversed, Whitworth taking the Vare with 72.38, while Mann was leading money winner with a then record $49,152. Mann had eight wins, Whitworth, seven.

Mann served as the president of the LPGA in 1974. Inducted into the LPGA Hall of Fame in 1977, Mann retired after 1981. At 6'3", or as she prefers to put it, 5'15", Mann is the tallest woman to play successful tournament golf. She is a naturally left-handed person who plays right-handed.

Tournament Record: 1958: Winner of Western Junior and Chicago Junior. 1960: Winner of Chicago Women's Amateur. 1964: Winner of Western Open. 1965: Winner of Lady Carling Open and U.S. Women's Open. 1966: Winner of Raleigh Invitational, Peach Blossom Invitational, Baton Rouge Invitational, and Waterloo Invitational. 1967: Winner of Tall City Open, Buckeye Savings International, and Supertest Open. 1968: Winner of Lady Carling Open, Raleigh Invitational, Shreveport Invitational, Bluegrass Invitational, Pabst Classic, Buckeye Savings Invitational, Supertest Canadian Open, Shirley Englehorn Invitational, Quality Chek'd Classic, and Willow Park Invitational. 1969: Winner of Raleigh Invitational, Dallas Civitan Open, Lady Carling Open, Southgate Open, Tournament of Champions, Molson's Canadian Open, Mickey Wright Invitational, and Corpus Christi Open. 1970: Winner of Burdines Invitational. 1972: Winner of Orange Blossom Classic and Lady Carling Open. 1973: Winner of Sears Women's Classic. 1974: Winner of Naples—Lely Classic and S&H Green Stamp Classic. 1975: Winner of Borden Classic, George Washington Classic, Dallas Civitan Open, and Lawson's Open.

MCDERMOTT, JOHN J. Born in Philadelphia, PA, August 12, 1891. Died August 1, 1971. America's first great homebred professional, a man who came virtually out of nowhere to win two straight U.S. National Opens, then disappeared from the scene almost as rapidly. McDermott tied for first in the 1910 Open, lost the play-off, then won the next two years. Three years later, however, he was out of golf, the victim of mental illness. He was full of ego and determination, feared no one, and let everybody know it. He was bitterly disappointed by losing the 1910 play-off to Alex Smith, and he told Alex the situation would be corrected the following year. It was. He also played in two British Opens because he wanted to convince the British he was no accident. So bright was the flame within McDermott that many said he simply burned himself out in his unparalleled drive to be better than everyone else. At any rate, he raised himself from a run-of-the-mill player to the championship class in only one season.

Tournament Record: 1910: Runner-up in U.S. Open. 1911, 1912: Winner of U.S. Open. 1913: Winner of Western Open, Shawnee Open, and Philadelphia Open.

John McDermott. *Courtesy U.S.G.A.*

MIDDLECOFF, DR. CARY. Born in Halls, TN, January 6, 1921. Winner of two U.S. Open titles and the biggest money winner in American golf in the fifteen years following World War II. Middlecoff also lost in a play-off for the Open and, in addition, won one Masters and was runner-up twice. Although he had a fine amateur record, Middlecoff did not attract widespread notice until 1945, when he defeated the pros in the North and South Open. At the time he was an officer in the Army Medical Corps, having followed his father into the practice of dentistry. After his discharge, he gained the quarterfinals of the 1946 U.S. Amateur and was named to the Walker Cup Team, but withdrew in order to turn professional. He won one tourney in 1947 and the next year won twice and was runner-up in the Masters. In 1949, he won the Open and five other tournaments, and a new star had emerged. Over the next seven years he won at least one tournament a year—sometimes as many as six—and was never lower than sixth on the money list. Although he drew criticism for his excruciatingly slow play, no one denied Middlecoff's talent. He was a great striker of the ball, was very long off the tee, and did an excellent job around the greens.

Tournament Record: 1937: Winner of Tennessee High School title. 1938, 1939: Winner of Memphis Amateur. 1940: Winner of Tennessee Amateur and West Kentucky Open. 1941: Winner of Tennessee Amateur, West Kentucky Open, and Southeastern Intercollegiate. 1942, 1943: Winner of Tennessee Amateur. 1945: Winner of North and South Open. 1947: Winner of Charlotte Open. 1948: Winner of

Miami Four-Ball and Hawaiian Open; runner-up in Masters. 1949: Winner of U.S. Open, Rio Grande Valley Open, Miami Four-Ball, Reading Open, Jacksonville Open, and Greenbrier Invitational; tied for first in Motor City Open. 1950: Winner of Houston Open, Seminole Pro-Amateur, Jacksonville Open, and St. Louis Open. 1951: Winner of Lakewood Park Open, Colonial Invitational, All-American Open, Eastern Open, St. Louis Open, and Kansas City Open. 1952: Winner of El Paso Open, Motor City Open, St. Paul Open, and Kansas City Open. 1953: Winner of Houston Open, Palm Beach Round Robin, and Carling Open. 1954: Winner of Motor City Open. 1955: Winner of Masters, Bing Crosby Invitational, Western Open, Miller Open, and Cavalcade of Golf. 1956: Winner of U.S. Open, Bing Crosby Invitational, and Phoenix Open. 1957: Winner of Bing Crosby Pro-Am; runner-up in U.S. Open. 1958: Winner of Miller Open. 1959: Winner of St. Petersburg Open; runner-up in Masters. 1961: Winner of Memphis Open.

Cary Middlecoff. *Morgan Fitz*

MILLER, John Laurence. Born in San Francisco, CA, April 29, 1947. Johnny Miller won the USGA Junior in 1964. Two years later he was all set to caddie in the U.S. Open, to be held at the course he'd grown up on, the Olympic Club. The last minute withdrawal of one of the players gave him a place in the field. He tied for eighth and wound up as low amateur at the age of nineteen. In 1969, he graduated from Brigham Young University, where he played varsity golf. He immediately turned professional.

By 1970, Miller had risen to fortieth on the money list, and the next year he won his first tournament, finishing eighteenth on the list. He also came close to winning his first major—the Masters. Miller closed with two 68s, but errors over the last few holes turned his lead of two strokes with four holes to go into a final deficit of two. In 1972, he won another tournament and finished seventeenth on the money list.

In the 1973 U.S. Open at Oakmont, Miller had begun well with 71 and 69. Then he shot 76. This left him six strokes behind the leaders, Arnold Palmer, Julius Boros, John Schlee, and Jerry Heard. Miller started his final round with four birdies, and suddenly he was back in the picture. He did bogey one hole, but continued to fire his irons at the stick, making five more birdies. He finished with a 63 for 279 to win by one stroke over Schlee.

Johnny Miller.

Suddenly, Miller was a superstar and polished this image still further when he provided the only real competition to Tom Weiskopf in the British Open at Troon. Miller finished second. He also won the World Cup individual and team (with Jack Nicklaus). However, at this point in his career Miller still had to prove he was more than just a golfer on a hot streak.

Miller provided the answer in 1974 in dramatic fashion. He started the year by winning the first three events on the PGA Tour. Having won the Crosby, Miller fired 69, 69, 66, 67 at Phoenix, and at Tucson, a 7,305 yard track, he began his victory march with a 62. Although he did not win the next tournament, he did post a sequence of twenty-three rounds of par or better. Miller went on to win the Heritage and Tournament of Champions, which meant that after eleven tournaments, he had been victorious in five. Later, he won Westchester with 69, 68, 65, 67. The 65 was the outstanding round of the year—Miller hit every green in one or two strokes and only missed one fairway. In September, he won in a play-off at the World Open (his total score included a 63), then at the end of the month, he won the Kaiser by eight strokes. Miller finished the year by winning the Dunlop Masters (Japan) by seven strokes.

Suddenly, Miller's play put him on a higher level than any golfer other than Jack Nicklaus. Miller's eight Tour victories set a then record for money winnings of $353,021, and he was PGA Player of the Year. Since 1974, no one has won as many events in one season—the closest was Tom Watson's six victories in 1980.

Miller started the 1975 season even better. At Phoenix, he won with a 24-under par score of 67, 61,

68, 64—260. His winning margin, fourteen strokes, has only been bettered once, by Bobby Locke's sixteen strokes in 1948. At Tucson, Miller posted 66, 69, 67, 61—263, nine strokes ahead of the field. In the Masters, his final rounds of 66 and 66 brought him from ten strokes to one behind the winner, Nicklaus. He also won the Bob Hope Desert Classic, repeated in the Kaiser and finished third in the British Open. He again won the World Cup individual and team championship (with Lou Graham).

In 1976, he won Tucson for the third time in a row and repeated in the Bob Hope Desert Classic. By this time Miller was known as the "Desert Fox." However, the highlight of the year was his victory in the British Open at Birkdale. Miller caught and passed Seve Ballesteros with a final-round 66 to win by six strokes.

However, 1976 saw the start of the most unfortunate, and best-publicized, slump ever to befall a player of Miller's stature. From second on the PGA Tour money list in 1975, Miller slipped to fourteenth. From there he plunged to 48th in 1977 and 111th in 1978.

For the beleaguered Miller, 1979 brought a slight improvement—to seventy-sixth on the list. He showed a flash of his old form in shooting a final-round 63 in the Hall of Fame Classic to tie Tom Watson, but lost the play-off, and at the end of the year, he won the Lancôme Trophy (France). Back in the United States for the 1980 season, Miller finished high in several events, then won the Inverrary in March. His recovery continued in 1981, with two wins and twelfth place in money. He also won the 1981 $1 million Sun City Challenge, defeating Seve Ballesteros in a nine-hole play-off. In 1982 and 1983, he continued the string with one victory each year, but then hit a dry spot before his latest win, in the 1987 AT&T Pebble Beach Pro-Am. A leg ailment forced Miller into part-time status in 1988, and by 1990 he was off the Tour for good.

Miller was a member of the 1975 and 1981 Ryder Cup teams.

At his best, Miller was known as one of the finest medium and short iron players of all time, hitting the ball so close to the pin with these clubs that his peers could only shake their heads in wonder at his performance.

Tournament Record: 1964: Winner of U.S. Junior Championship. 1971: Winner of Southern Open.

1972: Winner of Heritage Classic and Otago Classic (New Zealand). 1973: Winner of U.S. Open, Lancome Trophy (France), and World Cup individual and team (with Jack Nicklaus). 1974: Winner of Bing Crosby National Pro-Am, Phoenix Open, Tucson Open, Heritage Classic, Tournament of Champions, Westchester Classic, World Open, Kaiser International, and Dunlop Phoenix (Japan). 1975: Winner of Phoenix Open, Tucson Open, Bob Hope Desert Classic, Kaiser International, World Cup individual and team (with Lou Graham). 1976: Winner of Tucson Open, Bob Hope Desert Classic, and British Open. 1979: Winner of Lancome Trophy (France). 1980: Winner of Inverrary Classic. 1981: Winner of Tucson Open, Los Angeles Open, and Sun City Million-Dollar Challenge (South Africa). 1982: Winner of San Diego Open. 1983: Winner of Inverrary Classic and Chrysler Team Invitational (with Jack Nicklaus). 1984: Winner of Spalding Invitational. 1987: Winner of AT&T Pebble Beach Pro-Am.

MORRIS, THOMAS (OLD TOM). Born in St. Andrews, Scotland, June 26, 1821. Died May 27, 1908. A leading figure in Scottish golf for more than half a century and the first four-time winner of the British Open. Morris was apprenticed at the age of eighteen to Allan Robertson, the leading player of the day, in the ball-making trade. He was employed at Prestwick from 1851 to 1865, then returned to St. Andrews as greenskeeper, a post he held until 1904. Morris teamed with Robertson to win many great matches, and later he and his son, Tom, Jr., were virtually invincible. At his death, Morris was possibly the most revered man in the game. His British Open victories came in 1861, 1862, 1864, and 1867.

MORRIS, THOMAS, JR. (YOUNG TOM). Born in St. Andrews, Scotland, in 1850. Died December 25, 1875. The greatest player in the early recorded history of the game. Young Tom was a championship player at the age of sixteen, and by the time he was eighteen he won the first of his four British Open titles, all of which came in succession. By winning in 1868, 1869, and 1870, he gained permanent possession of the championship belt. The tournament was then held in abeyance for a year, and when the present cup was put up for competition in 1872, Morris won again. He and his father formed a formidable combination on the links, and it was during their match with Willie and Mungo Park that Young Tom re-

Old and Young Tom Morris. *Courtesy U.S.G.A.*

ceived news of the sudden death of his wife. He never recovered from the shock and died a few months later, at the age of twenty-five.

NELSON, JOHN BYRON, JR. Born in Fort Worth, TX, February 4, 1912. One of the greatest players in the history of golf, a man whose true greatness can never accurately be gauged because of the circumstances that prevailed when he was at his peak. Nelson proved his ability by winning the U.S. Open, the Masters, two PGA Championships and finishing second in two other PGAs between 1937 and 1942. But it was in 1944 and 1945, with most of the top players off to war (Nelson had been rejected because of a blood disorder), that he really hit his stride. In 1944 he won seven tournaments, was the leading money winner, averaged 69.67 strokes for 85 rounds, and was voted athlete of the year. Even that record paled before his performance in 1945, when he won nineteen tournaments (eleven in succession), was leading money winner, averaged an incredible 68.33 strokes for 120 rounds, and again was named athlete of the year. By the end of that span he had finished in the money in 113 consecutive tournaments and, at Seattle in 1945, had tied an 18-hole record of 259. During those years—and since—the argument raged: was he the greatest player who ever lived or were his records to be discounted because he set them when there was no competition?

At any rate, Nelson retired during the 1946 season because, like Bobby Jones before him, he was simply worn out from the strain of constant competition; it was getting to be too much of an effort to gear up emotionally to meet the challenge week after week.

Tournament Record: 1930: Winner of Southwest Amateur. 1935: Winner of New Jersey Open. 1936: Winner of Metropolitan Open. 1937: Winner of Masters, Belmont Open, Thomasville Open, and Central Pennsylvania Open. 1938: Winner of Thomasville Open and Hollywood Open. 1939: Winner of U.S. Open, Western Open, North and South Open, Phoenix Open, and Massachusetts Open; runner-up in PGA Championship. 1940: Winner of PGA Championship, Texas Open, Miami Open, and Ohio Open. 1941: Winner of Miami Open, Greensboro Open, Ohio Open, All-American Open, and Seminole Pro-Amateur; runner-up in PGA Championship and Masters. 1942: Winner of Masters, All-American Open, Oakland Open, Ohio Open, and Charles River Invita-

Byron Nelson.

tional. 1943: Winner of Kentucky Open. 1944: Winner of All-American Open, San Francisco Open, Knoxville Open, Red Cross Open, Golden Valley Open, Beverly Hills Open, and Nashville Open; runner-up in PGA Championship. 1945: Winner of PGA Championship, Canadian Open, Canadian PGA, All-American Open, San Antonio Open, Phoenix Open, Corpus Christi Open, New Orleans Open, Miami Four-Ball, Charlotte Open, Greensboro Open, Durham Open, Atlanta Open, Philadelphia *Inquirer* Open, Spring Lake Invitational, Chicago Victory Open, Knoxville Open, Esmeralda Open, Spokane Open, Seattle Open, and Fort Worth Open. 1946: Winner of Los Angeles Open, San Francisco Open, New Orleans Open, Houston Invitational, Columbus Invitational and Chicago Victory Open; tied for second in U.S. Open. 1947: Tied for second in Masters. 1948: Winner of Texas PGA. 1951: Winner of Bing Crosby Invitational. 1955: Winner of French Open.

NELSON, LARRY GENE. Born in Ft. Payne, AL, September 10, 1947. Unlike practically all great golfers, Nelson did not take up golf until he was an adult. He had been a good athlete in high school, lettering in baseball and basketball. He attended Southern Tech for a year before he was drafted and served two years in the military. After his discharge, he attended Kennesaw Junior College in Georgia, from which he graduated in 1970. He also worked as an illustrator at the Lockheed plant near his home.

It was not until 1969 that Nelson went to a driving range one day. He liked hitting balls so much, he went to work in pro Bert Seagraves' shop at the Pine Tree Club in Kennesaw. Seagrave and Ben Hogan's book *The Modern Fundamentals of Golf* were his sole teachers. They did their job well. Nelson tried the mini-tours briefly, and in 1972, finished bogey–bogey to lose the Florida State Open by a shot. This was his sole 72-hole event before he earned his PGA Tour playing card that fall.

Nelson climbed steadily up the Tour's ladder, rising from ninety-third on the money list in 1974 to sixty-sixth in 1975, forty-first in 1976, and twenty-sixth in 1977, all without winning a tournament. In 1977, however, he had shown promise of good things to come, with three ties for second at San Diego, Greensboro, and Hartford, and a third-place finish at Phoenix.

After falling back a little the next year, Nelson broke through in 1979. His first win came in the

Larry Nelson. *Andy Sharp*

In 1983, Nelson was not having a good year heading into the U.S. Open at Oakmont. For the first two rounds, he stayed in the background, shooting 75, 73, to put him seven strokes off the pace. Then, he shot a six-under par 65, good enough to pull him up to within one stroke of the leaders, Tom Watson and Seve Ballesteros. During the rain-interrupted final round, the battle was between Nelson and Watson. Play was halted late in the afternoon, with Nelson on the 16th tee, and Watson on the 15th green. The next morning, Nelson hit a 4-wood to the back level of the green on the 226-yard hole, a little over thirty yards from the cup. Nelson hoped he wouldn't three-putt, but instead made the putt for a birdie and went on to win by one stroke over Watson. His 10-under par effort on the last two rounds set a U.S. Open record.

1987 proved to be Nelson's best year financially; he earned $501,292, fourteenth on the money list. He also added a third major and made his third appearance in the Ryder Cup. At the PGA Championship at the PGA National in Palm Beach Gardens, Florida, Nelson was hardly the favorite. At the age of thirty-nine, he had gone through some injuries, and he had spent a lot of time off the Tour, much of it on his course architecture business. He also hadn't been playing very well, and had only earned a little over $53,000, 101st on the money list, when the championship started on August 6. Conditions—severe heat and humidity—also didn't favor an older man. However, Nelson, always known for his patience and mental toughness, shot steady golf—70, 72, 73, 72, 287, one under par—to tie Lanny Wadkins. It was a short play-off. Nelson holed his putt from six feet for a par. Wadkins missed from four feet, and that was that.

With his simple, rhythmic swing, Nelson's forte is a drive straight down the middle (he ranked fifth in driving accuracy in the PGA Tour's cumulative statistical rankings from 1980–1991).

Inverrary. He also won the Western Open, finished fourth in the U.S. Open and tied for second in the World Series. All told, he had nine Top 10 finishes and was second leading money winner. In Ryder Cup team play, Nelson helped to gain five points for the U.S.

To date, Nelson's finest moments have come in 1981, 1983, and 1987.

In 1981, he trailed Mark Hayes by two strokes coming to the 72nd hole of the Greensboro Open. Hayes was on the back of the green in two, Nelson in so bad a lie in a bunker that he doubted he could even get the ball onto the green. He holed it to go into a play-off, which he won on the second extra hole. At the PGA Championship at the Atlanta Athletic Club, before a hometown crowd that included many of his friends, he shot 70, 66, 66, 71—273 to win at a canter (by four shots). In the Ryder Cup play, he piled up another four points for the U.S. team.

Tournament Record: 1979: Winner of Inverrary Classic and Western Open. 1980: Winner of Atlanta Classic and Tokai Classic (Japan). 1981: Winner of Greater Greensboro Open and PGA Championship. 1983: Winner of U.S. Open and Dunlop International (Japan). 1984: Winner of Walt Disney World Golf Classic. 1987: Winner of PGA Championship and Walt Disney World–Oldsmobile Classic. 1988: Winner of Georgia Pacific–Atlanta Classic.

NICHOLS, ROBERT HERMAN. Born in Louisville, KY, April 14, 1936. Bobby Nichols got into golf as a caddie at the age of nine. When at St. Xavier High School, he was a promising football and basketball star as well as a fine golfer. On September 23, 1952, a car in which he and several other boys were riding failed to make a curve while traveling at 107 m.p.h. Sustaining a concussion, broken pelvis, back injury, and internal injuries, he lay unconscious for thirteen days and was hospitalized for three months. Despite these injuries, Nichols was soon able to play golf again, although his football and basketball days were over. However, while winning state high school and junior titles he met Bear Bryant, then the football coach of the University of Kentucky. When Bryant moved on to Texas A. and M., he arranged a football scholarship for Nichols, even though he knew Nichols couldn't play for him. In 1956, Nichols returned the favor by winning the Southwest Conference golf title.

After graduating in 1958 with a degree in business, Nichols worked in the oil fields for a few months before serving two years in the Army. When an assistant professional at the Midland Country Club, Nichols' game so impressed some of the club's members that they sponsored him on the Tour. Coming out in 1960, he soon was known as the "Louisville Slugger" for his booming tee shots, his affiliation with Hillerich and Bradsby, and his Louisville background.

From 1960 to 1975, Nichols was never out of the top sixty money winners—eight times he was in the top twenty. He won twelve events. His best year was 1964, when he finished fifth, while taking his sole major, the PGA Championship at the Columbus Country Club (in Ohio).

Nichols's victory really began the Sunday before the championship. During a party at Owl Creek Country Club near his Louisville home, he found a used putter in a barrel in the pro shop. He liked it and plunked down the $5 asking price. It was the best investment he ever made.

In the first round, Nichols shot a championship record 64 to take a three-shot lead. The round included eight birdies, four of the birdie putts being from outside ten feet. He took only thirteen putts on the back nine. In the second round, Nichols fell back a bit to a one-over 71. One behind was Arnold Palmer.

Nichols then shot a 69, for 204, to cling to a one-

shot lead over Palmer. However, without some spectacular recoveries and the $5 putter, the round could easily have been 80 or worse.

In the final round, Palmer pulled even after nine, but Nichols still bore a charmed life. At the second hole, his drive had seemed certain to go out of bounds when it bounced off a tree back into play. At the 526-yard 10th, he got home in two, and sank a thirty-five-footer for an eagle. He holed a fifteen-footer for a birdie at the 15th, a twelve-footer for par at 16, and then the cruncher—a fifty-one-footer at 17. He posted 271 for a three-stroke victory over Palmer and Jack Nicklaus.

In 1975, Nichols survived another disaster. He was struck by lightning at the Western Open, and was taken to hospital with Lee Trevino and Jerry Heard. Although Nichols continued to compete, he never won another Tour event.

Nichols joined the Senior Tour in 1986, and has won one individual event, the 1989 Southwestern Bell Classic.

Tournament Record: 1956: Winner of Southwestern Conference Championship. 1962: Winner of St. Petersburg Open and Houston Classic. 1963: Winner of Seattle Open. 1964: Winner of PGA Championship and Carling World Open. 1965: Winner of Houston Classic. 1966: Winner of Minnesota Golf Classic. 1968: Winner of PGA Team Championship (with George Archer). 1970: Winner of Dow Jones Open. 1973: Winner of Westchester Classic. 1974: Winner of San Diego and Canadian Open. 1986: Winner of The Showdown Classic (with Curt Byrum). 1989: Winner of Southwestern Bell Classic.

NICKLAUS, JACK WILLIAM. Born in Columbus, OH, January 21, 1940. Nicklaus started to play golf at age ten. The first nine holes he ever played, he shot 51. His first golf hero was Bobby Jones, who won the 1926 U.S. Open at Nicklaus's home course at the Scioto Country Club in Columbus. Jones's record of thirteen major championships helped Nicklaus establish his own goal—to win as many majors as he could. When he was thirteen years old, Nicklaus broke 70 for the first time and carried a handicap of three. In 1956, Nicklaus won the Ohio State Open; the next year he won the National Jaycee Junior.

Nicklaus came to the Tour with awesome credentials. His wins included: two U.S. Amateurs (1959, 1961), two Trans-Mississippi's (1958, 1959), the

Jack Nicklaus. *AP/Wide World Photos*

North and South (1959), the Western Amateur (1961) and the NCAA Championship (1961). He also played on two Walker Cup teams (1959, 1961) and was medalist in the World Amateur Team Championship in 1960, shooting 269 at Merion. Against the pros, he finished in forty-first place in the U.S. Open in 1958, was runner-up by only two strokes in 1960, and tied for fourth in 1961. In 1958, he took twelfth place in the Rubber City Open. In 1961, he played in three PGA events, making the cut in each, his highest finish a tie for twenty-third in the Buick Open. He turned pro in November 1961.

On the PGA Tour, Nicklaus has won seventy times, a figure bettered only by Sam Snead, with eighty-one. He has fifty-eight second-place and thirty-six third-place finishes. He shares the record with Arnold Palmer for most consecutive years winning a tourna-

ment at seventeen (1962–1978). During these years, he was always among the top four money-winners, while finishing first eight times. He reached $4 million in prize money won in 1977. He also had the lowest scoring average on the Tour eight times (1964, 1965, 1971, 1972, 1973, 1975, and 1976) and was runner-up six times. He was PGA Player of the Year in 1967, 1972, 1973, 1975, and 1976. He was named "Player of the Century" in *GOLF* Magazine's celebration of the Centennial of Golf in America in 1988.

Around the world, Nicklaus has won eighty-eight times. He also has played on six Ryder Cup teams (1969–1977, 1981) and captained the 1983 and 1987 teams. He was a member of six winning World Cup teams (1963, 1964, 1966, 1967, 1971, and 1973), he won the individual title in 1963, 1964, and 1971. He won the 1970 World Match Play.

Impressive as the above figures are, they pale in comparison to what Nicklaus has achieved in the major championships. At present, his victories total a record twenty, including: six Masters (1963, 1965, 1966, 1972, 1975, and 1986); five PGA Championships (1963, 1971, 1973, 1975, and 1980); four U.S. Opens (1962, 1967, 1972, and 1980), three British Opens (1966, 1970, and 1978); and two U.S. Amateurs (1959 and 1961). Even if later golf historians decide that, say, the amateur championships should not be counted as "majors," Nicklaus's total is not likely to shrink—it might even grow, because Nicklaus has taken three Tournament Players Championships, now known as The Players Championship, in 1974, 1976, and 1978. This tournament could, in the future, be deemed a major. Also, he has won his own Memorial tournament twice (1977 and 1984).

Nicklaus's first victory on the PGA Tour was also a major, the 1962 U.S. Open at Oakmont. This was not a popular win at the time, because Nicklaus tied Arnold Palmer, then and now the "The People's Choice," and won the play-off. In 1963, he won the Masters and PGA. Then, in the 1965 Masters, he gave what Bobby Jones called "the greatest performance in golf history," shooting 67, 71, 64, 69—271, to break Hogan's record of 274. He won by nine strokes, a new record margin of victory. In 1966, he successfully defended his Masters title. He also won his first British Open. The fairways at Muirfield had been narrowed to 25 yards at about 250 yards from the tee. The rough was waist high. So Nicklaus elected to take irons off the tee, and this strategy carried him to victory. He shot 70, 67, 75, 70—282 to win by a stroke over Doug Sanders and David Thomas. He now became one of only four golfers to win all four majors (the other three were Gary Player, Ben Hogan and Gene Sarazen). In the 1967 U.S. Open at Baltusrol, an amateur, Marty Fleckman, led after three rounds with 209, with Nicklaus and Palmer tied at 210. In the final round Nicklaus pulled away with a 65, to win by four strokes from Palmer. Fleckman shot 80. Nicklaus's total of 275 set a new championship record.

At this point Nicklaus's golf slipped a little, by his standards. In 1968, he "only" won two Tour events. In 1969, he had won at San Diego early in the year, but by late summer, with no further victories, the fashionable question was: "What's wrong with Nicklaus?" The answer was, "Nothing." A trimmer Nicklaus returned to the Tour in the fall (down 15 lbs. from a high of around 205 lbs.) and won two tournaments in a row. With his drop in weight, Nicklaus became more fashion-conscious, letting his hair grow and abandoning the baggy trousers of his youth. He also was entering one of his most prolific periods in terms of major wins.

In 1970, he won the British Open at St. Andrews, beating Doug Sanders in a play-off after Sanders had missed a short putt on the 72nd hole for the win. He went on to win seven majors from then until 1975. Especially memorable were his PGA victory of 1973, which put him one ahead of Jones's total of thirteen victories in majors, and the 1975 Masters. The press cited the latter tournament as "the greatest of all time."

Nicklaus got away to a fast start with 68, 67, to lead Tom Weiskopf by 6 and Johnny Miller by 11. Then Nicklaus faltered, scoring 73, while Weiskopf had a 66 to take a one stroke lead and Miller made up eight shots with his 65. On the 16th hole of the last round, Nicklaus holed one of the most critical putts of his life, an uphill forty-footer with a big break. This gave him a one-stroke lead, and he held on to beat Weiskopf by one stroke and Miller by two. It was Nicklaus's fifth Masters.

In 1979, Nicklaus had his worst season to that date on the Tour, failing to win a tournament, and finishing seventy-first on the money list. Again, the soothsayers were nodding wisely and saying the great man was finished.

Nicklaus went back to the drawing board that winter, and worked hard on his short game with Phil Rodgers. At the 1980 U.S. Open at Baltusrol, Nicklaus proved the experts wrong again by opening with a 63, then shooting 71, 70, 68—272, to beat Isao Aoki by two strokes and his own record for the championship by three. A little later, at Oak Hill, he scored 70, 69, 66, 69—274, to win the PGA by seven strokes over Andy Bean.

Nicklaus's latest major exploit was in the 1986 Masters. After the third round, Greg Norman led the field with 210. Fourteen players were within four strokes of Norman, including Nicklaus, at 214. In the last round, Nicklaus played one of his greatest rounds, shooting 65 for a total of 279. In the end, Tom Kite had a twenty-foot birdie putt for a tie on the 72nd green and missed. Norman only needed a par, but after a great drive, he made a poor swing on his 4-iron approach, pushing the ball twenty yards to the right of the green. From there he failed to get up and down. And Nicklaus had won his sixth Masters at the age of forty-six.

What is it that makes Nicklaus so great a player? His main strengths are long, straight driving, exceptional long and medium irons, and great clutch putting. In his twenties, Nicklaus was awesome off the tee. Often his length was enough to overpower most courses, leaving him with only a short shot into most par-4's and an easy iron into many par-5's. After he slimmed down, he did lose a few yards off the tee. However, as late as 1980, he still remained a long, accurate hitter compared with others on the PGA Tour. That year he ranked tenth in driving distance (averaging 269 yards), thirteenth in driving accuracy and led the Tour in hitting greens in regulation. In the five years from 1980 to 1985, he was second in greens hit and had the seventh best scoring average. His sole Achilles heel used to be his short game and wedge play, but that improved dramatically after the sessions with Rodgers. However, more important than any technique or skill are Nicklaus's desire and concentration. The player mentioned most frequently as being his equal in these departments is Ben Hogan. That's the highest possible praise.

Nicklaus became eligible for the Senior Tour in 1990, but he continued playing the majors and a few other regular Tour events, finishing sixth at age fifty in the 1990 Masters. In his first two years of eligibility, he won five of the nine Senior tournaments he entered.

Tournament Record: 1953: Winner of Ohio State Junior (13–15 Division), and Columbus Junior Match Play Championship. 1954: Winner of Columbus Junior Match Play and Stroke Play Championships. 1955: Winner of Columbus Junior Match Play and Stroke Play Championships, Ohio Jaycees, and Columbus District Amateur Championship. 1956: Winner of Ohio State Open, Ohio State Junior Championship, and Ohio Jaycees. 1957: Winner of National Jaycee Junior, Central Ohio High School District Championship, Ohio High Schools State Championship, and Ohio Jaycees. 1958: Winner of Trans-Mississippi Amateur and Queen City Open. 1959: Winner of U.S. Amateur, Trans-Mississippi Amateur, North and South Amateur, and Royal St. George's Challenge Vase (England). 1960: Winner of International Four-Ball (with Deane Beman) and Colonial Invitational Amateur. 1961: Winner of U.S. Amateur, Western Amateur, and NCAA Championship. 1962: Winner of U.S. Open, World Series, Seattle World's Fair, and Portland Open. 1963: Winner of World Series of Golf, Masters, PGA Championship, Sahara Invitational, Palm Springs Classic, and Tournament of Champions. 1964: Winner of Phoenix Open, Portland Open, Whitemarsh Open, Tournament of Champions, and Australian Open. 1965: Winner of Masters, Portland Open, Memphis Open, Thunderbird Classic, and Philadelphia Classic. 1966: Winner of Masters, British Open, Sahara Invitational, and PGA National Team Championship (with Arnold Palmer). 1967: Winner of U.S. Open, Bing Crosby, Western Open, Sahara Invitational, World Series of Golf, and Westchester Classic. 1968: Winner of Western Open, Australian Open, and American Golf Classic. 1969: Winner of San Diego Open, Sahara Invitational, and Kaiser International Open. 1970: Winner of Byron Nelson Classic, British Open, Piccadilly World Match Play Championship, World Series of Golf, and National Four-Ball Championship (with Arnold Palmer). 1971: Winner of PGA Championship, Tournament of Champions, Byron Nelson Classic, Walt Disney World Open, National Team Championship (with Arnold Palmer), Australian Dunlop, and Australian Open. 1972: Winner of Bing Crosby, Doral–Eastern Open, Masters, U.S. Open, Westchester Classic, U.S. Professional Match Play Championship, and Walt Disney World Open. 1973: Winner of Bing Crosby, New Orleans Open, Tournament of Champions, Atlanta Classic, PGA Championship, Ohio Kings Island Open, and Walt Disney. 1974: Winner of Hawaiian Open, and Tournament Players Championship. 1975: Winner of Doral–Eastern Open, Heritage Classic, Masters, PGA Championship, World Open, and Australian Open. 1976: Winner of Tournament

Players Championship, World Series of Golf, and Australian Open. 1977: Winner of Inverrary Classic, Tournament of Champions, and Memorial Tournament. 1978: Winner of Inverrary Classic, Tournament Players Championship, British Open, Philadelphia Classic, and Australian Open. 1980: Winner of U.S. Open, and PGA Championship. 1982: Winner of Colonial National Invitation. 1983: Winner of Chrysler Team Invitational (with Johnny Miller). 1984: Winner of Memorial. 1986: Winner of Masters. 1990: Winner of Tradition at Desert Mountain and Mazda Senior TPC. 1991: Winner of Tradition at Desert Mountain, PGA Seniors Championship, and U.S. Senior Open.

NORMAN, GREG. Born in Queensland, Australia, February 10, 1955. Norman never played golf until he was 16. Then, one day, he caddied for his mother, a three-handicapper. When she finished her round, he borrowed her clubs and played a few holes on his own. In two years, Norman went from a 27 handicap to scratch. His mother bought him two golf books

Greg Norman.
Fred Vuich

written by Jack Nicklaus—*Golf My Way* and *My 55 Ways to Lower Your Golf Score.* "I didn't try to copy Jack," says Greg, "but just learn the basics." Like Nicklaus, Norman learned to hit hard first, then learned to straighten it out.

He turned professional in 1976, and won in only his fourth start as a pro, in the West Lakes Classic in Australia. He had a 10-stroke lead after three rounds. Later the same year, he was chosen to play for Australia in the World Cup.

In 1977, he came to Europe, and won one event, the Martini, at Wentworth, England. He finished twentieth in the Order of Merit. That year marked his first U.S. appearance, in the Memorial; he missed the cut. In 1978, he did not win in Europe, but moved up to fifteenth in the Order of Merit. He won in Fiji, as well as in the New South Wales Open. He was first in the Australian Order of Merit that year. In 1980, he started showing the electrical bursts of low scoring for which he's now famed. In the French Open, he fired 67, 66, 68, 67, winning by 10 strokes. Then, in the Scandinavian Enterprise Open, he began with a 76, but won with 66, 70, 64. In the World Match Play, at Wentworth, England, he defeated Nick Faldo, Bernard Gallacher, then Sandy Lyle for the title. Lyle was leading money winner in Europe that year, with Norman second. Then Norman went home and annexed his most important title to date, the Australian Open. It was there that he earned the nickname "The Great White Shark" because of his shark-hunting stories.

In 1980, he was again first in the Australian Order of Merit. In Europe, he won twice and finished fourth in the Order of Merit. He also won the Australian Masters. In 1982, he won three events and was Europe's leading money winner with £66,405.

In 1983, he devoted more time to golf in the U.S., competing in nine events, and finishing in the top ten in each of them. His best finish was in his first tournament, the Bay Hill Classic, where he came from six strokes off the pace on the final day to tie Mike Nicolette, but lost the play-off on the first hole. Worldwide he had a fabulous year, winning seven events.

In 1984, after a so-so start, he went on a tear. He took the Kemper Open easily, leading by seven strokes after three rounds, and winning by five. At the U.S. Open at Winged Foot, he shot 70, 68, 69, 69 to tie Fuzzy Zoeller, but lost the play-off, 67 to 75. After a tie for tenth at Atlanta, Norman won the Canadian Open in a tense duel with Nicklaus. Then in the Western Open, he lost in another play-off to Tom Watson. He finished the year ninth on the money list, with $310,230. In Australia, he won their Masters and the Victoria Open.

Norman competed in sixteen events on the PGA Tour in 1985, but didn't win any of them. His best finishes were seconds in the Canadian Open and Bank of Boston Classic.

However, in 1986, Norman had an incredible record, leading all four majors going into the final round, and winning his first major, the British Open. In the Masters, Norman led by a stroke after three rounds with 210, but took three to get down on the last hole and so lost to Nicklaus. At the U.S. Open at Shinnecock Hills, Norman led the field by one stroke with 210, then fell away with a 75 to finish 12th. Then in the British Open, at the Ailsa course in Turnberry, Scotland, Norman was again out in front by a stroke after three rounds. This time, he hung on with a 69 for 280 and his first major win. Then, at the PGA Championship at the Inverness Club, in Toledo, Ohio, Norman led Bob Tway by four strokes after three rounds, but lost when Tway holed a bunker shot on the last hole.

Norman also won two PGA Tour events in 1986 and ended the year as the leading money winner with $653,296. Norman was also victorious in the European Open and Suntory World Match Play and then went on to win three in a row in Australia.

After all that success, 1987 had to be a disappointment for Norman. He didn't win on the PGA Tour, losing the Masters in a play-off when Larry Mize holed an incredible forty-yard pitch-and-run on the 11th hole. At home, however, he did win the Australian Masters and Australian Open.

In 1988, Norman was back in the winner's circle on the PGA Tour, winning the MCI Heritage Classic, but lost two tournaments in play-offs. He also injured his wrist in the second round of the U.S. Open when his club struck a boulder on the 9th hole at The Country Club in Brookline, Massachusetts. The injury put him out of action for nearly two months.

Norman won two PGA Tour events in 1989 and two more in 1990, playing with such consistency that he won the Vardon Trophy for low scoring average in each year. He also led the money list in 1990 with $1,165,477, despite suffering the disappointment of losing two more tournaments by one stroke when opponents holed shots from off the green on the 72nd hole—Robert Gamez at the Nestle Invitational and David Frost at the USF&G Classic.

Despite his impressive totals of money earnings and international titles, and the strong following he has gained because of his charisma and all-out style of play, Norman has fallen short of greatness in one crucial area—the major championships. Through 1992, he had only one major title to show for his many chances in the big ones, and had lost play-offs in the Masters, U.S. Open, and British Open. Still, no player had a greater impact on the game in the 1980s.

Tournament Record: 1976: Winner of West Lakes Classic. 1977: Winner of Martini International. 1978: Winner of New South Wales Open and Fiji Open. 1979: Winner of Martini International and Hong Kong Open. 1980: Winner of French Open, Scandinavian Enterprise Open, World Match Play, and Australian Open. 1981: Winner of Martini International, Dunlop Masters, and Australian Masters. 1982: Winner of Dunlop Masters, State Express Classic, and Benson & Hedges International Open. 1983: Winner of Kapalua International, Australian Masters, Queensland Open, New South Wales Open, Cannes (France) Invitational, Hong Kong Open, and World Match Play. 1984: Winner of Kemper Open, Canadian Open, Australian Masters, and Victoria Open. 1985: Winner of Dunhill Cup (with David Graham and Graham Marsh). 1986: Winner of Panasonic Las Vegas Invitational, Kemper Open, British Open, European Open, World Match Play, Dunhill Cup (with Rodger Davis and David Graham), Queensland Open, New South Wales Open, South Australian Open, and West Australian Open. 1987: Winner of Australian Masters and Australian Open. 1988: Winner of MCI Heritage Classic. 1989: Winner of The International and Greater Milwaukee Open. 1990: Winner of Doral Ryder Open and The Memorial. 1992: Winner of Canadian Open.

NORTH, ANDREW STEWART. Born in Thorp, WI, March 9, 1950. Andy North got into golf in an unusual way, through illness. When in the seventh grade in Madison, a bone in his knee had stopped growing and was disintegrating. He was on crutches for 18 months. During that period, he was told that he had to give up his favorite sports—basketball and football. He was allowed, however, to play golf if he used a golf cart. Andy's father was a low-handicap

Andy North. *Fred Vuich*

golfer, and Andy progressed quickly. Later, he did return to basketball, and was all-state as a high school senior, but by then golf was his main game.

North won the Wisconsin high school championship in 1966 and 1967, lost in the final of the U.S. Junior in 1967, and won the State Amateur in 1969. He took second place in the Wisconsin Open in 1968 and 1969. While at the University of Florida, he was chosen All-American in 1970, 1971, and 1972, and won the 1971 Western Amateur.

Joining the Tour in 1973, North made the top sixty on the money list in his rookie year. He made a dramatic improvement in earnings when he broke through to win his first Tour event, the 1977 Westchester Classic, and finished eighteenth on the money list that year.

In 1978, North sprang into the limelight by winning the U.S. Open at Cherry Hills Country Club in Denver, Colorado. The first three rounds, North scored 70, 70, 71, good for a one-shot lead. He made his position more secure by establishing a four-stroke margin with five holes to play, but then he frittered away most of his lead. He ended up sinking a four-foot bogey putt on the final hole to win by one stroke.

North was not to win again until 1985. Although he earned respectable money through 1982, he sank back into obscurity the next two years, due largely to an elbow injury.

Then he did it again—winning the 1985 U.S. Open at Oakland Hills Country Club in Birmingham, Michigan. For the first three rounds, the leader was Tze-Chung (T.C.) Chen from Taiwan. Meanwhile, North had shot 70, 65, 70, and only trailed by two strokes entering the final round. While Chen struggled to a final-round 77 that included a quadruple bogey eight on the fifth hole, North managed a 74 that was good for a one-stroke victory. An up-and-down for a par from a bunker on the 17th sent North to the last hole with a two-shot lead, and again a closing bogey was good enough.

Then the bottom again fell out of North's game. He hasn't finished among the top 125 money winners since 1985. A knee operation in 1987 was a contributing factor to his lack of success.

Tournament Record: 1966: Winner of Wisconsin High School Championship. 1967: Winner of Wisconsin High School Championship. 1969: Winner of Wisconsin Amateur Championship. 1971: Winner of Western Amateur Championship. 1972: Winner of Little Crosby. 1977: Winner of Westchester Classic. 1978: Winner of U.S. Open. 1985: Winner of U.S. Open.

OKAMOTO, AYAKO. Born in Hiroshima, Japan, April 2, 1951. First, Ayako Okamoto conquered Japan. That accomplished, she came to the United States, and established herself as one of the top players on the LPGA Tour. She's claimed sixteen Tour victories

Ayako Okamoto.
Courtesy LPGA

since coming to the U.S. in 1981, including four in 1987, when she was the LPGA Player of the Year.

Okamoto didn't take up golf until she was twenty-three years old. Before that, she was one of the top women's softball pitchers in Japan. In fact, she was so unfamiliar with golf that when she was in Hawaii for a softball tournament at the age of twenty, Okamoto and some of her teammates were chased off a golf course next to their hotel because they were sitting on the green—they didn't know what it was.

Okamoto turned pro just three years after taking up the game and won twenty Japanese LPGA events between 1975 and 1981, including eight in 1981. She came to the U.S. in part to meet the challenge of playing against the world's best and in part to escape the pressures of the superstar status she had attained in Japan.

Okamoto's stature has only increased in Japan since she came to America. In every tournament she is followed by a cadre of Japanese media, and they have had plenty to report.

Since 1982, her first full season in the U.S., Okamoto has failed to win an LPGA event only in 1985, a year she was plagued by a back ailment. She has a fine all-around game, combining surprising power with a deft touch around the greens.

Her first multiple-victory year in the United States was 1984, when she won three times and was third on the money list. She won twice in 1986 and had her best year in 1987 with four victories and $466,034 to lead the money list. In the process, Okamoto became the first foreigner to win LPGA Player of the Year honors. Okamoto had her career best scoring average in 1988 at 70.94 and won three times, though she slipped to sixth in money earnings. She ran her streak to five straight years among the top ten money winners in 1989 and 1990, winning once each year.

The only blemish on Okamoto's career has been her inability to capture a major championship. She's come close many times, including the 1987 U.S. Women's Open, where she lost to Laura Davies in a play-off.

Tournament Record: 1982: Winner of Arizona Copper Classic. 1983: Winner of Rochester International. 1984: Winner of J&B Scotch Pro-Am, Mayflower Classic, and Hitachi Ladies British Open. 1986: Winner of Elizabeth Arden Classic, and Cellular One–Ping Championship. 1987: Winner of Kyocera Inamori Classic, Chrysler-Plymouth Classic,

Jose Maria Olazabal. *Fred Vuich*

Lady Keystone Open, and Nestlé World Championship. 1988: Winner of Orient Leasing Hawaiian Ladies Open, San Diego Inamori Classic, and Greater Washington Open. 1989: Winner of Corning Classic. 1990: Winner of Sara Lee Classic. 1992: Winner of McDonald's Championship.

OLAZABAL, JOSE MARIA. Born in Fuenterrabia, Spain, February 5, 1966. Olazabal, the son of a greenskeeper, grew up next to a golf course. After putting together an impressive amateur record, he joined the European Tour when he was twenty years old, and quickly went about the task of fulfilling his ample promise.

In 1983, at age seventeen, Olazabal won the Spanish and Italian Amateurs and the British Boys' Championship, the next year he won the Spanish and British Amateurs, and in 1985 was the low amateur at the British Open, stamping himself as the hottest prospect from Spain since Seve Ballesteros. He didn't disappoint. Soon after turning pro, he established himself as one of the best players in Europe by winning two tournaments in his rookie year of 1986. He added two more European titles in 1988, two in 1989, three in 1990, and was a key member of the European Ryder Cup team in 1987, 1989, and 1991.

Olazabal, who has always played with maturity, even at an early age, and has no discernible weaknesses in his game, earned respect in the United States with his performance in the 1990 NEC World Series of Golf. He opened with an astounding 61 at Firestone Country Club, Akron, Ohio, and followed with three 67s to win by 12 shots over a strong field.

Tournament Record: 1986: Winner of Ebel European Masters–Swiss Open and Sanyo Open. 1988: Winner of Volvo Belgian Open and German Masters. 1989: Winner of Tenerife Open, KLM Dutch Open, and Visa Taiheiyo Masters. 1990: Winner of Benson & Hedges International, Carrolls Irish Open, Lancome Trophy, and NEC World Series of Golf. 1991: Winner of International, Open Catalonia and Epson Grand Prix of Europe. 1992: Winner of Open de Tenerife and Open Mediterrania.

OUIMET, FRANCIS DESALES. Born in Brookline, MA, May 8, 1893. Died September 2, 1967. America's first real golfing hero, the man who defeated Harry Vardon and Ted Ray in a play-off for the U.S. Open title in

Francis Ouimet. *Courtesy U.S.G.A.*

1913 and thereby removed whatever stigma there might have been against golf being a game for the common man. Ouimet was a former caddie and the son of a man of modest means, and after his stunning victory, Americans no longer regarded golf as a game for the idle rich. Although Ouimet went on to win two U.S. Amateurs and many other tournaments and to build an impeccable reputation at home and abroad, he will always be remembered as the man who stopped the British with the shots heard round the golfing world. Ouimet followed his historic victory by winning the U.S. Amateur in 1914. Then came the war, and then came Bobby Jones, and it was 1931 before he won the Amateur again, although he was a semifinalist many times. Ouimet was player or captain of every team America sent against Britain from 1921 through 1949, with the result that he became a very respected figure overseas. The British showed their opinion of him in 1951 when they made him captain of the Royal and Ancient Golf Club at St. Andrews, the first American to receive the honor.

Tournament Record: 1909: Winner of Boston Interscholastic. 1913: Winner of U.S. Open and Massachusetts Amateur. 1914: Winner of U.S. Amateur, French Amateur, and Massachusetts Amateur. 1915: Winner of Massachusetts Amateur. 1917: Winner of Western Amateur. 1919: Winner of Massachusetts Amateur. 1920: Winner of North and South Amateur; runner-up in U.S. Amateur. 1922: Winner of Massachusetts Amateur and Houston Invitational. 1923: Winner of St. George's Challenge Cup. 1924: Winner of Crump Memorial. 1925: Winner of Massachusetts Amateur and Gold Mashie Tournament. 1927: Winner of Crump Memorial. 1931: Winner of U.S. Amateur. 1932: Winner of Massachusetts Open.

PALMER, ARNOLD DANIEL. Born in Latrobe, PA, September 10, 1929. One of the most dynamic and popular individuals in all the history of sports, a man who almost singlehandedly raised golf to its present level of popularity. From his earliest amateur days, Palmer was a go-for-broke player, and this style, coupled with his great ability, quickly produced victories on the pro tour and attracted fans by the thousands. Other players had hitched up their trousers and knocked in fifty-foot putts, but none had done so quite like Palmer. His emotions were plain to see, after good shots and bad, and his "army" suffered

Arnold Palmer. *UPI/Bettmann*

with him, in person or through the medium of television. His galleries finally became so huge, it was a definite handicap to his playing partners, many of whom felt they had been trampled in the rush. With all this color, Palmer also provided skill. He won four Masters, one U.S. Open, and two British Opens in addition to the U.S. Amateur and dozens more. All this netted him more money than anyone before him made playing golf—over a million dollars by 1968—plus countless more dollars through a variety of businesses set up for him by his friend and manager, Mark McCormack. Much of this activity was grouped under the heading of Arnold Palmer Enterprises and was sold to RCA for several millions of dollars in the mid-1960s. All this did not help his golf game, and it was a virtually unanimous feeling among observers of the sport that his widespread interests left him without enough time to hone his skill. Certainly, as he passed the age of thirty-five, his play became a little less forceful and he ceased making every putt he looked at. Meanwhile, he was flitting about the world in his private jet, attending to business, playing exhibitions, appearing at various functions—and trying to squeeze in some tournament golf when possible. Despite his failure to win a major championship after 1964, his galleries remained the largest on the course and his supporters continued to greet every birdie with a cry of "Charge!" even when he obviously was not in contention. The adulation of his fans was so great that the slightest injury or indisposition became of national concern. There were many who no doubt felt he could walk on water if the situation demanded it, and there had been a time when it seemed he almost could. That was in 1960, when his reputation as a "charger" was established. In the Masters that year he birdied the last two holes to win by a stroke, and in the U.S. Open at Cherry Hills he went out the last round and shot the front nine in 30 strokes, finishing with a 65 for what had seemed an impossible victory. Palmer was voted in 1970 the Associated Press Athlete of the Decade as well as winning the Golfer of the Decade poll.

On the Senior PGA Tour, Palmer won the first official tournament he entered, the 1980 PGA Seniors, by defeating Paul Harney on the first play-off hole. He repeated in 1984. He also won the 1981 U.S.G.A. Senior Open at Oakland Hills Country Club in Birmingham, Michigan, in an 18-hole play-off with Billy Casper and Bob Stone. He ran away with the 1985 Senior Tournament Players Championship, winning by a record 11-stroke margin. This was his second straight title at Cleveland's Canterbury Golf Club.

Palmer's latest victory on the Senior Tour came in the 1988 Crestar Classic.

Tournament Record: 1947: Winner of Western Pennsylvania Amateur. 1953: Winner of Ohio Amateur. 1954: Winner of U.S. Amateur and Ohio Amateur. 1955: Winner of Canadian Open. 1956: Winner of Panama Open, Colombia Open, Insurance City Open, Eastern Open, and San Diego Open. 1957: Winner of Houston Open, Azalea Open, and Rubber City Open. 1958: Winner of St. Petersburg Open, Masters, and Pepsi Open. 1959: Winner of Thunderbird Invitational, Oklahoma City Open, and West

Palm Beach Open. 1960: Winner of Bob Hope Desert Classic, Texas Open, Baton Rouge Open, Pensacola Open, Masters, U.S. Open, Insurance City Open, Mobile Open, and Canada Cup (with Sam Snead). 1961: Winner of San Diego Open, Phoenix Open, Baton Rouge Open, Texas Open, British Open, and Western Open. 1962: Winner of Bob Hope Desert Classic, Phoenix Open, Masters, Texas Open, Tournament of Champions, Colonial National Invitation, British Open, American Golf Classic, and Canada Cup (with Sam Snead). 1963: Winner of Los Angeles Open, Phoenix Open, Pensacola Open, Thunderbird Classic, Cleveland Open, Western Open, Whitemarsh Open, Canada Cup (with Jack Nicklaus), and Australian Wills Masters. 1964: Winner of Masters, Oklahoma City Open, Canada Cup (with Jack Nicklaus), and World Match Play. 1965: Winner of Tournament of Champions. 1966: Winner of Los Angeles Open, Tournament of Champions, Australian Open, Houston Champions International, PGA Team Championship (with Jack Nicklaus), and Canada Cup (with Jack Nicklaus). 1967: Winner of Los Angeles Open, Tucson Open, American Golf Classic, Thunderbird Classic, World Cup (with Jack Nicklaus), World Cup Individual Trophy, and World Match Play. 1968: Winner of Bob Hope Desert Classic and Kemper Open. 1969: Winner of Heritage Classic and Danny Thomas Diplomat Classic. 1970: Winner of PGA Team Championship (with Jack Nicklaus). 1971: Winner of Bob Hope Desert Classic, Citrus Open, Westchester Classic, PGA Team Championship (with Jack Nicklaus), and Lancome Trophy (France). 1973: Winner of Bob Hope Desert Classic. 1975: Winner of Spanish Open and British PGA Championship. 1980: Winner of Canadian PGA Championship and PGA Seniors Championship. 1981: Winner of U.S. Senior Open. 1982: Winner of Marlboro Senior Classic and Denver Post Champions of Golf. 1983: Winner of Boca Grove Senior Classic. 1984: Winner of PGA Seniors Championship, Doug Sanders Celebrity Pro-Am, Senior Tournament Players Championship, and Quadel Classic. 1985: Winner of Senior Tournament Players Championship. 1988: Winner of Crestar Classic.

PALMER, SANDRA JEAN. Born in Fort Worth, TX, March 10, 1941. Palmer started playing golf at age thirteen in Bangor, Maine, where she was a caddie. As an amateur, she was a three-time winner of the West Texas Women's Championship, and was state champion in 1963. While at North Texas State, she was runner-up in the 1961 National Collegiate Championship.

Since turning professional in 1964, Palmer has been a premier player. She enjoyed only modest success until 1968, but from that year until 1977, she was never worse than ninth on the money list. In the twenty years from 1967 through 1986, she has been in the top twenty money winners sixteen times.

Her first victory, the 1970 Japan Women's Open, was unofficial. In 1971, she made a big splash on national television as she holed a sand shot for an eagle on the final hole of the Sealy Classic, then the richest event on the Tour, to beat Donna Caponi. From 1971 to 1977, she won two or more events a year. Her first major came in 1972, when she won the Titleholders Championship. In 1975, she won her second, the U.S. Women's Open at the Atlantic City Country Club in Northfield, N.J. Scoring 295, she finished four strokes ahead of Nancy Lopez (then an amateur), JoAnne Carner, and Sandra Post. Palmer

Sandra Palmer. *UPI/Bettmann*

also won the Colgate–Dinah Shore that year and led the money-winning list with $76,374. In 1973, she was third on the list, with five Tour victories and twenty-three top ten finishes. She has a total of twenty-one LPGA wins to her credit, her last victory coming in the 1986 Mayflower Classic.

Tournament Record: 1960: Winner of West Texas Women's Amateur Championship. 1962: Winner of West Texas Women's Amateur Championship. 1963: Winner of West Texas Women's Amateur Championship and Texas Women's Amateur Championship. 1970: Winner of Japan's Women's Open. 1971: Winner of Sealy Classic and Heritage Open. 1972: Winner of Titleholders Championship and Angelo's Four-Ball. 1973: Winner of Pompano Beach Classic, St. Paul Open, National Jewish Hospital Open, Cameron Park Open, and Angelo's Four-Ball. 1974: Winner of Burdine's Invitational, and Cubic Corporation Classic. 1975: Winner of U.S. Women's Open and Colgate–Dinah Shore Winner's Circle. 1976: Winner of Bloomington Classic, National Jewish Hospital Open, and Jerry Lewis Muscular Distrophy Classic. 1977: Winner of Kathryn Crosby–Honda Classic and Women's International. 1981: Winner of Whirlpool Championship of Deer Creek. 1982: Winner of Boston Five Classic. 1986: Winner of Mayflower Classic.

PATE, JEROME KENDRICK. Born in Macon, GA, September 16, 1953. Jerry Pate took up golf at age six and had a brilliant amateur career. While still in high school, he met up with golf coach Conrad Rehling, and when Rehling went to the University of Alabama, Pate followed. In 1973, he won the International Intercollegiate. The following year, he won the U.S. Amateur as well as the Florida Amateur, Buckeye Intercollegiate, and All-American Sun Bowl. In 1974, he also tied for the lowest individual score, 294, while playing on the winning U.S. team in the World Amateur Team Championship. In 1975, he was runner-up in the NCAA Championship. However, on the 1975 Walker Cup Team, he lost every match in which he played. He also was knocked out in the first round of the British Amateur. He finished the year as medalist in the Tour's Fall qualifying school.

With such credentials, Pate's first full year on the PGA Tour, 1976, was closely watched. It was quite a year. He finished tenth on the money list, set a record for first-year winnings of $153,102, and was chosen

Jerry Pate.
UPI/Bettmann

Rookie of the Year. In addition, he won twice, one a major. In the U.S. Open at the Atlanta Athletic Club, he shot 71, 69, 68, 68 to defeat Tom Weiskopf and Al Geiberger by two strokes. In doing so, he hit the shot of the year. On the 72nd hole, he was faced with a 5-iron shot from rough over water to a tightly placed pin. He left it two feet away. In the Canadian Open, he was no less impressive, closing with a 63 to defeat Jack Nicklaus by four strokes. He then went off to the British Open at Royal Birkdale. However, he did not match Lee Trevino's capture of these three titles in 1971. He produced the highest score of the championship, an 87, in the third round, including an 8 and three 7s on the second nine. However, a later venture to Japan was successful as he won the Pacific Masters. Despite his ups and downs, one thing seemed self-evident: Here was a star of the first magnitude.

Unfortunately, this judgment was proven wrong. Pate did finish in the top eleven of the money list in six of his first seven years on Tour, but came close to winning only one more major. He three-putted the final green of the 1978 PGA Championship to tie Tom Watson and John Mahaffey, but lost the play-off. He had eight wins in those seven years through 1982, but after that his career was ruined by injuries.

Nevertheless, there were bursts of brilliance and highlights of fun along the way. When he won the 1981 Memphis Classic, he celebrated by diving in full golf gear into the large lake to the left of the 18th green. When he won the 1982 Tournament Players Championship, at the Tournament Players Club at Sawgrass, Florida, he did it in dramatic fashion by canning a fifteen-foot putt for a birdie on the treacherous little "island" 17th hole, then birdied 18 by hitting a 5-iron to within two feet of the hole. His total of 280 won it for him by two strokes over Scott Simpson and Brad Bryant. Not content with merely diving into the lake during the presentation ceremonies, he inveigled Tour Commissioner Deane Beman and Pete Dye, the architect of the TPC at Sawgrass, to the edge of the bulkhead, and pushed both of them in. He then joined them with a perfectly executed racing dive. It was one of the rare occasions when the sequel bettered the original.

After that, Pate's game fell on evil times. A severe neck injury in mid-1982 put his career on hold. It wasn't until the spring of 1985 that Dr. Jim Andrews of Columbus, GA, discovered a torn cartilage in his left shoulder. An operation to remove about half of the cartilage was performed in June, and Pate returned to the Tour in October. However, from 1986 to the present, Pate has not finished better than 200th on the money list.

Tournament Record: 1973: Winner of International Intercollegiate. 1974: Winner of U.S. Amateur, Florida Amateur, Buckeye Intercollegiate, and All-American Sun Bowl. 1976: Winner of U.S. Open, Canadian Open, and Pacific Masters (Japan). 1977: Winner of Phoenix Open, Southern Open, and Mixed Team Championship (with Hollis Stacey). 1978: Winner of Southern Open. 1981: Winner of Memphis Classic, Pensacola Open, and Brazil Open. 1982: Winner of Tournament Players Championship and Colombian Open.

PEETE, CALVIN. Born in Detroit, MI, July 18, 1943. Unlike most Tour golfers, Peete did not touch a golf club until he was twenty-three. One of nineteen children, Peete moved from Detroit to a Pahokee, Florida farm when he was ten years old. At twelve, he fell out of a tree, breaking his left elbow in three places. He never was able to straighten his left arm again. At thirteen, he was forced to leave school and pick beans for $5 to $10 a day. Four years later, he took to selling goods to migrant farm workers. The field hands had little chance of getting to the city stores, so Peete would pack clothes, rings, watches, jewelry and anything else he could squeeze into his station wagon. Wherever the workers went, Peete followed. He became known as the "Diamond Man," from a diamond set in one of his front teeth. Peete had friends in Rochester, N.Y., and every year they would invite him to play golf. "I always turned them down," he says. "I thought the game was silly. Who wants to chase a little white ball around under the hot sun?" Then in 1966, rather than wait in the car for his friends to finish their game—it was 95 degrees, and the heat in the car was stifling—Peete decided to join them and was soon hooked on the game. He never had formal lessons, but bought instructional books by Ben Hogan and Sam Snead and taught himself. He began playing regularly, and soon was shooting in the low 80s. Then, he happened to see Jack Nicklaus and Lee Elder in their epic five-hole play-off for the 1968 American Golf Classic on television. When he heard Elder was going to make a "good chunk of money," he decided, "If he can do it, so can I, if I work hard." He turned professional in 1971 and qualified for the Tour at his third attempt in the spring of 1975.

Peete took a while to settle into his new life, only earning about $20,000 in each of his first three sea-

Calvin Peete.
Courtesy PGA

sons. He broke through at the 1979 Greater Milwaukee Open, and compiled an impressive record over the next eight years, when he won twelve PGA events. He earned more than $90,000 every year, and has had four $300,000-plus years (1982, 1983, 1985, and 1986). From tee to green there hasn't been a steadier golfer on Tour. Peete led the Tour's cumulative statistical rankings from 1980 through 1990 in two key categories: In driving accuracy, he hit .815 of all fairways, and hit .704 of all greens in regulation figures. The average on the 1990 Tour in these categories was .654 and .644 respectively. He won the Vardon Trophy in 1984 with a scoring average of 70.56.

The one flaw in his record is that, while he won more Tour events than anyone else from 1982 through 1986, he didn't win any majors. The nearest he came to a major victory was his impressive win in the 1985 Tournament Players Championship. He shot 70, 69, 69, 66—274, 14 under par, to win by three shots over D.A. Weibring.

Yet, when Peete was on a roll, there was an inevitability about his play—and the result—that only a few golfers in the history of the game could match. For example, when he won the 1986 USF&G Classic at New Orleans, his game was almost monotonous in its perfection—his smooth swing propelling the ball unerringly onto the short grass, then onto each green. He finished with a 19-under-par 269, five strokes ahead of the field.

In 1987, Peete suffered from lower back problems, which kept him on the sidelines for much of the year. He ranked no better than eighty-seventh on the money list after that, and essentially quit the Tour in 1991.

Tournament Record: 1979: Winner of Greater Milwaukee Open. 1982: Winner of Greater Milwaukee Open, Anheuser-Busch Classic, B.C. Open, and Pensacola Open. 1983: Winner of Georgia-Pacific Atlanta Classic and Anheuser-Busch Classic. 1984: Winner of Texas Open. 1985: Winner of Phoenix Open and Tournament Players Championship. 1986: Winner of Tournament of Champions and USF&G Classic.

PICARD, HENRY G. Born in Plymouth, MA, November 28, 1907. Winner of the 1938 Masters and 1939 PGA Championship, Picard possessed one of the fin-

Henry Picard. *UPI/Bettmann*

est swings in golf and ranked high among the stars of the 1930s. Picard's first victory of consequence came in the 1934 North and South Open. In 1935 he became professional at Hershey, Pennsylvania, and almost immediately he moved to the fore among the touring pros. That season, labeled "The Chocolate Soldier" by writers after his move to Hershey, he won six tournaments. Although at his peak, Picard began to curtail his tournament play as early as 1940. He made only a few token appearances after World War II and thus was a disappointment to his many followers, who felt he could have stayed at the top for many more years.

Tournament Record: 1925, 1926, 1932, 1933: Winner of Carolina Open and Charleston Open. 1934: Winner of North and South Open. 1935: Winner of Atlanta Open, Agua Caliente Open, Charleston Open, Metropolitan Open, Miami Four-Ball, and Inverness Four-Ball. 1936: Winner of North and South Open, Hershey Open, Miami Four-Ball, and Charleston Open. 1937: Winner of Miami Four-Ball, Hershey Open, Argentine Open, and Charleston Open. 1938: Winner of Masters and Pasadena Open. 1939: Winner of PGA, New Orleans Open, Thomasville Open, Inverness Four-Ball, Scranton Open, and Metropolitan Open. 1941: Winner of New Orleans Open and Harlingen Open. 1945: Winner of Miami Open.

PLAYER, GARY JIM. Born in Johannesburg, South Africa, November 1935. When Gary Player was a few months short of fifteen, his father asked him to come and play golf with him. Player replied, "I don't play golf, Dad, that's a sissy game." However, his father persuaded him, and Player started with three pars before his beginner's luck deserted him. He did get the golf bug, though, and in sixteen months he was a scratch golfer, and had the urge to play professionally.

He turned pro in 1953, and two years later headed for England. En route, he won the first tournament he played in outside South Africa, the Egyptian Match Play. It was a good omen for a man who, over the next thirty years, would log over six million travel miles in his quest for golf titles.

In 1956, he won the British Dunlop title. In 1957, he won his first Australian tournament, the PGA, beating Peter Thomson in the final. In 1958, he won for the first time in the United States at the Kentucky Derby Open. He was now an established international player, a winner on four continents.

His first major championship win came in 1959 in the British Open. After 36 holes at Muirfield, he was eight strokes behind after shooting 75, 71, but then fired 70, 68 to win by two strokes. In many ways, it was typical effort: Player never gives up.

In 1961 he won three PGA events, including his first Masters, and finished the year as leading money winner. The finish at Augusta was especially dramatic. Player was in the right bunker at the last hole, and got up and down. A few minutes later, Arnold Palmer was in the same bunker, needing to get up and down to win, and took four. The next year, Player added his third major, the PGA. Then, in 1965, he won the U.S. Open at Bellerive, after a play-off with Kel Nagle. With this victory, he became one of only three golfers to win all four majors—at the time only Gene Sarazen and Ben Hogan had achieved the feat. Since then, only Jack Nicklaus has added his name to this select list.

In 1965, he also won the World Match Play held at Wentworth, England, for the first time. In the semifinal, he made one of the most incredible comebacks in all of golf's history. Down to Tony Lema by seven

Gary Player. *Fred Vuich*

holes with 17 to play, he squared the match, and won on the first extra hole. He then beat Thomson in the final. He went on to win four more Match Plays (1966, 1968, 1971, and 1973), twice beating Jack Nicklaus in the final.

In 1968, he added another win in the British Open at Carnoustie, after a great battle with Nicklaus in the last round. He edged Nicklaus by two strokes, 289 to 291. In 1972, he took his second PGA at Oakland Hills Country Club in Birmingham, Michigan. Shooting 71, 71, 67, Player took a one-stroke lead into the final round. The 16th hole decided the outcome. Player's 150-yard approach shot was blocked by a tall tree, and had to carry a water hazard fronting the green. He hit a 9-iron to three feet, and made the birdie putt to take a two-stroke that he didn't relinquish. He finished with two pars for 71.

In 1974, he took two majors, the only time he has done it in his career. At the Masters, he was five strokes off the lead after two rounds, but then shot a 66 to get back in contention. With nine holes to play on the final day, some eight golfers had a chance until Player hit his 9-iron approach six inches from the pin on 17. He won by two strokes. At the British Open at Royal Lytham, Player was a wire-to-wire winner, shooting 282 four strokes ahead of Peter Oosterhuis. However, Player did have some adventures in the last round. At the 17th, his 6-iron approach landed in deep rough, and the ball was only found by a marshall sixty seconds short of the five-minute limit. Then at 18, his 5-iron second shot went through the green and finished against the wall of the clubhouse. Player managed a left-handed stroke with his putter to ten feet from the hole. At the end of the year, Player recorded a 59, the lowest score ever in a national championship, en route to winning the Brazilian Open. His card read: Out: 3, 4, 3, 3, 4, 2, 3, 3, 4—29. In: 2, 4, 3, 4, 4, 4, 2, 4, 3—30. With the victory he also reached 100 wins worldwide.

In 1978, he won the Masters for the third time, his ninth major. After three rounds of 72, 72, 69, he was seven strokes behind. After eight holes in the final round, nothing much had changed, and the huge galleries were paying attention to Hubert Green, Tom Watson, and Rod Funseth, one of whom would be the apparent winner. At this point, Player turned to Seve Ballesteros, his playing companion, and said, "These people don't think I can win. I'll show them." And he did, recording seven birdies in the last ten holes to shoot 64 and win by a stroke. Player went on to win the next two events on Tour, the Tournament of Champions and the Houston Open.

After turning fifty in November 1985, Player won the first senior event he played, the Quadel; then in 1986, he won three more events, including his first senior "major," the PGA Seniors. Player has been promoting the idea of senior "majors" ever since. Although there is no "official" senior majors, four tournaments, according to Player, should be given that status: the U.S. Senior Open, PGA Seniors, Senior Tournament Players Championship, and British Senior Open. Player currently has two U.S. Senior Opens, three PGA Seniors, one Senior Tournament Players Championship, and two British Senior Opens.

Tournament Record: 1955: Winner of East Rand Open and Egyptian Match Play. 1956: Winner of East Rand Open, South African Open, Dunlop Tournament, and Ampol Tournament. 1957: Winner of Australian PGA and Coughs Harbour Tournament. 1958: Winner of Natal Open, Kentucky Derby Open, Australian Open, Ampol Tournament, and Coughs Harbour Tournament. 1959: Winner of Transvaal Open, South African PGA, Natal Open, Western Province Open, Dunlop Masters, British Open, and Victoria Open. 1960: Winner of South African Open, South African PGA, Dunlop Masters, Transvaal Open, Natal Open, and Western Province Open. 1961: Winner of Masters, Lucky International Open, Sunshine Open, Yomiuri Open, and Ampol Tournament. 1962: Winner of Transvaal Open, Natal Open, PGA Championship, and Australian Open. 1963: Winner of Sponsored 5000, Transvaal Open, Liquid Air Tournament, Richelieu Grand Prix (Capetown), Richelieu Grand Prix (Johannesburg), Dunlop Masters, San Diego Open, and Australian Open. 1964: Winner of Dunlop Masters, Pensacola Open, and "500" Festival Open. 1965: Winner of South African Open, U.S. Open, World Series of Golf, World Match Play, NTL Challenge Cup, World Cup International Trophy, and Australian Open. 1966: Winner of South African Open, Natal Open, Transvaal Open, and World Match Play. 1967: Winner of Dunlop Masters and South African Open. 1968: Winner of South African Open, Natal Open, Western Province Open, World Series of Golf, British Open, World Match Play, and Australian Wills Masters. 1969: Winner of South African Open, South African PGA, Tournament of Champions, Australian Open, and Australian Wills Masters. 1970: Winner of Greensboro Open, Australian Open, and Dunlop International. 1971: Winner of General Motors Open, Western Province Open, Dunlop Masters, Jacksonville Open, National Airlines Open, and World Match Play. 1972: Winner of Dunlop Masters, South African Open, Western Province Open, Dunlop Masters, PGA Championship, World Series of Golf, New Orleans Open, Japan Airlines Open, and Brazilian Open. 1973: Winner of General Motors Open, Southern Open, and World Match Play. 1974: Winner of Dunlop Masters, Rand International Open, General Motors International Classic, Masters, Memphis Classic, British Open, Ibergolf Tournament, La Manga Tournament, Australian Open, and Brazilian Open. 1975: Winner of South African Open and General Motors Classic. 1976: Winner of Dunlop Masters (75/76), South African Open, Dunlop Masters (76/77), and General Motors Open. 1977: Winner of South African Open, ICL Transvaal, and World Cup

Individual. 1978: Winner of Masters, Tournament of Champions, and Houston Open. 1979: Winner of South African Open, South African PGA, Kronenbrau Masters, and Sun City. 1980: Winner of Trophee Boigny and Chilean Open. 1981: Winner of South African Open and Tooth Gold Coast Classic. 1982: Winner of South African PGA. 1984: Winner of Johnnie Walker Trophy. 1985: Winner of Quadel Seniors Classic. 1986: Winner of PGA Seniors Championship, United Hospital Seniors, and *Denver Post* Champions of Golf. 1987: Winner of Senior Tournament Players Championship, U.S. Senior Open, and Paine Webber World Seniors Invitational. 1988: Winner of PGA Seniors Championship, Aetna Challenge, Southwestern Bell, U.S. Senior Open, British Senior Open, and GTE North Classic. 1989: Winner of GTE North Classic and RJR Championship. 1990: Winner of PGA Seniors Championship. 1991: Winner of Royal Caribbean Classic.

RANKIN, JUDY (TORLUEMKE). Born February 18, 1945, in St. Louis, MO. Rankin started to play golf at the age of six under her father's tutelage, and by the time she was eight, she had won a string of four St. Louis PeeWee titles. At fourteen, she was the youngest ever to win a Missouri State championship. She was low amateur in the 1960 U.S. Open, when she was fifteen, and was a semifinalist in the U.S. Girls'

Judy Rankin. *UPI/Bettmann*

Junior. And she was only seventeen when she joined the professional ranks—one of the youngest ever.

Success didn't come easily as a pro, however. She had six years of waiting for her first tour victory in 1968. And her next one didn't come until 1970. But then she was on her way. She won three that year and went on to a total of twenty-eight in the 1970s. She was also the first woman to exceed more than $100,000 in prize money in one season, achieving this in 1976.

She was one of the smallest players on the women's tour, but one of the most consistent performers. She was named the LPGA's Player of the Year in 1976 and was elected president of LPGA that same year.

Tournament Record: 1968: Winner of Corpus Christi Civitan Open. 1970: Winner of George Washington Classic, Springfield Jaycee Open, and Lincoln-Mercury Open. 1971: Winner of Quality-First Classic. 1972: Winner of Lady Eve Open and Heritage Village Open. 1973: Winner of Raleigh Open, Lady Carling Open, Columbus Open, and GAC Classic. 1974: Winner of Colgate-European Open and Baltimore Classic. 1975: Winner of National Jewish Hospital Open. 1976: Winner of Burdine's Invitational, Colgate–Dinah Shore Winners Circle, Karsten-Ping Open, Babe Zaharias Invitational, Borden Classic, and Colgate-Hong Kong Open. 1977: Winner of Orange Blossom Classic, Bent Tree Classic, Mayflower Classic, Peter Jackson Classic, Colgate-European Open, and LPGA Team Championship (with JoAnne Carner). 1978: Winner of WVI Classic. 1979: Winner of WVI Classic.

RAWLS, ELIZABETH EARLE (BETSY). Born May 4, 1928, in Spartanburg, SC. A four-time winner of the U.S. Women's Open and one of the biggest money winners in the history of the LPGA tour. Betsy did not start playing golf until she was seventeen, but within four years she was good enough to win the Trans-National Amateur and the Texas Women's Amateur. The next year, 1950, she was again winning tournaments and was able to finish second in the U.S. Open as an amateur. In 1951, by now a Phi Beta Kappa graduate in physics from the University of Texas, she turned professional and immediately won the first of her four Open championships. Over the next two decades, Betsy won more than fifty tournaments and accumulated almost a quarter-million dollars in prize money. In July 1975, she retired as an active player and became Tournament Director of

Betsy Rawls. *UPI/Bettmann*

the LPGA Tour. In September 1981, she left the LPGA post to serve as the Executive Director for the McDonald's Championship.

Tournament Record: 1949: Winner of Texas Amateur and Trans-National Amateur. 1950: Winner of Texas Amateur and Broadmoor Invitational. 1951: Winner of U.S. Women's Open, Sacramento Open, and Hollywood Four-Ball. 1952: Winner of Houston Weathervane, Cross-Country Weathervane, Eastern Open, Western Open, Carrollton Open, and Thomasville Open. 1953: Winner of U.S. Women's Open, Sacramento Open, Eastern Open, and Texas Open. 1954: Winner of Tampa Open, St. Louis Open, Texas Open, and Inverness Four-Ball. 1955: Winner of Carollton Open. 1956: Winner of Tampa Open, Peach Blossom Open, and Sarasota Open. 1957: Winner of U.S. Women's Open, Tampa Open, Lake Worth Open, Peach Blossom Open, and Reno Open. 1958: Winner of Tampa Open and St. Petersburg Open.

1959: Winner of LPGA Championship, Lake Worth Open, Royal Crown Open, Babe Zaharias Open, Land of Sky Open, Mt. Prospect Open, Western Open, Waterloo Open, Opie Turner Open, and Triangle Round Robin. 1960: Winner of U.S. Women's Open, Babe Zaharias Open, Cosmopolitan Open, and Asheville Open. 1961: Winner of Cosmopolitan Open and Bill Brannin's Swing Parade. 1962: Winner of J.E. McAuliffe Memorial. 1963: Winner of Sunshine Open. 1964: Winner of Dallas Civitan and Vahalla Open. 1965: Winner of Pensacola Invitational and Waterloo Open. 1968: Winner of Mickey Wright Invitational. 1969: Winner of LPGA Championship. 1970: Winner of Dallas Civitan Open and Cincinnati Open. 1972: Winner of GAC Classic.

RAY, EDWARD (TED). Born in Jersey, England, March 28, 1877. Died July 1970. Ray won the U.S. Open championship at Inverness in 1920, but is best remembered by Americans for the 1913 Open in which he and Harry Vardon were beaten by the then unknown Francis Ouimet. Ray also won the British Open in 1912 and was in the top ten on eleven other occasions. Ray was a big man who wore a large

Allen Robertson. *Bettmann/Hulton*

mustache, always played in a hat instead of the traditional cap, and usually smoked a pipe on the course. He was one of the longest hitters of his day.

Tournament Record: 1899: Winner of Hampshire Amateur–Professional. 1903: Winner of Leeds Challenge Cup. 1906: Winner of Northern Section Tournament. 1910: Winner of Leeds Challenge Cup. 1911: Winner of Leeds Challenge Cup, Cruden Bay Tournament, and Northern Section Tournament; runner-up in French Open. 1912: Winner of British Open and Cramond Brig Tournament; runner-up in Belgian Open and German Open. 1913: Winner of Tooting Bec Cup; runner-up in British Open; tied for second in U.S. Open. 1919, 1922: Winner of Herts Open. 1923: Winner of *Daily Mail* Tournament and Herts Open. 1924: Winner of Herts Open. 1925: Tied for second in British Open. 1928, 1930, 1931, 1933, 1935: Winner of Herts Open.

ROBERTSON, ALLAN. Born in St. Andrews, Scotland, in 1815. Died September 1858. An almost legendary golfer who supposedly was never beaten in an indi-

Ted Ray.
Courtesy U.S.G.A.
Museum

vidual stake match. He was a ball maker by trade, and it was he to whom Tom Morris was apprenticed in 1839. These two titans apparently never faced each other in a significant match, so there is no basis for comparing them. It is recorded, however, that they were never beaten as a team. They seem to have come to the parting of the ways in a dispute over the new gutta-percha ball. Robertson fought the new innovation, seeing it as a threat to his trade in the feather-stuffed ball. Morris chose to adopt the new ball. Robertson died of an attack of jaundice in 1858, just two years before the first British Open. His fame rests on his feat of playing thirty-six holes at St. Andrews in 147 strokes, an incredible score in those days.

ROGERS, WILLIAM CHARLES. Born in Waco, TX, September 10, 1951. Bill Rogers started in the game at age nine and took the conventional road to the Tour by competing for a top golf college, the University of Houston. On the way, he won the 1972 Southern Amateur and 1973 All-American Collegiate Tournament. He was a member of the 1973 Walker Cup team.

Joining the Tour in 1974, he rose to twenty-ninth on the money list by 1977, and in that year won the Pacific Masters in Japan. His first victory on the Tour came in 1978, the Bob Hope Desert Classic, and earned over $100,000 for the year. In 1979, he set a Tour record for the most money earned in a single season by a player without a tournament win, $230,500. However, he did win outside the United States, taking the World Match Play at Wentworth, England. In 1980, he again was without a victory in the United States, but won the Suntory Open in Japan.

His finest year came in 1981. He won the Sea Pines Heritage, then finished joint second in the U.S. Open. He then began to feel he could be a major championship winner, and was persuaded by his good friend Ben Crenshaw to enter the British Open at Royal St. Georges. He opened with a 72, but followed with a 66, which gave him a one-shot lead. A third round of 67, and he enjoyed a five-stroke lead. Then, in the final round, he bogeyed the sixth hole, and double-bogeyed the seventh to see his lead wither to a stroke. He then pulled himself together, birdied three of the next four holes for a 71 and a four-stroke victory. He went on to take the World Series, repeat in Japan in the Suntory Open, win the Texas Open,

then went to Australia to win their Open and the New South Wales Open. Five wins in six events. He finished the year with $315,411 in money on the PGA Tour, good for fifth place on the list.

He was to win one more time in the U.S., the 1983 USF&G Classic, and earned over $100,000 that year and the previous year on the Tour. However, he never again finished among the top 100 money-winners on Tour, and retired in 1989.

Tournament Record: 1972: Winner of Southern Amateur. 1973: Winner of All-American Collegiate Tournament. 1977: Winner of Pacific Masters. 1978: Winner of Bob Hope Desert Classic. 1979: Winner of World Match Play Championship. 1980: Winner of Suntory Open (Japan). 1981: Winner of Sea Pines Heritage, British Open, World Series, Suntory Open, Texas Open, New South Wales Open, and Australian Open. 1983: Winner of USF&G Classic.

RODRIGUEZ, JUAN "CHI CHI." Born in Puerto Rico, October 23, 1935. Chi Chi gravitated to golf as a boy of nine, hitting tin cans with limbs from a guava tree. Later, Ed Dudley was his mentor and coach. Dudley gave him a job as shoeshine boy and then made him caddie-master. At the age of seventeen he led the Puerto Rico Open by six strokes, but faltered to finish a shot behind. He joined the Army to help support his large family when he was nineteen.

He joined the PGA Tour in 1960, but earned less than $11,000 his first three years. Then, in 1963 he won his first tournament, the Denver Open, and finished the year forty-eighth on the money list. After that, he was out of the top sixty money winners only three times up to 1978. His best year was in 1964, when he won two tournaments and finished ninth on the list. He won eight PGA Tour events during his career.

Throughout his career, Chi Chi has always been a showman. When he holed a birdie putt, he would drop his hat over the hole, and play to the crowd by taking bows and walking around the green with his arms raised. He was known as the "Clown Prince of the Tour." However, not all his colleagues liked his behaviour, feeling that his antics could be distracting. Fortunately, they have not quenched Chi Chi's thirst for fun. He still often plays to the crowd by pantomiming a matador wiping off and then sheathing his sword when he holes a birdie putt.

In 1986, his first full year since joining the PGA

Chi Chi Rodriguez. *Fred Vuich*

Senior Tour, Rodriguez won three events—the Senior Tournament Players Championship, the Digital Seniors Classic, and the United Virginia Bank Seniors. He also had six second-place finishes to take second on the money list with $399,172.

In 1987, Rodriguez became the first senior to earn more than $500,000 in one season. He won seven tournaments, including three straight, and four in a row that he entered.

At 5′ 7″ and 130 lbs, Chi Chi is extremely small by Tour standards. However, pound for pound he is still a long hitter, and by enthusiastically hurling his slight frame at the ball he can often hit 300 yards. Rodriguez has one of the best pairs of hands in the golf business—he is a consummate shotmaker and one of the few sand players who is mentioned in the same breath as Gary Player.

Tournament Record: 1963: Winner of Denver Open. 1964: Winner of Lucky International and Western Open. 1967: Winner of Texas Open. 1968:

Winner of Sahara Invitational. 1972: Winner of Byron Nelson Golf Classic. 1973: Winner of Greater Greensboro Open. 1976: Winner of Pepsi Mixed Team Championship (with JoAnn Washam). 1979: Winner of Tallahassee Open. 1986: Winner of Senior Tournament Players Championship, Digital Seniors Classic and United Virginia Bank Seniors. 1987: Winner of General Foods PGA Seniors, Vantage at the Dominion, United Hospitals Senior, Silver Pages Classic, Senior Players Reunion, Digital Seniors Classic, and GTE Northwest Classic, 1988: Winner of Doug Sanders Kingwood Classic and Digital Seniors Classic. 1989: Winner of Crestar Classic. 1990: Winner of Las Vegas Senior Classic, Ameritech Senior Open, and SunWest Bank–Charley Pride Senior Classic. 1991: Winner of GTE West Classic, Vintage ARCO Invitational, Las Vegas Senior Classic, and Murata Senior Reunion.

SANDERS, GEORGE DOUGLAS. Born in Cedartown, GA, July 24, 1933. When Doug Sanders came out on tour, his colleagues teased him by saying his swing was so short, he could tee off in a telephone booth. Sanders learned his unique action, he says, "When I started to play at the Cherokee G&CC in Cedartown, caddies weren't allowed to play, but we used to sneak on the course, and the hole we played had honeysuckle on one side and a creek on the other. I developed a short swing so I wouldn't lose any golf balls." Certainly, that swing served him well. With it, he developed into a most gifted shotmaker, especially noted for his ability to play low "quail high" irons, which made him a fantastic wind player.

As an amateur, Sanders won the 1951 International Jaycee Junior, the 1953 Southeastern Amateur, then the 1955 Mexican, "World," and All-American Championships. In 1956, he became the first amateur to win the Canadian Open, beating Dow Finsterwald in a playoff. He turned pro the same year.

Sanders won nineteen more Tour events between 1958 and 1972. He remained better than twenty-third on the money list from 1959 through 1967, and continued to do well until 1974. His best year was in 1961, when he won five events and finished third on the money list. He also finished seventh in 1962, fourth in 1965 and 1966, and sixth in 1967.

In the majors, Sanders knew only disappointment. He tied for second in the 1959 PGA, for third in 1960 and was third in 1961. In the 1961 U.S. Open, he tied for second, one stroke behind Gene Littler, whom he had led by three strokes going into the final round. Sanders also came close to greatness in the British Open. In 1966, he tied for second behind Jack Nicklaus at Muirfield, and tied for fourth at the same course in 1972. But, the one that really got away was the 1970 British Open at St. Andrews.

Sanders appeared to have the championship in his pocket when he played a great bunker shot at the 17th, known as the Road Hole. The pin was cut so close to the bunker that his explosion had to barely carry the lip to be close. He played the shot like a champion and got his 4, but at the 18th, he missed a four-foot putt for par and was tied by Nicklaus. In the play-off, Sanders played a perfect run-up into 18 and birdied the hole. However, by then Nicklaus had a one-stroke lead, and kept it by holing a birdie putt of his own.

Sanders joined the Senior PGA Tour in 1983, and that year won the World Seniors Invitational. Always known for his colorful outfits, he is one of the few players who has the courage to wear mauve outfits, down to the shoes, and carry it off.

Tournament Record: 1951: Winner of International Jaycee Junior. 1953: Winner of Southeastern Amateur. 1955: Winner of Mexican Championship, "World" Championship, and All-American Championship. 1956: Winner of Canadian Open. 1958: Winner of Western Open. 1959: Winner of Coral Gables Open. 1961: Winner of New Orleans Open, Colonial National Invitation, Hot Springs Open, Eastern Open, and Cajun Classic. 1962: Winner of Pensacola Open, St. Paul Open, and Oklahoma City Open. 1963: Winner of Greensboro Open. 1965: Winner of Pensacola Open and Doral Open. 1966: Winner of Bob Hope Desert Classic, Greensboro Open, and Jacksonville Open. 1967: Winner of Doral Open. 1970: Winner of Bahama Islands Open. 1972: Winner of Kemper Open. 1983: Winner of World Seniors Invitational.

SARAZEN (SARACENI), GENE. Born in Harrison, NY, February 27, 1902. One of America's greatest players during the 1920s and 1930s, and a man who went from grade school dropout to world renown during his more than fifty years in the game. Sarazen was one of four men to win the four major titles open to professionals, and his record shows two U.S. Opens, three PGA Championships, a Masters, and a British Open in addition to membership on six Ryder Cup Teams and victory in dozens of lesser tournaments. Sarazen was a brash young man who had plenty of

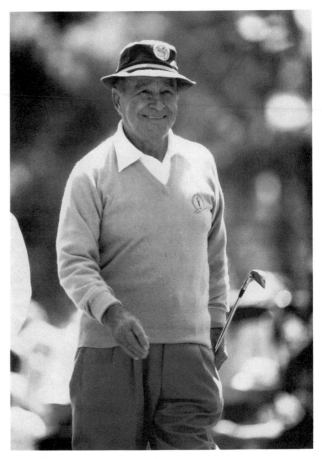

Gene Sarazen. *Leonard Kamsler*

confidence—and the skill to back it up. He won the U.S. Open when he was only twenty, and a year later he defeated the mighty Hagen in the final of the PGA. Only a few years earlier he had been forced to leave school to help support the family and had turned to caddying. He and Ed Sullivan were among the caddies at Apawamis in 1913 when Francis Ouimet beat the British and became the idol of all youngsters. Sarazen later became known as much for his longevity as for his skill, because he was still playing in all four major championships decades after his contemporaries had passed from the scene. Then he moved into a new career as television commentator on Shell's "Wonderful World of Golf," which led him to remark that more people saw him in one hour on television than watched him play in all his decades as a tournament player.

Sarazen was something of a come-from-behind player, and some of his feats will be remembered as long as the game is played. In 1922 he closed with a 68 to win the U.S. Open. In 1932 he played the last twenty-eight holes in 100 strokes to come from no-where and win the Open again. In 1935 he made his famed double-eagle in the Masters to make up a three-shot deficit on Craig Wood, whom he defeated in a play-off the next day. Sarazen also was an idea man, who was always good copy for writers. His best idea was the sand wedge, which he produced after a series of experiments in his Florida garage around 1930. Such is the popularity of the wedge today that Sarazen could well consider its invention as his most notable achievement.

Tournament Record: 1922: Winner of U.S. Open, PGA Championship, and New Orleans Open. 1923: Winner of PGA Championship, and North of England Professional. 1925: Winner of Metropolitan Open. 1927: Winner of Metropolitan PGA, Long Island Open, Miami Open, and Miami Beach Open. 1928: Winner of Miami Open, Miami Four-Ball, Metropolitan PGA, Miami Beach Open, and Bahamas Open; runner-up in British Open. 1929: Winner of Miami Open, Agua Caliente Open, Miami Beach Open, and Sands Point Invitational. 1930: Winner of Western Open, Miami Open, and Middle Atlantic Open; runner-up in PGA Championship. 1931: Winner of Florida West Coast Open, New Orleans Open, and Lannin Memorial. 1932: Winner of U.S. Open, and British Open. 1933: Winner of PGA Championship. 1934: Runner-up in U.S. Open. 1935: Winner of Masters and Massachusetts Open. 1936: Winner of Australian Open and St. Augustine Pro-Amateur. 1937: Winner of Florida West Coast Open and Chicago Open. 1938: Winner of Lake Placid Open. 1939: Winner of Metropolitan PGA. 1940: Runner-up in U.S. Open. 1941: Winner of Miami Four-Ball. 1953: Runner-up in PGA Senior Championship. 1954, 1958: Winner of PGA Senior Championship.

SHEEHAN, PATTY. Born in Middlebury, VT, October 27, 1956. Sheehan had a good amateur career, winning the Nevada State Amateur from 1975 through 1978 and the California Amateur in 1978 and 1979. She was a quarter-finalist in the 1976 U.S. Women's Amateur, and a finalist in 1979, losing to Carolyn Hill. In 1980, she played on the Curtis Cup team, winning all four of her matches, and won the AIAW National Championship. As a 13-year old, Sheehan was also a nationally ranked junior skier.

Joining the LPGA Tour in July 1980, Sheehan quickly made her mark, taking sixty-third on the money list after playing in only six events. In 1981,

she jumped to eleventh on the money list with $118,463, winning the Mazda Japan Classic and was Rookie-of-the-Year. Since then, she has earned over $200,000 each year. She has finished second in money four times (1983, 1984, 1988, and 1990) and never has finished worse than seventh. She earned twenty-five victories in her first ten full years on Tour, including two majors, the 1983 and 1984 LPGA Championships. She won the 1984 Vare Trophy with a 71.40 average, and was 1983 Player of the Year.

Sheehan's finest year financially came in 1990, when she earned $732,618, and won a career-high five tournaments in one campaign. Until 1992, her main disappointments came in the U.S. Women's Open. She finished second in 1983, 1988 and 1990, losing a six-shot lead after two rounds in the latter year. She finally won the championship in 1992 at Oakmont, shooting four-under-par 280 and then defeating Juli Inkster in an 18-hole playoff.

Patty Sheehan. *Reuters/Bettmann*

Tournament Record: 1975: Winner of Nevada State Amateur. 1976: Winner of Nevada State Amateur. 1977: Winner of Nevada State Amateur. 1978: Winner of Nevada State Amateur and California Amateur. 1980: Winner of AIAW National Championship. 1981: Winner of Mazda Japan Classic. 1982: Winner of Orlando Lady Classic, Safeco Classic, and Inamori Classic. 1983: Winner of Corning Classic, LPGA Championship, Henredon Classic, and Inamori Classic. 1984: Winner of Elizabeth Arden Classic, LPGA Championship, McDonald's Kids' Classic, and Henredon Classic. 1985: Winner of Sarasota Classic and J&B Scotch Pro-Am. 1986: Winner of Sarasota Classic, Kyocera Inamori Classic, and Konica San Jose Classic. 1988: Winner of Sarasota Classic and Mazda Japan Classic. 1989: Winner of Rochester International. 1990: Winner of Jamaica Classic, McDonald's Championship, Rochester International, Ping–Cellular One Championship, and Safeco Classic. 1991: Winner of Orix Hawaiian Ladies Open. 1992: Winner of Rochester International, Jamie Farr Toledo Classic, Women's British Open and U.S. Women's Open.

SHUTE, HERMAN DENSMORE. Born in Cleveland, OH, October 25, 1904. Died May 13, 1974. One of the finest players in the world during the 1930s, when he won the British Open and two PGA Championships, was also runner-up in both the PGA and the U.S. Open, and played on four Ryder Cup Teams. Shute was a fine player in all departments, but never quite caught the fancy of the public. One reason was that he did not play the tour as regularly as some of the others and, as a result, did not get as much public exposure. But beyond that, he was a reserved person who had little color. He simply went his own steady way which, more often than not, put him at or near the top in the championships. Shute turned pro in 1928 and within three years had been a strong contender in two U.S. Opens, had won two Tour tournaments, and had been named to the Ryder Cup Team. This set the tone for the next decade, during which Shute was winning, or almost winning, a title every year. Like most of the stars of the 1930s, Shute played little competitive golf after the war.

Tournament Record: 1923, 1925: Winner of West Virginia Amateur. 1927: Winner of Ohio Amateur. 1929: Winner of Ohio Open and Ohio PGA. 1930: Winner of Los Angeles Open, Texas Open, and Ohio Open. 1931: Winner of Ohio Open; runner-up in

Denny Shute.

PGA. 1932: Winner of Miami Biltmore Open, Glens Falls Open, and Akron Open. 1933: Winner of British Open and Gasparilla Open. 1934: Winner of Miami Four-Ball. 1936: Winner of PGA Championship and Tropical Open. 1937: Winner of PGA Championship. 1939: Winner of Glens Falls Open and St. Augustine Pro-Amateur. 1941: Runner-up in U.S. Open. 1950: Winner of Ohio Open. 1956: Winner of Akron Open.

SMITH, ALEX. Born in Carnoustie, Scotland, in 1872. Died April 20, 1930. One of five brothers who came to the United States in the mid-1890s and were destined to have a great impact on American golf. Alex was in many ways the complete professional. Not only was he an experienced club-maker and greens-keeper; he was good enough to win the U.S. Open twice, and he later taught Jerry Travers and Glenna Collett, who won eleven U.S. titles between them. Alex came to the United States in 1898 and took a job as assistant to Fred Herd in Washington Park in Chicago. Later that year, Herd won the U.S. Open and Alex was second. He was able to tie for fifth twenty-three years later, giving him a U.S. Open record of two wins, three seconds, three thirds, a fourth, and a fifth. Alex was a convivial man and a very fast one on the golf course, where his motto was "miss 'em quick." His brother Willie also won the U.S. Open, and the youngest of the family, Macdonald, was an outstanding player for three decades.

Tournament Record: 1898, 1901: Runner-up in U.S. Open. 1903: Winner of Western Open. 1905: Winner of Metropolitan Open; runner-up in U.S. Open. 1906: Winner of U.S. Open and Western Open. 1909: Winner of Metropolitan Open. 1910: Winner of U.S. Open and Metropolitan Open. 1913: Winner of Metropolitan Open.

Horton Smith.

Alex Smith. *Courtesy PGA World Hall of Fame*

SMITH, HORTON. Born in Springfield, MO, May 22, 1908. Died October 13, 1963. A player of infinite promise who burst on the tournament scene in the winter of 1928–1929 to capture eight tournaments and become the year's leading money winner. Smith went on to win other tournaments, including the Masters twice, but he never again matched that first glorious burst. In fairness to Smith, it should be said that it would be almost impossible to duplicate his rookie season. However, he did tamper with his fine swing through constant experimentation, and later he turned more to rules and administration, and his duties as a PGA officer did not help his game. He was a member of the PGA tournament committee as early as 1932, and he worked his way up until he became national president in 1952. Later, he was president of the PGA Seniors. Smith was stricken with Hodgkin's disease in 1957 and underwent several operations over the next few years. However, he continued on the job despite his ailments and was given the Ben Hogan Award in 1961 for carrying on despite a physical handicap.

Tournament Record: 1928: Winner of Oklahoma City Open and Catalina Open. 1929: Winner of French Open, LaGorce Open, Jacksonville Open, North and South Open, Pasadena Open, Pensacola Open, and Fort Myers Open; runner-up in German Open. 1930: Winner of Savannah Open, Oregon Open, Berkeley Open, and Orlando Open. 1931: Winner of St. Paul Open. 1932: Winner of Capital

City Open, Tri-State Open, and Michigan City Open. 1933: Winner of Miami Four-Ball. 1934: Winner of Masters and Louisville Open. 1935: Winner of Miami Biltmore Open, Palm Springs Open, and Pasadena Open. 1936: Winner of Masters and Victoria Open. 1937: Winner of North and South Open, Inverness Four-Ball, and Oklahoma City Four-Ball. 1940: Winner of St. Augustine Pro-Amateur, Colorado Open, and Massachusetts Open. 1941: Winner of Belleair Open and St. Paul Open. 1948, 1954: Winner of Michigan PGA.

SMITH, MACDONALD. Born in Carnoustie, Scotland, 1892. Died in 1949. Youngest brother of Alex and Willie Smith and considered by many to be the best golfer in the family, although he never won a major championship. Mac Smith, often called the greatest player who never won an Open, had a beautiful swing and a game good enough to win him dozens of tournaments, but no big ones. From 1910, when he tied his brother Alex and Johnny McDermott for the U.S. Open title, until 1936, when he was fourth in the same event, Mac was within three strokes of winning the U.S. or British Open a staggering twelve times. However, he always seemed to be throwing away a sure thing on the last round or else turning in a fantastic closing score that left him just short of winning. At any rate, he was a magnificent player, and it was generally conceded that he deserved more than three Western Opens and a Canadian Open beside his name. Smith worked in a shipyard during World War I and did not return to tournament golf until 1923.

Tournament Record: 1910: Winner of Claremont Open, Presidio Open, and California Open; runner-up in U.S. Open. 1912: Winner of Western Open. 1914: Winner of Metropolitan Open and Pennsylvania Open. 1916: Winner of Florida West Coast Open. 1924: Winner of Miami Four-Ball, Northern California Open, and California Open. 1925: Winner of Western Open, North and South Open, Long Island Open, and California Open. 1926: Winner of Canadian Open, Miami Four-Ball, Metropolitan Open, Texas Open, Dallas Open, and Chicago District Open. 1927: Winner of Chicago District Open. 1928: Winner of Los Angeles Open, South Central Open, and Palos Verdes Open. 1929: Winner of Los Angeles Open and Long Island Open. 1930: Winner of Long Island Open; runner-up in U.S. Open; tied for second

in British Open. 1931: Winner of Metropolitan Open and Long Island Open. 1932: Winner of Los Angeles Open; runner-up in British Open. 1933: Winner of Western Open. 1934: Winner of Los Angeles Open. 1935: Winner of Oakmont Open and Oakmont-Nassau Tournament. 1936: Winner of Seattle Open.

SMITH, MARILYN LOUISE. Born in Topeka, KS, April 13, 1929. Both Smith's father and professional Mike Murra in Wichita encouraged her to take up the game at age twelve. Before turning pro, she won the Kansas State Amateur three successive years (1946–1948). She also won the National Collegiate title in 1949 while at the University of Kansas.

Smith was a founder and charter member of the LPGA in 1950. She won her first tournament, the Fort Wayne Open, in 1954, and her last in 1972, the Pabst Open. She was a multiple winner on Tour on six occasions, including 1963, when she was named Most Improved Player. She won two majors, the 1963 and 1964 Titleholders, and twenty other Tour events. Her best playing years were from 1962 through 1972. During this period, she was among the top ten money winners eight times. Her best placings were fourth on the list in 1963, 1968, and 1970.

Smith served as President of the LPGA from 1958 to 1960. She was presented with the first Patty Berg award, in 1979, for outstanding service to women's golf.

Tournament Record: 1946: Winner of Kansas State Amateur. 1947: Winner of Kansas State Amateur. 1948: Winner of Kansas State Amateur. 1949: Winner of National Collegiate Championship. 1954: Winner of Fort Wayne Open. 1955: Winner of Heart of America Open and Mile High Open. 1957: Co-Winner of Homestead Four-Ball. 1958: Winner of Jacksonville Open. 1959: Winner of Memphis Open. 1962: Winner of Sunshine Open and Waterloo Open. 1963: Winner of Titleholders Championship, Peach Blossom Open, Eugene Open, and Cavern City Open. 1964: Winner of Titleholders Championship and Albuquerque Pro-Am. 1965: Winner of Peach Blossom Invitational. 1966: Winner of St. Petersburg Open and Delray Beach Invitational. 1967: Winner of St. Petersburg Open and Babe Zaharias Open. 1968: Winner of O'Sullivan Open. 1970: Winner of Golf Charities Open. 1972: Winner of Pabst Open.

SNEAD, SAMUEL JACKSON. Born in Hot Springs, VA, May 27, 1912. The greatest natural player in the history of golf, a man who won well over a hundred tournaments in his career, only to be best remembered for his failure to win the U.S. Open. Snead won the PGA three times, the Masters three times, and the British Open once—a remarkable record; but for years he struggled in vain to win the biggest one of all. He was second in 1937, the first year he ever competed in the Open, and everyone figured he was bound to win it, probably more than once. Then, in 1939, he came to the last hole needing a 5 to win and took an awful 8. That failure stuck with him for the remainder of his career. In 1947 he tied Lew Worsham for the title, but lost the play-off, and he was also second in 1949 and 1953. Sam also won the

Sam Snead. *Will Hertzberg*

Vardon Trophy four times, was leading money winner three times, was a member of eight Ryder Cup Teams and captain once.

On May 16, 1959, in the third round of the Sam Snead Festival at the Greenbrier, White Sulphur Springs, West Va., Snead shot a 59 en route to a winning total of 259, which left the field 11 strokes behind. Snead had one eagle, nine birdies and six pars on the par 70, 6,427 yard course. The round is not a PGA Tour record since the tournament was not official.

Snead came out of the West Virginia mountains in 1937 and was totally unknown. When he startled the golf world by winning the Oakland Open in early 1937, people (including the official tournament scorer) did not even know how to spell his name. Although Snead was no fool and soon displayed a great talent for making—and keeping—money, he was known for years as a hillbilly type who always had a vast storehouse of pungent jokes. He made no effort to disprove the claim that he had all his money buried in tin cans somewhere on his property in West Virginia. His smooth, graceful swing became a legend, and rightly so, because for more than thirty years it was held up as a model of how the club should be handled. Although Snead developed severe putting troubles and eventually adopted croquet and, later, sidesaddle putting techniques, his swing was as powerful and effortless as ever. He holds the record for official Tour victories with eighty-one.

As a senior, Snead won six PGA Senior Championships and five World Seniors. He has won the Legends of Golf twice, in 1978 with Gardner Dickinson as his partner, and in 1982, with Don January. He also won the 1980 Commemorative Pro-Am.

Tournament Record: 1936: Winner of West Virginia Closed Pro. 1937: Winner of Oakland Open, Bing Crosby Invitational, St. Paul Open, Nassau Open, and Miami Open; runner-up in U.S. Open. 1938: Winner of Bing Crosby Invitational, Greensboro Open, Inverness Four-Ball, Goodall Round Robin, Chicago Open, Canadian Open, Westchester Open, and White Sulphur Springs Open; runner-up in PGA Championship. 1939: Winner of St. Petersburg Open, Miami Four-Ball, Miami Open, and Ontario Open; runner-up in Masters. 1940: Winner of Canadian Open, Inverness Four-Ball, and Anthracite Open; runner-up in PGA Championship. 1941: Winner of Bing Crosby Invitational, St. Petersburg Open, North and South Open, Rochester Open, Henry Hurst Invitational, and Canadian Open. 1942: Winner of PGA Championship, St. Petersburg Open, and Corduba Open. 1944: Winner of Richmond Open and Portland Open. 1945: Winner of Los Angeles Open, Gulfport Open, Pensacola Open, Jacksonville Open, Dallas Open, and Tulsa Open. 1946: Winner of British Open, Jacksonville Open, Greensboro Open, Viriginia Open, Miami Open, and World Championship. 1947: Winner of Tulsa Invitational, Bing Crosby Pro-Am; runner-up in U.S. Open. 1948: Winner of Texas Open, Seminole Pro-Amateur, West Virginia PGA, Havana Invitational, and West Virginia Open. 1949: Winner of Masters, PGA Championship, Greensboro Open, Washington *Star* Open, Dapper Dan Open, National Celebrities Invitational, Western Open, and Decatur Open; tied for second in U.S. Open. 1950: Winner of Los Angeles Open, Texas Open, Miami Beach Open, Greensboro Open, Western Open, Colonial Invitational, Inverness Four-Ball, Reading Open, North and South Open, and Miami Open. 1951: Winner of PGA Championship, Greenbrier Invitational, and Miami Open. 1952: Winner of Masters, Seminole Pro-Amateur, Greenbrier Invitational, Goodall Round Robin, Inverness Four-Ball, All-American Open, Eastern Open, and Julius Boros Invitational. 1953: Winner of Orlando Two-Ball, Baton Rouge Open, and Greenbrier Invitational; runner-up in U.S. Open. 1954: Winner of Masters, Panama Open, and Palm Beach Round Robin. 1955: Winner of Bayshore Open, Greensboro Open, Palm Beach Round Robin, Insurance City Open, and Miami Open. 1956: Winner of Greensboro Open. 1957: Winner of Dallas Open, West Virginia Open, and Palm Beach Round Robin; runner-up in Masters. 1958: Winner of Greenbrier Invitational and Dallas Open. 1959: Winner of Sam Snead Festival. 1960: Winner of DeSoto Open, Greensboro Open, and West Virginia Open. 1961: Winner of Tournament of Champions and Sam Snead Festival. 1964: Winner of Haig and Haig Mixed Foursome Invitational (with Shirley Englehorn), PGA Senior Championship, and World Senior. 1965: Winner of Greensboro Open, PGA Senior Championship, and World Senior. 1967: Winner of PGA Senior Championship. 1968: Winner of West Virginia Open. 1970: Winner of PGA Senior Championship and World Senior. 1971: Winner of PGA Club Pro's Championship. 1972: Winner of PGA Senior Championship and World Senior. 1973: Win-

ner of PGA Senior Championship and World Senior. 1978: Winner of Legends of Golf (with Gardner Dickinson). 1980: Winner of Commemorative Pro-Am. 1982: Winner of Legends of Golf (with Don January).

STACY, HOLLIS. Born in Savannah, GA, March 16, 1954. Stacy set a record early in her national career that was tough to beat. She won the U.S. Girls Junior three years in a row. In her last victory, in 1971, she was four under par for the nineteen holes she needed to defeat Amy Alcott. Stacy also won the 1970 North and South, and played on the 1972 Curtis Cup team.

Coming on Tour in 1974, Stacy won in every year from 1977 through 1985. She won her first U.S. Women's Open in 1977 and finished fifth on the money list. The next year, she finished sixth, and again won the U.S. Women's title. Besides her back-to-back wins in the U.S. Open, she has also repeated in the West Virginia Classic (1981–1982) and the S&H Golf Classic (1982–1983).

Hollis Stacy. *Courtesy LPGA*

In 1984, Stacy won her third U.S. Open. Her victory at Salem Country Club in Peabody, Massachusetts, came in dramatic fashion as she eagled the 13th hole, holing out from 123 yards. She won one other major, the 1983 Peter Jackson Classic.

Six of Stacy's eighteen wins have come in suddendeath play-off. She lost only one of these, giving her a record success rate of .857.

Tournament Record: 1969: Winner of U.S. Girls Junior Championship. 1970: Winner of U.S. Girls Junior Championship and North and South Amateur. 1971: Winner of U.S. Girls Junior Championship. 1977: Winner of Rail Charity Golf Classic, Lady Tara Classic, and U.S. Women's Open. 1978: Winner of U.S. Women's Open and Birmingham Classic. 1979: Winner of Mayflower Classic. 1980: Winner of CPC International. 1981: Winner of West Virginia LPGA Classic and Inamori Classic. 1982: Winner of Whirlpool Championship of Deer Creek, S&H Golf Classic, and West Virginia LPGA Classic. 1983: Winner of S&H Golf Classic, CPC International, and Peter Jackson Classic. 1984: Winner of U.S. Women's Open and individual title at Nichirei Ladies Cup Team Matches. 1985: Winner of Mazda Classic of Deer Creek. 1991: Winner of Crestar Classic.

STADLER, CRAIG. Born in San Diego, CA, June 2, 1953. Stadler started in the game at age five, but did not become really interested, he says, "before age eight or nine." In 1971, he won the World Junior Championship. In 1973, he won the U.S. Amateur, defeating the defending champion Vinny Giles in the semifinals, and David Strawn in the final by 6 and 5. As a student at the University of Southern California, he was an All-American choice in 1974 and 1975, winning eleven college tournaments. Playing for the U.S. in the 1975 Walker Cup team matches, Stadler won all three matches he played.

Stadler's transition to the Tour was not an easy one. He failed to qualify at his first attempt, and when he did qualify for the second half of the 1976 season, he was, as he admits, "just awful." At that time and for a few years after, Stadler, as other perfectionists before him, was known for his temper and periodic club-throwing. However, he did climb on the money list, just failing to make the top sixty in 1977, and continued to do so over the next couple of years, but his highest finishes were no better than fourth. His only win was in the 1978 Magnolia Classic, a second-

Craig Stadler. *Fred Vuich*

ary event for those not invited to the Masters. In 1980 and 1981, he became a top player, winning the 1980 Bob Hope Desert Classic and Greensboro Open, and the 1981 Kemper Open. In both years, he finished eighth on the money list, winning in excess of $200,000.

His best year was 1982. He got off the mark quickly, winning the first event of the season, the Tucson Open. In the Crosby, he should have won, but took a couple of 6s in his final round and finished second to Jim Simons. In the Masters, he opened with 75, 69, then a 67, in which he birdied the last three holes and gave him a three-stroke lead going into the final round. After eleven holes, he had stretched his lead to 5, but faltered. He dropped shots on the 12th, 14th and 16th holes, and three-putted the 18th to go into a tie with Dan Pohl, who shot a last-round 67 to Stadler's 73. However, Stadler parred the first play-off hole, and Pohl didn't, and

Stadler was Masters Champion. Later in the year, Stadler won his second Kemper Open and also won the World Series of Golf, to become the second man to earn over $400,000 in a single season.

Although Stadler went from 1984 through 1990 without winning on the PGA Tour, he has still done well financially. He was eleventh on the money list in 1985, worth nearly $300,000, and finished between 25th and 53rd on the money list in each year from 1986 through 1990. He was second in 1991 when he won the Tour Championship.

Because of his ample figure and fine moustache, Stadler has come to be known as "the Walrus," a nickname he finds amusing. In fact, he and his wife Sue have quite a collection of walrus art in just about every conceivable medium. He may not look like an athlete at rest, but as the older PGA Tour pros used to say, "he puts some hurtin' on the ball." He's a marvelous shotmaker, and blessed with an excellent touch around the greens. He was a member of the 1983 and 1985 Ryder Cup teams.

Tournament Record: 1971: Winner of World Junior. 1973: Winner of U.S. Amateur. 1978: Winner of Magnolia Classic. 1980: Winner of Bob Hope Desert Classic and Greater Greensboro Open. 1981: Winner of Kemper Open. 1982: Winner of Tucson Open, Masters, Kemper Open, and World Series of Golf. 1984: Winner of Byron Nelson Classic. 1985: Winner of European Masters. 1986: Winner of Jerry Ford Invitational. 1987: Winner of Dunlop Phoenix (Japan). 1990: Winner of Scandanavian Enterprise Open. 1991: Winner of Tour Championship. 1992: Winner of NEC World Series of Golf.

STEPHENSON, JAN. Born in Sydney, Australia, December 22, 1951. Stephenson started in golf at age nine. As an amateur, Stephenson won five consecutive New South Wales (NSW) Schoolgirl Championships (1964–1968), four NSW Juniors (1969–1972), three Australian Junior Championships (1967, 1968, and 1971) and two NSW Amateurs (1971–1972). Turning professional in 1973, she won the Australian Open and three other events.

Coming to America and joining the LPGA Tour in July 1974, she was an immediate success, placing twenty-eighth on the money list and Rookie-of-the-Year honors. In 1976, she won her first LPGA event, the Sarah Coventry, then added the Birmingham Classic to finish eighth on the money list. She ranked among the top fifteen money winners every year through 1988, with the exception of 1980, when she had back problems. In 1981, she set the LPGA all-time 54-hole scoring record in a winning performance at the Mary Kay Classic. Her 18-under-par 198 total included twenty birdies. She now has sixteen official wins to her credit, including victories in three different majors.

Stephenson's first major came in the 1981 Peter Jackson Classic at Quebec. After rounds of 69, 66, 72, she had to hole a fourteen-foot birdie putt on the last hole to finish in 73 and win by a stroke from Nancy Lopez and Pat Bradley. In 1982, she took the LPGA Championship at the Jack Nicklaus Sports Center, in Kings Island, Ohio, shooting 69, 69, 70, 71, to win by two strokes from JoAnne Carner. Then in the 1983

Jan Stephenson. *Will Hertzberg*

U.S. Women's Open held at the Cedar Ridge Country Club in Tulsa, Oklahoma, Stephenson again bested Carner, edging her and Patty Sheehan by a stroke. Stephenson carded 72, 73, 71, 74.

Stephenson's most financially rewarding years occurred more recently. In 1987, she managed three victories despite an automobile accident, which occurred the evening of the third round of the S&H Golf Classic. Several of her ribs were broken, and she had to withdraw. She was leading the tournament at the time. She finished the year with $227,303, fourth on the money list. In 1988, she didn't win, but had ten top-five finishes; these included two second-place finishes—at the Chrysler-Plymouth Classic, where she shot a tournament record round of 64, equaling her personal lowest career score, and at the Boston Five Classic, where she lost in a play-off. She earned $236,739 for the year, ninth on the money list. Stephenson finished second in the Vare Trophy race, a scant .03 of a stroke behind Colleen Walker. Stephenson suffered a setback when she missed half of the 1990 season after her ring finger was broken in a mugging.

Tournament Record: 1964: Winner of New South Wales (NSW) Schoolgirl Championship. 1965: Winner of NSW Schoolgirl Championship. 1966: Winner of NSW Schoolgirl Championship. 1967: Winner of NSW Schoolgirl Championship and Australian Junior. 1968: Winner of NSW Schoolgirl Championship and Australian Junior. 1969: Winner of NSW Junior. 1970: Winner of NSW Junior. 1971: Winner of NSW Junior, Australian Junior and NSW Amateur. 1972: Winner of NSW Junior and NSW Amateur. 1973: Winner of Australian Open. 1976: Winner of Sarah Coventry—Naples Classic and Birmingham Classic. 1977: Winner of Australian Open. 1978: Winner of Women's International. 1980: Winner of Sun City Classic and Rolex World Mixed Team Championship (with David Graham). 1981: Winner of Peter Jackson Classic, Mary Kay Classic, United Virginia Bank Classic, and World Ladies. 1982: Winner of LPGA Championship and Lady Keystone. 1983: Winner of Tucson Conquistadores LPGA Open, Lady Keystone, U.S. Women's Open, and JC Penney Mixed Team (with Fred Couples). 1985: Winner of GNA Classic, Nichirei Ladies Cup, and Hennessy French Open. 1987: Winner of Santa Barbara Open, Safeco Classic, and Konica San Jose Classic.

Payne Stewart.
Fred Vuich

STEWART, PAYNE. Born in Springfield, MO, January 30, 1957. Stewart learned the game from his father, Bill, a fine amateur player who twice won the Missouri Amateur. Payne won that same title in 1979. He also won the Southwest Conference championship for Southern Methodist University that year, but he did not compile an outstanding amateur record on the national scene.

Stewart failed in his first couple of tries at qualifying for the PGA Tour, but in 1981 he won two tournaments on the Asian Tour and finished third in the Order of Merit. He made it to the PGA Tour in the summer of 1981 and has been one of the top money winners ever since, accumulating over $4.5 million through 1990. He has one of the sweetest swings and finest overall games on Tour and is a regular contender week in and week out, so his total of eight victories through 1992 is considered somewhat disappointing.

Stewart did win tournaments in his first two years, the Quad Cities Open in 1982 and the Walt Disney World Classic in 1983. Then came a frustrating period of more than three years without a victory despite numerous chances. He finished second eight times before finally breaking through with a win at the 1987 Hertz Bay Hill Classic. The year before, he finished third on the money list without winning an event.

After another winless campaign in 1988, Stewart broke into the top echelon of players by winning two events in 1989 and two more in 1990. He earned a total of over $2 million in those two years, ranking second and third on the money list. He took his first major title at the 1989 PGA Championship, shooting a closing 67 to catch and pass Mike Reid. Stewart added another major in 1991 when he defeated Scott Simpson in a playoff for the U.S. Open.

Tournament Record: 1981: Winner of Indian Open and Indonesian Open. 1982: Winner of Magnolia Classic and Quad Cities Open. 1983: Winner of Walt Disney World Classic. 1987: Winner of Hertz Bay Hill Classic. 1989: Winner of MCI Heritage Classic and PGA Championship. 1990: Winner of MCI Heritage Classic and GTE Byron Nelson Classic. 1991: Winner of U.S. Open.

STOCKTON, DAVE. Born in San Bernadino, CA, November 2, 1941. Stockton has a proud family heritage, being a direct descendant of Richard Stockton, who signed the Declaration of Independence for New Jersey. As a boy, Stockton was on his way to becoming an all-around athlete, but, at fifteen, he cracked six verterbrae in his back while surfing. He took up golf seriously at seventeen, and went on to play at the University of Southern California, from which he graduated with a degree in general man-

Dave Stockton.
Fred Vance

agement in 1964. He captained the golf team at USC and gained All-American ranking.

Stockton joined the Tour in 1964. His first win was in the 1967 Colonial, where he opened with a tournament record, 65, 66, then coasted in with 74, 73 to take the title. From that year he was in the top sixty money winners through 1978. His biggest money year was 1974, with three Tour wins and a total of $155,105 in prize money, good for sixth on the list. He was in the top twenty in 1967, 1968, 1970, 1971, 1973, and 1974. Overall, he won a total of eleven events.

Stockton won his first major championship, the PGA Championship at Southern Hills in Tulsa, Oklahoma, in 1970. Stockton shot 70, 70, 66 to take a three-stroke lead. He then had to fight off extreme heat and a stretch challenge by Arnold Palmer which fell short by two strokes. He won the PGA again in 1976 at the Congressional Country Club in Bethesda, Maryland. After shooting 70, 72, 69, he was four strokes back, but took the lead entering the back nine, and on the last green holed a thirteen-foot putt for a 71, to beat Ray Floyd and Don January by one stroke.

Stockton also had two close misses in two other majors, finishing tied for second in both the 1974 Masters and 1978 U.S. Open. He played on the 1970 and 1976 World Cup teams, and the 1971 and 1977 Ryder Cup teams. He was the non-playing captain of the 1991 Ryder Cup team.

In his prime, Stockton was never a long hitter, but at his best, he was very accurate. He has always been an outstanding scrambler and a deadly putter. He once played a stretch of ten rounds on Tour never using more than 28 putts.

Tournament Record: 1967: Winner of Colonial National Invitational and Haig Scotch Foursome (with Laurie Hammer). 1968: Winner of Cleveland Open and Milwaukee Open. 1970: Winner of PGA Championship. 1971: Winner of Massachusetts Classic. 1973: Winner of Milwaukee Open. 1974: Winner of Los Angeles Open, Quad Cities Open, and Hartford Open. 1976: Winner of PGA Championship.

STRANGE, CURTIS NORTHRUP. Born Norfolk, VA, January 30, 1955. Strange started in the game at age seven. "By the time I was eight," he says, "I was playing every day." Fortunately, he had the benefit of expert teaching, his father, Tom, being the profes-

Curtis Strange. *Fred Vuich*

sional and owner of the White Sands Country Club in Virginia Beach, VA. His father died of cancer when Curtis and his twin brother, Allan, were 14. Thereafter, Strange explains, "Chandler Harper, the Hall of Famer, became my teacher."

Strange grew up to be one of the best amateurs in the country. In 1973, at eighteen, he won the Southeastern Amateur. As a freshman at Wake Forest, he won the 1974 Western Amateur and the NCAA Championship, and reached the semifinals of the U.S. Amateur. In the NCAA Championship, he eagled the last hole to win the team title for his college, and the individual title for himself. He was 1974 College Player of the Year. That year, he also played on the winning U.S. World Amateur team.

In college, Strange was a long hitter, and earned the nickname "Brutus," after the big, rough sailer in the Popeye cartoons. However, even then, Strange had his eye on the Tour. "That swing could go bad," he says, "and I wanted one that would work every day. I shortened it, and gave away thirty yards off the tee just so as to make it dependable."

In 1975 and 1976, Strange won back-to-back vic-

tories in both the North and South as well as the Virginia State Amateur. He also won the 1975 Eastern Amateur; this was a very special win for him, because, as he said, "My father won the very first Eastern in 1957." In the 1975 U.S. Amateur, he reached the fifth round. He played on the winning U.S. team in the 1975 Walker Cup at St. Andrews, Scotland; he won twice in foursome play, and won one single and halved another.

Strange left Wake Forest in his junior year and turned professional in 1976. Surprisingly, he failed to get his Tour card that fall. So, he played on the British–European Tour, where his best finish was a tie for second in the Moroccan Grand Prix at Rabat. He qualified for the Tour in the spring of 1977.

After a disappointing 1978, Strange's game came together in 1979; by late summer he had earned over $100,000, and in the year's final individual event, the Pensacola Open, he won his first Tour victory. He finished that year twenty-first on the money list.

In 1980, he did even better, winning two Tour events and finishing third in money. While victory eluded him in 1981 and 1982, he continually knocked at the door, while taking ninth and tenth places on the money lists, respectively. In 1983, he returned to the winner's circle again, and enjoyed another victory in 1984.

Still, Strange wasn't having much success in the major championships. Even in 1985, when he won three tournaments and led the money list, he was remembered more for finishing second in the Masters. He opened with an 80, recovered with brilliant rounds of 65 and 68 to take the lead, but then lost it in the final round by hitting shots into the water on both the 13th and 15th holes.

The next year, 1986, was somewhat of an off year as Strange slipped to thirty-second on the money list, though he did win a tournament. He more than made up for it the next two years, winning three events in 1987 and four in 1988, and leading the money list both years. He also distinguished himself in the 1987 Dunhill Cup matches, shooting a record-breaking 62 on the Old Course, St. Andrews, Scotland.

Most importantly, Strange broke through with his first major title in 1988, when he defeated Nick Faldo in a play-off to win the U.S. Open at The Country Club in Brookline, Massachusetts. Strange led by one stroke through three rounds, but fell into a tie when he three-putted the 17th hole for a bogey in the final round. He preserved a spot in the play-off by getting up and down for par on the 18th hole, then won the play-off by four strokes with an even-par 71.

Strange also won the Independent Insurance Agent Open and season-ending Nabisco Championships in play-offs that year, while winning the Memorial Tournament in regulation. He finished with earnings of $1,147,644 and was PGA Player of the Year.

In 1989, Strange became the first player to win back-to-back U.S. Opens since Ben Hogan in 1950 and 1951. Strange shot a 64 in the second round, but trailed Tom Kite by three strokes after three rounds. While Kite faltered on Sunday, Strange won it with an even-par 70 that included sixteen pars, one birdie, and one bogey. He finished seventh on the money list in 1989, but slumped in 1990 with his first winless campaign in eight years.

Strange has compiled seventeen PGA Tour victories to date and competed on the 1983, 1985, 1987 and 1989 Ryder Cup teams.

Tournament Record: 1970: Winner of Virginia State Junior. 1973: Winner of Southeastern Amateur. 1974: Winner of NCAA Championship and Western Amateur. 1975: Winner of Eastern Amateur, North and South Amateur, and Virginia State Amateur. 1976: Winner of North and South Amateur, Virginia State Amateur. 1979: Winner of Pensacola Open. 1980: Winner of Michelob–Houston Open and Manufacturers Hanover Westchester Classic. 1983: Winner of Sammy Davis, Jr.–Greater Hartford Open. 1984: Winner of LaJet Classic. 1985: Winner of Honda Classic, Panasonic–Las Vegas Invitational, Canadian Open. 1986: Winner of Houston Open and ABC Cup (Japan). 1987: Winner of Canadian Open and Federal Express–St. Jude Classic. 1988: Winner of Independent Insurance Agent Open, Memorial Tournament, U.S. Open, Nabisco Championships. 1989: Winner of U.S. Open.

SUGGS, LOUISE. Born in Atlanta, GA, September 7, 1923. Winner of fifty tournaments on the Ladies' PGA tour following a successful amateur career that included victories in both the U.S. and British championships. Louise Suggs turned professional in 1948 and subsequently won the U.S. Open twice and the LPGA Championship once. Her record also included being the tour's leading money winner twice. She first played golf at the age of ten under the tutelage of her father and went on to develop one of the smooth-

Louise Suggs.

est swings in the game. Her best year was 1953, when she won eight tournaments and collected almost $20,000, an unusually large sum on the women's tour in those days.

Tournament Record: 1941: Winner of Southern Amateur. 1942: Winner of North and South. 1946: Winner of Western Amateur and North and South. 1947: Winner of Southern Amateur, Western Amateur, and U.S. Amateur. 1948: Winner of North and South and British Amateur. 1949: Winner of U.S. Women's Open, Western Open, and All-American Open. 1951: Winner of Carrollton Open. 1952: Winner of Jacksonville Open, Tampa Open, Stockton Open, U.S. Women's Open, All-American Open, and Betty Jameson Open. 1953: Winner of Western Open, Tampa Open, Betsy Rawls Open, San Diego Open, San Francisco Weathervane, Bakersfield Open, Philadelphia Weathervane, and Cross-Country Weathervane. 1954: Winner of Titleholders Championship, Sea Island Open, Betsy Rawls Open, Carrollton Open, and Babe Zaharias Open. 1955: Winner of Los Angeles Open, Oklahoma City Open, Eastern Open, Triangle Round Robin, and St. Louis Open. 1956: Winner of Titleholders Championship, Havana Open, and All-American Open. 1957: Winner of LPGA Championship and Heart of America Invitational. 1958: Winner of Babe Zaharias Open, Gatlinburg Open, French Lick Open, and Triangle Round Robin. 1959: Winner of Titleholders Championship, St. Petersburg Open, and Dallas Civitan Open. 1960:

Winner of Dallas Civitan Open, Triangle Round Robin, Youngstown Kitchen Open, and San Antonio Civitan Open. 1961: Winner of Sea Island Invitational, DeSoto Lakes Open, Dallas Civitan Open, Kansas City Open, and San Antonio Open. 1962: Winner of St. Petersburg Open.

SUTTON, HAL EVAN. Born in Shreveport, LA, April 28, 1958. Sutton started in golf at age 11 when a friend of his father's sent him a set of golf clubs. For the next two years, he would take his father's golf cart and "sometimes play seventy-two holes a day." Sutton's first important win was in the 1976 Cotton States Invitational. In 1978, he won the Dixie Amateur and was second in the North and South. The next year, he won the Western Amateur and Rice Planters', and repeated in the Dixie. He also played on the Walker Cup Team. In 1980, he won the North and South, Northeastern, Western, and U.S. Amateurs, and lost the NCAA Championship in a play-off. He took the individual title in the 1980 World Amateur team championship by nine strokes at Pinehurst, scoring a record twelve under par 276. In

Hal Sutton. *Fred Vuich*

1981, he again played in the Walker Cup and turned professional. He qualified for the Tour in the fall 1981 School.

Sutton's first year was little short of sensational. In 1982, he set a record for rookie earnings of $237,434 to finish eleventh on the money list. In thirty-one starts, he compiled eight top ten finishes and made the cut in twenty-five. Just before going into the Disney, he finished second in the Pensacola Open. He then won the Disney in a play-off over Bill Britton with a birdie on the fourth extra hole. When he was asked what he could do for an encore, Sutton replied, "I would like to continue to improve my game, win a major championship, and be the year's leading money winner." He did just that.

In 1983, Sutton won the Tournament Players Championship at Ponte Vedra, Florida. He opened with 73, 71, 70, which left him four strokes off the pace set by John Cook. In the final round, Cook fell to a 75, while Sutton shot 69, edging Bob Eastwood by a stroke. In the PGA Championship at the Riviera Country Club in California, Sutton led all the way, firing 65, 66, eleven under par, for the first two rounds, good for a three-stroke lead. He cooled off a little in the final two rounds, carding 72, 71. However, his 274 total was good enough to fight off a late challenge by Jack Nicklaus, whose last round effort of 66 fell short by a stroke. With twelve top ten finishes for the year, Sutton was leading money winner with $426,668. He also was the PGA Player of the Year.

Although Sutton did not win in 1984, he had two victories a year in both 1985 and 1986. Then the bottom dropped out of his promising career, and Sutton hasn't won since.

Tournament Record: 1974: Winner of Louisiana State Juniors. 1976: Winner of Cotton States Invitational. 1978: Winner of Dixie Amateur. 1979: Winner of Dixie Amateur, Western Amateur, and Rice Planters' Amateur. 1980: Winner of North and South Amateur, Northeastern Amateur, Western Amateur, and U.S. Amateur. 1982: Winner of Walt Disney World Golf Classic. 1983: Winner of Tournament Players Championship and PGA Championship. 1985: Winner of St. Jude–Memphis Classic, Southwest Classic, and Chrysler Team Championship (with Raymond Floyd). 1986: Winner of Phoenix Open and Memorial Tournament.

TAYLOR, JOHN HENRY. Born in Northam, North Devon, England, March 19, 1871. Died in February 1963. A five-time winner of the British Open Championship and, with Braid and Vardon, a member of the game's famed "triumvirate." J.H., as he was generally known, won the Open in 1894, 1895, 1900, 1909, and 1913. He also was second five times and third once. He accompanied Vardon to the United States in 1900 and was second to the Great Man in the U.S. Open that year. He also won the French Open twice and the German Open once and captured the British PGA title in 1904 and 1908. Taylor represented England against Scotland nine times and frequently partnered Vardon or Braid in matches on which a large sum was at stake.

THOMSON, PETER. Born in Melbourne, Australia, August 23, 1929. Winner of the British Open five times, a player who commanded great respect throughout the international golfing world, but was always badly underestimated by Americans. Thomson played in the United States on several occasions, but he finally began to make his visits few and far between. Americans never seemed to take to him, and the reverse was also true. He had a game that was ideally suited to seaside courses and to places that required improvisation and a certain finesse. On American courses, which were lush and well watered and demanded great accuracy with the pitching wedge, Thomson was never at home. Thus it was difficult for Americans to understand how he could win the British Open five times and still fail to win over here. Thomson could hit the low hook and get great distance on hard, wind-swept links, while the same shot left him far short on lush terrain. Nevertheless, his great record outside the United States, made on a wide variety of courses under all conditions, is evidence of his right to be classed among the great players. Thomson won the Texas Open and was fourth in the U.S. Open and in the 1956 and 1957 Masters. In the British Open, he had the almost unbelievable record of finishing either first or second for seven straight years from 1952 through 1958.

Thomson had more success in America on the Senior Tour, which he joined in 1982. He won eleven times, including the PGA Seniors Championship of 1984. Nine of his victories came in 1985 when he was the leading money-winner with $386,724. In contrast, when he won the Texas Open

Pete Thomson.
UPI/Bettmann

back in 1956, he won $13,478 and finished the year in ninth place with $20,413.

Tournament Record: 1950: Winner of New Zealand Open. 1951: Winner of Australian Open and New Zealand Open. 1952: Runner-up in British Open. 1953: Winner of New Zealand Open and New Zealand Professional; tied for second in British Open. 1954: Winner of British Open, Ampol Tournament, World Cup (with Kel Nagle), and *News of the World* Tournament. 1955: Winner of British Open and New Zealand Open. 1956: Winner of British Open and Texas Open. 1957: Runner-up in British Open. 1958: Winner of British Open and Dunlop Professional; tied for first in Daks Tournament. 1959: Winner of New Zealand Open, Italian Open, World Cup (with Kel Nagle), and Spanish Open. 1960: Winner of German Open, South China Open, Hong Kong Open, New Zealand Open, and Daks Tournament. 1961: Winner of New Zealand Open, Dunlop Masters, and *News of the World* Tournament; tied for first in Esso Golden Tournament. 1962: Winner of Martini International and Piccadilly Tournament. 1963: Winner of India Open. 1964: Winner of Philippine Open. 1965: Winner of British Open, New Zealand Open, Hong Kong Open and Daks Tournament. 1966: Winner of *News of the World* Tournament and India Open. 1967: Winner of Australian Open, Alcan International, Australian Professional, Hong Kong Open, and *News of the World* Tournament. 1968: Winner of Dunlop Masters, Victoria Open, and South Australian Open. 1971: Winner of International Japan Airlines Open, New Zealand Open, International Dunlop, and Tournament Wizard Championship (Japan). 1972: Winner of Australian Open. 1973: Winner of Australian Open. 1984: Winner of World Senior Invitational and General Foods PGA Seniors Championship. 1985: Winner of Vintage Invitational, Carta Blanca Johnny Mathis Classic, MONY Tournament of Champions, Champions Classic, Senior Players Reunion Pro-Am, Syracuse Seniors Classic, du Maurier Champions, United Virginia Bank Seniors and Barnett Suntree Classic.

TRAVERS, JEROME DUNSTAN. Born in New York, NY, May 19, 1887. Died in 1951. The only man besides Bobby Jones to win as many as five U.S. Amateur titles and one of only five amateurs ever to win the U.S. National Open. Travers was the son of a rich man and was able to devote all the time necessary to develop-

Jerome Travers. *Courtesy PGA World Hall of Fame*

ing a good game. His teacher was Alex Smith, who once said he thought Travers' golf temperament was even superior to that of Walter Hagen. Travers was a great putter, and his short game and competitive spirit more than offset any trouble he might have with his driver. His greatest demonstration of ability probably came in the 1915 U.S. Open, which he won despite severe driving problems. Prior to that victory he had done little at stroke play, and people were of the opinion he was strictly a match player. Travers ran into financial troubles in later years and eventually turned professional, although he never competed as a pro.

Tournament Record: 1904: Winner of Nassau Invitational. 1906: Winner of Metropolitan Amateur and Eastern Scholastic. 1907: Winner of U.S. Amateur, Metropolitan Amateur, and New Jersey Amateur. 1908: Winner of U.S. Amateur and New Jersey Amateur. 1911: Winner of Metropolitan Amateur and New Jersey Amateur. 1912: Winner of U.S. Amateur and Metropolitan Amateur. 1913: Winner of U.S. Amateur, Metropolitan Amateur, and New Jersey Amateur. 1914: Runner-up in U.S. Amateur. 1915: Winner of U.S. Open.

TRAVIS, WALTER J. Born in Maldon, Victoria, Australia, January 10, 1862. Died in 1927. One of the most remarkable figures in golf in that he did not take up the game until his mid-thirties, yet became a championship player within two years. Travis won his first U.S. Amateur at the age of thirty-eight, then went on to win two more of them, plus the British Amateur and dozens more. He was still good enough to win the tough Metropolitan Amateur at the age of fifty-three. After Travis had won three U.S. Amateurs in four years, he decided to take a crack at the British championship, and he almost caused an international incident. He was a taciturn man on the course and a stickler for the rules, and, for whatever reason, he quickly alienated the British. He won the tournament, mainly on the strength of his work with the Schenectady putter, and the British never forgave him. They banned the putter, accused Travis of surly behavior, and otherwise made clear their feelings. For his part, Travis thought he had been treated shabbily, and if he was responsible for his treatment by his own brusque manner, he could never make himself believe it. In later years Travis turned to

Walter Travis.
Courtesy U.S.G.A.

course architecture and also was the editor of the magazine *American Golfer* for many years.

Tournament Record: 1900: Winner of U.S. Amateur and Metropolitan Amateur. 1901: Winner of U.S. Amateur. 1902: Winner of Metropolitan Amateur; tied for second in U.S. Open. 1903: Winner of U.S. Amateur. 1904: Winner of British Amateur and North and South Amateur. 1906: Winner of Florida Open. 1909: Winner of Metropolitan Amateur. 1910, 1912: Winner of North and South Amateur. 1913, 1914: Winner of Cuban Amateur. 1915: Winner of Metropolitan Amateur and Southern Florida Amateur. 1916: Winner of Southern Florida Amateur.

TREVINO, LEE B. Born in Dallas, TX, December 1, 1939. An incredible aspect of Lee Trevino's rags-to-riches saga is that he attained fame only a few years after he was polishing clubs and shining shoes as an assistant in Texas. In the spring of 1967, his wife sent his entry to the local qualifier for the U.S. Open. They could ill afford the $20 fee. Lee went all the way, finished fifth at Baltusrol, and won $6,000. In subsequent years he did everything but walk across the water.

Raised near Dallas by his grandfather, a grave-digger, Lee went as far as the eighth grade before he had to work. He became a handyman at a pitch-and-putt course and also learned to play. But it was during a four-year hitch in the Marines that his game developed. After the Marines, it was back to a $30-a-week assistant's post in El Paso, where he played in some local events and finally, a fateful entry for the 1967 Open. If the golf world wondered about Trevino at Baltusrol, all the questions were answered when he won the 1968 U.S. Open.

After three rounds, Bert Yancey led with 205, but Trevino was only one stroke behind on rounds of 69, 68, 69. Jack Nicklaus was seven behind at 212. In the final round, Yancey started missing putts, and fell away to 76 and third place. Meanwhile, Trevino's last round 69 held off Nicklaus, who closed with a 67 and finished second to Trevino, four strokes behind. Trevino was the first player in U.S. Open history to play all four rounds in under par and in the 60s. He also equalled the record score of 275, established by Nicklaus in 1967.

In 1970, Trevino's steadiness became apparent as he won two Tour events, was leading money winner and won the Vardon Trophy. He also finished tied for third in the British Open, a final round of 77 costing him the championship.

In 1971, Trevino set a record that has never been equalled since. In a matter of four weeks, he won the U.S. Open, Canadian Open, and British Open. In the U.S. Open at the Merion Golf Club in Ardmore, Pennsylvania, he tied Nicklaus at 280, then won the play-off, 68 to 71. In the Canadian Open at Richelieu Valley Golf and Country Club, Montreal, Quebec, he again tied for first, this time with Art Wall, at 275. Trevino won with a birdie at the first play-off hole. Then, in the British Open at Royal Birkdale, Trevino, after taking a 7 at the 17th hole, finished at 278, one stroke ahead of Lu Liang Huan. In addition, Trevino won three other events on the PGA Tour, and finished second on the money list. He again won the Vardon Trophy, and was honored as PGA Player of the Year.

The following year, Trevino repeated in the British Open, held at Muirfield. He was paired with Tony Jacklin in the final two rounds. The climax of the tournament came at the par-5 17th hole. Leading by a stroke over Tony Jacklin, Trevino duck-hooked his drive into a bunker, made a weak recovery, hooked a fairway wood into the rough, then bladed a sand wedge clear across the green. Mad with himself, Trevino grabbed a 9-iron and hit the ball without even planting his feet. The chip went right into the hole. When Tony Jacklin missed his putt for a five, Trevino regained his lead, and finished with 278, one stroke ahead of Jack Nicklaus. In the Vardon Trophy, he made it three in a row.

In 1974, Trevino won the first of his PGA Championships. At Tanglewood Golf Club in Winston-Salem, North Carolina, he opened with a 73, but passed everyone with subsequent rounds of 66, 68, 69. Jack Nicklaus finished second, one stroke behind. Trevino again took home the Vardon Trophy. He won it again in 1980.

By the time he won the 1984 PGA, he had been without a victory for three-and-a-half years. The problem had been back injury, possibly caused when he was struck by lightning at the 1975 Western Open. He underwent an operation for a herniated disc late in 1976. In 1981, he had a nerve ending deadened. This killed the pain, but it took a while for

Lee Trevino. *AP/Wide World Photos*

Trevino to get back his confidence. It all came together for Lee at Shoal Creek, in Birmingham, Alabama. He was in marvelous form, shooting 69, 68, 67, 69 to outlast Gary Player and Lanny Wadkins and win by four strokes. At the age of forty-four, it was Trevino's twenty-seventh Tour victory, and his sixth major championship.

Trevino made a strong defense of his title at Cherry Hill, Colorado. He carded a four-under par 280, but Hubert Green outlasted him in the stretch, and won by two strokes.

Trevino played on the 1968, 1969, 1970, 1971, and 1974 World Cup teams, and in the Ryder Cup matches, appeared in 1969, 1971, 1973, 1975, 1979, and 1981. He captained the 1985 Ryder Cup team.

Trevino spent much of the 1980s working as a commentator for NBC, but he turned full-time to playing again when he turned fifty on December 1, 1989, becoming eligible for the Senior Tour. In 1990, he won seven senior events, including the U.S. Senior Open, where he finished two strokes ahead of Jack Nicklaus. Trevino posted a 68.89 scoring average to lead by a full stroke and topped the money list with $1,190,518. He became the first senior to earn more than the PGA Tour's leading money winner.

Trevino's swing is hardly orthodox. He has a strong grip, aims left, closes the blade at the top, and then pulls through strongly with the left hand to fade the ball. But his swing repeats and repeats, and that quality wins a lot of championships.

Tournament Record: 1968: Winner of U.S. Open and Hawaiian Open. 1969: Winner of Tucson Open. 1970: Winner of Tucson Open and National Airlines Open. 1971: Winner of Tallahassee Open, Danny Thomas–Memphis Classic, U.S. Open, Canadian Open, British Open, and Sahara Invitational. 1972: Winner of Danny Thomas–Memphis Classic, British Open, Greater Hartford Open, and Greater St. Louis Golf Classic. 1973: Winner of Jackie Gleason-Inverrary Classic, and Doral-Eastern Open. 1974: Winner of New Orleans Open, PGA Championship, and World Series of Golf. 1975: Winner of Florida Citrus Open and Mexican Open. 1976: Winner of Colonial National Invitation. 1977: Winner of Canadian Open and Morocco Grand Prix. 1978: Winner of Colonial National Invitation, Benson & Hedges, and Lancôme Trophy. 1979: Winner of Canadian Open and Canadian PGA. 1980: Winner of Tournament Players Championship, Danny Thomas–

Memphis Classic, and San Antonio–Texas Open. 1981: Winner of MONY Tournament of Champions. 1983: Winner of Canadian PGA Championship. 1984: Winner of PGA Championship. 1990: Winner of Royal Caribbean Classic, Aetna Challenge, Vintage Chrysler Invitational, Doug Sanders Kingwood Celebrity Classic, NYNEX Commemorative, U.S. Senior Open, and Transamerica Senior Championship. 1991: Winner of Aetna Challenge, Vantage at The Dominion, Liberty Mutual Legends of Golf (with Mike Hill), and Sunwest–Charley Pride Classic. 1992: Winner of Vantage at The Dominion, Tradition at Desert Mountain, PGA Seniors Championship, Liberty Mutual Legends of Golf (with Mike Hill), Las Vegas Senior Classic and Bell Atlantic Classic.

TWAY, ROBERT RAYMOND. Born in Oklahoma City, OK, May 4, 1959. Bob Tway started to play golf at age five. "I'd follow my grandfather and father around the course," he says. "I played in my first junior event at seven." At Oklahoma State, he was All-American from 1979 through 1981, and was awarded the 1981 Fred Haskins award for outstanding college golfer of the year. He was a member of the 1978 and 1980 NCAA championship teams. He was also a member of the 1980 World Cup team.

Tway turned professional in 1981. The first three times Tway tried to qualify for the PGA Tour, he failed. However, he did manage to play a few Tour events each year, and played anywhere else he could to pick up experience. He competed on the Asian and European Tours. He also played in the "minor league" Tournament Player Series, and won the 1983 Sandpiper–Santa Barbara Open. He qualified for the Tour in the fall of 1984.

In 1985, Tway had a strong first year, finishing second in the Quad Cities Open and registering three other top ten finishes. He was forty-fifth on the money list with $164,023.

In 1986, Tway broke through to the top ranks, tying Bernhard Langer in the rain-shortened Andy Williams at 204, then winning the play-off. He took the Westchester Classic with 272, edging his friend Willie Wood by a stroke. In the Georgia-Pacific Atlanta Classic, he came from four strokes off the pace with a final-round 64 to win his third title of the year. Then, in the PGA Championship, played at the Inverness Club, Toledo, OH, Tway was four behind Greg Norman with one round to go—202 to 206. Deadlocked with Norman coming to the par-4 72nd hole,

Bob Tway. *Fred Vuich*

Tway's second shot found a bunker, Norman's second hit the green but then sucked back into rough. It looked as though there could be a tie. Then Tway played the twenty-five-foot bunker shot perfectly, the ball gently landing eight feet short of the cup, then rolling in for a birdie. When Norman hit his sand wedge chip twelve feet past, and two-putted for a five, Tway was PGA Champion. Tway was later named PGA Player of the Year, and finished as the second leading money winner with $652,780, just $516 behind Norman.

Tway was not able to maintain such lofty status. He slumped to forty-seventh on the money list in 1987, then lost twice in play-offs in 1988. He finally broke back into the winner's circle at the 1989 Memorial Tournament and won again in 1990, earning more than $480,000 each of those two years.

When he was growing up, Tway says, "I modeled my swing on Tom Weiskopf. He was a great one and since we have about the same build, I copied his swing as best I could." Tway did a pretty good job. He does lean over a little more from the hips than his model, but his sound, rhythmic swing has a lot of Weiskopf in it.

Tournament Record: 1978: Winner of Trans-Mississippi Amateur. 1979: Winner of Southern Amateur. 1983: Winner of Sandpiper–Santa Barbara Open. 1986: Winner of Shearson Lehman Brothers–Andy Williams Open, Manufacturers Hanover Westchester Classic, Georgia-Pacific Atlanta Classic, and PGA Championship. 1989: Winner of Memorial Tournament. 1990: Winner of Las Vegas Invitational.

VARDON, HARRY. Born in Grouville, Isle of Jersey, England, May 7, 1870. Died March 20, 1937. The chief figure of Britain's famed "triumvirate" and considered by many to be the greatest player who ever lived. Vardon won six British Opens (a record), was runner-up four times, and was in the top five on six other occasions—sixteen times in the top five over a span of twenty-one years. He was just as impressive in America, which he toured on several occasions. He won the U.S. Open in 1900, tied for first and lost the play-off in 1913, and tied for second in 1920 at the age of fifty. He also won the British PGA in 1912 and the German Open in 1911 with a score of 279. The overlapping grip was first used by Vardon in the

Harry Vardon.
AP/Wide World Photos

1890's and was named for him, although J. H. Taylor is said to have employed it first. Vardon was a master fairway wood player, and historians without exception dwell at length on his ability to hit full brassie shots stiff to the pin. Certainly he had as graceful a swing as could be imagined, and for later generations of golfers, the highest compliment was to have one's swing compared to Vardon's. He is credited with sixty-two tournament wins. He once won fourteen events in a row.

VENTURI, KENNETH. Born in San Francisco, CA, May 15, 1931. The son of a San Francisco golf professional, Ken Venturi first played golf when he was twelve years old. In 1948, he won the San Francisco Interscholastic crown and was runner-up in the USGA Junior. In the following season, he won the San Francisco City Championship, and later was a two-time California Amateur champion. He first met Byron Nelson in 1952. Nelson completely remodeled Venturi's swing and continued to coach him during his career. Venturi played on the 1953 Walker Cup team, winning his foursome match with Sam Urzetta by 6 and 4, and his single by 9 and 8. In 1956, after an overseas hitch with the U.S. Army, he won the San Francisco City Championship again, beating Harvie Ward, and was invited to the Masters. He came very close to winning it. Venturi opened with 66, 69 to lead by four strokes. It looked as though Venturi would "blow up" quickly in the third round—he took 40 strokes to the turn. Then he pulled himself together, birdied 13, 14 and 15, and finished with 75, retaining his four-stroke lead. In the last round, Venturi went out in 38, with three three-putts, and needed a 40 on the back nine to win. He still couldn't buy a putt, however, and took 42, including six bogies. He lost by a stroke to Jack Burke Jr. Later in 1956, Venturi turned professional.

By the time he came to the 1960 Masters, Venturi was a seasoned pro, and known as a superb iron player. He had won nine Tour events. Again, he just failed to win Augusta's pride. Venturi lay one stroke behind Arnold Palmer after three rounds and posted a 283, but Palmer birdied the final two holes to win by a stroke.

About that time, Venturi decided that he needed more length from the tee, and started working on a draw, for more run. He lost consistency, and then found he couldn't get back his old method. Also, he had physical problems with his hands, the onset of the circulatory ailment that was ultimately to put an end to his career. From second on the money list in 1960, he slipped to fourteenth in 1961, sixty-sixth in 1962 and ninety-fourth in 1963.

Then, in 1964, Venturi's game started to come back. In a scenario made for Hollywood, Venturi's irons started homing in on the stick again, and he tied for ninth at Pensacola. Then, successive high finishes in the Thunderbird Classic (tied for third) and Buick Open (tied for sixth) sent him to the U.S. Open site at Congressional in the right frame of mind. He started with 72, 70, which placed him six behind Tommy Jacobs and five behind Palmer. Two rounds had to be played on the final day. Venturi carded 66, which put him four ahead of Palmer, but still two behind Jacobs. Venturi came into the clubhouse exhausted by the severe heat, and dehydrated to the point that a doctor accompanied him on the final round. Ironically, it was the other golfers who faded. Venturi plodded his weary way to a 70, and a total of 278, beating Jacobs and Palmer by four. Venturi added two more wins that year, and five other times was seventh or better, giving him his best year on Tour,

Ken Venturi. *UPI/Bettmann*

sixth on the money list with $62,465. He was later named PGA Player of the Year.

Venturi's health collapsed again in 1965. He had to undergo surgery on his wrists to relieve circulatory problems. He was sidelined almost the whole of the year, winning less than $300. The following year, he came back to win the Lucky International, but that was the end of his career. He's now a golf commentator for CBS.

Tournament Record: 1957: Winner of St. Paul Open and Miller Open. 1958: Winner of Thunderbird Invitational, Phoenix Open, Baton Rouge Open, and Gleneagles–Chicago Open. 1959: Winner of Los Angeles Open and Gleneagles–Chicago Open. 1960: Winner of Bing Crosby Pro-Am and Milwaukee Open. 1964: Winner of U.S. Open, Insurance City Open, and American Golf Classic. 1966: Winner of Lucky International.

WADKINS, JERRY LANSTON. Born in Richmond, VA, December 5, 1949. Lanny Wadkins got a fast start to his golf career, winning the 1963 and 1964 Pee Wee Championships. In 1966, at age sixteen, he shot 294 in the U.S. Amateur, nine strokes behind the winner. While attending Wake Forest on an Arnold Palmer golf scholarship, he had an outstanding amateur career. In 1968, he won the Southern Amateur. The following year, he took the Eastern Amateur and played on the Walker Cup team. In 1970, he had his best year, winning the U.S. Western, Southern Amateurs and playing on the World Amateur Cup team. He also finished second in a Tour event, the Heritage Classic. He was All-American that year, as well as in 1971. He was a member of the 1971 Walker Cup team, and played number one in the singles, winning both times; a great "scalp" was his defeat of five-time British Amateur champion Michael Bonallack by 3 and 1. Wadkins turned pro later that year.

In his first full year on Tour, Wadkins won the Sahara Invitational and earned $116,616, tenth on the money list. He was Rookie of the Year. The next year, he won two events, and rose to fifth on the list with $200,456. It looked as though the Tour had a new superstar. However, since then, Wadkins' progress has been uneven, to put it mildly. When he's on form, there is no player more brilliant, but when he's off, he can be way off.

Afflicted with gall-bladder problems in 1974, he dropped to fifty-fourth on the list. He came back to

Lanny Wadkins. *Fred Vuich*

the Tour too soon, he feels, and in 1975 and 1976 dropped out of the top sixty money-winners.

One of his finest years was 1977, when he won the PGA Championship. He carded 69, 71, 72, 70—excellent scores on Pebble Beach—and tied Gene Littler. Wadkins won on the third play-off hole. Wadkins also won the World Series that year, taking home $244,882 for the year, third on the money list.

The next year, Wadkins dropped out of the top sixty again, but did win two foreign events. He took the Canadian PGA by twelve strokes and also the Garden State PGA in Australia.

In 1979, Wadkins gave one of his finest performances in winning the Tournament Players Champi-

onship at Sawgrass. Wadkins opened with 67, 68, to lead George Burns by three strokes. He retained this lead even after a third round of 76, mostly due to high winds. In the final round, conditions verged on the unplayable, with wind gusts up to forty-five miles per hour. Wadkins's round—a wonderful 72—brought him home five strokes ahead of runner-up Tom Watson. To get an idea of how well Wadkins played in the final two rounds, one need look no farther than Burns's scores for the last two rounds—76, 83.

After another falling off in 1980 and 1981, in recent years Wadkins's Tour records shows a much more solid, as well as brilliant, player. From 1982 through 1992, he had fourteen victories, and finished in the top thirteen money winners every year except 1984, 1986, 1989 and 1992.

Wadkins was selected as PGA Player of the Year in 1985. He also played on the Ryder Cup team in 1977, 1979, 1983, 1985, 1987, 1989 and 1991, and on the World Cup team in 1977, 1984, and 1985.

Wadkins is a great crowd pleaser because of his attacking game. "I get a big kick out playing that way," he says, "You know, going for the green in two on a par-5 when the second shot is over water, but I never take a chance if it's a bad lie." Wadkins can be bold because he is one of the most accomplished shotmakers in the game. "Some people don't know I have those shots. They see me lashing away (Wadkins' tempo is fast and furious), but don't understand what I'm doing. I'm always working the ball. Every shot is calculated."

Tournament Record: 1963: Winner of National Pee Wee Championship. 1964: Winner of National Pee Wee Championship. 1968: Winner of Southern Amateur. 1969: Winner of Eastern Amateur. 1970: Winner of U.S. Amateur, Western Amateur, and Southern Amateur. 1972: Winner of Sahara Invitational. 1973: Winner of Byron Nelson Classic and USI Classic. 1977: Winner of PGA Championship and World Series of Golf. 1978: Winner of Canadian PGA Championship and Garden State PGA (Australia). 1979: Winner of Los Angeles Open, Tournament Players Championship, and Bridgestone Open. 1982: Winner of Phoenix Open, Tournament of Champions, and Buick Open. 1983: Winner of Greensboro Open and Tournament of Champions. 1984: Winner of World Nissan Championship. 1985: Winner of Bob Hope Classic, Los Angeles Open, and Walt Disney

World–Oldsmobile Classic. 1987: Winner of Doral–Ryder Open. 1988: Winner of Hawaiian Open and Colonial National Invitation. 1990: Winner of Anheuser-Busch Classic. 1991: Winner of Hawaiian Open. 1992: Winner of Canon–Greater Hartford Open.

WATSON, THOMAS. Born in Kansas City, MO, September 4, 1949. After playing collegiate golf at Stanford University, where he earned his B.A. in psychology in 1971, Watson immediately became a professional. His rookie season on the Tour, 1972, was hardly spectacular, although he came within a stroke of winning the Quad Cities Open. In 1973, he had victory within his grasp twice but let it get away, and this began to be his reputation. In 1974, he led the U.S. Open for three rounds but closed with a 79 and lost it. But he came charging back the next week to score his first pro victory in the tough Western Open, making up six shots in the closing round.

His big breakthrough came in 1975, when he won the British Open at Carnoustie and finished in the top ten in the other events that make up the Big Four. Three strokes off the lead on the final day, he rallied to gain a tie with Jack Newton. He won the play-off the next day. He was in seventh place on the money list with $153,795, and observers agreed that he was on his way.

He didn't win in 1976, although he finished in the top ten in eleven events and earned over $138,000. In 1977, he became the game's best player. He beat Jack Nicklaus in the Masters and the British Open with spectacular play and won three other events. He exceeded $300,000 in prize money and was the PGA Player of the Year.

In many ways 1978 was a repeat performance. Watson won five Tour events, raised his money winnings to $362,429 and was again PGA Player of the Year. The following year, he increased the Tour money-winning record to $462,636, while again winning five Tour events and being selected as PGA Player of the Year.

Besides being leading money winner and Player of the Year each year from 1977 through 1979, Watson also won the Vardon Trophy all three years, with stroke averages of 70.32, 70.16, and 70.27. No one else has achieved this triple distinction.

Still, his best year was yet to come. In 1980, Watson played in twenty-two Tour events, won money

Tom Watson. *UPI/Bettmann*

in all of them, and was in the top ten sixteen times. More important, he won six Tour events, setting a new money-winning record of $530,808. He was PGA Player of the Year. He also won his third British Open at Muirfield, where his rounds of 68, 70, 64, 69 left Lee Trevino four strokes behind.

In 1981, Watson says, "I fought myself and my swing." Nevertheless, he won three times on Tour, including his second Masters. He was third on the money list and topped $300,000 for the fifth time in a row.

In 1982, he made it six times in a row and again was selected as PGA Player of the Year. Watson also won his first U.S. Open that year. After a pair of 72s at Pebble Beach, Watson's third round 68 took him into a tie for the lead with Bill Rogers. Jack Nicklaus was three strokes behind. Nicklaus finished first, and with two holes to play, Watson needed to par in for a tie. On the 209-yard 17th, he hit a 2-iron into five-inch rough about five yards to the left of the hole. He then applied the cruncher—a deftly played, soft little sand wedge shot that rolled right into the hole. On 18, all he needed was a par to win, but holed a twenty-foot birdie putt for a final round of 70, and victory by two strokes. In the British Open at Troon, Watson was seven strokes behind after two rounds. His 69, 71 would normally have put him in or close to the lead, but not with Bobby Clampett shooting 67, 66. Watson's third round of 74 should have been a disappointment, but Clampett gave all his pursuers hope by taking 78. In the last round, Watson's 70 was good enough for a one-stroke victory and his fourth British Open win.

On the PGA Tour, 1983 was a disappointment for Watson. His best finishes were tied for second in the U.S. Open at Oakmont and in the Western Open. However, he did win his fifth British Open at Royal Birkdale, which puts him within grasp of one day tying the record of six (held by Harry Vardon). Watson took a one-stroke lead after the third round, on scores of 67, 68, 70, then added another 70 to win by a stroke.

In 1984, Watson returned to the top position on the PGA Tour, winning three times and earning $476,260. He didn't add to his list of majors, but came close, finishing second in both the Masters and British Open.

In 1985 and 1986, however, Watson began to slip, going without a victory and finishing eighteenth and twentieth on the money list. He made a bit of a comeback in 1987, finishing second at the U.S. Open, where Scott Simpson birdied three of the last six holes to win by one stroke, and winning the season-ending Nabisco Championships. But that was his lone victory in the six-year period from 1985 through 1990. Once the best putter on Tour, that part of his game abandoned him, and he especially had trouble with short putts. He also lost some of the desire that had driven him early in his career, and he cut back his schedule.

Still, Watson's position as one of the greatest players of all time was already secure. He has won thirty-two times on the PGA Tour and owns eight majors—five British Opens, two Masters, and one U.S. Open. He has won the Vardon Trophy three times, was PGA Player of the Year six times (1977, 1978, 1979, 1980, 1982, and 1984) and was a member of the 1977, 1981, 1983, and 1989 Ryder Cup teams.

Tournament Record: 1974: Winner of Western Open. 1975: Winner of Byron Nelson Golf Classic, British Open and World Series of Golf. 1977: Winner of Bing Crosby National Pro-Am, San Diego Open, Masters, Western Open, and British Open. 1978: Winner of Tucson Open, Bing Crosby National Pro-Am, Byron Nelson Golf Classic, Colgate Hall of Fame

Classic, and Anheuser-Busch Classic. 1979: Winner of Sea Pines Heritage Classic, Tournament of Champions, Byron Nelson Golf Classic, Memorial Tournament, and Colgate Hall of Fame Classic. 1980: Winner of San Diego Open, Los Angeles Open, Tournament of Champions, New Orleans Open, Byron Nelson Golf Classic, British Open, World Series of Golf, and Dunlop Phoenix (Japan). 1981: Winner of Masters, New Orleans Open, and Atlanta Classic. 1982: Winner of Los Angeles Open, Sea Pines Heritage Classic, U.S. Open, and British Open. 1983: Winner of British Open. 1984: Winner of Tucson Match Play, Tournament of Champions, and Western Open. 1987: Winner of Nabisco Championships.

WEISKOPF, Thomas Daniel. Tom Weiskopf took up the game when he was fifteen and shot in the 70s a year later. He won the Western Amateur in 1963.

Tom Weiskopf. *Courtesy PGA*

When he came to the Tour in 1965, Weiskopf was compared to Jack Nicklaus. Both came out of Ohio State University, both were exceptionally long hitters, and both had fine golf swings, Weiskopf's swing being heralded as the best of the modern era. But there the resemblance ended. Although Weiskopf had a career that most Tour pros would envy, he never had the burning ambition of a Nicklaus. He took time away from the Tour to be with his family, and also to pursue wildlife trophies, mostly sheep and elk.

Nevertheless, through 1982, Weiskopf won fifteen Tour events. For seventeen years, from 1966 through 1982, he was in the top sixty money winners, and from 1968 through 1978, in the top thirty. In 1968, 1973, and 1975, he was third on the money list. Eleven times he earned over $100,000. He played on the 1973 and 1975 Ryder Cup teams, and the 1972 World Cup team. He also took one major, the 1973 British Open.

Weiskopf's best year was undoubtedly 1973. His performance gave a tantalizing glimpse of what he might have achieved with, say, Nicklaus's or Hogan's head on his shoulders. He won the Colonial in May, and two weeks later finished second to Nicklaus at Atlanta. Then he won the Kemper Open, followed by the Philadelphia Classic. In the U.S. Open, Weiskopf finished third, one of those left in the wake of Johnny Miller's last-round 63. In July, Weiskopf went to Troon for the British Open. He started with a 68 to take the lead, and then added a 67, to lead Miller and Bert Yancey by three. In the third round, Miller took 32 to the turn, to Weiskopf's 37, but Weiskopf took 34 on the back nine to Miller's 37, to retain a one stroke lead. In the final round, Weiskopf increased his lead to three on the first hole, and was four ahead after nine. He finished with a 70, a comfortable winner by three strokes. Later in July, Weiskopf also won the Canadian Open and World Series. Worldwide, he won about $350,000 for the year.

When Weiskopf left the Tour in 1984, the reason was physical—a torn rotator cuff in his right shoulder. In the meantime, he has become a respected golf course architect, working mainly with Jay Morrish.

Tournament Record: 1963: Winner of Western Amateur. 1968: Winner of San Diego Open and Buick Open. 1971: Winner of Kemper Open and Philadelphia Classic. 1972: Winner of Inverrary Classic and World Match Play. 1973: Winner of Colonial National Invitation, Kemper Open, Philadelphia Classic, British Open, Canadian Open, World Series of Golf, and South African PGA Championship. 1975: Winner of Greensboro Open and Canadian Open. 1977: Winner of Kemper Open. 1978: Winner of Doral—Eastern Open. 1979: Winner of Argentine Open. 1981: Winner of LaJet Classic and Benson & Hedges International (England). 1982: Winner of Western Open and Jerry Ford Invitational.

WETHERED, JOYCE (LADY HEATHCOAT-AMORY). Born November 17, 1901. Rated for many years as being without question the greatest female golfer in the history of the game. Despite the rise of women's golf and the large number of outstanding players being developed, she still is rated as no worse than equal with Babe Didrikson Zaharias, Mickey Wright and Kathy Whitworth. Miss Wethered came on the

Joyce Wethered. *Courtesy U.S.G.A.*

tournament scene in 1920 and was virtually unbeatable from the start. She won the English Ladies championship five straight times beginning in 1920, and in the British women's championship, the premier event of its day, she played six times, winning four, being runner-up once and semifinalist once. As a matter of fact, she retired after 1925, having had her fill of competition at an early age, but the lure of St. Andrews brought her back one more time, in 1929, and she defeated Glenna Collett in the final. Thereafter, she limited her tournament play to an annual appearance in the foursomes at Worplesdon, which she won eight times in fifteen years. Her brother Roger was one of Britain's finest amateurs during the 1920s.

WHITWORTH, KATHRYNNE ANN. Born in Monahans, TX, September 27, 1939. Kathy Whitworth has compiled the most impressive record of any woman professional golfer. She started golf at fifteen years of age, and won the New Mexico State Amateur in 1957 and 1958 before turning professional in 1958. Whitworth was leading money winner eight times (1965–1968, 1970–1973), Player of the Year seven times (1966–1969, 1971–1973), and Vare Trophy winner seven times (1965–1967, 1969–1972). She holds the U.S. record for most official career professional wins, eighty-eight, surpassing Mickey Wright's eighty-two and Sam Snead's eighty-one. She also has won five majors: the 1965 and 1966 Titleholders Championships, the 1967 LPGA Championship and Western Open, and the 1971 LPGA Championship. The first LPGA player to reach career earnings of $1 million (in 1981), Whitworth had her finest year financially in 1983, when she won one event, but earned $191,492, good for fifth on the money list. Her most dominant period on the Tour was from 1963 through 1973, when she won seventy events. Like Sam Snead, the only "flaw" in her record has been her failure to win the national Open.

Whitworth feels that the main reason for her success was her ability to "keep the ball in play" and avoid destructive shots. She was also one of the finest putters of modern times.

Tournament Record: 1957: Winner of New Mexico State Amateur. 1958: Winner of New Mexico State Amateur. 1962: Winner of Kelly Girl Open and Phoenix Thunderbird Open. 1963: Winner of Carvel Open, Wolverine Open, Milwaukee Jaycee Open,

Kathy Whitworth. *UPI/Bettmann*

Ogden Open, Spokane Open, Hillside Open, San Antonio Civitan Open, and Gulf Coast Invitational. 1964: Winner of San Antonio Civitan Open. 1965: Winner of St. Petersburg Invitational, Shreveport Kiwanis Club Invitational, Bluegrass Invitational, Midwest Open, Yankee Open, Buckeye Savings Invitational, Mickey Wright Invitational, and Titleholders Championship. 1966: Winner of Tall City Open, Clayton Federal Invitational, Milwaukee Open, Supertest Invitational, Lady Carling (Sutton), Lady Carling (Baltimore), Las Cruces Open, Amarillo Open, and Titleholders Championship. 1967: Winner of Venice Open, Raleigh Invitational, St. Louis Invitational, LPGA Championship, Lady Carling (Columbus), Western Open, Los Angeles Open, and Alamo Open. 1968: Winner of Orange Blossom Classic, Dallas Civitan, Baltimore Lady Carling, Gino Paoli Open, Holiday Inn Classic, Kings River Classic, River Plantation Classic, Canyon Classic, Pensacola Invitational, and Louise Suggs Invitational. 1969: Winner of Orange Blossom Classic, Port Charlotte Invitation,

Port Malabar Invitational, Lady Carling (Atlanta), Patty Berg Classic, Wendell West Open, and River Plantation Open. 1970: Winner of Orange Blossom Classic, and Quality Chek'd Classic. 1971: Winner of Raleigh Classic, Suzuki Internationale, Lady Carling, LPGA Four-Ball Championship (with Judy Kimball), and LPGA Championship. 1972: Winner of Alamo Open, Raleigh Classic, Knoxville Open, Southgate Open, and Portland Open. 1973: Winner of Naples–Lely Classic, S&H Green Stamp Classic, Dallas Civitan, Southgate Open, Portland Open, Waco Tribune Herald Classic, and Lady Errol Classic. 1974: Winner of Orange Blossom Classic. 1975: Winner of Baltimore Championship, Colgate Triple Crown, and Southgate Open. 1976: Winner of Bent Tree Classic and Patty Berg Classic. 1977: Winner of Colgate–Dinah Shore Winner's Circle, American Defender Classic, and Coca-Cola Classic. 1978: Winner of National Jewish Hospital Open and Ping Classic (with Donna Caponi). 1980: Winner of Portland Ping Team Championship (with Donna Caponi). 1981: Winner of Coca-Cola Classic and Portland Ping Team Championship (with Donna Caponi). 1982: Winner of CPC International and Lady Michelob. 1983: Winner of Women's Kemper Open. 1984: Winner of Rochester International, Safeco Classic, and Smirnoff Ladies Irish Open. 1985: Winner of United Virginia Bank Classic.

WOOD, CRAIG RALPH. Born in Lake Placid, NY, November 18, 1901. Died May 8, 1968. A long-hitting, extremely popular player, who finally got a well-deserved championship to his credit when he won both the 1941 U.S. Open and Masters at the age of thirty-nine. Wood had begun to win tournaments on the winter tour as early as 1928, but it was thirteen years before he would take a major title. In between, he was runner-up in the Masters twice and in the U.S. Open, PGA Championship, and British Open. On the first hole at St. Andrews, Wood drove the ball into the Swilcan Burn, a belt of more than 350 yards. Wood operated an automobile agency for many years after World War II, then returned to golf in the early 1960s as pro at the Lucayan Beach Club on Grand Bahama Island, a position he held at his death.

Tournament Record: 1925: Winner of Kentucky Open. 1926: Winner of Kentucky PGA. 1928: Winner of Pasadena Open and New Jersey PGA. 1929: Winner of Oklahoma City Open, Hawaiian Open, and

Craig Wood.
Wide World Photos

New Jersey PGA. 1930: Winner of Harlingen Open, Reddy Tee Tournament, and New Jersey PGA. 1932: Winner of Pasadena Open, San Francisco Match Play, Radium Springs Open, and New Jersey PGA. 1933: Winner of Los Angeles Open; runner-up in British Open. 1934: Winner of Galveston Open and New Jersey Open; runner-up in Masters and PGA Championship. 1935: Runner-up in Masters. 1936: Winner of General Brock Open. 1939: Winner of Augusta Open; runner-up in U.S. Open. 1940: Winner of Miami Four-Ball and Metropolitan Open. 1941: Winner of U.S. Open and Masters. 1942: Winner of Canadian Open and Metropolitan PGA. 1943: Winner of Golden Valley Four-Ball. 1944: Winner of Durham Open.

WOOSNAM, IAN. Born in Oswestry, Wales, March 2, 1958. Woosnam, a scrappy 5'4" Welshman, gradually climbed the ladder of success until firmly establishing himself as one of the best players in the world with his victory in the 1991 Masters.

Woosnam turned pro at the age of twenty, but

after four years having earned a total of less than $10,000 on the European Tour, he was almost ready to quit and take a club job. Suddenly, though, his game fell into place while playing on the Safari Tour in Africa in early 1982, and he went on to win the Swiss Open and finish eighth in the European Order of Merit that year.

For the next four campaigns, Woosnam remained a once-a-year winner. Then in 1987, he took another big step up, winning five events in Europe to lead the Order of Merit and adding three more wins overseas. He put together yet another five-win season in Europe in 1990 to lead the Order of Merit for a second time and surpass Seve Ballesteros as Europe's career money leader.

Still, Woosnam had yet to win in the United States, where he'd made only limited appearances, nor had he won a major championship. He took care of both in a three-week span in the spring of 1991. First he won the USF&G Classic in New Orleans, then he

Ian Woosnam. *Fred Vuich*

earned his first major by outlasting Jose Maria Olazabal and Tom Watson down the stretch in the Masters.

Tournament Record: 1982: Winner of Swiss Open. 1983: Winner of Silk Cut Masters. 1985: Winner of Zambian Open. 1986: Winner of Lawrence Batley TPC and Kenya Open. 1987: Winner of Jersey Open, Cepsa Madrid Open, Bell's Scottish Open, Lancome Trophy, Suntory World Match Play Championship, Hong Kong Open, World Cup, Sun City Challenge. 1988: Winner of Volvo PGA Championship, Carrolls Irish Open, Panasonic European Open. 1989: Winner of Carrolls Irish Open. 1990: Winner of Amex Mediterranean Open, Torras Monte Carlo Open, Bell's Scottish Open, Epson Grand Prix, and Suntory World Match Play Championship. 1991: Winner of Mediterranean Open, Monte Carlo Open, USF&G Classic, and Masters. 1992: Winner of Monte Carlo Open.

WRIGHT, MARY KATHRYN (MICKEY). Born in San Diego, CA, February 14, 1935. Generally ranked with Joyce Wethered, Babe Didrikson Zaharias, and Kathy Whitworth at the head of any list of great women golfers. Miss Wright's domination of the LPGA tour in the early 1960s was complete, and from 1960 through 1964 she was leading money winner four times and Vare Trophy winner five times. She won thirteen tournaments in 1963 to set a record, and in two other years she won ten tournaments each. Her career total of eighty-two pro victories includes four U.S. Opens and four LPGA Championships. Like many great players before her, Miss Wright began to find the grind too much for her in the mid-1960s, and she announced her retirement to enter college at Southern Methodist University. However, she was back in action next season, although she never again played the entire schedule.

Tournament Record: 1952: Winner of 1952 U.S. Girls Junior Championship. 1954: Winner of World Amateur. 1956: Winner of Jacksonville Open. 1957: Winner of Sea Island Open, Jacksonville Open, and Wolverine Open. 1958: Winner of Sea Island Open, Opie Turner Open, Dallas Civitan Open, LPGA Championship, and U.S. Women's Open. 1959: Winner of Jacksonville Open, Cavalier Open, Alliance Machine International Open, and U.S. Women's Open. 1960: Winner of Sea Island Open, Tampa Open, Grossinger Open, Eastern Open, Memphis Open, and LPGA

Championship. 1961: Winner of St. Petersburg Open, Miami Open, Columbus Open, Waterloo Open, Spokane Open, Sacramento Valley Open, U.S. Women's Open, LPGA Championship, Titleholders Championship, and Mickey Wright Invitational. 1962: Winner of Sea Island Invitational, Titleholders Championship, Western Open, Milwaukee Open, Heart of America Invitational, Albuquerque Swing Parade, Salt Lake City Open, Spokane Open, San Diego Open, and Carlsbad Cavern City Open. 1963: Winner of Sea Island Invitational, St. Petersburg Open, Alpine Civitan Open, Muskogee Civitan Open, Dallas Civitan, Babe Zaharias Open, Western Open, Waterloo Open, Albuquerque Swing Parade, Idaho Centennial Open, Visalia Open, Mickey Wright Invitational, and LPGA Championship. 1964: Winner of Peach Blossom Invitational, Alexandria Open, Squirt Open, Muskogee Civitan Open, Lady Carling Eastern Open, Waldemar Open, U.S. Women's Open, Milwaukee Jay-Cee Open, Visalia Open, Tall City Open, and Gulf Coast Invitational. 1965: Winner of Baton Rouge Invitational and Dallas Civitan. 1966: Winner of Venice Open, Shreveport Kiwanis Invitational, Bluegrass In-

vitational, Western Open, Pacific Classic, Shirley Englehorn Invitational, and Mickey Wright Invitational. 1967: Winner of Shreveport Invitational, Bluegrass Invitational, Lady Carling (Baltimore), and Pensacola Invitational. 1968: Winner of Port Malabar Invitational, Palm Beach County Open, Tall City Open, and "500" Classic. 1969: Winner of Bluegrass Invitational. 1973: Winner of Colgate–Dinah Shore Winner's Circle.

ZAHARIAS, MILDRED DIDRIKSON (BABE). Born in Port Arthur, TX, June 26, 1914. Died September 27, 1956. Voted the greatest woman athlete of all time in every poll ever taken. Besides her golf exploits, she was the star of the 1932 Olympic Games and excelled at virtually every sport she tried, including baseball. At golf, Zaharias became so proficient as to be mentioned in the same breath as Joyce Wethered. She climaxed a fine amateur career by winning the U.S. women's championship in 1946 and the British title a year later, becoming the first American to win the British championship. The Babe dominated the budding women's tour almost as soon as she left the amateur ranks, and she was the leading money winner in each of her first four years as a professional. She also won three U.S. Opens and captured the Vare Trophy in 1954. The Babe, who was married to George Zaharias, was the first woman to hold the post of head professional at a golf club, was voted Woman Athlete of the Half Century (1949) by the Associated Press, and was voted Woman Athlete of the Year by AP ballot in 1932, 1945, 1946, 1947, and 1950. None of her accomplishments stirred the public as did her fight against cancer, for which she first underwent surgery in 1953. She supposedly was not going to be able to play again, but she came back to win the 1954 U.S. Open by a record twelve strokes. She won four other events that year and two more in 1955 before her condition deteriorated to a degree her courage and determination could not overcome.

Tournament Record: 1946: Winner of U.S. Women's Amateur. 1947: Winner of British Ladies Open Amateur Championship. 1948: Winner of All-American Open, World Championship, and U.S. Women's Open. 1949: Winner of World Championship and Eastern Open. 1950: Winner of All-American Open, World Championship, U.S. Women's Open, Titleholders Championship, Weathervane Open and Western Open. 1951: Winner of

Mickey Wright. *AP/Wide World Photos*

Babe Zaharias. *Courtesy U.S.G.A.*

All-American Open, World Championship, Ponte Verde Open, Tampa Open, Fresno Open, Richmond Open and Texas Open. 1952: Winner of Titleholders Championship, Fresno Open, Texas Open and Miami Weathervane. 1953: Winner of Sarasota Open and Babe Zaharias Open. 1954: Winner of All-American Open, U.S. Women's Open, Sarasota Open, Serbin Open and National Capital Open. 1955: Winner of Tampa Open and Serbin Open.

ZOELLER, Frank Urban. Born in New Albany, IN, November 11, 1951. Fuzzy Zoeller's nickname derives from his initials. He grew up alongside a fairway at the Valley View Country Club in New Albany and started swinging a golf club at age three. He entered his first tournament two years later. He enjoyed all sports while growing up, but when he was about eight, his father said to him, "Son, all we're doing is running back and forth between the golf course and the baseball diamond. You had better choose one." Zoeller chose golf. In 1972, while at Edison Junior College, he was the Florida State Junior College

champion. He also went to the University of Houston. In 1973, he won the Indiana State Amateur. He turned professional in 1973, and qualified for the Tour in the Fall of 1974.

Zoeller first came to national attention when he shot a 63 in the first round of the 1976 Quad Cities Open. The score included eight birdies in a row, which tied the record for consecutive birdies on Tour set in 1961 by Bob Goalby. In 1979, Zoeller had his first Tour win, in the San Diego Open, and qualified for the Masters. After three rounds, Ed Sneed led the tournament by five strokes over Tom Watson and Craig Stadler. Zoeller, on rounds of 70, 71, 69 was six behind. After Sneed had birdied the 15th at Augusta he looked a sure winner, but he lost strokes at each of the last three holes, and tied with Watson and Zoeller. All parred the first play-off hole. On the next hole, Zoeller birdied to earn the green jacket.

Zoeller's second major came in the 1984 U.S. Open at Winged Foot Golf Club in Mamaroneck, N.Y.

Fuzzy Zoeller. *Fred Vuich*

It also involved a play-off, with Greg Norman, although this one had little or no drama to it, Zoeller winning, 67 to 75.

Although Zoeller has won ten Tour events and played on three Ryder Cup Teams (1979, 1983, and 1985), his record might have been much better if he had a healthy back. After winning the 1984 U.S. Open, Zoeller had to pull out of the PGA Championship with a bad back. A month or so later he underwent surgery in New York City for two ruptured discs. "The back problem started when I was playing high school basketball," Zoeller says. "I was submarined and the back has bothered me from time to time ever since." Zoeller recovered to win once in 1985 and three times in 1986, but those were his last victories.

Zoeller was a very long hitter before his back problems curtailed his swing. His style is most unorthodox. He leans well over the ball, addressing it out of the neck of the club, with his hands very low. On the downswing, he compensates by raising his back into a more erect position, meanwhile hitting the heck out of the ball with his hands. Such a swing is tricky to time and demands the utmost in talent.

"The Fuzz" also has a marvelous twinkle in his eye. In an age when golfers complain that too many of the top players are dull, Zoeller stands out as refreshingly different and a lot of fun.

Tournament Record: 1972: Winner of Florida State Junior College Championship. 1973: Winner of Indiana State Amateur Championship. 1979: Winner of San Diego Open and Masters. 1981: Winner of Colonial National Invitation. 1983: Winner of Sea Pines Heritage Classic and Las Vegas Pro-Celebrity Classic. 1984: Winner of U.S. Open. 1985: Winner of Bay Hill Classic and Skins Game. 1986: Winner of AT&T Pebble Beach National Pro-Am, Sea Pines Heritage Classic, and Anheuser-Busch Golf Classic.

MONEY-WINNING RECORDS

Money prizes are what the professional touring golfer plays for. Over the years, like playing equipment and course design, prize money in golf has greatly improved. The first prize award in the U.S. Open when started in 1895 was $150. During the 1930's a tournament winner received on an average of $1,500. The $10,000 of the 1940s was a major step toward better winnings, and in the early 1950's,

when George S. May presented the $100,000 All-American and World Championship at Tam O'Shanter, golf was on its way to the big money era. Below is a listing of men's tournament prize money, in tour events only, in the modern era of golf:

Year	Events	Total Purse	Average Purse
1950	33	$ 459,950	$ 13,938
1951	30	$ 460,200	$ 15,340
1952	32	$ 498,016	$ 15,563
1953	32	$ 562,704	$ 17,585
1954	26	$ 600,810	$ 23,108
1955	36	$ 782,010	$ 21,723
1956	36	$ 847,070	$ 23,530
1957	32	$ 820,360	$ 25,636
1958	39	$ 1,005,800	$ 25,789
1959	43	$ 1,187,340	$ 27,613
1960	41	$ 1,187,340	$ 28,959
1961	45	$ 1,461,830	$ 32,485
1962	49	$ 1,790,320	$ 36,537
1963	43	$ 2,044,900	$ 47,497
1964	41	$ 2,301,063	$ 56,123
1965	36	$ 2,848,515	$ 79,403
1966	36	$ 3,074,445	$ 85,401
1967	37	$ 3,979,162	$ 108,356
1968	45	$ 5,077,600	$ 112,835
1969	47	$ 5,465,875	$ 116,295
1970	47	$ 6,259,501	$ 126,689
1971	52	$ 6,587,976	$ 112,968
1972	46	$ 6,954,649	$ 151,188
1973	75	$ 8,657,225	$ 115,429
1974	57	$ 8,165,941	$ 143,262
1975	51	$ 7,895,450	$ 154,812
1976	49	$ 9,157,522	$ 186,888
1977	48	$ 9,688,977	$ 201,853
1978	48	$10,337,332	$ 215,361
1979	46	$12,801,200	$ 278,286
1980	45	$13,371,786	$ 279,150
1981	45	$14,175,393	$ 315,008
1982	46	$15,089,576	$ 328,034
1983	45	$17,588,242	$ 390,850
1984	46	$21,251,382	$ 461,896
1985	47	$25,290,526	$ 538,096
1986	46	$25,442,242	$ 553,092
1987	46	$32,106,093	$ 697,959
1988	47	$36,959,307	$ 786,368
1989	44	$41,288,787	$ 938,382
1990	44	$46,251,831	$1,051,178
1991	44	$49,628,203	$1,127,914

Note: In 1973 and 1974 in particular, the number of Second Tour events included, twenty-six and fourteen, respectively, distort the average purse figure.

LEADING MONEY WINNERS (MEN) PRIOR TO 1955

(Yearly Record)

Year	Player	Money	Year	Player	Money
1934	Paul Runyan	$ 6,767	1945	Byron Nelson	$63,335
1935	Johnny Revolta	$ 9,543	1946	Ben Hogan	$42,556
1936	Horton Smith	$ 7,682	1947	Jim Demaret	$27,936
1937	Harry Cooper	$14,138	1948	Ben Hogan	$32,112
1938	Sam Snead	$19,543	1949	Sam Snead	$31,593
1939	Henry Picard	$10,303	1950	Sam Snead	$35,758
1940	Ben Hogan	$10,655	1951	Lloyd Mangrum	$26,088
1941	Ben Hogan	$18,358	1952	Julius Boros	$37,032
1942	Ben Hogan	$13,143	1953	Lew Worsham	$34,002
1943	No statistics compiled		1954	Bob Toski	$65,819
1944	Byron Nelson	$37,967			

MODERN-ERA LEADING MONEY WINNERS (MEN)

(In Regular PGA Tour Events)

1955

	Player	Money
1.	Julius Boros	$63,121
2.	Cary Middlecoff	39,567
3.	Doug Ford	33,503
4.	Mike Souchak	29,462
5.	Gene Littler	28,974
6.	Ted Kroll	25,117
7.	Sam Snead	23,464
8.	Tommy Bolt	22,585
9.	Fred Haas, Jr.	22,372
10.	Jerry Barber	18,865

1956

	Player	Money
1.	Ted Kroll	$72,835
2.	Dow Finsterwald	29,513
3.	Cary Middlecoff	27,352
4.	Fred Hawkins	24,805
5.	Jack Burke, Jr.	24,085
6.	Gene Littler	23,833
7.	Ed Furgol	23,125
8.	Mike Souchak	21,486
9.	Peter Thomson	20,413
10.	Doug Ford	19,389

1957

	Player	Money
1.	Dick Mayer	$65,835
2.	Doug Ford	45,378
3.	Dow Finsterwald	32,872
4.	Sam Snead	28,260
5.	Arnold Palmer	27,802
6	Paul Harney	21,735
7.	Art Wall, Jr.	20,831
8.	Al Balding	20,824
9.	Billy Casper, Jr.	20,807
10.	Ken Venturi	18,761

1958

	Player	Money
1.	Arnold Palmer	$42,607
2.	Billy Casper, Jr.	41,323
3.	Ken Venturi	36,267
4.	Dow Finsterwald	35,393
5.	Art Wall, Jr.	29,841
6.	Julius Boros	29,817
7.	Tommy Bolt	26,940
8.	Jay Hebert	26,834
9.	Bob Rosburg	25,170
10.	Doug Ford	21,874

1959

	Player	Money
1.	Art Wall, Jr.	$53,167
2.	Gene Littler	38,296
3.	Dow Finsterwald	33,906
4.	Billy Casper, Jr.	33,899
5.	Arnold Palmer	32,461
6.	Mike Souchak	31,807
7.	Bob Rosburg	31,676
8.	Doug Ford	31,009
9.	Jay Hebert	26,034
10.	Ken Venturi	25,886

1960

	Player	Money
1.	Arnold Palmer	$75,262
2.	Ken Venturi	41,230
3.	Dow Finsterwald	38,541
4.	Billy Casper, Jr.	31.060
5.	Jay Hebert	29,748
6.	Mike Souchak	28,903
7.	Doug Ford	28,411
8.	Gene Littler	26,837
9.	Bill Collins	26,496
10.	Doug Sanders	26,470

MODERN-ERA LEADING MONEY WINNERS (MEN)(continued)

(In Regular PGA Tour Events)

1961

	Player	Money
1.	Gary Player	$64,450
2.	Arnold Palmer	61,191
3.	Doug Sanders	57,428
4.	Billy Casper, Jr.	37,776
5.	Jay Hebert	35,583
6.	Johnny Pott	32,267
7.	Gay Brewer, Jr.	31,149
8.	Bob Goalby	30,918
9.	Gene Littler	29,245
10.	Billy Maxwell	28,335

1962

	Player	Money
1.	Arnold Palmer	$81,448
2.	Gene Littler	66,200
3.	Jack Nicklaus	61,868
4.	Billy Casper, Jr.	61,842
5.	Bob Goalby	46,240
6.	Gary Player	45,838
7.	Doug Sanders	43,385
8.	Dave Ragan, Jr.	37,327
9.	Bobby Nichols	34,311
10.	Dow Finsterwald	33,619

1963

	Player	Money
1.	Arnold Palmer	$128,230
2.	Jack Nicklaus	100,040
3.	Julius Boros	77,356
4.	Tony Lema	67,112
5.	Gary Player	55,455
6.	Dow Finsterwald	49,862
7.	Mason Rudolph, Jr.	39,120
8.	Al Geiberger	34,126
9.	Don January	33,754
10.	Bobby Nichols	33,604

1964

	Player	Money
1.	Jack Nicklaus	$113,284
2.	Arnold Palmer	113,203
3.	Billy Casper, Jr.	90,653
4.	Tony Lema	74,130
5.	Bobby Nichols	74,012
6.	Ken Venturi	62,465
7.	Gary Player	61,449
8.	Mason Rudolph, Jr.	52,568
9.	Juan Rodriguez	48,338
10.	Mike Souchak	39,559

1965

	Player	Money
1.	Jack Nicklaus	$140,752
2.	Tony Lema	101,816
3.	Billy Casper, Jr.	99,931
4.	Doug Sanders	72,182
5.	Gary Player	69,964
6.	Bruce Devlin	67,657
7.	Dave Marr	63,375
8.	Al Geiberger	59,699
9.	Gene Littler	58,898
10.	Arnold Palmer	57,770

1966

	Player	Money
1.	Billy Casper, Jr.	$121,944
2.	Jack Nicklaus	111,419
3.	Arnold Palmer	110,467
4.	Doug Sanders	80,096
5.	Gay Brewer	75,687
6.	Phil Rodgers	68,360
7.	Gene Littler	68,345
8.	R. H. Sikes	67,348
9.	Frank Beard	66,041
10.	Al Geiberger	63,220

1967

	Player	Money
1.	Jack Nicklaus	$188,988
2.	Arnold Palmer	184,065
3.	Billy Casper, Jr.	129,423
4.	Julius Boros	126,785
5.	Dan Sikes, jr.	111,508
6.	Doug Sanders	109,455
7.	Frank Beard	105,778
8.	George Archer	84,344
9.	Gay Brewer, Jr.	78,548
10.	Bob Goalby	77,106

1968

	Player	Money
1.	Billy Casper, Jr.	$205,168
2.	Jack Nicklaus	155,285
3.	Tom Weiskopf	152,946
4.	George Archer	150,972
5.	Julius Boros	148,310
6.	Lee Trevino	132,127
7.	Arnold Palmer	114,602
8.	Dan Sikes, Jr.	108,330
9.	Miller Barber	105,845
10.	Bob Murphy	105,595

1969

	Player	Money
1.	Frank Beard	$175,224
2.	Dave Hill	156,423
3.	Jack Nicklaus	140,167
4.	Gary Player	123,898
5.	Bruce Crampton	118,956
6.	Gene Littler	112,737
7.	Lee Trevino	112,418
8.	Ray Floyd	109,957
9.	Arnold Palmer	105,128
10.	Billy Casper, Jr.	104,689

MODERN-ERA LEADING MONEY WINNERS (MEN)(continued)

(In Regular PGA Tour Events)

1970

	Player	Money
1.	Lee Trevino	$157,037
2.	Billy Casper, Jr.	147,372
3.	Bruce Crampton	142,609
4.	Jack Nicklaus	142,149
5.	Arnold Palmer	128,853
6.	Frank Beard	124,690
7.	Dick Lotz	124,539
8.	Larry Hinson	120,897
9.	Bob Murphy	120,639
10.	Dave Hill	118,415

1971

	Player	Money
1.	Jack Nicklaus	$244,490
2.	Lee Trevino	231,202
3.	Arnold Palmer	209,603
4.	George Archer	147,769
5.	Gary Player	120,016
6.	Miller Barber	117,359
7.	Jerry Heard	112,389
8.	Frank Beard	112,337
9.	Dave Eichelberger	108,312
10.	Billy Casper, Jr.	107,276

1972

	Player	Money
1.	Jack Nicklaus	$320,942
2.	Lee Trevino	214,805
3.	George Archer	145,027
4.	Grier Jones	140,177
5.	Jerry Heard	137,198
6.	Tom Weiskopf	129,422
7.	Gary Player	120,719
8.	Bruce Devlin	119,768
9.	Tommy Aaron	118,924
10.	Lanny Wadkins	116,616

1973

	Player	Money
1.	Jack Nicklaus	$308,362
2.	Bruce Crampton	274,266
3.	Tom Weiskopf	245,463
4.	Lee Trevino	210,017
5.	Lanny Wadkins	200,455
6.	Miller Barber	184,014
7.	Hale Irwin	130,388
8.	Billy Casper, Jr.	129,474
9.	Johnny Miller	127,833
10.	John Schlee	118,017

1974

	Player	Money
1.	Johnny Miller	$353,021
2.	Jack Nicklaus	238,178
3.	Hubert Green	211,709
4.	Lee Trevino	203,422
5.	J. C. Snead	164,486
6.	Dave Stockton	155,105
7.	Hale Irwin	152,520
8.	Jerry Heard	145,788
9.	Brian Allin	137,950
10.	Tom Watson	135,474

1975

	Player	Money
1.	Jack Nicklaus	$298,149
2.	Johnny Miller	226,118
3.	Tom Weiskopf	219,140
4.	Hale Irwin	205,380
5.	Gene Littler	182,883
6.	Al Geiberger	175,693
7.	Tom Watson	153,795
8.	John Mahaffey	141,475
9.	Lee Trevino	134,206
10.	Bruce Crampton	132,532

1976

	Player	Money
1.	Jack Nicklaus	$266,438
2.	Ben Crenshaw	257,759
3.	Hale Irwin	252,718
4.	Hubert Green	228,031
5.	Al Geiberger	194,821
6.	J. C. Snead	192,645
7.	Ray Floyd	178,318
8.	David Graham	176,174
9.	Don January	163,622
10.	Jerry Pate	153,102

1977

	Player	Money
1.	Tom Watson	$310,653
2.	Jack Nicklaus	284,509
3.	Lanny Wadkins	244,882
4.	Hale Irwin	221,456
5.	Bruce Lietzke	202,156
6.	Tom Weiskopf	197,639
7.	Ray Floyd	163,261
8.	Miller Barber	148,320
9.	Hubert Green	140,255
10.	Bill Kratzert	134,758

1978

	Player	Money
1.	Tom Watson	$362,429
2.	Gil Morgan	267,459
3.	Andy Bean	267,241
4.	Jack Nicklaus	256,672
5.	Hubert Green	247,406
6.	Lee Trevino	228,723
7.	Hale Irwin	191,666
8.	Bill Kratzert	183,683
9.	Gary Player	177,336
10.	Jerry Pate	172,999

MODERN-ERA LEADING MONEY WINNERS (MEN) (continued)

(In Regular PGA Tour Events)

1979

	Player	Money
1.	Tom Watson	$462,636
2.	Larry Nelson	281,022
3.	Lon Hinkle	247,693
4.	Lee Trevino	238,732
5.	Ben Crenshaw	236,770
6.	Bill Rogers	230,500
7.	Andy Bean	208,253
8.	Bruce Lietzke	198,439
9.	Fuzzy Zoeller	196,951
10.	Lanny Wadkins	195,710

1980

	Player	Money
1.	Tom Watson	$530,808
2.	Lee Trevino	385,814
3.	Curtis Strange	271,888
4.	Andy Bean	269,033
5.	Ben Crenshaw	237,727
6.	Jerry Pate	222,976
7.	George Burns	219,928
8.	Craig Stadler	206,291
9.	Mike Reid	206,097
10.	Ray Floyd	192,993

1981

	Player	Money
1.	Tom Kite	$375,699
2.	Ray Floyd	359,360
3.	Tom Watson	347,660
4.	Bruce Lietzke	343,446
5.	Bill Rogers	315,411
6.	Jerry Pate	280,627
7.	Hale Irwin	276,499
8.	Craig Stadler	218,829
9.	Curtis Strange	201,513
10.	Larry Nelson	193,342

1982

	Player	Money
1.	Craig Stadler	$446,462
2.	Ray Floyd	386,809
3.	Tom Kite	341,081
4.	Calvin Peete	318,470
5.	Tom Watson	316,483
6.	Bob Gilder	308,648
7.	Lanny Wadkins	306,827
8.	Wayne Levi	280,681
9.	Jerry Pate	280,141
10.	Curtis Strange	263,378

1983

	Player	Money
1.	Hal Sutton	$426,668
2.	Fuzzy Zoeller	417,597
3.	Lanny Wadkins	319,271
4.	Calvin Peete	313,845
5.	Gil Morgan	306,133
6.	Rex Caldwell	284,434
7.	Ben Crenshaw	275,474
8.	Mark McCumber	268,294
9.	Tom Kite	257,066
10.	Jack Nicklaus	256,158

1984

	Player	Money
1.	Tom Watson	$476,260
2.	Mark O'Meara	465,873
3.	Andy Bean	422,995
4.	Denis Watson	408,562
5.	Tom Kite	348,640
6.	Bruce Lietzke	342,853
7.	Fred Couples	334,573
8.	Craig Stadler	324,241
9.	Greg Norman	310,230
10.	Peter Jacobsen	295,025

1985

	Player	Money
1.	Curtis Strange	$542,321
2.	Lanny Wadkins	446,893
3.	Calvin Peete	384,489
4.	Jim Thorpe	379,091
5.	Ray Floyd	378,989
6.	Corey Pavin	376,506
7.	Hal Sutton	365,340
8.	Roger Maltbie	360,554
9.	John Mahaffey	341,595
10.	Mark O'Meara	340,840

1986

	Player	Money
1.	Greg Norman	$653,296
2.	Bob Tway	652,780
3.	Payne Stewart	535,389
4.	Andy Bean	491,938
5.	Dan Pohl	436,630
6.	Hal Sutton	429,434
7.	Tom Kite	394,164
8.	Ben Crenshaw	388,169
9.	Ray Floyd	380,508
10.	Bernhard Langer	379,800

1987

	Player	Money
1.	Curtis Strange	$925,941
2.	Paul Azinger	822,481
3.	Ben Crenshaw	638,194
4.	Scott Simpson	621,032
5.	Tom Watson	616,351
6.	Larry Mize	561,407
7.	Greg Norman	535,450
8.	Tom Kite	525,516
9.	Chip Beck	523,003
10.	Mark Calcavecchia	522,398

MODERN-ERA LEADING MONEY WINNERS (MEN)(continued)
(In Regular PGA Tour Events)

1988

	Player	Money
1.	Curtis Strange	$1,147,644
2.	Chip Beck	916,818
3.	Joey Sindelar	813,732
4.	Ken Green	779,181
5.	Tom Kite	760,405
6.	Mark Calcavecchia	751,912
7.	Sandy Lyle	726,934
8.	Ben Crenshaw	696,895
9.	David Frost	691,500
10.	Lanny Wadkins	616,596

1989

	Player	Money
1.	Tom Kite	$1,395,278
2.	Payne Stewart	1,201,301
3.	Paul Azinger	951,649
4.	Greg Norman	835,096
5.	Mark Calcavecchia	897,741
6.	Tim Simpson	761,597
7.	Curtis Strange	752,587
8.	Steve Jones	745,578
9.	Chip Beck	694,087
10.	Scott Hoch	670,680

1990

	Player	Money
1.	Greg Norman	$1,165,477
2.	Wayne Levi	1,024,647
3.	Payne Stewart	976,281
4.	Paul Azinger	944,731
5.	Jodie Mudd	911,746
6.	Hale Irwin	838,249
7.	Mark Calcavecchia	834,281
8.	Tim Simpson	809,772
9.	Fred Couples	757,999
10.	Mark O'Meara	707,175

1991

	Player	Money
1.	Corey Pavin	$979,430
2.	Craig Stadler	827,628
3.	Fred Couples	791,749
4.	Tom Purtzer	750,568
5.	Andrew Magee	750,082
6.	Steve Pate	727,997
7.	Nick Price	714,389
8.	Davis Love III	686,361
9.	Paul Azinger	685,603
10.	Russ Cochran	684,851

1992

	Player	Money
1.	Fred Couples	$1,344,188
2.	Davis Love	1,191,630
3.	John Cook	1,165,606
4.	Nick Price	1,135,773
5.	Corey Pavin	980,934
6.	Tom Kite	957,445
7.	Paul Azinger	929,863
8.	Brad Faxon	812,093
9.	Lee Janzen	795,279
10.	Dan Forsman	763,190

ALL-TIME LEADING MONEY WINNERS (MEN)

(In Official PGA Tour Events)

Player	From Year	Total Winnings	Player	From Year	Total Winnings
1. Tom Kite	1972	$7,612,918	14. Mark O'Meara	1981	$4,648,751
2. Tom Watson	1972	$6,028,927	15. Hale Irwin	1968	$4,586,940
3. Curtis Strange	1977	$5,779,864	16. Craig Stadler	1976	$4,577,982
4. Lanny Wadkins	1971	$5,632,713	17. Corey Pavin	1984	$4,254,051
5. Fred Couples	1981	$5,466,915	18. Mark Calcavecchia	1981	$3,859,956
6. Payne Stewart	1981	$5,394,968	19. Gil Morgan	1973	$3,815,867
7. Jack Nicklaus	1962	$5,309,130	20. Wayne Levi	1977	$3,811,295
8. Paul Azinger	1982	$5,302,850	21. Nick Price	1983	$3,747,934
9. Greg Norman	1983	$6,247,909	22. John Mahaffey	1971	$3,569,106
10. Ben Crenshaw	1973	$5,129,901	23. John Cook	1980	$3,502,931
11. Ray Floyd	1963	$4,907,480	24. Lee Trevino	1967	$3,478,449
12. Bruce Lietzke	1975	$4,712,701	25. Scott Hoch	1980	$3,464,953
13. Chip Beck	1979	$4,701,257			

MODERN-ERA LEADING MONEY WINNERS (WOMEN)

(In Regular LPGA Tour Events)

Year	Player	Money	Year	Player	Money	Year	Player	Money
1950	Babe Zaharias	$14,800	1965	Kathy Whitworth	28,658	1979	Nancy Lopez	197,489
	Patty Berg	5,442		Marlene Hagge	21,532		Sandra Post	178,751
1951	Babe Zaharias	15,087	1966	Kathy Whitworth	33,517	1980	Beth Daniel	231,000
	Patty Berg	13,237		Sandra Haynie	30,157		Donna Caponi	220,620
1952	Betsy Rawls	14,505	1967	Kathy Whitworth	32,937	1981	Beth Daniel	206,978
	Betty Jameson	12,660		Sandra Haynie	26,543		JoAnne Carner	206,649
1953	Louise Suggs	19,816	1968	Kathy Whitworth	48,379	1982	JoAnne Carner	310,400
	Patty Berg	18,623		Carol Mann	45,921		Sandra Haynie	245,432
1954	Patty Berg	16,011	1969	Carol Mann	49,152	1983	JoAnne Carner	291,404
	Babe Zaharias	14,452		Kathy Whitworth	48,171		Patty Sheehan	250,939
1955	Patty Berg	16,497	1970	Kathy Whitworth	30,235	1984	Betsy King	266,771
	Louise Suggs	13,729		Sandra Haynie	26,606		Patty Sheehan	255,185
1956	Marlene Hagge	20,235	1971	Kathy Whitworth	41,182	1985	Nancy Lopez	416,472
	Patty Berg	12,560		Sandra Haynie	36,219		Pat Bradley	387,377
1957	Patty Berg	16,272	1972	Kathy Whitworth	65,063	1986	Pat Bradley	492,021
	Fay Crocker	12,019		Jane Blalock	57,323		Betsy King	290,195
1958	Bev Hanson	12,639	1973	Kathy Whitworth	82,864	1987	Ayako Okamoto	466,034
	Marlene Hagge	11,890		Judy Rankin	72,989		Betsy King	460,385
1959	Betsy Rawls	26,774	1974	JoAnne Carner	87,570	1988	Sherri Turner	350,851
	Mickey Wright	18,182		Jane Blalock	87,266		Patty Sheehan	326,171
1960	Louise Suggs	16,892	1975	Sandra Palmer	76,374	1989	Betsy King	654,132
	Mickey Wright	16,380		JoAnne Carner	64,842		Beth Daniel	504,851
1961	Mickey Wright	22,236	1976	Judy Rankin	150,734	1990	Beth Daniel	863,578
	Betsy Rawls	15,672		Donna Caponi	106,553		Patty Sheehan	732,618
1962	Mickey Wright	21,641	1977	Judy Rankin	122,890	1991	Pat Bradley	763,118
	Kathy Whitworth	17,044		JoAnne Carner	113,711		Meg Mallon	633,802
1963	Mickey Wright	31,269	1978	Nancy Lopez	189,813	1992	Dottie Mochrie	693,335
	Kathy Whitworth	26,858		Pat Bradley	118,057		Betsy King	551,320
1964	Mickey Wright	29,800						
	Ruth Jessen	23,431						

ALL-TIME LEADING MONEY WINNERS (WOMEN)

(In Official LPGA Tour Events)

Player	From Year	Total Winnings	Player	From Year	Total Winnings
1. Pat Bradley	1974	$4,347,706	14. Kathy Whitworth	1958	$1,722,440
2. Betsy King	1977	$3,906,643	15. Hollis Stacy	1974	$1,717,707
3. Beth Daniel	1979	$3,692,665	16. Dottie Mochrie	1988	$1,670,635
4. Patty Sheehan	1980	$3,591,290	17. Judy Dickinson	1978	$1,557,612
5. Nancy Lopez	1977	$3,562,371	18. Sally Little	1971	$1,500,437
6. Amy Alcott	1975	$2,850,188	19. Donna Caponi	1965	$1,387,920
7. JoAnne Carner	1970	$2,649,642	20. Danielle Ammaccapane	1988	$1,382,010
8. Ayako Okamoto	1981	$2,621,857	21. Kathy Postlewait	1974	$1,332,669
9. Jan Stephenson	1974	$2,014,186	22. Sandra Palmer	1964	$1,328,664
10. Juli Inkster	1983	$1,840.006	23. Jane Blalock	1969	$1,290,944
11. Colleen Walker	1982	$1,753,740	24. Chris Johnson	1980	$1,234,412
12. Rosie Jones	1982	$1,748,402	25. Meg Mallon	1987	$1,232,383
13. Jane Geddes	1983	$1,732,505			

PGA HALL OF FAME

The great sports writer Grantland Rice suggested a Hall of Fame for golfers through his nationally syndicated sports columns. Today, there are three recognized Halls of Fame: One established by the PGA, located at the association's headquarters in Palm Beach Gardens, Florida; one by the LPGA, located at its official home in Daytona Beach, Florida; plus the PGA World Golf Hall of Fame at Pinehurst, North Carolina.

Election to the PGA Hall of Fame is for overall contributions to golf. Nominees must be at least fifty years old, and since 1981, if being considered on the basis of playing ability, must have won at least two major championships. The selection committee is made up of Hall of Fame members, officials of major golf associations and editors. The PGA Hall of Fame is expected to be merged into the PGA World Golf Hall of Fame in Pinehurst.

Players elected to the PGA Hall of Fame are:

Year	Player	Year	Player	Year	Player
1940	Willie Anderson	1956	Craig Wood	1964	Lloyd Mangrum
	Tommy Armour	1957	Denny Shute		Ed Dudley
	Jim Barnes	1958	Horton Smith	1965	Vic Ghezzi
	Chick Evans[a]	1959	Harry Cooper	1966	Billy Burke
	Walter Hagen		Jock Hutchison, Sr.	1967	Bobby Cruikshank
	Bob Jones[a]		Paul Runyan	1968	M. R. "Chick" Harbert
	John McDermott	1960	Mike Brady	1969	Chandler Harper
	Francis Ouimet[a]		Jimmy Demaret	1974	Julius Boros
	Gene Sarazen		Fred McLeod		Cary Middlecoff
	Alex Smith	1961	Johnny Farrell	1975	Jack Burke, Jr.
	Jerry Travers[a]		W. Lawson Little		Doug Ford
	Walter Travis		Henry Picard	1976	Babe Zaharias
1953	Ben Hogan	1962	E. J. Harrison	1978	Patty Berg
	Byron Nelson		Olin Dutra	1979	Roberto De Vicenzo
	Sam Snead	1963	Ralph Guldahl	1980	Arnold Palmer
1954	Macdonald Smith		Johnny Revolta	1982	Gene Littler
1955	Leo Diegel				Billy Casper

[a] Amateur

LPGA HALL OF FAME

At the 1967 annual meeting of the Ladies' Professional Golf Association in Corpus Christi, Texas, it was decided to establish a Ladies PGA Hall of Fame for its members only. The members who had previously been elected to the Hall of Fame established in Augusta, Georgia, in 1951 were automatically inducted into this new Hall of Fame.

The LPGA Hall of Fame remained in Augusta for ten years. Then, in 1977 it moved into a wing of the World Hall of Fame in Pinehurst. It moved again with the LPGA Tour headquarters, to Sugarland, Texas, in 1983, and then to Daytona Beach, Florida, in 1989.

Present rules of eligibility for the LPGA Hall of Fame are that a player must have been a member in good standing in the LPGA for ten consecutive years, then either have won at least thirty official events, including two different major championships, or have won thirty-five official events including one major or forty official events.

Players who have qualified for the LPGA Hall of Fame are:

Year	Player	Year	Player	Year	Player
1951	Patty Berg	1969	Betsy Rawls	1982	JoAnne Carner
	Betty Jameson	1964	Mickey Wright	1987	Nancy Lopez
	Louise Suggs	1974	Kathy Whitworth	1991	Pat Bradley
	Mildred (Babe) Didrikson	1977	Carol Mann		
	Zaharias		Sandra Haynie		

a Amateur

PGA WORLD GOLF HALL OF FAME

The World Golf Hall of Fame, standing on the rim of the famous Pinehurst No. 2 course, was dedicated by President Gerald R. Ford on September 11, 1974. On that day the original thirteen enshrinees were formally inducted into the Hall of Fame, with all eight living members in attendance.

Eligibility to the World Golf Hall of Fame is based on playing ability or service to the game. Nominees of the modern era are elected by a vote of the Golf Writers Association of America. Pre-modern and distinguished service categories are elected by vote of special committees. Since 1986, the World Golf Hall of Fame has been operated by the PGA.

Those elected to the PGA World Golf Hall of Fame are:

Year	Player	Year	Player	Year	Player
1974	Patty Berg	1976	Tommy Armour	1983	Bob Hope*
	Walter Hagen		Jerome Travers		Jimmy Demaret
	Ben Hogan		James Braid	1985	JoAnne Carner
	Robert T. Jones, Jr.		Mickey Wright	1986	Cary Middlecoff
	Byron Nelson		Thomas Morris, Sr.	1987	Robert Trent Jones*
	Jack Nicklaus	1977	John Ball, Jr.		Betsy Rawls
	Francis Ouimet		Herb Graffis*	1988	Tom Watson
	Arnold Palmer		Bobby Locke		Peter Thomson
	Gary Player		Donald Ross*		Bob Harlow*
	Gene Sarazen	1978	Billy Casper	1989	Raymond Floyd
	Sam Snead		Harold Hilton		Nancy Lopez
	Harry Vardon		Dorothy Campbell Hurd		Roberto De Vicenzo
	Mildred (Babe) Zaharias		Howe		Jim Barnes
1975	Willie Anderson		Bing Crosby*	1990	Gene Littler
	Fred Corcoran*		Clifford Roberts*		Paul Runyan
	Joseph C. Dey*	1979	Louise Suggs		Horton Smith
	Charles (Chick) Evans		Walter Travis		William Campbell
	Thomas Morris, Jr.	1980	Lawson Little	1992	Hale Irwin
	John H. Taylor		Henry Cotton		Chi Chi Rodriguez
	Glenna Collett Vare	1981	Lee Trevino		Richard Tufts
	Joyce Wethered		Ralph Guldahl		Harry Cooper
		1982	Julius Boros		
			Kathy Whitworth		

* For distinguished service.

TROPHY AND AWARD WINNERS

In addition to prize money, professional golfers take great pride in winning the various awards and trophies given annually. Here are major trophies and awards:

THE PGA VARDON TROPHY

The PGA Vardon Trophy, named in honor of the internationally famous British golfer Harry Vardon, was placed in competition among American professionals in 1937 as a successor to the Harry E. Radix Trophy, which, prior to that time, had been awarded annually to the professional having the finest tournament record in competitive play in this country.

Today, the Vardon Trophy is awarded each year to the member of the PGA of America maintaining the best playing average in those events co-sponsored or so designated by the PGA.

The minimum number of official tournament rounds required for consideration for the Vardon Trophy is sixty in any one year. The Vardon Trophy has not always been awarded on a basis of seasonal playing average. From 1937 through 1941, the winner was decided on a point basis. Under this system, the leading players in each event received a predetermined number of points, and at the end of the year, the player with the greatest number of points was named the winner.

Year	Winner	Average	Year	Winner	Average	Year	Winner	Average
1934	Ky Laffoon[a]		1955	Sam Snead	69.86	1975	Bruce Crampton	70.51
1935	Paul Runyan[a]		1956	Cary Middlecoff	70.35	1976	Don January	70.89
1936	Ralph Guldahl[a]		1957	Dow Finsterwald	70.30	1977	Tom Watson	70.32
1937	Harry Cooper	500	1958	Bob Rosburg	70.11	1978	Tom Watson	70.16
1938	Sam Snead	520	1959	Art Wall, Jr.	70.35	1979	Tom Watson	70.27
1939	Byron Nelson	473	1960	Billy Casper, Jr.	69.95	1980	Lee Trevino	69.73
1940	Ben Hogan	423	1961	Arnold Palmer	69.85	1981	Tom Kite	69.80
1941	Ben Hogan	494	1962	Arnold Palmer	70.27	1982	Tom Kite	70.21
1942	Ben Hogan[a]		1963	Billy Casper, Jr.	70.58	1983	Raymond Floyd	70.61
1943–1944 Not played			1964	Arnold Palmer	70.01	1984	Calvin Peete	70.56
1945	Byron Nelson[a]		1965	Billy Casper, Jr.	70.58	1985	Don Pooley	70.36
1946	Ben Hogan[a]		1966	Billy Casper, Jr.	70.27	1986	Scott Hoch	70.08
1947	Jimmy Demaret	69.90	1967	Arnold Palmer	70.18	1987	Dan Pohl	70.25
1948	Ben Hogan	69.30	1968	Billy Casper, Jr.	69.82	1988	Chip Beck	69.46*
1949	Sam Snead	69.37	1969	Dave Hill	70.34	1989	Greg Norman	69.49
1950	Sam Snead	69.23	1970	Lee Trevino	70.64	1990	Greg Norman	69.10
1951	Lloyd Mangrum	70.05	1971	Lee Trevino	70.28	1991	Fred Couples	69.59
1952	Jack Burke, Jr.	70.54	1972	Lee Trevino	70.89	1992	Fred Couples	69.38
1953	Lloyd Mangrum	70.22	1973	Bruce Crampton	70.57			
1954	Dutch Harrison	70.41	1974	Lee Trevino	70.53			

[a] Radix Trophy awarded.

* Starting in 1988, scores adjusted relative to average score of field each week.

THE LPGA VARE TROPHY

The Vare Trophy was presented to the Ladies' Professional Golf Association by Betty Jameson in 1952 in honor of the great American player Glenna Collett Vare. Miss Jameson requested that this trophy be awarded to the player with the lowest scoring average at the end of each year. Vare Trophy scoring averages are computed on the basis of a player's total yearly score in official rounds she played during the year. A further requirement is that a player must compete in seventy official rounds of tournament competition during the LPGA Tour year.

Year	Winner	Average	Year	Winner	Average	Year	Winner	Average
1953	Patty Berg	75.00	1967	Kathy Whitworth	72.74	1981	JoAnne Carner	71.75
1954	Babe Zaharias	75.48	1968	Carol Mann	72.04	1982	JoAnne Carner	71.49
1955	Patty Berg	74.47	1969	Kathy Whitworth	72.38	1983	JoAnne Carner	71.41
1956	Patty Berg	74.57	1970	Kathy Whitworth	72.26	1984	Patty Sheehan	71.40
1957	Louise Suggs	74.64	1971	Kathy Whitworth	72.88	1985	Nancy Lopez	70.73
1958	Bev Hanson	74.92	1972	Kathy Whitworth	72.38	1986	Pat Bradley	71.10
1959	Betsy Rawls	74.03	1973	Judy Rankin	73.08	1987	Betsy King	71.14
1960	Mickey Wright	73.25	1974	JoAnne Carner	72.87	1988	Colleen Walker	71.26
1961	Mickey Wright	73.55	1975	JoAnne Carner	72.40	1989	Beth Daniel	70.38
1962	Mickey Wright	73.67	1976	Judy Rankin	72.25	1990	Beth Daniel	70.54
1963	Mickey Wright	72.81	1977	Judy Rankin	72.16	1991	Pat Bradley	70.63
1964	Mickey Wright	72.46	1978	Nancy Lopez	71.76	1992	Dottie Michrie	70.80
1965	Kathy Whitworth	72.61	1979	Nancy Lopez	71.20			
1966	Kathy Whitworth	72.60	1980	Amy Alcott	71.51			

PGA Player-of-the-Year Award

Each year the PGA of America presents the PGA Player-of-the-Year Award, based on a system which awards points for victories, standing on the money list and Vardon Trophy scoring average.

Year	Player	Year	Player	Year	Player	Year	Player
1948	Ben Hogan	1960	Arnold Palmer	1972	Jack Nicklaus	1984	Tom Watson
1949	Sam Snead	1961	Jerry Barber	1973	Jack Nicklaus	1985	Lanny Wadkins
1950	Ben Hogan	1962	Arnold Palmer	1974	Johnny Miller	1986	Bob Tway
1951	Ben Hogan	1963	Julius Boros	1975	Jack Nicklaus	1987	Paul Azinger
1952	Julius Boros	1964	Ken Venturi	1976	Jack Nicklaus	1988	Curtis Strange
1953	Ben Hogan	1965	Dave Marr	1977	Tom Watson	1989	Tom Kite
1954	Ed Furgol	1966	Billy Casper, Jr.	1978	Tom Watson	1990	Nick Faldo
1955	Doug Ford	1967	Jack Nicklaus	1979	Tom Watson	1991	Corey Pavin
1956	Jack Burke, Jr.	1968	No winner	1980	Tom Watson	1992	Fred Couples
1957	Dick Mayer	1969	Orville Moody	1981	Bill Rogers		
1958	Dow Finsterwald	1970	Billy Casper, Jr.	1982	Tom Watson		
1959	Art Wall, Jr.	1971	Lee Trevino	1983	Hal Sutton		

LPGA Player-of-the-Year Award

Year	Player	Year	Player	Year	Player	Year	Player
1966	Kathy Whitworth	1973	Kathy Whitworth	1980	Beth Daniel	1987	Ayako Okamoto
1967	Kathy Whitworth	1974	JoAnne Carner	1981	Joanne Carner	1988	Nancy Lopez
1968	Kathy Whitworth	1975	Sandra Palmer	1982	JoAnne Carner	1989	Betsy King
1969	Kathy Whitworth	1976	Judy Rankin	1983	Patty Sheehan	1990	Beth Daniel
1970	Sandra Haynie	1977	Judy Rankin	1984	Betsy King	1991	Pat Bradley
1971	Kathy Whitworth	1978	Nancy Lopez	1985	Nancy Lopez	1992	Dottie Mochrie
1972	Kathy Whitworth	1979	Nancy Lopez	1986	Pat Bradley		

PGA GOLF PROFESSIONAL-OF-THE-YEAR AWARD

Awarded annually by the PGA of America, the PGA Golf Professional-of-the-Year Award was established in 1955. This unique award, originally suggested by Richard S. Tufts of Pinehurst, North Carolina, former President of the United States Golf Association, was established to honor PGA club professionals for outstanding achievements.

Year	Winner
1955	Bill Gordon, Tam O'Shanter Country Club, Niles, Ill.
1956	Harry Shepherd, Mark Twain Country Club, Elmira, N.Y.
1957	Dugan Aycock, Lexington (N.C.) Country Club
1958	Harry Pezzullo, Mission Hills Golf Club, Northbrook, Ill.
1959	Eddie Duino, San Jose (Calif.) Country Club
1960	Warren Orlick, Tom O'Shanter Country Club, Orchard Lake, Mich.
1961	Don Padgett, Green Hills Golf and Country Club, Selma, Ind.
1962	Tom LoPresti, Haggin Oaks Golf Course, Sacramento, Calif.
1963	Bruce Herd, Flossmer (Ill.) Country Club
1964	Lyle Wehrman, Merced (Calif.) Golf and Country Club
1965	Hubby Habjan, Onwentsia Club, Lake Forest, Ill.
1966	Bill Strausbaugh, Jr., Turf Valley Country Club, Ellicott City, Md.
1967	Ernie Vossler, Quail Creek Golf and Country Club, Oklahoma City, Okla.
1968	Hardy Loudermilk, Oak Hills Country Club, San Antonio, Texas
1969	A. Hubert Smith, Jr., Arnold Center Golf Club, Tullahoma, Tenn.
1970	Grady C. Shumate, Tanglewood Golf Club, Clemmons, N.C.
1971	Ross T. Collins, Dallas Athletic Club, Dallas, Texas
1972	Howard Morrette, Twin Lakes Country Club, Kent, Ohio
1973	Warren Smith, Cherry Hills Country Club, Englewood, Colo.
1974	Paul Harvey, Paul Harvey's Golf Club, Hatchville, Mass.
1975	Walker Inman, Jr., Scioto Country Club, Columbus, Ohio
1976	Ron Letellier, Cold Spring Harbor Country Club, Cold Spring Harbor, N.Y.
1977	Don Soper, Royal Oak Golf Club, Royal Oak, Mich.
1978	Walter Lowell, Canton Golf Club, Canton, Conn.
1979	Gary Ellis, Pittsburgh Field Club, Pittsburgh, Pa.
1980	Stan Thirsk, Kansas City Country Club, Shawnee Mission, Kan.
1981	John Gerring, Atlanta Country Club, Marietta, Ga.
1982	Bob Popp, Omaha Country Club, Omaha, Neb.
1983	Ken Lindsay, Colonial Country Club, Jackson, Miss.
1984	Jerry Mowlds, Columbia-Edgewater Country Club, Portland, Ore.
1985	Jerry Cozby, Hillcrest Country Club, Bartlesville, Okla.
1986	David Ogilvie, Flossmoor Country Club, Flossmoor, Ill.
1987	Bob Ford, Oakmont Country Club, Oakmont, Pa.
1988	Hank Majewski, Wakefield Valley Country Club, Westminster, Md.
1989	Tom Addis III, Singing Hills Country Club, El Cajon, Cal.
1990	Jim Albus, Piping Rock Club, Locust Valley, N.Y.
1991	Joe Jemsek, Cog Hill GC, Lemont, Ill.

Horton Smith Trophy

This trophy is awarded by the PGA to a golf professional who has made outstanding contributions in the field of golf professional education.

1965	Emil Beck, River CC, Port Huron, Mich.
1966	Gene C. Mason, Columbia-Edgewater CC, Portland, Ore.
1967	Donald E. Fischesser, Evansville CC, Evansville, Ind.
1968	R. William Clarke, Hillendale CC, Phoenix, Md.
1969	Paul Hahn, Miami, Fla.
1970	Joe Walser, Oklahoma City CC, Oklahoma City, Okla.
1971	Irvin Schloss, Dunedin, Fla.
1972	John Budd, New Port Richey, Fla.
1973	George Aulbach, Pecan Valley CC, San Antonio, Tex.
1974	Bill Hardy, Chevy Chase Club, Chevy Chase, Md.
1975	John P. Heinrich, Elma Meadows GC, Elma, N.Y.
1976	Jim Bailey, Adams Park GC, Brighton, Ohio
1977	Paul Runyan, Green Gables CC, Denver, Colo.
1978	Andy Nusbaum, Siwanoy CC, Bronxville, N.Y.
1979	Howard E. Smith, Diamond Bar, Cal.
1980	Dale Mead, Del Rio G&CC, Modesto, Cal.
1981	Tom Addiss III, Singing Hills CC, El Cajon, Cal.
1982	Kent Cayce, Evansville CC, Evansville, Ind.
1983	Bill Strausbaugh, Columbia CC, Chevy Chase, Md.
1984	Don Essig III, The Hoosier Links, New Palestine, Ind.
1985	Larry Startzel, Country Club of Lansing, Mich.
1986	Mark Darnell, West Lake CC, Augusta, Ga.
1987	Ken Lindsay, Colonial CC, Jackson, Miss.
1988	Guy Wimberly, Arroyo Del Oso GC, Albuquerque, N.M.
1989	Verne D. Perry, Cedars GC, Brush Prairie, Wash.
1990	Mike Hebron, Smithtown Landing CC, St. James, N.Y.
1991	Joe Terry, Gulf Shores GC, Gulf Shores, Atla.

LPGA Teacher-of-the-Year Award

The Ladies' Professional Golf Association established this award in 1958. It is made annually to the woman professional who has most exemplified her profession during the year.

Year	Winner	Year	Winner	Year	Winner	Year	Winner
1958	Helen Dettweiler	1967	Jackie Pung	1976	Marge Burns	1985	Annette Thompson
1959	Shirley Spork	1968	Gloria Fecht	1977	De De Owens	1986	Barbara Crawford-O'Brient
1960	Barbara Rotvig	1969	Joann Winter	1978	Shirley Englehorn		
1961	Peggy Kirk Bell	1970	Gloria Armstrong	1979	Bobbie Ripley	1987	Linda Craft
1962	Ellen Griffin	1971	Jeannette Rector	1980	Betty Dodd	1988	Judy Whitehouse
1963	Vonnie Colby	1972	Lee Spencer	1981	Jane Read	1989	Sharon Miller
1964	Sally Doyle	1973	Penny Zavichas	1982	Barbara Romack	1990	Dana Rader
1965	Goldie Bateson	1974	Mary Dagraedt	1983	Rina Ritson	1991	Betsy Clark
1966	Ann Johnstone	1975	Carol Johnson	1984	Shirley Spork		

BEN HOGAN TROPHY

Given annually by Golf Writers Association of America to the individual who has continued to be active in golf despite a physical handicap.

1954	Babe Zaharias	1964	Bob Morgan	1974	Gay Brewer, Jr.	1984	Jay Sigel
1955	Ed Furgol	1965	Ernest Jones	1975	Patty Berg	1985	Rod Funseth
1956	Dwight Eisenhower	1966	Ken Venturi	1976	Paul Hahn	1986	Fuzzy Zoeller
1957	Clint Russell	1967	Warren Pease	1977	Desmond Sullivan	1987	Charles Owens
1958	Dale Bourisseau	1968	Shirley Englehorn	1978	Dennis Walters	1988	Pat Browne
1959	Charlie Boswell	1969	Curtis Person	1979	John Mahaffey	1989	Sally Little
1960	Skip Alexander	1970	Joe Lazaro	1980	Lee Trevino	1990	Linda Craft
1961	Horton Smith	1971	Larry Hinson	1981	Kathy Linney	1991	Pat Bradley
1962	Jimmy Nichols	1972	Ruth Jessen	1982	Al Geiberger	1992	Jim Nelford
1963	Bobby Nichols	1973	Gene Littler	1983	Calvin Peete		

THE WILLIAM D. RICHARDSON AWARD

Given annually by Golf Writers' Association of America to the individual who has made consistently outstanding contributions to golf.

Year	Winner	Year	Winner	Year	Winner	Year	Winner
1948	Robert A. Hudson	1960	Fred Corcoran	1972	Leo Fraser	1983	William C. Campbell
1949	Scotty Fessenden	1961	Joseph C. Dey, Jr.	1973	Ben Hogan	1984	Sam Snead
1950	Bing Crosby	1962	Walter Hagen	1974	Byron Nelson	1985	Lee Trevino
1951	Richard S. Tufts	1963	Herb and Joe Graffis	1975	Gary Player	1986	Kathy Whitworth
1952	Chick Evans	1964	Clifford Roberts	1976	Herbert Warren Wind	1987	Frank Hannigan
1953	Bob Hope	1965	Gene Sarazen	1977	Mark Cox	1988	Roger Barry
1954	Babe Zaharias	1966	Robert E. Harlow	1978	Jack Nicklaus	1989	Ben Crenshaw
1955	Dwight Eisenhower	1967	Max Elbin	1979	Jim Gaquin	1990	P. J. Boatwright
1956	George S. May	1968	Charles Bartlett	1980	Jack Tuthill	1991	Tom Watsan
1957	Francis Ouimet	1969	Arnold Palmer	1981	Robert Trent Jones	1992	Deane R. Beman
1958	Bob Jones	1970	Roberto De Vicenzo	1982	Chi Chi Rodriguez		
1959	Patty Berg	1971	Lincoln Werden				

CHARLES BARTLETT AWARD

Given by the Golf Writers' Association of America to a playing professional for unselfish contribution to the betterment of society.

Year	Winner	Year	Winner	Year	Winner	Year	Winner
1971	Billy Casper, Jr.	1977	Lee Elder	1983	No award	1989	Mary Bea Porter
1972	Lee Trevino	1978	Bert Yancey	1984	Gene Sarazen	1990	No award
1973	Gary Player	1979	No award	1985	No award	1991	No award
1974	Chi Chi Rodriguez	1980	No award	1986	No award	1992	John Daly
1975	Gene Littler	1981	No award	1987	No award		
1976	Arnold Palmer	1982	Patty Berg	1988	Patty Sheehan		

BOB JONES AWARD

Given annually by the United States Golf Association
for distinguished sportsmanship in golf.

Year	Winner	Year	Winner	Year	Winner
1955	Francis Ouimet	1969	Gerald H. Micklem	1981	JoAnne Carner
1956	William C. Campbell	1970	Roberto De Vicenzo	1982	William J. Patton
1957	Babe Zaharias	1971	Arnold Palmer	1983	Mrs. Maureen Garrett
1958	Margaret Curtis	1972	Michael F. Bonallack	1984	Jay Sigel
1959	Findlay S. Douglas	1973	Gene Littler	1985	Fuzzy Zoeller
1960	Charles Evans, Jr.	1974	Byron Nelson	1986	Jess Sweetser
1961	Joe Carr	1975	Jack Nicklaus	1987	Tom Watson
1962	Horton Smith	1976	Ben Hogan	1988	Isaac Grainger
1963	Patty Berg	1977	Bing Crosby	1989	Chi Chi Rodriguez
1964	Charles R. Coe		Bob Hope	1990	Peggy Kirk Bell
1965	Mrs. Glenna Collett Vare	1978	Bing Crosby	1991	Ben Crenshaw
1966	Gary Player		Bob Hope	1992	Gene Sarazen
1967	Richard S. Tufts	1979	Tom Kite		
1968	Robert B. Dickson	1980	Charles Yates		

FRED HASKINS AWARD (OUTSTANDING COLLEGIATE GOLFER)

Year	Winner	Year	Winner
1971	Ben Crenshaw (Texas)	1982	Willie Wood (Oklahoma State)
1972	Ben Crenshaw (Texas)	1983	Brad Faxon (Furman)
1973	Ben Crenshaw (Texas)	1984	John Inman (North Carolina)
1974	Curtis Strange (Wake Forest)	1985	Sam Randolph (Southern California)
1975	Jay Haas (Wake Forest)	1986	Scott Verplank (Oklahoma State)
1976	Phil Hancock (Florida)	1987	Bill Mayfair (Arizona State)
1977	Scott Simpson (Southern California)	1988	Bob Estes (Texas)
1978	Lindy Miller (Oklahoma State)	1989	Robert Gamez (Arizona)
1979	Bobby Clampett (Brigham Young)	1990	Phil Mickelson (Arizona State)
1980	Bobby Clampett (Brigham Young)	1991	Phil Mickelson (Arizona State)
1981	Bob Tway (Oklahoma State)	1992	Phil Mickelson (Arizona State)

Golf Equipment

THE EVOLUTION OF GOLF EQUIPMENT

One reason you see better golf scores today than ever before in the history of the game is the availability of better equipment. There is simply no comparison between today's golf clubs and the old hickory-shafted ones—woods with heads the size of sledge hammers and irons forged by blacksmiths—that were in use as late as the early 1930s. But a look back at the evolution of golf equipment reveals how the game has progressed.

THE GOLF BALL

The golf ball has dictated the design of the other golf equipment. Actually, as was stated in Section I, modern golf time is divided into periods based on the type of ball that was in use.

The Wooden and Feather Ball Period. Golf, as we know it, was probably first played with inexpensive wooden balls. The Dutch played a form of golf (called *colf*) from as early as 1297 until the early 1700s. Initially, they used balls made from beech or elm; from examples excavated in Amsterdam, these balls had a diameter of two inches and weighed about one and half ounces. Later they adopted a leather ball, stuffed with cow's hair, originally made

for *Kaatzen* (hand tennis), a game still played in Holland. These balls have a diameter of about 1.6 inches and weigh ³/₄ of an ounce. Then, the wooden ball and leather balls stuffed with wool or feathers coexisted side by side for several centuries. Although the featherie ball—a leather ball stuffed with feathers—eventually became the ball of choice in Scotland, apparently wooden balls were still being used in both Holland and Scotland well into the seventeenth century.

According to Steven van Hengel, the Dutch golf historian, the first mention in Holland of leather balls stuffed with feathers (featheries) came in 1657 in a poem by J. Six van Chandelier. Some lines from the poem indicate this and the connection with the Scottish game: "The golfer . . . braces himself and strikes his ash weighted with lead (Editor's note: the Dutch made club) or his *Scottish* cleek of boxwood, three fingers wide, one thick with lead in it, at the *feather ball.*"

Although the first reference to leather balls in Scotland is in 1554, we don't know whether they were stuffed with wool or feathers. However, we do know that in 1506 golf balls cost King James IV fourpence a dozen. In 1618, the grant by James I to James Melvill of a monopoly in golf balls for twenty-one years fixed the price at fourpence *each.* A noted golf historian, Robert Browning, feels, therefore, that

327

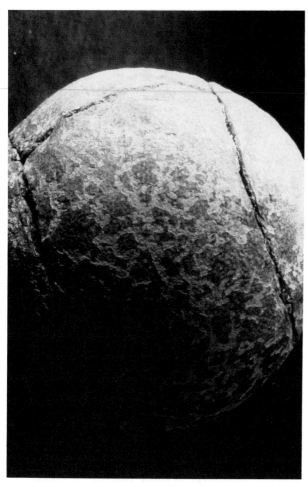

The featherie golf ball, used roughly from the 1500s until 1848, was nothing more than a leather sack filled with a top-hat's worth of goose feathers.

Courtesy Spalding Sports Worldwide

it is reasonable to deduce that between 1506 and 1618, the rise in price represents the difference between the cost of wooden balls and the more elaborate, stuffed leather balls. Only with the publication of Thomas Mathison's poem "The Goff" in 1743, in which the manufacture of golf balls is described, is it clear that the leather balls then in use were stuffed with feathers. In Scotland, the feather ball came in just about any size you wanted. They were numbered from 25–33 dram weight (1.56–2.06 oz.), the most popular being 26–28 (1.62–1.75 oz.). The diameter of a feather ball averaged around 1½ inches, but one of the largest balls to survive is nearly 2 inches in diameter. The feather ball remained in use until about 1848.

The making of feather balls was a tedious and wearisome task, and most ball makers could produce only four to six top-quality ones a day. The leather was softened with alum and water and cut into four, three, or two pieces. These were stitched together with waxed threads outside-in and reversed when the stitching was nearly completed. A small hole was left for the insertion of boiled goose feathers. The ball maker held the leather cover in his hand, in a recessed ball holder, and pushed the first feathers through the hole with a stuffing rod, a tapered piece of wrought iron sixteen to twenty inches long and fitted with a wooden crosspiece to be braced against the ball maker's chest. When the stuffing iron failed, an awl was used, and a volume of feathers that would fill the crown of a beaver hat eventually was inserted into the leather cover. The hole was then stitched up, and the ball was hammered hard and round and given three coats of paint.

Feather balls were seldom exactly round. In wet weather, they tended to become sodden and fly apart. They were easily cut on the seams. A player was fortunate if his ball endured two rounds. The best balls sold for up to five shillings apiece; in bulk, rarely less than one pound for a dozen.

Originally, there appear to have been ball makers in each golfing community, but in the middle of the eighteenth century the Gourlay family, of Leith and Musselburgh, Scotland, became pre-eminent, and a "Gourlay" was accepted as the best and most expensive of all the feather balls on the market. The patriarch of the family was Douglas Gourlay, at Leith, but it was his son, at Musselburgh, who brought the family name its greatest renown. Their principal competitor was Allan Robertson of St. Andrews.

We have no records on the distances that wooden balls could be driven. However, a skillful player at pall-mall could drive similar balls (with a diameter of around 2½ inches) 400 yards, albeit over a hard, smooth, prepared surface. In World War II, due to scarcity of golf balls, a Wooden Ball Championship was played at Potchefstroom, South Africa. By facing wood clubs with about ³/₁₆ths of an inch of balata belting or rubber, players could hit the ball 200 yards.

As to the distances featheries could be driven, we have fairly exact information. Records of the Glasgow club show that in 1786 a player named John Gibson hit a series of drives with the featherie. The distances ranged from 182 to 222 yards. The record drive with a featherie was established in 1836 by M. Samuel Messieux, a French professor at University of St. Andrews. On a slightly frosty day at St. Andrews, with a gentle wind behind him, Messieux drove a feather ball 361 yards, from the Hole o'Cross green (now shared by the 5th and 13th holes) into Hell bunker (in front of the 14th green).

The Gutta-Percha Ball Period. The first gutta-percha ball is believed to have been made in 1845 by the Rev. Dr. Robert Adams Paterson from gutta-percha that was used as packing around a black marble statue of Vishnu which had been sent from India. The statue is now at the University of St. Andrews.

However, not all writers accept this story. The verdict of *Golf Illustrated* (3/1/1901) was that no one person can be credited with the ball's invention and that the idea probably occurred to several different people at different times around 1845. What is known for certain is that the gutta-percha ball first made its appearance at the beginning of 1848, when it was played in a match at Blackheath, near London, England.

The earliest balls were produced under the name "Paterson's Patent." They were brown in color and were made with the hand by rolling the gutta-percha on a flat board. They had smooth surfaces, lined to simulate the seaming of a feather ball, and ducked quickly in flight until they had been marked and cut in play. Thus they were not introduced into the game generally until 1848, by which time the makers had learned to apply effective permanent markings to the surface so that they would fly properly.

The introduction of the gutta ball occasioned one of the great rejuvenations in the history of the game. Its lower cost, longer life, improved flight, truer run on the greens, and the fact that it did not fall apart in the rain, attracted an enormous number of new players, and the featherie was quickly replaced, despite the best propaganda efforts of its makers to protect their livelihood.

The influx of new players, in turn, forced the conversion of the Old Course at St. Andrews to a full eighteen holes. Until the gutta ball was developed, golfers played "out" along what is now known as the left-hand course, until they reached the End Hole. There they turned around and played "in" to the same holes. If two groups approached a green simultaneously, preference was given to those playing "out." However, as golfers multiplied with the ad-

vent of the gutta ball, the links proved too narrow to accommodate them, and about 1857 it was widened sufficiently to turn the greens into double ones so that eighteen holes could be cut instead of nine.

Gutta balls were generally as large as, if not larger than, the modern United States ball of diameter not less than 1.68 inches. They were marked 26, 26½, 27, 27½, 28, 28½, or 29 to designate their weight. These numbers probably referred to pennyweights in the troy weight scale. In this scale, 20 pennyweights equals an ounce.

Gutta balls were far easier to make than featheries, since they consisted solely of the single lump of gutta-percha, properly molded. Gutta-percha is a sap

In 1848, the "gutty" appeared. It was molded from gutta percha, the hardened sap of an East Asian tree. The gutty's long life and low cost made golf a game that could be enjoyed by the masses for the first time.
Courtesy Spalding Sports Worldwide

The first modern ball was the "Haskell," which incorporated a small rubber core wrapped with rubber windings. It flew further and straighter than previous balls and could be mass-produced in quantity.
Courtesy Spalding Sports Worldwide

produced by various trees and has the property of becoming soft and impressible at the temperature of boiling water and of retaining its shape when cooled. It is not affected by water except at boiling temperature.

Gutta-percha was procured from overseas in long, round rods about 1½ inches in diameter. Sufficient gutta-percha was cut from this rod, with the aid of a gauge, to make a ball of the desired size and weight. This piece was softened in hot water, shaped and rolled by hand, then nicked with the thin end of a hammer. Later, iron molds, or ball presses, were introduced, first with plain molding surfaces and subsequently with indented surfaces to create markings

on the ball. When first painted, gutta balls were given several coats, until it was noticed that this tended to fill the indentations of the markings. The number of coats was then reduced to two. It became customary, after applying the first coat, to let the balls season on racks for weeks before finishing them off.

The best-known balls were the hand-marked private brands of the club makers, such as the Auchterlonies, Old Tom Morris, and Robert Forgan, and the bramble and patent brands, such as the *Eureka*, *Melfort*, *White Melfort* (of white gutta-percha), *White Brand*, *Henley*, *O.K.*, *Ocobo*, *Silvertown No. 4*, *A.1*, *Clan*, *Thornton*, *Park's Special*, and *Agrippa*. The *Agrippa*, with bramble marking, became a great favorite. The *A.1* floated, but guttas in general did not.

In the earlier part of this period, there was a rival to the gutta ball, commonly called the putty ball to distinguish it from the "gutty." It was named the *Eclipse* and was made of undisclosed ingredients, possibly including India rubber and cork fillings. It had a shorter carry, but longer run and better wearing qualities. However, by the 1890s it had lost favor.

Accurate measurements of the distances that gutta balls flew were recorded. The longest drives recorded with a gutta are two made during the summer of 1892 at St. Andrews by amateur Edward Blackwell. On one drive, he hit from the 16th tee and drove the ball to within a few yards of the first hole. The spot was marked with a peg and measured the next day. He also drove from the 18th tee to the steps of the clubhouse; a west wind was blowing and the condition of the course was that of a normal summer. Both drives measured 366 yards. In another match that summer, Blackwell averaged 259 yards in reaching the 5th green in two shots—520 yards—and the 14th green in two shots—516 yards. The holes were in opposite directions so that the westerly wind, from the left on the 5th and the right on the 14th, could not have affected the result.

The longest distances a top-class golfer could expect with a gutta ball under normal conditions is shown by a match between Douglas Rolland, undoubtedly the biggest hitter among the professionals of that era, and amateur John Ball, winner of the British Open in 1890 and a record eight-time winner of the British Amateur. At the meeting for the British Open of 1894, a match was held between professionals and amateurs. The drives of Rolland and Ball were marked and later measured. Rolland's longest tee shot was 235 yards; his average for the round was 205 yards. Ball's average was 198 yards.

The earliest covers were of black gutta-percha, lightly lined by hand. Paint tended to fill the indentations, causing the balls to duck in flight just as had the first, smooth gutta balls. Dave Foulis, a Chicago professional, put one in an *Agrippa* mold and produced the raised bramble marking that was common to both the late gutta and early rubber balls.

The next important advancement was the development of the rubber Haskell ball, developed by a wealthy businessman from Cleveland, Coburn Haskell. In 1898, he experimented with a small, solid rubber core wrapped with rubber windings. The resulting sphere flew and rolled farther than the gutta balls.

Haskell balls were placed on the market by the B.F. Goodrich Rubber Co. in 1899 and became known as "Bounding Billies." It is estimated that they traveled about twenty-five yards farther than the gutta. The consensus at first, however, was that the distance a player gained did not offset the difficulty of controlling the lively ball on the green.

The debate was soon resolved. Walter J. Travis, considered the best putter of his day, won the 1901 U.S. Amateur with the Haskell. The next year, Laurie Auchterlonie won the U.S. Open with the ball, scoring in the 70s in every round, the first time this feat had been accomplished. Also in 1902, the British Open was won by Sandy Herd, significantly his only victory in the championship. Herd used a Haskell to defeat Harry Vardon (who three-putted the last green) and James Braid by one stroke. Vardon and Braid both played guttas. Then, in 1904, Travis, a short hitter playing a Haskell, beat Edward Blackwell, a long hitter playing a gutta, in the final of the British Amateur. The gutta thereafter became a relic of the past, and the game was again revolutionized and popularized as it had been with the advent of the gutta.

The day of the ball made by hand in the professional's shop was ending. A. G. Spalding & Brothers, at Chicopee, Massachusetts, a manufacturer of sporting goods, had undertaken production of the first gutta ball in the United States, the *Vardon Flyer*, in 1898 and obtained a license to produce its first rubber ball, the *Spalding Wizard*, in 1903. Soon thereafter the balata cover was developed for Spalding, and its improved adhering qualities made it an important innovation. In 1905 Spalding also introduced the first

"true" white golf balls. Previously, golf balls were black and they showed ugly dark patches when the white paint was nicked. The all-white material did away with these patches by offering a cover of approximately the same color as the paint.

Earliest experiments with the rubber ball concerned the core. It was determined that the best cores, for resilience, were mobile cores which offered least resistance to distortion of the ball caused by club-head impact. Operating on this theory, the Kempshall Golf Ball Company produced the Kempshall Water Core, in which a small sac of water was substituted for solid rubber. The competition to produce a longer ball was under way. Manufacturers tried adding lead to the solution, to combine weight with a mobile core, but lead proved injurious to curious children and animals. Zinc oxide was substituted, but the pigment tended to settle and unbalance the ball. In the 1920s, solutions involving glue, glycerin, and water were developed for first-line balls.

More telling improvements have been made in winding rubber bands around the core, the critical factor in the modern ball. Machines replaced men and were constantly improved for this process. The race was to him who could obtain the greatest tension—to him who could most closely approach the breaking point of rubber thread. The earliest thread was of wild rubber from the Amazon River Basin; development of plantation rubber greatly improved the quality of thread for this race.

Early rubber balls were made with the bramble and reverse mesh markings of the gutta ball, but experiments developed improvements as they revealed the best relationship of both depth and area of indentation to the ball's total surface. William Taylor, in England, reversed the markings on his molds to produce the first true "dimple," in contrast to the bramble, in 1908. The mesh, in contrast to the original reverse mesh, was a natural aftermath.

Early Haskell balls were light and large—about 1.55 ounces in weight and 1.71 inches in diameter, and they floated. In the absence of regulations governing size or weight, manufacturers pursued one another's leads in the quest for the most efficient combination. Heavy solutions in the core increased the weight to about 1.72 ounces in the first decade. Then both size and weight underwent a gradual reduction to 1.62 ounces by 1.63 inches about the time the Haskell patent expired in 1915.

Expiration of this patent increased the competition, which had tended to make courses obsolete. Therefore, in 1920 the USGA and the Royal and Ancient Golf Club of St. Andrews, Scotland, agreed jointly that (1) after May 1, 1921, balls used in their championships must weigh not more than 1.62 ounces and measure not less than 1.62 inches and (2) the two organizations would take whatever steps they deemed necessary in the future to limit the power of the ball. The ball actually was unchanged by this regulation; it continued to measure 1.63 inches, .01 inch above the minimum.

In 1923, the USGA decided that the power should be reduced. A series of experiments under William C. Fownes, Jr., and Herbert Jaques, Jr., led to introduction in the United States in 1930 of the so-called "balloon ball," weighing not more than 1.55 ounces and measuring not less than 1.68 inches. This ball, with no regulation of its velocity, became standard in the United States on January 1, 1931, and was the first deviation from the British ball. It proved too light to hold on line in flight in a wind or on a green as it lost momentum, and it survived only one year.

The present slightly heavier ball, weighing not more than 1.62 ounces and measuring not less than 1.68 inches, became standard in the United States on January 1, 1932. The velocity of this ball was not regulated, however, until the USGA completed a satisfactory testing machine in 1941. Since January 1, 1942, the USGA has required that the velocity of the ball be not greater than 250 feet per second when measured on the Association's machine under specified conditions. Since that time, the ball has remained substantially the same, thanks to USGA standardization.

In 1976, the USGA introduced a distance standard for balls. It states that a golf ball, when tested under the conditions specified by the USGA and on apparatus approved by the USGA on its outdoor range at Far Hills, N.J. (the driving machine is known as "Iron Byron," because the first of these machines, made by True Temper, were modeled after the swing of Byron Nelson), shall not cover an average distance in carry and roll exceeding 280 yards plus a tolerance of eight per cent, since reduced to six per cent (for a total of nearly 297 yards). The ball must also perform as if it were spherically symmetrical.

In the early 1970s, there was a strong move to get the R&A and USGA to adopt a uniform ball of an intermediate diameter between the British (1.62 inches) and American-size (1.68) balls. The effort failed, but from that day to this the American-size ball has gradually taken over. The American-size ball has been mandatory on the European Tour since 1968, the British Open has demanded the larger ball since 1974, and most other national championships have been decided with the larger ball for some years. The American ball is used in the Ryder Cup matches.

However, on the amateur side, the situation is different. The British ball is illegal in the U.S. because USGA rules state the size "must not be less than 1.68 inches in diameter." But the American ball can be used in countries who abide by R & A rules because they, too, deal in minimums. R & A rules state the ball must not be less than 1.62 inches in diameter—there's nothing to say it cannot be more. In Walker Cup play up to 1985, contestants could use either ball. In 1987, the American ball became mandatory.

The British-size ball will soon be relegated to a "collectible" item, and who knows, after a decent interval of years, may be worth some serious money, as featheries and guttas have proved before. As of January 1, 1990, the R&A adopted the American-size 1.68 inch ball and an Overall Distance Standard. The Rules of Golf are now the same in all respects the world over.

Rather closely related to the history of the ball is the tee. In Holland, Steven Van Hengel's research has revealed that players of the Dutch *colf* mostly teed the ball on a mound of soil. However, a "peg" type of tee, closely resembling a modern tee, can be seen in an engraving of a painting by Pieter van der Borscht of about 1590, and also on a seventeenth-century Dutch tile.

In the early days in Scotland, your caddie teed up your ball, making the tee from sand. Usually, he carried a small bag with damp sand in it—dry sand made a poor tee. It was then quite an art to make a tee, requiring a dexterous twist of the caddie's fingers to produce a small pyramid-shaped heap of sand on which to rest the ball.

Toward the end of the nineteenth century, tee boxes containing sand began appearing at every teeing ground. Sometimes this sand was dampened, sometimes water containers were attached to the tee boxes.

The caddie would be directed to pile the sand by the tapping of the driver on the ground on the precise spot. This, we must add, was a European custom, practiced by the more pompous gentlemen. When it was first tried in the United States, so one story goes, the American caddies saw fit to refuse "to bow down to the foreigners," and there were a few embarrassing moments until the "stand-off" was amicably settled. Soon, someone fashioned a mold resembling an elongated thimble that removed much of the guesswork as to size of the sand mound and the making of a tee became a do-it-yourself science for everyone.

Originally, the use of the word "tee" did not refer to the implement as we now know it but to the teeing ground—and even the teeing ground was not then as we now know it. When the Regulations for the Game of Golf were adopted by the St. Andrews Society of Golfers at their meeting on Friday, May 1, 1812, Rule 1 stated: "The ball must be teed not nearer the hole than two club lengths, not farther from it than four." This meant the golfers of that time were hitting their drives from within 8 to 15 feet of the cup. Naturally, this did the putting surface no good at all, and it was not long before they designated another spot for the purpose of "teeing off."

The origin of the wooden tee is a bit vague. A forerunner was the rubber tee advertised by A. G. Spalding as far back as 1893. A patent for a tee with a wooden stem and flexible tubular head was granted to a man named Grant in 1899. But the first marketable all-wooden tee was the *Reddy Tee* invented in 1920 by a dental surgeon named William Lowell. Its popularity was abetted by a huge order from the powerful F. W. Woolworth chain; its adoption by amateurs and pros was spurred on by none other than Walter Hagen, who would place one conspicuously behind his ear and walk down the fairway in full view of the gallery.

Today, the *wooden* tee is made in an astounding variety of shapes, sizes, and materials, and a check of your own supply will undoubtedly expose them in many colors, lengths, and head dimensions. You will probably find tall tees, for those who like to hit up on the ball, or for use on courses with lush grass in the tee-off area; short tees to help correct a tendency to hook or for use on hard tees with little grass; or tees with large cavities, called by many "hurricane tees," so the ball will not be easily blown off by the high winds common to seaside courses, or links.

THE GOLF CLUB

The history of the golf club is *very* closely integrated with the history of the ball. In fact, the club evolved in response to developments in the ball, and thus its history is divided into the same three periods of golf "time."

Wooden and Feather Ball Period. During this era, the full, free style known as the "St. Andrews swing" was developed. The clubs, which were at first rudimentary, tended toward the end of the period to be long, thin, and graceful; the featherie was swept from the ground with a full swing, which also tended to be long and graceful. The shafts were whippy and the grips thick. There was a considerable elegance to these clubs. The foremost club makers, Hugh Philp and Douglas McEwan, have become known as the Chippendale and Hepplewhite of club making.

The earliest known club maker was William Mayne, of Edinburgh, who received a Royal Warrant as club maker and spear maker from James VI in 1603. An old notebook records payments for the repair of "play clubis," "bonker clubis," and an "irone club." There are no known examples of these clubs, although some were pictured in the art of the times, showing their rudimentary nature.

Among the oldest known clubs is a set of six woods and two irons preserved in a case in the Big Room at the Troon Golf Club, Troon, Scotland. These were found in a walled-up closet of a house at Hull, England, with a copy of a Yorkshire paper dated 1741. It is possible that they are of Stuart times. All six woods and two irons are shafted with ash. Only one wood and one iron have grips. The woods are leaded and boned, the lead extending from near the toe two-thirds of the way to the heel. Although the stamp is too worn for identification, they could have been made by Andrew Dickson, of Leith, or Henry Mill, of St. Andrews, who were well-known club makers of the Stuart era and next in our line of knowledge after Mayne.

Club making reached its zenith in the last century of the feather-ball era, with the advent of the real artists: Simon Cossar of Leith; the successive generations of McEwans (James, Peter, and Douglas) of Leith and Musselburgh; Hugh Philp, of St. Andrews, and his assistant, James Wilson; and Harold White, of St. Andrews. Cossar, Philp, Wilson, and the McEwans were noted for their woods; Cossar, Wilson, and White for cleeks and irons. White is credited with giving Allan Robertson and Young Tom Morris such refined irons that they were able to introduce a wide range of new strokes into the game.

Early sets of clubs were primarily woods, which were the choice for most shots of any distance. Irons were used to dig the ball out of ruts and other troublesome lies, as well as on and around the putting surface. *The Bettmann Archive*

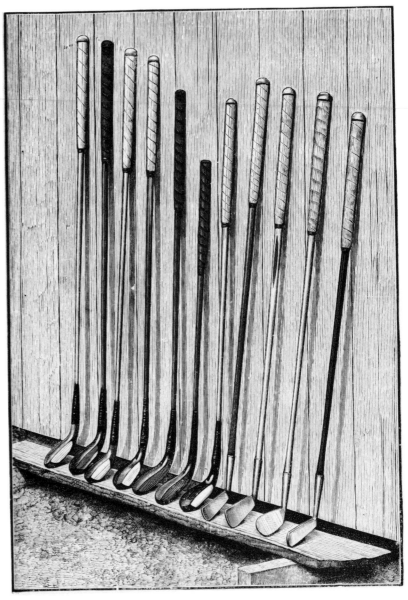

Douglas McEwan made his club heads from small cuts of hedgethorne, which had been planted horizontally on sloping banks so that the stems grew at an angle at the root and created a natural bend for the neck. The shafts, spliced onto the heads, were made of split ash.

By the first half of the nineteenth century, clubs had come to be divided into four classes: drivers, spoons, irons, and putters. Drivers were distinguished by their long, tapering, and flexible shafts and their small, raking heads. They comprised "play clubs," which had little loft and were designed for use over safe ground only, and "grassed drivers," which had more loft and were designed to lift a ball from a heavy or downhill lie or over a hazard.

Spoons were of four types: long spoons, middle spoons, short spoons, and baffing spoons, the distinctions being in the degree of loft. For a time there was also a fifth spoon, the niblick, a well-lofted club with a small head designed to drive a ball out of a wagon-wheel rut or similar man-made hazard.

Irons were three in number: driving irons, cleek, and bunker irons. There were two types of putters: driving putters, for approach work over unencumbered terrain, and green putters, for use on putting greens. With these sets, players negotiated their feather balls over holes measuring 80 to 400 yards.

The Gutta-Percha Ball Period. The gutta-percha ball was harder than the feather ball and put a considerable strain on the slender clubs with which feather balls had been stroked. Thus wooden heads gradually became shorter and squatter in shape. Hard thorn was discarded for the softer apple, pear, or beech in the heads, and leather inserts appeared in the faces. Hickory, which for golf originally came from Russia and later from Tennessee, replaced ash in the making of shafts.

Iron clubs increased in both number and variety and became vastly more refined. The superlative play of Young Tom Morris at St. Andrews is credited with popularizing the iron clubs he used so deftly. A full range of clubs during the gutta-ball period consisted of seven woods (driver, bulger driver, long spoon, brassie, middle spoon, short spoon, and putter) and six irons (cleek, midiron, lofting iron, mashie, niblick, and cleek putter). From these the golfer usually selected about eight. The range of clubs which Willie Park, Jr., had in winning the British Open Championships of 1887 and 1889 was bulger driver, straight-faced driver, spoon, brassie niblick, wooden putter, cleek, iron, mashie, iron niblick, and Parks Patent putter. The increase in the number of clubs brought about another innovation in the early nineties, that of a simple sailcloth bag for carrying them. Previously, the few clubs a player might need had been carried loose under the arm. Thus, the golf bag got its start in the gutta-percha era.

The introduction of the gutta ball did not change the club makers; it simply required them to develop new designs and materials. Douglas McEwan lived until 1896 and bridged both the feathery and the gutta periods. His son Peter in turn became a club maker and was followed by his four sons, who constituted the fifth generation of club-making McEwans. James Wilson, who had made clubs for the feather ball under Hugh Philp, set up his own shop at St. Andrews in 1852, and Philp then took in his nephew, Robert Forgan. Forgan and his son Thomas continued the business under their own name after Philp's death and achieved their own fame.

Robert Forgan was the first to appreciate the merit of hickory shafts after bolts of the wood had come up the Clyde to Glasgow for conversion to handles for pick, shovel, rake, hoe, and ax. Thomas Forgan produced the slightly oversized bulger driver and the ebony putter. Old Tom Morris, the Andersons, and the Auchterlonies were other noted club makers at St. Andrews, and there were Ben Sayers at North Berwick, Willie Park of Musselburgh, the Simpsons of Carnoustie, and many more.

In 1893, Willie Dunn, son of Willie of the famed Dunn twins of Scotland, arrived in the United States. He remained in this country to make clubs and also designed some fifteen to twenty courses. Other Scottish professionals emigrated in the 1890s and contributed to the establishment of the trade of American club making.

The trade itself was little changed. Wooden heads were cut out of a block, filed, spokeshaved, chiseled, gouged, leaded, boned, glass-papered, sometimes stained, and treated with a hare's foot dipped in a mixture of oil and varnish. Where the club heads used by Allan Robertson in the mid-1800s were only $5/16$ of an inch deep, the depth gradually increased to one inch and, for a time, two inches.

Iron heads were hand-forged from a bar of mild iron, heated, hammered, tempered, emery-wheeled, and polished, and the socket pierced for the rivet and nicked. Hickory shafts were seasoned, then cut, filed, planed, scraped, and glass-papered down to the required length, shape, and degree of whippiness, which was the real art. Shafts for wooden heads were finished in a splice, glued onto the heads, and whipped with tarred twine. Shafts for irons were finished with a prong to fit into the socket and holed for the iron cross rivet. Strips of untanned leather, shaped with a chisel, were nailed to the top of the shafts, wound on spirally over a cloth foundation, rolled tight between two polished boards, and nailed at the bottom. Both ends of the grip were bound with tarred twine, and the whole grip was then varnished.

Caliber of play improved greatly with the advent of the gutta ball. Allan Robertson shattered all precedent by scoring a 79 at St. Andrews in 1858, and this record stood until Young Tom Morris made a 77 in 1869. The British Open Championship was instituted at Prestwick, Scotland, in 1860 and was played there through 1872. Willie Park, Sr., won the first Open with a score of 174 for thirty-six holes, and Young Tom Morris retired the belt, emblematic of the Championship, by winning his third successive Championship, with a score of 149, in 1870. The first golf in the United States was played with gutta balls; the USGA Amateur, Open, and Women's Championships originated in 1895, three years before the invention of the rubber ball.

The Rubber-Ball Period. Golf was being overtaken by the Industrial Revolution when the rubber ball came into the game at the beginning of the twentieth century. These two factors wrought major changes in the clubs and the methods by which they were produced as craftsmanship moved out of the individual professional's shop and into the factory.

The softer rubber ball brought about the use of persimmon heads. Later, heads of laminated (layered) wood also were used. Hard insets appeared in the faces. Increased demand led to the adaptation of shoe-last machine tools for the fashioning of wooden club heads. Sockets were bored in the hosels, and shafts were inserted rather than spliced.

Drop forging almost completely replaced hand forging in the fashioning of iron clubs, and faces were deepened to accommodate the livelier ball and were machine-lined to increase the spin on the ball in flight. Stainless steels replaced carbon steels. Seamless steel shafts took the place of hickory. Composition materials were developed as an alternative to leather in grips, and the grip foundations were molded in so many ways that they were regulated in 1947. Inventive minds created novel clubs, not only center-shafted and aluminum putters and the sand wedge but also types which were such radical departures from the traditional form and make that they could not be approved by the USGA or by the Royal and Ancient Golf Club of St. Andrews, Scotland.

These changes had their genesis in the United States when Julian W. Curtiss, of A. G. Spalding & Bros., purchased some clubs in London in 1892 for resale in his company's retail stores. Two years later, Spalding employed some Scottish club makers and began producing its own clubs.

Hand modeling of woods and hand forging of irons naturally did not long survive the demands of factory production. Within the first decade, the Crawford, McGregor & Canby Company in Dayton, Ohio, a maker of shoe lasts, was turning out wooden heads, foundries were converting drop-forging processes to iron heads, and Allan Lard, in Chicopee, Massachusetts, was experimenting with perforated steel rods for shafts.

A. W. Knight, of Schenectady, New York, joined this inventive movement and produced an aluminum-headed putter with the shaft attached near the center, instead of at the heel. Walter J. Travis used this "Schenectady" putter in winning the British Amateur in 1904, and center-shafted clubs immediately were banned in Britain. It was not until 1933 that center-shafted putters were legalized.

During the twenty-nine years of its prohibition in England, the putter's popularity spread throughout the United States and brought forth an endorsement from William H. Taft, then President of the United States. President Taft sent a letter to Travis, telling how much he enjoyed using the Schenectady putter and that it had improved his game. So far as is known, this is the only time a President has lent endorsement to a golf club. (In the 1950s, President Dwight D. Eisenhower, whose enthusiasm for the game helped fuel the golf boom of that decade, was known to use Spalding clubs. This equipment was given to the president by his friend Bobby Jones, who became an adviser to Spalding shortly after retiring from competitive play in 1930.)

Seven years after he had patented the putter, Knight made his second contribution, the steel shaft. Again, that invention was brought about by Knight's desire to improve his own game. Seeking to get a greater "whip" to his driver, Knight reduced the diameter of his wooden shaft, making his driver unreliable for direction. It was then he began experimenting with steel. He found that the steel shaft produced the desired results and helped to improve his game.

The import of all these developments was such that, in promulgating its revised code of rules in September 1908, the Royal and Ancient Golf Club of St. Andrews appended the notation that it would not sanction any substantial departure from the traditional and accepted form and make of golf clubs. This principle has been invoked many times in an effort to preserve the original form of the game.

When Jock Hutchison won the British Open in 1921 with deeply slotted faces on his pitching clubs, the Royal and Ancient Golf Club immediately banned such faces, and the USGA concurred with a regulation governing markings, which became effective in 1924. After Horton Smith had so effectively used a sand wedge with a concave face designed by E. M. MacClain, of Houston, Texas, and Bobby Jones had used it in winning the 1930 British Open, the second leg of the Grand Slam, the principle of concavity was banned in 1931. However, late in 1931, Gene Sarazen designed a straight-faced sand wedge on which he lowered the back of the sole—today this is called "bounce"—so that the club would skid through the sand rather than dig into it. When he used it to win the British and U.S. Opens of 1932, he completed the revolution in bunker play.

Experiments with steel shafts went through several phases. Lard's perforated steel rod was no substi-

Three early sand wedges. The club on the far right has a concave face, designed to scoop the ball out of a bunker. Deviation in the shape of the clubface was ruled illegal in 1931, just about the time the modern sand wedge was invented.
Olmans' Guide to Golf Antiques

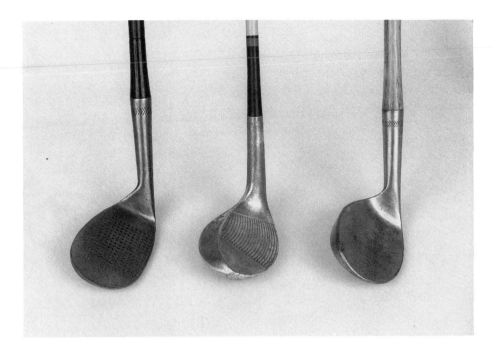

tute for hickory, and the locked-seam shaft of Knight proved not the answer, either, although the USGA approved such shafts in 1924. However, in 1924, the Union Hardware Company, of Torrington, Connecticut, drew a seamless shaft of high carbon steel which could be heat-treated and tempered. This came into the game in the late twenties, was approved by the Royal and Ancient Golf Club in 1929, and substantially replaced hickory in the early thirties. Importing its steel from Sweden, Union soon cornered almost the entire market, furnishing shafts to such old-line companies as Bristol, Kroydon, and Heddon and to Spalding, Wilson, MacGregor, as well as to Hillerich & Bradsby, Northwestern, Dubow, and Professional Golf.

Improvement of the steel shaft was accompanied by the general introduction of numbered clubs, rather than named clubs, and by the merchandising of matched sets, rather than individual clubs; clubs had become more numerous and more finely manufactured to specifications for flexibility and point of flex. Where formerly a golfer seeking new clubs went through a rack of mashies until he found one that "felt right" and then tried to find other clubs of similar feel, he now bought a whole set manufactured to impart the same feel. The merchandising aspect of this development was perhaps something more than a happy coincidence for the manufacturers. In any case, the merchandising opportunities

inherent in the numbered and matched sets were carried to an extreme, and in 1938 the USGA limited to fourteen the number of clubs a player might use in a round. The Royal and Ancient Golf Club concurred in a similar edict the next year.

The superiority of the steel shaft went unchallenged until the fifties, with introduction of glass shafts. The Fiberglas WonderShaft produced by the Shakespeare Company, Kalamazoo, Michigan, received a great deal of attention and publicity (Fiberglas is a registered trademark of Owens-Corning Fiberglas Corporation), mostly through the success of its chief proponent, Gary Player. He used this shaft in winning the 1965 U.S. Open, among other tournaments. However, the Shakespeare shaft eventually proved to have far too much torque (or twist) for professionals, whose consistency suffered as a result.

The Shakespeare Fiberglas shaft consisted of more than a half-million glass fibers bonded in parallel into a double-built tubular shaft, with the fibers running lengthwise on the shaft around a central spiral Fiberglas wall.

In 1965, after ten years of experimentation, an aluminum shaft more than ten percent stronger in tensile strength than steel alloy shafts but lighter by thirty percent was brought onto the market. The first to learn of this highest-strength aluminum on the market were all the major golf manufacturers, to whom sample shafts were shipped by Le Fiell Prod-

These intricately designed woods were fitted with early steel shafts, which came into general use in the 1930s. Steel shafts made clubs feel and play more alike, which led to the creation of "matched sets."

Olman's Guide to Golf Antiques

ucts, Inc., of Sante Fe Springs, California. It caught their fancy from the start. Here was lightweight material strong enough to hold the club head in position in relation to the hands, without torque. Was this it, then? Was this the shaft of the future?

From the present perspective, more than twenty-five years later, the answer has to be a decided no. At first, aluminum took off like a rocket. The great Arnold Palmer used an aluminum-shafted set early in 1968, and even won a tournament with them, which certainly didn't hurt sales. Also a factor were the distance claims made for the aluminum shaft. Since the shaft was about half an ounce lighter than the original or regular steel shaft, this meant, according to the manufacturer, that some of the weight saved in the shaft could be added to the club head, giving the golfer a club that weighed less overall but with a slightly heavier club head. Since the club head—the object being swung—was heavier, and the golfer could swing a slightly lighter overall weight faster, more distance was assured. How much distance? Around one club stronger than steel, say, ten yards longer per club.

What happened? After the dust settled, the following conclusions could be drawn: (1) The lighter overall weight did suit seniors and women golfers, and many of these did in fact experience a slight distance bonus; (2) On the other hand, most average golfers found that distance claims had been exagger-

ated, at least so far as they were concerned; (3) Aluminum gave a "softer" hit than steel. Some golfers liked it, but many more found it "dead" compared to the more lively impact feel they were used to in steel; (4) For better golfers, the softer feel of aluminum dulled feedback on a shot—with steel they knew if they had hit the ball well or badly, with aluminum, they did not.

In 1973, the graphite shaft (graphite fibers bonded together by resin in similar fashion to Fiberglas) was introduced. Because a graphite shaft is one-and-a-half to two ounces lighter than a regular steel shaft, and from one to two ounces lighter than aluminum or lightweight steel shafts, again much promotional hay was made in regard to distance. Highly exaggerated claims of twenty to fifty additional yards off the tee were made. Aluminum revisited, one might call it. And again, when the clubs got into the hands of average golfers, the distance bonus just wasn't there, except for seniors and women. Another problem was the price—a full set of early graphite-shafted clubs retailed for $1,100 to $1,800.

Graphite hung around for a few years in the 1970s until complaints of breakage, inconsistency, and high price lessened its appeal. But graphite was not dead, only dormant. Beginning in the mid-1980s, it was reintroduced in shafts, and clubheads as well, primarily by Japanese equipment companies entering the United States market. Many of these firms worked with graphite in other fields, and had learned how to control its manufacture. Graphite became more common, particularly fitted on drivers, and today it is seen regularly in the bags of players from professional tour ranks to rank amateurs.

Helping graphite's resurgence was a cost closer to, but still a few dollars more than, steel. But graphite has won its niche, whether with seniors and women looking for a few more yards from their slower swings, or big hitters who want to hit it even bigger.

Other shaft materials that have come along recently include titanium (again, lighter but more expensive than steel), lighter-weight steel, and exotic composites such as boron and Kevlar, which are mixed with graphite for strength and specific shot-making attributes.

While graphite and exotic materials appeal to some golfers, there is hardly a player today who hasn't been affected by changes in the manufacture of woods and irons since the 1960s. Much as the development of first the gutta and then the wound ball changed the face of the game, so did the emergence of investment-cast irons and metal woods.

In the early 1960s, investment-casting—pouring molten metal into molds—became popular especially in the aerospace industry, where exacting tolerances are required. The ability to easily mold metal rather than forge it under thousands of pounds of pressure allowed imaginative entrepreneurs the chance to resurrect an old idea in club design, spreading the weight out around the face. Moving the club's mass away from a small, centralized spot behind the center created a cavity in the backside, but more important, enlarged the so-called "sweet spot," so shots hit out toward the toe or in toward the heel of the club still would fly farther and straighter than if hit poorly off unforgiving forged irons.

Investment-casting also spurred a new design in woods, the oxymoronically named "metal woods." Metal woods are hollow, allowing weight to be moved around the outside of the head; the internal cavity then is filled with foam or some other lightweight material to add a little weight, deaden the shock of impact, and muffle the sound.

Both metal woods and investment-cast irons made golf immediately more enjoyable for millions of hackers. Clubs that actually helped correct mishits? They can't stop a severe slice from bending, but they do add yardage and temper the ill effects of poor shots.

The final piece of the more golfer-friendly puzzle was the creation of a new ball, the two-piece. The wound (or three-piece—solid core, rubber windings, balata cover) ball remained the sphere of choice into the early 1970s. Along the way it was improved with aerodynamic dimple patterns and thinner and/or more resilient cover materials. But the concept remained basically unchanged from Haskell's "Bounding Billy" of 1898.

Then, in 1968, Spalding unveiled its two-piece Top-Flite, a solid core of thermoplastic wrapped in a

The cavity-back iron, introduced in the 1960s, was the first true "game-improvement" club. Distributing the weight around the edges of the clubface rather than concentrating it in the center produced longer, straighter shots—even off mishits.
Courtesy Karsten Manufacturing

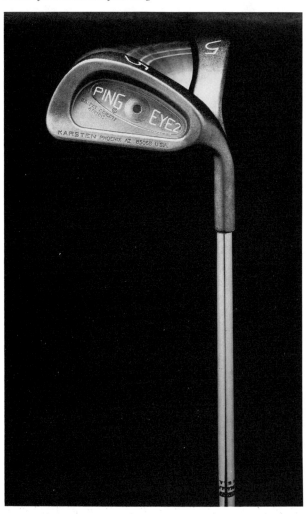

Metal woods produce the same game-improvement results as cavity-back irons. The heads are hollow, with the weight moved out to the club's perimeter. The intended result is more distance and more accuracy for golfers of all skill levels. *Courtesy Spalding Sports Worldwide*

tough cover. The ball won quick acceptance thanks to its longer distance and longer life: A poor shot wouldn't cut the cover as happened to the soft balata that shrouded three-piece balls. Furthermore, the two-piecer proved a perfect match for cast clubs, which made golfers more concerned with hitting it long and straight than with "feel" and "shotmaking."

In time, three-piece balls were covered with Du-Pont's Surlyn and other resilient materials. Advances in ball technology have created more distance, more feel, improved aerodynamic qualities that let the golfer "buy" a higher or lower shot, everything but the power to hit straighter shots. And that was tried by a company called Polara, which patterned its dimples in such a way as to fight the golfer's worst efforts to hit a slice or hook. The USGA banned the Polara, a

lawsuit followed, and the organization's right to ensure the traditional character of equipment was upheld.

TYPES OF GOLF CLUBS

Golf clubs today are generally classified in two categories, namely, *woods* and *irons*. Clubs of each category are designed for a particular type of stroke. Today, most clubs are only identified by a number—the exceptions are the driver, wedges, putters. However, up until the early 1930s, clubs had names—these names are shown next to the numbers on the following pages. More recently, some utility woods are often called by the manufacturer's names for the club. Examples are the "Ginty," equipped with a keel-like sole and made by Stan Thompson, and the "Baffler," which has twin runners on its sole and is made by Cobra.

THE WOODS

Until recently, the club head of this type of club was made from wood; hence the name. Today, woods can be made from metal—the very popular "metal woods"—where an investment-cast steel shell is packed with foam (to give a better sound). Metal woods can be perimeter weighted because they're hollow, which makes it easier to get the ball airborne and allows the club to be forgiving on mishits. Today's woods can also have heads made of graphite, ceramics, or ground glass in an advanced mix of epoxy resins. However, whatever the head is made of, woods are designed primarily for distance. This does not mean that a player should not try to be as accurate with them as he possibly can. But the average golfer cannot expect pinpoint accuracy with them.

The distance range given for the various woods here is a guide to what can be accomplished by an average golfer rather than an expert. Adjust to your capacity and ability, based on your own experience. In addition, remember that weather and course conditions can also have a great effect on distance that can be obtained from the various strokes.

No. 1 Wood or Driver. Used from the tee for maximum distance. Has a large head and deep face that is almost vertical. For the average player, the driver's range from a tee is 210 yards and up.

Normal Distance for Average Golfers.

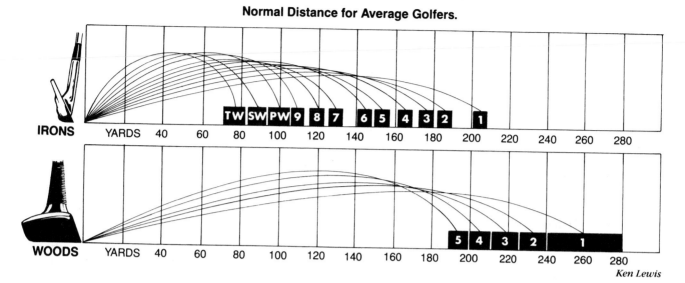

Ken Lewis

No. 2 Wood or Brassie. Named because of the brass plate traditionally found on the sole of the club. It has more loft to the face than a driver and hits the ball higher into the air. Its normal use is from the fairway, when the ball is sitting up well on fairway grass. Under certain circumstances, it is used in driving from the tee, even by expert players. Distance range: 200 to 235 yards.

No. 3 Wood or Spoon. Its face has more loft than a brassie or driver. The club sometimes has a shorter shaft than the driver or brassie. It is used for rather long shots from poor lies in the fairway or off the tee when a high ball is desired to go long with a favorable wind. Distance range: 190 to 220 yards.

No. 4 Wood or Cleek. This has a smaller head, shallower face, and more loft than a spoon. Customary use is from bad lies in fairways where a rather long shot with fairly high arc of flight is desired. Distance range: 180 to 210 yards.

No. 5 Wood or Baffy. This wood has more loft than the other woods mentioned and is used from the fairway and rough when the player is confronted with a poor lie. It gets the ball up quickly. It is an excellent club for women golfers. The No. 5 wood, incidentally, is becoming an increasingly popular club with all golfers, and the No. 2 wood seems to be obsolete. Distance range: 160 to 200 yards.

No. 6 Wood. This is used much the same as No. 5 wood. It provides a little more loft on the ball. Distance range: 150 to 190 yards.

No. 7 Wood. Many clubmakers now make a No. 7 wood because some golfers prefer, say, a 5 and 7 wood, to the more difficult long irons. The more lofted woods also are much more useful from the rough. Complete sets of woods are available for those golfers who "can't hit an iron" or fear a shank. Range: 140 to 180 yards.

THE IRONS

Iron clubs were so named because originally all iron heads were forged, from iron. Today, they can be forged carbon steel (which is chrome-plated), forged stainless steel, investment-cast stainless steel, or something more exotic. Graphite-headed irons have recently appeared, as well as heads made from bronze and beryllium copper. Some aren't even solid any more—"hollow irons," as their name implies, have cavities like metal woods and offer the same game-improvement advantages.

Iron clubs are intended for shots where accuracy rather than distance is the prime consideration and for shots that are lying in grass or on sand where the face of the club must get down and hit the ball up quickly. The irons fall into three general categories: long, medium, and short. The Nos. 1, 2, and 3 irons are classified as the long irons; the Nos. 4, 5, and 6 are regarded as medium irons; and the Nos. 7, 8, 9, and wedges rate as the short irons.

Iron clubs have shorter shafts than wood clubs and

have the shafts joined to the club heads at more upright angles than in wood club design. Consequently, to play the irons correctly, the player must stand closer to the ball than when playing a wood. By making sure that the bottom (the sole) of the club is squarely on the ground when taking the stance, the player will see from the location of the grip where to stand to use the club in the manner for which it is designed. The distance that can be made with any particular club depends on the individual. Again the ranges given here are representative of distances obtained by the average golfer.

No. 1 Iron or Driving Iron. A club seldom used or carried by the average golfer. (Most manufacturers no longer include the No. 1 iron in their standard matched sets.) It is a club with very little loft to its face and is used when a low ball is desired, such as when hitting into the wind. Distance range: 190 to 210 yards.

No. 2 Iron or Midiron. An all-around club for long shots from the fairway, tee, and sometimes rough. However, the No. 2 iron is a rather difficult club for the beginner to master because of the little loft and the extra strength required to obtain the proper distance. This iron is being replaced in many golfers' bags by the No. 5 wood. Distance range: 165 to 190 yards.

No. 3 Iron or Mid Mashie. Has a greater loft than the No. 2 iron and is much easier to use. It is generally the longest iron that most beginning players can handle with any degree of certainty. Distance range: 150 to 175 yards.

No. 4 Iron or Mashie Iron. A useful iron for shots from the fairway, rough, or bad lies. Used off the tee on many par-3 holes. Distance range: 140 to 165 yards.

No. 5 Iron or Mashie. For fairly long, high shots from the fairway or rough and off the tee on some par-3 holes. A popular and relatively easy club to use in pitching the ball high to the green so it will stop after hitting the ground. Also may be used for pitch-and-run shots from 30 to 50 yards off the green when it is desired that the ball travel part way through the air and roll the rest of the distance to the objective. Distance range: 130 to 155 yards.

No. 6 Iron or Spade Mashie. For pitch-and-run shots to the green and for playing the ball from high grass or difficult lies. It is useful from a clean lie in the sand trap when some distance is needed. It is also employed from the fairway. It has greater loft than the No. 5 iron. Distance range: 100 to 145 yards.

No. 7 Iron or Mashie Niblick. More loft, less distance than spade mashie. Used for short pitch or chip shots onto the green and to get out of traps, over trees, and so on. Imparts plenty of backspin to the ball to hold the green. Distance range: 100 to 135 yards.

No. 8 Iron or Pitching Niblick. Used much the same as No. 7 iron. For pitch shots from the fairway, rough, or quick-rising pitches over hazards and bunkers. Distance range: 80 to 120 yards.

No. 9 Iron or Niblick. For sand shots from traps and some shots from bad rough. The face has a great deal of loft, and the head is heavy to carry it through long tough grass or heavy sand. Distance range: 80 to 110 yards.

Putter. A club with straight or nearly straight face for rolling ball on green. There are many styles of putters, and the one you select is a matter of preference.

Special Clubs. Most complete sets come with a pitching wedge, slightly heavier and with more loft than the 9-iron. As its name implies, it's for pitch shots from, say, 100 yards and closer to the green. However, it can also be useful for some sand shots, for example, when the ball is buried. The sand wedge, usually the heaviest iron, and with a broader flange than the pitching wedge, is primarily designed for sand play, but also is useful for short pitches from rough or fairway. Recently, the "third" wedge has appeared, with more loft than the regular sand wedge. The standard loft on a men's sand wedge is 56 degrees. The third wedge's loft is often 60 degrees, but could vary from 58–62 degrees depending on an individual's needs. (Women's specifications would be one degree more in each case.) The club makes short pitches over hazards far easier, as one can use a fuller swing and thus play the shot more firmly.

At one time, dual-purpose wedges (for use in bunkers as well as from the fairway) were quite popular. However, they are rare today, because they were essentially an unhappy compromise between a pitching wedge and sand wedge and had broad, flat soles. What makes a good sand club makes that club less versatile from grass and vice versa.

A good sand wedge has "bounce"—the rear of the flange is lower than the leading edge so that the club will skid through the sand, taking a shallow cut without digging in. From the fairway, that same bounce makes the sand wedge hazardous to play from a tight or especially a bare lie, and particularly if you wish to open the blade for more loft on the shot. Most pitching wedges have essentially flat soles, which will cope with tight or bare lies. However, from sand, the pitching wedge will dig down into the sand too much on a good bunker lie.

In recent years, specialty woods have become popular. Most of them have the length of a 4 wood and the loft of a 7 wood. They are heavily sole-weighted, and some have a "keel" or "rails" on the soles designed to extricate the ball from rough. If wind is not a factor on their home course, many golfers can get along quite nicely with this club and their driver as their only woods.

Two specialty irons still sold today are the "rough iron" and "chipper." The former is a well-lofted, shallow-faced club usually about 5-iron length, the latter, used on short pitch-and-run shots, is about putter length, with lofts anywhere from that of a 4 to 7 iron. Some chippers and putters come as a matched pair.

Continuous sets. In the last few years, a few major manufacturers have designed continuous sets—the whole set is designed to have the same "look," a cross between a wood and an iron. As mentioned earlier, those who dislike irons have for some years been able to buy complete sets of woods. The continuous set takes that thought a step farther. The manufacturers employ metal wood and hollow iron technology to give excellent perimeter weighting. They also make the clubs equivalent to long irons extremely easy to hit. However, while one manufacturer retains a broad sole and a "wood-like" appearance from the driver down to the wedges, the other gradually narrows the sole as you go to the higher-numbered clubs, giving close to a traditional profile on the short irons. The clubs are especially good for higher-handicap players who normally have difficulty with any longer iron than, say, a 5 iron. They look—and are—very easy to hit.

It is very important to remember that a total of fourteen clubs is the limit permitted by the Rules of Golf. Many golfers will want to own more than fourteen clubs to deal with specific conditions. For ex-

ample, a narrow-soled sand wedge is best from hard bunkers while a broader-soled one is best from soft sand. Certain courses may favor use of a utility wood or iron, and so on. Before any round, select the fourteen most suitable clubs, but do not go over that number. If you deviate from the Rules of Golf, you may be playing a game with golf clubs and balls, but you're not playing golf.

MANUFACTURE OF GOLF EQUIPMENT

In no other game or sport is there quite the ignorance about the equipment with which it is played. In a sense, this is understandable. There are more than 200 operations that go into the making of a wood, more than 150 in an iron, several dozen in a ball. As a result, most golfers buy equipment on blind faith. To have some idea of what you are going to purchase, or of what you have already purchased, the following account may help to clarify the manufacturing mysteries behind golf equipment.

THE GOLF CLUBS

Possibly the most common misconception about club making is the notion that expensive clubs are handmade and that inexpensive clubs are manufactured by machine. All clubs, regardless of their price, are handmade. They are put together in a multistage process by craftsmen as skilled as surgeons. The difference, of course, comes in how much you want to spend for a set of clubs. Higher-priced custom-made sets get the individual treatment and styling of a tailor-made suit; lower-grade clubs are mass-produced on an assembly-line basis.

Woods. The business end of a wood, the head, is made either of wood, metal, or a composite material such as graphite. The method of manufacture is determined by that material.

In a wooden head, the material either is a solid piece, usually from the persimmon tree, a species known for its toughness, or a laminated block consisting of a number of layers glued together. Wooden clubheads are solid all the way through, except for the hollowed out neck into which the shaft is fitted.

The wooden block is shaped, then soaked in a bath of a specially produced wood pregnator that allows a moisture content of eight to ten percent. Too much moisture will lead to eventual swelling and popping

Although modern club manufacture is a largely high-tech process, certain steps are performed by hand. Careful installation of grips means the golfer can take a secure hold on the club, then set it down properly behind the ball.
Courtesy Karsten Manufacturing

of the face insert; too little moisture and the club will shatter at impact.

Metal woods are investment cast, their heads formed by pouring molten metal into molds. The heads are hollow, for perimeter weighting, although the cavity is filled with foam that gives the head balance and moderates the sound of impact.

Graphite heads are made either by wrapping long fibers into shape, or else compressing graphite powder, under intense heat and pressure, into a solid form. In all cases, extra weight is sometimes added to a wood, metal, or graphite head to change the club's playing characteristics. Some clubs even let the player insert small lead plugs under the heel or toe for customized playability.

Wooden heads usually carry a face insert and sole plate. Inserts (most commonly made of Cycolac, a strong plastic, but sometimes epoxy, aluminum, fiber, graphite, or other materials) are glued and

sometimes screwed into the head. (Often screws in the face of an insert are there purely for cosmetics.) The heads are then soled with brass or aluminum plates.

Clubheads of all materials are available to help correct a golfer's most common mistakes. Slicers might request a "hook-faced" wood, in which the face is cut back toward the heel; open-face woods add a slight left-to-right curve.

By the time a shaft is inserted into the neck of the head, excess weight has been trimmed off or else polished off in a metal tumbler, that also might be used to give a metal head a shiny finish. When the shaft and wooden head are put together, metal or plastic rings, called ferrules, are slipped around the neck to keep it from splitting. Once the ferrule is in place, a resilient thread—called whipping—is wrapped around the neck. Some graphite heads are fitted with ferrules and whipping, but metal woods aren't because there is little chance of the neck splitting from use.

Irons. The various stages of putting an iron together closely parallel those in putting together a wood. The difference, of course, is in the head. Each company has its own dies for its iron heads, which are forged by a steel company. When the club is assembled, the irons are ground and polished and, of course, checked for weight every bit as carefully as the woods are. The relation of one club to another with regard to weight can be explained like this: As each iron gets one inch shorter, it must pick up a quarter-ounce more in weight in its head in order to arrive at a correct balance. As a rule, the stainless-steel heads are a little more expensive than the chrome-plated carbon steel ones, but are more durable and retain their shine longer.

Beginning in the 1960s, investment-cast irons became increasingly available, and by the mid-1980s they were the overwhelming preference of amateur golfers, particularly those who realized that their games could use a little help.

Investment casting was not a new idea, although it did receive a big boost in the 1950s as the aerospace industry began to produce precision-made parts of lightweight, strong metal. When the innovators began experimenting with casting of golf clubs, they were picking up on an idea that was promoted as far back as the late 1800s: If the clubhead's weight could be spread out, distributed away from the small "sweet spot" in the center, less-than-perfect contact would still produce acceptable shots. Moving the weight toward the edges created a cavity on the back side of the club, hence the names "cavity-back" or "perimeter-weighted" irons.

Today, cavity-back clubs can be found in the hands of players of all skill levels, including touring professionals. Traditional forged blades still have a sizable market, and often are touted as the choice for the better player, meaning one who can make consistent contact on the small sweet spot. The other argument often heard is that forged clubs transmit more "feel" to the golfer than investment-cast clubs.

In the mid-1980s, a hybrid appeared, the "forged cavity-back" (FCB), an iron head that was forged into a perimeter-weighted shape. Many companies quickly designed their own versions. At the end of the decade, the FCB had carved out a small niche in iron sales.

THE GOLF BALL

No article of recreation is more abused, cursed, and dispatched to such inglorious reward than the innocent-looking, dimple-faced golf ball. In order to appreciate fully any factor of the golf ball or of its performance, it would be wise to consider the basic structure of the wound ball.

The center of the ball probably has experienced more change than any other part of the modern ball. Over the years such varied substances as steel, fiberglass, pills, glass, rubber, silicone, water, blood, iodine, mercury, tapioca, dry ice, gelatin, arsenic, and viscous pastes have been used in the center.

After the center has been made, it must be frozen to prepare it for winding. This is important because to wind a true sphere, the center must retain its shape until it is completely surrounded by the thread of the winding operation. It is necessary in the case of liquid-filled centers to have them completely full, with the air entirely eliminated. If there is any air present, the center will collapse when it thaws out and go off shape. This can result in erratic performance of the finished ball.

After the center has been made, it is wound with rubber thread into a core. This winding, which supplies the power, is considered by some to be the greatest achievement in ball manufacture. The thread has been greatly improved through modern technology, and the chemicals that have been added make this new isoprene thread more uniform in feel and resiliency. As it is applied under tension, the thread stores up an abundance of energy. It has been said that there is enough energy in the thread to lift a 150-pound man two feet off the ground.

The center of the ball is placed under very high pressure by the winding. This effect can be illustrated by wrapping a rubber band around your finger. One turn and you can notice the pressure. If you build up several layers, it continues to get tighter and tighter. This is what happens to the golf ball center. The pressure on the center actually builds up to about 2,500 pounds per square inch. In other words, the center as a whole is sustaining a total pressure of from 7,000 to 8,000 pounds.

All types of winding machines have automatic stops, so that when a ball has been wound to its predetermined size the machine will shut off. However, this is not completely reliable, and after the balls have been wound they must be measured. This may be done by various means. The balls of proper size are then surrounded by two hemispherical cups and are ready for molding.

The cups of cover stock that are placed around the wound balls prior to molding are made either of a compound containing balata as its principal component or in recent years of a DuPont thermoplastic called Surlyn. Surlyn and other synthetics now dominate the market because of their proven resistance to cutting. As a rule, balata-covered balls are used solely by Tour professionals, club professionals, and low-handicap amateurs because these skilled players can put more backspin on the ball (than one with a synthetic cover) and thus control approach shots

In constructing a "wound"—or three-piece—ball, the core is wrapped at high speed with rubber windings, then sheathed in a thin cover.

Courtesy Spalding Sports Worldwide

better. Such golfers also prefer the balata ball because they can also put more sidespin on it, and thus they can more easily hit intentional slices and hooks.

There are several methods for molding the cups from the prepared stock. In one of the methods, the heated stock is tubed into strips and cut into blanks of the proper size. The blanks are allowed to cool and are placed in cavities of a cold multiple-cavity cup-forming mold. The loaded mold is then heated, and sufficient hydraulic pressure is applied to cause the heated blanks to take the shape of the mold. After the stock has been heated and pressed out, the mold is chilled. This cools the formed cups, enabling the operator to remove them from the mold.

In another method, instead of using cold blanks, warm sheets or strips of stock are placed in a cold mold, hydraulic pressure is applied to cause the stock to take the shape of the mold, and then the mold is chilled and opened, permitting the removal of the formed cups. In some methods the cups are molded individually, while in others they are formed as a sheet. Therefore, it may or may not be necessary to die out or cut out these cups, depending on the method of molding used. In most cases, the flash or surplus stock can be reused.

After the covers have been formed around the cores, the balls must be cleaned and treated in preparation for spray-painting. Years ago, there was a variety of paints used on golf balls, depending on the selection by the manufacturer according to the way the balls were prepared. In recent years, practically all the golf ball manufacturers have progressively adopted the same basic type of paint, known as a polyurethane. The balls are generally sprayed with two or three coats of white polyurethane paint, at the choice of the individual manufacturer. The length of drying time between coats may also vary due to the conditions under which the painted balls are dried. The golf balls are then packaged for sale.

The method just described is the one most generally followed in the construction of the wound or three-part golf ball (so named because of its three main parts: the center core, the highly tensioned thread winding, and the outside cover).

More recently, the solid ball made a comeback. Although the Faultless Rubber Co. did produce a solid ball back in 1922–1923—a compound of rubber, sulfur, glue, and zinc oxide, which was then dipped in balata—the ball never caught on and was only used at driving ranges. It was not until 1966 that

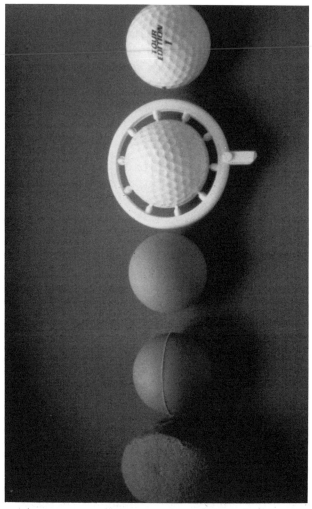

The two-piece, "solid" ball begins with a solid center. That is encased in a durable thermoplastic shell, which is compressed under heat and pressure.

Courtesy Spalding Sports Worldwide

Spalding produced the first high-performance two-piece ball—the Executive—with a solid core and custom-polymer blended cover. The following year, Surlyn was introduced. It made a superbly tough cover. Today, the two-piece ball has a injection molded core, made of a polybutadiene/silica/monomer system with a Surlyn cover.

Many claims, including virtual indestructibility, truer flight, and less hook and slice, are made by manufacturers of solid balls. However, one thing seems certain. Average golfers have taken to the "solid" balls and Surlyn-covered wound balls in droves because of their long-distance and long-

wearing properties. Today only low-handicappers and pros use balata-covered wound balls.

In the fall of 1985, Spalding introduced the "Tour Edition" ball, which blurs the difference between balata and two-piece balls. Although the ball is two-piece, it has a new synthetic cover made of a material called "Zinthane." The material is softer than Surlyn so that the ball spins nearly as fast as balata. So, the better golfer can get the backspin he wants and can work the ball, yet the ball is also durable. Other ball manufacturers have since come out with balls with similar benefits. It seems likely that this type of ball will ultimately replace balata-covered wound balls. In fact, the wound ball itself may be well on its way to extinction.

Incidentally, regardless of construction, the dimples on all balls, while distinctive, are not intended to be a mere attractive design. They directly affect the aerodynamics of the flight of the ball. From the impact and force of the tee shot, backspin is imparted on the ball, causing it to rotate at a rate of 4,000 to 5,000 revolutions per minute. As the ball backspins, the rotation causes air to pile under the ball while sucking it away from the top of the ball. This creates a pressure underneath and a vacuumlike condition above, similar to the vacuum over the wings of an airplane in flight. This condition causes the rise of the ball and keeps it airborne. The number, size, and depth of the dimples influence the lift and flight of the ball.

Over the years, there have been many experiments with the number, depth, shape, and arrangement of dimples to give a better trajectory. For a long time, there was one conventional dimple pattern: Called the Atti pattern, it featured 336 dimples arranged in circular rows. This created eight large triangular dimple groupings on the ball, so that this pattern is also called *octahedral.* Today, the number of dimples can vary from 324 all the way up to 492, and there are several additional patterns: *icosahedral*—dimples arranged in twenty triangular groups; variations of icosahedral; MacGregor's tetra-icosahedral or deltahedral—twenty-four triangular groups; and Dunlop's dodecahedral (DDH)—twelve pentagonal groups.

In general, the smaller or deeper the dimple, the lower the ball's trajectory, and vice versa. However, since ball manufacturers use dimple design and pattern to "fine-tune" the ultimate performance of any individual ball, dimples are usually only a reliable indicator of performance if you're comparing balls with the same construction and cover, and made by the same company.

Such an analysis might appear to the uninitiated to be a belaboring of the task of making a little white ball. But this is hardly the case. Indeed, some of the procedures have been minimized for clarity in the foregoing description. One manufacturer claims that eighty-five separate steps are required in the production of his ball—a sobering thought for anyone who has teed up a new ball and neatly dispatched it to a watery grave.

The ball maker's burden, of course, is weighted considerably by the necessity of working within the restrictions imposed by the USGA. It would be quite simple to produce a ball that would travel 500 yards or more when properly hit. But Rule 5-1 states: "The ball the player uses shall conform to specifications . . . on maximum weight, minimum size, spherical symmetry, initial velocity and overall distance when tested under specified conditions." The desire to fulfill the average golfer's demand for a ball that will travel far and handsome, while staying within the USGA's limitations, has presented the manufacturers with a challenge.

In fairness to the governing fathers of the game, it should be made clear that some measure of flexibility is extended to the ball makers. There is no rule that specifies what materials must be used or in what amounts. The ball simply must be no smaller than 1.680 inches in diameter and no heavier than 1.620 ounces (and, of course, pass the velocity, symmetry, and distance tests). Beyond these controls, the manufacturers are free to design any ball that will appeal to the golfer; and this is what they have been doing at a fast pace.

SELECTION OF GOLF EQUIPMENT

Anyone who has a real interest in becoming proficient in golf owes it to himself to obtain the best equipment he can afford. It is false economy to shop for bargains without giving very careful consideration to their suitability. The value of your time devoted to learning golf makes the purchase of correctly fitted equipment the cheapest part of your investment in learning the sport. This is particularly true with regard to the selection of your clubs—the most basic equipment items.

A SET OF CLUBS

The average golfer who goes out to buy a set of clubs usually winds up doing something like this: he goes to a pro shop or a sporting-goods store, waggles clubs from several different sets, and then buys the set most comfortable to his grip and pocketbook. That is like buying a new car in a dark room.

Before you go out to buy that next (or first) set of golf clubs, here are some questions to ask yourself: Should you get a stiff shaft, or do you need the extra flex provided by a regular, or even ladies' flex? Do you know what your swing weight is? Should the head of your driver lie in or lie out, and should it have a deep face or a shallow face? The foregoing are not just a lot of mumbo-jumbo terms trumped up by canny manufacturers who are after your dollar. They represent some of the characteristics that are built into every intelligently purchased golf club to fit your particular swing.

There is much more to swinging a golf club than meets the eye. You must remember that the key to good golf is a grooved swing, and the only thing that will permit a grooved swing is a set of clubs that are matched within themselves and fit the person's playing requirements. There are several important factors in the selection of golf clubs for each player. Among them are:

1. Your physical specifications and aptitudes.
2. Your athletic and occupational background.
3. Your age.
4. Club shaft flexibility, length, weight, and so on.

These are factors that an experienced golf professional considers in prescribing clubs for your individual needs. He knows precisely the club specifications that most conform to your golf swing. Just like the doctor who makes a diagnosis and then writes out a medical prescription for your ailment, the golf professional does the same thing in the matter of prescribing the proper golf clubs most suitable for you. Still, it can be helpful to both you and your pro only if you are able to discuss your needs with him on a knowledgeable basis.

When purchasing golf clubs, you may select from standard matched sets or have a set of custom clubs made. By a matched set of clubs is meant that the woods and irons are of a specific swing weight, the shaft lengths are graduated, and there is uniformity

Nomenclature of the Woods.

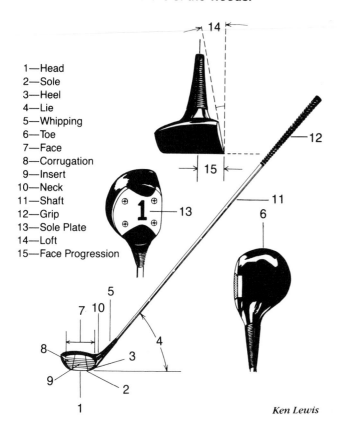

1—Head
2—Sole
3—Heel
4—Lie
5—Whipping
6—Toe
7—Face
8—Corrugation
9—Insert
10—Neck
11—Shaft
12—Grip
13—Sole Plate
14—Loft
15—Face Progression

Ken Lewis

in the flexibility of the shafts. This, in a general way, reduces the problem of selection for the ordinary golfer to knowing what swing weight, grip, shaft flex, and so on are right for him.

The difference, of course, between custom club makers and regular club manufacturers is that the former make clubs on order to fit certain specifications furnished by the buyer, through his professional, whereas the regular manufacturers turn out their clubs to certain standard specifications. Until recently, this customization only came at a significant extra price. Now, however, most major clubmakers offer a selection of lies, shafts, grips, lengths, and other specifications. The manufacturers have realized both the playing—and marketing—advantages in giving golfers clubs that better fit their needs.

Remember that the selection of good clubs is a long-time investment. They are long-lived, and, over a period of years that you will be using them, the amount of money saved at the time of purchase will dwindle into relative insignificance.

Shaft Flexibility. Shaft flexibility, or flex, as it is often called, refers to the amount of stiffness built into a club's shaft. Since the center of a golf shaft is hollow, flex variation between shafts is accomplished by making slight changes in the diameters of the hollow metal. Stiffer shafts have larger diameters than more flexible shafts.

The golf shaft is designed to do more than connect the grip end of the club to the hitting end: it is capable of power, of movement, of giving assistance to the hit, of getting the club head squarely into the ball. If there is a magic wand in golf, it could well be the golf shaft itself.

The club shaft bends on both the backswing and the downswing. Just how much of this flexing will occur depends basically on two factors: (1) the stiffness of the shaft and (2) the speed of the swing. Actually, the speed of your swing dictates the type of shaft you should use. Generally, the fast swinger needs the stiffer shaft because he has the power to flex it properly. The slower swinger needs a more flexible shaft so that it can actually add controlled clubhead speed at the moment of impact. The most pronounced flexing of the shaft occurs during the downswing. Usually the club head lags behind the hands until they approach the impact position. Then the shaft, like a spring, begins to straighten until the club head overtakes the hands and slams into the ball. To get maximum accuracy and power from your swing, the clubhead has to be slightly ahead of the shaft at impact.

If a shaft is too stiff for a particular individual, it will not deflect enough and there will be less spring effect. The clubhead tends to lag behind the hands, reducing the effective loft and leaving the clubface open. As a result, symptoms that can indicate too stiff a shaft include consistently pushing the ball to the right and hitting it too low. Others are loss of distance and a hard, unsolid feeling on all but center-face hits.

If the shaft is too flexible, the golfer will experience a "whippy" feeling during the swing. The shaft deflects and then springs through too much and thus the clubhead is too far ahead of the hands at impact, adding loft and closing the face. If the ball is consistently hit too high and hooked too often, the problem may be a shaft that is too flexible. The same is true if the golfer experiences poor directional control and loses distance.

Although shaft designations vary with different

manufacturers, most companies make clubs with the following five flexibilities:

1. Extra stiff or "X" shaft, used by strong tournament professionals;
2. Stiff or "S" shaft, used usually by professionals, low-handicap amateurs, and other strong players;
3. Medium flex, also known as Regular or "R" flex, suited to most men and very strong women;
4. Flexible or "A" shaft, suited to senior men and stronger women;
5. Ladies or "L" shaft, a very whippy shaft suited for average women and younger juniors.

The growing availability of graphite and other composite shafts has brought more than these five basic shaft flexes to the public's attention. Subtle changes in manufacturing mean shafts now are available in regular-stiff, softer grades, and other middle classifications.

Shaft Length. The shaft lengths of a set of clubs, although different from the short putter to the long driver, are "matched" to each other and to the spe-

cific function of each club. The proper method of clubfitting for shaft length starts with determining your exact driver length requirement as the basis for determining the proper shaft length for every club in your set.

The length of club you use is dependent, not on your height, but on two other factors: the length of your arms and your strength. The average man who plays golf is 5 feet 11 inches and has a distance of approximately 27 inches from his fingertips to the ground while standing in a normal position. A shorter player with short arms, but with enough strength in them, can often gain extra arc in his swing by employing a longer shaft. Most tall golfers with long arms can generally use standard-length clubs without any difficulty.

Here is a quick way to determine whether your present clubs are built with the right shaft length for you: place a golf ball on the floor and imagine that you are about to use your driver. Without a driver in your hands, get into position to hit the ball and be sure to take a position for a full swing. This will take some concentration, but you will be surprised how well you can do this even without having the driver in your hands.

After you have done this, keep your feet in position and have someone remove the golf ball after inconspicuously marking the spot on which it was placed. Now, take your driver, grip it where you normally would, and still without moving your feet, again get in position to hit a drive. When you have regained a comfortable—and natural—position, sole your driver and have the golf ball replaced on its original spot. If the golf ball now lines up too much with the toe of your club, your driver may be too short for you. If the ball lines up with the heel of the club, your driver may be too long for your most natural swing.

A golf professional can analyze your swing and stance in more detail to determine the correct driver shaft length for you. In doing so, he will take stock of your physical make-up—the length of your arms, legs, and torso—and how you stand up to the ball, all of which determine the distance of your hands from the ground as you address the ball. Generally, the closer your hands are to the ground at address, the less shaft length you will need.

Your golf professional also will be interested in the plane of your swing to determine if it is upright, medium, or flat. If your swing is upright, you move

Nomenclature of the Irons.

1—Head
2—Sole
3—Face
4—Lie
5—Ferrule
6—Hosel
7—Toe
8—Shaft
9—Grip
10—Back Stamping
11—Heel
12—Corrugation
13—Loft
14—Face Progression

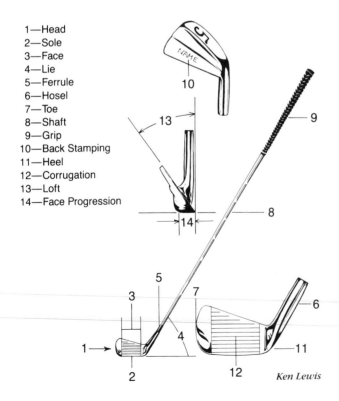

Ken Lewis

Shaft Length (Inches)

Woods	Men's	Women's
Driver	43	42
No. 2	42½	41½
No. 3	42	41
No. 4	41½	40½
No. 5	41	40
No. 6	40½	39½
No. 7	40	39
No. 8	30½	38½
No. 9	39	38

Irons	Men's	Women's
No. 1	39½	38½
No. 2	39	38
No. 3	38½	37½
No. 4	38	37
No. 5	37½	36½
No. 6	37	36
No. 7	36½	35½
No. 8	36	35
No. 9	35½	34½
Pitching Wedge	35½	34½
Sand Wedge	35½	34½
Putter	34-35	33-34

the clubhead back on a plane which is relatively vertical. At the top of the backswing, your hands are positioned well above your right shoulder. As an upright swinger, you require less shaft length than the flat swinger because you stand closer to the ball when you address it. On the other hand, a golfer with a naturally flat swing moves the clubhead around his body in a more horizontal plane, and his hands do not get as high at the top of the backswing. A flat swing needs more shaft length than the upright swing in order for the club to reach out for the ball.

A medium swing, of course, falls between these two extremes. Once your driver length has been established, all other clubs in your set can be properly "matched" to this length. The chart below shows the "average" shaft lengths for the most popular golf clubs in a set. Club length corrections are made using these specifications as the base measurement.

Swing Weight. There are two weights—swing weight and total weight—to consider when selecting golf clubs. The difference between the two can be explained as follows: *swing weight* is the weight which the golfer feels in the head of the club when he swings it as opposed to the *total weight* he would feel if he simply picked it up. That is, the swing weight indicates the distribution of the weight of a club. It is the proportion of the weight in the head compared to the shaft and grip, and it is measured on either of two different scales. One is called the official standard scale, which is graded numerically. The other, which is more commonly employed, is the lorythmic scale, which is designated by letters A, B, C, D, and E and by ten numerical gradations in each letter designation, from 0 through 9. These designations are computed from the official swing weight scale.

A reading of, say, 20.05 on the official scale equals a reading of D-0 on the lorythmic scale. A swing weight of 21.75, or D-9, would be very strong and quite probably a club which could be handled only by someone such as a powerful professional golfer. A reading of 18.75 (C-0), on the other hand, would represent a weak club with plenty of whip and would be suitable only for a small woman. That is, A and B swing weights are exceptionally light and are seldom employed in standard clubs. C swing weights are those used by most women golfers, the average ranging between C-4 and C-7. Stronger women and men players employ clubs in the D range, the swing weight for most men falling in the D-1 to D-5 area. Incidentally, to get an idea how much head weight change is involved in a three-point adjustment, the weight of a quarter coin when added to the head of a No. 5 iron will increase the club's swing weight by three points.

Stiffer-shafted clubs usually require slightly higher swing weights to achieve proper "head feel." Slight increases in head weight also improve the flex characteristics of these stronger shafts. The proper swing weight on a club with a stiff shaft will therefore be proportionately heavier than a club with a regular

Shaft flex	Suggested Swing Weight Range
Extra stiff	D-1—D-8
Stiff	D-0—D-6
Medium	C-9—D-5
Flexible	C-7—D-3
Ladies	C-4—D-0

shaft. But remember that if you use a club with too stiff a shaft and too heavy a swing weight for your strength, not only will you tend to top or slice but also you will develop hitches in your swing. Too whippy a shaft and too light a swing weight will cause loss of distance and a tendency to hook the ball.

The total weight (or club weight) is not significant in itself. The overall weight of a club must always be in proportion to the swing weight to give true feel. In other words, a heavy club will normally have a greater swing weight than a light club, although there would be an overlapping in swing weight for slight changes in overall weight. Generally speaking, the heavier the club head, the more force it will impart to the ball at impact, assuming, of course, that the clubhead is moving at a fixed rate of speed. Balancing that is the fact that you can swing a lighter clubhead faster than you can a heavier one. (The principle there is that if two subjects are moved with equal force, the lighter one will be moved faster.) Actually, it is due to this that the lightweight shafts offer so much promise to the average player. That is, by using lighter shafts, the manufacturer has been able to decrease the overall weight of the golf club, thereby allowing the golfer to generate greater clubhead speed with the same amount of effort. Increased clubhead speed means greater distance. Also, clubhead weight has been increased, giving the golfer more weight where he can best use it, which also helps achieve more distance.

Manufacturers claim that most golfers will find they will be using one less club with lightweight shafts. In other words, where you would normally hit a No. 6 iron with a steel-shafted club, you should be able to accomplish the same thing with a No. 7 iron equipped with a lightweight shaft.

Lightweight shafts today come in a profusion of materials. Besides the lightweight steel shafts and newer super-lightweight steel shafts, there are graphite shafts, as well as those made from exotic materials such as titanium. For the purposes of comparison, here are the weights of more commonly available shafts (figures are for driver-length shafts: lower numbers represent more flexible shafts, higher numbers, stiffer shafts): Original steel shaft, 4¼ to 4½ oz.; lightweight steel shaft and aluminum shaft, 3¾ to 4 oz.; graphite shaft, 2¼ to 3¼ oz.; titanium shaft, 2½ to 3½ oz.; very lightweight steel shaft, 2⅞ to 3¾ oz.

In recent years, frequency matching of clubs has been introduced as another way of matching clubs. Frequency matching determines the stiffness feel of a club *dynamically* as opposed to static methods, such as measuring swingweight and total weight.

Three factors influence this stiffness feel: the length of a club; the weight of the clubhead (and the distribution of weight within the head); and the shaft itself—its stiffness, weight, and the distribution of weight within the shaft.

For example, if you shorten any club, it will feel stiffer than it was originally. If you lengthen it, it will feel more flexible. Similarly, if you take weight out of a clubhead, the shaft will feel stiffer; adding weight makes it feel more flexible. As regards the shaft itself, the stiffer the flex, obviously the stiffer the shaft is going to feel.

Determining the frequency of a golf club (or set of golf clubs) requires the use of a special machine that measures vibration cycles as a function of time. These units are called "cycles-per-second," or "cycles-per-minute."

Although several frequency machines are in use, a common machine is the one devised by True Temper, in which a golf club is rigidly fastened by the butt end of the shaft. The clubhead is pulled down and released. While the shaft vibrates, phototransistors pick up the impulses, relay these through the logic control and display them in cycles per minute. In a well-matched set of clubs, the differences in frequency between successive clubs in a set are the same.

Grip Size and Type. If the golf shot were not such a powerful stroke, the size of the grips on your clubs might not be too important. But the stroke is a violent one, and if your grips are too small or too large for your hands, something in that connecting link is going to give at the precise moment everything should be firm. Keep in mind that the clubhead that is traveling 150 miles an hour or more at impact cannot be held delicately, or be allowed to slip from your grasp, or be so big there is no feel.

The grip of the club must fit your hands so that there is a firm bond between golfer and club. One that is too small will be hard to hold and will permit the club to twist during the hit. You will lose all control and feel of the shot. However, if the grip is too thick for your hands, you will be forced to hold the club in the meaty part of your hand; all feel is choked away, and circulation is cut off at the wrist. The arms then get tired, and the correct approach to the swing disappears.

How do you know if your grips really fit? Generally, if the fingers of the left hand dig into the heel of the palm, the grips are too thin. If there is a noticeable separation between the fingers and the palm, they are too thick. A perfect grip would find the finger tips *barely* touching the palm.

The right-size grip gives your hands that "feel" of your clubs that is essential to good club control. "Feel" in your hands is so sensitive that you can actually notice the difference when the diameter of your grip is changed by a mere $1/32$ inch.

The thickness of the grip also affects what is called "hand action." On the downswing, the hands and arms must rotate counterclockwise to square the clubface at impact. If the grip is too large, it inhibits hand action; the hands and arms then rotate too slowly, and the clubface is likely to be left open at impact, with a slice or push the result. If the grip is too small, it tends to make the hand action too lively; then, the hands and arms rotate too quickly and the clubface is likely to be closed at impact, leading to a hook or pull. Golfers who tend to slice or push the ball consistently should experiment with slightly thinner grips and those who tend to hook or pull should try thicker ones.

By the way, manufacturers have a unique method of specifying the size of their grips. The standard men's grip measures $28/32$ inch in diameter at a point $2^1/2$ inches from the top of the shaft and is tapered to $25/32$ inch at a point $5^1/2$ inches from the top. An undersize grip is described as "$1/32$ inch under," which means $1/32$ inch below standard. An oversize is "$1/32$ inch over," and a full oversize is "$1/16$ inch over."

There are a variety of styles of grips available. Whichever type you select, be sure that you are able to grip the club firmly with your fingers. You also need a grip with good traction—a grip that will not slip or turn in any weather. Moisture, whether from perspiration or the elements, must also be dispersed. On the cork and rubber grips, the golfer gets traction from the material itself and the surface design. Pockets or indentations in the grip displace moisture and prevent slipping, without the golfer's having to grip harder.

Leather grips rely on their tackiness to get traction, with an assist from the small round perforations made in the leather. These tiny holes help drain away sweat or moisture, which then evaporates. The edges of the grips are skived (thinned), so that when they are wound on they form ridges or grooves down the grip, which also help to stop slipping.

Under the Rules, the grip must be "substantially straight and plain in form and shall not be molded for any part of the hands" (Rule 4-1c). This statement makes it clear that grips that place the hands in more or less locked-in positions are strictly training grips; they can't be used during a round of golf. Also, Appendix II of the Rules of Golf states how Rule 4-1c is interpreted by the USGA. For clubs other than putters, the grip must be generally circular in cross-section. The only exception permitted is that a "continuous, straight, slightly raised rib" can be incorporated along the "full length of the grip." The USGA does permit the grip to be tapered. However, it must not have any bulge or waist. The association also requires that the axis of the grip coincide with the axis of the shaft, except for putters. A putter may have a noncircular cross-section as long as the cross-section has no concavity and remains generally similar throughout the length of the grip.

Perhaps you have wondered why most grips taper down from top to bottom. This has been the conventional shape for grips from time immemorial. The reason can be better understood by making this experiment. Stretch out your arms, with the hands together, as when holding a club. Your arms form a "V," and you will note that the opening in your hands—where the grip would be—is conically shaped and naturally fitting the conventional grip. This conical grip, therefore, is designed to conform to the hands in action.

In choosing new clubs, or new grips for your clubs, remember this: your grips should feel good in your hands—at all times, in all climates. They should have a good, positive feel and not hurt your hands. They should enable you to grasp the club correctly, firmly, and easily to maintain control, power, and club-face alignment.

The Loft and Lie of a Clubhead. The loft angle of a golf club is the angle between the face of the club and a vertical line from the sole of the club. It is the angle that gives elevation to a golf shot. The higher the number of the club, the more loft angle and more elevation you can expect, but also less distance.

The difference in the loft of the same club number from one manufacturer to another may vary slightly.

Also a few manufacturers put out half sizes; that is, they make a No. 2 wood with a loft of 13 degrees and No. 2½ wood (which is still called a brassie) with a 14½ degree loft. If you have any difficulty in hitting the ball into the air, you may find it best to employ the club with the greater loft.

Players who have no trouble getting the ball into the air regardless of the iron they use may prefer a "strong" set of clubs. They have the clear option of specifying lofts that are one-half club less than standard. In other words, the No. 5 iron in such a set would have 30-degree loft, the No. 8 iron would have 42-degree loft, and so forth. This selection provides for a set of iron clubs from which each properly hit shot will deliver somewhat greater distance than can be obtained from a set with standard loft angles. However, the margin for error in such a set is reduced, particularly on the long irons; and the set can be hard to handle, and mishit shots can often result.

Many times higher-handicap players are better served by a slightly "lofted" set in which each club has one-half club or more loft than standard. Such a set of clubs will be easier to handle, particularly for players who have trouble obtaining elevation on their iron shots.

These options are also of particular interest to players who have some difficulty handling their long irons. In these cases, the player can have his three long irons specified with "lofted" angles and the rest of the clubs in the set made "standard."

The lie of a golf club is the angle between the center line of the shaft and the horizontal. It is important in the proper fit method because it is the correctness of this angle for your swing that allows you to bring the hitting surface of the club head square to the ball at the moment of impact.

If the lie angle of the club is too flat, that is, too small, then at impact the heel of the club is off the ground. This tilts the plane of the clubface to the right and the ball is pushed or sliced to the right. Similarly, if the lie of the club is too upright, that is, too large, the plane of the clubface is tilted to the left and the ball is pulled or hooked to the left. These built-in equipment errors can be corrected by the player through unnatural adjustments in his stance or swing. Clubs with proper lie angles make such adjustments unnecessary.

The best way to determine whether your clubs have the correct lie is to hit balls off a piece of plywood about four and one-half feet square, painted

Standard Loft Angles (in number of degrees)

Woods	Men's	Women's
No. 1	11	12
No. 2	13	14
No. 3	16	17
No. 4	19	20
No. 5	22	23
No. 6	25	26
No. 7	28	29
No. 8	31	32
No. 9	34	35

Irons	Men's	Women's
No. 1	17	18
No. 2	20	21
No. 3	24	25
No. 4	28	29
No. 5	32	33
No. 6	36	37
No. 7	40	41
No. 8	44	45
No. 9	48	49
Pitching Wedge	52	53
Sand Wedge	56	57
Putter	1–5	1–5

a dark color. Select representative clubs, such as the 2-iron, 5-iron and 9-iron, and put a strip of ½- or ¾-inch white masking tape on the sole of each club. Then go ahead and hit some balls with each club. The impact with the board will leave a scuffmark on the tape. If the mark is the middle of the sole, the lie is correct. If it is toward the heel, the club has too upright a lie; if toward the heel, too flat a lie. If these tests show that your clubs are too upright or too flat, have your professional bend them in a loft and lie machine to the correct lie. Be careful: Forged clubs can be readjusted this way with little worry. Investment-cast clubs, however, are more brittle due to their method of manufacture, and easily could snap. Don't do any bending of clubs yourself, and if in any doubt, return them to the manufacturer for "tweaking."

In general, players of short stature need flat or medium flat lies, and tall players need upright or medium upright lies. However, the acid test is to hit balls from plywood board as described above.

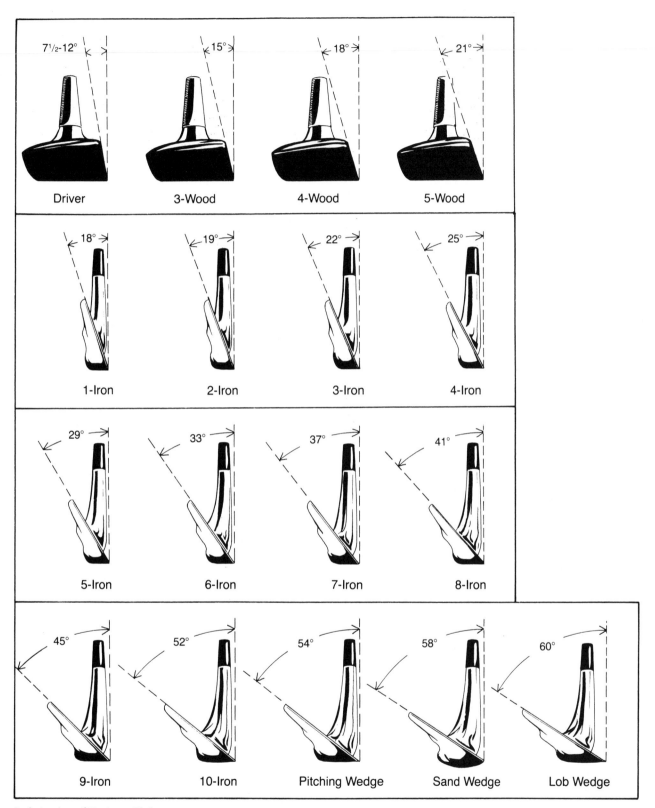

Loft Angles of Various Clubs. *Ken Lewis*

Standard Lie Angles (in number of degrees)

Woods	Men's	Women's
No. 1	55	53
No. 2	55$\frac{1}{2}$	53$\frac{1}{2}$
No. 3	56	54
No. 4	56$\frac{1}{2}$	54$\frac{1}{2}$
No. 5	57	55
No. 6	57$\frac{1}{2}$	55$\frac{1}{2}$
No. 7	58	56
No. 8	58$\frac{1}{2}$	56$\frac{1}{2}$
No. 9	59	57

Irons	Men's	Women's
No. 1	55	53
No. 2	56	54
No. 3	57	55
No. 4	58	56
No. 5	59	57
No. 6	60	58
No. 7	61	59
No. 8	62	60
No. 9	63	61
Pitching Wedge	63	61
Sand Wedge	63	61
Putter	68–78	68–78

Wood Club Facing. The "facing" of a wood club refers to the angle between the club face and a line exactly perpendicular to the desired line of flight. If this angle is "zero," the club is said to be faced "straight." A right-handed club is said to be "open" when the club face looks slightly to the right. It is said to be "closed" when the club face looks slightly to the left. The true facing of a club is often difficult for most golfers to recognize because the club maker is dealing with slight but important angles when he faces the club.

To see just how important these slight angles can be, consider the fact that a two-degree modification in face angle will affect the left-to-right position of a 200-yard drive by as much as twenty-one feet. This degree of error results from the off-line hit effect of an open or closed face at the moment of impact. It does not allow for the added slice or hook effect, which can be as much or greater, bringing the combined error close to fifteen yards. How many times have you wished your ball was a little to the left or right on your drive? Proper club facing can help you keep the ball where it belongs, in the fairway.

The club maker "closes" the face of a club to compensate for a natural slicing tendency on the part of a player. Since the "average" golfer has the tendency to slice, most standard wood sets are made with slightly closed faces. This built-in hook in a standard set, no matter how slight, can be disastrous if the player happens to have a natural hook, for it only accentuates the problem. And it probably will not be sufficiently helpful to a natural slicer who usually needs more of a built-in hook than happens in a standard set.

Clubhead Design. Most club manufacturers offer at least two or three different club-head designs in their top-grade clubs. These can vary from traditional woods and irons to the more modern metal woods, cavity-back and hollow irons. When shopping for new clubs, it's important to understand how head design affect your shots. Although, for clarity, the design features are treated in isolation here, manufacturers often combine them to produce clubs that perform well.

All other design elements being the same, the deeper the head of a club, the lower the ball will fly. This is because the center of gravity rises as the head becomes deeper. Shallow heads have low centers of gravity and will therefore send the ball higher.

Soleweighting is another design feature that affects the height of the ball's trajectory. Woods and irons with a lot of soleweighting have low centers of gravity and send the ball high. Some examples are heavy-soled woods with runners or V-soles and irons with wide soles. Traditional woods with their conventional soleplates and traditional irons with their narrow soles have higher centers of gravity and the ball flies lower.

The term "hosel offset" or simply "offset" is often found in advertisements or other literature on modern clubs. "Offset" occurs when the leading edge of an iron or metal wood is set behind the forward-most portion of the hosel. You measure the amount of offset on a club from the farthest front portion of the hosel to the farthest front portion of the face on its centerline. Offset affects the trajectory of the ball by controlling the exact moment of impact. The more the offset on a club, the later the ball is contacted and the lower the ball will fly. A club with less or no offset will contact the ball sooner, sending the ball higher.

"Progressive offset," where the long irons have moderate (from $\frac{1}{8}$ to $\frac{1}{4}$ inch) to extreme offset (over ¼ inch) and the more lofted clubs have little or no offset, is considered a "game improvement" feature for average golfers. Offset helps in hitting the long and middle irons more solidly because it tends to keep the golfer's hands ahead of the clubface on the downswing, leading to a more effective "down-and-through" hit on these hard-to-hit clubs. On short irons, offset also aids in correct alignment.

Traditional woods usually have the face in front of the shaft. This is referred to as "face progression," which is measured from the centerline of the shaft to the farthest front portion of the face on its centerline. Face progression also affects the moment the club-face contacts the ball. With two woods that were otherwise identical, the more the face progression, the earlier the ball would be contacted, and the higher the ball would fly. Less face progression gives lower ball flight.

Another feature often found on traditional woods is "backweighting"—usually a brass weight on the back of the head. This has a similar effect to soleweighting and produces a higher trajectory.

Two other features found on many modern clubs are beveled leading edges and radiused soles. The leading edge is that portion of the clubface closest to the target in the address position. When the edge is sharp, it can cause "digging" into the ground. However, if the leading edge is beveled (rounded off), it will not dig in as much. A radiused sole is one that is curved from toe to heel and/or from front to back. The toe-to-heel radius makes it easier to hit from poor or sidehill lies than a club with a flat sole. The front to back radius tends to prevent a club from digging. Most weekend golfers are better off with beveled leading edges and radiusing on woods and irons alike.

When selecting your clubs, be sure that you keep all the factors—shaft flexibility, length, swing weight, grip design, loft, and clubhead design—in mind. Remember that no other sport is so exacting as golf in that so many specifications must be met to a precision fit of implement and player.

Correcting Faults. Now that you know the most important factors in clubfitting, you can realize that many faults can be helped solely by a change in equipment. However, it's important to realize that altering the specifications on your clubs or getting new clubs with different specifications can't correct *all* faults. For example, if you sky the ball or hit it very fat, a lesson from your professional is the only remedy. Also, how many corrections you need depends on the severity of your problem. A huge slice, for example, might need several corrections, whereas a few yards of slice may need only one. A professional can help you experiment with various specifications and decide the most useful equipment changes for your game. The pro can determine whether your present set can be modified to improve your game or whether a new set is indicated.

If you pull or hook the ball, both faults are caused by a closed clubface at impact, so what cures a pull will also cure a hook. The corrections are to: Try a stiffer shaft, a flatter lie, and a larger size grip. Also, try woods with more open clubfaces than your present set. Similarly, pushes and slices are caused by an open clubface at impact. Try a more flexible shaft, a more upright lie, and smaller grips. Try woods with more closed faces than your present set.

If you hit the ball too high, you can correct this problem with clubs that have stronger lofts, stiffer shafts, less face progression in woods and offset irons, even offset woods. Also, try deeper-faced clubs and avoid woods with brass backweights. If you've been using clubs with low centers of gravity, such as woods with heavy soles or metal woods and irons with heavy sole or perimeter weighting, go to more traditional clubs with higher centers of gravity.

Reverse the corrections if you hit the ball too low. Try clubs with more loft, more flexible shafts, more face progression on woods, or woods with brass backweights. Certainly, you shouldn't use woods or irons with a lot of offset. If you are, then go to clubs with less or no offset. Also hit some clubs with shallower faces than your present clubs and avoid traditional woods and irons with their higher centers of gravity.

If you consistently hit a lot of shots thin, then the hit is low on the clubface. You again need clubs with lower centers of gravity than you're using at present. If you've been playing with traditional woods and irons, try shallower faced clubs, soleweighted woods and irons, metal woods, and perimeter-weighted irons such as cavity-back and hollow irons.

If you get many off-center hits, then change from traditional clubs to those with heel-toe weighting or perimeter weighting. Slightly increased lofts will help you get the ball up even if you don't hit the ball on the sweet spot. Also, experiment with clubs that are half-an-inch to an inch shorter than your present clubs.

Set Makeup. At one time, sets of clubs most commonly consisted of a driver, 3-wood, 4-wood, 2–9 irons, pitching wedge, sand wedge, and a putter. However, this traditional set makeup doesn't suit everybody. So, manufacturers today offer other options—higher-lofted woods, utility woods, rough irons, chippers, and "third wedges" with extra loft. You're allowed fourteen clubs under the Rules of Golf. It makes sense to pick the fourteen clubs that play up *your* strengths and cover up *your* weaknesses.

To help you and your professional determine the best set makeup for you, keep records of what clubs you actually use over several rounds. You can note these facts on your scorecards.

For example, on your first hole, you hit a driver, a 4-iron that misses the green, a sand wedge pitch, and two putts. You'd note on the card D (for driver), 3 (for 3-iron), SW (for sand wedge), and 2P (for two putts). A fairway wood can be noted as 3W, a utility woods as U, rough irons as R, a pitching wedge as PW, and so on. If you hit a shot badly, circle the notation for that shot.

After a few rounds, you can easily see which clubs you use most often, those you hardly use at all, those you hit well, and those you invariably mishit. Your decisions, you'll find, are almost made for you. For example, you could find that you hardly ever hit your driver well. Okay, get rid of it and try a driver that is easier to hit—one with more loft or with a shallower face, or a metal wood. You see that you never hit your 3-wood well. Okay, get rid of it, too. If you hit your 4-wood well, use that instead of a 3-wood through the green. If you hit your long irons badly, you could have the lofts on these clubs increased or substitute long irons that are easier to hit (with shallower faces, more soleweight, heel-toe or perimeter weighting), even go to 5- and 7-woods. You could also try one of the "continuous sets," where the clubs filling in for the long irons look like woods. If you seldom play the rough well, put a utility wood or rough iron in your bag. If you play a lot of short pitch shots to tight pin placements, add a "third wedge." If your chipping is bad, try a chipper. And so on.

Be utterly ruthless and coldly logical in making these choices. Playing with the right set makeup for you can make a big dent in your handicap. So don't let false pride get in the way of making the right choice! At the 19th hole, they'll never ask you whether you crushed a 2-iron at the long par-3 13th, or eased a little 7-wood onto the green! It's how many that counts, not how!

THE PUTTER

Putters—the clubs, that is—are as individual as neckties. There are literally dozens of types of putters on the market, each as distinctly different to the eye as a polka dot is from a red stripe. At one time you were blissfully limited to a choice of six—Calamity Jane, Blade Type Mallet, Blue Goose, Mills, Schenectady, and Cash-in—but today the choice is considerably wider, although many of them are but subtle variations on these original six.

Probably the most significant change in putter design in recent years is the heel-toe-weighted putter. In the mid-1960s, Karsten Solheim's famous "Ping" putter made its appearance (closely followed by "Ping" irons). Today, there's hardly a major club manufacturer that doesn't have a heel-toe-weighted putter in its line. They come in all sizes of head, from normal size to oversize, the latter made popular by Jack Nicklaus's winning the 1986 Masters with such a putter.

As with other heel–toe weighted clubs, the heel–

This 1930s-model putter is a copy of "Calamity Jane," which Bobby Jones used throughout most of his career. Jones was one of the first golf stars to design and lend his name to clubs. *Olmans' Guide to Golf Antiques*

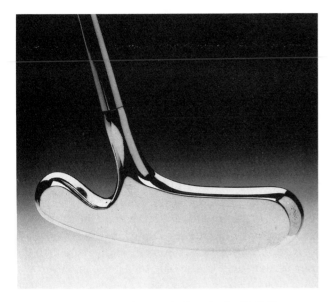

One of golf's most enduring designs is the BullsEye putter. It debuted in the 1930s and is still popular today.
Courtesy Titleist

toe weighted putter is more "forgiving" on mishits. If a conventional putter is struck on the toe side of its sweet spot, the toe is kicked back, opening the blade. There's a loss of force and the ball will finish short and to the right of its intended target. Similarly, if the ball is struck to the heel side of the sweet spot, the ball finishes short and left. The farther the ball is struck away from the sweet spot, the more misdirected and short the putt becomes. It's been found that when a putt that would normally roll twenty feet is struck half an inch from the sweet spot, it will only travel some sixteen to eighteen feet. Putters with good heel-toe weight distribution will hit such putts farther and straighter than conventional putters. However, the distance will always be less than a sweet spot hit.

With all this going for it, the question arises as to why the whole world doesn't putt with a heel-toe-weighted putter? Also, why did Jack Nicklaus, for example, after putting so well in the 1986 Masters, abandon his oversized heel-toe-weighted putter and return to a conventionally weighted weapon? It's because, in the world of club design, practically every design feature is a trade-off. With heel-toe-weighted clubs, whether putters or otherwise, you do obtain a correction on mishits. However, you also get less feedback on a mishit than with a conven-

tional club, and thus your stroke can become quite sloppy and inaccurate without your realizing it. In fact, Jack Nicklaus cited this reason for his return to a conventional putter. With a conventionally weighted putter (or other club), you're "punished" on mishits, but you do know you have mishit it! Therefore, you know what to work on to improve your stroke.

Another important innovation in recent years has been the development of putters and putting styles that overcome an age-old problem that afflicts many more mature golfers—the dreaded "yips." This putting disease afflicts the smaller muscles, particularly those of the right hand and wrist, on short putts. At best, the golfer uses a "scooping" action of the right hand, thinning and mishitting every "knee-knocker" he looks at. At worst, the involuntary twitch of the right hand can jerk the ball right off the green! (In Britain, this disease is also known as the "twitches.")

Famous golfers, including Harry Vardon, Tommy Armour, Leo Diegel, Sam Snead, and Ben Hogan have suffered from the "yips" late in their careers. For example, Vardon sadly recounted how he became unable to look at the ball on short putts. Instead, his gaze was riveted on his right hand, and he would helplessly watch for his right hand to "jump." Leo

The original "Ping" putter from the early 1960s. Placing the weight at the heel and toe kept the head from twisting at impact, producing truer roll. Today, heel–toe designs dominate the putter market.
Courtesy Karsten Manufacturing

Diegel even went as far as to create a totally new style of putting in the 1920s in an attempt to overcome his problem.

However, despite this and other efforts, the consensus of opinion from Vardon's time to Hogan's was, in the words of English golfing scribe Henry Longhurst, "Once you've had 'em, you've got 'em!" In other words, there was no known permanent cure.

Today, thankfully, this is no longer true. In recent years, new putters and methods have overcome the "yips." What makes them work is that they take the "yipping" muscles out of the stroke completely.

The first solution was the "croquet" putter, where you faced the hole, straddled the line of putt, and putted between the legs. When straddling the line was made illegal, Sam Snead came up with a variation of the "croquet" style, which he called the "sidesaddle." He placed his feet together, positioned the ball slightly forward of and to the right of the right foot. He held the putter at the top with his left hand, the thumb curled over the butt. With his right hand he held the putter well down the shaft, the right arm extended. He stroked with the whole right arm, with no wrist action.

More recently, Charlie Owens, a noted performer on the Senior PGA Tour, designed an extra long (about fifty inches depending on the height of the user) and heavy (three-and-a-half pounds) putter and a new putting method to go along with it. You stand to the side of the ball, as you would normally. However, you anchor the top end of the putter with your left hand against your breastbone, the left forearm across the chest. The right hand is down the shaft, the right arm extended as in Snead's method. And again, you stroke with the whole right arm. Many senior professionals formerly afflicted with the "yips" are now putting well again with this putter or similar models.

Whether you select a heel-toe or conventionally weighted putter, a normal length or extra-long putter, only you can decide what putter is best for you. However, to help you make your selection, keep these factors in mind: (1) feel in your hands, (2) proper balance, (3) lie and loft, (4) weight, (5) shaft length, and (6) shape of the head.

You should be able to tell if the putter has good feel and balance merely by swinging it back and forth a few times and hitting a few balls with it on the practice green. Select a putter that is easy to line up and easy to look at. You should not have much trouble finding a putter to suit your particular needs and putting habits if you spend a little time looking over the various models.

The lie is the angle of inclination between the head and shaft, measured with sole (bottom) of the putter lying flat on a level surface. The average lie is about 72 degrees. Putters are, of course, available nowadays with any lie you specify; the exception is any very upright putter, which would not conform to the Rules. Appendix II states that "the axis of the shaft from the top to a point not more than 5 inches above the sole must diverge from the vertical in the toe-heel plane by at least 10 degrees in relation to the horizontal line determining length of head."

A good way to determine correct lie is to take the putter and stand to the ball, on a hard, level surface, as you normally would to putt. If the sole is approximately flush with the surface on which you're standing, the lie is basically right for you.

Just how much loft there should be on a matter is a matter of controversy even among experts. However, most agree that the most important factor is the type of greens on which you're playing. If the greens are smooth and fast, you need less loft to get the ball rolling properly without it hopping or bouncing after impact. The rougher and slower the greens, the more loft you need to get the ball up on top of the grass and rolling smoothly. In the old days, when greens were rougher than they are today, there was at least 4 and sometimes as much as 12 degrees of loft on putters. However, on today's better greens, a good guide would be to use 1–2 degrees of loft on fast, smooth greens, about 4–5 degrees on slow, rougher greens.

As to putter weight, a conventional-length putter of normal length weighs between fifteen and eighteen ounces. Shaft lengths range from thirty-two to thirty-eight inches, with the average men's putter length about thirty-four to thirty-five inches, and average women's, thirty-three to thirty-four inches.

Although the final decision on the weight of the putter is up to you, the golf course where you expect to do most of your playing again should enter into your consideration. If the greens are fast, the lightweight putter is probably best for you. But if the greens are particularly slow, a heavier putter may be better. Heavier putters cut down on your touch, while light ones can require almost too firm a "hit" even for short three- or four-footers. Medium-weight putters work equally well on fast and slow greens.

Most putters have alignment aids on the top of the putter—usually a line or series of lines—or a marking on the face. These should indicate the sweet spot (also called the "center of gravity") of the putter. Although most heel-toe-weighted putters have the sweet spot correctly marked, this is not true on many older styles of putters. An extreme case would be an old blade putter with a long hosel, where the sweet spot might be, say, only an inch out from the hosel toward to the toe. On many putters, the line is placed in the middle of the blade, but the sweet spot is actually toward the heel from that point. This hurts you if you mistakenly align and strike the ball on this line, thinking it is actually the sweet spot.

The easiest way to determine a putter's sweet spot is to hold the putter by its handle loosely between the thumb and index finger. Then gently tap along the clubface with the eraser end of a pencil. When you tap at the toe end, the clubhead twists as the toe is knocked back; at the heel end, the clubhead twists as the heel is knocked back. Continue tapping along the face with the pencil until you find the point where the head does not twist, but is knocked straight back. Mark this spot, which is approximately the putter's sweet spot.

THE GOLF BALL

Golf balls vary in price to some extent, but you get what you pay for. Use the best brand and model consistent with your type of game.

Nearly all manufacturers agree that the first concern in choosing a golf ball should be its construction—a two-piece ball or a wound ball. Most two-piece balls spin more slowly coming off the clubface. In comparison to the wound ball, it doesn't fly as high or have as much bite on landing. That means less distance in the air, but more roll once it hits the ground. On average, two-piece balls travel a few yards farther overall than most wound balls.

With its synthetic cover, a two-piece ball also is more durable. It's designed for the average golfer, someone who mishits often enough to make durability necessary. But even when mishit, the two-piece ball has an advantage. Because it spins less, you get less sidespin; that makes it more forgiving, reducing the severity of unintended slices and hooks.

A wound ball spins faster than a two-piece, which gives it a higher trajectory and slightly more carry, but the additional backspin also makes it stop more

quickly after landing. Although it's rare for any ball to lose its shape during play (unless you hit it as hard as a pro or into trees), a wound ball with a balata cover is slightly more susceptible to going out-of-round than a two-piece, with a synthetic-covered wound ball falling somewhere in the middle.

Most manufacturers say that two-piece balls are longer than wound balls, but they aren't as consistent in length. The better player often prefers to give up a little distance for a ball that is more consistent.

Besides durability, cover materials affect a ball's spin. Balata spins more quickly than Surlyn, and better players, who don't worry about mis-hitting, prefer the control balata gives them. Many also say they can "feel" the difference between the harder synthetic and balata. In the last few years, most ball manufacturers have introduced "softer" synthetics, making two-piece balls that feel and spin more like wound balls without sacrificing durability.

Feel is something that all players want, but it is a quality that can't be measured. The hardness of a cover material will tell you something about feel, so will compression. All wound balls and some two-piece balls are measured for compression, but it is still the most misunderstood dimension of ball design. Many people have no idea—or the wrong idea—about what compression is and what it means.

Technically, compression is a measure of a golf ball's resistance to deformation, or "flattening" when force is applied, which is what happens when the ball is struck by a club. At impact, a ball actually changes shape, "compressing" against the clubface. Compression simply measures how much the shape of the ball changes (or, as the scientists put it, "deflects") under a constant weight.

Those balls that are measured for compression are rated on 0–200 scale. A standard weight is applied to each ball. A ball that didn't compress at all would be rated at a compression of 200. A ball that deflected 200/1,000ths ($\frac{1}{5}$) inch would have a compression of zero. Between those extremes, for every 1/1,000th of an inch the ball compresses, it drops one point from 200.

It was once assumed that a higher compression ball always went farther—that a 100 compression would always outperform a 90, a 90 an 80, and so on. Most experts now say that compression has almost nothing to do with distance. There is some evidence that golfers with slower swing speeds get more yardage from a 90 compression than a 100, but the increase is said to be slight and primarily on iron shots. What compression does indicate, the experts say, is feel off the club and sound, and to many golfers it has to do with their thinking that they're controlling the ball. But not everyone. The consensus is that many players can't feel a difference, say, between a 90 and 100 compression. The pros on the Tour do, however (or so they claim), and most of them choose 100 compression because with their high impact speeds, a 90 is too soft. There is some evidence that a 90 ball spins faster than a 100 because the 90 stays on the clubface a microsecond longer at impact. However, the acid test for most male golfers is to try both compressions and see which they prefer.

How about 80 compression balls for women? One major manufacturer makes them for women, and obviously thinks that it's the best ball for them. Others feel that 80s are too soft for anyone, that they're simply balls that don't measure up and must be gotten rid of somehow. As with the men, women must experiment with different compression balls to see what suits them.

The situation for both men and women is complicated by the fact that not every ball marked 90 compression actually measures 90! In fact, balls aren't made in batches of 100s, 90s, and 80s. They're simply manufactured, then sorted by compression. If they fall roughly 3–5 points on either side of 90, that's what they are; the same applies to 100s and 80s. The rest are sold as range balls or "second quality" balls.

How a ball is made and what it's made of aren't the only factors determining performance. Outside influences can have a big effect. One of the most telling is weather.

If you're playing in the wind, go with a low trajectory ball of your choice. Surlyn, which spins more slowly than balata so it has a lower trajectory, also is great in a wind. Johnny Miller won the British Open in 1976 using a Surlyn-covered wound ball. He says, "The Surlyn ball bores through a headwind almost unaffected. In crosswinds, you only have to aim off very slightly."

There's less you can do in rain. Water gets between club and ball, reducing your chance of imparting spin; that's why you get fliers from wet grass, where the ball flies and rolls farther than usual.

In hot weather, wound balls feel softer, so go to a higher compression to compensate. In cold, a wound ball seems to lose some of its resiliency and feel.

Two-piece balls feel harder in the cold, but actually they are little affected by temperature extremes.

Where you play is another big factor in ball selection. Well-watered, lush courses yield little roll, so plan to get your distance in the air, not on the ground. On a course with elevated greens, where you can't run the ball on, you want a ball that gets up in the air, too. However, on a flat, dry course, a low-flying ball will run and run. For example, in the South and Southwest, where you're playing on bermudagrass with harder ground and sandier soil, carry is less important because the hard ground makes for a good roll. In the East and Midwest, you need more carry because the ground is softer, the grass lusher, and consequently there's less roll.

Don't neglect the effect different clubs have on balls either. Two-piece balls are well-suited to metal and graphite woods; the hard material of the club meeting the hard material of the ball results in a slower spin, which makes for lower trajectory, more distance, and less sideways movement. Wooden clubs impart more spin on the ball, particularly clubs with soft inserts such as fiber. Two-piece balls also team well with investment-cast irons: The ball jumps off the face, and since both club and ball are more forgiving of mishits, and slices and hooks, you have a better chance of staying in play.

Watch out for low center of gravity irons teamed with wound balls; the ball will go high, but probably not as far. Better players, who probably hit forged irons and wound balls, will find that the ball goes exactly where it's hit; there's little forgiveness in that combination.

Even the ball's color can be of help. Colored balls can be useful in the desert because the grass isn't as green and white balls tend to blend into browned-out fairway. Also, if you're playing late in the day, hitting into the sun, it's easier to see a colored ball than a white one; the colored ball turns black against the sun so you can follow it.

If one color is helpful, how about two? Besides conventional one-color balls, Karsten Manufacturing makes two-color balls. According to the manufacturer, such balls "flicker" in the air, making them easier to see.

Construction, cover, compression, dimpling, weather, clubs, and courses are all important, and taken together, the golf ball can be made to do almost anything. But how can you find the best ball for you? Probably, the soundest method is to honestly analyze your game and then talk it over with your pro. Take the two or three balls you two agree on, and go hit them. You'll soon see which ball you prefer.

THE GOLF BAG

A bag to carry your clubs in can be very simple or very elaborate. Bags are made from leather, vinyl or nylon plastic, or canvas, or they can be a combination of materials. They also come in a variety of shapes, colors, and prices. It is usually wise to purchase one large enough to hold all the extra items—rain gear, hand towel, Band-Aids, salt tablets, insect repellent, pencils, extra matches, extra glove, balls, and tees—that come in so handy. Thus, be sure the bag is of ample size. Too often a small bag is used, and the golfer has to jam his clubs into too small a space, raising havoc with the grips and endangering the shafts as well. Also, if you plan to carry the bag yourself, use a lighter basic bag—sometimes called a "Sunday bag"—but one that still has room enough for the important accessories.

GOLF CARTS

The pull or "caddie" cart was invented in the late 1930s to answer the demand of golfers on public links who wanted to play but could not afford caddies. The pull cart was a cheap way to take the load off your back, and the influx of new players (combined with the financially debilitating effects of the Depression) created an instant market. The first pull carts were heavy, unwieldy, and nonfolding, but they sold. Manufacturers, convinced that they were onto a good thing, streamlined their carts after the war, making them lighter, folding, and easy to carry.

The pull-cart industry has even withstood the advent of the electric golf car and the concomitant resistance of some private clubs to allow pull carts on their courses. A fleet of golf cars is a virtual gold mine for any club, and many of them have forbidden the use of pull carts because they would cut into this certain income. A few clubs also feel that pull carts tend to give off the air of a "public links" course and are thus undesirable at a country club. But the dearth of caddies has offset the strictures of private clubs, and the rise in the median standard of living has cracked the rigid status system of golf, freed more people to play, built more public courses, and broken the captive market of the clubs with their stables

of electric cars. There are new players and new courses—and new markets for pull carts. For the beginner, a pull cart is certainly preferable to the golf car because of its cost.

If you are familiar with the wheel, you should not need much instruction on the mechanical operation of a pull cart. But every beginning golfer should realize that pull carts are becoming a major source of concern for golf course superintendents and agronomists. Loaded down with a heavy bag, fourteen clubs, extra clothing, balls, and tees, and sometimes the player too (when the cart includes a fold-out seat to rest on), the pull cart is a mass of weight centered on two wheels. The wheels dig into the turf, cause ruts, and enrage greenskeepers. From the outset, manufacturers agreed to establish a minimum diameter for the wheels, setting the standard of 10 inches. The larger wheels spread the dead weight of the cart over a bigger area, reducing the tendency of the tires to plow channels in the turf.

Electric or gasoline golf cars are fine for the senior golfers or ones who cannot take the rigors of the golf course walk. In selecting one of these mechanized vehicles, use the same care and techniques as you would in purchasing an automobile.

GOLF CLOTHING AND GOLFING ACCESSORIES

Forty years ago or more knickers were considered the style for men playing golf. Today any sport clothes, such as slacks, sport shirts, and sweaters are acceptable. Many golf clubs even permit their players to wear shorts—but usually not "short" shorts—while on the course. Whatever clothes you wear, be sure that you are comfortable and have freedom of movement. It is a good idea to wear a bright-colored cap or hat. It helps other players to spot you.

Shoes with steel or tungsten spikes on the heel and sole are essential parts of your equipment. They provide the necessary surer footing, thereby permitting you a more solid foundation from which to hit the ball. Without them, you will slip and slide when making your shots.

A look at the majority of top touring professionals would seem to rate a golf glove as an important piece of equipment. True, a fine glove can offer a sensitive feel of the club and more confidence in your grip. On the fashion side, golf gloves are becoming attractive accessories. With the growing range of hues available, gloves now can provide bright color accents or be matched to a color-coordinated outfit.

There are many accessories that you will wish to have available in your golf bag. Rain gear of some type—at least a water-repellent jacket and hat—is advisable to have in your bag. A golf umbrella is also a good rain accessory. Club covers for woods are an accessory that pays dividends by keeping the clubs in good condition. Actually golf is a game of gimmicks and gadgetry. There is no limit to the accessories that you can acquire.

CARE OF GOLF EQUIPMENT

Undeniably, the golf equipment of today is the finest ever. A not surprising corollary to this statement is that it is also the most expensive. To protect your sizable investment, it makes good sense to take good care of it.

GOLF CLUBS

While in play, you can save your clubs a lot of grief by just a little thought. For instance, never bang the club on the ground in a fit of temper. This shock and vibration will bend the shaft where it is not meant to be bent, and it will be incapable of flexing properly. Remember that an error of one degree at the outset can amount to as much as a thirty-foot error at the target 200 yards away. This shattering experience to the club can also cause the inside wall of the shaft to flake off or to loosen some of the impregnated lead inside, making an audible noise as the club is taken from the bag and brought into address position. It has been known to crack heads.

Dirt and grime left on your clubs can have an effect on your game. For example, the addition of one-eighth of an ounce to the club head can change the swing weight one point. The wear of the grip can also change the swing weight. Therefore, replace any grip that has begun to wear out before it gets too thin. If you wait too long to replace a worn grip, the new one will not feel right to your hands, and it will be a long time before you regain your touch.

Do not attempt to repair any damage to any of the components, and do not tinker with sole plates, shafts, or heads. Major alterations are the job of skilled craftsmen qualified to handle the particular brand of club you are using.

Wash composition club grips occasionally with a soapy water solution and then rinse and dry. Clean leather grips with naptha, followed by two light applications of a good leather preservative.

The irons have also undergone some changes, but the reasons for and the methods of keeping them clean remain the same. You cannot expect to play your best golf with clubs that are clogged with dirt or bits of grass; not only will the ball react crazily after being hit but the actual "feel" of the club will be altered. To control the shot and get proper backspin on the ball, keep the scoring free of dirt and the clubface clean. To do this, first clean the corrugations in the club face with a toothpick or tee. Then give the clubs a thorough washing in a soap and water solution, rinse, and dry. That is all. Never use any harsh brushes, steel wool, or abrasives.

Grip adjustment, breakage of clubs, or bent shafts pertaining to the woods apply to irons as well. Do not take any unnecessary chances: have a qualified professional do the repairing, or have the club sent back to the manufacturer.

GOLF BALLS

Golf balls require very little care, but here are several tips to remember: Always store balls in a dark, cool place, below room temperature if possible. Deterioration of golf balls is a chemical action, and such deterioration slows down in a cool, dark area. However, most new balls retain their playability for many years, regardless of how you store them.

Keep all balls clean. Mud on a ball will directly affect its flight, since it may close up the dimpled surface.

GOLF BAG AND ACCESSORIES

The care of the golf bag depends on the type of material it is made of. For example, duck and canvas bags are easy to wash. Just immerse them fully in soapy detergent. Rub with a brush if exceptionally dirty. Then rinse thoroughly and allow to dry.

Nylon and most other plastic bags can be washed with a good soapy detergent to get out mud, grass stains, and other spots. Rust marks are almost impossible to remove, but good, hard rubbing will improve them a lot. (Never clean a nylon bag with a dry-cleaning fluid, as it may dissolve the rubber backing which gives body to the nylon and waterproofs it.)

Leather bags should be cleaned with saddle soap or a good leather conditioner to prevent cracking and excessive wear and to add to the looks. Do not oil a leather bag, as it will pick up dirt and dust too easily.

Regardless of material, replace the strap when there is evidence of wear and prevent the inconvenience of a possible strap break in the middle of a round. Also check the condition of the zippers and avoid the expense of losing costly items. Do not allow anyone to sit on the bag and destroy the rings that give it its shape and strength, and be a little careful in inserting or removing clubs. Pulling them out or thrusting them in forcibly causes abrasions to the finish of both woods and irons.

Prolonging the Life of a Golf Umbrella. A golf umbrella is a handy addition to a golfer's complement of supplies. Remember to open it when it rains and again when it is time to dry. Do not pound it into the bag compartments. You will break the ribs and damage the fabric. Keep the umbrella in its sheath when possible.

Caring for the Golf Shoe. All golfers would agree that the right golf shoes can have a great effect on their game. Yet, most either neglect to or do not know how to properly care for these valuable items of equipment.

Remove grass and dirt from the spikes, or cleats, and soles before placing them in your locker, carryall bag, or car trunk. The temperature changes from outside to locker room and especially the variations in the trunk of the car would crack and stiffen any leather articles and tend to deteriorate rubber products. Keep the shoes treated and polished with a good leather conditioner, and always use good shoe trees to keep the shoes in shape.

Remember that mud and early morning dew are the greatest enemies of golf shoes. Continual exposure to this moisture, as well as an improper drying process, breaks down the fibers of the soles, and they will get out of shape eventually. Avoiding moisture is virtually impossible for the golfer. However, you can follow a simple procedure to protect your shoes. After golf shoes get wet, upon return to the clubhouse, immediately put well-ventilated wooden shoe trees in them, and dry at room temperature—never on a radiator or in a hot automobile trunk. When they are thoroughly dry, spray on a coat of silicone around the welts and polish with a good grade of shoe wax before wearing again.

Check the golf shoes periodically for loose or missing spikes. Take measures to correct the situation. Also, when the spikes on the metatarsal bone are worn half down, it is time to replace the entire set.

When storing during the winter months or for extended periods of time, the golf shoes should be dried on shoe trees, sprayed with a coat of silicone, polished, and stored in a dry area of normal room temperature. It is also a good idea to replace spikes and worn shoelaces at this time so the shoes are ready for wear the next season.

Prolonging the Life of a Golf Glove. Leather golf gloves should be handled with the same care given to any fine piece of apparel. A few simple rules will assure long service from any high-quality leather golf glove:

1. Slip glove on by gently pulling at the cuff from both the front and back alternately. Flexing the fingers helps work them into the glove. Then smooth each finger and the thumb, beginning at the finger tip and working the leather toward the palm.

2. Slip the glove off one finger at a time. Then smooth it out to help retain its shape and size, particularly if it is damp. Do not allow a damp glove to dry in excessive heat or sunlight, which could destroy its suppleness.

3. Leather golf gloves should be washed before they become too soiled. Use rich suds of mild, neutral soap or flakes in lukewarm water. Rinse thoroughly in clear, lukewarm water. Then use a very light suds rinse. This will help to keep the glove pliable and soft. Do not squeeze or wring. Roll the glove in a heavy towel to blot. Unroll at once and blow into the glove to shape it. Dry gradually again, avoiding excessive heat and sunshine. When the glove is slightly damp, work it between your fingers or on your hand to soften the leather. In fact, some manufacturers even suggest that you shampoo the glove while it is on your hand. To improve the leather's luster after the glove is dry, buff lightly with a soft cloth.

Principles of Golf

There is no getting away from it; golf is a difficult game to play, but most people make it a good deal more difficult at the very beginning because they simply don't take the trouble to learn the fundamentals of the swing.

The first priority of a beginning golfer must be to acquire a sound, consistent swing. If his swing is sound, he will have a firm foundation on which to build.

However, if the beginner's swing has major flaws, playing the game will be a continual struggle. The frustrated player usually starts to look for quick cures and often winds up adopting and discarding endless pieces of advice in an everlasting attempt to correct his swing.

Whether you're a beginner or an experienced golfer discouraged by lack of progress, the best way to learn a fundamentally correct swing is through a series of lessons from a PGA professional. His trained eyes can see where you're going wrong, and he can then set you on the right path. It's truly the short way home.

Instructional ideas from books, magazines, and videos can supplement live instruction from your professional and increase your understanding of golf technique but can never replace it.

THE GRIP

Because the hands are the golfer's only connection with the club, it's vital that they be placed on the grip of the club correctly.

The most reliable method is called a neutral grip, with both Vs (formed by the index fingers and thumbs of both hands) pointing to the right ear at address. When you've taken this grip, you should be able to bring the hands and club up in front of your eyes and see two-and-a-half to three knuckles of the left hand. This type of grip encourages a swing that is neither too flat nor too steep, where the club approaches the ball from the inside, then squares up at impact, before returning to the inside just after impact.

The slicer's grip is known as the "weak" grip. In this grip, the hands are turned to the left. The Vs point up to your chin, or even left of it, at address. When you bring the hands and club up in front of you with a weak grip, you'll see one or no knuckles of the left hand, and two or three knuckles of the right hand. Such a grip encourages a move to the outside going back, with the right side dominant, and leads to a closing of the clubface at the top of the swing. The forearms tend to roll to the left or counterclockwise, closing the clubface. On the downswing, the forearms tend to make an equal and opposite action—they roll clockwise, opening the clubface. This action, besides leading to a slice, restrains or "blocks" the proper release and inhibits the swing. It slows down the club and by itself causes a loss of power. In a hook grip, the hands are turned to the right. The Vs point to the tip of the right shoulder and three knuckles of the left hand are visible at address.

This encourages you to take the club back on the inside with the left side in charge. You also tend to roll the forearms to the right (clockwise), which opens the club a little. On the downswing, again your forearms will make an equal and opposite action— they'll roll counterclockwise, closing the club through impact, and whipping the club through the ball. This most often produces a right-to-left spinning shot, better known as a hook.

For most male golfers, the neutral grip is best. However, most women and senior players, with slower hand action should consider a slightly strong grip, to help them release the club through the ball. The majority of LPGA Tour players have strong grips. As for the Senior Tour pros, many had weak grips as an anti-hook measure when in their twenties and thirties, but to a man, they've returned to stronger grips as seniors.

TAKING THE GRIP

Where you position the club in the hands is also very important. In the left hand, the grip of the club should run from under the butt of the hand across the middle joint of the left index finger. The left thumb should run straight down the right side of the grip. To avoid looseness, draw the left thumb toward the index finger so that you firm up the big muscle at the base of the V.

A very good test of the left-hand grip is to take your grip, then bring the club up so that it is horizontal. If the grip of the club is in the correct position in the hand, then you should be able to remove the back three fingers of the hand, and support the club between the butt of the hand and the index finger.

If the grip of the club slips into the lifeline at the base of the thumb, your grip is too much in the palm. With such a left-hand grip, the club will slip around in the hand, even if you use a glove. Wear on your glove in this area is a sure sign of this problem.

In the correct grip, the club is firmly pinned between the last three fingers and butt of the hand. If anything, it is preferable to hold the club slightly too much in the fingers than in the palm. The more the grip is in the fingers, the more wrist action you get, and the more power. The more the grip is in the palm, the more you cut down on wrist action; you'll probably be more accurate, but have less power. Many long-hitting Tour players grip the club slightly more in the fingers than advised here. Experiment to see the exact position that is best for you.

The right-hand grip should be strictly in the fingers. You should lay the club at the base of the middle two fingers, then position the lifeline of the right hand on top of the left thumb. Rest the right thumb slightly on the left side of the shaft. As with the left hand, there should be no looseness between the thumb and index finger, so draw the right thumb toward the index finger so that you firm up the muscle at the base of the V.

PALMS PARALLEL

Another important fundamental of the correct grip is that the palms must be positioned parallel to each other. Only when the palms are parallel can the hands work together during the swing, as they should.

Periodically, test your grip by taking it with the club resting on the ground, then opening your hands so that your fingers extend. You can then readily see whether the palms are parallel.

GRIP PRESSURE

The correct grip pressure is also critical. You must grip the club firmly enough to control it, but not so tightly that you "white-knuckle" it.

If you grip too loosely, you may let go of the club at the top of the swing with the last three fingers of the left hand, or the club may drop into the open V of the right hand. Such looseness leads to loss of control, and usually you will hit too early with the right hand and lose power. On the other hand, too tight a grip tightens the muscles of the forearms and locks the wrists. This prevents the forearms from rotating and the wrists from cocking and uncocking. As with too weak a grip, there's not enough hand action through the ball, with the result that you will usually leave the clubface open at impact, and fade or slice the ball.

Formerly, many teachers emphasized that you should feel the most pressure in the last three fingers of the left hand and the middle two fingers of the right hand. While it's true that these fingers must grip securely, the trend today is more toward feeling an equal grip tension in all the fingers of both hands. In this way, you will feel as though one "large hand" were swinging the club, which is ideal.

A very good way to test your grip pressure is in the waggle. If you waggle and can't feel the weight of the clubhead in your hands as you do so, then you're gripping too tightly. If you waggle and the hands separate from the club, then the grip is too weak. However, if you waggle and your hands stay on the club, yet you retain good clubhead feel, your grip pressure is correct.

It's worth noting that the grip pressure will automatically tighten as the outward pull of centrifugal force increases, especially during the downswing. Many male amateurs, especially, seem unaware of this fact, and as a result, grip far too tightly at address. For them, it's best to think of gripping as lightly as they can, without of course letting go of the club.

GRIP TYPE

The two most common grips in use today are the overlap (or Vardon) grip and the interlock grip.

In the overlap, the right little finger overlaps the left index finger. If your fingers are long, you may wish to rest the little finger on top of the left index finger. If they're shorter, wrapping the right little finger around the large knuckle of the left index finger may be more comfortable. Whichever method you adopt, the overlap grip takes the little finger of the right hand off the shaft. This has the effect of slightly weakening the right hand. Since most golfers are right-handed, the overlap grip tends to balance the strength of the hands so that they function as a unit during the swing. The overlap is by far the most popular grip, and is used by the majority of golfers, amateurs and professionals alike.

In the interlock grip, the little finger of the right hand rests between the index and adjoining finger of the left hand and interlocks with the left index finger. This grip is particularly useful for golfers with smaller hands or those whose fingers are short in relation to the length of their palms. However, this is not to say that these are the only golfers who should interlock. Golfers should experiment with both overlap and interlock grips to determine which is better for them. Like the overlap grip, the interlock unifies the hands so that they work together during the swing. The most famous golfer using the interlock grip is Jack Nicklaus.

Three other types of grip deserve mention. These are particularly helpful in solving specific physical problems.

In the ten-finger grip (sometimes called the "baseball" grip), there is no overlap or interlock, and all the fingers hold onto the club. Although several top-class golfers have used this grip, it is seldom seen today on the PGA Tour because of the risk of the hands working independently in the swing, or of the right hand overpowering the left. However, for golfers with very weak or small hands, neither of these problems is likely to emerge. For them, the ten-finger grip can be an excellent way to develop maximum power.

If a golfer's right hand is so strong it's always overpowering the left, or if the golfer has a problem developing left-side leadership in the swing, overlapping with two fingers of the right hand can be a good temporary or even permanent grip.

If a golfer develops arthritis in the left thumb or the thumb is injured in such a way that to place it down the shaft is painful, then wrapping it around the shaft may be the only solution. Hall of Famer Gene Sarazen used an interlock grip with his left thumb around the shaft throughout his long and successful career. Harrison R. "Jimmy" Johnston, who was an excellent amateur back in the 1920s and won the U.S. Amateur in 1929, used a ten-finger grip with his left thumb around the shaft. Wrapping the thumb around the shaft puts the grip of the club more in the palm than with the thumb down the shaft, so it's advisable to use a thicker grip than usual under the left hand to avoid looseness.

ADDRESS

The correct address doesn't ensure the correct swing. However, it is true to say that you're far more likely to swing correctly if your address is correct than if it is faulty.

To hit the ball straight you should aim the club straight at the target and adopt a square stance, with your feet, hips, and shoulders aligned parallel to an imaginary line extending from the ball to your target.

Along with the neutral grip, this will put you in the best possible position from which to make a solid swing.

STANCE WIDTH

There are several considerations that influence stance width. The wider the stance, the more weight you can shift to the right foot in the backswing, and back to the left foot in the downswing. The correct weight shift is what gives you leverage in the swing, and is a very important component of power. However, too wide a stance inhibits the hip turn and shoulder turn, another power component.

The narrower the stance, the more you can turn the hips and shoulders to the right going back and to the left coming through the ball. However, a narrow stance limits your ability to shift your weight, at least while retaining your balance.

For a driver, you want to take the widest stance you can while retaining your ability to turn the body and shift the weight. The exact width of stance you take, therefore, is personal.

At one end of the scale, take a young, powerful, flexible golfer. He might do best with a stance that is slightly wider than shoulder width (measured from between the insides of the heels). He has the athletic ability and flexibility to make a good shoulder turn and strong weight shift even though the stance is wide, and he is swinging so strongly with such active leg action that he needs a wide stance to retain his balance.

At the other end of the scale, take a senior golfer. If he's lost something in terms of athletic ability and flexibility, then he'll probably do better with a narrower stance, say, one of shoulder width or even slightly narrower. This stance allows him to make the fullest shoulder and hip turn of which he's capable, yet it's still wide enough so that he can shift enough weight to the right foot for leverage. The narrower stance also makes it easier for him to return the weight from the right foot to the left going through the ball. Finally, his leg action is usually not as strong as when he was younger, so he doesn't need as wide a stance to retain balance as he did when younger.

Once you've established your correct stance width for the driver, you should progressively narrow the stance as you play the shorter and more lofted clubs. With a driver, the wider stance places more weight behind the ball and puts you in position to deliver the clubhead through the ball with the necessary "sweeping" type of blow. However, when you're playing the ball from the grass, you need a more descending blow and a more compact swing for accuracy. Narrowing the stance puts your body weight more over the ball; this reduces the backswing length and enables you to hit down on the ball.

Varying the width of the stance varies the amount of weight you'll feel on each foot at address. As a rough rule of thumb, with a driver feel as though you've put about sixty percent of the weight on the right foot and forty percent on the left, with a 5-iron feel as though the weight is about equally divided, and with a wedge, feel about sixty percent of the weight on the left foot.

FOOT POSITION

The way you position your feet is also important because it directly affects the body action during the swing. As a rule, you should place the right foot at right angles or "square" to the intended line of swing. This braces the right leg so that it can resist the turn of the upper body during the backswing. As you complete your turn, you create a lot of tension in the right leg. This tension is released at the start of the downswing and is what transfers the weight from the right foot back to the left.

However, while you don't want a lot of tension in the left leg during the backswing, you do want the left side to turn out of the way, or "clear" as it is called, in the downswing. Turning the left foot slightly outward will accomplish both objectives for most golfers. However, golfers who aren't very flexible may find turning the left foot outward restricts their backswing too much. For them, a squarer or even a square left foot may be the answer. One great player who played with both feet square to the line throughout his career was Englishman Henry Cotton, who won the British Open three times (1934, 1937, and 1948), despite World War II robbing him of some of his best years.

BALL POSITION

In the 1960s and 1970s, much was made of "keeping things simple" in terms of ball position. At the time, many PGA Tour professionals advocated playing every club from the same position, about off the left heel.

For a very strong player, playing all the clubs from the same position is feasible. His strong leg action makes it easy for him to return the weight to the left foot by impact and make a solid hit. However, most amateurs need more help in making a descending blow than can be provided by merely narrowing the stance. Because their leg action isn't as strong, they need to progressively move the ball back in the stance as well.

Assuming you find that your best ball position for the driver is, say, a couple of inches inside the left heel, then position the ball with a 5-iron about an inch farther back in the stance, and with a wedge about an inch farther back than the 5-iron.

POSTURE

Good posture begins with good knee flex. The address position is a "ready" position akin to a tennis player awaiting a serve or an infielder in baseball before the pitch. If the legs are straight or stiff, your body is not ready to make an athletic move. This applies in golf just as much as in other sports. If you set up with straight legs, your legs won't function properly in the swing, and you'll be reduced to hitting the ball with just the upper body. Without the leverage that good leg action provides, you'll lose a significant amount of power.

Besides being flexed, the legs should be slightly knock-kneed, with the weight set on the insides of the feet. In the backswing, the left knee should work forward and behind the ball while the right leg resists. On the downswing, the right knee should work forward, toward the ball and then through to the left. Setting the knees slightly inward puts them in the correct position to function in this way during the swing.

With the correct set of the knees, you should feel firmly connected to the ground. In fact, it should be possible for you to take your address and, when a friend tries to push you off balance, be able to resist a push—from any direction—without any difficulty. If you do lose your balance when pushed, the direction in which you lose your balance tells you the necessary correction. If you can be pushed off balance forward, then your weight initially was too much on your toes, if backward, too much on the heels. Strive to have the weight balanced between the balls and heels of each foot. If you can be pushed to the left, you had too much weight on the left foot, and vice

versa. In most cases, you'll find that lack of knee flex also has contributed to loss of balance.

Going along with the flexed knees, the rear end should be lowered into a slightly sit-down position. The rear end counterbalances the upper body, which is leaning forward. To have good posture, you should stand tall, head erect, then lean forward from the hips, keeping the back straight and letting the arms hang down from the shoulders. Position the hands directly over the ball (when viewed in a mirror) so that there is a slight forward tilt of the shaft.

Johnny Miller describes good posture thus: "I stand with my feet about shoulder width apart, my arms hanging by my sides, and feel as though I could jump 10 feet up in the air, just like a cougar about to jump on his prey." A marvelous image. Put another way, the feelings of good posture are to feel *down* on your legs, *up* with the upper body, along with the relaxed *down* feeling of the hanging arms.

To accommodate the different lengths and lies of the various clubs, adjust the position of your hands and arms. With the driver, the longest club in the bag and the one with the flattest lie, you must stand farthest from the ball and position the hands and arms farthest away from the body. As the clubs become shorter and their lies more upright, gradually move the hands and arms closer to the body while standing closer to the ball. As a rough guide, with a driver, position the hands about two handwidths away from the body and with a wedge, one handwidth.

THE ROUTINE

Many golfers set up to the ball in a haphazard fashion. They'll set their feet, then, when they try to set the clubhead behind the ball, find they're too close or too far from the ball, and have to shuffle around. Alternatively, they find themselves out of position after taking address. For example, they'll find that the ball is too far forward or back in the stance, or the body aligned too far right or left. Thus, they're forced to make too many last-minute adjustments, each one carrying with it the seeds of doubt and reduced confidence.

In contrast, a professional or low-handicap amateur always seems to set up in the same way every time and with a minimum of fuss. He steps into the ball the same way, takes the same number of waggles, and so on. This is no accident. The better player has schooled himself to follow an unvarying routine in setting up. Repeating this routine every time breeds consistency. That's why developing your own routine is vital to success.

Although no two golfers will use exactly the same routine, here are the basic steps that are common to most good golfers.

With your selected club in hand, start from a point about three yards behind the ball, looking toward the target. From this position, you can see your target and form a clear picture of the shot you want to hit. It also allows you to determine your intended line of swing. For a straight shot, the best point is directly behind the ball, with your ball and the target in a straight line.

With your eyes on the intended line, step diagonally left, then turn and face the ball. Take your grip and put the clubhead behind the ball square to the intended line of swing.

Initially, set up to the ball with your feet together. You'll then find it easy to establish the correct ball position by first moving the left foot to the left and second, moving the right foot to the right into the correct stance width.

Once you've taken your address, keep in constant motion. Shift the weight slightly from the right foot to the left and back again until you're satisfied that all is correct. You may also want to take a waggle or two.

The type of waggle you select is personal. It can be a break of the wrists, a short back and forth movement of the clubhead with firm wrists, a little pumping action of the clubhead up and down behind the ball, or even a small circular movement of the clubhead. The reasons for the waggle are first, to keep your hands and the clubhead moving so that your wrists remain free, and second, to establish clubhead feel in the hands. So, experiment to find the type of waggle that best achieves these goals for you. However, whichever waggle you select, always take the same number of waggles at the same points in the routine. Also, try to restrict the number of waggles you take to a maximum of three. If you waggle more than three times, you give yourself too much time to second-guess yourself about the shot. Then, doubt can induce tension that will ruin the swing.

The one fault you must avoid is to come to a full stop before starting your swing. The longer you stand motionless over the ball, the more likely it is that tension will creep into the body. The ideal is to keep in motion, and after your last waggle and glance

at the target, settle the clubhead behind the ball for only the briefest of moments before starting back.

A very good thing to build into your routine just before you start your backswing is a forward press. Like the waggle, it's also a tension-breaker designed to help you start the swing smoothly. One of the best forward presses is to flex the right knee inward, shifting a little weight to the left foot. This sets up a reverse press, with the weight flowing to the right foot as you swing the club away from the ball. However, you can do that only if you rest the clubhead on the ground before the swing. If, like Jack Nicklaus, you prefer to hover the clubhead behind the ball at address, that is you never do ground it, you'll probably find it best to emulate Nicklaus, whose forward press consists of firming up the whole left side as he turns his head slightly to the right.

Even if you decide to use the forward press with the right knee, you should take a leaf out of Nicklaus's book and include a firming of the left side in the movement. To do this, extend the left arm, while lightly pressing the upper left arm against the left pectoral muscle in the chest. You thus connect the left arm and shoulder and ensure that they work together in the takeaway and backswing.

Both types of forward press have their adherents, so again experimentation is the only way to determine what's right for you.

THE SWING

Even though you've now learned the correct grip, alignment, and address, the first move back can make or break the whole effort. Get the takeaway right and you'll be well on your way to a successful shot. Get it wrong and you'll have to compensate somewhere in the swing to hit the ball solidly.

Most golfers know the minute they start back the swing whether it will be successful or not. That's how important the correct takeaway is.

THE ONE-PIECE TAKEAWAY

For the first couple of feet, you should swing the club back in "one piece," with the club, the left hand, arm, shoulder, and knee working together.

This takeaway picks up where the correct address and forward press left off. It ensures that the swing starts back straight from the ball. It starts the shoulders and hips turning immediately, which helps you make a wide, full backswing that will stretch and wind up the muscles of the left side. It also initiates the weight shift to the right foot.

Working on the one-piece takeaway is particularly important for reformed slicers, who must break their habit of picking the club up with the right hand and wrist and taking the club outside the line.

To the Top

As the backswing progresses, the body winds up from the bottom up. The first part of the body to complete its backward movement is the lower body, the second is the upper body, which coils around the right leg, the third are the arms and hands, which swing the club up, and lastly the wrists complete their cocking (or hinging).

The one-piece backswing initiates the weight shift to the right foot, and this continues until most of the weight is on the right foot at the top of the swing. The amount of weight shifted to the right foot depends on the club being used. With a driver, for example, where you start with a wide stance and much of the weight behind the ball, shift the weight to the flat of the right foot; at the top, you should feel a little pressure in the right heel. With a short iron, where you start with a narrower stance and the weight more over the ball, shift the weight less, to the inside of the right foot.

The right leg is an important key to a successful windup. You set it inward at address in a braced position. During the backswing, you should make an effort to keep it in the same position while retaining the same amount of knee flex as at address. One of the most important power sources is the coiling action of the upper body—shoulder and hip turn—into and against the right leg. The action is very much like winding up a spring. Keeping the right knee as still as possible anchors the lower end of this "spring."

The resistance of the right leg also prevents too big a weight shift to the right foot. If you find your weight is on the outside of the right foot at the top of the swing, then it means that the muscles in your right leg are too slack and the right knee has moved very much to the right, with your upper body also swaying far to the right. This will make it very difficult to shift the weight back to the left foot in the downswing. If the weight remains too much on the right foot, you'll tend to hit behind the ball. If you overcompensate, and shift too much weight to the

left foot too early, your body will get ahead of the ball and you could hit the ball too low or even top it.

This is not to say that there shouldn't be any lateral movement of the head in the backswing. Especially with woods and longer irons, you must make a big weight shift, and along with it there should be some lateral movement of the head to the right. Very powerful players—Seve Ballesteros is a notable example—have up to six inches of lateral movement when they go after the long ball, and Curtis Strange has played his best golf with a mini-sway. The length of the lateral movement depends on the amount of power desired and therefore the amount of weight shift needed for leverage. However, whether you use a lot of lateral head movement or only a little so as to obtain more control, the right knee must remain firm and retain its original flex so as to provide a stable platform for the coil.

The action of the left leg during the backswing should be fairly automatic. The one-piece backswing started the turning of the hips and shoulders and as the backswing continues, the left knee should work behind the ball more on long clubs, slightly less on shorter clubs, and the left heel will rise—pulled up by the hip turn. However, it's worth pointing out that, if you restrict the hip turn by forcing the left heel to remain on the ground, it tightens the coil of the upper body against the lower body and can give you more power—*if* you have the physique to handle it.

If you work on restricting the hip turn, the amount of your shoulder turn and weight shift to the right foot depends directly on your flexibility. If you're flexible, you may be able to restrict the hip turn to, say, twenty degrees, yet still make a ninety-degree shoulder turn, which most teachers agree is the minimum shoulder turn that will develop adequate power with a driver. If you're very flexible, like some young Tour players, you may be able to make a shoulder turn of as much as 120 degrees. Flexible players can also make a good weight shift while restricting their hips.

It's worth noting that if you're working on restricting the hip turn, this modifies the "one-piece" takeaway. Instead of including the left knee in the movement, you anchor the left heel and key on moving just the club, left hand, arm, and shoulder back together.

If you're not flexible, restricting the hip turn to twenty degrees will drastically reduce your shoulder turn, often to much less than ninety degrees. You then don't create a long enough backswing to develop adequate power and you probably won't make a good weight shift. The opposite is also true: A bigger hip turn, say around forty-five degrees, allows you to make a bigger shoulder turn, a longer backswing and a better weight shift. So, if you're not flexible, you're far better off allowing the left heel to be pulled from the ground by the hip turn. That way, you develop a bigger hip and shoulder turn and the lower body leverage you need for good power. The shoulders, arms, hands, and club are basically carried back in one piece.

Here's a good checkpoint at the end of the correct takeaway. Swing back until the clubshaft is horizontal to the ground and parallel to your intended line of swing. Then stop your swing and check the clubface. If the toe of the club points straight up in the air, you are in the correct position.

The action of the arms and wrists adds a significant amount of power to the shot. On the backswing, the arms not only rotate, the left arm stays extended, while the right arm folds into the side. On the downswing, the left arm stays extended, while the right arm straightens, from about hip high in the downswing, through impact. This straightening action of the right arm adds significant force to the blow. The cocking and uncocking action of the wrists amplifies this power.

To understand arm and wrist action, try the following "baseball" style drill. It exaggerates the correct action so that you can both see and feel it.

Using a sand wedge, take your normal address. Now raise the upper body to an erect position along with your hands and club until the shaft is parallel to the ground. If it helps, imagine you're going to address a ball perched in a bush in front of you. Then swing back and through continuously, keeping your grip light so that your body and arms can move freely and you develop plenty of clubhead speed.

You'll find that on the backswing, you'll turn the body to the right and rotate the arms and clubhead to the right (clockwise). The left arm will stay extended, while the weight of the sand wedge forces the right arm to fold into the side. The heavy sand wedge also will make the wrists cock at the end of the backswing. If you study the clubface, you'll see that it's facing upward. On the forward swing, the left arm stays extended through impact. However, the right arm starts to extend half-way through the swing, and is fully extended just after impact. Thereafter, in the follow-through, the left arm folds into

the side. Also, the arms rotate to the left (counterclockwise) in the forward swing and follow-through, and in the finish the clubface faces downward. Work on this drill until the correct arm and wrist action is automatic.

Putting the power elements together, the first part of the body to be fully wound is the lower body, with the hips turned up to forty-five degrees and the weight shifted into the firm right leg. The upper body is the second part to be fully wound up, with the shoulders turned ninety or more degrees. Third are the arms and hands which swing the club up to a position above the right shoulder. Lastly, the cocking of the wrists allows the clubshaft to reach a horizontal position or even slightly beyond horizontal with a flexible player.

THE DOWNSWING

Coming down, the body unwinds in the order that it was wound up. If the backswing is correct, the downswing will most likely be correct as well.

The lower body unwinds first, the right knee thrusting forward and toward the ball. This starts the shifting of the weight to the left foot and the turning of the hips to the left. The lower body action initiates the unwinding of the upper body, and the shoulders start to turn to the left. However, up to this point the arms, wrists, hands, and club "do nothing"; they're simply pulled down into what is called the "late hit" position—where the clubshaft is vertical, the left arm is still extended, the right arm is into the right side, and the wrists are still cocked. Then, as the hips and shoulders continue turning to the left, the arms release, rotating to the left as the right arm straightens, and lastly the wrists uncock at impact. In the follow-through, the body continues to turn to the left, the right arm extends fully as the left arm folds, and the right arm rolls over the left arm. At the finish, the golfer is in an erect position, his body fully turned to the left, and almost all the weight on the outside of the left heel.

STRONG HANDS

An important aspect of learning the swing is to strengthen and educate the hands. Often, what sets the professional's game above those of most amateurs is that: (1) The professional's hands are trained to find the back of the ball, with the clubhead striking the ball flush; (2) His hands are strong enough to absorb the shock of impact, so that there's very little turning of the blade on a mishit; and (3) His hands and arms can whip the club through the ball with enough speed to obtain good distance. In contrast, most amateurs lack strong hand action. Even if they have a functionally sound swing, what's usually missing is a strong release of the hands and arms—from hip high in the downswing to hip high in the follow-through. It's the release that accounts for the acceleration and crispness of the professional's hit.

Most Tour professionals develop their hands by practicing and playing golf every day. However, even if you only play once or twice a week, there are ways to keep the hands strong and tuned to their task.

The pioneer in this area was British champion and top teacher Henry Cotton. Here are some of his best "hands" drills, several of which can be done at home in a basement, garage, or backyard.

FIND THE BALL

If you're a golfer who presently hits the ball off the toe or heel rather than the sweet spot, then you need to train your hands to "find" the back of the ball.

As a first drill, walk down the fairway and knock a ball along with just your right hand holding the club. Stop. Then hit the ball with both hands. You'll hit the ball flush straight away because your right hand now knows where the clubhead is. Once you have mastered this, do the same drill with just your left hand. If you're right-handed, your left hand will need more work, and initially, choke down on the club to make it easier to make good contact. Finally, do it with both hands together. When you do this drill, make a point of walking up to the ball and hitting it from any stance. Hit the ball wherever your feet are when you reach it. Hit it from there.

Another variant of this drill is to scatter some balls on the practice ground, then go up to each ball and hit short shots. Again, step up to each ball and hit it from whatever stance you happen to be in when you reach the ball. Do this drill also holding the club with just your left hand or right hand, then with both hands together.

Some readers will be shocked to be asked to hit balls without first lining up their feet. Of course, lining up the feet—and body—makes it easier to hit the ball flush. However, the drill helps you acquire the ability to make a flush hit whatever the circum-

stances. When you consider the number of times in a round that you're forced to play the ball from an uneven stance, it's obvious that this is a skill that every golfer should acquire.

To show that the great golfers can hit the ball flush whatever their stance, Cotton used to tell a story about Harry Vardon. When Vardon was at his best, students of the game believed his phenomenal accuracy was due to his ability to duplicate his stance every time. An experiment showed this was not true. Vardon hit a series of identical drives, and on each drive he took a slightly different foot position, even though all the drives dropped within a few feet of the target. The accuracy lay in his trained hands.

FULL SHOTS WITH EACH HAND

More advanced work in finding the back of the ball is to hit full shots with the left hand and right hand alone. If you're right-handed, you'll probably find that the right hand does reasonably well. At first, you may find it difficult to control the right elbow on the backswing, which has a tendency to fly away from the body too much. However, if you work on the correct folding of the right arm in the backswing, you'll eventually master the correct movement, which is very similar to throwing a ball underhand.

The left-handed swing gives one the opportunity to experience and feel the "back-handed" swing that left side must make, and you'll appreciate how the extended left arm forms the radius of a good swing. However, for right-handers, the left side will need far more work than the right. To show you what can be done, when Cotton was in his prime, he developed his left hand to the point where he could hit 4-irons 150 yards and 4-woods off the fairway about 200 yards. Johnny Miller, who also believes strongly in the value of single-handed swings, can hit the ball similar distances.

Although hitting the ball with each hand is hard work, it's surprising how soon the hands get to know their proper roles. When you start, make it easy on yourself by using a short iron and slightly teeing several balls in a row. Start with half-swings and work up to full swings.

A side benefit of this practice is that it ruthlessly exposes a poor grip. If you're presently holding the club badly, you'll find you're forced to change to a sound grip. It also teaches the correct amount of grip tension in each hand. If the club turns in your hand, your grip is too loose. If you can't develop enough clubhead speed, the grip is too tight. Holding too tightly also leads to the fingers tiring during the stroke and letting go at impact.

HIT AND STOP

When you're practicing, hit some balls in the following manner: Swing back, hit the ball, then swish the club straight back, that is, away from the target. This teaches you to hold onto the club at impact, because it puts a double strain on the hands, wrists, and forearms. When in his prime, Cotton could hit a drive within twenty yards of his maximum distance with this technique.

SCYTHE THE ROUGH

Go into the deepest long grass you can find and "scythe" it with an iron. Stand in the rough, swing back and through, then step forward and repeat the action. Do this with both hands alone and with both hands on the grip. Try to develop as much clubhead speed as possible through the grass. This is a great drill for strengthening the hands.

HIT THE TIRE

As Cotton often lamented, on many courses these days you can't find rough that is deep enough for the "scythe" exercise. Happily, some 35 years ago, he hit on an excellent substitute. While parking his car at the club, he saw an old abandoned car tire, and kicked it out of his way. As he did so, he instantly realized that here was the ideal way to strengthen and educate the hands.

He went into his shop and began striking the outside of the tire. It worked so well that he had only one regret—he had discovered the tire's benefits after his best playing days were over!

The best club to use on the tire is an old one-iron, because it allows you to hit the tire squarely with the clubface. Hit the tire using your left hand alone, your right hand, and both hands. Take a full swing, and whack it hard.

Cotton compared hitting the outside of the tire to the heavy bag used in boxing. The boxer doesn't just hit the light bag; otherwise his hands wouldn't be prepared to take the impact of a punch. He must use the heavy bag for this purpose. The tire does the same for your golf. It overtrains the hands and allows you to cope with the impact of a golf ball very easily. The impact with the tire is at least twenty times stronger than that with a ball.

The tire produces amazing results. Most golfers can hit short and medium irons, because the loft on the clubs diminishes the force of impact. But they can't hit a long iron, since the impact is so strong. However, if you start using the tire drill, your long iron play will dramatically improve.

There are only two caveats with the tire drill, said Cotton. It's very powerful, and one or two minutes is enough for one session—more and you'll wear yourself out. Also, don't do the tire drill immediately before going out to play golf. You must rest in between.

INSIDE THE TIRE

At one time, teachers used to tell you that a golfer's natural clubhead speed through impact could not be improved. In other words, you were stuck with the clubhead speed you were born with. Cotton believed this contention was not true. He developed a series of drills that can, in fact, make a significant improvement in this area.

What you need for these drills is a "headless" club, an old iron from which the clubhead has been removed. You then whip the club to and fro inside the tire.

Start by taking the headless club in your right hand only, and swish it back and forth as fast as you can so that it sharply strikes each side of the tire. If you're right-handed, you'll probably find that your right hand can perform the drill reasonably well.

However, the left hand will probably be considerably weaker. In very little time, it will slow down. Instead of whipping the club back and forth with the hand and wrist, you'll find that all the effort is coming from the upper left arm. The tip of the club slows until it is, so to speak, "stirring a pudding."

What you're looking for, of course, is a fast whipping motion with the forearm and hands, with plenty of wrist action. So, when either of your hands starts to "stir the pudding," stop and rest before continuing. You can do the drill up to the point of initial tiredness, but doing it with tired muscles will do more harm than good.

Cotton emphasized this point because, as he says, most golfers are going to find that they're using muscles that have seen little or no action in their golfing lives. As the Romans used to say: *Festina lente*, Hurry slowly!

Also do this drill with both hands on the headless club, and while you're doing it, check that both hands are working in harmony. As stated earlier, in the grip the palms of both hands must be set parallel to each other so that they can work together during the swing. You can't have the left hand whipping the club with a lively wrist while the right hand is pushing with a firmer wrist. Mix your actions and the hands will be fighting each other.

CONTRAS

One of the problems of golf, said Cotton, is that it twists the spine and can create back problems unless you take steps to prevent it. Injuries occur because you must start in a lopsided position; the right hand is lower than the left on the grip so you must address the ball with the right side relaxed and the right shoulder lower than the left.

The problem is magnified for the Tour golfer who plays and practices so much. Often, when a young amateur star turns professional, his manager will say to him, "If you really work at your game, you'll be great." So he does, and instead of improving, he gets worse, because he overworks his spine and golf muscles to the point where fatigue sets in and destroys whatever talent he may possess.

This problem of back injury will also strike the weekend golfer on vacation. He practices and plays every day, and finds that on his last day he's playing worse than he did on his first. Conversely, many golfers play better after a rest. The spine and golf muscles return to normal once the one-sided deforming pull on the body stops.

Happily, Cotton discovered the remedy— "contras." If you're a right-hander, make some left-handed swings part of your practice program. For example, if you're working on the outside of the tire, turn around from time to time and hit the tire with the back of the one-iron. Do this with both hands and with each hand alone.

A few years ago, before the 1980 British Open, Gary Player complained to Cotton that his back was hurting. Cotton suggested "contras," and since that day Player has always included them in his swing exercises.

SHOTMAKING

Once you've learned the basic swing, you're ready to move on to the second stage in learning golf, that is, learning how to vary the swing in order to cope with different situations encountered on the course.

On occasion, you'll need to hit a hook, or even an outright slice. You'll need higher shots and lower shots than usual. These shots allow you to play around, over, or under an obstacle such as a tree between you and the target, or start the ball at the middle of a green and then work it with a hook or slice toward a pin cut behind a bunker. They're also invaluable in a wind. Often, knowing how to play such shots can mean the difference between having a shot you can play, and having to chip out of trouble sideways. Certainly, no golfer's education is complete until he has learned how to play them.

DRAWS AND HOOKS

You control the amount of curve with your grip. If you want a gentle draw, use a strong grip, if a hook, a stronger grip. To make a ball curve from right to left you must set up "closed," with your feet, hips, and shoulders aligned slightly to the right of your target. Your clubface remains square, pointed at your target.

FADES AND SLICES

Assuming you're now hitting the ball with a draw, to produce a fade or slice you must weaken the grip. Aim the club at the target, then set up with the feet, hips, and shoulders on a line to the left of the target. If you want a fade, aim slightly left and weaken your grip just a little; if a slice, aim farther left and weaken it a lot.

When playing a slice, remember that in opening the blade, you're putting extra loft on the club. If you try to slice a well-lofted iron such as the 9-iron or wedge, the amount of backspin you put on the ball will prevent the slice from taking effect. All you'll get will be a high fade. So, if you want to slice the ball, it's a good rule to select nothing more lofted than a 7-iron. It's also important to remember that a slice is a *weak* shot. On a fade, you might need to take, say, one club stronger than usual, for a big slice, perhaps as much as three clubs stronger.

When you attempt a very big slice, you may find

that you shank the ball with an iron because you have to pull the club across the ball so much from out to in. If this happens to you, take a leaf out of Lee Trevino's book, and slice a 3- or 4-wood. If you want less than the full distance of the club, choke down on it. Trevino is a master of this shot.

HIGH AND LOW SHOTS

An easy way to hit the ball high and low is by simply adjusting your ball position and weight distribution at address.

To hit the ball higher than usual, put the ball more forward in the stance. However, don't move the hands forward with the clubhead when you address the ball. Position them behind the ball so that the shaft leans slightly away from the hole (when viewed in a mirror). This has the effect of increasing the effective loft on the club. Also, put more weight on the right foot than usual, and allow the right shoulder to be a little lower than usual. In the swing, key on keeping the weight back on the right foot so that you hit the ball with the increased loft.

When playing the high shot, you must be careful about your lie. If the lie is good to excellent, then you won't have a problem. However, off a tight lie, you could easily top the ball. If you need a higher shot than usual off a tight lie, the only answer is to fade the ball, using the slice techniques described earlier.

To hit the ball lower, simply do the reverse. Put the ball back in the stance, but don't move the hands back with the clubhead. Rather, position them ahead of the ball so that the shaft leans toward the hole, reducing the effective loft on the club. Also, put more weight on the left foot than usual. In the swing, concentrate on keeping the weight on the left foot.

When playing the low shot, be careful to select a club that will have enough loft to get the ball up. If you try to play a 2-iron very much back in the stance, the ball won't leave the ground!

Another way of hitting the ball high or low is by altering your grip pressure and with it the type of swing you produce. This method, though slightly more difficult, has the advantage of giving you better control.

To hit the ball high, grip much lighter than usual. Otherwise, the address is normal. However, if you find it effective, you can play the ball just a little forward in the stance and put a little more weight on the right foot than usual. The lighter grip has the effect of making you take a longer swing and increasing the amount of wrist cock at the top of the swing. On the downswing, you'll also tend to use the hands and wrists more than usual. However, the hand action is a little different from normal. Through impact, work the right hand under and slightly ahead of the left hand, "throwing" the ball up in the air.

To hit the ball low, you take a normal address, but grip the club more firmly than usual. Again, if you find it effective, you may want to put a little more weight on the left foot, and play the ball back just a bit. The tighter grip has the effect of shortening the backswing and reducing the cocking of the wrists. With a shorter backswing and less hand action you'll put less backspin on the ball at impact so that it flies lower.

TROUBLE SHOTS

Nobody likes them. It's difficult to hit the ball successfully from tough lies or under poor weather conditions. However, if you know the correct techniques, you'll find yourself relishing the challenge presented by these shots. Instead of thinking of them as "trouble shots," you'll classify them as part of shotmaking. This is in fact the best attitude. Instead of bemoaning your fate, you'll find yourself studying the lie or the conditions and calmly making the necessary adjustments. That's the road that leads to success.

ROUGH

When your ball goes into the rough, the first thing to consider is your lie. The lie dictates what sort of shot to play and, in some cases, even what club you must use. So, don't make the mistake of selecting a club based solely on the distance and then going into the rough and trying to make it work. See what the lie permits you to do, then think about yardage, wind, club selection, and so on.

If your ball is lying in light rough, say up to about two inches in height, you usually can use your normal technique. If you need distance, then by all means use a well-lofted wood like a 5- or a 7-wood or one of the newer utility woods, which usually have the loft of a 7-wood but the length of a 4-wood. A wood will spread the grass as it moves through it and so slide through rough far more easily than an iron. If you have only a 4-wood in your bag, and need more loft than the club provides, then play for a fade, aiming a little left of target, and using a weaker grip than usual.

However, while your technique need not change in light rough, your club selection should vary from normal. If your ball is lying normally just off the ground, you'll probably get at least five yards extra roll and you may get what is called a "flyer." Because you can't squeeze the ball between the clubface and ground at impact as you do normally, the shot can "fly" on you, and travel up to twenty yards farther than normal. So, play this shot with a weaker club than normal. If it "flies," you'll be on the green. If it doesn't, you'll be on the front of the green in position to chip or putt for your par.

It's worth adding that you can get "flyers" in the fairway, too. If you have a particularly fluffy lie, or if the grass is wet, with the ball sitting just above the ground, guard against a "flier." If your ball lies in clover, then you can almost count on the ball "flying."

If your ball is on hard ground, the best way to play the shot is with a fade. However, in addition to aiming left, and weakening the grip, it's a good idea to firm up your left-hand grip. This prevents the club from twisting in the hands on impact with the hard dirt.

If you encounter a "perched" lie, where the ball is teed up on top of the grass, then a change in technique is indicated. Choke down on the club so that you raise the clubhead to ball level. Whatever club you're using, set up with the weight evenly balanced between the feet so that you can make a sweeping type of blow and catch the ball cleanly. The common mistakes with this lie are either to press the club down into the grass in back of the ball at address, or to hit down on the ball too steeply. Either mistake can result in your going completely under the ball and skying the shot.

If the rough is severe, and you know you must use an iron, then grip more firmly than usual to prevent the club turning in the hands at impact. Your goal should be to put the clubhead on the ball with the least amount of grass possible getting between the face and the ball. To do that, you must make a steeper descent on the ball than usual. Play the ball farther back in the stance, the hands ahead of the ball, and break your wrists in the takeaway. This takes the club

up on a more upright plane so that you can hit down firmly on the ball. It's particularly important in heavy rough to power the club through the heavy grass as strongly as possible. To do that, key on driving the right side through the ball and you'll surprise yourself with the distance you can get. Also, don't forget that playing the ball back in your stance reduces the effective loft on the club so use a more lofted club than usual.

In very severe rough, despite gripping more firmly, the clubhead can catch in the grass, sending the ball left. One way that is often advocated to cope with this is to simply open the blade. However, with this technique, the grass can grab the heel of the club and close it violently, leading to the very thing you're trying to avoid—a smothered shot to the left. Instead, use the technique advocated by Arnold Palmer and Johnny Miller—take a more lofted club than normal and close the blade before taking your grip. This ensures a cleaner hit because the toe of the club cuts into the grass first.

To play the shot, aim and set up at an imaginary target, say, ten yards right of your actual target. Position the ball back in the stance. Then, gripping firmly, close the blade so that the leading edge is square to the target. Swing back along the line established by your closed shoulders at address with an early wrist break, but on the downswing deliberately pull the ball, coming over the top with the right shoulder so you hit down and through straight at the target. As in baseball, this "pulled" shot is very strong. However, it will roll when it hits the ground.

Incidentally, you can use exactly the same technique if your ball lies in a divot hole. Use a more lofted iron than usual for the distance, close the blade slightly, and pull the ball.

If your ball comes to rest next to a tree, you can usually either hit a low shot or high shot as described earlier. But if your ball is so close to a tree that you can't take a normal right-handed swing, then there are two ways to handle the situation.

Undoubtedly, the easiest shot to hit is simply to turn your back on the target, your feet fairly close together, and position the ball a little to the right of your right foot. Using a short iron, grip it at the lower end of the handle, and punch the ball behind you with a firm right wrist and arm. Practice this shot a little, and you'll find you can add a little wrist to the shot and this will increase the distance you can obtain.

Much more difficult is to attempt a left-handed shot. This is especially true if you're trying to play the shot by turning the blade of a short iron upside down so that the clubface is directed at the target. Most right-handers have absolutely no idea how to make a left-handed swing. It's not too difficult to reverse the static fundamentals: take a left-handed grip and set up with a strong right side, the right shoulder higher than the left, the right arm extended to form a straight line down the right arm and the clubshaft, and the left arm bent and into the side. However, the resulting swing can be completely ineffective. Most high-handicappers will just whiff the ball. So, unless you have plenty of golfing talent, and are prepared to practice this shot, go with the shot where you turn your back on the hole.

It's important to add that, if you happen to use a putter with a plain back so that it has a little loft or even one with a slightly rounded back which can give you effective loft, then this makes the left-handed stroke far easier. However, even with the aid of such a putter, most amateurs would be well advised to limit the left-handed stroke to a firm "punching" action with very little wrist in it.

Sloping Lies

There are four types of sloping lie: Uphill, downhill, ball above feet, and ball below feet. Each lie requires a change in the way you set up and swing. However, a few hints apply to all of them.

On all sloping lies, it's tough to retain your balance. The harder the swing you make, the more easily you can lose your balance and mishit the ball. Therefore, it's a good idea to swing easily any time you're playing from one of these lies. Also, stay centered, and keep the head very steady. To encourage an easy swing, take a stronger club than usual on all but downhill lies.

If the lie is very severe, you have to be especially careful to retain your balance. If you were to make a big body turn and weight shift, you could easily fall over. So, keep the lower body quiet and cut down on your turn by playing the shot mostly with your hands and arms. You'll lose some power with this technique, so take a much stronger club than usual, except, of course, on downhill lies.

On an uphill lie, the key is to make the club swing through the ball on a path that is parallel to the slope. To do this, you have to tilt your body to the right so there's more weight on the right foot than the left at address. If you concentrate on putting the left shoulder a little higher than usual, this will help you get the right set up. This position will increase the effective loft on the club. This is why you need a stronger club than usual. This technique works fine on all but severe uphill lies.

If the lie is very much uphill, it becomes very difficult, if not impossible, to tilt the body far enough to the right, because to do so would make you fall down the slope to the right. So, bend the left knee a little so you can set up in a better balanced position. Then set your legs firmly and stay over the ball using the "hands-and-arms" swing.

Besides hitting the ball higher, most golfers will have the tendency to hook the ball off an uphill lie. This is because, with so much weight set on the right foot, it's difficult to shift the weight to the left foot in the downswing. As a result, the left hip will turn to the left sooner, causing the hands and arms to release earlier, closing the blade. In such a situation, allow for the hook by aiming a little right of target.

On a downhill lie, the key to success is the same as with an uphill lie—swing through parallel to the slope. To do this, think of setting up with the left shoulder lower than usual, and you'll put more weight on the left foot as you should. To avoid catching the slope with the club in your backswing, it's a good idea to play the ball back in your stance. However, these adjustments will reduce the effective loft on the club, so use a more lofted club than usual.

On a severe downhill lie, you'll find it impossible to keep your balance unless you bend the right knee a little at address and make more of "hands-and-arms" swing. To avoid catching the slope on your backswing, break the wrists in the takeaway. This will take the club up on a steeper than usual path.

Most people find that they slice from a downhill lie. This is because it's extremely difficult to prevent your upper body going down the slope with the lower body in the downswing. Your body tends to slide past the ball, and prevents you from fully releasing the hands and arms by impact, and you leave the clubface open. Allow for the slice in your aim.

Playing a wood from a downhill lie is hazardous. However, it can be done if you need the distance and the slope is fairly mild. Just remember to take a wood with enough loft. If you have a 5-wood, a 7-wood or a utility wood, these are particularly good clubs to use. However, if the most lofted wood you have is a 4-wood, then the best way to make it work is to go with the natural tendency of the slope and deliberately fade the shot. With a slight slice swing, you make a steeper descent on the ball, and the open clubface at impact increases the club's effective loft.

On a lie with the ball above your feet, most golfers know that you must allow for a hook, but few understand why. Cast your mind back to the baseball-style drill discussed earlier, where you were asked to imagine that the ball was up in a bush in front of you. This represents about the most severe "ball-above-feet" lie imaginable, and it induces the most drastic open to closed action, causing a hook. The less severe the slope, the less hook you get.

From this type of lie, you're forced to stand more erect than usual, and this in turn will make you swing on a flatter plane and hook the ball. To reduce the amount of hook, choke well down on the club and select a stronger club than you'd usually use for the distance. Put more weight on the balls of your feet to avoid falling down the slope during the swing.

On a very severe ball-above-feet lie, you'll have to choke down even more. You must also cut down on your usual amount of body turn. Again, playing the shot with more of a "hands-and-arms swing" is the answer.

On a lie with the ball below your feet, the most important point is to "sit down" to the ball. On this lie, you tend to lean over the ball very much and put too much weight on the toes. This can lead to falling forward during the swing, and you could slice or even shank the ball. However, if you flex your knees and put your weight on the heels, you can minimize this tendency. Holding the club at the end of the grip and bringing the ball in closer to the body will also help you set up in the most comfortable position possible. Despite these adjustments, the ball will still tend to fly to the right on this lie, so aim a little left to allow for it.

It's extremely difficult to get a good body turn on this type of lie. So, whether the ball is a little or a lot below your feet, it's safest to swing mainly with the arms and hands. It is also very easy with this lie to come out of your knee flex in the downswing and top the ball. This is a shot where you must stay down to the ball.

WIND AND WET

In foul weather, a little knowledge is far from being a dangerous thing; it can be a lifesaver. If you try to play your normal game in poor conditions, you're in

for a frustrating time. In a strong wind, for example, if your ball is blown off course a couple of times early in the round, it can ruin your whole day. You get down on yourself, and the double-bogeys multiply. However, if you know the adjustments to make, you can get to the point where you enjoy the challenge of the elements.

Even so, don't expect to score normally in poor conditions, as so many golfers do. You are going to miss more shots than usual. The trick is to try to keep these mistakes to a minimum. Realize that the conditions are the same for everyone, that everyone is going to score worse than usual, and you'll have the right mental attitude to become a good player under wet or windy conditions.

In a wind, make the low ball your basic weapon. You must avoid hitting the ball high, because then the wind will toss it around, and you'll have no control. To hit the low shot remember what was said earlier: The key is to take a shorter, easier backswing so that you reduce the amount of backspin you put on the ball. As a general rule, instead of taking your normal 9-iron for a shot, take a 7-iron, choke down on it, and swing easily. You'll get the same distance as you normally would with a 9-iron, but the ball will fly lower and out of the wind.

Hitting the low ball is particularly important when playing into the wind. It's also extremely difficult to do because your every instinct tells you to hit harder to try to make up for the expected loss of distance. Don't fall into this trap. If you do, you'll put so much backspin on the ball that it will soar high in the air and you may lose as much as a third of your normal distance. Worse, if you hook or slice the ball, the wind will exaggerate the sidespin, and your ball will be blown far off course.

With a driver, don't follow the common advice of teeing the ball low. What usually happens is that you then swing down steeply on the ball, put too much backspin on it, and, rather than flying low, it gets up too high. Tee the ball normally, and concentrate on making a good sweeping type of contact on the back of the ball.

When playing into the green, take into account that the wind is going to make the ball stop more quickly than usual. So, select a stronger club than you normally would. If you have to carry a bunker or other hazard in front of the green, play it safe and take a much stronger club, one that will land the ball at the back of the green. Then, even if you hit too hard and the ball gets up too high, or even if you mishit it, you'll at least carry the hazard and be safely on the green.

Most golfers would feel they need little help in hitting a downwind tee shot. Yet, simple as it should be, it's surprising how many times this sort of shot goes awry. Usually, the error is simply swinging too hard. You think, "Here's my chance for the longest drive of the day," then you swipe at the ball and mishit it. Instead, concentrate on making a good, solid swing. That will allow the wind to give you the extra distance.

Remember that the wind will knock some of the backspin off the ball, so teeing the ball a little higher than usual can help you get it up in the air. However, if the wind is very strong, say over twenty-five miles an hour, and you hit a driver, the wind will knock the ball down so much you won't obtain adequate carry. In such circumstances, use a 3-wood from the tee.

Playing into the green, avoid the "knock-down" effect of the wind by keeping the ball low. In other words, if there's an opening into the green between bunkers, hit a low, running shot that will land short and roll up to the flag. Take a stronger club than you'd normally use, choke down on it and play the ball back in your stance. Also, firm up your grip so that you reduce the length of the backswing and wrist action and produce a "punching" effect. However, if you have to play a shot of normal height, to carry a bunker for example, then you must use a normal swing so that you put as much backspin on the ball as possible. If you're trying to decide which of two clubs to use, taking the weaker club and hitting it firmly will normally give the best result.

In crosswinds, and assuming you hit the ball fairly straight, it's usually best to keep things simple. If the wind is blowing from right to left, simply aim a little farther to the right than normal and let the wind bring the ball back. If it's blowing from left to right, just aim a little farther to the left.

However, if your normal shot is a hook, then the sidespin will fight a left to right wind and the ball will fly straighter, but shorter than usual. In a right-to-left wind, the hook will "ride" the wind and go farther than usual. If your normal shot is a slice, the opposite happens; your ball will fight a right-to-left wind and "ride" a left-to-right wind. Bear these factors in mind when playing into the green, and club yourself accordingly.

If you've reached a level of skill where you can draw or fade the ball at will, you have more options open. Off the tee of a long, wide-open hole, where distance is your prime goal, riding the wind can give you a significant distance advantage. However, on a drive to a narrow landing area, or an approach shot, making the ball fight the wind will give you maximum accuracy.

On a rainy day, you want the utmost accuracy off the tee. So, it's a good idea to choke down a little on the driver, and concentrate on making a smooth, solid swing to the middle of the fairway. To keep the ball airborne longer in the heavy air, tee the ball a little higher than usual.

Through the green, the wet grass makes the less lofted clubs more difficult to hit. It robs you of backspin, and therefore you'll find it more difficult to loft the ball. Instead of playing a 3-wood from the fairway, select a 5-wood. Instead of playing a 2- or 3-iron, use a 7-wood, choking down on the club on shorter shots. Also, look at the top of the ball rather than the back of it. This will help to hit the ball, if anything, a little thin. You must avoid hitting fat. With wet dirt as well as wet grass getting between the clubface and the ball at impact, the ball can go anywhere. You shouldn't expect to get your normal distance on a wet day, so use at least one club stronger than normal.

Playing out of wet rough is particularly difficult. It's essential to take a more lofted club than you would normally, and, if anything, play safe in selecting your target area.

In the short game, the watchword is: Be up. On pitch shots, aim for the top of the flag. On chip shots, where you'd normally allow the ball to roll, take a more lofted club and carry the ball up to the hole. Trying to roll the ball through wet grass is difficult to judge and should be avoided where possible. In putting, remember that wet greens are slower than normal. So, take less break than you normally would and aim to leave the ball a good foot past the hole.

SAND PLAY

The average golfer seldom practices from sand. As a result, he rarely masters bunker technique. When he gets into a bunker, it can be a traumatic experience. A good bunker player is successful because he has taken the time to learn the necessary shots. However, it's one thing to know the correct techniques, but quite another to have confidence in them. If you have the necessary confidence, you can go into any bunker and *know* you can execute the shot. Without it, you'll be lost. The number one cause of missed bunker shots is a tentative swing. You won't be tentative if you devote even a small part of your practice time to hitting bunker shots.

NORMAL EXPLOSION SHOT

Most amateurs don't understand that the regular explosion shot from a good lie in a bunker is simply a slice swing made with a club designed to skid through the sand. Too often they simply attempt to play the shot as they would an iron from the fairway, setting up with a square blade and the shoulders square to the intended line. They then try to hit down behind the ball and control the distance by the amount of sand they take.

There's no margin for error with this technique. Sometimes, the sand wedge digs in too much behind the ball, and they leave the ball in the bunker, or, if they attempt to correct this and hit the shot thin, they either top the ball or send it over the green.

On every shot from a good lie in a greenside bunker, you should set up so as to put some slice spin on the ball. Position the ball about two inches inside the left heel, then open the blade before taking your grip, so that the leading edge aims to the right of target. Then take an open stance with the feet, hips, and shoulders aimed to the left of your target.

You should also set up with slightly more weight on the left foot. This will encourage you to cock the wrists early going back. An early wrist cock is essential in a bunker so that you take the club up quickly enough to clear the sand on your backswing. You swing the club up steeply, hit down firmly, about two inches behind the ball, and then swing through to a full finish.

The swing follows the open alignment of the body. You swing back outside the line and swing through across the line, from out to in. The feeling is one of hitting a shot to the left of target. However, the open blade compensates for the out-to-in swing. The large amount of loft on the sand wedge prevents any curve in the air, so the ball flies straight, about halfway between the direction in which the clubface is pointing and the line of swing. Be aware, however, that this usually puts slice spin on the ball, which tends to make the ball jump to the right on landing, and take this action into account when aiming your shot.

As with any slice-type swing, you must keep the blade open through impact. To do this, you may want to weaken the grip as Tom Watson and others do. However, if you find it more comfortable to retain your usual strong grip, there is another way to do it. Simply allow the strong grip to open the blade in the usual manner going back, but on the downswing, pull through strongly with the heel of the left hand, delaying the normal roll-over of the right hand and arm over the left. Johnny Miller suggests imagining that you're going to balance a champagne glass on the clubface. This image will also help you keep the clubface open through impact.

You might think that, with such a steep swing, the sand wedge would dig deep into the sand. This is not the case, however, because of the bounce on the sole of the club. When you address a ball with the face of the wedge square, the leading edge is raised above the ground; this design is what constitutes bounce. The soles on most sand wedges are angled, with the back end lower than the front. Others have rounded soles, with a radius on the sole from front to back, which has the same effect as angling the sole. When you set the blade open, you increase the effective bounce on the sand wedge. Thus, even with a steep downward hit, the club will ride through the sand, taking a shallow cut.

The shallow cut is what provides the margin for error. Although you should plan to enter the sand about two inches behind the ball, you have quite a lot of leeway. If you inadvertently hit down in the sand slightly closer to the ball, you hit the ball slightly harder, and the ball carries a little farther. However, you also have less sand between the clubface and ball at impact, so you put more backspin and sidespin on the ball and it pulls up quicker. The harder hit is offset by the increased backspin. The compensation works in reverse if you hit slightly too far behind the ball. You have more sand between the clubface and ball at impact, therefore less backspin, but you don't hit the ball quite as hard. The result is a shot that carries less far, but rolls more.

It's worth adding that you shouldn't go to extremes in the distance you aim to enter the sand behind the ball. If you enter the sand very close to the ball, just a thin layer of sand gets between the ball and clubface at impact. The sand then acts much like sandpaper would, in that the club grips the ball, putting a tremendous amount of spin on it. Skillful sand players can play shots that take advantage of this fact. However, they're dangerous, since you're obviously close to skulling the ball. If you enter the sand far behind the ball, you'll put little or no backspin on the ball and have very little control. Furthermore, you'll risk taking too much sand and leaving the ball in the bunker.

Actually, hitting about two inches behind the ball is just a starting point. If you study the reaction of the ball when it lands on the green, you'll be able to determine whether you're getting too much or too little spin, and thus whether you are hitting too close or far behind the ball. Work toward the ideal shot, which is a happy medium between the extremes, one where the ball lands, checks, and then slowly rolls toward the hole.

Basically, you should vary the distance obtained on the shot in two ways: the length of the backswing, and how much slice spin you put on the ball.

On a short shot, make a short swing. On a longer shot, make a longer swing. If you try to use too long a swing on a short shot, it is all too easy to decelerate into the ball, which is fatal on any sand shot. On a longer shot, a short swing won't give you enough force to get up to the hole.

To vary the amount of slice spin you put on the ball, vary your address. The shorter the shot, the more you open the stance and shoulders, and the more you open the blade. This increases the effective loft on the club and the higher and shorter the ball flies, with more slice spin. The longer the shot, the less you align your body left and the less you open the blade. This reduces the amount of slice spin, and, with a less open clubface, the ball flies lower and farther.

On longer shots, you should also play the ball back farther in the stance and aim to enter the sand closer to the ball, say about an inch.

The amount you open the clubface to the right and open the body to the left should always correspond exactly. In other words, if you aim the clubface eight feet right of the hole, then aim the body eight feet left. Then the open clubface and body will always offset each other and the ball will fly straight between the path of the swing and clubface aim.

If the sand is wet, then the clubhead will not cut into the sand as much as usual. So you need to hit the ball with less clubhead speed. You can do this in two ways. Either take a shorter, easier swing or take your normal length of swing while opening the clubface a little less than usual and hitting slightly farther behind the ball.

THE BURIED LIE

When your ball is buried, the only way to get it up and out is to hit down deeply under the ball. Therefore, the shallow cut set up by the open face in the regular explosion shot won't do the job. You need to square the blade so that you convert your sand wedge from a skidding to a digging weapon. Squaring the blade eliminates the bounce on the wedge so that it digs into the sand.

Controlling distance from a buried lie is more difficult than on a regular explosion because you can't put much spin on the shot. What you have to do is vary your angle of descent on the ball.

On short shots, where you want the ball to stop as quickly as possible, set up with a square blade, a narrow, very open stance and shoulder alignment and play the ball about in the middle of the stance. (If you carry a third wedge, with a loft of sixty degrees or more, this is a good time to put it to use.) Position almost all your weight on the left foot. Then, pick the club up steeply with a very quick wrist break and hit down as steeply as you can, entering the sand as close to the ball as possible, and cutting underneath it. You almost literally plunge the clubhead into the sand behind the ball, and there won't be much, if any, follow-through. Because of the steepness of the downswing, the ball will jump up high in the air. Although you won't get much backspin, the ball will drop softly onto the green, and won't roll far.

On longer shots, set up with a wider, more normal stance, and only open up the body slightly. Play the ball back toward the right foot, and have the weight slightly on the left foot. This setup helps you break your wrists early, take the club up steeply and hit down firmly. However, the ascent and descent is not as steep as on the short shot. Hit down about two inches behind the ball. The amount of sand that gets between the clubface and ball on this shot prevents you from putting any spin on the ball, so that it will run after it lands on the green.

It's worth adding that if your ball comes to rest in a water hazard, and you decide to play it, you should use the same technique as for longer shots from a buried lie in a bunker. Because the club will skid through the water, you should always hit down about two inches behind the ball. Don't attempt to play a ball lying in more than two inches of water. The water will distort your sight of the ball and it's all too easy to miss the shot. In fact, if you want to play really safe, it's better to take a drop for a one stroke penalty unless at least a portion of the ball is above the surface.

HILLY BUNKER LIES

If you have a sidehill, uphill, or downhill lie in a bunker, the techniques previously described are applicable. The following tips will help in a bunker situation.

On a ball-above-feet lie, the large amount of loft on the sand wedge will prevent the ball from hooking. However, because you're swinging on a flatter plane than usual, you will tend to pull the ball. To compensate, aim farther right of target than usual. It's also a good idea to choke down on the club so you don't have to swing on as flat a plane as if you held the club normally.

With the ball below your feet, you're forced to make a more upright swing, and you'll tend to push the ball. So, compensate by aiming farther left of target than usual. The worst lie of this type is when your feet are outside the bunker, but the ball lies within the bunker. Then, make an extra effort to stand as close to the ball as possible, holding the club at the end. Widen your stance, and bend your knees to get down to the ball. Key on keeping the same amount of knee flex through impact. It's all too easy on this shot to straighten your legs and top the ball.

On an uphill lie, you'll find that, if you take the same amount of sand as usual, you'll tend to hit the ball too high and it will finish short of the hole. So instead, aim to enter the sand closer to the ball, about one inch instead of two.

On a downhill lie, there's a tendency to hit the ball thin or even skull it. So it's a good idea to hit farther behind the ball than usual, about three inches instead of two.

LONGER BUNKER SHOTS

When you reach the point where you can no longer get the ball up to the hole with a sand wedge, it's best to go to a stronger club—a pitching wedge, 9-iron, or 8-iron. Use the same technique as for the longer explosion shot: slightly open stance, slightly open blade, the ball back in the stance, and aim to enter the sand about one inch behind the ball. Even though these clubs have relatively flat soles compared to a sand wedge, by opening the blade, you create some bounce on them, so that they'll skid through the sand and give you some margin for error.

When you need a full shot with an iron, the worst mistake you can make is to hit the ball fat: the ball simply won't go anywhere. It's safest to play the ball well back in the stance, just inside the right heel, with the hands in their normal position off the inside of the left leg. Also, put slightly more weight on the left foot. This setup makes it nearly impossible to hit behind the ball. However, for insurance, select a spot about an inch in front of the ball, and look at that, rather than the ball, during the swing. In selecting a club for this shot, remember you'll be hooding the club, and therefore taking about two club's worth of loft off the ball. So, if the shot normally calls for a 4-iron, use a 6-iron.

The safest technique with a fairway wood is to create some bounce on the club by opening the clubface about an inch before taking your grip. Opening the clubface lowers the back of the sole so that the club will skid through the sand, rather than digging in. Then aim well left of your target and align your feet and shoulders parallel to that aim. Position the ball well forward in the stance, about off the left heel. Then go ahead and swing. The result will be a big, high slice. Even if you hit slightly behind the ball, the bounce you've created on the club will ensure a reasonable result.

SHORT GAME

The short game covers all shots where you have to make less than a full swing; for most golfers this is from around 100 yards into the green. There are basically two types of shots you'll need—pitches and chips.

PITCH SHOTS

The pitch shot is played with a lofted club such as a pitching wedge, sand wedge, or nine-iron. It's used when you want to carry the ball onto the green and then have it stop by the hole. Although you're using less than a full swing, the fundamentals of pitching are very similar to those of the full swing.

In the same way that you narrowed the stance from the driver down to the short irons, you continue to narrow the stance as you get closer to the hole. To some extent, this is because you wish to make a descending hit on the ball. However, it's also because the shorter the shot, the more you should use the hands and arms rather than a big body turn and weight shift. Setting the feet closer together encourages this type of swing.

For a normal pitch shot, set up with the blade set squarely at the hole, and take a narrow, slightly open stance. Your shoulders should also be slightly open with the hands a little ahead of the ball, which is positioned about four inches inside the left heel. As with the bunker shot, put a little more weight on your left foot to encourage a quicker wrist break and a more upright swing than normal.

The swing follows your shoulder alignment. Swing back slightly outside the line, breaking the wrists. It's particularly important to brace the right knee firmly inward, and keep it still throughout the backswing. Although there will be a slight weight shift to the right foot, especially on the longer pitches, the weight should only shift to the inside of the foot. If you allow the right knee to waver, the shot will lack precision. Essentially, what you should do is swing the club back with the hands and arms around a firm right leg, then hit down and slightly across the ball.

On all pitch shots, you want to make sure that the clubface stays open well into the follow-through. As with the bunker shot, you have your choice of grips. You can take a slightly weak grip or retain your neutral grip and pull through strongly with the butt of the left hand.

The distance of the shot is controlled in two ways; the length of the swing and the extent to which you choke down on the club, which narrows the radius of the swing.

If you have a long pitch, you might swing your hands back to shoulder height. On a very short pitch, you might swing them just past your right leg. On a pitch of medium length, you might swing them back in between these extremes, say, to about waist height. Although no exact guides can be given on choking down (you'll develop a feel for this as you develop as a shotmaker), a rough rule of thumb would be that on a shoulder-height swing, choke down about an inch, on a waist-height swing, about two inches, and on a swing just past your right leg, about three inches.

The follow-through should mirror the length of the backswing. If you swing back to shoulder height, swing through to shoulder height; if back to waist height, through to waist height, and so on. In pitching as in the long game, decelerating through the ball can be fatal.

If you're a beginner, it's a good idea to experiment hitting shots with these different lengths of swing using each of the pitching clubs, the wedges, and 9-iron. Once you're familiar with the distances and amount of stop you can expect with each club, you'll have made a good start on acquiring touch.

To play a higher or lower shot than usual, use the techniques outlined earlier. Either play the ball farther forward or back in the stance or use a lighter or firmer grip with the ball played only slightly forward or back in the stance.

Occasionally, you'll want a shot that flies extra high and stops very quickly. Then, play the shot like a short bunker shot, with the ball up off the left heel, and a very open blade and stance. Only attempt this shot with a lofted wedge or sand wedge, and only when you have an excellent lie. Otherwise, the bounce on the club could lead to bellying the ball. In such a case, use a pitching wedge.

If you're in rough close to the green, or the ball is lying poorly on ground you can cut through, you can actually use exactly the same technique as for an explosion from a bunker, including hitting down behind the ball. Since this will take some of the force out of the shot, imagining you're actually in a bunker can give you a good idea of how hard to swing. Use either a sand wedge or lofted (third) wedge.

If you have a bad lie, then you'll have to play the ball back in your stance nearer the right foot. The hands will be ahead of the ball, hooding the blade. This helps you make more of a downward hit. Also, break the wrists quickly on this shot so as to steepen the swing. You will find that the ball will fly lower, and run more, so allow for this in planning your stroke. Play the same shot if you must pitch into the wind. In that case, the ball will probably stop normally because of the wind.

If you encounter hard ground, you have to guard against the wedge sticking in the ground if you hit fat. Just open the blade of the wedge a trifle at address, rather than setting it square, and you'll ensure that it will skid through.

If your ball comes to rest in a cuppy lie, don't make the mistake of pressing the clubhead down behind the ball at address. The clubhead can then become snagged by the back of the cuppy area in the takeaway, and cause you to miss the shot. Instead, hover the blade behind the ball at address, then hit down firmly on it.

From time to time, you'll want a shot that flies high but rolls once it lands on the green. To do that, set up with a slightly open stance, but square the shoulders to the intended line of swing. In the downswing, instead of keeping the blade open through impact, allow the hands and arms to release normally so that the right hand and arm roll over the left. This slightly closes the blade at impact and puts run on the ball. The technique is very similar to a draw in miniature.

Chip Shot Strategy

On chips, which are short shots from around the green, you can use any club from a 4-iron down to a lofted wedge. Some great golfers have always chipped with just one club. At the opposite end of the scale, other greats have advocated chipping with every club in the bag except the long irons. For the average golfer, neither method is usually the answer.

Amateurs don't practice as often as the pros, so they often haven't put in enough time to become familiar with all the suitable irons, and they usually don't have the skill to manipulate one club so that all sorts of chips can be made with it. A compromise is usually the best solution. Experiment with all the irons, then pick the fewest that give you complete coverage. As an example, you might decide that a 5-iron, 7-iron, 9-iron, and the wedges are enough to do the job for you. Certainly, this method will let you use fewer clubs without having to resort very often to manipulating the blade.

The club you should choose on any individual shot will depend on the ball's lie, the amount and type of ground between the ball and the green, the amount of green you have to play with, and whether the green itself is hard or soft. As an aid in selecting the right club and visualizing the shot, always pick out the spot on which you want the ball to land. In your mind's eye, see the ball flying through the air, landing on the spot, then rolling to the flag.

As a general rule, always land the ball on the green, which will give a predictable bounce, rather than on the fringe. Also, take the club with the least amount of loft that will get the job done. The less the loft on a club, the easier it is to chip the ball solidly. Also, if you mishit a less lofted club slightly, the result will usually be pretty good, whereas with a very lofted club, such as a wedge, a mishit can leave you halfway to the hole.

Putting these factors together, think in terms of selecting the least lofted club that will land the ball at least a yard on the green—to provide a margin of safety—and stop the ball by the hole.

For example, if the hole is about thirty feet away and your ball lies just off the green, you shouldn't need a more lofted club than, say, a 5-iron. If you have to carry about five feet of fringe, you would need about a 7-iron. If you had fifteen feet of fringe, you'd need a more lofted club, such as a wedge. However, don't make the mistake of reaching for a lofted club if you have a lot of green with which to work. For instance, suppose your ball lay fifteen feet back from the fringe, but you had sixty feet of green between the fringe and hole, then you could use one of the less lofted clubs, land the ball on the green and have it roll to the hole. Put another way, play a lofted chip only if you're forced to by the situation at hand.

It's also worth mentioning that you can land the ball short of the green as long as the ground is firm and you know the ball will bounce predictably. You can also be forced to do this if the green is too firm or the slope is too steep to allow you to land the ball on the green and stop it by the hole.

Chipping Styles

When you get close to the green, you need so little force in the stroke, as in putting, that there is room for individuality in technique. You can chip with just your arms and shoulders, with no wrists in the stroke, or make a wristy stroke. You can play the ball with the club soled normally, or by crowding the ball, play it with the shaft more upright and the heel of the club off the ground. You can play the ball from the middle of the stance, back off the right foot, or even outside the right foot. All these styles have been used successfully by top professionals in recent years, so that none of them can be said to be wrong. Equally well, none of them is necessarily best for any particular individual. So, even if you happen to use one style, a little experimentation is in order to see if another style might not do even better for you.

A key factor in deciding which type of stroke you should use is to pick the one that lets you hit the ball most solidly. The worst sin in chipping is to hit the ball fat. This is usually caused by a scooping action of the right hand through impact. The hands and wrists release too early, and the result is either a fat hit or a top. The best styles in chipping have built-in preventives against this fault. Of the methods that follow, the first two could be described as traditional and the second two as modern.

Arm and Shoulder Stroke

The popularity of the arm-and-shoulder putting stroke on Tour has led many of the pros to use the same method in chipping. Set up for this stroke with a narrow, slightly open stance, choking well down on the club for control and putting a little more weight on the left foot. However, because you want the ball to roll, and therefore sidespin is undesirable, the shoulders should be square to the intended line. Position the ball about in the middle of the stance, the hands ahead of the ball, with the left arm and shaft forming a straight line. Hold the club firmly enough so that you can eliminate wrist action and make the shot with your arms and shoulders. The feeling you'll get is one of making the stroke with the forearms, with the shoulders rocking back and through as a result. A good key in developing the stroke is to think of taking the "Y" formed by the arm and club back and through together. To generate the necessary force, swing the club back and through the same distance, like the swing of a pendulum.

In this type of stroke, the ball is swept away. This works well from a good lie. However, if the lie is poor, you'll have to play the ball farther back in your stance, hooding or delofting the club a little. You must allow for this hooding in your club selection.

WRISTY STROKE

The setup is similar to the arm and shoulder stroke— a narrow, slightly open stance, square shoulders, hands well down the club, and the left arm and clubshaft in line. However, the ball is slightly farther back in the stance, and most of the weight is kept firmly on the left foot. Going back, break the wrists quickly. As with the pitch, your right knee must be virtually immovable, otherwise you won't hit the ball as precisely as you want. The feel of the wristy chip is that you hit the ball with your hands, with the wrists going along for the ride, and with just enough arm and shoulder action to make the action smooth. There's very little follow-through on the wristy stroke. That's why it's often described as a "tap," a "pop," a "jab," or even a "stab." Cutting off the follow-through helps prevent any scooping with the right hand. When the right hand catches up with the left, the stroke ends. One of the advantages of the wristy stroke is that, because of the early wrist break, you can make exactly the same stroke from poor as well as good lies.

It's worth pointing out that, even if you normally use the arm and shoulder stroke, it can be well worth your while to acquire the wristy stroke as a shot to deal with very poor lies. Also, if you like to use a wristy putting stroke, you may prefer to standardize your short game by chipping in the same way. A great golfer who does just that is Gary Player.

BALL BACK STROKE

When golfers first saw Hubert Green chipping a few years ago, many of them probably wrote off his style as unorthodox and probably not the right way to go. Green leans well over the ball, which is positioned several inches to the right of his right foot. He uses a very narrow, open stance and body alignment, and chokes down to the steel of the club. The hands are opposite the inside of the left leg, an extremely hooded position of the blade. His backswing is all wrist, then he hits down firmly on the ball. Green only allows his arms and shoulders to get into the act after impact, when they extend the club out toward the target.

However, there's a lot of method to Green's apparent madness. Also, his record of nineteen victories on the PGA Tour, including the 1977 U.S. Open and 1985 PGA Championship, speaks for itself. The following are the advantages Green feels his chipping style possesses.

He plays the ball to the right of his right foot because the only way he can miss the shot is to hit it a trifle thin, and a thin shot produces practically the same result as a good stroke. If he were to play the ball in the center of his stance, he could hit the ball fat or even top it. His stance is narrow, because he can keep the legs out of the shot and stay over the ball. He stands open to get a better view of the line, and give plenty of room for his arms to swing through the ball. He chokes down to the steel because the closer he gets to the ball, the better feel he has, almost like tossing the ball toward the hole. He's a wrist chipper because he then avoids all movement of the arms, shoulders, and legs up until impact, and it's these parts of the body that could make him sway.

It's different, but Green's method has stood the test of time. For a golfer who continually hits his chip shots fat, it's worth trying.

HEEL-UP STROKE

Another very different chipping method is one recently pioneered by Phil Rodgers. In all the previous chipping styles, the blade of the club is soled normally. Rodgers plays the ball back in a slightly open stance, opposite his right foot, but only six inches from it. To play the ball that far back in the stance and that close to the body, Rodgers chokes down to the steel of the club and holds his hands high. The clubshaft is an extension of the left arm and therefore closer to vertical than it's natural lie. Only the toe of the club rests on the grass; the heel is up in the air. The advantage of this positioning is that it prevents the heel of the club snagging in the grass at impact as can happen if the club is soled flat.

Rodgers uses a ten-finger grip for chipping, because he feels that doing so gives him better control. He also turns both hands very much outwards (the left hand very weak and the right very strong), with the arms out and away from the body and parallel to the intended line. This tends to eliminate any wrist action. He keeps the butt end of the club against the inside of the left forearm as a further preventive against wrist action. Although Rodgers strokes with the arms and shoulders, with no wrists, he doesn't feel that much, if any, follow-through is necessary.

More recently, Johnny Miller went to a similar style of chipping with the thought that he would make his chipping style as much like his putting style as possible. He uses his putting grip, a reverse overlap, and chokes down on the grip to putter length. He takes a narrow, slightly open stance, with the ball about four inches from the feet and positioned just inside the right heel on normal shots. Like Rodgers, Miller stands the club on its toe, his hands arched downward to prevent wristiness. He then uses an arm-and-shoulder stroke.

Important advantages of playing the ball close to the feet and setting the club on its toe as in the Rodgers and Miller styles are that the club travels almost straight back and straight through (in a conventional style, the club swings back to the inside, then comes through the ball from inside to square and then back to the inside) and that the clubface stays squarer to the intended line, rather than opening and closing.

THE TEXAS WEDGE

Using the putter from off the green, known as the Texas wedge, can often be the best percentage shot. Arnold Palmer once put it this way, "Your worst putt (from just off the green) is often better than your best chip." In the same way that using a lower-lofted club gives you a better chance of playing a successful chip than a higher-lofted club, so using a putter gives you a higher rate of success than even a lower-lofted club, provided the conditions are right.

As a general rule, you should consider using the putter if your ball is just off the green and you only have to putt through a few feet of fringe. However, if the ball is farther off the green, it's usually better to chip, because it becomes difficult to judge how much harder to strike the ball in order to roll it through the fringe. Ideally, the fringe should be well manicured. However, the putter can give you a very safe, if not elegant, shot if the ground is bare and you're afraid of mishitting a chip. If the ball is lying down in a depression, a good chipper will probably prefer to chip. Again, however, playing the putter will at least give you a safe shot, even if it does hop about a bit before settling down. If the fringe is very lush and the ball is sitting down in the grass a little, play the ball an inch or so forward in your stance, but leave your hands in their normal position so that the shaft is leaning a little to your right. This increases the effective loft of the putter, and will help you get the ball up and out of the grass for a good roll. In other cases, use your normal putting stroke.

PUTTING

The average club golfer takes approximately thirty-eight to forty-two putts per round. Against a regulation thirty-six putts for eighteen holes, this means he is taking at least two to six three-putt greens a round. A good professional, on the other hand, takes six or seven less than regulation. To win a tournament on the PGA tour today, you usually have to average less than thirty putts per round.

Why the massive difference between the club golfer's performance and that of the tournament winner? Confidence? Practice? Natural ability? Yes, all these are factors in the development of a successful putter. But what about those players who practice their putting from dawn till dark, yet cannot buy a putt? Actually, successful putting can be broken down into three interdependent elements: (1) reading greens; (2) judging distance and break; and (3) proper stroking of the ball.

READING THE GREENS

The length and type of the grass, its dryness or wetness, and its level (downhill or up) are very important considerations when putting. Another factor, often overlooked by many golfers, is the direction of the grain on a putting green. It has a definite effect not only on how far a putt will roll but also on which direction it will bend. On some greens the grain can alter by as much as 25 percent how hard a putt should be struck—the amount depending on whether you're putting with or against it.

It is, of course, illegal to roughen the grass on a green to find out which way the grass lies. Generally, however, the grass just off a green, on its fringe, will have the same grain as on the green itself, and it is legal to brush your putter across the fringe and thus determine the direction of the grain. But the safest method of determining the grain of a green is to look for its shine. When looking toward the hole, should you notice a shiny reflection of the sun on the green, you are usually looking with the grain, and thus your ball will roll a great deal more freely and much farther than you might normally expect. This sheen is caused by the mowers clipping the fibrous runners of the grass. Conversely, if the surface of the green appears dull from where you stand, you are looking against the grain, and you must hit the ball much harder than you might generally consider necessary.

Another way you can determine the grain is to study the growth around the edge of the hole. When you look closely at it, you notice that the grass around three-quarters of its circumference is sharp, distinct, and cleanly cut. On the remaining portion, the grass will be more ragged and inconsistent. This is because the grass on the side of the cup toward which the grass lies will readily die due to the fact that more of the root system is severed on the "down-grain" side of the hole when the green is cut. It means that when standing on the same side of the hole as the rough edge and looking across the cup, you will be looking into the grain. Should you have to putt over this rough edge, you are stroking against the grain and will have to hit harder.

When you putt with the grain, your ball meets little resistance from the grass, which already bends in the direction of the putt. Such a putt must be hit approximately fifteen to twenty-five percent more softly than a putt rolling against the grain. The grain that runs directly across the line of your putt will have a similarly strong effect, and you must allow for some right or left roll even on an almost absolutely flat surface. For example, a long putt breaking right on a green with its grain growing left to right would probably require you to allow two or three more inches of break, depending on the amount of slope.

The type of grass employed on the green also has an effect on your putting. There are two basic types of grass used on golf courses: Bermuda and bent. There are almost infinite varieties of these two, but these are the fundamental strains. The easiest way to tell the two apart is to remember that bent grass does exactly what its name implies: it bends. Bent grass is allowed to grow longer than Bermuda, and the tops of the leaves curl over and lie flat, so that the length of the blade is bent almost double. Bermuda grass, on the other hand, looks like a crew cut. It is much shorter than bent, and it is bristly and stubby to touch. The two grasses have very different characteristics.

Bermuda grass is used mainly in the South and Southwest because it stands up well under hot, dry conditions. Bermuda is generally more grainy than bent, and the grain it does have is usually more consistent. The grain on some Bermuda greens is produced almost entirely by the cutting pattern of a lawn mower. Bermuda grass is thick, and its large, coarse leaf makes for a slow putting green. Bermuda greens have less break, too, because the heavy leaves keep the ball from sliding off. The grain on a Bermuda green, however, can radically affect the break or speed of a putt. Going with the grain, a 10-foot putt is equal to a 6-footer, and putting across the grain can double the amount of break, pulling a straight ten-footer a full two feet off line. Because Bermuda greens tend to be slow and bumpy, try to contact the ball at the bottom of your putting stroke in order to get the ball rolling smoothly. Also, make allowances for the grain. If you are putting with it, play the ball toward the center of your stance to avoid getting overspin, and play the ball more forward when going against the grain. Through the green, there are several things to keep in mind. Bermuda greens are closely cropped and are usually hard. You may have to land the ball in front of them and let it roll on. Because Bermuda is thick and full, it makes excellent fairways that yield perfect lies. But for the same reason, it becomes an impenetrable rough when left to grow. In tangled, matted grass, do not try for distance. Take what you need to get back to the fairway, and play it safe. Bermuda rough grabs the clubhead, and you may leave the ball right where you found it.

Bent grass is found mainly in the North, although a few southern courses (Augusta National and Pinehurst) use it. It is a cool-weather grass, and its fine leaf makes for a smooth, true, and slick putting surface. Bent grass can be very grainy, especially near mountains and water, and a good hint to remember is that the grain on such courses will grow toward the mountains and away from the water. Because bent greens are so fast, play the ball more toward the center of your stance as you would on a straight downhill putt. Incidentally, bent fairways are not as easy to hit off as Bermuda. Because the grass is thin and soft, and the turf soft, too, there is a tendency for the player to hit every shot fat. And on some bent fairways, especially in the Midwest, patches of clover creep into the bent, producing flier lies. Confronted with his ball lying in clover, the player should take one club less and try to pick the ball clean.

JUDGING DISTANCE AND BREAK

One of the first things you should do when your ball arrives on the green is inspect it carefully. The *Rules of Golf* permit you to pick up the ball and remove any foreign matter from it. The Rules also allow you to repair ball marks on the green and to remove any loose impediments, such as leaves, either by picking them up or brushing them aside with your hand or club. Although the Rules permit you to repair ball marks, you may not repair other imperfections in the putting surface. To do so, the USGA feels, would further slow down the game; golf is slow enough as it is without making it worse.

Study the grass around the edge of the hole very carefully for any footprints, spike scuffs, or ragged edges that could seriously impede the line of your putt. If there is more damage to the grass on one edge than on the other side, chances are good that your putt will roll to that side. Also your ball, because it will be traveling more slowly at the end of its stroke as it nears the hole, is more subject to the slightest imperfections on the green. Thus, when such imperfections are found, it is usually advisable to hit the ball more firmly so that it will be able to overcome these rough spots.

When putting on a green with a slope or slant, you must be able to judge the break of your ball as it comes toward the hole. Generally, you can determine this break by getting well away from the ball and taking a good look at the entire green surface. If this does not answer your break question, examine the cup itself. If one side looks lower than the other,

the green does slope toward that side. Judging the break of your ball and how to read slopes of a green comes only with experience and practice. But keep in mind that a putt which must break twice is going to break much more sharply off the second turn than the first. This is again due to the fact that your ball will have slowed down sufficiently so that it will be affected more by the contour of the green. For this same reason, a putt that has to roll across a slant at the near conclusion of its roll will break more sharply at that point than it would have if the slope were met shortly after the ball was stroked. In other words, on putts that must roll over several slopes, be sure to allow for more of a break nearer the cup than at the beginning of the stroke.

Wet greens are slower as a rule than dry ones; therefore you must stroke your ball more firmly. Remember that putts will not break as far as normal on a sloping green when it is wet; also, you are permitted to move your ball on a green if casual water impedes the line of your putt.

To line up a putt, try to picture in your mind just where the ball is going to have to go to reach the hole and at what speed it is going to have to travel. Look over the ball position from all conceivable angles. This means not only from behind the ball but also from behind the cup and from the sides. You should note not only the grain of the grass and side roll but also the degree of downward or upward slant between your ball and the cup. The final judgment of the distance between the ball and the hole, its proper line, and the power needed to sink your putt comes, of course, with practice and experience. In this book, a long putt is referred to as one over twelve feet; a short putt as one from two to twelve feet; and a very short putt as one two feet or less.

The plumb-bob technique of lining up in which the player uses his putter in the manner of a surveyor's instrument is becoming more and more popular. In using the system, you must stand so that a straight line extends from your dominant eye to the ball and then on to the hole. The other eye must be kept closed. Your dominant eye is the eye which allows you to see one object superimposed over another in the same way both eyes can see the superimposition. The putter should be held perpendicular at arm's length with the thumb and forefinger gripping it at the bottom of the grip. It is best to stand from three to six feet back of the ball when lining up. As a rule, the shorter the putt, the closer you stand to the ball. Cover the ball with the lower part of the putter shaft and then run your dominant eye up the shaft. If the shaft covers the hole, the putt is straight. If the shaft falls to the left of the hole, the putt will break from left to right. If the shaft falls to the right of the hole, the putt will break from right to left. The system works best on putts of fifteen feet or less.

PUTTING STROKES

As in chipping, the force required in the putting stroke is so small compared to a full swing that there is a lot of room for individuality. Some great putters, such as Bobby Locke, have putted from a very closed stance, but then there's Chi Chi Rodriguez, who has recently taken a new lease of life on the Senior Tour and putts brilliantly from a very open stance. Some, like Tom Watson, have a quick tempo. Others, like Jack Nicklaus, stroke deliberately. Some use a wristless stroke powered by the arms and shoulders, Bob Charles is a notable example. Others, such as Gary Player, uses a wristy stroke. In fact, great putters use such diverse styles that one could conclude that anything goes in building a putting stroke.

However, despite this diversity, it is possible to find fundamentals to which most, if not, all great putters adhere. They can form a good foundation for your own efforts to build a good stroke.

PUTT LIKE YOU SWING

Overall, the great putters tend to adopt a putting style that is very close to that of their full swing. This fact by itself tends to explain most of the different styles you see. As stated, Bobby Locke putted from a very closed stance, but he also set up very closed in the long game, with a big draw as his normal flight. Gary Player does the same thing, except that he plays his full shots with a gentle draw. Tom Watson has a quick tempo in putting, but also swings fast on full shots. Jack Nicklaus is deliberation itself in both phases of the game. Ben Crenshaw has a smooth, flowing putting stroke, and his full swing has the same characteristics. Bob Charles's putting stroke is stiff-wristed and his full swing tends to be firm-wristed, too.

There's very good reasons why this is so. Every golfer wants to simplify his game, so putting with a style similar to your full swing makes a lot of sense. Equally well, every golfer must find a style that suits his physique and temperament. Why, for example, adopt a fast tempo in putting if a slow tempo comes naturally to you? You're going against your own nature. However, the most compelling reason for putting in a similar way to your full swing is consistency. If you adopt a putting style that is contrary to your full swing, the characteristics of your putting style can "leak" into your full swing.

For example, if your full swing is from open (going back) to closed (in the follow-through) and you decide to adopt a new putting stroke, where you work the blade from shut to open, you may well find yourself shutting the blade on the backswing of a full shot, with disastrous consequences. Equally well, if you have a long, smooth, full swing such as Ben Crenshaw's and try to adopt the rapid tempo of a Tom Watson on the green, the faster tempo could find its way into your full swing, and you could totally lose your timing.

REPEAT AND REPEAT

One characteristic that all great putters share is consistency. Earlier, the importance of having a routine for every shot up to the green was emphasized. An unvarying routine is equally important on the green. Some great putters read the putt only from behind the ball looking toward the hole. Others also read it from behind the hole looking back toward the ball. Some use the plum-bob technique; others don't. Some take a couple of practice swings before stepping into the ball; some take none. Some take one more look at the line to the hole when over the ball; others take two or three. However, whatever the components of their individual routines, the great putters always repeat their routines—exactly—before every putt. Consistency in setting up focuses the mind for proper concentration and helps consistency of stroke. A great putter's stroke repeats and repeats. Whatever the type of stroke you settle on, make certain it is one that you personally can repeat, too.

GRIP STYLE

The most popular style of grip is the reverse overlap, where the left index finger is extended down across the fingers of the right hand. It's designed to make the hands work as a unit during the putting swing, and it's certainly a good place to start. However, the reverse overlap can't be regarded as the only grip to use because other grips have been used by the great putters.

For example, Bobby Locke always used his regular overlap grip in putting, seeing no need to change it for putting. Byron Nelson used an interesting hybrid grip in putting, called the double-reverse overlap. Nelson held the club with the last three fingers of the left hand and the first three of the right, with the little finger of the right hand overlapping the middle finger of the left hand, and the left index finger extended across the first three fingers of the right hand. This is an effective grip that affords plenty of feel as well as unifying the hands. A distinctive touch Nelson added to this grip was to dig the end of the right thumb and fingernail into the grip. He said this helped him keep the putter blade square during the swing. Phil Rodgers uses and advocates a ten-finger grip for putting as well as chipping, and for the same reason, more control. Hubert Green, ever the individualist, uses a split-handed grip, the right hand several inches below the left. Later in his career, Gene Sarazen advocated extending the right forefinger down the right side of the shaft. He said it was especially useful for golfers who normally putt stiff-wristed, but who find that they're inadvertently breaking their wrists.

There also have been grips specifically devised against the "yips." A golfer with the yips is not able to control the muscles of the right hand and wrist. At first, it's merely a "scooping" action, which leads to hitting "up" on the ball; thus you mishit the ball, half-topping it, and start missing short putts. The disease can develop into an uncontrollable twitch that can knock a short putt right off the green. Many exotic grips have been devised against the yips, the most common being the cross-handed grip, with the left hand below the right on the shaft. This grip puts the left hand in such a strong position that it's far more difficult for the right hand to misbehave.

GRIP POSITION

There's also no absolute in the positioning of the handle in the hands. Some great putters have positioned the club in the hands as in the full swing grip, the palms parallel to each other. Others, to eliminate wristiness and the possibility of yipping, turn both hands outward on the grip and, going along with this, position the arms away from the body in a bent

position, with the left forearm or both forearms parallel to the intended line. Another grip that will eliminate wristiness is to position the club more in the palms, with the wrists arched downward more than in the regular grip for the full swing. While an extreme palm grip—where, say, the grip of the club lies in the lifeline of the left hand—is fatal in the full swing, because you don't get the support from the butt of the hand, it is fine in the shorter putting stroke, and in fact many excellent putters use it.

About the only constant among the grips of the great putters is that they all place the thumbs straight down or at least on the center of the shaft, rather than the sides. This positioning gives maximum feel.

STANCE WIDTH

Although extremely wide stances, such as Ruth Jessen's a few years ago, and very narrow stances, such as Ray Floyd's, are seen, the majority of great putters set up with a reasonably wide stance, with the feet positioned about a foot apart between the heels. Such a stance affords stability as well as comfort for most golfers. If you decide to adopt a narrower stance, remember that, in a wind, you will probably have to widen it for stability.

PUTTING POSTURE

In posture, too, the great putters differ very widely. Some, like Jack Nicklaus, like to get down to their work and lean well over the ball. Others, like Ray Floyd and Ben Crenshaw, prefer to stand more erect and make a stroke from a position close to that for a traditional chip shot. To some extent, the posture you adopt will depend on the length and lie of the putter you use. However, in general, it's better to adopt a posture that suits you and then select a putter whose length and lie fits that posture rather than the other way round.

HEAD POSITION

Most great putters position their heads so that their eyes are directly over the ball or at least over the intended line of putt. They argue that only if your head is in this position do you get a true picture of the line; thus you're more likely to aim and stroke correctly. If you are too close to the ball so that your eyes are outside the line of putt, you tend to take the club back outside the line and swing from shut to open. If you're too far away so that your eyes are inside the line of putt, you tend to swing the club inside the line and swing from open to closed. However, if your eyes are over the line, you tend to keep the head of the putter squarer during the stroke.

A good way to determine where your head is positioned is to take your putting stance, then, without moving your feet or head, lay the putter on one side and drop another ball from the bridge of your nose.

It's worth mentioning that, if you decide to adopt a more erect posture in putting you may prefer to position your head slightly inside the target line, as it would be on a chip. The stance that Ben Crenshaw takes while putting is a good example.

A GOOD ROLL

One of the factors that great putters emphasize in putting is to "put a good roll on the ball." However, it's important to realize that the ball doesn't start to roll immediately as it leaves the face of the putter. It actually skids across the surface of the green before the friction between its cover and the grass slows it down and it begins to roll. This skidding phase of the putt is about twenty percent of the distance, say, four feet in a twenty-foot putt. However, the main point to understand is that for most of its travel, a putt is simply rolling toward the hole. Therefore, any topspin or backspin you apply to the ball will have no effect on it for the greater part of its journey. This is why it's pointless and in fact harmful to attempt to put these spins on a putt.

If you hit down on a putt, the ball is driven into the ground, and will jump up before skidding and settling down to roll. This makes the roll more unpredictable. If you hit up on a putt, this acts as a half-top would, again driving the ball into the ground. This leads to an important point: To put the best roll on the ball, you must hit the ball at the bottom of the swing (when the clubhead is neither descending nor ascending) and the shaft should also be vertical. With the shaft vertical, the true loft of the putter meets the ball and lifts it up on top of the grass into the skidding phase. Thus, it's fundamental that you set up with the shaft vertical and position the ball in your stance so that you strike it at the bottom of the arc.

The skidding aspect of a putt also explains why it's pointless to try to put sidespin on a putt. Once again,

after a short distance, the ball is simply rolling across the green.

NEVER CUT A PUTT

It's interesting to note that, back at the turn of the century, the great putters *did* attempt to cut their putts by swinging from out to in and drawing the putter across the ball, and hook them by swinging from in to out. However, those were the days of the stymie, and this was done in an attempt to work the ball around an opponent's ball lying on your line and into the side of the hole. Even then, old-timers such as James Braid knew enough to add that such a stroke shouldn't be attempted unless the break were favorable. In fact, it's certain that if any ball did fall in, it was the break that was responsible, not cutting or hooking the ball.

Today, because there are no stymies, there's no need for this, and so all great putters try to put the best roll on the ball that they can. To do that, you must avoid an out-to-in swing, which can make you pull the ball to the left of the hole, as well as making the ball slide too much rather than roll, or a swing that is very much in-to-out that would cause a push. Theoretically, the best strokes are either straight back along the intended line, and then through along the line, or back to the inside, straight through the ball, and then back to the inside.

ALIGNMENT

A great aid to stroking the ball correctly is to set up with a square stance. If your feet are square to the intended line, it's easier to visualize the correct swing path through the ball. Even if you prefer a closed or open stance, it's a good idea to at least set up with the shoulders square. With open or closed shoulders, it's all too easy to stroke from out-to-in or in-to-out.

DON'T MOVE THE HEAD OR BODY

The putting stroke is the ultimate precision stroke in golf. Thus, just about every great putter has made a point of keeping the body—with special emphasis on the legs and head—absolutely still during the stroke. Arnold Palmer's famous knock-kneed stance came about for this reason, as does the common advice to place slightly more weight on the left foot.

Gary Player even went so far one time as to suggest you feel as though your legs were set in concrete. Also, one of golf's oldest tips, "hit and hark" (listen for the sound of the ball rattling in the hole before you lift your head) comes from an effort to keep the head down, and therefore still.

Only two great putters have been noted for allowing the body to move—Bobby Jones, who permitted his knees to work much as in a full shot, though in miniature, and Bobby Locke, who learned how to play golf from a book authored by Jones. It's worth noting, however, that both Jones and Locke played in an era when greens were slower and long putts almost required a bit of help from the lower body.

NEVER DECELERATE

You'll see great putters stroking the ball with an even tempo back and through the ball, with backswings and follow-throughs of equal length. You'll see some others visibly accelerating through—often taking a shorter backswing than follow-through. However, you'll never see a great putter decelerate through, except when he's putting badly. Deceleration is fatal in the full swing, and it's equally fatal in putting. If you allow the putter to decelerate, you won't roll the ball well and invariably leave it short of the hole. Usually, deceleration comes from taking too long a backswing, then trying to compensate for it.

WRISTY OR WRISTLESS

Probably the biggest question that the golfer has to decide in putting is whether he will putt with a wristy style or an arm-and-shoulder (wristless) style. Both have proved successful on Tour, although arm-and-shoulder putters predominate today. This is chiefly due to the improvement in greens over the last twenty to thirty years.

Rough greens or greens with a great deal of grain, such as common Bermuda greens, almost force you to adopt a wristy style. However, on today's finely manicured greens, with bent grass predominating and the advent of dwarf Bermudas with finer leaves, the arm-and-shoulder style has taken over on the PGA Tour. Today, the wristy style is seen mostly on the PGA Senior Tour, because many of the older golfers grew up on rough or grainy greens and developed a wristy style. However, it's also worth noting that long putters—which encourage the wristless,

sweeping stroke—have gained in popularity as a result of their use by several senior tour players.

In the wristy style of putting, you take the club to the inside with just wrist action. Then you stroke the ball firmly, giving it a firm rap. There's little or no follow-through. A feature of many great wristy putters' styles is that they hood the blade by turning the wrists slightly counterclockwise as they take the club back. Hooding is thought to make it easier to release the putter through the ball, which in turn puts a better roll on the ball. Great wrist putters that hood the blade include Arnold Palmer, Gary Player, and Billy Casper.

In the arm-and-shoulder style of putting, there's no wrist action. As in chipping, you take the "Y" formed by the arms and club and swing it back and through in one piece, with the shoulders turning in sympathy with the arm and club movement. However, in the arm-and-shoulder style you can also experiment to see whether hooding the blade is effective. Bob Charles, often cited as one of the finest exponents of the arm-and-shoulder, hoods the blade. Other fine putters, like Ben Crenshaw, don't, simply taking the "Y" back and through.

On long putts, both the wristy and arm-and-shoulder styles must be modified. With a wristy stroke, you won't generate enough force to get the ball up to the hole, especially if the greens are slow. Then, you have to supplement the wrist action with some arm-and-shoulder action. Similarly, arm-and-shoulder putters often use a little wrist action on long putts. It gives you better feel and supplies the additional force you need.

ANTI-YIP STROKES

The first remedy for the yips was simply to hold on to the club tightly with the left hand. Then came "Diegeling," named after Leo Diegel, the 1928 and 1929 PGA champion, who fought the yips by forcing both elbows well away from his body while turning the hands very much outward—the ultimate "wristless" stroke. Other champions of the period tried such things as holding the club with only the right hand on short putts.

More recently, Sam Snead's "sidesaddle" style has attracted a lot of attention among yippers. From a stance facing the hole with his feet together, Snead plays the ball slightly forward of and to the right of his right foot. He holds the putter with the thumb of the left hand on top of the butt, with his right hand well below the left, the right arm extended. The stroke is made with the whole right arm swinging back and forth like a pendulum, the left hand and forearm rotating to act as a hinge. This removes the yipping muscles of the right hand and wrist from the stroke. However, the problem with this style for most golfers is that, lacking Snead's flexibility, it's uncomfortable for them to lean slightly to the right from the waist, as one must in this style. Some golfers also find it difficult to judge the strength necessary for long putts.

However, in the last few years, the putting style and special putter devised by Charlie Owens has become popular on the Senior PGA Tour. The putter is long (about fifty inches, depending on your height) and heavy (three-and-a-half pounds). You stand to the side of the ball as you would normally, but stand very erect. You anchor the top end of the putter in a hook formed by the left thumb and forefinger with the left forearm across the chest, holding very lightly with the other three fingers. The left hand is braced against the center of the chest, with the left forearm across the chest. The right arm, as in Snead's method, is extended and makes the swing so that, again, the yipping muscles of the right hand and wrist are taken out of the stroke. However, the method does not suffer from the disadvantages of the Snead method. Several Senior Tour players have had success with this method, and in 1991 Rocco Mediate became the first player on the regular PGA Tour to score a victory using the long putter.

GOLF STRATEGY

Golf is largely a mental game—a game played mostly between your ears. For example, you should never just walk up to the ball and hit away. Every shot you make while out on the course should have a purpose. When you step up to the tee or come up to your ball elsewhere on the course, try to visualize the way the shot should be played and where you want to place your ball. Keep in mind that some holes and shots can be played aggressively; others should be played more conservatively. Weigh the risks and consequences against conditions, the situation, and your normal playing ability, and then make the shot accordingly. Often the longest hit is not the best hit; always consider the next shot. If you do not have the

honor, carefully watch your partner and/or opponents shoot and see what happens to their shots. Consider especially the wind and terrain, and be aware of any hazards. Speaking of hazards, remember that they should always be approached with the positive-thinking psychology. That is, when you approach the shot with a sinking feeling in the pit of your stomach at the thought of an approaching obstacle, your ball always seems to be attracted to that hazard as if it had some sort of a strong magnet. To prevent this, concentrate on where you want to put the ball, not on where you do not want to hit it.

As you stand on the tee, remember that it is extremely important to control your drive position, because substantial error can affect all subsequent shots. In a fairway that is very narrow, for example, it often pays to tee the ball a little lower and not to swing too hard. This encourages you to stay down on the ball better and to hit through it. Also when hitting drives, employ the club in which you have the most confidence. There is a misconception among beginning players that they must use a driver from the tee. This is not true. Actually, if you are not hitting the No. 1 wood well, try the No. 3 wood. In this way, you will have a better chance to get the ball up into the air, and there is actually little difference in the resulting distance: about fifteen to thirty yards between the two clubs. Remember that it is going to take at least two shots to get on the green anyway, so why not play safe and get on in two? It is wise to play the percentages; it usually pays.

On short par-3 holes, it is a good idea to use a tee, even if you are using an iron, because the ball will come off it the same way every time. If you play it from the turf on the tee, you will not have as predictable a shot as you have from a tee.

In addition to planning each shot carefully, be sure that its alignment is proper. Before addressing the ball, stand behind it and study the situation carefully. This will give you a better overall perspective of the shot, a chance to formulate a plan and to draw an imaginary target line. Then, as you walk toward the ball, keep looking at your target. This will focus in your mind a clear mental picture of what you are going to attempt to do when you take your stroke. When you get to your ball, you will be able to take the proper stance and swing to carry out the desired plan for the shot. Actually, this deliberate lining-up procedure should be followed on all shots since it will aid greatly in carrying out your planned strategy.

Even when winter rules permit teeing up in the fairway, do not do it unless the lie is very bad. Play the ball where it lies, because when you tee the ball up this practice encourages a scooping action that is bad for your fairway game. If you are in the rough or must play out of trouble, play it safe and do not gamble recklessly. One stroke lost is not going to make too great a difference in your final score. So, if you are in trouble, play a safety shot into the fairway and try to salvage a par from there. Many times, an 80-shooter will end up with a score of over 90 because he gambled on shots where the odds were totally against him.

When you get close to the green, keep in mind the flagstick position. But, on longer approach shots, it is still safer and generally a more effective course of action to play to the center of the green rather than the pin. On short pitches and chips to a sloping green, it is usually better to be on the low side of the hole. Study putts carefully; then stroke decisively and give your ball a chance to drop in on a putt. Do not, however, be overbold; keep your putt moving, but dying, at the cup. Remember that three-putt greens should be avoided at all cost.

Most good golfers follow the old philosophy that it takes only one good shot a hole to get a par. An excellent drive to the green on a par-3 hole, for example, will place your ball on the green within two putts of par. A well-executed approach shot can make up for a poor drive. Sinking a long putt may erase the missed iron shot out on the fairway. So, if you do not become discouraged after a poor shot, but go after the next one to make up for it, you will often end with a par on the hole. But never become ruffled, stubborn, or angry. Although every player needs a little temper to keep him fired up, too many allow their tempers to get the better of them. The result, of course, is that they have trouble visualizing their shots and just swing harder and harder. For this reason, keep your temper under control. Remember that next to a good swing, a cool head, coupled with good judgment, is the most valuable asset in golf.

"Playing within yourself" means you must know your own game and its limitations. In golf, there is no point in fooling yourself. If you are not a professional, you are an amateur; if you are an amateur, you are probably an average golfer. And an average golfer simply cannot be expected to play scratch golf. If you can admit that fact to yourself, you are on the way to knowing your game and playing in character.

One good method to genuine improvement and knowing your game is to estimate your own par before you step on the first tee this weekend. Par, for instance, for the 18-handicapper is not 72; it is 90. Most courses have four short holes (par-3), four long holes (par-5), and ten other holes of varying lengths over which the scratch player's par is four. Therefore, the sensible amateur must figure the numbers printed on the card so that they come within his own abilities. For example, a long par-4 will be a par-5 for him, and if he gets a four he has, in effect, made a personal birdie. The same applies, of course, to those difficult par-3 holes. They become par-4s for the average golfer. Now, using a little arithmetic on this imaginary game, you should reach the following conclusion. If you take fours at all the short holes, fives at all the long holes, and fives again on all the par-4s, your total will be 86. That's playing 14-handicap golf, and 14-handicap golf is a good deal better than average.

Be sure to select the club which will allow you to stay well within your swing's capabilities. Many players do not do this because they overrate their strength. This means they must swing too hard to get the full distance. It would be better to take one more club (for example, the No. 4 iron instead of No. 5 iron) to make the shot. By not swinging as hard, you will make more solid contact and, of course, have greater accuracy. Remember that it is better to sacrifice distance for accuracy. You will generally score better.

You must, of course, overclub with care, and there are cases where it is even unwise. For example, if there is an out-of-bounds, a water hazard, a big sand trap, or woods beyond a green, do not overclub. Here, it would be better to take the club that, if hit perfectly, will put you on the green. Should you take more club, in this instance, and hit the shot perfectly, you would be in deep trouble. On the other hand, if there is a big trap in front of the green and no trouble behind it, the opposite strategy would usually hold true. In this case, you should take ample club and, if you mishit the shot slightly, you will still reach the green or be hole-high. Even if you hit the shot perfectly and go over the green, you won't be in so much trouble as if you were short of the green. In other words, select the club that puts you in the best position for your next shot and that will keep you out of worse trouble.

There are certain shots for which location of the

green will determine the amount of club to employ. For instance, when hitting from an elevated position to the green, use one club less than normal, whereas when hitting to elevated greens, take one more club. But, in normal situations, it is best to use ample club for your shot.

Always make the easiest possible shot. Do not try to show off and impress your partner or opponents. For example, do not take short cuts on doglegs. It does not pay except in extraordinary situations. It is always wise to play the hole as it is designed, and you will have a better angle from which to play your next shot. Although it may sound very elementary, play the shot the easiest possible way, and you will enjoy your round of golf a great deal more.

As you can see, attacking a golf course for the lowest possible score demands more than strength, timing, and a repeating golf swing. You must (1) know your own game, (2) know your limitations, (3) play within them, and (4) think! And you must never forget that the name of the game is "Keep the ball in play."

PRACTICE STRATEGY

The importance of a short practice session before a game of golf cannot be emphasized too strongly. Athletes in all other sports warm up before they start actual competition. Lack of warm-up is one reason why a golfer will find himself playing better on the back nine than on the opening nine. He actually spends the first nine holes warming up, although he is probably unaware of it. He loses valuable strokes, and he runs the danger of compounding his first simple mistakes into larger errors as the game progresses.

Arrive on the practice driving range about forty-five minutes before your golf game. Do not take friends or acquaintances along, because even their most well-meaning suggestions and comments are a distraction. Assume the attitude that you are about to give yourself a brief private review lesson in basic golf techniques. As you proceed through the warm-up, check yourself for a smooth swing; proper stance, balance, grip, and hand-and-arm action; straight drives, accurate putting, and sharp timing. It is important to remember that the warm-up is only a conditioner. It is not the occasion to experiment with new ideas, or an opportunity to practice difficult shots, or a chance to try blasting your way out of

a sand trap. Your chief concern is to perfect the basic shots. You can spend time on these more difficult problems in your practice sessions during the week. Some courses have practice driving ranges; others do not. If your course does not have one, the best thing to do is stop off at one en route to the course.

In putting, begin one foot away from the cup. It is very important to practice short putts; but unfortunately, golfers do not seem to practice them often enough. Remember: the most important putts are the short ones. When you are sinking the one-footers regularly, try putting from two feet out; then three, four, five, and so on. Continue this procedure until you are scoring from about twenty feet away and you are confident that you are putting accurately.

Follow your practice putts with brief exercises. For example: (1) Hold a club straight out in your left hand and raise it up and down several times. (2) Take several hard swings with two woods at the same time. (3) Place a wood behind your back and wrap your arms around the shaft. Twist your trunk from left to right; loosen up your waist, your knees, your arms, and your back. To conclude the practice, take the club which feels the most comfortable (maybe the No. 5 iron or No. 4 wood) and hit a few lusty shots with it. This will give you an added feeling of confidence in your ability and serve to brighten your mental outlook for the coming game.

Warming up may sound like a hard routine. Actually, it normally should take you less than a half-hour to complete the entire practice. This will enable you to relax for about fifteen minutes prior to the match.

HOW TO TAKE A LESSON

Much has been written about the art of teaching golf; however, the importance of the art of taking a lesson has been generally overlooked. While it does not require any physical skill, you must use a modicum of common sense.

First and foremost, be honest with your golf professional and tell him exactly what you are trying to accomplish. Do you want a complete picture of the golf swing, or do you just want to play for the exercise? Are you willing to practice, or don't you have the time? Is this lesson to be one of a series, or a one-shot deal? Having your objectives clear at the start and making them known to the instructor can save both of you a lot of grief. But being honest with the pro doesn't stop there. Reveal any physical handicaps you may have, however minor, that could affect the way you swing.

Another problem with many of the players is that they are not good listeners. Their one idea is to belt as many balls as they can in the allotted time. Remember, it is impossible to get your money's worth if you insist on hitting while the instructor is explaining something. Only by listening will you be able to absorb it. Also remember that listening to your golf professional entails carrying out what he is telling you—even if it does not feel comfortable for a time. When you do anything new, it is bound to feel strange at first. It means listening to *him*, not listening to well-meaning, but mostly uninformed, advice from your golf buddies.

A good listener also has patience. Do not expect miracles in five minutes or worry unduly just because you cannot hit each shot perfectly. Do not be impatient when your pro tells you he liked the swing, even when you missed! What he means is that you are that much nearer to really swinging the club. So keep at it, and, with hard work and patience, you will be surprised how good you can become.

Never be afraid to ask your pro a question. After all, that is what he is there for. This applies to any point he is making, not just golf language. If he knows you do not understand, he can usually find another way of putting it which will be clear to you.

Many people are too anxious when they go for a lesson. They tighten up and can hardly hit a shot. Remember that fear and the golf swing do not mix. Confidence, on the other hand, is one of the best tonics for a golf swing.

So next time you take a lesson:

1. Be honest with your pro and state your objectives.
2. Listen to him—and only him—and do what he tells you.
3. Be patient; the golf swing, like Rome, is not built in a day.
4. Be confident. Remember: fear will make a paralyzed rabbit out of anyone!
5. Ask your pro questions; he will not bite!

The Rules of Golf

1992
Rules of
Golf

And The Rules of Amateur Status

USGA

INCLUDES QUADRENNIAL REVISION TO THE RULES

**THE
RULES
OF
GOLF**

as approved by
THE UNITED STATES GOLF ASSOCIATION®
and
**THE ROYAL AND ANCIENT GOLF CLUB
OF ST. ANDREWS, SCOTLAND**

Effective January 1, 1992

PRINTED IN THE UNITED STATES OF AMERICA

CHANGES SINCE 1991

DEFINITIONS

Casual Water and Loose Impediments
Expanded to state that frost is neither casual water nor a loose impediment.

Equipment
Expanded to state more clearly the status of a cart shared by two or more players.

Line of Play
A Definition has been added to state that the "line of play" is the direction which the player wishes his ball to take after a stroke, plus a reasonable distance on either side of the intended direction. The line of play extends vertically upwards from the ground, but does not extend beyond the hole.

Line of Putt
A Definition has been added to state that the "line of putt" is the line which the player wishes his ball to take after a stroke on the putting green. Except with respect to Rule 16-1e, the line of putt includes a reasonable distance on either side of the intended line. The line of putt does not extend beyond the hole.

RULES

4-2. Clubs; Playing Characteristics Changed
Amended to state that the playing characteristics of a club shall not be purposely changed by adjustment or by any other means.

4-4. Maximum of Fourteen Clubs
Amended to prohibit the addition or replacement of a club by borrowing any club selected for play by any other person playing on the course.

5-3. Ball Unfit for Play
Amended to clarify procedure in determining if a ball is unfit for play and the penalty for failing to comply with this procedure.

8. Advice; Indicating Line of Play
The Note was amended permitting a team captain or coach to give advice to members of a team in a team competition whether or not there is a concurrent individual competition.

9-2. Information as to Strokes Taken; Match Play
Expanded to state that a player does not have to inform his opponent that he has incurred a penalty if he is obviously proceeding under a Rule involving a penalty and this has been observed by his opponent.

11-5. Playing from Wrong Teeing Ground
New Rule 11-5 has been added to cover a ball played from a wrong teeing ground. The provisions of Rule 11-4 will apply.

12-2. Identifying Ball
Amended to clarify procedure for a player in identifying his ball and the penalty for failing to comply with this procedure.

13-2. Improving Lie, Area of Intended Swing or Line of Play
Expanded to prohibit improving a reasonable extension of the line of play beyond the hole.

13-4. Ball Lying in or Touching Hazard
Former Exceptions 1 and 2 have been deleted and replaced with new Exception 1 and a Note. New Exception 1 states there is no penalty if a player touches ground in any hazard or water in a water hazard as a result of or to prevent falling, in removing an obstruction, in measuring or in retrieving or lifting a ball under any Rule or if he places his clubs in a hazard, provided nothing is done which constitutes testing the condition of the

hazard or improves the lie of the ball. The Note permits the player to touch with a club or otherwise any obstruction, any construction declared by the Committee to be an integral part of the course or any grass, bush, tree or other growing thing at any time, including at address or in the backward movement for the stroke.

16-1c. The Putting Green; Repair of Hole Plugs, Ball Marks and Other Damage
Expanded to prohibit the repair of damage to the putting green, other than old hole plugs or ball marks, which might assist the player in his subsequent play of the hole.

16-1g. The Putting Green; Playing Stroke While Another Ball in Motion
Amended to state that a player incurs no penalty for playing a stroke while another ball is in motion after a stroke from the putting green provided that it was his turn to play.

20-2b. Dropping and Re-Dropping; Where to Drop
Amended to provide that when a ball is to be dropped, it must be dropped as near as possible to a specific spot which shall be estimated if it is not precisely known.

A second paragraph has been added stating that a ball when dropped must first strike a part of the course where the applicable Rule requires it to be dropped. Corresponding changes have been made in Rule 20-2a, Rule 20-2c(vi) and the penultimate paragraph of Rule 20-2c.

23-1. Loose Impediments; Relief
Amended to prohibit the removal of a loose impediment which might influence the movement of a ball while the ball is in motion.

24-1. Movable Obstruction
Amended to prohibit the removal of a movable obstruction which might influence the movement of a ball

while the ball is in motion, other than an attended flagstick or equipment of the players.

24-2c. Immovable Obstruction; Ball Lost
Added to provide relief for a ball lost in an immovable obstruction. Previously a ball lost in an immovable obstruction was a lost ball and the provisions of Rule 27-1 applied.

25-1a. Casual Water, Ground Under Repair and Certain Damage to Course; Interference
Amended to state that a player is entitled to relief from casual water, ground under repair or a hole, cast or runway made by a burrowing animal, a reptile or a bird only when such a condition is on the course and interferes with the player's stance or the area of his intended swing.

26-2a. Ball Played Within Water Hazard; Ball Comes to Rest in Hazard
Amended to allow a player who drops a ball in the hazard under Rule 26-1a, to elect not to play the ball and either (a) proceed under Rule 26-1b, adding the additional penalty of one stroke prescribed by that Rule; or (b) proceed under Rule 26-1c, if applicable, adding the additional penalty of one stroke prescribed by that Rule; or (c) add an additional penalty of one stroke and play a ball as nearly as possible at the spot from which the last stroke from outside the hazard was played.

26-2b. Ball Played Within Water Hazard; Ball Lost or Unplayable Outside Hazard or Out of Bounds
An additional Note has been added stating that when proceeding under this Rule, the player is not required to drop a ball under Rule 27-1 or 28a. If he does drop a ball, he is not required to play it and he may alternatively proceed under Clause (ii) or (iii) of this Rule.

28. Ball Unplayable
Amended to clarify that if the unplayable ball lies in a bunker, the player may proceed under Clause a, b, or c.

32. Bogey, Par and Stableford Competitions
Expanded to state that four under the fixed score has a value of six points.

33-7. Disqualification Penalty; Committee Discretion
Expanded to state that any penalty less than disqualification shall not be waived or modified.

34-1b. Claims and Penalties; Stroke Play
Expanded to state that competitors who agree to waive the Rules (Rule 1-3) shall be disqualified even after the competition has closed.

APPENDIX I
LOCAL RULES

Preamble
Expanded to state that additional information regarding acceptable and prohibited Local Rules is provided in the *Decisions on the Rules of Golf* under Rule 33-8.

Lifting an Embedded Ball
An Exception has been added to the Local Rule prohibiting relief for a ball embedded in its own pitch-mark in the ground if (a) it is clearly unreasonable for the player to play a stroke because of interference by any other condition or (b) interference would occur only through use of an unnecessarily abnormal stance, swing or direction of play.

Protection of Young Trees
Added to provide text for a Local Rule when a Committee desires to prevent damage to young trees.

APPENDIX II

4-1a. Design of Clubs; General
Added to address adjustability in the design of clubs.

7

4-1c(v). Design of Clubs; Grip
Added to state that the cross-sectional dimension of a grip shall not exceed 1.75 inches (45mm).

4-1c(vi). Design of Clubs; Grip
Added to clarify that a putter may have more than one grip, provided each is circular in cross-section. A Note has also been added permitting the use of putters, which were approved for use or marketed prior to January 1, 1992 which are in breach of this Clause, until December 31, 1992.

4-1e. Club Face; Impact Area Markings
Amended heading to indicate that this section deals specifically with "Impact Area Markings." The former heading was just "Markings."

4-1e. Club Face; Putter Face Markings
Added to clearly indicate that the specifications in **4-1e. Club Face; Impact Area Markings and Decorative Markings** do not apply to putters.

APPENDIX III

c. Spherical Symmetry
Amended to reflect a change in determining whether a ball performs as if it were generally spherically symmetrical.

SUPPORT THE USGA MEMBERS PROGRAM

For information about supporting the USGA through its Members Program, call 1-800-223-0041. From New Jersey call 1-908-234-2300.

8

CONTENTS

9   10

11

THE RULES OF GOLF

Section I
ETIQUETTE

Courtesy on the Course

Safety

Prior to playing a stroke or making a practice swing, the player should ensure that no one is standing close by or in a position to be hit by the club, the ball or any stones, pebbles, twigs or the like which may be moved by the stroke or swing.

Consideration for Other Players

The player who has the honor should be allowed to play before his opponent or fellow-competitor tees his ball.

No one should move, talk or stand close to or directly behind the ball or the hole when a player is addressing the ball or making a stroke.

In the interest of all, players should play without delay.

No player should play until the players in front are out of range.

Players searching for a ball should signal the players behind them to pass as soon as it becomes apparent that the ball will not easily be found. They should not search for five minutes before doing so. They should not continue play until the players following them have passed and are out of range.

When the play of a hole has been completed, players should immediately leave the putting green.

Priority on the Course

In the absence of special rules, two-ball matches should have precedence over and be entitled to pass any three- or four-ball match, which should invite them through.

A single player has no standing and should give way to a match of any kind.

12

Etiquette

Any match playing a whole round is entitled to pass a match playing a shorter round.

If a match fails to keep its place on the course and loses more than one clear hole on the players in front, it should invite the match following to pass.

Care of the Course

Holes in Bunkers

Before leaving a bunker, a player should carefully fill up and smooth over all holes and footprints made by him.

Replace Divots; Repair Ball-Marks and Damage by Spikes

Through the green, a player should ensure that any turf cut or displaced by him is replaced at once and pressed down and that any damage to the putting green made by a ball is carefully repaired. Damage to the putting green caused by golf shoe spikes should be repaired *on completion of the hole*.

Damage to Greens — Flagsticks, Bags, etc.

Players should ensure that, when putting down bags or the flagstick, no damage is done to the putting green and that neither they nor their caddies damage the hole by standing close to it, in handling the flagstick or in removing the ball from the hole. The flagstick should be properly replaced in the hole before the players leave the putting green. Players should not damage the putting green by leaning on their putters, particularly when removing the ball from the hole.

Golf Carts

Local notices regulating the movement of golf carts should be strictly observed.

Damage Through Practice Swings

In taking practice swings, players should avoid causing damage to the course, particularly the tees, by removing divots.

13

Defs.

Section II
DEFINITIONS

Addressing the Ball

A player has "addressed the ball" when he has taken his <u>stance</u> and has also grounded his club, except that in a <u>hazard</u> a player has addressed the ball when he has taken his stance.

Advice

"Advice" is any counsel or suggestion which could influence a player in determining his play, the choice of a club or the method of making a <u>stroke</u>.

Information on the Rules or on matters of public information, such as the position of hazards or the flagstick on the putting green, is not advice.

Ball Deemed to Move

See "Move or Moved."

Ball Holed

See "Holed."

Ball Lost

See "Lost Ball."

Ball in Play

A ball is "in play" as soon as the player has made a <u>stroke</u> on the <u>teeing ground</u>. It remains in play until holed out, except when it is <u>lost</u>, <u>out of bounds</u> or lifted, or another ball has been substituted under an applicable Rule, whether or not such Rule permits substitution; a ball so substituted becomes the ball in play.

Bunker

A "bunker" is a <u>hazard</u> consisting of a prepared area of ground, often a hollow, from which turf or soil has been removed and replaced with sand or the like. Grass-covered ground bordering or within a bunker is not part

14

of the bunker. The margin of a bunker extends vertically downwards, but not upwards.

Caddie

A "caddie" is one who carries or handles a player's clubs during play and otherwise assists him in accordance with the Rules.

When one caddie is employed by more than one player, he is always deemed to be the caddie of the player whose ball is involved, and equipment carried by him is deemed to be that player's equipment, except when the caddie acts upon specific directions of another player, in which case he is considered to be that other player's caddie.

Casual Water

"Casual water" is any temporary accumulation of water on the course which is visible before or after the player takes his stance and is not in a water hazard. Snow and natural ice, other than frost, are either casual water or loose impediments, at the option of the player. Manufactured ice is an obstruction. Dew and frost are not casual water.

Committee

The "Committee" is the committee in charge of the competition or, if the matter does not arise in a competition, the committee in charge of the course.

Competitor

A "competitor" is a player in a stroke competition. A "fellow-competitor" is any person with whom the competitor plays. Neither is partner of the other.

In stroke play foursome and four-ball competitions, where the context so admits, the word "competitor" or "fellow-competitor" includes his partner.

Course

The "course" is the whole area within which play is permitted. See Rule 33-2.

15

Equipment

"Equipment" is anything used, worn or carried by or for the player except any ball he has played at the hole being played and any small object, such as a coin or a tee, when used to mark the position of a ball or the extent of an area in which a ball is to be dropped. Equipment includes a golf cart, whether or not motorized. If such a cart is shared by two or more players, the cart and everything in it are deemed to be the equipment of the player whose ball is involved except that, when the cart is being moved by one of the players sharing it, the cart and everything in it are deemed to be that player's equipment.

Note: A ball played at the hole being played is equipment when it has been lifted and not put back into play.

Fellow-Competitor

See "Competitor."

Flagstick

The "flagstick" is a movable straight indicator, with or without bunting or other material attached, centered in the hole to show its position. It shall be circular in cross-section.

Forecaddie

A "forecaddie" is one who is employed by the Committee to indicate to players the position of balls during play. He is an outside agency.

Ground Under Repair

"Ground under repair" is any portion of the course so marked by order of the Committee or so declared by its authorized representative. It includes material piled for removal and a hole made by a greenkeeper, even if not so marked. Stakes and lines defining ground under repair are in such ground. The margin of ground under repair extends vertically downwards, but not upwards.

16

Note 1: Grass cuttings and other material left on the course which have been abandoned and are not intended to be removed are not ground under repair unless so marked.

Note 2: The Committee may make a Local Rule prohibiting play from ground under repair.

Hazards

A "hazard" is any bunker or water hazard.

Hole

The "hole" shall be 4¼ inches (108mm) in diameter and at least 4 inches (100mm) deep. If a lining is used, it shall be sunk at least 1 inch (25mm) below the putting green surface unless the nature of the soil makes it impracticable to do so; its outer diameter shall not exceed 4¼ inches (108mm).

Holed

A ball is "holed" when it is at rest within the circumference of the hole and all of it is below the level of the lip of the hole.

Honor

The side entitled to play first from the teeing ground is said to have the "honor."

Lateral Water Hazard

A "lateral water hazard" is a water hazard or that part of a water hazard so situated that it is not possible or is deemed by the Committee to be impracticable to drop a ball behind the water hazard in accordance with Rule 26-1b.

That part of a water hazard to be played as a lateral water hazard should be distinctively marked.

Note: Lateral water hazards should be defined by red stakes or lines.

17

Line of Play

The "line of play" is the direction which the player wishes his ball to take after a stroke, plus a reasonable distance on either side of the intended direction. The line of play extends vertically upwards from the ground, but does not extend beyond the hole.

Line of Putt

The "line of putt" is the line which the player wishes his ball to take after a stroke on the putting green. Except with respect to Rule 16-1e, the line of putt includes a reasonable distance on either side of the intended line. The line of putt does not extend beyond the hole.

Loose Impediments

"Loose impediments" are natural objects such as stones, leaves, twigs, branches and the like, dung, worms and insects and casts or heaps made by them, provided they are not fixed or growing, are not solidly embedded and do not adhere to the ball.

Sand and loose soil are loose impediments on the putting green, but not elsewhere.

Snow and natural ice, other than frost, are either casual water or loose impediments, at the option of the player. Manufactured ice is an obstruction.

Dew and frost are not loose impediments.

Lost Ball

A ball is "lost" if:

a. It is not found or identified as his by the player within five minutes after the player's side or his or their caddies have begun to search for it; or

b. The player has put another ball into play under the Rules, even though he may not have searched for the original ball; or

c. The player has played any stroke with a provisional ball from the place where the original ball is likely to be or from a point nearer the hole than that place,

18

Defs.

whereupon the provisional ball becomes the ball in play.

Time spent in playing a wrong ball is not counted in the five-minute period allowed for search.

Marker

A "marker" is one who is appointed by the Committee to record a competitor's score in stroke play. He may be a fellow-competitor. He is not a referee.

Matches

See "Sides and Matches."

Move or Moved

A ball is deemed to have "moved" if it leaves its position and comes to rest in any other place.

Observer

An "observer" is one who is appointed by the Committee to assist a referee to decide questions of fact and to report to him any breach of a Rule. An observer should not attend the flagstick, stand at or mark the position of the hole, or lift the ball or mark its position.

Obstructions

An "obstruction" is anything artificial, including the artificial surfaces and sides of roads and paths and manufactured ice, except:

    a. Objects defining out of bounds, such as walls, fences, stakes and railings;

    b. Any part of an immovable artificial object which is out of bounds; and

    c. Any construction declared by the Committee to be an integral part of the course.

Out of Bounds

"Out of bounds" is ground on which play is prohibited.

When out of bounds is defined by reference to stakes or a fence or as being beyond stakes or a fence, the out of bounds line is determined by the nearest inside points

19

Defs.

of the stakes or fence posts at ground level excluding angled supports.

When out of bounds is defined by a line on the ground, the line itself is out of bounds.

The out of bounds line extends vertically upwards and downwards.

A ball is out of bounds when all of it lies out of bounds.

A player may stand out of bounds to play a ball lying within bounds.

Outside Agency

An "outside agency" is any agency not part of the match or, in stroke play, not part of the competitor's side, and includes a referee, a marker, an observer or a fore-caddie. Neither wind nor water is an outside agency.

Partner

A "partner" is a player associated with another player on the same side.

In a threesome, foursome, best-ball or four-ball match, where the context so admits, the word "player" includes his partner or partners.

Penalty Stroke

A "penalty stroke" is one added to the score of a player or side under certain Rules. In a threesome or foursome, penalty strokes do not affect the order of play.

Provisional Ball

A "provisional ball" is a ball played under Rule 27-2 for a ball which may be lost outside a water hazard or may be out of bounds.

Putting Green

The "putting green" is all ground of the hole being played which is specially prepared for putting or otherwise defined as such by the Committee. A ball is on the putting green when any part of it touches the putting green.

20

Defs.

Referee

A "referee" is one who is appointed by the Committee to accompany players to decide questions of fact and apply the Rules of Golf. He shall act on any breach of a Rule which he observes or is reported to him.

A referee should not attend the flagstick, stand at or mark the position of the hole, or lift the ball or mark its position.

Rub of the Green

A "rub of the green" occurs when a ball in motion is accidentally deflected or stopped by any outside agency (see Rule 19-1).

Rule

The term "Rule" includes Local Rules made by the Committee under Rule 33-8a.

Sides and Matches

Side: A player, or two or more players who are partners.

Single: A match in which one plays against another.

Threesome: A match in which one plays against two, and each side plays one ball.

Foursome: A match in which two play against two, and each side plays one ball.

Three-Ball: A match play competition in which three play against one another, each playing his own ball. Each player is playing two distinct matches.

Best-Ball: A match in which one plays against the better ball of two or the best ball of three players.

Four-Ball: A match in which two play their better ball against the better ball of two other players.

Stance

Taking the "stance" consists in a player placing his feet in position for and preparatory to making a stroke.

Stipulated Round

The "stipulated round" consists of playing the holes of the course in their correct sequence unless otherwise

21

Defs.

authorized by the Committee. The number of holes in a stipulated round is 18 unless a smaller number is authorized by the Committee. As to extension of stipulated round in match play, see Rule 2-3.

Stroke

A "stroke" is the forward movement of the club made with the intention of fairly striking at and moving the ball, but if a player checks his downswing voluntarily before the clubhead reaches the ball he is deemed not to have made a stroke.

Teeing Ground

The "teeing ground" is the starting place for the hole to be played. It is a rectangular area two club-lengths in depth, the front and the sides of which are defined by the outside limits of two tee-markers. A ball is outside the teeing ground when all of it lies outside the teeing ground.

Through the Green

"Through the green" is the whole area of the course except:

    a. The teeing ground and putting green of the hole being played; and

    b. All hazards on the course.

Water Hazard

A "water hazard" is any sea, lake, pond, river, ditch, surface drainage ditch or other open water course (whether or not containing water) and anything of a similar nature.

All ground or water within the margin of a water hazard is part of the water hazard. The margin of a water hazard extends vertically upwards and downwards. Stakes and lines defining the margins of water hazards are in the hazards.

Note: Water hazards (other than lateral water hazards) should be defined by yellow stakes or lines.

22

R. 1

Wrong Ball

A "wrong ball" is any ball other than:
 a. The ball in play,
 b. A provisional ball or
 c. In stroke play, a second ball played under Rule 3-3 or Rule 20-7b.

Note: Ball in play includes a ball substituted for the ball in play when the player is proceeding under an applicable Rule which does not permit substitution.

Section III
THE RULES OF PLAY

THE GAME
Rule 1. The Game

1-1. General

The Game of Golf consists in playing a ball from the teeing ground into the hole by a stroke or successive strokes in accordance with the Rules.

1-2. Exerting Influence on Ball

No player or caddie shall take any action to influence the position or the movement of a ball except in accordance with the Rules.

PENALTY FOR BREACH OF RULE 1-2:
Match play — Loss of hole; Stroke play — Two strokes.

Note: In the case of a serious breach of Rule 1-2, the Committee may impose a penalty of disqualification.

1-3. Agreement to Waive Rules

Players shall not agree to exclude the operation of any Rule or to waive any penalty incurred.

23

R. 2

PENALTY FOR BREACH OF RULE 1-3:
Match play — Disqualification of both sides; Stroke play — Disqualification of competitors concerned.

(Agreeing to play out of turn in stroke play — see Rule 10-2c.)

1-4. Points Not Covered by Rules

If any point in dispute is not covered by the Rules, the decision shall be made in accordance with equity.

Rule 2. Match Play

2-1. Winner of Hole; Reckoning of Holes

In match play the game is played by holes.

Except as otherwise provided in the Rules, a hole is won by the side which holes its ball in the fewer strokes. In a handicap match the lower net score wins the hole.

The reckoning of holes is kept by the terms: so many "holes up" or "all square," and so many "to play."

A side is "dormie" when it is as many holes up as there are holes remaining to be played.

2-2. Halved Hole

A hole is halved if each side holes out in the same number of strokes.

When a player has holed out and his opponent has been left with a stroke for the half, if the player thereafter incurs a penalty, the hole is halved.

2-3. Winner of Match

A match (which consists of a stipulated round, unless otherwise decreed by the Committee) is won by the side which is leading by a number of holes greater than the number of holes remaining to be played.

The Committee may, for the purpose of settling a tie, extend the stipulated round to as many holes as are required for a match to be won.

24

R. 3

2-4. Concession of Next Stroke, Hole or Match

When the opponent's ball is at rest or is deemed to be at rest under Rule 16-2, the player may concede the opponent to have holed out with his next stroke and the ball may be removed by either side with a club or otherwise.

A player may concede a hole or a match at any time prior to the conclusion of the hole or the match.

Concession of a stroke, hole or match may not be declined or withdrawn.

2-5. Claims

In match play, if a doubt or dispute arises between the players and no duly authorized representative of the Committee is available within a reasonable time, the players shall continue the match without delay. Any claim, if it is to be considered by the Committee, must be made before any player in the match plays from the next teeing ground or, in the case of the last hole of the match, before all players in the match leave the putting green.

No later claim shall be considered unless it is based on facts previously unknown to the player making the claim and the player making the claim had been given wrong information (Rules 6-2a and 9) by an opponent. In any case, no later claim shall be considered after the result of the match has been officially announced, unless the Committee is satisfied that the opponent knew he was giving wrong information.

2-6. General Penalty

The penalty for a breach of a Rule in match play is loss of hole except when otherwise provided.

Rule 3. Stroke Play

3-1. Winner

The competitor who plays the stipulated round or rounds in the fewest strokes is the winner.

25

R. 3

3-2. Failure to Hole Out

If a competitor fails to hole out at any hole and does not correct his mistake before he plays a stroke from the next teeing ground or, in the case of the last hole of the round, before he leaves the putting green, *he shall be disqualified.*

3-3. Doubt as to Procedure

a. PROCEDURE

In stroke play only, when during play of a hole a competitor is doubtful of his rights or procedure, he may, without penalty, play a second ball. After the situation which caused the doubt has arisen, the competitor should, before taking further action, announce to his marker or a fellow-competitor his decision to invoke this Rule and the ball with which he will score if the Rules permit.

The competitor shall report the facts to the Committee before returning his score card unless he scores the same with both balls; if he fails to do so, *he shall be disqualified.*

b. DETERMINATION OF SCORE FOR HOLE

If the Rules allow the procedure selected in advance by the competitor, the score with the ball selected shall be his score for the hole.

If the competitor fails to announce in advance his decision to invoke this Rule or his selection, the score with the original ball or, if the original ball is not one of the balls being played, the first ball put into play shall count if the Rules allow the procedure adopted for such ball.

Note: A second ball played under Rule 3-3 is not a provisional ball under Rule 27-2.

3-4. Refusal to Comply with a Rule

If a competitor refuses to comply with a Rule affecting the rights of another competitor, *he shall be disqualified.*

3-5. General Penalty

The penalty for a breach of a Rule in stroke play is two strokes except when otherwise provided.

26

CLUBS AND THE BALL

The United States Golf Association and the Royal and Ancient Golf Club of St. Andrews reserve the right to change the Rules and make and change the interpretations relating to clubs, balls and other implements at any time.

Rule 4. Clubs

If there may be any reasonable basis for doubt as to whether a club which is to be manufactured conforms with Rule 4 and Appendix II, the manufacturer should submit a sample to the United States Golf Association for a ruling, such sample to become its property for reference purposes. If a manufacturer fails to do so, he assumes the risk of a ruling that the club does not conform with the Rules of Golf.

A player in doubt as to the conformity of a club should consult the United States Golf Association.

4-1. Form and Make of Clubs

A club is an implement designed to be used for striking the ball.

A putter is a club designed primarily for use on the putting green.

The player's clubs shall conform with the provisions of this Rule and with the specifications and interpretations set forth in Appendix II.

a. GENERAL

The club shall be composed of a shaft and a head. All parts of the club shall be fixed so that the club is one unit. The club shall not be designed to be adjustable except for weight. The club shall not be substantially different from the traditional and customary form and make.

(See also Appendix II.)

b. SHAFT

The shaft shall be generally straight, with the same bending and twisting properties in any direction, and

27

shall be attached to the clubhead at the heel either directly or through a single plain neck or socket. A putter shaft may be attached to any point in the head.

c. GRIP

The grip consists of that part of the shaft designed to be held by the player and any material added to it for the purpose of obtaining a firm hold. The grip shall be substantially straight and plain in form and shall not be molded for any part of the hands.

d. CLUBHEAD

The distance from the heel to the toe of the clubhead shall be greater than the distance from the face to the back. The clubhead shall be generally plain in shape.

The clubhead shall have only one face designed for striking the ball, except that a putter may have two such faces if their characteristics are the same, they are opposite each other and the loft of each is the same and does not exceed 10 degrees.

e. CLUB FACE

The face shall not have any degree of concavity and, in relation to the ball, shall be hard and rigid. It shall be generally smooth except for such markings as are permitted by Appendix II.

f. WEAR

A club which conforms with Rule 4-1 when new is deemed to conform after wear through normal use. Any part of a club which has been purposely altered is regarded as new and must conform, in the altered state, with the Rules.

g. DAMAGE

If a player's club ceases to conform with Rule 4-1 because of damage sustained in the normal course of play, the player may:

28

(i) use the club in its damaged state, but only for the remainder of the stipulated round during which such damage was sustained; or

(ii) without unduly delaying play, repair it.

A club which ceases to conform because of damage sustained other than in the normal course of play shall not subsequently be used during the round.

(Damage changing playing characteristics of club — see Rule 4-2.)

(Damage rendering club unfit for play — see Rule 4-4a.)

4-2. Playing Characteristics Changed

During a stipulated round, the playing characteristics of a club shall not be purposely changed by adjustment or by any other means.

If the playing characteristics of a player's club are changed during a round because of damage sustained in the normal course of play, the player may:

(i) use the club in its altered state; or

(ii) without unduly delaying play, repair it.

If the playing characteristics of a player's club are changed because of damage sustained other than in the normal course of play, the club shall not subsequently be used during the round.

Damage to a club which occurred prior to a round may be repaired during the round, provided the playing characteristics are not changed and play is not unduly delayed.

4-3. Foreign Material

No foreign material shall be applied to the club face for the purpose of influencing the movement of the ball.

PENALTY FOR BREACH OF RULE 4-1, -2 or -3:
Disqualification.

29

4-4. Maximum of Fourteen Clubs

a. SELECTION AND REPLACEMENT OF CLUBS

The player shall start a stipulated round with not more than fourteen clubs. He is limited to the clubs thus selected for that round except that, without unduly delaying play, he may:

(i) if he started with fewer than fourteen, add as many as will bring his total to that number; and

(ii) replace, with any club, a club which becomes unfit for play in the normal course of play.

The addition or replacement of a club or clubs may not be made by borrowing any club selected for play by any other person playing on the course.

b. PARTNERS MAY SHARE CLUBS

Partners may share clubs, provided that the total number of clubs carried by the partners so sharing does not exceed fourteen.

PENALTY FOR BREACH OF RULE 4-4a or b,
REGARDLESS OF NUMBER OF EXCESS CLUBS CARRIED:

Match play — At the conclusion of the hole at which the breach is discovered, the state of the match shall be adjusted by deducting one hole for each hole at which a breach occurred. Maximum deduction per round: two holes.

Stroke play — Two strokes for each hole at which any breach occurred; maximum penalty per round: four strokes.

Bogey and par competitions — Penalties as in match play.

Stableford competitions — See Note to Rule 32-1b.

c. EXCESS CLUB DECLARED OUT OF PLAY

Any club carried or used in breach of this Rule shall be declared out of play by the player immediately upon

30

R. 5

discovery that a breach has occurred and thereafter shall not be used by the player during the round.

PENALTY FOR BREACH OF RULE 4-4c: *Disqualification.*

Rule 5. The Ball

5-1. General

The ball the player uses shall conform to specifications set forth in Appendix III on maximum weight, minimum size, spherical symmetry, initial velocity and overall distance when tested under specified conditions.

5-2. Foreign Material

No foreign material shall be applied to a ball for the purpose of changing its playing characteristics.

PENALTY FOR BREACH OF RULE 5-1 or 5-2: *Disqualification.*

5-3. Ball Unfit for Play

A ball is unfit for play if it is visibly cut, cracked or out of shape. A ball is not unfit for play solely because mud or other materials adhere to it, its surface is scratched or scraped or its paint is damaged or discolored.

If a player has reason to believe his ball has become unfit for play during the play of the hole being played, he may during the play of such hole lift his ball without penalty to determine whether it is unfit.

Before lifting the ball, the player must announce his intention to his opponent in match play or his marker or a fellow-competitor in stroke play and mark the position of the ball. He may then lift and examine the ball without cleaning it and must give his opponent, marker or fellow-competitor an opportunity to examine the ball.

If he fails to comply with this procedure, *he shall incur a penalty of one stroke.*

If it is determined that the ball has become unfit for play during play of the hole being played, the player may

31

R. 6

substitute another ball, placing it on the spot where the original ball lay. Otherwise, the original ball shall be replaced.

If a ball breaks into pieces as a result of a stroke, the stroke shall be cancelled and the player shall play a ball without penalty as nearly as possible at the spot from which the original ball was played (see Rule 20-5).

*PENALTY FOR BREACH OF RULE 5-3:
Match play — Loss of hole; Stroke play — Two strokes.

**If a player incurs the general penalty for breach of Rule 5-3, no additional penalty under the Rule shall be applied.*

Note: If the opponent, marker or fellow-competitor wishes to dispute a claim of unfitness, he must do so before the player plays another ball.

(Cleaning ball lifted from putting green or under any other Rule — see Rule 21.)

PLAYER'S RESPONSIBILITIES
Rule 6. The Player

Definition

A "marker" is one who is appointed by the Committee to record a competitor's score in stroke play. He may be a fellow-competitor. He is not a referee.

6-1. Conditions of Competition

The player is responsible for knowing the conditions under which the competition is to be played (Rule 33-1).

6-2. Handicap

a. MATCH PLAY

Before starting a match in a handicap competition, the players should determine from one another their respective handicaps. If a player begins the match having declared a higher handicap which would affect the number

32

R. 6

of strokes given or received, *he shall be disqualified*; otherwise, the player shall play off the declared handicap.

b. STROKE PLAY

In any round of a handicap competition, the competitor shall ensure that his handicap is recorded on his score card before it is returned to the Committee. If no handicap is recorded on his score card before it is returned, or if the recorded handicap is higher than that to which he is entitled and this affects the number of strokes received, *he shall be disqualified* from that round of the handicap competition; otherwise, the score shall stand.

Note: It is the player's responsibility to know the holes at which handicap strokes are to be given or received.

6-3. Time of Starting and Groups

a. TIME OF STARTING

The player shall start at the time laid down by the Committee.

b. GROUPS

In stroke play, the competitor shall remain throughout the round in the group arranged by the Committee unless the Committee authorizes or ratifies a change.

PENALTY FOR BREACH OF RULE 6-3: *Disqualification.*

(Best-ball and four-ball play — see Rules 30-3a and 31-2.)

Note: The Committee may provide in the conditions of a competition (Rule 33-1) that, if the player arrives at his starting point, ready to play, within five minutes after his starting time, in the absence of circumstances which warrant waiving the penalty of disqualification as provided in Rule 33-7, the penalty for failure to start on time is *loss of the first hole in match play or two strokes at the first hole in stroke play* instead of disqualification.

6-4. Caddie

The player may have only one caddie at any one time, *under penalty of disqualification.*

33

R. 6

For any breach of a Rule by his caddie, the player incurs the applicable penalty.

6-5. Ball

The responsibility for playing the proper ball rests with the player. Each player should put an identification mark on his ball.

6-6. Scoring in Stroke Play

a. RECORDING SCORES

After each hole the marker should check the score with the competitor and record it. On completion of the round the marker shall sign the card and hand it to the competitor. If more than one marker records the scores, each shall sign for the part for which he is responsible.

b. SIGNING AND RETURNING CARD

After completion of the round, the competitor should check his score for each hole and settle any doubtful points with the Committee. He shall ensure that the marker has signed the card, countersign the card himself and return it to the Committee as soon as possible.

PENALTY FOR BREACH OF RULE 6-6b: *Disqualification.*

c. ALTERATION OF CARD

No alteration may be made on a card after the competitor has returned it to the Committee.

d. WRONG SCORE FOR HOLE

The competitor is responsible for the correctness of the score recorded for each hole. If he returns a score for any hole lower than actually taken, *he shall be disqualified.* If he returns a score for any hole higher than actually taken, the score as returned shall stand.

Note 1: The Committee is responsible for the addition of scores and application of the handicap recorded on the card — see Rule 33-5.

Note 2: In four-ball stroke play, see also Rule 31-4 and -7a.

34

R. 6

6-7. Undue Delay

The player shall play without undue delay. Between completion of a hole and playing from the next teeing ground, the player shall not unduly delay play.

PENALTY FOR BREACH OF RULE 6-7:
Match play — Loss of hole; Stroke play — Two strokes. For repeated offense — Disqualification.
If the player unduly delays play between holes, he is delaying the play of the next hole and the penalty applies to that hole.

6-8. Discontinuance of Play

a. WHEN PERMITTED
The player shall not discontinue play unless:
  (i) the Committee has suspended play;
  (ii) he believes there is danger from lightning;
  (iii) he is seeking a decision from the Committee on a doubtful or disputed point (see Rules 2-5 and 34-3); or
  (iv) there is some other good reason such as sudden illness.
Bad weather is not of itself a good reason for discontinuing play.
If the player discontinues play without specific permission from the Committee, he shall report to the Committee as soon as practicable. If he does so and the Committee considers his reason satisfactory, the player incurs no penalty. Otherwise, *the player shall be disqualified.*
Exception in match play: Players discontinuing match play by agreement are not subject to disqualification unless by so doing the competition is delayed.

Note: Leaving the course does not of itself constitute discontinuance of play.

b. PROCEDURE WHEN PLAY SUSPENDED BY COMMITTEE
When play is suspended by the Committee, if the players in a match or group are between the play of two holes, they shall not resume play until the Committee has

35

R. 7

ordered a resumption of play. If they are in the process of playing a hole, they may continue provided they do so without delay. If they choose to continue, they shall discontinue either before or immediately after completing the hole, and shall not thereafter resume play until the Committee has ordered a resumption of play.
When play has been suspended by the Committee, the player shall resume play when the Committee has ordered a resumption of play.

PENALTY FOR BREACH OF RULE 6-8b: *Disqualification.*

c. LIFTING BALL WHEN PLAY DISCONTINUED
When during the play of a hole a player discontinues play under Rule 6-8a, he may lift his ball. A ball may be cleaned when so lifted. If a ball has been so lifted, the player shall, when play is resumed, place a ball on the spot from which the original ball was lifted.

PENALTY FOR BREACH OF RULE 6-8c:
Match play — Loss of hole; Stroke play — Two strokes.

Rule 7. Practice

7-1. Before or Between Rounds

a. MATCH PLAY
On any day of a match play competition, a player may practice on the competition course before a round.

b. STROKE PLAY
On any day of a stroke competition or play-off, a competitor shall not practice on the competition course or test the surface of any putting green on the course before a round or play-off. When two or more rounds of a stroke competition are to be played over consecutive days, practice between those rounds on any competition course remaining to be played is prohibited.

36

R. 7

Exception: Practice putting or chipping on or near the first teeing ground before starting a round or play-off is permitted.

PENALTY FOR BREACH OF RULE 7-1b: *Disqualification.*

Note: The Committee may in the conditions of a competition (Rule 33-1) prohibit practice on the competition course on any day of a match play competition or permit practice on the competition course or part of the course (Rule 33-2c) on any day of or between rounds of a stroke competition.

7-2. During Round

A player shall not play a practice stroke either during the play of a hole or between the play of two holes except that, between the play of two holes, the player may practice putting or chipping on or near the putting green of the hole last played, any practice putting green or the teeing ground of the next hole to be played in the round, provided such practice stroke is not played from a hazard and does not unduly delay play (Rule 6-7).

Exception: When play has been suspended by the Committee, a player may, prior to resumption of play, practice (a) as provided in this Rule, (b) anywhere other than on the competition course and (c) as otherwise permitted by the Committee.

PENALTY FOR BREACH OF RULE 7-2:
Match play — Loss of hole; Stroke play — Two strokes. In the event of a breach between the play of two holes, the penalty applies to the next hole.

Note 1: A practice swing is not a practice stroke and may be taken at any place, provided the player does not breach the Rules.

Note 2: The Committee may prohibit practice on or near the putting green of the hole last played.

37

R. 8

Rule 8. Advice; Indicating Line of Play

Definitions

"Advice" is any counsel or suggestion which could influence a player in determining his play, the choice of a club or the method of making a stroke.
Information on the Rules or on matters of public information, such as the position of hazards or the flagstick on the putting green, is not advice.
The "line of play" is the direction which the player wishes his ball to take after a stroke, plus a reasonable distance on either side of the intended direction. The line of play extends vertically upwards from the ground, but does not extend beyond the hole.

8-1. Advice

A player shall not give advice to anyone in the competition except his partner. A player may ask for advice from only his partner or either of their caddies.

8-2. Indicating Line of Play

a. OTHER THAN ON PUTTING GREEN
Except on the putting green, a player may have the line of play indicated to him by anyone, but no one shall stand on or close to the line while the stroke is being played. Any mark placed during the play of a hole by the player or with his knowledge to indicate the line shall be removed before the stroke is played.

Exception: Flagstick attended or held up — see Rule 17-1.

b. ON THE PUTTING GREEN
When the player's ball is on the putting green, the player, his partner or either of their caddies may, before but not during the stroke, point out a line for putting, but in so doing the putting green shall not be touched. No mark shall be placed anywhere to indicate a line for putting.

38

R. 9

PENALTY FOR BREACH OF RULE:
Match play — Loss of hole; Stroke play — Two strokes.

Note: In a team competition with or without concurrent individual competition, the Committee may in the conditions of the competition (Rule 33-1) permit each team to appoint one person, *e.g.*, team captain or coach, who may give <u>advice</u> (including pointing out a line for putting) to members of that team. Such person shall be identified to the Committee prior to the start of the competition.

Rule 9. Information as to Strokes Taken

9-1. General

The number of strokes a player has taken shall include any penalty strokes incurred.

9-2. Match Play

A player who has incurred a penalty shall inform his opponent as soon as practicable, unless he is obviously proceeding under a Rule involving a penalty and this has been observed by his opponent. If he fails so to inform his opponent, he shall be deemed to have given wrong information, even if he was not aware that he had incurred a penalty.

An opponent is entitled to ascertain from the player, during the play of a hole, the number of strokes he has taken and, after play of a hole, the number of strokes taken on the hole just completed.

If during the play of a hole the player gives or is deemed to give wrong information as to the number of strokes taken, he shall incur no penalty if he corrects the mistake before his opponent has played his next stroke. If the player fails so to correct the wrong information, *he shall lose the hole.*

If after play of a hole the player gives or is deemed to give wrong information as to the number of strokes taken

39

R. 10

on the hole just completed and this affects the opponent's understanding of the result of the hole, he shall incur no penalty if he corrects his mistake before any player plays from the next <u>teeing ground</u> or, in the case of the last hole of the match, before all players leave the <u>putting green</u>. If the player fails so to correct the wrong information, *he shall lose the hole.*

9-3. Stroke Play

A competitor who has incurred a penalty should inform his marker as soon as practicable.

ORDER OF PLAY
Rule 10. Order of Play

10-1. Match Play

a. TEEING GROUND

The side entitled to play first from the <u>teeing ground</u> is said to have the "honor."

The side which shall have the honor at the first teeing ground shall be determined by the order of the draw. In the absence of a draw, the honor should be decided by lot.

The side which wins a hole shall take the honor at the next teeing ground. If a hole has been halved, the side which had the honor at the previous teeing ground shall retain it.

b. OTHER THAN ON TEEING GROUND

When the balls are in play, the ball farther from the hole shall be played first. If the balls are equidistant from the hole, the ball to be played first should be decided by lot.

Exception: Rule 30-3c (best-ball and four-ball match play).

40

R. 10

c. PLAYING OUT OF TURN

If a player plays when his opponent should have played, the opponent may immediately require the player to cancel the stroke so played and, in correct order, play a ball without penalty as nearly as possible at the spot from which the original ball was last played (see Rule 20-5).

10-2. Stroke Play

a. TEEING GROUND

The competitor entitled to play first from the <u>teeing ground</u> is said to have the "honor."

The competitor who shall have the honor at the first teeing ground shall be determined by the order of the draw. In the absence of a draw, the honor should be decided by lot.

The competitor with the lowest score at a hole shall take the honor at the next teeing ground. The competitor with the second lowest score shall play next and so on. If two or more competitors have the same score at a hole, they shall play from the next teeing ground in the same order as at the previous teeing ground.

b. OTHER THAN ON TEEING GROUND

When the balls are in play, the ball farthest from the hole shall be played first. If two or more balls are equidistant from the hole, the ball to be played first should be decided by lot.

Exceptions: Rules 22 (ball interfering with or assisting play) and 31-5 (four-ball stroke play).

c. PLAYING OUT OF TURN

If a competitor plays out of turn, no penalty is incurred and the ball shall be played as it lies. If, however, the Committee determines that competitors have agreed to play in an order other than that set forth in Clauses 2a and 2b of this Rule to give one of them an advantage, *they shall be disqualified.*

41

R. 11

(Incorrect order of play in threesomes and foursomes stroke play — see Rule 29-3.)

10-3. Provisional Ball or Second Ball from Teeing Ground

If a player plays a <u>provisional ball</u> or a second ball from a <u>teeing ground</u>, he should do so after his opponent or fellow-competitor has played his first <u>stroke</u>. If a player plays a provisional ball or a second ball out of turn, Clauses 1c and 2c of this Rule shall apply.

10-4. Ball Moved in Measuring

If a ball is moved in measuring to determine which ball is farther from the hole, no penalty is incurred and the ball shall be replaced.

TEEING GROUND
Rule 11. Teeing Ground

Definition

The "teeing ground" is the starting place for the hole to be played. It is a rectangular area two club-lengths in depth, the front and the sides of which are defined by the outside limits of two tee-markers. A ball is outside the teeing ground when all of it lies outside the teeing ground.

11-1. Teeing

In teeing, the ball may be placed on the ground, on an irregularity of surface created by the player on the ground or on a tee, sand or other substance in order to raise it off the ground.

A player may stand outside the <u>teeing ground</u> to play a ball within it.

11-2. Tee-Markers

Before a player plays his first stroke with any ball from the teeing ground of the hole being played, the tee-

42

markers are deemed to be fixed. In such circumstances, if the player moves or allows to be moved a tee-marker for the purpose of avoiding interference with his stance, the area of his intended swing or his line of play, *he shall incur the penalty for a breach of Rule 13-2.*

11-3. Ball Falling Off Tee

If a ball, when not in play, falls off a tee or is knocked off a tee by the player in addressing it, it may be re-teed without penalty, but if a stroke is made at the ball in these circumstances, whether the ball is moving or not, the stroke counts but no penalty is incurred.

11-4. Playing from Outside Teeing Ground

a. MATCH PLAY

If a player, when starting a hole, plays a ball from outside the teeing ground, the opponent may immediately require the player to cancel the stroke so played and play a ball from within the teeing ground, without penalty.

b. STROKE PLAY

If a competitor, when starting a hole, plays a ball from outside the teeing ground, *he shall incur a penalty of two strokes* and shall then play a ball from within the teeing ground.

If the competitor plays a stroke from the next teeing ground without first correcting his mistake or, in the case of the last hole of the round, leaves the putting green without first declaring his intention to correct his mistake, *he shall be disqualified.*

Strokes played by a competitor from outside the teeing ground do not count in his score.

11-5. Playing from Wrong Teeing Ground

The provisions of Rule 11-4 apply.

43

PLAYING THE BALL

Rule 12. Searching for and Identifying Ball

Definitions

A "hazard" is any bunker or water hazard.

A "bunker" is a hazard consisting of a prepared area of ground, often a hollow, from which turf or soil has been removed and replaced with sand or the like. Grass-covered ground bordering or within a bunker is not part of the bunker. The margin of a bunker extends vertically downwards, but not upwards.

A "water hazard" is any sea, lake, pond, river, ditch, surface drainage ditch or other open water course (whether or not containing water) and anything of a similar nature.

All ground or water within the margin of a water hazard is part of the water hazard. The margin of a water hazard extends vertically upwards and downwards. Stakes and lines defining the margins of water hazards are in the hazards.

12-1. Searching for Ball; Seeing Ball

In searching for his ball anywhere on the course, the player may touch or bend long grass, rushes, bushes, whins, heather or the like, but only to the extent necessary to find and identify it, provided that this does not improve the lie of the ball, the area of his intended swing or his line of play.

A player is not necessarily entitled to see his ball when playing a stroke.

In a hazard, if a ball is covered by loose impediments or sand, the player may remove by probing, raking or other means as much thereof as will enable him to see a part of the ball. If an excess is removed, no penalty is incurred and the ball shall be re-covered so that only a part of the ball is visible. If the ball is moved in such removal, no penalty is incurred; the ball shall be replaced

44

and, if necessary, re-covered. As to removal of loose impediments outside a hazard, see Rule 23.

If a ball lying in casual water, ground under repair or a hole, cast or runway made by a burrowing animal, a reptile or a bird is accidentally moved during search, no penalty is incurred; the ball shall be replaced, unless the player elects to proceed under Rule 25-1b.

If a ball is believed to be lying in water in a water hazard, the player may probe for it with a club or otherwise. If the ball is moved in so doing, no penalty is incurred; the ball shall be replaced, unless the player elects to proceed under Rule 26-1.

PENALTY FOR BREACH OF RULE 12-1:
Match play — Loss of hole; Stroke play — Two strokes.

12-2. Identifying Ball

The responsibility for playing the proper ball rests with the player. Each player should put an identification mark on his ball.

Except in a hazard, the player may, without penalty, lift a ball he believes to be his own for the purpose of identification and clean it to the extent necessary for identification. If the ball is the player's ball, he shall replace it. Before lifting the ball, the player must announce his intention to his opponent in match play or his marker or a fellow-competitor in stroke play and mark the position of the ball. He must then give his opponent, marker or fellow-competitor an opportunity to observe the lifting and replacement. If he lifts his ball without announcing his intention in advance, marking the position of the ball or giving his opponent, marker or fellow-competitor an opportunity to observe, or if he lifts his ball for identification in a hazard, or cleans it more than necessary for identification, *he shall incur a penalty of one stroke* and the ball shall be replaced.

45

If a player who is required to replace a ball fails to do so, *he shall incur the penalty* for a breach of Rule 20-3a, but no additional penalty under Rule 12-2 shall be applied.

Rule 13. Ball Played as It Lies; Lie, Area of Intended Swing and Line of Play; Stance

Definitions

A "hazard" is any bunker or water hazard.

A "bunker" is a hazard consisting of a prepared area of ground, often a hollow, from which turf or soil has been removed and replaced with sand or the like. Grass-covered ground bordering or within a bunker is not part of the bunker. The margin of a bunker extends vertically downwards, but not upwards.

A "water hazard" is any sea, lake, pond, river, ditch, surface drainage ditch or other open water course (whether or not containing water) and anything of a similar nature.

All ground or water within the margin of a water hazard is part of the water hazard. The margin of a water hazard extends vertically upwards and downwards. Stakes and lines defining the margins of water hazards are in the hazards.

The "line of play" is the direction which the player wishes his ball to take after a stroke, plus a reasonable distance on either side of the intended direction. The line of play extends vertically upwards from the ground, but does not extend beyond the hole.

13-1. Ball Played as It Lies

The ball shall be played as it lies, except as otherwise provided in the Rules.

(Ball at rest moved — see Rule 18.)

13-2. Improving Lie, Area of Intended Swing or Line of Play

Except as provided in the Rules, a player shall not improve or allow to be improved:

46

R. 13

the position or lie of his ball,
the area of his intended swing,
his <u>line of play</u> or
a reasonable extension of that line beyond the hole or
the area in which he is to drop or place a ball
by any of the following actions:
> moving, bending or breaking anything growing or
> fixed (including immovable <u>obstructions</u> and objects
> defining <u>out of bounds</u>) or
> removing or pressing down sand, loose soil, replaced
> divots, other cut turf placed in position or other
> irregularities of surface
except as follows:
> as may occur in fairly taking his <u>stance</u>,
> in making a <u>stroke</u> or the backward movement of his
> club for a stroke,
> on the <u>teeing ground</u> in creating or eliminating
> irregularities of surface, or
> on the <u>putting green</u> in removing sand and loose soil
> as provided in Rule 16-1a or in repairing damage as
> provided in Rule 16-1c.

The club may be grounded only lightly and shall not
be pressed on the ground.

Exception: Ball lying in or touching hazard — see Rule
13-4.

13-3. Building Stance
A player is entitled to place his feet firmly in taking
his stance, but he shall not build a stance.

13-4. Ball Lying in or Touching Hazard
Except as provided in the Rules, before making a <u>stroke</u>
at a ball which lies in or touches a <u>hazard</u> (whether a
<u>bunker</u> or a <u>water hazard</u>), the player shall not:
> a. Test the condition of the hazard or any similar
> hazard,
> b. Touch the ground in the hazard or water in the
> water hazard with a club or otherwise, or

47

R. 14

> c. Touch or move a <u>loose impediment</u> lying in or
> touching the hazard.

Exceptions:

1. Provided nothing is done which constitutes testing
the condition of the hazard or improves the lie of the ball,
there is no penalty if the player (a) touches the ground
in any hazard or water in a water hazard as a result of
or to prevent falling, in removing an <u>obstruction</u>, in
measuring or in retrieving or lifting a ball under any Rule
or (b) places his clubs in a hazard.

2. The player after playing the stroke, or his <u>caddie</u> at
any time without the authority of the player, may smooth
sand or soil in the hazard, provided that, if the ball still
lies in the hazard, nothing is done which improves the
lie of the ball or assists the player in his subsequent play
of the hole.

Note: At any time, including at address or in the
backward movement for the stroke, the player may touch
with a club or otherwise any obstruction, any construction declared by the Committee to be an integral part
of the course or any grass, bush, tree or other growing
thing.

PENALTY FOR BREACH OF RULE:
Match play — Loss of hole; Stroke play — Two strokes.

(Searching for ball — see Rule 12-1.)

Rule 14. Striking the Ball

Definition
A "stroke" is the forward movement of the club made
with the intention of fairly striking at and moving the ball,
but if a player checks his downswing voluntarily before
the clubhead reaches the ball he is deemed not to have
made a stroke.

48

R. 14

14-1. Ball to Be Fairly Struck At
The ball shall be fairly struck at with the head of the
club and must not be pushed, scraped or spooned.

14-2. Assistance
In making a <u>stroke</u>, a player shall not accept physical
assistance or protection from the elements.

PENALTY FOR BREACH OF RULE 14-1 OR -2:
Match play — Loss of hole; Stroke play — Two strokes.

14-3. Artificial Devices and Unusual Equipment
*If there may be any reasonable basis for doubt as to
whether an item which is to be manufactured would, if
used by a player during a round, cause the player to be
in breach of Rule 14-3, the manufacturer should submit
a sample to the United States Golf Association for a ruling, such sample to become its property for reference
purposes. If a manufacturer fails to do so, he assumes the
risk of an unfavorable ruling.*

*A player in doubt as to whether use of an item would
constitute a breach of Rule 14-3 should consult the United
States Golf Association.*

Except as provided in the Rules, during a <u>stipulated</u>
<u>round</u> the player shall not use any artificial device or
unusual equipment:
> a. Which might assist him in making a stroke or in
> his play; or
> b. For the purpose of gauging or measuring distance
> or conditions which might affect his play; or
> c. Which might assist him in gripping the club, except
> that plain gloves may be worn, resin, tape or gauze may
> be applied to the grip (provided such application does
> not render the grip non-conforming under Rule 4-1c)
> and a towel or handkerchief may be wrapped around
> the grip.

PENALTY FOR BREACH OF RULE 14-3: *Disqualification.*

49

R. 15

14-4. Striking the Ball More than Once
If a player's club strikes the ball more than once in the
course of a <u>stroke</u>, the player shall count the stroke and
add a penalty stroke, making two strokes in all.

14-5. Playing Moving Ball
A player shall not play while his ball is moving.

Exceptions:
> Ball falling off tee — Rule 11-3.
> Striking the ball more than once — Rule 14-4.
> Ball moving in water — Rule 14-6.

When the ball begins to move only after the player has
begun the <u>stroke</u> or the backward movement of his club
for the stroke, he shall incur no penalty under this Rule
for playing a moving ball, but he is not exempt from any
penalty incurred under the following Rules:
> Ball at rest moved by player — Rule 18-2a.
> Ball at rest moving after address — Rule 18-2b.
> Ball at rest moving after loose impediment touched —
> Rule 18-2c.

14-6. Ball Moving in Water
When a ball is moving in water in a <u>water hazard</u>, the
player may, without penalty, make a <u>stroke</u>, but he must
not delay making his stroke in order to allow the wind
or current to improve the position of the ball. A ball
moving in water in a water hazard may be lifted if the
player elects to invoke Rule 26.

PENALTY FOR BREACH OF RULE 14-5 OR -6:
Match play — Loss of hole; Stroke play — Two strokes.

Rule 15. Playing a Wrong Ball
Definition
A "wrong ball" is any ball other than:
> a. The <u>ball in play</u>,
> b. A <u>provisional ball</u> or

50

c. In stroke play, a second ball played under Rule 3-3 or Rule 20-7b.

Note: Ball in play includes a ball substituted for the ball in play when the player is proceeding under an applicable Rule which does not permit substitution.

15-1. General

A player must hole out with the ball played from the teeing ground unless a Rule permits him to substitute another ball. If a player substitutes another ball when proceeding under an applicable Rule which does not permit substitution, that ball is not a wrong ball; it becomes the ball in play and, if the error is not corrected as provided in Rule 20-6, *the player shall incur a penalty of loss of hole in match play or two strokes in stroke play.*

15-2. Match Play

If a player plays a stroke with a wrong ball except in a hazard, *he shall lose the hole.*

If a player plays any strokes in a hazard with a wrong ball, there is no penalty. Strokes played in a hazard with a wrong ball do not count in the player's score. If the wrong ball belongs to another player, its owner shall place a ball on the spot from which the wrong ball was first played.

If the player and opponent exchange balls during the play of a hole, the first to play the wrong ball other than from a hazard shall lose the hole; when this cannot be determined, the hole shall be played out with the balls exchanged.

15-3. Stroke Play

If a competitor plays a stroke or strokes with a wrong ball, *he shall incur a penalty of two strokes,* unless the only stroke or strokes played with such ball were played when it was lying in a hazard, in which case no penalty is incurred.

51

The competitor must correct his mistake by playing the correct ball. If he fails to correct his mistake before he plays a stroke from the next teeing ground or, in the case of the last hole of the round, fails to declare his intention to correct his mistake before leaving the putting green, *he shall be disqualified.*

Strokes played by a competitor with a wrong ball do not count in his score.

If the wrong ball belongs to another competitor, its owner shall place a ball on the spot from which the wrong ball was first played.

(Lie of ball to be placed or replaced altered — see Rule 20-3b.)

THE PUTTING GREEN

Rule 16. The Putting Green

Definitions

The "putting green" is all ground of the hole being played which is specially prepared for putting or otherwise defined as such by the Committee. A ball is on the putting green when any part of it touches the putting green.

The "line of putt" is the line which the player wishes his ball to take after a stroke on the putting green. Except with respect to Rule 16-1e, the line of putt includes a reasonable distance on either side of the intended line. The line of putt does not extend beyond the hole.

A ball is "holed" when it is at rest within the circumference of the hole and all of it is below the level of the lip of the hole.

16-1. General

a. TOUCHING LINE OF PUTT

The line of putt must not be touched except:

52

(i) the player may move sand and loose soil on the putting green and other loose impediments by picking them up or by brushing them aside with his hand or a club without pressing anything down;

(ii) in addressing the ball, the player may place the club in front of the ball without pressing anything down;

(iii) in measuring — Rule 10-4;

(iv) in lifting the ball — Rule 16-1b;

(v) in pressing down a ball-marker;

(vi) in repairing old hole plugs or ball marks on the putting green — Rule 16-1c; and

(vii) in removing movable obstructions — Rule 24-1.

(Indicating line for putting on putting green — see Rule 8-2b.)

b. LIFTING BALL

A ball on the putting green may be lifted and, if desired, cleaned. A ball so lifted shall be replaced on the spot from which it was lifted.

c. REPAIR OF HOLE PLUGS, BALL MARKS
AND OTHER DAMAGE

The player may repair an old hole plug or damage to the putting green caused by the impact of a ball, whether or not the player's ball lies on the putting green. If the ball is moved in the process of such repair, it shall be replaced, without penalty. Any other damage to the putting green shall not be repaired if it might assist the player in his subsequent play of the hole.

d. TESTING SURFACE

During the play of a hole, a player shall not test the surface of the putting green by rolling a ball or roughening or scraping the surface.

e. STANDING ASTRIDE OR ON LINE OF PUTT

The player shall not make a stroke on the putting green from a stance astride, or with either foot touching, the line of putt or an extension of that line behind the ball.

53

f. POSITION OF CADDIE OR PARTNER

While making a stroke on the putting green, the player shall not allow his caddie, his partner or his partner's caddie to position himself on or close to an extension of the line of putt behind the ball.

g. PLAYING STROKE WHILE ANOTHER BALL IN MOTION

The player shall not play a stroke while another ball is in motion after a stroke from the putting green, except that, if a player does so, he incurs no penalty if it was his turn to play.

(Lifting ball interfering with or assisting play while another ball in motion — see Rule 22.)

PENALTY FOR BREACH OF RULE 16-1:
Match play — Loss of hole; Stroke play — Two strokes.

16-2. Ball Overhanging Hole

When any part of the ball overhangs the lip of the hole, the player is allowed enough time to reach the hole without unreasonable delay and an additional ten seconds to determine whether the ball is at rest. If by then the ball has not fallen into the hole, it is deemed to be at rest. If the ball subsequently falls into the hole, the player is deemed to have holed out with his last stroke, and *he shall add a penalty stroke to his score* for the hole; otherwise there is no penalty under this Rule.

(Undue delay — see Rule 6-7.)

Rule 17. The Flagstick

17-1. Flagstick Attended, Removed or Held Up

Before and during the stroke, the player may have the flagstick attended, removed or held up to indicate the position of the hole. This may be done only on the authority of the player before he plays his stroke.

54

R. 17

If, prior to the stroke, the flagstick is attended, removed or held up by anyone with the player's knowledge and no objection is made, the player shall be deemed to have authorized it. If anyone attends or holds up the flagstick or stands near the hole while a stroke is being played, he shall be deemed to be attending the flagstick until the ball comes to rest.

17-2. Unauthorized Attendance

a. MATCH PLAY

In match play, an opponent or his caddie shall not, without the authority or prior knowledge of the player, attend, remove or hold up the flagstick while the player is making a stroke or his ball is in motion.

b. STROKE PLAY

In stroke play, if a fellow-competitor or his caddie attends, removes or holds up the flagstick without the competitor's authority or prior knowledge while the competitor is making a stroke or his ball is in motion, *the fellow-competitor shall incur the penalty* for breach of this Rule. In such circumstances, if the competitor's ball strikes the flagstick, the person attending it or anything carried by him, the competitor incurs no penalty and the ball shall be played as it lies, except that, if the stroke was played from the putting green, the stroke shall be cancelled, the ball replaced and the stroke replayed.

PENALTY FOR BREACH OF RULE 17-1 or -2:
Match play — Loss of hole; Stroke play — Two strokes.

17-3. Ball Striking Flagstick or Attendant

The player's ball shall not strike:

a. The flagstick when attended, removed or held up by the player, his partner or either of their caddies, or by another person with the player's authority or prior knowledge; or

55

R. 18

b. The player's caddie, his partner or his partner's caddie when attending the flagstick, or another person attending the flagstick with the player's authority or prior knowledge or anything carried by any such person; or

c. The flagstick in the hole, unattended, when the ball has been played from the putting green.

PENALTY FOR BREACH OF RULE 17-3:
Match play — Loss of hole; Stroke play — Two strokes, and the ball shall be played as it lies.

17-4. Ball Resting Against Flagstick

If the ball rests against the flagstick when it is in the hole, the player or another person authorized by him may move or remove the flagstick and if the ball falls into the hole, the player shall be deemed to have holed out with his last stroke; otherwise, the ball, if moved, shall be placed on the lip of the hole, without penalty.

BALL MOVED, DEFLECTED OR STOPPED
Rule 18. Ball at Rest Moved

Definitions

A ball is deemed to have "moved" if it leaves its position and comes to rest in any other place.

An "outside agency" is any agency not part of the match or, in stroke play, not part of the competitor's side, and includes a referee, a marker, an observer or a fore-caddie. Neither wind nor water is an outside agency.

"Equipment" is anything used, worn or carried by or for the player except any ball he has played at the hole being played and any small object, such as a coin or a tee, when used to mark the position of a ball or the extent of an area in which a ball is to be dropped. Equipment includes a golf cart, whether or not motorized. If such a cart is shared by two or more players, the cart and

56

R. 18

everything in it are deemed to be the equipment of the player whose ball is involved except that, when the cart is being moved by one of the players sharing it, the cart and everything in it are deemed to be that player's equipment.

Note: A ball played at the hole being played is equipment when it has been lifted and not put back into play.

A player has "addressed the ball" when he has taken his stance and has also grounded his club, except that in a hazard a player has addressed the ball when he has taken his stance.

Taking the "stance" consists in a player placing his feet in position for and preparatory to making a stroke.

18-1. By Outside Agency

If a ball at rest is moved by an outside agency, the player shall incur no penalty and the ball shall be replaced before the player plays another stroke.

(Player's ball at rest moved by another ball — see Rule 18-5.)

18-2. By Player, Partner, Caddie or Equipment

a. GENERAL

When a player's ball is in play, if:

(i) the player, his partner or either of their caddies lifts or moves it, touches it purposely (except with a club in the act of addressing it) or causes it to move except as permitted by a Rule, or

(ii) equipment of the player or his partner causes the ball to move,

the player shall incur a penalty stroke. The ball shall be replaced unless the movement of the ball occurs after the player has begun his swing and he does not discontinue his swing.

Under the Rules no penalty is incurred if a player accidentally causes his ball to move in the following circumstances:

57

R. 18

In measuring to determine which ball farther from hole — Rule 10-4

In searching for covered ball in hazard or for ball in casual water, ground under repair, etc. — Rule 12-1

In the process of repairing hole plug or ball mark — Rule 16-1c

In the process of removing loose impediment on putting green — Rule 18-2c

In the process of lifting ball under a Rule — Rule 20-1

In the process of placing or replacing ball under a Rule — Rule 20-3a

In complying with Rule 22 relating to lifting ball interfering with or assisting play

In removal of movable obstruction — Rule 24-1.

b. BALL MOVING AFTER ADDRESS

If a player's ball in play moves after he has addressed it (other than as a result of a stroke), the player shall be deemed to have moved the ball and *shall incur a penalty stroke.* The player shall replace the ball unless the movement of the ball occurs after he has begun his swing and he does not discontinue his swing.

c. BALL MOVING AFTER LOOSE IMPEDIMENT TOUCHED

Through the green, if the ball moves after any loose impediment lying within a club-length of it has been touched by the player, his partner or either of their caddies and before the player has addressed it, the player shall be deemed to have moved the ball and *shall incur a penalty stroke.* The player shall replace the ball unless the movement of the ball occurs after he has begun his swing and he does not discontinue his swing.

On the putting green, if the ball or the ball-marker moves in the process of removing any loose impediment, the ball or the ball-marker shall be replaced. There is no penalty provided the movement of the ball or the ball-marker is directly attributable to the removal of the loose

58

R. 18

impediment. Otherwise, *the player shall incur a penalty stroke* under Rule 18-2a or 20-1.

18-3. By Opponent, Caddie or Equipment in Match Play

a. DURING SEARCH

If, during search for a player's ball, it is moved by an opponent, his caddie or his equipment, no penalty is incurred and the player shall replace the ball.

b. OTHER THAN DURING SEARCH

If, other than during search for a ball, the ball is touched or moved by an opponent, his caddie or his equipment, except as otherwise provided in the Rules, *the opponent shall incur a penalty stroke.* The player shall replace the ball.

(Ball moved in measuring to determine which ball farther from the hole — see Rule 10-4.)

(Playing a wrong ball — see Rule 15-2.)

(Ball moved in complying with Rule 22 relating to lifting ball interfering with or assisting play.)

18-4. By Fellow-Competitor, Caddie or Equipment in Stroke Play

If a competitor's ball is moved by a fellow-competitor, his caddie or his equipment, no penalty is incurred. The competitor shall replace his ball.

(Playing a wrong ball — see Rule 15-3.)

18-5. By Another Ball

If a ball in play and at rest is moved by another ball in motion after a stroke, the moved ball shall be replaced.

PENALTY FOR BREACH OF RULE:
Match play — Loss of hole; Stroke play — Two strokes.
If a player who is required to replace a ball fails to do so, he shall incur the general penalty for breach of Rule 18 but no additional penalty under Rule 18 shall be applied.

59

R. 19

Note 1: If a ball to be replaced under this Rule is not immediately recoverable, another ball may be substituted.

Note 2: If it is impossible to determine the spot on which a ball is to be placed, see Rule 20-3c.

Rule 19. Ball in Motion Deflected or Stopped

Definitions

An "outside agency" is any agency not part of the match or, in stroke play, not part of the competitor's side, and includes a referee, a marker, an observer or a fore-caddie. Neither wind nor water is an outside agency.

"Equipment" is anything used, worn or carried by or for the player except any ball he has played at the hole being played and any small object, such as a coin or a tee, when used to mark the position of a ball or the extent of an area in which a ball is to be dropped. Equipment includes a golf cart, whether or not motorized. If such a cart is shared by two or more players, the cart and everything in it are deemed to be the equipment of the player whose ball is involved except that, when the cart is being moved by one of the players sharing it, the cart and everything in it are deemed to be that player's equipment.

Note: A ball played at the hole being played is equipment when it has been lifted and not put back into play.

19-1. By Outside Agency

If a ball in motion is accidentally deflected or stopped by any outside agency, it is a rub of the green, no penalty is incurred and the ball shall be played as it lies except:

a. If a ball in motion after a stroke other than on the putting green comes to rest in or on any moving or animate outside agency, the player shall, through the green or in a hazard, drop the ball, or on the putting

60

R. 19

green place the ball, as near as possible to the spot where the outside agency was when the ball came to rest in or on it, and

b. If a ball in motion after a stroke on the putting green is deflected or stopped by, or comes to rest in or on, any moving or animate outside agency except a worm or an insect, the stroke shall be cancelled, the ball replaced and the stroke replayed.

If the ball is not immediately recoverable, another ball may be substituted.

(Player's ball deflected or stopped by another ball — see Rule 19-5.)

Note: If the referee or the Committee determines that a player's ball has been purposely deflected or stopped by an outside agency, Rule 1-4 applies to the player. If the outside agency is a fellow-competitor or his caddie, Rule 1-2 applies to the fellow-competitor.

19-2. By Player, Partner, Caddie or Equipment

a. MATCH PLAY

If a player's ball is accidentally deflected or stopped by himself, his partner or either of their caddies or equipment, *he shall lose the hole.*

b. STROKE PLAY

If a competitor's ball is accidentally deflected or stopped by himself, his partner or either of their caddies or equipment, *the competitor shall incur a penalty of two strokes.* The ball shall be played as it lies, except when it comes to rest in or on the competitor's, his partner's or either of their caddies' clothes or equipment, in which case the competitor shall through the green or in a hazard drop the ball, or on the putting green place the ball, as near as possible to where the article was when the ball came to rest in or on it.

Exception: Dropped ball — see Rule 20-2a.

61

R. 19

(Ball purposely deflected or stopped by player, partner or caddie — see Rule 1-2.)

19-3. By Opponent, Caddie or Equipment in Match Play

If a player's ball is accidentally deflected or stopped by an opponent, his caddie or his equipment, no penalty is incurred. The player may play the ball as it lies or, before another stroke is played by either side, cancel the stroke and play a ball without penalty as nearly as possible at the spot from which the original ball was last played (see Rule 20-5).

If the ball has come to rest in or on the opponent's or his caddie's clothes or equipment, the player may through the green or in a hazard drop the ball, or on the putting green place the ball, as near as possible to where the article was when the ball came to rest in or on it.

Exception: Ball striking person attending flagstick — see Rule 17-3b.

(Ball purposely deflected or stopped by opponent or caddie — see Rule 1-2.)

19-4. By Fellow-Competitor, Caddie or Equipment in Stroke Play

See Rule 19-1 regarding ball deflected by outside agency.

19-5. By Another Ball

If a player's ball in motion after a stroke is deflected or stopped by a ball at rest, the player shall play his ball as it lies. In stroke play, if both balls lay on the putting green prior to the stroke, *the player incurs a penalty of two strokes.* Otherwise, no penalty is incurred.

If a player's ball in motion after a stroke is deflected or stopped by another ball in motion, the player shall play his ball as it lies. There is no penalty unless the player was in breach of Rule 16-1g, in which case *he shall incur the penalty for breach of that Rule.*

62

R. 20

Exception: Ball in motion after a stroke on the putting green deflected or stopped by moving or animate outside agency — see Rule 19-1b.

PENALTY FOR BREACH OF RULE:
Match play — Loss of hole; Stroke play — Two strokes.

RELIEF SITUATIONS AND PROCEDURE
Rule 20. Lifting, Dropping and Placing; Playing from Wrong Place

20-1. Lifting

A ball to be lifted under the Rules may be lifted by the player, his partner or another person authorized by the player. In any such case, the player shall be responsible for any breach of the Rules.

The position of the ball shall be marked before it is lifted under a Rule which requires it to be replaced. If it is not marked, *the player shall incur a penalty of one stroke* and the ball shall be replaced. If it is not replaced, *the player shall incur the general penalty* for breach of this Rule but no additional penalty under Rule 20-1 shall be applied.

If a ball or the ball-marker is accidentally moved in the process of lifting the ball under a Rule or marking its position, the ball or the ball-marker shall be replaced. There is no penalty provided the movement of the ball or the ball-marker is directly attributable to the specific act of marking the position of or lifting the ball. Otherwise, *the player shall incur a penalty stroke* under this Rule or Rule 18-2a.

Exception: If a player incurs a penalty for failing to act in accordance with Rule 5-3 or 12-2, no additional penalty under Rule 20-1 shall be applied.

Note: The position of a ball to be lifted should be marked by placing a ball-marker, a small coin or other

63

similar object immediately behind the ball. If the ball-marker interferes with the play, stance or stroke of another player, it should be placed one or more clubhead-lengths to one side.

20-2. Dropping and Re-dropping

a. BY WHOM AND HOW
A ball to be dropped under the Rules shall be dropped by the player himself. He shall stand erect, hold the ball at shoulder height and arm's length and drop it. If a ball is dropped by any other person or in any other manner and the error is not corrected as provided in Rule 20-6, *the player shall incur a penalty stroke.*

If the ball touches the player, his partner, either of their caddies or their equipment before or after it strikes a part of the course, the ball shall be re-dropped, without penalty. There is no limit to the number of times a ball shall be re-dropped in such circumstances.

(Taking action to influence position or movement of ball — see Rule 1-2.)

b. WHERE TO DROP
When a ball is to be dropped as near as possible to a specific spot, it shall be dropped not nearer the hole than the specific spot which, if it is not precisely known to the player, shall be estimated.

A ball when dropped must first strike a part of the course where the applicable Rule requires it to be dropped. If it is not so dropped, Rules 20-6 and -7 apply.

c. WHEN TO RE-DROP
A dropped ball shall be re-dropped without penalty if it:
(i) rolls into a hazard;
(ii) rolls out of a hazard;
(iii) rolls onto a putting green;
(iv) rolls out of bounds;
(v) rolls to a position where there is interference by the condition from which relief was taken under Rule

64

R. 20

24-2 (immovable obstruction) or Rule 25-1 (abnormal ground condition);
(vi) rolls and comes to rest more than two club-lengths from where it first struck a part of the course; or
(vii) rolls and comes to rest nearer the hole than its original position or estimated position (see Rule 20-2b) unless otherwise permitted by the Rules.

If the ball when re-dropped rolls into any position listed above, it shall be placed as near as possible to the spot where it first struck a part of the course when re-dropped.

If a ball to be re-dropped or placed under this Rule is not immediately recoverable, another ball may be substituted.

20-3. Placing and Replacing

a. BY WHOM AND WHERE
A ball to be placed under the Rules shall be placed by the player or his partner. If a ball is to be replaced, the player, his partner or the person who lifted or moved it shall place it on the spot from which it was lifted or moved. In any such case, the player shall be responsible for any breach of the Rules.

If a ball or the ball-marker is accidentally moved in the process of placing or replacing the ball, the ball or the ball-marker shall be replaced. There is no penalty provided the movement of the ball or the ball-marker is directly attributable to the specific act of placing or replacing the ball or removing the ball-marker. Otherwise, *the player shall incur a penalty stroke* under Rule 18-2a or 20-1.

b. LIE OF BALL TO BE PLACED OR REPLACED ALTERED
If the original lie of a ball to be placed or replaced has been altered:
(i) except in a hazard, the ball shall be placed in the nearest lie most similar to the original lie which is not

65

R. 20

more than one club-length from the original lie, not nearer the hole and not in a hazard;
(ii) in a water hazard, the ball shall be placed in accordance with Clause (i) above, except that the ball must be placed in the water hazard;
(iii) in a bunker, the original lie shall be recreated as nearly as possible and the ball shall be placed in that lie.

c. SPOT NOT DETERMINABLE
If it is impossible to determine the spot where the ball is to be placed or replaced:
(i) through the green, the ball shall be dropped as near as possible to the place where it lay but not in a hazard;
(ii) in a hazard, the ball shall be dropped in the hazard as near as possible to the place where it lay;
(iii) on the putting green, the ball shall be placed as near as possible to the place where it lay but not in a hazard.

d. BALL FAILS TO REMAIN ON SPOT
If a ball when placed fails to remain on the spot on which it was placed, it shall be replaced without penalty. If it still fails to remain on that spot:
(i) except in a hazard, it shall be placed at the nearest spot not nearer the hole or in a hazard where it can be placed at rest;
(ii) in a hazard, it shall be placed in the hazard at the nearest spot not nearer the hole where it can be placed at rest.

PENALTY FOR BREACH OF RULE 20-1, -2 or -3:
Match play — Loss of hole; Stroke play — Two strokes.

20-4. When Ball Dropped or Placed Is in Play

If the player's ball in play has been lifted, it is again in play when dropped or placed.

66

A substituted ball becomes the ball in play if it is dropped or placed under an applicable Rule, whether or not such Rule permits substitution. A ball substituted under an inapplicable Rule is a wrong ball.

20-5. Playing Next Stroke from Where Previous Stroke Played

When, under the Rules, a player elects or is required to play his next stroke from where a previous stroke was played, he shall proceed as follows: If the stroke is to be played from the teeing ground, the ball to be played shall be played from anywhere within the teeing ground and may be teed; if the stroke is to be played from through the green or a hazard, it shall be dropped; if the stroke is to be played on the putting green, it shall be placed.

PENALTY FOR BREACH OF RULE 20-5:
Match play — Loss of hole; Stroke play — Two strokes.

20-6. Lifting Ball Wrongly Dropped or Placed

A ball dropped or placed in a wrong place or otherwise not in accordance with the Rules but not played may be lifted, without penalty, and the player shall then proceed correctly.

20-7. Playing from Wrong Place

For a ball played from outside the teeing ground or from a wrong teeing ground — see Rule 11-4 and -5.

a. MATCH PLAY

If a player plays a stroke with a ball which has been dropped or placed in a wrong place, *he shall lose the hole.*

b. STROKE PLAY

If a competitor plays a stroke with (i) his original ball which has been dropped or placed in a wrong place, (ii) a substituted ball which has been dropped or placed under an applicable Rule but in a wrong place or (iii) his ball in play when it has been moved and not replaced in a case where the Rules require replacement, *he shall*, provided

67

a serious breach has not occurred, *incur the penalty prescribed by the applicable Rule* and play out the hole with the ball.

If, after playing from a wrong place, a competitor becomes aware of that fact and believes that a serious breach may be involved, he may, provided he has not played a stroke from the next teeing ground or, in the case of the last hole of the round, left the putting green, declare that he will play out the hole with a second ball dropped or placed in accordance with the Rules. The competitor shall report the facts to the Committee before returning his score card; if he fails to do so, *he shall be disqualified.* The Committee shall determine whether a serious breach of the Rule occurred. If so, the score with the second ball shall count and *the competitor shall add two penalty strokes to his score with that ball.*

If a serious breach has occurred and the competitor has failed to correct it as prescribed above, *he shall be disqualified.*

Note: If a competitor plays a second ball, penalty strokes incurred by playing the ball ruled not to count and strokes subsequently taken with that ball shall be disregarded.

Rule 21. Cleaning Ball

A ball on the putting green may be cleaned when lifted under Rule 16-1b. Elsewhere, a ball may be cleaned when lifted except when it has been lifted:

a. To determine if it is unfit for play (Rule 5-3);

b. For identification (Rule 12-2), in which case it may be cleaned only to the extent necessary for identification; or

c. Because it is interfering with or assisting play (Rule 22).

68

If a player cleans his ball during play of a hole except as provided in this Rule, *he shall incur a penalty of one stroke* and the ball, if lifted, shall be replaced.

If a player who is required to replace a ball fails to do so, *he shall incur the penalty* for breach of Rule 20-3a, but no additional penalty under Rule 21 shall be applied.

Exception: If a player incurs a penalty for failing to act in accordance with Rule 5-3, 12-2 or 22, no additional penalty under Rule 21 shall be applied.

Rule 22. Ball Interfering with or Assisting Play

Any player may:

a. Lift his ball if he considers that the ball might assist any other player or

b. Have any other ball lifted if he considers that the ball might interfere with his play or assist the play of any other player,

but this may not be done while another ball is in motion. In stroke play, a player required to lift his ball may play first rather than lift. A ball lifted under this Rule shall be replaced.

If a ball is accidentally moved in complying with this Rule, no penalty is incurred and the ball shall be replaced.

PENALTY FOR BREACH OF RULE:
Match play — Loss of hole; Stroke play — Two strokes.

Note: Except on the putting green, the ball may not be cleaned when lifted under this Rule — see Rule 21.

Rule 23. Loose Impediments

Definition

"Loose impediments" are natural objects such as stones, leaves, twigs, branches and the like, dung, worms

69

and insects and casts or heaps made by them, provided they are not fixed or growing, are not solidly embedded and do not adhere to the ball.

Sand and loose soil are loose impediments on the putting green but not elsewhere.

Snow and natural ice, other than frost, are either casual water or loose impediments, at the option of the player. Manufactured ice is an obstruction.

Dew and frost are not loose impediments.

23-1. Relief

Except when both the loose impediment and the ball lie in or touch a hazard, any loose impediment may be removed without penalty. If the ball moves, see Rule 18-2c.

When a ball is in motion, a loose impediment which might influence the movement of the ball shall not be removed.

PENALTY FOR BREACH OF RULE:
Match play — Loss of hole; Stroke play — Two strokes.

(Searching for ball in hazard — see Rule 12-1.)
(Touching line of putt — see Rule 16-1a.)

Rule 24. Obstructions

Definition

An "obstruction" is anything artificial, including the artificial surfaces and sides of roads and paths and manufactured ice, except:

a. Objects defining out of bounds, such as walls, fences, stakes and railings;

b. Any part of an immovable artificial object which is out of bounds; and

c. Any construction declared by the Committee to be an integral part of the course.

70

R. 24

24-1. Movable Obstruction

A player may obtain relief from a movable obstruction as follows:

a. If the ball does not lie in or on the obstruction, the obstruction may be removed. If the ball moves, it shall be replaced, and there is no penalty provided that the movement of the ball is directly attributable to the removal of the obstruction. Otherwise, Rule 18-2a applies.

b. If the ball lies in or on the obstruction, the ball may be lifted, without penalty, and the obstruction removed. The ball shall <u>through the green</u> or in a <u>hazard</u> be dropped, or on the <u>putting green</u> be placed, as near as possible to the spot directly under the place where the ball lay in or on the obstruction, but not nearer the hole.

The ball may be cleaned when lifted under Rule 24-1.

When a ball is in motion, an obstruction which might influence the movement of the ball, other than an attended flagstick or equipment of the players, shall not be removed.

24-2. Immovable Obstruction

a. INTERFERENCE

Interference by an immovable <u>obstruction</u> occurs when a ball lies in or on the obstruction, or so close to the obstruction that the obstruction interferes with the player's <u>stance</u> or the area of his intended swing. If the player's ball lies on the <u>putting green</u>, interference also occurs if an immovable obstruction on the putting green intervenes on his line of putt. Otherwise, intervention on the line of play is not, of itself, interference under this Rule.

b. RELIEF

Except when the ball lies in or touches a <u>water hazard</u> or a <u>lateral water hazard</u>, a player may obtain relief from interference by an immovable <u>obstruction</u>, without penalty, as follows:

71

R. 24

(i) *Through the Green:* If the ball lies <u>through the green</u>, the point on the <u>course</u> nearest to where the ball lies shall be determined (without crossing over, through or under the obstruction) which (a) is not nearer the hole, (b) avoids interference (as defined) and (c) is not in a <u>hazard</u> or on a <u>putting green</u>. The player shall lift the ball and drop it within one club-length of the point thus determined on ground which fulfils (a), (b) and (c) above.

Note: The prohibition against crossing over, through or under the <u>obstruction</u> does not apply to the artificial surfaces and sides of roads and paths or when the ball lies in or on the obstruction.

(ii) *In a Bunker:* If the ball lies in or touches a <u>bunker</u>, the player shall lift and drop the ball in accordance with Clause (i) above, except that the ball must be dropped in the bunker.

(iii) *On the Putting Green:* If the ball lies on the <u>putting green</u>, the player shall lift the ball and place it in the nearest position to where it lay which affords relief from interference, but not nearer the hole nor in a hazard.

The ball may be cleaned when lifted under Rule 24-2b.

(Ball rolling to a position where there is interference by the condition from which relief was taken — see Rule 20-2c(v).)

Exception: A player may not obtain relief under Rule 24-2b if (a) it is clearly unreasonable for him to play a stroke because of interference by anything other than an immovable obstruction or (b) interference by an immovable obstruction would occur only through use of an unnecessarily abnormal stance, swing or direction of play.

Note: If a ball lies in or touches a <u>water hazard</u> (including a <u>lateral water hazard</u>), the player is not entitled to relief without penalty from interference by an immovable

72

R. 25

obstruction. The player shall play the ball as it lies or proceed under Rule 26-1.

c. BALL LOST

Except in a <u>water hazard</u> or a <u>lateral water hazard</u>, if there is reasonable evidence that a ball is lost in an immovable obstruction, the player may, without penalty, substitute another ball and follow the procedure prescribed in Rule 24-2b. For the purpose of applying this Rule, the ball shall be deemed to lie at the spot where it entered the obstruction. If the ball is lost in an underground drain pipe or culvert the entrance to which is in a <u>hazard</u>, a ball must be dropped in that hazard or the player may proceed under Rule 26-1, if applicable.

PENALTY FOR BREACH OF RULE:
Match play — Loss of hole; Stroke play — Two strokes.

Rule 25. Abnormal Ground Conditions and Wrong Putting Green

Definitions

"Casual water" is any temporary accumulation of water on the <u>course</u> which is visible before or after the player takes his <u>stance</u> and is not in a <u>water hazard</u>. Snow and natural ice, other than frost, are casual water or <u>loose impediments</u>, at the option of the player. Manufactured ice is an <u>obstruction</u>. Dew and frost are not casual water.

"Ground under repair" is any portion of the <u>course</u> so marked by order of the Committee or so declared by its authorized representative. It includes material piled for removal and a hole made by a greenkeeper, even if not so marked. Stakes and lines defining ground under repair are in such ground. The margin of ground under repair extends vertically downwards, but not upwards.

Note 1: Grass cuttings and other material left on the course which have been abandoned and are not intended

73

R. 25

to be removed are not ground under repair unless so marked.

Note 2: The Committee may make a Local Rule prohibiting play from ground under repair.

25-1. Casual Water, Ground Under Repair and Certain Damage to Course

a. INTERFERENCE

Interference by <u>casual water</u>, <u>ground under repair</u> or a hole, cast or runway made by a burrowing animal, a reptile or a bird occurs when a ball lies in or touches any of these conditions or when such a condition on the <u>course</u> interferes with the player's <u>stance</u> or the area of his intended swing.

If the player's ball lies on the <u>putting green</u>, interference also occurs if such condition on the putting green intervenes on his line of putt.

If interference exists, the player may either play the ball as it lies (unless prohibited by Local Rule) or take relief as provided in Clause b.

b. RELIEF

If the player elects to take relief, he shall proceed as follows:

(i) *Through the Green:* If the ball lies <u>through the green</u>, the point on the <u>course</u> nearest to where the ball lies shall be determined which (a) is not nearer the hole, (b) avoids interference by the condition, and (c) is not in a <u>hazard</u> or on a <u>putting green</u>. The player shall lift the ball and drop it without penalty within one club-length of the point thus determined on ground which fulfils (a), (b) and (c) above.

(ii) *In a Hazard:* If the ball lies in or touches a <u>hazard</u>, the player shall lift and drop the ball either:

(a) Without penalty, in the hazard, as near as possible to the spot where the ball lay, but not nearer

74

the hole, on ground which affords maximum available relief from the condition;

or

(b) *Under penalty of one stroke*, outside the hazard, keeping the point where the ball lay directly between the hole and the spot on which the ball is dropped.

Exception: If a ball lies in or touches a water hazard (including a lateral water hazard), the player is not entitled to relief without penalty from a hole, cast or runway made by a burrowing animal, a reptile or a bird. The player shall play the ball as it lies or proceed under Rule 26-1.

(iii) *On the Putting Green:* If the ball lies on the putting green, the player shall lift the ball and place it without penalty in the nearest position to where it lay which affords maximum available relief from the condition, but not nearer the hole nor in a hazard.

The ball may be cleaned when lifted under Rule 25-1b.

(Ball rolling to a position where there is interference by the condition from which relief was taken — see Rule 20-2c(v).)

Exception: A player may not obtain relief under Rule 25-1b if (a) it is clearly unreasonable for him to play a stroke because of interference by anything other than a condition covered by Rule 25-1a or (b) interference by such a condition would occur only through use of an unnecessarily abnormal stance, swing or direction of play.

c. BALL LOST UNDER CONDITION COVERED BY RULE 25-1

It is a question of fact whether a ball lost after having been struck toward a condition covered by Rule 25-1 is lost under such condition. In order to treat the ball as lost under such condition, there must be reasonable evidence to that effect. In the absence of such evidence, the ball must be treated as a lost ball and Rule 27 applies.

(i) *Outside a Hazard* — If a ball is lost outside a hazard under a condition covered by Rule 25-1, the player may take relief as follows: the point on the course nearest to where the ball last crossed the margin of the area shall be determined which (a) is not nearer the hole than where the ball last crossed the margin, (b) avoids interference by the condition and (c) is not in a hazard or on a putting green. He shall drop a ball without penalty within one club-length of the point thus determined on ground which fulfils (a), (b) and (c) above.

(ii) *In a Hazard* — If a ball is lost in a hazard under a condition covered by Rule 25-1, the player may drop a ball either:

(a) Without penalty, in the hazard, as near as possible to the point at which the original ball last crossed the margin of the area, but not nearer the hole, on ground which affords maximum available relief from the condition

or

(b) *Under penalty of one stroke*, outside the hazard, keeping the point at which the original ball last crossed the margin of the hazard directly between the hole and the spot on which the ball is dropped.

Exception: If a ball lies in a water hazard (including a lateral water hazard), the player is not entitled to relief without penalty for a ball lost in a hole, cast or runway made by a burrowing animal, a reptile or a bird. The player shall proceed under Rule 26-1.

25-2. Embedded Ball

A ball embedded in its own pitch-mark in the ground in any closely mown area through the green may be lifted, cleaned and dropped, without penalty, as near as possible to the spot where it lay but not nearer the hole. "Closely

mown area" means any area of the course, including paths through the rough, cut to fairway height or less.

25-3. Wrong Putting Green

A player must not play a ball which lies on a putting green other than that of the hole being played. The ball must be lifted and the player must proceed as follows: The point on the course nearest to where the ball lies shall be determined which (a) is not nearer the hole and (b) is not in a hazard or on a putting green. The player shall lift the ball and drop it without penalty within one club-length of the point thus determined on ground which fulfils (a) and (b) above. The ball may be cleaned when so lifted.

Note: Unless otherwise prescribed by the Committee, the term "a putting green other than that of the hole being played" includes a practice putting green or pitching green on the course.

PENALTY FOR BREACH OF RULE:
Match play — Loss of hole; Stroke play — Two strokes.

Rule 26. Water Hazards (Including Lateral Water Hazards)

Definitions

A "water hazard" is any sea, lake, pond, river, ditch, surface drainage ditch or other open water course (whether or not containing water) and anything of a similar nature.

All ground or water within the margin of a water hazard is part of the water hazard. The margin of a water hazard extends vertically upwards and downwards. Stakes and lines defining the margins of water hazards are in the hazards.

Note: Water hazards (other than lateral water hazards) should be defined by yellow stakes or lines.

A "lateral water hazard" is a water hazard or that part of a water hazard so situated that it is not possible or is deemed by the Committee to be impracticable to drop a ball behind the water hazard in accordance with Rule 26-1b.

That part of a water hazard to be played as a lateral water hazard should be distinctively marked.

Note: Lateral water hazards should be defined by red stakes or lines.

26-1. Ball in Water Hazard

It is a question of fact whether a ball lost after having been struck toward a water hazard is lost inside or outside the hazard. In order to treat the ball as lost in the hazard, there must be reasonable evidence that the ball lodged in it. In the absence of such evidence, the ball must be treated as a lost ball and Rule 27 applies.

If a ball lies in, touches or is lost in a water hazard (whether the ball lies in water or not), the player may *under penalty of one stroke:*

a. Play a ball as nearly as possible at the spot from which the original ball was last played (see Rule 20-5);

or

b. Drop a ball behind the water hazard, keeping the point at which the original ball last crossed the margin of the water hazard directly between the hole and the spot on which the ball is dropped, with no limit to how far behind the water hazard the ball may be dropped.

or

c. *As additional options available only if the ball lies in, touches or is lost in a lateral water hazard,* drop a ball outside the water hazard within two club-lengths of (i) the point where the original ball last crossed the margin of the water hazard or (ii) a point on the opposite margin of the water hazard equidistant from the hole. The ball must be dropped and come to rest

R. 26

not nearer the hole than the point where the original ball last crossed the margin of the water hazard.

The ball may be cleaned when lifted under this Rule.

(Ball moving in water in a water hazard — see Rule 14-6.)

26-2. Ball Played Within Water Hazard

a. BALL COMES TO REST IN HAZARD

If a ball played from within a water hazard comes to rest in the hazard after the stroke, the player may:

(i) proceed under Rule 26-1; or

(ii) *under penalty of one stroke,* play a ball as nearly as possible at the spot from which the last stroke from outside the hazard was played (see Rule 20-5).

If the player proceeds under Rule 26-1a, he may elect not to play the dropped ball. If he so elects, he may:

a. Proceed under Rule 26-1b, *adding the additional penalty of one stroke* prescribed by that Rule;

or

b. Proceed under Rule 26-1c, if applicable, *adding the additional penalty of one stroke* prescribed by that Rule;

or

c. *Add an additional penalty of one stroke* and play a ball as nearly as possible at the spot from which the last stroke from outside the hazard was played (see Rule 20-5).

b. BALL LOST OR UNPLAYABLE OUTSIDE HAZARD OR OUT OF BOUNDS

If a ball played from within a water hazard is lost or declared unplayable outside the hazard or is out of bounds, the player, after taking *a penalty of one stroke* under Rule 27-1 or 28a, may:

(i) play a ball as nearly as possible at the spot in the hazard from which the original ball was last played (see Rule 20-5); or

79

R. 27

(ii) proceed under Rule 26-1b, or if applicable Rule 26-1c, *adding the additional penalty of one stroke* prescribed by the Rule and using as the reference point the point where the original ball last crossed the margin of the hazard before it came to rest in the hazard; or

(iii) *add an additional penalty of one stroke* and play a ball as nearly as possible at the spot from which the last stroke from outside the hazard was played (see Rule 20-5).

Note 1: When proceeding under Rule 26-2b, the player is not required to drop a ball under Rule 27-1 or 28a. If he does drop a ball, he is not required to play it. He may alternatively proceed under Clause (ii) or (iii).

Note 2: If a ball played from within a water hazard is declared unplayable outside the hazard, nothing in Rule 26-2b precludes the player from proceeding under Rule 28b or c.

PENALTY FOR BREACH OF RULE:
Match play — Loss of hole; Stroke play — Two strokes.

Rule 27. Ball Lost or Out of Bounds; Provisional Ball

If the original ball is lost in an immovable obstruction (Rule 24-2) or under a condition covered by Rule 25-1 (casual water, ground under repair and certain damage to the course), the player may proceed under the applicable Rule. If the original ball is lost in a water hazard, the player shall proceed under Rule 26.

Such Rules may not be used unless there is reasonable evidence that the ball is lost in an immovable obstruction, under a condition covered by Rule 25-1 or in a water hazard.

Definitions

A ball is "lost" if:

80

R. 27

a. It is not found or identified as his by the player within five minutes after the player's side or his or their caddies have begun to search for it; or

b. The player has put another ball into play under the Rules, even though he may not have searched for the original ball; or

c. The player has played any stroke with a provisional ball from the place where the original ball is likely to be or from a point nearer the hole than that place, whereupon the provisional ball becomes the ball in play.

Time spent in playing a wrong ball is not counted in the five-minute period allowed for search.

"Out of bounds" is ground on which play is prohibited.

When out of bounds is defined by reference to stakes or a fence, or as being beyond stakes or a fence, the out of bounds line is determined by the nearest inside points of the stakes or fence posts at ground level excluding angled supports.

When out of bounds is defined by a line on the ground, the line itself is out of bounds.

The out of bounds line extends vertically upwards and downwards.

A ball is out of bounds when all of it lies out of bounds.

A player may stand out of bounds to play a ball lying within bounds.

A "provisional ball" is a ball played under Rule 27-2 for a ball which may be lost outside a water hazard or may be out of bounds.

27-1. Ball Lost or Out of Bounds

If a ball is lost outside a water hazard or is out of bounds, the player shall play a ball, *under penalty of one stroke,* as nearly as possible at the spot from which the original ball was last played (see Rule 20-5).

81

R. 27

PENALTY FOR BREACH OF RULE 27-1:
Match play — Loss of hole; Stroke play — Two strokes.

27-2. Provisional Ball

a. PROCEDURE

If a ball may be lost outside a water hazard or may be out of bounds, to save time the player may play another ball provisionally as nearly as possible at the spot from which the original ball was played (see Rule 20-5). The player shall inform his opponent in match play or his marker or a fellow-competitor in stroke play that he intends to play a provisional ball, and he shall play it before he or his partner goes forward to search for the original ball. If he fails to do so and plays another ball, such ball is not a provisional ball and becomes the ball in play *under penalty of stroke and distance* (Rule 27-1); the original ball is deemed to be lost.

b. WHEN PROVISIONAL BALL BECOMES BALL IN PLAY

The player may play a provisional ball until he reaches the place where the original ball is likely to be. If he plays a stroke with the provisional ball from the place where the original ball is likely to be or from a point nearer the hole than that place, the original ball is deemed to be lost and the provisional ball becomes the ball in play *under penalty of stroke and distance* (Rule 27-1).

If the original ball is lost outside a water hazard or is out of bounds, the provisional ball becomes the ball in play, *under penalty of stroke and distance* (Rule 27-1).

c. WHEN PROVISIONAL BALL TO BE ABANDONED

If the original ball is neither lost outside a water hazard nor out of bounds, the player shall abandon the provisional ball and continue play with the original ball. If he fails to do so, any further strokes played with the provisional ball shall constitute playing a wrong ball and the provisions of Rule 15 shall apply.

82

R. 28/29

Note: If the original ball lies in a water hazard, the player shall play the ball as it lies or proceed under Rule 26. If it is lost in a water hazard or unplayable, the player shall proceed under Rule 26 or 28, whichever is applicable.

Rule 28. Ball Unplayable

The player may declare his ball unplayable at any place on the course except when the ball lies in or touches a water hazard. The player is the sole judge as to whether his ball is unplayable.

If the player deems his ball to be unplayable, he shall, *under penalty of one stroke:*

a. Play a ball as nearly as possible at the spot from which the original ball was last played (see Rule 20-5);
or

b. Drop a ball within two club-lengths of the spot where the ball lay, but not nearer the hole;
or

c. Drop a ball behind the point where the ball lay, keeping that point directly between the hole and the spot on which the ball is dropped, with no limit to how far behind that point the ball may be dropped.

If the unplayable ball lies in a bunker, the player may proceed under Clause a, b or c. If he elects to proceed under Clause b or c, a ball must be dropped in the bunker. The ball may be cleaned when lifted under this Rule.

PENALTY FOR BREACH OF RULE:
Match play — Loss of hole; Stroke play — Two strokes.

OTHER FORMS OF PLAY
Rule 29. Threesomes and Foursomes

Definitions
Threesome: A match in which one plays against two, and each side plays one ball.

83

Foursome: A match in which two play against two, and each side plays one ball.

29-1. General
In a threesome or a foursome, during any stipulated round the partners shall play alternately from the teeing grounds and alternately during the play of each hole. Penalty strokes do not affect the order of play.

29-2. Match Play
If a player plays when his partner should have played, *his side shall lose the hole.*

29-3. Stroke Play
If the partners play a stroke or strokes in incorrect order, such stroke or strokes shall be cancelled and *the side shall incur a penalty of two strokes.* The side shall correct the error by playing a ball in correct order as nearly as possible at the spot from which it first played in incorrect order (see Rule 20-5). If the side plays a stroke from the next teeing ground without first correcting the error or, in the case of the last hole of the round, leaves the putting green without declaring its intention to correct the error, *the side shall be disqualified.*

Rule 30. Three-Ball, Best-Ball and Four-Ball Match Play

Definitions
Three-Ball: A match play competition in which three play against one another, each playing his own ball. Each player is playing two distinct matches.
Best-Ball: A match in which one plays against the better ball of two or the best ball of three players.
Four-Ball: A match in which two play their better ball against the better ball of two other players.

84

R. 30

30-1. Rules of Golf Apply
The Rules of Golf, so far as they are not at variance with the following special Rules, shall apply to three-ball, best-ball and four-ball matches.

30-2. Three-Ball Match Play

a. BALL AT REST MOVED BY AN OPPONENT
Except as otherwise provided in the Rules, if the player's ball is touched or moved by an opponent, his caddie or equipment other than during search, Rule 18-3b applies. *That opponent shall incur a penalty stroke in his match with the player,* but not in his match with the other opponent.

b. BALL DEFLECTED OR STOPPED BY AN OPPONENT ACCIDENTALLY
If a player's ball is accidentally deflected or stopped by an opponent, his caddie or equipment, no penalty shall be incurred. In his match with that opponent the player may play the ball as it lies or, before another stroke is played by either side, he may cancel the stroke and play a ball without penalty as nearly as possible at the spot from which the original ball was last played (see Rule 20-5). In his match with the other opponent, the ball shall be played as it lies.

Exception: Ball striking person attending flagstick — see Rule 17-3b.

(Ball purposely deflected or stopped by opponent — see Rule 1-2.)

30-3. Best-Ball and Four-Ball Match Play

a. REPRESENTATION OF SIDE
A side may be represented by one partner for all or any part of a match; all partners need not be present. An absent partner may join a match between holes, but not during play of a hole.

85

R. 30

b. MAXIMUM OF FOURTEEN CLUBS
The side shall be penalized for a breach of Rule 4-4 by any partner.

c. ORDER OF PLAY
Balls belonging to the same side may be played in the order the side considers best.

d. WRONG BALL
If a player plays a stroke with a wrong ball except in a hazard, *he shall be disqualified for that hole,* but his partner incurs no penalty even if the wrong ball belongs to him. If the wrong ball belongs to another player, its owner shall place a ball on the spot from which the wrong ball was first played.

e. DISQUALIFICATION OF SIDE
(i) *A side shall be disqualified* for a breach of any of the following by any partner:
Rule 1-3 — Agreement to Waive Rules.
Rule 4-1, -2 or -3 — Clubs.
Rule 5-1 or -2 — The Ball.
Rule 6-2a — Handicap (playing off higher handicap).
Rule 6-4 — Caddie.
Rule 6-7 — Undue Delay (repeated offense).
Rule 14-3 — Artificial Devices and Unusual Equipment.
(ii) *A side shall be disqualified* for a breach of any of the following by all partners:
Rule 6-3 — Time of Starting and Groups.
Rule 6-8 — Discontinuance of Play.

f. EFFECT OF OTHER PENALTIES
If a player's breach of a Rule assists his partner's play or adversely affects an opponent's play, *the partner incurs the applicable penalty in addition to any penalty incurred by the player.*

86

R. 31

In all other cases where a player incurs a penalty for breach of a Rule, the penalty shall not apply to his partner. Where the penalty is stated to be loss of hole, the effect shall be to disqualify the player for that hole.

g. ANOTHER FORM OF MATCH PLAYED CONCURRENTLY

In a best-ball or four-ball match when another form of match is played concurrently, the above special Rules shall apply.

Rule 31. Four-Ball Stroke Play

In four-ball stroke play two competitors play as partners, each playing his own ball. The lower score of the partners is the score for the hole. If one partner fails to complete the play of a hole, there is no penalty.

31-1. Rules of Golf Apply

The Rules of Golf, so far as they are not at variance with the following special Rules, shall apply to four-ball stroke play.

31-2. Representation of Side

A side may be represented by either partner for all or any part of a stipulated round; both partners need not be present. An absent competitor may join his partner between holes, but not during play of a hole.

31-3. Maximum of Fourteen Clubs

The side shall be penalized for a breach of Rule 4-4 by either partner.

31-4. Scoring

The marker is required to record for each hole only the gross score of whichever partner's score is to count. The gross scores to count must be individually identifiable; otherwise *the side shall be disqualified.* Only one of the partners need be responsible for complying with Rule 6-6b.

87

R. 31

(Wrong score — see Rule 31-7a.)

31-5. Order of Play

Balls belonging to the same side may be played in the order the side considers best.

31-6. Wrong Ball

If a competitor plays a stroke with a wrong ball except in a hazard, *he shall add two penalty strokes to his score for the hole* and shall then play the correct ball. His partner incurs no penalty even if the wrong ball belongs to him.

If the wrong ball belongs to another competitor, its owner shall place a ball on the spot from which the wrong ball was first played.

31-7. Disqualification Penalties

a. BREACH BY ONE PARTNER

A side shall be disqualified from the competition for a breach of any of the following by either partner:
Rule 1-3 — Agreement to Waive Rules.
Rule 3-4 — Refusal to Comply with Rule.
Rule 4-1, -2 or -3 — Clubs.
Rule 5-1 or -2 — The Ball.
Rule 6-2b — Handicap (playing off higher handicap; failure to record handicap).
Rule 6-4 — Caddie.
Rule 6-6b — Signing and Returning Card.
Rule 6-6d — Wrong Score for Hole, *i.e.*, when the recorded score of the partner whose score is to count is lower than actually taken. If the recorded score of the partner whose score is to count is higher than actually taken, it must stand as returned.
Rule 6-7 — Undue Delay (repeated offense).
Rule 7-1 — Practice Before or Between Rounds.
Rule 14-3 — Artificial Devices and Unusual Equipment.

88

R. 32

Rule 31-4 — Gross Scores to Count Not Individually Identifiable.

b. BREACH BY BOTH PARTNERS

A side shall be disqualified:

(i) for a breach by both partners of Rule 6-3 (Time of Starting and Groups) or Rule 6-8 (Discontinuance of Play), or

(ii) if, at the same hole, each partner is in breach of a Rule the penalty for which is disqualification from the competition or for a hole.

c. FOR THE HOLE ONLY

In all other cases where a breach of a Rule would entail disqualification, *the competitor shall be disqualified only for the hole at which the breach occurred.*

31-8. Effect of Other Penalties

If a competitor's breach of a Rule assists his partner's play, *the partner incurs the applicable penalty in addition to any penalty incurred by the competitor.*

In all other cases where a competitor incurs a penalty for breach of a Rule, the penalty shall not apply to his partner.

Rule 32. Bogey, Par and Stableford Competitions

32-1. Conditions

Bogey, par and Stableford competitions are forms of stroke competition in which play is against a fixed score at each hole. The Rules for stroke play, so far as they are not at variance with the following special Rules, apply.

a. BOGEY AND PAR COMPETITIONS

The reckoning for bogey and par competitions is made as in match play. Any hole for which a competitor makes no return shall be regarded as a loss. The winner is the competitor who is most successful in the aggregate of holes.

89

R. 32

The marker is responsible for marking only the gross number of strokes for each hole where the competitor makes a net score equal to or less than the fixed score.

Note: Maximum of 14 clubs — Penalties as in match play — see Rule 4-4.

b. STABLEFORD COMPETITIONS

The reckoning in Stableford competitions is made by points awarded in relation to a fixed score at each hole as follows:

Hole Played In	Points
More than one over fixed score or no score returned	0
One over fixed score	1
Fixed score	2
One under fixed score	3
Two under fixed score	4
Three under fixed score	5
Four under fixed score	6

The winner is the competitor who scores the highest number of points.

The marker shall be responsible for marking only the gross number of strokes at each hole where the competitor's net score earns one or more points.

Note: Maximum of 14 clubs (Rule 4-4) — Penalties applied as follows: From total points scored for the round, deduction of two points for each hole at which any breach occurred; maximum deduction per round: four points.

32-2. Disqualification Penalties

a. FROM THE COMPETITION

A competitor shall be disqualified from the competition for a breach of any of the following:
Rule 1-3 — Agreement to Waive Rules.
Rule 3-4 — Refusal to Comply with Rule.

90

R. 33

Rule 4-1, -2 or -3 — Clubs.
Rule 5-1 or -2 — The Ball.
Rule 6-2b — Handicap (playing off higher handicap; failure to record handicap).
Rule 6-3 — Time of Starting and Groups.
Rule 6-4 — Caddie.
Rule 6-6b — Signing and Returning Card.
Rule 6-6d — Wrong Score for Hole, except that no penalty shall be incurred when a breach of this Rule does not affect the result of the hole.
Rule 6-7 — Undue Delay (repeated offense).
Rule 6-8 — Discontinuance of Play.
Rule 7-1 — Practice Before or Between Rounds.
Rule 14-3 — Artificial Devices and Unusual Equipment.

b. FOR A HOLE
In all other cases where a breach of a Rule would entail disqualification, *the competitor shall be disqualified only for the hole at which the breach occurred.*

ADMINISTRATION
Rule 33. The Committee

33-1. Conditions; Waiving Rule
The Committee shall lay down the conditions under which a competition is to be played.
The Committee has no power to waive a Rule of Golf.
Certain special rules governing stroke play are so substantially different from those governing match play that combining the two forms of play is not practicable and is not permitted. The results of matches played and the scores returned in these circumstances shall not be accepted.
In stroke play the Committee may limit a referee's duties.

91

R. 33

33-2. The Course

a. DEFINING BOUNDS AND MARGINS
The Committee shall define accurately:
(i) the course and out of bounds,
(ii) the margins of water hazards and lateral water hazards,
(iii) ground under repair, and
(iv) obstructions and integral parts of the course.

b. NEW HOLES
New holes should be made on the day on which a stroke competition begins and at such other times as the Committee considers necessary, provided all competitors in a single round play with each hole cut in the same position.

Exception: When it is impossible for a damaged hole to be repaired so that it conforms with the Definition, the Committee may make a new hole in a nearby similar position.

c. PRACTICE GROUND
Where there is no practice ground available outside the area of a competition course, the Committee should lay down the area on which players may practice on any day of a competition, if it is practicable to do so. On any day of a stroke competition, the Committee should not normally permit practice on or to a putting green or from a hazard of the competition course.

d. COURSE UNPLAYABLE
If the Committee or its authorized representative considers that for any reason the course is not in a playable condition or that there are circumstances which render the proper playing of the game impossible, it may, in match play or stroke play, order a temporary suspension of play or, in stroke play, declare play null and void and cancel all scores for the round in question. When play has been temporarily suspended, it shall be resumed from where it was discontinued, even though resumption

92

R. 33

occurs on a subsequent day. When a round is cancelled, all penalties incurred in that round are cancelled.

(Procedure in discontinuing play — see Rule 6-8.)

33-3. Times of Starting and Groups
The Committee shall lay down the times of starting and, in stroke play, arrange the groups in which competitors shall play.
When a match play competition is played over an extended period, the Committee shall lay down the limit of time within which each round shall be completed. When players are allowed to arrange the date of their match within these limits, the Committee should announce that the match must be played at a stated time on the last day of the period unless the players agree to a prior date.

33-4. Handicap Stroke Table
The Committee shall publish a table indicating the order of holes at which handicap strokes are to be given or received.

33-5. Score Card
In stroke play, the Committee shall issue for each competitor a score card containing the date and the competitor's name or, in foursome or four-ball stroke play, the competitors' names.
In stroke play, the Committee is responsible for the addition of scores and application of the handicap recorded on the card.
In four-ball stroke play, the Committee is responsible for recording the better-ball score for each hole and in the process applying the handicaps recorded on the card, and adding the better-ball scores.
In bogey, par and Stableford competitions, the Committee is responsible for applying the handicap recorded on the card and determining the result of each hole and the overall result or points total.

93

R. 34

33-6. Decision of Ties
The Committee shall announce the manner, day and time for the decision of a halved match or of a tie, whether played on level terms or under handicap.
A halved match shall not be decided by stroke play. A tie in stroke play shall not be decided by a match.

33-7. Disqualification Penalty; Committee Discretion
A penalty of disqualification may in exceptional individual cases be waived, modified or imposed if the Committee considers such action warranted.
Any penalty less than disqualification shall not be waived or modified.

33-8. Local Rules

a. POLICY
The Committee may make and publish Local Rules for abnormal conditions if they are consistent with the policy of the Governing Authority for the country concerned as set forth in Appendix I to these Rules.

b. WAIVING PENALTY
A penalty imposed by a Rule of Golf shall not be waived by a Local Rule.

Rule 34. Disputes and Decisions

34-1. Claims and Penalties

a. MATCH PLAY
In match play if a claim is lodged with the Committee under Rule 2-5, a decision should be given as soon as possible so that the state of the match may, if necessary, be adjusted.
If a claim is not made within the time limit provided by Rule 2-5, it shall not be considered unless it is based on facts previously unknown to the player making the claim and the player making the claim had been given

94

R. 34

wrong information (Rules 6-2a and 9) by an opponent. In any case, no later claim shall be considered after the result of the match has been officially announced, unless the Committee is satisfied that the opponent knew he was giving wrong information.

b. STROKE PLAY

In stroke play no penalty shall be rescinded, modified or imposed after the competition has closed, except that a penalty of disqualification shall be imposed at any time after the competition has closed if a competitor:

(i) returned a score for any hole lower than actually taken (Rule 6-6d) for any reason other than failure to include a penalty which he did not know he had incurred; or

(ii) returned a score card on which he had recorded a handicap which he knew was higher than that to which he was entitled, and this affected the number of strokes received (Rule 6-2b); or

(iii) was in breach of Rule 1-3.

A competition is deemed to have closed when the result has been officially announced or, in stroke play qualifying followed by match play, when the player has teed off in his first match.

34-2. Referee's Decision

If a referee has been appointed by the Committee, his decision shall be final.

34-3. Committee's Decision

In the absence of a referee, any dispute or doubtful point on the Rules shall be referred to the Committee, whose decision shall be final.

If the Committee cannot come to a decision, it shall refer the dispute or doubtful point to the Rules of Golf Committee of the United States Golf Association, whose decision shall be final.

If the dispute or doubtful point has not been referred to the Rules of Golf Committee, the player or players

95

App. I

have the right to refer an agreed statement through the Secretary of the Club to the Rules of Golf Committee for an opinion as to the correctness of the decision given. The reply will be sent to the Secretary of the Club or Clubs concerned.

If play is conducted other than in accordance with the Rules of Golf, the Rules of Golf Committee will not give a decision on any question.

Appendix I
LOCAL RULES;
CONDITIONS OF THE COMPETITION
Local Rules

Rule 33-8 provides:

"The Committee may make and publish Local Rules for abnormal conditions if they are consistent with the policy of the Governing Authority for the country concerned as set forth in Appendix I to these Rules.

"A penalty imposed by a Rule of Golf shall not be waived by a Local Rule."

Information regarding acceptable and prohibited Local Rules is provided in the *Decisions on the Rules of Golf* under Rule 33-8. Among the matters for which Local Rules may be advisable are the following:

1. Obstructions

Clarifying the status of objects which may be obstructions (Rule 24).

Declaring any construction to be an integral part of the course and, accordingly, not an obstruction, *e.g.*, built-up sides of teeing grounds, putting greens and bunkers (Rules 24 and 33-2a).

2. Roads and Paths

Providing relief of the type afforded under Rule 24-2b from roads and paths not having artificial surfaces and sides if they could unfairly affect play.

96

App. I

3. Preservation of Course

Preservation of the course by defining areas, including turf nurseries and other parts of the course under cultivation, as ground under repair from which play is prohibited.

4. Water Hazards

Lateral Water Hazards. Clarifying the status of sections of water hazards which may be lateral water hazards (Rule 26).

Provisional Ball. Permitting play of a provisional ball for a ball which may be in a water hazard of such character that it would be impracticable to determine whether the ball is in the hazard or to do so would unduly delay play. In such case, if a provisional ball is played and the original ball is in a water hazard, the player may play the original ball as it lies or continue the provisional ball in play, but he may not proceed under Rule 26-1.

5. Defining Bounds and Margins

Specifying means used to define out of bounds, hazards, water hazards, lateral water hazards and ground under repair.

6. Ball Drops

Establishment of special areas on which balls may be dropped when it is not feasible or practicable to proceed exactly in conformity with Rule 24-2b (immovable obstructions), Rule 25-1b or -1c (ground under repair), Rule 26-1 (water hazards and lateral water hazards) and Rule 28 (ball unplayable).

7. Temporary Conditions — Mud, Extreme Wetness

Temporary conditions which might interfere with proper playing of the game, including mud and extreme wetness warranting lifting an embedded ball anywhere through the green (see detailed recommendation below) or removal of mud from a ball through the green.

* * *

97

App. I

Following are the suggested texts for other Local Rules which are authorized by the USGA:

Lifting an Embedded Ball

Rule 25-2 provides relief without penalty for a ball embedded in its own pitch-mark in any closely mown area through the green.

On the putting green, a ball may be lifted and damage caused by the impact of a ball may be repaired (Rules 16-1b and c).

When permission to lift an embedded ball anywhere through the green would be warranted, the following Local Rule is suggested:

Anywhere "through the green," a ball which is embedded in its own pitch-mark in the ground, except in loose sand, may be lifted without penalty, cleaned and dropped as near as possible to the spot where it lay but not nearer the hole. (See Rule 20.)

("Through the green" is the whole area of the course except:

a. Teeing ground and putting green of the hole being played;

b. All hazards on the course.)

Exception: A player may not obtain relief under this Rule if it is clearly unreasonable for him to play a stroke because of interference by anything other than the condition covered by this Rule.

Practice Between Holes

When, between the play of two holes, it is desired to prohibit practice putting or chipping on or near the putting green of the hole last played, the following Local Rule is recommended:

98

Between the play of two holes, a player shall not play any practice stroke on or near the putting green of the hole last played. (For other practice, see Rules 7 and 33-2c.)

PENALTY FOR BREACH OF LOCAL RULE:
Match play — Loss of next hole; Stroke play — Two strokes at next hole.

Marking Position of Lifted Ball

When it is desired to require a specific means of marking the position of a lifted ball on the putting green, the following Local Rule is recommended:

Before a ball on the putting green is lifted, its position shall be marked by placing a small coin or some similar object immediately behind the ball; if the ball-marker interferes with another player, it should be moved one or more putterhead-lengths to one side. If the position of the ball is not so marked, *the player shall incur a penalty of one stroke* and the ball shall be replaced. If the ball is not replaced, *the player shall incur the penalty* for breach of Rule 20-3a, but no additional penalty under this Local Rule shall be applied. (This modifies Rule 20-1.)

Prohibition Against Touching Line of Putt with Club

When it is desired to prohibit touching the line of putt with a club in moving loose impediments, the following Local Rule is recommended:

The line of putt shall not be touched with a club for any purpose except to repair old hole plugs or ball marks or during address. (This modifies Rule 16-1a.)

PENALTY FOR BREACH OF LOCAL RULE:
Match play — Loss of hole; Stroke play — Two strokes.

99

Protection of Young Trees

When it is desired to prevent damage to young trees, the following Local Rule is recommended:

Protection of young trees identified by _____ — If such a tree interferes with a player's stance or the area of his intended swing, the ball must be lifted, without penalty, and dropped in accordance with the procedure prescribed in Rule 24-2b(i) (Immovable Obstruction). The ball may be cleaned when so lifted.

Temporary Obstructions

When temporary obstructions are installed for a competition, the following Local Rule is recommended:

1. Definition

Temporary immovable obstructions include tents, scoreboards, grandstands, refreshment stands and lavatories. Any temporary equipment for photography, press, radio and television is also a temporary immovable obstruction, provided it is not mobile or otherwise readily movable.

Excluded are temporary power lines and cables and mats covering them and temporary telephone lines and stanchions supporting them (from which relief is provided in Clause 5) and mobile or otherwise readily movable equipment for photography, press, radio or television (from which relief is obtainable under Rule 24-1).

2. Interference

Interference by a temporary immovable obstruction occurs when (a) the ball lies in or on the obstruction or so close to the obstruction that the obstruction interferes with the player's stance or the area of his intended swing or (b) the obstruction intervenes between the player's ball and the hole or the ball lies within one club-length of a spot where such intervention would exist.

100

3. Relief

A player may obtain relief from interference by a temporary immovable obstruction as follows:

a. THROUGH THE GREEN

Through the green, the point on the course nearest to where the ball lies shall be determined which (a) is not nearer the hole, (b) avoids interference as defined in Clause 2 of this Local Rule and (c) is not in a hazard or on a putting green. He shall lift the ball and drop it without penalty within one club-length of the point thus determined on ground which fulfils (a), (b) and (c) above. The ball may be cleaned when so lifted.

b. IN A HAZARD

If the ball lies in a hazard, the player shall lift and drop the ball either:

(i) in the hazard, without penalty, on the nearest ground affording complete relief within the limits specified in Clause 3a above or, if complete relief is impossible, on ground within the hazard affording maximum relief, or

(ii) outside the hazard, *under penalty of one stroke,* as follows: The player shall determine the point on the course nearest to where the ball lies which (a) is not nearer the hole, (b) avoids interference as defined in Clause 2 of this Local Rule and (c) is not in a hazard. He shall drop the ball within one club-length of the point thus determined on ground which fulfils (a), (b) and (c) above.

The ball may be cleaned when so lifted.

Exception: A player may not obtain relief from a temporary immovable obstruction under Clause 3a or 3b if (a) it is clearly unreasonable for him to play a stroke, or in the case of intervention to play a stroke directly toward the obstruction, because of interference by anything other than the obstruction or (b) interference would

101

occur only through use of an unnecessarily abnormal stance, swing or direction of play.

4. Ball Lost in Temporary Immovable Obstruction

If there is reasonable evidence that a ball is lost within the confines of a temporary immovable obstruction, the player may take relief without penalty as prescribed in Rule 24-2c.

5. Temporary Power Lines and Cables

The above Clauses do not apply to (1) temporary power lines or cables or mats covering them or (2) temporary telephone lines or stanchions supporting them. If such items are readily movable, the player may obtain relief under Rule 24-1. If they are not readily movable, the player may, if the ball lies through the green, obtain relief as provided in Rule 24-2b(i). If the ball lies in a bunker or a water hazard, the player may obtain relief under Rule 24-2b(i), except that the ball must be dropped in the bunker or water hazard.

Note: The prohibition in Rule 24-2b(i) against crossing over, through or under the obstruction does not apply.

If a ball strikes a temporary power line or cable which is elevated, it must be replayed, without penalty (see Rule 20-5). If the ball is not immediately recoverable, another ball may be substituted.

Exception: Ball striking elevated junction section of cable rising from the ground shall not be replayed.

6. Re-Dropping

If a dropped ball rolls into a position covered by this Local Rule, or nearer the hole than its original position, it shall be re-dropped without penalty. If it again rolls into such a position, it shall be placed where it first struck a part of the course when re-dropped.

PENALTY FOR BREACH OF LOCAL RULE:
Match play — Loss of hole; Stroke play — Two strokes.

102

App. I

"Preferred Lies" and "Winter Rules"

The USGA does not endorse "preferred lies" and "winter rules" and recommends that the Rules of Golf be observed uniformly. Ground under repair is provided for in Rule 25. Occasional abnormal conditions which might interfere with fair play and are not widespread should be defined accurately as ground under repair.

However, adverse conditions are sometimes so general throughout a course that the Committee believes "preferred lies" or "winter rules" would promote fair play or help protect the course. Heavy snows, spring thaws, prolonged rains or extreme heat can make fairways unsatisfactory and sometimes prevent use of heavy mowing equipment.

When a Committee adopts a Local Rule for "preferred lies" or "winter rules," it should be in detail and should be interpreted by the Committee, as there is no established code for"winter rules." Without a detailed Local Rule, it is meaningless for a Committee to post a notice merely saying "Winter Rules Today."

The following Local Rule would seem appropriate for the conditions in question, but the USGA will not interpret it:

A ball lying on a "fairway" may be lifted and cleaned, without penalty, and placed within one club-length of where it originally lay, not nearer the hole, and so as to preserve as nearly as possible the stance required to play from the original lie. A ball so lifted is back in play when the player addresses it or, if he does not address it, when he makes his next stroke at it.

Before a Committee adopts a Local Rule permitting "preferred lies" or "winter rules," the following facts should be considered:

1. Such a Local Rule conflicts with the Rules of Golf and the fundamental principle of playing the ball as it lies.

103

App. I

2. "Winter rules" are sometimes adopted under the guise of protecting the course when, in fact, the practical effect is just the opposite — they permit moving the ball to the best turf, from which divots are then taken to injure the course further.

3. "Preferred lies" or "winter rules" tend generally to lower scores and handicaps, thus penalizing the players in competition with players whose scores for handicaps are made under the Rules of Golf.

4. Extended use or indiscriminate use of "preferred lies" or "winter rules" will place players at a disadvantage when competing at a course where the ball must be played as it lies.

Handicapping and "Preferred Lies"

Scores made under a Local Rule for "preferred lies" or "winter rules" may be accepted for handicapping if the Committee considers that conditions warrant.

When such a Local Rule is adopted, the Committee should ensure that the course's normal scoring difficulty is maintained as nearly as possible through adjustment of tee-markers and related methods. However, if extreme conditions cause extended use of "preferred lies" or "winter rules" and the course management cannot adjust scoring difficulty properly, the club should obtain a Temporary Course Rating from its district golf association.

Conditions of the Competition

Rule 33-1 states: "The Committee shall lay down the conditions under which a competition is to be played." Conditions should include such matters as method of entry, eligibility requirements, format, the method of deciding ties, the method of determining the draw for match play and handicap allowances for a handicap competition.

104

App. I

How to Decide Ties

Rule 33-6 empowers the Committee to determine how and when a halved match or a stroke play tie shall be decided. The decision should be published in advance. The USGA recommends:

1. Match Play

A match which ends all square should be played off hole by hole until one side wins a hole. The play-off should start on the hole where the match began. In a handicap match, handicap strokes should be allowed as in the prescribed round.

2. Stroke Play

(a) In the event of a tie in a scratch stroke play competition, an 18-hole play-off is recommended. If that is not feasible, a hole-by-hole play-off is recommended.

(b) In the event of a tie in a handicap stroke play competition, a play-off over 18 holes with handicaps is recommended. If a shorter play-off is necessary, the percentage of 18 holes to be played should be applied to the players' handicaps to determine their play-off handicaps. It is advisable to arrange for a percentage of holes that will result in whole numbers in handicaps; if this is not feasible, handicap stroke fractions of one-half stroke or more should count as a full stroke and any lesser fraction should be disregarded.

(c) In either a scratch or handicap stroke play competition, if a play-off of any type is not feasible, matching score cards is recommended. The method of matching cards should be announced in advance. An acceptable method of matching cards is to determine the winner on the basis of the best score for the last nine holes. If the tying players have the same score for the last nine, determine the winner on the basis of the last six holes, last three holes and finally the 18th hole. If such a method is used in a handicap stroke play competition, one-half, one-third, one-sixth, etc. of the handicaps should be deducted.

105

App. I

(d) If the conditions of the competition provide that ties shall be decided over the last nine, last six, last three and last hole, they should also provide what will happen if this procedure does not produce a winner.

Draw for Match Play

Although the draw for match play may be completely blind or certain players may be distributed through different quarters or eighths, the General Numerical Draw is recommended if flights are determined by a qualifying round.

General Numerical Draw

For purposes of determining places in the draw, ties in qualifying rounds other than those for the last qualifying place shall be decided by the order in which scores are returned, the first score to be returned receiving the lowest available number, etc. If it is impossible to determine the order in which scores are returned, ties shall be determined by a blind draw.

UPPER HALF	LOWER HALF	UPPER HALF	LOWER HALF
64 QUALIFIERS		32 QUALIFIERS	
1 vs. 64	2 vs. 63	1 vs. 32	2 vs. 31
32 vs. 33	31 vs. 34	16 vs. 17	15 vs. 18
16 vs. 49	15 vs. 50	8 vs. 25	7 vs. 26
17 vs. 48	18 vs. 47	9 vs. 24	10 vs. 23
8 vs. 57	7 vs. 58	4 vs. 29	3 vs. 30
25 vs. 40	26 vs. 39	13 vs. 20	14 vs. 19
9 vs. 56	10 vs. 55	5 vs. 28	6 vs. 27
24 vs. 41	23 vs. 42	12 vs. 21	11 vs. 22
4 vs. 61	3 vs. 62	16 QUALIFIERS	
29 vs. 36	30 vs. 35	1 vs. 16	2 vs. 15
13 vs. 52	14 vs. 51	8 vs. 9	7 vs. 10
20 vs. 45	19 vs. 46	4 vs. 13	3 vs. 14
5 vs. 60	6 vs. 59	5 vs. 12	6 vs. 11
28 vs. 37	27 vs. 38	8 QUALIFIERS	
12 vs. 53	11 vs. 54	1 vs. 8	2 vs. 7
21 vs. 44	22 vs. 43	4 vs. 5	3 vs. 6

106

App. I

Handicap Allowances

The USGA recommends the following handicap allowances in handicap competitions:

Singles match play: Allow the higher-handicapped player the full difference between the handicaps of the two players.

Four-ball match play: Reduce the handicaps of all four players by the handicap of the low-handicapped player, who shall then play from scratch. Allow each of the three other players 100 percent of the resulting difference.

Individual stroke play: Allow the full handicap.

Four-ball stroke play: Men — Allow each competitor 90 percent of his handicap. Women — Allow each competitor 95 percent of her handicap.

Best-ball-of-four, stroke play: Men — Allow each competitor 80 percent of his handicap. Women — Allow each competitor 90 percent of her handicap.

Optional Conditions

The following are some conditions which a Committee may wish to make:

List of Conforming Golf Balls

The USGA periodically issues a List of Conforming Golf Balls. If it is desired to require use of a brand of golf ball on the List, the List should be posted and the following issued as a condition of the competition:

Only brands of golf balls on the USGA's latest List of Conforming Golf Balls may be used. Penalty for use of brand not on the List: Disqualification.

One-Ball Rule

If it is desired to prohibit changing brands of golf balls during a stipulated round, the following condition is recommended; it is suggested that it be considered only for competitions involving expert players:

107

App. I

Limitation on Golf Balls Used During Round
(Condition: Rules 5-1 and 33-1)

1. BALLS WITH IDENTICAL MARKINGS TO BE USED

Throughout a stipulated round, the player is limited to golf balls with identical markings, except that the player-identification numbers may differ by number only, not by color.

PENALTY FOR BREACH OF CONDITION:

Match play — At the conclusion of the hole at which the breach is discovered, the state of the match shall be adjusted by deducting one hole for each hole at which a breach occurred. Maximum deduction per round: two holes. Stroke play — Two strokes for each hole at which any breach occurred; maximum penalty per round: four strokes.

2. PROCEDURE WHEN BREACH DISCOVERED

When a player discovers that he has used a ball in breach of this condition, he shall abandon that ball before playing from the next teeing ground and complete the round using a proper ball; otherwise, *the player shall be disqualified.* If discovery is made during play of a hole and the player elects to substitute a proper ball before completing that hole, the player shall place a proper ball on the spot where the ball used in breach of this condition lay.

Time of Starting

If the Committee desires to adopt the condition in the Note under Rule 6-3a, the following wording is recommended:

Rule 6-3a provides: "The player shall start at the time laid down by the Committee." The penalty for breach of Rule 6-3a is disqualification. However, it is a condition of the competition that, if the player arrives at his starting point, ready to play, within five minutes after his starting time, in the absence of circumstances which

108

App. I

warrant waiving the penalty of disqualification as provided in Rule 33-7, the penalty for failure to start on time is loss of the first hole in match play or two strokes at the first hole in stroke play instead of disqualification.

Practice

The Committee may make regulations governing practice in accordance with the Note to Rule 7-1, Clause (c) of the Exception under Rule 7-2 and Rule 33-2c.

Advice in Team Competitions

If the Committee desires to adopt the condition in the Note under Rule 8, which applies to a team competition with or without concurrent individual competition, the following wording is recommended:

In accordance with the Note to Rule 8 of the Rules of Golf, each team may appoint one person (in addition to the persons from whom advice may be asked under Rule 8-1) who may give advice (including pointing out a line for putting) to members of that team. Such person [if it is desired to put a restriction on who may be appointed, insert such restriction here] shall be identified to the Committee prior to the start of the competition.

Automotive Transportation

If it is desired to prohibit automotive transportation in a competition, the following condition is suggested:

Players shall not use automotive transportation during play.

PENALTY FOR BREACH OF CONDITION:

Match play — At the conclusion of the hole at which the breach is discovered, the state of the match shall be adjusted by deducting one hole for each hole at which a breach occurred. Maximum deduction per round: two holes.

109

App. II

Stroke play — Two strokes for each hole at which any breach occurred; maximum penalty per round: four strokes.

Match or stroke play — Use of any unauthorized automotive vehicle shall be discontinued immediately upon discovery that a breach has occurred. Otherwise, the player shall be disqualified.

Appendices II and III

Any design in a club or ball which is not covered by Rules 4 and 5 and Appendices II and III, or which might significantly change the nature of the game, will be ruled on by the United States Golf Association and the Royal and Ancient Golf Club of St. Andrews.

Note: Equipment approved for use or marketed prior to January 1, 1988 which conformed to the Rules in effect in 1987 but does not conform to the 1988 and subsequent Rules may be used until December 31, 1995; thereafter all equipment must conform to the current Rules.

110

Appendix II
DESIGN OF CLUBS

Rule 4-1 prescribes general regulations for the design of clubs. The following paragraphs, which provide some detailed specifications and clarify how Rule 4-1 is interpreted, should be read in conjunction with this Rule.

4-1a. General

ADJUSTABILITY — EXCEPTION FOR PUTTERS

Clubs other than putters shall not be designed to be adjustable except for weight.

Some other forms of adjustability are permitted in the design of a putter, provided that:

(i) the adjustment cannot be readily made;

(ii) all adjustable parts are firmly fixed and there is no reasonable likelihood of them working loose during a round; and

(iii) all configurations of adjustment conform with the Rules.

The disqualification penalty for purposely changing the playing characteristics of a club during a stipulated round (Rule 4-2) applies to all clubs, including a putter.

Note: It is recommended that all putters with adjustable parts be submitted to the United States Golf Association for a ruling.

4-1b. Shaft

GENERALLY STRAIGHT

The shaft shall be at least 18 inches (457mm) in length. It shall be straight from the top of the grip to a point not more than 5 inches (127mm) above the sole, measured along the axis of the shaft and the neck or socket.

BENDING AND TWISTING PROPERTIES

The shaft must be so designed and manufactured that at any point along its length:

CLUBS

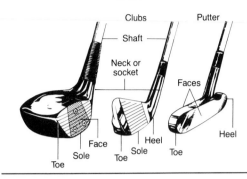

GRIPS

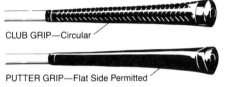

CLUB GRIP—Circular

PUTTER GRIP—Flat Side Permitted

GROOVES

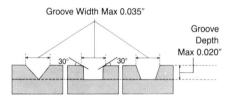

Groove Width Max 0.035″

Groove Depth Max 0.020″

30°   30°

(i) it bends in such a way that the deflection is the same regardless of how the shaft is rotated about its longitudinal axis; and

(ii) it twists the same amount in both directions.

ATTACHMENT TO CLUBHEAD

The neck or socket must not be more than 5 inches (127mm) in length, measured from the top of the neck or socket to the sole along its axis. The shaft and the neck or socket must remain in line with the heel, or with a point to the right or left of the heel, when the club is viewed in the address position. The distance between the axis of the shaft or the neck or socket and the back of the heel must not exceed 0.625 inches (16mm).

Exception for Putters: The shaft or neck or socket of a putter may be fixed at any point in the head and need not remain in line with the heel. The axis of the shaft from the top to a point not more than 5 inches (127mm) above the sole must diverge from the vertical in the toe-heel plane by at least 10 degrees when the club is in its normal address position.

4-1c. Grip

(i) For clubs other than putters the grip must be generally circular in cross-section, except that a continuous, straight, slightly raised rib may be incorporated along the full length of the grip.

(ii) A putter grip may have a non-circular cross-section, provided the cross-section has no concavity and remains generally similar throughout the length of the grip.

(iii) The grip may be tapered but must not have any bulge or waist.

(iv) For clubs other than putters the axis of the grip must coincide with the axis of the shaft.

(v) The cross-sectional dimension of a grip measured in any direction shall not exceed 1.75 inches (45mm).

(vi) A putter may have more than one grip, provided each is circular in cross-section and the axis of each coincides with the axis of the shaft.

Note: Putters approved for use or marketed prior to January 1, 1992 which are in breach of Clause (vi) may be used until December 31, 1992.

4-1d. Clubhead

DIMENSIONS

The dimensions of a clubhead (see diagram) are measured, with the clubhead in its normal address position, on horizontal lines between vertical projections of the outermost points of (i) the heel and the toe and (ii) the face and the back. If the outermost point of the heel is not clearly defined, it is deemed to be 0.625 inches (16mm) above the horizontal plane on which the club is resting in its normal address position.

PLAIN IN SHAPE

The clubhead shall be generally plain in shape. All parts shall be rigid, structural in nature and functional.

Features such as holes through the head, windows or transparencies, or appendages to the main body of the head such as plates, rods or fins for the purpose of meeting dimensional specifications, for aiming or for any other purpose are not permitted. Exceptions may be made for putters.

Any furrows in or runners on the sole shall not extend into the face.

4-1e. Club Face

GENERAL

Except for specified markings, the surface roughness must not exceed that of decorative sandblasting. Markings must not have sharp edges or raised lips, as determined by a finger test. The material and construction of the face shall not be designed or manufactured to have

App. II

the effect at impact of a spring, or to impart significantly more spin to the ball than a standard steel face, or to have any other effect which would unduly influence the movement of the ball.

IMPACT AREA MARKINGS

Markings within the area where impact is intended (the "impact area") are governed by the following:

(i) *Grooves.* A series of straight grooves with diverging sides and a symmetrical cross-section may be used. (See diagram.) The width and cross-section must be generally consistent across the face of the club and along the length of the grooves. Any rounding of groove edges shall be in the form of a radius which does not exceed 0.020 inches (0.5mm). The width of the grooves shall not exceed 0.035 inches (0.9mm), using the 30 degree method of measurement on file with the United States Golf Association. The distance between edges of adjacent grooves must not be less than three times the width of a groove, and not less than 0.075 inches (1.9mm). The depth of a groove must not exceed 0.020 inches (0.5mm).

(ii) *Punch Marks.* Punch marks may be used. The area of any such mark must not exceed 0.0044 square inches (2.8 sq. mm). A mark must not be closer to an adjacent mark than 0.168 inches (4.3mm), measured from center to center. The depth of a punch mark must not exceed 0.040 inches (1.0mm). If punch marks are used in combination with grooves, a punch mark may not be closer to a groove than 0.168 inches (4.3mm), measured from center to center.

DECORATIVE MARKINGS

The center of the impact area may be indicated by a design within the boundary of a square whose sides are 0.375 inches (9.5mm) in length. Such a design must not unduly influence the movement of the ball. Decorative markings are permitted outside the impact area.

115

App. III

NON-METALLIC CLUB FACE MARKINGS

The above specifications do not apply to clubs on which the impact area of the face is non-metallic and whose loft angle is 24 degrees or less, but markings which could unduly influence the movement of the ball are prohibited. Clubs with this type of face and a loft angle exceeding 24 degrees may have grooves of maximum width 0.040 inches (1.0mm) and maximum depth 1½ times the groove width, but must otherwise conform to the markings specifications above.

PUTTER FACE MARKINGS

The specifications above with regard to club face markings do not apply to putters.

Appendix III
THE BALL

a. WEIGHT

The weight of the ball shall not be greater than 1.620 ounces avoirdupois (45.93gm).

b. SIZE

The diameter of the ball shall be not less than 1.680 inches (42.67mm). This specification will be satisfied if, under its own weight, a ball falls through a 1.680 inches diameter ring gauge in fewer than 25 out of 100 randomly selected positions, the test being carried out at a temperature of $23\pm1°C$.

c. SPHERICAL SYMMETRY

The ball must not be designed, manufactured or intentionally modified to have flight properties which differ from those of a spherically symmetrical ball.

Furthermore the ball will not conform to the Rules of Golf if it fails to satisfy the performance specifications outlined below:

116

App. III

As described in procedures on file at the United States Golf Association, each ball type will be tested using 40 balls of that type, in 20 pairs. One ball of each pair will be launched spinning about one specified axis; the other ball of each pair will be launched spinning about a different, but also specified axis. Differences in carry and time of flight between the two balls of each pair will be recorded. If the mean of the differences in carry is greater than 3.0 yards, and that value is significant at the 5% level, OR if the mean of the differences in time of flight is greater than 0.20 seconds, and that value is significant at the 5% level, the ball type will not conform to the Rules of Golf.

Note: Methods of determining whether a ball performs as if it were generally spherically symmetrical may be subject to change as instrumentation becomes available to measure other properties accurately, such as aerodynamic coefficient of lift, coefficient of drag and moment of inertia.

d. INITIAL VELOCITY

The velocity of the ball shall not be greater than 250 feet (76.2m) per second when measured on apparatus approved by the United States Golf Association. A maximum tolerance of 2% will be allowed. The temperature of the ball when tested shall be $23\pm1°C$.

e. OVERALL DISTANCE STANDARD

A brand of golf ball, when tested on apparatus approved by the USGA on the outdoor range at the USGA Headquarters under the conditions set forth in the Overall Distance Standard for golf balls on file with the USGA, shall not cover an average distance in carry and roll exceeding 280 yards plus a tolerance of 6%. *Note:* The 6% tolerance will be reduced to a minimum of 4% as test techniques are improved.

117

App. IV

Appendix IV
MISCELLANEOUS
Par Computation

"Par" is the score that an expert golfer would be expected to make for a given hole. Par means errorless play without flukes and under ordinary weather conditions, allowing two strokes on the putting green.

Yardages for guidance in computing par are given below. They should not be applied arbitrarily; allowance should be made for the configuration of the ground, any difficult or unusual conditions and the severity of the hazards.

Each hole should be measured horizontally from the middle of the tee area to be used to the center of the green, following the line of play planned by the architect in laying out the hole. Thus, in a hole with a bend, the line at the elbow point should be centered in the fairway in accordance with the architect's intention.

YARDAGES FOR GUIDANCE

PAR	MEN	WOMEN
3	up to 250	up to 210
4	251 to 470	211 to 400
5	471 and over	401 to 575
6		576 and over

Flagstick Dimensions

The USGA recommends that the flagstick be at least seven feet in height and that its diameter be not greater than three-quarters of an inch from a point three inches above the ground to the bottom of the hole.

Protection of Persons Against Lightning

As there have been many deaths and injuries from lightning on golf courses, all clubs and sponsors of golf

118

competitions are urged to take every precaution for the protection of persons against lightning.

Attention is called to Rules 6-8 and 33-2d.

The USGA suggests that players be informed that they have the right to stop play if they think lightning threatens them, even though the Committee may not have specifically authorized it by signal.

The USGA generally uses the following signals and recommends that all Committees do similarly:

Discontinue Play: Three consecutive notes of siren, repeated.

Resume Play: One prolonged note of siren, repeated.

Posters containing detailed information on protection from lightning are available from the USGA.

RULES OF AMATEUR STATUS

Any person who considers that any action he is proposing to take might endanger his amateur status should submit particulars to the United States Golf Association for consideration.

Definition of an Amateur Golfer

An amateur golfer is one who plays the game as a non-remunerative or non-profit-making sport.

Rule 1. Forfeiture of Amateur Status at Any Age

The following are examples of acts at any age which are contrary to the Definition of an Amateur Golfer and cause forfeiture of amateur status:

1. Professionalism

a. Receiving payment or compensation for serving as a professional golfer or identifying oneself as a professional golfer.

119

b. Taking any action for the purpose of becoming a professional golfer.

Note: Such actions include applying for a professional's position; filing application to a school or competition conducted to qualify persons to play as professionals in tournaments; receiving services from or entering into an agreement, written or oral, with a sponsor or professional agent; agreement to accept payment or compensation for allowing one's name or likeness as a skilled golfer to be used for any commercial purpose; and holding or retaining membership in any organization of professional golfers.

2. Playing for Prize Money

Playing for prize money or its equivalent in a match, tournament or exhibition.

Note: A player may participate in an event in which prize money or its equivalent is offered, provided that prior to participation he irrevocably waives his right to accept prize money in that event. (See USGA Policy on Gambling for definition of prize money.)

3. Instruction

Receiving payment or compensation for giving instruction in playing golf, either orally, in writing, by pictures or by other demonstrations, to either individuals or groups.

Exceptions:

1. Golf instruction may be given by an employee of an educational institution or system to students of the institution or system and by camp counselors to those in their charge, provided that the total time devoted to golf instruction during a year comprises less than 50 percent of the time spent during the year in the performance of all duties as such employee or counselor.

2. Payment or compensation may be accepted for instruction in writing, provided one's ability or reputation

120

as a golfer was not a major factor in one's employment or in the commission or sale of one's work.

4. Prizes, Testimonials and Gifts

a. Acceptance of a prize or testimonial of the following character (this applies to total prizes received for any event or series of events in any one tournament or exhibition, including hole-in-one or other events in which golf skill is a factor):

(i) Of retail value exceeding $500; or

(ii) Of a nature which is the equivalent of money or makes it readily convertible into money.

Exceptions:

1. Prizes of only symbolic value (such as metal trophies).

2. More than one testimonial award may be accepted from different donors even though their total retail value exceeds $500, provided they are not presented so as to evade the $500 value limit for a single award. (Testimonial awards relate to notable performances or contributions to golf, as distinguished from tournament prizes.)

b. Conversion of a prize into money.

c. Accepting expenses in any amount as a prize.

d. Because of golf skill or golf reputation, accepting in connection with any golfing event:

(i) Money, or

(ii) Anything else, other than merchandise of nominal value provided to all players.

5. Lending Name or Likeness

Because of golf skill or golf reputation, receiving or contracting to receive payment, compensation or personal benefit, directly or indirectly, for allowing one's name or likeness as a golfer to be used in any way for the advertisement or sale of anything, whether or not used in or appertaining to golf, except as a golf author or broadcaster as permitted by Rule 1-7.

121

6. Personal Appearance

Because of golf skill or golf reputation, receiving payment or compensation, directly or indirectly, for a personal appearance, except that reasonable expenses actually incurred may be received if no golf competition or exhibition is involved.

7. Broadcasting and Writing

Because of golf skill or golf reputation, receiving payment or compensation, directly or indirectly, for broadcasting concerning golf, a golf event or golf events, writing golf articles or books, or allowing one's name to be advertised or published as the author of golf articles or books of which one is not actually the author.

Exceptions:

1. Broadcasting or writing as part of one's primary occupation or career, provided instruction in playing golf is not included except as permitted in Rule 1-3.

2. Part-time broadcasting or writing, provided (a) the player is actually the author of the commentary, articles or books, (b) instruction in playing golf is not included except as permitted in Rule 1-3 and (c) the payment or compensation does not have the purpose or effect, directly or indirectly, of financing participation in a golf competition or golf competitions.

8. Golf Equipment

Because of golf skill or golf reputation, accepting golf balls, clubs, golf merchandise, golf clothing or golf shoes, directly or indirectly, from anyone manufacturing such merchandise without payment of current market price.

9. Membership and Privileges

Because of golf skill or golf reputation, accepting membership or privileges in a club or at a golf course without full payment for the class of membership or privileges involved unless such membership or privileges have been awarded (1) as purely and deservedly honorary,

122

Amateur Status

(2) in recognition of an outstanding performance or contribution to golf and (3) without a time limit.

10. Expenses

Accepting expenses, in money or otherwise, from any source other than from a member of the player's family or legal guardian to engage in a golf competition or exhibition, or to improve golf skill.

Exceptions: A player may receive a reasonable amount of expenses as follows:

1. JUNIOR COMPETITIONS
As a player in a golf competition or exhibition limited exclusively to players who have not reached their 18th birthday.

2. INTERNATIONAL TEAMS
As a representative of a recognized golf association in an international team match between or among golf associations when such expenses are paid by one or more of the golf associations involved or, subject to the approval of the USGA, as a representative in an international team match conducted by some other athletic organization.

3. USGA PUBLIC LINKS CHAMPIONSHIPS
As a qualified contestant in the USGA Amateur Public Links Championships proper, but only within limits fixed by the USGA.

4. SCHOOL, COLLEGE, MILITARY TEAMS
As a representative of a recognized educational institution or of a military service in (1) team events or (2) other events which are limited to representatives of recognized educational institutions or of military serices, respectively. In each case, expenses may be accepted from only an educational or military authority.

123

Amateur Status

5. INDUSTRIAL OR BUSINESS TEAMS
As a representative of an industrial or business golf team in industrial or business golf team competitions, respectively, but only within limits fixed by the USGA. (A statement of such limits may be obtained on request from the USGA.)

6. INVITATION UNRELATED TO GOLF SKILL
As a player invited for reasons unrelated to golf skill, e.g., a celebrity, a business associate or customer, a guest in a club-sponsored competition, etc., to take part in a golfing event.

Note 1: Except as otherwise provided in Exception 6 to Rule 1-10, acceptance of expenses from an employer, a partner or other vocational source is not permissible.

Note 2: Business Expenses — It is permissible to play in a golf competition while on a business trip with expenses paid provided that the golf part of the expenses is borne personally and is not charged to business. Further, the business involved must be actual and substantial, and not merely a subterfuge for legitimizing expenses when the primary purpose is golf competition.

Note 3: Private Transport — Acceptance of private transport furnished or arranged for by a tournament sponsor, directly or indirectly, as an inducement for a player to engage in a golf competition or exhibition shall be considered accepting expenses under Rule 1-10.

11. Scholarships

Because of golf skill or golf reputation, accepting the benefits of a scholarship or grant-in-aid other than in accord with the regulation of the National Collegiate Athletic Association, the Association of Intercollegiate

124

Amateur Status

Athletics for Women, the National Association for Intercollegiate Athletics, or the National Junior College Athletic Association.

12. Conduct Detrimental to Golf

Any conduct, including activities in connection with golf gambling, which is considered detrimental to the best interests of the game.

Rule 2. Advisory Opinions, Enforcement and Reinstatement

1. Advisory Opinions

Any person who considers that any action he is proposing to take might endanger his amateur status may submit particulars to the staff of the United States Golf Association for advice. If dissatisfied with the staff's advice, he may request that the matter be referred to the Amateur Status and Conduct Committee for decision. If dissatisfied with the Amateur Status and Conduct Committee's decision, he may, by written notice to the staff within 30 days after being notified of the decision, appeal to the Executive Committee, in which case he shall be given reasonable notice of the next meeting of the Executive Committee at which the matter may be heard and shall be entitled to present his case in person or in writing. The decision of the Executive Committee shall be final.

2. Enforcement

Whenever information of a possible act contrary to the Definition of an Amateur Golfer by a player claiming to be an amateur shall come to the attention of the United States Golf Association, the staff shall notify the player of the possible act contrary to the Definition of an Amateur Golfer, invite the player to submit such information as the player deems relevant and make such other investigation as seems appropriate under the circumstances. The staff shall submit to the Amateur Status and

125

Amateur Status

Conduct Committee all information provided by the player, their findings and their recommendation, and the Amateur Status and Conduct Committee shall decide whether an act contrary to the Definition of an Amateur Golfer has occurred. If dissatisfied with the Amateur Status and Conduct Committee's decision, the player may, by written notice to the staff within 30 days after being notified of the decision, appeal to the Executive Committee, in which case the player shall be given reasonable notice of the next meeting of the Executive Committee at which the matter may be heard and shall be entitled to present his case in person or in writing. The decision of the Executive Committee shall be final.

Upon a final decision of the Amateur Status and Conduct Committee or the Executive Committee that a player has acted contrary to the Definition of an Amateur Golfer, such Committee may require the player to refrain or desist from specified actions as a condition of retaining his amateur status or declare the amateur status of the player forfeited. Such Committee shall notify the player, if possible, and may notify any interested golf association of any action taken under this paragraph.

3. Reinstatement

a. AUTHORITY AND PRINCIPLES
Either the Executive Committee or its Amateur Status and Conduct Committee may reinstate a player to amateur status and prescribe the waiting period necessary for reinstatement or deny reinstatement. In addition, the Amateur Status and Conduct Committee may authorize the staff of the USGA to reinstate a player to amateur status and prescribe the waiting period necessary for reinstatement in situations where the acts contrary to the Definition of an Amateur Golfer are covered by ample precedent.

Each application for reinstatement shall be decided on its merits with consideration normally being given to the following principles:

126

Amateur Status

(i) Awaiting Reinstatement

The professional holds an advantage over the amateur by reason of having devoted himself to the game as his profession; other persons acting contrary to the Rules of Amateur Status also obtain advantages not available to the amateur. They do not necessarily lose such advantage merely by deciding to cease acting contrary to the Rules.

Therefore, an applicant for reinstatement to amateur status shall undergo a period awaiting reinstatement as prescribed.

The period awaiting reinstatement shall start from the date of the player's last act contrary to the Definition of an Amateur Golfer unless it is decided that it shall start from the date of the player's last known act contrary to the Definition of an Amateur Golfer.

(ii) Period Awaiting Reinstatement

A period awaiting reinstatement of two years normally will be required. However, that period may be *extended or shortened*. Longer periods normally will be required when applicants have played extensively for prize money or have been previously reinstated; shorter periods often will be permitted when applicants have acted contrary to the Rules for one year or less. A probationary period of one year normally will be required when an applicant's only act contrary to the Definition of an Amateur Golfer was to accept a prize of retail value exceeding $500.

(iii) Players of National Prominence

Players of national prominence who have acted contrary to the Definition of an Amateur Golfer for more than five years normally will not be eligible for reinstatement.

127

Policy on Gambling

(iv) Status During Period Awaiting Reinstatement

During the period awaiting reinstatement an applicant for reinstatement shall conform with the Definition of an Amateur Golfer.

He shall not be eligible to enter competitions limited to amateurs except that he may enter competitions solely among members of a club of which he is a member, subject to the approval of the club. He may also, without prejudicing his application, enter, as an applicant for reinstatement, competitions which are not limited to amateurs but shall not accept any prize reserved for an amateur.

b. Form of Application

Each application for reinstatement shall be prepared, in duplicate, on forms provided by the USGA.

The application must be filed through a recognized amateur golf association in whose district the applicant resides. The association's recommendation, if any, will be considered. If the applicant is unknown to the association, this should be noted and the application forwarded to the USGA, without prejudice.

c. Objection by Applicant

If dissatisfied with the decision with respect to his application for reinstatement, the applicant may, by written notice to the staff within 30 days after being notified of the decision, appeal to the Executive Committee, in which case he shall be given reasonable notice of the next meeting of the Executive Committee at which the matter may be heard and shall be entitled to present his case in person or in writing. The decision of the Executive Committee shall be final.

USGA Policy on Gambling

The Definition of an Amateur Golfer provides that an amateur golfer is one who plays the game as a non-

128

Policy on Gambling

remunerative or non-profit-making sport. When gambling motives are introduced, problems can arise which threaten the integrity of the game.

The USGA does not object to participation in wagering among individual golfers or teams of golfers when participation in the wagering is limited to the players, the players may only wager on themselves or their teams, the sole source of all money won by players is advanced by the players and the primary purpose is the playing of the game for enjoyment.

The distinction between playing for prize money and gambling is essential to the validity of the Rules of Amateur Status. Participation in wagering among individual golfers and participation in wagering among teams constitutes golf wagering and not playing for prize money.

On the other hand, organized amateur events open to the general golfing public and designed and promoted to create cash prizes are not approved by the USGA. Golfers participating in such events without irrevocably waiving their right to cash prizes are deemed by the USGA to be playing for prize money.

The USGA is opposed to and urges its Member Clubs, all golf associations and all other sponsors of golf competitions to prohibit types of gambling such as: (1) Calcuttas, (2) other auction pools, (3) pari-mutuels and (4) any other forms of gambling organized for general participation or permitting participants to bet on someone other than themselves or their teams.

The Association may deny amateur status, entry in USGA Championships and membership on USGA teams for international competitions to players whose activities in connection with golf gambling, whether organized or individual, are considered by the USGA to be contrary to the best interests of golf.

129

Index

INDEX TO THE RULES OF GOLF

130

DECISIONS ON THE RULES OF GOLF

The *Decisions on the Rules of Golf* shows how the Rules have been applied over the years. Here you'll find out how to handle even the most unusual situations on the golf course. Packed with more than 500 pages of individual rulings, the *Decisions* book is the perfect complement to the *Rules of Golf*. Each decision is cross-referenced so that you'll be able to find answers quickly.

To order your copy of the *Decisions on the Rules of Golf*, just call the USGA Order Department at 1-800-336-4446, or send $15 for a single copy order plus $3.45 for shipping and handling to:

USGA Order Department
P.O. Box 2000
Far Hills, NJ 07931-2000

For information on other USGA publications and videos, including *Golf Rules in Brief* and a video on the *Rules of Golf*, please contact the USGA Order Department.

> 1992
>
> DECISIONS
> on the
> RULES OF GOLF
>
> by the
> United States Golf Association
> and the
> Royal and Ancient Golf Club
> of St. Andrews

143

144

PRICES OF RULES OF GOLF BOOKLET

1 to 249 copies — $1 each
250 to 999 copies — 85 cents each
1,000 to 9,999 copies — 70 cents each
10,000 and up — 55 cents each
(New Jersey shipments — add 7% sales tax)

Shipping Charges

Total Amount of Order	Shipping and Handling Charges
$0.00 - 1.50	$1.25
$1.51 - 5.00	$2.25
$5.01 - 15.00	$3.45
$15.01 - 30.00	$4.50
$30.01 - 40.00	$5.50
$40.01 - 50.00	$6.00
$50.01 - 75.00	$7.25
$75.01 - 100.00	$8.50
Over $100	Actual Shipping Charges will be Invoiced

To order, call the USGA Order Department at 1-800-336-4446 or send payment with your order to:

USGA Order Department
P.O. Box 2000
Far Hills, NJ 07931-2000

Competitions for 1992

Championship or Team Event	Dates of Event	Location
Curtis Cup	June 5-6	**Royal Liverpool Golf Club** Hoylake, England
Open	June 18-21	**Pebble Beach Golf Links** Pebble Beach, California
Women's Amateur Public Links	June 24-28	**Haggin Oaks Golf Course** Sacramento, California
Senior Open	July 9-12	**Saucon Valley Country Club** Bethlehem, Pennsylvania
Amateur Public Links	July 13-18	**Edinburgh USA** Brooklyn Park, Minnesota
Women's Open	July 23-26	**Oakmont Country Club** Oakmont, Pennsylvania
Junior Amateur	July 28 - Aug. 1	**Wollaston Golf Club** Milton, Massachusetts
Girls' Junior	Aug. 3-8	**Meridian Hills Country Club** Indianapolis, Indiana
Women's Amateur	Aug. 10-15	**Kemper Lakes Golf Course** Hawthorne Woods, Illinois
Amateur	Aug. 25-30	**Muirfield Village Golf Club** Dublin, Ohio
Mid-Amateur	Sept. 19-24	**Detroit Golf Club** Detroit, Michigan
Senior Women's Amateur	Sept. 23-25	**Tucson Country Club** Tucson, Arizona
Women's World Amateur Team	Oct. 1-4	**Marine Drive Golf Club** Vancouver, B.C., Canada
World Amateur Team	Oct. 8-11	**Capilano Golf & Country Club** Vancouver, B.C., Canada
Women's Mid-Amateur	Oct. 10-15	**Old Marsh Golf Club** Palm Beach Gardens, Florida
Senior Amateur	Oct. 19-24	**The Loxahatchee Club** Jupiter, Florida

Handicap Index Limits:
Open — 2.4
Senior Open — 5.4
Women's Open — 4.4
Junior Amateur — 9.4
Girls' Junior — 12.4
Women's Amateur — 5.4
Amateur — 3.4
Mid-Amateur — 5.4
Women's Mid-Amateur — 9.4
Senior Women's Amateur — 12.4
Senior Amateur — 8.4
Others — No Limit

Age Limits:
Senior Open — must be 50 on or before June 29
Junior Amateur — cannot be 18 on or before August 1
Girls' Junior — cannot be 18 on or before August 8
Senior Amateur — must be 55 on or before September 1
Senior Women's Amateur — must be 50 on or before September 23
Mid-Amateur — must be 25 on or before September 1
Women's Mid-Amateur — must be 25 on or before September 15

These are the only official *Rules of Golf* recognized by the governing bodies of golf in the United States and in every part of the world in which golf is played. The *Rules of Golf* are approved by the United States Golf Association and the Royal and Ancient Golf Club of St. Andrews, Scotland. Golf—whether in competition or not—played by any other rules (excepting local rules, see below) is *not* golf. Many beginning golfers, who have not had the opportunity to study the official rules of the game, erroneously tend to regard these rules as restrictive and designed primarily for the tournament player. The more experienced player, regardless of his golfing ability, will always vouch for the fact that playing by the rules adds much to the enjoyment of the game.

It is impossible for the *Rules of Golf* to anticipate the special physical peculiarities of individual golf courses, with the result that it is often unfair, undesirable, or actually impossible to follow these rules literally. In such cases, local rules are recommended by the USGA and should be made, printed on the scorecard, and posted at the first tee. Where practical, limits of zones to which local rules apply should be marked with stakes. The USGA has made specific recommendations regarding local rules in the appendix to the *Rules of Golf.* You can obtain a *Rules of Golf* booklet from the USGA, Golf House, P.O. Box 708, Far Hills, N.J. 07931. The price is $1.00.

GOLF ETIQUETTE

Etiquette is your observance of the code for correct behavior in respect to other players and to the course itself. The rules of golf etiquette, as stated in Section I of the *Rules of Golf*, should govern your conduct on the course whether you are playing competitive golf or not. This code for correct behavior is a pleasant one, easily understood, and designed for all-round enjoyment of the game. The principle of the etiquette of golf is consideration for fellow players, be they opponents or partners.

It is pleasant to possess skill at golf, and a degree of skill may be attained by all willing to strive for it. But the degree of skill attained is not of greatest importance; golf's chief contribution to the enjoyment of living is the means it provides for making friends, playing in the outdoors, improving health, and developing a high reputation for honor through the observance of the following points of etiquette of the game of golf.

1. *No one should move, talk, or stand close to or directly behind the ball or the hole when a player is addressing the ball or making a stroke.* Unexpected movements and noises tend to disturb a golfer making a stroke. Also, most golfers are thrown off by having someone standing directly behind them when they are swinging or putting. Thus, you are expected to make yourself as unobtrusive as possible while another player is playing. In addition, remember that no attempt, however indirect, should be made to hamper the play of your opponent. In this respect, golf differs from most other competitive sports. In baseball, for example, it is considered part of the game to jockey or needle the opposing players and try to force them into making mistakes. In golf, this strategy should *never* be employed.

2. *The player who has the honor should be allowed to play before his opponent or fellow competitor tees his ball.* Give your fellow player the whole tee to himself when it is his turn to play. It helps him to concentrate. Also, when a golfer hits a tee shot out of bounds, he should step aside and not shoot again until all his fellow players have driven. This is really a good rule to follow, since if you have driven out of bounds, you will have time to compose yourself and probably make a better second try.

3. *No player should play until the players in front are out of range.* Never underestimate your hitting limits. A golf ball is hard and travels with tremendous speed. Many golfers have been severely injured by players who did not know they could "hit so far." Do not be impatient to drive; you will catch up. When you hit a ball, and there is the slightest chance of its hitting someone, immediately and loudly cry, "Fore."

4. *In the interest of all, players should play without delay.* As you approach your ball, plan your upcoming shot: what club you should use, where you want to put the ball, and how hard to hit it. This will eliminate unnecessary delay and perhaps forestall annoyance on your fellow competitors' part. If the group behind is obviously playing faster than yours, or if they have fewer players, of course, invite them to play through.

5. *Players searching for a ball should allow other players coming up to pass them; they should signal to the players following them to pass and should not continue their play until those players have*

passed and are out of range. If it appears that your original ball may be difficult to find, it is a good idea to play a provisional one. This saves the time required to walk back and play another ball if the original one is not found. Also, if your opponent hits a ball toward a difficult location, help him by following the shot and visually marking its position by some kind of landmark. Remember that nothing indicates a sportsman golfer quicker than his willingness to help find an opponent's lost ball. All in the group should co-operate. In all cases, the *Rules of Golf* allow only five minutes for a search for a ball.

6. *Before leaving a bunker, a player should carefully fill up all holes made by him therein.* In other words, upon leaving a sand bunker, always take the time to smooth your tracks. It is difficult enough to play efficiently from loose sand without having to dig your ball from a depression as you strike at it. Remember the other fellow, and fill in your heel marks. And the considerate golfer enters a trap where the bank is lowest, since he does less damage there than if he clambers down a steep sand slope.

7. *Through the green, a player should ensure that any turf cut or displaced by him is replaced at once and pressed down, and that, after the players have holed out, any damage to the putting green made by the ball or the player is carefully repaired.* Out of consideration both for those playing behind you and for those on the days to follow, you should take pride in preserving the turf as carpetlike as possible. Nothing is more exasperating than to find that your ball has ended in a divot scar after a perfect shot. Also, you have an obligation as a golfer to help maintain the course in as good a condition as possible. Divot marks and loose divots lying around are unsightly as well as injurious to the course.

8. *Players should ensure that, when dropping bags or the flagstick, no damage is done to the putting green, and that neither they nor their caddies damage the hole by standing close to the hole or in handling the flagstick or in removing the ball from the hole. The flagstick should be properly replaced in the hole before the players leave the putting green.* Perhaps the most frequent and flagrant abuses of etiquette occur on the putting green. With the use of caddies on the decline, golfers in the same group are frequently called upon to tend flagstick for a partner or opponent. Proper etiquette here simply calls for being as considerate of your opponents as of your partner—or as you would expect to be treated

yourself. Do not step in the line of a putt. Ask whether the player would prefer to have the flagstick tended or removed. Take note of the fact that if the player is shooting from the fringe of the green, rather than the actual putting surface, he is entitled to have the pin left in the cup and will not incur a penalty if the ball hits the flagstick. If he is fairly close to the hole despite being off the putting surface, he may want the flagstick tended, taken out, or left in the cup. Ask him what his preference is. On the putting green, remember not to drag, twist, or scuff your golf shoes, as this will mar the green and may affect a following player's putt. Pick up your feet so that everyone will have a fair chance to putt. Also do not get into the habit of leaning heavily on your putter as you stand on the green or reach for your ball in the hole. This will produce indentations on the green that may affect another player's putt. Remember that the *Rules of Golf* prevent pressing down the surface of the green to give yourself a smoother line to the hole. You may, however, remove any loose objects between the ball and the hole, either by picking them up or by brushing them aside with the putter. But in the latter case, use the putter in a brushing motion across the line of your putt, with no downward pressure exerted with its head. Also, you may, under the *Rules of Golf,* repair ball marks on your line left by balls hitting on the putting green, but you are only permitted to repair the pit mark, not to improve your line to the cup. To repair a ball mark on the green, insert a sharp-pointed object (a peg tee or knife) just outside the area; at several positions (1) tend to lift the center of the ball mark; then (2) tend to pull the turf toward the center of the pit mark; and (3) smooth the area after the repair. Smoothing may be done in any reasonable manner.

9. *When the play of a hole has been completed, players should immediately leave the putting green.* Be sure to place bags or golf carts on the side or back of the green nearest the next tee; never in front of the green. Record scores on the way to the next tee or on the tee itself. Remember that delays on the putting green will obstruct the flow of play and interrupt the pace of players behind you.

Good golf etiquette is really nothing more than common courtesy on the course. Sure, there are times when the temptation to break golf ethics and etiquette exists. However, since the golfer is completely on his honor, he must police himself as carefully and thoroughly when he is not being observed as when he is. If he moves the ball by accident, or grounds his club in a bunker, he should at once call the proper penalty on himself. He should never attempt to improve his lie in the fairway or rough by exerting downward pressure behind the ball with his foot or the sole of his club. When he marks his ball on the green, he should replace it exactly and not try to gain an inch in the direction of the hole or take a better lie to one side or the other of his spot. Generally, a golfer who slyly cheats hurts his own game most since the time he spends gaining unfair advantage could be more effectively applied to making better shots himself.

The simple rules of etiquette just mentioned serve three main purposes: (1) to reduce the probability of personal injury on the course; (2) to sustain the enjoyment of the game; and (3) to speed up play. Today, slow play is a major problem at most clubs and a concern of all golf committees. To guard against this major breach of golf etiquette, give yourself the following self-examination:

1. On the putting green, am I overcareful in reading the line from several angles? Do I imagine I see things that are not really there? Do I pick up unimportant things? Do I lift the ball to "clean" it when it could not possibly need it? Do I have other balls lifted needlessly, as a matter of routine, or only when they might really interfere? In stroke play, do I putt out whenever feasible, instead of lifting and marking my ball? Do I retry putts while others wait?

2. Before starting, do I know the handicap allowances and local rules?

3. Do I always know when it is my turn to play? And am I ready to play?

4. While others are playing, do I size up my shot and decide what club to use? Or am I indecisive in selecting clubs?

5. When I hit one off the fairway, do I line it up with objects in the area where it went and thus save time in searching?

6. With a double caddie, when I go a different way from the player sharing the caddie, do I take two or three clubs with me to speed my selection?

7. Do I have a second ball handy in case I need it?

8. Do I practice-swing or waggle unnecessarily?

9. Do I let following players through whenever there is an open hole ahead or when I am looking for a ball?

10. Does my idle chatter distract and delay others?

11. Do I try to give a lesson to others during a round?

12. After a bad shot, do I analyze it for my companions' edification and re-examine my swing needlessly?

13. If I use a cart, do I park it in the right place for saving time without hurting the course?

14. Do I waste time between nines?

Priority on the Course. In the absence of special local rules, a group of two players should have precedence and should be entitled to pass any other kind of match. A single player has no standing and should give way to a match of any kind.

Any match playing a whole round (eighteen holes) is entitled to pass a match playing a shorter round. If a match fails to keep its place on the course and loses more than one clear hole on the players in front, it should allow the match following to pass.

THE CADDIE AND THE GOLFER

The dictionary says that a caddie is "one who assists a golfer especially by carrying his clubs." With a good caddie, it is the "assists" that is important, and carrying the clubs is only incidental to his main purpose: helping his golfer any way he can. The player and his caddie make up "the side," and it is the one trace of teamwork in an otherwise individual sport.

Ideally, of course, the caddie should *help*, but it is up to the golfer to use him wisely.

Try to evaluate your caddie. If you think he is capable and knowledgeable, ask his advice, but ask it before you voice your own decision, so he will be objective. In quizzing him about distances to the green, ask him how many yards it is, not what club he thinks you need. Only *you* know how far you can hit with each club; only *you* know whether you are going to hit the shot full or punch it. Above all, remember that you may ask advice only of your caddie or your playing partner and his caddie, and you are permitted by the *Rules of Golf* to have only one caddie.

The player may send his caddie ahead to a hill to show the line to the green, but he may not mark the spot when the player hits. Similarly on the putting green, the caddie may point to the desired line, but he may not touch the line with a club or other marker to indicate how much break should be played. Anything that the player is forbidden to do, such as repairing spike marks on the green, his caddie is prohibited from doing also. If the golfer's shot hits his caddie, he loses the hole in match play and is penalized two strokes in medal play. If this situation occurs in best-ball, only the offending player is affected. He is disqualified for the hole, but his partner is not penalized.

Caddies around the world are a colorful group, ranging from the wise old Scottish caddies who always say "we" when talking about their player, to the lovely geishas of Japan and the formidable women of Belgium. In the United States, several former caddies have become Open champions (Ouimet, Hagen, Sarazen, Hogan, Nelson, and Mangrum), and many have become excellent golfers.

GOLF CARS AND THE GOLFER

Electric golf cars and hand-drawn pull carts have replaced the caddie in many areas of the United States. While the caddie always added a trace of camaraderie to a sport that is basically lonely, the golf cars are less expensive overall and are more readily available. Proper handling of a golf cart or car is essential to course maintenance, pace of play, personal safety, and, of course, golf etiquette. Here are some points to keep in mind when handling a golf car:

1. On starting out, check to see if your car is in gear to go forward and not backward.

2. Do not start until everyone has driven from the tee.

3. Do not drive out ahead of the ball which is closest to the tee. If you have a gasoline car, turn off the engine while your companion is addressing and playing the ball. Never keep driving ahead when someone is playing a shot.

4. When appropriate, advance to your own ball. Always stop even with the ball and park to the side on which your clubs (or your companion's clubs) are carried.

5. Always park reasonably close to the ball so the player can size up his shot, make his selection of clubs, and even change clubs without undue delay.

6. If you have to park a distance from your ball, size up the distance to the green from your car as best you can. Then take one or two extra clubs with you so as to save a trip back and forth to the car.

7. When hunting for a lost ball, park your car in the rough; do not leave it in the fairway in the way of the following group.

8. In driving a car, be careful not to injure fairways, greens, or traps. Never drive close to traps or greens. Stay on paved paths when possible.

9. Never park in front of a green while putting. If possible, park high on the side of the green nearest the next tee, out of the way of the next group.

10. Never drive a car in muddy places, through puddles of water, or in any place that might injure it.

11. Do not drag your feet outside the car. Keep them inside until the car is stopped.

12. Do not get in or out of the car when it is moving.

13. Do not drive parallel to the top of a hill or rise in such a way that the car will be on a pronounced slant. It might overturn.

14. When you are going up or down, always approach a hill or rise in a straight line. If you want to turn at the bottom of a hill, keep going straight for a time after you have reached the bottom. Then turn slowly and at a big angle.

15. Never make a sharp turn, even on a straightaway.

16. Never ride with a companion you consider an inexperienced or incompetent driver.

17. Try to avoid holes or slight bumps on the fairway.

18. Be sure to set brakes before you leave the car.

ETIQUETTE AND THE SPECTATOR

Because more people are attending tournaments, it is important that golfing galleryites know the rules of being good spectators. If you recognize the following rules and obey them, you will enjoy the game more, and so will the players. Like the rules of etiquette for players, the ones for golf spectators are based on common courtesy and fairness.

1. Do not talk or move when someone is making a shot. Any distraction can break a player's concentration.

2. Do not speak to the players during their rounds unless they speak to you first.

3. Stay behind the gallery ropes which surround the tees and greens, and do not crowd the players. Cross fairways only at places where crosswalks are indicated.

4. Never call out loudly, even though no one in the group you are following is making a shot. There may be players in adjoining fairways.

5. Obey the commands of the marshals at all times. They are there for your protection as well as that of the players.

6. Remember that there may be players behind and in front of the group you are following, so watch out for them. Do not leave a green until all players have holed out.

The rules of etiquette are based on courtesy and common sense, and they apply to tournament spectators as well as players. *Fred Vuich*

7. Give all players the same courtesy. Actually, one of the worst breaches of spectator etiquette occurs when a particular gallery favorite is paired with some player in whom the spectators are less interested. The gallery tends to wait only until the favorite has putted out and then rush away to find a vantage point for watching the next hole. Quite often this leaves the other player putting while the crowd is streaking pell-mell toward the next tee and noisily discussing its favorite's performance on that hole. This is grossly unfair to the other player and leaves him at a distinct disadvantage in the competition. Stay in place until all have finished the hole. Be silent and immobile while a shot is being played, regardless of who is playing it.

8. Groups with little or no gallery deserve the same courtesies as the other players. They are playing for a living, too.

9. Keep the circle around the green or tee as large as possible. In this way more people will have a chance to enjoy each shot.

10. Show consideration to your fellow spectators by kneeling if you are in the front row and the gallery is large.

11. Do not walk through traps or on tees and greens.

12. Do not roam the course aimlessly, or you may be hit.

13. Never run, or you may create a stampede and someone may get hurt.

14. Wear low-heeled shoes or golf shoes. Ladies should never wear high heels, as they damage the golf course.

15. Do not be a litterbug. Use the litter baskets at all times.

16. Leave the camera at home, unless you are watching a practice round. Don't try to conceal a camera in your pocket—it might be confiscated.

17. Display your admission ticket or badge conspicuously.

18. Treat the players as you would want to be treated if you were in their shoes.

It is necessary to formulate a plan to achieve optimum value from watching a major golf tournament. For instance, if you are lucky enough to attend a four-day tournament, the formula is simple. The first two days, when the crowds are smaller, afford excellent opportunity to get to know the course by walking, say, four or five holes with different groups. Only by understanding and evaluating the architecture can you appreciate the merit of the leading scores.

By walking the entire course you have an opportunity to study the pros' psychology. If you watch carefully you will find many of the seasoned campaigners playing well within themselves off the tees, perhaps even reverting to a three-wood on a hole within a particularly narrow fairway or where accuracy pays greater dividends than length. You will find that they will loosen the reins when it comes to a long par-5 in the hope of picking up a birdie.

You get a chance to study the way they attack the flagstick, not merely selecting a club which will reach the green; how they make use of, or allow for, the wind; how they have a pre-shot routine which seldom varies. Also, during the first two days, before the guillotine falls, it is often profitable to follow some of the younger players. Although they may not have acquired the necessary consistency to bridge the big money gulf, they are still fine strikers of the ball—often, in itself, a joy to watch.

The last two days of the tournament, when the galleries, especially those following the leaders, grow dense, hole-by-hole watching becomes more difficult. The vital spot at any hole, of course, is the green. Consequently, as soon as the players have holed out you should head for the next green. Usually you will find that you will be down about level with their drives by the time they have all driven off, and can stop for a moment to contemplate their next shot. You ought to be well in position at the green on a par-4 by the time they hit their second shots. While you are waiting for the players to reach the green, move around so that you are in the most advantageous position to head for the next hole.

Some well-banked greens offer natural grandstands. These are the best spots at which to take a breather or wait for other pairings to come by. If you are short, and skeptical about your chances of seeing much in a large crowd, we offer these suggestions. A light three-legged stool is no trouble to carry and forms an ideal portable grandstand; or better still, there are, on the market, aluminum, three-legged seat-sticks which have been used on many occasions to see over the heads of galleries even twenty-deep. They act as walking-sticks when closed, a seat while waiting, and are perfectly balanced to stand on when necessary. If neither of these is available, cardboard periscopes are the next best thing to direct vision.

Being a spectator at golf is a highly individual pastime. No two people can nip in and out of a crowd or break away as quickly as one. One may want to watch a tee shot, the other to make for the green. You lose one another momentarily, and a couple of thousand people have reached a bottleneck ahead of you. The only way, therefore, to see what *you* want is to be a lone wolf.

Most tournament programs carry a map of the course so you can see at a glance how best to flit from one vantage point to another to pick up players two or three holes away. When you join a new group always looks for the official scorer's board to find out how the players stand in relation to par. Never take the word of a "know-all," for you can bet your bottom dollar that he will be wrong.

If you can only spare one day at a tournament, then plan to get there early. All the competitors at one time or another will be warming up in the practice area, and here is where you can really study their methods in detail. Do not just stand idly by watching where the balls go—take that for granted. Concentrate on one player and watch each particular facet of his swing in turn and in detail. At no time should a spectator interfere with or talk to a competitor even on the practice ground. This is his one opportunity to tune up his concentration as well as his game, and it is a gross breach of etiquette to question him at such a time.

A great deal can be gleaned from watching the top players, amateur or professional, if one goes in the right frame of mind and digests what one sees. Conversely, a knowledgeable gallery can give a tremendous boost to the morale of a player if they show they are rooting for him. Whether a player is leading the field or not, he appreciates the recognition of a good shot, but he is either appalled or embarrassed by a ripple of applause for a shot which is clearly inadequate, or for the completion of a tap-in putt. A golf tournament is not meant primarily as an entertainment. It is an exhibition of skill, and as with any subject, the more acquainted one is with it, the more one can appreciate the finer points.

SAFETY FIRST ON THE GOLF COURSE

Safety should come first on the golf course. Carelessness, overzealousness, ignorance of the rules—all can lead not only to embarrassment but to serious injury or worse. Accidents will happen, but most can be avoided if the player exercises common sense. The safety checkpoints below cover common situations encountered on the golf course.

Playing

In Range. Never hit a golf ball if others are within range.

Workers. If workers are ahead, warn them before you take your stroke.

Blind Hole. If a hole is blind (either dogleg or overhill), do not hit until you are certain that the party ahead is out of range.

Practice. Save your practice shots for the practice tee; you may hit an unwary companion. Besides, practice shots during play of a hole are against the rules. Do not practice-swing when it is not your turn to play.

Stand Away. Stand well away from a player making a shot, preferably to the right (if he is right-handed); do not get ahead of the ball; some of us *do* shank.

Anger. Anger can hurt your game; club-throwing can hurt your companions.

Shagging. If a caddie is shagging for you, avoid having him face the sun; it may blind him to a falling ball.

Wood and Stones. Warn others nearby when you play from woods or stony rough.

Lightning

Get Off! If a thunderstorm threatens, get off the golf course if at all possible.

Sheltering. If you cannot leave the course, find a shelter, a grove of trees (never a single one), or below ground level protection in a ditch or bunker.

Golf Cars

Hills. Never drive a golf car on a sidehill or up a steep slope. It can topple over.

Turns. Avoid sharp turns, even where the ground is level.

Legs. Keep your feet and legs in the car.

Common Sense. Drive sensibly: not too fast or too close to other players.

General

Insects. Beware of bees and hornets; some people are allergic to their sting.

Pets, Children. Pets and young children belong at home. Golf courses are not nurseries.

Sun. Wear a hat when the sun shines brightest; salt tablets may help.

Act Your Age. Remember—and act—your age.

COMPETITIVE GOLF

One of the most important features of golf, accounting in large measure for its almost universal popularity as an outdoor participating sport, is its adaptability to competition between players of varying abilities. In almost every other sport, there is seldom any real contest when one player is distinctly better than another. But in golf, the "duffer," or beginner, can play on equal terms with the expert golfer, thanks to a handicapping system.

Over the years many handicap systems have been devised, but today the United States Golf Association handicap system is almost universally used. Even this system, as fair as it is, is subject to annual review and revision by the Handicap and Executive committees of the USGA and must meet the needs of the more than twenty million golfers of varying ability in the United States. Complete details regarding the USGA Golf Handicap System are contained in the USGA golf booklet, *USGA Golf Handicap System with USGA Course Rating System and Golf Committee Manual,* which costs $3.00 a copy and is available from the USGA, Golf House, P.O. Box 708, Far Hills, N.J. 07931.

THE INTRODUCTION OF SLOPE

Until recently, there has been a basic inequity in the USGA Golf Handicap System. It favored the expert golfer and discriminated against the higher handicapper. It made the basic assumption that golfers that have earned similar handicaps on different courses will have an equal chance of winning in head-to-head competition. This was not correct, because handicaps at that time did not sufficiently reflect the difficulty of the course being played.

For example, a 10 handicapper from a short, easy course had to stay with his 10 handicap even when playing from the back tees of a very tough course such as Pine Valley, where his score would skyrocket. If he were playing against a local member with a 10 handicap, he would have to play him level, even though he actually needed several strokes to have a fair chance of winning. This was termed a "portability problem" by the USGA, which realized that handicaps did not travel well.

Moreover, the traditional course-rating system was calculated largely on yardage and the handicaps that came out of the system told what the expert (scratch) golfer was going to score, but did not provide for less skilled golfers. The average golfer has about a 17 handicap and doesn't hit the ball as far or as straight as an expert. When he gets into trouble, he doesn't recover as well. So the higher-handicapper needs more strokes to play against a low-handicapper on tough courses.

The new "Slope System" considers the bogey golfer as well as the scratch player and involves a rating system that measures the relative difficulty of a course for both calibers of golfers. This is called a USGA Slope Rating and is a number used to adjust a handicap to a particular course. The more difficult a course, the higher the slope rating, and the more strokes the golfer receives; the easier the course, the lower the slope rating and the fewer strokes received. The highest slope rating is 155, the lowest is 55. The average slope rating for men and women is 113.

In addition to considering yardage, the new USGA Slope Rating considers elevation, prevailing wind, rough, trees, bunkers, water hazards, undulations on greens, and even psychological effects, such as a long carry over water to a small, tightly bunkered green. The ratings then help determine a player's USGA Handicap Index, which represents the golfer's ability on a course of average difficulty (113 in the new rating system).

However, because few courses are of exactly average difficulty, the golfer hardly ever plays off his USGA Handicap Index. Instead, he uses it to determine how many strokes he gets on a particular course. He does this by consulting a chart posted at each course. It lists the course slope rating and shows by how many strokes a player must adjust his Handicap Index to arrive at his "Course Handicap," the handicap he will use on that particular course.

For example, a player with a USGA Handicap Index of 10 will play from 8 on the easier Darlington course (Slope Rating: 90), off 10 at Hatherly (Slope Rating: 113), but gets 13 strokes at Pine Valley (Slope Rating: 150). Note: A scratch golfer is expected to score scratch figures wherever he plays.

The USGA adopted the "Slope System" effective January 1, 1987, and it is now in use by all regional golf associations in the country.

COMPUTATION OF HANDICAPS

Where the Slope System is in effect, a player's USGA Handicap Index is arrived at as follows:

1. Determine the handicap differentials by subtracting the appropriate USGA Course Rating from each of the last twenty adjusted gross scores and multiply each resulting figure by 113. Divide this result in each case by the corresponding USGA Slope Rating and round off to the nearest tenth.
2. Total the lowest ten handicap differentials and multiply the result by .096. Delete all numbers after the tenths digit, i.e., don't round off to the nearest tenth.

What follows is the scoring record of a player showing how his USGA Handicap Index is determined.

Date M D Y	Adjusted Score	USGA Course Rating	Score Minus Course Rating	USGA Slope Rating	Handicap Differential
12 21 86	90	70.1	19.9	116	19.4
12 12 86	91	70.1	20.9	116	20.4
11 24 86	94	72.3	21.7	123	19.9
11 20 86	88	70.1	17.9	116	*17.4
11 18 86	89	70.1	18.9	116	18.4
11 17 86	90	72.3	17.7	123	*16.3
11 16 86	91	72.3	18.7	123	*17.2
10 12 86	91	70.1	20.9	116	20.4
10 10 86	91	70.1	20.9	116	20.4
9 8 86	86	68.7	17.3	105	18.6
9 4 86	90	70.1	19.9	116	19.4
9 1 86	92	72.3	19.7	123	*18.1
8 24 86	85	68.0	17.0	107	*18.0
8 16 86	78	68.7	9.3	105	*10.0
8 12 86	82	70.1	11.9	116	*11.6
8 2 86	84	70.1	13.9	116	*13.5
7 14 86	94	72.3	21.7	123	19.9
7 5 86	93	72.3	20.7	123	19.0
7 4 86	89	72.3	16.9	123	*15.3
7 1 86	88	70.1	17.9	116	*17.4

* 10 lowest handicap differentials

Total of 10 lowest handicap differentials 154.8
Total multiplied by .096 .... 14.861
Delete all numbers after the tenths digit 14.8
USGA Handicap Index is 14.8

A USGA Handicap Index must not be issued to a player who has returned fewer than five acceptable rounds. When at least five but fewer than twenty acceptable scores are available, the formula used to determine a USGA Handicap Index is as follows:

(1) Determine the number of differentials to be used from the following table

Column I Differentials Available		Column II Differentials to Be Used
5 or 6	....	Lowest 1
7 or 8	....	Lowest 2
9 or 10	....	Lowest 3
11 or 12	....	Lowest 4
13 or 14	....	Lowest 5
15 or 16	....	Lowest 6
17	....	Lowest 7
18	....	Lowest 8
19	....	Lowest 9

(2) Determine handicap differentials
(3) Average the lowest handicap differentials to be used from column II.
(4) Multiply this result by .96
(5) Delete all numbers after the tenths digit (do not round off).

Example: 11 scores available (Column I)—

Total of lowest 4 differentials (Column II)	103.5
Average (103.5 divided by 4)	25.875
Multiply average by .96	24.84
Delete all numbers after tenths digit	24.8
USGA Handicap Index is	24.8

SLOPE AND COURSE RATING

Courses are rated by authorized golf associations, not by individual clubs. To establish the Slope Rating for a course, there are three basic steps. First, the Yardage Rating for the course is calculated, then the USGA Course Rating, and finally the Bogey Rating and Slope Rating.

Yardage Rating is the evaluation of the playing difficulty of a course based on yardage only. It is the score a scratch player on his game is expected to make when playing a course of average difficulty.

Yardage ratings are obtained by using the following formulae:

a. YARDAGE RATING FOR MEN

$$\text{Yardage Rating} = \frac{\text{Length of Course}}{220} + 40.9$$

Example: If the length of the course is 6,419 yards, Yardage Rating for men is calculated as follows:

$$\text{Yardage Rating} = \frac{6,409}{220} + 40.9 = 29.18 + 40.9$$

$$\text{Yardage Rating} = 29.2 + 40.9 = 70.1$$

(*Note: It is recommended that the division by 220 be carried two places and rounded off to the nearest tenth and added to 40.9*)

b. YARDAGE RATING FOR WOMEN

$$\text{Yardage Rating} = \frac{\text{Length of Course}}{180} + 40.1$$

The second step is to establish the USGA Course Rating. This is an evaluation of the playing difficulty of a course for scratch players. It is expressed in strokes and decimal fractions of a stroke, and is based on yardage and other obstacles to the extent that they affect the scoring ability of a scratch player.

To determine the Course Rating, the rating team first applies the total yardage of the course to the USGA Yardage Rating Formula, as described above. The Course Rating is determined by a modification of the Yardage Rating based on ten obstacle factors. On each hole, each factor is evaluated by the rating team on a scale of zero to ten. When the rating process has been completed, units for each factor are totaled and multiplied by a relative weight factor. The resulting figures are then totaled and applied to a formula from which a number is produced. This number, which may be positive or negative, is applied to the Yardage Rating to produce the USGA Course Rating.

Following are the obstacle factors to be considered:

1. Topography. Difficulty of stance in the landing area and the vertical angle of shot from the landing area into the green.
2. Fairway. The effective width and depth of the landing area, which can be reduced by a dogleg, trees, or fairway slope.
3. Recoverability and Rough. The existence of rough and other penalizing factors in the proximity of the landing area and around the green.
4. Out of Bounds. The existence of out of bounds in the proximity of the landing area and around the green.

5. Water Hazards. The existence of water hazards in the proximity of the landing area and around the green.
6. Trees. The strategic location, size, height, and number of trees.
7. Bunkers. The existence of bunkers in the proximity of the landing area and around the green.
8. Green Target. The size, firmness, shape, and slope of a green in relation to the normal length of the approach shot.
9. Green Surface. The contour and normal speed of the putting surface.
10. Psychological. The mental effect on play created by the proximity of obstacles to a target area.

The Rating Team must also consider factors that cause a course to play significantly longer or shorter than its measured length, as follows:

1. Roll. Unirrigated and thin fairways and downhill landing areas result in the ball rolling farther than the normal twenty-five yards. Irrigated and lush fairways and uphill landing areas result in the ball rolling less than twenty-five yards.
2. Elevation. Holes that are uphill from tee to green play longer than those that are downhill from tee to green.
3. Doglegs. Holes in which the fairway bends short of the normal drive zone will force the player to hit less than a full tee shot.
4. Prevailing Wind. Even though there may be as many holes with the wind as against, a constant wind, as on a seaside course, makes play more difficult.
5. Altitude Above Sea Level. The ball will carry a greater distance in high altitudes. The Yardage Rating of a course at an altitude of 2,000 feet or higher is adjusted downward to compensate.

The first step in the determination of the USGA Slope Rating is to establish a Bogey Rating, accomplished by evaluating the obstacle factors from the standpoint of the bogey golfer. A "bogey golfer" is one with a USGA Handicap Index of 17.5 to 22.4 strokes developed on a course of average difficulty. A male bogey golfer can hit tee shots an average of 200 yards and can reach a 370-yard hole in two shots. A female bogey golfer can hit tee shots of 160 yards and can reach a 300-yard hole in two shots. The "Bogey Rating" is equivalent to the average of the better half of a bogey golfer's scores under normal playing conditions. The USGA Slope Rating is then determined by multiplying the difference between the Bogey Rating and the USGA Course Rating by 5.381 for men and 4.24 for women.

Proper course measurement is an integral part of course rating. Permanent markers should be imbedded in the middle of the tee and the hole measured from this point to the center of the green. Measurements should be horizontal (air-line) with steel tape or surveying instruments along the planned line of play (usually down the center of the fairway). If more than one set of tees are in common use, separate measurements and rating markers should be established for each. The yardage markers should be of the same color as the tee markers which will be balanced around them. Where men's tees are used by women, there must be a women's course rating from those tees in order for scores to be used for handicap purposes. There is no equitable way of automatically adjusting women's Course and Slope Ratings from forward tees to any other set of tees.

The USGA recommends the following standard colors and terms for tee markers; the club scorecard should show the course rating from each set of markers, as in this example:

USGA COURSE AND SLOPE RATINGS

Tees	Terms	Men's USGA Ratings		Women's USGA Ratings	
		Course	Slope	Course	Slope
BACK	BLUE (or Championship) COURSE	72.0	119	—	—
MIDDLE	WHITE COURSE	71.3	113	73.7	122
FORWARD	RED COURSE	69.5	105	72.0	118

To facilitate players recording eighteen-hole scores made by combining consecutive nine-hole scores, Course Ratings for each nine holes from each set of tee-markers should be posted at the place where scores are recorded. Players may then combine the applicable nine-hole Course Ratings to record the appropriate 18-hole USGA Course Rating along with the adjusted eighteen-hole score.

On a nine-hole course, if separate tees or tee-markers are used for each nine of an eighteen-hole round, separate measurements and permanent yardage markers shall be established for each nine. The yardage markers (and their respective tee-markers) should be identified with "1" or "I" for the first nine and "2" or "II" for the second nine.

Stroke Holes The higher-handicapped players receive the full difference between handicaps. For example, when a golfer with a 12 plays a golfer with a handicap of 7 strokes, he gets a handicap of 5 strokes. In match play these strokes must be taken on the holes indicated on the scorecard. (Note the italicized numbers on the sample card shown here.)

A handicap stroke is in the nature of an equalizer and should be available on a hole where it most likely will be needed. In allocating the order of handicap strokes to the eighteen holes of a course, consideration should be given to the likelihood of the strokes' being of use as equalizers and not solely as winning strokes to the one receiving them. To do this, you should assign the odd-numbered strokes to the holes on the first nine and the even-numbered strokes to

the holes on the second nine. This equalizes as nearly as possible the distribution of handicap strokes over the entire eighteen holes. (In a case in which the second nine is decidedly more difficult than the first nine, consider allocating odd-numbered strokes to the second nine.)

Allocate the first stroke to the hole on the first nine on which the higher-handicapped player most needs a stroke as an equalizer and the second stroke to the hole on the second nine on which the higher-handicapped player most needs a stroke as an equalizer. Continue alternating in this way for the full eighteen holes.

It is felt that the higher-handicapped player most needs strokes as equalizers on difficult par-5 holes, followed in sequence by difficult par 4s, other par 5s, other par 4s, and finally par 3s. An exceptionally difficult par 3 might warrant being allocated a stroke before an exceptionally easy par 4 or par 5.

A difficult par 5 is one on which a majority of golfers normally cannot reach the green in three strokes. A difficult par 4 is one on which a majority of golfers normally cannot reach the green in two strokes. An exceptionally difficult par 3 is one on which a majority of golfers normally cannot reach the green in one stroke.

In our example, the player would receive three handicap strokes on the first nine, the other two on the second nine, on the holes listed 1, 2, 3, 4, and 5, in the order of need of an equalizing stroke. On the sample card, the five strokes would apply on holes 5, 16, 2, 13, and 1.

SAMPLE SCORECARD

Hole	1	2	3	4	5	6	7	8	9	
Par	4	5	4	4	5	3	4	3	4	36
Yards	444	525	380	391	572	177	401	228	368	3,486
Handicap	5	3	11	9	1	17	7	15	13	OUT
Hole	10	11	12	13	14	15	16	17	18	
Par	4	3	4	5	3	4	5	4	4	36
Yards	378	167	435	499	210	410	568	358	428	3,453
Handicap	12	18	6	4	16	10	2	14	8	IN

		Total Yards	6,939
		Total Par	72

Handicapping the Unhandicapped. The USGA Golf Handicap System is the approved method for determining handicaps, but it will not solve unusual problems such as that of determining fair allowances for convention and resort tournaments which attract novice and occasional players. Obviously, the man who never plays except during his vacation or at an annual trade tournament wants a fair chance in the competition for net prizes.

A standard way of solving such a matter is to conduct a kickers' tournament. Each player selects his own handicap and then shoots at a score which has been drawn blind.

Another method for stroke play is the Callaway Handicap System, devised by Lionel F. Callaway. It is not adaptable to match play tournaments and is not a substitute for the USGA Golf Handicap System.

Under the Callaway System a player's handicap is determined after each round by deducting from his gross score for eighteen holes the scores of the worst individual holes during the first sixteen holes. The table below shows the number of "worst hole"

scores he may deduct and the adjustment to be made, based on his gross score. For instance, if his gross score for eighteen holes is 96, he turns to the table and opposite that score finds that he may deduct the total for his three worst holes scored on Holes 1 through 16, inclusive. Thus, if he has one 9, one 8, and a 7, his handicap totals 24. From this total further plus or minus adjustment is then made according to the adjustment shown at the bottom of each column. For a gross score of 96 the adjustment requires a deduction of 2, resulting in a final handicap of 22. Thus 96 minus 22 handicap equals a net score of 74.

Another one-round system is the Peoria handicapping system. While no golfer in Peoria knows who gave birth to the notion, it is simple and works fairly well in events where players have no playing records on which handicaps are based. After the players tee off, six holes are selected for handicap computation purposes. A player's scores on these six holes are selected and multiplied by 3, and par is subtracted to determine the handicap.

CALLAWAY HANDICAP SYSTEM

If Your Score Is					*Deduct*
		70	71	72	scratch; no adjustment
73	74	75	—	—	$\frac{1}{2}$ worst hole and adjustment
76	77	78	79	80	1　worst hole and adjustment
81	82	83	84	85	$1\frac{1}{2}$ worst holes and adjustment
86	87	88	89	90	2　worst holes and adjustment
91	92	93	94	95	$2\frac{1}{2}$ worst holes and adjustment
96	97	98	99	100	3　worst holes and adjustment
101	102	103	104	105	$3\frac{1}{2}$ worst holes and adjustment
106	107	108	109	110	4　worst holes and adjustment
111	112	113	114	115	$4\frac{1}{2}$ worst holes and adjustment
116	117	118	119	120	5　worst holes and adjustment
121	122	123	124	125	$5\frac{1}{2}$ worst holes and adjustment
126	127	128	129	130	6　worst holes and adjustment
					Maximum Handicap: 50

		Adjustment			
−2	−1	0	+1	+2	Add to or Deduct from Handicap

Notes: 1. No hole may be scored at more than twice its par.
　　　2. Half strokes count as a whole.
　　　3. The 17th and 18th holes are never deducted.
　　　4. In the case of ties, lowest handicap takes preference.

TYPES OF PLAY

As was stated in Section I, there are two basic types of play.

Stroke Play. In stroke play (formerly called medal play) scoring is based on the number of strokes a player requires to complete 18 holes, or one full round of golf. This form of play is used principally for one-day competitions and in the qualifying rounds of tournaments lasting for longer periods, where it is necessary to reduce a large field of competitors to a certain number of players. In tournaments of this kind, all who enter play eighteen or thirty-six holes of stroke play, and the eight, sixteen, thirty-two, or sixty-four players with the lowest scores then continue at match play. One-day tournaments are usually on a handicap basis to equalize the playing abilities of the golfers entered. Actually, stroke play competition is the most severe test of golf, for when a player has trouble on one or two holes in a good field of players, he has a very serious problem to overcome.

Match Play. Individual competition is involved in match play. There may be one or two players on a side. In most tournament play a match is between two players only. In such a match the player who wins the greatest number of holes from his opponent wins the match; the total number of strokes involved does not count. Thus a player may require several strokes more on the entire round than his opponent and still beat him in the number of holes won. Each hole counts one point and is decided by the number of strokes required to complete the individual hole. If both players get identical scores on a hole, that hole is said to be "halved."

Match play is used in most tournaments following the qualifying round. The eight, sixteen, thirty-two, or sixty-four players having the lowest scores at stroke play in the qualifying round continue at match play. Players are paired for matches in accordance with the General Numerical Draw (see page 427). If there are insufficient players to complete a flight, byes may be used for the last places (or highest numbers) in the general numerical draw. The lowest score is No. 1, the second lowest score No. 2, and so on until the names of all qualifiers are listed. Thereafter, byes are added to complete the flight. If the defending champion is exempted from qualifying and the general numerical draw is used, it is customary for him to be given the No. 1 position in the draw. The matter should be settled in advance.

TOURNAMENTS AND COMPETITIONS

One of golf's appeals is that so many different types of competitions can be arranged. Just a few of the more popular types are given here.

Age Contest

Twenties	Ages 20–29
Thirties	Ages 30–39
Forties	Ages 40–49
Fifties	Ages 50–59
Sixties	Ages 60 and over

All enter under the same conditions, play on the same day on the same course, and use their full handicaps. Each may choose his partner, who must be in the same class as himself. There are eighteen holes of stroke play, and prizes are awarded in each class.

Average Score. Stroke play. Partners average their gross scores for each hole and deduct half their combined handicap from their eighteen-hole total. Half-strokes count as whole strokes after totaling.

Best-Ball and Aggregate (Low-Ball, Low-Total). This is a variation of the regular four-ball match. Two points are involved on each hole, one point for the best ball and one point for the low aggregate score of a side.

Best-Ball Match. Each player plays his own ball. Two of the contestants are partners and play their best ball against the score of a third and generally better player.

Best-Ball Twosome. Taking handicaps as they fall on the card, two players play as a team. The lowest score recorded on each hole, with handicap, counts toward the team's best-ball score for the round. Although both players play their own ball, only the lowest score on each hole is counted. The team having the lowest best-ball score wins the event.

Best-Ball Foursome. This is the same as the best-ball twosome, except that the teams are now composed of four players. The lowest score, with handicap, on each hole counts as the team's score. This can also be played using the best two-ball or best three-ball scores of the foursome where the two low scores or three low scores, respectively, are used in determining the team's total.

Bingle-Bangle-Bungle. Three points on each hole. One point to player whose ball first comes to rest on clipped surface of green. A second point to the player whose ball is nearest the cup after all players are on the green. The third point to the player who first sinks his putt. On short holes, where it is possible to reach the green from the tee, no point is awarded for first on the green, since the player with the honor has too great an edge; instead, this point goes to the player whose ball is second nearest to the pin after all balls are on the green. In settling up, each player wins the difference between his total points and the total points of each player with fewer points.

Blind-Holes Tournament. The winning score is based on only nine holes, selected individually from among the eighteen to be played. The holes are not selected until after all players have left the first tee, so that the players have no knowledge of the holes that will count until they have finished play. Half-handicap is generally used to compile net totals.

Blind Low-Net Foursome. Contestants play eighteen holes with whom they please. At conclusion of play, committee draws names from hat and groups players into foursomes; net scores are added to determine winning foursome.

Blind Partners. This is an eighteen-hole stroke play round with 100 percent handicaps. Players may play with anyone of their choice, but partners are not drawn until the last group has teed off, so a player does not know his partner until he has finished. Winner is the team with the lowest better-ball score after deducting both handicaps.

Breakfast Team Tourney. All interested golfers assemble at the club for breakfast, then are split by handicaps into two equal teams. Low-handicap golfer of Team A plays against low man of Team B, and so on, until all contestants are paired. Play is in foursomes, stroke play, no handicaps. Use Nassau

scoring to determine victors in each foursome, who get their breakfasts bought by losers.

Club Championships. Class and club championships may be played on either a match play or stroke play basis. No handicaps are figured. If the championship is to be played on a match play basis, usually a qualifying round of eighteen or thirty-six holes is played with either the low eight or the low sixteen players qualifying for match play. If the championships are to be decided on a stroke play basis, this can be done by playing either seventy-two holes or thirty-six holes. Some clubs decide their championships on one day, with the contestants playing thirty-six holes; others decide theirs on seventy-two holes, over four weekends of play. Some clubs match their players according to handicaps without a qualifying round.

Consolation Tournament. This is held at the end of the season on any basis desired. The only players eligible to compete, however, are those who have not won a tournament prize during the season. Some clubs give a prize to every player in the tournament.

Costume Tournament. Mixed Scotch Foursomes. Each player dresses in some sort of costume of his own selection. Prizes can be awarded for best costumes as well as best scores.

Drop-Out Tournament. Each player is allowed his full handicap, the strokes to be taken as they come on the card. The player then plays against par. A player remains in the contest only until he loses a hole to par. The winner is the player going farthest around the course.

Fewest Putts. Only strokes taken on the putting surface are counted. No handicaps are used. The winner is the player using fewest putts.

Flag Tournament. Each player is given a small flag, with his name attached to the flagstick. Using his full handicap, he plays until he has used the number of strokes equaling par plus his handicap. He plants the flag after using his quota of strokes, playing an extra hole or two if necessary. The winner is the player who plants his flag farthest around the course. A variation is to award equal prizes to all players who hole out at the 18th green within their allotted number of strokes.

Four-Ball Stroke Play. This is similar to individual handicap stroke play except that players are paired in two-man teams, and their better ball on each hole is the team score. Allow each player 100 percent of his handicap, the strokes to be taken as they come on the card. Many of the other tournaments listed above for individuals can be adapted to four-ball play.

Get-Acquainted Tourney. Eighteen-hole stroke play with handicaps. Each entrant must play with a partner with whom he has never before been teamed.

Goat Tournament. Each member of the club is given an inexpensive token in the form of a goat, with his name on the reverse side. Any player may then challenge another to a handicap match, the winner to get the loser's "goat." After a player has lost his goat, he may continue to challenge in an attempt to get another player's goat. However, if he should lose and not have a goat with which to pay, he must purchase a "kid" for a nominal amount from the professional and give up the kid. The kid is convertible into merchandise in the professional's shop. Only players with a goat in their possession may be challenged, and players usually are not required to accept a challenge more often than once a week. Records of goat play and the current location of each goat are usually posted so that a player may know who has his goat and who has the most goats. The winner is the player holding the most goats at the end of the season.

Handicap Stroke Play. Players play eighteen holes at stroke play. Prizes may be awarded for best gross and net scores. Full handicaps are used.

High and Low Ball. Two points are involved on each hole. One point is scored for the best ball and one for the better of the two poorest balls, in regular four-ball match. For example, A and B are partners, and C and D are partners. A scores 5 and B scores 3 on a hole. C and D each score 4 on the same hole. A and B win a point for the best ball, and C and D win a point because their second best ball is better than A.

Husband and Wife Two-Ball Match. This is to be played the same as a Two-Ball Mixed Foursome, but the partners must be husband and wife.

Intra-Club Matches. Members of a club are divided into teams, and matches are played on a point system with a regular schedule.

The following is the set-up of a league; variations can be made depending on the club or the organization: Players are divided according to classes. Each team should have one member from A, B, C, and D classes. In this way, a player plays against an opponent of his own class and reduces the number of strokes given to a minimum. Play is on a point basis, with the Nassau Point System recommended.

In some cases, the league is divided into five-man teams, with the fifth man acting as alternate. The alternate member of the team plays when one of the other members of the team is absent. A new alternate should be designated for each team match.

Junior Tourney. Open to children of members below the age of eighteen with separate divisions for boys and girls. Stroke play, eighteen or thirty-six holes, no handicap. In addition to an award for low score among the entire field, it is a good idea to have several flights by age groupings.

Kickers' Tournament (sometimes called Blind Bogey). The committee draws a number, advising players that it was, for example, between sixty and seventy. Players select their own handicaps without knowing exactly the number drawn. The player whose net score equals, or is closest to, the number drawn is the winner. This is a good type of tournament to schedule when accurate handicap information for a large percentage of the players is not available.

Kickers' Replay Tournament. Each player is allowed to replay any (and only) two shots in a round. The player must continue with the replayed ball once it is called. Full handicap to apply.

Ladder Tournament. The names of all players are listed in order, according to handicaps, at the start of the season, those having the same handicap being listed alphabetically. A player may challenge any one of the three players immediately above him to an eighteen-hole match. If he wins, they exchange places. If he loses, he may not challenge again until he has defended his own position against a challenge from below. Play is usually carried out without handicaps.

Long and Short Tourney. Many players have good long games and poor short games, and vice versa. This event combines the abilities of these two types of golfers. One player does the driving and long work; his partner does the approaching and putting. Players select their own partners.

Low-Net Foursome. The total score of the four players, less handicaps, determines the winning foursome in the field of contestants.

Match vs. Par. Players, using their handicaps as they fall on the card, play against par. For example, if a player's net score on a par-4 hole is higher than 4, the player would be 1 down to par. The winner of the event is the player who is most "up" on par at the finish of the round.

Medal Sweepstakes. Players play eighteen holes, and the winner is the player with the lowest net score. Also, a prize may be given to the player with the lowest gross score in order to encourage participation of low-handicappers.

Miniature Tourney. A thirty-six-hole event. Contestants, using three-quarters of their handicaps, play nine holes in the morning to qualify. Entire field then divided into flights of eight players each, the eight low net players forming the first flight, the next eight low net players forming the second flight, and so on. Three match play rounds of nine holes each are then played to determine a winner and runner-up for each flight.

Mixed Foursomes. These are a standard Sunday afternoon feature at many clubs, and they are now played in three ways. The official way is for the partners to alternate driving from each tee and then to play alternate shots until the ball is holed. The game is perhaps more enjoyable for average golfers if both partners drive from each tee and select which ball to play thereafter. In a third method, the partners both drive from each tee, and then each plays a second shot with the other's ball. After the second shots, a choice is made regarding the ball with which the hole will be completed, alternate shots being continued, of course.

Most 3s. Or 4s or 5s. Use net or gross scores, as you prefer. Can also be used in combination with other events.

Mystery Event. Send players out without telling them what type of contest they are entering, except that it is either match or stroke play. After all scores are in, release news of what the event was, and determine winner.

Nassau Tournament. This is similar to the handicap stroke play, except that handicap strokes are taken hole by hole as they fall on the card, and prizes are awarded for the best first nine, the best second nine, and the best eighteen holes. The advantage is that a player making a poor start or tiring at the finish may still win a prize for his play on the other nine.

No Alibi Tournament. Instead of deducting his handicap at the end of the round, each player is allowed to replay during the round the number of shots equaling three-quarters of his handicap. A stroke replayed must be used even if it is worse than the original; it cannot be replayed a second time.

Odd and Even Tournament. This tournament is played in foursomes, two players making up one team. One player to play all even holes and the other all odd holes. Use one-half of combined handicap; no more than ten strokes difference in handicap of partners. Low net is the winner.

Par Battle. Played under full handicap. Advise players that on a certain ten holes of the course five points will be won if par or better is shot. On three other holes award ten points for par or better. On three other holes there is a five-point penalty for players who do not score par or better, and on the remaining two holes, the penalty is ten points for failing to make par. Winner is player with most points at end of round.

Parent and Child Tournament. Parent may play with one or more children. Selected drive, alternate strokes; one-half combined handicap is used for eighteen holes.

Pari-Mutuels. Play in these events is in foursomes with full handicaps. Score for each hole is determined by the two best balls on each hole (net). The score of the best two balls is used rather than the score for the best ball, as the two-ball procedure keeps more players in the competition, playing out each hole.

When it is legal, bets on the foursomes to win, place, or show are taken in units of one dollar. After the last foursome has left the first tee, the betting is closed and the total money, less ten percent (the pro's cut for running the event), is divided into forty parts. The money is then split as follows:

	Win	Place	Show
Winning foursome	16 parts	8 parts	4 parts
Second-place foursome		6 parts	3 parts
Third-place foursome			3 parts

All the bettors who have bet on the winning foursome to win divide the win-money. For instance, if the win-money was $100 and eight men had bet $1 on them to win and one man had bet $2 on them to win, the $1 bettors would receive $10 each and the $2 bettor would receive $20.

Point Accumulation Tournament. To be scored as follows:

Any score equaling par or better, 5 points

Any score from 1 to 4 strokes inclusive over par, 3 points

Any score from 5 to 7 strokes inclusive over par, 1 point

The 18th fairway is measured off at 150 yards, 175 yards, 200 yards, and 250 yards.

A player with a handicap of 12 or less scores:

5 points for driving over 250 yards
4 points for driving over 200 yards
3 points for driving over 175 yards
1 point for driving in fairway

A player with a handicap of 13 or more scores:

5 points for driving over 200 yards
4 points for driving over 175 yards
3 points for driving over 150 yards
1 point for driving in fairway

(All drives, in order to score points, must be in the fairway.)

Point Tournament. Players use full handicaps, taking the strokes as they come on the card. Four points are awarded for an eagle, three for a birdie, two for a par, and one for a score one over par, on a net basis. The winner is the player with the highest number of points.

Pros vs. Members. The club professional agrees to play a handicap match against each member as he is challenged, making a nominal charge for each round. The professional plays from scratch. The member making the best showing in his match receives a prize from the professional at the end of the season.

Pyramid Tournament. This is another form of the ladder tournament, featuring a different arrangement of the tournament board used. Entries are arranged in pyramidal form, with one name at the peak, two names in the next lower level, three names in the third level, etc. The pyramid can be as large or as small as the number of entries requires.

At the very beginning of the tournament, each entry must challenge and defeat at least one player on his own level before being eligible to challenge entries on the next higher level. After this initial win, all challenges are to the next higher level. The challenger, if he wins, exchanges places on the pyramid with the loser of the match. In all other respects, the rules of play are the same as required for the ladder tournament.

Relay Event. Partners select one of their scores for the first nine, the other score for the second nine, to get their eighteen-hole total. Allow one-half or three-eighths combined handicap.

Replay Tournament. This is a variation of the No Alibi Tournament. Instead of allowing a player to replay a given number of his worst strokes, an opponent is designated for each player, and the opponent is allowed to recall a given number of the player's best shots and ask that they be replayed. For Class A players, nine strokes may be recalled; Class B, six strokes; Class C, three strokes. If the competition is conducted at stroke play, each opponent must, of course, exercise all his recall options.

Remorseful Golf. In this contest each player has the privilege of making his opponent play over any four shots during the round.

Ringer Tournament. A player builds his total over the season by posting his lowest score on each hole. Scoring is on a gross basis.

Round Robin Tournament. Each entrant plays every other entrant at handicap match play during the season; allow the full difference between handicaps in each match. A time limit is usually set for completion of each round; a player who cannot meet an opponent within the time limit forfeits the match, but may continue in the tournament. The winner is the player winning most matches.

Scorefest. Two teams, of any size. Losing team is the one that scores the least points on following system:

Net scores over 100	2 points
Net scores 90 to 100	5 points
Net scores 85 to 89	10 points
Net scores 80 to 84	15 points
Net scores 75 to 79	25 points
Net scores 70 to 74	40 points
Net scores under 70	75 points

Scrip Tourney. Furnish each player with $10,000 in stage money. Each player has a partner; play in foursomes. Pair with the most scrip after play is over wins. Wins and losses settled whenever incurred during round. Awards are such matters as: low ball each hole, $100; low aggregate each hole, $200; birdies, $300; eagles, $500; first ball on each green, $100; first putt sunk, $200; and so on, as the ingenuity of the committee can devise. Penalties include: ball in rough, $100; ball in wrong fairway, $300; ball hitting tree and rebounding into fairway being played, $500; ball in water, $200; fanning, $300; swearing, $400; swearing at caddie, $1,000, and so forth.

Selected Score. Each player plays thirty-six holes. From his two cards, he selects his best score on each hole. The winner is the player with the lowest total score for the selected eighteen holes. If net prizes are awarded, three-quarters of handicaps are usually enough. This event may be completed in a day or extended over a weekend.

Senior Tourney. Stroke play, eighteen holes. Open to players fifty or more years of age. Played without regular club handicaps, but older players get a stroke advantage as follows: fifty to fifty-four years old, scratch; fifty-five to fifty-nine, two strokes; sixty to sixty-four, four strokes; sixty-five to sixty-nine, six strokes; seventy and over, eight strokes. There should be a prize for low gross player, no matter what his age.

Shotgun Tournament. At least one team is stationed on each tee of the eighteen holes at a specific time; the longer holes may accommodate two teams. The start of play for everyone is signaled by a shotgun blast or a suitable substitute that can be heard throughout the course. All groups should finish playing the eighteen holes at about the same time.

Six- or Twelve-Hole Elective. Either nine or eighteen holes stroke play, at the end of which each player selects as his score the total scores made on his six or twelve best holes. Two-thirds of the regular club handicap is used for eighteen holes; one-third for nine holes.

Six-Point Match. Six points are at stake on each hole. In reality there are two points being fought for by each pair in the threesome; A vs. B, B vs. C, and A vs. C. Low score each hole wins 4 points, middle score wins 2 points, high man wins nothing. If all tie, 2 points apiece. Two players tie for low, 3 points each. One player low, other two tied, the split is 4-1-1. Generally the point allocation is obvious, but when a player gets a stroke from one of his opponents and not from the other one, it is harder to figure the number of points each player wins. In such cases, merely compute results of each match (AB, BC, and AC) separately and the point split is readily determined.

Speck Tournament. Players are teamed as in four-ball match play. Each team is credited on each hole with one speck (*a*) for the longest drive in the fairway, (*b*) for getting the first ball on the green, (*c*) for having the closest ball to the pin on the approach shot, (*d*) for a one-putt green, and (*e*) for the lowest score on the hole. The team having the most specks at the end of the 18 holes wins.

Splash Contest. No entry fee, but players must contribute one new ball for every time they play into a water hazard during the round. A player entering the contest but failing to turn in his score is charged three balls, on suspicion. Award balls to the three low net players on a 60-30-10 split-up.

String Tournament. Each player or each side is given a piece of string in lieu of handicap strokes. The string is measured to allow one foot for each handicap stroke. The player or side may advance the ball by hand to a more favorable spot at any time, measuring the distance the ball was moved with the string and cutting off the length used. When the string is used up, the player is on his own. The string may be used on the putting green to advance the ball into the hole, or it may be used to inch away from a difficult lie through the green or in a hazard.

Sweepstakes. Stroke (or medal) play, full handicap. Each player in tourney signs up for one new golf ball.

Golfer with low net score wins half the balls, second best net takes one-third, third place wins one-sixth.

Syndicate Tournament. The field is divided into classes according to handicaps: Class A may be men with handicaps of 7 and under; Class B, 8 to 15; Class C, 16 to 24; and the like. The player who makes the lowest score in his class on a hole wins a syndicate. Syndicates may be cumulative; in the event that one or more holes are tied, those syndicates go to the player next winning a hole.

Net Syndicate Tournament. Played with full handicap. Golfers post their scores, then put a ring around their score on each hole where they are entitled to a stroke by their handicap. This is to aid the committee, which looks over the scores of the entire field and picks the man whose net score is lowest for the first hole. If no one has tied him, he wins the hole from the entire field and wins $1/18$th of the prize money. If two or more players tie for low on the first hole, the committee examines the second hole, and so on, until a hole is reached where one golfer has a clear net win. Tied holes carry forward to next win hole. On eighteenth hole, if no syndicate is won, tying low players split whatever entry money remains.

Team Match–Nassau System. Regular eighteen-hole matches are played by two or more teams, but the scoring is on the Nassau System basis: 1 point for the first nine holes and 1 point for the second nine holes and 1 point for the match.

Three-Ball Matches. In this match three players play together. Each may play against both of the others, or where one player is better than either of the other two he will play against the best ball of the two poorer players.

One-Half Aggregate Score. This is a variation of the Three-Ball Match described above and is used where the players are of equal playing ability and one of them is not enough better than the other two to justify his playing their best ball. In this case the scores of the two partners are added, and one-half thereof counts against the odd player's score. For example, one of the partners takes a 4 and the other a 3, making a total of 7, their score for the hole being $3^1/2$. The odd player must beat this in order to win.

Threesome Match. One player, hitting every shot, opposes two players who stroke alternately at a sin

gle ball. A traditional event in the British Isles, this contest does not seem to have much popularity this side of the ocean.

Two-Ball Foursome. Two players constitute a team, and only one ball is used by each team; the partners alternate in playing the shots. One partner drives from all the even-numbered tees and the other partner drives from all the odd-numbered tees, regardless of which one made the last stroke on the previous hole. If this event is played on a handicap basis, one-half of the combined handicaps is used.

SPECIAL OR NOVELTY EVENTS

Approaching and Putting Contest. This is a very popular form of competition for a Sunday or holiday afternoon as it can be played in front of the clubhouse either on the 9th or 18th hole, or both. Each contestant approaches and holes out three balls from 25, 50, and 100 yards off the green. In each case each ball should be played from a different direction. The winner is the one holing out the three balls in the fewest number of strokes.

"Can You Take It?" Tournament. This tournament is played in foursomes using regular handicaps. The idea is to create noise and disturbance throughout the round to disturb and distract your partners. It is advisable to place one practical joker in each foursome to start the fireworks and get the other three members of the party into the right spirit. Contestants are not allowed, however, to interfere with the actual swinging of the club or with the lie or flight of the ball.

Any contestant who cannot take it good-naturedly is fined according to his misbehavior. These fines are set before the match and are applied, when paid, to the tournament fund to buy more prizes for the winners.

Consecutive Club Tourney. Each player allowed only four clubs: 3-wood, 5-iron, 8-iron, and putter. All players use the 3-wood off the first tee, thereafter they must use 5-iron, 8-iron, and putter in that sequence for all subsequent shots, no matter what the lie of the ball. To even up player ability, allow only half handicaps.

Cross-Country Tournament No. 1. Start about a mile from the course and play directly across country, finishing on one of the greens of the course near the clubhouse, if possible, but designated in advance. The ball must be played from wherever it lies. If found in an unplayable position, the player is permitted to lift and tee up with the loss of two strokes. This contest furnishes many exciting and unusual situations.

Cross-Country Tournament No. 2. This contest is played entirely on the golf course, skipping about, however, from one hole to another, not in the usual rotation. Play might start at the 1st tee and go to hole No. 6, then start at the 7th tee and go to hole No. 14, and so on, until at least nine holes have been played.

Driving Contest. Pick a wide-open flat fairway. Each contestant gets five drives, with only the best three counting. Only shots ending in fairway count. For quick determination of distance, erect marker flags each 25 yards from 125 yards to 300 yards. Judges stationed down the fairway can estimate yardage beyond nearest marker. A variation of this event allows only three drives and deducts 10 percent from the distance for all shots ending up in the rough.

Forfeit Round. This is not for serious play. At each green, post directions for a forfeit to be paid during the play of the next hole by the player whose score for the hole just completed is highest. Suggested: (*a*) take off shoes and play shots with shoes dangling between arms, laced around neck; (*b*) carry all clubs out of bag; (*c*) use only putter, tee to green; (*d*) at the "drink" hole, treat the foursome; (*e*) walk backward, tee to green; (*f*) laugh from instant of finishing drive until ball is holed out; (*g*) whistle (or sing) from tee to green; (*h*) low man, not high scorer, pays penalty prescribed for previous hole; (*i*) play all shots standing on one foot. No forfeit is paid on holes where high score is tied.

Monkey Foursome. Each member of the foursome carries a single club of his choice. One ball is played. Each member of the foursome, in rotation, plays the ball from wherever it happens to lie and with whatever club he has chosen to carry.

Monkey Foursome, Captain's Choice. Played as above, except that each foursome elects a captain who selects the player to make each shot as the strategy of the hole dictates.

Obstacle Tourney. Played with or without handicap. Each hole presents some obstacle, such as a stake off to one side of the fairway that must be played around, or a barrel just short of the green that must be played through.

One-Club Event. Each player carries only one club, which must be used for all shots. Club may be specified by committee or selected by player. Low net wins. Variation may permit two clubs or even three.

Putting Contest. A putting contest is played entirely on a putting course or green. A qualifying round is played, and then the qualifiers compete on a match play basis. The whole tournament can be run off in one afternoon. An obstacle putting contest is one where obstacles are placed around the putting green.

Putting Tourney. An eighteen-hole event on the practice putting green. Winner determined by total putts. In case of ties, all tying contestants play extra holes at sudden death.

Razzle-Dazzle Tournament. Two teams are picked by the club professional from the field of players that shows up on the day of play. A captain is selected by each team. Each team numbers its players from 1 up with a cardboard pinned on back or chest of each player. Only one ball is played by each team. Player No. 1 shoots first, then No. 2, and so on, until every player has shot. Then start over again with No. 1.

Play with regular razzle-dazzle rules; that is, make all the noise you want, at any time you want to razz the opposing team, without touching them.

Solo-Club Team Match. Two teams, each with twelve men and a nonplaying captain, are chosen. The players are numbered, and each player uses only the club assigned to him as follows:

Player No. 1 uses driver
Player No. 2 uses 3-wood
Player No. 3 uses 4-wood
Player No. 4 uses 2-iron
Player No. 5 uses 3-iron
Player No. 6 uses 4-iron
Player No. 7 uses 5-iron
Player No. 8 uses 6-iron
Player No. 9 uses 7-iron
Player No. 10 uses 8-iron
Player No. 11 uses 9-iron or wedge
Player No. 12 uses putter

The captain directs the team and decides the club to be used on each shot, the club specified to be used only by the man assigned to it. In other words, each man carries and uses only one club.

Throw-Out Tournament. At the conclusion of play, each player is allowed to reject his three (or any designated number) worst holes. Handicaps usually are reduced in proportion to the number of holes which may be rejected. The winner is the player with the lowest score for the fifteen holes (or the designated number) finally selected.

How to Win Golf Matches

Confidence and bold playing win golf matches. To gain confidence, it is essential to have and follow a plan of action. Think out the course you are going to play beforehand, and decide such things as where you will go strong off the tee and where you will just keep the ball in play. Having devised your plan, do not deviate from it unless, of course, it means losing the hole.

Now that you have a plan of attack thought out, let us consider the match itself. Here are twelve golden rules for success:

1. Know your own game. Never count on doing better than your average. You will have some good holes and some bad holes. Your opponent will too. This sort of thinking will keep you from blowing up when things go wrong or being too elated when they are right.

2. Study the course conditions: they will radically affect your play. On a dry course, play run-up shots. On a wet day, play pitch shots right to the hole. On a windy day, you again want to play low, bouncing shots. Remember that the speed of the greens can change during the day. In the early morning the dew will make them slow. In the afternoon, when the sun has dried them out, they will be faster.

3. Play the shot you know you can make—not a fancy shot out of a book. In other words, forget trying to hit your "career shot" and play it safe and sane. Always plan one shot *ahead* to make your next shot easier.

4. Study your opponent's style during the first few holes. It can often give you a lot of confidence! A player with several faults will surely come ungrooved before the end. Also, in the psychology department, it is well to study your opponent to determine his little idiosyncrasies. Some players cannot stand to be outhit, in which case if possible let it fly on the first few holes to get him pressing. If you drive for equal distance, it may be a good idea to ease up just a little so that you get the first shot at the green. Seeing you on there, particularly if you are close, can burst a lot of them apart at the seams.

5. Disregard your opponent's shots as much as humanly possible and concentrate on playing your own game. That is, play your game shot by shot, and do not worry about your bad shots. Remember that a bad shot in match play can, at worst, mean *one* lost hole. Never give up on a hole and waste strokes. In singles many a hole is won with a bogey. It is important, too, to keep comments about your play to yourself. If you goof a shot and it still comes off, do not let anybody know you blew it, but let them think you simply have a wide variety of shots. Your opponent may get a mental lift if you start complaining about your game, and, even worse, you may convince yourself.

6. Play position with *every* shot. Disregarding your opponent's shots from tee to green is, of course, virtually impossible. Yet you can conquer this to some extent by not even watching when he hits, but going about the business of mentally planning your own shot. Do everything in your power to concentrate merely on shooting the best score you can. Naturally you will be aware of the fact when an opponent hits the ball out of bounds or, as an example, into a water hazard. This is going to give you shots to play with, and your first instinct is to put the crusher on him by flogging it far down the fairway. Do not do it. In such a case, sacrifice distance for accuracy. Take the club with which you are dead certain you can keep the ball straight and safely in play.

7. Do not let the opposition profit from your club selection, but, if possible, learn from their shots. Much of the time an alert opponent will be watching you to profit from how much club you use on a short hole or on your approaches. To foil the fellow who makes a habit of looking in your bag, you can cross him up by hitting half or three-quarter shots. And if you are addicted to the same practice, you will see how far down the grip he holds the

club and how much of a swing he takes; otherwise, he may be giving you the same business.

8. Do everything you can to keep the pressure on your opponent and off yourself. For example, try to hole everything from thirty yards in. Not that you *will* hole all of them, but because this positive attitude will leave you closer to the hole than a wishy-washy effort. Once in a while, one will drop and really shake your opponent.

9. Play away from trouble. We know this sounds obvious; but many players will dispatch a beautiful drive straight into a fairway bunker, when with a little care they could have been in good shape.

10. Do watch your opponent carefully when he putts, and keep the putting pressure on him at every opportunity. While this may sound like a contradiction of Rule 5, remember this: If you have the same line and are inside of him you can "go to school" on how his ball rolls, but also be sure to watch how firmly he strokes the putt. Also be certain to observe the putt as it slides past the cup so that you can get a line on how the green will break coming back.

11. Always play at your own pace. If you usually play slowly, do not allow your opponent to speed up the game and throw you off your normal pace. If you normally play fast and your opponent is playing slowly, keep yourself in motion by walking forward and studying your next shot some more.

12. Do not let up when you are ahead. This is *fatal.* Keep playing each hole according to your plan.

Now, when it comes to playing a four-ball, you and your partner should start from the first tee with the idea of playing for birdies. A slow start can be very costly, because in this type of match it mostly takes a birdie to *win* a hole. Holes are very seldom won with pars. Also, at the start, elect a captain for the side, usually the player with more experience. It is this player's job to make the tactical decisions. Here are three golden rules that will surely help in four-ball play:

1. Never stop building your partner's confidence.
2. Find out such seemingly trivial things as whether your partner likes to hit first. Many players prefer to have the other team member hit first, finding it comforting to know that he is on the fairway. This helps particularly on the 3-pars if your partner likes advice as to what club you used and how well you hit it.
3. Give your opponents fits!

All other considerations flow from these three.

On par-3s the better iron player should shoot first. Having the accurate iron player already on the green can give the weaker iron shooter confidence. If you have the honor, this puts the pressure on your opponents. Actually, before teeing off on *any* key hole, the side's strategy should be discussed and decided. Of course, the state of the match will sometimes reverse your original plans for any key hole.

One of the things amateurs forget is that if your side is away *either* of you can shoot next. Do not confine your use of this option to the putting green. It can work in your favor on *any* approach shot, or even on seconds on par-5s. Remember: the idea is to give your partner confidence. So, when your side is away, *the player with the best chance of making the shot should play first.* A successful shot on his part will encourage his partner to make a success of the more difficult shot. And two successful shots can really put the pressure on your opponents.

While we are on this subject of options, there may be times when you prefer not to surrender the option. By this we mean have the player who is nearer the hole play first, regardless of the difficulty of the shot. The thinking here is to get two shots near the hole before your opponents have the chance to match your shots. Where options and the matter of giving confidence to your partner conflict, each case will have to be decided on its merits. But always think about the situation before making a decision. A clear plan can give each partner a better picture of what he has to do and increase his chances of making a successful shot.

Confidence will not come from ignorance, but will be fostered by planned knowledge. Playing bold does not mean playing with the blinders on, but rather knowing what you must do and then doing it!

WHY GOLFERS BET—AND HOW

Why do people bet at golf? Almost everyone bets on sports events, but the peculiar thing about golf wagers is that the *participants* in the game do most of the betting. This situation is almost unique in sports, for the people who play a game do not as a rule have something staked on the outcome. Sports such as baseball, basketball, boxing, and football, which are ideal for spectator gambling, do not seem to produce betting by the players themselves. Then, why is the bet a *seemingly* necessary part of golf?

The answer seems to lie in the very nature of sport itself. Competition is a natural concomitant of most sports, but golf is an exception since, for all practical purposes, it can really be played alone, with only the course and one's best previous score as the opponent. People bet when they play golf to produce that element of competition with a tangible opponent that is inherent in most other sports. Without the wager, two players often feel that they are only randomly involved in any sort of game, and each of them may actually feel that he is playing by himself. The bet is the connecting link between the two golfers. It establishes the competition, creates it so that no longer is the player struggling only with himself, but with a flesh-and-blood rival. Any game that can be played alone generally *requires* a wager to state the competition. Thus, people bet on pool, free-throw shooting, and golf, but not on ping-pong, basketball, and tennis. Betting on golf also relieves the frustrations of the game, for the player is no longer fighting himself, but a palpable challenger. And so betting is a paradoxical factor in golf. It is the element that makes golf unique (because it is the participants who are doing the betting), but at the same time, it is the catalyst that makes golf like other sports because it establishes the competition with another player. Remember that we are always referring to casual, weekend golf in this write-up, and not tournament play.

On a less philosophical level, the high incidence of betting in golf is surely attributable to the game's admirable handicapping system. It is necessary for a good bet that the opponents be roughly equal in ability so that there is some doubt as to the outcome of the contest; golf's handicapping techniques effect such an equality, even between two players of disparate skills.

If you are going to bet at golf, you had better be like a poker player and know the house rules before you start. Most wagers are won or lost on the first tee when the game is made up, so know what you are playing, and above all, know your opponents. Here is a brief guide to the types of bets you may encounter:

Nassau. The most common kind of bet. At match play, as previously mentioned in this section, three points are scored: one for the first nine, one for the second, and one for the eighteen. If a golfer is playing a "one-dollar Nassau," he has three individual one-dollar bets.

Bisque. A handicap stroke that may be taken on any hole at the player's option. Strictly speaking, a stroke that is given to an opponent must be taken at the hole indicated on the scorecard as being that particular handicap number. Thus, if a player is given "five strokes," he must use those strokes on the holes marked one to five on the card. The handicap numbers are usually circled to differentiate them from the hole numbers. A bisque, on the other hand, may be taken anywhere.

Skins. A skin is awarded to the winner of each hole, provided that he is not tied by another player. If two tie, all tie. A deadlier version of this game (and not one for those who play a steady, unspectacular game) is called cumulative skins. In this little hair-raiser, holes not won by anyone are accumulated and awarded to the first winner of a hole. Also called "scats" or "syndicates."

Greenie. This is a shot that ends up closest to the hole on par-3s. Again, the winner collects from the other members of the foursome.

Team Skins. Those loyal partners who do not wish to win greenies and skins from one another play for team skins. If either member wins a skin, it is awarded to the team and not to the individual.

Bobs and Birds. Bobs are points scored for closest to the pin on par-3 holes only. Birds are points scored for birdies on any hole; double for eagles.

Bingle-Bangle-Bungle. A fast-paced item with lots of action. Three points on each hole: one for the player who reaches the green first, one for the player nearest to the cup after all are on the green, and one for the player who first holes out.

Low Ball and Total. A four-ball team bet in which the best ball of each team wins one point, and the low total of the partners wins another. This game is a method of getting a good bet out of the situation in which there is one very good player with a poor one against two average players.

Low and High Ball. A four-ball team bet in which two points are scored on each hole; low score wins a point, and high score loses a point. If both partners score lower on a hole than their opponents, they can win two points.

Calcutta Pool or Auction. A calcutta is played according to the usual rules and regulations that always apply to a tournament. All competitors are registered according to their official handicaps. Then, on the eve of the tournament, the calcutta auction is held. Each twosome is sold to the highest bidder, with the result that after a percentage of the total pool has been taken out, usually for a charitable cause, the rest goes to winning team and their "owner or owners."

Press or Extra. A new bet on the remaining holes. If someone wants to take a "dollar extra" on the 17th tee, he wants to play the last two holes for the dollar.

The best advice on betting is never to wager more than you can comfortably afford to lose, or else you may be putting yourself under unnecessary pressure that will probably hurt your game. Do not rush into an extra bet when you are losing unless you have been playing unusually badly and have suddenly discovered the cure, or you have been hitting the ball well, but have been unlucky.

COUNTRY CLUB MEMBERSHIP

Say the words "country club" to someone, and he will more than likely conjure up a certain dreamy image: Suddenly, it is the days of F. Scott Fitzgerald, and men immaculately dressed in long white ducks, straw boaters, and blue blazers with the crest of their club emblazoned prominently over their chest pockets, stroll with elegant women about the grounds; here and there a few are playing golf on a green course that seems to run right up to the blue-pooled sky; the tennis courts are full; the veranda of the clubhouse is crowded with sportsmen clustering around a portable bar; and at night the clubhouse becomes a ballroom, and the men and the women, even more elegant than before, are swirling on the floor under papier-mâché streamers soaked with sprinkling lights. Ah yes, the country club!

The image is no longer intact, for many country clubs exist today primarily as *golf clubs,* and they fulfill that function very well. A golfer who is thinking of joining a private club should be aware that he will be paying his money for several privileges and advantages.

Immediately on joining, he is no longer a public links player, but one of the exclusive twenty-three percent of golfers in the United States who play at private clubs. This exclusiveness is of more than nominal value, too. Public course players make up seventy-seven percent of the total numbers of golfers in this country, but only sixty-one percent of the courses are open to them, and those are usually crowded. The twenty-three percent who are private club members, on the other hand, play on thirty-nine percent of the nation's courses, and for them, five-hour waiting lines simply don't occur.

The club golfer gets some more things for his money, too. Inevitably, private club courses are in better condition and are more challenging than the average municipal layout. Private clubs spend a nationwide average of $490,136 a year on maintenance operating costs, or $11,500 a hole for a regulation eighteen-hole course. They spend 14.6 percent more than municipal courses and 71.6 percent more than daily fee courses. Their maintenance job is made easier by the absence of the crushing traffic that the public courses must withstand.

Country clubs are expensive, and statistics supplied by Pannell Kerr Forster, an accounting firm that audits the accounts of over 300 private clubs nationwide, reveal how much. In 1991, annual dues across the country by themselves averaged $1,970. However, it's interesting to note that, in general, the larger the membership of a club, the less dues members pay. In clubs with over 700 members, dues averaged $1,677 but those with 551–700 members averaged $2,324, those with 400 to 550 members averaged $2,407, and those with under 400 members averaged $3,065. Breaking down the national average of $1,970 regionally, dues averaged $2,147 in the East, $1,623 in the South, $2,532 in the Mid-West, and $2,103 in the Far West.

Although annual dues is the most common yardstick of country club cost, it's usually only the tip of the iceberg. In the first year, a member will probably have to pay an initiation fee, and may have to purchase a club bond or certificate. Besides annual dues, old and new members alike have to pay some or all of the following: Annual assessments, service charges, and minimum charges (many clubs charge a minimum for bar and restaurant whether or not a member uses them).

For example, at country clubs in the New York metropolitan area, the cost of first-year membership in 1992 varied from a low of $1,000 to a high of

$125,000. (In recent years, many private clubs have allowed new members to spread the costs of initiation fees, bonds, and certificates over a one- to five-year period.) However, once the new member has paid these startup costs, the picture is somewhat brighter. Annual costs excluding initiation fees, bonds, and certificates varied from a low of $1,000 to a high of $11,000.

The costs described above are for full memberships. Other types of memberships in country clubs are also available. Nongolfing members enjoy every privilege of the club except golf, and they can usually play by paying a greens fee, though there may be a limit to the number of rounds they can play a year. There are also special memberships for widows, clergy, seniors, nonresidents, and juniors (usually for members' sons who are over twenty-one, but have not yet reached the requisite age for full, regular membership, normally between twenty-five and thirty). All of these special memberships go at a reduced rate and are bargains.

It should also be pointed out that there are other choices, such as the semi-private or, more recently, the town-owned course. The latter is usually a former country club acquired by a town that offers reasonable fees to town residents. In 1992, typical green fees at such courses ranged from a low of $5 to a high of $50.

Lastly, private clubs may not be quite as elegant as they were in the past, when they were the bastions of the nabobs of the community. But the golf courses are better and harder, and the golfers are more enthusiastic than ever. If a new member, wistfully searching for past glories and faded dreams, were to don his white ducks and blazer, he would probably be stared at, but if you do join and happen to run into Scott Fitzgerald's ghost lurking about the old place, you will know it is a country club.

Golf Architecture

In all sports, two parameters define the nature of the game—the code of rules, and the dimensions of the playing field. One of the things that sets golf apart is that golf courses have no fixed dimensions. Necessary playing skills may change from one course to another, based on the geography of the site and on one individual's concept of how the game should be played—the architect of the golf course.

The first golf architects were the players themselves, who of necessity "designed" their holes as they went. In the earliest days of golf in Scotland, there were no formal courses at all—play was over whatever strip of common ground was available close to town, where balls could easily be found and played again, and outside interference was at a minimum. Most of these golfing grounds tended to be on the sandy ground or "linksland" that occurs near coastal towns, which was unfit for farming or other utilitarian purpose.

On linksland, three main hazards had to be confronted—bare, sandy patches where grass did not grow (bunkers), thickets of long grass or heather or whins that could not easily be played out of, and the variable winds common to the Scottish coast. Often there was also a small stream (known to the Scots as a "burn"), which in fact had much to do with the natural formation of the links, but since balls were valuable the water hazard did not play a major

role. As the golfers perfected their skills they gradually chose targets closer to the hazards and interesting holes were born. Eventually, players agreed on one "course" that provided the most interesting play and it was formalized, with the first players out each morning assigned the duty of cutting a new hole somewhere within the prescribed area or "green." But courses were still far from standardized, ranging from five holes at Leith and six at Perth, to a dozen crisscrossing holes at Prestwick, to twenty-five holes at Montrose, and twenty-two (eleven holes out to a point and then back in reverse to the starting point) at St. Andrews.

The Scots took their native game with them to other parts of the world. There was a rudimentary course at Blackheath, near London, as early as 1608, but generally speaking golf did not gain a foothold outside Scotland until the middle of the nineteenth century. Then, in rapid succession, came courses at Calcutta, India (1829); Pau, France (1856); Westward Ho!, England (1864); Montreal, Canada (1875); Yonkers, N.Y. (1888); Hong Kong (1889); and Melbourne, Australia (1891). By the turn of the century, golf had become known in the far corners of the world.

But most of these early courses outside Scotland were disappointing, because they lacked the natural challenges and advantages of linksland that had been the key to the appeal of the game. Above all, they lacked the fine, well-drained turf that was such a joy to play from and the natural bunkers that offered some scope for a fine recovery if properly played. At first, the advice of leading players was sought to improve playing interest, but eventually there was a realization that what was needed were specialists in laying out courses. Those who showed foresight in choosing a site for the course, and a flair for constructing and placing their hazards to simulate the challenges of the links quickly rose to prominence.

The period from 1900, when Willie Park, Jr. discovered that good golf could be adapted to the sandy heaths southwest of London until 1930 and the start of the worldwide Depression has been referred to as the Golden Age of golf architecture. Designers of the day freely exchanged theories and techniques as they improved their craft, and the booming world economy provided the opportunity to create excellent courses everywhere golf had spread—the eastern and western United States, Canada, England, Europe, Australia, New Zealand, and Japan. After 1930, though, progress ground to a halt due to the consecutive plagues of the Depression and World War II.

The postwar period saw another boom in course construction. Many prewar courses had to be reconstructed after years without care and, in some instances, under fire; afterwards, the production of new courses was accelerated. Although great improvements had been made in earthmoving technology, these were offset by the deaths of many leading architects of the prewar era, leaving relatively few designers with experience in the days of more "natural" design. Additionally, the sheer volume of work and ease of travel prompted the best architects to take on more work than ever before. Overall quality improved, but fewer projects received the individual attention and care necessary to achieve greatness.

Since the turn of the century, many individuals have had a pronounced influence on the theory and practice of golf architecture. Several of the most prominent designers are profiled in the following pages. But if it were necessary to select the single most profound influence on the development of golf architecture up until the present, the choice would have to go not to a man but to a golf course—the Old Course at St. Andrews.

THE IMPORTANCE OF THE OLD COURSE AT ST. ANDREWS

The influence of St. Andrews on the development of golf is a combination of natural and historic advantages. We know the modern town as the headquarters of the Royal & Ancient Golf Club and the "Home of Golf," but these titles are not bestowed as a simple matter of chronology—the earliest recorded golf course was a six-holer at Perth, the oldest continuous golf club and author of the first code of rules is the Honourable Company of Edinburgh Golfers (ten years the senior of the R & A), and in fact the great Open and Amateur championships conducted today by the Royal & Ancient were founded at Prestwick and Royal Liverpool, respectively.

But in the world of golf architecture, the Old Course is indeed the mother of all courses because of the variety of natural advantages it possessed. The natural plateaux that were selected as green sites were ideally spaced apart, so that most holes were of a good length, requiring two full shots. The contours of the ground, continuously rolling yet never severe, made for interesting play without requiring any of the blind shots over sandhills that were once popular, but which are frowned upon today. The profusion of natural bunkers contributed to an unusual complexity in the strategy of play, ensuring that the course never grew uninteresting, and there was always more to learn about it. In addition, the natural turf conditions, particularly at some of the chosen green sites, were far better than those of most other links. The Old Course became regarded as so superior that when its routing was finally set at eighteen holes, other Scottish courses soon converted to the same number.

The contributions of local golfers also made St. Andrews outstanding. It produced three of the outstanding champions of early competitive days, Allan Robertson and the two Tom Morrises. St. Andrews was the first links to consider turf maintenance; Robertson was instructed in 1842 to oversee the care of the course. As a part of this program, Robertson carried out the widening of the Old Course in 1848, a move designed to reduce the congestion of traffic and play that at the same time created more variety of strategic play—players since have had the option of choosing a longer route to the green less congested by hazards, or risking long carries and close

The mother of all courses—and the cradle of the game—the Old Course at St. Andrews. The view here, circa 1940, is of the 17th green (foreground right) with holes one and 18 in the broad expanse beyond. At rear left is the clubhouse of the Royal & Ancient Golf Club. *UPI/Bettmann*

passages of hazards to shoot for pars and birdies. Later, Robertson and "Old Tom" Morris added some hazards to the course of their own, either to stabilize a worn-out area of turf as a bunker, or just to make play more interesting, as Robertson attempted with the construction of a new 17th green and bunker about 1850—the famous Road hole.

St. Andrews' pre-eminence among the ancient links, and its resulting popularity, has led it to be studied and imitated by the majority of the world's eminent architects. Macdonald and Tillinghast learned the game as students at the University of St. Andrews; Donald Ross got to know the course while serving his apprenticeship in Tom Morris's shop; and Colt, MacKenzie, Fowler, and Tom Simpson were among the Old Course's keenest students, Simpson calling it "the only enduring text on golf course design." And, of course, every noteworthy player (with the single exception of Hogan) for generations has come to know the Old Course during one or another of the many championships it has hosted, including, among others, Braid, Jones, Thomson, and Nicklaus, all of whom went on to contribute to the

progress of course design with an Open Championship at St. Andrews under their belts.

The practice of golf course architecture has evolved in leaps and bounds over the past 150 years, but where it has been most successful, architects have sought to recreate the natural challenges of St. Andrews and the other early links over which the game evolved.

BIOGRAPHIES OF INFLUENTIAL GOLF ARCHITECTS

CHARLES H. ALISON (1882–1952)

A journalist and secretary at Stoke Poges GC near London, Alison became an apprentice and later a partner of that course's designer, H. S. Colt. After World War I, Alison carried out most of the firm's work in North America and the Far East, and is best remembered as the designer of Japan's early landmark courses. His trademarks as a designer were the deep, sculptured bunkers called "Alisons" in Japan in his honor, and the detailed plans and sketches of his designs that were left for construction personnel to execute.

Landmark courses: Hirono GC, Kobe, Japan; Kawana GC (Fuji course), Japan; Huntingdale GC, Melbourne, Australia; Sea Island GC (Seaside nine), Georgia; Century CC, White Plains, New York; Bob O'Link GC, Highland Park, Illinois.

JAMES BRAID (1870–1950)

Braid had definite ideas on what constituted good course design, and following the end of his brilliant competitive career and World War I, he designed or remodeled countless courses in the British Isles with the assistance of contractor John R. Stutt. In his redesign work Braid paid particular attention to adding bunkers that would strengthen a hole's test of driving play: at many clubs, including Nairn in Scotland, a particularly strong fairway bunker about 230 yards out in the left-center of a fairway is known as "Braid's Bunker." Braid also did fine courses on his own, and later in partnership with C. K. Hutchison and Stutt.

Landmark courses: Carnoustie, Scotland [finalized present championship course]; Gleneagles (King's and Queen's courses), Scotland; Boat of Garten, Scotland; St. Enodoc GC, Cornwall, England.

HARRY S. COLT (1869–1951)

As secretary of the newly formed Sunningdale GC near London, Colt became interested in course design during the final shaping of Willie Park's Old Course, and began to dabble in the design of several other early heathland courses nearby. Gradually, he became recognized as an expert in the field, receiving the great accolade of being chosen to design the Eden course at St. Andrews in 1913. After World War I, Colt expanded his design business to a worldwide scale, taking on projects in Europe, Canada, America, and the Far East in partnership with C. H. Alison and, briefly, Alister Mackenzie. Colt was perhaps the first important golf architect to have made his mark without a reputation as a professional player; one of the first to prepare detailed plans of his designs; and was responsible for the design of a second set of "championship" tees at Sunningdale to compensate for the introduction of the Haskell ball in 1902.

Landmark courses: Sunningdale (New Course), England; St. George's Hill GC, Weybridge, England;

Swinley Forest GC, Ascot, England; St. Andrews (Eden Course), Scotland; St. George's G & CC, Ontario, Canada; GC du Touquet, France; Royal Portrush GC, Northern Ireland; Haagsche GC, Wassenar, The Netherlands; also made contributions to the routing of Muirfield, Scotland, and Pine Valley GC, Clementon, New Jersey [with George Crump].

GEORGE A. CRUMP (1871–1918)

The least prolific and most accomplished golf architect of all time, Crump was a wealthy Philadelphia hotel owner and avid golfer, who became obsessed with the dream of building the world's finest course in the New Jersey pine barrens. In 1912, he convinced a group of friends to invest in the project, sold his hotel, and went about building the Pine Valley Golf Club.

Crump obtained the assistance of architect H.S. Colt in laying out the course, and discussed the design in general with several other designers he counted among his friends, including A. W. Tillinghast and Hugh Wilson; but it was Crump who devoted the last six years of his life to the construction of the course, and he who established the island landing areas that give the course its uniquely heroic scale.

Crump died in 1918 with only fourteen holes of his masterpiece complete; the design was completed to his plans by Hugh Wilson and C. H. Alison in 1922.

PAUL "PETE" DYE (1925–)

A fine amateur golfer, Dye left his successful business in 1959 to start a career in golf design. He became enamored with small greens, pot bunkers, and railroad ties after a visit to Scotland in 1963, and they soon became trademark elements of his own designs. In an age of mass-produced designs, Dye prided himself on limiting the number of his projects and being actively involved with their construction, designing his greens on the ground instead of on paper. Dye's wife, Alice, a former Curtis Cup player, also played a major role in his business, stressing the need for a set of extreme forward tees for the average woman player. His Tournament Players Club at Sawgrass, Florida, became the model for the PGA Tour's "Stadium Golf" facilities of the 1980s, and gave Dye the reputation as "the designer players love to hate." His use of several different grasses on the same course to

Pete Dye, a hands-on designer and one of the most influential figures in modern golf architecture.

present color and textural differences is also noteworthy.

Landmark courses: Crooked Stick GC, Carmel, Indiana; The Golf Club, Columbus, Ohio; Harbour Town Links, Hilton Head, South Carolina; Casa de Campo (Teeth of the Dog course), Dominican Republic; Oak Tree GC, Edmond, Oklahoma; Tournament Players Club at Sawgrass, Ponte Vedra, Florida; Long Cove Club, Hilton Head, South Carolina; The Honors Course, Ooltewah, Tennessee; PGA West (Stadium Course), La Quinta, California; Old Marsh GC, Jupiter, Florida; Kiawah Island (Ocean Course), Kiawah Island, South Carolina.

GEORGE FAZIO (1912–1986)

Fazio was a popular professional golfer of his day, who served as club professional at Pine Valley for several years. The highlight of his playing career was a play-off loss to Ben Hogan in the U.S. Open of 1950. Fazio entered the business of golf course design in 1959 and quickly rose to prominence. He was joined by his nephew Tom in 1962. George Fazio's designs were notable for a cookie-cutter style of bunkering and the use of small, multiple teeing grounds providing a variety of angles as well as lengths of play; several of his projects are also noted for their extreme difficulty.

Landmark courses: Jupiter Hills GC, Tequesta, Florida; Moselem Springs GC, Fleetwood, Pennsylvania; Butler National GC, Oak Brook, Illinois; The National GC of Canada, Ontario, Canada.

TOM FAZIO (1945–)

Involved in the construction of his uncle's golf courses by the age of eighteen, Tom Fazio quickly assumed the primary responsibility for seeing that George Fazio's designs were carried out in detail in the field. By the mid-1970s, Tom was an equal partner in the design of the firm's courses, and in ten years he was himself considered one of the "big three" of modern course design, along with Dye and Nicklaus. Tom Fazio's work is noted for fine routing plans emphasizing the natural features of the site, the multi-tee style he inherited from his uncle, and artistic bunkering and construction work carried out by a large in-house staff.

Landmark courses: Wild Dunes GC, Isle of Palms, South Carolina; The Vintage Club, Indian Wells, California; Lake Nona GC, Orlando, Florida; Wade Hampton Club, Cashiers, North Carolina; Black Diamond Ranch, Lecanto, Florida.

WILLIAM S. FLYNN (1891–1945)

After assisting Hugh Wilson with the completion of the East course at Merion in the role of greenskeeper, Flynn formed a partnership with engineer Howard Toomey and completed many fine courses throughout the United States between World War I and World War II. Most of his courses are classic parkland layouts with the traditional old-style small greens, but Flynn had no unique design trademark that characterizes his courses. A number of Flynn's assistants later became prominent architects in their own right, including William Gordon, "Red" Lawrence, and Dick Wilson.

Landmark courses: Shinnecock Hills GC, Southampton, NY; Cherry Hills CC, Denver, Colorado; Upper Cascades Course, Hot Springs, Virginia; The Country Club, Pepper Pike, Ohio; Philadelphia CC, Gladwyne, Pennsylvania; Rolling Green CC, Springfield, Pennsylvania; Indian Creek CC, Miami, Florida.

W. HERBERT FOWLER (1856–1941)

A fine amateur player after taking up golf at the age of thirty-five, Fowler's first attempt at course design was financed by his brother-in-law, and the resulting Walton Heath layout met with instant acclaim. Fowler was considered among his contemporaries an instinctively gifted designer, with the ability to take in all the possibilities of a site quickly and without the aid of plans. His courses are especially notable for the severity of their bunkering, typically including cross-bunkers on at least a couple of long two-shot holes.

During his career Fowler was a partner at one time with Tom Simpson, and later with J. F. Abercromby.

Landmark courses: Walton Heath GC (Old and New Courses), Tadworth, England; The Berkshire GC (Red and Blue Courses), Ascot, England; Saunton GC, Devon, England; Royal North Devon GC, Westward Ho!, England; Eastward Ho CC, Chathamport, Massachusetts.

HENRY C. FOWNES (1856–1935) AND WILLIAM C. FOWNES (1878–1950)

The Fownes family [father and son] owned a steel manufacturing business in Pittsburgh, Pennsylvania, and used some of the profits of its sale to found Oakmont Country Club, which Henry Fownes laid out in its present form in 1903, a tremendously long and difficult course for its day. The younger Fownes became a very accomplished player, winning the 1910 U.S. Amateur, and as chairman of the club's green committee worked to increase the standard of the course to his own philosophy that "A shot poorly played, should be a shot irrevocably lost." Over the years holes were lengthened, ditches dug to serve as drainage and hazard, and as many as 220 bunkers were created, all of them raked in furrows to make up for the subsoil-enforced lack of depth. William Fownes was also an early proponent of lightning-fast putting greens, and Oakmont's remain among the most severe in golf. His creation was a landmark of "penal" design and the first concerted effort by a golf architect to compensate in design for the radical improvements in golf equipment that occurred around the turn of the century.

ROBERT TRENT JONES (1906–)

The first golf architect to prepare himself for the profession through a specialized program of collegiate study (at Cornell University), Jones entered into a partnership with Canadian designer Stanley Thompson in 1930, and found early jobs constructing public golf courses during the Depression era, funded by the federal Works Progress Administration program. Following the Second World War, Jones came to the forefront of a new era of course design, as the revolution in the development of modern earthmoving equipment made golf possible on thousands of sites previously unsuited to the game.

Trent Jones's career leapt forward around 1950,

No architect has been more prolific than Robert Trent Jones, the producer of more than 400 courses plus two sons who followed him into the business.

after his landmark design with Robert Tyre "Bobby" Jones at Peachtree, and his retention by several prominent clubs, including Oakland Hills, Baltusrol, and Oak Hill, to revamp their courses in anticipation of major tournaments. His business grew to worldwide proportions, ultimately producing more than 400 courses in 42 states and 25 countries. Jones's trademark style, featuring long runway-style tees, elevated greens, and high flashes of sand in his bunkers, became recognized as the American style of design throughout the world for more than twenty years.

Trent Jones was followed into the business by his two sons, Rees and Bob, Jr., who became established as leading designers in their own right by the late 1970s.

Landmark courses: Peachtree GC, Atlanta, Georgia [with Bobby Jones]; Bellerive CC, St. Louis, Missouri; Spyglass Hill GC, California; Golden Horseshoe GC, Williamsburg, Virginia; Point O'Woods G & CC, Benton Harbor, Michigan; Mauna Kea GC, Hawaii; El Rincon, Bogota, Colombia; Dorado Beach, Puerto Rico; Sotogrande, Cadiz, Spain; Royal Dar-es-Salaam (Red Course), Rabat, Morocco; Ballybunion GC (New Course), Ireland.

Alister Mackenzie, the architect of Cypress Point and Augusta National, originally trained as a medical doctor. *Courtesy U.S.G.A.*

Landmark redesign efforts: Oakland Hills (South Course), Birmingham, Michigan; Baltusrol GC (Lower Course), Springfield, New Jersey; Oak Hill CC (East Course), Rochester, New York; Firestone CC (South Course), Akron, Ohio.

CHARLES BLAIR MACDONALD (1856–1939)

Generally recognized as the father of golf course design in America, Macdonald had become an accomplished golfer while attending the University of St. Andrews and designed his first course, Chicago Golf Club, for a group of wealthy friends. After the publication of a discussion of the best of British golf architecture, he devoted much time and energy to the creation of an ideal course that would compare favorably with the best British links: the National Golf Links of America, founded, designed, and constructed by Macdonald himself.

After the completion of The National, Macdonald went on to create a dozen other courses over the next fifteen years, most of which were built by his associates Seth Raynor and Charles Banks, who continued the business after Macdonald's interest waned. Macdonald's designs are immediately recognizable for their deep bunkers with steep grass faces, and, typically, several holes patterned after outstanding British links holes he had observed in his travels.

Landmark courses: The National Golf Links of America, Southampton, New York; Chicago Golf

Club, Wheaton, Illinois; Yale University GC, New Haven, Connecticut; Mid Ocean Club, Bermuda; Lido GC, Lido Beach, New York [no longer existing]; Piping Rock Club, Locust Valley, New York; St. Louis CC, Missouri.

ALISTER MACKENZIE (1870–1934)

A man of many talents, Mackenzie originally trained as a medical doctor, and helped to develop the art of camouflage for the British Army. His first involvement with golf course design came in 1907, when he was invited to assist H. S. Colt on the design of Alwoodley GC in Mackenzie's hometown of Leeds, because of his keen interest in the study of natural contours. Mackenzie won acclaim as a designer in a 1914 competition sponsored by the British journal, *Country Life*, and entered the profession full-time after World War I, working literally around the world from England to California to South America, Australia, and New Zealand.

The flowing lines of his bunkers and complex, multi-level contours of his greens, combined with a well-considered philosophy of design emphasizing the natural features of the given site and variety in the play, lend a distinct and artistic signature to Mackenzie's golf courses.

Landmark courses: Cypress Point Club, Pebble Beach, California; Augusta National GC, Augusta, Georgia [with Bob Jones]; Royal Melbourne GC (West Course), Victoria, Australia; Victoria GC, Melbourne, Australia; Kingston Heath GC, Melbourne, Australia; New South Wales GC, Sydney, Australia; Titirangi GC, Auckland, New Zealand; Crystal Downs CC, Frankfort, Michigan; Pasatiempo GC, Santa Cruz, California; Lahinch GC, Co. Clare, Ireland; Moortown GC, Leeds, England.

PERRY D. MAXWELL (1879–1952)

Oklahoman banker Maxwell was of Scottish descent, but did not take up golf until he was thirty. In 1913, he constructed a rudimentary nine-hole course for his hometown of Ardmore, Oklahoma, and after retiring from his business in 1920, he went to work for Alister Mackenzie on the construction of Crystal Downs, the Ohio State University Golf Courses, and Augusta National.

After Mackenzie's death, Maxwell blossomed into a successful designer on his own in the midwestern United States, though his productivity was severely curtailed by the Depression. His talent for designing demanding, undulating greens was widely acclaimed, and as a result he was retained to install "Maxwell Rolls" in selected greens at several prominent clubs, including Augusta National, Merion, and Pine Valley.

Landmark courses: Southern Hills CC, Tulsa, Oklahoma; Prairie Dunes CC, Hutchinson, Kansas; Dornick Hills G & CC, Ardmore, Oklahoma; Colonial CC, Fort Worth, Texas [revisions]; Crystal Downs CC, Frankfort, Michigan [with Mackenzie].

"OLD TOM" MORRIS (1821–1908)

As a fine champion and gentleman and as professional and greenkeeper to the Royal & Ancient Golf Club of St. Andrews, Tom Morris was the logical choice for early British clubs to consult in laying out and formalizing links courses. He knew little about constructing artificial hazards that blended into the terrain, but showed some talent for routing courses to take advantage of natural features, and was the first designer to lay out courses in two loops of nine holes to break up long stretches playing in line with prevailing winds.

Landmark courses: Muirfield, Scotland [original routing plan]; Royal County Down GC, Newcastle, Northern Ireland; Prestwick, Scotland; Elie, Scotland; Royal Dornoch, Scotland [original routing].

JACK W. NICKLAUS (1940–)

Interested in course design even as a young player, Nicklaus began to pursue design work while still at the height of his playing career, working in collaboration with Pete Dye and, later, Desmond Muirhead, with whom he planned Muirfield Village GC in his hometown of Columbus, Ohio. Upon the success of this project, Nicklaus founded his own firm, Golforce, Inc., and, with the help of senior designers Bob Cupp and Jay Morrish, became recognized as one of the most eminent architects of his day. His design style has already undergone considerable changes, from a more natural style on his early courses to an increasing reliance on artificial hazards and landscape features. Nicklaus's early courses, Glen Abbey and Muirfield Village, were instrumental in the move toward providing gallery mounds for tournament spectators. His courses were also known for an immaculate standard of maintenance, which his company oversaw under contract.

Landmark courses: Muirfield Village GC, Dublin, Ohio; Glen Abbey GC, Oakville, Ontario, Canada; Shoal Creek Club, Birmingham, Alabama; Desert Highlands GC, Scottsdale, Arizona; Castle Pines GC, Castle Rock, Colorado; Loxahatchee Club, Jupiter, Florida; Bear Creek GC, Temecula, California.

WILLIE PARK, JR. (1864–1925)

Twice Open champion during his successful playing career, Willie Park turned to golf architecture near the turn of the century, and many consider him the first artistically accomplished golf architect. Park revolutionized the practice of course design by carefully constructing rolling putting surfaces and naturally shaped bunkers artificially where natural features were found wanting and by bringing golf to the heathlands of suburban London and other areas previously thought unsuitable. Among his innovations were the first artificial two-tiered green, the 13th at Huntercombe, England, and the first artificial water hazard, a small pond guarding the 5th green at Sunningdale.

Landmark courses: Sunningdale GC (Old Course), Ascot, England; Huntercombe, England; Notts Golf Club, Hollinwell, England; Olympia Fields CC (North Course), Illinois; Maidstone Club, East Hampton, New York.

DONALD J. ROSS (1872–1948)

Born in Dornoch, Scotland, Donald Ross learned golf as an apprentice to Old Tom Morris at St. Andrews,

Scotsman Donald Ross learned his golf at the knee of Old Tom Morris, then displayed his design talents through dozens of subtly challenging courses across the Eastern U.S. and Canada.

Courtesy U.S.G.A. Museum

and developed a unique understanding of golf course design from his experiences at St. Andrews and under the tutelage of John Sutherland, the club secretary responsible for the intricate greens design of the Royal Dornoch links. After emigrating to the United States to serve as professional and greenkeeper at Oakley CC near Boston, Ross was persuaded by the Tufts family to develop three new resort courses at Pinehurst, North Carolina; and the reputation he achieved for these courses created a demand for his talents just as the golf boom in America began to take off. From 1912 to his death in 1948, Ross is credited with the development of several hundred courses throughout the eastern U.S. and Canada, including many of our eminent championship venues. His design style was noted for subtle contouring of the approaches and putting surfaces, which featured small plateaus falling away to hollows at the sides or even to the rear, emphasizing strategic approaches and tricky recovery play.

Landmark courses: Pinehurst CC (No. 2 Course), Pinehurst, North Carolina; Seminole GC, North Palm Beach, Florida; Beverly CC, Chicago, Illinois; Salem CC, Peabody, Massachusetts; Oakland Hills CC (South Course), Birmingham, Michigan; Oak Hill CC (East and West Courses), Rochester, New York; Plainfield CC, New Jersey; Scioto CC, Columbus, Ohio; Northland CC, Duluth, Minnesota; Aronimink GC, Newtown Square, Pennsylvania; Essex G & CC, Windsor, Ontario, Canada.

THOMAS C. SIMPSON (1877–1964)

Educated as a lawyer but also a scratch golfer, Simpson became intrigued with the problems of golf architecture during the celebrated redesign of his home club at Woking, England, by members John Low and Stuart Paton. In 1910, he went into partnership with Herbert Fowler. Tom Simpson prided himself on supervising the construction of his designs, but despite the limits on his productivity, he was instrumental in bringing outstanding courses to Europe in the 1920s and 1930s. Simpson is also well-remembered for his thoughtful essays on architectural theory and philosophy, and for his beautifully rendered design illustrations.

Landmark courses: Chantilly, France; Morfontaine GC, Senlis, France; Royal Antwerp, Belgium; Ashridge GC, England; Cruden Bay G & CC, Scotland; The Berkshire GC (Red and Blue Courses), Ascot,

England [with Fowler]; major revisions to Muirfield, Scotland, and Ballybunion GC (Old Course), Ireland.

GEORGE C. THOMAS, JR. (1873–1932)

A banker by trade, Thomas devoted much of his time to his two hobbies: horticulture (he was an expert on the breeding of roses) and golf architecture. He observed the work of Donald Ross and A. W. Tillinghast as a member of the greens committees of new courses they were building around Philadelphia, and also became a friend of George Crump and Hugh Wilson while they were at work on their own courses. Thomas completed a couple of courses on his own while still in Philadelphia, but became prominent after moving to southern California in 1919, where he designed the top courses in the Los Angeles area. Thomas's courses are recognizable both for their distinctive, sprawling, amorphous bunker shapes, and the fact that they often begin with two short par-5s, which Thomas felt helped get players away and which would serve as a good 19th and 20th holes for play-offs. Perhaps Thomas's most lasting contribution, though, was his definitive text, *Golf Architecture in America: Its Strategy and Construction.*

Landmark courses: Los Angeles CC (North Course), California; Riviera CC, Pacific Palisades, California [with Billy Bell]; Bel Air CC, Los Angeles, California; Ojai Valley CC, Ojai, California; Whitemarsh Valley CC, Chestnut Hill, Pennsylvania.

STANLEY THOMPSON (1894–1952)

One of five Scottish brothers, all accomplished players, Stanley Thompson emigrated with his family to Canada prior to World War I, and began his design career in the early 1920s. After modest early success, he was commissioned by the two national railway companies to build courses for Banff Springs and Jasper Park resorts in the Canadian Rockies, and the spectacular results cemented his reputation as Canada's premier designer. Thompson's work was punctuated by his liberal use of large, flared bunkers, and his genius for routing a course to take advantage of splendid natural backdrops. He also spared no expense in the construction of his courses: Banff Springs, in 1925, was the first golf course that cost more than one million dollars to construct. Thompson should also be given credit for producing a stable of young assistants who went on to fine

careers of their own, including Howard Watson, Geoffrey Cornish, and Robert Trent Jones.

Landmark courses: Banff Springs GC, Alberta, Canada; Jasper Park GC, Alberta; Capilano G & CC, North Vancouver, British Columbia; Cape Breton Highlands Golf Links, Ingonish, Nova Scotia; Mississauga G & CC, Toronto, Ontario; La Gavea G & CC, Rio de Janiero, Brazil.

ALBERT W. TILLINGHAST (1874–1942)

Tillinghast took up golf after a visit to St. Andrews, Scotland, following his college graduation, and designed his first course after the turn of the century for a family friend at Shawnee, Pennsylvania, on the Delaware River. The success of this course encouraged him to set up business, with an office in New York and advertisements in national golfing publications, and his next job, building a course for San Francisco Golf Club, earned him a strong national reputation. After World War I, he settled back in the East and built a string of excellent courses along the eastern seaboard. His design philosophy allowed some latitude for wayward driving but none in approaching his trademark small, well-guarded greens; Tillinghast took particular pride in his design of par-3 holes. He was also a frequent contributor to (and eventually became editor of) *Golf Illustrated*, in the pages of which he often discussed design issues.

Landmark courses: San Francisco GC, California; Winged Foot GC (East and West Courses), Mamaroneck, New York; Baltusrol GC (Upper and Lower Courses), Springfield, New Jersey; Somerset Hills CC, Bernardsville, New Jersey; Baltimore CC (Five Farms East Course), Maryland; Bethpage GC (Black Course), Farmingdale, New York; Brook Hollow GC, Dallas, Texas; Ridgewood GC, Ridgewood, New Jersey.

L. S. "DICK" WILSON (1904–1965)

Wilson was first involved with golf construction at the age of ten, serving as water boy to the construction crews on the West Course at Merion. After his education was completed he went directly to work for the firm of Toomey and Flynn, and is credited with substantial contributions to the design of Shinnecock Hills and Indian Creek CC in Miami during his tenure. After World War II, he began his own practice, which was based in Florida, and along with Robert Trent Jones moved to the forefront of the profession. Wilson is mistakenly considered a flat-course architect because he worked so much in Florida, but the real hallmarks of his design are a profusion of dogleg holes and elevated greens requiring a high, carrying approach shot in keeping with the modern approach to the game.

Landmark courses: Doral CC (Blue Course), Miami, Florida; Pine Tree GC, Boynton Beach, Florida; Bay Hill Club, Orlando, Florida; NCR CC (South Course), Dayton, Ohio; Cog Hill GC (No. 4 Course), Lemont, Illinois; Laurel Valley CC, Ligonier, Pennsylvania; Meadow Brook Club, Jericho, New York; Deepdale GC, Manhasset, New York; Royal Montreal GC (Blue Course), Ile Bizard, Quebec, Canada; Lagunita CC, Caracas, Venezuela.

HUGH I. WILSON (1879–1925)

An avid amateur golfer, Wilson was selected by the committee of Merion Cricket Club to make a study of the great British links in preparation for the design of a new Merion course, partly because the committee thought the trip might improve his failing health. After seven months' study overseas, he returned to complete the design of the club's new East and West courses himself, showing a remarkable natural talent for bunker placement and greens contouring to complement the natural features of each hole. He might have been the most gifted of his contemporaries—Crump, Thomas, and Tillinghast among them—but because of his poor health he never pursued the career, remaining only a consultant to his protégé, William Flynn, until his own death in 1925.

THE GREAT COURSES

The contrast between the early Scottish links and some products of modern architecture could hardly be more dramatic. Where it would have been inconceivable to the early Scots to artificially construct and contour greens, or spend much time on course maintenance, today it is not uncommon to move hundreds of thousands of cubic yards of earth in shaping a course to its designer's specifications, and a similar number of dollars on annual course maintenance. Yet, modern layouts like Pevero (hewn from the rocky hills of Sardinia by Robert Trent Jones) and the Tournament Players Club (reclaimed from a Florida swamp by Pete Dye) stand side-by-side with

Sandwich, Troon, and St. Andrews in rankings of the world's great courses.

The essence of a golf course is that it provide interesting play, hole after hole, for all classes of golfers. At one end of the scale, it should provide a complete and equitable test of the game's many requisite skills for competitive play, right up to the championship level; at the other, it should live up to the architect MacKenzie's credo that "even the absolute beginner should be able to enjoy his round, in spite of the fact that he is piling up a big score." The first requirement demands a challenging and well-balanced test; the second adds a versatile layout, the provision of variety, and esthetic appeal to the list of demands.

If a golf course were just another park, then its esthetic appeal might be the most important litmus test of quality; however, because its primary purpose is to provide for the playing of golf, its shotmaking requirements must come first in the analysis. In this respect, two emphatic definitions of quality leap to mind. The first is the renowned architect A. W. Tillinghast's definition of shot values: "The relationship between the properly placed shot to the fairway and the following one to the green is the real standard of measuring the merit of any course." To elaborate, add to this Bob Jones's explanation of the rationale behind the design of the Augusta National: "There should be presented to each golfer an interesting problem which will test him without being so impossibly difficult that he will have little chance of success. There must be something to do, but that something must always be within the realm of reasonable accomplishment."

So, at least in part, the quality of a course can be broken down to an analysis of its individual holes. Certainly the possession of great holes, such as Tillinghast's 10th at Winged Foot West, or better still a stretch of great holes like Jones and MacKenzie's "Amen Corner" at the Augusta National, is a contributing factor to all the best courses. But these cannot be created as a compromise while other holes suffer, as Tillinghast elaborated: "This is sure: Every hole must have individuality and must be sound. . . . If it has nothing about it that might make it respectable, it has to have quality knocked into it until it can hold its head up in polite society." Thus, MacKenzie's spectacular 16th hole at Cypress Point adds to the reputation of an already outstanding course, but Robert Trent Jones's 3rd at Mauna Kea in Hawaii (across a similar expanse of the Pacific Ocean) does not by itself elevate that course to the status of the elite.

A great course is, however, more than a collection of good holes: if that were all it takes, a course comprising eighteen replicas of the 16th at Cypress would be the pinnacle of architecture. We demand more: namely, a *variety* of interesting holes and hazards, and a *balance* among the holes so that no particular style of play is favored.

In some aspects of design, variety is taken for granted. For example, it generally goes without saying that we want a good mix of par-3, par-4, and par-5 holes within the eighteen, and a more discriminating critic would demand a variety of lengths within each class so that during a round the player would be required to use every club in his bag. Ideally, too, a course should offer the traditional hazards native to the links—contour, bunkers, a bit of water—plus whatever the given site has to offer. But only the truly great designers have taken their assignment of providing variety to its logical conclusion—a variety of green sites (plateaux, ground level, elevated, punchbowl, tilted, multi-tiered, and so on) to favor differing styles of approach shots, the variety of fairway lies and stances common to the links, and a routing plan like that of Muirfield or Portmarnock that ensures that the wind will have to be countered from all quarters. The designer who can create eighteen distinctly memorable holes of quality, and in fact a new challenge on every shot, while at the same time giving a harmony and character to the course as a whole, is a master of the profession.

As if all that were not enough to ask of our architects, we would also ask them to provide us with a well-balanced course. Ideally, there should be the same number of doglegs (and major hazards) to the left of the course as to the right, so that neither the fader nor hooker is favored in competitive play. And the perfect course would also strike the proper balance between all the requisite skills of the game: strength, accuracy, and proper tactics (one might also label these as talent, execution, and intelligence) being the first three.

Of course, every architect has his own ideas about just where the ideal balance of golfing skills falls, so even the great courses vary considerably in their demands. Oakland Hills, for example, places great demands on long and straight driving to narrow targets between fairway bunkers, while the Augusta National provides acres of fairways but demands a jeweler's touch around the greens. Winged Foot West is emphatically a second-shot course, and also requires talent with the sand wedge when an approach is missed; while the huge greens and bone dry ground of St. Andrews insist that the golfer be reasonably adept at laying approach putts dead from sixty feet. However, we only have room for only a few courses that provide the kind of "do-or-die" test that Pine Valley or Oakmont or the Tournament Players Club provides; the course that provides a balance of penal, strategic, and heroic play, as well as between the long and short games, such as Pinehurst No. 2, is much harder to achieve.

For some, course conditioning is also crucial to enjoying the play; and certainly the verdant fairways of Augusta and the pool-table smoothness of the greens at Royal Melbourne add to their luster. But while the greens must be true and reasonably well-paced, and the fairways fair, asking for much more may just be a waste of money; in truth, a "turf nursery" atmosphere can detract from the natural spirit of the game. The ancient links are replete with poor lies, requiring character on the part of the player to take them as they come, and this is part of the true spirit of game. If the soil below our feet is well-drained, the turf crisp, and we get no greater share of difficult lies than our opponent, we should be well satisfied.

Those are the principal playing attributes of golf courses, and there are some who would have us believe that the discussion of great courses should end right there. Fortunately, few of us must play for our suppers, so instead of spending all of our three-and-one-half hours (or, sadly, often longer) staring at the ground in front of us and pacing off yardages, we can afford lapses of concentration long enough to look around us and enjoy the scenery and atmosphere the course has to offer. Indeed, it is often the only consolation the course can offer us when we are not playing as well as we would like.

Scenery, of course, does not count for more than good golf: if it did, then surely there would have been room in our list of great courses for Banff in the Canadian Rockies, Ireland's magical Killarney, Robert Trent Jones, Jr.'s Arrowhead in the Red Rocks near Denver, or the remote Bamburgh Castle layout (all 5,465 yards of it) in the northeast of England. But scenery and atmosphere most certainly do add something to every one of the world's best courses, and the best architects use it to maximum advantage in their designs.

Scenic appeal is largely a matter of individual preference, but beauty in golf must also have a functional dimension—a stream flowing across a golf hole is only beautiful if it crosses at a point that creates interesting play, and care must be taken in the routing to ensure this. If the architect is a true master, the routing will wander the property and take in all its many facets as well. A good example is Prairie Dunes: the course begins through a valley, mounts the crest of a dune, plays down from the top and around the entire dune, then across rolling ground and back, off on a long stretch into some cottonwoods at the far end of the property, and back out of the trees and around another dune to finish beside the clubhouse. On the best courses one has the sense that the routing was a part of the ground to begin with, instead of the work of the designer, and that, as Alistair Cooke once suggested, the golf course is a microcosm of the landscape.

Unfortunately, rare is the property that offers a neat loop of eighteen natural holes complete with natural hazards to hold the player's interest. So the architect must create whatever hazards are necessary while blending them into the landscape, so that, as Pete Dye was instructed in building The Golf Club, "The course ought to look as though it's been there forever from the day it opens." But it must be admitted that the advantages of a good piece of property outweigh much of what the architect can accomplish artificially—none of the ten top-ranked courses in *Golf Magazine's 100 Greatest Courses in the World* was made by bulldozers.

The great architects have all been able to do beautiful construction work that stands by itself. Pete Dye's use of native grasses of differing textures adds definition to the edges of fairways and hazards and makes the golf holes stand out to the eye. The contours of greens by Donald Ross and Perry Maxwell have a beauty all their own, especially when viewed from close range with a putter in hand. And the sculptured bunkers of George Thomas's Riviera, Tillinghast's San Francisco Golf Club, MacKenzie's Kingston Heath, or Ross's Seminole, are perhaps the most memorable features of the properties in general.

The atmosphere of a course and its surroundings also play a role in its enjoyment. Some may argue that this is not an inherent feature of the architecture, but for many, one of the enticements of the game is the escape it offers from the everyday world. This escape is enhanced when the setting evokes memories of great tournaments past (such as at Merion or St. Andrews), or is quiet and remote (whether it be the lonely peninsula of Falsterbo in southern Sweden, the enclosed individual holes at the exclusive Pine Valley, or just an oasis amidst the more urban setting of Royal Lytham), or when the clubhouse is comfortable and the companions congenial.

In the end, the great courses are the ones that stand apart in the memory, offering a unique character and challenge derived from the beauty of the setting, and which, to quote Dr. MacKenzie once more, "like good music or good anything else … grows on the player the more frequently he visits it."

GOLF MAGAZINE'S 100 GREATEST COURSES IN THE WORLD

Rank	Course	Location	Architects	Year	Par	Yds.
1	Pine Valley	Clementon, NJ	George Crump/H. S. Colt	1918	70	6,765
2	Cypress Point	Pebble Beach, CA	Alister Mackenzie	1928	72	6,536
3	Augusta National	Augusta, GA	Alister Mackenzie/ Bobby Jones	1932	72	6,904
4	Muirfield	Gullane, SCOTLAND	Old Tom Morris, H. S. Colt, Tom Simpson	1891, 1926	71	6,894
5	Pebble Beach	Pebble Beach, CA	Jack Neville/Douglas Grant	1919	72	6,825
6	Royal Melbourne (Composite)	Melbourne, AUSTRALIA	Alister Mackenzie/ Alex Russell	1926	71	6,946
7	St. Andrews (Old)	St. Andrews, SCOTLAND		16th century	72	6,950
8	Royal County Down	Newcastle, N. IRELAND	Old Tom Morris, Tom Dunn, Harry Vardon	1889, 1905, 1919	72	6,968
9	Shinnecock Hills	Southampton, NY	William Flynn/Howard Toomey	1931	70	6,912
10	Merion (East)	Ardmore, PA	Hugh Wilson	1911	70	6,544

GOLF MAGAZINE'S 100 GREATEST COURSES IN THE WORLD (continued)

Rank	Course	Location	Architects	Year	Par	Yds.
11	Royal Dornoch	Dornoch, SCOTLAND	Old Tom Morris, John Sutherland, George Duncan	1896, 1922, 1947	70	6,577
12	Ballybunion (Old)	Ballybunion, SCOTLAND	P. Murphy, James Braid, Tom Simpson	1906, 1936	71	6,700
13	Pinehurst (No. 2)	Pinehurst, NC	Donald Ross	1903, 1935	72	7,051
14	Prairie Dunes	Hutchinson, KS	Perry Maxwell, Press Maxwell	1935, 1956	70	6,542
15	Winged Foot (West)	Mamaroneck, NY	A. W. Tillinghast	1923	72	6,956
16	Crystal Downs	Frankfort, MI	Alister Mackenzie/Perry Maxwell	1932	70	6,518
17	Royal Portrush (Dunluce)	Portrush, N. IRELAND	H. S. Colt	1920	73	6,810
18	Seminole	North Palm Beach, FL	Donald Ross, Dick Wilson	1929, 1947	72	6,752
19	Oakmont	Oakmont, PA	William and Henry Fownes	1903	71	6,989
20	Turnberry (Ailsa)	Turnberry, SCOTLAND	P. Mackenzie Ross	1947	71	7,060
21	Royal Birkdale	Southport, ENGLAND	George Lowe, Fred Hawtree/J. H. Taylor	1889, 1931	72	7,001
22	Oakland Hills (South)	Birmingham, MI	Donald Ross, Robert Trent Jones	1917, 1950	72	7,067
23	Olympic (Lake)	San Francisco, CA	Wilfrid Reid, Sam Whiting, Robert Trent Jones	1917, 1924, 1953	71	6,808
24	Portmarnock	Portmarnock, IRELAND	George Ross/W. C. Pickeman, Fred Hawtree	1894, 1964	72	7,103
25	Baltusrol (Lower)	Springfield, NJ	A. W. Tillinghast, Robert Trent Jones	1922, 1953	72	7,069
26	The Country Club (Open)	Brookline, MA	Willie Campbell, William Flynn, Rees Jones	1895, 1927, 1986	71	7,010
27	Casa de Campo (Teeth of the Dog)	La Romana, DOMIN REP	Pete Dye	1971	72	6,888
28	Kingston Heath	Melbourne, AUSTRALIA	Des Soutar, Alister Mackenzie	1925, 1928	72	6,814
29	Muirfield Village	Dublin, OH	Jack Nicklaus/Desmond Muirhead	1974	72	7,106
30	Woodhall Spa	Woodhall Spa, ENGLAND	S. V. Hotchkin/ C. K. Hutchinson	1926	73	6,866
31	Riviera	Pacific Palisades, CA	George Thomas/Billy Bell	1926	72	7,101
32	Carnoustie (Championship)	Carnoustie, SCOTLAND	Allan Robertson, Willie Park Jr, Tom Morris, James Braid	1842, 1926	72	7,200
33	The Golf Club	New Albany, OH	Pete Dye	1967	72	7,037
34	San Francisco GC	San Francisco, CA	A. W. Tillinghast	1915	71	6,623
35	Royal St. George's	Sandwich, ENGLAND	Laidlaw Purves, Allister Mackenzie, Frank Pennink	1887, 1925, 1975	70	6,829
36	Harbour Town	Hilton Head, SC	Pete Dye/Jack Nicklaus	1969	71	6,652
37	Southern Hills	Tulsa, OK	Perry Maxwell	1935	71	7,037
38	Oak Hill (East)	Rochester, NY	Donald Ross, Robert Trent Jones, George and Tom Fazio	1926, 1955, 1978	70	6,964
39	Chicago Golf Club	Wheaton, IL	Charles Blair Macdonald, Seth Raynor	1895, 1925	70	6,553

GOLF MAGAZINE'S 100 GREATEST COURSES IN THE WORLD (continued)

Rank	Course	Location	Architects	Year	Par	Yds.
40	Quaker Ridge	Scarsdale, NY	A. W. Tillinghast, Robert Trent Jones	1926, 1960	70	6,745
41	Royal Troon (Old)	Troon, SCOTLAND	Willie Ferrie, James Braid	1878, etc.	72	7,067
42	National GL of America	Southampton, NY	Charles Blair Macdonald	1911	73	6,745
43	Sunningdale (Old)	Sunningdale, ENGLAND	Willie Park, H. S. Colt	1901, 1920	72	6,566
44	Hirono	Kobe, JAPAN	Charles Alison	1932	72	6,925
45	Colonial	Fort Worth, TX	John Bredemus, Perry Maxwell	1935, 1940	70	7,142
46	Medinah (No. 3)	Medinah, IL	Tom Bendelow, Harry Collis, Roger Packard	1928, 1932, 1986	72	7,365
47	Los Angeles CC (North)	Los Angeles, CA	George Thomas	1921	71	6,811
48	Kasumigaseki (East)	Kawagoe, JAPAN	Kinya Fujita/ Charles Alison	1929	72	6,934
49	Garden City GC	Garden City, NY	Devereux Emmet, Walter Travis	1902, 1906	73	6,840
50	Shoal Creek	Birmingham, AL	Jack Nicklaus	1977	72	7,029
51	Inverness	Toledo, OH	Donald Ross, George and Tom Fazio	1919, 1977	71	6,982
52	Durban CC	Durban, SOUTH AFRICA	Laurie Waters, S. V. Hotchkin	1922, 1928	72	6,576
53	Royal Adelaide	Adelaide, AUSTRALIA	Alistar Mackenzie, Peter Thomson/Michael Wolveridge	1904, 1926	73	7,010
54	Cherry Hills	Englewood, CO	William Flynn	1923	72	7,148
55	Fishers Island	Fishers Island, NY	Seth Raynor	1917	72	6,445
56	El Saler	Valencia, SPAIN	Javier Arana	1967	72	7,108
57	Camargo	Cincinnati, OH	Seth Raynor	1921	70	6,406
58	New South Wales	Sydney, AUSTRALIA	Alister Mackenzie	1928	72	6,688
59	Shadow Creek	North Las Vegas, NV	Tom Fazio/Steve Wynn	1989	72	7,090
60	Lake Nona	Orlanda, FL	Tom Fazio	1986	72	7,011
61	Long Cove	Hilton Head, SC	Pete Dye	1981	71	6,900
62	Cascades (Upper)	Hot Springs, VA	William Flynn	1923	71	6,568
63	Wild Dunes (Links)	Isle of Palms, SC	Tom Fazio	1979	72	6,708
64	Somerset Hills	Bernardsville, NJ	A. W. Tillinghast	1918	71	6,524
65	Scioto	Columbus, OH	Donald Ross, Dick Wilson	1912, 1963	71	6,917
66	Morfontaine	Senlis, FRANCE	Tom Simpson	1927	70	6,632
67	The Honors Course	Ooltewah, TN	Pete and P. B. Dye	1984	72	7,024
68	Royal Lytham & St. Annes	St. Annes on Sea, ENGLAND	George Lowe	1886	71	6,673
69	Wentworth (West)	Virgina Water, ENGLAND	H. S. Colt/J. S. F. Morrison	1924	74	6,997
70	Troon	Scottsdale, AZ	Jay Morrish/Tom Weiskopf	1986	72	7,026
71	Yale University	New Haven, CT	Charles Blair Macdonald/ Seth Raynor	1926	70	6,628
72	National GC of Canada	Woodbridge, Ont., CANADA	George and Tom Fazio	1976	71	6,975
73	TPC at Sawgrass (Stadium)	Ponte Vedra, FL	Pete Dye	1980	72	6,950
74	Baltimore (Five Farms East)	Timonium, MD	A. W. Tillinghast	1926	70	6,675
75	Black Diamond	Lecanto, FL	Tom Fazio	1987	72	7,159

GOLF MAGAZINE'S 100 GREATEST COURSES IN THE WORLD (continued)

Rank	Course	Location	Architects	Year	Par	Yds.
76	Maidstone	East Hampton, NY	Willie and John Park, Willie Tucker	1891, 1899	72	6,325
77	Firestone (South)	Akron, OH	Robert Trent Jones, Jack Nicklaus	1960, 1986	70	7,173
78	Royal Dar-es-Salaam (Red)	Rabat, MOROCCO	Robert Trent Jones	1971	73	7,462
79	Royal Liverpool	Hoylake, ENGLAND	George Morris/Chambers, H. S. Colt, Frank Pennink	1869, 1925, 1965	72	6,979
80	Capilano	North Vancouver, B.C., CANADA	Stanley Thompson	1937	72	6,538
81	Paraparaumu Beach	Paraparaumu Beach, NEW ZEALAND	Alex Russell	1949	71	6,438
82	Commonwealth	Melbourne, AUSTRALIA	S. Bennett, Charles Lane/ Sloan Morpeth	1919, 1926	72	6,719
83	Canterbury	Cleveland, OH	Herbert Strong	1922	71	6,852
84	Victoria	Melbourne, AUSTRALIA	Alister Mackenzie	1927	72	6,842
85	Ganton	Ganton, ENGLAND	Dunn, Vardon, Braid, Colt, Hutchinson	1891, 1930	72	6,677
86	Butler National	Oak Brook, IL	George and Tom Fazio	1974	72	7,302
87	Walton Heath (Old)	Tadworth, ENGLAND	Herbert Fowler	1904	73	6,813
88	El Rincon	Bogota, COLOMBIA	Robert Trent Jones	1960	72	7,516
89	Kiawah Island (Ocean)	Kiawah Island, SC	Pete Dye	1991	72	7,752
90	Oak Tree GC	Edmond, OK	Pete Dye	1976	71	7,015
91	Lahinch	Lahinch, IRELAND	Old Tom Morris, Gibson, Alister Mackenzie	1893, 1910, 1927	72	6,538
92	Sotogrande (Old)	Cadiz, SPAIN	Robert Trent Jones	1965	72	6,910
93	Forest Highlands	Flagstaff, AZ	Jay Morrish/Tom Weiskopf	1988	71	7,051
94	Saucon Valley (Grace)	Bethlehem, PA	William and David Gordon	1957	72	7,051
95	Kawana (Fuji)	Shizuoka, JAPAN	Charles Alison, Kinya Fujita	1936	70	6,970
96	The Australian	Sydney, AUSTRALIA	Jack Nicklaus	1978	72	7,148
97	Royal Montreal (Blue)	Ile Bizard, Que, CANADA	Dick Wilson	1959	70	6,738
98	Jupiter Hills (Hills)	Tequesta, FL	George and Tom Fazio	1970, 1974	72	6,905
99	Congressional (Blue)	Bethesda, MD	Devereux Emmet, Robert Trent Jones, Rees Jones	1924, 1957, 1962	72	7,270
100	Peachtree	Atlanta, GA	Robert Trent Jones/ Bobby Jones	1948	72	7,043

GOLF MAGAZINE'S 100 GREATEST COURSES IN THE U.S.

Rank	Course	Location	Architects	Year	Par	Yds.
1	Pine Valley	Clementon, NJ	George Crump/H. S. Colt	1918	70	6,765
2	Cypress Point	Pebble Beach, CA	Alister Mackenzie	1928	72	6,536
3	Augusta National	Augusta, GA	Alister Mackenzie/ Bobby Jones	1932	72	6,905
4	Pebble Beach	Pebble Beach, GA	Jack Neville/Douglas Grant	1919	72	6,825
5	Shinnecock Hills	Southampton, NY	William Flynn/Howard Toomey	1931	70	6,912
6	Merion (East)	Ardmore, PA	Hugh Wilson	1911	70	6,544
7	Pinehurst (No. 2)	Pinehurst, NC	Donald Ross	1903, 1935	72	7,051
8	Prairie Dunes	Hutchinson, KS	Perry Maxwell, Press Maxwell	1935, 1956	70	6,542
9	Winged Foot (West)	Mamaroneck, NY	A. W. Tillinghast	1923	72	6,956
10	Crystal Downs	Frankfort, MI	Alister Mackenzie/Perry Maxwell	1932	70	6,518
11	Seminole	North Palm Beach, FL	Donald Ross, Dick Wilson	1929, 1947	72	6,752
12	Oakmont	Oakmont, PA	William and Henry Fownes	1903	71	6,989
13	Oakland Hills (South)	Birmingham, MI	Donald Ross, Robert Trent Jones	1917, 1950	72	7,067
14	Olympic (Lake)	San Francisco, CA	Wilfrid Reid, Sam Whiting, Robert Trent Jones	1917, 1924, 1953	71	6,808
15	Baltusrol (Lower)	Springfield, NJ	A. W. Tillinghast, Robert Trent Jones	1922, 1953	72	7,069
16	The Country Club (Open)	Brookline, MA	Willie Campbell, William Flynn, Rees Jones	1895, 1927, 1986	71	7,010
17	Muirfield Village	Dublin, OH	Jack Nicklaus/Desmond Muirhead	1974	72	7,106
18	Riviera	Pacific Palisades, CA	George Thomas/Billy Bell	1926	72	7,101
19	The Golf Club	New Albany, OH	Pete Dye	1967	72	7,037
20	San Francisco GC	San Francisco, CA	A. W. Tillinghast	1915	71	6,623
21	Harbour Town	Hilton Head, SC	Pete Dye/Jack Nicklaus	1969	71	6,652
22	Southern Hills	Tulsa, OK	Perry Maxwell	1935	71	7,037
23	Oak Hill (East)	Rochester, NY	Donald Ross, Robert Trent Jones, George and Tom Fazio	1926, 1955, 1978	70	6,964
24	Chicago Golf Club	Wheaton, IL	Charles Blair Macdonald, Seth Raynor	1895, 1925	70	6,553
25	Quaker Ridge	Scarsdale, NY	A. W. Tillinghast, Robert Trent Jones	1926, 1960	70	6,745
26	National GL of America	Southampton, NY	Charles Blair Macdonald	1911	73	6,745
27	Colonial	Fort Worth, TX	John Bredemus, Perry Maxwell	1935, 1940	70	7,142
28	Medinah (No. 3)	Medinah, IL	Tom Bendelow, Harry Collis, Roger Packard	1928, 1932, 1986	72	7,365
29	Los Angeles CC (North)	Los Angeles, CA	George Thomas	1921	71	6,811
30	Garden City GC	Garden City, NY	Devereux Emmett, Walter Travis	1902, 1906	73	6,840
31	Shoal Creek	Birmingham, AL	Jack Nicklaus	1977	72	7,029
32	Inverness	Toledo, OH	Donald Ross, George and Tom Fazio	1919, 1977	71	6,982
33	Cherry Hills	Englewood, CO	William Flynn	1923	72	7,148

GOLF MAGAZINE'S 100 GREATEST COURSES IN THE U.S. (continued)

Rank	Course	Location	Architects	Year	Par	Yds.
34	Fishers Island	Fishers Island, NY	Seth Raynor	1917	72	6,445
35	Camargo	Cincinnati, OH	Seth Raynor	1921	70	6,406
36	Shadow Creek	North Las Vegas, NV	Tom Fazio/Steve Wynn	1989	72	7,090
37	Lake Nona	Orlando, FL	Tom Fazio	1986	72	7,011
38	Long Cove	Hilton Head, SC	Pete Dye	1981	71	6,900
39	Cascades (Upper)	Hot Springs, VA	William Flynn	1923	71	6,568
40	Wild Dunes (Links)	Isle of Palms, SC	Tom Fazio	1979	72	6,708
41	Somerset Hills	Bernardsville, NJ	A. W. Tillinghast	1918	71	6,524
42	Scioto	Columbus, OH	Donald Ross, Dick Wilson	1912, 1963	71	6,917
43	The Honors Course	Ooltewah, TN	Pete and P. B. Dye	1984	72	7,024
44	Troon	Scottsdale, AZ	Jay Morrish/Tom Weiskopf	1986	72	7,026
45	Yale University	New Haven, CT	Charles Blair Macdonald/ Seth Raynor	1926	70	6,628
46	TPC at Sawgrass (Stadium)	Ponte Vedra, FL	Pete Dye	1980	72	6,950
47	Baltimore (Five Farms East)	Timonium, MD	A. W. Tillinghast	1926	70	6,675
48	Black Diamond	Lecanto, FL	Tom Fazio	1987	72	7,159
49	Maidstone	East Hampton, NY	Willie and John Park, Willie Tucker	1891, 1899	72	6,325
50	Firestone (South)	Akron, OH	Robert Trent Jones, Jack Nicklaus	1960, 1986	70	7,173
51	Canterbury	Cleveland, OH	Herbert Strong	1922	71	6,852
52	Butler National	Oak Brook, IL	George and Tom Fazio	1974	72	7,302
53	Kiawah Island (Ocean)	Kiawah Island, SC	Pete Dye	1991	72	7,752
54	Oak Tree GC	Edmond, OK	Pete Dye	1976	71	7,015
55	Forest Highlands	Flagstaff, AZ	Jay Morrish and Tom Weiskopf	1988	71	7,051
56	Saucon Valley (Grace)	Bethlehem, PA	William and David Gordon	1957	72	7,051
57	Jupiter Hills (Hills)	Tequesta, FL	George and Tom Fazio	1970, 1974	72	6,905
58	Congressional (Blue)	Bethesda, MD	Devereux Emmett, Robert Trent Jones, Rees Jones	1924, 1957, 1962	72	7,270
59	Peachtree	Atlanta, GA	Robert Trent Jones/ Bobby Jones	1948	72	7,043
60	Doral (Blue)	Miami, FL	Dick Wilson	1962	72	6,939
61	PGA West (Stadium)	La Quinta, CA	Pete Dye	1986	72	7,271
62	Ridgewood (West-East)	Ridgewood, NJ	A. W. Tillinghast	1929	71	6,938
63	Winged Foot (East)	Mamaroneck, NY	A. W. Tillinghast	1923	72	6,665
64	Bellerive	Creve Coeur, MO	Robert Trent Jones	1959	71	7,311
65	Haig Point	Daufuskie Island, SC	Rees Jones	1987	72	7,114
66	Point O'Woods	Benton Harbor, MI	Robert Trent Jones	1958	71	6,884
67	Pine Tree	Boynton Beach, FL	Dick Wilson	1962	72	7,123
68	Spyglass Hill	Pebble Beach, CA	Robert Trent Jones	1966	72	6,810
69	Ohio State (Scarlet)	Columbus, OH	Alister Mackenzie/Perry Maxwell	1934	72	7,104
70	Laurel Valley	Ligonier, PA	Dick Wilson	1960	72	7,060
71	Salem	Peabody, MA	Donald Ross	1926	72	6,787
72	Pasatiempo	Santa Cruz, CA	Alister Mackenzie	1929	71	6,483
73	Plainfield	South Plainfield, NJ	Donald Ross	1920	72	6,859
74	Eugene	Eugene, OR	Robert Trent Jones	1967	72	6,837

GOLF MAGAZINE'S 100 GREATEST COURSES IN THE U.S. (continued)

Rank	Course	Location	Architects	Year	Par	Yds.
75	Champions (Cypress Creek)	Houston, TX	Ralph Plummer	1959	72	7,181
76	Indianwood (Old)	Lake Orion, MI	Wilfrid Reid/William Connellan, Bob Cupp	1928, 1987		
77	The Dunes	Myrtle Beach, SC	Robert Trent Jones	1949, 1979	72	7,021
78	CC of North Carolina (Dogwood)	Pinehurst, NC	Ellis Maples/Willard Byrd	1963	72	7,154
79	NCR (South)	Kettering, OH	Dick Wilson	1954	71	6,824
80	Crooked Stick	Carmel, IN	Pete Dye	1964, 1986	72	7,516
81	Meadow Brook	Jericho, NY	Dick Wilson	1955	72	7,101
82	The Kiele Course	Lihue, Kauai, HI	Jack Nicklaus	1989	72	7,070
83	PGA West (Jack Nicklaus Private)	La Quinta, CA	Jack Nicklaus	1988	72	6,933
84	Saucon Valley (Old)	Bethlehem, PA	Herbert Strong, William Gordon	1922, 1951	71	6,799
85	Troon North	Scottsdale, AZ	Jay Morrish/Tom Weiskopf	1990	72	7,008
86	Aronimink	Newton Square, PA	Donald Ross, Dick Wilson	1928, 1961	70	6,974
87	The Country Club	Pepper Pike, OH	William Flynn/Howard Toomey	1931	72	6,908
88	Olympia Fields (North)	Olympia Fields, IL	Willie Park	1932	70	6,867
89	Mauna Kea	Kamuela, Big Island, HI	Robert Trent Jones	1965	72	7,114
90	Hazeltine National	Chaska, MN	Robert Trent Jones, Rees Jones	1962, 1978, 1989	72	7,149
91	Old Warson	Ladue, MO	Robert Trent Jones	1955	71	6,946
92	Bay Hill	Orlando, FL	Dick Wilson, Arnold Palmer	1961, 1980	72	7,173
93	Stanford University	Palo Alto, CA	Billy Bell, Robert Trent Jones	1930, 1968	71	6,770
94	Bethpage (Black)	Farmingdale, NY	A. W. Tillinghast	1936		
95	The Prince Course	Princeville, Kauai, HI	Robert Trent Jones, Jr.	1989	72	7,309
96	Kittansett	Marion, MA	Fred Hood	1923	71	6,545
97	Interlachen	Edina, MN	Willie Watson, Donald Ross, Robert Trent Jones	1910, 1919, 1962		
98	Spanish Bay	Pebble Beach, CA	Robert Trent Jones, Jr./ Sandy Tatum/Tom Watson	1987	72	6,820
99	Desert Forest	Carefree, AZ	Red Lawrence	1962	72	6,981
100	Wannamoisett	Rumford, RI	Donald Ross	1916	69	6,631

PROFILES OF THE THIRTY GREATEST COURSES

(1) PINE VALLEY, CLEMENTON, NEW JERSEY

Founded and designed by the Philadelphian George Crump amidst the pine barrens of southern New Jersey, the island target areas and generally heroic scale of Pine Valley make it unique among the world's golf courses. The unsurpassed collection of individual holes includes three of the best drive-and-pitch holes in golf, and two gargantuan par-five holes that are not meant to be reached in two shots. The island fairways and greens are relatively wide targets, but the native sand and scrub that surrounds them is so fearsome that even top players have become unnerved, and stories of scoring disasters abound, not least of them that of the 3-handicapper who made the turn in 38 only to take 38 more strokes on the 145-yard 10th hole after tangling with the notorious pot bunker at the front of the green. The private nature of the club and lack of room for spectators has limited its role as a tournament venue to the Walker Cup Matches of 1936 and 1985.

(2) CYPRESS POINT, PEBBLE BEACH, CALIFORNIA

Described by former USGA president Frank Tatum as "the Sistine Chapel of golf," this exclusive neighbor of Pebble Beach is perhaps the most compellingly beautiful of all the world's courses. Designed by the eminent architect Dr. Alister MacKenzie, its routing wanders back among a forest of pine and cypress, and then across more open links-style terrain, before emerging onto the rocky cliffs from which it derives its name. Despite the inclusion of consecutive par-5 (the 5th and 6th) and consecutive par-3 (the 15th and 16th) holes, and a modest length of just over 6,500 yards from the back tees, the course remains a searching test for all levels of golfers, and the famous 233-yard par-3 16th hole across a cove of the Pacific Ocean stands alone as the most spectacular hole in the game.

(3) AUGUSTA NATIONAL, AUGUSTA, GEORGIA

Founded by the legendary Bobby Jones and his friend Clifford Roberts as a national club for their friends from around the country, the Augusta National has become world famous as host to The Masters Tournament each April. Located on the site of a nursery that dates back to Civil War days, the course is noted for its brilliant floral displays as well as for the quality of the design by Jones and his hand-picked golf architect, Dr. Alister MacKenzie, which requires strength and strategic position play in order to set up birdie opportunities. The style of the course, featuring wide, verdant fairways with very little rough, large rolling greens, and the heroic use of water hazards, was adopted by a generation of American designers. Of many outstanding holes, the stretch from the 11th through 13th (nicknamed the "Amen Corner") are probably the course's best.

(4) MUIRFIELD, GULLANE, E. LOTHIAN, SCOTLAND

Home to the oldest golf club in the world, the Honourable Company of Edinburgh Golfers, the private Muirfield course overlooking the Firth of Forth was established in 1891 after the club's tenure at Leith and Musselburgh. The routing, finalized in the late 1920s after thirty-five years of refinements, is outstanding among British links for its constant changes of direction within two loops. The tenacity of the rough and depth of the sod-faced bunkers are legendary for their severity. The slight separation from the sea and gentler contours give it a somewhat more tame appearance than some other Open championship links, but among those who have played it the course's reputation is beyond dispute.

(5) PEBBLE BEACH, PEBBLE BEACH, CALIFORNIA

The quintessential American seaside course, the Pebble Beach layout stretches along the high bluffs along the southern coast of the Monterey Peninsula, overlooking Carmel Beach and the Pacific. Completed by novice architects Jack Neville and Douglas Grant in 1919, the figure-eight routing follows the spectacular coastline as much as possible, with the edge of the sea in play to the right from the 6th through 10th holes and to the left for the two famous finishing holes, all of these among the great holes the game has to offer. The service of the course as host to the annual Bing Crosby Pro-Am and to the thrilling U.S. Opens of 1972, 1982 and 1992 has added to its notoriety even among non-golfers.

The ultimate American course—and the site of three U.S. Opens—Pebble Beach Golf Links on California's Monterey Peninsula. This is the par-five 18th.

(6) *ROYAL MELBOURNE* (COMPOSITE COURSE), BLACK ROCK, VICTORIA, AUSTRALIA

Australia's premier championship venue, the tournament course at Royal Melbourne is a composite of twelve holes from Alister Mackenzie's West course and six from the newer East course, designed by Mackenzie's protégé, Alex Russell. Indeed, not all of the best of the thirty-six holes are included in the composite routing; the purpose of the amalgamated layout was to eliminate the need for tournament galleries to cross the public roads that divide the East and West courses. However, the composite layout does feature a wonderful selection of two-shot holes in the classic Royal Melbourne tradition, with sprawling diagonal fairway bunkers providing many

options of line from the tee according to the player's objective and nerve and the conditions of the day. With such fearsome bunkers, and greens world-renowned for their speed and contour, the designers could allow plenty of latitude for poorer players with wide fairways, and the lack of natural water on the property is scarcely noticed except at the finish, when it dawns on you that you have played all the way round with one ball.

(7) *ST. ANDREWS* (OLD COURSE), FIFE, SCOTLAND

Home to the Royal & Ancient Golf Club, but like St. Andrews' three other courses owned by the town, the Old Course sets the standard by which subsequent courses are judged. A difficult course to appreciate at first, owing to the complex array of hazards and a lack of visual definition, it has nevertheless withstood the test of time and retained its strategic interest through revolutions in equipment, course maintenance, and playing technique. Its unique evolution resulted in parallel fairways, seven double greens that serve two holes each, and hazards of many different origins, all of which until recent times allowed the course to be played entirely backwards (from 1st tee to 17th green, 18th tee to 16th green, and so on). Several holes, including the 11th, 14th, 16th and the famous "Road Hole," the 17th, are still considered among the best in the game. Even setting history aside, the Old Course sets a standard against which few other courses can compete.

(8) *ROYAL COUNTY DOWN*, NEWCASTLE, CO. DOWN, NORTHERN IRELAND

One of the most demanding tests of driving the game has to offer, Royal County Down's splendid setting near the foot of the Mountains of Mourne, halfway between Belfast and Dublin, has ironically cast it as a holiday course instead of a venue for championships. Originally laid out among the sandhills along Dundrum Bay by Old Tom Morris in 1889, the main feature of the course is the extreme naturalness of the design, with several blind drives aimed over marker stones at the peaks of the great dunes, to narrow fairways flanked by deep rough, a smattering of bunkers, and large banks of gorse. The greens are rather flat and less well conceived than the rest of the course, but the tee-to-green test of golf remains equal to the setting as one of the most searching in the game. The first nine holes (which return to the clubhouse) are especially fine.

(9) *SHINNECOCK HILLS*, SOUTHAMPTON, NEW YORK

Finally emerging into the spotlight as host to the 1986 U.S. Open Championship, it took only ninety-five years for Shinnecock to find its place in the public awareness. Founded in 1891, the club was one of five charter members of the United States Golf Association four years later, and hosted the second Open championship in 1896 on an early layout. The present course was designed by William Flynn and his young assistant Dick Wilson in 1931, and bears no resemblance to the earlier course. Described as America's most links-like course, because of its wavy

fescue rough and the added challenge of variable winds, the course is on higher, more rolling ground than a true links. This is especially true at the 9th hole, whose typically small and sloping green sits atop a high hill beside the oldest clubhouse in America, designed by Stanford White in 1893.

(10) *MERION* (EAST COURSE), ARDMORE, PENNSYLVANIA

Designed by club member Hugh Wilson after an extensive tour of the classic British courses, Merion's East course settles snugly on just 126 acres in Philadelphia's Main Line suburbs, with an architectural polish to match the neighborhood. A short course at only 6,544 yards, its skillfully contoured greens and large bunkers (sprinkled liberally in some cases with beachgrass and broom, and known locally as the "white faces of Merion") demand position play and fail to be overcome by displays of raw power. Among its other storied hazards are a narrow brook close beside the 11th green, and an overgrown worked-out quarry that must be overcome on each of the three finishing holes. The course's service as the setting for Bob Jones's completion of the Grand Slam in the 1930 U.S. Amateur, Ben Hogan's dramatic play-off win in the 1950 Open, and Lee Trevino's play-off victory over Jack Nicklaus in the 1971 event reserve a special niche for the course in American championship history.

(11) *ROYAL DORNOCH*, SUTHERLAND, SCOTLAND

Fully six hundred miles to the north of London, Royal Dornoch's remote location (on the same latitude as Hudson's Bay) has been a handicap to attracting championships and has assured it the distinction of being the world's least-played great course. The narrow strip of linksland is flanked by a gorse-covered bluff that comes into play at the near and far ends of the course, with splendid bunkering and large, natural plateau greens forming the framework of a test that emphasizes position play without severe penalties for the average player. The outward nine is generally considered to be the cream of the course, but the bunkerless par-4 14th hole (nicknamed "Foxy"), routed through a shallow valley to an offset plateau green, is the most storied hole. The small Royal burgh also commands a place in history as birthplace of Donald Ross, who learned the game over these links before emigrating to America to become one of the game's outstanding architects.

(12) *BALLYBUNION* (OLD COURSE), CO. KERRY, IRELAND

Among the most spectacular examples of golf architecture to be found anywhere, Ballybunion's Old Course is set high among gargantuan sand dunes overlooking the Atlantic Ocean on Ireland's sparsely populated west coast. After some relatively modest opening holes, the design takes a turn for the dramatic at the clifftop par-4 7th hole, and from there wanders back and forth from the dunes to the ocean's edge for a succession of breathtaking holes, of which the par-4 11th is perhaps most memorable. The design places a premium on rifle-straight approaches to the greens, many of which are narrow targets elevated above bunkers and hollows or nestling beside steep dunes.

(13) *PINEHURST* (NO. 2 COURSE), PINEHURST, NORTH CAROLINA

The earliest of America's winter golfing resorts, Pinehurst was founded at the turn of the century by the Tufts family, who brought the young professional and budding golf architect Donald Ross down from Massachusetts to oversee its development. Seven courses are now operated by the resort, but foremost among them is Ross's No. 2, which was carved from the forests of pine and dogwood that colonized the sandhill country and nurtured through forty years of refinements by the architect-in-residence. Its small, elevated greens and carefully contoured surrounds are the hallmark of Ross's work, striking what many believe to be the perfect balance between the long game and recovery play; while the sparse lovegrass and beds of pine needles that characterize the roughs require technique instead of power in escaping.

(14) *PRAIRIE DUNES*, HUTCHINSON, KANSAS

With its open, rolling, dunelike terrain and roughs tangled with plum thickets and wild yucca, not to mention the windy climate that made Dorothy famous, Prairie Dunes is often compared to the links of Britain even though it lies more than 1,000 miles from any ocean. In fact, however, none of the British links can boast of the small, severely humpbacked

Ballybunnion's Old Course winds through sand dunes on Ireland's west coast. *Fred Vuich*

Small, elevated greens are the salient characteristic at Donald Ross's Pinehurst Number 2. This is the 17th.
Jim Moriarty/Courtesy Pinehurst Country Club

Perry Maxwell greens or the occasional interruption of cottonwoods that lend the course much of its character. The original nine holes laid out by Perry Maxwell in 1937 (including the magnificent, rolling 420-yard 8th) form the greater part of the challenge, with the course expanded to eighteen holes by Press Maxwell in 1956.

(15) *WINGED FOOT* (*WEST COURSE*), *MAMARONECK, NEW YORK*

This difficult parkland layout, closely lined by huge specimen trees, is one of two outstanding courses designed by A. W. Tillinghast for the suburban New York club. Its architect described the nature of the challenge as follows: "The holes . . . are of a sturdy breed. . . . It is only the knowledge that the next shot must be played with rifle accuracy that brings the realization that the drive must be placed. The holes are like men, all rather similar from foot to neck, but

with the greens showing the same varying characters as human faces." The severely contoured, pear-shaped greens and the high-faced bunkers that flank them create the brunt of the challenge. The 190-yard par-3 10th hole and the 448-yard finisher are considered two of the classic holes in American golf.

(16) *CRYSTAL DOWNS*, *FRANKFORT, MICHIGAN*

Overlooked for years because of its remote location in northwest lower Michigan, this collaboration of Dr. Alister Mackenzie and construction superintendent Perry Maxwell is just beginning to receive its due as one of the great layouts in America. The front nine holes fill a huge undulating bowl of ground below the clubhouse, separated by wispy native rough while the back nine wanders away from the clubhouse and back through woods and across an old orchard, just removed from the spectacular bluff overlooking Lake Michigan, which provides a commanding view from the clubhouse. Of many fine holes, perhaps the most notable are the four outstanding short two-shotters, none measuring more than 353 yards, and the two par-5s that are both true three-shot holes.

(17) ROYAL PORTRUSH (DUNLUCE COURSE), CO. ANTRIM, NORTHERN IRELAND

The least-known of the great Irish links, owing to its location on the Antrim coast north of Belfast, the Dunluce links of Royal Portrush is one of the few links courses that is entirely a product of the Golden Age of design, being laid out by H. S. Colt in the 1920s. Consequently, it possesses not only the natural links undulations of the fairways and spectacular views of the water that nature provided it, but a balance and variety of holes and a great set of putting greens that are the hallmark of a virtuoso designer. The most memorable of the holes are the dogleg 5th, downhill to a green at the edge of the cliffs known as Whiterocks, with a view up the coast to Dunluce Castle after which the course is named, and the 211-yard "Calamity Corner" 14th, requiring a long carry across a grassy chasm to a summit of green: an awesome hole in the typical west wind.

(18) SEMINOLE, NORTH PALM BEACH, FLORIDA

Overlooking the Atlantic Ocean some twenty miles north of Palm Beach, Seminole is the posh private golf club that serves as the playground of the elite, as well as a winter haven for top players the likes of Ben Hogan, who spent a month here each spring tuning up his game for The Masters. The course is neither unreasonably long nor uncomfortably tight, and the medium-sized greens are fairly modest in contour, yet the orientation of the greens and thoughtful bunkering emphasize position play, with tactics dictated by the wind of the day. Unusually for Florida, there is some elevation change to the property, which was thoughtfully employed by the architect Donald Ross on several holes. Among the individual holes, the 390-yard 6th was pronounced by Hogan to be "the best par-4 in the world."

(19) OAKMONT, OAKMONT, PENNSYLVANIA

Founded by the father-and-son team of Henry and William Fownes on the outskirts of Pittsburgh in 1903, Oakmont has become synonomous with the penal philosophy of golf course design according to the younger Fownes's standard that "A shot poorly played should be a shot irrevocably lost." Laid out over hilly terrain sliced in two by a narrow gorge through which the Pennsylvania Turnpike unobtrusively transects the course, Oakmont is distinctive for its sprawling bunkers (nearly 200 in number), including the famous Church Pews between the 3rd and 4th fairways, with several narrow grassy strips breaking up a huge bunker into several rows of trouble. Originally a saber-toothed rake was used to furrow the sand and make recovery extra-difficult, but thankfully it is gone and the course is somewhat less fearsome than when club member Sam Parks was the only competitor in the 1935 U.S. Open to break 300 for the four rounds. The huge, rolling greens are legendary for their contour and speed.

(20) TURNBERRY (AILSA COURSE), AYRSHIRE, SCOTLAND

With its stretch of eight holes right along the coast, evoking memories of Pebble Beach, the Ailsa is probably Scotland's most scenic and spectacular championship links. A golf course has existed on this site since as early as 1903, but the present course had to be shaped with heavy machinery after the construction of an air base during World War II had devastated the site; consequently, the design is somewhat modern in theory compared to most other links, but some of the typical linksland roll of the fairways was never recovered. The course is dominated by views of the lonely rock of the Ailsa Craig offshore, and the tall lighthouse that stands sentinel over the powerhouse 9th and 10th holes, as well as the violently changeable moods of the weather at this particular spot on the coastline. Its first service as the venue for a major championship produced the epic Tom Watson–Jack Nicklaus confrontation in the 1977 Open.

(21) ROYAL BIRKDALE, SOUTHPORT, MERSEYSIDE, ENGLAND

Routed through towering sand dunes on England's Lancashire coast, Royal Birkdale is probably the most contemporary in style and most respected of the links courses that serve as host to the British Open

Championship. Its holes are confined to the valleys between the dunes that are covered by native willow scrub, with modestly contoured fairways and well-defined greens presenting more of a "target golf" challenge than most classic links courses, which are generally noted for a lack of visual definition. It is also one of only two courses on the Open roster (Muirfield is the other) that returns to the clubhouse at the 9th in the classic form of modern routing. The dramatic long finish includes three par-5s and the 473-yard par-4 18th in the last six holes.

(22) OAKLAND HILLS (SOUTH COURSE), BIRMINGHAM, MICHIGAN

Originally a fine Donald Ross layout over rolling farmland in the western suburbs of Detroit (considered highly enough to have hosted the U.S. Open championships of 1924 and 1937), the South course at Oakland Hills took on a sterner character after its redesign by Robert Trent Jones for the 1951 Open. By Jones's description at the time, "the game had outrun architecture"; his response was to lengthen the course and locate huge fairway bunkers to either side of the professionals' landing areas from the tee to make the course one of the world's great driving tests, as well as enlarging and recontouring some of the greens to make putting more hazardous. The course has mellowed somewhat since that championship, won by Hogan with a total of 7 over par despite a final-round 67, but it remains one of America's premier championship venues. The sharply doglegged par-4 16th, which hooks around a pond landscaped by willow trees, is considered one of America's classic holes.

(23) OLYMPIC (LAKESIDE COURSE), SAN FRANCISCO, CALIFORNIA

Originally laid out by Wilfrid Reid on a bare hillside just over the crest from the Pacific Slope, Olympic's Lakeside course has since evolved into one of the tightest driving courses in American golf with the growth of a thick forest of pine and eucalyptus that lines every fairway. The modest overall length is deceiving, because the hilly terrain, wet climate, and number of doglegs all conspire to make the course play relatively long. The fairways are so narrow that only one fairway bunker was deemed necessary for the entire eighteen holes, but the tiny greens are liberally bunkered. The club's secondary Ocean

course, part of which tunnels under Skyline Boulevard and overlooks the ocean itself, has been threatened by landslides in recent years.

(24) PORTMARNOCK, CO. DUBLIN, IRELAND

One of the most testing of all links courses, its location on a low-lying spit of land just to the north of Dublin harbor has established Portmarnock as Ireland's definitive championship venue. With more modest undulations than other noted Irish links, it is less striking to the eye but completely at the mercy of capricious winds, and the routing takes full advantage of the conditions with constant changes of direction. Severe pot bunkers reminiscent of Muirfield or St. Andrews defend several greens, most memorably at the 8th, 10th, and 14th holes; but the 192-yard 15th which skirts the beach is the most celebrated hole. The clubhouse with its red-tiled roof is noted for its hospitality, which is especially welcome after a tangle with the elements.

(25) BALTUSROL (LOWER COURSE), SPRINGFIELD, NEW JERSEY

This club, named after a farmer who was found murdered on the property, holds the unique distinction of having hosted U.S. Open championships on each of its two courses, both of which were originally designed by A.W. Tillinghast in 1922. The Lower Course (named because it sits lower on the hillside that rises behind the huge clubhouse) was remodeled by Robert Trent Jones in preparation for the 1954 U.S. Open, and is today the choice for championship play. It is considerably the longer of the two courses and has a somewhat restrained overall design, although the finish of back-to-back par 5s (including the 630-yard 17th, the longest hole in major championship history) is unusual, and the water-infested par-3 4th hole is another spectacular exception. The sloping, unaltered Upper course was also host to the 1936 U.S. Open, and the U.S. Women's Open Championship as recently as 1985.

(26) THE COUNTRY CLUB (OPEN COURSE), BROOKLINE, MASSACHUSETTS

The Country Club was chartered in 1860 when golf hadn't even arrived on U.S. shores and there was no need for a more distinctive name. Willie Campbell laid out the original nine-hole course in 1893, and

Robert Trent Jones added fairway bunkers to make Oakland Hills' South Course a sterner test. *Fred Vuich*

two years later the club was one of the founding members of the USGA. The course was expanded to eighteen holes in 1910 and to twenty-seven holes in 1927. A composite course including the par-4 11th, which combines two holes of the third nine, hosted the U.S. Open in 1963 and again in 1988, after a restoration by Rees Jones enhanced the course's reputation. Yet the rolling terrain, old-fashioned bunkering and occasional rock outcroppings still play the same prominent role in the design that they did in 1913, when a twenty-year-old former caddie at the club, Francis Ouimet, beat the English touring professionals Harry Vardon and Ted Ray in a play-off to become the first amateur and the second native American to win the U.S. Open.

(27) *CASA DE CAMPO* (TEETH OF THE DOG COURSE), LA ROMANA, DOMINICAN REPUBLIC

The golfing jewel of the Caribbean, Casa de Campo was literally hand-carved from the native coral by an army of native laborers under the direction of architect Pete Dye. Like a links, the course is laid out parallel with the sea (and straddling the resort's pri-

vate airstrip), but the clubhouse is located at the center of the figure-eight routing. Two dramatic stretches of holes, Nos. 5–8 and 15–17, play along the clifftops, and no fewer than six shots must be played across the edge of the surf, prompting one observer to remark that "Pebble Beach may have seven holes along the sea, but only Casa de Campo has seven holes *in* the sea." Such proximity does have its drawbacks, however. The island tee at the 8th hole has been rebuilt several times and the par-3 5th hole had to be completely changed from its original form following severe storms that crashed into the coastline.

(28) *KINGSTON HEATH*, CHELTENHAM, MELBOURNE, AUSTRALIA

Just one of several excellent courses in the Sand Belt region on the outskirts of Melbourne, Kingston Heath was laid out by Des Soutar in 1925. It really came to life when its magnificent clusters of bunkers were added by Alister Mackenzie three years later, while he was at work on nearby Royal Melbourne. The course had to be confined within a very small area, and so several parallel holes were created. Subsequent plantings and growth have, however, ensured that the course never feels cramped—though it is certainly not a course on which one will survive a bad day with the driver. There are only three par-3 holes, but each one is unforgettable for the bunkers that surround it, with the uphill 15th (which was changed completely by Mackenzie) being the most arresting of the group.

(29) MUIRFIELD VILLAGE, DUBLIN, OHIO

Built in the suburbs of his hometown of Columbus, the Muirfield Village course was Jack Nicklaus's first complete effort as a golf course architect and is named after the famous Scottish course over which he captured his first British Open championship in 1966. Laid out on rolling, wooded terrain dotted by natural streams, the course is especially noteworthy for the effort that was expended to provide complete visibility of the target areas and all surrounding hazards, as well as for the number of truly outstanding holes it contains. Deep bunkers around the greens place great emphasis on the approaches, while the low spectator mounds around the last few greens are an early forerunner of the "Stadium Golf" concept providing for Nicklaus's own Memorial Tournament.

(30) WOODHALL SPA, LINCOLNSHIRE, ENGLAND

An oasis of heathland on the dull plain of Lincolnshire, the relatively untested Woodhall Spa course is one of the most demanding inland courses in Britain, emphatically so in the tee-to-green play. Designed by Colonel S.V. Hotchkin in 1926, and still privately owned by his family, the course features bunkers of unparalleled depth among inland courses, particularly at the three one-shot holes that are all surrounded by deep pits. Elsewhere, narrow fairways lined first with heather, then thick beech trees and a lush growth of ferns, place a premium on long and straight driving.

EIGHTEEN GREAT HOLES

In golf architecture, like the game it provides for, while it is possible to achieve a very high standard, there is no standard of perfection. An architect may design eighteen outstanding holes out of eighteen (although it is not often done), but in doing so he will by no means have exhausted the possibilities of design to the point where one could state he had done the best job possible.

With more than 400,000 golf holes around the world to choose from, no two of them precisely alike in any respect except length, the selection of just eighteen to make up an "ideal" course is a prodigious, and necessarily subjective, task. To place some bounds on our imagination, we have limited our composite course to no more than one hole from any single course (even though many have more than one outstanding candidate), and in our routing we have been faithful to the actual numbers of the holes on the courses they come from, so that our opening hole is indeed an ideal *opening* hole, and the 18th is a tournament-tested finisher. Many outstanding holes had to be passed over, either because they didn't fit in with a preceding or following hole that had already been decided upon, or because they were too similar to another selected hole, or they biased the overall balance of the course, or they weren't quite good enough. Our final defense, therefore, is not that there are not other holes that belong on an "ideal" course, but that all of the holes we have chosen *do*.

The selection of holes must succeed on two levels. Individually, they must stand on their own merits: difficult enough to provide a challenge for the best players in the world, yet versatile in their design to allow for less accomplished players or severe weather. Each should possess an original character and a unique challenge, ideally a product of the terrain over which it is laid out. And the hazards should be so arranged that every shot remains interesting in the strategy as well as the play.

Simultaneously, each hole selected should contribute something unique to the balance and variety of the golf course as a whole. Thus, the lake to the left of the 5th fairway balances the ocean to the right of the 11th; the left-hand swing of the 15th contrasts with the sharp right turn at the 8th and the straightaway 3rd, our two complementary par-5s; the uphill drive and downhill approach at the 13th offset the downhill drive and uphill approach at the 9th, and so forth. No two greens are alike in size or contour, from the wildly undulating 1st and huge two-tiered second to the tiny, tilted 10th, but each is perfectly adapted to the shot it receives. And, of course, the lengths of the holes vary as much as possible, so that the golfer should have to use every club in his bag and every shot in his repertoire, from the fairway-wood second shot at the 15th to the cut wedge approach at the 10th.

The holes come from all around the world, and span the generations from St. Andrews to Muirfield Village. Each is a showpiece on its own, but together they provide a compelling course.

SCORECARD—EIGHTEEN GREAT HOLES

No.	Course	Par	Yards
1	National Golf Links	4	320
2	Carnoustie	4	439
3	Durban CC	5	506
4	Cruden Bay G & CC	3	193
5	Mid Ocean Club	4	433
6	Seminole GC	4	390
7	Pebble Beach GL	3	107
8	Crystal Downs CC	5	550
9	Lahinch GC	4	382
10	Riviera CC	4	311
11	Ballybunion GC (Old)	4	449
12	Augusta National GC	3	162
13	Pine Valley GC	4	446
14	Muirfield Village GC	4	363
15	Hirono GC	5	555
16	Cypress Point Club	3	233
17	St. Andrews Old Course	4	461
18	Royal Lytham & St. Anne's	4	386
Out		36	3320
In		35	3366
Total		71	6686

HOLE NO. 1, NATIONAL GOLF LINKS OF AMERICA SOUTHAMPTON, NEW YORK
320 YARDS

Ideally, an opening hole ought to afford the player some leeway on his opening tee shot, but give full advantage to the more confident and reliable player. C. B. Macdonald must have had this in mind when he designed the opening hole of his own ideal course, The National, in 1909. A nest of bunkers lies in the corner of the dogleg, tempting the player to try a 200-yard carry to set up a straight-in approach to the wildly undulating green. There is a safer line from the tee into a bowl of fairway on the right, but from that angle the length of the approach over a cross-bunker is very deceptive. It is not even unthinkable for the strongest of players to drive level with the

green, but that was not the hot-tempered architect's intention: he wrote a son-in-law out of his will for demonstrating this perceived weakness of the design.

HOLE NO. 2, CARNOUSTIE, SCOTLAND
439 YARDS

Now that the player has fully loosened up his muscles, we may intensify the challenge of the course, here with a long par 4 curving gently to the right along the course of a natural gulley among dunes. A critically placed pot bunker lies within the boundaries of the fairway just to the left of center, at the length of a good drive; it is named after the architect, Braid, who fashioned a similar hazard on many of the courses throughout Scotland and England in which he had a hand. One must play closely beside the bunker if there is to be any hope of getting up to the back portion of the long, two-tiered green with the approach.

HOLE NO. 3, DURBAN COUNTRY CLUB, SOUTH AFRICA
506 YARDS

Two paramount virtues of a great hole are that it presents an exhilarating challenge from the tee, and clearly sets out its problems for the golfers to see. The 3rd at Durban, frequently cited as Africa's best hole, is a textbook example. From the tee, elevated atop a high dune, the hole unfolds through a sharply undulating valley and past three deep bunkers on the way to an elevated green set into a tree-covered dune at the valley's far end. To the right, there is the prospect of a beautiful beach and the Indian Ocean, just far enough removed to be a calming rather than frightening influence. As with most good short par 5s, the hole is not overwhelming if played cautiously with three fairly straight shots, but the elevation of the tee and bowl of fairway tempt many into the fatal mistake of swinging too hard, whence they discover that the native kikuyu grass carpeting the dunes will smother the expected bounce and result in a hanging lie.

HOLE NO. 4, CRUDEN BAY, SCOTLAND
193 YARDS

Great golf holes abound on our most celebrated courses, but not all of the best holes in the world are as famous. This is especially true among the lesser-known links of Scotland and England, such as Cruden Bay, thirty miles to the north of Aberdeen, where architects Fowler and Simpson carved some wonderful and some bizarre holes out of some of the highest sand dunes in British golf.

The fourth, a lengthy par 3, is definitely among the first category of hole. It crosses a wrinkled bowl of fairway to a shelf of green set high in the dunes along the North Sea, protected by a single bunker at the left front of the green and a series of grassy depressions around the right-hand side to the back. Into the wind there may be days when it is virtually unreachable from the medal tee, but it always remains playable, and there is the added attraction of everyday life passing by in the tiny fishing village of Port Erroll, whose shops lie across Cruden Water no more than a 9-iron shot away from the tee.

HOLE NO. 5, MID OCEAN CLUB, BERMUDA
433 YARDS

Charles Blair Macdonald became famous as a golf architect for his adaptations of celebrated British links holes within his own designs, but he was proudest of his original design, which he called the "Cape" hole, that encouraged the player to attempt a prodigious carry across water to an angled fairway in order to set up a shorter approach to the green. His 5th at Mid Ocean is the ultimate expression of the type. The tee sits high atop a hill, with glorious views of the sparkling Atlantic; the drive must bite off a portion of Mangrove Lake to a sharply banked fairway. An overly safe drive to the right leaves a long second from a sidehill lie, to a well-protected green; but the penalty for overestimating one's strength from the tee is humbling and total.

HOLE NO. 6, SEMINOLE GOLF CLUB, NORTH PALM BEACH, FLORIDA
390 YARDS

Like most of its kin at Donald Ross's exclusive Florida masterpiece, the 6th at Seminole is neither imposingly long nor narrow, but only two well-placed and well-struck shots are rewarded. Sited along the crest of a ridge at the high point of the property, the hole calls for a semi-blind drive across a diagonal stretch of bunkers, with the long carry down to the left side being rewarded by an open approach. A safer drive down the right necessitates that more sprawling sand be carried on the pitch; in addition, there is

much less room for error in stopping the approach on the slightly crowned green from this angle. No greater accolade could be bestowed upon a hole than the testimony of Ben Hogan, who called the 6th simply "the best par 4 in the world."

HOLE NO. 7, PEBBLE BEACH GOLF LINKS, PEBBLE BEACH, CALIFORNIA
107 YARDS

There are no rules of golf architecture, and no arbitrary minimum length for a one-shot hole has been set. Even the shortest of pitches can be a frightening shot if the target is sufficiently small and the hazards that guard it imposing; such a hole is the 7th at Pebble Beach. Though sometimes overshadowed by other holes from the spectacular stretch overlooking Carmel Bay, it is perhaps the most exacting shot to be found on any major championship course, not to mention the shortest. Length is of little concern unless the drop from the tee distracts, but there is only a sliver of green to aim at with bunkers all around, not to mention the Pacific Ocean that will come into play on the right in a crosswind. It takes courage to drill a medium or long iron shot in the direction of Big Sur when the wind is against, and in really severe conditions the wisest option might be that once employed by Sam Snead, who putted down the hill into the front bunker, blasted out and made sure of his four.

HOLE NO. 8, CRYSTAL DOWNS COUNTRY CLUB, FRANKFORT, MICHIGAN
550 YARDS

For some reason there seem to be an unusual number of outstanding 8th holes to choose from in making up an eclectic course; but in the search for a good three-shot par-5, Dr. MacKenzie's little-known masterpiece in northern Michigan provides a candidate without peer. Extremely long hitters may flirt with a huge, dense silver maple in the corner of the dogleg with fleeting thoughts of getting home in two, but wise members will satisfy themselves with a straightaway tee shot to the crest of a wildly undulating fairway, leaving a good lie and stance from which to place the second shot along the spine of the fairway at the right. With any wind about, the uphill pitch to the tiny summit of green is still most exacting, with a steep bank at the front edge and a shrub-covered hillside beyond the green.

HOLE NO. 9, LAHINCH GOLF CLUB, IRELAND
382 YARDS

One of Ireland's most hallowed links, Lahinch has become celebrated more for its unusual blind holes than for strategic architecture, but the 9th begins an exceptional run of holes carved from the dunes by Mackenzie in his 1926 re-routing of the course. The exceedingly long and narrow green sits along a narrow shelf between a bunker and knob to the right and a steep fall to the left, obviously calling for a straight-in approach; but on this line a very long carry over a deep bowl in the fairway is critical to a flat lie for the pitch. A less demanding carry is in order if the drive is away to the right, but then the approach must carry the corner of the bunker in front and check up quickly before it disappears over the slight rise at the left edge of the green, and down toward the next tee.

HOLE NO. 10, RIVIERA COUNTRY CLUB, PACIFIC PALISADES, CALIFORNIA
311 YARDS

One of the idealistic concepts of golf architecture is that all the hazards of a hole should be in plain view from the tee so that even the first-time visitor can map out the proper playing strategy; but there is no rule that the best strategy ought to be immediately obvious, and certainly there ought to be one hole on any course where local knowledge helps the score. One of the cleverest holes along these lines is Riviera's 10th. All the hazards are in view from the tee, and the straightaway route to the green looks broad and inviting; but the putting green is tilted away from a bunker just in front, so that even a well-struck wedge shot from the wrong angle of approach may skip right through. The trick here is to play the tee shot well down the *left* side of the fairway, and cut a 9-iron or wedge shot into the reverse slope of the green. The longer the drive, the more to the right one can leave it, but on this hole patience is a virtue most frequently rewarded.

HOLE NO. 11, BALLYBUNION (OLD COURSE), IRELAND
449 YARDS

After the subtle challenge of the 10th, there could be no greater contrast than this, one of the most spectacular holes the game has to offer. The small championship tee perches right atop the edge of a sand dune, with a fifty-foot drop to the beach and the Atlantic immediately at hand; the drive must skirt the cliff edge to settle on a modest patch of fairway between still higher sandhills to the left and the sea. The approach, over a deep valley of fairway and through a narrow gap between guardian dunes to a knob of green, leaves some margin for error at the front and back, but if the target is missed to one side just holding the pitch on the green will require an excellent touch. Not a single bunker was necessary to complicate the demands of the hole.

HOLE NO. 12, AUGUSTA NATIONAL GOLF CLUB, AUGUSTA, GEORGIA
162 YARDS

Centerpiece of the fabulous "Amen Corner," the 12th at Augusta is that rare short hole where even the best professionals at the peak of their game are inclined to opt for safety and aim away from the pin. Its angled green nestles behind Rae's Creek in the shadow of a steep hillside to the rear, with a deep bunker in front and two more diabolical bunkers excavated from the slope behind. When the pin is set on the right corner of the green (where it always resides on Masters Sunday), a fraction of an under-club or push will find the creek, while a pull with the right club will leave a frightening explosion out of the back bunker with nothing but the creek to stop a runaway shot. Swirling winds in this corner of the course add to the risky nature of the shot, and veteran competitors usually take their chances with a long putt or chip from the left side of the green if they have any lead to protect.

HOLE NO. 13, PINE VALLEY GOLF CLUB, CLEMENTON, NEW JERSEY
446 YARDS

The singling out of one hole from George Crump's treasury in the New Jersey pine barrens is a difficult choice, because it requires us to pass over a dozen other outstanding candidates, but there is comfort in the knowledge that the quality of whichever hole we finally select will be beyond dispute. The long 13th is the class of the course's long two-shot holes. From a low-lying championship tee, the drive is uphill over the classic Pine Valley wastelands to a crown of fairway; only a long drive straight along its spine will clear the way for a medium-iron approach across more wasteland to the huge, tilted green. For the less accomplished player, there is a safe patch of fairway short and to the right of the green at which to aim the second shot, but every extra yard of safety the player takes with his lay-up shot results in a more difficult pitch as the green falls steeply away.

HOLE NO. 14, MUIRFIELD VILLAGE GOLF CLUB, DUBLIN, OHIO
363 YARDS

The narrow brook that interrupts the fairway about a hundred yards short of the green requires longer hitters to play a fairway wood or long iron from the tee, but it in no way lessens the demands of this outstanding short par 4. The fairway is enclosed in a wooded valley but is not exceptionally narrow, giving the player the option of a straight and narrow tee shot with his driving iron, or a longer tee shot over the shoulder of a hill on the right so the pitch can be played more into the slope of the long green, which tilts toward the creek. There is no safe side to favor on the approach: the creek at the right means disaster, while an explosion from one of the bunkers on the left threatens more of the same.

HOLE NO. 15, HIRONO GOLF CLUB, JAPAN
550 YARDS

In a country where heavy earthmoving is now considered essential in the construction of golf courses, no better case could be found for the advantages of natural golfing ground and thoughtful layout than the 15th at Hirono, our longest hole. Each of the three shots to the green must clear valleys of varying depth to reach the next target area; of these the central ravine is the most severe, requiring a fair carry for the weaker player to clear its bunker-studded far face, or a good shot from the stronger player who has left his drive behind the lone pine tree in the left side of the fairway, or in the long strip of fairway bunker to the right. A slight dip before the elevated green and its flanking bunkers ensures the approach must carry to the heart of the target and resists most attempts to reach home with a long second, though Jack Nicklaus once succeeded here with a drive and a long spoon.

HOLE NO. 16, CYPRESS POINT GOLF CLUB, PEBBLE BEACH, CALIFORNIA
233 YARDS

Perched atop the cliffs at the headland of the Monterey Peninsula, the 16th at Cypress Point is certainly the most dramatic hole in golf, perhaps the most beautiful, and among the most difficult to complete in regulation figures. The direct line to the green is all carry across the frothing Pacific surf and a tangle of the fleshy iceplant native to the cliffs, from which there is little chance of escape. In all conditions, but particularly attractive when the wind is against, one may play a safe mid-iron over a narrower part of the cove to the neck of the point, followed by a pitch along it to the green, a totally unthrilling alternative but nearly always the correct choice in stroke competition. However, this safety does not extend to a pull with the driver, for a cove on the far side of the narrow spit can jump up to claim the error. From there, as Jimmy Demaret once observed, "The only place you can drop the ball over your shoulder is in Honolulu."

HOLE NO. 17, ST. ANDREWS (OLD COURSE), SCOTLAND
461 YARDS

Even more infamous than the 16th at Cypress is famous, the Road Hole at St. Andrews epitomizes the fine line between success and disaster that is characteristic of the greatest holes. Contrary to folklore, the hole did not evolve as a result of purely natural forces; it was instead designed by the local professional Allan Robertson about 1850, who almost certainly would not have escaped retribution for his plan had the hole not been clearly a three-shotter in those days of the gutty ball. Today, however, the hole is within range of two shots, exceptional though they must be. The drive is across out-of-bounds territory that once was the railway stationmaster's garden and back onto the course far downrange; the boundary wall angles away to the right, and every extra foot that can be carried is crucial for those who wish to reach the green in two. The long approach must thread the needle between a cruel pot bunker chewing its way into the heart of the plateau green on the left, and the paved road which parallels the rear flank of the green. On this hole as the last, the par figure is a rather overly optimistic standard, but the ruthless separation of excellent play from that which is not quite so good, when combined with the option of a safer but less rewarding alternate route, is the hallmark of golf architecture at its best.

HOLE NO. 18, ROYAL LYTHAM & ST. ANNES, ENGLAND 386 YARDS

Among modern designers the 440-yard finishing hole flanked by a water hazard has become almost a cliché of design; its insistence upon two solid shots to complete the round is commendable, but in tournament play it often produces the anticlimax of a giveaway finish, and almost precludes the possibility of a crowning birdie thrust. Much better is the home hole at Lytham, where a headwind and two diagonal rows of cross-bunkers demand nothing less than a perfect final drive, but leaves open the possibility of an attacking approach to the long, narrow green once the drive is accomplished. Combined with a supremely difficult 16th and 17th, this hole would be the crowning glory of a heroic finish, and offers the added bonus of having the clubhouse immediately at hand behind the home green, so close in fact that Gary Player was once required to putt left-handed from beside its walls after misjudging the final approach of his 1974 Open triumph.

GOLF MAGAZINE'S 100 GREATEST HOLES IN AMERICA

Hole	Course	Par/Yardage/ Architects	Hole	Course	Par/Yardage/ Architects
No. 12	AUGUSTA NATIONAL GC Augusta, Ga.	Par 3, 155 yds. Mackenzie	No. 5	COLONIAL CC Fort Worth, Tex.	Par 4, 466 yds. Maxwell
No. 13	AUGUSTA NATIONAL GC Augusta, Ga.	Par 5, 465 yds. Mackenzie/Nicklaus	No. 18	COLONIAL CC Fort Worth, Tex.	Par 4, 434 yds. Bredemus
No. 4	BALTUSROL GC (LOWER) Springfield, N.J.	Par 3, 192 yds. Tillinghast/Jones	No. 18	CONGRESSIONAL CC Bethesda, Md.	Par 4, 465 yds. Jones
No. 17	BALTUSROL GC (LOWER) Springfield, N.J.	Par 5, 630 yds. Tillinghast/Jones	No. 2	CRAG BURN GC East Aurora, N.Y.	Par 5, 607 yds. Jones
No. 18	BAY HILL CLUB Orlando, Fla.	Par 4, 456 yds. D. Wilson/Palmer	No. 6	CROOKED STICK GC Carmel, Ind.	Par 3, 189 yds. Dye
No. 4	BEAR CREEK GOLF Temecula, Cal.	Par 4, 435 yds. Nicklaus	No. 8	CRYSTAL DOWNS CC Frankfort, Mich.	Par 5, 550 yds. Mackenzie
No. 18	BEAR CREEK GOLF WORLD (MASTERS) Houston, Tex.	Par 4, 442 yds. Riviere	No. 16	CYPRESS POINT CLUB Pebble Beach, Cal.	Par 3, 233 yds. Mackenzie
No. 10	BEL AIR CC Los Angeles, Cal.	Par 3, 198 yds. Thomas	No. 17	CYPRESS POINT CLUB Pebble Beach, Cal.	Par 4, 375 yds. Mackenzie
No. 5	BETHPAGE STATE PARK (BLACK) Farmingdale, N.Y.	Par 4, 438 yds. Tillinghast	No. 10	COUNTRY CLUB OF DETROIT Grosse Pointe Farms, Mich.	Par 5, 581 yds. Colt
No. 16	BROOK HOLLOW GC Dallas, Tex.	Par 3, 228 yds. Tillinghast	No. 18	DORAL CC (BLUE) Miami, Fla.	Par 4, 437 yds. D. Wilson
No. 18	BUTLER NATIONAL GC Oak Brook, Ill.	Par 4, 466 yds. G. & T. Fazio	No. 13	THE DUNES GOLF & BEACH CLUB Myrtle Beach, S.C.	Par 5, 575 yds. Jones
No. 18	CANTERBURY CC Cleveland, Ohio	Par 4, 438 yds. Strong	No. 18	EDGEWOOD TAHOE GC Stateline, Nev.	Par 5, 591 yds. G. Fazio
No. 2	CHICAGO GC Wheaton, Ill.	Par 4, 440 yds. Macdonald/Raynor	No. 17	FIRESTONE CC (NORTH) Akron, Ohio	Par 3, 218 yds. Jones
No. 12	CHICAGO GC Wheaton, Ill.	Par 4, 405 yds. Macdonald/Raynor			

GOLF MAGAZINE'S 100 GREATEST HOLES IN AMERICA (continued)

Hole	Course	Par/Yardage/ Architects	Hole	Course	Par/Yardage/ Architects
No. 16	FIRESTONE CC (SOUTH) Akron, Ohio	Par 5, 625 yds. Jones	No. 9	MYOPIA HUNT CLUB South Hamilton, Mass.	Par 3, 136 yds. Leeds
No. 8	FISHERS ISLAND CLUB Fishers Island, N.Y.	Par 5, 460 yds. Raynor	No. 4	NATIONAL GL OF AMERICA Southampton, N.Y.	Par 3, 196 yds. Macdonald
No. 2	THE GREENBRIER COURSE White Sulphur Springs, W. Va.	Par 4, 403 yds. Nicklaus	No. 17	NATIONAL GL OF AMERICA Southampton, N.Y.	Par 4, 368 yds. Macdonald
No. 18	HALF MOON BAY GL Half Moon Bay, Cal.	Par 4, 428 yds. Palmer/Duane	No. 3	OAK TREE GC Edmond, Okla.	Par 5, 584 yds. Dye
No. 15	HARBOUR TOWN LINKS Hilton Head, S.C.	Par 5, 562 yds. Dye/Nicklaus	No. 16	OAKLAND HILLS CC (SOUTH) Birmingham, Mich.	Par 4, 405 yds. Ross/Jones
No. 17	HARBOUR TOWN LINKS Hilton Head, S.C.	Par 3, 179 yds. Dye/Nicklaus	No. 15	OAKMONT CC Oakmont, Pa.	Par 4, 453 yds. Fownes
No. 12	INDIAN CREEK CC Bal Harbour, Fla.	Par 3, 190 yds. Flynn/D. Wilson	No. 3	THE GOLF CLUB OF OKLAHOMA Broken Arrow, Okla.	Par 4, 415 yds. T. Fazio
No. 12	INTERLACHEN CC Edina, Minn.	Par 5, 541 yds. Watson/Ross	No. 16	OLYMPIC CLUB (LAKE) San Francisco, Cal.	Par 5, 604 yds. Reid/Whiting
No. 7	INVERNESS CLUB Toledo, Ohio	Par 4, 452 yds. Ross	No. 18	OLYMPIC CLUB (LAKE) San Francisco, Cal.	Par 4, 338 yds. Reid/Whiting
No. 9	JUPITER HILLS CLUB (HILLS) Tequesta, Fla.	Par 3, 190 yds. G. & T. Fazio	No. 7	PALMETTO GC Aiken, S.C.	Par 3, 161 yds. Mackenzie
No. 17	KEMPER LAKES GC Hawthorn Woods, Ill.	Par 3, 203 yds. Killian/Nugent	No. 8	PEBBLE BEACH GL Pebble Beach, Cal.	Par 4, 425 yds. Neville/Grant
No. 3	KITTANSETT CLUB Marion, Mass.	Par 3, 170 yds. Hood	No. 18	PEBBLE BEACH GL Pebble Beach, Cal.	Par 5, 548 yds. Neville/Grant
No. 3	LINVILLE GC Linville, N.C.	Par 4, 455 yds. Ross	No. 9	PGA WEST (STADIUM) La Quinta, Cal.	Par 4, 450 yds. Dye
No. 7	LONG COVE CLUB Hilton Head, S.C.	Par 4, 439 yds. Dye	No. 18	PHILADELPHIA CRICKET CLUB Flourtown, Pa.	Par 4, 472 yds. Tillinghast
No. 9	MAIDSTONE CLUB East Hampton, N.Y.	Par 4, 410 yds. Park	No. 9	PHILMONT CC (NORTH) Philadelphia, Pa.	Par 5, 574 yds. Flynn
No. 14	MAIDSTONE CLUB East Hampton, N.Y.	Par 3, 140 yds. Park	No. 13	PINE VALLEY GC Pine Valley, N.J.	Par 4, 446 yds. Crump/H. Wilson
No. 3	MAUNA KEA GC Kamuela, Hawaii	Par 3, 215 yds. Jones	No. 15	PINE VALLEY GC Pine Valley, N.J.	Par 5, 603 yds. Crump/H. Wilson
No. 17	MEDINAH CC (NO. 3) Medinah, Ill.	Par 3, 220 yds. Bendelow/Killian	No. 2	PINEHURST CC (NO. 2) Pinehurst, N.C.	Par 4, 441 yds. Ross
No. 11	MERION GC (EAST) Ardmore, Pa.	Par 4, 369 yds. H. Wilson/Flynn	No. 5	PINEHURST CC (NO. 2) Pinehurst, N.C.	Par 4, 445 yds. Ross
No. 16	MERION GC (EAST) Ardmore, Pa.	Par 4, 428 yds. H. Wilson	No. 9	POINT O'WOODS G&CC Benton Harbor, Mich.	Par 3, 203 yds. Jones
No. 12	MUIRFIELD VILLAGE GC Dublin, Ohio	Par 3, 152 yds. Nicklaus/Muirhead	No. 8	PRAIRIE DUNES CC Hutchinson, Kan.	Par 4, 420 yds. Maxwell
No. 14	MUIRFIELD VILLAGE GC Dublin, Ohio	Par 4, 363 yds. Nicklaus/Muirhead	No. 10	PRAIRIE DUNES CC Hutchinson, Kan.	Par 3, 169 yds. Maxwell
No. 4	MYOPIA HUNT CLUB South Hamilton, Mass.	Par 4, 392 yds. Leeds			

GOLF MAGAZINE'S 100 GREATEST HOLES IN AMERICA (continued)

Hole	Course	Par/Yardage/ Architects	Hole	Course	Par/Yardage/ Architects
No. 7	PRESTON TRAIL GC Dallas, Tex.	Par 4, 422 yds. Plummer	No. 18	SOUTHERN HILLS CC Tulsa, Okla.	Par 4, 449 yds. Maxwell
No. 6	QUAKER RIDGE GC Scarsdale, N.Y.	Par 4, 446 yds. Tillinghast	No. 3	THE COUNTRY CLUB Brookline, Mass.	Par 4, 446 yds. Campbell
No. 18	RIVIERA CC Pacific Palisades, Cal.	Par 4, 443 yds. Thomas	No. 9	THE COUNTRY CLUB Pepper Pike, Ohio	Par 3, 188 yds. Flynn
No. 9	ROCKAWAY HUNTING CLUB Cedarhurst, N.Y.	Par 4, 465 yds. Tillinghast	No. 13	THE GOLF CLUB New Albany, Ohio	Par 4, 369 yds. Dye
No. 7	SAN FRANCISCO GC San Francisco, Cal.	Par 3, 180 yds. Tillinghast	No. 17	TPC AT SAWGRASS Ponte Vedra, Fla.	Par 3, 132 yds. Dye
No. 10	SAUCON VALLEY CC (GRACE) Bethlehem, Pa.	Par 5, 534 yds. Gordon	No. 18	TPC AT SAWGRASS Ponte Vedra, Fla.	Par 4, 440 yds. Dye
No. 4	SEA ISLAND GC (SEASIDE) St. Simons Island, Ga.	Par 4, 382 yds. Colt/Alison	No. 15	TROON G&CC Scottsdale, Ariz.	Par 3, 139 yds. Weiskopf/Morrish
No. 6	SEMINOLE GC North Palm Beach, Fla.	Par 4, 390 yds. Ross	No. 16	THE VINTAGE CLUB (MOUNTAIN) Indian Wells, Cal.	Par 4, 379 yds. T. Fazio
No. 17	SEMINOLE GC North Palm Beach, Fla.	Par 3, 175 yds. Ross	No. 9	WHITINSVILLE GC Whitinsville, Mass.	Par 4, 440 yds. Ross
No. 11	SHINNECOCK HILLS GC Southampton, N.Y.	Par 3, 158 yds. Flynn/D. Wilson	No. 18	WILD DUNES Isle of Palms, S.C.	Par 5, 540 yds. T. Fazio
No. 14	SHINNECOCK HILLS GC Southampton, N.Y.	Par 4, 444 yds. Flynn/D. Wilson	No. 10	WINGED FOOT GC (WEST) Mamaroneck, N.Y.	Par 3, 190 yds. Tillinghast
No. 11	SHOREACRES Lake Bluff, Ill.	Par 4, 349 yds. Raynor	No. 18	WINGED FOOT GC (WEST) Mamaroneck, N.Y.	Par 4, 448 yds. Tillinghast
No. 15	SOMERSET HILLS CC Bernardsville, N.J.	Par 4, 385 yds. Tillinghast	No. 4	YALE UNIVERSITY GC New Haven, Conn.	Par 4, 443 yds. Macdonald
No. 12	SOUTHERN HILLS CC Tulsa, Okla.	Par 4, 444 yds. Maxwell	No. 9	YALE UNIVERSITY GC New Haven, Conn.	Par 3, 228 yds. Macdonald

Glossary of Golf Terms

THE LANGUAGE OF golf is almost as romantic and interesting as the history and play of the game itself. True, many words (those that can be printed) of the golfer are self-explanatory and do not require lengthy definitions. But there are others whose derivations, like the early history of the sport, are lost in antiquity. For instance, no one is sure where the word "golf" itself comes from. However, golf historian Robert Browning feels that the word is derived from the German *kolbe,* which means "club." Thus, golf, the Belgian game of *chole,* the Dutch games of *colf* and *kolf* all mean "club," and each is in its own way the "game of the club."

There is even some controversy over why eighteen holes constitute a round of golf. Sure, there are any number of counterfeit theories. One of the more spurious is based on the notion that there are approximately eighteen shots of whisky in a fifth of Scotch. As golfers plied their way across the Scottish moors centuries ago—so the story goes—they celebrated the completion of each "hole" by imbibing a swig. Hence, when the bottle had been emptied, the round was considered finished.

Actually, golf became an eighteen-hole game at St. Andrews, Scotland, a little more than 200 years ago, according to Browning (among other authorities).

During the latter half of the eighteenth century, the rules, standards, and fashions of golf were set by the Honourable Company of Edinburgh Golfers, who played their golf over the Links of Leith. However, this leadership was gradually taken over by the members of the Royal and Ancient Golf Club, who played their golf over the links of St. Andrews. Until the middle of the eighteenth century, golf had been played over courses of no established length. Leith, for example, had only five holes. Blackheath, another ancient club, had seven, which was the most fashionable number; but other courses had as many as twenty-five. Possibly seven would have remained the traditional number for a round had it not been for the example of St. Andrews.

At the time, St. Andrews had twelve holes. The first eleven traveled straight out to the end of a small peninsula. After playing these, the golfers returned to the clubhouse by playing the first ten greens backward, plus a solitary green by the clubhouse. Thus, a "round" of golf at St. Andrews, consisted of twenty-two holes. In 1764, however, the Royal and Ancient resolved that the first four holes should be converted into two. Since this change automatically converted the same four holes into two on the way back, the "round" was reduced from twenty-two holes to eighteen. And since St. Andrews was the arbiter of all that was correct about golf, 18 holes soon came to be accepted as standard throughout Scotland and England and, eventually, the world. Thus, this is the accepted reason why a round consists of eighteen holes.

We know the derivations of many other golf terms. In 1891, in England, for example, one Hugh Rotherman suggested that a certain "ground score" be established for each golf course so that players could compete against a fixed and certain score. At the Great Yarmouth Club, the secretary, Dr. T. Browne, initiated a series of matches based on a relatively stable score for each hole, and the device proved to be eminently popular. For the first time, players could devise systems of handicapping and course comparisons and, at the same time, roughly analyze how they were performing on particular days. During this same year, a popular music-hall song was sweeping Britain, and the words were catchy and naggingly unforgettable: "Hush, hush," it went, "here comes the Bogey Man." And so quite naturally, as such stories go, a Major C. Wellman grew especially angry after a bad round and fired at Dr. Browne the immortally mordant remark, "That score of yours is a regular 'Bogey Man.' "

In those days, the term "bogey" became synonymous with our "par," meaning the score that an average good player should make on a given hole. But unlike American "par," "bogey" might change from day to day according to weather conditions and other influences. Eventually, there evolved a more demanding standard—"Old Man Par," as Bobby Jones was wont to call it. Par was and is an unvarying score: it never takes three putts, and never gets down in one. It is immutable and impervious to any mere change in conditions. And therein lies its terror—and its challenge.

The word "birdie," meaning one under par, had a similarly unusual birth in the United States. In 1903, A. H. Smith of Atlantic City, after holing out, is said to have commented, "That's a bird of a shot." The terms "eagle," for two under par, and "albatross," for three under par, came about by natural amplification of Smith's original metaphor, but "double eagle" has completely replaced the awkward "albatross."

The term "caddie," for bag carrier, can be traced back to the days of Mary, Queen of Scots. An avid golfer, the queen played the game while attending school in France, using *cadets* (pronounced ka-day), younger sons of nobility who served as pages, to carry her unwieldy clubs. The close cognate was transposed, with the French pronunciation intact, and it has lasted since the seventeenth century.

Here are some of the most common phrases that are frequently used in golf:

Ace. A hole made in one stroke. Same as a hole in one.

Address. The position taken by a player in preparing to start a stroke. Same as *addressing the ball*.

Advice. Counsel which could influence how a shot is played or what club is used.

Albatross. Score for a hole of three strokes under par. See *double eagle*.

Amateur. One who plays golf as a sport, without monetary compensation.

Approach. A stroke played to the putting green, or to the pin if possible. Usually refers to a medium- or short-term shot.

Apron. Grass area immediately bordering the putting surface, generally mowed about halfway. Same as *fringe*.

Automatics. An extra Nassau bet permitted any time a player is two points behind.

Away. The ball farthest from the hole when more than one golfer is playing. The golfer whose ball is "away" shoots first.

Back door. The rear of the hole. A putt that "drops in the back door" is one that goes all the way around the hole and at the moment when it seems to have no chance to fall in, plops in the back of the cup.

Back side. The second nine holes in an eighteen-hole course.

Backspin. A reverse spin put on the ball to make it stop on the putting green.

Backswing. The backward portion of the swing starting from the ground and going back over the head.

Ball. The round object struck by the golf club. The golf ball is 1.68 inches in diameter and has a weight of 1.62 ounces.

Ball deemed to move. A ball is deemed to have "moved" if it leaves its position and comes to rest in any other place.

Ball holed. A ball is "holed" when it lies within the circumference of the hole and all of it is below the level of the lip of the hole.

Ball in play. A ball is "in play" as soon as the player has made a stroke on the teeing ground. It remains in play as his ball until holed out, except when it is out of bounds, lost, or lifted or when another ball is substituted in accordance with the official rules or local rules.

Ball lost. A ball is "lost" if (1) it cannot be found within five minutes after the player's side or his or their caddies have begun to search for it; (2) it be declared lost by the player without searching five minutes; (3) after a search of five minutes the player is unable to identify a ball as his ball; (4) The player has played any stroke with a provisional ball from the place where the original ball is likely to be or from a point nearer the hole than that place, whereupon the provisional ball becomes the ball in play. Time spent in playing a wrong ball is not counted in the five-minute period allowed for search. Play of a wrong ball does not constitute abandonment of the ball in play.

Ball marker. A small coin or facsimile used to spot a ball position on the putting green.

Banana ball. A flagrantly bad slice, curving to the right in the shape of a banana.

Barranca. A deep ravine.

Beach. Any sand hazard on the golf course.

Belt one. To hit a ball well while applying a little extra power.

Bend one. To hook or slice.

Bent. Type of grass primarily used on northern courses.

Bermuda. Type of grass primarily used on southern courses.

Best-ball. A match in which one plays against the better ball of two or the best ball of three players. Also the lower score by either of two match partners.

Birdie. One stroke under the designated par of a hole.

Bite. Backspin imparted to a ball.

Blade. A type of putter.

Blade one. To hit a topped shot. See *top*.

Bladesman. An admiring description applied to an excellent putter.

Blast. Hitting out of a sand trap and taking large quantities of sand with the shot. Same as *explode*.

Blind Bogey. A competition in which a score is drawn out of a hat, and the player coming closest to it wins.

Blind hole. A hole is said to be "blind" when its putting green cannot be seen by the player as he approaches.

Block. To manipulate the swing to force a clubhead arc from inside to outside at impact.

Bogey. One stroke over the designated par of a hole.

Bold. Strong, too long, as in "he was bold with the putt, and it went six feet past." Also a firmly played approach to a well-protected flagpin in a difficult position.

Borrow. In putting, to play to one side or the other from a direct line to the hole in order to compensate for slope or curve in the green.

Bunker. An area of bare ground, often a depression, which is usually covered with sand. It falls under the category of "hazard" in the *Rules of Golf*, although grass-covered ground bordering or within a bunker is not part of the hazard. Oddly enough, "bunkers" were once havens, but only for sheep. The original bunkers in Scotland were holes hollowed out by flocks of sheep for protection against the strong winds on seaside courses.

Bunt. Hitting an intentional short shot.

Burn. A Scottish term for a creek or stream.

Bye. A term used in tournament pairings. Those who draw a "bye" advance to the next round without having to play an opponent.

Caddie. A person who carries or handles a player's clubs during play and otherwise assists him in accordance with the rules.

Can. To hole a putt.

Cap. Top end of a club grip and shaft.

Carry. Distance from the place where the ball is struck to the place where it first strikes the ground.

Casting. A swing-damaging error of starting the downswing with the hands dominating the action. Same as *hitting from the top*.

Casual water. Any *temporary* accumulation of water which is visible before or after the player takes his stance and which is not a hazard of itself or is not in a water hazard. Snow and natural ice are either casual water or loose impediments, at the option of the player. Manufactured ice is an obstruction. Dew is not casual water. A player may lift his ball from "casual water" without penalty.

Championship. A tournament representing title to a trophy offered for competition, usually annually, by a recognized golfing body, such as the United States Golf Association or the Royal and Ancient Golf Club of St. Andrews, Scotland.

Chip shot. A short approach of low trajectory, usually from near the putting green, hit with overspin or bite, depending on the distance from the putting green, or from the cup.

Choke. To grip down farther on the handle. Also, to collapse under great pressure.

Chop. To hit a ball with a hacking motion to impart extra spin.

Chump. An easy opponent.

Closed stance. The left foot extends over the line of flight while the right foot is back.

Club. Used to hit a golf ball. Also a group of golfers.

Clubbing a player. To advise a partner which club to use for a particular shot.

Club head. The hitting portion of the club.

Clubhouse. A building that houses such facilities as lockers, restaurant, bar, and meeting rooms.

Clubhouse lawyer. An over-officious caller of the *Rules of Golf*; or a self-appointed arbiter.

Cocked wrists. The bend of the wrists in the swing.

Committee. The "committee" is the group in charge of the competition.

Competitor. A player in a stroke competition. A "fellow competitor" is any player with whom the competitor plays. Neither is partner of the other. In stroke play, foursome, and four-ball competitions where the context so admits, the word "competitor" or "fellow competitor" shall be held to include his partner.

Controlled shot. A stroke made with less than full power.

Course. The whole area within which play is permitted. A "golf course" usually indicates nine or eighteen holes, each hole consisting of a tee, fairway, and putting green.

Course Rating. The evaluation of the playing difficulty of a course compared with other rated courses. It is expressed in strokes and decimal fractions of a stroke, and is based on yardage and the ability of a scratch golfer.

Cross-bunker. A narrow bunker that crosses a hole at a right angle to the player's line of flight to the putting green.

Cup. See *hole*.

Cuppy. A lie in which the ball is positioned in a small depression in the ground.

Cut shot. A controlled stroke that results in a high, soft shot that sits (stops rolling) almost immediately when it hits the green.

Dead. A ball is said to be dead when it lies so close to the hole that there is no doubt that it will be sunk with the next stroke. Also a ball which lands on the green with so much backspin it stops without running forward.

Deuce. A hole made in two strokes.

Dimple. Round, scientifically made indentations in the cover of a ball which keep its flight through the air steady and true.

Divot. Piece of turf cut out by a club head during a stroke (always to be replaced and pressed down).

Dog-it. To play poorly under stress.

Dogleg. A bend in the fairway either to the right or to the left.

Dormie. When a player or side is as many holes ahead as remain to be played in a match. Opponent(s) must win every remaining hole to tie the match.

Double bogey. A score of two over par for a single hole.

Double eagle. A score of three under par.

Down. The number of holes (match play) or strokes (stroke play) a player is behind an opponent.

Draw. A controlled "hook" stroke used to gain shot-making position or get out of trouble. Also the pairing for match play.

Drive. To hit a ball from a tee.

Driver. No. 1 wood. Usually used only off the teeing surface when maximum distance is required.

Dub. A poorly executed shot; a missed shot.

Duck hook. A violent hook caused either by an over-closed club face or by severe pronation of the hands. Ball normally travels low and hits the ground quickly.

Duffer. An unskilled golfer. Same as a *hacker*.

Dunk. To hit a ball into a water hazard.

Eagle. Two strokes under the designated par for a hole.

Equipment. This is anything used, worn, or carried by or for the player except his ball in play.

Explode. Hitting out of a sand trap and taking large quantities of sand with the shot. Same as *blast*.

Extra. A new or additional bet on the remaining holes. If someone wants to take a "dollar extra" on the 17th tee, he wants to play the last two holes for the dollar. Same as a *press*.

Face. Hitting surface of the club head.

Fade. A term used to indicate a slight turn from left to right at the end of the ball's flight. Also a controlled "slice" shot.

Fairway. The well-kept portion of terrain between the tee and putting green, affording the player a favorable lie for the ball.

Fan. To miss the ball completely. Same as *whiff*.

Fat shot. Refers to the club first hitting the ground behind the ball. Ball should be struck first with ensuing divot in front. Causes high or low shots and loss of distance.

Feather. To hit a long high shot with a gentle left-to-right flight which brings the ball down very lightly and without much roll.

Field. All the contestants in a tournament or championship.

Flagstick. A movable marker placed in the hole on the green to show its location. Same as *flag* or *pin*.

Flange. Additional surface of the club head which protrudes at the sole.

Flash trap. A small, shallow sand bunker.

Flat. A very obtuse angle between the sole of a club and the shaft.

Flat swing. Occurs when the club head is carried back in a flat manner, usually in an inside-out manner.

Flier. A ball that leaves the club face without spin and travels farther than normal.

Flier lie. A "lie" in clover or tufted grass. Also a good "lie" in the rough.

Flight. A division of players for tournament play. Players of equal ability are placed in the same flight. The flights may consist of any number of players; however, sixteen is the usual number. Also a term given to a ball hit into the air.

Flub. A poor shot, usually caused by hitting the ground before hitting the ball.

Follow-through. The continuation of the swing after the ball has been struck.

Fore. An expression called out in warning to those in danger from the flight of the ball. From the British phrase, "Look out before!"

Forecaddie. A person employed by the committee to indicate or mark the position of a player's ball on the course.

Four-ball. A match in which two play their better ball against the better ball of two other players.

Foursome. A match in which two play against two, and each side plays one ball. Often erroneously used to describe a four-ball match. Used most often in international competition, such as the Walker, Ryder, and Curtis Cups. Also a term given to four players playing together.

Fried egg. See *plugged lie.*

Fringe. See *apron.*

Frog hair. Short grass bordering the edge of the green.

Front side. The first nine holes of an eighteen-hole course.

Gimme. A putt so short that it will most likely be conceded by an opponent.

Go-to-school. To help determine the roll of a green by observing the path of a prior putt over the same area.

Grain. The direction in which grass on a putting green grows, and therefore lies, after it is closely cut.

Grasscutter. A hard-hit ball, traveling low and skimming the grass.

Green. The whole links or golf course. A "putting green," on the other hand, is all the ground of the hole being played which is specially prepared for putting or otherwise defined by the committee. Hence, the terms "green fee," "green committee," "greenkeeper," and so on should always be used in the singular rather than the plural. While this is true according to the *Rules of Golf,* the term "green" popularly means the putting surface, the closely cut area which contains the hole or cup, and means the same as *putting green.*

Green fee. The fee paid for the privilege of playing on the golf course.

Grip. The part of the shaft, covered with leather or other material, by which the club is grasped. Also the grasp itself.

Gross. A player's score before his handicap is deducted. That is, the total number of strokes taken to complete a designated round.

Ground under repair. Any portion of the course so marked by order of the committee. It includes material piled for removal and a hole made by a greenkeeper, even if not so marked. Stakes and lines marking such an area are not in such ground.

Hacker. An unskilled golfer. Same as *duffer.*

Halved. A hole is "halved" when each side has played it in the same number of strokes. Also to play a match to no decision.

Handicap. The stroke or strokes which a player may deduct from his gross, or actual, score. Actually, it is the number of strokes a player receives to adjust his scoring ability to the common level of a scratch or zero-handicap golfer.

Handicap allowance. The portion of the handicap usable in a given form of play.

Handicap differential. The difference between a player's gross score and the course rating of the golf course on which the score was made.

Hanging lie. A ball resting on a downhill slope.

Hazard. A hazard is any bunker or water hazard. A "bunker" is a hazard consisting of a prepared area of ground, often a hollow, from which turf or soil has been removed and replaced with sand or the like. Grass-covered ground bordering or within a bunker is not part of the bunker. A "water hazard" is any sea, lake, pond, river, ditch, surface drainage ditch, or other open water course (whether or not containing water) and anything of a similar nature. All ground or water within the margin of a water hazard is part of the water hazard. The margin of a water hazard is deemed to extend vertically upwards. Stakes and lines defining the margins of water hazards are in the hazards. A "lateral water hazard" is a water hazard or that part of a water hazard running approximately parallel to the line of play and so situated that it is not possible or is deemed by the committee to be impracticable to drop a ball behind the water hazard and keep the spot at which the ball last crossed the hazard margin between the player and the hole.

Heel. Part of the club head nearest the shaft. Also to hit from this part and send the ball at right angles to the line of play.

Hole. A round receptacle in the green, $4\frac{1}{4}$ inches in diameter and at least 4 inches deep and usually metal-lined. Same as *cup.* Also units of play from tee to putting green; a *round* consists of eighteen holes or units.

Hole-high. A ball even with the hole, but off to one side.

Hole in one. A hole made in one stroke. Same as *ace.*

Hole out. To put the ball into the cup to complete the play for one hole.

Home. The green.

Home pro. A professional who maintains his position at a golf club to teach and plays only in local events. Same as *club professional.*

Honor. The right or privilege of hitting first from the tee, which goes to the winner of the preceding hole or the last hole won (or, on the first hole, by tossing a coin).

Hook. To hit a ball in a curve to the left of the intended target.

Hosel. The hollow part of the iron club head into which the shaft is fitted.

Hustler. An adept golfer who purposely maintains a higher handicap in order to make more favorable wagers.

In. An expression used to describe the second nine of golf course, as opposed to *out*—the first nine holes.

Insert. Part of the club face of wooden clubs.

In-the-leather. A term in friendly matches allowing (or giving) a putt that lies no farther from the cup than the length of the leather wrapping on the player's putter.

Iron. Club with a metal head. Irons are usually classified long irons (Nos. 1, 2, 3), middle irons (Nos. 4, 5, 6) and short irons (Nos. 7, 8, 9, and wedge). Progressing from the No. 1 through the wedge, the iron face becomes larger and more lofted.

Lag. Putting with the intention of leaving the ball close to the hole in a position for surely holing out with the next stroke.

Lateral hazard. Any water hazard running approximately parallel to the line of play. Same as *parallel hazard*.

Lie. The position in which the ball rests on the ground. Also the angle which the shaft makes with the ground when the club is sitting in its natural position.

Line. The direction in which the player *intends* the ball to travel after it is hit. Same as *line of flight* or *line of play*.

Links. A term originally given to a seaside golf course; now, any golf course.

Lip. The top edge or rim of the hole or cup.

Lob shot. An extremely high and soft type of shot requiring a good deal of "feel" in the hands. It goes straight up and comes almost straight down with a minimum of overspin or forward momentum. Very useful in tight situations where not much green is available to work with.

Loft. The elevation of the ball into the air. Also the angle at which the club face is set from the vertical and is employed to lift the ball into the air.

Lofter. A highly lofted iron club that was a forerunner of the niblick. It is now obsolete.

Long game. Any of those shots in which considerable distance is important.

Looping. A backswing error in which the head and shoulders move forward and to the left so that they are more over the ball than is correct. This makes the club head return to the ball from the outside and causes shanking.

Loose impediments. Natural objects that are not fixed or growing or adhering to the ball. Includes stones that are not solidly imbedded, twigs, leaves, branches, and the like, molehills, dung, worms, and insects, and the casts or heaps made by them.

Low ball and total. A four-ball team bet in which the best ball of each team wins one point, and the low total of the partners wins another.

LPGA. Abbreviation for Ladies' Professional Golf Association.

Make the cut. To score well enough in allocated number of rounds to qualify for final one or two rounds in professional tournament competition.

Marker. An object on the tee which determines the forward limits from which to drive. Same as *tee marker*. Also a scorer in stroke play who is appointed by the committee to record a competitor's score. He may be a fellow competitor.

Marshal. A person appointed by the committee to handle spectators and keep order during a tournament.

Match. A golf competition played by holes—each hole is a separate contest—rather than the total score. The team or player winning the greatest number of holes is the winner.

Match Play. Competition by holes. The winner of the first hole is said to be "one up," and even if he wins that hole by two or more strokes, he is not more than "one up." He can increase his lead by one every time he wins another hole. A competition decided according to match play ends when one player is more holes "up" than there are left to play—as in 4&3, four up with three to play.

Medal. The low qualifying score for a match-play tournament or championship.

Medalist. The player with the lowest qualifying score in a tournament.

Medal Play. A competition decided by total, overall score, with every stroke counting and being significant. Same as *stroke play*.

Mixed foursome. A foursome with two pairs of golfers, each consisting of a male and a female player.

Mulligan. A second shot, usually off the first tee, that is sometimes permitted in a casual social game, but never in a competition played strictly by the *Rules of Golf*.

Nassau. A competition, either match or stroke play, in which a point is allotted for the first nine holes, another point for the second nine, and still another for the overall eighteen.

Neck. The part of the club where the shaft joins the head. Same as *socket*.

Net. A player's score after his handicap is subtracted.

NGF. Abbreviation for National Golf Foundation.

Observer. A person appointed by the committee to assist the referee, to decide questions of fact, and to report to the referee any breach of the rules. An observer should not attend the flagstick, stand at or mark the position of the hole, or lift the ball or mark its position.

Obstruction. Anything artificial, whether erected, placed, or left on the course, except objects defining course boundaries or artificially constructed roads and paths.

Open. A tournament open to both amateurs and professionals.

Open stance. The left foot is dropped back of the imaginary line of the direction of the ball, enabling the golfer to face more in the direction toward which he wishes to hit.

Out. An expression used to describe the first nine of a golf course, as opposed to *in*—the second nine holes. See *side*.

Out of bounds. The ground outside of the course, on which play is prohibited. This area requires a penalty of "stroke" and "distance" each time a player hits into it. In other words, the player has to replay the shot with a one-stroke penalty.

Outside agency. Any agency not part of the match or, in stroke play, not part of a competitor's side; includes marker, observer, referee, or a forecaddie.

Overclubbing. Use of a club giving too much distance.

Par. The theoretical number of strokes a player should take for a hole; golf's standard of good performance. The par for each hole is usually indicated on the scorecard.

Partner. A player associated with another player on the same side in a match.

Penalty stroke. A stroke added to a player's score for violation of certain rules.

PGA. Abbreviation for Professional Golfers Association.

Pin. See *flagstick*.

Pin-high. See *hole-high*.

Pinehurst. Partners play each other's drive, then select one ball with which to finish the hole. Usually in stroke play.

Pitch. A short shot up to the putting green, generally made by lofting the ball in a high arc and landing with backspin.

Pitch and run. The same shot as the pitch, but executed with a lower-numbered club, thus preventing the high arc and backspin and thereby permitting the ball to run after it hits the putting green.

Pitching wedge. An iron designed primarily for making short pitching shots.

Play club. An ancient driver; now obsolete.

Playing through. Occurs when a group of players are permitted to pass another group playing ahead.

Plugged lie. A "lie" generally in a bunker in which the ball is buried in the sand. Same as a *fried egg*.

Plus handicap. The number of strokes a player gives to adjust his scoring ability to the common level.

Pot bunker. A small, deep sand trap.

Preferred lie. Under local rules which permit a player to improve the lie of the ball in a specified way without penalty.

Press. An extra bet.

Professional. Usually called a *pro*. A player who teaches (the *teaching pro*) or plays in tournaments (the *touring pro*) for monetary compensation.

Pro shop. A place to buy golf equipment; it is operated by the club professional.

Provisional ball. A ball played after the previous ball may be lost or out of bounds.

Pull. A ball, when hit, that goes to the left of the target with little or no curving.

Punch. A low, controlled shot straight into the wind, executed by slamming the club down into the ball with a short swing.

Push. A ball, when hit, that goes to the right of the target with little or no curving.

Putt. Stroking the ball toward the hole when on the putting green.

Putter. Club with straight face, used on the putting green.

Putting green. The "putting green" is all the ground of the hole being played which is specially prepared for putting or otherwise defined as such by the committee.

Quail high. A long shot that has low trajectory.

R & A. Abbreviation for Royal and Ancient Golf Club of St. Andrews.

Referee. A person who has been appointed by the committee to accompany players to decide questions of fact and of golf law. He shall act on any breach of rules which he may observe or which may be reported to him by an observer.

Ringer score. The cumulative scores of a player's lowest number of strokes per hole set on a given course over a given period of time.

Roll-on-a-shot. To turn the wrists too much at impact.

Rookie. A former amateur golfer on his first year of playing the professional tour.

Rough. Areas, usually of relatively long grass, adjacent to the tee, fairway, putting green, or hazards.

Round. See *hole* (last sentence).

Round robin. A controlled tournament in which every player plays one match against every other player.

Rub of the green. A "rub of the green" occurs when a ball in motion is stopped or deflected by an outside agency, which is any agency not part of the match or, in stroke play, not part of a competitor's side. Also, "tough luck," or "that's the way the ball bounces."

Run. The distance the ball rolls after striking the ground or on the ground.

Running iron. An iron used primarily for short running shots.

Run-up. An approach shot in which the ball travels close to the ground or on the ground.

Sand trap. A colloquial expression for bunker. See *hazard*.

Sand wedge. An iron designed primarily to get out of sand traps. It has a heavy flange on the bottom.

Scoop. An improper swing in which the clubhead has a dipping or digging action.

Scotch foursome. A match in which partners alternate hitting one ball, alternately driving regardless of which one holed out on the previous hole. A "mixed" Scotch foursome refers to a man and woman as partners.

Scratch. To play at par.

Scratch player. One who receives no handicap allowance.

Scuffing. The name given to the error of hitting the ground behind the ball.

Set. A full complement of golf clubs.

Shaft. That part of the club which is not the head.

Shagging. Gathering of golf balls hit from practice tees.

Shank. To hit a ball on the hosel of the club causing it to go sharply off line, generally to the right.

Short game. The shots of pitching, chipping, and putting.

Side. A player, or two or more players who are partners. Also when speaking of the eighteen holes on a golf course, "side" can mean the first nine holes (*front side*, or "out"), or last nine holes (*back side*, or "in").

Skulling. An error, generally in a chip or pitch shot, of hitting the ball too hard and obtaining too great distance. This is caused by hitting the ball at or above its center.

Sky. To hit underneath the ball, sending it higher than intended, like a "pop fly" in baseball. Same as a *rainmaker*.

Slice. A shot which curves to the right of the target.

Snake. A very long putt, usually one over several breaks in the green.

Snipe. A sharply hooked ball that dives quickly.

Socket. The opening in the neck of an iron club into which the shaft is fitted. Also, in Great Britain, to shank a shot. See *neck*.

Sole. The bottom of the club head. Also the act of placing the club on the ground at address.

Sole plate. The metal plate located on the bottom of wooden-head clubs.

Spray. To hit a ball far off line.

Square. A match that is all even.

Square stance. A stance in which both feet are in a line parallel to the direction in which the player wishes to hit the ball.

Stab. A half-hearted swing, or one lacking the proper arc.

Stance. Position of the feet when addressing the ball.

Stand please. The shout used to request spectators to remain motionless and silent while a player is shooting.

Stipulated round. Playing all eighteen holes of a course in their correct sequence.

Stony. To hit it "stony" is to hit a ball close to the flagstick.

Stroke. Any forward motion of the club head made with intent to hit and move the ball, successful or not.

Stroke hole. The hole on which a player applies a handicap stroke. The numerical order in which handicap strokes are allocated to the holes of the golf course should be shown on the scorecard.

Stroke play. Competition in which the winner is determined by the low number of strokes taken for one stipulated round; or for the number of stipulated rounds constituting a given tournament. Same as *medal play*.

Stymie. In match play, a situation in which an opponent's ball is in the line of a player's putt. Since the stymie is no longer played (the blocking ball may be lifted), the word is used generally when there is a tree in the way of a shot to the green; such a golfer would be "stymied."

Sudden death. The continuation of a match or stroke competition that is deadlocked at the end of the allotted number of holes. Competition continues until one or the other of the players wins a hole.

Summer rules. Ordinary playing rules of golf apply.

Sweet spot. Dead center of the face of the club. Used to define the reason for a well-hit shot.

Swing. The action by a player in stroking the ball.

Take the pipe. Collapsing under tension at critical stage of golf competition.

Takeway. The beginning of the backswing.

Tee. A wooden peg on which the ball is placed for driving. Also the area from which the ball is driven on the first shot of each hole. Same as *teeing ground*.

Tee marker. See *marker*.

Texas wedge. The putter, when used from off the putting green.

Thread. A shot on which the ball steered through a narrow opening.

Three-ball. A match in which three play against one another, each playing his own ball.

Threesome. A match in which two players play alternate strokes with the same ball and oppose a single player. Also, a colloquialism for three players engaged in stroke play.

Through the green. The whole area of the course except the teeing ground, putting green, and hazards.

Toe. The portion of the club head farthest from where it joins the shaft.

Toe job. A shot hit too far toward the toe of the club.

Top. To hit a ball above center, causing it to roll or hop rather than to rise off the ground.

Tournament. A competition at either match or stroke play.

Track iron. A club with a small, round head, used in the early days of golf, mainly to extricate the ball from cart tracks; club is, of course, now obsolete.

Trouble shot. A recovery stroke taken from a trouble position such as a bunker or rough, or from behind trees.

Turn. Starting the second or back nine.

Underclubbing. Using a club giving too short distance.

Unplayable lie. A ball in a position where it cannot be played; for example, between rocks or in a thicket of trees.

Up. The number of holes or strokes a player is ahead of his opponent.

Upright. That angle between the head of a club and its shaft which is less obtuse than a flat lie.

Upright swing. A swing in which the club head is carried more directly backward and upward from the ball.

USGA. Abbreviation for United States Golf Association.

Waggle. The preliminary action before hitting the ball of flexing the wrists, causing the club to swing forward and backward.

Water hazard. See *hazard*.

Water hole. A hole which has a stream or pond adjacent to it or in the middle of it, usually forcing the players to shoot over it.

Wedge. A high-lofted iron used for short shots.

Whiff. To miss the ball completely. Same as *fan*.

Whins. A British term for heavy rough or brush.

Whipping. The thread or twine used in wrapping the space where the head and shaft are joined.

Wind cheater. An intentionally low-hit ball into the wind.

Winter rules. Rules used when the players are permitted to improve the lie of their ball on the fairway. They are usually local golf rules.

Wood. A club with a large head, used for hitting the ball longer distance. Can be made of wood or metal.

Yardage Rating. The evaluation of the playing difficulty of a hole or a course based on yardage only.

Yips. Convulsive shakes that cause the player to badly miss a short putt.

I N D E X

509